Calculus

with Trigonometry and Analytic Geometry

Second Edition

Calculus

with Trigonometry and Analytic Geometry

Second Edition

John H. Saxon Jr.

Frank Y. H. Wang

Revised by:

Bret L. Crock

James A. Sellers

Calculus with Trigonometry and Analytic Geometry
Second Edition

ISBN 978-1-56577-146-8   ISBN 1-56577-146-X

Editorial staff: Brian Rice, Matt Maloney, Clint Keele, Eric Scaia

Copyediting staff: Chris Davey, Susan Toth

Production staff: Angela Johnson, Carrie Brown, Eric Atkins, Brenda Bell, Jane Claunch, David LeBlanc, Adriana Maxwell, Chad Morris, Tonea Morrow, Nancy Rimassa, Debra Sullivan, Darlene Terry, Jason Vredenburg

Manufacturing Code: 8   0868   13 12 11
4500323499

─── *Reaching us via the Internet* ───

www.saxonpublishers.com

E-mail: info@saxonpublishers.com

Table of Contents

	Preface	*xi*
Lesson 1	The Real Numbers • Fundamental Concept Review	1
Lesson 2	More Concept Review • The Graphing Calculator	6
Lesson 3	The Contrapositive • The Converse and Inverse • Iff Statements	13
Lesson 4	Radian Measure of Angles • Trigonometric Ratios • Four Quadrant Signs • Simplifying Trigonometric Expressions	16
Lesson 5	Word Problem Review	21
Lesson 6	Functions: Their Equations and Graphs • Functional Notation • Domain and Range	25
Lesson 7	The Unit Circle • Centerline, Amplitude, and Phase Angle of Sinusoids • Period of a Function • Important Numbers • Exponential Functions	35
Lesson 8	Pythagorean Identities • Functions of $-\theta$ • Trigonometric Identities • Cofunctions • Similar Triangles	46
Lesson 9	Absolute Value as a Distance • Graphing "Special" Functions • Logarithms • Base 10 and Base e • Simple Logarithm Problems	54
Lesson 10	Quadratic Polynomials • Remainder Theorem • Synthetic Division • Rational Roots Theorem	62
Lesson 11	Continuity • Left-hand and Right-hand Limits	69
Lesson 12	Sum and Difference Identities • Double-Angle Identities • Half-Angle Identities • Graphs of Logarithmic Functions	74
Lesson 13	Inverse Trigonometric Functions • Trigonometric Equations	83
Lesson 14	Limit of a Function	88
Lesson 15	Interval Notation • Products of Linear Factors • Tangents • Increasing and Decreasing Functions	92
Lesson 16	Logarithms of Products and Quotients • Logarithms of Powers • Exponential Equations	97

Lesson 17 Infinity as a Limit • Undefined Limits   102

Lesson 18 Sums, Differences, Products, and Quotients of Functions • Composition
of Functions   105

Lesson 19 The Derivative • Slopes of Curves on a Graphing Calculator   111

Lesson 20 Change of Base • Graphing Origin-Centered Conics on a Graphing
Calculator   118

Lesson 21 Translations of Functions • Graphs of Rational Functions I   122

Lesson 22 Binomial Expansion • Recognizing the Equations of Conic Sections   129

Lesson 23 Trigonometric Functions of $n\theta$ • Graphing Conics on a Graphing
Calculator   134

Lesson 24 New Notation for the Definition of the Derivative • The Derivative of x^n 138

Lesson 25 The Constant-Multiple Rule for Derivatives • The Derivatives of Sums
and Differences • Proof of the Derivative of a Sum   141

Lesson 26 Derivatives of e^x and $\ln |x|$ • Derivatives of $\sin x$ and $\cos x$ •
Exponential Growth and Decay   146

Lesson 27 Equation of the Tangent Line • Higher-Order Derivatives   152

Lesson 28 Graphs of Rational Functions II • A Special Limit   155

Lesson 29 Newton and Leibniz • Differentials   160

Lesson 30 Graph of $\tan \theta$ • Graphs of Reciprocal Functions   163

Lesson 31 Product Rule • Proof of the Product Rule   169

Lesson 32 An Antiderivative • The Indefinite Integral   173

Lesson 33 Factors of Polynomial Functions • Graphs of Polynomial Functions   176

Lesson 34 Implicit Differentiation   182

Lesson 35 Integral of a Constant • Integral of $kf(x)$ • Integral of x^n 187

Lesson 36 Critical Numbers • A Note about Critical Numbers   191

Lesson 37 Differentiation by u Substitution   196

Lesson 38 Integral of a Sum • Integral of $\dfrac{1}{x}$ 200

Lesson 39 Area Under a Curve (Upper and Lower Sums) • Left, Right, and
Midpoint Sums   203

Lesson 40 Units for the Derivative • Normal Lines • Maximums and Minimums
on a Graphing Calculator   211

Lesson 41 Graphs of Rational Functions III • Repeated Factors   216

Lesson 42 The Derivative of a Quotient • Proof of the Quotient Rule   220

Lesson 43 Area Under a Curve as an Infinite Summation   224

Lesson 44 The Chain Rule • Alternate Definition of the Derivative •
The Symmetric Derivative   230

Lesson 45 Using f' to Characterize f • Using f' to Find Maximums and Minimums 236

Lesson 46 Related-Rates Problems 241

Lesson 47 Fundamental Theorem of Calculus, Part 1 • Riemann Sums • The Definite Integral 246

Lesson 48 Derivatives of Trigonometric Functions • Summary of Rules for Derivatives and Differentials 252

Lesson 49 Concavity and Inflection Points • Geometric Meaning of the Second Derivative • First and Second Derivative Tests 258

Lesson 50 Derivatives of Composite Functions • Derivatives of Products and Quotients of Composite Functions 264

Lesson 51 Integration by Guessing 269

Lesson 52 Maximization and Minimization Problems 272

Lesson 53 Numerical Integration of Positive-Valued Functions on a Graphing Calculator 277

Lesson 54 Velocity and Acceleration • Motion Due to Gravity 281

Lesson 55 Maclaurin Polynomials 285

Lesson 56 More Integration by Guessing • A Word of Caution 290

Lesson 57 Properties of the Definite Integral 295

Lesson 58 Explicit and Implicit Equations • Inverse Functions 302

Lesson 59 Computing Areas • More Numerical Integration on a Graphing Calculator 309

Lesson 60 Area Between Two Curves • Area Between Curves Using a Graphing Calculator 313

Lesson 61 Playing Games with f, f', and f'' 318

Lesson 62 Work, Distance, and Rates 321

Lesson 63 Critical Number (Closed Interval) Theorem 326

Lesson 64 Derivatives of Inverse Trigonometric Functions • What to Memorize 331

Lesson 65 Falling-Body Problems 336

Lesson 66 u Substitution • Change of Variable • Proof of the Substitution Theorem 342

Lesson 67 Areas Involving Functions of y 347

Lesson 68 Even and Odd Functions 351

Lesson 69 Integration by Parts I 356

Lesson 70 Properties of Limits • Some Special Limits 361

Lesson 71 Solids of Revolution I: Disks 366

Lesson 72 Derivatives of a^x • Derivatives of $\log_a x$ • Derivative of $|f(x)|$ 372

Lesson 73 Integrals of a^x • Integrals of $\log_a x$ 377

Lesson 74 Fluid Force 380

Lesson 75   Continuity of Functions   386

Lesson 76   Integration of Odd Powers of sin x and cos x 392

Lesson 77   Pumping Fluids   395

Lesson 78   Particle Motion I   400

Lesson 79   L'Hôpital's Rule   404

Lesson 80   Asymptotes of Rational Functions   409

Lesson 81   Solids of Revolution II: Washers   414

Lesson 82   Limits and Continuity • Differentiability   420

Lesson 83   Integration of Even Powers of sin x and cos x 426

Lesson 84   Logarithmic Differentiation   429

Lesson 85   The Mean Value Theorem • Application of the Mean Value Theorem
               in Mathematics • Proof of Rolle's Theorem • Practical Application of
               the Mean Value Theorem   434

Lesson 86   Rules for Even and Odd Functions   441

Lesson 87   Solids of Revolution III: Shells   445

Lesson 88   Separable Differential Equations   450

Lesson 89   Average Value of a Function • Mean Value Theorem for Integrals •
               Proof of the Mean Value Theorem for Integrals   456

Lesson 90   Particle Motion II   461

Lesson 91   Product and Difference Indeterminate Forms   466

Lesson 92   Derivatives of Inverse Functions   470

Lesson 93   Newton's Method   475

Lesson 94   Solids of Revolution IV: Displaced Axes of Revolution   480

Lesson 95   Trapezoidal Rule • Error Bound for the Trapezoidal Rule   486

Lesson 96   Derivatives and Integrals of Functions Involving Absolute Value   492

Lesson 97   Solids Defined by Cross Sections   498

Lesson 98   Fundamental Theorem of Calculus, Part 2 • The Natural Logarithm
               Function   502

Lesson 99   Linear Approximations Using Differentials   508

Lesson 100   Integrals of Powers of tan x • Integrals of Powers of cot x • Integrals
               of sec x and csc x 511

Lesson 101   Limit of $\dfrac{\sin x}{x}$ for Small x • Proof of the Derivative of sin x 516

Lesson 102   Derivatives of ln x and e^x • Definition of e 521

Lesson 103   Proof of the Fundamental Theorem of Calculus • Epsilon-Delta Proofs   524

Lesson **104**   Graphs of Solutions of Differential Equations • Slope Fields • Recognizing Graphs of Slope Fields   529

Lesson **105**   Sequences • Limit of a Sequence • Graphs of Sequences • Characteristics of Sequences   537

Lesson **106**   Introduction to Parametric Equations • Slope of Parametric Curves   545

Lesson **107**   Polar Coordinates • Polar Equations   550

Lesson **108**   Introduction to Vectors • Arithmetic of Vectors • Unit Vectors and Normal Vectors   556

Lesson **109**   Arc Length I: Rectangular Equations   565

Lesson **110**   Rose Curves   569

Lesson **111**   The Exponential Indeterminate Forms 0^0, 1^∞, and ∞^0 575

Lesson **112**   Foundations of Trigonometric Substitution   578

Lesson **113**   Trigonometric Substitution   581

Lesson **114**   Arc Length II: Parametric Equations   587

Lesson **115**   Partial Fractions I • Logistic Differential Equations   591

Lesson **116**   Series   597

Lesson **117**   Geometric Series • Telescoping Series   600

Lesson **118**   Limaçons and Lemniscates   604

Lesson **119**   Parametric Equations—Second Derivatives and Tangent Lines   610

Lesson **120**   Partial Fractions II   614

Lesson **121**   Convergence and Divergence • Series Indexing • Arithmetic of Series   617

Lesson **122**   Integration by Parts II   621

Lesson **123**   Vector Functions   625

Lesson **124**   Implicit Differentiation II   628

Lesson **125**   Infinite Limits of Integration   632

Lesson **126**   Partial Fractions III   637

Lesson **127**   *p*-Series   639

Lesson **128**   Basic Comparison Test • Integral Test • Proof of *p*-Test   642

Lesson **129**   Area Bounded by Polar Curves   646

Lesson **130**   Ratio Test • Root Test   651

Lesson **131**   Infinite Integrands   654

Lesson **132**   Limit Comparison Test   657

Lesson **133**   Euler's Method   660

Lesson **134**   Slopes of Polar Curves   664

Lesson **135**   Absolute Convergence   669

Lesson **136**   Using the Chain Rule with the Fundamental Theorem of Calculus   672

Lesson **137**   Piecewise Integration   674

Lesson **138**   Conditional Convergence and Leibniz's Theorem   677

Lesson **139**   Alternating Series Approximation Theorem   680

Lesson **140**   Projectile Motion   684

Lesson **141**   Taylor Series   688

Lesson **142**   Velocity and Acceleration as Vector Functions   691

Lesson **143**   Binomial Series   694

Lesson **144**   Remainder Theorem   696

Lesson **145**   Convergence of Power Series   699

Lesson **146**   Term-by-Term Differentiation and Integration of Power Series   703

Lesson **147**   Substitution into Power Series   706

Lesson **148**   Integral Approximation Using Power Series   708

              Index   711

              Answers to Odd-Numbered Problems   721

Preface

about this edition

This textbook is designed for prospective mathematics majors and students interested in engineering, computer science, physics, business, or the life sciences. It is divided into 148 lessons designed to be taught sequentially and without omission over three semesters. Following a condensed, intensive review of the algebra, trigonometry, and analytic geometry topics necessary for success in calculus, the lessons cover topics in the syllabus for the College Board's Advanced Placement (AP) program for calculus. The topics in the AP Calculus AB syllabus are generally found in the first two thirds of the textbook, while the Calculus BC syllabus topics are generally found in the final third of the textbook. Other important topics not found in the AP calculus course descriptions are interspersed throughout.

Several features distinguish this textbook from the preceding edition. Most significantly, its content is greatly expanded. Much of the Calculus BC course material is new. A new strand of lessons covers many aspects of sequences and series. In particular, lessons on the following topics have been added: types of series, tests for convergence, approximating functions with series, and term-by-term differentiation and integration of power series. The approximation strand has been improved by the addition of lessons on Newton's method, Euler's method, and the trapezoidal rule. Other new topics include slope fields, parametric equations, polar functions, vector functions, logistic growth, arc length, piecewise integration, projectile motion, and volumes of solids defined by cross sections.

Use of graphing calculators also enhances the instruction in this new edition. Students are introduced to several features of the TI-83 and are shown how to confirm answers by graphical and numerical means. While the graphing calculator is a powerful instructional tool, most of the problems and exercises in the book can be solved without one. When problems require a calculator, we usually indicate so with the word *approximate* (or one of its variations). However, before taking advantage of technology, students must understand how to solve the problem without it. **In no case should use of a computing device replace learning proper techniques or showing one's work.**

This textbook also includes an innovation that we call *lesson reference numbers* (LRNs). Appearing in parentheses below each problem, LRNs direct students to lessons they should review when they experience difficulty solving a problem.

philosophy

The abstractions of calculus are not usually understood with limited exposure. To ensure long-term retention and solid skills development, our textbook uses two methods we call *incremental development* and *continual practice and review*. **Incremental development** is the process of building knowledge in pieces over time. In calculus, as with all mathematics, the ability to comprehend a new topic depends on retention of previous material. Therefore, when we present an increment of a topic, we practice it for several days before expanding on it. **Continual practice and review** is the process of exercising learned skills again and again throughout the year. This procedure reinforces students' foundational knowledge and prepares them to learn subsequent, more complex elements.

The benefits of our methodology are best illustrated by example. *Beginning with Problem Set 11, several carefully designed problems on limits appear in most of the next 105 problem sets.* This ensures that students practice limits regularly for twenty-five weeks or more. Students, therefore, have a unique advantage when they reach Lessons 105 and 116, which introduce sequences and series respectively. Traditional textbooks separate limits from sequences and series by hundreds of pages in which they cover derivatives, integrals, and related applications. **Students using traditional textbooks often forget limit rules before they reach the discussion of sequences, and they must often scramble to relearn them.** Instead of being able to focus on the new concept, they must concentrate on concepts and skills they were taught much earlier. **Continual practice and review helps students reinforce rather than forget concepts or skills to which they have been introduced.**

For those new to Saxon, I highlight several key qualities of this and other Saxon mathematics textbooks.

1. **The problem sets are carefully constructed. They are the core of the textbook.** Problem sets are designed to review previously covered material and to prepare students for future lessons. Therefore, students should not skip any problem in the problem sets.

2. **We do not aim for mastery during the initial presentation of a concept.** Instead, we afford students the opportunity to achieve mastery over time. This helps build student confidence and leads to a deeper understanding of the concepts and skills being taught.

3. **We often apply techniques before demonstrating the theory behind them.** John Saxon was fond of saying "Doing, more often than not, precedes understanding." This is not to say the textbook is devoid of theory. It simply means that theory may be deferred until students have mastered the application of technique.

4. **Topics that are usually presented as a unit in other textbooks are often introduced gradually in this one.** For example, as part of the incremental design, techniques of integration are discussed in twenty-one separate lessons spread from Lesson 32 to Lesson 148.

acknowledgments Updating and expanding the original edition of this textbook was a laborious task requiring the considerable efforts of a number of key individuals. At the core of the process was Bret Crock, a long-time classroom teacher who used the first edition of this textbook in the Douglas County School District in Parker, Colorado. His need for a curriculum that addressed the Calculus BC criteria motivated Bret to create lesson plans, examples, and problem sets that allowed his students to continue their study of calculus beyond the 117 lessons in the first edition. His original class notes, lesson outlines, examples, and problem sets form the basis for this new edition.

Bret's materials were transformed into complete lessons by Dr. James Sellers, professor of mathematics at Cedarville University in Ohio. Charged with ensuring mathematical precision and rigor, James both constructed the new lessons and reviewed the original material from the first edition, reorganizing and imposing mathematical sophistication where necessary.

After James enhanced the manuscript, I made editorial changes. My work was followed by the work of our upper grades mathematics editor, Brian Rice, and his associate editors, Clint Keele, Matt Maloney, and Eric Scaia. Then, with a final polish, our supervising copy editor, Chris Davey, prepared the manuscript for publication.

Perhaps the most demanding work was done by our production staff, led by Carrie Brown. Carrie was assisted by Eric Atkins, Brenda Bell, Jane Claunch, David LeBlanc, Adriana Maxwell, Chad Morris, Tonea Morrow, Nancy Rimassa, Debra Sullivan, Darlene Terry, and Jason Vredenburg.

I am proud of all who worked so tirelessly to bring this project to fruition. All of us at Saxon Publishers hope that our efforts were for a good purpose. We are grateful and flattered that you— either classroom teacher or student—have chosen our calculus textbook for your studies. Best wishes!

Frank Y. H. Wang, Ph.D.
President, Saxon Publishers, Inc.
Norman, Oklahoma

LESSON 1 *The Real Numbers • Fundamental Concept Review*

1.A

the real numbers

The numbers that we naturally use to count make up the set called the **natural numbers,** the **counting numbers,** or the **positive integers.** We use the symbol $\mathbb{N}$ to represent this set.

$$\mathbb{N} = \{1, 2, 3, \dots\}$$

When we include the number 0 with these numbers, we get the whole numbers.

$$\text{Whole Numbers} = \{0, 1, 2, \dots\}$$

The negatives of the natural numbers are called the **negative integers.** The number zero together with the positive and the negative integers forms the set of **integers.** The symbol $\mathbb{Z}$ is often used to represent this set. (This symbol comes from the first letter in the German word *Zahlen,* which means "integers.")

$$\mathbb{Z} = \{\dots, -3, -2, -1, 0, 1, 2, 3, \dots\}$$

Any number that can be expressed as a quotient (fraction) using two integers is called a **rational number.** (Remember that zero cannot be a divisor.) We use the symbol $\mathbb{Q}$ (for quotient) to designate this set. The following numbers are rational numbers:

$$0, 4, 0.0021, -\frac{7}{23}, \frac{45}{14}, -4.16\overline{32}, 1.12121212\dots$$

Any decimal number that cannot be written as a quotient of integers is called an **irrational number.** We do not have a symbol for the set of irrational numbers. Examples of irrational numbers are:

$$\sqrt{2}, \pi, e, \sqrt[3]{13}, \sqrt[5]{41}$$

The set of **real numbers** includes all members of the set of rational numbers and all members of the set of irrational numbers. We use the symbol $\mathbb{R}$ to represent the set of real numbers. Using the symbol $\subset$ to mean "is a subset of," we can write

$$\mathbb{N} \subset \mathbb{Z} \subset \mathbb{Q} \subset \mathbb{R}$$

Every natural number is an integer. Every integer is a rational number. And every rational number is a real number.

In the chart below, we summarize what we have learned.

REAL NUMBERS

IRRATIONAL NUMBERS Real numbers that cannot be expressed as a fraction using two integers, such as: $\sqrt[3]{5}, \sqrt{2}, -\sqrt{2}, 2\sqrt{2}, \pi, 3\pi$, etc.	RATIONAL NUMBERS Real numbers that can be expressed as a fraction using two integers, such as: $\frac{1}{2}, 0.3, -\frac{2}{3}$, etc.
	INTEGERS Set of whole numbers and the opposites of the natural numbers: $\dots, -4, -3, -2, -1, 0, 1, 2, 3, 4, \dots$
	WHOLE NUMBERS Set of natural numbers and the number 0 $0, 1, 2, 3, 4, \dots$
	NATURAL OR COUNTING NUMBERS $1, 2, 3, 4, \dots$

Students are advised against using this chart to draw conclusions about how large a set is relative to other sets. Rather, use it as a reference to remember what kinds of numbers are in each set and to get information about which sets are subsets of others.

The real numbers are an ordered set, for the members of the set of real numbers can be arranged in order, which we indicate when we draw a real number line.

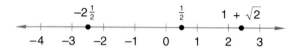

Each point on the number line is associated with a unique number called the **coordinate** of the point. When we graph a number, we place a dot on the number line to indicate the position of the point that has this number as its coordinate. On the number line above, the numbers $\frac{1}{2}$, $1 + \sqrt{2}$, and $-2\frac{1}{2}$ are graphed. Below we list the order properties of the real numbers.

ORDER PROPERTIES OF THE REAL NUMBERS

Let x, y, and z represent real numbers.

1. **Trichotomy.** Exactly one of the following is true:
$$x < y \quad \text{or} \quad x = y \quad \text{or} \quad x > y$$

2. **Transitivity.** If $x < y$ and $y < z$, then $x < z$.

3. **Addition.** If $x < y$, then $x + z < y + z$.

4. **Multiplication.** If z is positive and $x < y$, then $xz < yz$. If z is negative and $x < y$, then $xz > yz$.

5. **Reciprocal.** If x and y are positive and $x < y$, then $\frac{1}{x} > \frac{1}{y}$.

The real numbers also constitute a **field.** The properties of fields are shown below. Note that the symbol $\in$ means "is an element of."

FIELD PROPERTIES

Let x, y, and z be elements of a field F.

1. **Closure laws.** $x + y \in F$ and $xy \in F$

2. **Commutative laws.** $x + y = y + x$ and $xy = yx$

3. **Associative laws.**
$$x + (y + z) = (x + y) + z \quad \text{and} \quad x(yz) = (xy)z$$

4. **Distributive law.** $x(y + z) = xy + xz$

5. **Identity elements.** There are two distinct numbers 0 and 1 satisfying $x + 0 = x$ and $x \cdot 1 = x$.

6. **Inverses.** Each number x has an additive inverse (also called a negative), $-x$, satisfying $x + (-x) = 0$. Also, each number x except 0 has a multiplicative inverse (also called a reciprocal), x^{-1}, satisfying $x \cdot x^{-1} = 1$.

1.B

fundamental concept review

To be a successful calculus student, you must review some fundamental concepts from algebra. Rather than present an expository review, we work problems whose solutions require us to apply the concepts.

example 1.1   Solve $y = v\left(\dfrac{a}{x} + \dfrac{b}{mc}\right)$ for c.

solution   The solution can be found using six steps: (1) eliminate parentheses, (2) multiply by the least common multiple of the denominators, (3) simplify, (4) put all terms containing c on one side of the equals sign, (5) factor c, and (6) divide. In each step we assume that no denominator equals zero.

(1) $\qquad\qquad y = \dfrac{va}{x} + \dfrac{vb}{mc}$ $\qquad\qquad$ eliminated parentheses

(2) $\qquad xmc \cdot y = xmc \cdot \dfrac{va}{x} + xmc \cdot \dfrac{vb}{mc}$ $\qquad$ multiplied by LCM of denominators

(3) $\qquad\qquad xmcy = mcva + xvb$ $\qquad\qquad$ simplified

(4) $\quad xmcy - mcva = xvb$ $\qquad\qquad$ rearranged

(5) $\quad c(xmy - mva) = xvb$ $\qquad\qquad$ factored

(6) $\qquad\qquad c = \dfrac{xvb}{xmy - mva}$ $\qquad\qquad$ divided

example 1.2   Simplify: (a) $\dfrac{x}{a + \dfrac{m}{1 + \dfrac{c}{d}}}$ (b) $\dfrac{\dfrac{a}{x^2} + \dfrac{b}{x}}{\dfrac{m}{x^2} + \dfrac{k}{xc}}$

solution   (a)   When there is no equals sign, the denominators cannot be eliminated. However, this expression can be written as a simple fraction using the following four steps: (1) add, (2) simplify, (3) add, and (4) simplify.

(1) $\qquad\qquad \dfrac{x}{a + \dfrac{m}{\dfrac{d + c}{d}}}$ $\qquad\qquad$ added

(2) $\qquad\qquad \dfrac{x}{a + \dfrac{md}{d + c}}$ $\qquad\qquad$ simplified

(3) $\qquad\qquad \dfrac{x}{\dfrac{a(d + c) + md}{d + c}}$ $\qquad\qquad$ added

(4) $\qquad\qquad \dfrac{x(d + c)}{a(d + c) + md}$ $\qquad\qquad$ simplified

(b)   There is no equals sign in this expression, so the denominators cannot be eliminated. We (1) add in the numerator and denominator and (2) simplify.

(1) $\qquad\qquad \dfrac{\dfrac{a + bx}{x^2}}{\dfrac{mc + kx}{x^2c}}$ $\qquad\qquad$ added

(2) $\qquad\qquad \dfrac{c(a + bx)}{mc + kx}$ $\qquad\qquad$ simplified

example 1.3   Simplify: $\dfrac{4 + \sqrt{2}}{3 - 2\sqrt{2}}$

solution   We multiply above and below by $3 + 2\sqrt{2}$, which is the conjugate of the denominator, and then simplify.

$$\frac{4 + \sqrt{2}}{3 - 2\sqrt{2}} \cdot \frac{3 + 2\sqrt{2}}{3 + 2\sqrt{2}} = \frac{16 + 11\sqrt{2}}{9 - 8} = \mathbf{16 + 11\sqrt{2}}$$

example 1.4   Simplify: $3\sqrt{\dfrac{3}{2}} - 4\sqrt{\dfrac{2}{3}} - \sqrt{24}$

solution   First we rationalize the denominators.

$$3 \cdot \frac{\sqrt{3}}{\sqrt{2}} \cdot \frac{\sqrt{2}}{\sqrt{2}} - 4 \cdot \frac{\sqrt{2}}{\sqrt{3}} \cdot \frac{\sqrt{3}}{\sqrt{3}} - 2\sqrt{6} = \frac{3\sqrt{6}}{2} - \frac{4\sqrt{6}}{3} - 2\sqrt{6}$$

We finish by adding these three terms, using 6 as a common denominator.

$$\frac{9\sqrt{6}}{6} - \frac{8\sqrt{6}}{6} - \frac{12\sqrt{6}}{6} = -\frac{\mathbf{11}\sqrt{6}}{\mathbf{6}}$$

example 1.5   Simplify: (a) $\dfrac{y^{x+3}\,y^{x/2-1}\,z^a}{y^{(x-a)/2}\,z^{(x-a)/3}}$ (b) $x^{3/4}\sqrt{xy}\,x^{1/2}\sqrt[3]{x^4}$

solution   (a) First we collect powers of like bases. Then we add the exponents.

$$y^{x+3+x/2-1-x/2+a/2}\,z^{a-x/3+a/3} = \mathbf{y^{x+2+a/2}\,z^{4a/3-x/3}}$$

(b) We replace the radicals with fractional exponents. Then we add the exponents of like bases.

$$x^{3/4}x^{1/2}y^{1/2}x^{1/2}x^{4/3} = \mathbf{x^{37/12}\,y^{1/2}}$$

example 1.6   Factor: $4a^{3m+2} - 16a^{3m}$

solution   If each term is written in factored form, the common factor $4a^{3m}$ can be determined by inspection. We extract the common factor and finish by factoring $a^2 - 4$.

$$(4a^{3m})a^2 - (4)(4a^{3m}) = 4a^{3m}(a^2 - 4) \qquad \text{common factor}$$
$$= \mathbf{4a^{3m}(a + 2)(a - 2)} \qquad \text{factored } a^2 - 4$$

example 1.7   Factor: (a) $8a^3 - b^3c^6$ (b) $m^3 + x^3y^6$

solution   (a) The difference of two cubes $F^3 - S^3$ can be factored as $(F - S)(F^2 + FS + S^2)$.

$$8a^3 - b^3c^6 = (2a)^3 - (bc^2)^3$$
$$= \mathbf{(2a - bc^2)(4a^2 + 2abc^2 + b^2c^4)}$$

(b) The sum of two cubes $F^3 + S^3$ has similar factorization:

$$F^3 + S^3 = (F + S)(F^2 - FS + S^2)$$

Therefore:

$$m^3 + x^3y^6 = (m)^3 + (xy^2)^3$$
$$= \mathbf{(m + xy^2)(m^2 - mxy^2 + x^2y^4)}$$

example 1.8   Simplify: (a) $\dfrac{14!}{6!\,11!}$ (b) $\dfrac{N!}{(N-2)!}$ (c) $\displaystyle\sum_{j=0}^{3} \frac{2^j}{j+1}$ (d) $\displaystyle\sum_{i=1}^{4} 3$

solution   Recall that $N!$, read "N factorial," is defined to be the product of the integers from 1 to N.

$$N! = N \cdot (N - 1) \cdot (N - 2) \cdot \cdots \cdot 3 \cdot 2 \cdot 1$$

(a) $\dfrac{14!}{6!\,11!} = \dfrac{\overset{7}{\cancel{14}} \cdot 13 \cdot \cancel{12} \cdot \cancel{11!}}{6 \cdot 5 \cdot \cancel{4} \cdot \cancel{3} \cdot \cancel{2} \cdot 1 \cdot \cancel{11!}} = \dfrac{7 \cdot 13}{30} = \dfrac{91}{30}$

(b) $\dfrac{N!}{(N-2)!} = \dfrac{N \cdot (N-1) \cdot (N-2)!}{(N-2)!} = N \cdot (N-1) = N^2 - N$

The symbol Σ indicates summation.

(c) $\displaystyle\sum_{j=0}^{3} \dfrac{2^j}{j+1} = \dfrac{2^{(0)}}{(0)+1} + \dfrac{2^{(1)}}{(1)+1} + \dfrac{2^{(2)}}{(2)+1} + \dfrac{2^{(3)}}{(3)+1} = 1 + 1 + \dfrac{4}{3} + 2 = \dfrac{16}{3}$

(d) $\displaystyle\sum_{i=1}^{4} 3 = 3 + 3 + 3 + 3 = \mathbf{12}$

example 1.9 Compare (assume $a \neq 0$): A. $\dfrac{1}{a}$ B. a^{-1}

In comparison problems throughout this text, the answer is A if quantity A is greater, B if quantity B is greater, C if quantities A and B are equal, and D if insufficient information is provided to determine which quantity is greater.

solution Quantities A and B are equal since a^{-1} is another way of writing $\dfrac{1}{a}$. Therefore, the answer is **C**.

problem set 1 In Saxon textbooks it is customary to give problems that cover only those concepts discussed in the text itself. However, in the early problem sets we will not follow this custom. For example, in Problem Set 1, problems 1–4, 13, 24, and 25 are not discussed in the lesson. Students who have difficulty with any of the review problems in these early lessons should refer to earlier texts in the Saxon series.

For problems 1–4, the answer is A if quantity A is greater, B if quantity B is greater, C if quantities A and B are equal, and D if insufficient information is provided to determine which quantity is greater.

1. Compare: A. $7\dfrac{1}{4}$ ft^2 B. 0.8 yd^2

2. Given that $x = t$, compare: A. $7(2t - 2x)$ B. $-6(3t - 3x)$

3. Given that $4 < x < 9$ and $2 < y < 14$, compare: A. x B. y

4. Given that a is the average of 3 and 6, compare: A. $3a$ B. $a + 6$

5. Solve for R_1: $\dfrac{m}{x} = y\left(\dfrac{1}{R_1} + \dfrac{a}{R_2}\right)$

Simplify the expressions in problems 6–13.

6. $a + \dfrac{1}{a + \dfrac{1}{a}}$

7. $\dfrac{1}{a + \dfrac{1}{x + \dfrac{1}{m}}}$

8. $\dfrac{x^2 y}{1 + m^2} + \dfrac{x}{y}$

9. $\dfrac{4 - 3\sqrt{2}}{8 - \sqrt{2}}$

10. $\dfrac{x^a y^{a+b}}{x^{-a/2} y^{b-1}}$

11. $\dfrac{m^{x+2} b^{x-2}}{m^{2x/3} b^{-3x/2}}$

12. $\sqrt{xy}\, x^{2/3} y^{-3/2}$

13. Solve: $\begin{cases} 2x + 3y = -4 \\ x - 2z = -3 \\ 2y - z = -6 \end{cases}$

Factor the expressions in problems 14–19.

14. $a^2x - a^2 - 4b^2x + 4b^2$ **15.** $16a^{4m+3} - 8a^{2m+3}$ **16.** $a^2b^{2x+2} - ab^{2x+1}$

17. $9x^2 - y^4$ **18.** $a^6 - 27b^3c^3$ **19.** $x^3y^6 + 8m^{12}$

Simplify the expressions in problems 20–23.

20. $\dfrac{12!}{8!\,4!}$ **21.** $\dfrac{n(n!)}{(n+1)!}$ **22.** $\displaystyle\sum_{i=1}^{3} 4$ **23.** $\displaystyle\sum_{m=0}^{3} \dfrac{3^m}{m+1}$

24. Find the surface area of a sphere whose volume is $\dfrac{4}{3}\pi$ cubic meters.

25. Find the volume of a right circular cone whose base has an area of 4π square centimeters and whose height is 4 centimeters.

LESSON 2   *More Concept Review • The Graphing Calculator*

2.A

more concept review

We continue reviewing fundamental concepts.

example 2.1   Find the coordinates of the point halfway between $(-4, 7)$ and $(13, 5)$.

solution   The x-coordinate of the midpoint is the average of the x-coordinates, and the y-coordinate of the midpoint is the average of the y-coordinates.

$$x_m = \frac{-4+13}{2} = \frac{9}{2} \qquad y_m = \frac{7+5}{2} = 6$$

example 2.2   Find the distance between $(4, 3)$ and $(-2, -1)$.

solution   First we graph the points. The distance between the points is found by using the distance formula, which is an extension of the Pythagorean theorem. We arbitrarily choose point $(-2, -1)$ to be P_1 and $(4, 3)$ to be P_2.

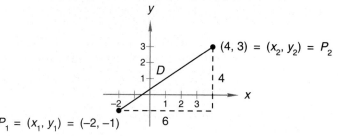

The distance between P_1 and P_2 is

$$\sqrt{(x_1 - x_2)^2 + (y_1 - y_2)^2} = \sqrt{(-2-4)^2 + (-1-3)^2}$$
$$= \sqrt{(-6)^2 + (-4)^2}$$
$$= \sqrt{52} = 2\sqrt{13}$$

example 2.3   Use the point-slope form of the equation of a line to write the slope-intercept form of the equation of the line that passes through $(-2, 4)$ and has a slope of $-\frac{2}{3}$.

solution   We begin with the point-slope form and substitute.

$$(y - y_1) = m(x - x_1)$$

point-slope form of a line where m is the slope and the line passes through point (x_1, y_1)

$$y - (4) = -\frac{2}{3}[x - (-2)]$$

substituted values for m, x_1, and y_1

$$3y - 12 = -2x - 4$$

simplified

$$y = -\frac{2}{3}x + \frac{8}{3}$$

rearranged to obtain the form $y = mx + b$

example 2.4   Write the slope-intercept form of the equation of the line through $(-4, 2)$ that is perpendicular to $-2x + 3y + 1 = 0$.

solution   First we find the slope of the given line. The slope of a line in general form, or $ax + by + c = 0$, is given by $-\frac{a}{b}$. Another way to find the slope is to rewrite the equation in slope-intercept form so that the coefficient of x is the slope.

$$y = \frac{2}{3}x - \frac{1}{3}$$

The line perpendicular to this line has a slope of $-\frac{3}{2}$ (the negative reciprocal of $\frac{2}{3}$). If we use $-\frac{3}{2}$ as the slope and use -4 and 2 for x and y, we can solve for b.

$$2 = -\frac{3}{2}(-4) + b$$

$$b = -4$$

Thus, the line that satisfies the conditions of the problem has the equation

$$y = -\frac{3}{2}x - 4$$

example 2.5   Solve $x^2 - 3x + 1 = 0$ by completing the square.

solution   We use six steps.

(1) $\qquad\qquad x^2 - 3x = -1$ $\qquad\qquad\qquad$ subtracted

(2) $\quad x^2 - 3x + \left(-\frac{3}{2}\right)^2 = -1 + \left(-\frac{3}{2}\right)^2$ $\qquad$ squared $\frac{1}{2}$ of the coefficient of the x-term and added that to both sides

(3) $\quad x^2 - 3x + \left(-\frac{3}{2}\right)^2 = \frac{5}{4}$ $\qquad\qquad$ simplified right-hand side

(4) $\qquad\quad \left(x - \frac{3}{2}\right)^2 = \frac{5}{4}$ $\qquad\qquad$ recognized left-hand side as the square of a binomial

(5) $\qquad\qquad x - \frac{3}{2} = \pm\frac{\sqrt{5}}{2}$ $\qquad\qquad$ difference of two squares theorem

(6) $\qquad\qquad\quad x = \frac{3}{2} \pm \frac{\sqrt{5}}{2}$ $\qquad\qquad$ solved for x

example 2.6   Solve $x^2 - 3x + 1 = 0$ by using the quadratic formula.

solution   The quadratic formula determines the values of x such that

$$ax^2 + bx + c = 0$$

The solutions of the quadratic equation shown above in terms of a, b, and c are

$$x = \frac{-b \pm \sqrt{b^2 - 4ac}}{2a}$$

In this example $a = 1$, $b = -3$, and $c = 1$. So the solutions to $x^2 - 3x + 1 = 0$ are

$$x = \frac{3 \pm \sqrt{9 - 4(1)(1)}}{2(1)}$$

Therefore, the values of x for which $x^2 - 3x + 1 = 0$ are

$$x = \frac{3 + \sqrt{5}}{2} \quad \text{and} \quad x = \frac{3 - \sqrt{5}}{2}$$

Note: These are the same answers obtained in example 2.5.

example 2.7   Divide $x^3 - y^3$ by $x - y$.

   solution

$$
\require{enclose}
\begin{array}{r}
x^2 + xy + y^2 \\
x - y \enclose{longdiv}{x^3 - y^3} \\
\underline{x^3 - x^2y} \\
x^2y \\
\underline{x^2y - xy^2} \\
xy^2 - y^3 \\
\underline{xy^2 - y^3} \\
\end{array}
$$

The answer is $x^2 + xy + y^2$.

example 2.8   Solve: $\begin{cases} x^2 + y^2 = 9 \\ y - x = 1 \end{cases}$

   solution   We solve the bottom equation for y, square both sides, and substitute for y^2 in the top equation.

$$y = x + 1 \qquad\qquad \text{solved bottom equation for } y$$
$$y^2 = x^2 + 2x + 1 \qquad\qquad \text{squared both sides}$$
$$x^2 + (x^2 + 2x + 1) = 9 \qquad\qquad \text{substituted for } y^2 \text{ in top equation}$$

Then we simplify and use the quadratic formula to solve for x.

$$x^2 + x - 4 = 0 \qquad\qquad \text{simplified}$$
$$x = \frac{-1 \pm \sqrt{1 - 4(1)(-4)}}{2} \qquad\qquad \text{used quadratic formula}$$
$$x = -\frac{1}{2} \pm \frac{\sqrt{17}}{2} \qquad\qquad \text{simplified}$$

We finish by substituting each of the values of x into the equation $y = x + 1$ to find the corresponding values of y.

$$y = \left(-\frac{1}{2} + \frac{\sqrt{17}}{2}\right) + 1 \qquad y = \left(-\frac{1}{2} - \frac{\sqrt{17}}{2}\right) + 1 \qquad \text{substituted}$$

$$y = \frac{1}{2} + \frac{\sqrt{17}}{2} \qquad\qquad y = \frac{1}{2} - \frac{\sqrt{17}}{2} \qquad\qquad \text{simplified}$$

Thus, the ordered pairs of x and y that satisfy the given system are

$$\left(-\frac{1}{2} + \frac{\sqrt{17}}{2}, \frac{1}{2} + \frac{\sqrt{17}}{2}\right) \quad \text{and} \quad \left(-\frac{1}{2} - \frac{\sqrt{17}}{2}, \frac{1}{2} - \frac{\sqrt{17}}{2}\right)$$

Some may recognize $x^2 + y^2 = 9$ as the equation of a circle of radius 3 centered at the origin. The equation $y - x = 1$ is the equation of a line. The values of x and y that satisfy both equations are the coordinates of the points of intersection between the circle and the line. However, to solve the problem as given does not require this knowledge. The figure below shows the graphs of the equations $x^2 + y^2 = 9$ (circle) and $y - x = 1$ (line). The two intersection points (indicated by dots) are the points whose coordinates satisfy both equations.

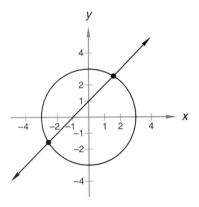

2.B

the graphing calculator

The graphing calculator, now widely used in the classroom, can be a powerful and useful tool for analyzing functions and their graphs. These handheld calculators can perform calculations and tasks that once required computers the size of a room.

A number of graphing calculators are available on the market. In this text we use the Texas Instruments TI-83 graphing calculator as our instructional tool. Although there are more powerful models, the TI-83 performs the functions needed for a precollege calculus course. We have selected the TI-83 from among several alternatives simply for ease of presentation.

One of the most powerful aspects of the graphing calculator is its ability to produce the graph of a function quickly and accurately. We demonstrate this with the polynomial function $f(x) = x^2 - 3x + 1$. Graphing a function almost always requires three keys. Below we show these keys and their corresponding actions.

Y=	opens the *function editor* screen
X,T,θ,n	inserts the independent variable
GRAPH	graphs the function

For the function $f(x) = x^2 - 3x + 1$, we press

to obtain the graph below.

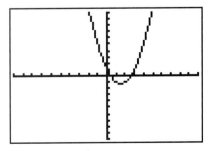

The appearance of the graph can be altered in two ways. The first is to change the window settings directly. This requires the WINDOW key, which opens the *window editor* screen, and the ◖, ◗, ▲, and ▼ keys, which are used to scroll through the list. We desire a better view of what the graph does near the origin. Thus we change the window settings as seen below on the left-hand side and press GRAPH to get the graph on the right-hand side.

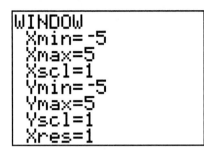
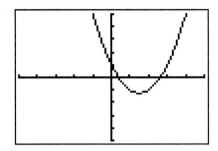

The second way to adjust the appearance of a graph is with the ZOOM menu. We press ZOOM to see the following:

Two useful options are 2:Zoom In and 3:Zoom Out. The former allows us to choose a portion of the graph to view more closely. The latter lets us select a point from which to pan away for a broader view. For now, we choose 5:ZSquare, which adjusts the WINDOW settings to get a uniform scale for the x- and y-axes. (This can be done either by scrolling down to 5:ZSquare and pressing ENTER or simply by pressing 5 .)

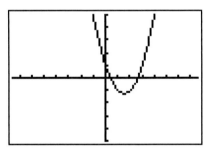

example 2.9   Use the graphing calculator to find the zeros of the polynomial function $f(x) = x^2 - 3x + 1$.

solution   This is the function graphed in the previous demonstration. To quickly obtain some of the points on the graph, we press the TRACE key. The rule for the function appears in the top left corner of the screen. The bottom portion of the screen contains x- and y-coordinates for the point of the graph marked by a small, flashing cursor (which looks like a small square). By using the left and right arrow keys, we move the cursor along the graph, and the displayed coordinates change accordingly. Moving the cursor so that it is near the zeros allows us to see that one zero is somewhere between 0.32 and 0.49, while the other is between 2.58 and 2.75.

To find better estimates, we utilize the CALCULATE feature, which gives numerical approximations for various aspects of functions. The following keys are needed:

                    implements the secondary role of the next key pressed

CALC
TRACE   displays the CALCULATE screen if preceded by 2nd †

---

†The secondary function of each key is listed above and to the left of the key. Note that the characters' color corresponds to the color of the 2nd key.

When we press these buttons in sequence, the following screen appears:

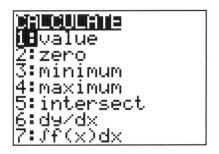

We press ❷ to select 2:zero, the feature that finds zeros of functions. The calculator prompts for a left bound (or lower bound) for *x*, so we move the cursor to the left of the lesser zero and press ENTER. Then the calculator asks for a right bound (or upper bound) for the zero, so we move the cursor to the right of the lesser zero (making sure not to move it beyond the other zero). Again, we press ENTER. Finally, the calculator asks for a guess. After moving the cursor nearer to the lessor zero, we press ENTER. The answer given is X=.38196601, Y=0. This means that if *x* = 0.38196601, then *y* is very near 0. (It may be that *y* = 0 when *x* = 0.38196601, but that is not certain.) We repeat the procedure to find that the larger zero is approximately 2.618034. We compare these answers with the numerical approximations of the exact answers found in examples 2.5 and 2.6.

$$\text{Larger zero: } x = \frac{3}{2} + \frac{\sqrt{5}}{2} \approx 2.618033989$$

$$\text{Smaller zero: } x = \frac{3}{2} - \frac{\sqrt{5}}{2} \approx 0.3819660113$$

Unless otherwise stated, we will give answers to four decimal places when estimating. When we round the numerical values of the answers in examples 2.5 and 2.6, we find that they are identical to the (rounded) graphing calculator answers found above.

zeros: $x \approx$ **0.3820** and **2.6180**

example 2.10   Use the graphing calculator to find the coordinates of the intersection points of the graphs of the functions $y = x^2 - 3x + 1$ and $y = x + 1$.

solution   We begin by defining the functions as Y1 and Y2 on the function editor screen:

$$Y_1 = X^2 - 3X + 1$$

$$Y_2 = X + 1$$

Pressing ZOOM 6 graphs the functions in the standard window. The CALCULATE menu is used to find intersection points. From this menu we select 5:intersect.

The calculator requires that one graph be designated as the first curve. Pressing ⌃ or ⌄ toggles between the two curves. We arbitrarily decide the parabola is the first curve and select it by pressing ENTER when the flashing cursor is on the parabola only. Similarly, we mark the line as the second curve. After designating the curve, the calculator requires a guess for the intersection point. It wants to know a point on the second curve near the intersection. We use the ◖ and ◗ keys to move the cursor near the leftmost intersection and press ENTER. The answer given is X=0, Y=1. After repeating the procedure for the other intersection, the calculator gives X=4, Y=5. Thus, as determined by the graphing calculator, the coordinates of the points of intersection are

(0, 1) and **(4, 5)**

We can easily check that the ordered pairs above represent the points of intersection by substituting *x*- and *y*-values of the coordinates of each intersection point (*x*, *y*) into the original equations to confirm that they satisfy both equations.

In this case the coordinates are integers. They could be determined algebraically without the graphing calculator. However, in some cases algebraically finding the exact values of the coordinates of the intersection points is difficult (if not impossible).

problem set
2

†
1. Find the distance from the midpoint of the segment joining $(4, 2)$ and $(10, -2)$ to the point $(6, 8)$.
$_{(2)}$

2. Find: y
$_{(R)}$

3. Write the linear equation whose general
$_{(2)}$ form is $2x - 3y + 2 = 0$ in the slope-intercept form $y = mx + b$.

4. Find the equation of the line that is perpendicular to the line $4y + 3x - 2 = 0$ and that passes
$_{(2)}$ through the point $(1, -1)$.

Solve the equations in problems 5 and 6 by completing the square.

5. $x^2 - 3x - 4 = 0$
$_{(2)}$

6. $2x^2 = x + 3$
$_{(2)}$

7. Solve $3x^2 - x - 7 = 0$ by using the quadratic formula.
$_{(2)}$

8. Divide $2x^3 - 3x + 5$ by $x - 3$.
$_{(2)}$

9. Solve: $\begin{cases} xy = -4 \\ y = -x - 2 \end{cases}$
$_{(2)}$

10. Use a graphing calculator to approximate the value(s) of x where the graph of the parabola
$_{(2)}$ $y = x^2 + 3x - 1$ crosses the x-axis.

11. Use a graphing calculator to approximate the value(s) of x where the graph of the cubic
$_{(2)}$ function $y = x^3 + 3x^2 - 3$ crosses the x-axis.

12. Use a graphing calculator to approximate the coordinates of the intersection point(s) of the
$_{(2)}$ graphs of $y = x^2 - 3x + 1$ and $y = x^3 + 3x^2 - 3$.

13. Solve for x: $k^2 = \dfrac{1}{bc}\left(\dfrac{x}{3} - \dfrac{6y}{d}\right)$
$_{(1)}$

Simplify the expressions in problems 14–17.

14. $\dfrac{ax}{b + \dfrac{c}{d + \dfrac{m}{t}}}$
$_{(1)}$

15. $3\sqrt{\dfrac{2}{5}} - 4\sqrt{\dfrac{5}{2}} + 3\sqrt{40}$
$_{(1)}$

16. $\dfrac{y^{a-2}z^{4a}}{y^{-2a-1}z^{a/3+2}}$
$_{(1)}$

17. $\sqrt{x^3y^3}\,y^{1/3}x^{2/3}$
$_{(1)}$

18. Solve: $\begin{cases} x + y + z = 4 \\ 2x - y - z = -1 \\ x - y + z = 0 \end{cases}$
$_{(R)}$

Factor the expressions in problems 19 and 20.

19. $14x^{4b-2} - 7x^{2b}$
$_{(1)}$

20. $x^3y^6 - 8x^6y^{12}$
$_{(1)}$

Simplify the expressions in problems 21–23.

21. $\dfrac{n!}{(n-1)!}$
$_{(1)}$

22. $\displaystyle\sum_{n=1}^{3}(n^2 - 2)$
$_{(1)}$

23. $\displaystyle\sum_{j=-2}^{1}\dfrac{2j-3}{3}$
$_{(1)}$

24. Find the volume of a trough 5 meters long whose ends are equilateral triangles, each of whose
$_{(R)}$ sides has a length of 2 meters.

25. Given that $x^2 = y^2$, compare: A. x B. y
$_{(1)}$

---

†The italicized numbers within parentheses below each problem number refer to the lesson in which the concepts
for that problem are discussed. Review problems are indicated with an R.

LESSON 3 *The Contrapositive • The Converse and Inverse • Iff Statements*

3.A
the contrapositive

Often in mathematics we make if-then statements, which are called **conditionals.** The following are examples:

- If quadrilateral *ABCD* is a square, then quadrilateral *ABCD* is a rectangle.
- If *f* is a polynomial function, then *f* is a continuous function.

The same exact statements can be made another way by turning the statements around and using negatives. The alternative statement is called a **contrapositive.** Two steps are necessary to form the contrapositive. The first step is to negate both the *if* statement and the *then* statement. The second step is to reverse the order of the resulting statements so that the *if* portion becomes the *then* portion and the *then* portion becomes the *if* portion.

If a conditional statement is true, then its contrapositive is also true. If a conditional is false, its contrapositive is also false. A conditional statement and its contrapositive are said to be **equivalent statements.** In other words, **a conditional statement and its contrapositive are different ways of saying the same thing.**

example 3.1 Write the contrapositive of each of the two previous examples.

solution To write the contrapositive of an if-then statement, we must first negate each part of the statement.

"If quadrilateral *ABCD* is not a square"
"then quadrilateral *ABCD* is not a rectangle."

We now reverse the order of the *if* and *then* statements, changing the *if* statement to a *then* statement and the *then* statement to an *if* statement:

If quadrilateral *ABCD* is not a rectangle,
then quadrilateral *ABCD* is not a square.

We do the same thing for the second statement.

If *f* is not a continuous function,
then *f* is not a polynomial function.

example 3.2 The following conditional statement is true:

If function *f* is differentiable at point *P*,
then function *f* is continuous at point *P*.

Make an equivalent statement that is true.

solution The contrapositive of a conditional statement is equivalent to the conditional statement. Without worrying about what the conditional statement means, we simply form its contrapositive.

If function *f* is not continuous at point *P*,
then function *f* is not differentiable at point *P*.

example 3.3 State the contrapositive of the following conditional:

If *x* is a rational number,
then *x* is an irrational number.

solution From Lesson 1, we know this conditional is false, but that is not important here. We only worry about writing its contrapositive.

If *x* is not an irrational number,
then *x* is not a rational number.

This statement is equivalent to the previous conditional, and, like the first, it is also false.

3.B
the converse and inverse

In the previous section we learned how to write the contrapositive of a conditional statement. We also learned that a conditional statement and its contrapositive are equivalent. Therefore, if a conditional statement is true, its contrapositive is also true; also, if the contrapositive of a conditional statement is true, the conditional statement itself is true.

In this section we learn how to write the **converse** and **inverse** of a conditional statement. The converse of a conditional statement can simply be obtained by reversing the order of the *if* and *then* statements of a conditional statement. In other words, the converse can be obtained by making the *if* statement a *then* statement and the *then* statement an *if* statement. To get the inverse of a conditional statement requires negating both the *if* and the *then* statements.

When we try to find the contrapositive of the converse of a statement, we get the inverse of the statement. Since a conditional statement and its contrapositive are equivalent, **the converse and inverse of a conditional statement are equivalent.** Therefore, if the converse of a conditional statement is true (false), then the inverse of the conditional statement is also true (false).

example 3.4   Write the converse of the statement

> "If quadrilateral *ABCD* is a square,
>
> then quadrilateral *ABCD* is a rectangle."

solution   We write the converse of the statement by reversing the *if* and *then* statements.

> **If quadrilateral *ABCD* is a rectangle,**
>
> **then quadrilateral *ABCD* is a square.**

We see from this example that **the converse of a true conditional statement is not necessarily true.**

example 3.5   Write the inverse of the original conditional statement in example 3.4.

solution   We write the inverse of a conditional statement by negating the *if* and *then* portions of the statement.

> **If quadrilateral *ABCD* is not a square,**
>
> **then quadrilateral *ABCD* is not a rectangle.**

Another way to obtain the inverse of the original conditional statement is to find the contrapositive of its converse. Taking the answer from example 3.4 we see that the first step in finding the contrapositive negates the components of the original statement. The second step undoes finding the converse. Since the converse of the conditional statement is false, the inverse of the conditional statement is also false.

3.C
iff statements

In the previous section we learned that the converse of a true conditional statement is not necessarily true. There are instances, however, when both a statement and its converse are true. In such instances, the shorthand word *iff,* read "if and only if," can be used to write a single statement expressing both the statement and its converse together. For example, the following conditional statement about $\triangle ABC$ and its converse are true.

Statement: If $m\angle A = m\angle B$, then $BC = AC$.

Converse: If $BC = AC$, then $m\angle A = m\angle B$.

We can reduce these two statements to one statement by using *iff:*

$$m\angle A = m\angle B \text{ iff } BC = AC$$

The statement above can be written in words as:

> Two angles of a triangle are equal in measure if and only if the sides opposite these two angles are equal in length.

example 3.6   Use *iff* to express both conditional statements in one sentence.

> If a triangle is equilateral, then it is equiangular.
>
> If a triangle is equiangular, then it is equilateral.

solution   We combine both these statements using "iff."

> **A triangle is equilateral iff the triangle is equiangular.**

We could have also written:

> A triangle is equiangular iff the triangle is equilateral.

problem set 3

1. State the converse of the following conditional statement:
(3)
> If the light is on, then the switch is on.

2. State the inverse of the following conditional statement:
(3)
> If the light is on, then the switch is on.

3. State the contrapositive of the following conditional statement:
(3)
> If the light is on, then the switch is on.

4. The following conditional statement is true:
(3)
> If x is a real number, then x is a complex number.

Make an equivalent statement that is true.

5. Write the slope-intercept form of the equation of the line that passes through the point $(2, 2)$ and
(2) is perpendicular to the line $2y - x - 1 = 0$.

6. Complete the square to rewrite $x^2 = -6x - 13$ in the form $(x + a)^2 + b = 0$, where a and
(2) b are constants.

7. Use the quadratic formula to find all the values of x that make $x^2 - 3x - 7$ equal zero.
(2)

8. Solve: $\begin{cases} 2y^2 - x^2 = 1 \\ y + 1 = x \end{cases}$
(2)

9. Divide $x^3 - 13x^2 + 10x - 8$ by $x - 1$.
(R)

9. Divide $x^3 - 13x^2 + 10x - 8$ by $x - 1$.
(2)

10. Use a graphing calculator to approximate the zero(s) of the function
(2) $f(x) = x^3 - 3x^2 - 3x + 1$.

11. Use a graphing calculator to approximate the coordinates of the intersection point(s) of the
(2) graphs of the functions $f(x) = x^3 - 3x^2 - 3x + 1$ and $g(x) = x - 1$.

12. Solve for R_1: $\dfrac{m + b}{c} = \dfrac{1}{k}\left(\dfrac{a}{R_1} + \dfrac{b}{R_2}\right)$
(1)

Simplify the expressions in problems 13–17.

13. $\dfrac{4 - 2\sqrt{3}}{2 - \sqrt{3}}$
(1)

14. $5\sqrt{\dfrac{3}{7}} - 2\sqrt{\dfrac{7}{3}} + \sqrt{84}$
(1)

15. $\sqrt{x^3 y^5}\, y^{1/4} x^{3/2}$
(1)

16. $\dfrac{1}{1 + \dfrac{1}{1 + \dfrac{1}{1 + \dfrac{1}{2}}}}$
(1)

17. $\dfrac{m}{x + \dfrac{p}{1 - \dfrac{y}{m}}}$
(1)

Factor the expressions in problems 18 and 19.

18. $a^3b^3 - 8x^6y^9$
(I)

19. $2x^3 + 3x^2 - 2x$
(R)

Simplify the expressions in problems 20–23.

20. $\displaystyle\sum_{j=1}^{4}(j^2 - 2j)$
(I)

21. $\dfrac{41!}{38!\,3!}$
(I)

22. $\dfrac{a^2 - b^2}{a + b}$
(R)

23. $\dfrac{n!\,(n + 1)!}{(n + 2)!}$
(I)

24. An inverted right circular cone is partially
(R) filled with liquid as shown. What is the volume of the liquid if the diameter of the base of the cone is 4 cm, the height of the cone is 6 cm, and the depth of the liquid is 2 cm?

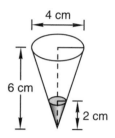

25. Assuming $x > y$ and neither x nor y equals 0, compare the following: A. $\dfrac{1}{x}$ B. $\dfrac{1}{y}$
(I)

LESSON 4   *Radian Measure of Angles • Trigonometric Ratios • Four Quadrant Signs • Simplifying Trigonometric Expressions*

4.A
radian measure of angles

If an arc of a circle has the same length as a radius of the circle, the central angle is said to measure 1 radian.

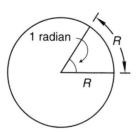

Arc length = 1 radius

The relationship between arc length and central angle is given by $s = \theta R$ where s is the arc length, θ is the measure of the central angle in radians, and R is the radius of the circle. The arc length of a full circle equals the circumference, so $s = 2\pi R = \theta R$. Thus $\theta = 2\pi$, which means the central angle measures 2π radians. Since we already know that the central angle of a circle measures $360°$, we can create the following unit multipliers for degree-to-radian conversion and radian-to-degree conversion:

$$\frac{\pi \text{ radians}}{180 \text{ degrees}} \quad \text{and} \quad \frac{180 \text{ degrees}}{\pi \text{ radians}}$$

example 4.1   Convert 40° to radian measure. Express the answer to four decimal places.

solution   We use the unit multiplier

$$\frac{\pi \text{ radians}}{180 \text{ degrees}}$$

Since π radians equals 180 degrees, the value of this fraction is 1. Any number multiplied by it equals itself. Unit multipliers are useful because they allow one quantity expressed in terms of a certain unit to be converted to another unit of measure.

$$40° = 40 \text{ degrees} \cdot \frac{\pi \text{ radians}}{180 \text{ degrees}} = \frac{(40 \text{ degrees})(\pi \text{ radians})}{180 \text{ degrees}}$$

Cancelling the degrees from both numerator and denominator, we get

$$40° = \frac{40\pi \text{ radians}}{180} \approx \mathbf{0.6981 \text{ radians}}$$

Note that we did not use the approximation 3.14 for π. Instead we used the value stored in the calculator. If we had used 3.14, our final answer would not be accurate to four decimal places.

Radians are the preferred unit of measure in calculus because radians are considered "unitless." When we say "sin 3.2" we mean the value of the sine function at 3.2 radians, not at 3.2 degrees. If no unit is specified, the unit of measure is assumed to be radians.

4.B
trigonometric ratios

Most people find a mnemonic helpful in remembering the definitions of the trigonometric ratios that we call the **sine, cosine,** and **tangent.** The letters that make up the mnemonic **Soh Cah Toa** can be used to help remember the definitions shown here.

$$\text{Sine} = \frac{\textbf{O}\text{pposite}}{\textbf{H}\text{ypotenuse}} \qquad \text{Cosine} = \frac{\textbf{A}\text{djacent}}{\textbf{H}\text{ypotenuse}} \qquad \text{Tangent} = \frac{\textbf{O}\text{pposite}}{\textbf{A}\text{djacent}}$$

$$\sin \theta = \frac{a}{c} \qquad \cos \theta = \frac{b}{c} \qquad \tan \theta = \frac{a}{b}$$

The tangent of an angle can also be expressed in terms of the sine of the angle and the cosine of the angle.

$$\tan \theta = \frac{\sin \theta}{\cos \theta}$$

The reciprocal functions of the sine, cosine, and tangent are the **cosecant, secant,** and **cotangent** respectively, as shown here:

$$\csc \theta = \frac{1}{\sin \theta} \qquad \sec \theta = \frac{1}{\cos \theta} \qquad \cot \theta = \frac{1}{\tan \theta}$$

Mathematics books often evaluate the trigonometric functions at $\frac{\pi}{3}$, $\frac{\pi}{4}$, and $\frac{\pi}{6}$ (60°, 45°, and 30° respectively), because the exact values of the functions at these angles can be determined quickly by using the two right triangles shown here:

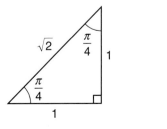 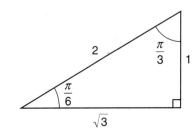

example 4.2   Evaluate: $\sin^2 \dfrac{\pi}{3} - \tan \dfrac{\pi}{4} + \cos \dfrac{\pi}{6}$

solution   We use the triangles to find $\sin^2 \dfrac{\pi}{3}$, $\tan \dfrac{\pi}{4}$, and $\cos \dfrac{\pi}{6}$.

$$\sin^2 \frac{\pi}{3} - \tan \frac{\pi}{4} + \cos \frac{\pi}{6} = \left(\frac{\sqrt{3}}{2}\right)^2 - 1 + \frac{\sqrt{3}}{2} \qquad \text{substituted}$$

$$= \frac{3}{4} - 1 + \frac{\sqrt{3}}{2} \qquad \text{squared}$$

$$= -\frac{1}{4} + \frac{\sqrt{3}}{2} \qquad \text{simplified}$$

$$= \frac{-1 + 2\sqrt{3}}{4} \qquad \text{added}$$

example 4.3   Evaluate: $\sec 30° + \csc \dfrac{\pi}{6}$

solution   We begin by rewriting $\sec 30°$ and $\csc \dfrac{\pi}{6}$ in terms of sine and cosine.

$$\sec 30° = \frac{1}{\cos 30°}, \quad \csc \frac{\pi}{6} = \frac{1}{\sin \dfrac{\pi}{6}} \qquad \text{definitions}$$

$$\sec 30° + \csc \frac{\pi}{6} = \frac{1}{\dfrac{\sqrt{3}}{2}} + \frac{1}{\dfrac{1}{2}} \qquad \text{substituted}$$

$$= \frac{2}{\sqrt{3}} + 2 \qquad \text{simplified}$$

$$= \frac{2\sqrt{3}}{3} + 2 \qquad \text{rationalized}$$

$$= \frac{2\sqrt{3} + 6}{3} \qquad \text{added}$$

4.C
four quadrant signs

The signs of the trigonometric functions of an angle in the first quadrant are all positive. The signs of these functions in the other three quadrants can be determined by drawing triangles in each of the quadrants as we show below. The hypotenuse is always positive.

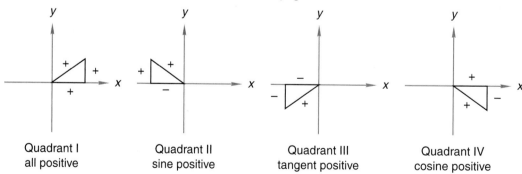

Quadrant I   Quadrant II   Quadrant III   Quadrant IV
all positive   sine positive   tangent positive   cosine positive

The three basic trigonometric functions are positive in the first quadrant, and only one of these functions is positive in each of the other three quadrants. The first letters of the sentence

All Students Take Calculus

can be used to help remember that **A**ll three functions are positive in the first quadrant, the **S**ine is positive in the second quadrant, the **T**angent is positive in the third quadrant, and the **C**osine is positive in the fourth quadrant.

example 4.4   Evaluate: $2 \sin \dfrac{19\pi}{6} + 3 \sin -\dfrac{4\pi}{3}$

solution   Functions of angles greater than 360° or 2π radians can be reduced to functions of angles less than 360° or 2π radians by subtracting multiples of 360° or 2π from the angle. We begin by subtracting 2π from $\frac{19\pi}{6}$ to get an equivalent angle that is less than 2π. The result is $\frac{7\pi}{6}$. Then we draw two diagrams.

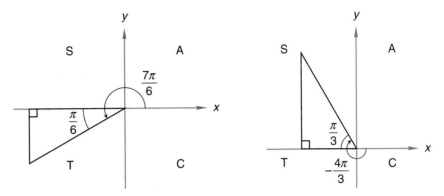

The sine is negative in the third quadrant, so $\sin \frac{7\pi}{6}$ equals $-\sin \frac{\pi}{6}$. The sine is positive in the second quadrant, so $\sin -\frac{4\pi}{3}$ equals $\sin \frac{\pi}{3}$. Thus, we have

$$2 \sin \frac{19\pi}{6} + 3 \sin -\frac{4\pi}{3} = 2\left(-\sin \frac{\pi}{6}\right) + 3 \sin \frac{\pi}{3} \qquad \text{simplified argument}$$

$$= 2\left(-\frac{1}{2}\right) + 3\left(\frac{\sqrt{3}}{2}\right) \qquad \text{evaluated}$$

$$= \frac{-2 + 3\sqrt{3}}{2} \qquad \text{added}$$

example 4.5   Evaluate: $4 \tan -\dfrac{11\pi}{6} + 2 \sec -\dfrac{\pi}{4}$

solution   We begin by drawing the necessary diagrams.

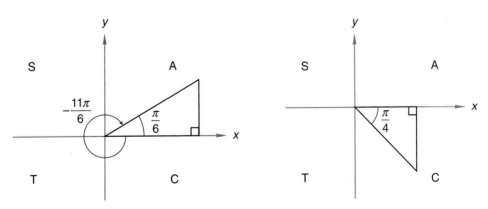

The tangent is positive in the first quadrant, so $\tan -\frac{11\pi}{6}$ equals $\tan \frac{\pi}{6}$. The cosine is positive in the fourth quadrant, so the secant is also positive. Thus $\sec -\frac{\pi}{4}$ equals $\sec \frac{\pi}{4}$. So we have

$$4 \tan -\frac{11\pi}{6} + 2 \sec -\frac{\pi}{4} = 4\left(\frac{1}{\sqrt{3}}\right) + \frac{2}{\dfrac{1}{\sqrt{2}}} = \frac{4\sqrt{3}}{3} + 2\sqrt{2} = \frac{4\sqrt{3} + 6\sqrt{2}}{3}$$

4.D

simplifying trigonometric expressions

Many trigonometric expressions can be simplified if we remember that $\tan \theta$ is the ratio of $\sin \theta$ to $\cos \theta$ and that $\cot \theta$, $\sec \theta$, and $\csc \theta$ are the reciprocals of $\tan \theta$, $\cos \theta$, and $\sin \theta$ respectively.

example 4.6   Simplify: $(\cos^2 \theta)(\sec \theta)(\tan \theta)$

solution   We remember that $\cos^2 \theta$ means $(\cos \theta)^2$, not $\cos (\theta^2)$. The function $\sec \theta$ is the reciprocal of $\cos \theta$, and $\tan \theta$ equals $\sin \theta$ divided by $\cos \theta$. Thus, we substitute and get

$$\cancel{(\cos^2 \theta)}\left(\frac{1}{\cancel{\cos \theta}}\right)\left(\frac{\sin \theta}{\cancel{\cos \theta}}\right) = \sin \theta$$

example 4.7   Simplify: $\dfrac{\cot \theta \cos \theta}{\csc \theta}$

solution   We substitute equivalent expressions for $\cot \theta$ and $\csc \theta$ and get $\cos^2 \theta$ as our answer.

$$\frac{\left(\dfrac{\cos \theta}{\sin \theta}\right)\left(\dfrac{\cos \theta}{1}\right)}{\dfrac{1}{\sin \theta}} = \cos^2 \theta$$

problem set 4

1.   Use a graphing calculator to approximate the x-intercept(s) of the graph of the function
(2) $f(x) = x^4 + 2x^3 - 3x^2 - 4x - 1$.

2.   Use a graphing calculator to approximate the coordinates of the intersection point(s) of the
(2)   graphs of $y = x - 1$ and $y = x^4 + 2x^3 - 3x^2 - 4x - 1$.

Evaluate the expressions in problems 3–6.

3. $\cos^2 \dfrac{\pi}{3} - \cot \dfrac{\pi}{4} + \sin \dfrac{\pi}{6}$
(4)

4. $\sec 60° + \csc^2 \dfrac{\pi}{3}$
(4)

5. $3 \cos \dfrac{17\pi}{6} + 2 \cos -\dfrac{5\pi}{3}$
(4)

6. $4 \tan -\dfrac{3\pi}{4} + \sin -\dfrac{\pi}{4}$
(4)

Simplify the expressions in problems 7 and 8.

7. $(\sin^2 \theta)(\csc \theta)(\cot \theta)$
(4)

8. $\dfrac{\tan \theta \sin \theta}{\sec \theta}$
(4)

9.   Write the contrapositive of the following conditional statement:
(3)
             A function is not one-to-one if it is both increasing and decreasing.

10.   State the contrapositive, converse, and inverse of the following conditional:
(3)
             If you hit your thumb with a hammer, then your thumb hurts.

11.   Write the point-slope form and the general form of the equation of the line that is parallel to the
(2)   line $\frac{x}{3} + 2 = -3y$ and passes through the point $(-9, -3)$.

12.   Factor to find the values of x that satisfy the equation $-2x^2 = 7x - 15$.
(2)

13.   Solve $x^2 + x = 1$ by using the quadratic formula.
(2)

14.   Multiply $3x^2 - 4x + 5$ by $2x - 1$.
(R)

15.   Using algebra, find the ordered pairs of x and y that satisfy both the equation $x^2 + y^2 = 8$ and
(2)   the equation $x + y = 0$.

16. Solve for r: $\dfrac{1}{r} = v\left(\dfrac{1}{r_1} + \dfrac{1}{r_2}\right)$
(1)

Simplify the expressions in problems 17–21.

17. $\dfrac{(n-1)!\,n!}{(n-2)!}$
(1)

18. $5\sqrt{\dfrac{1}{5}} - 3\sqrt{5} + \sqrt{50}$
(1)

19. $\dfrac{x^3 - y^3}{x^2 + xy + y^2}$
(1)

20. $\displaystyle\sum_{i=-1}^{1} (2^i + i)$
(1)

21. $\dfrac{1}{1 + \dfrac{1}{1 + \dfrac{1}{3}}}$
(1)

22. Find the surface area of a rectangular solid whose height is h, whose width is w, and whose
(R) length is L.

23. An isosceles triangle is situated in the xy-plane so that the vertices of its base are the origin and
(R) the point $(10, 0)$. If the height of the triangle is half the length of the base of the triangle, what are
the coordinates of its third vertex? You may assume the missing vertex is in the first quadrant.

24. Let x be a positive real number. Compare: A. x B. x^{10}
(1)

25. In $\triangle ABC$, $AB = BC$. Compare:
(1)
   A. x B. y

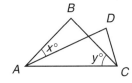

LESSON 5 *Word Problem Review*

In this lesson we present a variety of word problems similar to those that arise later. We have found
that many students have difficulty solving word problems that require calculus. Their struggles are
often not with the calculus required to solve the problems, but with the mechanics and algebra of
setting up the problems. Therefore, we practice this skill in a variety of problems whose solutions are
not dependent on calculus in preparation for solving similar problems that do require calculus.

example 5.1   Boyle's Law says that if the temperature of a quantity of ideal gas is unchanged, the product of the
pressure and the volume equals a constant k. When there are 1000 m^3 of a particular ideal gas, the
pressure is $5\ \frac{\text{N}}{\text{m}^2}$. What would the pressure be if the volume were 200 m^3, assuming the temperature is
the same?

solution   We begin by designating variables P and V for pressure and volume. Boyle's Law says that if
temperature is constant, then

$$PV = k$$

The problem tells us that for a given temperature, 1000 m^3 of the gas has a pressure of $5\ \frac{\text{N}}{\text{m}^2}$. We can
solve for k:

$$\left(5\ \frac{\text{N}}{\text{m}^2}\right)(1000\ \text{m}^3) = k \qquad \text{substitution}$$

$$5000\ \text{N}\cdot\text{m} = k \qquad \text{simplification}$$

Using this value of *k,* we can find the pressure when the volume is 200 m³.

$$PV = 5000 \text{ N} \cdot \text{m}$$
$$P(200 \text{ m}^3) = 5000 \text{ N} \cdot \text{m} \qquad \text{substitution}$$
$$P = \frac{5000 \text{ N} \cdot \text{m}}{200 \text{ m}^3} \qquad \text{solved for } P$$
$$P = \mathbf{25} \, \frac{\mathbf{N}}{\mathbf{m}^2} \qquad \text{simplified}$$

Thus, when the volume is 200 m³, the pressure is $25 \, \dfrac{\text{N}}{\text{m}^2}$.

example 5.2   Dagney and Lael found that the cost varied directly with the number who worked and inversely with the Sabercat index. The cost was $400 when 5 people worked and the index was 8. What was the cost when 13 people worked and the index was 2?

solution   This problem allows us practice with variation relationships whose equations contain variables and a constant of proportionality. Let *W* represent the number of workers, *S* represent the Sabercat index, and *k* be the constant of proportionality. Then

$$\text{Cost} = \frac{kW}{S}$$

This is a three-step problem. The first step is to find *k*.

$$400 = \frac{k5}{8} \qquad \text{substituted}$$
$$k = 640 \qquad \text{solved for } k$$

The second step is to substitute for *k* in the equation.

$$\text{Cost} = \frac{640W}{S} \qquad \text{substituted}$$

The last step is to substitute for *W* and *S*.

$$\text{Cost} = \frac{(640)(13)}{2} = \mathbf{\$4160}$$

example 5.3   The cost varied linearly with the number of workers. When there were 10 workers, the cost was $70. When there were 20 workers, the cost was $120. What was the cost when there were only 2 workers?

solution   The words *varied linearly* tell us that the equation is a linear equation.

$$\text{Cost} = mW + b$$

We have two unknowns, so we need two equations. We get one equation by using 70 for cost and 10 for *W* and get the other equation by using 120 for cost and 20 for *W*. Then we solve this system of equations.

$$\begin{array}{rcl} 70 = m(10) + b & \longrightarrow & 140 = 20m + 2b \\ 120 = m(20) + b & \longrightarrow & \underline{-120 = -20m - b} \\ & & 20 = b \qquad \text{solved for } b \end{array}$$

We let $b = 20$ in the first equation to solve for *m*.

$$70 = m(10) + 20 \qquad \text{substituted}$$
$$m = 5 \qquad \text{solved}$$

Finally we have the linear equation.

$$\text{Cost} = 5W + 20$$

By substituting, we find that when there were 2 workers, the cost was $30.

$$\text{Cost} = 5(2) + 20 = \mathbf{\$30}$$

example 5.4   Farmer Jill wants to use 100 meters of fence to enclose a rectangular region that borders a river. If L is the length of the side of fence parallel to the river, what is the area of the fenced region in terms of L? (Assume the river's border is straight and no fence is needed along the river.)

solution   We begin by drawing a picture of the problem and show all the information in the problem. We choose the letter W to denote the width of the region.

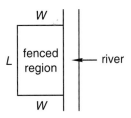

The total amount of fencing used is 100 meters. Therefore,

$$L + 2W = 100 \qquad (1)$$

The area of the fenced region is simply LW:

$$A = LW$$

Since we want A in terms of L only, we solve equation (1) for W.

$$L + 2W = 100$$

$$W = \frac{100 - L}{2} = 50 - \frac{1}{2}L \qquad \text{solved for } W$$

By substitution we get

$$A = L\left(50 - \frac{1}{2}L\right)$$

$$= 50L - \frac{1}{2}L^2$$

problem set 5

1. The time necessary to complete a project varies inversely with the number of engineers who
   (5) work on the project and directly with the amount of money invested. When 2 engineers work and $1000 is invested, the project takes 5 days. How many days will it take to complete the project if 3 engineers work and $3000 is invested?

2. The cost of a Jimmy Built building varies linearly with the number of floors the building has. If
   (5) a 10-story Jimmy Built building costs $12 million and a 4-story Jimmy Built building costs $6 million, how much does a 7-story Jimmy Built building cost?

3. Michelle wants to enclose a rectangular region that borders a river. The region to be enclosed
   (5) must have an area of 100 m². If L is the length of the side of the rectangular region that is parallel to the river, how much fence must be used in terms of L? (Assume the riverbank is straight and no fence is needed along the river.)

4. Use a graphing calculator to approximate the root(s) of the function $f(x) = x^3 - 2x^2 + x + 1$.
   (2)

5. Use a graphing calculator to approximate the coordinates of the intersection point(s) of the
   (2) graphs of the functions $f(x) = x^3 - 2x^2 + x + 1$ and $g(x) = x^2 - 2$.

6. Express 50° in radian measure to four decimal places.
   (4)

Evaluate the expressions in problems 7–9.

7. $2\cos\left(-\dfrac{5\pi}{4}\right) - \sec\dfrac{\pi}{4}$
(4)

8. $\tan^2\dfrac{\pi}{3} - \cot^2\dfrac{\pi}{3}$
(4)

9. $\sin^2\left(-\dfrac{2\pi}{3}\right) - \csc\left(-\dfrac{\pi}{2}\right)$
(4)

Simplify the expressions in problems 10 and 11.

10. $(\sin^2 x)(\csc x)(\cos x)$
(4)

11. $\dfrac{\cos\alpha\,\sec\alpha}{\csc\alpha}$
(4)

12. State the contrapositive of the following conditional statement:
(3)

> If the polygon is a triangle, then the polygon has four sides.

13. Use the quadratic formula to find the values of x for which the value of the polynomial
(2) $2x^2 - 3x + 1$ is zero.

14. Write the general form of the equation of the line that is parallel to the y-axis and passes through
(2) the point $(2, 3)$.

15. Solve algebraically: $\begin{cases} y = x^2 + 1 \\ y - 2x = 0 \end{cases}$
(2)

16. Given that $x^2 = \sqrt{y + 1}$, solve for y in terms of x.
(1)

Simplify the expressions in problems 17–21.

17. $\dfrac{x^3 - a^3}{x - a}$
(1)

18. $\dfrac{\sqrt{3} + \sqrt{2}}{\sqrt{3} - \sqrt{2}}$
(1)

19. $\dfrac{4}{m + \dfrac{a}{x - 1}}$
(1)

20. $\dfrac{18!}{16!\,2!}$
(1)

21. $\displaystyle\sum_{n=1}^{4}\left((-2)^n + 1\right)$
(1)

22. Find the total surface area of a right circular cone whose volume is 12π cm³ and whose base has
(R) an area of 9π cm².

23. Find the distance between the point $(3, -4)$ and the line $y = -\frac{4}{3}x + \frac{25}{3}$ using the
(2) following steps:

(a) Find the slope of the line perpendicular to $y = -\frac{4}{3}x + \frac{25}{3}$.

(b) Find the equation of the line through the point $(3, -4)$ that is perpendicular to the line $y = -\frac{4}{3}x + \frac{25}{3}$.

(c) Find the intersection point of the line found in (b) and the line $y = -\frac{4}{3}x + \frac{25}{3}$.

(d) Find the distance between the point found in (c) and the point $(3, -4)$.

24. An isosceles triangle is situated in the xy-plane so that the vertices of its base are the origin and
(2) the point $(8, 6)$. If the height of the triangle is half the length of the base of the triangle, what are the coordinates of the third vertex of the isosceles triangle? You may assume the missing vertex is in the first quadrant.

25. Assuming x and y are both less than zero and $x < y$, compare: A. $-x$ B. $-y$
(1)

LESSON 6   *Functions: Their Equations and Graphs • Functional Notation • Domain and Range*

6.A

functions: their equations and graphs

Modern mathematicians have found that a process that produces exactly one answer for each value chosen for the input is extremely useful, and they use the word **function** to describe any process that does this. Thus, an equation is not necessary. All that is needed is a rule that tells: (1) what numbers can be used and (2) how to find the answer for each number. The rule allows us to match each member of a specified set, called the **domain** (the input values), with exactly one member of a second set, called the **range** (the output values). The individual members of the range are called the **images.** A function **maps** each member of the domain to exactly one member of the range.

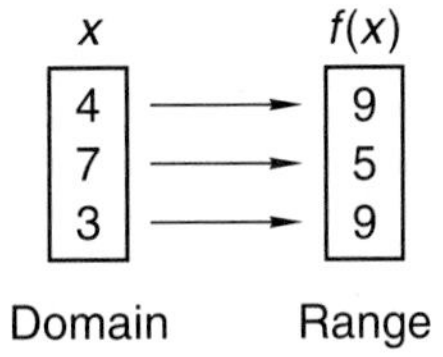

$$
\begin{array}{ccc}
x & & f(x) \\
\boxed{\begin{array}{c} 4 \\ 7 \\ 3 \end{array}} & \longrightarrow & \boxed{\begin{array}{c} 9 \\ 5 \\ 9 \end{array}} \\
\text{Domain} & & \text{Range}
\end{array}
$$

The diagram shows that if x is 4, the image (answer) is 9. If x is 7, the image is 5, and if x is 3, the image is 9. Since we have exactly one image for each value of x, we have a function. The image for both 4 and 3 is 9, but since 4 has only one image and 3 has only one image, the requirement that each member of the domain have exactly one image is satisfied. In this example we used a diagram rather than an equation to specify the images. The only values of x that can be used are 4, 7, and 3, because in this example it was arbitrarily decided that the domain would contain only these three numbers.

The rule for a function may also be stated by a list of ordered pairs such that every first member is paired with exactly one second member. The following set of ordered pairs defines a **relation** but does not define a function:

$$(4, 3), \ (5, 7), \ (9, 3), \ (4, -5), \ (8, 14), \ (6, -3)$$

This is not a function because the first and the fourth pairs have different images for 4. The following set of ordered pairs *does* define a function:

$$(4, 3), \ (5, 7), \ (9, 3), \ (4, 3), \ (8, 14), \ (6, -3)$$

Even though there are two 4's, they both map to 3, which means this can still be a function.

In this book we concentrate almost exclusively on functions whose rules can be written as equations. Note, however, that a function is defined by an equation, but a function is not the equation itself. As an alternative to the standard function notation, a colon and an arrow can indicate the pairing or mapping.

$$
\begin{array}{ll}
f(x) = x^2 + 4 & f: x \longrightarrow x^2 + 4 \\
g(x) = x^3 - 2x + 1 & g: x \longrightarrow x^3 - 2x + 1
\end{array}
$$

The f function rule is that x maps to $x^2 + 4$, and the g function rule is that x maps to $x^3 - 2x + 1$. The notations on the left are read "f of x equals $x^2 + 4$" and "g of x equals $x^3 - 2x + 1$." The notations on the right are read "f maps x to $x^2 + 4$" and "g maps x to $x^3 - 2x + 1$."

Thus we see that the word *function* is used to describe the idea of a particular kind of mapping or pairing and that this idea has different aspects. One aspect is algebraic, another aspect is arithmetic, and a third aspect is geometric.

> We use the word *function* to describe a mapping from each member of the input set, which is called the *domain,* to exactly one member of the output set, which is called the *range.* Thus the word *function* brings to mind the following:
>
> 1. The numbers that are acceptable as inputs and the algebraic rule (if one exists) that can be used to find the unique output that is paired with each input.
>
> 2. A table of ordered pairs of inputs and outputs where each input member is paired with exactly one output and all equal inputs have the same outputs.
>
> 3. The graph of the geometric points whose coordinates are the ordered pairs just described.

What functions are and how they interrelate can be explained by using a box called a **function machine.** The function machine uses a rule to produce exactly one output for every input. Consider the two functions that follow:

$$f(x) = 4x \qquad g(x) = x^2 + 2$$

The f rule is to multiply any input by 4, and the g rule is to square any input and then add 2. This may be easier to understand if we remove the x from parentheses. The f function multiplies whatever is in the parentheses by 4, and the g function squares whatever is in the parentheses and then adds 2.

example 6.1 Given $f(x) = x^2 + 5$, find (a) $f(-2)$, (b) $f(x + 2)$, and (c) $f(x + \Delta x)$.

solution We use the function machine thought process:

This function machine squares the input and then adds 5.

(a) Insert (-2) and get $(-2)^2 + 5 = $ **9.**

(b) Insert $(x + 2)$ and get $(x + 2)^2 + 5 = x^2 + 4x + 9.$

(c) Insert $(x + \Delta x)$ and get $(x + \Delta x)^2 + 5 = x^2 + 2x(\Delta x) + (\Delta x)^2 + 5.$

example 6.2 Use a graphing calculator to estimate the value of

(a) $f(\pi)$ (b) $f(\sqrt{2})$ (c) $f(\cos 5\sqrt{3})$

where $f(x) = \dfrac{1}{\sqrt{1 + x^2}}$.

solution The first step is to define the function in the calculator. The Y= button opens the function editor window where we define f as follows:

$$Y_1 = 1/\sqrt{(1+X^2)}$$

Another useful preliminary step is to adjust the WINDOW settings. We do so as seen on the left and press GRAPH to get the screen on the right.

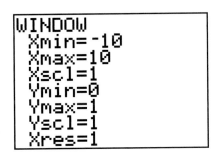

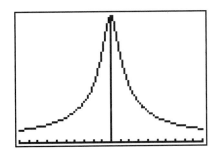

(a) As with previous examples using the graphing calculator, we need the CALCULATE menu. This time we select 1:value. In the lower left-hand corner, X= appears, followed by a flashing rectangular region. We press

to insert π and get the following:

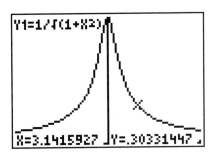

From the Y=.30331447 found in the lower right-hand corner, we know $f(\pi) \approx \mathbf{0.3033.}$

(b) Similarly, we find $f(\sqrt{2})$.

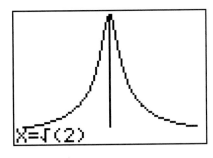

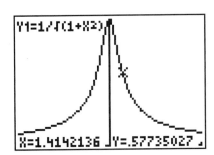

$f(\sqrt{2}) \approx \mathbf{0.5774}$

(c) First we make sure the calculator is in radian mode. Then we compute $f(\cos 5\sqrt{3})$.

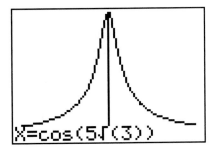

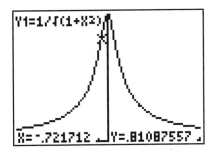

$f(\cos 5\sqrt{3}) \approx \mathbf{0.8109}$

example 6.3   Use the graphing calculator to find $f(1)$, $f(2)$, $f(3)$, ..., $f(10)$ where $f(x) = \dfrac{1}{\sqrt{1 + x^2}}$.

solution   To quickly obtain a table of output values for a function, we use the key sequences shown below.

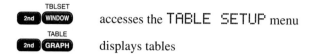

This function is the same one as in the previous example, so it should already be defined as Y_1 in the calculator. First, we access the TABLE SETUP menu. We want the table to start with $f(1)$, so we set TblStart=1. ∆Tbl defines the increment for the independent variable x. Since our desired input values differ by 1, we set ∆Tbl=1. Next, we display the table.

X	Y₁
1	.70711
2	.44721
3	.31623
4	.24254
5	.19612
6	.1644
7	.14142

X=1

The column whose heading is X lists the input values, while the column marked Y_1 shows the output values $f(1)$, $f(2)$, $f(3)$, ..., $f(10)$. Of course, we must scroll down to see all the values required.

6.B
functional notation

Functional notation is useful because it indicates that the relationship is single-valued and because it can be used with letters of our choice to name or identify particular single-valued relationships. To name the equations

$$y = 2x + 3 \qquad y = e^t \qquad y = \ln u \qquad y = \sin(2s + 2)$$

we could use the letters f, θ, g, and h to write

$$f(x) = 2x + 3 \qquad \theta(t) = e^t \qquad g(u) = \ln u \qquad h(s) = \sin(2s + 2)$$

From this we see that $f(x)$, $\theta(t)$, $g(u)$, and $h(s)$ mean the same thing that y means, but these notations provide more information. It allows us to name each equation differently. It indicates that the expressions are single-valued. Functional notation also allows us to identify the input value used to get a particular answer. Below, the old notation tells us that the answer is 11. The functional notation tells us that if we use the f equation and let x equal 4, the answer is 11.

$$y = 11 \qquad f(4) = 11$$

The additional information provided by functional notation explains why it is so widely used.

Functional notation is also useful on a graph. If we have a graph of the f equation in x, we use the single letter f to identify the graph and $f(x)$ to represent the y-value of the f equation when x equals some unspecified value. We use $f(a)$ to designate the y-value of the f equation when x equals the constant a. For example, $f(4)$ designates the y-value of the equation when x equals 4. On the graph, $f(4)$ represents the directed vertical distance from the x-axis to the graph when x equals 4. (The input value of any point on the graph is represented by its distance to the right or left of the y-axis. The output value for the same point is represented by its distance above or below the x-axis.) We know how to use ordered pairs of x and y written as (x, y). Now we can designate the same ordered pairs with x and $f(x)$ by writing

$$(x, f(x))$$

The graph of the function is the graph of the ordered pairs of inputs x and outputs $f(x)$.

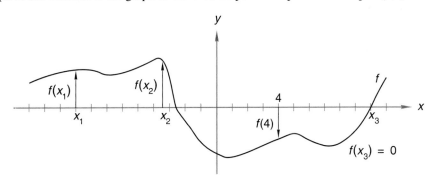

Functional notation and xy-notation are used interchangeably in this lesson and in the rest of the book whenever convenient. We even use both notations in the same problem to emphasize this interchangeability. For example, note that the vertical axis in the diagram above is labeled y instead of $f(x)$.

example 6.4   Which of the following are not graphs of functions?

A.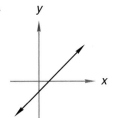

B.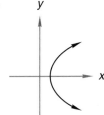

C.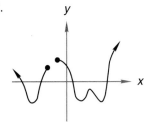

D.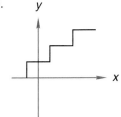

solution   Since a function is single-valued, there can be only one y-value for any value of x. **If at any value of x we can draw a vertical line that touches the graph more than once, then the graph is not the graph of a function.** This means the graph of a function cannot loop back anywhere and cannot contain any vertical segments.

A.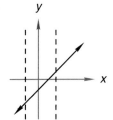

B.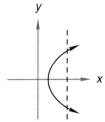

C.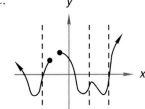

D.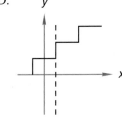

Figures A and C show graphs of functions because it is impossible to draw a vertical line that touches the graph in more than one place. (Note that in C, the graph of the function is broken, or in mathematical terms, **discontinuous.** This does not matter as the definition of a function only requires that for every input there is exactly one output. In the case of C, some values of x lead to no values of y. So those values of x are not in the domain of the function.)

Figure B is not the graph of a function, for we have found a value of x at which a vertical line touches the graph in two places. The graph in **figure D** fails the vertical line test because it contains vertical segments.

example 6.5 Which of the following sets of points could lie on the graph of a function?

A. $\{(1, 2), (2, 3), (3, 4), (4, 5)\}$ B. $\{(1, 2), (2, 3), (1, 3), (4, 5)\}$

C. $\{(4, 3), (2, 2), (4, 3), (3, 3)\}$ D. $\{(1, -1), (4, -1), (-1, -1), (3, -2)\}$

solution Only sets of ordered pairs in which every first number is paired with a unique second number can lie on the graph of a function. So we look for duplicate initial numbers. In set A all the initial numbers are different and each is paired with a second number, so **set A** could lie on the graph of a function. Set B fails because two ordered pairs have 1 as the first number, but the second numbers are different. **Set C** works because although this set has two ordered pairs in which 4 is the first number, both of these ordered pairs have 3 as the second number. In set D three of the second numbers are −1, but **set D** still passes the criteria because all the initial numbers are different.

example 6.6 Determine whether the following statement is true or false and justify your answer: The mapping

$$f: x \longrightarrow x^4 + x^2$$

is not a function because it maps both +1 and −1 to +2.

solution **False. The mapping is a function.** A function is a mapping in which every value of x is mapped to exactly one value of y. Two different values of x can be mapped to the same value of y.

example 6.7 Determine whether the following statement is true or false and explain your answer: The equation $y = \frac{1}{2}x^2 + 2$ is not the equation of a function because there is a vertical line that intersects the graph of this equation at more than one point.

solution **False.** Any number used for x results in just one answer for y. Thus, every vertical line intersects the graph at only one point. The graph of $y = \frac{1}{2}x^2 + 2$ is the following:

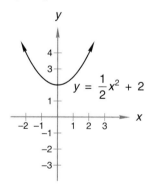

The graph does not fail the vertical line test.

6.C

domain and range The definition of a function has two parts. One part is a rule that tells how to find the output value $f(x)$ for each value of the input x. **The other part is the description of the set of input values that may be used for x. This set is the domain for the function.** The domain for a function may be determined by the person who makes up the function. Here we show the rules and the domains for functions made up by Selby and Bruce.

SELBY'S FUNCTION	BRUCE'S FUNCTION
$f(x) = 2x + 3$	$g(x) = 2x + 3$
domain: $D = \{\text{reals}\}$	domain: $D = \{\text{integers}\}$

The algebraic part of the rule for each of these functions is the same, but the functions are different functions because the domains are different. We do not know why Selby and Bruce chose different domains. We must accept the domains they have specified, because the person who designates the algebraic part of the functions also gets to choose the domain. However, when the domain of a function is not specified, it is customary to assume it to be the largest possible set of numbers for which the function can be defined.

Whenever we encounter a problem, we must determine the algebraic rule for the function implied by the statement of the problem and the acceptable domain for the function. Sometimes a problem is stated in such a way that we cannot use certain numbers as input values. If boxes cost $25 each, we could use the following function machine to find the cost of x boxes.

$$\text{Cost} = 25(\ )$$

$x \longrightarrow$		$\longrightarrow 25x$
$4 \longrightarrow$	$25(\ )$	$\longrightarrow 100$
$7 \longrightarrow$		$\longrightarrow 175$

Four boxes cost $100 and seven boxes cost $175. We would not try to use this equation to find the cost of $7\frac{1}{2}$ boxes, -3 boxes, or π boxes because we assume that only whole numbers of boxes can be purchased. Trying to buy $7\frac{1}{2}$ boxes, -3 boxes, or π boxes does not make sense. No statement about the domain was made, but it seems that the set of whole numbers is the implied domain for this problem. We can buy no boxes, one box, two boxes, etc. Therefore,

$$\text{Domain} = \{0, 1, 2, 3, \dots\}$$

Even if the equation being considered is not the result of a real problem, we still need to determine the domain. **In this book we deal with functions of real numbers. The domains of the functions, unless otherwise specified, are understood to be the set of real numbers that produce images that are also real numbers.**

The **range** of a function is the set of all images obtained when all values in the domain are used as inputs for the function. Thus we do not specify the range when we have an algebraic expression for the function. We mentally insert all members of the domain and investigate the set of outputs that results.

One way to determine the domain and range of a function is to look at the graph of the function. The x-coordinates of the points on the graph constitute the domain, and the y-coordinates of the points on the graph constitute the range. Consider the following figures:

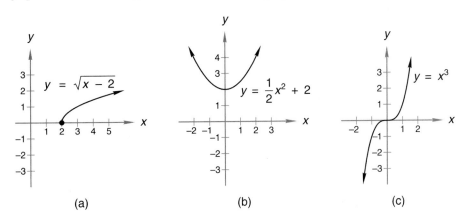

(a)   (b)   (c)

In figure (a) the x-values on the graph begin at 2 and increase without bound, so the domain is the set of all real numbers greater than or equal to 2. The y-values on the graph begin at zero and increase without bound, so the range is the set of all real numbers greater than or equal to zero. In figure (b) the x-values on the graph go from negative infinity to positive infinity, so the domain is the set of real numbers. The y-values begin at $+2$ and increase without bound, so the range is the set of all real numbers greater than or equal to 2. In figure (c) the values of x include all real numbers, and the values of y include all real numbers. Thus, for this function, the set of real numbers is both the domain and range.

Strictly speaking, when determining the range of a function, we are required to show that there is a value (or values) of the domain that maps to each and every value of the range. For our purposes, we do not require such rigor. Determining the range simply by reading off the set of y-values from the graph of a function suffices.

example 6.8 Find the domain and range of the function $f(x) = \sqrt{x + 5}$.

solution The values of x in the domain of this function are real numbers that produce images that are also real numbers. These must be values of x that make $x + 5 \geq 0$. (If $x + 5 < 0$, then the square root is an imaginary number.) Thus, the domain consists of the real numbers x that satisfy $x \geq -5$.

To designate domains, we use set notation: { } indicates a set, the symbol $\in$ means *is an element of*, the symbol $\mathbb{R}$ represents the real numbers, and a vertical line means *such that*. Thus, we write

$$\text{Domain of } f = \{x \in \mathbb{R} \mid x \geq -5\}$$

This is read as follows: "The domain of f is the set of all real numbers x such that x is greater than or equal to -5."

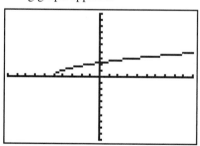

$$y = \sqrt{x + 5}$$

On the graph we see that there are no negative values of y, so the range consists of all real numbers equal to or greater than zero.

$$\text{Range of } f = \{y \in \mathbb{R} \mid y \geq 0\}$$

example 6.9 Use the (TRACE) feature of the TI-83 to verify the domain of f found in example 6.8.

solution We define $Y1$ as

$$Y1 = \sqrt{(X+5)}$$

and select $6:ZStandard$ under the (ZOOM) menu, which means the window shows the x- and y-axes from -10 to 10. The following graph appears:

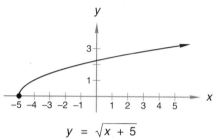

We use the (TRACE) feature to trace out points on the curve. Shown below are points on the graph and their respective coordinates:

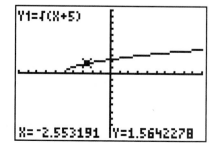

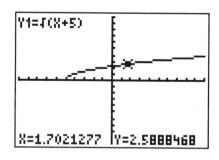

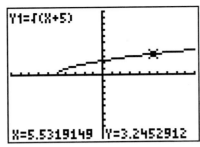 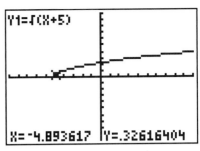

Note that if we press the ◖ key until we get a value of x less than –5, then we get no value of y. This confirms that y simply does not exist for values of x less than –5, as stated in example 6.8.

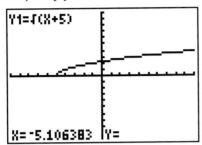 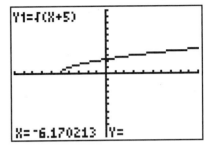

example 6.10 Find the domain and range of $f(x) = \dfrac{\sqrt{x}}{x - 2}$.

solution From the numerator of the function we see that x cannot be a negative number because the square root of a negative number is an imaginary number. From the denominator of the function we see that x cannot equal 2, because this would make the denominator zero. Thus,

$$\text{Domain} = \{x \in \mathbb{R} \mid x \geq 0,\ x \neq 2\}$$

Finding the range of some functions is easier if we graph the functions.

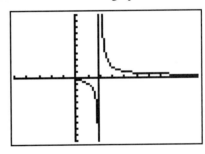

The graph of this function shows that the values of y include all positive and negative real numbers. Zero also appears to be a y-value, but this must be verified "by hand" in case it is an asymptotic value. In this case it is easy to check, since $f(0) = 0$. Therefore

$$\text{Range} = \mathbb{R}$$

problem set 6

1. The pressure of an ideal gas varies directly with the temperature and inversely with the volume. The
   (5) initial pressure, volume, and temperature were 5 newtons per square meter, 5 liters, and 100 Kelvin. What would the pressure be if the volume were 4 liters and the temperature were 1000 Kelvin?

2. A rectangular box with a square base has a total surface area of 100 cm². If x is the length of a
   (5) side of the base, what is the volume of the box in terms of x?

3. Use a graphing calculator to approximate the value(s) of x for which $x^3 + 3x^2 - 1$ equals 0.
   (2)

4. Approximate the coordinates of the intersection point(s) of the graphs of the functions
   (2) $f(x) = e^x$ and $g(x) = x^3 + 3x^2 - 1$ in the interval [–4, 2]. (The value of e, an irrational number, is approximately 2.7182818284.)

5. Convert 1.570796327 radians to degrees. Round your answer to the nearest degree.
   (4)

6. Which of the following sets of points could lie on the graph of a function?
(6)

A. $\{(2, -2), (-3, 2), (2, -3), (3, 3)\}$

B. $\{(1, 2), (2, 2), (3, 2), (4, 2)\}$

C. $\{(1, 2), (1, 3), (6, 7), (-1, 13)\}$

D. $\{(-1, 2), (2, -1), (-1, 4), (5, 8)\}$

7. Shown is the graph of a function ψ.
(6) Estimate the value of each of the following:

(a) $\psi(1)$ (b) $\psi(-1)$ (c) $\psi(-2)$

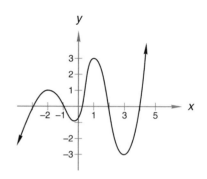

8. Shown is a function machine f where only
(6) a few input and output values are given. Which of the following could be the equation for f?

A. $f(x) = 2x + 1$

B. $f(x) = 2x^2 - 2$

C. $f(x) = x^2 + 1$

D. $f(x) = 2x$

9. If $f(x) = 2x^2 - 1$, what is $f(x + \Delta x)$?
(6)

10. Express the domain and range of the function $f(x) = \sqrt{x - 1}$ using set notation.
(6)

11. Express the domain and range of the function $y = \dfrac{\sqrt{x + 1}}{x}$ using set notation.
(6)

12. Use a graphing calculator to approximate the values of y when $x = \pi$ and when $x = \sqrt{2}$
(2) given the equation $y = \dfrac{\sqrt{x + 1}}{x}$.

Evaluate the expressions in problems 13–15.

13. $2 \cos^2 -\dfrac{5\pi}{4} - \sec^2 \dfrac{\pi}{4}$
(4)

14. $\cot \dfrac{\pi}{6} + \sin -\dfrac{\pi}{3}$
(4)

15. $\sin \dfrac{\pi}{6} \cos -\dfrac{\pi}{3}$
(4)

Simplify the expressions in problems 16 and 17.

16. $(\cot^2 x)(\sec^2 x)(\sin x)$
(4)

17. $\dfrac{(\cot \theta)(\sec \theta)}{(\csc \theta)}$
(4)

18. State the converse and inverse of the following statement:
(3)

If I live in Norman, then I live in Oklahoma.

19. Suppose $y = mx + b$ and $y = nx + c$ are the equations of two perpendicular lines. What is
(2) the numerical value of mn?

20. Solve algebraically for s: $\sqrt{s} - \sqrt{s - 8} = 2$
(1)

21. Compute: $\displaystyle\sum_{i=-1}^{1} 3^i$
(1)

22. Simplify: $\dfrac{\sqrt{3} - \sqrt{2}}{\sqrt{3} + \sqrt{2}}$
(1)

23. Find the total surface area of a right circular cylinder whose volume is 9π cubic centimeters and
(R) whose height is 1 centimeter.

24. Assuming *x*, *y*, and *z* are lengths as shown,
(1) compare the following:

A. $x + y$ B. z

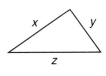

25. Use the fact that the measure of an
(R) inscribed angle equals one half the
measure of the subtended arc to find *x*
given

$$m\angle ABC = 5x - 10 \text{ and}$$
$$m\widehat{ADC} = x^2 - 20$$

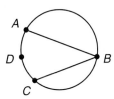

LESSON 7 ***The Unit Circle • Centerline, Amplitude, and Phase Angle of Sinusoids • Period of a Function • Important Numbers • Exponential Functions***

7.A
the unit circle

In a right triangle the sine of an acute angle θ is the ratio of the length of the side opposite angle θ to the length of the hypotenuse. Thus, if we draw a triangle whose hypotenuse is 1 unit long, the sine of angle θ will be the length of the side opposite this angle divided by 1. A circle whose radius is 1 is called a **unit circle.** If we center a unit circle at the origin as shown below and measure the central angles counterclockwise from the positive *x*-axis, the *y*-coordinate of any point on the unit circle equals the sine of the central angle because *y* is the length of the side opposite angle θ in the triangle. On the right-hand side we graph $y = \sin \theta$ and note that the horizontal axis is the θ-axis.

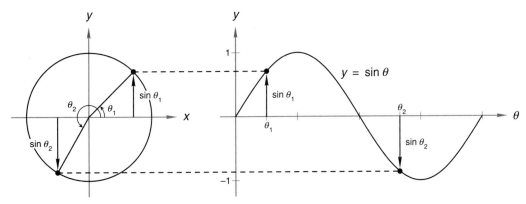

The sines of θ_1 and θ_2 equal the **directed lengths** of the **vertical** sides of the triangles since the length of every hypotenuse equals 1. This agrees with the graph of $y = \sin \theta$ on the right, where the vertical distance from the θ-axis to the graph also equals $\sin \theta$. When the graph is above the θ-axis, the sine is positive, and when the graph is below the θ-axis, the sine is negative. Note that when θ equals zero, the sine is zero, and as θ increases from 0° to 360°, or 2π radians, the value of the sine goes from 0 to 1 to 0 to −1 and back to 0. In this discussion we use θ to represent the independent variable to emphasize that the input represents an angle. In mathematics the variable *x* is most often used as the independent variable and is also used to represent angles. In this graph of the sine curve, the horizontal axis was chosen to be the θ-axis. Sometimes we use θ and sometimes we use *x*.

We see that the *y*-coordinate of any point on a unit circle equals the sine of the central angle θ measured counterclockwise from the positive *x*-axis.

$$y = \sin \theta$$

The same unit circle can be used to discuss the values of the cosine, because the value of cos θ equals the length of the adjacent side over the length of the hypotenuse. When the length of the hypotenuse equals 1, the **directed length** of a **horizontal** side of a triangle in the unit circle equals the cosine of the angle. Thus, the x-coordinate of any point on the unit circle equals the cosine of the central angle measured counterclockwise from the positive x-axis. To show the projection of the cosine function from the unit circle, we graph the function using a vertical orientation.

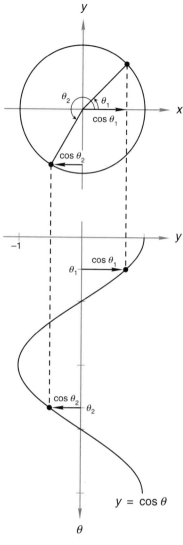

On the graph of $y = \cos \theta$ at right, the values of cos θ correlate with the directed lengths of the horizontal sides of the tria-ngle in the circle on top. From this we see that the x-coordinate of any point on a unit circle equals the cosine of the central angle θ measured counterclockwise from the positive x-axis.

$$x = \cos \theta$$

Note that the value of cos $0°$ is 1, and as θ goes from $0°$ to $360°$, the value of the cosine goes from 1 to 0 to -1 to 0 and back to 1.

Below, we simply rotate the graph of the cosine function so that the θ-axis is horizontal.

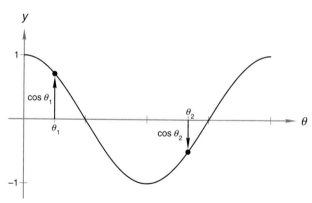

example 7.1   Shown is a unit circle centered at the origin. Find the coordinates of points P_1 and P_2.

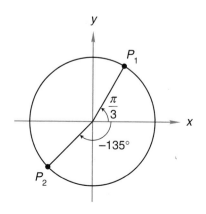

solution   The central angle for P_1 is $\theta = \dfrac{\pi}{3}$, so

$$x = \cos \frac{\pi}{3} = \frac{1}{2}$$

$$y = \sin \frac{\pi}{3} = \frac{\sqrt{3}}{2}$$

For P_2, $\theta = -135°$, so

$$x = \cos -135° = -\frac{\sqrt{2}}{2}$$

$$y = \sin -135° = -\frac{\sqrt{2}}{2}$$

Therefore, $P_1 = \left(\dfrac{1}{2}, \dfrac{\sqrt{3}}{2} \right)$ and $P_2 = \left(-\dfrac{\sqrt{2}}{2}, -\dfrac{\sqrt{2}}{2} \right)$.

7.B
centerline, amplitude, and phase angle of sinusoids

Below we show more complete graphs of the sine and cosine functions.

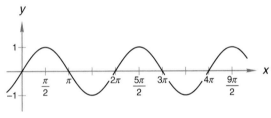

$y = \sin x$

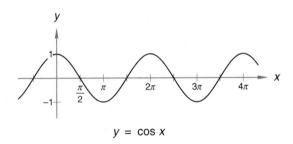

$y = \cos x$

Because the graph of the cosine function looks much like the graph of the sine function, we call both of these functions **sinusoids.** (The Greek suffix *-oid* means "having the shape of." For example, something that has the shape of a crystal is crystalloid.) The equations of the sine function and the cosine function whose period is $2\pi^{\dagger}$ have the following forms.

$$y = A + B \sin (\theta - D) \qquad y = A + B \cos (\theta - D)$$

The constant A is the y-value of the horizontal *centerline* of the graph, and the constant B denotes the *amplitude,* which is the value of the maximum deviation of the graph from the centerline.

In the left-hand figure below, the centerline is the θ-axis, and the graph goes 4 units above and 4 units below the centerline. In the equation below the figure, we note that $A = 0$ and $B = 4$. In the

---
†More on this in the next section.

right-hand figure, the centerline is $y = +2$, as indicated by the $+2$ value of A in the equation. Since B is 4, this curve also goes 4 units above and below its centerline.

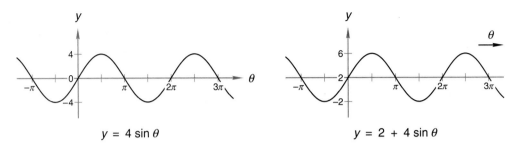

$y = 4 \sin \theta$ $y = 2 + 4 \sin \theta$

The constant D denotes the *phase angle*. Note that the negative of the phase angle appears in the argument of the trigonometric function. The phase angle for a sine function is the value of θ at any point where the graph crosses the centerline on the way up as the curve is traced from left to right, though it is customary to use the crossing point nearest the origin as the phase angle.

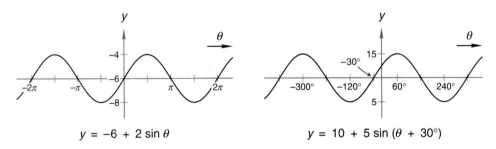

$y = -6 + 2 \sin \theta$ $y = 10 + 5 \sin (\theta + 30°)$

In the left-hand figure above, the centerline is $y = -6$ and the amplitude is 2. Since the curve crosses the centerline on the way up where θ equals zero, the phase angle is 0. In the right-hand figure above, the centerline is 10, the amplitude is 5, and the phase angle is $-30°$. The equations of the cosine functions for the same curves are identical except that the phase angle for the cosine function is a value of θ at which the graph is at its highest point.

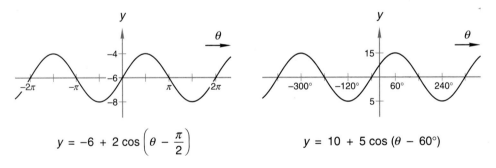

$y = -6 + 2 \cos \left(\theta - \dfrac{\pi}{2} \right)$ $y = 10 + 5 \cos (\theta - 60°)$

Again we note that the negative of the phase angle appears in the argument.

We can write the equation of the curve on the right-hand side as a negative sine function and as a negative cosine function. If we make the coefficient B a negative number, the phase angle for the sine function is a value of θ where the graph crosses its centerline on the way down, and the phase angle for the cosine function is a value of θ where the graph is at its lowest point.

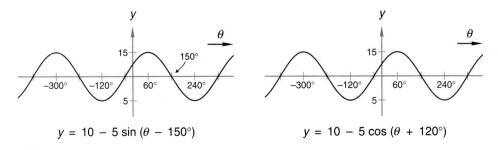

$y = 10 - 5 \sin (\theta - 150°)$ $y = 10 - 5 \cos (\theta + 120°)$

example 7.2   Graph: $y = -3 + 5 \cos (\theta - 45°)$

solution   The easiest way to graph a sinusoid is to draw a model, as we do on the left-hand side below.

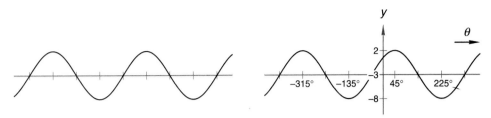

Then, on the right-hand side, we mark the centerline as –3. Since the graph goes up 5 and down 5, the peak values are +2 and –8. The argument is $(\theta - 45°)$, so the phase angle is +45°. This is a value of θ where the graph has a maximum point. The graph crosses the θ-axis every 180°, and this information can be used to locate other points on the axis, as shown.

example 7.3   Graph: $y = -3 - 4 \sin (x + 45°)$

solution   We draw the model curve on the left and then incorporate the labels in the figure on the right. The centerline is $y = -3$ and the amplitude is 4, so the curve goes up to +1 and down to –7. The phase angle is –45°, which is a value of x where the graph of a negative sine function crosses its centerline on the way down.

example 7.4   Graph: $y = 2 - 3 \cos (\theta - 30°)$

solution   Again we draw the curve and put the labels on it. This time the centerline is $y = 2$, and the curve goes up 3 to 5 and down 3 to –1. The phase angle is +30°, which is a value of θ where the graph of a negative cosine function reaches a minimum point.

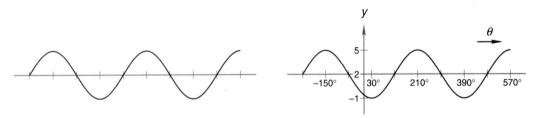

example 7.5   Use the graphing calculator to graph the equation defined in example 7.4 so that the plotted graph shows the same x- and y-values as the graph shown in the solution to example 7.4.

solution   First, we remember to set the calculator to degree mode. On a TI-83 this can be done by pressing the [MODE] key and selecting Degree.

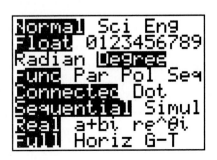

We then define $Y_1=2-3\cos(X-30)$. (Notice that X must be used instead of θ.) In the graph shown in the solution to Example 7.4, the θ-axis varies from $\theta = -240°$ to $\theta = 570°$, and the y-axis varies from -1 to 5. We set the window as such and then press GRAPH.

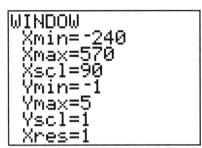 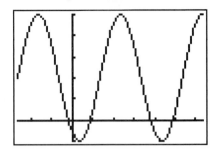

If we want to show the centerline, we define $Y_2=2$ and graph this horizontal line along with the graph of Y_1.

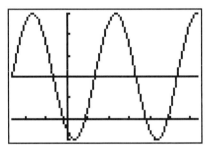

7.C

period of a function

Both the sine and cosine functions are periodic functions whose period is 360°, or 2π radians, since the values of $\sin\theta$ and $\cos\theta$ repeat in regular patterns as θ increases or decreases through multiples of 360°, or 2π radians. The sine of 30° is $\frac{1}{2}$. Since $30° + 360°$ equals once around a circle plus 30° more, the sine of $30° + 360°$ is the same as the sine of 30°. The angle $30° + 720°$ means twice around a circle and 30° more, so the sine of this angle is also the same as the sine of 30°. Thus, the values of $\sin 30°$, $\sin(30° + 360°)$, and $\sin(30° + 720°)$ are all $\frac{1}{2}$. We can go around a circle as many times as we please and then go 30° more, and the sine of all of these angles is $\frac{1}{2}$. If n is an integer,

$$\sin(\theta + n360°) = \sin\theta$$

We say that the *period* of $\sin\theta$ is 360° because the values repeat every 360°. If another function repeats its values every 180°, we say that the period of that function is 180°. Using p for the period and n for an integer, we say that a function is a periodic function if, for any θ and n,

$$f(\theta) = f(\theta + np)$$

The functions $y = \sin\theta$ and $y = \sin(2\theta)$ are periodic functions because the graphs of both functions repeat the same patterns again and again as θ increases.

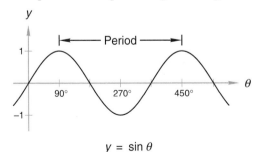 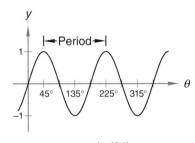

$$y = \sin\theta \qquad\qquad y = \sin(2\theta)$$

The graph of $y = \sin(2\theta)$ repeats the pattern twice as often as $y = \sin\theta$ does, so the period of $\sin(2\theta)$ is one half the period of $\sin\theta$. The period of a function is the horizontal distance on the graph between any two corresponding points. Thus the θ distance between two successive peak values can be used to determine the period. In the graph on the left, we see that the period is $450° - 90°$, or 360°. Thus the period for $y = \sin\theta$ is 360°, or 2π radians. In the graph on the right, the period is $225° - 45°$, or 180°. In the graph of $y = \sin(2\theta)$, the pattern repeats twice as often as

$y = \sin \theta$ and the period is 180°, or π radians. In the graph of $y = \sin(3\theta)$, the pattern repeats 3 times as often as $y = \sin \theta$, and the period is 120°, or $\frac{2\pi}{3}$ radians. The graph $y = \sin\left(\frac{1}{3}\theta\right)$ repeats one third as often, and its period is 360° ÷ $\left(\frac{1}{3}\right)$ = 1080°, or (2π) ÷ $\left(\frac{1}{3}\right)$ = 6π radians. From these observations we see that the constant C in $y = \sin(C\theta)$ equals 360° divided by the period in degrees, or 2π radians divided by the period in radians.

$$\text{Constant } C = \frac{360°}{\text{period}} \qquad \text{Constant } C = \frac{2\pi}{\text{period}}$$

Thus the general equations of the sine function and the cosine function are

$$y = A + B \sin\big[C(\theta - D)\big] \qquad \text{and} \qquad y = A + B \cos\big[C(\theta - D)\big]$$

where A is the y-value of the centerline, B is the amplitude, C equals 360° or 2π divided by the period, and D is the phase angle.

example 7.6   Graph: $y = -10 + 4\cos(3\theta - 135°)$

solution   **The first step is to factor the argument so that the coefficient of θ is 1. Then the phase angle can be read directly.** We factor and get

$$y = -10 + 4\cos\big[3(\theta - 45°)\big]$$

Next we draw a model sinusoid.

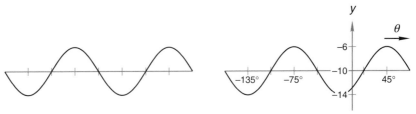

On the right-hand side we show that the y-coordinate of the centerline is -10 and the amplitude is 4. The phase angle is $+45°$, so one peak value of the graph occurs when $\theta = +45°$. The constant C is 3, so the period is 360° divided by 3, or 120°. Thus, from $+45°$ we move 120° to the left and mark the θ value below the next peak as $45° - 120°$, or $-75°$. Now, if we wish, we can locate other points of interest on the θ-axis by noting that each hump of the graph spans half a period, or 60°.

example 7.7   Use the graphing calculator to draw the graph shown in the solution of example 7.6.

solution   We set $\texttt{Y1=-10+4cos(3x-135)}$ and then press $\boxed{\texttt{WINDOW}}$ to set $\texttt{Xmin=-165, Xmax=75,}$ $\texttt{Xscl=15, Ymin=-14, Ymax=-6,}$ and $\texttt{Yscl=1}$. The resulting graph is

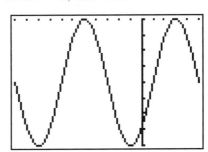

If we define $\texttt{Y2=-10}$, we can draw the centerline of the curve.

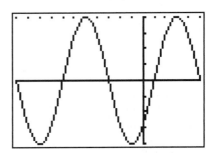

7.D
important numbers

Possibly the most important numbers in mathematics are the numbers 0, 1, π, and e. Zero is important because it is the additive identity. The sum of any number and 0 is the number itself. The number 1 is the multiplicative identity because the product of any number and 1 is the number itself.

The number π is an irrational number because it cannot be written as a fraction of integers. Thus it cannot be written as a decimal numeral with a finite number of digits.

$$\pi = 3.1415926535897932384\ldots$$

This merely shows the first 20 digits of π. The digits of π go on and on in a non-repeating pattern. Irrational numbers made the ancients most uncomfortable, and for centuries many insisted that these numbers were not real numbers. But irrational numbers occur naturally. For example, π represents the number of times the diameter of a circle divides into the circumference.

$$\frac{\text{Circumference}}{\text{Diameter}} = \pi$$

The number e, called the natural number, is also an irrational real number. The three-digit approximation of e is 2.72, but as with any irrational number, the decimal expansion of e consists of an infinite number of digits that do not repeat in a pattern.

$$e = 2.7182818284590452353\ldots$$

In calculus the number e is the preferred base for logarithms and exponentials because its use makes many operations much easier.

7.E
exponential functions

An exponential function has the form

$$y = b^x$$

The base b can be any positive number except 1. We do not use 1 as a base, because 1 raised to any power is 1.

$$y = 1^x \qquad \text{means} \qquad y = 1 \qquad \text{for all } x \in \mathbb{R}$$

We want all values of x and y to be real numbers, so the base cannot be a negative number, because this leads to an imaginary value for y for some values of x. For example, if -2 is the base and x equals $\frac{3}{2}$, the y-value is $2\sqrt{-2}$, which is unacceptable.

$$\begin{aligned}
y &= (-2)^{3/2} & &\text{base is } -2 \\
y &= [(-2)^3]^{1/2} & &\text{equivalent expression} \\
y &= \sqrt{-8} & &\text{simplified} \\
y &= 2\sqrt{-2} & &\text{simplified}
\end{aligned}$$

If the base is a number between 0 and 1, the graph of the equation is a continuous curve similar to the curves shown on the left-hand side below. If the base is a number greater than 1, the graph of the equation is a continuous curve similar to the curves shown on the right-hand side.

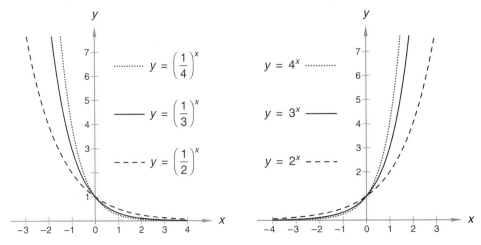

Note that all the graphs cross the y-axis 1 unit above the origin at $(0, 1)$ because $b^0 = 1$. Graphing exponential functions is easy because these graphs have one of the two basic shapes shown here.

example 7.8   Sketch the graphs of (a) $y = 1.3^x$ and (b) $y = 4^x$.

solution   We can get three quick points on the graph of $y = 1.3^x$ by letting x equal 0, 1, and –1.

$$y = (1.3)^0 \qquad y = (1.3)^1 \qquad y = (1.3)^{-1}$$

$$= 1 \qquad\qquad = 1.3 \qquad\qquad = \frac{1}{1.3}$$

Thus the coordinates of these three points are $(0, 1)$, $(1, 1.3)$, and $(-1, \frac{1}{1.3})$. **This shows us that in any exponential function $y = b^x$, if we let x equal 0, 1, and –1, the y-values are 1, b, and 1 over b, respectively.** This means that three points on the graph of $y = 4^x$ are $(0, 1)$, $(1, 4)$, and $(-1, \frac{1}{4})$.

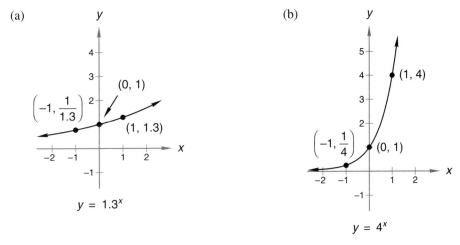

When we look at the sketches, we see that $y = 4^x$ rises more quickly than $y = 1.3^x$. The graph of $y = 4^x$ must rise rather abruptly to reach a y-value of 4 when $x = 1$. The graph of $y = 40^x$ is even steeper because a y-value of 40 must be reached when $x = 1$. Although it is not apparent from the graph of $y = 1.3^x$ in (a), this function does grow steeper and steeper as x increases.

example 7.9   Using a graphing calculator, sketch the graphs of (a) $y = -e^x$ and (b) $y = e^{-x}$.

solution   A negative sign can only be placed in two places in the function $y = e^x$, before the e or before the x. One placement causes the graph of $y = e^x$ to be reflected in the x-axis (flipped about the x-axis), and the other causes the graph of $y = e^x$ to be reflected in the y-axis.

(a) With the following key sequence, we define the function in the calculator:

Then we press ⟨ZOOM⟩ and select 6: ZStandard to yield the graph.

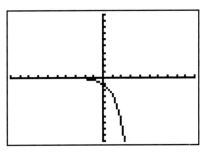

The minus sign in $-e^x$ changes the sign of each y-value in $y = e^x$ from positive to negative and causes the graph of $y = -e^x$ to be a reflection of the graph of $y = e^x$ about the x-axis (flipped about the x-axis).

(b) For the second function we use the key sequence

followed by GRAPH to obtain

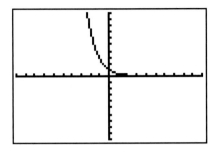

The minus sign in e^{-x} changes the sign of each x and causes the graph of $y = e^x$ to be reflected about the y-axis (flipped about the y-axis). Since $y = e^{-x}$ is the same as $y = \left(\frac{1}{e}\right)^x$, the minus sign has the effect of changing the base from e to $\frac{1}{e}$. (It can be shown that the graphs of all pairs of exponential functions whose bases are reciprocals are reflections of each other about the y-axis.)

example 7.10   Sketch the graph of $y = -e^{-x}$.

solution   This equation has two minus signs, so the graph is reflected in both axes, one first then the other. This can be a little confusing, but we can always fall back on the expedient of finding three quick points.

$$y = -e^{-x}$$

x	0	1	−1
y	−1	$-\dfrac{1}{e}$	$-e$

We show the graph of $y = e^x$ on the left and $y = -e^{-x}$ on the right.

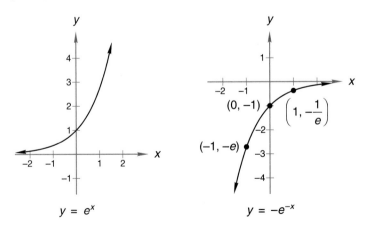

$$y = e^x \qquad\qquad y = -e^{-x}$$

problem set 7

1. The accomplishment number varies directly with the effort index and inversely with the time
   (5)   squandered. If the accomplishment number is 5 when the effort index is 20 and the time squandered is 8 hours, what is the accomplishment number when the effort index is 12 and the time squandered is 6 hours?

2. The number of wombats varies linearly with the number of fangles. If there are 170 wombats
   (5)   when there are 10 fangles, and 95 wombats when there are 5 fangles, then how many fangles are there when there are 50 wombats?

3. Squares are cut out of each corner of a
(5) 6-inch by 8-inch rectangular piece of sheet
metal. The resulting flaps are folded up to
form an open-topped rectangular box. If
the length of the sides of the cut-out square
is x, what is the volume V of the box in
terms of x?

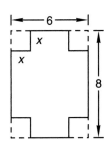

4. Find the coordinates of the intersection point(s) of the graphs of $y = 0$ and
(2) $y = x^4 - 2x^3 + x^2 - x - 1$.

5. Shown is a unit circle centered at the
(7) origin of the coordinate plane. Without
using a calculator, find the coordinates of
P_1 and P_2.

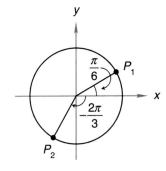

6. Sketch the graphs of $y = 2^x$ and $y = 2^{-x}$ on the same set of axes.
(7)

7. Sketch the graphs of $y = e^x$ and $y = -e^x$ on the same set of axes.
(7)

8. Graph: $y = -3 + 5 \sin [3(x - 45°)]$
(7)

9. Write the equation of the sinusoid shown
(7) in terms of the cosine function.

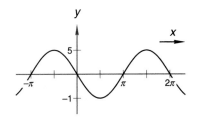

10. Determine whether the following statement is true or false and explain why:
(6)
> The equation $y = x^2 + 1$ cannot be the equation of a function of x,
> because $x = -8$ and $x = 8$ both map to the same value of y.

11. Let $f(x) = x^2 - x$. Find $f(x + h)$.
(6)

12. State the domain and the range of the function $y = \sin x$.
(6)

Evaluate the expressions in problems 13 and 14.

13. $\sin^2 -\dfrac{\pi}{4} \cos^2 \dfrac{3\pi}{4}$
(4)

14. $\tan -\dfrac{2\pi}{3} + 2 \sin \dfrac{\pi}{3}$
(4)

Simplify the expressions in problems 15 and 16.

15. $\dfrac{\cos \theta \sin \theta}{\tan \theta}$
(4)

16. $(\cot \theta)(\sin \theta) - \cos \theta$
(4)

For problems 17 and 18, suppose θ is an angle such that $\tan \theta = \dfrac{7}{3}$.

17. In which quadrants could θ lie?
(4)

18. Compute: $\cot \theta$
(4)

19. State the contrapositive, converse, and inverse of the following conditional statement:
(3)
$$\text{If } n \text{ is an odd number, then } n + 2 \text{ is an even number.}$$

20. Find the values of y that satisfy the equation $x^2 + y^2 = 9$ when $x = 1$.
(2)

21. Simplify: $\dfrac{\dfrac{1}{x+h} - \dfrac{1}{x}}{h}$
(1)

22. Which of the following assertions is true regarding the numbers e and π?
(7)
   A. Both numbers are rational numbers.

   B. Neither number can be expressed as the ratio of two whole numbers.

   C. Both numbers can be expressed as the ratio of two whole numbers.

   D. Both numbers are greater than 3.

23. Could this machine be a function machine?
(6) Justify your answer.

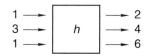

24. Find the length of the diagonals of a rectangle whose length is 12 and whose width is 5.
(2)

25. Given the figure shown, compare:
(1)
   A. $x + y$ B. z

LESSON 8 *Pythagorean Identities • Functions of $-\theta$ • Trigonometric Identities • Cofunctions • Similar Triangles*

8.A
Pythagorean identities

We can use the triangle on the left below to prove the basic trigonometric identity shown on the right.

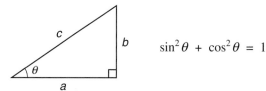

First we substitute for $\sin\theta$ and $\cos\theta$. [*Note:* $\sin^2\theta$ means $(\sin\theta)^2$, not $\sin(\theta^2)$.]

$$\sin^2\theta + \cos^2\theta = \left(\frac{b}{c}\right)^2 + \left(\frac{a}{c}\right)^2$$

Next we add the fractions and get

$$\frac{b^2 + a^2}{c^2}$$

By the Pythagorean theorem, the sum of the squares of the legs, $b^2 + a^2$, equals the square of the hypotenuse, which is c^2. Thus we can substitute c^2 for $b^2 + a^2$. Therefore,

$$\sin^2\theta + \cos^2\theta = \left(\frac{b}{c}\right)^2 + \left(\frac{a}{c}\right)^2 = \frac{b^2 + a^2}{c^2} = \frac{c^2}{c^2} = 1$$

We could use the same triangle to prove the two other trigonometric identities, which are

$$1 + \cot^2\theta = \csc^2\theta \qquad \text{and} \qquad \tan^2\theta + 1 = \sec^2\theta$$

Instead, we develop these identities from $\sin^2\theta + \cos^2\theta = 1$. To get the first one, we divide every term by $\sin^2\theta$. To get the second, we divide by $\cos^2\theta$.

$$\sin^2\theta + \cos^2\theta = 1 \qquad\qquad \sin^2\theta + \cos^2\theta = 1$$

$$\frac{\sin^2\theta}{\sin^2\theta} + \frac{\cos^2\theta}{\sin^2\theta} = \frac{1}{\sin^2\theta} \qquad\qquad \frac{\sin^2\theta}{\cos^2\theta} + \frac{\cos^2\theta}{\cos^2\theta} = \frac{1}{\cos^2\theta}$$

$$1 + \cot^2\theta = \csc^2\theta \qquad\qquad \tan^2\theta + 1 = \sec^2\theta$$

These three identities are called **Pythagorean identities.** They are frequently used in calculus problems involving trigonometry.

> PYTHAGOREAN IDENTITIES
>
> $$\sin^2\theta + \cos^2\theta = 1$$
> $$\tan^2\theta + 1 = \sec^2\theta$$
> $$\cot^2\theta + 1 = \csc^2\theta$$

In each of the three Pythagorean identities, θ must be a real number for which each of the terms is defined. In the identity $\sin^2\theta + \cos^2\theta = 1$, each function and term is defined for any real θ. However, in the identities $\tan^2\theta + 1 = \sec^2\theta$ and $\cot^2\theta + 1 = \csc^2\theta$, there are values of θ for which the terms $\tan^2\theta$, $\sec^2\theta$, $\cot^2\theta$, and $\csc^2\theta$ are not defined. For these as well as other identities, θ cannot be a value that results in an undefined term.

example 8.1   Evaluate: $\sin^2 17° + \cos^2 17°$

solution   The Pythagorean identity

$$\sin^2\theta + \cos^2\theta = 1$$

is true for any value of θ. Thus it is true when $\theta = 17°$.

$$\sin^2 17° + \cos^2 17° = \mathbf{1}$$

8.B
functions of −θ

It is often necessary to use one of the following identities:

$$\sin -\theta = -\sin\theta \qquad\qquad \csc -\theta = -\csc\theta$$
$$\cos -\theta = \cos\theta \qquad\qquad \sec -\theta = \sec\theta$$
$$\tan -\theta = -\tan\theta \qquad\qquad \cot -\theta = -\cot\theta$$

These relationships hold true for all values of θ. We need a way to recall them quickly and accurately. We can do this if we visualize the following unit circle with angles θ and $-\theta$.

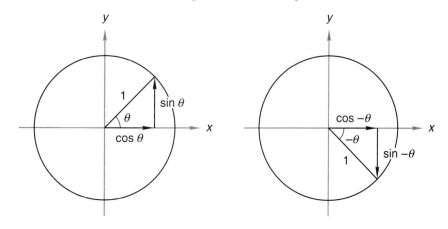

The cosine of $-\theta$ and the cosine of θ are represented by the horizontal sides of the triangles, which are identical in length and in direction. Thus the cosines of θ and $-\theta$ are equal. The secant is the reciprocal of the cosine, so this also gives us the sign relationship between $\sec -\theta$ and $\sec \theta$.

$$\cos -\theta = \cos \theta \quad \longrightarrow \quad \sec -\theta = \sec \theta$$

Functions like the cosine and secant functions are called **even functions.** A function f is even if

$$f(-x) = f(x) \qquad \text{for all } x \text{ in the domain of } f$$

The sine of $-\theta$ and the sine of $+\theta$ are represented by the vertical sides of the triangles. These vertical lengths are equal but are on opposite sides of the x-axis. So $\sin (-\theta)$ has the same magnitude as $\sin \theta$, but its sign is different. The cosecant of an angle is the reciprocal of the sine of the angle, and this also gives us the sign relationship between $\csc (-\theta)$ and $\csc \theta$.

$$\sin -\theta = -\sin \theta \quad \longrightarrow \quad \csc -\theta = -\csc \theta$$

Functions like the sine function are called **odd functions.** A function f is odd if

$$f(-x) = -f(x) \qquad \text{for all } x \text{ in the domain of } f$$

The tangent relationship can be determined using the fact $\tan \theta = \dfrac{\sin \theta}{\cos \theta}$.

$$\tan -\theta = \frac{\sin -\theta}{\cos -\theta} = \frac{-\sin \theta}{\cos \theta} = -\frac{\sin \theta}{\cos \theta} = -\tan \theta$$

Since the cotangent function is the reciprocal of the tangent function,

$$\cot -\theta = -\cot \theta$$

Therefore, the tangent function and the cotangent function are odd functions.

example 8.2   Simplify: $\dfrac{(\sin -\theta)(\cos -\theta)}{\tan -\theta}$

solution   We simplify the expression by rewriting functions of $-\theta$ in terms of functions of θ. We replace $\sin -\theta$ with $-\sin \theta$, $\cos -\theta$ with $\cos \theta$, and $\tan -\theta$ with $-\tan \theta$.

$$\begin{aligned}
\frac{(\sin -\theta)(\cos -\theta)}{\tan -\theta} &= \frac{(-\sin \theta)(\cos \theta)}{-\tan \theta} \\[2mm]
&= \frac{\sin \theta \cos \theta}{\dfrac{\sin \theta}{\cos \theta}} \\[2mm]
&= (\cos \theta)^2 \\[2mm]
&= \mathbf{\cos^2 \theta}
\end{aligned}$$

example 8.3   Show that $(\tan -\theta)(\cos -\theta) - (\sin -\theta) = 0$ for all values of θ that make sense.[†]

solution   First we substitute as necessary to get functions of θ rather than functions of $-\theta$.

$$(-\tan \theta)(\cos \theta) - (-\sin \theta)$$

Then we replace $\tan \theta$ with $\sin \theta$ over $\cos \theta$ and simplify.

$$-\left(\frac{\sin \theta}{\cos \theta}\right)(\cos \theta) + \sin \theta = -\sin \theta + \sin \theta = 0$$

8.C

trigonometric identities

In calculus it is often helpful to change trigonometric expressions to a simpler equivalent form. An equation involving two equivalent trigonometric expressions is called a **trigonometric identity.** Problems designed to permit practice in changing trigonometric expressions from one form to another consist of two expressions connected by an equals sign. Our job is to work with one of the expressions

---

[†] Values of θ that do not make sense are those values for which one of the expressions is not defined.

and manipulate it until it takes on the form of the other expression. Although an equals sign is present, we cannot use the rules for equations, which allow us to add the same quantity to both sides or multiply both sides by the same quantity. We must restrict ourselves to three techniques. We may:

1. Substitute an equivalent expression for all or any part of a given expression.

2. Multiply the numerator and denominator of any expression or the numerator and denominator of a part of any expression by the same nonzero quantity.

3. Combine terms that have equal denominators.

There is no one correct way to show that two expressions are equivalent. We try one thing and if that does not work, we try something else. After much practice these transformations will become familiar and not at all troublesome. In this lesson we will consider expressions that can be simplified by using one of the Pythagorean identities. In these expressions we will learn to look for terms such as $\sin^2 x + \cos^2 x$, $1 - \sin^2 x$, $1 - \cos^2 x$, $1 + \cot^2 x$, $\csc^2 x - 1$, $\tan^2 x + 1$, and $\sec^2 x - 1$.

example 8.4   Show that the following relation is true for all real numbers x where the functions are defined:

$$\frac{\cos^2 x + 4 + \sin^2 x}{5 \sec^2 -x} = \cos^2 x$$

solution   If we look carefully at the numerator of the left-hand side, we can find $\sin^2 x + \cos^2 x$, which equals 1, hiding there. So we decide to work with the left-hand side. We rearrange the numerator and we replace $\sec^2 -x$ with $\sec^2 x$ in the denominator.

$$\frac{(\sin^2 x + \cos^2 x) + 4}{5 \sec^2 x} \qquad \text{rearranged and replaced}$$

$$= \frac{5}{5 \sec^2 x} \qquad \sin^2 x + \cos^2 x = 1$$

$$= \cos^2 x \qquad \frac{1}{\sec^2 x} = \cos^2 x$$

example 8.5   Show that $\cos^2 x \sec^2 x - \cos^2 x = \sin^2 x$ for all real numbers x where the functions are defined.

solution   Again we begin with the expression on the left. This time we factor first.

$$(\cos^2 x)(\sec^2 x - 1) \qquad \text{factored}$$

$$= (\cos^2 x)(\tan^2 x) \qquad \sec^2 x - 1 = \tan^2 x$$

$$= (\cos^2 x)\left(\frac{\sin^2 x}{\cos^2 x}\right) \qquad \text{substituted}$$

$$= \sin^2 x \qquad \text{simplified}$$

8.D

cofunctions   The sum of the angles in any triangle is $180°$, or π radians. If a triangle is a right triangle, the right angle has a measure of $90°$, or $\frac{\pi}{2}$ radians. If one acute angle is θ, the other acute angle must be $90° - \theta$, or $\frac{\pi}{2} - \theta$. When we write $90° - \theta$, it is understood that θ is measured in degrees, and when we write $\frac{\pi}{2} - \theta$, it is understood that θ is measured in radians. If the sum of two angles is $90°$, or $\frac{\pi}{2}$, the angles are called **complementary angles.** Thus, when θ is measured in degrees, $90° - \theta$ is the complement of angle θ; and when θ is measured in radians, $\frac{\pi}{2} - \theta$ is the complement of angle θ.

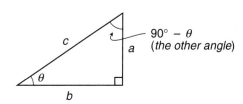

In the right triangle shown above, the sine of θ equals a over c, and the cosine of the other angle also equals a over c.

$$\sin \theta = \frac{a}{c} \qquad \cos (90° - \theta) = \frac{a}{c}$$

The cosine of θ equals b over c, and the sine of the other angle equals b over c.

$$\cos \theta = \frac{b}{c} \qquad \sin (90° - \theta) = \frac{b}{c}$$

The tangent and cotangent have similar relationships.

$$\tan \theta = \frac{a}{b} \qquad \cot (90° - \theta) = \frac{a}{b}$$

$$\cot \theta = \frac{b}{a} \qquad \tan (90° - \theta) = \frac{b}{a}$$

The secant and cosecant also have similar relationships.

$$\sec \theta = \frac{c}{b} \qquad \csc (90° - \theta) = \frac{c}{b}$$

$$\csc \theta = \frac{c}{a} \qquad \sec (90° - \theta) = \frac{c}{a}$$

Thus every trigonometric function of θ has the same value as the trigonometric cofunction of $(90° - \theta)$. We can remember this if we always think of $(90° - \theta)$ as *the other angle*.

$(90° - \theta)$ **is the other angle**

It is interesting to note that the words *cosine, cotangent,* and *cosecant* are abbreviations for "the sine of the complementary angle" (the other angle), "the tangent of the complementary angle" (the other angle), and "the secant of the complementary angle" (the other angle). Thus

cosine	**means**	**the sine of the other angle**
cotangent	**means**	**the tangent of the other angle**
cosecant	**means**	**the secant of the other angle**

Now we have four procedures that we can use to simplify trigonometric expressions.

1. Replace functions of $-\theta$ with equivalent functions of $+\theta$.
2. Replace functions of $90° - \theta$ or $\frac{\pi}{2} - \theta$ with their cofunctions of θ.
3. Look for forms of the Pythagorean identity that can be replaced.
4. Replace $\tan x$, $\cot x$, $\sec x$, and $\csc x$ with equivalent expressions that use $\sin x$ and $\cos x$.

example 8.6   Show that $(\sin^2 -\theta)(\csc^2 \theta - 1)\left[\cot \left(\dfrac{\pi}{2} - \theta\right)\right] = \sin \theta \cos \theta$.

solution   **We must be careful when we substitute for a function that is raised to a power.** Since $\sin -\theta = -\sin \theta$, we might be tempted to write

$$\sin^2 -\theta = -\sin^2 \theta \qquad \text{NO! NO! NO!}$$

We remember that $\sin^2 -\theta$ means $(\sin -\theta)(\sin -\theta)$, and since $\sin -\theta = -\sin \theta$, we have

$$\sin^2 -\theta = (\sin -\theta)(\sin -\theta) = (-\sin \theta)(-\sin \theta) = \sin^2 \theta$$

Now we substitute $\sin^2 \theta$ for $\sin^2 -\theta$ and replace $\cot \left(\dfrac{\pi}{2} - \theta\right)$ with its cofunction, $\tan \theta$, to get

$$(\sin^2 \theta)(\csc^2 \theta - 1)(\tan \theta)$$

The middle factor looks like it may be a part of a Pythagorean identity. To investigate, we begin with the basic Pythagorean identity.

$$\sin^2 \theta + \cos^2 \theta = 1$$

If we divide by $\sin^2 \theta$, we get

$$1 + \cot^2 \theta = \csc^2 \theta$$

Aha! Now we see that $\csc^2 \theta - 1 = \cot^2 \theta$, so we make this replacement. Then we replace $\cot^2 \theta$ with $\cos^2 \theta$ over $\sin^2 \theta$ and $\tan \theta$ with $\sin \theta$ over $\cos \theta$.

$$(\sin^2 \theta)(\cot^2 \theta)(\tan \theta) = (\sin^2 \theta)\left(\frac{\cos^2 \theta}{\sin^2 \theta}\right)\left(\frac{\sin \theta}{\cos \theta}\right) = \sin \theta \cos \theta$$

8.E

similar triangles

Two polygons are similar if their corresponding angles have equal measures and if the lengths of their corresponding sides are proportional. Triangles are three-sided polygons, and the angles in one triangle equal the angles in another triangle if and only if (iff) the corresponding sides are proportional. This relationship between angles and sides in similar triangles makes similar triangles especially useful.

example 8.7   Find: b

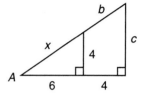

solution   First we use the Pythagorean theorem to find x.

$$6^2 + 4^2 = x^2$$
$$x = 2\sqrt{13}$$

The big triangle and the little triangle are similar because the corresponding angles are equal. Since corresponding sides of similar triangles are proportional,

$$\frac{\text{hypotenuse of big triangle}}{\text{hypotenuse of little triangle}} = \frac{\text{horizontal leg of big triangle}}{\text{horizontal leg of little triangle}}$$

Therefore

$$\frac{x + b}{x} = \frac{6 + 4}{6}$$
$$\frac{2\sqrt{13} + b}{2\sqrt{13}} = \frac{10}{6}$$
$$b = \frac{4\sqrt{13}}{3}$$

example 8.8   Solve for p in terms of h, x, and d.

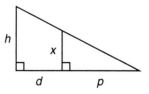

solution   We use the vertical and horizontal sides to write a proportion. Then we cross multiply.

$$\frac{x}{h} = \frac{p}{d + p}$$
$$ph = xd + xp$$

Now we solve for p.

$$ph - xp = xd$$
$$p(h - x) = xd$$
$$p = \frac{xd}{h - x}$$

example 8.9   Solve for y in terms of a, b, and x.

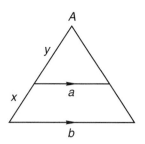

solution   The big triangle and the little triangle are similar because both contain angle A and because corresponding angles are equal when parallel lines are cut by a transversal. We write the proportion and cross multiply.

$$\frac{y}{y + x} = \frac{a}{b}$$

$$yb = ay + ax$$

Now we solve for y.

$$yb - ay = ax$$

$$y(b - a) = ax$$

$$y = \frac{ax}{b - a}$$

example 8.10   Find x, y, and z.

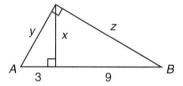

solution   There are three triangles in the figure. They are similar triangles because all of them contain a right angle and all of them contain an angle that has the same measure as angle A. We can write the proportions easily if we can remember which sides to use. A sure way is to redraw the figure as three separate triangles, one big, one small, and one medium.

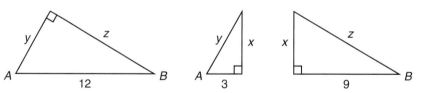

Now, taking two triangles at a time, we can write the ratios of corresponding sides. Below on the left, we use the outer triangles. In the center, we compare the first two triangles. On the right, we use the last two triangles.

$$\frac{z}{12} = \frac{x}{y} = \frac{9}{z} \qquad \frac{y}{12} = \frac{3}{y} = \frac{x}{z} \qquad \frac{z}{y} = \frac{x}{3} = \frac{9}{x}$$

Now we try to find a way to use these proportions to get the answers we need. We can use two ratios from each group and write:

$$\frac{z}{12} = \frac{9}{z} \qquad\qquad \frac{y}{12} = \frac{3}{y} \qquad\qquad \frac{x}{3} = \frac{9}{x}$$

$$z^2 = 108 \qquad\qquad y^2 = 36 \qquad\qquad x^2 = 27$$

$$z = 6\sqrt{3} \qquad\qquad y = 6 \qquad\qquad x = 3\sqrt{3}$$

problem set 8

1. The density of a horizontally oriented 10-foot-long rod varies linearly with the distance x from
   (5) the left end of the rod. If the density is 5 at the left end of the rod and 17 at the right end, what is the density of the rod 4 feet from the rod's left end?

2. A rectangular box has a total surface area of 500 cm². The edges of its square base measure x cm.
$_{(5)}$ Express the volume V of the box in terms of x.

3. The equation of a certain parabola is $y = x^2 + 2x - 3$.
$_{(2)}$

    (a) Complete the square to rewrite the equation of the parabola in the form $y = (x - a)^2 + b$.

    (b) Graph the parabola.

    (c) Does the parabola open upward or downward?

    (d) Write the equation of the line that divides the parabola into two symmetric halves.

    (e) What are the coordinates of the vertex of the parabola?

4. Use a graphing calculator to graph the function $y = x^2 + 2x - 3$. Use the trace feature of the
$_{(2)}$ calculator to find approximate coordinates of various points on the graph. In particular, find the
approximate coordinates of the lowest point on the graph.

5. The basic Pythagorean identity is $\sin^2 \theta + \cos^2 \theta = 1$.
$_{(8)}$

    (a) Divide the basic identity by $\sin^2 \theta$ to develop another Pythagorean identity.

    (b) Divide the basic identity by $\cos^2 \theta$ to develop another Pythagorean identity.

Evaluate the expressions in problems 6 and 7.

6. $\sin^2 \dfrac{\pi}{7} + \cos^2 \dfrac{\pi}{7}$
$_{(8)}$

7. $\sec^2 \dfrac{5\pi}{4} + 2 \tan -\dfrac{\pi}{4}$
$_{(4)}$

For problems 8–10, assume that θ is an angle such that $\sin \theta = -\frac{4}{5}$. Without using a calculator,
compute each of the following:

8. $\sin -\theta$
$_{(8)}$

9. $\cos \left(\dfrac{\pi}{2} - \theta \right)$
$_{(8)}$

10. $\sec \left(\dfrac{\pi}{2} - \theta \right)$
$_{(8)}$

For problems 11–13, show that the trigonometric identity holds for all real numbers x where the
functions are defined.

11. $\dfrac{\sin^2 x + 2 + \cos^2 x}{3 \csc^2 -x} = \sin^2 x$
$_{(8)}$

12. $\left[\sec \left(\dfrac{\pi}{2} - x \right) \right] (\sin -x) = -1$
$_{(8)}$

13. $(\sin x) \left[\cos \left(\dfrac{\pi}{2} - x \right) \right] + (\cos -x)(\cos x) = 1$
$_{(8)}$

14. Find the zeros of the quadratic polynomial $x^2 - 3x + 2$.
$_{(2)}$

15. Solve for x in terms of L.
$_{(8)}$

16. Solve for h in terms of x and a.
$_{(8)}$

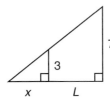

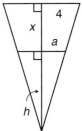

17. The unit circle shown is centered at the
$_{(7)}$ origin. Find the coordinates of the point P.

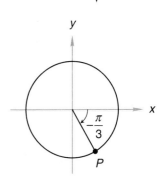

18. Graph: $y = -3 + 2 \cos\left[2\left(x - \dfrac{\pi}{4}\right)\right]$
(7)

19. Write the equation of the sinusoid shown
(7) in terms of the sine function.

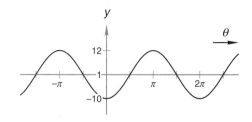

20. Which of the following sets of points could lie on the graph of a function?
(6)
    A. $\{(1, 5), (6, 2), (4, 3), (6, -3)\}$ B. $\{(2, 4), (1, 5), (3, 1), (6, 3)\}$

    C. $\{(1, -1), (-1, 1), (1, 3), (4, \pi)\}$ D. $\{(14, 12), (-1, -7), (8, 12), (10, -3)\}$

21. Simplify: $\dfrac{(x + h)^2 - x^2}{h}$
(R)

22. Graph $y = \cos(x^3)$ and $y = x^2$ on a graphing calculator using the radian mode.
(2) Approximate the coordinates of the intersection point(s) of the two functions.

23. Use x as the independent variable to write the equation of the quadratic function f whose zeros
(R) are -3 and -2 and whose leading coefficient is 2. (*Hint:* If k is a zero of a function, then $x - k$ is a factor of the function.)

24. Given that x, y, and z are real numbers and $xy > zy$, compare: A. x B. z
(1)

25. Given that $a + b = 10$ and $ab = 5$, compute the value of $a^2 + b^2$. (*Hint:* Begin by
(R) squaring both sides of the first equation.)

LESSON 9   *Absolute Value as a Distance • Graphing "Special" Functions • Logarithms • Base 10 and Base e • Simple Logarithm Problems*

9.A

absolute value as a distance

A real number has two qualities. One is the quality of being positive or negative. The number zero does not possess this quality, as it is neither positive nor negative. Every other real number is either a positive number or a negative number. The second quality of a real number is called the **absolute value** of the number. Some people think of the absolute value of a number as describing the "bigness" of the number. We can think of +3 and −3 as both having the same degree of bigness, which is 3.

$$|+3| = 3 \qquad |-3| = 3$$

Using the word *bigness* to describe the absolute value of a real number is not a good idea, because a number does not have a physical size. But numbers can be arranged in order, and we can use the position of the graph of a number on the number line to describe the absolute value of the number. Thus we think of absolute value as the distance between the graph of a number and the origin on the number line. Looking at this number line,

we see that +3 and −3 are both the same distance from the origin. Thus they have the same absolute value.

If we write that the absolute value of x is less than 4, we indicate that x is a number whose graph is less than 4 units from the origin. If we write that the absolute value of x is greater than 4, we indicate that x is a number whose graph is more than 4 units from the origin. So the graphs of the solution sets to $|x| < 4$ and $|x| > 4$ are as shown. (*Note:* The circles in the graphs are empty because 4 and −4 are not in the solution set.)

Inequalities such as those shown here

$$|x - 7| > 3 \qquad |x + 4| < 3 \qquad |x - 5| < 3$$

are satisfied by numbers whose graphs lie in certain regions on the number line. It is helpful to have a way to describe the solution sets of these inequalities. The numbers that satisfy the inequality on the left-hand side below are the numbers whose graphs are within 5 units of the graph of a on the number line.

$$|x - a| < 5 \qquad |x - a| > 5$$

The numbers that satisfy the inequality on the right-hand side above are the numbers whose graphs are more than 5 units away from the graph of a on the number line.

example 9.1 Graph the following set on a number line: $\{x \in \mathbb{R} \mid |x - 5| < 2\}$.

solution We must indicate all *real numbers* that satisfy the inequality. The solution set consists of the numbers less than 2 units from +5 on the number line.

$$|x - 5| < 2$$

(number line graph with open circles at 3 and 7, marks at 3, 5, 7)

example 9.2 Graph the following set on a number line: $\{x \in \mathbb{Z} \mid |3x - 1| > 2\}$.

solution We must indicate all *integers* that satisfy the inequality. We begin by factoring the inequality so that the x has a coefficient of 1.

$$\left|3\left(x - \frac{1}{3}\right)\right| > 2 \qquad \text{factored inside absolute value}$$

$$|3|\left|x - \frac{1}{3}\right| > 2 \qquad \text{property of absolute value}$$

$$3\left|x - \frac{1}{3}\right| > 2 \qquad \text{simplified}$$

$$\left|x - \frac{1}{3}\right| > \frac{2}{3} \qquad \text{multiplied by } \frac{1}{3}$$

The graph of every integer except 0 and +1 is more than $\frac{2}{3}$ from $\frac{1}{3}$. Thus, our graph indicates all integers except 0 and +1.

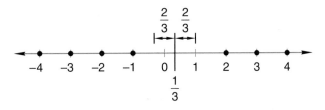

9.B

graphing "special" functions

In later lessons we discuss the fact that a curve does not have a defined slope at a point where the curve makes a sudden change in direction. Graphs of many absolute value functions come to one or more points called **cusps** where the graph changes direction suddenly. These graphs are ideal for discussing graphs of functions that do not have a defined slope at some point. The graph of the absolute value of a function is easy to draw if we use two steps. The first step is to graph the function defined with the absolute value notation removed. The second step is to draw the graph of the absolute value function by plotting above the x-axis the reflection of all points originally graphed below the x-axis. The graph of the opposite of the absolute value of a function is the mirror image in the x-axis of the graph of the absolute value. The following graphs demonstrate these facts.

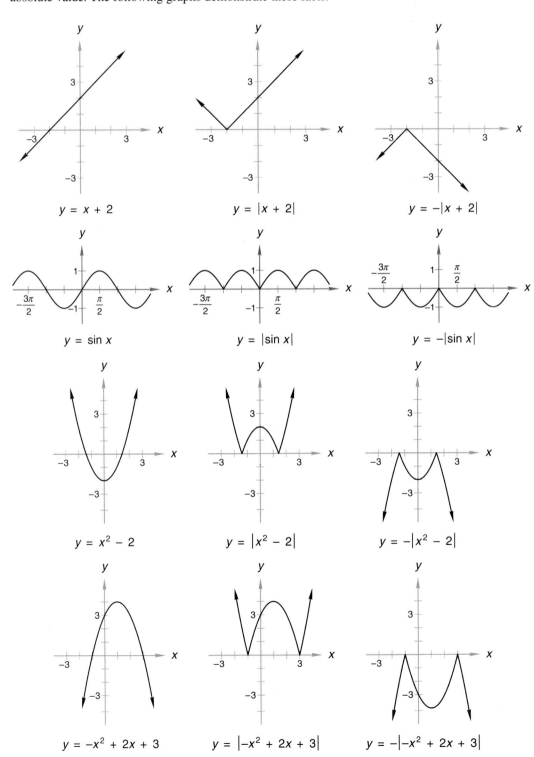

$y = x + 2$ $y = |x + 2|$ $y = -|x + 2|$

$y = \sin x$ $y = |\sin x|$ $y = -|\sin x|$

$y = x^2 - 2$ $y = |x^2 - 2|$ $y = -|x^2 - 2|$

$y = -x^2 + 2x + 3$ $y = |-x^2 + 2x + 3|$ $y = -|-x^2 + 2x + 3|$

example 9.3   Graph: $y = |-\sin x|$

solution   On the left we show the graph of $y = -\sin x,$ and on the right we make every negative value of y positive.

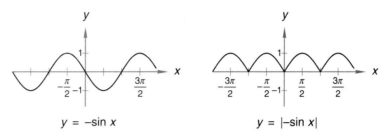

$y = -\sin x$ $y = |-\sin x|$

Note: This graph is identical to the graph of $y = |\sin x|$ shown earlier in the lesson.

example 9.4   Graph: (a) $y = \sqrt{x}$ (b) $y = \sqrt[3]{x}$ (c) $y = \sqrt[3]{x^2}$

solution   These functions can be written with fractional exponents as follows:

$$\text{(a) } y = x^{1/2} \qquad \text{(b) } y = x^{1/3} \qquad \text{(c) } y = x^{2/3}$$

The square root of x is a function whose graph terminates abruptly. Negative values of x are not in the domain of $\sqrt{x}$ because negative numbers do not have real square roots. All real numbers have cube roots, so the graph of $y = x^{1/3}$ exists for all real values of x. We can turn the graph of $y = x^{1/3}$ into a graph with a cusp by squaring the function to get $y = (x^{1/3})^2,$ which is the same as $y = x^{2/3}.$

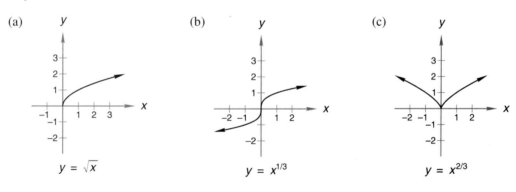

(a) $y = \sqrt{x}$ (b) $y = x^{1/3}$ (c) $y = x^{2/3}$

example 9.5   Graph: $y = [x]$

solution   The symbol $[x]$ stands for the **greatest integer function of x.** The value of $[x]$ is the greatest integer less than or equal to x. Note that the graph jumps to a new value as each greater integer is reached, moving from left to right.

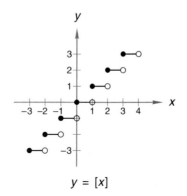

$y = [x]$

example 9.6   Write an equation for the function whose graph is shown.

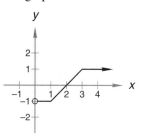

solution   This type of function is called a **piecewise function.** It is constructed by stringing together pieces of several functions. This graph has three pieces. For the left-hand piece (when x is between 0 and 1), $y = -1$. For the middle piece (when x is between 1 and 3), $y = x - 2$. For the right-hand piece (when x is greater than 3), $y = 1$. To describe the function, we must write the equation for each piece of the graph.

$$y = \begin{cases} -1 & \text{if } 0 < x \le 1 \\ x - 2 & \text{if } 1 < x \le 3 \\ 1 & \text{if } x > 3 \end{cases}$$

Of course, minor adjustments are possible. For example, the first x-range could be $0 < x < 1$ if the second x-range were changed to $1 \le x \le 3$. However, these simple changes are not always possible.

9.C
logarithms

Any positive number can be written as any positive base raised to some power, either positive or negative. We use the letter N to represent the number and the letter b to represent the base. The letter L represents the logarithm, which is the exponent.

$$N = b^L$$

This is read by saying "N equals b to the L." We could also read this by saying "the logarithm for b to yield N is L." We abbreviate the word **logarithm** with **log** and write this in compact form as

$$\log_b N = L$$

We read this as "the logarithm of N to the base b equals L." Thus

$$N = b^L \qquad \text{and} \qquad \log_b N = L$$

are two ways to write the same thing.

When discussing exponential functions, we restrict ourselves to positive bases b because certain powers of negative numbers are undefined. For example, $(-1)^{1/2}$ and $(-1)^{1/4}$ are undefined in the real number system. Indeed, $(-1)^{1/n}$ is undefined for all even integers n. Because of such considerations, we restrict ourselves to positive bases b. Since b is positive, N must also be positive. This is the reason we do not find logarithms of negative numbers.

example 9.7   Write $4 = 5^y$ in logarithmic form.

solution   We remember that a logarithm is the exponent, and here the exponent is y. Therefore we begin by writing

$$\log = y$$

Next we indicate the base, which in this case is 5.

$$\log_5 = y$$

Now the only thing left is the number 4. We insert it and have

$$\log_5 4 = y$$

9.D
base 10 and base *e*

Logarithms that use 10 as a base are called **common logarithms.** Before slide rules and calculators were invented, most scientific calculations were made using tables of common logarithms. Though tables are outdated, common logarithms are still used today. Other bases are also used for special purposes. For example, in information theory a base of 2 is sometimes used. The most important base in higher mathematics is the base e. Logarithms with a base of e are called **natural logarithms.**

It is customary to designate that the base is 10 by writing log with no subscript, and it is customary to designate that the base is e by using the letters ln with no subscript. For example,

$$\log 42 \quad \text{means} \quad \log_{10} 42$$
$$\ln 42 \quad \text{means} \quad \log_e 42$$

Tables of logarithms give common logarithms and natural logarithms to four or five digits, and calculators are usually accurate to seven or eight. When accuracy is desired, logarithms can be obtained from these sources; but since beginners often tend to get lost in the arithmetic of logarithm problems, we sometimes round off logarithms to two decimal places and concentrate on understanding rather than on arithmetic accuracy.

example 9.8   Write 2.4 as a power of the base   (a) 10   (b) e.

solution   (a) We are trying to find L such that

$$2.4 = 10^L$$

This means $\log_{10} 2.4 = L$. On the TI-83, $\log_{10} 2.4$, or log 2.4, is determined by pressing [LOG] [2] [.] [4] [)] [ENTER]. The answer is approximately 0.38. So, $2.4 \approx 10^{0.38}$.

(b) Here we want to find L such that

$$2.4 = e^L \quad \text{or} \quad \log_e 2.4 = L$$

This is the same as $\ln 2.4 = L$. We press [LN] [2] [.] [4] [)] [ENTER] to get 0.88, approximately. Therefore, $2.4 \approx e^{0.88}$.

9.E
simple logarithm problems

The ability to change from the logarithmic form of an equation to the exponential form is most useful. Some logarithmic equations can be solved by rewriting them as exponential equations.

example 9.9   Solve $\log_{1/3} P = 2$ for P.

solution   We rewrite the equation in exponential form and then solve.

$$\left(\frac{1}{3}\right)^2 = P \qquad \text{exponential form}$$

$$\frac{1}{9} = P \qquad \text{solved}$$

example 9.10   Solve $\log_x (6x - 9) = 2$ for x.

solution   We rewrite the equation in exponential form and then solve.

$$x^2 = 6x - 9 \qquad \text{exponential form}$$
$$x^2 - 6x + 9 = 0 \qquad \text{rearranged}$$
$$(x - 3)^2 = 0 \qquad \text{factored}$$
$$x = 3 \qquad \text{solved}$$

Since the argument of a logarithm can never be zero or negative, we check to see if using 3 for x makes $6x - 9$ nonpositive.

$$6(3) - 9 = 9 \qquad \text{check}$$

Since x is the base, we must also make sure x is positive. Of course 3 is positive, so **3** is an acceptable value for x.

example 9.11 Solve $\log_b 9 = -\dfrac{1}{2}$ for b.

solution We rewrite the equation in exponential form and solve by raising both sides to the appropriate power.

$$b^{-1/2} = 9 \qquad \text{exponential form}$$
$$(b^{-1/2})^{-2} = 9^{-2} \qquad \text{raised both sides to } -2 \text{ power}$$
$$b = \frac{1}{81} \qquad \text{simplified}$$

example 9.12 Solve $\log_3 \dfrac{1}{27} = 2m + 1$ for m.

solution We rewrite the equation in exponential form and then solve.

$$3^{2m+1} = \frac{1}{27} \qquad \text{exponential form}$$
$$3^{2m+1} = 3^{-3} \qquad \text{changed form}$$
$$2m + 1 = -3 \qquad \text{equal bases implies equal exponents}$$
$$m = \mathbf{-2} \qquad \text{solved}$$

problem set 9

1. In an oil field, as more wells are drilled each oil well pumps less oil; however, the total amount of oil pumped may increase. Suppose an oil field with 20 wells produces 10,000 barrels of oil daily. For each additional well, the production capacity of every well decreases by 10 barrels per day. Express the total volume V of oil pumped per day in terms of x, where x is the number of wells added.
(5)

2. (a) Graph the function from problem 1 on a graphing calculator in a window that clearly shows the peak in the graph.
(2)

(b) Use the trace feature of the calculator to find the coordinates of the high point on the graph.

(c) How many additional wells should be drilled to produce the maximum amount of oil?

(d) How many barrels of oil would be produced?

3. A rectangular box has a volume of 125 cubic centimeters. Its square base has edges that measure x centimeters. The material for the base costs \$5 per square centimeter and the material for the top and the four sides costs \$2 per square centimeter. Express the total cost of material required to make the box in terms of x.
(5)

4. Find the coordinates of the vertex and the axis of symmetry of the parabola $y = x^2 - 3x + 4$ by completing the square and rewriting the equation in the form $y = (x - a)^2 + b$.
(2)

5. Find the coordinates of the point halfway between $(-5, -8)$ and $(0, 4)$.
(2)

6. Write 7.3 as a power of the base (a) 10 (b) e
(9)

7. If $3^y = 4$, then y equals
(9)

A. $\dfrac{4}{3}$ B. $\log_3 4$ C. $\log_4 3$ D. $\sqrt[3]{4}$

8. Simplify: $\dfrac{y^3 y^{3/4 - 2} z^2}{y^{(3-2)/3} z^{(3-2)/6}}$
(1)

9. Find both a symbolic representation and a numerical approximation for x when:
(9)
(a) $10^x = 3$ (b) $e^x = 5$

10. Solve $\log_3 27 = 2b + 1$ for b.
(9)

11. Solve $\log_x (3x - 2) = 2$ for x.
(9)

12. Let $f(x) = [x]$.
(9)

    (a) Graph f.

    (b) Calculate $f(1.2)$ and $f(-1.2)$.

13. Graph: $y = |\cos x|$
(9)

14. Graph g where $g(x) = \begin{cases} x^2 \text{ when } x < 1 \\ 2x \text{ when } x \geq 1. \end{cases}$
(9)

15. Describe the set of all real values of x such that $|x - 3| < 0.001$.
(9)

16. Write the piecewise definition of the function f whose graph is shown.
(9)

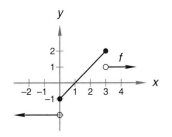

17. Write the equation of the sinusoid shown in terms of the sine function.
(7)

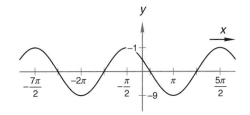

18. Sketch the graphs of $y = 2^x$ and $y = \left(\dfrac{1}{2}\right)^x$ on the same coordinate plane.
(7)

19. Simplify: $(\tan -x)\left[\sec^2\left(\dfrac{\pi}{2} - x\right)\right](\sin -x)$
(8)

20. Solve for L in terms of x.
(8)

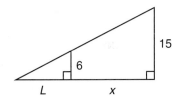

21. The unit circle shown is centered at the origin. Find the y-coordinates of P_1, P_2, and P_3.
(7)

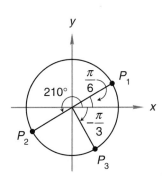

22. Determine whether or not the mapping $f: x \longrightarrow \pm\sqrt{x}$ is a function and explain your answer.
(6)

23. Given $f(x) = x^2$, find $f(x + h) - f(x)$.
(6)

24. Evaluate: $\dfrac{\displaystyle\sum_{i=1}^{10} i}{10}$
(1)

25. Given the figure shown, compare:
(R)
    A. The sum of the areas of squares A and B

    B. The area of square C

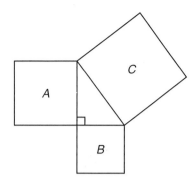

LESSON **10**   *Quadratic Polynomials • Remainder Theorem • Synthetic Division • Rational Roots Theorem*

10.A

quadratic polynomials

Below we show examples of a quadratic polynomial, a quadratic polynomial equation, and a quadratic polynomial function.

QUADRATIC POLYNOMIAL	QUADRATIC POLYNOMIAL EQUATION	QUADRATIC POLYNOMIAL FUNCTION
$x^2 - 3x + 2$	$x^2 - 3x + 2 = 0$	$y = x^2 - 3x + 2$
$(x - 1)(x - 2)$	$(x - 1)(x - 2) = 0$	$y = (x - 1)(x - 2)$
zeros are 1, 2	**roots** are 1, 2	**x-intercepts** of graph are $x = 1, 2$

The **zeros** of a polynomial are the values of the variable, in this case x, that make the value of the polynomial 0. The **roots** of a polynomial equation are the values of the variable that make the equation true. The **x-intercepts** of the graph of a polynomial function are the x-values where the graph crosses the x-axis.

The graph of a quadratic function is a parabola. If a quadratic function is rewritten in the form

$$y = a(x - h)^2 + k$$

its graph can easily be sketched. For a quadratic function written in this form,

    (h, k) are the coordinates of the vertex.

    $x = h$ is the axis of symmetry.

    If $a > 0$, then the graph of the parabola opens upward.

    If $a < 0$, then the graph of the parabola opens downward.

    If x is set to 0, the resulting value of y is the y-intercept of the graph.

If a quadratic function is written in the form

$$y = a(x - r)(x - s)$$

then the graph of the function has x-intercepts $x = r$ and $x = s$.

example 10.1   Graph the parabola $f(x) = -2x^2 - 8x - 5$.

solution   The negative coefficient of x^2 tells us that the graph opens down, and the constant -5 gives us the value of the y-intercept. However, we need more information, so we change the form of the equation by completing the square. We begin by placing parentheses around the nonconstant terms.

$f(x) = (-2x^2 - 8x \quad) - 5$	used parentheses
$f(x) = -2(x^2 + 4x \quad) - 5$	factored
$f(x) = -2(x^2 + 4x + 4) - 5 + 8$	completed the square
$f(x) = -2(x + 2)^2 + 3$	simplified

The $(x + 2)$ tells us that the axis of symmetry is $x = -2$, and the $+3$ gives us the y-value of the vertex. Knowing this and knowing that the y-intercept is -5 permits us to sketch the parabola.

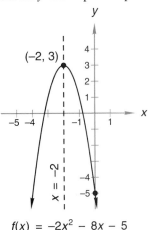

$$f(x) = -2x^2 - 8x - 5$$

example 10.2   Find the quadratic function whose x-intercepts are -3 and $+2$ and whose y-intercept is $+3$. Then graph the function.

solution   Since the x-intercepts are -3 and $+2$, we know that two of the factors of the polynomial are $(x + 3)$ and $(x - 2)$, but we do not know the value of the constant factor a.

$$y = a(x + 3)(x - 2)$$
$$y = ax^2 + ax - 6a$$

We can substitute the coordinates of any point on the curve to solve for a. The point $(0, 3)$ is on the curve because the y-intercept is $+3$. When we use these coordinates for x and y, we find that $+3 = -6a$ because the x-terms have a value of zero after we substitute.

$$3 = a(0)^2 + a(0) - 6a \qquad \text{substituted}$$

$$a = -\frac{1}{2} \qquad \text{simplified}$$

Now we have

$$y = -\frac{1}{2}(x + 3)(x - 2) \qquad \text{or} \qquad y = -\frac{1}{2}x^2 - \frac{1}{2}x + 3$$

Since a is a negative number, we know that the parabola opens down. The graph of this function is shown on the left-hand side below.

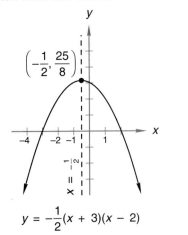

$$y = -\frac{1}{2}(x + 3)(x - 2)$$

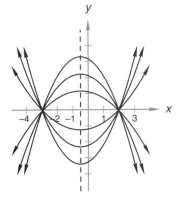

$$y = k(x + 3)(x - 2)$$

As we see in the figure on the right-hand side, there are an infinite number of parabolas whose graphs cross the x-axis at -3 and $+2$. (Notice that their y-intercepts differ.) All of them can be written with factors of $(x + 3)$ and $(x - 2)$. The shape of the graphs can be changed by using different numbers for the constant factor a.

10.B
remainder theorem

We saw in Lesson 2 how the graphing calculator can be used to evaluate a function at certain values of its domain. Now we study some powerful theoretical tools for evaluating polynomials. One such tool is the **remainder theorem.**

REMAINDER THEOREM

When a polynomial $f(x)$ is divided by $x - c$ where c is a constant, the remainder equals the value of the polynomial evaluated at c.

In other words, $f(c)$ is the remainder when $f(x)$ is divided by $x - c$.

To look at a specific example, we manufacture a cubic polynomial by multiplying the factors $x + 1$, $x - 2$, and $x + 3$, as shown on the left-hand side below. Since one of the factors of the polynomial is $x - 2$, $x - 2$ divides the polynomial evenly (that is, without remainder), as shown on the right-hand side.

$$f(x) = (x + 1)(x - 2)(x + 3)$$
$$f(x) = x^3 + 2x^2 - 5x - 6$$

$$\require{enclose}
\begin{array}{r}
x^2 + 4x + 3 \\
x - 2 \enclose{longdiv}{x^3 + 2x^2 - 5x - 6} \\
\underline{x^3 - 2x^2} \\
4x^2 - 5x \\
\underline{4x^2 - 8x} \\
3x - 6 \\
\underline{3x - 6} \\
0
\end{array}$$

The value of a polynomial is zero if x is replaced by a number that is a zero of the polynomial. The factored form and the unfactored form of the f polynomial of this example are equivalent expressions, and both equal zero when x is replaced by 2, which is consistent with the theorem.

$$\begin{aligned}
f(2) &= (2 + 1)(2 - 2)(2 + 3) & f(2) &= (2)^3 + 2(2)^2 - 5(2) - 6 \\
&= (3)(0)(5) & &= 8 + 8 - 10 - 6 \\
&= 0 & &= 0
\end{aligned}$$

Now we add 10 to the f polynomial. This produces a new polynomial, which we call g. The g polynomial does not have $x - 2$ as a factor. When we divide the g polynomial by $x - 2$, the remainder is 10.

$$g(x) = (x + 1)(x - 2)(x + 3) + 10$$
$$g(x) = x^3 + 2x^2 - 5x + 4$$

$$\require{enclose}
\begin{array}{r}
x^2 + 4x + 3 \\
x - 2 \enclose{longdiv}{x^3 + 2x^2 - 5x + 4} \\
\underline{x^3 - 2x^2} \\
4x^2 - 5x \\
\underline{4x^2 - 8x} \\
3x + 4 \\
\underline{3x - 6} \\
10
\end{array}$$

Both the factored and unfactored forms of the g equation have a value of 10 when x is replaced by 2. Again, this is consistent with the theorem.

$$\begin{aligned}
g(2) &= (2 + 1)(2 - 2)(2 + 3) + 10 & g(2) &= (2)^3 + 2(2)^2 - 5(2) + 4 \\
&= (3)(0)(5) + 10 & &= 8 + 8 - 10 + 4 \\
&= 10 & &= 10
\end{aligned}$$

example 10.3 What is the remainder when the polynomial $x^3 + x^2 - x + 1$ is divided by $x + 2$?

solution According to the remainder theorem, the remainder when a polynomial is divided by $x - c$ equals the polynomial evaluated at $x = c$. Therefore, the remainder when $x^3 + x^2 - x + 1$ is divided by $x + 2$, or $x - (-2)$, equals $x^3 + x^2 - x + 1$ evaluated at $x = -2$.

$$(-2)^3 + (-2)^2 - (-2) + 1 = -1$$

So the remainder is **–1.** We verify this by dividing.

$$
\begin{array}{r}
x^2 - x + 1 \\
x + 2 \overline{)\,x^3 + x^2 - x + 1} \\
\underline{x^3 + 2x^2} \\
-x^2 - x \\
\underline{-x^2 - 2x} \\
x + 1 \\
\underline{x + 2} \\
-1
\end{array}
$$

As a reminder, we could also calculate this value with a graphing calculator. After defining

$$\mathtt{Y_1 = X^3 + X^2 - X + 1}$$

we access the `CALCULATE` menu, choose `1:value`, and enter `(-)` `2` when prompted for a value of `X`. The calculator quickly returns `Y= -1`.

10.C
synthetic division

Because dividing a polynomial by $x - c$ gives such useful information, synthetic division was invented to allow this type of division to be done quickly. Synthetic division can be used to divide a polynomial by $x - 4$ or $x + 3$, but it cannot be easily used to divide by terms such as $2x + 4$ or $x^2 - 5$. Both the coefficient and the exponent of x in the divisor must be 1 in order to use synthetic division.

example 10.4   Let $p(x) = 2x^3 + 3x^2 - 4x - 7$. Use synthetic division to divide $p(x)$ by $x + 1$.

solution   To divide by $x + 1$, we use –1 as a divisor. We write the coefficients of the polynomial and bring down the first constant, which is 2.

$$
\begin{array}{r|rrrr}
-1 & 2 & 3 & -4 & -7 \\
& \downarrow & & & \\
\hline
& 2 & & &
\end{array}
$$

The next step is to multiply 2 by the divisor, –1, for a product of –2, which we record under the 3.

$$
\begin{array}{r|rrrr}
-1 & 2 & 3 & -4 & -7 \\
& \downarrow & -2 & & \\
\hline
& 2 & & &
\end{array}
$$

Then we add 3 and –2 to get 1. We multiply 1 by the divisor, –1, and record the product under the –4. Then we add, multiply, record, and add again.

$$
\begin{array}{r|rrrr}
-1 & 2 & 3 & -4 & -7 \\
& \downarrow & -2 & -1 & 5 \\
\hline
& 2 & 1 & -5 & \boxed{-2}
\end{array}
$$

The first three numbers below the line are the coefficients of the quotient polynomial, and the remainder is –2. The greatest exponent of the quotient polynomial is always 1 less than the greatest exponent of the dividend. Thus, we may write

$$\frac{p(x)}{x + 1} = 2x^2 + x - 5 - \frac{2}{x + 1}$$

example 10.5   Use synthetic division to evaluate $3x^3 - 4x - 2$ when $x = 2$.

solution   We enter the coefficients, remembering to write zero for the coefficient of the x^2 term.

$$
\begin{array}{r|rrrr}
2 & 3 & 0 & -4 & -2 \\
& \downarrow & 6 & 12 & 16 \\
\hline
& 3 & 6 & 8 & \boxed{14}
\end{array}
$$

The numbers 3, 6, and 8 are the coefficients of the quotient polynomial, and 14 is the remainder. Thus, the value of $3x^3 - 4x - 2$ when $x = 2$ is **14**, so 2 is not a zero of the polynomial.

$$3x^3 - 4x - 2 = (3x^2 + 6x + 8)(x - 2) + 14$$

10.D
rational roots theorem

If a number is a zero of a polynomial, the number is also a root of the polynomial equation formed by setting the polynomial equal to zero. We know that we can find rational and irrational zeros of quadratic polynomials by completing the square or by using the quadratic formula. However, these two tools are useful only on quadratic polynomials. Other tools must be utilized for polynomials of higher degree. The **rational roots theorem** allows us to list all possible rational roots of any polynomial, but it does not tell which, if any, of these potential roots are really roots. There is no comparable theorem for irrational roots. This is unfortunate because most polynomial equations have irrational roots. However, finding or estimating irrational roots is time consuming. Therefore, the polynomials encountered in this book are contrived to have integral roots such as $\pm 1, \pm 2,$ and ± 3. The rational roots theorem is useful in helping us decide which of these roots to investigate.

RATIONAL ROOTS THEOREM

If a polynomial whose coefficients are integers has a rational root, then this number is a fraction whose numerator is some integral factor of the constant term and whose denominator is some integral factor of the term of highest degree.

Thus, the possible rational roots of $4x^{14} + 3x^8 + 7x + 3$ can be found by forming all the fractions whose numerators are integer factors of 3 and whose denominators are integer factors of 4.

$$\frac{\text{Factors of 3}}{\text{Factors of 4}} = \frac{1, -1, 3, -3}{1, -1, 2, -2, 4, -4}$$

If we do this, we can list all possible rational roots of $4x^{14} + 3x^8 + 7x + 3$.

$$1, -1, \frac{1}{2}, -\frac{1}{2}, \frac{3}{4}, -\frac{3}{4}, \frac{1}{4}, -\frac{1}{4}, \frac{3}{2}, -\frac{3}{2}, 3, -3$$

example 10.6 Find the zeros of the function $f(x) = x^3 + 2x^2 - 2x - 4$.

solution We could use a computer to estimate the zeros, but since this is a problem in a beginning calculus book, we presume that there is at least one rational zero of the polynomial. If so, it can be found from the following list:

$$\pm\frac{1}{1}, \pm\frac{2}{1}, \pm\frac{4}{1} \longrightarrow +1, -1, +2, -2, +4, -4$$

We use synthetic division to see which, if any, of these numbers are zeros.

$$\underline{1|}\ \ 1 \quad 2 \quad -2 \quad -4 \qquad\qquad \underline{-1|}\ \ 1 \quad 2 \quad -2 \quad -4$$
$$\quad\quad\quad\ \ 1 \quad 3 \quad 1 \qquad\qquad\qquad\quad\ \ -1 \quad -1 \quad 3$$
$$\quad\quad 1 \quad 3 \quad 1 \quad \boxed{-3} \qquad\qquad\quad 1 \quad 1 \quad -3 \quad \boxed{-1}$$

$$\underline{2|}\ \ 1 \quad 2 \quad -2 \quad -4 \qquad\qquad \underline{-2|}\ \ 1 \quad 2 \quad -2 \quad -4$$
$$\quad\quad\quad\ \ 2 \quad 8 \quad 12 \qquad\qquad\qquad\quad\ \ -2 \quad 0 \quad 4$$
$$\quad\quad 1 \quad 4 \quad 6 \quad \boxed{8} \qquad\qquad\qquad 1 \quad 0 \quad -2 \quad \boxed{0}$$

The last remainder is zero; so -2 is a zero of the polynomial function, and $x + 2$ is a factor of the polynomial.

$$x^3 + 2x^2 - 2x - 4 = (x + 2)(x^2 - 2)$$

We find the other zeros of the equation by factoring $x^2 - 2$.

$$x^2 - 2 = 0$$
$$(x + \sqrt{2})(x - \sqrt{2}) = 0$$
$$x = \pm\sqrt{2}$$

Thus, the factors of the original polynomial are $(x + 2)$, $(x - \sqrt{2})$, and $(x + \sqrt{2})$, and the zeros are **$-2, \sqrt{2},$ and $-\sqrt{2}.$**

example 10.7   Find the roots of $x^3 - 7x - 6 = 0$.

solution   First we list the possible rational roots.

$$+1, -1, +2, -2, +3, -3, +6, -6$$

Then we use synthetic division. Note that we include a zero for the coefficient of the x^2 term in the dividend.

$$
\begin{array}{r|rrrr}
\underline{1} & 1 & 0 & -7 & -6 \\
  &   & 1 & 1 & -6 \\
\hline
  & 1 & 1 & -6 & \boxed{-12}
\end{array}
\qquad
\begin{array}{r|rrrr}
\underline{-1} & 1 & 0 & -7 & -6 \\
  &   & -1 & 1 & 6 \\
\hline
  & 1 & -1 & -6 & \boxed{0}
\end{array}
$$

Zero is the remainder when we divide by -1, so -1 is a root of the polynomial. The reduced polynomial is $x^2 - x - 6$, and we can use the quadratic formula to find its roots.

$$x = \frac{1 \pm \sqrt{1 - (4)(1)(-6)}}{2} = \frac{1 \pm \sqrt{25}}{2} = -2, 3$$

Thus the roots of the polynomial equation are **-2, -1,** and **3**.

example 10.8   Use the rational roots theorem to find the possible rational roots of the equation $2x^3 + 2x^2 - 3x - 3 = 0$.

solution   The possible rational roots of the equation are all numbers of the form $\frac{a}{b}$, where a is a factor of 3 and b is a factor of 2. Therefore, the possible rational roots of the polynomial equation are the following:

$$\pm\frac{3}{1}, \pm\frac{3}{2}, \pm\frac{1}{2}, \pm\frac{1}{1} \quad\longrightarrow\quad +3, -3, +\frac{3}{2}, -\frac{3}{2}, +\frac{1}{2}, -\frac{1}{2}, +1, -1$$

example 10.9   Use a graphing calculator to estimate the zeros of the function $f(x) = x^3 + 2x^2 - 2x - 4$.

solution   First we graph the function.

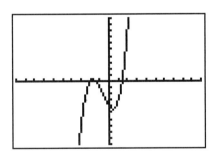

It is difficult at this point to tell the exact number of real zeros so we change the WINDOW settings to zoom in near the x-axis.

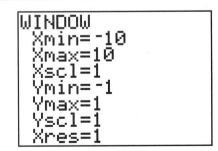
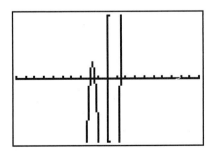

Admittedly, we now have a distorted view of the graph, but it shows the portion of the graph that interests us. We can see that there are three different zeros. As in Lesson 2, we utilize the option $\mathsf{2:zero}$ in the $\mathsf{CALCULATE}$ menu to approximate the zeros. They are

$$-2, -1.4142, 1.4142$$

Notice that these agree with the results of example 10.6, where we found the exact zeros to be

$$-2, -\sqrt{2}, \sqrt{2}$$

**problem set
10**

1. Two vehicles leave an intersection at the same time. One vehicle travels due north at 30 mph and
(5) the other travels due east at 40 mph. Find the straight-line distance between the vehicles two
hours after they leave the intersection.

2. (a) A rectangular box has a volume of 100 cubic units. Let x be the length of the sides of its
(5) square bases. Express the surface area A of the box in terms of x.

   (b) What is the domain of the function A?

3. Develop the three Pythagorean identities.
(8)

4. One hundred feet of fence is used to enclose a large rectangular corral and to divide the corral
(5) into two smaller rectangular areas with a piece of fence parallel to the shorter sides of the
rectangle. Express the total area enclosed in terms of x, where x is the length of the short sides.

5. Determine the remainder when $x^5 - 2x^4 + x^3 - x^2 + 3x + 1$ is divided by $x - 1$.
(10)

6. Let $f(x) = x^4 - 2x^2 + 2x + 1$. Use synthetic division to determine the following:
(10)

   (a) $f(-1)$ (b) $f(1)$ (c) $f(3)$

7. Use the rational roots theorem to list the possible rational roots of the function
(10) $f(x) = x^3 - x^2 - 4x + 4$.

8. Determine all the rational zeros of $f(x)$, where $f(x) = x^3 - x^2 - 4x + 4$.
(10)

9. Use a graphing calculator to evaluate the polynomial $x^4 - 22x^3 + \pi x^2 - x + \sqrt{2}$ at the
(10) following:

   (a) $x = \dfrac{1}{3}$ (b) $x = \sqrt{3}$ (c) $x = \dfrac{\pi}{2}$

10. How many radians are there in $47°$?
(4)

11. Graph each of the following functions:
(9)

   (a) $y = [x]$ (b) $y = \left| x^2 + x - 2 \right|$

12. Solve $\log_{1/3} 9 = 2x + 1$ for x.
(9)

13. Solve $\ln(b^3) = 2$ for b.
(9)

14. Find x: (a) $10^x = 4$ (b) $e^x = 4$
(9)

15. Sketch the graph of $y = x^{2/3}$.
(9)

16. Write the equation of the sinusoid shown
(7) in terms of the sine function.

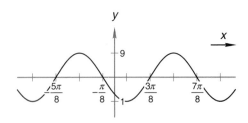

17. Sketch the graphs of $y = e^x$ and $y = -e^{-x}$ on the same coordinate plane.
(7)

18. On a number line, graph the set of all integers x such that $|2x - 3| < 4$.
(9)

19. Given the figure shown, express $\sec \alpha$ in
₍₄₎ terms of a and b.

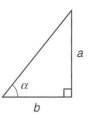

20. Show that $\dfrac{\sin^2 -\theta \;+\; \cos^2 \theta \;+\; 2}{3 \tan -\theta} = -\cot \theta$ for all values of θ where the functions are defined.
₍₈₎

21. Show that $\sin x \;-\; \sin x \cos^2 x = \sin^3 x$ for all values of x.
₍₈₎

22. Let f be a quadratic function such that $f(2) = f(-3) = 0$ and $f(3) = 6$. Find the
₍₁₀₎ equation for f.

23. Let $f(x) = x^2$. Write an expression for $\dfrac{f(x + \Delta x) - f(x)}{\Delta x}$ and simplify it.
₍₆₎

24. The base angles of an isosceles triangle have twice the measure of the vertex angle of the
_(R) triangle. Find the measure of the vertex angle.

25. Recalling that the measure of an exterior angle of a triangle equals the sum of the measures of
_(R) the remote interior angles, solve for x given the figure and information shown below.

$$m\angle CAB = 5x - 40$$
$$m\angle ABC = 3x$$
$$m\angle ACD = 4x + 60$$

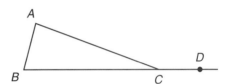

LESSON 11 *Continuity • Left-hand and Right-hand Limits*

11.A

continuity   We begin discussing **continuity** with an intuitive definition that can be interpreted graphically. A function is **continuous** on an interval between the *x*-values a and b if the function is defined for all values of x between a and b and if a small change in x does not produce a sudden jump in the value of y. If a function is not continuous at a value of x, we say that the function has a **discontinuity** at that value of x. The graphs of the continuous functions considered in this book can be drawn on an interval on which the function is defined without lifting the pencil from the paper. Continuous functions, such as polynomial functions and exponential functions, are highly useful in calculus, but these functions do not exhibit the aberrant behavior necessary for a discussion of some of the fundamental concepts of calculus. Thus, we consider more complicated functions. Usually we just draw the graph of the function we need without bothering to find an equation for the function. The following graphs exhibit typical discontinuities.

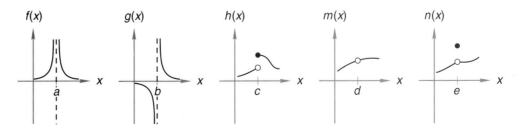

The functions whose graphs are shown here have discontinuities at a, b, c, d, and e. A **vertical asymptote** is a vertical line approached but never touched by the graph of a function. Often a vertical asymptote is represented by a vertical dashed line. The two graphs on the left have vertical asymptotes at a and b, so the functions are not defined for these values of x. Therefore, f is not continuous at a, and g is not continuous at b. In the third graph, the function is defined at c, but the graph shows that a small change in x produces a "jump" in the value of $h(x)$, so the function is not continuous at c. In the fourth graph, there is a hole in the graph at d, so the function is not defined at d. Therefore, the function is not continuous at d. In the rightmost graph the function is defined at e, but there is a sudden jump in the value of $n(x)$ at e, so the function is not continuous at e. Graphs like the three on the right are useful for explanations of continuity and limits—the topic of the next section. (Note that in these three graphs, the dots and holes shown have a physical size; however, in reality these dots and holes represent points that have no physical dimension. The dots and holes are drawn in an exaggerated fashion to clearly show endpoints and points of discontinuity.)

11.B

left-hand and right-hand limits

The study of calculus is based on a concept called the **limit** of a function. The limit of a function is the number the value of the function approaches as x gets very close to some designated number. Two of the most important limits concern the values of the following expressions as the value of x gets closer and closer to zero:

$$(1 + x)^{1/x} \qquad \text{and} \qquad \frac{\sin x}{x}$$

If we replace x with zero in these two expressions, we get results that cannot be evaluated.

$$(1 + 0)^{1/0} \qquad \text{and} \qquad \frac{\sin 0}{0} = \frac{0}{0}$$

But if we let x get extremely close to zero, we find that the value of $(1 + x)^{1/x}$ gets extremely close to the number e. If x is in radians, the value of $\sin x$ divided by x gets extremely close to 1.

To discuss limits, it is helpful to think of x as a dot on the x-axis that we can move right or left as we choose. From any selected position of the x-dot, we move vertically to the graph of the function and then horizontally to read the output value of $f(x)$ on the y-axis. We show this in the left-hand figure below. In the right-hand figure we show the graph of a function that has no value when $x = 5$.

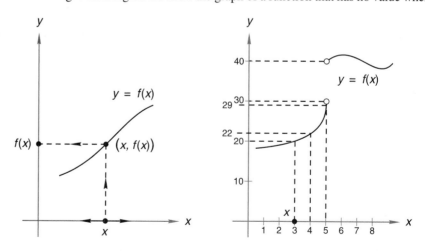

In the figure on the right-hand side we place the x-dot at 3 and see that the output value $f(x)$ is 20. When the x-dot moves from 3 to 4, the output value of $f(x)$ increases from 20 to 22. When the x-dot moves from 4 to 4.9, the output value $f(x)$ increases from 22 to 29. As x **approaches** 5 from the left, we see that the value of $f(x)$ gets closer and closer to 30. We use the notation 5^- to show that x approaches 5 from the left, and we write

$$\lim_{x \to 5^-} f(x) = 30$$

We say that 30 is the left-hand limit of $f(x)$ as x approaches 5. If we let the x-dot move along the x-axis and approach 5 from the right-hand side, $f(x)$ gets closer and closer to 40. We use the notation 5^+ to show that x approaches 5 from the right, and we write

$$\lim_{x \to 5^+} f(x) = 40$$

We say that the right-hand limit of $f(x)$ as x approaches 5 is 40.

The limit of $f(x)$ as x approaches some number a from the right or the left is the number $f(x)$ gets closer and closer to as x gets closer and closer to a. When discussing limits, we do not even consider the value of $f(x)$ when $x = a$.

example 11.1   Given this graph of f, estimate:

(a) $\lim f(x)$ as x approaches 3^+

(b) $\lim f(x)$ as x approaches 3^-

(c) $\lim f(x)$ as x approaches 1^-

(d) $\lim f(x)$ as x approaches 1^+

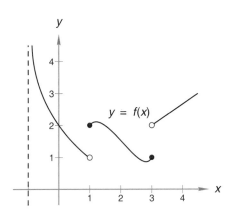

solution   (a) As x approaches 3 from the right, the value of $f(x)$ gets closer and closer to 2, so

$$\lim_{x \to 3^+} f(x) = \mathbf{2}$$

(b) As x approaches 3 from the left, the value of $f(x)$ gets closer and closer to 1, so

$$\lim_{x \to 3^-} f(x) = \mathbf{1}$$

(c) As x approaches 1 from the left, the value of $f(x)$ approaches 1, so

$$\lim_{x \to 1^-} f(x) = \mathbf{1}$$

(d) As x approaches 1 from the right, the value of $f(x)$ approaches 2, so

$$\lim_{x \to 1^+} f(x) = \mathbf{2}$$

example 11.2   Estimate: (a) $\lim\limits_{x \to 3^+} f(x)$ (b) $\lim\limits_{x \to 3^-} f(x)$

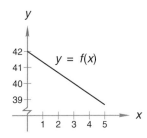

solution   The value of $f(x)$ as x approaches 3 from the right or from the left appears to be about 40. Thus, we estimate that the right-hand limit and left-hand limit are both about 40.

(a) $\lim\limits_{x \to 3^+} f(x) \approx \mathbf{40}$ (b) $\lim\limits_{x \to 3^-} f(x) \approx \mathbf{40}$

The fact that the value of $f(3)$ also appears to be 40 is of no concern to us, as we are only interested in values of $f(x)$ when x is extremely close to 3.

example 11.3   Given that

$$f(x) = \begin{cases} 1 & \text{when } x \geq 0 \\ -1 & \text{when } x < 0 \end{cases}$$

sketch the graph of f and find:

(a) $\lim\limits_{x \to 0^+} f(x)$ (b) $\lim\limits_{x \to 0^-} f(x)$

solution   (a) On the graph we see that as x approaches
zero from the right the value of $f(x)$ is 1 and
continues to be 1. Thus the right-hand limit
of $f(x)$ as x approaches zero is 1.

$$\lim_{x \to 0^+} f(x) = 1$$

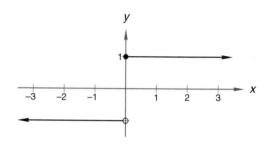

(b) The left-hand limit of $f(x)$ as x approaches
zero is -1 because $f(x)$ is -1 and continues
to be -1 as x approaches zero from the left.

$$\lim_{x \to 0^-} f(x) = -1$$

**problem set
11**

1. The number of sophists varied inversely as the square of the number of xenophobes present. If
(5)   there were 8 sophists when there were 5 xenophobes present, how many sophists would there be
if there were 2 xenophobes present?

2. Find the length in inches of the shadow cast by an L-foot-tall building when a nearby R-inch pole
(8)   casts a 1-foot shadow.

3. Given this graph of a function f, evaluate
(11)   the following limits:

(a) $\lim\limits_{x \to 0^+} f(x)$ (b) $\lim\limits_{x \to 0^-} f(x)$

(c) $\lim\limits_{x \to -1^-} f(x)$ (d) $\lim\limits_{x \to -1^+} f(x)$

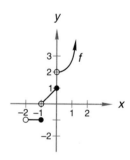

4. Graph the function g where $g(x) = [x] + 1$. Then evaluate the following limits:
(9,11)
(a) $\lim\limits_{x \to 1^+} g(x)$ (b) $\lim\limits_{x \to 1^-} g(x)$

5. Let $f(x) = 2x^5 - 4x^4 + 3x^3 - 2x^2 + x - 1$. Determine the following values by using
(10)   synthetic division:
(a) $f(-1)$ (b) $f(2)$ (c) $f(-2)$

6. (a) Use the rational roots theorem to list the possible rational roots of the function
(10) $h(x) = 6x^3 - 19x^2 + 2x + 3$.

(b) Determine all the actual zeros of the function h.

7. Using your graphing calculator, estimate the zeros of the function $f(x) = x^3 + 3x^2 - 2x - 6$.
(10)

8. Solve $\log_x (2x - 7) = 1$ for x.
(9)

9. Find x given that $e^x = 10$.
(9)

10. Graph: $y = -|\sin x|$
(9)

11. The standard form of the equation of a circle with center (h, k) and radius r is
(2) $(x - h)^2 + (y - k)^2 = r^2$. Write the standard form of the equation of the circle that goes through $(-2, 6)$ and whose center is $(1, 2)$.

12. Find the range of $f(x) = x^2$ when the domain is $\{x \in \mathbb{R} \mid |x| < 2\}$.
(6)

13. Use a graphing calculator to approximate the coordinates where the graphs of $y = \frac{1}{x}$
(2,7) and $y = \ln(x^2)$ intersect.

14. Sketch the graphs of $y = e^x$ and $y = e^{-x}$ on the same coordinate plane.
(7)

15. Show that $-(\sin -x)(\sec x)\left[\cot\left(\frac{\pi}{2} - x\right)\right] + 1 = \sec^2 x$ for all values of x where the functions
(8) are defined.

16. Simplify: $\dfrac{\sin x - \sin x \cos^2 x}{\sec^2 x - 1}$
(4)

17. Find the coordinates of the vertex of the graph of the quadratic function $y = x^2 - 2x + 4$.
(10)

18. Solve for L in terms of x and H for
(8) this figure.

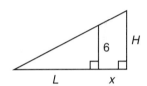

19. On a number line, graph all real values of x that satisfy the equation $|3x + 6| < 15$.
(9)

20. Graph: $y = -1 + 2\sin\left[\dfrac{2}{3}\left(x - \dfrac{\pi}{2}\right)\right]$
(7)

21. Find the equation for the quadratic function f such that $f(-1) = f(2) = 0$ and $f(0) = -4$.
(10)

22. Describe the domain and range of $y = \sqrt{x^2 - 1}$ using set notation.
(6)

23. Let $f(x) = \dfrac{1}{x}$. Write the simplified expression for $\dfrac{f(x + \Delta x) - f(x)}{\Delta x}$.
(6)

24. Find the area of a triangle whose three sides have lengths 5, 6, and 7. *Note:* Heron's formula
(R) states that the area A of a triangle whose sides have lengths a, b, and c is

$$A = \sqrt{s(s - a)(s - b)(s - c)} \qquad \text{where} \qquad s = \frac{1}{2}(a + b + c)$$

25. Let x, y, and z be lengths of the sides of a triangle of area 10. Compare the following:
(1)
A. x B. $y + z$

LESSON 12   *Sum and Difference Identities • Double-Angle Identities • Half-Angle Identities • Graphs of Logarithmic Functions*

12.A
sum and difference identities

If we use a calculator to approximate the sine of 10°, the sine of 20°, and the sine of 30°, we get $\sin 10° \approx 0.1736$, $\sin 20° \approx 0.3420$, and $\sin 30° \approx 0.5000$. We note to our dismay that the sine of 10° plus the sine of 20° does not equal the sine of 30°.

$$
\begin{array}{ll}
\sin 10° \approx 0.1736 & \sin 30° \approx 0.5000 \\
+ \ \sin 20° \approx 0.3420 & \\
\hline
\ 0.5156 &
\end{array}
$$

To find the output of trigonometric functions for sums and differences, we must use the appropriate trigonometric identities. Many trigonometric identities are used in calculus, and it is difficult to memorize all of them. The two identities

$$
\tan \theta = \frac{\sin \theta}{\cos \theta} \qquad \text{and} \qquad \sin^2 \theta + \cos^2 \theta = 1
$$

are reasonably easy to remember. If, in addition to these, one memorizes the identities for the sine and cosine of the sum and difference of two angles, the other identities can be developed quickly when required.

The identities for $\sin (A + B)$ and $\cos (A + B)$ are given below:

$$
\sin (A + B) = \sin A \cos B + \cos A \sin B
$$
$$
\cos (A + B) = \cos A \cos B - \sin A \sin B
$$

To help us memorize these identities, we note that the letter pattern in both cases from left to right is *AB, AB, AB*. We also note that if sine comes first on the left-hand side of the equation, then it also comes first on the right-hand side of the equation. If cosine comes first on the left-hand side of the equation, then it also comes first on the right-hand side of the equation. Next, we write the expressions for $\sin (A - B)$ and $\cos (A - B)$. These are exactly the same as the identities for the sine and the cosine of $(A + B)$ except that the signs are changed.

$$
\sin (A - B) = \sin A \cos B - \cos A \sin B
$$
$$
\cos (A - B) = \cos A \cos B + \sin A \sin B
$$

A complete list of the key trigonometric identities is shown below.

KEY TRIGONOMETRIC IDENTITIES

$$
\tan \theta = \frac{\sin \theta}{\cos \theta}
$$

$$
\sin^2 \theta + \cos^2 \theta = 1
$$

$$
\sin (A + B) = \sin A \cos B + \cos A \sin B
$$

$$
\sin (A - B) = \sin A \cos B - \cos A \sin B
$$

$$
\cos (A + B) = \cos A \cos B - \sin A \sin B
$$

$$
\cos (A - B) = \cos A \cos B + \sin A \sin B
$$

Note: **Students should practice writing this list of identities several times daily until the identities can be reproduced in less than thirty seconds. Writing these identities is also a** suggested first step for taking trigonometry-oriented examinations, because these identities can be used to develop other identities accurately and quickly.

example 12.1   Simplify: $\sin\left(\theta + \dfrac{\pi}{4}\right)$

solution   This is the sine of a sum. It requires the use of the identity for $\sin(A + B)$.

$$\sin(A + B) = \sin A \cos B + \cos A \sin B$$

We replace A with θ and B with $\dfrac{\pi}{4}$.

$$\sin\left(\theta + \frac{\pi}{4}\right) = \sin\theta\cos\frac{\pi}{4} + \cos\theta\sin\frac{\pi}{4}$$

Both the sine and the cosine of $\dfrac{\pi}{4}$ equal $\dfrac{\sqrt{2}}{2}$, so

$$\sin\left(\theta + \frac{\pi}{4}\right) = (\sin\theta)\left(\frac{\sqrt{2}}{2}\right) + (\cos\theta)\left(\frac{\sqrt{2}}{2}\right)$$

$$= \frac{\sqrt{2}}{2}(\sin\theta + \cos\theta)$$

example 12.2   Find the exact value of $\cos 15°$ by using a trigonometric identity and the fact that $60° - 45° = 15°$.

solution   This problem provides practice in the use of the identity for $\cos(A - B)$, which is

$$\cos(A - B) = \cos A \cos B + \sin A \sin B$$

We replace A with $60°$ and B with $45°$.

$$\cos(60° - 45°) = \cos 60° \cos 45° + \sin 60° \sin 45°$$

$$\cos 15° = \left(\frac{1}{2}\right)\left(\frac{\sqrt{2}}{2}\right) + \left(\frac{\sqrt{3}}{2}\right)\left(\frac{\sqrt{2}}{2}\right)$$

$$= \frac{\sqrt{2}}{4} + \frac{\sqrt{6}}{4} = \frac{\sqrt{2} + \sqrt{6}}{4}$$

example 12.3   Develop an identity for $\tan(A + B)$.

solution   We know that $\tan(A + B)$ equals $\sin(A + B)$ divided by $\cos(A + B)$.

$$\tan(A + B) = \frac{\sin(A + B)}{\cos(A + B)} = \frac{\sin A \cos B + \cos A \sin B}{\cos A \cos B - \sin A \sin B}$$

There are many forms of tangent identities. We concentrate on forms in which the first entry in the denominator is the number 1. To change $\cos A \cos B$ to 1, we must divide it by itself. To do this, we must also divide every other term in the whole expression by $\cos A \cos B$ so that the value of the expression does not change.

$$\tan(A + B) = \frac{\dfrac{\sin A \cancel{\cos B}}{\cos A \cancel{\cos B}} + \dfrac{\cancel{\cos A} \sin B}{\cancel{\cos A} \cos B}}{\dfrac{\cancel{\cos A}\,\cancel{\cos B}}{\cancel{\cos A}\,\cancel{\cos B}} - \dfrac{\sin A \sin B}{\cos A \cos B}}$$

We cancel as shown and end up with

$$\tan(A + B) = \frac{\tan A + \tan B}{1 - \tan A \tan B}$$

example 12.4 Develop an identity for tan $(A - B)$.

solution The procedure is the same except we use the identities for $(A - B)$ instead of the ones for $(A + B)$.

$$\tan (A - B) = \dfrac{\dfrac{\sin A \cancel{\cos B}}{\cos A \cancel{\cos B}} - \dfrac{\cancel{\cos A} \sin B}{\cancel{\cos A} \cos B}}{\dfrac{\cancel{\cos A} \cancel{\cos B}}{\cancel{\cos A} \cancel{\cos B}} + \dfrac{\sin A \sin B}{\cos A \cos B}}$$

We cancel as shown and end up with

$$\tan (A - B) = \frac{\tan A - \tan B}{1 + \tan A \tan B}$$

This identity gives the tangent of the angle of intersection of two lines. The two lines (1 and 2) shown below form angles A and B with a horizontal line. Since the slope of a line is the tangent of the angle the line makes with a horizontal line, we can replace tan A with m_1 (the slope of Line 1) and tan B with m_2 (the slope of Line 2) and write the expression for tan ϕ shown on the right-hand side.

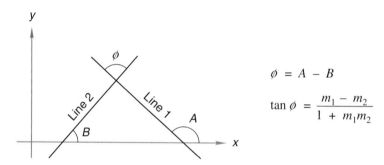

$$\phi = A - B$$

$$\tan \phi = \frac{m_1 - m_2}{1 + m_1 m_2}$$

12.B
double-angle identities

We can use the sum and difference identities for the sine and the cosine to develop many other identities quickly and accurately. To develop an identity for sin $(2A)$, we use the identity for sin $(A + B)$ and replace B with A.

$$\sin (A + B) = \sin A \cos B + \cos A \sin B$$

$$\sin (A + A) = \sin A \cos A + \cos A \sin A$$

$$\boxed{\sin (2A) = 2 \sin A \cos A}$$

To develop an identity for cos $(2A)$, we use the identity for cos $(A + B)$ and replace B with A.

$$\cos (A + B) = \cos A \cos B - \sin A \sin B$$

$$\cos (A + A) = \cos A \cos A - \sin A \sin A$$

$$\boxed{\cos (2A) = \cos^2 A - \sin^2 A}$$

We can get two other identities for cos $(2A)$ by substituting from the basic Pythagorean identity $\sin^2 A + \cos^2 A = 1$. We solve the Pythagorean identity for $\cos^2 A$ as we show on the left-hand side below and for $\sin^2 A$ as we show on the right-hand side.

$$\cos^2 A = 1 - \sin^2 A \qquad \sin^2 A = 1 - \cos^2 A$$

Now we substitute these expressions into the identity for cos (2A).

$$\cos (2A) = \cos^2 A - \sin^2 A \qquad\qquad \cos (2A) = \cos^2 A - \sin^2 A$$
$$\cos (2A) = (1 - \sin^2 A) - \sin^2 A \qquad\qquad \cos (2A) = \cos^2 A - (1 - \cos^2 A)$$

$$\boxed{\cos (2A) = 1 - 2\sin^2 A} \qquad\qquad \boxed{\cos (2A) = 2\cos^2 A - 1}$$

In calculus we often encounter expressions that contain $\sin x$ and $\sin (2x)$ or $\cos x$ and $\cos (2x)$. The double-angle identities enable us to simplify those expressions by replacing $\cos (2x)$ or $\sin (2x)$ with expressions that contain $\cos x$ or $\sin x$.

example 12.5   Develop the identity for tan (2A).

solution   The procedure is the same one we used to find sin (2A) and cos (2A). We just replace B with A in the identity for tan (A + B).

$$\tan (A + B) = \frac{\tan A + \tan B}{1 - \tan A \tan B}$$

$$\tan (A + A) = \frac{\tan A + \tan A}{1 - \tan A \tan A}$$

$$\boxed{\tan (2A) = \frac{2 \tan A}{1 - \tan^2 A}}$$

We now have five double-angle identities: one for sin (2A), three for cos (2A), and one for tan (2A).

$$\boxed{\begin{aligned} \sin (2A) &= 2 \sin A \cos A \\[4pt] \cos (2A) &= \cos^2 A - \sin^2 A \\[4pt] \cos (2A) &= 2 \cos^2 A - 1 \\[4pt] \cos (2A) &= 1 - 2 \sin^2 A \\[4pt] \tan (2A) &= \frac{2 \tan A}{1 - \tan^2 A} \end{aligned}}$$

12.C

half-angle identities

The double-angle identities can be manipulated to obtain half-angle identities. Consider, for example, the last two identities for cos (2A). If we solve these for $\sin^2 A$ and $\cos^2 A$, we get

$$\sin^2 A = \frac{1}{2} - \frac{1}{2} \cos 2A \qquad\qquad \cos^2 A = \frac{1}{2} + \frac{1}{2} \cos 2A$$

Replacing A with $\frac{x}{2}$ and taking the square root of both sides yields two half-angle identities.

$$\sin^2 \frac{x}{2} = \frac{1}{2} - \frac{1}{2} \cos \left[2\left(\frac{x}{2}\right) \right] \qquad\qquad \cos^2 \frac{x}{2} = \frac{1}{2} + \frac{1}{2} \cos \left[2\left(\frac{x}{2}\right) \right]$$

$$\boxed{\sin \frac{x}{2} = \pm\sqrt{\frac{1}{2} - \frac{\cos x}{2}}} \qquad\qquad \boxed{\cos \frac{x}{2} = \pm\sqrt{\frac{1}{2} + \frac{\cos x}{2}}}$$

It is important to remember that these half-angle identities are rearranged forms of the identities for cos (2A) with A replaced by $\frac{x}{2}$.

example 12.6   Show that $\dfrac{\sin x}{\sin (2x)} = \dfrac{\sec x}{2}$ for all values of x that make sense.

solution   When simplifying expressions containing a trigonometric function of $2x$, it is advisable to use a double-angle identity.

$$\frac{\sin x}{\sin (2x)} = \frac{\sin x}{2 \sin x \cos x} \qquad \text{double-angle identity}$$

$$= \frac{1}{2 \cos x} \qquad \text{simplified}$$

$$= \frac{\sec x}{2} \qquad \text{definition of } \sec x$$

12.D

graphs of logarithmic functions   We know that 10 raised to the power 2 equals 100. We can say this in the language of logarithms if we call the exponent a logarithm and say that the logarithm of 100 for the base 10 equals 2.

$$100 = 10^2 \qquad \text{is equivalent to} \qquad \log_{10} 100 = 2$$

Using b for the base, N for the number, and L for the logarithm, we can write

$$N = b^L \qquad \text{or} \qquad L = \log_b N$$

On the left-hand side below, we graph an exponential function whose base is greater than 1. On the right-hand side below, we show the graph of the logarithmic function having the same base.

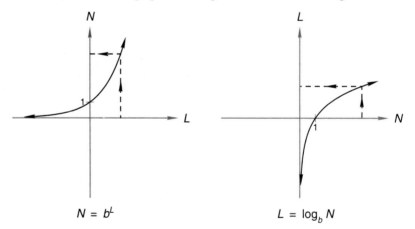

$$N = b^L \qquad\qquad\qquad L = \log_b N$$

To reduce confusion in mathematics, we use the horizontal axis for the independent variable and the vertical axis for the dependent variable (the answer). Thus, as shown in the left-hand figure and equation, we begin with a value of L and find the answer, which is the corresponding value of N. In the right-hand figure and equation, we begin with a value of N, and the answer is the corresponding value of L. It is customary to use x for the independent variable in both equations. If we do this, we can graph both functions on the same set of coordinate axes and find that they are mirror images of each other about the line $y = x$.

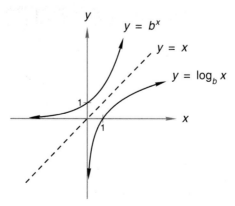

It is important to remember that only positive numbers have logarithms. (We discussed this in Lesson 9.) Keep this in mind when graphing logarithmic functions.

example 12.7   Sketch the graph of $y = \log_4 x$.

solution   We do not have a table of logarithms to the base 4, but we do know how to quickly get three points on the graph of an exponential function by using 0, 1, and –1 for x. To quickly obtain three points on the graph of $y = \log_4 x$, we rewrite the logarithmic equation in exponential form and substitute 0, 1, and –1 for y.

$$y = \log_4 x \qquad \text{is equivalent to} \qquad 4^y = x$$

y	1	0	–1
x	4	1	$\dfrac{1}{4}$

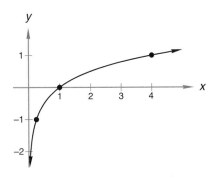

$$y = \log_4 x$$

example 12.8   Sketch the graph of $y = -\log_4 x$.

solution   First we move the negative sign across the equals sign. Then we substitute 1, 0, and –1 for y in the exponential form of the equation and solve for x.

$$-y = \log_4 x \qquad \text{is equivalent to} \qquad 4^{-y} = x$$

y	1	0	–1
x	$\dfrac{1}{4}$	1	4

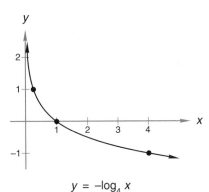

$$y = -\log_4 x$$

The graph of $y = -\log_4 x$ is the mirror image about the x-axis of the graph of $y = \log_4 x$ that was shown in example 12.7.

example 12.9   Assuming b is greater than 1, graph the following:

(a) $y = \log_b x$ (b) $y = -\log_b x$ (c) $y = \log_b -x$ (d) $y = -\log_b -x$

solution   **The logarithmic function is one of the most important functions in all mathematics, and it is important to be able to quickly sketch its graph without resorting to point-by-point plotting.** We must memorize the shape of the graph of $y = \log_b x$ for $b > 1$, which we show at (a) below. This graph can be altered three ways by including minus signs in the equation. The graph of (b) $y = -\log_b x$ is a reflection of the first graph in the x-axis (a flip about the x-axis) because every value of y is the negative of its value in $y = \log_b x$. The graph of (c) $y = \log_b -x$ is a reflection of the first graph in the y-axis because every value of x is the negative of its value in $y = \log_b x$. In (d) $y = -\log_b -x$, both minus signs are present, so both reflections take place.

(a)

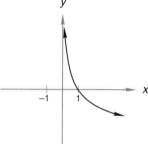

$$y = \log_b x$$

(b)

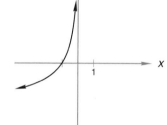

$$y = -\log_b x$$

(c)

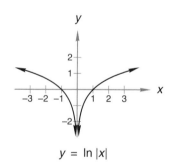

$$y = \log_b -x$$

(d)

$$y = -\log_b -x$$

These are the graphs for values of b satisfying the inequality $b > 1$. If $0 < b < 1$, the graphs in parts (a), (b), (c), and (d) would be different.

example 12.10   Graph: $y = \ln |x|$

solution   As seen in the previous example, the graph of $y = \log_b x$ lies to the right of the y-axis because $\log_b x$ is only defined for positive values of x, whereas the graph of $y = \log_b -x$ lies to the left of the y-axis because $\log_b -x$ is only defined for negative values of x. The graphs of $y = \ln x$ and $y = \ln -x$ are reflections of each other about the y-axis. The graph of $y = \ln |x|$ is a composite of the graphs of $y = \ln x$ and $y = \ln -x$, and this function is defined for all values of x except zero.

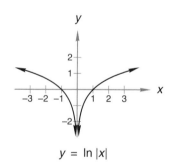

$$y = \ln |x|$$

A graphing calculator comment is in order. The graphing calculator denotes the absolute value function by `abs(`, and it is accessed with the key sequence (MATH) (▶) (1). (*Note:* Pressing (MATH) (▶) accesses the `NUM` menu. This menu provides a selection of operations applied to numbers.) By defining `Y₁=ln(abs(X))` and graphing with `ZStandard` settings, the following screen appears:

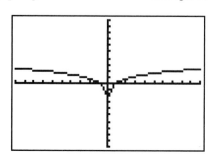

It looks as if the graph has a sharp corner on the y-axis. From the above example, we know this is not true. Zooming in on the origin produces a less deceiving graph.

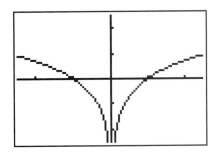

The point is this: Be careful when using a graphing calculator to visualize graphs. It may lead you to false conclusions.

example 12.11   Sketch the graph of $y = -\log_{1/4} x$.

solution   First we move the negative sign across the equals sign and write $-y = \log_{1/4} x$. Next we write the exponential form of this equation and use 1, 0, and –1 for y and solve for x.

$$\left(\frac{1}{4}\right)^{-y} = x$$

y	1	0	−1
x	4	1	$\dfrac{1}{4}$

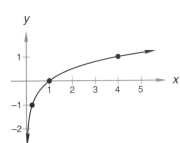

$$y = -\log_{1/4} x$$

This graph is identical to the graph of $y = \log_4 x$ in example 12.7.

example 12.12   Sketch the graph of $y = \log_2 -x$.

solution   We write the exponential form of this equation and use 1, 0, and –1 for y to find three points on the graph.

$$2^y = -x \qquad \text{changed to exponential form}$$
$$-2^y = x \qquad \text{multiplied by (–1)}$$

y	1	0	−1
x	−2	−1	$-\dfrac{1}{2}$

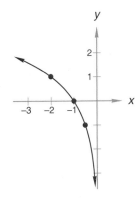

$$y = \log_2 -x$$

problem set
12

1. The area of a particular rectangle is 8 times the area of a certain square, and the width of the
(5) rectangle is twice the length of a side of the square. Given that the perimeter of the rectangle is
16 units greater than the perimeter of the square, find the dimensions of both the rectangle and
the square.

2. A 10-foot ladder leans against a vertical wall. The base of the ladder is x feet away from the base
(5) of the wall. Find an expression in terms of x whose value equals the vertical distance from the
top of the ladder to the ground.

3. Write the key trigonometric identities, and then develop one identity for $\sin (2A)$ and three
(12) identities for $\cos (2A)$.

4. Suppose $\cos \alpha = \dfrac{1}{5}$. Use a double-angle identity to find the value of $\cos (2\alpha)$.
(12)

5. Using $\tan \theta = \frac{\sin \theta}{\cos \theta}$ and the sum and difference identities for sine and cosine, develop the
(12) identities for (a) $\tan (A + B)$ and (b) $\tan (A - B)$.

6. Use the sum identity for the tangent function to find the exact value of $\tan 75°$.
(12)

7. Show that $(\sin x + \cos x)^2 = 1 + \sin (2x)$ for all values of x.
(12)

8. Graph $f(x) = \begin{cases} x + 1 & \text{when } x \neq 1 \\ 3 & \text{when } x = 1. \end{cases}$
(9)

9. Evaluate the following limits for $f(x) = \begin{cases} x + 1 & \text{when } x \neq 1 \\ 3 & \text{when } x = 1. \end{cases}$
(11)

    (a) $\lim\limits_{x \to 1^+} f(x)$ (b) $\lim\limits_{x \to 1^-} f(x)$

10. Use the rational roots theorem to determine all the rational roots of the function
(10) $y = 2x^3 - 7x^2 - 5x + 4$.

11. Solve $\log_4 (3x + 1) = \dfrac{1}{2}$ for x.
(9)

12. Sketch the graph of $y = x^{1/4}$.
(9)

13. Sketch the graphs of $y = 2^x$ and $y = 2^{-x}$ on the same coordinate plane.
(7)

14. Sketch the graphs of $y = 2^x$ and $y = \log_2 x$ on the same coordinate plane.
(7,12)

15. Sketch the graphs of $y = \log_2 x$ and $y = \log_2 -x$ on the same coordinate plane.
(12)

16. Simplify: $\left[\sin \left(\dfrac{\pi}{2} - x \right) \right](\csc -x)(\sin x)(\cos -x)$
(8)

17. Find the equation of the quadratic function whose graph has x-intercepts at $x = -1$ and $x = 2$
(10) and a y-intercept at $y = -2$.

18. Solve for y in terms of x for the
(8) figure shown.

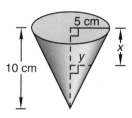

19. Graph: $y = 2 + 3 \sin \left[3 \left(x - \dfrac{\pi}{4} \right) \right]$
(7)

20. Let $f(x) = 2x^2$. Simplify the expression $\dfrac{f(x + h) - f(x)}{h}$.
(6)

21. (a) Develop an identity for $\cos \dfrac{x}{2}$.   (b) Develop an identity for $\sin \dfrac{x}{2}$.
(12)

22. Find the real values of x for which $\sqrt{1 - x}$ is a real number.
(6)

23. State the contrapositive of the following statement: If two angles of a triangle have equal
(3) measures, then the sides opposite them have equal lengths.

24. Find x, y, and z in the figure shown using
(R) the fact that the measure of an inscribed
angle equals half the measure of the arc it
subtends.

$$m\,\overset{\frown}{AC} = x$$
$$m\,\overset{\frown}{AB} = y$$
$$m\,\overset{\frown}{BC} = z$$

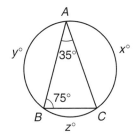

25. One base of a trapezoid is the same length as the height of the trapezoid, and the other base of
(R) the trapezoid is twice the height. The area of the trapezoid is 12. Find the height of the trapezoid.

LESSON 13   *Inverse Trigonometric Functions •*
Trigonometric Equations

13.A
inverse trigonometric functions

We can determine the sine of any angle since the sine of any angle has only one value. If we write

$$\sin 30° = ?$$

the answer is $\frac{1}{2}$. We can turn things around and ask for an angle whose sine is $\frac{1}{2}$ three different ways.

$$\sin^{-1} \frac{1}{2} = ? \qquad \arcsin \frac{1}{2} = ? \qquad \text{The angle whose sine is } \frac{1}{2} = ?$$

All three of these statements refer to the **inverse sine** of $\dfrac{1}{2}$. The notations

$$\arcsin \frac{1}{2} \qquad \sin^{-1} \frac{1}{2} \qquad \text{inverse sine } \frac{1}{2}$$

all mean the same thing. There is an infinite number of angles whose sine equals $\frac{1}{2}$. The sine of 30° is $\frac{1}{2}$, the sine of (30° + 360°) is $\frac{1}{2}$, the sine of [30° + 2(360°)] is $\frac{1}{2}$, and the sine of [30° + n(360°)] is $\frac{1}{2}$ as long as n is an integer. Also, the sine of 150° is $\frac{1}{2}$, the sine of (150° + 360°) is $\frac{1}{2}$, and the sine of [150° + n(360°)] is $\frac{1}{2}$ as long as n is an integer.

   When we ask for the inverse sine, the inverse cosine, or the inverse tangent of an angle, we would like to have only one possible answer so that the inverses are functions. We can achieve this by restricting ourselves to portions of the graphs of $\sin x$, $\cos x$, or $\tan x$ where the function is always decreasing or always increasing and where all values in the range of the function are included.

Mathematicians choose the portion between $-\frac{\pi}{2}$ and $\frac{\pi}{2}$ radians to define the range of the inverse sine function, because this portion is closest to the origin. Between these values of x, the graph is always ascending and all values of $\sin x$ between -1 and $+1$ are encountered.

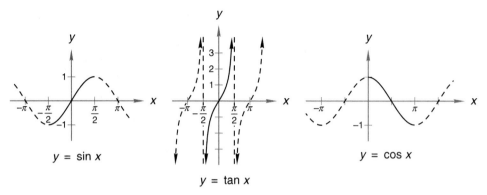

$$y = \sin x \qquad y = \tan x \qquad y = \cos x$$

In the center we see that the portion of the graph of $y = \tan x$ closest to the origin is ascending everywhere and that this portion includes all values of $\tan x$ between $-\infty$ and ∞. This is the portion between $-\frac{\pi}{2}$ and $\frac{\pi}{2}$, so mathematicians restrict the output of the inverse tangent function to this range of values. To choose the portion to be used for the inverse cosine function, we note that the portion between $-\pi$ and 0 is ascending everywhere and the portion between 0 and π is descending everywhere and that both portions are the same distance from the origin. Mathematicians choose the portion of the graph between 0 and π to define the range of the inverse cosine because this range of values includes the first-quadrant angles, which are the angles used most often.

The points on the graphs of the inverse sine function, the inverse cosine function, and the inverse tangent function have the same coordinates as points on the sine function, the cosine function, and the tangent function, but in reverse order. For example, the point $\left(\frac{\pi}{2}, 1\right)$ is on the graph of $y = \sin x$, and the point $\left(1, \frac{\pi}{2}\right)$ is on the graph of $y = \sin^{-1} x$.

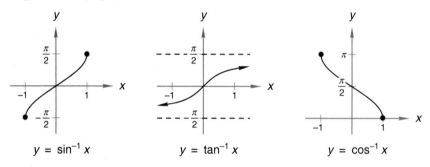

$$y = \sin^{-1} x \qquad y = \tan^{-1} x \qquad y = \cos^{-1} x$$

Note that the graphs of the inverse sine function and the inverse cosine function terminate abruptly because these functions are only defined for x-values from -1 to 1. The inverse tangent function, however, is defined for all real values of x.

example 13.1   Evaluate: $\sin^{-1} \dfrac{\sqrt{2}}{2}$

solution   We seek the angle between $-\frac{\pi}{2}$ and $\frac{\pi}{2}$ whose sine is $\frac{\sqrt{2}}{2}$. The sine of $\frac{\pi}{4}$ equals $\frac{1}{\sqrt{2}}$, which equals $\frac{\sqrt{2}}{2}$. Thus, the answer is $\frac{\pi}{4}$, or $45°$.

$$\sin^{-1} \frac{\sqrt{2}}{2} = \frac{\pi}{4}$$

Note that $\sin^{-1} x$ is not the reciprocal of $\sin x$.

$$\sin^{-1} x \neq \frac{1}{\sin x}$$

Writing $\sin^{-1} x$ indicates the inverse function of $\sin x$. To express the reciprocal of $\sin x$ we write $(\sin x)^{-1}$.

example 13.2   Evaluate: $\cos^{-1} -\dfrac{\sqrt{3}}{2}$

solution   We seek the angle between 0° and 180° whose cosine is $-\frac{\sqrt{3}}{2}$. The cosine is negative between 90° and 180°, so we need a second-quadrant angle.

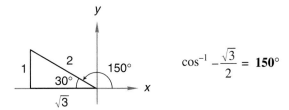

13.B

trigonometric equations

Since there is an infinite number of angles whose sine equals $\dfrac{1}{2}$, the equation

$$\sin x = \frac{1}{2}$$

has an infinite number of solutions. We can indicate that we are only interested in values of x between 0° and 360° if we follow the equation with the notation $0° \le x < 360°$.

example 13.3   Solve: $\sec x = -2$ $(0° \le x < 360°)$

solution   We must find all values of x between 0° and 360° whose secant is −2. Secant is the reciprocal of cosine, so we can write

$$\sec x = -2 \qquad \text{or} \qquad \cos x = -\frac{1}{2}$$

There are two angles between 0° and 360° whose cosine equals $-\frac{1}{2}$. They are **120°** and **240°,** as seen in the figures below.

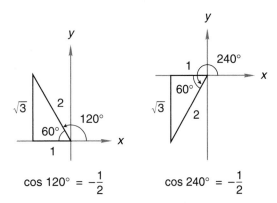

example 13.4   Solve: $\sin^2 x = 1$ $(0 \le x < 2\pi)$

solution   We must find the radian measures of x between 0 and 2π that satisfy the given equation. If we move the 1 to the left side, we get a factorable expression. We set each of the factors equal to zero and solve.

$$\sin^2 x - 1 = 0 \qquad\qquad \text{added } -1 \text{ to both sides}$$

$$(\sin x - 1)(\sin x + 1) = 0 \qquad\qquad \text{factored}$$

$$\sin x = 1 \quad \text{or} \quad \sin x = -1 \qquad\qquad \text{zero factor theorem}$$

$$x = \frac{\pi}{2} \qquad\qquad x = \frac{3\pi}{2} \qquad\qquad \text{solved}$$

example 13.5   Solve: $\tan^2 x = 3$ $(0° \leq x < 360°)$

solution   We rearrange and factor.

$$\tan^2 x - 3 = 0 \qquad \text{rearranged}$$
$$(\tan x - \sqrt{3})(\tan x + \sqrt{3}) = 0 \qquad \text{factored}$$
$$\tan x = \sqrt{3} \quad \text{or} \quad \tan x = -\sqrt{3} \qquad \text{zero factor theorem}$$

The tangent is positive in the first and third quadrants. The angles in these quadrants whose tangent is $\sqrt{3}$ are 60° and 240°. The tangent is negative in the second and fourth quadrants. The tangents of both 120° and 300° are $-\sqrt{3}$. Thus, there are four answers.

$$x = \mathbf{60°, 120°, 240°, 300°}$$

example 13.6   Solve: $\cos^2 x + 2 \sin x - 2 = 0$ $(0° \leq x < 360°)$

solution   The trick here is to replace $\cos^2 x$ with $1 - \sin^2 x$. The resulting equation in $\sin x$ can be factored.

$$(1 - \sin^2 x) + 2 \sin x - 2 = 0 \qquad \text{substituted}$$
$$\sin^2 x - 2 \sin x + 1 = 0 \qquad \text{simplified}$$
$$(\sin x - 1)(\sin x - 1) = 0 \qquad \text{factored}$$
$$\sin x = 1 \qquad \text{zero factor theorem}$$
$$x = \mathbf{90°} \qquad \text{solved}$$

example 13.7   Solve: $2 \sin^2 \theta = 3 + 3 \cos \theta$ $(0° \leq \theta < 360°)$

solution   Substitutions that lead to factorable expressions can be made. We rearrange this equation, substitute $(1 - \cos^2 \theta)$ for $\sin^2 \theta$, factor, and solve.

$$2 \sin^2 \theta - 3 \cos \theta - 3 = 0 \qquad \text{rearranged}$$
$$2(1 - \cos^2 \theta) - 3 \cos \theta - 3 = 0 \qquad \text{substituted}$$
$$-2 \cos^2 \theta - 3 \cos \theta - 1 = 0 \qquad \text{simplified}$$
$$2 \cos^2 \theta + 3 \cos \theta + 1 = 0 \qquad \text{changed signs}$$

This expression has the form $2u^2 + 3u + 1$, which can be factored as $(2u + 1)(u + 1)$. Thus the equation can be written in a similar factored form.

$$(2 \cos \theta + 1)(\cos \theta + 1) = 0 \qquad \text{factored}$$

$$\cos \theta = -\frac{1}{2} \quad \text{or} \quad \cos \theta = -1 \qquad \text{zero factor theorem}$$

The only angle in the domain specified whose cosine equals –1 is 180°, but the cosines of both 120° and 240° equal $-\frac{1}{2}$. Thus there are three answers.

$$\theta = \mathbf{120°, 180°, 240°}$$

problem set 13

1. The strength of a beam with a rectangular cross section varies jointly with the square of the depth of its cross section and with the width of its cross section. If the strength is 40 when the width is P inches and the depth is M cm, what is the strength when the width is A inches and the depth is 3 cm?
(5)

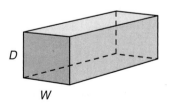

2. Two boats leave a buoy at the same time. One of the boats travels south at a rate of $3a$ miles per hour, and the other boat travels west at a rate of $4a$ miles per hour. What is the distance between the two boats 3 hours after they leave the buoy?
(5)

Evaluate the expressions in problems 3 and 4. Express your answers in radians.

3.
(13)
$\sin^{-1} -\dfrac{\sqrt{2}}{2}$

4.
(13)
$\cos^{-1} \dfrac{\sqrt{3}}{2}$

Solve the equations in problems 5–7 for x.

5.
(13)
$\csc x = -2 \ (0° \leq x < 360°)$

6.
(13)
$\cos^2 x = 1 \ (0 \leq x < 2\pi)$

7.
(13)
$\sin^2 x + 2 \cos x - 2 = 0 \ (0 \leq x < 2\pi)$

8.
(7)
Sketch the graphs of $y = \sin x$ and $y = \sin (2x)$ on the same coordinate plane.

9.
(12)
Sketch the graphs of $y = \ln x$, $y = -\ln x$, and $y = \ln -x$ on the same coordinate plane.

10.
(12)
Use the sum formula for $\sin (A + B)$ to show the following:

$$\frac{\sin (x + \Delta x) - \sin x}{\Delta x} = \sin x \left(\frac{\cos \Delta x - 1}{\Delta x} \right) + \cos x \left(\frac{\sin \Delta x}{\Delta x} \right)$$

11.
(12)
Write the key trigonometric identities from Lesson 12, and develop three identities for $\cos (2A)$.

12.
(12)
One of the sum identities for the tangent function is

$$\tan (A + B) = \frac{\tan A + \tan B}{1 - \tan A \tan B}$$

(a) Develop this identity from the sum identities for sine and cosine.

(b) Determine the value of $\tan (2A)$ given that $\tan A = \dfrac{1}{2}$.

13.
(9)
Graph f where $f(x) = \begin{cases} 2x - 1 & \text{when } x > 1 \\ 3 & \text{when } x = 1 \\ x^2 & \text{when } x < 1. \end{cases}$

14.
(11)
Evaluate the following for $f(x) = \begin{cases} 2x - 1 & \text{when } x > 1 \\ 3 & \text{when } x = 1 \\ x^2 & \text{when } x < 1: \end{cases}$

(a) $\lim\limits_{x \to 1^+} f(x)$ (b) $\lim\limits_{x \to 1^-} f(x)$ (c) $f(1)$

15.
(2,6)
(a) Use a graphing calculator to graph $y = \sqrt{9 - x^2}$. (Graph this using the ZDecimal option.)

(b) If we square both sides of the equation, we get $y^2 = 9 - x^2$ or $x^2 + y^2 = 9$, which is the equation of a circle centered at the origin with a radius of 3. Explain why the graph obtained in (a) is only the graph of a semicircle.

(c) Explain how the graph of a complete circle might be obtained on the graphing calculator.

16.
(10)
The roots of a quadratic function $y = f(x)$ are $x = 2$ and $x = -6$. Find the axis of symmetry of the graph of f.

17.
(9)
Write in standard form the equation of a circle whose center is $(1, -2)$ and whose area is 4π.

18.
(6)
Let $f(x) = \dfrac{2}{x}$. Simplify the expression $\dfrac{f(x + \Delta x) - f(x)}{\Delta x}$.

19.
(2)
Use a graphing calculator to approximate the value(s) of x for which $x^3 + x^2 - 2x + 2$ equals zero.

20. Use a graphing calculator to graph $y = 5$ and $y = e^x$ simultaneously.
(2,9)

(a) Approximate to three decimal places the coordinates of the point where these two graphs intersect.

(b) Determine the exact coordinates of the point of intersection.

21. Determine the domain of the function $y = \dfrac{\sqrt{x-2}}{x}$.
(6)

22. $\triangle ABC$ is an equilateral triangle. Assume $AB = 3$ and $\overline{DE}$ is parallel to $\overline{AB}$. Find the length of $\overline{DE}$ in terms of h.
(8)

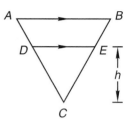

23. Given $f(x) = x^2$, compute $\dfrac{1}{4}\displaystyle\sum_{n=1}^{4} f(1)$.
(1,6)

24. In $\triangle ABC$, $m\angle A > m\angle B$. Compare: A. CB B. AC
(1)

25. Given that $x^2 + y^2 = 3$ and $x^2 - y^2 = 4$, find the value of $x^4 - y^4$.
(R)

LESSON 14 *Limit of a Function*

A function has a limit at a particular value of x if it has both a right-hand limit and a left-hand limit at that value of x and these two limits are equal.

The limit of a continuous function as x approaches a is the value of the function when $x = a$, because the graphs of continuous functions never "break." Thus, the limits of the following functions as x approaches 3 are the values of the functions when $x = 3$.

$$\lim_{x \to 3} (x + 6) = 9 \qquad \lim_{x \to 3} (x^2 + 3) = 12$$

The limit of the sum, product, or difference of functions when x approaches a is the sum, product, or difference of the individual limits. The limit of the quotient of two functions is the quotient of the limits if the limit of the function in the denominator is not zero.

$$\lim_{x \to 3} \left[(x + 6) + (x^2 + 3)\right] = 9 + 12 \qquad \lim_{x \to 3} \left[(x + 6)(x^2 + 3)\right] = (9)(12)$$
$$= 21 \qquad\qquad\qquad = 108$$

$$\lim_{x \to 3} \left[(x + 6) - (x^2 + 3)\right] = 9 - 12 \qquad \lim_{x \to 3} \frac{x + 6}{x^2 + 3} = \frac{9}{12} = \frac{3}{4}$$
$$= -3$$

These examples are not good examples to teach the idea of a limit, because the limit of these functions as x approaches 3 is the value of the function when x equals 3. A better example would be a function that has a limit as x approaches 3, but that has no defined value when the value of x equals 3. Consider, for example, the function

$$f(x) = \frac{x^2 - x - 6}{x - 3}$$

Since $x^2 - x - 6 = (x - 3)(x + 2)$, we see that

$$\frac{x^2 - x - 6}{x - 3} = x + 2$$

for all values of x except $x = 3$. Therefore, the graphs of $f(x)$ and $x + 2$ look quite similar. On the left-hand side below we show the graph of the line $y = x + 2$, and on the right-hand side we show the graph of f. The only difference between the two is the discontinuity at $x = 3$ in the graph of f.

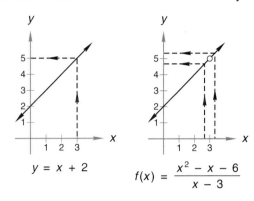

$$y = x + 2$$

$$f(x) = \frac{x^2 - x - 6}{x - 3}$$

The function f has no value when x equals 3, because the denominator equals zero when x equals 3, but it has the same values as $x + 2$ for all other values of x. Therefore,

$$\lim_{x \to 3^-} \frac{x^2 - x - 6}{x - 3} = 5 \qquad \text{and} \qquad \lim_{x \to 3^+} \frac{x^2 - x - 6}{x - 3} = 5$$

Since the left-hand and right-hand limits exist and are equal,

$$\lim_{x \to 3} f(x) = \lim_{x \to 3} \frac{x^2 - x - 6}{x - 3} = 5$$

even though $f(3)$ **does not exist.**

example 14.1   Evaluate: $\lim\limits_{x \to 2} \dfrac{x^2 - 4}{x - 2}$

solution   When $x = 2$, this function has no value because the denominator equals zero. If we factor the numerator, we get

$$\lim_{x \to 2} \frac{(x - 2)(x + 2)}{(x - 2)}$$

For any value of x other than 2, the two $x - 2$ factors cancel, so

$$\lim_{x \to 2} \frac{x^2 - 4}{x - 2} = \lim_{x \to 2} (x + 2) = \mathbf{4}$$

example 14.2   Evaluate: $\lim\limits_{x \to 3} \dfrac{x^2 + 2x}{x + 1}$

solution   This problem is trivial because there is no discontinuity at $x = 3$.

$$\lim_{x \to 3} \frac{x^2 + 2x}{x + 1} = \frac{9 + 6}{3 + 1} = \frac{\mathbf{15}}{\mathbf{4}}$$

example 14.3   Evaluate: $\lim\limits_{x \to 3} \dfrac{x^2 + 6x}{x - 3}$

solution   This function has no limit as x approaches 3, because the denominator approaches zero while the numerator approaches some nonzero number.

$$\lim_{x \to 3} \frac{x(x + 6)}{x - 3} \ [\neq] \ \frac{27}{0} \qquad \text{\textbf{Thus, the limit does not exist.}}$$

We use the symbol [$\neq$] because we do not wish to indicate that $\dfrac{27}{0}$ is the limit.

example 14.4   Evaluate: $\lim\limits_{t \to 2} \dfrac{t - 2}{t^2 + 4}$

solution   In this problem, the independent variable is t instead of x. As t approaches 2, the numerator approaches zero and the denominator approaches 8.

$$\lim\limits_{t \to 2} \frac{t - 2}{t^2 + 4} = \frac{0}{8} = 0$$

Thus, the limit exists and equals **0.**

example 14.5   Evaluate: $\lim\limits_{s \to -1} \dfrac{2s^2 + 5s + 3}{s + 1}$

solution   When $s = -1$, the denominator equals 0, which can be problematic. We hope the numerator has a factor of $s + 1$. After factoring we see that it does.

$$\lim\limits_{s \to -1} \frac{(2s + 3)(s + 1)}{(s + 1)}$$

For all values of s except -1, this function is identical to $2s + 3$. We do not care about the value of the function when $s = -1$; we are only interested in the function values when s is close to -1.

$$\lim\limits_{s \to -1} \frac{2s^2 + 5s + 3}{s + 1} = \lim\limits_{s \to -1} (2s + 3) = \mathbf{1}$$

example 14.6   Evaluate: $\lim\limits_{x \to 2} \dfrac{x^3 - 8}{x - 2}$

solution   The denominator equals zero when $x = 2$. Thus, we hope that $x - 2$ is a factor of the numerator.

$$\lim\limits_{x \to 2} \frac{(x - 2)(x^2 + 2x + 4)}{x - 2} \qquad \text{factored numerator}$$

$$= \lim\limits_{x \to 2} (x^2 + 2x + 4) \qquad \text{canceled}$$

$$= 2^2 + 2(2) + 4 \qquad \text{substituted}$$

$$= \mathbf{12} \qquad \text{simplified}$$

example 14.7   Evaluate: $\lim\limits_{x \to 0} \dfrac{(3 + x)^2 - 3^2}{x}$

solution   We expand the numerator and hope that each term in the resulting numerator has a factor of x so we can cancel the x in the denominator.

$$\lim\limits_{x \to 0} \frac{9 + 6x + x^2 - 9}{x} \qquad \text{expanded}$$

$$= \lim\limits_{x \to 0} \frac{6x + x^2}{x} \qquad \text{simplified}$$

$$= \lim\limits_{x \to 0} (6 + x) \qquad \text{canceled}$$

$$= \mathbf{6} \qquad \text{substituted}$$

example 14.8   Use a graphing calculator to confirm that $\lim\limits_{x \to 0} \dfrac{(3 + x)^2 - 3^2}{x} = 6$.

solution   The graphing calculator can be used as a tool to intelligently guess the value of a limit. There are at least two ways to accomplish this task. First, we could graph the function

$$\text{Y1=((3+X)}^2\text{-9)/X}$$

and use the ⬚TRACE⬚ feature of the calculator to estimate the function values as the x-values approach 0. This provides a nice visualization of the limit.

A second option is to build a table of values of the function for x-values near 0. For this we need two key sequences:

TBLSET
2nd WINDOW   accesses the TABLE SETUP menu

TABLE
2nd GRAPH   displays tables

After defining the function as above, we access the TABLE SETUP menu and set

$$\texttt{TblStart=0.5} \quad \text{and} \quad \texttt{\triangle Tbl=-0.1}$$

(Indpnt and Depend should be in Auto mode.) Next we display the table.

X	Y₁
.5	6.5
.4	6.4
.3	6.3
.2	6.2
.1	6.1
0	ERROR
-.1	5.9

X=.5

Notice the ERROR for the function when $x = 0$. This occurs because the function is undefined at 0 (due to division by 0). However, for x-values near 0, the y-values approach 6. This confirms (numerically) the algebraic work we performed in example 14.7.

problem set 14

1. (5) A rectangular garden that has an area of 100 ft² is bounded on three sides by a brick wall costing $50 per foot and on the fourth side by a fence costing only $20 per foot. Express the cost of the garden's enclosure in terms of the single variable x, where x is the length of the fenced side.

2. (5) Stig traveled for h hours at m miles per hour but arrived at the fjord 2 hours late. How fast should Stig have traveled to have arrived on time? (*Hint:* Figure out the distance Stig had to travel, and use the fact that distance is the product of rate and time.)

3. (14) Graph: $y = \dfrac{x^2 - 1}{x - 1}$

Evaluate the limits in problems 4–8.

4. (14) $\lim\limits_{x \to 3} \dfrac{x^2 + 2x}{x + 2}$

5. (14) $\lim\limits_{x \to 2} \dfrac{x^2 + x - 6}{x - 2}$

6. (14) $\lim\limits_{x \to a} \dfrac{x^2 - a^2}{x - a}$

7. (14) $\lim\limits_{x \to 0} \dfrac{(2 + x)^2 - 2^2}{x}$

8. (14) $\lim\limits_{x \to 0} \dfrac{\dfrac{1}{2 + x} - \dfrac{1}{2}}{x}$

9. (13) Solve: $2 \sin^2 x - 3 \cos x = 3 \ (0° \le x < 360°)$

10. (7) Determine the amplitude, the period, and the equation of the centerline for the function $y = 4 - 2 \sin (3x)$.

11. (7,12) Sketch $y = e^x$ and $y = \ln x$ on the same coordinate plane.

12. (12) Sketch $y = \ln x$ and $y = \ln -x$ on the same coordinate plane.

13. (12) (a) State three double-angle identities for $\cos (2x)$.

(b) Using one of these three identities, write $\cos^2 x$ in terms of $\cos (2x)$ without involving another trigonometric function.

14. (12) Use the identity for $\sin (A + B)$ to simplify the expression $\sin \left(\dfrac{\pi}{2} + x \right)$.

15. (a) Write the key trigonometric identities, and develop an identity for tan $(A - B)$.
(12)

(b) Use this identity for the tangent function to compute the exact value of tan 15°.

16. If $y - 1 = \ln x$, what does x equal?
(9)

17. Without the aid of a calculator, sketch the graph of $y = -|x^2 - 3x - 4|$.
(9)

18. Which of the following sets of points could lie on the graph of a function?
(6)

A. $\{(1, 1), (2, 2), (3, 3), (4, 4)\}$ B. $\{(1, 1), (1, -1), (2, 2)\}$

C. $\{(-1, 0), (0, -1), (1, -1), (-1, -1)\}$ D. $\{(0, 0), (0, 1)\}$

19. On the number line, graph the solution of the inequality $|x - 1| < 2$.
(9)

20. Use a graphing calculator to help approximate the value of $\lim_{x \to 0} \frac{\sin x}{x}$. Begin by graphing the
(14) function $y_1 = \frac{\sin x}{x}$. Then examine the coordinates of points on the graph of y_1 as x approaches 0.

21. Show that the following equivalence is true for all x where the functions are defined.
(8)

$$(\sec -x)\left[\sin\left(\frac{\pi}{2} - x\right)\right] + (\sin -x)\left[\cos\left(\frac{\pi}{2} - x\right)\right] = \cos^2 x$$

22. Which of the following equations represents a function y of the independent variable x?
(6)

A. $x^2 + y^2 = 9$ B. $x^2 = y$

C. $x = y^2$ D. $y = \pm\sqrt{x}$

23. Simplify the following expression so that it has a numerator of 1:
(1)

$$\left(\frac{\sqrt{x + h} - \sqrt{x}}{h}\right)\left(\frac{\sqrt{x + h} + \sqrt{x}}{\sqrt{x + h} + \sqrt{x}}\right)$$

24. Evaluate: $\sum_{x=1}^{4} \frac{1}{x}$
(1)

25. Given that x is a real number, compare the following: A. $\sqrt{x^2}$ B. $|x|$
(1)

LESSON 15 *Interval Notation • Products of Linear Factors • Tangents • Increasing and Decreasing Functions*

15.A

interval notation

The first graph on the left below designates the real numbers between −3 and 2 but does not include the endpoints −3 and 2. The second graph (the one in the upper right) designates the same numbers but includes −3 and 2. The other two graphs include one endpoint but exclude the other endpoint.

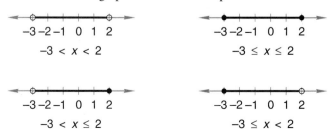

-3 < x < 2   -3 ≤ x ≤ 2

-3 < x ≤ 2   -3 ≤ x < 2

The notation below each graph designates the same set of values of x as does the graph. Each of the notations designates an **interval** on the set of real numbers. In calculus it is often necessary to designate such intervals, and we use **interval notation** for this purpose because it is more compact than the notation used above. We write the endpoint numbers separated with a comma and use a parenthesis if an endpoint number is not included in the interval or a bracket if the endpoint number is included. Therefore, the notations above can be expressed more compactly as follows:

OPEN INTERVAL	CLOSED INTERVAL	PARTIALLY CLOSED INTERVALS	
$-3 < x < 2$	$-3 \le x \le 2$	$-3 < x \le 2$	$-3 \le x < 2$
$(-3, 2)$	$[-3, 2]$	$(-3, 2]$	$[-3, 2)$

The notation for an open interval $(-3, 2)$ is exactly the same notation used to designate the ordered pair of x and y, $(-3, 2)$. Whether the notation designates an open interval or an ordered pair is an assessment that must be made by the reader based on the context in which the notation is used.

The notations

$$(-\infty, 4) \qquad (-\infty, 4] \qquad (4, \infty) \qquad [4, \infty)$$

designate the real numbers less than 4, the real numbers less than or equal to 4, the real numbers greater than 4, and the real numbers greater than or equal to 4. The symbols ∞ and $-\infty$ are the symbols for positive infinity and negative infinity. **Infinity** is not a number. It is the word used to designate a quantity that increases without bound. When the symbol ∞ or $-\infty$ is used in interval notation, it is always preceded or followed by a parenthesis, as seen in the notations above.

example 15.1   Designate the following intervals by using interval notation:

(a) $4 < x \le 30$ (b) $x \ge 22$ (c) $x < -42$

solution   We use the bracket when an equals sign appears in the description of the interval.

(a) **(4, 30]**   (b) **[22, ∞)**   (c) **(−∞, −42)**

example 15.2   On which intervals is this function positive?

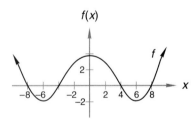

solution   The function has a positive value whenever the graph of the function is above the x-axis. Thus, this function is positive (greater than zero) on these intervals: **(−∞, −8), (−4, +4),** and **(8, ∞).**

15.B

products of linear factors

Consider the expression

$$x - 2$$

If x equals 2, this expression equals zero. If x is less than 2, this expression represents a negative number. If x is greater than 2, this expression represents a positive number. These seemingly trivial statements are of considerable importance in determining the signs of functions on designated intervals. If a function is defined as a product of nonrepeating linear factors, such as

$$f(x) = x(x + 3)(x + 6)(x - 2)(x - 5)$$

the function has a value of zero iff one of the factors equals zero. Thus, this function equals zero iff x equals 0, −3, −6, +2, or +5. **The value of the function changes sign at each of these zeros and can only do so at these zeros.**

example 15.3   Use (a) a number line and (b) interval notation to show the intervals on which the function

$$f(x) = x(x + 3)(x + 6)(x - 2)(x - 5)$$

is positive and the intervals on which the function is negative.

solution   (a) First we sketch a number line and graph the zeros of the function.

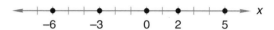

Now we must determine the sign of the function at some *x*-value that is not a zero of the function. We decide to use +1 for this value of *x*.

$$f(1) = 1(1 + 3)(1 + 6)(1 - 2)(1 - 5) = (+)(+)(+)(-)(-) = +$$

Thus, the sign of the function is positive when $x = +1$. From the graph we see that it must be positive for all *x*-values between 0 and 2. For products of nonrepeating linear factors, the sign changes at every zero, as shown below.

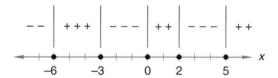

(b) We can use interval notation to give the same information by saying that the function has **positive values on the intervals (–6, –3), (0, 2), and (5, ∞) and negative values on the intervals (–∞, –6), (–3, 0), and (2, 5).** With the graphing calculator, we can confirm these results.

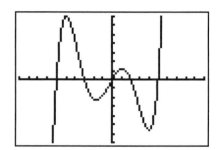

15.C

tangents   The word **tangent** comes from the Latin word *tangere,* which means "to touch." A tangent to a curve is a straight line that "touches" the curve. An accurate informal definition of a tangent is difficult to devise. A formal definition will be given in a later lesson. We introduce the tangent by considering the following figure:

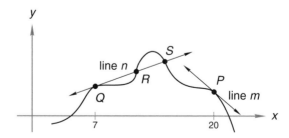

Line *m* is tangent to the curve at *P*. Line *n* is tangent to the curve at *Q* but not at *R* or *S*. We customarily designate points of tangency by giving the *x*-coordinate of the point. The points of tangency for the given lines and this curve are at $x = 7$ and $x = 20$. **The slope of a curve at a point is the slope of the line tangent to the curve at that point.**

example 15.4   For what values of x does this curve have a slope of zero?

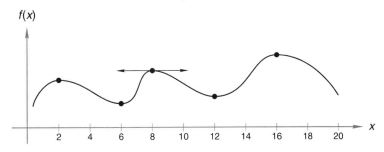

solution   The slope of a curve is zero when the tangent is horizontal. We estimate that the point of tangency of the horizontal tangent shown in the figure has an x-value of **8.** The other places where the curve appears to have horizontal tangents are at x-values of **2, 6, 12, and 16.**

15.D
increasing and decreasing functions

A function f is an **increasing function** on an interval (a, b) if every greater input value of x on this interval produces a greater output $f(x)$. A function is a **decreasing function** on an interval (a, b) if every greater input value of x on this interval produces a lesser output $f(x)$.

If the graph of a function is everywhere ascending as x increases from a to b, the function is an increasing function on the interval (a, b). If the graph is everywhere descending as x increases from a to b, the function is a decreasing function on the interval (a, b). The function graphed at right is increasing on the interval (a, b) and decreasing on the interval (b, c).

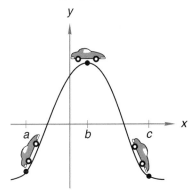

example 15.5   On which intervals does the function graphed here appear to be decreasing?

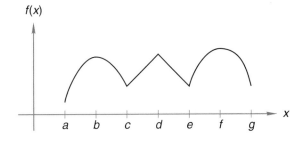

solution   The graph appears to be descending on the intervals (b, c), (d, e), and (f, g). Thus the function appears to be decreasing on these intervals.

example 15.6   Using a graphing calculator, estimate the intervals over which the function $f(x) = x(x + 3)(x + 6)(x - 2)(x - 5)$ appears to be increasing.

solution   We must estimate the values of x at which the graph reaches a high point or low point. This can be accomplished (with some accuracy) with the TRACE feature. Within the window whose parameters are shown

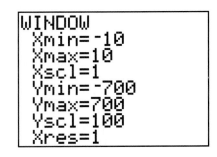

the TRACE feature indicates that the high and low points are located at (approximately) $x = -4.8936, -1.7021, 1.0638,$ and 4.0426. From these estimates, the function is increasing over the intervals $(-\infty, -4.8936)$, $(-1.7021, 1.0638)$, and $(4.0426, \infty)$.

problem set 15

1. Two pipes feed into a pool. The larger pipe can fill the pool in 2 hours. The smaller pipe can fill
(5) the pool in 6 hours. If both pipes are used together, how long would it take to fill the pool?

2. The sum of two numbers is 40. Let L be the larger number. Express the product of the two
(5) numbers in terms of L.

3. Shown is the graph of the function f.
(15)

(a) Use interval notation to describe the interval(s) on which f is positive.

(b) Use interval notation to describe the interval(s) on which f is negative.

(c) Use interval notation to describe the interval(s) on which f is increasing.

(d) Use interval notation to describe the interval(s) on which f is decreasing.

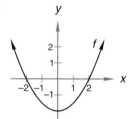

4. Using the rational root theorem, find the solutions of the equation $x^3 - 6x - 4 = 0$.
(15)

5. Let $f(x) = x(x - 2)(x + 3)$. Use a number line to show the intervals on which f is positive and
(15) the intervals on which f is negative. Also, indicate the values of x for which f is zero.

6. As accurately as possible, sketch the graph of $y = x^2$ $(0 \le x \le 2)$. Draw a line tangent to the
(15) graph at $x = 1$, and use this line to estimate the slope of the curve at $x = 1$.

Solve the equations in problems 7 and 8 for x $(0 \le x < 2\pi)$.

7. $\tan^2 x = 1$
(13)

8. $\sin^2 x - \sin x + \dfrac{1}{4} = 0$
(13)

9. Let $y = \arcsin x$. Solve for x in terms of y.
(13)

10. (a) Solve the equation $x^2 - 8y - 4x + 20 = 0$ for y.
(1,2)

(b) Graph the equation on a graphing calculator.

(c) Trace out points on the graph, and determine to one decimal place the coordinates of the lowest point on the graph. (You might try using different ZOOM modes.)

Evaluate the limits in problems 11–14.

11. $\lim\limits_{x \to 1} \dfrac{x^2 - 1}{x - 1}$
(14)

12. $\lim\limits_{x \to -1} \dfrac{x^2 + 1}{x - 1}$
(14)

13. $\lim\limits_{x \to 0} \dfrac{(1 + x)^2 - (1)^2}{x}$
(14)

14. $\lim\limits_{x \to -1} \dfrac{2x^2 + x - 1}{x + 1}$
(14)

15. Simplify: $\dfrac{[2(x + \Delta x) + 3] - (2x + 3)}{\Delta x}$
(1)

16. Find the value of k for which $y = \dfrac{1}{k} \sin (kx)$ has a period of 4π.
(7)

17. From the sum identity for the sine function, develop an expression for $\sin (2x)$.
(12)

18. Graph $y = e^x$, $y = -e^x$, and $y = \ln x$ on the same coordinate plane.
(7,12)

19. Suppose $\sin^2 A = \dfrac{1}{7}$. Determine the value of $\cos(2A)$ by using a double-angle identity.
(12)

20. Solve $\log_2\left(\dfrac{x-1}{x+1}\right) = 3$ for x.
(9)

21. If (x, y) is a point on the unit circle centered at the origin, what is the value of $x^2 + y^2$?
(7)

22. Find the values of y for which $|y - 3| < 0.01$.
(9)

23. Find the volume of a right prism whose height is L centimeters and whose bases are equilateral
(R) triangles with sides that are E centimeters long.

24. Find the next term of this sequence: 1, 4, 9, 16, ...
(R)

25. Determine the sum $x + y + z + t + s + v$ from the figure shown.
(R)

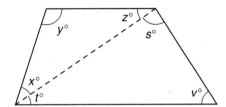

LESSON 16   *Logarithms of Products and Quotients • Logarithms of Powers • Exponential Equations*

16.A

logarithms of products and quotients

Remember that we multiply powers of the same base by adding the exponents as shown on the left-hand side below. We divide powers of the same base by subtracting the lower exponent from the upper exponent as shown on the right-hand side.

$$10^5 \cdot 10^2 = 10^{5+2} = 10^7 \qquad \frac{10^5}{10^2} = 10^{5-2} = 10^3$$

Since the common logarithm of 10^5 is 5 and the common logarithm of 10^2 is 2, we can use logarithmic notation and write

$$\log(10^5 \cdot 10^2) = \log 10^5 + \log 10^2 \qquad \log\left(\frac{10^5}{10^2}\right) = \log 10^5 - \log 10^2$$

$$= 5 + 2 = 7 \qquad\qquad\qquad = 5 - 2 = 3$$

These examples illustrate the fact that the logarithm of a product equals the sum of the logarithms and the logarithm of a quotient equals the difference of the logarithms.

$$\boxed{\log_b(MN) = \log_b M + \log_b N} \qquad \boxed{\log_b\left(\frac{M}{N}\right) = \log_b M - \log_b N}$$

Another important property of logarithms is stated below:

$$\boxed{\text{If } \log_b x = \log_b y, \text{ then } x = y.}$$

example 16.1   Solve $\log_4 (x + 2) + \log_4 5 = 2$ for x.

solution   The bases are the same, and the logs are added, so $(x + 2)$ and 5 can be multiplied. Thus we write

$$\log_4 (5(x + 2)) = 2$$

Now we write this equation in exponential form and solve.

$$5(x + 2) = 4^2 \qquad \text{exponential form}$$
$$5x + 10 = 16 \qquad \text{distributive property}$$
$$x = \frac{6}{5} \qquad \text{solved}$$

We must check to see that replacing x with $\frac{6}{5}$ does not cause $x + 2$ to be negative, because negative numbers do not have logarithms. Since $\frac{6}{5} + 2$ is a positive number, $x = \frac{6}{5}$ is a valid solution.

example 16.2   Solve $\ln (x - 1) - \ln (x + 2) = \ln 14$ for x.

solution   On the left the bases are the same, and the logs are subtracted. This means that the arguments can be divided.

$$\ln \frac{x - 1}{x + 2} = \ln 14 \qquad \text{difference rule for logarithms}$$
$$\frac{x - 1}{x + 2} = 14 \qquad \text{equal arguments}$$
$$x - 1 = 14x + 28 \qquad \text{multiplied}$$
$$-13x = 29 \qquad \text{simplified}$$
$$x = -\frac{29}{13} \qquad \text{solved, but we must check}$$

If $-\frac{29}{13}$ replaces x in the argument $x - 1$, the result is a negative number. Since negative numbers do not have logarithms, this value of x is unacceptable. **Thus the problem has no solution.**

16.B

logarithms of powers   The next rule for logarithms is useful and, for some, is the most difficult to remember. We note that the logarithm of 10^2 to the base 10 is 2, so 3 times this logarithm equals 6.

$$\log_{10} (10^2) = 2 \qquad \text{so} \qquad 3(\log_{10} 10^2) = 3(2) = 6$$

But this last result is the same as the logarithm of $(10^2)^3$.

$$\log_{10} \left[(10^2)^3 \right] \qquad \text{equals} \qquad \log_{10} 10^6 = 6$$

From this we see that the logarithm of a power of a number is the same as the exponent times the logarithm of the number. **This means that the use of logarithms permits us to change exponents to coefficients. The reverse is also true: A coefficient can be changed to an exponent.**

$$\boxed{\log_b (M^c) = c(\log_b M)}$$

example 16.3   Solve $2 \log_8 x + \log_8 4 = 1$ for x.

solution   **In the first term we change the coefficient to an exponent** and write

$$\log_8 (x^2) + \log_8 4 = 1$$

The logs are added, so the arguments can be multiplied.

$$\log_8 (4x^2) = 1$$

We finish by rewriting the equation in exponential form and solving.

$$4x^2 = 8^1 \qquad \text{exponential form}$$
$$x^2 = 2 \qquad \text{divided}$$
$$x = \pm\sqrt{2} \qquad \text{solved}$$

However, $-\sqrt{2}$ is not an acceptable value because $\log_8(-\sqrt{2})$ is undefined. Thus $x = \sqrt{2}$ is the only solution.

example 16.4   Solve $-2\ln 3 - \ln(x-1) = -\ln\dfrac{1}{4}$ for x.

solution   We begin by using the rule for powers to rewrite $-2\ln 3$ as $\ln 3^{-2}$ or $\ln\frac{1}{9}$ and $-\ln\frac{1}{4}$ as $\ln\left(\frac{1}{4}\right)^{-1}$ or $\ln 4$.

$$\ln\frac{1}{9} - \ln(x-1) = \ln 4 \qquad \text{power rule for logarithms}$$

$$\ln\frac{\frac{1}{9}}{x-1} = \ln 4 \qquad \text{difference rule for logarithms}$$

$$\frac{\frac{1}{9}}{x-1} = 4 \qquad \text{equal arguments}$$

$$\frac{1}{9} = 4x - 4 \qquad \text{simplified}$$

$$\frac{37}{36} = x \qquad \text{solved}$$

This value of x is acceptable since it does not make the argument negative.

16.C
exponential equations

Exponential equations are intimidating because the variable is in the exponent. **To find the solution, it is necessary to find a way to get the variable out of the exponent.** One way to do this is to write both sides of the equation as powers of the same base. If powers of the same base are equal, the exponents must be equal.

example 16.5   Solve $8^{3x+2} = 16$ without using logarithms.

solution   The trick is to write everything as a power of the same base. In this example the base is 2.

$$(2^3)^{3x+2} = 2^4 \qquad \text{same base}$$
$$2^{9x+6} = 2^4 \qquad \text{simplified}$$

Since the expressions are equal and the bases are equal, the exponents must be equal.

$$9x + 6 = 4 \qquad \text{exponents equal}$$
$$x = -\frac{2}{9} \qquad \text{solved}$$

example 16.6   Solve $10^{-2x+2} = 8$ for x.

solution   This problem looks similar to the preceding one, but it is very different because 8 and 10 cannot be written as powers of the same base unless we use logarithms. We choose the common logarithm, log base 10, because one of the bases in the problem is 10.

$$\log(10^{-2x+2}) = \log 8 \qquad \text{log of both sides}$$

On the left-hand side we apply the power rule for logarithms.

$$(-2x + 2)\log 10 = \log 8 \qquad \text{power rule for logarithms}$$

But log 10 is 1, so we end up with a simple algebraic equation.

$$-2x + 2 = \log 8 \qquad \text{equation}$$
$$-2x = \log 8 - 2 \qquad \text{added } -2 \text{ to both sides}$$
$$x = -\frac{\log 8 - 2}{2} \qquad \text{divided}$$

From the calculator we obtain the approximation $x \approx 0.5485$. It is wise to wait till the end of such a problem before using a calculator. This insures the greatest accuracy for the answer.

example 16.7   Solve $e^{-2x+3} = 5$ for x.

solution   Again the variables are in the exponent, and the bases cannot be written as powers of the same number without using logarithms. Since one base is already e, we decide to take the natural logarithms of both sides. We do this by writing ln in front of both expressions.

$$\ln\left(e^{-2x+3}\right) = \ln 5 \qquad \text{ln of both sides}$$

Now we use the power rule for logarithms on the left-hand side.

$$(-2x + 3)\ln e = \ln 5 \qquad \text{power rule for logarithms}$$

We remember that the natural logarithm of e is 1. This is the reason that we used base e instead of base 10 in this problem. Thus, we get

$$-2x + 3 = \ln 5 \qquad \text{simplified}$$
$$-2x = \ln 5 - 3 \qquad \text{added } -3$$
$$x = -\frac{\ln 5 - 3}{2} \qquad \text{divided}$$

Again, we have avoided using the calculator in the process of solving the equation. We do so now to get the most accurate approximation.

$$x \approx 0.6953$$

example 16.8   Solve $5^{2x-1} = 6^{x-2}$ for x.

solution   Again the variables are in the exponents. We can get the variables out of the exponents by taking the logarithms of both sides. Since neither of the bases is e or 10, there is no special reason to choose either base. We decide to take the common logarithms of both sides.

$$\log\left(5^{2x-1}\right) = \log\left(6^{x-2}\right) \qquad \text{log of both sides}$$

Next we use the power rule on both sides.

$$(2x - 1)\log 5 = (x - 2)\log 6 \qquad \text{power rule for logarithms}$$
$$(2\log 5)x - \log 5 = (\log 6)x - 2\log 6 \qquad \text{distributive property}$$
$$(2\log 5)x - (\log 6)x = \log 5 - 2\log 6 \qquad \text{combined like terms}$$
$$(2\log 5 - \log 6)x = \log 5 - 2\log 6 \qquad \text{factored}$$
$$x = \frac{\log 5 - 2\log 6}{2\log 5 - \log 6} \qquad \text{simplified}$$

This answer appears to be complicated, and the algebraic steps are difficult to follow with all the logs present. However, we have an exact solution. Only now should the calculator be employed to approximate the answer.

$$x \approx -1.3833$$

problem set 16

1. The number of vehicles Ronk sells varies linearly with the number of vehicles he shows to
   (5) potential buyers. If showing 100 cars results in his selling 25 of them while showing 120 cars results in his selling 29 of them, how many cars must he show in order to sell 30 cars?

2. Given that a rectangle has perimeter p and width w, find an expression for the area of the
   (5) rectangle in terms of p and w.

Solve the equations in problems 3–7 for x.

3. $\ln (x + 2) - \ln (x - 1) = \ln 5$
(16)

4. $2 \log_3 x - \log_3 4 = 2$
(16)

5. $27^{2x + 1} = 9$
(16)

6. $10^{x + 1} = e^{2x}$
(16)

7. $3^{-x + 1} = 4^{x + 2}$
(16)

For problems 8–10, $f(x) = |x^2 - 1|$.

8. Graph f.
(9)

9. On which intervals is f increasing, and on which intervals is f decreasing?
(15)

10. For what value(s) of x does the graph of f have a slope of zero?
(15)

11. Let $g(x) = x(x - 1)(x + 2)(x - 3)$. Show on a number line where $g > 0$ and where $g < 0$.
(15)

12. (a) Graph $g(x) = x(x - 1)(x + 2)(x - 3)$ on a graphing calculator. Set the parameters of the
(2) calculator display to show x-values from $x = -5$ to $x = 5$ and y-values from $y = -10$ to $y = 10$.

(b) For the interval from $x = -2$ to $x = 3$, determine the coordinates of the highest point. Give coordinates to one decimal place.

13. Solve: $4 \sin^2 x - 3 = 0$ $(0 \le x < 2\pi)$
(13)

14. Given $f(x) = 2x$, simplify the expression $\dfrac{f(x + \Delta x) - f(x)}{\Delta x}$.
(6)

15. Given $f(x) = x^2$, evaluate the expression $\displaystyle\lim_{\Delta x \to 0} \dfrac{f(x + \Delta x) - f(x)}{\Delta x}$.
(14)

Evaluate the limits in problems 16 and 17.

16. $\displaystyle\lim_{t \to 1} \dfrac{t^2 - 2t + 1}{t - 1}$
(14)

17. $\displaystyle\lim_{s \to 1} \dfrac{s - 1}{s^2 + 1}$
(14)

18. (a) Evaluate: $\displaystyle\lim_{x \to 0} (e^x + 1)$
(14)

(b) Enter the function $y = e^x + 1$ into a graphing calculator. Use the table feature to approximate the value y approaches when x approaches zero.

19. Write the equation of the sinusoid shown
(7) in terms of the sine function.

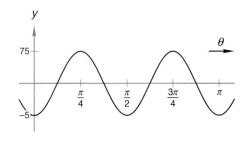

20. As accurately as possible, sketch the graph of $y = \ln x$. Draw a line tangent to the graph
(12) at $x = 1$, and use this line to estimate the slope of the curve at $x = 1$.

21. Describe the domain and range of $y = \ln -x$.
(6)

22. Without using a calculator, determine the value of $\sin^2 43° + \cos^2 43°$.
(8)

23. (a) Use the identities $\sin (2A) = 2 \sin A \cos A$ and $\cos (2A) = \cos^2 A - \sin^2 A$ to prove that
(12) $\tan (2A) = \frac{2 \tan A}{1 - \tan^2 A}$.

(b) Find the exact value of $\tan (2A)$ given that $\tan A = 2$.

24. Given $x > 0$, compare: A. $\dfrac{1}{\sqrt[3]{x^2}}$ B. $\sqrt[3]{x^{-2}}$
(1)

25. Given the figure shown, find
(R) $x + y + z + t$. (*Hint:* See problem 25 in
Problem Set 15.)

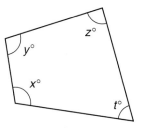

LESSON 17   *Infinity as a Limit • Undefined Limits*

17.A

infinity as a limit

The word **infinity** describes a quantity whose value is increasing without bound. If x represents a positive number that is getting smaller and smaller and is approaching zero from the positive side, the value of 1 over x $\left(\frac{1}{x}\right)$ is a positive number that is getting larger and larger. We use the symbol ∞ to indicate that a value is increasing positively without bound. If x represents a negative number that is getting smaller and smaller and approaching zero from the negative side, the value of 1 over x is a negative number whose absolute value is increasing without bound. We use the symbol $-\infty$ to indicate that a value is increasing negatively without bound. In mathematics, when we speak of the limit of a function, we usually mean a numerical limit. However, it is sometimes convenient to be able to use $+\infty$ or $-\infty$ when discussing limits. If we use limit notation, we can write the statements discussed in this paragraph as follows:

$$\lim_{x \to 0^+} \frac{1}{x} = \infty \qquad \text{and} \qquad \lim_{x \to 0^-} \frac{1}{x} = -\infty$$

x	0.1	0.01	0.001	0.0001	–0.1	–0.01	–0.001	–0.0001
$\dfrac{1}{x}$	10	100	1,000	10,000	–10	–100	–1,000	–10,000

It is important to remember that infinity is not a real number. Every real number has a fixed position on the number line. Infinity is a word used to help describe a quantity whose value is increasing without bound.

In the example above, we see the x-values approaching a finite number (zero) while the function values approach ∞ or $-\infty$. We may also consider what happens in a limit when the x-values are allowed to grow large (go to ∞ or $-\infty$).

example 17.1   Evaluate: $\displaystyle\lim_{x \to \infty} \frac{4x^2 + x + 6}{3x^2 + 1}$

solution   A good procedure for evaluating a quotient of polynomials as x approaches infinity is to divide every term in the numerator and in the denominator by the highest power of x in the denominator. If we divide every term by x^2 and simplify, we get

$$\lim_{x \to \infty} \frac{4 + \dfrac{1}{x} + \dfrac{6}{x^2}}{3 + \dfrac{1}{x^2}} = \frac{4 + 0 + 0}{3 + 0} = \frac{4}{3}$$

As x gets larger and larger, the value of each term with a power of x in the denominator gets smaller and smaller, and the value of these terms is zero in the limit.

example 17.2   Evaluate: $\lim\limits_{x \to -\infty} \dfrac{x^3 + 6x}{8x^2 + 5x}$

solution   In this example we divide every term by x^2, which gives

$$\lim_{x \to -\infty} \frac{x + \dfrac{6}{x}}{8 + \dfrac{5}{x}} = \lim_{x \to -\infty} \frac{x}{8} = -\infty$$

The fractional terms approach zero as x gets large, and we are left with x over 8, whose limit as x approaches negative infinity is **negative infinity.** Some authors do not use infinity as a limit. They say that the limit of this expression as x approaches infinity is undefined or does not exist.

example 17.3   Evaluate: $\lim\limits_{x \to \infty} \dfrac{5x + 7}{13x^2 + 10x + 2}$

solution   We divide every term by x^2, since it is the highest power term in the denominator.

$$\lim_{x \to \infty} \frac{\dfrac{5}{x} + \dfrac{7}{x^2}}{13 + \dfrac{10}{x} + \dfrac{2}{x^2}}$$

As x gets large, we have

$$\frac{0 + 0}{13 + 0 + 0} = 0$$

17.B
undefined limits

If the left-hand limit and the right-hand limit as x approaches a finite value are both $-\infty$ or both $+\infty$, we can say that the limit is $-\infty$ or $+\infty$, as with the function graphed on the left-hand side below.

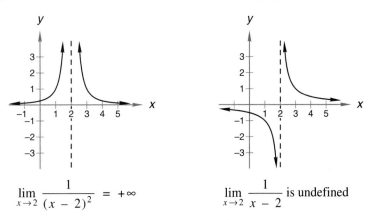

$$\lim_{x \to 2} \frac{1}{(x - 2)^2} = +\infty \qquad\qquad \lim_{x \to 2} \frac{1}{x - 2} \text{ is undefined}$$

The expression $(x - 2)^2$ approaches zero as x approaches 2. Since the expression is squared, its value is always positive. Thus the left-hand limit and the right-hand limit are both $+\infty$. In the graph on the right-hand side, the expression $x - 2$ is positive when x approaches 2 from the right (when x is greater than 2) and negative when x approaches 2 from the left (when x is less than 2). Thus the left-hand limit is $-\infty$ and the right-hand limit is $+\infty$. Since these limits are different, the limit of the function graphed on the right is undefined or does not exist.

example 17.4   Find the limit of $-\dfrac{1}{(x + 3)^2}$ as x approaches -3.

solution   We first graph the function in question.

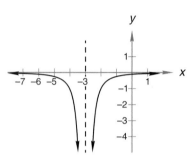

From the graph, we see

$$\lim_{x \to -3^-} -\frac{1}{(x + 3)^2} = -\infty \qquad \text{and} \qquad \lim_{x \to -3^+} -\frac{1}{(x + 3)^2} = -\infty$$

Since the left-hand limit and right-hand limit are equal, we say

$$\lim_{x \to -3} -\frac{1}{(x + 3)^2} = -\infty$$

We say that this limit is $-\infty$ in spite of the fact that we have defined a limit to be a real number. We make this exception because using the symbols $+\infty$ and $-\infty$ provides more information than the term *undefined* conveys.

problem set 17

1. Carlos drove the car at an average speed of 40 mph for M hours, and Miranda drove the car at an average speed of 60 mph for the next B hours. What was the average speed of the car for the entire trip? (Remember that average rate = total distance ÷ total time.)
(5)

2. A 400-square-foot rectangular garden is enclosed by fencing on all four sides, and the width of the garden is w. Express the total length of fencing used to enclose the garden in terms of w.
(5)

Evaluate the limits in problems 3–6.

3. $\displaystyle\lim_{x \to \infty} \frac{3x^3 - 2x + 4}{1 - 2x^3}$
(17)

4. $\displaystyle\lim_{x \to -\infty} \frac{x^3 - 6x}{5x + x^2}$
(17)

5. $\displaystyle\lim_{x \to a} \frac{x^2 - a^2}{x - a}$
(14)

6. $\displaystyle\lim_{x \to a} \frac{x - a}{x^2 + a^2}$
(14)

For problems 7–10, evaluate each limit given that f is the function whose graph is shown.

7. $\displaystyle\lim_{x \to -1} f(x)$
(17)

8. $\displaystyle\lim_{x \to 1^-} f(x)$
(17)

9. $\displaystyle\lim_{x \to 1^+} f(x)$
(17)

10. $\displaystyle\lim_{x \to 1} f(x)$
(17)

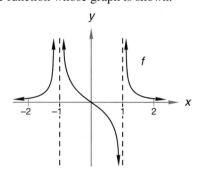

11. On what interval(s) is f increasing and on what interval(s) is f decreasing if f is the function graphed above? Express your answer using interval notation.
(15)

Solve the equations in problems 12–14 for x.

12. $\sin^2 x + 2 \cos x - 2 = 0 \ (0 \le x < 2\pi)$
(13)

13. $2 \ln x = \ln (x - 1) + \ln (x - 2)$ **14.** $4^{2x} = 16^{1-x}$
(16)   (16)

15. If $y = e^x$, what does x equal?
(9)

16. Determine the amplitude, the period, and the equation of the centerline of the graph of
(7) $y = -2 + 3 \sin (4x)$.

17. Write the key trigonometric identities, and use them to develop an expression that gives $\cos^2 A$
(12) as a function of $\cos (2A)$.

18. Show that $2 \sin \left(\dfrac{\pi}{2} - x \right) \dfrac{1}{\sec -x} - 1 = \cos (2x)$.
(12)

19. Let $f(x) = (1 + \frac{1}{x})^x$. Enter the equation for f into a graphing calculator. Create a table listing
(11,14) values of $f(x)$ for positive values of x near $x = 0$. Set the parameters of the table so that the x-values are multiples of 0.001. What is the value of $f(x)$ when x is 0.003? 0.002? 0.001? What do you think $\lim_{x \to 0^+} f(x)$ equals?

20. Find the distance between the point $(1, -1)$ and the line $2y - x + 3 = 6$. (*Hint:* See
(2) problem 23 in Problem Set 5.)

21. Solve $4^{2p-5} = 7^{3p+2}$ for p.
(16)

22. As accurately as possible, sketch the graph of $y = 2^x$. Draw a line tangent to the graph at
(7) $x = 1$, and use this line to estimate the slope of the curve at $x = 1$.

23. Evaluate the limit $\lim\limits_{h \to 0} \dfrac{f(x + h) - f(x)}{h}$, where $f(x) = 2x^2$.
(14)

24. Given x, y, z, a, and b as shown in the
(R) figure, compare the following:

   A. $x + y + z$ B. $y + a + b$

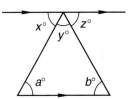

25. Given that x and y are both positive, $x^2 + y^2 = 20$, and $xy = 8$, find $x + y$. (*Hint:* Use the
(R) fact that $x^2 + 2xy + y^2$ is the square of the desired quantity.)

LESSON 18   *Sums, Differences, Products, and Quotients of Functions • Composition of Functions*

18.A

sums, differences, products, and quotients of functions

Two functions can be added, subtracted, multiplied, or divided to form a new function. The domain of the new function is the set of all numbers that were in the domains of both the original functions. Of course, any number that would cause the denominator of a quotient function to be zero is excluded from the domain of a quotient function.

example 18.1 Let $f(x) = x^2$ and $g(x) = \sqrt{x}$. Find the following, including the domain of each:

(a) $(f + g)(x)$ (b) $(f - g)(x)$ (c) $(fg)(x)$ (d) $\left(\dfrac{f}{g}\right)(x)$

solution (a) $(f + g)(x)$ means the same thing as $f(x) + g(x)$.

$$(f + g)(x) = x^2 + \sqrt{x}$$

(b) $(f - g)(x)$ means the same thing as $f(x) - g(x)$.

$$(f - g)(x) = x^2 - \sqrt{x}$$

(c) $(fg)(x)$ means the same thing as $f(x) \cdot g(x)$.

$$(fg)(x) = (x^2)(x^{1/2}) = x^{5/2}$$

(d) $\left(\dfrac{f}{g}\right)(x)$ means the same thing as $\dfrac{f(x)}{g(x)}$.

$$\left(\frac{f}{g}\right)(x) = \frac{x^2}{\sqrt{x}} = x^{3/2}$$

Since negative numbers are not members of the domain of $f(x) = \sqrt{x}$, negative numbers are excluded from the domains of all four of the new functions. The domains of $(f + g)$, $(f - g)$, and (fg) consist of the set of real numbers equal to or greater than zero.

$$\text{Domain of } (f \pm g) \text{ and } (fg) = \{x \in \mathbb{R} \mid x \geq 0\}$$

Since the denominator of $\frac{f}{g}$ can never be zero, we must also exclude any numbers that g maps to zero. The only such number is zero.

$$\text{Domain of } \left(\frac{f}{g}\right) = \{x \in \mathbb{R} \mid x > 0\}$$

18.B
composition of functions

We can also form new functions by a process called **composition**. To **compose** two functions we use the output of one function machine as the input of another function machine. Here we use the output of the f machine as the input of the g machine.

A composite function machine can do the work of both of these machines. First it multiplies the input by 5; then it takes the square root of the product.

The composite function is denoted by $g \circ f$, which is read "g circle f" or "g composed with f." Note that the g comes first but f is nearer to the argument, which indicates that we put the output $f(x)$ of the f machine into the g machine. That is, $(g \circ f)(x) = g(f(x))$. If -3 is used as an input of the f machine above, the output is -15. This is unacceptable as an input for the g machine, because the g machine takes the square root of any input. Thus neither -3 nor any other negative number can be used as an input of this composite machine. The domain for this composite machine is all real numbers equal to or greater than zero.

$$\text{Domain of } (g \circ f) = \{x \in \mathbb{R} \mid x \geq 0\}$$

The range is also the set of real numbers equal to or greater than zero.

$$\text{Range of } (g \circ f) = \{y \in \mathbb{R} \mid y \geq 0\}$$

In general, the domain of a composite function consists of all real numbers that produce outputs from the first machine that are acceptable as inputs for the second machine.

example 18.2   Use the functions $f(x) = x^2 + 2$ and $g(x) = 3x + 5$ to form the composite function $f \circ g$. State the domain of $(f \circ g)$.

solution   **We have to use the g function first.** If we put x into the g machine, we get $3x + 5$. Then we put $3x + 5$ into the f machine. The f machine squares any input and then adds 2.

$$x \longrightarrow \boxed{\overset{3(\ ) + 5}{g}} \longrightarrow (3x + 5) \longrightarrow \boxed{\overset{f(\ ) = (\ )^2 + 2}{f}} \longrightarrow (3x + 5)^2 + 2$$

The result of using both machines in turn is the composite function f circle g. We did g first since the notation $f \circ g$ indicates that f is applied to the output of the g machine.

$$(f \circ g)(x) = (3x + 5)^2 + 2$$
$$(f \circ g)(x) = 9x^2 + 30x + 27$$

The g machine accepts any real number as an input, and all of its real number outputs are acceptable to the f machine. Thus, the domain of f circle g is the set of all real numbers.

$$\text{Domain of } (f \circ g) = \mathbb{R}$$

example 18.3   Use the functions

$$f(x) = 2 + \sin x \quad \text{and} \quad g(x) = x - \frac{\pi}{2}$$

to find $f(g(x))$. State the domain and the range of the composite function.

solution   The notation $f(g(x))$ says to put $g(x)$ into the f machine, so we draw the g machine first.

$$x \longrightarrow \boxed{\overset{g(\ ) = (\ ) - \frac{\pi}{2}}{g}} \longrightarrow \left(x - \frac{\pi}{2}\right)$$

Now we put $x - \dfrac{\pi}{2}$ into the f machine.

$$\left(x - \frac{\pi}{2}\right) \longrightarrow \boxed{\overset{f(\ ) = 2 + \sin(\ )}{f}} \longrightarrow 2 + \sin\left(x - \frac{\pi}{2}\right)$$

$$f(g(x)) = 2 + \sin\left(x - \frac{\pi}{2}\right)$$
$$f(g(x)) = 2 - \cos x$$

We note that x can be any real number, and since the value of the cosine of any number is always between -1 and $+1$, $f(g(x))$ can be any number between 1 and 3.

$$\text{Domain of } (f \circ g) = \mathbb{R} \qquad \text{Range of } (f \circ g) = \{y \in \mathbb{R} \mid 1 \le y \le 3\}$$

example 18.4   The function $e^{-2x + 1}$ is a composite function. Use two function machines to show how it could be composed.

solution   The first function machine multiplies any input by -2 and then adds 1. The second function machine takes the output of the first machine and uses it as an exponent for e.

$$x \longrightarrow \boxed{\overset{-2(\ ) + 1}{f}} \longrightarrow (-2x + 1) \longrightarrow \boxed{\overset{e^{(\ )}}{g}} \longrightarrow e^{-2x + 1}$$

So we see that

$$e^{-2x + 1} = g(f(x))$$

where $f(x) = -2x + 1$ and $g(x) = e^x$. It should be noted that there are infinitely many ways to compose this function. This happens to be one of the "obvious ways."

example 18.5 The function $\sin(2x + 3)$ is a composite function. Use two function machines to show how it could be composed.

solution We see that the input of the sine machine is $2x + 3$. Thus,

$$x \longrightarrow \boxed{} \overset{2(\ )+3}{\longrightarrow} (2x + 3) \longrightarrow \boxed{} \overset{\sin(\ )}{\longrightarrow} \sin(2x + 3)$$

So we see that

$$\sin(2x + 3) = f(g(x))$$

where $f(x) = \sin x$ and $g(x) = 2x + 3$.

example 18.6 Let $f(x) = \sqrt{x}$ and $g(x) = 2x + 3$. Find the domain and range of $f \circ g$ and the domain and range of $g \circ f$.

solution We look at $f \circ g$ first.

$$x \longrightarrow \overset{2(\ )+3}{\boxed{g}} \longrightarrow (2x + 3) \longrightarrow \overset{\sqrt{(\ )}}{\boxed{f}} \longrightarrow \sqrt{2x + 3}$$

The g machine accepts any real number input and can produce any real number output. The f machine only accepts numbers that are not negative, so $g(x)$ must be equal to or greater than zero to be an acceptable input for f.

$$g(x) \geq 0$$
$$2x + 3 \geq 0$$
$$2x \geq -3$$
$$x \geq -\frac{3}{2}$$

Thus, the domain of $f \circ g$ is the set of all values of x equal to or greater than $-\frac{3}{2}$. Since the value of $\sqrt{2x + 3}$ is never negative, the range is the set of all real numbers greater than or equal to zero.

Domain of $(f \circ g) = \left\{ x \in \mathbb{R} \mid x \geq -\frac{3}{2} \right\}$

Range of $(f \circ g) = \{ y \in \mathbb{R} \mid y \geq 0 \}$

$$y = \sqrt{2x + 3}$$

Now we look at $g \circ f$.

$$x \longrightarrow \overset{f(\ )=\sqrt{(\ )}}{\boxed{f}} \longrightarrow \sqrt{x} \longrightarrow \overset{g(\ )=2(\ )+3}{\boxed{g}} \longrightarrow 2\sqrt{x} + 3$$

Again, the difficulty is with the f machine, because it accepts only nonnegative numbers. However, all its outputs are acceptable inputs for the g machine. Thus the domain of $g \circ f$ consists of zero and all of the positive real numbers. Since $\sqrt{x}$ is always greater than or equal to zero, $2\sqrt{x} + 3$ is always greater than or equal to 3. Thus the range of $g \circ f$ is the set of all real numbers greater than or equal to 3.

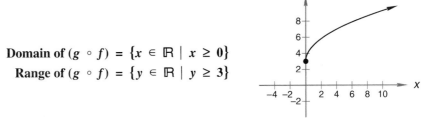

$$\text{Domain of } (g \circ f) = \{x \in \mathbb{R} \mid x \geq 0\}$$
$$\text{Range of } (g \circ f) = \{y \in \mathbb{R} \mid y \geq 3\}$$

$$y = 2\sqrt{x} + 3$$

Notice that $f \circ g$ is not the same function as $g \circ f$ and that their domains and ranges are different. This is often, but not always, the case. Be careful when working with composite functions. The order of the functions is often crucial.

example 18.7   Determine whether the following statement is true or false and explain why:

If $f(x) = x^2$ and $g(x) = \sqrt{x}$, then the domains of $f \circ g$ and $g \circ f$ are equal.

solution   The f machine accepts any real number and squares it. The resulting nonnegative numbers are acceptable to the g machine. Thus, all real numbers are acceptable to $g \circ f$. But since the g machine takes square roots, it does not accept negative numbers. Thus the domain of $f \circ g$ is the set of nonnegative real numbers.

$$\text{Domain of } (f \circ g) = \{x \in \mathbb{R} \mid x \geq 0\}$$
$$\text{Domain of } (g \circ f) = \mathbb{R}$$

Therefore, the statement is **false.**

problem set 18

1. When used alone, pipe A can fill the entire tank in 6 hours, and pipe B can fill the entire tank in 3 hours. If both pipes are used together, how long will it take to fill the entire tank?
   (5)

2. Farmer Jones wants to enclose a rectangular pasture and plans to use an existing stone wall as one side of the rectangle. The pasture is to have an area of 20,000 square meters. If the length of the segment of the fence parallel to the stone wall is P, what is the total length of fencing required in terms of the variable P.
   (5)

For problems 3–8, $f(x) = x^2 + 1$ and $g(x) = \sqrt{x - 1}$.

3. Write the equation for $f + g$ and evaluate $(f + g)(5)$.
   (18)

4. Write the equation for fg and evaluate $(fg)(5)$.
   (18)

5. Write the equation for $\dfrac{f}{g}$ and evaluate $\left(\dfrac{f}{g}\right)(5)$.
   (18)

6. Describe the domain of $\dfrac{f}{g}$.
   (18)

7. Write the equation for $f \circ g$ and evaluate $(f \circ g)(3)$.
   (18)

8. Describe the domain and range of $f \circ g$.
   (18)

9. The function $\cos(2x - \pi)$ is a composite function. Use two function machines to show how it could be composed.
   (18)

Evaluate the limits in problems 10 and 11.

10. $\displaystyle\lim_{x\to\infty} \frac{1 - x^2}{3x^2 + 2x - 4}$
(17)

11. $\displaystyle\lim_{x\to\infty} \frac{3x^2}{x^3 - 4x + 1}$
(17)

12. Given the graph of f shown, evaluate the
(17) following two limits:

    (a) $\displaystyle\lim_{x\to-2} f(x)$ (b) $\displaystyle\lim_{x\to1} f(x)$

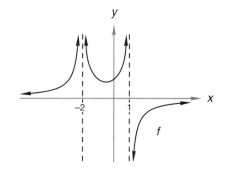

In problems 13 and 14 solve for x.

13. $\dfrac{\pi}{2} = \arcsin x$
(13)

14. $\ln x - \ln (x + 1) = \ln 2$
(16)

15. Given $g(x) = x(x - 2)(x + 3)$, use interval notation to designate the intervals on which the
(15) graph of g lies above the x-axis and the intervals on which the graph of g lies below the x-axis.

16. Graph: $y = -2 + \sin \left[2\left(x - \dfrac{\pi}{4} \right) \right]$ $(0 \le x \le 2\pi)$
(7)

17. On what interval(s) is the function in problem 16 increasing?
(15)

18. Enter the function $y = \frac{\sin x}{x}$ into the calculator. Set the mode of the calculator to radians. Set
(14) the parameters of the display to let x and y range from -1 to 1 with the scales measured in tenths. Graph the function. Use the trace feature to trace out points on the curve. What value does the y-coordinate seem to approach as the x-coordinate approaches 0? Is the function defined at $x = 0$?

19. Evaluate $\displaystyle\lim_{\Delta x\to0} \frac{f(x + \Delta x) - f(x)}{\Delta x}$, where $f(x) = 3x + 2$.
(14)

20. State the contrapositive of the following conditional statement:
(3)

$$\text{If } x = 2, \text{ then } x^2 = 4.$$

21. Show that $\dfrac{(\sec^2 x - 1)[\cos (-x)]}{(1 - \cos^2 x)(\tan^2 x + 1)} = \cos x$ for all values where both sides make sense.
(8)

22. Solve $7^{3x-2} = 13^{x+1}$ for x.
(16)

23. As accurately as possible, sketch the graph of $y = \sin x$. Draw a line tangent to the graph
(7) at $x = 0.5$, and use this line to estimate the slope of the curve at $x = 0.5$.

24. Find the area of $\triangle ABC$ in terms of x
(R) given the figure shown. (*Hint:* Use trigonometric functions and the fact that the measure of an inscribed angle equals one-half the measure of the sub-tended arc.)

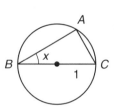

25. Find the next term of the sequence whose first six terms are 1, 1, 2, 4, 7, and 11.
(R)

LESSON 19   *The Derivative • Slopes of Curves on a Graphing Calculator*

19.A
the derivative   Lines, which are the graphs of linear functions, possess a quality called slope. The slope of a line tells us how steeply a line rises or falls (assuming we are moving from left to right).

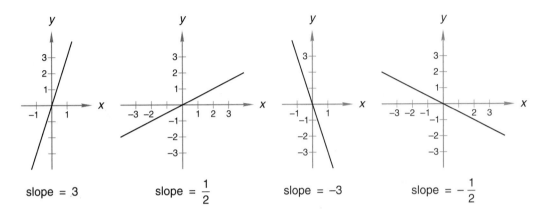

slope = 3   slope = $\dfrac{1}{2}$ slope = −3   slope = −$\dfrac{1}{2}$

For a line with equation $y = mx + b$, the slope is m. **For nonlinear equations, the slope of a curve at a point is determined by the slope of the line tangent to the curve at that point.** In the figure below, we draw lines tangent to the function $f(x) = x^2 + 2$ at points S, P, Q, and R.

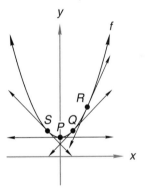

We see that the slope of f at points Q and R is positive and that the slope at R is greater than the slope at Q. The slope of f at P, which is the vertex of the parabola, is 0, and the slope at S is negative.

Consider curve C (shown below), which is the graph of a function $y = f(x)$, and let t be tangent to C at point P_1.

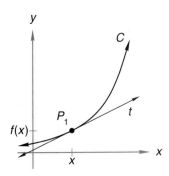

We denote the coordinates of the point P_1 by $(x, f(x))$. Then we draw a secant line that passes through P_1 and another point P_2 on the curve C not far from P_1, as shown below.

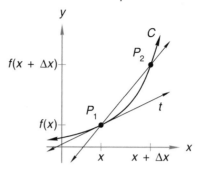

Notice that the coordinates of the point P_2 are $(x + \Delta x, f(x + \Delta x))$. So, the distance between the x-coordinates of P_1 and P_2 is Δx. Moreover, the slope of the secant line is

$$\frac{f(x + \Delta x) - f(x)}{(x + \Delta x) - x} \quad \text{or} \quad \frac{f(x + \Delta x) - f(x)}{\Delta x}$$

Now we let P_2 move down the curve toward P_1. As this happens, the value of Δx gets smaller and smaller and the slope of the secant line gets closer and closer to the slope of the tangent line at P_1.

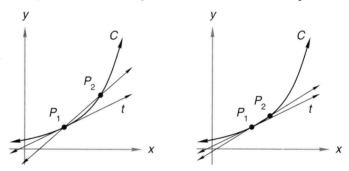

This motivates us to define a new function, called the **derivative,** which tells us the slope of the graph of f. By convention, we name the new function f', read "f prime."

DERIVATIVE OF A FUNCTION

The derivative of a function f at a point x is given by

$$f'(x) = \lim_{\Delta x \to 0} \frac{f(x + \Delta x) - f(x)}{\Delta x}$$

provided the limit exists.

If f is a function that has a derivative, then the tangent that can be drawn to the graph of f at $x = a$ has slope $f'(a)$. To find the derivative of a particular function, we write the difference of the values of y at x and at $x + \Delta x$ in the numerator and write Δx in the denominator. The rest of the process is an algebraic game of trying to find an equivalent expression that does not have Δx as a factor of the denominator so we can let Δx approach zero. (Otherwise, we appear to have division by 0 as Δx goes to 0, which is undesirable.)

The notations

$$\frac{d}{dx} \quad \text{and} \quad D_x$$

are operators that indicate taking a derivative. If the f function is $f(x) = x^2$, we can indicate the operation of taking the derivative of the f function by writing either

$$\frac{d}{dx} f(x) \quad \text{or} \quad D_x f(x)$$

We read both of these by saying "the derivative of f of x with respect to x." Since $f(x)$ equals x^2 in this example, we can also designate the same derivative by writing

$$\frac{d}{dx}x^2 \quad\text{or}\quad D_x x^2$$

If the function is described by using y instead of $f(x)$ and if it is written $y = x^2$, we could designate the derivative by writing

$$\frac{d}{dx}y \quad\text{or}\quad \frac{dy}{dx} \quad\text{or}\quad D_x y$$

We read each of these by saying "the derivative of y with respect to x." We can also read $\frac{dy}{dx}$ as "dee y dee x."

The derivative is one of the most essential topics of calculus. Students are encouraged to study this lesson carefully.

example 19.1   Let $y = x^2$. Find $\dfrac{dy}{dx}$.

solution   The derivative is the limit, as Δx approaches zero, of the difference in the y-coordinates of the graph of $y = x^2$ at $x + \Delta x$ and at x, divided by Δx. The y-coordinate of $y = x^2$ at x is x^2 and at $x + \Delta x$ is $(x + \Delta x)^2$. Thus we write

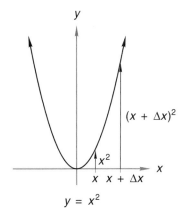

$$\frac{dy}{dx} = \lim_{\Delta x \to 0} \frac{(x + \Delta x)^2 - x^2}{\Delta x}$$

Next we expand the expression in the numerator and are pleased to find that the first and last terms in the resulting expression are x^2 and $-x^2$, which sum to zero.

$$\lim_{\Delta x \to 0} \frac{\boxed{x^2} + 2x\,\Delta x + (\Delta x)^2 \boxed{- x^2}}{\Delta x} = \lim_{\Delta x \to 0} \frac{2x\,\Delta x + (\Delta x)^2}{\Delta x}$$

Since Δx does not equal zero, we can divide both terms in the numerator by Δx and get

$$\frac{dy}{dx} = \lim_{\Delta x \to 0} (2x + \Delta x)$$

This new expression does not have a Δx as a factor of the denominator, so we can let Δx approach zero to get

$$\frac{dy}{dx} = 2x$$

This tells us that if x is 3, the slope of the graph of $y = x^2$ is 2 times 3, or 6. If x is 10, the slope of the graph of $y = x^2$ is 2 times 10, or 20.

example 19.2   Given $f(x) = x^2$, find the slope of the line tangent to the graph of f at $x = 4$.

solution   In example 19.1 we found that the derivative of the function $f(x) = x^2$ is $f'(x) = 2x$. The f' function tells us the slope of the tangent line that can be drawn to the graph of f for various values of x. The slope of the tangent line that can be drawn to the graph of f at $x = 4$ is simply

$$f'(4) = 2(4) = \mathbf{8}$$

example 19.3   Let $y = 4x$. Find $D_x y$.

solution   The goal is to find the derivative of the function. We already know that the slope of $y = 4x$ is 4 for every x, since $y = 4x$ is the equation of a line whose slope is 4. We can show that the definition of the derivative yields the same result. We define $y = f(x) = 4x$, so we may use the notation in the definition.

$$D_x y = \lim_{\Delta x \to 0} \frac{f(x + \Delta x) - f(x)}{\Delta x}$$

Next, we will replace $f(x)$ with $4x$ and replace $f(x + \Delta x)$ with $4(x + \Delta x)$.

$$D_x y = \lim_{\Delta x \to 0} \frac{4(x + \Delta x) - 4(x)}{\Delta x}$$

If we expand the numerator, we are again pleased to find that the first and last terms sum to zero.

$$D_x y = \lim_{\Delta x \to 0} \frac{\boxed{4x} + 4\,\Delta x \boxed{- 4x}}{\Delta x} = \lim_{\Delta x \to 0} \frac{4\,\Delta x}{\Delta x} = \lim_{\Delta x \to 0} 4$$

The number 4 equals 4 no matter what value Δx has or approaches, so

$$D_x y = \lim_{\Delta x \to 0} 4 = \mathbf{4}$$

which is the expected answer.

example 19.4   Use the definition of the derivative to show that the derivative of the constant function $f(x) = c$ is zero.

solution   The equations

$$y = 4 \qquad y = -17 \qquad y = 42$$

are equations of constant functions whose graphs are straight lines parallel to the x-axis; thus they have slopes of zero. Proving this by using the definition of a derivative might seem useless, but it provides good practice. We repeat the definition of the derivative here.

$$f'(x) = \lim_{\Delta x \to 0} \frac{f(x + \Delta x) - f(x)}{\Delta x}$$

The output of $f(x) = c$ is always c regardless of the input value. So $f(x)$ equals c and $f(x + \Delta x)$ also equals c. Thus, their difference is zero.

$$f'(x) = \lim_{\Delta x \to 0} \frac{c - c}{\Delta x} = \lim_{\Delta x \to 0} \frac{0}{\Delta x} = \lim_{\Delta x \to 0} 0 = \mathbf{0}$$

example 19.5   Let $y = \dfrac{1}{x}$. Find $\dfrac{dy}{dx}$.

solution   The definition of the derivative of a function $y = f(x)$ is

$$\frac{dy}{dx} = \lim_{\Delta x \to 0} \frac{f(x + \Delta x) - f(x)}{\Delta x}$$

For $f(x) = \dfrac{1}{x}$, this is

$$\frac{dy}{dx} = \lim_{\Delta x \to 0} \frac{\dfrac{1}{x + \Delta x} - \dfrac{1}{x}}{\Delta x}$$

The value of this expression cannot be determined when $\Delta x = 0$, so we use the rules of algebra to find an equivalent expression that does not have Δx as a factor of the denominator. First, we add the expressions in the numerator and get

$$\frac{\dfrac{x - (x + \Delta x)}{x(x + \Delta x)}}{\Delta x} = \frac{\dfrac{x - x - \Delta x}{x(x + \Delta x)}}{\Delta x} = -\frac{1}{x(x + \Delta x)} = -\frac{1}{x^2 + x\,\Delta x}$$

Now we have

$$\frac{dy}{dx} = \lim_{\Delta x \to 0} -\frac{1}{x^2 + x\,\Delta x}$$

In this expression Δx is not a factor of the entire denominator. As Δx approaches zero, the denominator approaches x^2, so we have

$$\frac{dy}{dx} = -\frac{1}{x^2}$$

example 19.6   Find the slope of the tangent line that can be drawn to the graph of $f(x) = \dfrac{1}{x}$ at $x = 2$.

solution   We show a sketch of the problem.

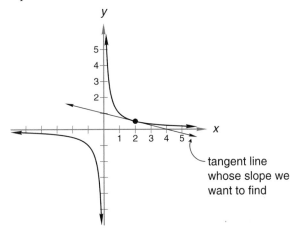

Note that it is not necessary to draw the sketch above to solve the problem. We do so simply for illustrative purposes. To find the slope of the tangent line that can be drawn to the graph of $f(x) = \frac{1}{x}$ at $x = 2$, we first compute the equation of the derivative f'. Then we evaluate f' at $x = 2$. From example 19.5 we know that

$$f'(x) = -\frac{1}{x^2} \qquad \longrightarrow \qquad f'(2) = -\frac{1}{2^2} = -\frac{1}{4}$$

Thus, the slope of the tangent line drawn to the graph of f at $x = 2$ is $-\dfrac{1}{4}$.

19.B
slopes of curves on a graphing calculator

While a graphing calculator should never be viewed as a replacement for understanding mathematical ideas, it is sometimes useful for quickly calculating desired values. In particular, the TI-83 can be used to quickly determine the slope of the graph of a function f at a certain point. Note that the TI-83 cannot find the derivative function in terms of x; it can only approximate the derivative for any given input value of x. This is a significant limitation, one that explains the importance of being able to find derivatives by the definition.

example 19.7   Use a graphing calculator to approximate the slope of the graph of $f(x) = \dfrac{1}{x}$ at the point $\left(4, \dfrac{1}{4}\right)$.

solution   From example 19.5 we already know that the slope of the curve at this point is $-\frac{1}{16}$. We confirm this with the calculator by pressing $\boxed{\text{MATH}}$ and then choosing option 8:nDeriv(. This can be accomplished by simply pressing the **8** key or scrolling down to this option with the down arrow key and then pressing **ENTER**. Once chosen, nDeriv(appears on the calculation screen, awaiting more input. We must tell the calculator the function under consideration, the independent variable, and the value of the independent variable at which the slope of the curve is to be calculated. In this case we press

1 **÷** **X,T,θ,n** **,** **X,T,θ,n** **,** **4** **)** **ENTER**

and the answer -.0625000039 appears. According to the TI-83 calculator, the slope of $\frac{1}{x}$ at the point $(4, \frac{1}{4})$ is **-0.0625000039**. But is this approximation correct? As mentioned above, the true answer is $-\frac{1}{16}$, which equals -0.0625. So we see that the calculator is correct to several decimal places. Keep in mind that the calculator is only giving an approximation, and that the 39 which appears at the end of its answer is incorrect. Even so, if we simply want an approximation of the slope, this method provides a quick way of finding it.

example 19.8   Use a graphing calculator to approximate the slope of the graph of $f(x) = \sin x$ at the point $(\pi, 0)$.

solution   We currently do not know how to find the derivative of $\sin x$, so we use our calculator as an aid. Keying

$$\pi$$
MATH **8** **SIN** **X,T,θ,n** **)** **,** **X,T,θ,n** **,** **2nd** **^** **)** **ENTER**

yields **-0.9999998333**, which is extremely close to -1. Indeed, the true slope is -1, which a later lesson will show. From a graphical point of view, the answer already makes sense. Below we graph the function $\sin x$ as well as the tangent to the graph at $x = \pi$.

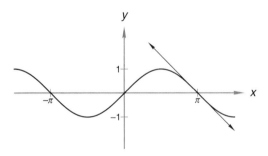

Note that at the point $(\pi, 0)$ the slope of the tangent line appears to be about -1.

**problem set
19**

1.   The intensity of a light source measured at a point P varies inversely as the square of the distance
(5)   from P to the light source. If the intensity measured at a point 5 meters from the light source is N, what would the intensity measure at a point M meters from the light source?

In problems 2–4 use the definition of the derivative to find $f'(x)$.

2. $f(x) = 3x + 2$ 3. $f(x) = x^3$ 4. $f(x) = x^2 + x$
(19)   (19)   (19)

5.   Find the slope of the line that can be drawn tangent to the graph of f at $x = 5$ given that
(19) $f(x) = \frac{2}{x}$.

6.   Use the trace feature or the table feature of a graphing calculator to find $\lim_{x \to 0} \frac{(2 + x)^2 - 2^2}{x}$.
(19)   (*Hint:* See example 14.8.)

7.   For $f(x) = \ln x$ and $g(x) = \frac{1}{x}$, write the equation for $f \circ g$ and describe the domain and
(18)   range of $f \circ g$.

8.   (a) List all the possible rational roots of the function $f(x) = x^3 - 3x^2 + 5x - 15$.
(10)
     (b) Graph the function on a graphing calculator and determine if any of the answers to Part (a) represent actual roots of the equation.

Evaluate the limits in problems 9 and 10.

9. $\displaystyle\lim_{x \to -\infty} \frac{2x - 15x^3}{14x^2 - 13x}$
(17)

10. $\displaystyle\lim_{x \to -\infty} \frac{3 - 14x^5 + 2x^3}{x^4 - x^5 + 1}$
(17)

In problems 11–13 f is the function whose graph is shown at the right.

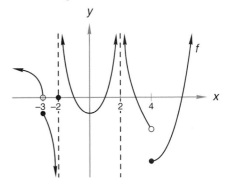

11. Evaluate: $\displaystyle\lim_{x \to 2} f(x)$
(17)

12. Evaluate: $\displaystyle\lim_{x \to -2} f(x)$
(17)

13. Use interval notation to describe the interval(s) on which f is increasing.
(15)

Solve the equations in problems 14–16 for x.

14. $e^{-x + 5} = 13^{2x + 3}$
(16)

15. $\log_2 x + \log_2 (x - 2) = \log_2 3$
(16)

16. $\sin x = \cos x \ \ (0 \le x < 2\pi)$
(13)

17. In the figure shown, find the area of $\triangle ABC$ in terms of x.
(8)

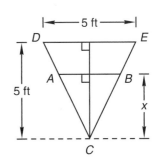

18. Describe the values of x for which $|x - 4| < \varepsilon$ if ε represents an unspecified small positive number.
(9)

19. Suppose $\sin A = \frac{3}{5}$, $\cos A = \frac{4}{5}$, $\sin B = \frac{12}{13}$, and $\cos B = \frac{5}{13}$. Find the value of $\sin (A + B)$.
(4,12)

20. Use a graphing calculator to approximate the point(s) of intersection of $g(x) = x^2 - 7$ and $f(x) = x^3 + x^2 - 5x - 5$.
(2)

21. Write the key trigonometric identities, and then develop an expression that gives $\sin^2 x$ as a function of $\cos (2x)$.
(12)

22. Use a graphing calculator to approximate the slope of the curve $y = \sin x$ at $x = 0.5$.
(19)

23. Use a graphing calculator to approximate the slope of the curve $y = 2^x$ at $x = 1$.
(19)

24. Find the length of the side of the largest square that can be circumscribed by a circle of radius 3. (*Note:* The diagonal of a square circumscribed by a circle is a diameter of the circle.)
(R)

25. Let A, B, and C be three distinct points. Compare:
(R)

   A. AC B. $AB + BC$

LESSON 20 *Change of Base • Graphing Origin-Centered Conics on a Graphing Calculator*

20.A

change of base   If we know the logarithm of a number to some base, we can find the logarithm to any other base by dividing the known logarithm by the appropriate constant. Because tables and calculators can be used to find values of $\ln x$ and $\log x$ for any x, we usually use either $\ln x$ or $\log x$ as a starting point to find logarithms to other bases. We can change a table of base 10 logarithms to a table of base 5 logarithms by dividing every entry in the base 10 table by $\log 5$, which is approximately 0.69897. We can change a table of base e logarithms to a table of base 5 logarithms by dividing every entry by $\ln 5$, which is approximately 1.6094. We change the bases of logarithms in this book, so it is helpful to have a procedure we can use automatically. To demonstrate, we show how to find the base 4 logarithm of 15 from the logarithms of a known base b. First we write

$$y = \log_4 15$$

Then we rewrite this equation in exponential form and take the base b logarithm of both sides. Finally we solve for y.

$$4^y = 15 \qquad\qquad \text{exponential form}$$
$$y \log_b 4 = \log_b 15 \qquad\qquad \log_b \text{ of both sides}$$
$$y = \frac{\log_b 15}{\log_b 4} \qquad\qquad \text{solved for } y$$

Since $y = \log_4 15$,

$$\log_4 15 = \frac{\log_b 15}{\log_b 4} \qquad\qquad \text{substituted}$$

Look carefully at the last step. The number 4 is the base we want to use and b is the base whose values we know. **All we have to do to change to the new base is use the known base to write the log of the argument on top and to write the log of the intended base on the bottom.**

$$\log_4 15 = \frac{\log_b 15}{\log_b 4}$$

Using this result, we can now numerically calculate $\log_4 15$. We do so by setting b equal to e or 10.

Set $b = e$:   Set $b = 10$:

$$\log_4 15 = \frac{\ln 15}{\ln 4} \approx 1.9534 \qquad\qquad \log_4 15 = \frac{\log_{10} 15}{\log_{10} 4} \approx 1.9534$$

example 20.1   Rewrite $\log_4 x$ using common logarithms.

solution   We always use either 10 or e as the new base, because these logarithms are available from a calculator. Here we use base 10. We put the x on top and the 4 below.

$$\log_4 x = \frac{\log_{10} x}{\log_{10} 4}$$

The logarithm of any number to the base 4 is the common logarithm of the number divided by the common logarithm of 4.

example 20.2   Estimate $\log_4 67$ using a calculator.

solution   From the previous example,

$$\log_4 67 = \frac{\log 67}{\log 4}$$

Because common logarithms can be found with a calculator, this is a useful rewriting of the problem.

$$\log_4 67 \approx \mathbf{3.0330}$$

We expected an answer near 3, since $\log_4 64 = 3$.

example 20.3   Use a calculator to approximate $4 \log_{15} 6 + 5 \log_4 7$.

solution   To use the calculator, the values of $\log_{15} 6$ and $\log_4 7$ must be expressed differently. In this example we use base e logarithms as the vehicle. Remember

$$\log_{15} 6 = \frac{\ln 6}{\ln 15} \qquad \text{and} \qquad \log_4 7 = \frac{\ln 7}{\ln 4}$$

As seen below, the calculator approximates the answer as **9.6650.**

```
4ln(6)/ln(15)+5l
n(7)/ln(4)
          9.664954889
```

example 20.4   If $\log_b 47 = 17$, what is b?

solution   This problem does not require a change of base. First, we rewrite the expression in exponential form.

$$b^{17} = 47 \qquad \text{exponential form}$$
$$\sqrt[17]{b^{17}} = \sqrt[17]{47} \qquad \text{root of both sides}$$
$$b = \sqrt[17]{47} \qquad \text{simplified}$$
$$b \approx \mathbf{1.2542} \qquad \text{calculated}$$

This approximation is found by pressing

20.B

graphing origin-centered conics on a graphing calculator

We now want to graph some conic sections on a graphing calculator. At this point, we are only interested in conic sections centered at the origin. For example, the circle of radius 2 centered at $(0, 0)$ is given by the equation $x^2 + y^2 = 4$. This equation does not define a function, because the x-value 0 produces two different y-values, 2 and -2. How do we graph such a curve on a calculator? We simply determine the functions needed to define the curve and plot them separately.

Notice that

$$x^2 + y^2 = 4$$
$$y^2 = 4 - x^2$$
$$y = \pm\sqrt{4 - x^2}$$

So there are two functions that combine to generate this circle:

$$y = \sqrt{4 - x^2} \qquad \text{and} \qquad y = -\sqrt{4 - x^2}$$

One builds the upper semicircle and the other builds the lower one. On the graphing calculator, we define

$Y1$ by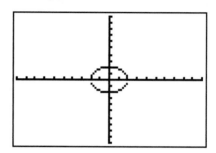

and $Y2$ by

Using ZStandard, the following appears:

A few comments are in order here. First, notice that the graph appears to be an ellipse, not a circle. This visual distortion arises because the horizontal and vertical axes are scaled differently. The TI-83 is not trying to show you a "square" screen with ZStandard. It is drawing the graph correctly, but not in a framework that clearly exhibits a circle. To correct this, we press ZOOM 5 to obtain the ZSquare view. The curve is somewhat small at this point, so we zoom in. The graph appears as follows:

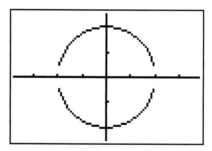

A second comment is in order. Do the functions

$$y = \sqrt{4 - x^2} \qquad \text{and} \qquad y = -\sqrt{4 - x^2}$$

intercept the x-axis? Of course they do, at $x = 2$ and $x = -2$. But the TI-83 does not show this. Both semicircles are separated from the x-axis slightly. Again, do not let the calculator fool you. Always check what the calculator shows with other mathematical knowledge to confirm the results.

example 20.5   Use a graphing calculator to graph the curve given by

$$\frac{x^2}{4} + \frac{y^2}{9} = 1$$

solution   This equation yields an ellipse centered at the origin. To draw it on the calculator, we must split it into two functions.

$$\frac{x^2}{4} + \frac{y^2}{9} = 1$$
$$9x^2 + 4y^2 = 36$$
$$4y^2 = 36 - 9x^2$$
$$y^2 = 9 - \frac{9x^2}{4}$$
$$y = \pm\sqrt{9 - \frac{9x^2}{4}}$$

So we simply define Y_1 and Y_2 on the calculator by

and

Using the ZStandard option and then the ZSquare option, we obtain the following:

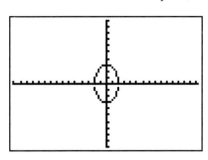

problem set 20

1. Express the distance from the point $(2, 3)$ to the point (x, y) on the line $y = 2x + 1$ in terms of x.
(2)

2. Express $\log_{10} x$ in terms of the natural logarithm.
(20)

3. Use a calculator to approximate the value of $\log_4 15$.
(20)

In problems 4–6 use the definition of the derivative to find the indicated derivative.

4. $\dfrac{d}{dx} f(x)$ where $f(x) = 5x - 3$
(19)

5. $\dfrac{d}{dx} y$ where $y = 3x^2$
(19)

6. $D_x f(x)$ where $f(x) = -\dfrac{1}{x}$
(19)

7. On a graphing calculator, graph the set of all points (x, y) that satisfy the equation $x^2 + y^2 = 9$. What are the two functions that must be graphed? Does your graph actually look like a circle? If not, what can be done to make it look like a circle?
(20)

8. Using a graphing calculator, graph the set of all points that lie on the ellipse $\dfrac{x^2}{9} + \dfrac{y^2}{4} = 1$. What are the two functions that must be graphed?
(20)

9. (a) On a graphing calculator, graph the function $g(x) = \dfrac{f(1 + x) - f(1)}{x}$ where $f(x) = -\dfrac{1}{x}$.
(19)
   (b) Using the trace or table feature, determine what $g(x)$ approaches as x approaches 0.
   (c) Evaluate the derivative of $f(x) = -\dfrac{1}{x}$ at $x = 1$, and compare it to the value found in (b).

10. Let $f(x) = \ln x$ and $g(x) = e^x$. Write an equation for $f \circ g$.
(18)

11. Let $f(x) = \sin x$ and $g(x) = 2x - \dfrac{\pi}{2}$. Write an equation for $f \circ g$.
(18)

12. Use a calculator to approximate the value of $3 \log_2 12 + \log_{16} 92$.
(20)

Evaluate the limits in problems 13–15.

13. $\displaystyle\lim_{x \to 2} \dfrac{2 - \dfrac{2}{x}}{4 - x^2}$
(17)

14. $\displaystyle\lim_{x \to 3} \dfrac{2x^2 - 2x - 12}{x - 3}$
(14)

15. $\displaystyle\lim_{x \to \infty} \dfrac{x^2 + 3x}{x^3}$
(17)

16. Use interval notation to describe the intervals for which the graph of f lies above the x-axis for the function $f(x) = x(x - 2)(x + 4)$.
(15)

Solve the equations in problems 17 and 18 for *x*.

17. $y = \arcsin \dfrac{x}{2}$
(13)

18. $\sin^2 x - 1 = 0 \ (0 \le x < 2\pi)$
(13)

19. Use synthetic division to find the value of k for which $x = -1$ is a zero of $x^3 + 2x^2 + 3x + k$.
(10)

20. Show that $[(\sec -x) - 1](\sec x + 1) = \tan^2 x$ for all values of x where the functions are defined.
(8)

21. Write $\dfrac{1 + \sqrt{3}}{2 - \sqrt{3}}$ with a rational denominator.
(1)

22. Write the key trigonometric identities and develop an identity for $\cos \dfrac{x}{2}$.
(12)

23. Use a graphing calculator to find the slope of the curve $y = \cos x$ at $x = 0$.
(19)

24. Given rectangle *ABCD* and triangle *AEB* where *E* is arbitrarily chosen on $\overline{DC}$, compare the following:
(R)

    A. the area of $\triangle AEB$

    B. the area of $\triangle ACB$

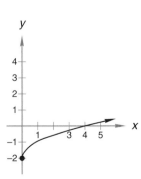

25. Find the sixth term of the geometric sequence whose first three terms are 1, 2, and 4.
(R)

LESSON 21 *Translations of Functions • Graphs of Rational Functions I*

21.A

translations of functions

If we add a constant to a function, the graph of the function is translated (shifted) vertically. If we add +2, the graph is shifted up 2 units. If we add –2, the graph is shifted down 2 units.

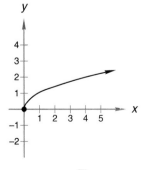

$y = \sqrt{x}$

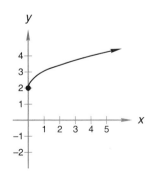

$y = \sqrt{x} + 2$

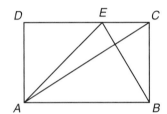

$y = \sqrt{x} - 2$

If we replace x with the sum of x and a constant, the graph of the function is shifted horizontally. If we replace x with $x + 2$, the graph of the function is shifted 2 units to the left. If we replace x with $x - 2$, the graph is shifted 2 units to the right.

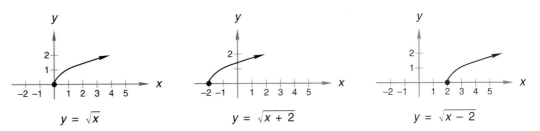

$$y = \sqrt{x} \qquad\qquad y = \sqrt{x + 2} \qquad\qquad y = \sqrt{x - 2}$$

Sometimes one forgets whether replacing x with $x + 2$ moves the graph to the left or the right. It is easy to check. In the left-hand equation above, $y = 0$ when $x = 0$. In the center equation, $y = 0$ when $x = -2$. Thus replacing x with $x + 2$ causes a two-unit shift of the graph to the left.

example 21.1 Graph the function $y = |x|$. Then change the equation to shift the graph 3 units to the left and down 2 units. Graph this new function.

solution To shift the graph 3 units to the left, we replace x with $x + 3$. To shift the graph down 2 units, we add -2 to the function.

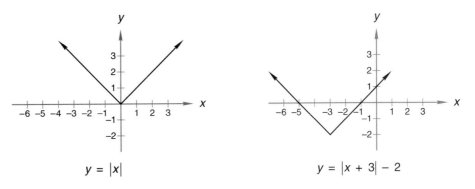

$$y = |x| \qquad\qquad\qquad y = |x + 3| - 2$$

example 21.2 Graph the function $y = \frac{1}{2}x^2$. Then change the equation to shift the curve 3 units to the right and up 2 units. Graph this new function.

solution To get a quick sketch, we select x-values of 0, 3, and -3 and find corresponding y-values of 0, 4.5, and 4.5. To shift the graph 3 units to the right, we replace x with $x - 3$, and we add $+2$ to the function to shift the graph up 2 units.

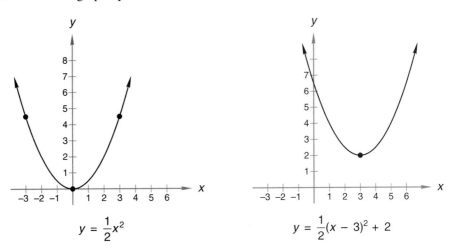

$$y = \frac{1}{2}x^2 \qquad\qquad\qquad y = \frac{1}{2}(x - 3)^2 + 2$$

example 21.3 Graph the function $y = \frac{1}{2}x$. Then change the equation to shift the graph 2 units to the left and down 1 unit.

solution In (a) we show the graph of $y = \frac{1}{2}x$. In (b) we show the graph of $y = \frac{1}{2}(x + 2)$, which is the original graph shifted 2 units to the left. In (c) we add -1 to the function to shift the center graph down 1 unit.

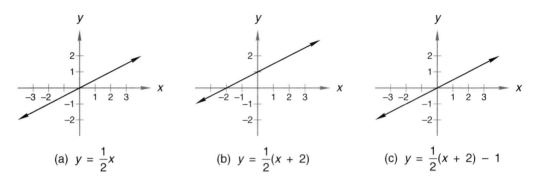

(a) $y = \dfrac{1}{2}x$ (b) $y = \dfrac{1}{2}(x + 2)$ (c) $y = \dfrac{1}{2}(x + 2) - 1$

This example illustrates a peculiarity of linear functions: a horizontal shift can have the same effect as a vertical shift. We note that in (b), the shift 2 units to the left could have been considered a vertical shift of $+1$ unit. Thus (c) is the same graph as (a). This should not be surprising, since the equation in (c) simplifies to the equation in (a).

$$y = \frac{1}{2}(x + 2) - 1 \qquad \text{equation in (c)}$$

$$y = \frac{1}{2}x + 1 - 1 \qquad \text{distributive property}$$

$$y = \frac{1}{2}x \qquad \text{simplified to equation in (a)}$$

example 21.4 Given $y = |4 \sin x|$, change the function to shift the graph down 2 units and $\dfrac{\pi}{2}$ units to the right.

solution To get the required transformation, we replace x with $x - \dfrac{\pi}{2}$ and add -2 to the function.

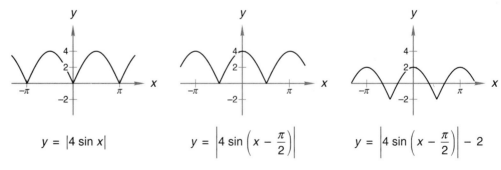

$y = |4 \sin x|$ $y = \left|4 \sin\left(x - \dfrac{\pi}{2}\right)\right|$ $y = \left|4 \sin\left(x - \dfrac{\pi}{2}\right)\right| - 2$

example 21.5 To the right are the Ꮓ5Ꮮaꞑꓒaꭱꓒ graphs of the functions

$$f(x) = x^3 - 3x^2 + 2x,$$

$$g(x) = x^3 - 3x^2 + 2x + 6, \quad \text{and}$$

$$h(x) = x^3 - 3x^2 + 2x - 3$$

For each graph, determine the corresponding function.

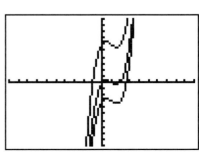

solution   Note that the graph in the middle has x-intercepts at $x = 0$ and $x = 2$. The only function above with a root at 0 is $f(x) = x^3 - 3x^2 + 2x$. So the middle graph must correspond to the function f. Then the upper graph must be the graph of $g(x) = x^3 - 3x^2 + 2x + 6$, which is $f(x) + 6$, and the lower graph must be the graph of $h(x) = x^3 - 3x^2 + 2x - 3$, which is $f(x) - 3$.

21.B
graphs of rational functions I

Some algebraic expressions consist of variables whose exponents are whole numbers and whose coefficients are real numbers. We call these expressions **polynomials.** The following expressions are polynomials in one variable.

$$5x^2 \qquad -3x^4 \qquad 7 \qquad \sqrt{2}x^3$$

All of these expressions have a real number coefficient and a whole number exponent. The number 7 is a polynomial because it can be written as $7x^0$. The polynomials above are also called **monomials,** because they have only one term. The indicated sum of two or more polynomials is also a polynomial. Thus, all three of the following expressions are polynomials:

$$5x^2 + 2x \qquad 3x + 5 \qquad 2x^2 + 2x + 3$$

Polynomials with exactly two terms are called **binomials,** and polynomials with exactly three terms are called **trinomials.** Thus the first two expressions are binomials, and the third expression is a trinomial. If a fraction has a polynomial for both the numerator and the denominator, we say that the fraction is a **rational polynomial expression.** Rational polynomial functions are called **rational functions,** and they appear often in the study of calculus. Thus the graphs of these functions are important.

example 21.6   Graph: $y = \dfrac{1}{x}$

solution   As noted in Lesson 17, when x is a large positive number, $\frac{1}{x}$ is a small positive number. When x is a large negative number, $\frac{1}{x}$ is a small negative number. We indicate this with the partial graph below.

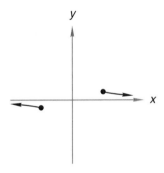

Note that these "ends" of the graph never touch the x-axis because $\frac{1}{x}$ can never equal zero. Admittedly, $\frac{1}{x}$ gets arbitrarily close to zero, but it **never** equals zero. This means that the x-axis is a **horizontal asymptote** for this function.

We can build a table of values for this function when x is near zero. (Since zero is not in the domain of $\frac{1}{x}$, we cannot let $x = 0$.)

x	y
1	1
0.5	2
0.1	10
0.01	100
0.001	1000

x	y
−1	−1
−0.5	−2
−0.1	−10
−0.01	−100
−0.001	−1000

So, as x gets close to zero from the right, y increases positively to $+\infty$. When x gets close to zero from the left, y increases negatively to $-\infty$. In terms of limits,

$$\lim_{x \to 0^+} \frac{1}{x} = +\infty \qquad \text{and} \qquad \lim_{x \to 0^-} \frac{1}{x} = -\infty$$

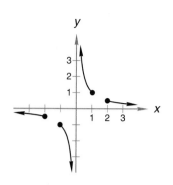

This is enough information to complete the sketch. In this example the y-axis is a **vertical asymptote,** which is a vertical line that the graph approaches but never touches. It is important to note that the graph goes up on one side of the asymptote and reappears from the lower end on the other side of the asymptote.

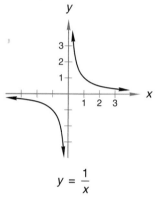

$$y = \frac{1}{x}$$

example 21.7   Graph: $y = \dfrac{1}{x - 3} + 2$

solution   The x in the preceding example has been replaced with $x - 3$, so the whole graph is shifted 3 units to the right. The +2 shifts the graph up 2 units.

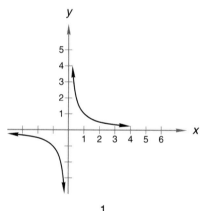

$$y = \frac{1}{x}$$

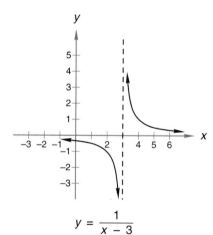

$$y = \frac{1}{x - 3}$$

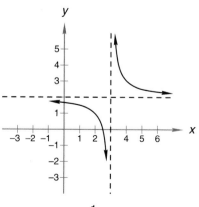

$$y = \frac{1}{x - 3} + 2$$

When we shift the graph 3 units to the right, the vertical asymptote becomes $x = 3$. We also see that $y = 2$ is a horizontal asymptote for this function, as the points on the "ends" of the graph get close to this line but never touch it.

example 21.8   Graph: (a) $y = -\dfrac{1}{x}$ (b) $y = \dfrac{1}{3 - x}$ (c) $y = \dfrac{1}{x^2}$

solution   (a) The graph of $y = -\frac{1}{x}$ is the "upside down" version of the graph of $y = \frac{1}{x}$. When x is $+2$, $\frac{1}{x}$ equals $+\frac{1}{2}$ and $-\frac{1}{x}$ equals $-\frac{1}{2}$. When x is -2, $\frac{1}{x}$ equals $-\frac{1}{2}$ and $-\frac{1}{x}$ equals $+\frac{1}{2}$. This pattern holds true for all values of x. We show the graph of $y = \frac{1}{x}$ on the left and the graph of $y = -\frac{1}{x}$ on the right. Each of these graphs is said to be a reflection in the x-axis of the other graph.

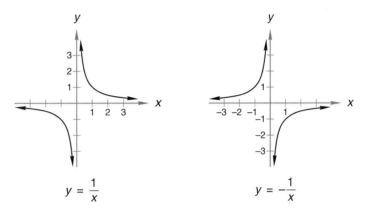

(b) This graph is easy to sketch if we rewrite the expression so that the sign of x is positive.

$$y = -\dfrac{1}{x - 3}$$

We see that this graph is the graph of $y = \frac{1}{x}$ shifted 3 units to the right and then flipped upside down about the x-axis.

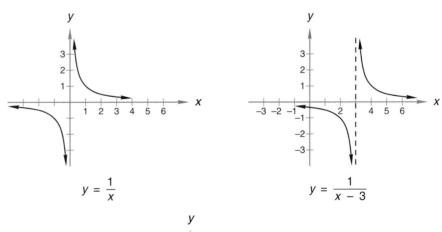

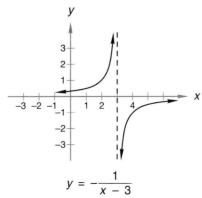

(c) Every value of x is squared so every value of y is positive. The graph looks like a "volcano," as we see on the left. The graph of the negative of the function is shown on the right; it looks like an "upside-down volcano."

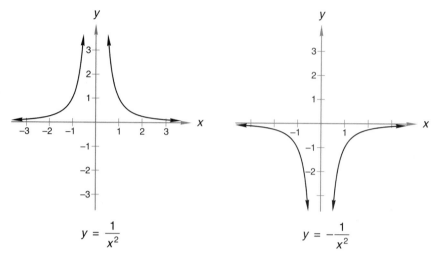

$$y = \frac{1}{x^2} \qquad\qquad\qquad\qquad y = -\frac{1}{x^2}$$

problem set 21

1. Jamar wants to use 100 meters of fence to enclose a rectangular region that will adjoin an existing wall. Therefore he only needs fence on 3 sides. The length of the side of the rectangular region that is parallel to the existing wall is L. Find the area of the region in terms of L.
   (5)

2. (a) Graph: $y = |x|$
   (21)
   (b) Change the function to shift the graph to the left 2 units and down 1 unit.

3. Graph $y = \sqrt{x}$, $y = \sqrt{x} + 2$, and $y = \sqrt{x} - 2$ on the same coordinate plane.
   (21)

4. Suppose $f(x) = \frac{1}{x}$. Let g be the function whose graph is the graph of f shifted 3 units to the left. Write the equation for g and graph g.
   (21)

Write the expressions in problems 5 and 6 entirely in terms of the natural logarithm.

5. $\log_{10} x$
   (20)

6. $\log_3 x$
   (20)

7. Approximate the solution(s) to the following system of equations:
   (2)
   $$\begin{cases} y = x^3 + 2x^2 - 3x - 5 \\ y = e^x \end{cases}$$

8. Use the definition of the derivative to find $\dfrac{dy}{dx}$ when $y = -x^2$.
   (19)

9. Use the definition of the derivative to find $\dfrac{d}{dx} f(x)$ when $f(x) = x^2 + 2x$.
   (19)

10. Use a graphing calculator to graph the set of points (x, y) that satisfy $\frac{x^2}{4} + y^2 = 1$. What are the two equations that must be used to produce the complete graph?
    (20)

11. On a graphing calculator, graph the function g defined by the equation $g(x) = \frac{f(2 + x) - f(2)}{x}$ where $f(x) = -x^2$.
    (14,19)

    (a) Using the trace feature or the table feature, determine what $g(x)$ approaches as x approaches zero.

    (b) Evaluate $D_x f(x)$ at $x = 2$. How does this answer compare with the answer to (a)?

Let $f(x) = x^2$ and $g(x) = e^x$ in problems 12 and 13.

12. Write the equation of $g \circ f$.
    (18)

13. Determine the domain and range of f and g, and then determine the domain and range of $g \circ f$.
    (18)

Evaluate the limits in problems 14–16.

14. $\lim\limits_{x \to 0} -\dfrac{1}{x}$
(17)

15. $\lim\limits_{x \to 0} \dfrac{1}{x^2}$
(17)

16. $\lim\limits_{x \to \infty} \dfrac{3x^3 - 14x^2 + 5}{1 - 2x^3}$
(17)

17. Find all values of x that satisfy the equation $10^{-2x} = 5$.
(16)

18. (a) Without using a graphing calculator, graph the function $f(x) = \left| x^2 - 3x + 2 \right|$.
(9,15)
    (b) Use interval notation to describe the values of x for which the graph of f is increasing. (*Note:* The x-coordinate of the vertex of the parabola $y = x^2 - 3x + 2$ is exactly halfway between the zeros of the function.)

19. Show that $\sin x - \sin x \cos^2 x = \sin^3 x$ for all real numbers x.
(8)

20. Use a graphing calculator to graph the function $y = \left| x^2 + 3x - 2 \right|$. Use the trace feature to
(2)
find the coordinates to one decimal place of the highest point on the graph between the two roots of the function.

21. Write the key trigonometric identities; then develop an expression that gives $\cos^2 x$ as a function
(12)
of $\cos (2x)$.

22. Let A and B be numbers such that $\sin A = \frac{3}{5}$ and $\sin B = \frac{4}{5}$. Find $\cos A$ and $\cos B$, assuming
(4)
both $\cos A$ and $\cos B$ are positive.

23. State an identity for $\tan (A + B)$. Then find the value of $\tan (A + B)$ where $\sin A = \frac{3}{5}$ and
(12)
$\sin B = \frac{4}{5}$.

24. Find the fourth term in the sequence whose first three terms are 1, 8, and 27.
(R)

25. Find the perimeter of the square that can be inscribed in a circle of radius $\sqrt{2}$.
(R)

LESSON 22   *Binomial Expansion • Recognizing the Equations of Conic Sections*

22.A
binomial expansion

The **binomial theorem** gives us a pattern that we can use to find the terms of the expansion of a binomial raised to a positive integer power. Let n be a positive integer. Then

$$(F + S)^n = F^n + \frac{n!}{(n-1)!\,1!}F^{n-1}S^1 + \frac{n!}{(n-2)!\,2!}F^{n-2}S^2 + \frac{n!}{(n-3)!\,3!}F^{n-3}S^3$$

$$+ \cdots + \frac{n!}{(n-k+1)!\,(k-1)!}F^{n-k+1}S^{k-1} + \cdots + S^n$$

We use F for the first term of the binomial and S for the second term. We can see the pattern of the exponents if we look at the exponents in the expansions of $(F + S)^n$. We let n equal 6 for one example and let n equal 10 for another example.

$$\boxed{1} \qquad \boxed{2} \qquad \boxed{3} \qquad \boxed{4} \qquad \boxed{n + 1}$$

$$(F + S)^6 = F^6 + \frac{6!}{5!\,1!}F^5S + \frac{6!}{4!\,2!}F^4S^2 + \frac{6!}{3!\,3!}F^3S^3 + \cdots + S^6$$

$$(F + S)^{10} = F^{10} + \frac{10!}{9!\,1!}F^9S + \frac{10!}{8!\,2!}F^8S^2 + \frac{10!}{7!\,3!}F^7S^3 + \cdots + S^{10}$$

The first term of both expansions is F^n. In each succeeding term, the exponent of F decreases by 1 and the exponent of S increases by 1. **The sum of the exponents in each term is n.** The last term is S^n. Note that the coefficients of both the first and last terms are 1. **The coefficients of the other terms have the factorial of n in the numerator and the product of the factorials of the exponents in the denominator.**

example 22.1   Write the expansion of $(x + \Delta x)^7$.

solution   First we write the exponents and leave a space to insert the coefficients.

$$(x + \Delta x)^7 = x^7 + \square x^6 \Delta x + \square x^5 (\Delta x)^2 + \square x^4 (\Delta x)^3 + \cdots + (\Delta x)^7$$

The coefficient of the first term and the last term is always 1. The coefficient of every other term has 7! in the numerator and the product of the factorials of the exponents of x and Δx in the denominator.

$$(x + \Delta x)^7 = x^7 + \frac{7!}{6!\,1!} x^6 \Delta x + \frac{7!}{5!\,2!} x^5 (\Delta x)^2 + \frac{7!}{4!\,3!} x^4 (\Delta x)^3$$

$$+ \frac{7!}{3!\,4!} x^3 (\Delta x)^4 + \frac{7!}{2!\,5!} x^2 (\Delta x)^5 + \frac{7!}{1!\,6!} x(\Delta x)^6 + (\Delta x)^7$$

Note: This expansion is crucial in determining the derivative of x^7.

example 22.2   Find the eighth term of the expansion of $(F + S)^{12}$.

solution   An easy way to begin is with the exponents of S. In the first term, the exponent of S is 0, then 1, etc.

Term Number:	1	2	3	4	...
Term:	F^{12}	$\dfrac{12!}{11!\,1!}F^{11}S$	$\dfrac{12!}{10!\,2!}F^{10}S^2$	$\dfrac{12!}{9!\,3!}F^9S^3$	...
Exponent of S:	0	1	2	3	...

Thus the exponent of S in the eighth term is 7, so the exponent of F must be 5 since the sum of the exponents must equal 12. Thus the variables are

$$F^5 S^7$$

The numerator of the coefficient is 12!, and the denominator of the coefficient is 5! 7!. Using this information we can write the eighth term of the expansion of $(F + S)^{12}$ as follows:

$$\frac{12!}{5!\,7!} F^5 S^7 = 792 F^5 S^7$$

example 22.3   Find the tenth term of the expansion of $(2x^3 - y)^{15}$.

solution   We begin by finding the tenth term of the expansion of $(F + S)^{15}$. Then we replace F with $2x^3$ and S with $-y$. The exponent of the variable S in the tenth term is 9, so the exponent of F must be 6, because the exponents must sum to 15.

$$F^6 S^9$$

Now we remember the pattern and write the coefficient.

$$\text{Tenth term} = \frac{15!}{6!\,9!} F^6 S^9 = 5005 F^6 S^9$$

We finish by replacing F with $2x^3$ and S with $-y$.

$$5005(2x^3)^6(-y)^9 = 5005\big[64x^{18}(-y^9)\big] = -320{,}320 x^{18} y^9$$

22.B
recognizing the equations of conic sections

The general equation of a conic section is

$$ax^2 + bxy + cy^2 + dx + ey + f = 0$$

where a, b, c, d, e, and f are real numbers. If the coefficients a, b, and c are zero and the coefficients d and e are not both zero, then the result is an equation such as

$$4x + 2y + 5 = 0$$

which is the equation of a straight line.

If the coefficients b and c are zero and the coefficients a and e are not zero, then the result is an equation such as

$$x^2 + 4x - y + 1 = 0$$

which is the equation of a parabola. We can change the form of this equation by completing the square and writing the equation in standard form as

$$y = (x + 2)^2 - 3$$

We can also get the equation of a parabola if a and b equal zero and if c and d do not equal zero.

If $b = 0$ and the coefficients a and c are equal, we get an equation such as

$$x^2 + y^2 - 8x - 4y + 11 = 0$$

This is the equation of a circle, and it can be rewritten in the following standard form:

$$(x - 4)^2 + (y - 2)^2 = 3^2$$

If $b = 0$, if a and c are both positive or both negative, and if a is not equal to c, then the equation describes an ellipse. The standard form can be determined by completing the square on the x-terms and y-terms.

GENERAL FORM   STANDARD FORM

$$4x^2 + 3y^2 + 4x - 2y = 0 \qquad \frac{\left(x + \frac{1}{2}\right)^2}{\frac{1}{3}} + \frac{\left(y - \frac{1}{3}\right)^2}{\frac{4}{9}} = 1$$

If $b = 0$ and if a and c have opposite signs, then the equation describes a hyperbola. In the following equation, the coefficients 4 and –3 have opposite signs, so it is the equation of a hyperbola that can be rewritten in standard form.

GENERAL FORM   STANDARD FORM

$$4x^2 - 3y^2 + 8x - 2y + 7 = 0 \qquad \frac{\left(y + \frac{1}{3}\right)^2}{\frac{10}{9}} - \frac{(x + 1)^2}{\frac{5}{6}} = 1$$

If b is not zero, the equation has an xy-term. In this case, the axes of the graph of the equation are inclined with respect to the x- and y-axes, which is the same as saying that the axes of the equation have been rotated. The following graphs illustrate equations that contain xy-terms.

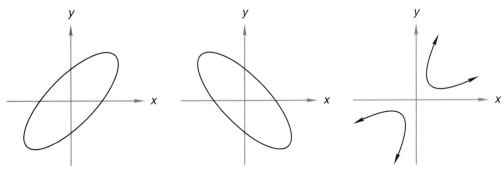

example 22.4   Indicate whether each equation is the equation of an ellipse, a hyperbola, a circle, or a parabola.

(a) $4x^2 + 36y^2 + 40x - 288y + 532 = 0$

(b) $9x^2 - 54x - 16y - 79 - 4y^2 = 0$

(c) $x - y^2 + 4y - 3 = 0$

(d) $x^2 + y^2 - 8x + 6y - 56 = 0$

(e) $x^2 + 36y^2 + 40 - 288y + 532 = 0$

solution   (a) **Ellipse.** The coefficients of x^2 and y^2 have the same sign but are not equal.

(b) **Hyperbola.** The coefficients of x^2 and y^2 have different signs.

(c) **Parabola.** The equation has an x-term and a y^2-term but no x^2-term.

(d) **Circle.** The coefficients of x^2 and y^2 are equal.

(e) **Ellipse.** The coefficients of x^2 and y^2 have the same sign but are not equal.

**problem set
22**

1. Square corners of equal size are cut from a
(5) 10- by 12-inch sheet as shown. The
resulting flaps are folded up to form a box
with no top. Express the volume of the box
in terms of x.

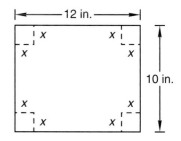

2. Find the coefficient of $x^{15}y^3$ in $(2y - 3x^5)^6$.
(22)

3. Use the binomial theorem to expand $(x + \Delta x)^6$.
(22)

4. Indicate whether each of the following is the equation of an ellipse, a hyperbola, a circle, or a
(22) parabola.

(a) $x^2 + 2y + 3x + 5 = 0$

(b) $2x^2 + 3x - 2y + 2y^2 + 3 = 0$

(c) $2x^2 - 3y^2 + 7x + 4y + 5 = 0$

(d) $9x^2 + 4y^2 + 36x - 24y + 36 = 0$

5. Identify the conic section whose equation is $x^2 - 2x - y^2 = 0$, and rewrite the equation in
(22) standard form.

6. Use a graphing calculator to graph the equation $x^2 + 2y + 3x + 5 = 0$. Estimate to one
(20) decimal place the coordinates of the highest point on the graph using the trace feature on the
calculator.

7. Without using a graphing calculator, graph the function $f(x) = |x^2 - 1|$, and then graph the
(21) function $g(x) = f(x - 1)$.

8. Write the equations of both of the asymptotes of the graph of $y = \dfrac{1}{x - 3}$.
(21)

9. Write $\log_3 x$ entirely in terms of natural logarithms.
(20)

10. Use a graphing calculator to solve the following system of equations: $\begin{cases} x^2 + y^2 = 16 \\ y = -2x + 1 \end{cases}$
(2)

Use the definition of the derivative in problems 11 and 12.

11. Let $f(x) = 3x + 5$. Find $\dfrac{d}{dx} f(x)$.
(19)

12. Let $y = -\dfrac{2}{x}$. Find $\dfrac{dy}{dx}$.
(19)

13. Let $f(x) = \ln x$ and $g(x) = x$. What domains are implied for f and g?
(6)

14. Find the axis of symmetry of the graph of the quadratic function whose x-intercepts are at
(10) $x = 2$ and $x = -1$ and whose y-intercept is -4.

15. Evaluate: $\displaystyle\lim_{x \to \infty} \dfrac{3 - 2x + x^3}{2 + 14x^3}$
(17)

16. Evaluate: $\sin^{-1}(\sin 270°)$
(13)

17. Find the values of x for which $\sec x = -2$ $(180° \le x < 360°)$.
(13)

18. If $\triangle ABC$ is an equilateral triangle and $\overline{ED}$
(8) is parallel to $\overline{AB}$, then what is x in
terms of h?

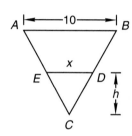

19. Describe the set of all the values of x for which $|2x - 3| < \varepsilon$, where ε stands for some
(9) unspecified small positive number.

20. On a graphing calculator, graph the function $f(x) = \frac{\sin x}{x}$. Use the trace feature or the table
(14) feature to estimate the value $f(x)$ approaches as x approaches 0.

21. Given the function $f(x) = \frac{x^4}{16} - x^3 + \frac{3x^2}{8} - x + 1$, estimate $f(\sqrt{2})$ and $f(\pi)$ by graphing
(6) the function on a graphing calculator and taking advantage of the CALCULATE menu option.

22. Use the diagram at the right to solve for x,
(8) y, and z.

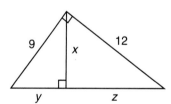

23. Find all values of x that satisfy the equation $\sqrt{2x + 3} = x$.
(2)

24. Find the sum of all the interior angles of
(R) the polygon shown.

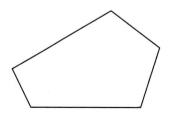

25. Supposing x is a real number, compare: A. x^2 B. x^3
(1)

LESSON 23 *Trigonometric Functions of nθ • Graphing Conics on a Graphing Calculator*

23.A
trigonometric functions of *nθ*

There are two angles between $0°$ and $360°$ whose sine is $\frac{1}{2}$. The sine is positive for angles in the first and second quadrants, and the angles whose sines are $\frac{1}{2}$ are $30°$ and $150°$. Thus the equation

$$\sin \theta = \frac{1}{2} \qquad (0° \le \theta < 360°)$$

has both $30°$ and $150°$ as solutions. The problem is more complex for functions of $n\theta$.

example 23.1 Solve: $\sin (3\theta) = \dfrac{1}{2}$ $(0° \le \theta < 360°)$

solution In this example the argument is 3θ. Since θ can be any angle between $0°$ and $360°$, 3θ can be any angle between $0°$ and $3(360°)$, or $1080°$. Thus 3θ can be $30°$ plus $360°$ (once around), which is $390°$, or $30°$ plus $720°$ (twice around), which is $750°$.

$$3\theta = 30° \qquad 3\theta = 390° \qquad 3\theta = 750°$$
$$\theta = \mathbf{10°} \qquad \theta = \mathbf{130°} \qquad \theta = \mathbf{250°}$$

Also, since 3θ can equal $150°$, 3θ can equal $150°$ plus $360°$, or $510°$; and 3θ can equal $150°$ plus $720°$, or $870°$.

$$3\theta = 150° \qquad 3\theta = 510° \qquad 3\theta = 870°$$
$$\theta = \mathbf{50°} \qquad \theta = \mathbf{170°} \qquad \theta = \mathbf{290°}$$

We see that if $\sin \theta = k$ has two solutions, then $\sin (3\theta) = k$ has six solutions, $\sin (4\theta) = k$ has eight solutions, and $\sin (n\theta) = k$ has $2n$ solutions.

We now illustrate the example graphically by plotting the functions $y = \sin (3x)$ and $y = \frac{1}{2}$. Graphically, our six solutions correspond to six points of intersection.

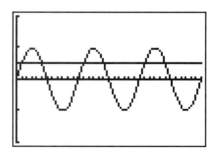

This graph has been drawn with the calculator in **DEGREE** mode, $0° \le x < 360°$, and **Xscl=10** so that a tick mark occurs every $10°$. A careful examination shows that the first intersection point occurs at the first tick mark $(x = 10°)$ and the second intersection point occurs at the fifth tick mark $(x = 50°)$. Finally, note that 3 cycles of the graph of the sine function appear on the interval $0° \le x < 360°$. (A **cycle** of a trigonometric function is the graph of one period of the function.) This is because the period of $\sin (3\theta)$ is $\frac{360°}{3} = 120°$, as we learned in Lesson 7.

example 23.2 Solve: $\tan (4\theta) - \dfrac{\sqrt{3}}{3} = 0$ $(0 \le \theta < 2\pi)$

solution The equation is given and the notation following the equation indicates that angles between 0 and 2π are acceptable. First we solve for $\tan (4\theta)$ by adding $\frac{\sqrt{3}}{3}$ to both sides.

$$\tan (4\theta) = \frac{\sqrt{3}}{3} \qquad \text{or} \qquad \tan (4\theta) = \frac{1}{\sqrt{3}}$$

There are two angles between 0 and 2π whose tangent is $\dfrac{\sqrt{3}}{3}$. These angles are $\dfrac{\pi}{6}$ and $\dfrac{7\pi}{6}$. Thus

$$4\theta = \frac{\pi}{6} \qquad \text{and} \qquad 4\theta = \frac{7\pi}{6}$$

Since θ must be between 0 and 2π, 4θ must be between 0 and $4(2\pi)$, or 8π. Thus $\frac{\pi}{6}$ and $\frac{7\pi}{6}$ can be increased by 2π for one full period, 4π for two full periods, and 6π for three full periods.

$$4\theta = \frac{\pi}{6} \qquad 4\theta = \frac{13\pi}{6} \qquad 4\theta = \frac{25\pi}{6} \qquad 4\theta = \frac{37\pi}{6}$$

$$\theta = \frac{\pi}{24} \qquad \theta = \frac{13\pi}{24} \qquad \theta = \frac{25\pi}{24} \qquad \theta = \frac{37\pi}{24}$$

$$4\theta = \frac{7\pi}{6} \qquad 4\theta = \frac{19\pi}{6} \qquad 4\theta = \frac{31\pi}{6} \qquad 4\theta = \frac{43\pi}{6}$$

$$\theta = \frac{7\pi}{24} \qquad \theta = \frac{19\pi}{24} \qquad \theta = \frac{31\pi}{24} \qquad \theta = \frac{43\pi}{24}$$

We can illustrate this example graphically by plotting the functions $y = \tan(4x)$ and $y = \frac{\sqrt{3}}{3}$ for $0 \le x < 2\pi$ and $-2 \le y \le 2$.

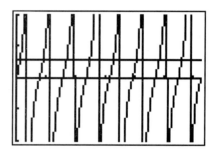

23.B
graphing conics on a graphing calculator

In Lesson 20 we saw that graphing a conic section centered at the origin requires finding the two functions that define the conic and then plotting them on the same set of axes. The same is true when the conics are not centered at the origin, but the algebra is slightly more complicated.

example 23.3   Using a graphing calculator, graph the ellipse defined by

$$x^2 + 2x + 4y^2 = 15$$

solution   We must solve this equation for y.

$$4y^2 = 15 - x^2 - 2x \qquad\qquad \text{subtraction}$$

$$y^2 = \frac{15 - x^2 - 2x}{4} \qquad\qquad \text{division by 4}$$

$$y = \pm\sqrt{\frac{15 - x^2 - 2x}{4}} \qquad\qquad \text{square root}$$

So we must plot the functions

$$\texttt{Y1=}\sqrt{\texttt{((15-X}^2\texttt{-2X)/4)}} \qquad \text{and}$$
$$\texttt{Y2=-Y1}$$

Note: The TI-83 allows functions to be defined in terms of other functions. To obtain $\texttt{Y1}$, press `VARS` and then use the $\blacktriangleright$ key to access the $\texttt{Y-VARS}$ menu. From the $\texttt{Y-VARS}$ menu, select $\texttt{1:Function...}$; then select $\texttt{1:Y1}$.

After applying ℤ𝖲𝗍𝖺𝗇𝖽𝖺𝗋𝖽 followed by ℤ𝖲𝗊𝗎𝖺𝗋𝖾, the following graph appears:

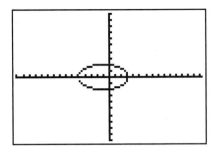

Does this graph make sense? It does appear to be an ellipse, which is a good sign. The center of the graph appears to be $(-1, 0)$. Is this correct? To check, we rewrite the original equation in standard form.

$$x^2 + 2x + 4y^2 = 15 \qquad \text{original equation}$$
$$x^2 + 2x + 1 + 4y^2 = 15 + 1 \qquad \text{completed the square}$$
$$(x + 1)^2 + 4y^2 = 16 \qquad \text{simplified}$$
$$\frac{(x + 1)^2}{16} + \frac{y^2}{4} = 1 \qquad \text{divided}$$

From this we see that the center is $(-1, 0)$, which further confirms our result.

example 23.4   Using a graphing calculator, graph the conic section defined by
$$x^2 + 4x + y^2 - 2y = 4$$

solution   We see that this defines a circle since the coefficients of x^2 and y^2 are equal. Moreover, the equation in standard form (after completing the square) is $(x + 2)^2 + (y - 1)^2 = 3^2$. So we have a circle of radius 3 centered at $(-2, 1)$. To graph this circle on a graphing calculator, we must solve the standard equation for y.

$$(x + 2)^2 + (y - 1)^2 = 9 \qquad \text{standard equation}$$
$$(y - 1)^2 = 9 - (x + 2)^2 \qquad \text{subtraction}$$
$$y - 1 = \pm\sqrt{9 - (x + 2)^2} \qquad \text{square root}$$
$$y = 1 \pm \sqrt{9 - (x + 2)^2} \qquad \text{addition}$$

So we must graph
$$\mathsf{Y_1=1+\sqrt{(9-(X+2)^2)}} \qquad \text{and} \qquad \mathsf{Y_2=1-\sqrt{(9-(X+2)^2)}}$$

Using ℤ𝖲𝗍𝖺𝗇𝖽𝖺𝗋𝖽 followed by ℤ𝖲𝗊𝗎𝖺𝗋𝖾, we see

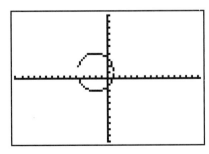

Note: We could not use $\mathsf{Y_1 = -Y_2}$ in this example.

problem set 23

1. The circumference of a circle equals the perimeter of a square. Which has the greater area, the circle or the square?
   (5)

In problems 2 and 3 solve for x $(0 \le x < 2\pi)$.

2. $\sin(3x) = -\dfrac{1}{2}$
(23)

3. $\tan(4x) + \dfrac{\sqrt{3}}{3} = 0$
(23)

4. Identify the conic section whose equation is $x^2 + 4y^2 - 16y + 12 = 0$.
(22)

5. Use the graphing calculator to graph $x^2 + 4y^2 - 16y + 12 = 0$.
(23)

6. Use the binomial theorem to expand $(x + \Delta x)^8$.
(22)

7. Let $f(x) = \sin x$. Graph the function $g(x) = 2 + 3f\left(x - \dfrac{\pi}{2}\right)$.
(7,21)

8. Write the equation of the function whose graph is identical to the graph of $y = \frac{1}{x}$ except that it
(21) is shifted left 2 units and up 3 units.

9. Write an expression for the exact value of x such that $4^x = 17$.
(16)

10. Use the definition of the derivative to determine $\dfrac{d}{dx}f(x)$, where $f(x) = -4x + 5$.
(19)

11. Use the definition of the derivative to determine $D_x y$, where $y = x^3$.
(19)

12. Let $f(x) = \sin x$ and $g(x) = x^2$. Find the domain and range of f and g.
(6)

13. For f and g as defined in problem 12, write the equation of $f \circ g$. Find the domain and range
(18) of $f \circ g$.

Evaluate the limits in problems 14–16.

14. $\displaystyle\lim_{x\to\infty} \dfrac{x^2 - 3x^3 + 14}{4x^3 - 7x^2 - 5}$
(17)

15. $\displaystyle\lim_{x\to1} \dfrac{x^2 + x - 2}{x^2 - 1}$
(14)

16. $\displaystyle\lim_{x\to\infty} \dfrac{x^2 + 6x - 4}{x^3 + 4x^2 - 1}$
(17)

17. On which interval(s) is the function $y = x^2 + x - 2$ increasing?
(15)

18. Sketch the graphs of $y = \ln x$ and $y = \ln(-x)$ on the same set of axes. Then sketch the graph
(12) of $y = \ln|x|$ on another set of axes.

19. Show that $(\cot^2 x + 1)(\sin^2 -x) + \left[\cos\left(\frac{\pi}{2} - x\right)\right](\sin -x) = \cos^2 x$ for all values of x where
(8) the functions are defined.

20. Use synthetic division to find the value of k for which $x = 1$ is a zero of the polynomial
(10) $x^3 - 3x^2 + 4x + k$.

21. (a) State an identity that gives $\cos^2 x$ as a function of $\cos(2x)$.
(12)

(b) Given that $\cos 30° = \cos(2 \cdot 15°) = \dfrac{\sqrt{3}}{2}$, use (a) to calculate $\cos^2(15°)$.

22. Approximate all of the zeros of $y = \ln(x^2) + \sin x - 3$.
(2)

23. Shown is a unit circle centered at the
(7) origin. Find the coordinates of the point P.

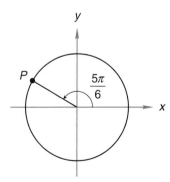

24. Find the length of a side of the equilateral triangle that can be inscribed in a circle of radius 4.
(R)

25. Assuming x and y are positive real numbers, compare the following:
(1)

A. x percent of y B. y percent of x

LESSON 24 *New Notation for the Definition of the Derivative •*
The Derivative of x^n

24.A

new notation for the definition of the derivative

Many modern calculus books use the letter h instead of Δx in the definition of the derivative. Thus they use the notation on the right-hand side instead of the notation on the left-hand side.

$$\frac{d}{dx}f(x) = \lim_{\Delta x \to 0} \frac{f(x + \Delta x) - f(x)}{\Delta x} \qquad \frac{d}{dx}f(x) = \lim_{h \to 0} \frac{f(x + h) - f(x)}{h}$$

example 24.1 Use the h notation for the definition of the derivative to find $g'(x)$ given that $g(x) = \sqrt{x}$.

solution First we write

$$\frac{d}{dx}\sqrt{x} = \lim_{h \to 0} \frac{\sqrt{x + h} - \sqrt{x}}{h}$$

We must find a way to get the h out of the denominator so we can let h approach zero. Sometimes one algebraic procedure works, and sometimes another algebraic procedure works. In this case, if we multiply above and below by the conjugate of the numerator, we get a factor of h in the numerator that cancels the h in the denominator.

$$\frac{d}{dx}\sqrt{x} = \lim_{h \to 0} \frac{\sqrt{x + h} - \sqrt{x}}{h} \cdot \frac{\sqrt{x + h} + \sqrt{x}}{\sqrt{x + h} + \sqrt{x}} \qquad \text{conjugate}$$

$$= \lim_{h \to 0} \frac{x + h - \sqrt{x + h}\sqrt{x} + \sqrt{x + h}\sqrt{x} - x}{h(\sqrt{x + h} + \sqrt{x})} \qquad \text{multiplied}$$

$$= \lim_{h \to 0} \frac{h}{h(\sqrt{x + h} + \sqrt{x})} \qquad \text{simplified numerator}$$

$$= \lim_{h \to 0} \frac{1}{\sqrt{x + h} + \sqrt{x}} \qquad \text{canceled}$$

In this expression we still have an h in the denominator, but h is not a factor of the denominator, so h can approach zero without the denominator approaching zero. Thus

$$\frac{d}{dx}\sqrt{x} = \lim_{h \to 0} \frac{1}{\sqrt{x + h} + \sqrt{x}} = \frac{1}{\sqrt{x} + \sqrt{x}} = \frac{1}{2\sqrt{x}} = \frac{1}{2}x^{-1/2}$$

24.B

the derivative of x^n

We remember the definition of the derivative of a function by remembering the geometrical interpretation. The slope of the secant through P_1 and P_2 in the figure on the left below is the rise divided by the run. In the figure on the right the y-value of P_2 is $f(x + h)$ and the y-value of P_1 is $f(x)$.

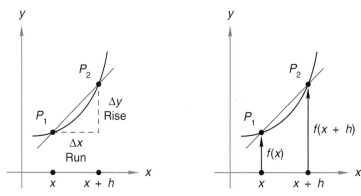

The value of the rise Δy is the difference of these two expressions. The run is Δx; so we can write the rise over the run as

$$\frac{\text{Rise}}{\text{Run}} = \frac{\Delta y}{\Delta x} = \frac{f(x + h) - f(x)}{h}$$

The derivative is the limit of this expression as h approaches zero. We remember that the trick is to rearrange the expression algebraically so that h is not a factor of the denominator when h approaches zero. If the function whose derivative we seek is x^3, we would proceed as follows.

$$\frac{d}{dx}x^3 = \lim_{h \to 0} \frac{(x + h)^3 - x^3}{h}$$

When we expand $(x + h)^3$ by using the binomial formula, we get x^3 as the first term, which cancels with the $-x^3$ term in the numerator.

$$\frac{d}{dx}x^3 = \lim_{h \to \infty} \frac{\cancel{x^3} + 3x^2h + 3xh^2 + h^3 - \cancel{x^3}}{h}$$

Furthermore, we note that the second term has h as a factor and that every other term has h^2 as a factor. If we divide by h, we no longer have an h in the denominator.

$$\frac{d}{dx}x^3 = \lim_{h \to 0} \left[3x^2 + (3xh + h^2) \right]$$

In this expression all of the terms after the first term have h as a factor. If we let h approach zero, then the value of all of these terms approaches zero. Thus,

$$\frac{d}{dx}x^3 = 3x^2$$

example 24.2   Find the derivative of x^n where n is 1, 2, 3, 4, ...

solution   We use the same diagrams to remember that the definition of the derivative is an algebraic expression of the limit of the rise over the run as the run approaches zero.

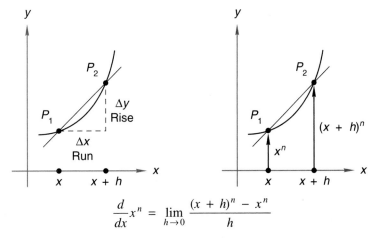

$$\frac{d}{dx}x^n = \lim_{h \to 0} \frac{(x + h)^n - x^n}{h}$$

When we expand the numerator, we get $x^n + nx^{n-1}h$ plus other terms whose coefficients we represent with empty boxes since their value is of no interest. The last term in the numerator is the last term in the numerator above.

$$\frac{d}{dx}x^n = \lim_{h \to 0} \frac{x^n + nx^{n-1}h + \square x^{n-2}h^2 + \square x^{n-3}h^3 + \cdots + h^n - x^n}{h}$$

Every term except the first two terms and the last term has h^2 as a factor. Thus

$$\frac{d}{dx}x^n = \lim_{h \to 0} \frac{x^n + nx^{n-1}h + [\text{terms that have } h^2 \text{ as a factor}] - x^n}{h}$$

The sum of the first term and the last term in the numerator is zero. If we divide the rest by h, the h in the second term is eliminated, and every term in the parentheses still has h as a factor.

$$\frac{d}{dx}x^n = \lim_{h \to 0}\left[nx^{n-1} + (\text{terms that have } h \text{ as a factor})\right]$$

When h approaches zero, the values of all of the terms in the parentheses approach zero, which means

$$\frac{d}{dx}x^n = nx^{n-1}$$

In this example we used the binomial expansion of $(x + h)^n$ to prove that the derivative of x^n is nx^{n-1} if n is a positive integer. This proof is only valid if n is a natural number. It does not work for a rational number such as $\frac{2}{3}$ or an irrational number such as π, because the binomial expansion cannot be used to expand expressions such as $(x + h)^{2/3}$ or $(x + h)^{\pi}$. **The rule above is valid, however, for any real number value of n.** We will use this fact even though the complete proof is not presented. This rule is called the **power rule** for derivatives.

problem set 24

1. A rectangular sheet of metal measuring 1 meter by 20 meters is to be made into a gutter by bending its two sides upward at right angles to the base. If both vertical sides of the gutter have the same height x, what is the capacity of the gutter in terms of x? (The capacity of the gutter is the maximum amount of fluid it could hold if it were closed at both ends.)
   ⁽⁵⁾

20 m

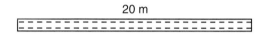

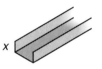

x

2. Find $\dfrac{dy}{dx}$ where $y = x^3$.
   ⁽²⁴⁾

3. Find $f'(x)$ where $f(x) = \sqrt[3]{x}$.
   ⁽²⁴⁾

4. Find $\dfrac{ds}{dt}$ where $s = \dfrac{1}{t^3}$.
   ⁽²⁴⁾

5. Find $D_x y$ where $y = \sqrt[4]{x^3}$.
   ⁽²⁴⁾

6. Find $\dfrac{dy}{dx}$ where $y = \dfrac{1}{x^2}$.
   ⁽²⁴⁾

7. Let $f(x) = x^2$ and define g by $g(x) = \dfrac{f(2 + x) - f(2)}{x}$.
   ^(14,24)

   (a) Graph g on a graphing calculator.

   (b) Use the trace feature or the table feature to determine the value $g(x)$ approaches as x approaches 0.

   (c) Find $f'(x)$ and evaluate f' at $x = 2$.

   (d) How do the answers to (b) and (c) compare?

8. Solve: $\cos(3\theta) = -\dfrac{1}{2}$ $(0 \le \theta < 2\pi)$
   ⁽²³⁾

9. Use the graphing calculator to graph $4y^2 + 8y - x + 5 = 0$.
   ⁽²³⁾

10. Find the coefficient of $x^4 y^3$ in the expansion of $(x - 2y)^7$.
    ⁽²²⁾

11. Let $f(x) = e^x$ and $g(x) = f(-x)$. Graph f and g on the same coordinate plane.
    ⁽⁷⁾

12. Let $f(x) = \cos x$ and $h(x) = 1 + f\left(x - \dfrac{\pi}{4}\right)$. Graph h.
    ^(7,21)

13. Sketch the graph of $y = \dfrac{1}{x^2}$.
(21)

14. Rewrite $y = \log x$ in terms of the natural logarithms.
(20)

15. Use the definition of the derivative to calculate $f'(x)$ where $f(x) = 2x^2$.
(19)

16. Let $f(x) = x^2$ and $g(x) = \sqrt{x - 4}$.
(18)

    (a) Write the equations of $f \circ g$ and $g \circ f$.

    (b) Find the domain and range of f, g, $f \circ g$, and $g \circ f$.

Evaluate the limits in problems 17 and 18.

17. $\displaystyle\lim_{x \to 3} \dfrac{x^3 - 27}{x - 3}$
(14)

18. $\displaystyle\lim_{x \to \infty} \dfrac{2x^3 - x^4}{2x^2 - 1}$
(17)

19. (a) Find the coordinates of the midpoint of the line segment joining the points $(2, -1)$ and $(4, 2)$.
(2)

    (b) Write the equation of the line that passes through the points $(2, -1)$ and $(4, 2)$.

    (c) Find the equation of the line consisting of all the points that are equidistant from the points $(2, -1)$ and $(4, 2)$.

20. Sketch the graph of $y = -\log_6 x$.
(12)

21. Given that $f(x) = \begin{cases} 2 & \text{when } x \geq 1 \\ -2 & \text{when } x < 1, \end{cases}$ sketch the graph of f and find:
(11)

    (a) $\displaystyle\lim_{x \to 1^+} f(x)$
                            (b) $\displaystyle\lim_{x \to 1^-} f(x)$

22. Let L represent a constant. Use interval notation to describe the values of y for which
(9) $|y - L| < 0.001$.

23. Show that $(1 - \cos^2 x)\csc^2 x + \tan^2 x = \sec^2 x$ for all values of x where the functions are
(8) defined.

24. Evaluate: $3 \tan^2 \dfrac{\pi}{6} + 2 \sin^2 \left(-\dfrac{\pi}{4}\right)$
(4)

25. If $m\angle ABC$ in the figure shown is $40°$, then
(R) what is the measure of angle ADC? Justify your answer.

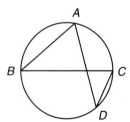

LESSON 25   *The Constant-Multiple Rule for Derivatives •*
The Derivatives of Sums and Differences • Proof of
the Derivative of a Sum

25.A
the constant-multiple rule for derivatives

If we form a new function by multiplying a given function by 5, the slope of the graph of the new function at every value of x is 5 times as steep as the slope of the graph of the original function. If we multiply a function by $-\frac{1}{3}$, the slope of the graph of the new function at every value of x is $-\frac{1}{3}$ as steep as the slope of the original function. If we multiply a function by any constant c, the slope of the graph of the new function at every value of x is c times the slope of the graph of the original function. The derivative of a function of x is the rate of change of the function with respect to x and has the same value as the slope of the graph of the function.

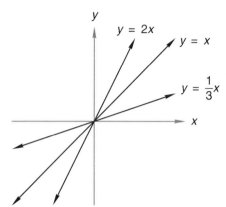

If $y = x$, $\dfrac{d}{dx}x = 1$.

If $y = 2x$, $\dfrac{d}{dx}(2x) = 2$.

If $y = \dfrac{1}{3}x$, $\dfrac{d}{dx}\left(\dfrac{1}{3}x\right) = \dfrac{1}{3}$.

The slope of the graph of $y = x$ is 1, and the derivative of x is 1. The slope of the graph of $y = 2x$ is 2, and the derivative of $2x$ is 2, which is twice the derivative of x. The slope of the graph of $y = \dfrac{1}{3}x$ is $\dfrac{1}{3}$, and the derivative of $\dfrac{1}{3}x$ is $\dfrac{1}{3}$. This is one-third the derivative of x. This explanation uses a linear function as an example, but the rule demonstrated is valid for any function.

CONSTANT-MULTIPLE RULE FOR DERIVATIVES

The derivative of the product of a constant and a function equals the product of the constant and the derivative of the function.

$$\frac{d}{dx}cf(x) = c\frac{d}{dx}f(x)$$

In Lesson 14 we noted that the limit of the product of two functions is the product of the individual limits. If one of the functions is a constant function, the limit of the product equals the constant times the limit of the other function. We can use this property of limits to prove the constant-multiple rule. To do this, we use $cf(x)$ in the definition of the derivative and factor out the c.

$$\frac{d}{dx}cf(x) = \lim_{h \to 0} \frac{cf(x + h) - cf(x)}{h}$$

$$= c \lim_{h \to 0} \frac{f(x + h) - f(x)}{h}$$

$$= c\frac{d}{dx}f(x)$$

This means that we can always move a constant factor from the right side of the derivative operator $\frac{d}{dx}$ to the left side of the derivative operator.

$$\frac{d}{dx}20x^{15} = 20\frac{d}{dx}x^{15} \qquad \text{and} \qquad \frac{d}{dx}(-13x^{-14}) = -13\frac{d}{dx}x^{-14}$$

example 25.1 Let $f(x) = 20x^3$. Find $f'(x)$.

solution The derivative of x^3 is $3x^2$, and the derivative of 20 times x^3 is 20 times $3x^2$.

$$f'(x) = \frac{d}{dx}20x^3 = 20\frac{d}{dx}x^3 = 20(3x^2) = \mathbf{60x^2}$$

It is not necessary to write the two steps, as we can find this derivative in one step by mentally multiplying the coefficient 20 by the exponent 3 and reducing the exponent by 1.

$$f'(x) = \frac{d}{dx}20x^3 = 60x^2$$

example 25.2   Find $f'(x)$ and $g'(x)$ given: (a) $f(x) = 3x^{\sqrt{2}}$ (b) $g(x) = -14x^{-5}$

solution   We mentally multiply the coefficients by the exponents and reduce the exponent by 1.

(a) $f'(x) = \dfrac{d}{dx}3x^{\sqrt{2}} = \mathbf{3\sqrt{2}\,x^{\sqrt{2}-1}}$ (b) $g'(x) = \dfrac{d}{dx}-14x^{-5} = \mathbf{70x^{-6}}$

25.B
the derivatives of sums and differences

The slope of the graph of $f(x) = 2x$ is 2. The slope of the graph of $g(x) = 10x$ is 10. If we add the functions, we get the function $(f + g)(x) = 12x$. The slope of the graph of this function is 12, which equals the sum of the individual slopes. We used these two linear functions to demonstrate a more general rule: **The slope of the graph of the sum or difference of two functions is the sum or the difference of the individual slopes.** This rule applies whether or not the functions are linear.

The slope of the graph of a function has the same value as the derivative of the function, which leads to the following box:

DERIVATIVES OF SUMS AND DIFFERENCES

The derivative of the sum or the difference of two functions equals the sum or the difference of the derivatives of the individual functions.

$$\frac{d}{dx}(f + g)(x) = \frac{d}{dx}f(x) + \frac{d}{dx}g(x) = f'(x) + g'(x)$$

$$\frac{d}{dx}(f - g)(x) = \frac{d}{dx}f(x) - \frac{d}{dx}g(x) = f'(x) - g'(x)$$

---

example 25.3   Find $\dfrac{dy}{dx}$ where $y = 4x^{-3} - 2x^{\sqrt{2}} + 4$.

solution   We take the derivative of each term and sum the derivatives. We remember that the derivative of 4 (or of any constant) is zero.

$$\frac{dy}{dx} = \mathbf{-12x^{-4} - 2\sqrt{2}\,x^{\sqrt{2}-1}}$$

example 25.4   Find $f'(x)$ where $f(x) = \dfrac{3}{x^4} - 2x^{\pi} + \dfrac{2}{x^{-2}} + 4$.

solution   The first step is to write $f(x)$ with no variables in the denominator.

$$f(x) = 3x^{-4} - 2x^{\pi} + 2x^2 + 4$$

The derivative of the sum equals the sum of the individual derivatives.

$$f'(x) = \mathbf{-12x^{-5} - 2\pi x^{\pi-1} + 4x}$$

example 25.5   Let $s = -16t^2 + 42t$. Find $\dfrac{ds}{dt}$.

solution   The derivative of a sum equals the sum of the individual derivatives.

$$\frac{ds}{dt} = \mathbf{-32t + 42}$$

25.C

proof of the derivative of a sum

This proof is straightforward. It requires the definition of the derivative and a few basic algebraic manipulations. The goal is to show that the derivative of a sum of two functions equals the sum of the individual derivatives. We want to show that

$$\frac{d}{dx}[f(x) + g(x)] = \frac{d}{dx}f(x) + \frac{d}{dx}g(x)$$

First we use the definition of the derivative to define the sum of the derivative of $f(x)$ and the derivative of $g(x)$.

$$\frac{d}{dx}f(x) + \frac{d}{dx}g(x) = \lim_{\Delta x \to 0} \frac{f(x + \Delta x) - f(x)}{\Delta x} + \lim_{\Delta x \to 0} \frac{g(x + \Delta x) - g(x)}{\Delta x} \qquad (1)$$

Next we write the definition of the derivative of $f(x) + g(x)$.

$$\frac{d}{dx}[f(x) + g(x)] = \frac{d}{dx}(f + g)(x) = \lim_{\Delta x \to 0} \frac{[(f + g)(x + \Delta x)] - [(f + g)(x)]}{\Delta x}$$

$$= \lim_{\Delta x \to 0} \frac{[f(x + \Delta x) + g(x + \Delta x)] - [f(x) + g(x)]}{\Delta x}$$

We rearrange the numerator and write this expression as the sum of two fractions.

$$\lim_{\Delta x \to 0} \left[\frac{f(x + \Delta x) - f(x)}{\Delta x} + \frac{g(x + \Delta x) - g(x)}{\Delta x} \right]$$

But the limit of a sum equals the sum of the individual limits, so we can write

$$\lim_{\Delta x \to 0} \frac{f(x + \Delta x) - f(x)}{\Delta x} + \lim_{\Delta x \to 0} \frac{g(x + \Delta x) - g(x)}{\Delta x}$$

This is the same expression as equation (1), which equals the sum of the individual derivatives. So the proof is complete.

$$\frac{d}{dx}[f(x) + g(x)] = \frac{d}{dx}f(x) + \frac{d}{dx}g(x)$$

The proof of the derivative of the difference of two functions is exactly the same except that the sign between the functions is a minus sign instead of a plus sign.

problem set 25

1. Express the distance between a point (x, y) on the graph of $y = x^2$ and the point $(3, 4)$ entirely in terms of x.
(2)

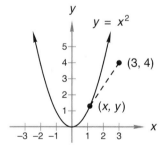

2. The pressure of an ideal gas varies directly as the temperature and inversely as the volume. If the initial pressure, volume, and temperature were N newtons per square meter, L liters, and K kelvins, what would the pressure be if the volume was 4 liters and the temperature was 1000 kelvins?
(5)

3. Use the definition of the derivative to determine $f'(x)$ when $f(x) = \sqrt{x}$.
(19)

4. Find $D_x y$ where $y = x^{14}$.
(24)

5. Find $\frac{dy}{dx}$ where $y = \frac{1}{x^3}$.
(24)

6. Find $f'(x)$ where $f(x) = \sqrt{x^3}$.
(24)

7. Find $\frac{ds}{dt}$ where $s(t) = \frac{1}{\sqrt{t}}$.
(24)

8. If $f(x) = \dfrac{1}{5}x^5 + 5x^{-2} + 6x^4 + 3$, what is $f'(x)$?
(25)

9. If $y = \dfrac{4}{u^2} - 3\sqrt{u}$, what is $\dfrac{dy}{du}$?
(25)

10. If $s(t) = v_0 t + \dfrac{1}{2}at^2$ (a and v_0 are constants), what is $s'(t)$?
(25)

11. Enter $y = \dfrac{f(2 + x) - f(2)}{x}$ into a graphing calculator where $f(x) = \sqrt{x}$.
(14,24)

   (a) Use the trace feature or the table feature to approximate to two decimal places the value y approaches as x approaches 0.

   (b) Use the power rule to find $f'(x)$.

   (c) Approximate $f'(2)$ to two decimal places.

   (d) How do the answers to (a) and (c) compare?

12. Find the values of θ between 0 and 2π for which $\cos(3\theta) = -1$.
(23)

13. Use the graphing calculator to graph $x^2 - 4x - y^2 = 0$.
(23)

14. (a) Use the graphing calculator to determine how many real zeros the polynomial $y = x^2 - x + 4$ has.
(2)

   (b) Justify your answer by algebraically finding the zeros of the polynomial.

15. Suppose $f(x) = e^x$ and $g(x) = f(x - 1)$. Graph both f and g on the same coordinate plane.
(21)

16. Determine the interval(s) on which the function $f(x) = \dfrac{1}{x - 3} + 2$ is increasing.
(15,21)

17. Graph $y = \sin^{-1} x$ on a graphing calculator where the window displays $x = [-1.5, 1.5]$ and $y = [-\pi, \pi]$. State the domain and range of the function.
(13)

18. Find all values of x for which $\ln(3x + 2) - \ln(2x - 1) = \ln 5$.
(16)

19. Let $f(x) = x(x - 2)(x + 4)(x + 1)$. On a number line, indicate the intervals on which f is positive and the intervals on which f is negative.
(15)

20. Show that $\dfrac{2\cos x}{\sin(2x)}\csc -x = -\csc^2 x$ for all values of x where the functions are defined.
(8,12)

21. Determine the exact value of k for which $e^{9k} = 2$.
(16)

22. Find the coefficient of x^3y^2 in the expansion of $(x - 2y)^5$.
(22)

23. Find the domain and range of the function $y = 1 + \sqrt{x}$.
(6)

24. Assume P lies outside circle O and $\overline{PA}$ and $\overline{PB}$ are two line segments that are tangent to points A and B on circle O. Compare the following:
(R)

   A. length of $\overline{PA}$ B. length of $\overline{PB}$

25. $\overline{BD}$ is the angle bisector of $\angle ABC$, as shown. $AB = x$, $BC = a$, $AD = c$, and $DC = a + b$. What is x in terms of a, b, and c? (*Hint:* The angle bisector of an angle in a triangle cuts the opposite side into lengths that are proportional to the adjacent sides.)
(R)

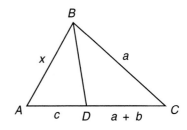

LESSON 26 *Derivatives of e^x and ln $|x|$ • Derivatives of sin x and cos x • Exponential Growth and Decay*

26.A

derivatives of e^x and ln $|x|$

The derivative of e^x is given by

$$\frac{d}{dx}e^x = \lim_{h\to 0}\frac{e^{x+h}-e^x}{h}$$

Unfortunately, there is no easy way to obtain a factor of h in the numerator to cancel out the h in the denominator. So determining $\frac{d}{dx}e^x$ at this point is difficult. However, we know that for small values of h the function

$$g(x) = \frac{e^{x+h}-e^x}{h}$$

closely approximates the derivative function. We can use this fact, along with our graphing calculators, to discover the derivative of e^x.

We define two functions:

$$Y_1 = e^\wedge(X)$$
$$Y_2 = (e^\wedge(X+H)-e^\wedge(X))/H$$

(The H is obtained by pressing `ALPHA` `∧`.) Notice that these are simply

$$e^x \quad \text{and} \quad \frac{e^{x+h}-e^x}{h}$$

Next, we assign a small value to H. In the main screen, enter

$$0.00001 \to H$$

This is accomplished using the `STO▸` key. By considering the difference quotient

$$\frac{e^{x+h}-e^x}{h}$$

with $h = 0.00001$, we should have an excellent approximation of the derivative function.

We build a table of values for both Y_1 and Y_2. For this we need two key sequences:

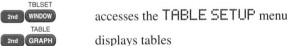

`2nd` `WINDOW`   accesses the `TABLE SETUP` menu

`2nd` `GRAPH`   displays tables

We access the `TABLE SETUP` menu and set both `TblStart` and `ΔTbl` to 1. Then we display the table of values.

X	Y₁	Y₂
1	2.7183	2.7183
2	7.3891	7.3891
3	20.086	20.086
4	54.598	54.598
5	148.41	148.41
6	403.43	403.43
7	1096.6	1096.6

X=1

We see that Y_1 and Y_2 are practically equal for all values of x. What does this mean? It means that

$$e^x \approx \frac{e^{x+h}-e^x}{h}$$

when $h = 0.00001$. Indeed, it can be shown that

$$e^x = \lim_{h\to 0}\frac{e^{x+h}-e^x}{h}$$

The right-hand side of this equation is the derivative of e^x. Therefore e^x is its own derivative.

$$\frac{d}{dx}e^x = e^x$$

We demonstrate this fact more rigorously later in the text. **Few functions are their own derivative, but e^x is one of them.**

  Now we turn to the function $f(x) = \ln x$. We wish to do the same calculator analysis to discover $\frac{d}{dx} \ln x$. First, we must define our difference quotient:

$$\texttt{Y1=(ln(X+H)-ln(X))/H}$$

If we keep $H = 0.00001$, deselect $\texttt{Y2}$, and retain the same $\texttt{TABLE SETUP}$, we get the following:

X	Y1
1	1
2	.5
3	.33333
4	.25
5	.2
6	.16667
7	.14286

X=1

Can a pattern be found here? Yes, if we compare the values of $\texttt{X}$ to the values of $\texttt{Y1}$. We note that the values of $\texttt{Y1}$ appear to be the reciprocals of the corresponding values of $\texttt{X}$.

So what is the pattern?

$$y_1 = \frac{1}{x}$$

Since $\texttt{Y1}$ is playing the role of the derivative of $\ln x$, we have our result.

$$\frac{d}{dx}\ln x = \frac{1}{x}$$

x	y_1
1	1
2	$\frac{1}{2}$
3	$\frac{1}{3}$
4	$\frac{1}{4}$
5	$\frac{1}{5}$

We will also demonstrate this fact more rigorously later in the book.

  It turns out that we can even make a more general statement about the derivative of the natural logarithm function. Below, we show the graph of $y = \ln |x|$.

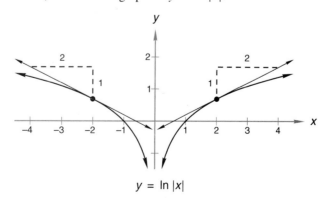

$$y = \ln |x|$$

We note that the graph of $y = \ln |x|$ is the graph of $y = \ln x$ on the right-hand side of the y-axis and the graph of $y = \ln -x$ on the left-hand side of the y-axis. The slope of this graph at any value of x is $\frac{1}{x}$. Thus, when $x = 2$, the slope of the graph of the function is $\frac{1}{2}$, and when $x = -2$, the slope is $-\frac{1}{2}$.

The derivative of ln x is $\frac{1}{x}$, and the derivative of ln $-x$ is $\frac{1}{x}$. Therefore, the derivative of ln $|x|$ is $\frac{1}{x}$. The function $y = \ln x$ is defined only for positive values of x. The function $y = \ln -x$ is defined only for negative values of x. The function $y = \ln |x|$ is defined for all positive and negative values of x and is the most comprehensive form of the natural logarithm function. It is only undefined at zero.

We summarize here.

The derivative of e^x is e^x. | The derivative of ln $|x|$ is $\dfrac{1}{x}$.

$$\frac{d}{dx}e^x = e^x \qquad\qquad \frac{d}{dx}\ln |x| = \frac{1}{x}$$

---

example 26.1 Find $\dfrac{dy}{dx}$ given that $y = 4 \ln x - 6e^x + 2x^2$.

solution The derivative of a sum equals the sum of the individual derivatives. Thus,

$$\frac{dy}{dx} = \frac{4}{x} - 6e^x + 4x$$

example 26.2 Find $\frac{dy}{dx}$ given that $y = 4 \ln |x| - 6e^x + 2x^2$, and tell how this derivative differs from the derivative in example 26.1.

solution The algebraic expression for the derivative is the same, because the derivative of $4 \ln |x|$ and the derivative of $4 \ln x$ are both $\frac{4}{x}$.

$$\frac{dy}{dx} = \frac{4}{x} - 6e^x + 4x$$

The difference is that both the function and the derivative in this problem are defined for both positive and negative values of x, while the function and the derivative in the preceding problem were defined only for positive values of x.

26.B
derivatives of sin x and cos x

The derivatives of sin x and cos x are also easy to remember. If x is measured in radians (rather than degrees), the slope of the sine function for any value of x equals the value of cos x. If x is measured in radians (rather than degrees), the slope of the cosine function for any value of x equals the value of $-\sin x$.

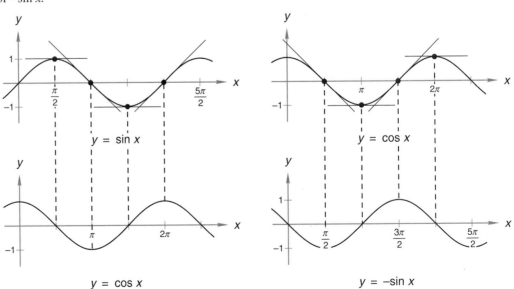

In the two figures above, the slope of the uppermost graph at any value of x equals the value of the function in the graph beneath it for that same value of x. In the top graph on the left-hand side we note that the slope of sin x is zero when x equals $\frac{\pi}{2}$ and $\frac{3\pi}{2}$. In the graph beneath it we see that the value of cos x is zero when x equals $\frac{\pi}{2}$ and $\frac{3\pi}{2}$. The slope of the graph of $y = \sin x$ is +1 when x equals 0 and is –1 when x equals π. The value of cos x is +1 when x equals 0 and –1 when x equals π. This correspondence between the slope of the graph of $y = \sin x$ and the value of cos x occurs for every value of x **if x is measured in radians.**

We have drawn tangent lines at four places in the top graph on the right-hand side. The slopes of these tangents equal the values of –sin x. This correspondence between the slope of the graph of $y = \cos x$ and the value of –sin x occurs for every value of x **if x is measured in radians.**

Since the slope of the graph equals the rate of change of the function, which we call the derivative, we have the following rules.

The derivative of sin x with respect to x is cos x.	The derivative of cos x with respect to x is –sin x.
$$\frac{d}{dx}\sin x = \cos x$$	$$\frac{d}{dx}\cos x = -\sin x$$

As with the exponential and natural logarithm functions, the graphing calculator can be used to confirm what we have stated here regarding the derivative of the sine and cosine functions. For reasons of space we do not do such a demonstration here, but we urge students to do so on their own. We use the definition of the derivative to prove these rules in a later lesson.

example 26.3   Find the derivative of $y = 3 \sin x - \cos x + 2e^x$.

solution   The derivative of a sum is the sum of the individual derivatives.

$$\frac{dy}{dx} = 3 \cos x - (-\sin x) + 2e^x$$

$$= \mathbf{3 \cos x + \sin x + 2e^x}$$

example 26.4   Find the derivative of $y = -3 \cos x + 3 \ln x - 2 \sin x$.

solution   The derivative of a sum is the sum of the individual derivatives.

$$\frac{dy}{dx} = -3(-\sin x) + 3\left(\frac{1}{x}\right) - 2 \cos x$$

$$= \mathbf{3 \sin x + \frac{3}{x} - 2 \cos x}$$

26.C
exponential growth and decay

Exponential equations of the form $A(t) = A_0 e^{kt}$ are often encountered in mathematics and science courses because such equations can be used to model the growth rate of bacteria, the voltage on a capacitor, radioactive decay, growth of money in a bank account, and other real-world situations. In the above equation, $A(t)$ is the amount present at any particular time t. A_0 is the initial amount present (the amount present at time $t = 0$), and k is a constant that must be determined for each problem. (k is closely related to the rate of growth.)

example 26.5   The number of bacteria present at noon was 400, and 9 hours later the bacteria numbered 800. Assume exponential growth and find the equation that describes the number of bacteria as a function of t, where t is measured in hours. Then find the number of bacteria present at noon the next day.

solution   We begin by writing the exponential equation for the number of bacteria present at some time t. The symbol $A(t)$ is used to represent this number.

$$A(t) = A_0 e^{kt}$$

For this problem, time began at noon. The number of bacteria was 400 when time equaled zero (noon), so $A_0 = 400$.

$$A(t) = 400 e^{kt}$$

Solving for k requires that we take the natural logarithm of both sides of the equation. To solve for k, we use 9 for t and 800 for $A(t)$.

$$A(t) = 400e^{kt} \qquad \text{equation}$$
$$800 = 400e^{9k} \qquad \text{substituted}$$
$$2 = e^{9k} \qquad \text{divided by 400}$$
$$\ln 2 = \ln e^{9k} \qquad \text{ln of both sides}$$
$$\ln 2 = 9k \qquad \text{simplified}$$
$$\frac{\ln 2}{9} = k \qquad \text{solved for } k$$
$$A(t) = \mathbf{400e^{(\ln 2)t/9}}$$

Now that we have k, we can complete the second part of the solution. We are asked for the number of bacteria present at noon the next day, when $t = 24$, which is the value of $A(t)$ when $t = 24$. All that is required is an evaluation of the exponential when t is replaced with 24.

$$A(24) = 400e^{(\ln 2)(24)/9} \qquad \text{substituted}$$
$$A(24) = \mathbf{2540} \qquad \text{evaluated and rounded}$$

problem set 26

1. The weight of a bag grew exponentially. At noon the bag weighed 150 grams, and one hour later
(26) the bag weighed 200 grams. Write an equation that describes the weight of the bag as a function of time t measured in hours. How much would the bag weigh at 3 p.m.?

2. The area of a spot decreased exponentially. At midnight the area of the spot was 1 square
(26) centimeter, and two hours later the area of the spot was 0.8 square centimeters. At what time would the area of the spot be 0.5 square centimeters?

3. The volume of a balloon increased exponentially. At 1 p.m. the volume of the balloon was
(26) 100 cm^3, and 2 hours later the volume of the balloon was 300 cm^3. What time was it when the volume of the balloon was 400 cm^3?

4. Let $f(t) = \dfrac{\sqrt{2}}{t^2} + 3t^{-3}$. Find $f'(t)$.
(25)

5. Let $y = 3x^4 - \dfrac{2}{\sqrt{x}} + 2$. Find $\dfrac{dy}{dx}$.
(25)

6. Find $f'(x)$ where $f(x) = e^x + \ln|x| - \sin x + \cos x$.
(26)

7. Find $\dfrac{dy}{du}$ where $y = \ln u - 2e^u + \sqrt{u}$.
(26)

8. Find $D_x y$ where $y = 2 \sin x + 14e^x - \dfrac{14}{x}$.
(26)

9. Find $s'(t)$ where $s(t) = x_0 + v_0 t + \dfrac{1}{2}at^2$ and x_0, v_0, and a are constants.
(25)

10. Find $f'(x)$ where $f(x) = 3e^x - 4 \cos x - \dfrac{1}{4} \ln|x|$.
(26)

11. Use the definition of the derivative to compute $D_x y$ where $y = -3x^2$.
(19)

12. Use a graphing calculator to graph $x^2 - y^2 - 2x - 4y - 4 = 0$. What are the coordinates of
(23) the vertices of the conic section?

13. Let $y = \sin x$. Change the equation to shift the graph up 2 units and right 3 units. Sketch the
(21) graph of the new equation.

14. Solve: $\sin^2 x + 2 \cos x - 2 = 0$ $(0 \le x < 2\pi)$
(13)

15. Sketch the graphs of $y = 2^x$ and $y = \log_2 x$ on the same coordinate plane.
(7,12)

16. Evaluate: $\displaystyle\lim_{x \to \infty} \frac{2x - 3x^2 + 4}{2x^2 + 14}$
(17)

17. Express the exact solution of $4 = 3^x$ in terms of natural logarithms.
(20)

18. Sketch the graphs of $g(x) = f(-x)$ and $h(x) = -f(x)$ given that $f(x) = e^x$.
(7)

19. Solve: $\log_5 (x + 3) + \log_5 10 = 3$
(16)

20. State the converse of the following statement: If a function has a derivative at $x = a$, then the
(3)   function is continuous at $x = a$.

21. Find all values of θ for which $0 \le \theta < 2\pi$ and $\tan(3\theta) = 1$.
(23)

22. Solve for x, y, and z in the figure shown.
(8)

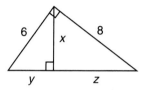

23. The equation of an ellipse whose center is (h, k), whose major axis is vertical with a length of
(22) $2a$, and whose minor axis is horizontal with a length of $2b$ is

$$\frac{(x - h)^2}{b^2} + \frac{(y - k)^2}{a^2} = 1$$

Write the equation of the ellipse whose center is the point $(-2, 3)$, whose major axis is vertical and 4 units long, and whose minor axis is 2 units long.

24. Find the area of the triangle whose sides have lengths 5, 7, and 10. (*Note:* Heron's formula
(R)   states that a triangle whose sides have lengths a, b, and c has area $\sqrt{s(s - a)(s - b)(s - c)}$,
where $s = \frac{1}{2}(a + b + c)$.)

25. A parallelogram is placed on the plane so
(2)   that one of its vertices is placed at the
origin and one of its sides lies on the x-axis.
The coordinates of all four vertices are as
shown. Find the midpoint of the line
segment that joins (b, c) and $(a, 0)$, and
find the midpoint of the segment that joins
$(0, 0)$ and $(a + b, c)$. Explain the
significance of your answer.

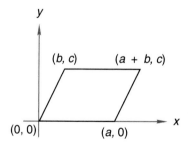

LESSON 27 *Equation of the Tangent Line • Higher-Order Derivatives*

27.A

equation of the tangent line

The slope of the line tangent to a curve at a designated value of x can be found by evaluating the derivative at that value of x.

example 27.1 Let $y = x^2 - 4x + 3$. Compute $\left. \dfrac{dy}{dx} \right|_3$.

solution The vertical line with the small 3 next to it indicates that the derivative should be evaluated at the x-value of 3. We can use functional notation to write the same problem by saying "Let $f(x) = x^2 - 4x + 3$. Find $f'(3)$."

$$\frac{dy}{dx} = 2x - 4 \qquad\qquad \left.\frac{dy}{dx}\right|_3 = 2(3) - 4 = \mathbf{2}$$

example 27.2 Find the equation of the line tangent to the graph of $y = x^2 - 4x + 3$ when $x = 3$.

solution We can find the equation of a line if we know the coordinates of a point on the line and the slope of the line. For this problem we know the tangent touches the graph when $x = 3$. We let x equal 3 and solve for y to get

$$y = (3)^2 - 4(3) + 3 = 0$$

Thus the point $(3, 0)$ is on the curve and on the tangent line. To find the slope when $x = 3$, we find $f'(3)$.

$$f'(x) = 2x - 4$$
$$f'(3) = 2(3) - 4 = 2$$

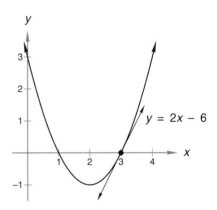

$y = 2x + b$	slope is 2
$0 = 2(3) + b$	passes through $(3, 0)$
$-6 = b$	solved for b
$y = 2x - 6$	equation of tangent line

example 27.3 Find the equation of the line tangent to $y = \sin x$ when $x = \dfrac{\pi}{6}$.

solution We can calculate the slope of this line using nDeriv on the TI-83.

$$\text{nDeriv(sin(X),X,}\pi\text{/6)}$$

(Remember to have the calculator in Radian mode.) The slope of the tangent line is given by the approximation 0.8660. Can we determine the exact value of the derivative? Certainly.

$$\frac{d}{dx}\sin x = \cos x$$

$$\left.\frac{d}{dx}\sin x\right|_{\pi/6} = \cos\left(\frac{\pi}{6}\right) = \frac{\sqrt{3}}{2}$$

$\dfrac{\sqrt{3}}{2}$ is the exact value of the slope, and $\dfrac{\sqrt{3}}{2} = 0.8660254038\ldots$

Now we can find the equation of the tangent line.

$$y = \frac{\sqrt{3}}{2}x + b \qquad\qquad \text{slope is } \frac{\sqrt{3}}{2}$$

$$\frac{1}{2} = \frac{\sqrt{3}}{2}\left(\frac{\pi}{6}\right) + b \qquad\qquad \text{passes through } \left(\frac{\pi}{6}, \frac{1}{2}\right)$$

$$b = \frac{1}{2} - \frac{\sqrt{3}\pi}{12} \qquad\qquad \text{solved}$$

$$y = \frac{\sqrt{3}}{2}x + \left(\frac{1}{2} - \frac{\sqrt{3}\pi}{12}\right) \qquad \text{equation}$$

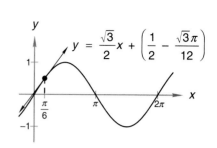

example 27.4   Find the equation of the line tangent to $f(x) = \sin x$ when $x = 1$.

solution   The calculator must be set in radian mode for this problem. One point on the tangent line is $(1, f(1))$, and the slope of the tangent line is $f'(1)$.

$$f(x) = \sin x \qquad\qquad f'(x) = \cos x$$
$$\sin(1) \approx 0.8415 \qquad\qquad \cos(1) \approx 0.5403$$

Thus the tangent line has a slope of 0.5403 and passes through the point $(1, 0.8415)$.

$$y = 0.5403x + b \qquad\qquad \text{slope is } 0.5403$$
$$0.8415 = 0.5403(1) + b \qquad\qquad (1, 0.8415)$$
$$b = 0.3012 \qquad\qquad \text{solved}$$

$$\mathbf{y = 0.5403x + 0.3012} \qquad \text{equation}$$

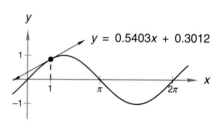

27.B
higher-order derivatives

If a function is differentiable, its derivative is another function called the **first derivative.** If the first derivative is differentiable, its derivative is a function called the **second derivative.** If the second derivative is differentiable, its derivative is a function called the **third derivative,** etc.

FUNCTION	FIRST DERIVATIVE	SECOND DERIVATIVE	THIRD DERIVATIVE
$f(x)$ or y	$f'(x)$ or $\dfrac{dy}{dx}$	$f''(x)$ or $\dfrac{d^2y}{dx^2}$	$f'''(x)$ or $\dfrac{d^3y}{dx^3}$

We read the notations for the second derivative as "f double prime of x" or as "dee squared y over dee x squared." We read the notations for the third derivative as "f triple prime of x" or as "dee cubed y over dee x cubed."

example 27.5   Let $y = 3u^5$. Find $\dfrac{d^2y}{du^2}\Big|_2$.

solution   We find the first derivative and then find the derivative of the first derivative.

$$y = 3u^5 \quad\longrightarrow\quad \frac{dy}{du} = 15u^4 \quad\longrightarrow\quad \frac{d^2y}{du^2} = 60u^3$$

Now we evaluate $60u^3$ at $u = 2$.

$$60u^3\Big|_2 = 60(2)^3 = \mathbf{480}$$

example 27.6 Let $f(x) = \dfrac{1}{x^2}$. Find $f'''(2)$.

solution We rewrite the function as $f(x) = x^{-2}$ and take the derivative three times.

$$f'(x) = -2x^{-3} \quad \longrightarrow \quad f''(x) = 6x^{-4} \quad \longrightarrow \quad f'''(x) = -24x^{-5}$$

If we evaluate $-24x^{-5}$ when $x = 2$, we get

$$-24x^{-5}\Big|_2 = -\frac{24}{(2)^5} = -\frac{24}{32} = -\frac{3}{4}$$

problem set 27

1. A certain company's assets increased exponentially. After 1 year in business the assets were
(26) worth \$1,530,000, and after 3 years in business the assets were worth \$3 million. Write an
equation that describes the growth of the assets of the business as a function of t, where t is the
number of years since the company started. Then determine the value of the assets after 7 years
in business.

2. Let $y = \dfrac{1}{\sqrt{x^3}} - \dfrac{1}{3}e^x + 4\cos x$. Find $\dfrac{dy}{dx}$.
(26)

3. Let $f(x) = \dfrac{1}{x} + 2\ln|x| - 3\sin x$. Find $f'(x)$.
(26)

4. Let $y = 2u^2 - \dfrac{\sqrt[3]{u}}{3} + c$ where c is constant. Find $D_u y$.
(25)

5. Use the definition of the derivative to find $f'(x)$ where $f(x) = -\dfrac{1}{x}$.
(19)

6. Find $\dfrac{d^3 y}{dx^3}$ where $y = 3e^x - 2x^3$.   **7.** Find $f''(t)$ where $f(t) = 3\sin t + \ln t$.
(27) (27)

8. If $f(x) = \ln|x|$, what is $f''(-14)$?
(27)

9. Find the equation of the line tangent to the graph of $y = x^2 + 3$ at $x = -1$.
(27)

10. Find an approximation of the slope of the line tangent to the graph of $y = \sin x - \cos x$
(27) at $x = -1$.

11. Find the equation of the line tangent to the graph of $y = 2e^x$ at $x = 2$.
(27)

12. Write the key trigonometric identities, and develop an expression that gives $\cos^2 \theta$ as a function
(12) of $\cos(2\theta)$.

13. Find all values of x between $0°$ and $360°$ that satisfy the equation $\sin(4x) + 1 = 0$.
(23)

14. Use a graphing calculator to graph $4y^2 - 9x^2 - 8y - 32 = 0$. What are the coordinates of the
(23) vertices of the conic section?

15. (a) Find an equation in terms of x for the slope of the line that passes through the points (x, y)
$(14,27)$ and $(\frac{\pi}{2}, 1)$ on the graph of $y = \sin x$. Call this function of x the slope function.

   (b) Graph the slope function on a graphing calculator.

   (c) Approximate to one decimal place the limit of the slope function as x approaches $\frac{\pi}{2}$ by using
       the trace feature or the table feature of a graphing calculator.

   (d) Evaluate $\dfrac{dy}{dx}\Big|_{\pi/2}$ for the function $y = \sin x$.

   (e) How do the answers to (c) and (d) compare?

16. Evaluate: $\log_3 5$
(20)

17. (a) Find the domain and range of f and g where $f(x) = \sqrt{x - 1}$ and $g(x) = x^2$.
(6,18)

    (b) Write the equation of $f \circ g$ and determine the domain and range of $f \circ g$.

18. Evaluate: $\dfrac{21! \, 4!}{5! \, 7! \, 18!}$
(1)

19. Use interval notation to designate the interval(s) on which the graph of f lies above the x-axis
(15) for $f(x) = (2 - x)(x + 3)(x - 1)$.

20. Graph the function $y = \dfrac{x^2 - 1}{x - 1}$ and find $\lim\limits_{x \to 1} \dfrac{x^2 - 1}{x - 1}$.
(14)

21. Suppose that $f(x)$ is a polynomial such that $f(x) = q(x)(x - 2) + 7$, where $q(x)$ is also a
(10) polynomial. What is the value of $f(2)$? (*Hint:* Review the statement of the remainder theorem.)

22. Use the rational roots theorem to find the zeros of the function $f(x) = x^3 - 2x^2 - 5x + 6$.
(10)

23. Find the equation of the quadratic function that has zeros at $x = 1$ and $x = -2$ and whose
(10) graph has a y-intercept at $y = -4$.

24. Find x in terms of a in the figure shown.
(R) (*Hint:* Use the fact that if two secants are drawn to a circle from a common point, as in the given figure, then the product of the length of one secant times the length of its external segment is equal to the product of the length of the other secant times the length of its external segment.)

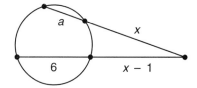

25. If $x - y = 4$ and $xy = 3$, what is the value of $x^2 + y^2$?
(R)

LESSON 28   *Graphs of Rational Functions II • A Special Limit*

28.A

graphs of rational functions II

A **rational function** is a fraction of polynomials whose coefficients are rational. For example, if a_1, a_2, a_3, a_4, b_1, b_2, b_3, b_4, and b_5 are rational numbers, then the function below is a rational function.

$$f(x) = \frac{a_1 x^3 + a_2 x^2 + a_3 x + a_4}{b_1 x^4 + b_2 x^3 + b_3 x^2 + b_4 x + b_5}$$

In this lesson we restrict our discussion to polynomials whose linear factors are all real linear factors. Thus it is possible to factor the numerator into a product of a constant k_1 and three linear factors of the form $(x + a)$. The denominator can be factored into the product of k_2 and four linear factors.

$$f(x) = \frac{k_1(x + a)(x + b)(x + c)}{k_2(x + d)(x + e)(x + f)(x + g)}$$

The zeros of the numerator are the zeros of the function, and the zeros of the denominator are the x-values where vertical asymptotes occur.

    We begin our investigation of the graphs of rational functions by considering the special case of functions that are factored into linear real factors occurring only once each. To ensure that the x-axis is the horizontal asymptote, the denominators of these functions must have more factors than the numerators.

   **Since a rational function that is composed of unique nonrepeating linear factors changes
signs at every zero of the numerator and the denominator, the graph must cross the *x*-axis at
each zero and must jump across the *x*-axis at each vertical asymptote.**

   The graphs of these functions can be sketched quickly if we begin by drawing dashed lines for
the vertical asymptotes and placing dots on the *x*-axis at the zeros. Next we determine whether the
function is positive or negative for large positive values of *x*. Then we work our way from right to left,
crossing the *x*-axis at the zeros and going off the paper vertically at the asymptotes.

   Suppose we have a function that has a small positive value when *x* is a large positive number,
and the zeros and the vertical asymptotes are as shown.

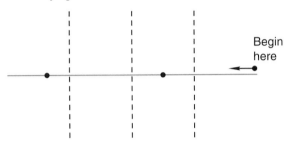

We begin on the right at a small positive value of *y* and move to the left. The graph cannot cross the
x-axis because there is no zero, so it goes off the figure vertically at the asymptote.

   The graph went off the figure at the top and to the right of this first asymptote. Thus the graph
must reappear from below on the left side of this asymptote. It sees a zero, so it crosses the *x*-axis and
goes off the figure at the top again.

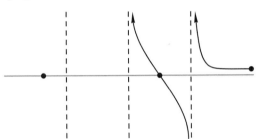

Again it must reappear from below on the left-hand side of the second asymptote. This time it sees no
zero, so it must not touch the *x*-axis. Thus it turns around and goes back down. (We show how to
determine exactly where the graph turns around later in the book. For now we just guess.)

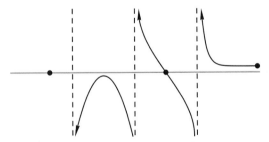

The graph must reappear on the left side of the third asymptote from above. Then it crosses at the zero
and comes back to approach the horizontal asymptote, which is the *x*-axis.

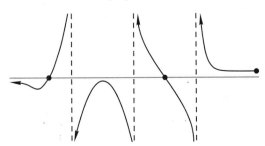

As a last step, we extend the graph to the right and add the missing arrowheads. We note that, in this example, the x-axis serves as a horizontal asymptote as x approaches +∞. The completed graph is shown below.

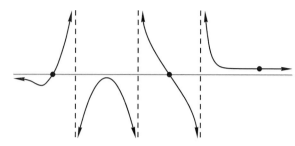

example 28.1 Graph: $f(x) = -\dfrac{x(x-7)}{(x+5)(x+2)(x-2)(x-5)}$

solution First we plot the zeros and the vertical asymptotes.

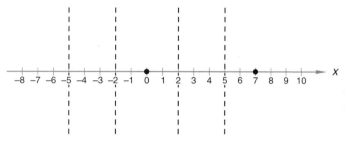

Next we must determine the starting point for the right end of the graph. The term of highest degree in a polynomial is the dominant term, because for large absolute values of x the value of the highest-degree term is greater than the absolute value of the sum of all the other terms in the polynomial. Thus, if x is a large positive number, we can estimate the value of a rational function whose denominator is of higher degree than the numerator by considering only the lead terms in the numerator and denominator.

$$f(x) = -\dfrac{x^2 + \text{(other terms)}}{x^4 + \text{(other terms)}}$$

As x takes on larger and larger positive values, both x^2 and x^4 are large positive numbers; since the term x^4 in the denominator has the higher degree and since there is a minus sign in front, the value of the fraction is a small negative number. This gives us our starting point on the right-hand end of the graph.

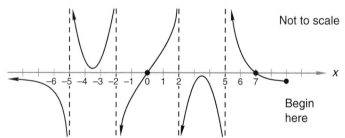

We complete the graph by extending it to the right and adding the missing arrowheads. In this case, the x-axis is the horizontal asymptote so the graph must rise and approach the x-axis.

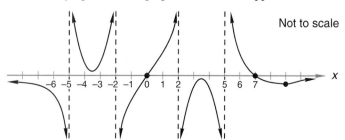

example 28.2   Graph: $y = \dfrac{(x + 5)(x - 3)(x - 1)}{(x - 4)(x + 2)(x + 4)(x - 1)}$

solution   First we simplify the expression by canceling the $x - 1$ factors above and below; but we must remember to put a hole in the graph when $x = 1$, because the function is not defined at that point. Then we plot the zeros and the vertical asymptotes. We begin our sketch on the right-hand end by noting that when x is a large positive number, y is a small positive number, because the ratio of the lead polynomial terms is $+\dfrac{x^2}{x^3}$.

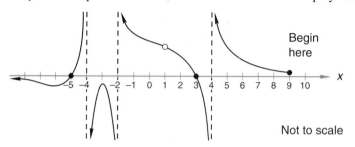

As with the previous examples, the x-axis is a horizontal asymptote, so we extend the graph to the right and finish by adding the missing arrowheads.

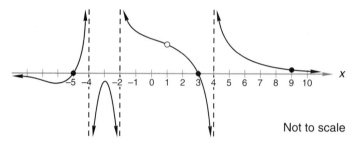

28.B

a special limit   Consider the following limits:

     (a) $\displaystyle\lim_{x \to 0} \frac{1}{x}$ (b) $\displaystyle\lim_{x \to 0} -\frac{1}{x^2}$ (c) $\displaystyle\lim_{x \to 0} \frac{4x + 8}{x + 2}$ (d) $\displaystyle\lim_{x \to 3} \frac{x^2 - 9}{x - 3}$

Limit (a) does not exist because the left-hand limit does not equal the right-hand limit. Limit (b) is $-\infty$. Limit (c) is 8 divided by 2 which equals 4. Limit (d) is 6 because the numerator is factorable. But what is the value of the following limit?

$$\lim_{h \to 0} \frac{\sin\left(\dfrac{\pi}{2} + h\right) - \sin\dfrac{\pi}{2}}{h}$$

This limit can be evaluated easily if we recognize that the expression is the definition of the derivative of $\sin x$ evaluated at $\frac{\pi}{2}$. The derivative of $\sin x$ can be written as follows.

$$\lim_{h \to 0} \frac{\sin(x + h) - \sin x}{h} = \cos x$$

If $x = \dfrac{\pi}{2}$, then $\cos x = 0$, so this limit equals zero when $x = \dfrac{\pi}{2}$.

     The ability to recognize limit problems that are derivatives in disguise is a critical skill. They appear in virtually all standardized calculus tests. Variations of the following limit problems appear in several future problem sets. Look for them.

$$\lim_{\Delta x \to 0} \frac{\ln(x + \Delta x) - \ln x}{\Delta x} \qquad\qquad \lim_{h \to 0} \frac{e^{x+h} - e^x}{h}$$

The limit on the left is the limit for the definition of the derivative of $\ln x$. The derivative of $\ln x$ is $\frac{1}{x}$, so the value of this limit is $\frac{1}{x}$. The limit on the right is the limit for the definition of the derivative of e^x. The derivative of e^x is e^x, so the value of this limit is e^x.

problem set
28

1. The amount of money in the treasury was decreasing at an exponential rate. If the treasury
(26) contained $2 million on the first of the month and contained only $100 on the thirtieth of the
month, during which day did the treasury contain $0.5 million?

Graph the functions of problems 2 and 3. Clearly show all x-intercepts and asymptotes. Other than
these features, the graphs need not be precise.

2. $f(x) = \dfrac{(x - 2)(x + 3)}{(x - 5)(x + 2)(x - 3)}$
(28)

3. $y = -\dfrac{x(x - 3)}{(x - 1)(x + 2)(x + 3)}$
(28)

4. Let $s(t) = x_0 + v_0 t + \dfrac{1}{2} g t^2$ where x_0, v_0, and g are constants. Find $s''(t)$.
(27)

5. Compute $\dfrac{d^2 y}{du^2}\bigg|_2$ for $y = \dfrac{1}{u}$.
(27)

6. Find $\dfrac{dy}{dx}\bigg|_2$ where $y = \dfrac{1}{5} e^x - 2 \cos x + 3 \ln |x|$.
(26,27)

7. Find the slope of the line tangent to the graph of $y = 2 \sin x + \cos x$ at $x = 4.2$.
(27)

8. Find the equation of the line tangent to the graph of $y = \dfrac{1}{x}$ at $x = 1$.
(27)

9. (a) Find the value of $\lim_{h \to 0} \dfrac{\sin\left(\frac{\pi}{2} + h\right) - \sin \frac{\pi}{2}}{h}$. (*Hint:* Think about the definition of the
(28)   derivative.)

   (b) Confirm your answer to (a) by entering the function $y = \dfrac{\sin\left(\frac{\pi}{2} + x\right) - \sin \frac{\pi}{2}}{x}$ in a graphing
       calculator. What value does y approach as x approaches 0? List the values of y when x is 0.1,
       -0.1, 0.01, and -0.01.

10. Use a graphing calculator to graph $x^2 + y^2 - 2x + 12y + 6 = 0$. What are the coordinates
(22,23) of the center of the conic section?

11. If one linear factor of $x^3 + x^2 - 2x - 2$ is $x + 1$, what are the other two linear factors?
(10)

12. Let $f(x) = \sqrt{x}$ and $g(x) = 1 + \sqrt{x - 2}$. Describe the graph of g in terms of the graph of f.
(21)

13. Suppose $f(x)$ is a polynomial and $f(x) = q(x)(x - 4) + 5$ where $q(x)$ is also a polynomial.
(10) What is the value of $f(4)$?

14. Find all real values of x for which $-2 \ln 2 + \ln (x - 2) = \ln (2x - 4)$.
(16)

15. Let $f(x) = \dfrac{x^2 + x - 6}{x + 3}$.
(14)

   (a) Sketch the graph of f.

   (b) Graph the function f on a graphing calculator. Use the trace feature to guess the value of
       $\lim_{x \to -3} f(x)$.

   (c) Find $\lim_{x \to -3} f(x)$. Compare this with your answer to (b).

16. Suppose $\log_b 53 = 31$. Find b.
(20)

17. If $\dfrac{dy}{dx} = 2x$, which of the following could equal y?
(24)

   A. 2   B. $2x$ C. x^2 D. x^3

18. Describe the set of all integer values of x for which $|3x - 1| < 16$.
(9)

19. Show that $\dfrac{(\sin x + \cos x)^2 - 1}{2 \sin -x} = -\cos x$ for all values of x where the functions are defined.
(8)

20. Evaluate: $\cos -\dfrac{13\pi}{3} \sin^2 \dfrac{\pi}{4}$
(4)

21. Rewrite $\dfrac{2 - \sqrt{3}}{1 - \sqrt{2}}$ so that the denominator is a rational number.
(1)

22. Write an equation that expresses the following idea: The distance d_1 from a point (x, y) to the point $(0, 1)$ is the same as the distance d_2 from the point (x, y) to the line $y = -1$.
(2)

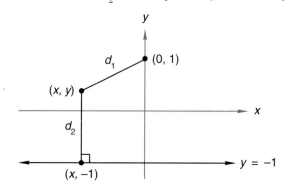

23. Solve the equation you found in problem 22 for y. It turns out that the set of all points satisfying the conditions described in problem 22 is a parabola. The point $(0, 1)$ is called the **focus** of the parabola and the line $y = -1$ is called the **directrix** of the parabola.
(2)

24. An arbitrarily drawn triangle is oriented on the coordinate plane so that one of its vertices lies at the origin and one of its sides lies on the x-axis. The coordinates of all three vertices of the triangle are as shown. Use the midpoint formula to find the coordinates of the midpoints shown. Write the equation of the line that passes through the midpoints. What does this imply about any line that bisects two sides of a triangle?
(2)

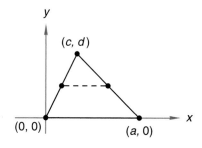

25. Find the number of distinct diagonals that can be drawn in a six-sided regular polygon.
(R)

LESSON 29 *Newton and Leibniz • Differentials*

29.A

Newton and Leibniz

The derivative of a function is the limit of the ratio of the change in y to the change in x as the change in x approaches zero. For a function $y = f(x)$,

$$\frac{dy}{dx} = \frac{d}{dx} f(x) = \lim_{\Delta x \to 0} \frac{\Delta y}{\Delta x} = \lim_{\Delta x \to 0} \frac{f(x + \Delta x) - f(x)}{\Delta x}$$

Sir Isaac Newton (1642–1727), an Englishman, and Gottfried Wilhelm Leibniz (1646–1716), a German, invented calculus independently of one another in the seventeenth century. To designate the derivative of a function, Newton placed a dot over the y and wrote $\dot{y}$ (read "y dot"). Over the years the dot changed to a prime, and now we write y' (read "y prime"). The derivative as conceived by Newton and indicated by his notation $\dot{y}$ was a single entity and had no numerator or denominator.

Leibniz designated the derivative with the fractional notation $\frac{dy}{dx}$ and considered the derivative to be a fraction of very small quantities dy and dx, which he called *infinitesimals* and which he moved about using the rules of algebra. Leibniz could multiply $\frac{dy}{dx}$ by dx and get dy by canceling the dx above and the dx below as shown here.

$$\frac{dy}{d\!\!\!/x} \, d\!\!\!/x = dy$$

Many scientists prefer Leibniz's notation because it facilitates the solution of practical problems whose solutions would be more difficult using the notation of Newton. In this book we will use both notations. We use Leibniz's notation more often, because it is easier for the beginner to understand.

29.B
differentials

We define differentials below.

DEFINITION OF DIFFERENTIALS

Let $y = f(x)$ be a function that can be differentiated. The **differential of x** (denoted by dx) is any nonzero real number. The **differential of y** (denoted by dy) is given by $dy = f'(x)\,dx$.

Below we show an illustration of this definition. As Δx gets small, P_2 gets closer to P_1 and $\frac{\Delta y}{\Delta x}$ becomes a better and better approximation of $\frac{dy}{dx}$.

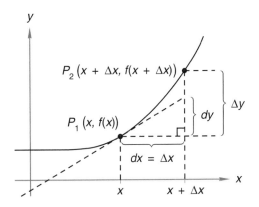

example 29.1   Let $y = 3x^{-2} + 2x^2 + 1$. Find dy.

solution   From the definition of differentials,

$$dy = f'(x)\,dx$$

Therefore

$$dy = (-6x^{-3} + 4x)\,dx$$

example 29.2   Let $y = \sin t + \cos t$. Find dy.

solution   In this example, y is a function of t. We apply the definition of differentials, keeping in mind that t plays the role of x in the definition.

$$dy = f'(t)\,dt$$
$$dy = (\cos t - \sin t)\,dt$$

problem set
29

1. At noon the bacteria colony covered 20 square centimeters. However, the area covered by the
(26) bacteria increased exponentially. If at 2 p.m. the bacteria covered 50 square centimeters, how
much area was covered by the bacteria at 5 p.m.?

Compute dy in problems 2–4.

2. $y = \dfrac{3}{x^2} + 2 \sin x + 2e^x$
(29)

3. $y = 2 \ln |u| - \dfrac{4}{\sqrt{u}}$
(29)

4. $y = \sqrt[3]{t} + 2$
(29)

5. Sketch the graph of $y = \dfrac{(x-3)(x+2)}{x(x-1)(x+1)}$.
(28)

6. Write the equation of the line tangent to the graph of $y = \sqrt{x}$ at $x = 4$.
(27)

7. Graph $y = \sqrt{x}$ and the equation of the tangent line found in problem 6 in the same window
(2) on a graphing calculator. (Set the WINDOW parameters so that only the first quadrant is
displayed.)

Approximate the solutions to problems 8 and 9.

8. Find $\dfrac{d^3 y}{dx^3}\bigg|_{3.5}$ where $y = \sin x$.
(27)

9. Find $\dfrac{du}{dx}\bigg|_{-1.78}$ where $u = 4 \ln |x| + 2e^x - \cos x$.
(26,27)

10. Write the key trigonometric identities; then develop an identity for $\tan(2A)$. If $\tan A = -\frac{1}{4}$,
(12) what is the value of $\tan(2A)$?

11. Solve: $4^{x^2 - 4x + 7} = 64$
(16)

12. Find all values of x such that $0 \le x < \pi$ and $\sin(4x) = -\dfrac{1}{2}$.
(23)

13. Use a graphing calculator to find all the roots of $y = \sin(4x) + \frac{1}{2}$ where $0 \le x < \pi$.
(2) Compare these answers to those found in problem 12.

14. Use a graphing calculator to graph $4y^2 - 9x^2 - 8y + 36x - 68 = 0$. What are the
(23) coordinates of the center of the conic section?

Evaluate the limits in problems 15 and 16.

15. $\displaystyle\lim_{\Delta x \to 0} \dfrac{\ln(x + \Delta x) - \ln x}{\Delta x}$
(28)

16. $\displaystyle\lim_{x \to \infty} \dfrac{2x^3 - x^2 + 1}{1 - 5x^3}$
(17)

17. Sketch the graphs of $y = \dfrac{1}{x}$ and $y = \dfrac{1}{(x-3)^2}$.
(21)

18. (a) Evaluate: $\sin^{-1} \dfrac{1}{2}$
(13)

(b) Solve: $\sin x = \dfrac{1}{2}$ $(0 \le x < 2\pi)$

19. Use two function machines to show how $f(x) = e^{5x^2 + x - 2}$ might be composed.
(18)

20. Sketch the graphs of $y = x^{1/3}$ and $y = x^{2/3}$.
(9)

21. Find the domain and range of $y = 1 + 2 \sin -x$.
(6,8)

22. Approximate the value of x for which $2^x = 5$.
(20)

23. Shown is a function machine f where only a few input and output values are given.
(6)

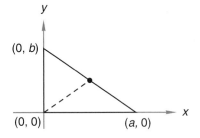

Which of the following could be the equation of f ?

A. $f(x) = 2x$ B. $f(x) = x + \dfrac{3}{2}$ C. $f(x) = 2^x$ D. $f(x) = x^2 + 1$

24. A right triangle is oriented on the Cartesian
(2) plane so that one of its legs coincides with
the x-axis and one of its legs coincides with
the y-axis. The coordinates of all three
vertices are as shown. Find the length of
the hypotenuse and the length of the
median drawn to the hypotenuse which is
shown by the dashed line. How are these
two lengths related?

25. Find the sum of the first 100 positive
(R) integers.

LESSON 30   *Graph of tan θ • Graphs of Reciprocal Functions*

30.A

graph of tan θ   As we have seen, the unit circle is an excellent visual aid for understanding the graphs of the sine function and the cosine function.

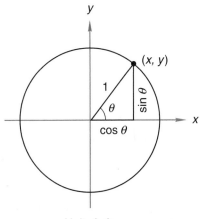

Unit circle

We can look at the unit circle and see that the y-coordinate of any point on the unit circle equals the value of sin θ and the x-coordinate equals the value of cos θ. **The value of tan θ is the value of sin θ divided by cos θ, and this ratio equals the slope of the hypotenuse of the triangle drawn in the**

unit circle. This fact is easy to remember because the slope of a line and the tangent of its angle with the horizontal have the same definition.

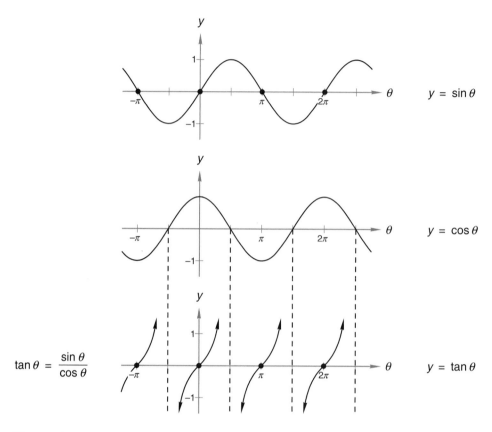

$$\tan \theta = \frac{\sin \theta}{\cos \theta}$$

The graph of $y = \tan \theta$ shown above is drawn directly under the graphs of $y = \sin \theta$ and $y = \cos \theta$. **Note that the graph of $y = \tan \theta$ crosses the x-axis at every point at which $\sin \theta$ equals zero (marked with dots on both graphs) and has a vertical asymptote at every point at which $\cos \theta$ equals zero (indicated by the dashed lines).** We note that the graphs of the sine and cosine functions repeat every 2π radians (360°), so the period of both the sine and cosine functions is 2π radians (360°). **The graph of the tangent function repeats every π radians (180°), so the period of the tangent function is half the period of the sine and cosine functions.**

30.B
graphs of reciprocal functions

If we know the graph of a function f, the graph of the reciprocal function can be sketched by inspection. The equation of the reciprocal function of f is given below.

$$\text{Reciprocal of } f(x) = \frac{1}{f(x)}$$

There are three things that are especially helpful in graphing a reciprocal function.

1. The vertical asymptotes and zeros of the original function change places and become the zeros and vertical asymptotes of the reciprocal function. Thus, the graph of the reciprocal function has a vertical asymptote at every point where the graph of the original function touches or crosses the x-axis, and the graph of the reciprocal function touches or crosses the x-axis at every vertical asymptote of the original function.

2. The points where the y-coordinate is +1 or −1 appear on both graphs. For example, if the points (4, 1) and (7, −1) are on the graph of the original function, then the same points are on the graph of the reciprocal function.

3. When the value of the original function is a large positive (negative) number, the value of the reciprocal function is a small positive (negative) number. When the value of the original function is a small positive (negative) number, the value of the reciprocal function is a large positive (negative) number.

example 30.1   Use the graph of $y = \sin x$ to sketch the graph of $y = \csc x$.

solution   The cosecant function is the reciprocal of the sine function. We sketch the graph of $y = \sin x$ on the left and draw dashed vertical lines where the sine graph crosses the x-axis. These become asymptotes in the graph of $y = \csc x$. We put dots at the points where $\sin x = \pm 1$, because $\csc x$ also passes through these points. That is enough information to sketch the graph of $\csc x$, which we do on the right.

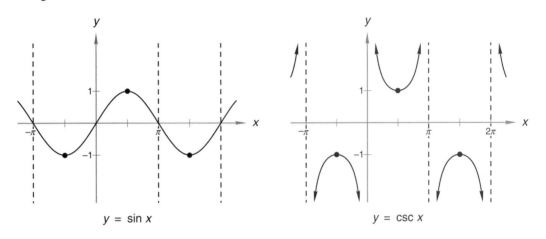

$y = \sin x$ $y = \csc x$

example 30.2   Use the graphs of $y = \cos x$ and $y = \tan x$ to sketch the graphs of $y = \sec x$ and $y = \cot x$.

solution   We sketch the graphs of $y = \cos x$ and $y = \tan x$, drawing dashed vertical lines where these curves cross the x-axis and dots at places where the functions have a value of ± 1. Then we use the asymptotes and the dots to sketch the reciprocal functions. Notice that the asymptotes in $y = \tan x$ become zeros in $y = \cot x$.

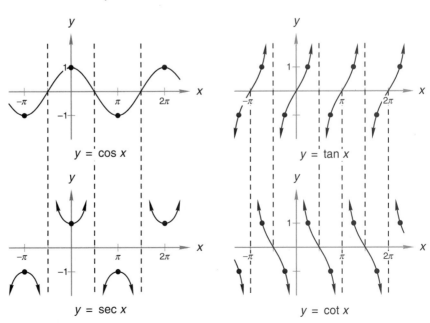

$y = \cos x$ $y = \tan x$

$y = \sec x$ $y = \cot x$

example 30.3   Graph: $y = \csc(\theta + 45°)$

solution   A quick way to graph a cosecant function is to use the graph of the corresponding sine function. On the left-hand side we graph $y = \sin(\theta + 45°)$. On the right-hand side we draw vertical asymptotes at the zeros of the sine function and place dots at the points where $\sin \theta$ has a value of $+1$ or -1. Then we use the asymptotes and dots to help us sketch the cosecant function.

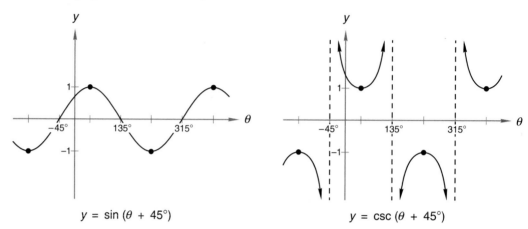

$y = \sin(\theta + 45°)$ $y = \csc(\theta + 45°)$

   (*Note:* Constants that shift the graph vertically should be ignored until the last step. For example, to sketch the graph of $y = 5 + \csc(\theta + 45°)$, we would find the graph of $y = \csc(\theta + 45°)$ and then shift this graph up 5 units.)

example 30.4   Graph: $y = \sec(x - 20°)$

solution   On the left-hand side we graph $y = \cos(x - 20°)$. On the right-hand side we use asymptotes and dots to graph the secant function.

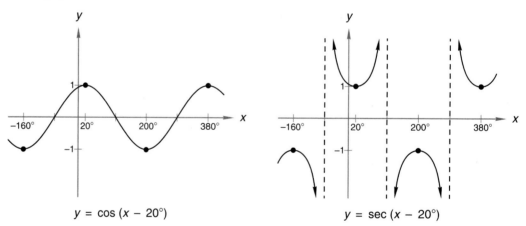

$y = \cos(x - 20°)$ $y = \sec(x - 20°)$

To sketch the graph of $y = A + \sec(x - 20°)$, we would use the graph on the right-hand side and relabel the centerline $y = A$.

example 30.5   Sketch the reciprocal function of the function shown in the figure.

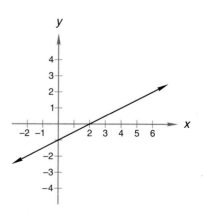

solution   The graph of the reciprocal function has a vertical asymptote at $x = 2$. The function graphed is large and positive when x is large and positive, so the reciprocal function is small and positive when x is large and positive. The original function is large and negative when x is large and negative, so the reciprocal function is small and negative for large negative input values. We remember to place dots on the original graph at y-values of ± 1 and to draw the graph of the reciprocal functions through the dots.

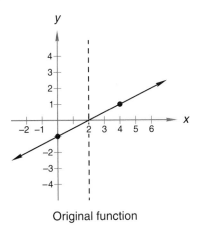

Original function   Reciprocal function

example 30.6   The graph of f is shown. Sketch the graph of the reciprocal function $\frac{1}{f}$.

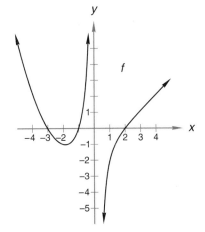

solution   The reciprocal function has vertical asymptotes when $x = -1$, -3, and $+2$. First we draw the asymptotes and place dots at y-values of ± 1. The y-axis is a vertical asymptote of the function, which indicates that the origin is a zero of the reciprocal function. This is enough information to sketch the reciprocal function.

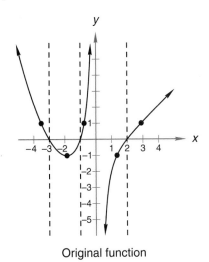

Original function   Reciprocal function

**problem set
30**

1. Dee and Hudson drove M miles per hour for H hours but got to the shore 2 hours late. How fast
(5) should they have driven to have arrived on time? Express the answer in terms of M and H.

2. Let $f(x) = 2x + 1$ and $g(x) = \dfrac{1}{f(x)}$. Sketch f and g on the same coordinate plane.
(30)

3. Sketch the graph of $y = \tan x$ $(-2\pi \le x \le 2\pi)$, clearly indicating all zeros and asymptotes.
(30)

4. Graph the following functions on the same coordinate plane:
(30)

$$y = \sin\left(x - \frac{\pi}{4}\right) \qquad \text{and} \qquad y = \csc\left(x - \frac{\pi}{4}\right)$$

5. For $y = 3 \sin t - \sqrt{2}\,e^t + \dfrac{1}{3}\ln|t|$, write the expression for the differential dy.
(29)

6. Sketch the graph of $y = \dfrac{(x - 3)(x + 2)}{(x + 5)x(x - 2)}$, clearly indicating all zeros and asymptotes.
(28)

7. Find the equation of the line tangent to the graph of $y = \ln x + \sin x$ when $x = 3$.
(27)

8. Approximate $\left.\dfrac{d^5 y}{dx^5}\right|_2$ where $y = 3e^x$.
(27)

Differentiate the functions given in problems 9 and 10.

9. $y = 14 \cos u + \dfrac{e^u}{2} - \ln u$
(26)

10. $y = \sqrt[3]{t^2} - \dfrac{3}{t}$
(25)

11. By inspection write the exact value of $\displaystyle\lim_{h \to 0} \dfrac{e^{(2+h)} - e^2}{h}$. (*Hint:* Recall the definition of the
(28) derivative.)

12. Using a graphing calculator, estimate to one decimal place the value of $y = \frac{e^{(2+x)} - e^2}{x}$ as x
(2) approaches 0. How does this answer compare to the answer of problem 11?

13. Use a graphing calculator to graph $4y^2 + x^2 - 2x - 3 = 0$. What are the coordinates of the
(23) center of the conic section?

14. Let $f(x) = \ln x$ and $g(x) = \sqrt{x + 1}$.
(18)

    (a) Write the equations of $f \circ g$ and $g \circ f$.

    (b) Find the domain and range for both composite functions.

15. Write the key trigonometric identities, and develop an identity for $\cos \dfrac{x}{2}$.
(12)

16. Let $f(x) = x(1 - x)(x + 3)(x + 1)$. Use interval notation to indicate the interval(s) on which
(15) the graph of f lies below the x-axis.

17. Let $f(x) = \ln x$ and $g(x) = e^x$. Graph the functions $y = f(-x)$ and $y = g(-x)$ on the same
(7,12) coordinate plane.

18. Graph the function whose equation is $y = 4 + \sec(\theta - 30°)$.
(30)

19. When the polynomial $f(x)$ is divided by $x - 3$, its remainder is 4. What is the value of $f(3)$?
(10)

20. Shown is the unit circle centered at the
    (7) origin. Find the coordinates of points
    P_1 and P_2.

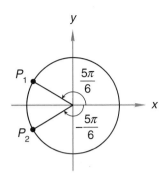

21. Sketch the graph of $y = -|\sin x|$.
    (9)

22. Let $f(x) = 2 + \sin x$ and $g(x) = f\left(x - \dfrac{\pi}{4}\right)$. Sketch the graph of g.
    (21)

23. Use a graphing calculator to solve the following system of equations: $\begin{cases} x^2 + y^2 = 8 \\ y = \ln x \end{cases}$
    (2)

24. Solve for x with the figure shown, given the following: $\begin{cases} AP = x \\ PC = x - 1 \\ BC = x - 2. \end{cases}$
    (R)

    Use the fact that if a tangent and a secant
    are drawn to a circle from a common point
    outside the circle, then the square of the
    length of the tangent segment is equal to
    the product of the length of the secant
    segment and the length of the external
    portion of the secant segment.

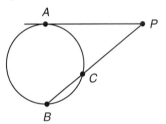

25. Assuming x, y, and z are real numbers, compare the following:
    (1)
    A. the average of x, y, and z   B. $x + y + z$

LESSON 31   *Product Rule • Proof of the Product Rule*

31.A

product rule   The slope of the graph of the sum of two functions is the sum of the slopes of the graphs of the individual functions. We know this because the derivative of a sum of two functions equals the sum of the derivatives of the individual functions.

$$f(x) = 2x + 5 \qquad g(x) = x^2 + 3x \qquad (f + g)(x) = x^2 + 5x + 5$$
$$\text{Slope} = 2 \qquad \text{Slope} = 2x + 3 \qquad \text{Slope} = 2x + 5$$
$$f'(x) = 2 \qquad g'(x) = 2x + 3 \qquad (f + g)'(x) = 2x + 5$$

Unfortunately, the derivative of the product of two functions does not equal the product of the individual derivatives. **The derivative of a product of two functions equals the first function times the derivative of the second, plus the second function times the derivative of the first.** For two functions f and g,

$$(fg)'(x) = f(x)g'(x) + g(x)f'(x)$$

This is called the **product rule** for derivatives. For f and g as defined at the beginning of the lesson,

$$(fg)'(x) = (2x + 5)(2x + 3) + (x^2 + 3x)(2) \qquad \text{substituted}$$
$$= 6x^2 + 22x + 15 \qquad \text{simplified}$$

Using a more common notation, we can call the functions u and v and their derivatives u' and v'. In this case the derivative of a product $y = uv$ is

$$\frac{d}{dx}(uv) = u\frac{dv}{dx} + v\frac{du}{dx}$$

or using the prime notation

$$\boxed{(uv)' = uv' + vu'}$$

This final notation is perhaps the cleanest of all. It shows clearly that if u and v are functions of x, the derivative of the product of u and v is the sum of two quantities. Each quantity has a factor that is one of the functions, and the second factor is the derivative of the other function.

The differential of a product of two functions is the first function times the differential of the second, plus the second function times the differential of the first. Thus, the differential of uv can be written as

$$d(uv) = u\,dv + v\,du$$

A mnemonic for remembering this is:

$$\boxed{\text{first dee second plus second dee first}}$$

example 31.1   Let $y = x^2 \sin x$. Find y'.

solution   The derivative of x^2 is $2x$, and the derivative of $\sin x$ is $\cos x$.

$$\frac{d}{dx}x^2 = 2x \qquad \frac{d}{dx}\sin x = \cos x$$

To find the derivative of the product, we write

$$y' = x^2(\cos x) + (\sin x)(2x) \qquad \text{product rule}$$
$$= \mathbf{x^2 \cos x + 2x \sin x} \qquad \text{rearranged}$$

example 31.2   Let $f(x) = x^2 e^x$. Find $f'(x)$.

solution   We write the first times the derivative of the second, plus the second times the derivative of the first.

$$f'(x) = x^2 e^x + e^x(2x) \qquad \text{product rule}$$
$$= \mathbf{xe^x(x + 2)} \qquad \text{factored}$$

example 31.3   Let $u = \ln x$, $v = 2e^x$, and $y = uv$. Find y'.

solution   This time we remember $(uv)' = uv' + vu'$.

$$y' = (\ln x)2e^x + 2e^x\frac{1}{x} \qquad \text{product rule}$$

$$= \mathbf{2e^x\left(\ln x + \frac{1}{x}\right)} \qquad \text{factored}$$

example 31.4   Let $f(x) = e^x \cos x$. Determine $f'(1.2)$.

solution   First we find $f'(x)$.

$$f'(x) = e^x(-\sin x) + (\cos x)e^x \qquad \text{product rule}$$
$$f'(x) = -e^x \sin x + e^x \cos x \qquad \text{rearranged}$$
$$f'(1.2) = -e^{1.2} \sin (1.2) + e^{1.2} \cos (1.2) \qquad \text{substituted}$$
$$f'(1.2) \approx \mathbf{-1.8914} \qquad \text{used calculator (in radian mode)}$$

We can also compute $f'(1.2)$ by using the TI-83's nDeriv(function (item 8 of the MATH menu.)

$$\text{nDeriv}(e^X \cos(X), X, 1.2)$$

The answer is the same to four decimal places.

The answer also has a graphical interpretation. We can now say that the slope of the graph at the point $(1.2, f(1.2))$ is about -1.8914. The slope of the line tangent to the graph at this point is also approximately -1.8914.

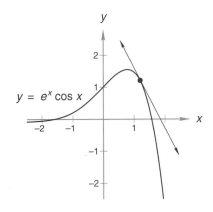

example 31.5   Let $s = x^2 y^3$. Find ds.

solution   The differentials of x^2 and y^3 are

$$d(x^2) = 2x\, dx \qquad \text{and} \qquad d(y^3) = 3y^2\, dy$$

The differential of a product of two functions equals the first function times the differential of the second, plus the second function times the differential of the first. Thus

$$ds = x^2(3y^2\, dy) + y^3(2x\, dx) = 3x^2 y^2\, dy + 2xy^3\, dx$$

example 31.6   If $y = s^2 \sin t,$ what is dy?

solution   The differentials of s^2 and $\sin t$ are

$$d(s^2) = 2s\, ds \qquad \text{and} \qquad d(\sin t) = \cos t\, dt$$

We write the differential of y as the first times the differential of the second, plus the second times the differential of the first.

$$dy = s^2(\cos t\, dt) + (\sin t)(2s\, ds) = s^2 \cos t\, dt + 2s \sin t\, ds$$

31.B
proof of the product rule

If we use the definition of the derivative to write an expression for $f'(x)$ and $g'(x)$, we get

$$f'(x) = \lim_{\Delta x \to 0} \frac{f(x + \Delta x) - f(x)}{\Delta x} \qquad \text{and} \qquad g'(x) = \lim_{\Delta x \to 0} \frac{g(x + \Delta x) - g(x)}{\Delta x}$$

We want to show that the derivative of a product of $f(x)$ and $g(x)$ is $f(x)$ times the derivative of $g(x)$, plus $g(x)$ times the derivative of $f(x)$. This means we want to show that

$$(fg)'(x) = f(x) \lim_{\Delta x \to 0} \left[\frac{g(x + \Delta x) - g(x)}{\Delta x} \right] + g(x) \lim_{\Delta x \to 0} \left[\frac{f(x + \Delta x) - f(x)}{\Delta x} \right]$$

We begin by noting the definition of $(fg)'(x)$.

$$(fg)'(x) = \lim_{\Delta x \to 0} \frac{(fg)(x + \Delta x) - (fg)(x)}{\Delta x}$$

The notation $(fg)(x)$ means $f(x)$ times $g(x)$, and thus we can write

$$(fg)'(x) = \lim_{\Delta x \to 0} \frac{f(x + \Delta x)g(x + \Delta x) - f(x)g(x)}{\Delta x}$$

Next we use an algebraic trick and add $-f(x + \Delta x)g(x) + f(x + \Delta x)g(x)$, which equals zero, to the numerator and regroup the terms to get

$$\lim_{\Delta x \to 0} \frac{f(x + \Delta x)g(x + \Delta x) - f(x + \Delta x)g(x) + f(x + \Delta x)g(x) - f(x)g(x)}{\Delta x}$$

$$= \lim_{\Delta x \to 0} \left[f(x + \Delta x)\left(\frac{g(x + \Delta x) - g(x)}{\Delta x} \right) \right] + \lim_{\Delta x \to 0} \left[g(x) \frac{f(x + \Delta x) - f(x)}{\Delta x} \right]$$

This is exactly what we wanted to show except that we wanted to get $f(x)$ instead of $f(x + \Delta x)$ as the first factor. But the limit of $f(x + \Delta x)$ as Δx approaches zero is $f(x)$. Thus we have

$$(fg)'(x) = f(x) \lim_{\Delta x \to 0} \frac{g(x + \Delta x) - g(x)}{\Delta x} + g(x) \lim_{\Delta x \to 0} \frac{f(x + \Delta x) - f(x)}{\Delta x}$$

This shows that the derivative of $(fg)(x)$ equals $f(x)$ times the derivative of $g(x)$, plus $g(x)$ times the derivative of $f(x)$, which completes the proof.

problem set 31

1. **(5)** Equal-sized squares are cut from the corners of a 10- by 10-inch sheet. The resulting flaps are folded up to form a box with no top. Assuming the lengths of the sides of the squares that are cut away are all x, write an expression for the volume of the box in terms of x.

2. **(26)** The volume was increasing exponentially. One minute after the little bang, the volume was 10 cubic kilometers, and three minutes after the little bang, the volume was 30 cubic kilometers. How many minutes after the little bang would the volume be 60 cubic kilometers?

3. **(31)** Find y' where $y = x^3 e^x$.

4. **(31)** Find $\dfrac{dy}{dt}$ where $y = -3t \cos t$.

5. **(31)** Evaluate $f'(-2)$ for $f(x) = x^2 \ln |x|$.

6. **(31)** Find ds where $s = 2x^2 y$.

7. **(27)** Assuming $s(x) = -\dfrac{1}{\sqrt{x}} + 2 \cos x$, find $s''(x)$.

8. **(27)** Assuming $f(t) = 3 \sin t - \sqrt{2} e^t$, find $f'''(t)$.

9. **(30)** Let $f(x) = x^2 - 1$ and $g(x) = \frac{1}{f(x)}$. Graph the functions f and g on the same coordinate axes. Do not use a calculator.

Graph the functions in problems 10 and 11, clearly indicating all zeros and asymptotes.

10. **(30)** $y = \tan x \ (0 \le x \le 2\pi)$

11. **(28)** $y = \dfrac{x - 1}{x(x + 2)(3 - x)}$

12. **(27)** Find the equation of the line tangent to the graph of $y = \sqrt[3]{x^2}$ at $x = 8$.

13. **(2)** Use a graphing calculator to graph $y = \sqrt[3]{x^2}$ and the line whose equation was found in problem 12. Adjust the WINDOW settings to clearly show both graphs at the point of tangency.

14. **(12)** State an identity for $\tan (A + B)$ in terms of $\tan A$ and $\tan B$. If $\tan A = \frac{1}{2}$ and $\tan B = 4$, what is the value of $\tan (A + B)$?

15. **(8)** The base of this right circular cone has a radius of 3 cm, and the height of the cone is 8 cm. Find the volume of the liquid in the cone if the depth of the liquid is 4 cm.

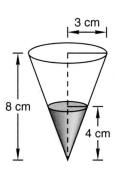

16. Without using a calculator, find all values of x between 0 and 2π for which $\sin(3x) = -\dfrac{\sqrt{2}}{2}$.
(23)

17. Let $f(x) = |x|$. Graph the equation $y = f(x - 1)$.
(21)

18. Use a graphing calculator to graph $4x^2 + y^2 - 2y - 3 = 0$. What are the coordinates of the
(22,23)   center of the conic section?

19. Solve $2 \ln x - \ln\left(x + \dfrac{1}{2}\right) = \ln 2$ for x.
(16)

20. Evaluate: $\displaystyle\lim_{x \to -2} \dfrac{2x^2 + 3x - 2}{x^2 + 4}$
(14)

21. Use the rational roots theorem to find all the real roots of the function $y = x^3 - x^2 + 2x - 2$.
(10)

22. Write the contrapositive of the following statement:
(3)
          If a conditional statement is true, then its contrapositive is also true.

23. Find all integer values of x that satisfy the inequality $|x - 2| > -1$.
(9)

24. Suppose P is a point that lies outside circle O, which has a radius of 3. If the distance from P to
(R)   the center of circle O is 6 and $\overline{PA}$ is tangent to circle O at A, what is the length of $\overline{PA}$? (*Note:* The
      radius drawn to the point where a tangent intersects a circle is perpendicular to the tangent.)

25. Find the sum of the infinite geometric series $1 + \dfrac{1}{3} + \dfrac{1}{9} + \cdots$. Use the fact that
(R)

$$a + ar + ar^2 + \cdots = \dfrac{a}{1 - r}$$

provided $|r| < 1$.

LESSON 32   *An Antiderivative • The Indefinite Integral*

32.A

an antiderivative

Multiplication and division are inverse operations because multiplication undoes division and division undoes multiplication. Differentiating a function produces a second function called the derivative of the original function. The inverse operation of differentiation is the operation of going back to the original function, and this operation is called **antidifferentiation.** Unfortunately, the process of "going back" or antidifferentiating cannot give a unique answer. Antidifferentiation yields a multitude of answers, all of which differ by a constant. To demonstrate, notice that the derivative of each of these three functions is $2x$.

(a) $\dfrac{d}{dx}x^2 = 2x$ (b) $\dfrac{d}{dx}(x^2 + 42) = 2x$ (c) $\dfrac{d}{dx}(x^2 - 165) = 2x$

Each of the original functions contains a constant term. The constant for (a) is zero because x^2 is the same as $x^2 + 0$. The constants on the ends of $x^2 + 42$ and $x^2 - 165$ are $+42$ and -165. Since the derivative of each of these functions is $2x$, we see that $2x$ has many antiderivatives, of which we have shown only three. **No single function is the antiderivative of $2x$, because there are infinitely many functions whose derivatives are $2x$.**

example 32.1   Let $f(x) = 2x$. Find a function F that is an antiderivative of f.

solution   If we differentiate x^2, we get $2x$. We also get $2x$ if we differentiate $x^2 + 157$. To make the point that any constant works, we choose $x^2 - $ **463** as our antiderivative. More generally, an antiderivative of f is $F(x) = x^2 + C$ where C is some number.

32.B

the indefinite integral   **Indefinite integration** is the process of finding the set of all antiderivatives of a given function. We call this set **the indefinite integral.** It is incorrect to speak of **the** antiderivative of a function, because there is more than one, but it is correct to speak of **the** indefinite integral of a function. We use an elongated *S* to indicate the process of finding the indefinite integral of a function, and we call this symbol an **integral symbol.** Thus, we can write the indefinite integral of 2*x* as

$$\int 2x \, dx = x^2 + \text{(any real number)}$$

We use a capital *C* to represent *any real number,* and we call *C* the **constant of integration.**

$$\int 2x \, dx = x^2 + C$$

The *dx* indicates that *x* is the **variable of integration** and that we are integrating with respect to *x*.

The derivative is defined as a limit approached by the value of the following expressions as Δx and *h* approach zero.

$$\frac{d}{dx} f(x) = \lim_{\Delta x \to 0} \frac{f(x + \Delta x) - f(x)}{\Delta x} \qquad \text{or} \qquad \frac{d}{dx} f(x) = \lim_{h \to 0} \frac{f(x + h) - f(x)}{h}$$

There is no corresponding definition of the indefinite integral of a function. Finding the indefinite integral of a function requires the ability to guess the answer based on experience with the derivative and the differential. We check a guess by finding its differential or derivative.

example 32.2   Find $\int \cos x \, dx$.

solution   We remember that the differential of sin *x* is cos *x dx*, so the integral of cos *x dx* is sin *x* + *C*.

$$\int \cos x \, dx = \sin x + C$$

We must check this guess.

$$d(\sin x + C) = d \sin x + d(C) = \cos x \, dx \qquad \text{check}$$

example 32.3   Find $\int -\sin t \, dt$.

solution   The differential of cos *t* is −sin *t dt*. Thus, the integral of −sin *t dt* is cos *t* + *C*.

$$\int -\sin t \, dt = \cos t + C$$

We must check this guess.

$$d(\cos t + C) = d \cos t + d(C) = -\sin t \, dt \qquad \text{check}$$

example 32.4   Find $\int e^x \, dx$.

solution   We guess the answer, knowing that the differential of e^x is $e^x \, dx$.

$$\int e^x \, dx = e^x + C$$

We must check this guess.

$$d(e^x + C) = de^x + d(C) = e^x \, dx \qquad \text{check}$$

example 32.5   Let $\dfrac{dy}{dx} = \cos x$. Find *y*.

solution   The derivative of *y* with respect to *x* equals cos *x*. Thus, *y* must equal some antiderivative of cos *x*.

$$y = \int \cos x \, dx = \sin x + C$$

We must check this guess.

$$\frac{d}{dx}(\sin x + C) = \cos x \qquad \text{check}$$

problem set 32

1. If the volume of a sphere doubles, what is the ratio of the surface area of the new, larger sphere to the old, smaller sphere?
(5)

2. A ladder that is 12 feet long leans so that it just touches the top of a 4-foot-tall brick wall and then rests against the side of a vertical wall beyond the brick wall. The brick wall is 4 feet from the wall beyond it. (See the diagram.)
(5)

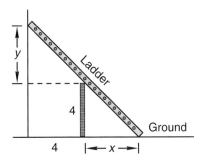

(a) Use the Pythagorean theorem to write an equation that relates the sides of the large triangle.

(b) Use the fact that the two smaller triangles are similar to write a proportion involving x and y.

Find an antiderivative of each expression in problems 3 and 4 with respect to the variable in the problem.

3. $5x^4$
(32)

4. $3t^2$
(32)

Antidifferentiate in problems 5–7.

5. $\displaystyle\int \cos x \, dx$
(32)

6. $\displaystyle\int e^t \, dt$
(32)

7. $\displaystyle\int -\sin x \, dx$
(32)

8. If $\dfrac{dy}{dx} = \dfrac{1}{x}$, find y.
(32)

9. Let $u = x^2 y$. Find du.
(31)

10. Let $f(x) = e^x$, $g(x) = \sin x$, and $h(x) = f(x)g(x)$. Find $h'(x)$.
(31)

11. Let $y = x \ln x$. Evaluate: $\left.\dfrac{dy}{dx}\right|_{2.5}$
(27,31)

12. Let $f(x) = x^2 + x - 2$ and $g(x) = \dfrac{1}{f(x)}$. Graph f and g on the same coordinate plane.
(30)

13. Sketch the graph of $y = \dfrac{x}{(x-2)(x+3)}$, clearly indicating all zeros and asymptotes.
(28)

14. Let $y = 2\sqrt[4]{x^3} - \dfrac{4}{x}$. Find $\dfrac{dy}{dx}$.
(25)

15. Use a graphing calculator to graph $x^2 - y^2 + 2y - 5 = 0$. What are the coordinates of the center of the conic section?
(22,23)

16. Develop identities for both $\sin \dfrac{x}{2}$ and $\cos \dfrac{x}{2}$.
(12)

17. Evaluate: $\displaystyle\lim_{x \to \infty} \dfrac{3x^3 - 5}{1 - x^2}$
(17)

18. A polynomial $f(x)$ is divided by $x - 3$, and the remainder is 5. What is the value of $f(3)$?
(10)

19. Let $f(x) = \begin{cases} \cos x & \text{if } x > 0 \\ \sin x & \text{if } x \leq 0. \end{cases}$ Graph f and evaluate $\lim_{x \to 0^+} f(x)$ and $\lim_{x \to 0^-} f(x)$.
(11)

20. Find the values of x for which $|x - 1| < 0.4$.
(9)

21. If A is a number such that $\sin A = \dfrac{1}{3}$ and $\cos A$ is positive, what is the exact value of $\cos A$?
(4)

22. If A is as defined in problem 21, what is the exact value of $(\sin -A)\left[\cos\left(\dfrac{\pi}{2} - A\right)\right](\cos A)$?
(8)

23. Find the real values of x for which $2 \log_2 x + \log_2 9 = 1$.
(16)

24. A square is oriented in the coordinate plane
(R) so that two of its sides lie on the coordinate axes. The length of each side is a, as shown in the figure. Find the slopes of the diagonals of the square. How are the slopes of the two diagonals related? What does this indicate?

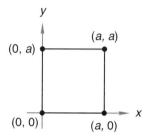

25. Find the sum of all the terms of the geometric sequence whose terms are the members of the set
(R) $\left\{1, \frac{1}{2}, \frac{1}{4}, \frac{1}{8}, \dots\right\}$.

LESSON 33 *Factors of Polynomial Functions • Graphs of Polynomial Functions*

33.A

factors of polynomial functions

Lesson 28 considered the graphs of rational polynomial functions. In this lesson we perform a more detailed investigation of the factors of polynomials and take a closer look at the graphs of second-, third-, and fourth-degree polynomial equations.

A polynomial is called a **real polynomial** if all its coefficients are real numbers. The **degree** of a polynomial is the value of its greatest exponent. For example, $f(x) = x^{15} + 19x^{12} - \pi x^5$ is a real polynomial of degree 15. The term of highest degree in a polynomial is the dominant term because, for large absolute values of x, the value of the highest-degree term is greater than the absolute value of the sum of all the other terms in the equation. The greater the absolute value of x, the greater the dominance of the highest-degree term. **Thus the behavior of the polynomial for large absolute values of x can be determined by looking at both the exponent of the highest-degree term and the sign of the coefficient of this term.**

The function $g(x) = x^2 + 4$ is called an **irreducible** quadratic because it cannot be factored. This function can never equal zero, because $x^2 + 4$ is a positive real number for all real number values of x. **Thus irreducible quadratic factors never cause a polynomial to equal zero.**

Any polynomial can be written as a product of real linear factors and irreducible quadratic factors. **The graph of a polynomial crosses the x-axis when a real linear factor occurs an odd number of times and touches but does not cross the x-axis when a real linear factor occurs an even number of times.**

Consider $h(x) = (x - 1)(x - 3)^2$. When $x = 1$, the $(x - 1)$ factor equals zero, and the graph of h crosses the x-axis at $x = 1$. When $x = 3$, the $(x - 3)^2$ factor equals zero, and the graph touches but does not cross the x-axis when $x = 3$, because the value of $(x - 3)^2$ never changes sign. If this expression does not equal zero, it equals some positive number. This would also be true if the exponent of $(x - 3)$ were 4, 6, 8, or any even number. The graph of h for $0 \leq x \leq 10$ is shown below:

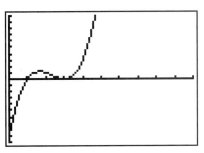

example 33.1   If $f(x) = (x + 4)(x + 2)^4(x^2 + 3)(x - 5)^3(x - 7)^2$, at what values of x does the graph of f touch the x-axis, and at what values of x does the graph cross the x-axis?

solution   The irreducible quadratic factor $x^2 + 3$ can never equal zero and can never cause the graph to touch the x-axis. One of the linear factors equals zero when $x = -4$; one of the linear factors equals zero when $x = -2$; one of the linear factors equals zero when $x = 5$; and another equals zero when $x = 7$. Thus the graph touches the x-axis at x-values of **−4, −2, 5,** and **7.** It only crosses the x-axis at zeros caused by linear factors that have an odd exponent, so the graph crosses the x-axis when x equals **−4** or **+5.** The graph touches but does not cross the x-axis when x equals 7 or −2, because the factors $(x - 7)$ and $(x + 2)$ occur an even number of times.

example 33.2   Which of the following graphs most resembles the graph of $y = (x - 1)^2(x + 2)^2$?

A.   B.

C.   D.

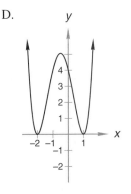

solution   The graph of the given equation must touch the x-axis at the zeros of the linear real factors. Thus the graph must touch the x-axis at x-values of +1 and −2. This eliminates A. and C. In the equation, both linear factors are squared, so the graph does not cross the x-axis at either +1 or −2. This eliminates B. Graph **D.** touches but does not cross the x-axis at +1 and −2, so this graph would most resemble the graph of the function.

33.B
graphs of polynomial functions

The discussion of factors of polynomials gives us some insight into the behavior of graphs of polynomial functions but is not of great value in graphing higher-order polynomial functions because of the great difficulty usually encountered in trying to find the factors.

Graphs of polynomial functions are smooth continuous curves that have no holes, no breaks, and no sharp points. **The turning point theorem tells us that the graph of a polynomial function has fewer turning points than the degree of the polynomial.** Thus the graph of a third-degree polynomial function has at most two turning points, the graph of a fourth-degree polynomial function has at most three turning points, and so on. Below we show the graphs of one second-, one third-, and one fourth-degree polynomial equation. Note the number of turning points in each graph.

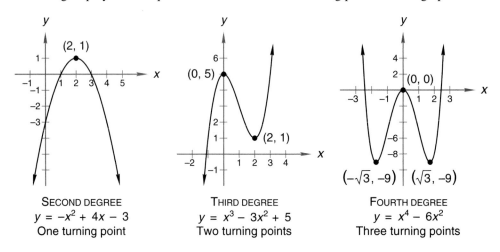

SECOND DEGREE
$y = -x^2 + 4x - 3$
One turning point

THIRD DEGREE
$y = x^3 - 3x^2 + 5$
Two turning points

FOURTH DEGREE
$y = x^4 - 6x^2$
Three turning points

example 33.3 Which of the following functions is most likely to produce this graph?

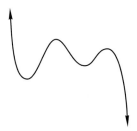

$$f(x) = x^7 - 4x^5 + 3x - 2$$
$$g(x) = -x^6 - 5x + 2$$
$$h(x) = -x^5 + 10x^4 - 35x^3 + 50x^2 - 24x$$

solution We know that $g(x) = -x^6 - 5x + 2$ is incorrect. Its dominant term $(-x^6)$ is negative for large absolute values of x. This means that both "ends" of the graph of g must point down. The graph in question has one end going up. The answer cannot be f either. The dominant term in $f(x)$ is x^7. If x is large and positive, then x^7 is also large and positive, so the right "end" of the graph of f goes up. Our graph goes down as x gets large and positive, so the answer must be $h(x) = -x^5 + 10x^4 - 35x^3 + 50x^2 - 24x$. Notice that it has the proper tendencies for large positive and negative values of x. It also has an acceptable number of turning points.

When we look at the equations of polynomial functions, it is nice to have some idea of what the graph of the function could look like. The general cubic equation has the form

$$f(x) = ax^3 + bx^2 + cx + d$$

The graph of a cubic function can have an inflection point only, or it can have an inflection point and two turning points. If the x^3 term has a positive coefficient (i.e., if a is a positive number), the graph has one of the two forms shown on the left-hand side below. If the x^3 term has a negative coefficient (i.e., if a is a negative number), the graphs are flipped upside down as shown on the right-hand side.

The shape of a graph is determined by the values of the coefficients a, b, and c. The vertical position of the graph can be changed by changing the value of d. In fact, d is the y-intercept of the graph of f.

The general equation of a quartic function is

$$y = ax^4 + bx^3 + cx^2 + dx + e$$

The first term is the dominant term, and the value of x^4 is a positive number for any value of x. If a is a positive number, the graph "opens up," as in these graphs.

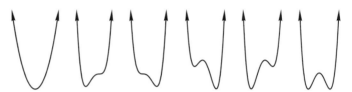

If the coefficient a of the first term is a negative number, the graph has one of the forms shown below.

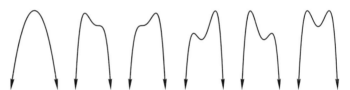

The graph of a quartic function can resemble the graph of a quadratic function. It can have one turning point and one inflection point. The graph can also have three turning points. The shape of the graph is determined by the values of the coefficients a, b, c, and d, and the vertical position of the graph is determined by the value of the constant e.

An in-depth study of polynomial functions reveals several interesting but seldom discussed properties of polynomials. The general form of an nth-degree polynomial function is

$$f(x) = ax^n + bx^{n-1} + cx^{n-2} + \cdots + k$$

The sum of all the roots is $-\frac{b}{a}$. The product of all the roots is $\frac{k}{a}$ if the degree of the polynomial is even; the product is $-\frac{k}{a}$ if the degree of the polynomial is odd. The average value of all the roots is given by

$$\bar{x} = -\frac{b}{na}$$

For a quadratic polynomial, $\bar{x}$ (read "x bar") equals the x-value of the vertex. For a cubic polynomial, $\bar{x}$ equals the x-value of the inflection point. For a quartic polynomial, the value of $\bar{x}$ gives us a good idea of the x-value of the "center" of the graph.

example 33.4   Sketch the graph of $y = -x^3 + 3x^2 - 2x + 3$.

solution   Every cubic polynomial has at least one real root, so the graph of every cubic polynomial function crosses the x-axis somewhere. We just need a rough sketch, so we do not search for this root. The x-value of the inflection point is $-\frac{b}{3a}$, which equals $\frac{3}{3}$, or 1. If we let x equal 1, we can solve for y.

$$y = -(1)^3 + 3(1)^2 - 2(1) + 3 = 3$$

Thus the inflection point is (1, 3). The coefficient of x^3 tells us the curve goes down on the right and up on the left.

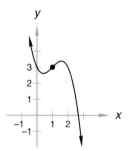 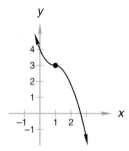

Since the y-intercept of this function, 3, is level with the inflection point, we can be certain that the left-hand graphic is more reasonable. In a later lesson we discuss how to use the derivative to discover which form the graph has and how to find the x-values of the turning points if the graph has turning points.

**problem set
33**

1. A right triangle is inscribed in a unit circle
(2,7)   as shown. Find the area of the triangle in
terms of y.

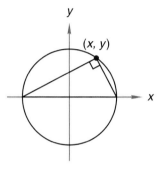

2. The intensity of the questioning increased exponentially. If the intensity was 10 at noon and 20
(26)   one hour later, what was the intensity of the questioning at 5 p.m.?

3. Sketch the graph of $y = (x - 1)(x + 1)^2$. Clearly show places where the graph either crosses
(33)   or touches the x-axis.

4. Use your knowledge of polynomials to make a rough sketch of the possible shapes of the graph
(33)   of $y = 3x^3 + ax^2 + bx + c$, where a, b, and c are unknown constants.

5. Which of the following could be the graph of $y = -x(x - 2)^2$?
(33)

A.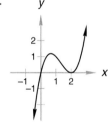

B.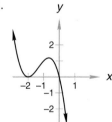

C.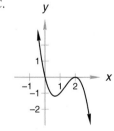

D.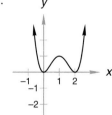

6. Find: $\int \cos u \, du$
(32)

7. Find a function that satisfies $\dfrac{dy}{dx} = e^x$.
(32)

8. Let $y = \sin x \cos x$. Find $\dfrac{dy}{dx}$.
(31)

9. Let $f(t) = 3e^t \cos t$. Approximate $f'(6)$.
(31)

10. Graph the following equations on the same coordinate plane:
(30)

$$y = \cos\left(x - \frac{\pi}{4}\right) \qquad \text{and} \qquad y = \sec\left(x - \frac{\pi}{4}\right)$$

11. Let $y = 2e^x - \ln u + 4 \sin t$. Find the differential dy.
(29)

12. Write the equation of the line tangent to the graph of $y = \sin x$ at $x = 16.3$.
(27)

13. Let $f(x) = 2 \sin x$. Find $f'(x)$, $f''(x)$, and $f'''(x)$.
(26,27)

14. (a) Use a graphing calculator to graph the top half of $(x + 4)^2 + (y + 4)^2 = 12^2$.
(23)

     (b) In the same window, graph $y = \frac{16}{x}$. (Do not be concerned if the portion of the graph in the third quadrant is only partially shown.)

     (c) Find the coordinates of the point(s) of intersection of the two graphs in the first quadrant.

15. Evaluate: $\displaystyle\lim_{h \to 0} \dfrac{e^{e+h} - e^e}{h}$
(28)

16. Use a calculator to approximate the value of $\log_3 10$.
(20)

17. Develop an identity for $\tan (2A)$.
(12)

18. Solve the following equation for x: $y = \arcsin x$.
(13)

19. Let $f(x) = 2 \sin x$ and $g(x) = |x|$. Graph h where $h(x) = g(f(x))$.
(9,18)

20. Show that $1 + 2(\sin -x)\left[\cos\left(\dfrac{\pi}{2} - x\right)\right] = \cos (2x)$.
(8)

21. Find all values of x between 0 and 2π that satisfy the equation $\cos (3x) = \dfrac{1}{2}$.
(23)

22. Evaluate: $\displaystyle\lim_{x \to 1} \dfrac{x^2 - 1}{x^2 + 2x - 3}$
(14)

23. (a) Find the minimum distance between the point (2, 3) and the line $5y = 12x + 4$.
(2,22)
     (*Hint:* See problem 23 in Problem Set 5.)

     (b) Write the equation of the circle that has the point (2, 3) as its center and is tangent to the line $5y = 12x + 4$.

24. Find the number of ways six different colored balls can be arranged in a row.
(R)

25. A fair coin is flipped and comes up tails eight times in a row. If the same coin is flipped a ninth time, what is the probability that it will come up tails again?
(R)

LESSON 34 *Implicit Differentiation*

An equation that defines y as a function of x is written in explicit form when it is in the "y equals" form with a single y on one side of the equals sign and no y's on the other side. Any other form of the equation is an implicit form. Below we show implicit and explicit forms of the same equation.

IMPLICIT   EXPLICIT

$$xy + 1 = 2x - y \qquad y = \frac{2x - 1}{x + 1}$$

We can use a method called **implicit differentiation** to find $\frac{dy}{dx}$ when y is defined implicitly. This procedure is useful because some equations cannot be written in explicit form. The equation $x^2 + y^2 = 25$ is the equation of a circle. This equation does not describe y as a function of x because there are two values of y for every value of x on the open interval $(-5, 5)$.

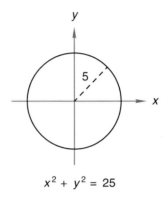

$$x^2 + y^2 = 25$$

While the equation of the circle does not define a function, implicit differentiation permits us to find the slope of the graph of the curve at any point on the graph.

Explicit differentiation always results in an expression for the derivative that contains only constants and the variable x. The derivatives found by using implicit differentiation often contain constants and both x and y. This outcome is not unwelcome, because it permits us to write expressions for the slopes of curves that are not graphs of functions. If the equation is not a function, the expression for the slope contains the y-variable so that the slope of the graph is defined at every point.

We will use differentials to begin our investigation of the derivatives of implicitly defined functions. The first step is always the same. We find the differential of each term. Then, if we want to find the derivative with respect to x, we divide each term of the differential expression by dx. If we want to find the derivative with respect to y, we divide each term by dy. Often we encounter problems in which both variables are functions of time. To find the derivatives with respect to time in these problems, we divide each term by dt.

example 34.1 Let $xy + 1 = 2x - y$. Find $\dfrac{dy}{dx}$.

solution We must use implicit differentiation. To do this, we always follow three steps. **The first step is always the same. We find the differential of every term on both sides of the equation.** We remember to use the product rule to find the differential of xy.

$$x\,dy + y\,dx + 0 = 2\,dx - dy \qquad \text{differentials}$$

Since we want to find the derivative with respect to x, the second step is to divide every term by dx.

$$x \frac{dy}{dx} + y \frac{dx}{dx} = 2 \frac{dx}{dx} - \frac{dy}{dx} \qquad \text{divided by } dx$$

The third step is to solve algebraically for $\frac{dy}{dx}$.

$$x \frac{dy}{dx} + y = 2 - \frac{dy}{dx} \qquad \frac{dx}{dx} \text{ simplifies to 1}$$

$$x \frac{dy}{dx} + \frac{dy}{dx} = 2 - y \qquad \text{rearranged}$$

$$\frac{dy}{dx}(x + 1) = 2 - y \qquad \text{factored}$$

$$\frac{dy}{dx} = \frac{2 - y}{x + 1} \qquad \text{divided by } x + 1$$

example 34.2 Given that $y^2 - xy = \sin x$ and that both x and y are functions of time, find:

(a) $\dfrac{dy}{dx}$ (b) $\dfrac{dx}{dy}$ (c) $\dfrac{dy}{dt}$

solution **The first step is always the same.** We find the differential of every term on both sides of the equation.

$$2y \, dy - x \, dy - y \, dx = \cos x \, dx$$

(a) To find $\dfrac{dy}{dx}$, we divide every term by dx and solve for $\dfrac{dy}{dx}$.

$$2y \frac{dy}{dx} - x \frac{dy}{dx} - y = \cos x \qquad \text{divided by } dx$$

$$\frac{dy}{dx}(2y - x) = y + \cos x \qquad \text{rearranged}$$

$$\frac{dy}{dx} = \frac{y + \cos x}{2y - x} \qquad \text{divided}$$

(b) To find $\dfrac{dx}{dy}$, we divide every term by dy and solve for $\dfrac{dx}{dy}$.

$$2y - x - y \frac{dx}{dy} = \cos x \frac{dx}{dy} \qquad \text{divided by } dy$$

$$\frac{dx}{dy}(y + \cos x) = 2y - x \qquad \text{rearranged}$$

$$\frac{dx}{dy} = \frac{2y - x}{y + \cos x} \qquad \text{divided}$$

We see that the expressions for $\dfrac{dy}{dx}$ and $\dfrac{dx}{dy}$ are reciprocals.

(c) To find $\dfrac{dy}{dt}$, we divide every term by dt and solve for $\dfrac{dy}{dt}$.

$$2y \frac{dy}{dt} - x \frac{dy}{dt} - y \frac{dx}{dt} = \cos x \frac{dx}{dt} \qquad \text{divided by } dt$$

$$\frac{dy}{dt}(2y - x) = \frac{dx}{dt}(y + \cos x) \qquad \text{rearranged}$$

$$\frac{dy}{dt} = \frac{y + \cos x}{2y - x} \frac{dx}{dt} \qquad \text{divided}$$

example 34.3   If $x^2y - ye^x = \cos x$, what is $\dfrac{dy}{dx}$?

solution   First we find the differential of each term on both sides of the equation.

$$x^2\,dy + y(2x\,dx) - y(e^x\,dx) - e^x\,dy = -\sin x\,dx \qquad \text{differentials}$$

Next we divide each term by dx.

$$x^2\frac{dy}{dx} + 2xy - ye^x - e^x\frac{dy}{dx} = -\sin x \qquad \text{divided by } dx$$

Then we solve for $\dfrac{dy}{dx}$.

$$\frac{dy}{dx}(x^2 - e^x) = -\sin x - 2xy + ye^x \qquad \text{rearranged}$$

$$\frac{dy}{dx} = \frac{-\sin x - 2xy + ye^x}{x^2 - e^x} \qquad \text{divided}$$

example 34.4   Find the slope of the line tangent to the graph of $x^2 + y^2 = 2$ at $(1, 1)$.

solution   First we find the differential of every term on both sides of the equation.

$$2x\,dx + 2y\,dy = 0 \qquad \text{differentials}$$

Then we divide each term by dx and solve for $\dfrac{dy}{dx}$.

$$2x + 2y\frac{dy}{dx} = 0 \qquad \text{divided}$$

$$2y\frac{dy}{dx} = -2x \qquad \text{rearranged}$$

$$\frac{dy}{dx} = -\frac{x}{y} \qquad \text{divided}$$

To evaluate the slope, we substitute 1 for x and 1 for y.

$$\frac{dy}{dx} = -\frac{1}{1} = -1 \qquad \text{evaluated}$$

The slope of the tangent at $(1, 1)$ is -1. We can see this from the graph as well.

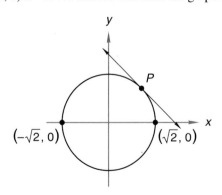

Both the x- and y-coordinate of point P had to be specified to compute the slope of the tangent line through P, because there is more than one point on the graph associated with its x-value.

example 34.5   Find the point(s) on the graph of $x^2 + y^2 = 2$ where:

(a) the tangent line is horizontal.   (b) the tangent line is vertical.

solution   (a) The tangent line is horizontal when its slope is 0.

$$\frac{dy}{dx} = -\frac{x}{y} = 0 \quad \longrightarrow \quad x = 0$$

Therefore, the points associated with $x = 0$ have tangent lines that are horizontal. If $x = 0$, then

$$0^2 + y^2 = 2$$
$$y^2 = 2$$
$$y = \pm\sqrt{2}$$

Thus, there are two points, $(0, -\sqrt{2})$ and $(0, \sqrt{2})$, where the tangent line is horizontal.

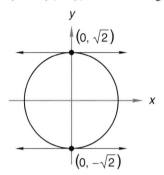

(b) Vertical tangent lines occur where the slope is undefined. In this case, the slope is undefined only when we divide by 0. So $y = 0$ gives the desired points.

$$x^2 + 0^2 = 2$$
$$x^2 = 2$$
$$x = \pm\sqrt{2}$$

The points $(0, -\sqrt{2})$ and $(0, \sqrt{2})$ are the points with vertical tangent lines.

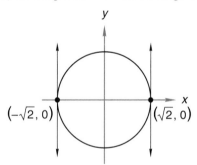

example 34.6   Given that x and y are both functions of time and $x^2 + y^2 = 2$, find:

(a) $\dfrac{dx}{dt}$

(b) $\dfrac{dx}{dt}$ at $(1, 1)$ when $\dfrac{dy}{dt} = 7$

solution   (a) First we find the differential of every term on both sides of the equation.

$$2x \, dx + 2y \, dy = 0 \qquad \text{differentials}$$

Next we divide each term by dt and solve for $\dfrac{dx}{dt}$.

$$2x\frac{dx}{dt} + 2y\frac{dy}{dt} = 0 \qquad \text{divided by } dt$$

$$\frac{dx}{dt} = -\frac{y}{x}\frac{dy}{dt} \qquad \text{solved}$$

(b) To find $\dfrac{dx}{dt}$ at $(1, 1)$ when $\dfrac{dy}{dt} = 7$, we substitute for x, y, and $\dfrac{dy}{dt}$.

$$\frac{dx}{dt} = -\frac{1}{1}(7) = -7$$

**problem set
34**

1. A ladder that is 12 feet long leans so that it just touches the top of a 4-foot-tall brick wall and
(8) then rests against the side of a vertical wall beyond the brick wall. The brick wall is 4 feet from
the wall beyond it. (See the diagram in problem 2 in Problem Set 32.)

   (a) Use the Pythagorean theorem to write an equation that relates the sides of the large triangle.

   (b) Use the fact that the two smaller right triangles are similar to write a proportion involving
   x and y.

   (c) Use a graphing calculator to graph the equations from (a) and (b), and find any first quadrant
   intersection points.

2. If $y^3 - xy - 1 = x^2 + y^2$, what is $\dfrac{dy}{dx}$?
(34)

3. Let x and y be functions of time. Find $\dfrac{dx}{dt}$ where $y^2 - x^2 = \cos x$.
(34)

4. Find the slope of the line that can be drawn tangent to the graph of the equation $x^2 + y^2 = 1$ at
(34) the point $\left(-\dfrac{\sqrt{2}}{2}, \dfrac{\sqrt{2}}{2}\right)$.

5. Sketch the graph of $y = x(x - 1)^2(x + 2)^3$. Clearly indicate where the graph touches or
(33) intersects the x-axis.

6. Use your knowledge of the graphs of polynomial functions to make a rough sketch of the graph
(33) of $y = -2x^3 + x^2 - 5x + 2$.

7. Let $f(x) = 3x^2$. Find a function F such that $F'(x) = f(x)$.
(32)

Integrate in problems 8–10.

8. $\displaystyle\int 5x^4\,dx$ 9. $\displaystyle\int e^t\,dt$ 10. $\displaystyle\int -\sin u\,du$
(32)   (32)   (32)

11. Let $y = x^3 \cos x$. Find y'.
(31)

12. Let $s = -3u^2v$. Find ds.
(31)

13. Find $\dfrac{dy}{dx}$ for $y = 2 \ln x + 4\sqrt[3]{x^2} - \dfrac{e^x}{3}$.
(26)

14. Find $s''(t)$ where $s(t) = s_0 + v_0 t + \dfrac{1}{2}gt^2$ and s_0, v_0, and g are constants.
(27)

15. Let $f(x) = x^2 - 2x - 1$ and $g(x) = \dfrac{1}{f(x)}$. Graph f and g on the same coordinate plane.
(30)

16. Sketch the graph of $y = \dfrac{(2 - x)(x + 1)}{(x - 1)(x + 3)x}$. Clearly indicate all asymptotes and zeros.
(28)

17. Suppose that $f(x)$ is a polynomial such that $\dfrac{f(x)}{x - 3} = x^3 + 2x + 2 + \dfrac{4}{x - 3}$. What is $f(3)$?
(10)

18. Let $f(x) = \sin x$ and $g(x) = f(2x)$. Graph g.
(7)

19. Use a graphing calculator to estimate $\displaystyle\lim_{x \to 0}\left[x^2 \sin\left(\dfrac{1}{x}\right)\right]$.
(14)

20. Solve $y = e^x$ for x.
(9)

21. Simplify: $(\sin -x)\left[\cos\left(\dfrac{\pi}{2} - x\right)\right]\left[\sec^2\left(\dfrac{\pi}{2} - -x\right)\right]$
(8)

22. Express the equation $y = \log_2 x$ entirely in terms of natural logarithms.
(20)

23. Use a graphing calculator to graph $y^2 - 4x^2 - 16 = 0$. What are the coordinates of the
(22,23)   vertices of the conic section?

24. How many distinguishable ways can 4 identical red balls and 3 identical green balls be arranged
(R)   in a row?

25. Let $m\widehat{AB} = x$ and $m\widehat{CD} = y$. Express
(R) $m\angle D$ and $m\angle B$ in terms of x and y. Then
express $m\angle CED$ in terms of $m\angle B$ and
$m\angle D$. Finally, express $m\angle CED$ in terms
of x and y. (*Hint:* The measure of an angle
inscribed in a circle is half the measure of
the subtended arc, and an exterior angle of
a triangle equals the sum of the remote
interior angles of the triangle.)

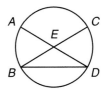

LESSON 35   *Integral of a Constant • Integral of kf(x) • Integral of x^n*

35.A
integral of a constant

The derivative of $5x$ is 5, and the differential of $5x$ is $5\,dx$.

$$\text{If } y = 5x, \text{ then } \frac{dy}{dx} = 5 \text{ and } dy = 5\,dx.$$

We can perform the inverse operation, antidifferentiation, as follows:

$$\int 5\,dx = 5x + C$$

The elongated S, $\int$, is called an integral symbol. The expression $\int 5\,dx$ is referred to as an indefinite
integral. Some may wonder why we do not call $\int$ an antidifferentiation symbol. We could do so;
however, by convention the symbol is called an integration symbol. The reason for this convention
will become apparent in a later lesson, where we show a remarkable connection between the process
of antidifferentiation and a process called *definite integration.* In this lesson and in succeeding
lessons, we use the terms integration, indefinite integration, and antidifferentiation interchangeably.

The expression $\int 5\,dx$ asks for the set of functions dependent upon x whose derivatives are 5.
The dx tells us quite plainly that x is the variable of integration. Sometimes the variable of integration
is t, v, or u and the presence of dt, du, or dv makes this clear.

$$\int dt = t + C \qquad \int 5\,dv = 5v + C \qquad \int 7\,du = 7u + C$$

We can generalize these examples into a rule for finding the integral of a constant. If k is a
constant, then

$$\boxed{\int k\,dx = kx + C}$$

where C is a constant of integration.

35.B

integral of
kf(x)

The derivative of a constant times a function is the constant times the derivative of the function. This means that a constant factor of a function can be moved across the operator $\frac{d}{dx}$. On the left-hand side below, we have the derivative of 4 times x^2. On the right-hand side, we have moved the 4 across the operator $\frac{d}{dx}$, so that the 4 is in front.

$$\frac{d}{dx}4x^2 = 4\frac{d}{dx}x^2$$

Now we find that the derivative of x^2 is $2x$; we multiply this result by 4.

$$4\frac{d}{dx}x^2 = 4(2x)$$

To undo what we have done requires antidifferentiation.

$$\int 4(2x)\,dx$$

The operator for antidifferentiation is the integral sign, and we can move the 4 across the integral sign to get

$$4\int 2x\,dx$$

We could have moved the 2 outside the integral symbol as well, but we know that an antiderivative of $2x$ is x^2. Recognition of when to move a constant comes with experience. Now we antidifferentiate and remember to write the C.

$$4(x^2 + C) = 4x^2 + 4C$$

But C is a symbol that we use to represent any number. Thus $4C$ is 4 times any number, which also can equal any number, so the 4 is not necessary. Thus, we do not multiply the constant of integration by 4 but instead write

$$4\int 2x\,dx = \mathbf{4x^2 + C}$$

The example above can be stated more generally. If k is a constant and f is a function of x, then

$$\boxed{\int kf(x)\,dx = k\int f(x)\,dx}$$

However, we provide the following caution:

> Be careful never to move a variable across the integral sign.

example 35.1   Find: $\int 4\cos t\,dt$

solution   We move the 4 across the integral sign.

$$\int 4\cos t\,dt = 4\int \cos t\,dt = \mathbf{4\sin t + C}$$

Now we check the answer by finding the differential.

$$d(4\sin t + C) = 4\cos t\,dt \qquad \text{check}$$

example 35.2   Find: $\int \sin u\,du$

solution   The ability to move a constant across the integral sign is quite helpful here. We know that the derivative of $\cos u$ is $-\sin u$, but we have $+\sin u$. The trick is to multiply $\sin u$ by $(-1)(-1)$ and move one -1 across the integral sign, as shown.

$$\int (-1)(-1)\sin u\,du = -\int (-\sin u)\,du = -(\cos u) + C = \mathbf{-\cos u + C}$$

Now we check the answer by finding the differential.

$$d(-\cos u + C) = -(-\sin u)\, du = \sin u\, du \qquad \text{check}$$

35.C
integral of x^n

The derivative of x^n with respect to x is nx^{n-1}. Thus, the derivative of x^4 with respect to x is $4x^3$. To antidifferentiate $4x^3$, we must get back to x^4.

$$\int 4x^3\, dx = x^4 + C$$

To do this, we must develop a procedure to get rid of the 4 in front and to change the exponent from 3 to 4. To get rid of the 4 in front, we can divide by $3 + 1$, and we can get back to the original exponent of 4 by writing $3 + 1$ as the new exponent.

$$\int 4x^3\, dx = 4\left(\frac{x^{3+1}}{3+1}\right) + C = x^4 + C$$

Since the derivative of $x^4 + C$ is $4x^3$, the answer is correct. We can generalize this example into a rule for finding the integral of x^n. To find the integral of x^n, we change the exponent n to $n + 1$ and divide by $n + 1$.

$$\boxed{\int x^n\, dx = \frac{x^{n+1}}{n+1} + C}$$

This rule works for all values of the exponent n except -1, which is a special case we discuss in Lesson 38.

example 35.3   Find: $\displaystyle\int 5s^{-20}\, ds$

solution   First we move the 5 across the integral sign and write

$$5\int s^{-20}\, ds$$

We must be careful with negative exponents; -20 increased by 1 is -19. We divide by $-20 + 1$ and make the new exponent $-20 + 1$. We also record the constant of integration.

$$5\int s^{-20}\, ds = 5\left(\frac{s^{-19}}{-19}\right) + C = -\frac{5s^{-19}}{19} + C$$

The derivative of this expression is $5s^{-20}$, so our answer is correct.

example 35.4   Find: $\displaystyle\int \frac{1}{3}\sqrt[3]{t^2}\, dt$

solution   To begin, we move the $\dfrac{1}{3}$ across the integral sign and rewrite $\sqrt[3]{t^2}$ with a fractional exponent.

$$\frac{1}{3}\int t^{2/3}\, dt$$

To antidifferentiate, we make the new exponent $\frac{2}{3} + 1$, divide by $\frac{2}{3} + 1$, and include the constant of integration.

$$\frac{1}{3}\int t^{2/3}\, dt = \frac{1}{3}\left(\frac{t^{2/3+1}}{\frac{2}{3}+1}\right) + C = \frac{1}{5}t^{5/3} + C$$

example 35.5   Find: $\displaystyle\int \frac{3\,du}{\sqrt{u}}$

solution   We move the 3 across the integral sign and write $\dfrac{1}{\sqrt{u}}$ as $u^{-1/2}$.

$$3\int u^{-1/2}\,du$$

Now we increase the exponent by 1 to get $-\dfrac{1}{2} + 1 = \dfrac{1}{2}$; then we divide by the same number.

$$3\int u^{-1/2}\,du = 3\left(\frac{u^{1/2}}{\dfrac{1}{2}}\right) + C = 6u^{1/2} + C$$

example 35.6   Find: $\displaystyle\int 5z^{\pi}\,dz$

solution   We move the 5 across the integral sign.

$$5\int z^{\pi}\,dz$$

Now we increase π by 1 to get $\pi + 1$, and we also divide by $\pi + 1$.

$$5\int z^{\pi}\,dz = \frac{5z^{\pi+1}}{\pi + 1} + C$$

**problem set
35**

1. The surface area of a rectangular solid is 100 cm^2. The length L and width w of the solid are
(5) equal. What is the volume of the solid in terms of L?

2. The speed of the seraphim increased exponentially. At noon their speed was 50 fathoms per
(26) second. At 1 p.m. their speed was 60 fathoms per second. What was their speed at 6 p.m.?

Integrate in problems 3–6.

3. $\displaystyle\int 3\sin x\,dx$ **4.** $\displaystyle\int \frac{2\,dt}{\sqrt{t}}$ **5.** $\displaystyle\int \frac{1}{2}\sqrt[3]{u}\,du$ **6.** $\displaystyle\int 3x\,dx$
(35)   (35)   (35)   (35)

7. Let $2x^2y + y^2 = \cos x$. Find $\dfrac{dy}{dx}$.
(34)

8. Suppose u and v are both functions of time. Find $\dfrac{du}{dt}$ given that $u^2 + v^2 = 2uv$.
(34)

9. Find the equation of the line tangent to the graph of the equation $y^2 - x^2 = 1$ at the point $(0, 1)$.
(34)

10. Which of the following graphs most resembles the graph of $y = x^3(x + 2)^2$.
(33)

A.

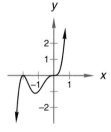

B.

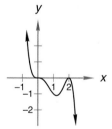

C.

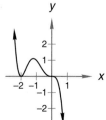

D.

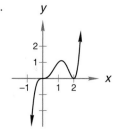

11. Make a rough sketch of the possible shapes of the graph of $y = -x^4 + ax^3 + bx^2 + cx + d$
(33)   where $a, b, c,$ and d represent unknown constants.

12. Approximate $s''(2)$ where $s(t) = \sqrt[3]{t} - 2\sqrt{t} + \dfrac{3}{t}$.
(27)

Evaluate the limits in problems 13–15.

13. $\displaystyle\lim_{\Delta x \to 0} \frac{e^{x+\Delta x} - e^x}{\Delta x}$
(28)

14. $\displaystyle\lim_{x \to 2} \frac{x^2 + x - 6}{x - 2}$
(14)

15. $\displaystyle\lim_{x \to \infty} \frac{x + 1}{x}$
(17)

16. Sketch the graph of $f(x) = x^3 + 1$, and determine the intervals on which f is increasing.
(33)

17. Solve: $8^{2x-1} = 4$
(16)

18. Find the value of k for which $x = -1$ is a zero of $y = 2x^3 + x + k$.
(10)

19. Let $f(x) = e^x$ and $g(x) = -f(-x)$. Graph f and g on the same coordinate plane.
(7)

20. Let $f(x) = \sin x$ and $g(x) = -3 + 2f\left(x - \dfrac{\pi}{3}\right)$. Graph g.
(7)

21. Find values of x between 0 and 2π such that $2\sin^2 x - 3\sin x + 1 = 0$.
(13)

22. Use the definition of the derivative to find $f'(x)$ where $f(x) = 2x^3 + 3x - 4$.
(19)

23. Use a graphing calculator to graph $x^2 + y^2 - 2x + 4y - 4 = 0$. What are the coordinates of
(22,23)   the center of this conic section?

24. Find the area of an equilateral triangle whose sides all have length 5.
(R)

25. If $x = 5 + y$, what is the value of $x^2 - 2xy + y^2$?
(R)

LESSON 36   *Critical Numbers • A Note about Critical Numbers*

36.A

critical numbers

The box below states the definition of a critical number.

> A **critical number** of a function f is a number c in the domain of f
> where either $f'(c) = 0$ or $f'(c)$ does not exist.

In other words, the critical numbers of a function f are those values of the domain of f where the derivative of f equals zero or does not exist.

Lesson 15 showed that the derivative of f equaled zero whenever the slope of the tangent line drawn to the graph of f is horizontal. This lesson shows instances where the derivative does not exist. Intuitively, these are places where the graph of the function comes to a sharp point (has a "corner") or where the tangent line to the graph becomes vertical. Three examples of functions where the derivative does not exist for some value of the function's domain are shown.

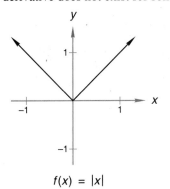

$f(x) = |x|$

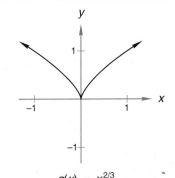

$g(x) = x^{2/3}$

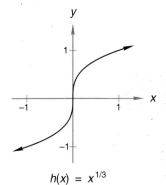

$h(x) = x^{1/3}$

It is not possible to draw a line tangent to either the graph of f or g at $x = 0$. In the graph of h the tangent line becomes vertical as we approach 0 along the x-axis.

Critical numbers are important because of the following fact:

> If f has a **local maximum** or a **local minimum** at c, then c is a critical number.

A proof of this fact is not shown, but we use the fact in this lesson. The figure below illustrates the statement in the box.

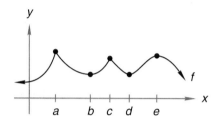

The numbers a, b, c, d, and e along the x-axis are critical numbers, as they are places where the derivative of the function f equals zero or does not exist. The derivative of f does not exist for either $x = a$ or $x = c$, because the graph of f comes to a sharp point. The derivative equals zero at $x = b$, $x = d$, and $x = e$, because lines drawn tangent to the graph of f are horizontal at these points. The corresponding values of f at a, b, c, d, and e are **local extrema** values, because they are values of f that are either greater or less than all other values of f for inputs in the neighborhoods of these numbers. More explicitly, f has a **local maximum,** or **relative maximum,** at a, c, and e, because $f(a)$, $f(c)$, and $f(e)$ are larger than the other values of f for inputs near a, c, and e. We can see this from the graph of f because f appears to have high points in the vicinity of a, c, and e. Similarly, f has a **local minimum,** or **relative minimum,** at b and d, because the values of f at b and d are smaller than values of f for inputs near b and d.

example 36.1   Find the critical numbers of the function $f(x) = x^3 + \frac{9}{2}x^2 + 6x + 5$. Also, find where the relative maximum and minimum values of f occur.

solution   Critical numbers are the numbers for which f' equals zero or does not exist. This is a polynomial function, and the derivative exists for every number on the interval $(-\infty, +\infty)$ for polynomial functions. Thus the critical numbers for this function are the **stationary numbers,** which are the numbers at which the derivative equals zero. First we find $f'(x)$.

$$f(x) = x^3 + \frac{9}{2}x^2 + 6x + 5 \qquad \text{equation}$$
$$f'(x) = 3x^2 + 9x + 6 \qquad \text{differentiated}$$
$$3x^2 + 9x + 6 = 0 \qquad \text{set } f'(x) = 0$$
$$3(x + 2)(x + 1) = 0 \qquad \text{factored}$$
$$x = -2, -1 \qquad \text{solved}$$

Thus f has critical numbers at $x = -2$ and $x = -1$.

We know that the graphs of cubic functions can take on three forms. The coefficient of the x^3 term is positive, so $f(x)$ has large positive values for large positive values of x.

The graph on the left has no critical points, for there are no places where the slope equals zero or is undefined. The graph in the center has one critical point (the slope is zero). The graph on the right has two critical points (the slope is zero) so we know it is the correct one. We have found that the x-values of P_1 and P_2 are -2 and -1. The equation of the function lets us find the y-values at these critical numbers.

When $x = -2$,

$$y = (-2)^3 + \frac{9}{2}(-2)^2 + 6(-2) + 5 = 3$$

When $x = -1$,

$$y = (-1)^3 + \frac{9}{2}(-1)^2 + 6(-1) + 5 = 2.5$$

Thus the local maximum point on the graph is **$(-2, 3)$,** and the local minimum point is **$(-1, 2.5)$.**

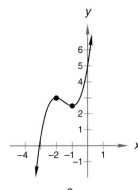

$$f(x) = x^3 + \frac{9}{2}x^2 + 6x + 5$$

example 36.2   Find the critical numbers of the function $f(x) = \frac{1}{4}x^4 - \frac{1}{3}x^3 - x^2 + 5$, and indicate where the relative maximum and minimum values occur.

solution   This is a polynomial function. Polynomial functions have a derivative for all x on the interval $(-\infty, +\infty)$. Thus the critical numbers are places where the derivative equals zero. To find these numbers, we differentiate the fourth-degree equation and get a third-degree equation. The critical numbers are found by factoring this cubic function.

$$f(x) = \frac{1}{4}x^4 - \frac{1}{3}x^3 - x^2 + 5 \qquad \text{original function}$$
$$f'(x) = x^3 - x^2 - 2x \qquad \text{differentiated}$$
$$x^3 - x^2 - 2x = 0 \qquad \text{set } f'(x) = 0$$
$$x(x - 2)(x + 1) = 0 \qquad \text{factored}$$
$$x = 2, 0, \text{ and } -1 \qquad \text{solved}$$

Therefore, **the critical numbers are $x = 2, 0,$ and -1.** The graph of a fourth-degree polynomial can have one, two, or three places where the slope is zero. Because the lead coefficient is positive, the graph could have one of the following forms.

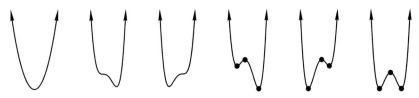

Since this function has three critical points, its graph must look like one of the three right-hand graphs. The x-coordinates of the critical points on the graph are -1, 0, and 2. Substituting these values into the equation of the function would give the *y*-values of the extreme points. Since the graph of *f* must resemble one of the three right-hand graphs, **f must attain local minimum values at *x* = –1 and *x* = 2 and a local maximum value at *x* = 0.**

We graph *f* on the TI-83 to show its shape.

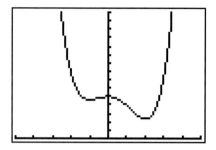

36.B

a note about critical numbers

The previous section stated that all local maximums or minimums occur at critical numbers. However, the converse of this statement is not true. **Not every critical number produces a local maximum or minimum.** For example, let $f(x) = x^3$. Then $f'(x) = 3x^2$, which means that $x = 0$ is a critical number. However, there is no local maximum or minimum at this point.

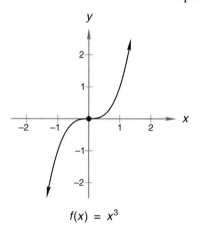

$$f(x) = x^3$$

As a second example, let $g(x) = x^{1/3}$.

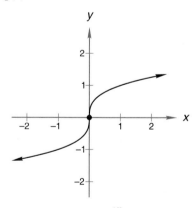

$$g(x) = x^{1/3}$$

From the power rule, $g'(x) = \dfrac{1}{3}x^{-2/3}$, or

$$g'(x) = \frac{1}{3x^{2/3}}$$

Notice that g' is not defined at $x = 0$, which means that 0 is a critical number of *g*. However, from the graph, we see that there is no local maximum or minimum at $x = 0$.

problem set
36

1. A cone is formed from a circle of radius 10 cm by removing a sector whose central angle has a
(4) measure of x radians and then joining the two edges of the remaining portion.

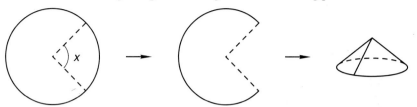

Find the radius and circumference of the circular base of the cone in terms of x.

2. Find the critical numbers of $y = \frac{1}{3}x^3 - x$. Use a rough sketch of the graph of the function y to
(36) determine the local maximum and minimum values of y and where they occur.

3. Find the critical numbers of the function $f(x) = x^3 - \frac{9}{2}x^2 + 6x + 3$. Use a rough sketch of
(36) the function to determine the local maximum and minimum values of y and where they occur.

Antidifferentiate in problems 4–6.

4. $\int \frac{\sqrt{u}}{20}\, du$ 5. $\int 2\cos t\, dt$ 6. $\int 3\, dx$
(35)   (35)   (35)

7. Let $y^3 + xy = e^x$. Find $\dfrac{dy}{dx}$.
(34)

8. Let $x = \sin y$. Find $\dfrac{dy}{dx}$.
(34)

9. If x and y are both functions of t and $2x - y^2 = \ln x$, what is $\dfrac{dx}{dt}$?
(34)

10. Approximate the slope of the line tangent to the graph of f at $x = -1$ where $f(x) = x \sin x$.
(19)

11. Let $y = 2x^2 + 3\sin x - 4\cos x + \ln x$. Find $\dfrac{dy}{dx}$.
(25)

12. Make a rough sketch of the possible shapes of $y = 3x^3 + ax^2 + bx + c$, where a, b, and c
(33) represent unknown constants.

13. Sketch the basic shape of $y = x(x - 1)(x + 2)^2$. Clearly indicate the behavior of the graph
(33) near the points where the graph intercepts the x-axis.

14. Sketch the graph of $y = \tan x$ $(-2\pi \le x \le 2\pi)$. Clearly indicate all asymptotes and zeros.
(30)

15. Sketch the graph of $y = \dfrac{x(x - 2)}{(x - 3)(x + 1)(x - 1)}$. Clearly indicate all asymptotes and zeros.
(28)

16. State an identity for $\tan(A + B)$, and use it to derive an identity for $\tan(2A)$.
(12)

17. (a) Find the value of x such that $x = \cos x$ by graphing the functions $y = x$ and $y = \cos x$
(2)   on a graphing calculator and finding the x-coordinate of the point of intersection.

    (b) Find the zeros of the function $y = x - \cos x$. How does this answer compare with your
        answer to (a)?

18. Use a graphing calculator to graph $y + 4x^2 + 8x - 6 = 0$. Determine the x-intercept(s) of the
(22,23) function.

19. Solve: $\log_b 27 = 3$ 20. Evaluate: $\displaystyle\lim_{t \to \infty} \frac{2t^2 + 3}{4 - 5t^2}$
(9)   (17)

21. Graph f where $f(x) = \begin{cases} x^2 & \text{when } x \leq 1 \\ 2x & \text{when } x > 1, \end{cases}$ and then find $\lim\limits_{x \to 1^+} f(x)$ and $\lim\limits_{x \to 1^-} f(x)$.
(9,11)

22. State the converse of the following statement: If $f' > 0$ on the interval $[a, b]$, then f is
(3) increasing on the interval $[a, b]$.

23. Let $f(x) = \sqrt{x}$ and $g(x) = f(x + 2) + 2$. Graph f and g on the same coordinate plane.
(21)

24. Find the radius of the circle that can be circumscribed around a square whose sides each have a
(R) length of 5 centimeters. Remember that the diagonal of a square inscribed in a circle is a diameter of the circle.

25. Assuming $x - y > 0$, compare the following: A. $x^2 - 2xy + y^2$ B. $x^2 + 2xy + y^2$
(1)

LESSON 37 *Differentiation by u Substitution*

One of the most powerful tools in mathematics is substitution.

> **SUBSTITUTION AXIOM**
>
> If two expressions a and b are of equal value, $a = b$, then a may replace b or b may replace a in another expression without changing the value of the expression. Also, a may replace b or b may replace a in any statement without changing the truth or falsity of the statement. Also, a may replace b or b may replace a in any equation or inequality without changing the solution set of the equation or inequality.

Substitution is especially useful in calculus, because it allows us to replace a complicated expression with a simple one. Then we work with the simple expression and make a reverse substitution as the last step. Knowing when to substitute and what to substitute comes with experience and practice. It is important to be able to look at a complicated expression and recognize the basic form of the expression. The basic form often suggests the substitution that should be used. In this lesson the letter u is used to write the basic form, and the substitution is called **u substitution.**

$$y = e^{x^2 + 2} \qquad\qquad \text{has the form of} \qquad y = e^u$$
$$y = (x^3 - 2x^2 + 1)^{100} \qquad \text{has the form of} \qquad y = u^{100}$$
$$y = \ln(x^2 + 42) \qquad\qquad \text{has the form of} \qquad y = \ln u$$
$$y = \sin(x^2 - 15) \qquad\qquad \text{has the form of} \qquad y = \sin u$$
$$y = (\sin x)^3 \qquad\qquad\qquad \text{has the form of} \qquad y = u^3$$

The derivative of many functions can be found using u substitution. To find the derivative of

$$y = e^{x^2 + 2}$$

we note that the basic form of this equation is

$$y = e^u$$

Then we compute the differential du and record both u and du in a box.

$$\boxed{\begin{aligned} u &= x^2 + 2 \\ du &= 2x\,dx \end{aligned}}$$

Next we find the differential of the basic form.

$$y = e^u \quad\longrightarrow\quad dy = e^u\,du \qquad \text{differential}$$

Then a second substitution is made. We replace u with $x^2 + 2$ and replace du with $2x\,dx$. The last step is to divide by dx.

$$dy = (e^{x^2+2})(2x\,dx) \qquad \text{substituted}$$

$$\frac{dy}{dx} = 2xe^{x^2+2} \qquad \text{divided by } dx$$

example 37.1 If $f(x) = (x^2 + 2x)^{10}$, what is $f'(x)$?

solution The first step is to recognize the basic form of the equation and use u to write the basic form.

$$y = u^{10} \qquad \text{basic form}$$

We record the substitution in a box, compute du, and record it in the same box.

$$y = u^{10} \qquad \boxed{\begin{aligned} u &= x^2 + 2x \\ du &= (2x + 2)\,dx \end{aligned}}$$

After that, we find the differential dy of the basic u expression, use the information in the box to make a second substitution, and finish by dividing both sides by dx.

$$dy = 10u^9\,du \qquad\qquad \text{differential}$$

$$dy = 10(x^2 + 2x)^9(2x + 2)\,dx \qquad \text{substituted}$$

$$f'(x) = \frac{dy}{dx} = 20x^9(x + 2)^9(x + 1) \qquad \text{divided by dx and factored}$$

example 37.2 If $h(x) = \sqrt[3]{x^2 + 2x}$, what is $h'(x)$?

solution **We always rewrite radical expressions as expressions with fractional exponents.** Doing this yields $y = (x^2 + 2x)^{1/3}$, which has the basic form $y = u^{1/3}$.

$$y = u^{1/3} \qquad \boxed{\begin{aligned} u &= x^2 + 2x \\ du &= (2x + 2)\,dx \end{aligned}}$$

We find the differential of y, make the reverse substitution, and then divide by dx.

$$dy = \frac{1}{3}u^{-2/3}\,du \qquad\qquad \text{differential}$$

$$dy = \frac{1}{3}(x^2 + 2x)^{-2/3}(2x + 2)\,dx \qquad \text{substituted}$$

$$h'(x) = \frac{dy}{dx} = \frac{2}{3}(x^2 + 2x)^{-2/3}(x + 1) \qquad \text{divided by } dx \text{ and factored}$$

example 37.3 Let $g(x) = \ln(x^2 - 42)$. Find $g'(x)$.

solution First u is used to write the basic form of $\ln(x^2 - 42)$. This is the first substitution. Then we compute du and record u and du in a box.

$$y = \ln u \qquad \boxed{\begin{aligned} u &= x^2 - 42 \\ du &= 2x\,dx \end{aligned}}$$

Next we find the differential of y, make the reverse substitution, and divide by dx.

$$dy = \frac{1}{u}\,du \qquad\qquad \text{differential}$$

$$dy = \frac{2x\,dx}{x^2 - 42} \qquad\qquad \text{substituted}$$

$$g'(x) = \frac{dy}{dx} = \frac{2x}{x^2 - 42} \qquad \text{divided by } dx$$

example 37.4   Suppose $f(t) = \sin(t^3 - 15)$. Find $f'(t)$.

solution   First we write the basic form of the equation using u. This is the first substitution. Then we compute du and record u and du in a box.

$$y = \sin(u) \qquad \boxed{\begin{aligned} u &= t^3 - 15 \\ du &= 3t^2\, dt \end{aligned}}$$

Next we find dy, make the reverse substitution, and divide by dt.

$$dy = \cos(u)\, du \qquad\qquad \text{differential}$$

$$dy = \left[\cos(t^3 - 15)\right](3t^2\, dt) \qquad\qquad \text{substituted}$$

$$f'(t) = \frac{dy}{dt} = \mathbf{3t^2 \cos(t^3 - 15)} \qquad\qquad \text{divided by } dt$$

example 37.5   If $y = \sin^3 x$, what is $\dfrac{dy}{dx}$?

solution   Remember that $\sin^3 x$ means $(\sin x)^3$. We substitute and record u and du in a box.

$$y = u^3 \qquad \boxed{\begin{aligned} u &= \sin x \\ du &= \cos x\, dx \end{aligned}}$$

Next we find dy, make the reverse substitution, and divide by dx.

$$dy = 3u^2\, du \qquad\qquad \text{differential}$$

$$dy = 3(\sin x)^2(\cos x\, dx) \qquad\qquad \text{substituted}$$

$$\frac{dy}{dx} = \mathbf{3\cos x \sin^2 x} \qquad\qquad \text{divided by } dx$$

example 37.6   Find $\dfrac{dy}{dx}$ where $y = \cos(e^x)$.

solution   This time we let $u = e^x$.

$$y = \cos(u) \quad\longrightarrow\quad dy = -\sin(u)\, du \qquad \boxed{\begin{aligned} u &= e^x \\ du &= e^x\, dx \end{aligned}}$$

We make the reverse substitution and divide by dx.

$$dy = \left[-\sin(e^x)\right](e^x\, dx) \qquad\qquad \text{substituted}$$

$$\frac{dy}{dx} = \mathbf{-e^x \sin(e^x)} \qquad\qquad \text{divided by } dx$$

example 37.7   Let $y = (e^x + 1)^{1/2}$. Find y'.

solution   This time we let $u = e^x + 1$.

$$y = u^{1/2} \quad\longrightarrow\quad dy = \frac{1}{2}u^{-1/2}\, du \qquad \boxed{\begin{aligned} u &= e^x + 1 \\ du &= e^x\, dx \end{aligned}}$$

We make the reverse substitution and divide by dx.

$$dy = \frac{1}{2}(e^x + 1)^{-1/2}(e^x\, dx) \qquad\qquad \text{substituted}$$

$$y' = \frac{dy}{dx} = \mathbf{\frac{e^x}{2(e^x + 1)^{1/2}}} \qquad\qquad \text{divided by } dx$$

example 37.8   Use u substitution to find $\dfrac{dy}{dx}$ where $y = \ln |\cos x|$.

solution   We write the basic form and record the substitution in a box.

$$y = \ln |u| \qquad \boxed{\begin{aligned} u &= \cos x \\ du &= -\sin x\, dx \end{aligned}}$$

Then we find the differential of the basic form, substitute again, and divide by dx.

$$dy = \frac{1}{u}\, du \qquad\qquad \text{differential}$$

$$dy = \frac{-\sin x\, dx}{\cos x} \qquad\qquad \text{substituted}$$

$$\frac{dy}{dx} = -\tan x \qquad\qquad \text{divided and simplified}$$

**problem set
37**

1. A ladder that is 12 feet long leans so that it just touches the top of a 4-foot-tall brick wall and
(5,8) then rests against the side of a vertical wall beyond the brick wall. The brick wall is 4 feet from
the wall beyond it. (See the diagram in problem 2 in Problem Set 32.)

   (a) Use the Pythagorean theorem to write an equation that relates the sides of the large triangle.

   (b) Use the fact that the two smaller right triangles are similar to write a proportion involving x and y.

   (c) Solve the proportion for y, and substitute the answer into the first equation found.

   (d) You now have an equation in terms of only the variable x. Find the values of x that make the equation true by using a graphing calculator to find the roots of the equation. Be sure to consider which values of x make sense in this problem.

2. Let $f(x) = (x^3 - 3x^2 + 1)^{20}$. Find $f'(x)$.
(37)

3. Let $y = \sin (t^3 + 1)$. Find $\dfrac{dy}{dt}$.
(37)

4. Let $g(x) = \cos^3 x$. Find $g'(x)$.
(37)

5. Let $y = \ln (x^2 + 1)$. Find $\dfrac{dy}{dx}$.
(37)

6. Let $h(x) = \sqrt[3]{x^3 + 2x - 1}$. Find $h'(x)$.
(37)

7. Let $y = \dfrac{1}{\sqrt{x^2 - 1}}$. Find $\dfrac{dy}{dx}$.
(37)

8. (a) Find the critical numbers of $f(x) = -3x^4 - 4x^3 + 12x^2 - 12$.
(36)

   (b) Use a rough sketch of the graph of f to determine where the local maximums and local minimums of f occur and what their values are.

Integrate in problems 9–11.

9. $\displaystyle\int \frac{3}{\sqrt{u}}\, du$
(35)

10. $\displaystyle\int -4\sqrt[3]{t^2}\, dt$
(35)

11. $\displaystyle\int x\sqrt{x}\, dx$ (*Hint:* Multiply first.)
(35)

12. If $xy^2 - 2y = e^x$, what is $\dfrac{dy}{dx}$?
(34)

13. Find the equation of the line tangent to the graph of $x^2 - 4y^2 = 0$ at the point $(4, 2)$.
(34)

14. Use the definition of the derivative to find $f'(x)$ where $f(x) = \sqrt{x}$.
(19)

15. Sketch the graph of $y = x(x - 3)^2(x + 2)^3$.
(33)

16. Let $f(x) = \ln x$ and $g(x) = \sqrt{x - 1}$. Find the domain and the range of f and g.
(6)

17. Let $f(x) = \ln x$ and $g(x) = \sqrt{x - 1}$. Find the equation of $f \circ g$ and determine the domain
(18)   of $f \circ g$.

18. Solve: $-\sqrt{3} + 2 \tan (3\theta) = 0$ $(0 \le \theta \le \pi)$
(23)

19. Use a graphing calculator to approximate $\lim\limits_{x \to \infty} \left(1 + \dfrac{1}{x}\right)^x$ to at least three decimal places.
(17)

20. Develop an expression that gives $\sin^2 x$ in terms of $\cos (2x)$.
(12)

21. Find the equation of the quadratic function whose x-intercepts are $x = -1$ and $x = 2$ and
(10)   whose y-intercept is $y = -4$.

22. Simplify: $(\sin -x)\left[\csc\left(\dfrac{\pi}{2} - x\right)\right]$
(8)

23. Evaluate: $\lim\limits_{n \to \infty} \dfrac{(n + 1)(n - 3)}{2 - n^2}$
(17)

24. If $\begin{vmatrix} a & b \\ c & d \end{vmatrix} = ad - bc$, what value of d makes $\begin{vmatrix} 2 & 3 \\ -1 & d \end{vmatrix} = 4$ true?
(R)

25. Assuming $x > y > 0$, compare the following: A. x^y B. y^x
(1)

LESSON 38 *Integral of a Sum • Integral of $\dfrac{1}{x}$*

38.A
integral of a sum

We remember that the derivative of a sum is the sum of the individual derivatives.

$$\frac{d}{dx}(x^2 + e^x + \sin x) = \frac{d}{dx}x^2 + \frac{d}{dx}e^x + \frac{d}{dx}\sin x$$

Taking these derivatives results in the following sum:

$$2x + e^x + \cos x$$

To undo what we have done, we must antidifferentiate each of these expressions separately. We may do so because the integral of a sum is the sum of the integrals.

$$\int (f(x) + g(x))\, dx = \int f(x)\, dx + \int g(x)\, dx$$

This lets us write

$$\int (2x + e^x + \cos x)\, dx = \int 2x\, dx + \int e^x\, dx + \int \cos x\, dx$$

Each of these indefinite integrals requires a constant of integration that represents some number.

$$\int 2x\, dx + \int e^x\, dx + \int \cos x\, dx = (x^2 + C_1) + (e^x + C_2) + (\sin x + C_3)$$

We rearrange this expression to get

$$x^2 + e^x + \sin x + C_1 + C_2 + C_3$$

Each letter C represents an arbitrary number, so $C_1 + C_2 + C_3$ is also an arbitrary number, which we can represent with the single letter C.

$$x^2 + e^x + \sin x + C$$

Thus we see that the constants of integration of a sum can be combined into a single constant of integration.

example 38.1 Integrate: $\int (6s^{12} + 5s + 3e^s + 4)\, ds$

solution The indefinite integral of a sum is the sum of the individual indefinite integrals, so we rewrite the integral as follows:

$$\int 6s^{12}\, ds + \int 5s\, ds + \int 3e^s\, ds + \int 4\, ds$$

Next we move the constants in front of the integral signs.

$$6\int s^{12}\, ds + 5\int s\, ds + 3\int e^s\, ds + 4\int ds$$

Then we integrate each term and write a single constant of integration at the end.

$$\frac{6}{13}s^{13} + \frac{5}{2}s^2 + 3e^s + 4s + C$$

example 38.2 Integrate: $\int (6\sin u + 5u^{-5} + 3e^u - 2)\, du$

solution We use just two steps this time. First we put the constants in front. (Notice how the signs in the first term are handled so we can integrate $-\sin u$, which is the derivative of $\cos u$.)

$$-6\int -\sin u\, du + 5\int u^{-5}\, du + 3\int e^u\, du - 2\int du$$

Then we integrate

$$-6\cos u - \frac{5}{4}u^{-4} + 3e^u - 2u + C$$

Remember that you can check your answer by differentiating the result. The derivative of your answer must be the function that you integrated.

38.B
integral of $\frac{1}{x}$

Recall from Lesson 26 that

$$\frac{d}{dx}\ln |x| = \frac{1}{x}$$

When we write

$$\int \frac{1}{x}\, dx$$

we are asking for the family of antiderivatives that is defined for all nonzero values of x. So

$$\int \frac{1}{x}\, dx = \ln |x| + C$$

If we were to write

$$\int \frac{1}{x} \, dx = \ln x + C$$

we would be designating a function that is defined only for positive values of x.

The integral of $\frac{1}{x^2}$ is found by rewriting it as x^{-2} and using the method that has been devised to integrate x^n.

$$\int \frac{1}{x^2} \, dx = \int x^{-2} \, dx = \frac{x^{-2+1}}{-2+1} + C = -x^{-1} + C$$

Attempting to integrate $\frac{1}{x}$ using this method results in a zero denominator.

$$\int \frac{1}{x} \, dx = \int x^{-1} \, dx = \frac{x^{-1+1}}{-1+1} = \frac{x^0}{0} \qquad ?????$$

From this we see that the rule for finding the integral of x^n cannot be used if $n = -1$. The rule can be used for any value of n except -1, which is a special case.

$$\int x^{-1} \, dx = \int \frac{1}{x} \, dx = \ln |x| + C$$

example 38.3 Integrate: $\displaystyle\int \left(\frac{4}{t} + 3t^{-1} + 4 \cos t + 3 \sin t \right) dt$

solution The integral of a sum is the sum of the integrals. First we write the constants in front of the integral signs.

$$4 \int \frac{dt}{t} + 3 \int \frac{dt}{t} + 4 \int \cos t \, dt - 3 \int -\sin t \, dt$$

(Notice how the signs on the last term are handled and that the first two terms can be combined.) So the integral is

$$\mathbf{7 \ln |t| + 4 \sin t - 3 \cos t + C}$$

**problem set
38**

1. The hole kept getting larger. In fact, the volume of the hole increased exponentially. At midnight
(26) the volume of the hole was 10 cubic meters. Two hours later the volume of the hole was 15 cubic meters. What time will it be when the volume of the hole gets to be 30 cubic meters?

2. A rectangular box with a square base has a volume of 64 cubic inches. Express the total surface
(5) area of the box in terms of x if the length of one of the sides of the base is x inches.

Integrate in problems 3 and 4.

3. $\displaystyle\int \left(2x^2 - \frac{3}{\sqrt{x}} + 3 \right) dx$
(38)

4. $\displaystyle\int \left(2 \cos u - \frac{2}{u} + 3 \sin u \right) du$
(38)

5. For $y = \cos (x^3 + 2x + 1)$, find $\dfrac{dy}{dx}$.
(37)

6. For $y = \ln |\sin x|$, find y'.
(37)

7. For $f(x) = \dfrac{1}{\sqrt{x^2 + 2x + 1}}$, find $f'(x)$.
(37)

8. For $s = 2 \ln |\sin t + 2e^t|$, find $\dfrac{ds}{dt}$.
(37)

9. Let $f(x) = 3x^4 - 8x^3 - 6x^2 + 24x - 1$.
(36)
  (a) Find the critical numbers of f.
  (b) Use a sketch of the graph of f to determine the values of all local maximums and minimums of f.

10. Graph the function $f(x) = 3x^4 - 8x^3 - 6x^2 + 24x - 1$ on a graphing calculator, and
(2) determine the zeros of the function.

11. What is $\dfrac{dy}{dx}$ if $xy - y^3 = \sin x$?
(34)

12. What is $f'(x)$ if $[f(x)]^2 - 2x\,f(x) = e^x$? (*Hint:* Replace $f(x)$ with y.)
(34)

13. What is $\dfrac{dx}{dt}$ if $x^3 - y^3 = e^t$? Assume x and y are functions of t.
(34)

Sketch the graphs of the functions given in problems 14–16.

14. $y = \sqrt{x^3}$
(9)

15. $y = \cot x \; (0 \le x \le 2\pi)$
(30)

16. $y = \dfrac{(2 - x)(x + 1)(x - 4)}{(x - 4)(x - 3)(x - 1)(x + 2)}$
(28)

17. Let $f(x) = \sin x$ and $g(x) = \dfrac{1}{f(x)}$. Sketch the graphs of f and g on the same coordinate plane.
(30)

18. Find the values of x that makes the equation $49^{x+1} = 7^{3x^2-6}$ true.
(16)

19. Let $f(x) = x(x + 2)(x - 3)(x + 1)$. On a number line, indicate the intervals on which f is
(15) positive and the intervals on which f is negative.

20. Determine the equation of the centerline, the period, and the amplitude of the function
(7) $y = -2 + 3\sin(4x - 3)$.

21. What is the sum of the first forty positive integers?
(R)

22. Determine the numerical value of $\tan^2 \dfrac{\pi}{15} - \sec^2 \dfrac{\pi}{15}$. Do not use a calculator.
(8)

23. Simplify: $\left[\sin\left(\dfrac{\pi}{2} - \theta\right)\right](\tan \theta)(\sin -\theta)$
(8)

24. Find the area of an equilateral triangle whose sides are 6 units long.
(R)

25. Assuming $x - y = 3$, compare the following: A. $x^2 + y^2$ B. $9 + 2xy$
(1)

LESSON 39 *Area Under a Curve (Upper and Lower Sums)* • *Left, Right, and Midpoint Sums*

39.A
area under a curve (upper and lower sums)

To describe the size of a surface in everyday life, we use the word *area*. Thus we might say "The area of this table is 1450 square centimeters." In the applied problems in this book, areas can also be used to represent distance, work, and total force. In mathematics it is helpful to strip away the units and consider area to be a real number that can be used to numerically describe an abstract quality associated with every closed planar geometric figure. This allows us to study the numerical aspect of area without having to consider the myriad units that can cause confusion. **For our basic definition of area, we define the area of a rectangle to be its length times its width.**

This definition is then used to help define the area of a triangle. The area of a triangle is then used to define the area of a trapezoid.

The expression πr^2 gives the area of a circle, but we have not exactly defined how to determine the area of a region with a curved boundary. Our investigation of areas bounded by curves begins by considering graphs of continuous functions that are everywhere increasing and are nonnegative on the interval $[a, b]$. This last restriction means that the graph of the function does not go below the x-axis between a and b. We consider the area bounded by the graph, the x-axis, and the lines $x = a$ and $x = b$. **This area is called the area under the curve on the interval $[a, b]$.**

The area of the rectangle shown below is 32. In the figure to its right, we can see the area A lies under the function f, above the x-axis, and between x-values of a and b. But what is the value of A?

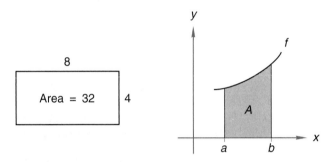

Can we prove that such a number A exists? If it does exist, can a method of finding it precisely be developed? This lesson concentrates on developing a definition of "the area under a curve." We begin by finding an approximation for the area by drawing rectangles and adding the areas of the rectangles. To demonstrate the procedure of adding the areas of rectangles, we will approximate the area of the region under the graph of $y = x^2 + 1$, above the x-axis, and between x-values of 0 and 2. This is the area of the region shaded in the figure on the left-hand side below. First, we divide the distance between 0 and 2 into four intervals of equal length, as shown in the center figure. This **partitions** the interval $[0, 2]$ into nonoverlapping parts. In the figure on the right-hand side, we draw vertical lines from the end of each partition to the graph of the function.

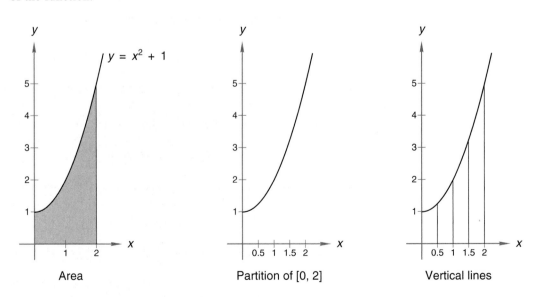

| Area | Partition of [0, 2] | Vertical lines |

Now we can draw rectangles. In the figure on the left-hand side below, the left side of each partition is used as the height of each rectangle, which makes all of the rectangles fall below the curve. In the figure on the right-hand side, the right side of each partition is used as the height of each rectangle, which puts the top of each rectangle above the curve.

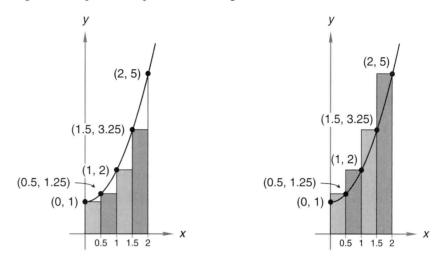

The sum of the areas of the four rectangles in the figure on the left is called a **lower sum,** because the least value of $f(x)$ on each interval was used as the height of the rectangle. We can compute the value of this sum, which we designate S_L. (The subscript L stands for *lower.*) The width of each rectangle is 0.5. Using the value of $f(x)$ at the left end of each interval as the height of the rectangle, we get

$$S_L = [f(0)](0.5) + [f(0.5)](0.5) + [f(1)](0.5) + [f(1.5)](0.5)$$
$$= (1)(0.5) + (1.25)(0.5) + (2)(0.5) + (3.25)(0.5) = 3.75$$

The sum of the areas of the four rectangles in the right-hand figure is called an **upper sum** because the greatest value of $f(x)$ on each interval was used as the height of the rectangle. We can compute the value of this sum, which we designate S_U. Again the width of each rectangle is 0.5. Using the value of $f(x)$ at the right end of each interval as the height, we get

$$S_U = [f(0.5)](0.5) + [f(1)](0.5) + [f(1.5)](0.5) + [f(2)](0.5)$$
$$= (1.25)(0.5) + (2)(0.5) + (3.25)(0.5) + (5)(0.5) = 5.75$$

The rectangles used in the computation of the lower sum all lie beneath the curve, so the lower sum is less than the exact area A, which is the number we are trying to approximate. The rectangles used in the computation of the upper sum all extend above the curve, so the upper sum is greater than A.

$$3.75 < A < 5.75 \quad \text{or} \quad S_L < A < S_U$$

The exact value of the number A that we are trying to approximate in this example is $4\frac{2}{3}$. (Lessons 43 and 47 show where this number comes from.) The lower sum of 3.75 is less than $4\frac{2}{3}$, and the upper sum of 5.75 is greater than $4\frac{2}{3}$.

The error in our lower sum is approximately 0.92, which is the sum of the four "triangular" areas below the curve in the left-hand figure. The error in our upper sum is approximately 1.1, which is the sum of the four "triangular" areas above the curve in the right-hand figure. If we were to use eight partitions instead of four partitions, the lower sum would be approximately 4.19 and the upper sum would be approximately 5.19.

$$4.19 < 4\frac{2}{3} < 5.19$$

The error in the new lower sum is approximately 0.48, and the error in the new upper sum is approximately 0.52. As the number of partitions on the interval increases, the errors become smaller and smaller, and the lower sum and the upper sum get closer and closer to $4\frac{2}{3}$, which is the actual value of A. This line of investigation will be explored more completely in Lesson 43. For now, we are content to find an approximation for the area under a curve using either an upper sum or a lower sum.

Even though we know that the answer obtained from an upper-sum or lower-sum computation is not sufficiently accurate (and we do in fact call it an approximation), it is fairly important that students realize a prescribed method is being followed. Thus, **everyone doing the problem should arrive at exactly the same answer.**

example 39.1   Use lower sums to estimate the area under $y = x^2 + 2$ on the interval $[1, 3]$ divided into $n = 4$ equal subdivisions.

solution   It is always a good idea to begin such a problem with a picture. It is not crucial that the picture be extremely accurate—in fact, it is sometimes helpful if the scale is exaggerated. It is important, however, that the picture be accurate enough to demonstrate the details needed to solve the problem.

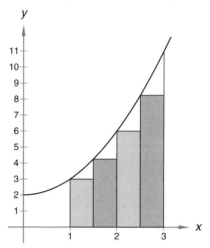

Since the function is increasing on the interval $[1, 3]$ and we are calculating a lower sum, the x-value at the left end of a particular subinterval produces the height of that rectangle.

The width of each subinterval is always

$$\Delta x = \frac{b - a}{n}$$

where $[a, b]$ describes the interval and n is the number of subintervals into which $[a, b]$ is subdivided.

$$\Delta x = \frac{3 - 1}{4} = \frac{1}{2}$$

The left-hand endpoints of the subintervals are the following:

$$x_0 = 1 \qquad x_1 = 1.5$$
$$x_2 = 2 \qquad x_3 = 2.5$$

We need the corresponding y-values at these points, as they are the heights of each of the rectangles.

$$y_0 = f(x_0) = f(1) = 3$$
$$y_1 = f(x_1) = f(1.5) = 4.25$$
$$y_2 = f(x_2) = f(2) = 6$$
$$y_3 = f(x_3) = f(2.5) = 8.25$$

We now add the areas of the lower rectangles to compute the lower sum.

$$S_L = \frac{1}{2}(3) + \frac{1}{2}(4.25) + \frac{1}{2}(6) + \frac{1}{2}(8.25)$$

$$= \frac{1}{2}(3 + 4.25 + 6 + 8.25)$$

$$= \mathbf{10.75}$$

Again, this value of 10.75 is only an approximation of the exact area. Still, it is a useful value to know.

example 39.2   Use upper rectangles to estimate the area under $y = -x^2 + 9$ on the interval $[1, 2]$ divided into $n = 5$ rectangles.

solution   As before, we begin with a picture.

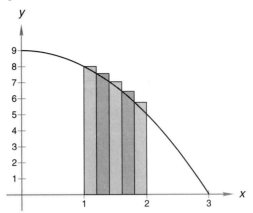

Because the function is decreasing on the interval of interest and the problem requires the use of upper rectangles, we have to use the left-hand endpoint of each subinterval. The width of each rectangle is

$$\frac{b - a}{n} = \frac{2 - 1}{5} = 0.2$$

The left-hand endpoints of each subinterval and their corresponding y-values are as follows:

$$x_0 = 1 \quad x_1 = 1.2 \quad x_2 = 1.4 \quad x_3 = 1.6 \quad x_4 = 1.8$$
$$y_0 = 8 \quad y_1 = 7.56 \quad y_2 = 7.04 \quad y_3 = 6.44 \quad y_4 = 5.76$$

The y-values constitute the heights of the upper rectangles, and each rectangle's width is 0.2. We add the areas of these rectangles to find the upper sum.

$$S_U = (0.2)(8) + (0.2)(7.56) + (0.2)(7.04) + (0.2)(6.44) + (0.2)(5.76)$$
$$= (0.2)(8 + 7.56 + 7.04 + 6.44 + 5.76)$$
$$= \mathbf{6.96}$$

Note that in this case the exact area is actually smaller than 6.96.

example 39.3   Use lower rectangles with $n = 6$ subintervals to estimate the area under $y = -x^2 + 2x$ on the interval $[0, 2]$.

solution   Again, we begin with a picture.

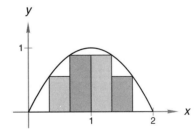

This problem requires careful consideration. On the interval of interest, the function has both increasing and decreasing portions. We have to use left-hand endpoints when the function is increasing and right-hand endpoints when the function is decreasing. The width of each interval is

$$\Delta x = \frac{b - a}{n} = \frac{2 - 0}{6} = \frac{1}{3}$$

So,

$$S_L = \frac{1}{3}f(0) + \frac{1}{3}f\left(\frac{1}{3}\right) + \frac{1}{3}f\left(\frac{2}{3}\right) + \frac{1}{3}f\left(\frac{4}{3}\right) + \frac{1}{3}f\left(\frac{5}{3}\right) + \frac{1}{3}f(2)$$

$$= \frac{1}{3}\left(0 + \frac{5}{9} + \frac{8}{9} + \frac{8}{9} + \frac{5}{9} + 0\right) = \frac{26}{27}$$

A few comments are in order here. Notice that $x = 1$ is not used as an endpoint. If a careful drawing is not made, details such as this are often missed. Also, be aware of situations such as this, where two of the rectangles are degenerate rectangles—they have a height of zero, and therefore no area. Most importantly, you must remember that this method only **estimates** the area under the curve.

But what are some ways to make more accurate estimations? The number of subintervals could be increased. It seems that this decreases the amount of error in either the upper or lower sum. Since the upper sum is too large and the lower sum is too small, perhaps a better approximation of the actual area under the curve would be the average of the two. Using trapezoids instead of rectangles often drastically reduces the error. (This will be the topic of Lesson 95.)

39.B
left, right, and midpoint sums

Until recent years, usually only upper and lower rectangles were studied to estimate the area under a curve. Now, with the availability of desktop computers and programmable graphing calculators, the study can be expanded. It would be a fairly simple task to write a program to make the calculation in example 39.1. The situation in example 39.3, in which the endpoints used switched from the left-hand end to the right-hand end, would be considerably more difficult to program. Because of situations such as these, the discussion of approximating the area under a curve usually includes left sums, right sums, and midpoint sums. As their names suggest, left sums always use the left-hand endpoint, right sums always use the right-hand endpoint, and midpoint sums always use the midpoint of each subinterval.

In example 39.1 lower rectangles were used. If this problem were to be repeated using left rectangles, the solution would be exactly the same. Example 39.2 called for upper rectangles. Again, this would be exactly the same as using left rectangles.

example 39.4   Repeat example 39.2, but use right rectangles instead of upper rectangles.

solution   As always, we begin with a drawing.

The drawing should make it obvious that whether lower rectangles or right rectangles are used, the problem is exactly the same.

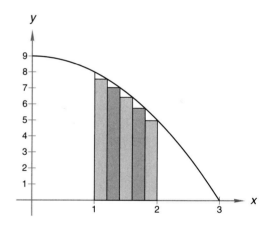

$$\Delta x = \frac{2 - 1}{5} = 0.2$$

The right-hand endpoints of the subintervals, along with their corresponding y-values, are as follows:

$x_1 = 1.2$	$x_2 = 1.4$	$x_3 = 1.6$	$x_4 = 1.8$	$x_5 = 2$
$y_1 = 7.56$	$y_2 = 7.04$	$y_3 = 6.44$	$y_4 = 5.76$	$y_5 = 5$

Therefore, $S_R = (0.2)(7.56 + 7.04 + 6.44 + 5.76 + 5) = $ **6.36.**

example 39.5   Repeat example 39.3, but use left rectangles instead of lower rectangles.

solution   We begin with a drawing.

The drawing indicates that using left rectangles is really a combination of using upper and lower rectangles.

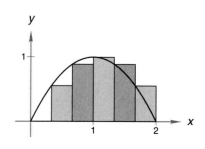

$$\Delta x = \frac{2 - 0}{6} = \frac{1}{3}$$

The left-hand endpoints and their y-values are as follows:

$$x_0 = 0 \qquad x_1 = \frac{1}{3} \qquad x_2 = \frac{2}{3} \qquad x_3 = 1 \qquad x_4 = \frac{4}{3} \qquad x_5 = \frac{5}{3}$$

$$y_0 = 0 \qquad y_1 = \frac{5}{9} \qquad y_2 = \frac{8}{9} \qquad y_3 = 1 \qquad y_4 = \frac{8}{9} \qquad y_5 = \frac{5}{9}$$

Therefore,

$$S_{Left} = \left(\frac{1}{3}\right)\left(0 + \frac{5}{9} + \frac{8}{9} + 1 + \frac{8}{9} + \frac{5}{9}\right) = \frac{35}{27}$$

Notice that in contrast to example 39.3 there is no ambiguity over which endpoints to choose here; we always use the left-hand endpoint. This is definitely an advantage. However, because some of the rectangles are completely below the graph while others go above the graph, we cannot state whether S_{Left} is greater than or less than the exact area. This is certainly a drawback.

example 39.6   Use midpoint rectangles with $n = 4$ subintervals to estimate the area under $y = \cos x$ on the interval $[0, \frac{\pi}{2}]$.

solution   We begin with a picture.

Here, the width of each of our rectangles is

$$\Delta x = \frac{\frac{\pi}{2} - 0}{4} = \frac{\pi}{8}$$

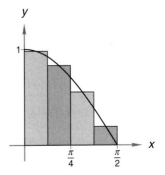

We are using the midpoints of each subinterval to determine the height of each rectangle. These midpoints are

$$x_0 = \frac{\pi}{16} \qquad x_1 = \frac{3\pi}{16} \qquad x_2 = \frac{5\pi}{16} \qquad x_3 = \frac{7\pi}{16}$$

The height of each rectangle is the cosine of each of these x-values:

$$y_0 \approx 0.9808 \qquad y_1 \approx 0.8315 \qquad y_2 \approx 0.5556 \qquad y_3 \approx 0.1951$$

(These approximations are simply found using a calculator.) Therefore the approximate area is

$$S_{Mid} \approx \left(\frac{\pi}{8}\right)(0.9808 + 0.8315 + 0.5556 + 0.1951)$$

$$S_{Mid} \approx \mathbf{1.0065}$$

The **exact** area under the curve $y = \cos x$ between $x = 0$ and $x = \frac{\pi}{2}$ is 1. So S_{Mid} with four subintervals is a fairly good approximation of the area here.

**problem set
39**

1.
(39)   Sketch the graph of $y = x^2 + 1$. Find a lower sum to estimate the area under the curve on the interval $[0, 4]$ divided into $n = 4$ subintervals.

2.
(39)   Estimate the area under the function described in problem 1 by using upper rectangles with $n = 4$ subintervals on the interval $[2, 4]$.

3.
(39)   Estimate the area under the function described in problem 1 by using $n = 4$ midpoint rectangles on the interval $[1, 3]$.

Integrate in problems 4 and 5.

4. $\int \left(4e^x - \dfrac{1}{\sqrt{x}} + 6 \right) dx$
(38)

5. $\int \left(3e^x - \dfrac{2}{x} + \sin x - \cos x - \dfrac{4}{\sqrt{x}} + 2x^5 \right) dx$
(38)

6. Find $f'(x)$ given $f(x) = e^{\cos x}$.
(37)

7. Find $\dfrac{dy}{dx}$ given $y = \sin (x^3 - 4x^2 + 2x - 5)$.
(37)

8. If $y = \sin^3 x$, what is $\dfrac{dy}{dx}$?
(37)

9. (a) Find all the critical numbers of $y = \dfrac{1}{4}x^4 + \dfrac{2}{3}x^3 - \dfrac{1}{2}x^2 - 2x + 5$.
(36)

     (b) Use a rough sketch of the graph of the function to determine the local maximum and minimum values of y and where they occur.

10. Let x and y be functions of t. Differentiate implicitly to find $\dfrac{dx}{dt}$ given $x^2 + y^2 = 9$.
(34)

11. Approximate the slope of the line tangent to the graph of $y = \ln |x| + e^x$ at $x = -2$.
(19,26)

12. Approximate the value of $f'''(3)$ where $f(x) = -3 \cos x$.
(27)

13. Let $f(x) = 12 \ln |x| \sin x$. Determine $f'(0.5)$.
(26,31)

14. Shown below is the graph of $f(x) = \ln x$ with the point $(2, \ln 2)$ marked on the graph as well
(19,26) as an arbitrary point $(x, \ln x)$. A line is drawn through these two points. As x approaches the value 2, the line drawn through the two points better and better approximates the line tangent to the graph of f at $x = 2$. The slope of the line through the two points is $s = \frac{\ln x - \ln 2}{x - 2}$.

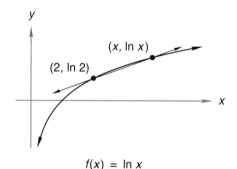

$f(x) = \ln x$

     (a) Use the trace or table feature on the graphing calculator to determine the limit of the slope function s as x approaches 2.

     (b) Determine the exact value of $f'(2)$ where $f(x) = \ln x$.

Evaluate the limits in problems 15–17.

15. $\lim\limits_{n \to \infty} \dfrac{3n^2}{1000n + n^2}$
(17)

16. $\lim\limits_{x \to 0} \dfrac{x + 1}{x}$
(17)

17. $\lim\limits_{n \to \infty} \dfrac{3n^3 - 4n^2}{n^2 - 5n}$
(17)

18. Indicate whether the following statement is true or false and justify your answer:
(11)

         If f is a function such that $\lim\limits_{x \to 1^+} f(x) = \lim\limits_{x \to 1^-} f(x) = 3$, then $f(1) = 3$.

19. Let $f(x) = \sqrt{x}$ and $g(x) = -1 + f(x - 2)$. Graph f and g on the same coordinate plane.
(21)

20. Find the values of a, b, and c in $f(x) = ax^2 + bx + c$ for which the graph of f will intersect
(10) the x-axis at -1 and 2 and the y-axis at -4.

21. Describe both the domain and the range of the function $y = \arcsin x$.
(13)

22. The sum of the squares of the first n positive integers is $\frac{n(n + 1)(2n + 1)}{6}$. Verify this formula for the
(R) sum of the squares of the first four positive integers. Apply this formula to find the sum of the
squares of the first 40 positive integers.

23. Evaluate: $\displaystyle\sum_{i=-1}^{1} -\left(\frac{1}{2}\right)^{i}$
(1)

24. Show that $(\sin x)\left[\cos\left(\dfrac{\pi}{2} - x\right)\right] + (\cos -x)\left[\sin\left(\dfrac{\pi}{2} - x\right)\right] = 1$ for all values of x.
(8)

25. A unit circle is centered at the origin. The center of the circle is the point O. If P is the point on
(13) the unit circle with coordinates $\left(\frac{1}{2}, \frac{\sqrt{3}}{2}\right)$, what is the angle θ that $\overline{OP}$ makes with the
positive x-axis.

LESSON 40 *Units for the Derivative • Normal Lines • Maximums and Minimums on a Graphing Calculator*

40.A
units for the derivative

For physical applications of calculus, it is necessary to consider the units of the independent variable
and the units of the dependent variable. When these units are considered, we find that the derivative
of a function also has units. Consider the graph of $V(t)$, where V is volume in cubic centimeters and t
is time in seconds.

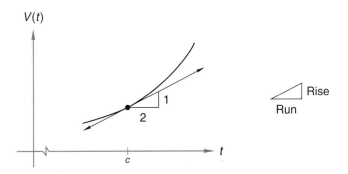

The graph shows that when $t = c$ the slope of V equals 1 cubic centimeter divided by 2 seconds, or

$$V'(c) = \frac{1 \text{ cm}^3}{2 \text{ s}} = \frac{1}{2}\frac{\text{cm}^3}{\text{s}}$$

As demonstrated, **the unit of the derivative of a function is the unit of the dependent variable
(unit on the vertical axis) divided by the unit of the independent variable (unit on the
horizontal axis).**

example 40.1 The distance s of the particle from the origin is given by the equation $s = t^2 + 3t + 7$, where s is in meters and time t is in minutes. What is the rate of change of the distance with respect to time when time equals 4 minutes?

solution The rate of change of s with respect to t when t equals 4 minutes is $\left.\dfrac{ds}{dt}\right|_4$.

$$s = t^2 + 3t + 7 \qquad \text{equation}$$

$$\frac{ds}{dt} = 2t + 3 \qquad \text{derivative}$$

$$\left.\frac{ds}{dt}\right|_4 = 2(4) + 3 = 11 \frac{\text{meters}}{\text{minute}} \qquad \text{evaluated}$$

The rate of change of distance with respect to time is **velocity,** so the velocity when $t = 4$ is

$$\left.\frac{ds}{dt}\right|_4 = 11 \ \frac{\textbf{meters}}{\textbf{minute}}$$

example 40.2 The velocity of a particle in meters per second is given by the quadratic equation $v = 4t^2 + 2t + 4$ where time t is in seconds. What is the acceleration of the particle when $t = 3$ seconds?

solution **Acceleration** is the rate of change of velocity with respect to time. We want the acceleration when $t = 3$, which is $\left.\dfrac{dv}{dt}\right|_3$.

$$v = \left(4t^2 + 2t + 4\right) \frac{\text{meters}}{\text{second}} \qquad \text{equation}$$

$$\text{Acceleration} = \frac{dv}{dt} = (8t + 2) \frac{\frac{\text{meters}}{\text{second}}}{\text{second}} \qquad \text{derivative}$$

$$\left.\frac{dv}{dt}\right|_3 = 8(3) + 2 = 26 \frac{\frac{\text{meters}}{\text{second}}}{\text{second}} \qquad \text{evaluated}$$

The units of velocity are meters/second, or meters per second. The units of acceleration are (meters/second)/second, or meters per second per second. This is often written as meters per second squared, or m/s^2. Thus the acceleration, which is the rate of change of velocity, is

$$26 \ \frac{\text{m}}{\text{s}^2}$$

40.B
normal lines In mathematics the word *normal* does not mean ordinary. It means perpendicular. This use of the word *normal* began with the ancient Romans, as the Latin word for a carpenter's square is *norma*.

example 40.3 Find the equation of the line normal to the graph of $y = e^x$ at $x = 1$.

solution When $x = 1$, $e^x = e^1$, or e, so the point of intersection is $(1, e)$. **The slope of the normal line is the negative reciprocal of the slope of the tangent line, because the normal line is perpendicular to the tangent line.** The slope of the tangent line at $x = 1$ equals the value of the derivative of e^x at $x = 1$.

$$\frac{dy}{dx} = e^x \quad \longrightarrow \quad \left.\frac{dy}{dx}\right|_1 = e$$

Since the slope of the tangent line is e, the slope of the normal line is $-\dfrac{1}{e}$.

$$y = -\frac{1}{e}x + b \qquad\qquad \text{slope is } -\frac{1}{e}$$

$$e = -\frac{1}{e}(1) + b \qquad\qquad \text{passes through } (1, e)$$

$$b = e + \frac{1}{e} = \frac{e^2 + 1}{e} \qquad\qquad \text{solved for } b$$

$$y = -\frac{1}{e}x + \frac{e^2 + 1}{e} \qquad\qquad \text{equation of the normal line}$$

The constants in this equation are exact because we used e instead of a decimal approximation of e. A calculator may be used to change the exact answer to an approximate answer with decimal numerals.

$$y = -0.3679x + 3.0862$$

Here we see the graphs of $y = e^x$, $y = -\frac{1}{e}x + \frac{e^2+1}{e}$ (the normal line at $x = 1$), and $y = ex$ (the tangent line at $x = 1$).

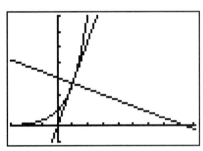

Remember that a ⟨ZSquare⟩ ⟨**ZOOM**⟩ should be employed in order to see the perpendicularity of the tangent and normal lines.

example 40.4   Use a calculator as necessary to approximate the equation of the line normal to the graph of $y = e^{\sin x}$ when $x = 2.7$.

solution   First we use a calculator to find the value of y when $x = 2.7$, being careful to have the calculator set to radians.

$$y = e^{\sin 2.7} \approx 1.5332$$

Thus the point of intersection of the normal line and the graph is approximately $(2.7, 1.5332)$.

Next we evaluate the derivative of $y = e^{\sin x}$ at 2.7 to find the slope of the tangent. First we write the basic form and record the substitution in a box.

$$y = e^u \qquad\qquad \boxed{\begin{array}{l} u = \sin x \\ du = \cos x \, dx \end{array}}$$

Now we find the differential of the basic form, substitute, and divide by dx.

$$dy = e^u \, du \qquad\qquad \text{differential}$$

$$dy = (e^{\sin x})(\cos x \, dx) \qquad\qquad \text{substituted}$$

$$\frac{dy}{dx} = (\cos x)e^{\sin x} \qquad\qquad \text{divided by } dx$$

Evaluating the derivative when $x = 2.7$ gives

$$\frac{dy}{dx}\bigg|_{2.7} = (\cos 2.7)e^{\sin 2.7} \approx -1.3862$$

This is the slope of the tangent line through the point (2.7, 1.5332). The slope of the normal line is

$$-\frac{1}{-1.3862} \approx 0.7214$$

If we use 2.7 for x, 1.5332 for y, and 0.7214 for m, we can solve for b.

$$
\begin{aligned}
y &= mx + b & &\text{equation} \\
1.5332 &\approx (0.7214)(2.7) + b & &\text{substituted} \\
b &\approx -0.4146 & &\text{solved}
\end{aligned}
$$

So the equation that approximates the normal line is

$$y = 0.7214x - 0.4146$$

40.C

maximums and minimums on a graphing calculator

There are occasions when a quick approximation of a relative maximum or minimum of a function in a certain closed interval is needed. Rather than taking the derivative and finding critical numbers, such approximations can be accomplished on a TI-83.

example 40.5   Approximate the value of the relative maximum of $y = \sin x$ on the interval $[0, \pi]$.

solution   It is often wise to try a new procedure on a problem that can be verified another way. Here we know the maximum is 1, which occurs when $x = \frac{\pi}{2}$. To find the maximum with the calculator, we define $\mathtt{Y1=\sin(X)}$. Using the $\mathtt{ZTrig}$ settings in the $\mathtt{ZOOM}$ menu yields the graph to the right.

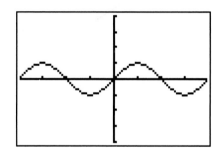

After pressing $\boxed{\text{2nd}}\ \boxed{\text{TRACE}}$ (CALC) to access the $\mathtt{CALCULATE}$ menu, we choose the option $\mathtt{4:maximum}$. The calculator awaits a left bound for the max. Using the $\blacktriangleleft$ and $\blacktriangleright$ buttons, we place the cursor to the left of the max and press $\boxed{\text{ENTER}}$. Then we place the cursor somewhere to the right of the max and press $\boxed{\text{ENTER}}$ again. Finally, we place the cursor near the max and press $\boxed{\text{ENTER}}$. The calculator returns a screen such as the one at right.

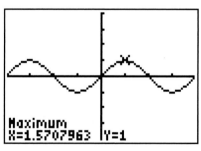

The calculator has found the maximum of **1** at $x = 1.5707963$. The x-value found by the graphing calculator is a decimal approximation for the exact input $x = \frac{\pi}{2}$.

example 40.6   Estimate the minimum of $y = x^3 + 4x^2 - 7x - 5$ over the interval $[0, 4]$.

solution   Using the $\mathtt{ZStandard}$ settings, we see the graph of the function as follows:

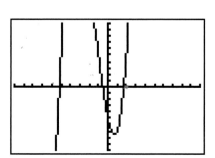

Although a portion of the graph is off the screen, the relevant portion over the interval [0, 4] is in plain view, so we are ready to go to the CALCULATE menu to obtain our estimate. After doing so, the calculator returns a minimum value of approximately **–7.5972.**

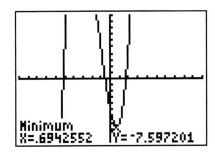

As we have stated, this is only an approximate value. To obtain the exact local minimum, you must algebraically determine the derivative, find the critical values, and evaluate the original function at these values. You should primarily use the calculator to give you the approximate maximums or minimums; exact answers should be found by hand.

problem set 40

1. The volume V (in cubic centimeters) of the balloon at time t (in seconds) is given by the equation
(40) $V(t) = 20e^t$. Find the rate of change of the volume when $t = 3$ seconds.

2. A particle is moving along the number line so that its distance from the origin at any time t (in
(40) seconds) is given by $s(t) = -2t^2 + t^3$. Find the velocity of the particle when $t = 1$ second.

3. Find the equation of the line normal to the graph of $y = -3 \ln |x|$ at $x = -3$.
(40)

4. (a) Find the critical numbers of f where $f(x) = x^3 + \dfrac{3}{2}x^2 - 6x + 2$.
(36)

   (b) Use this equation and a rough sketch of the graph of the function to determine where the local maximums and minimums of f occur and what their values are.

5. Sketch the graph of $y = -x^2 + 1$ and partition the interval [0, 1] into four subintervals of
(39) equal length. Estimate the area between the curve and the x-axis over the interval [0, 1] by calculating the upper sum.

6. Use a left sum to estimate the area under $y = -x^2 + 4$ on the interval [–1, 2] with $n = 6$
(39) subintervals.

7. Use a right sum to estimate the area under $y = -x^2 + 4$ on the interval [–1, 2] with $n = 6$
(39) subintervals.

8. Using a graphing calculator, graph $y = x^3 - 4x^2 + 2x - 1$. Find the approximate
(40) coordinates of the local minimum point and the local maximum point on the graph by using the CALCULATE menu on the calculator.

9. Use a graphing calculator to approximate the value of the derivative of $y = x^3$ at $x = 2$. Test
(29) the calculator's answer directly by computing the derivative of $y = x^3$ and evaluating it at $x = 2$.

Antidifferentiate in problems 10–12.

10. $\displaystyle\int \left(2 \sin x - 4x - \dfrac{3}{2}\sqrt{x} - 3 \right) dx$ **11.** $\displaystyle\int \left(\dfrac{\sqrt{2}}{t} + 3 \cos t + 1 \right) dt$
(38) (38)

12. $\displaystyle\int \left(\dfrac{x + 1}{x} \right) dx$ (*Hint:* Rewrite the integrand as the sum of two terms.)
(38)

Differentiate the functions in problems 13–15 with respect to x.

13. $y = \sqrt[3]{x^2 + 5}$ **14.** $s = \ln |\sin x|$ **15.** $y = -\sin^4 x$
(37) (37) (37)

16. Find $\dfrac{dy}{dx}$ where $\sin x + \cos y = xy$.
(34)

17. Find $\dfrac{dA}{dt}$ where $A = \dfrac{4}{3}\pi r^3$ and both the area A and the radius r are functions of time t.
(34)

18. Let $f(x) = 2\ln|x|$. Evaluate $f'''(-2)$.
(27)

19. Find $\dfrac{dy}{dx}$ where $y = e^x \ln|x|$.
(31)

20. Sketch the graph of g where $f(x) = x^2 + x - 2$ and $g(x) = \dfrac{1}{f(x)}$.
(30)

21. Determine the approximate value of $\log_3 5$.
(20)

22. Evaluate: $\displaystyle\lim_{x\to\infty} \dfrac{x^3 - 4x + 5}{1 - 2x^3}$
(17)

23. Simplify: $\dfrac{1 - \sin^2\theta}{\cos^2\left(\dfrac{\pi}{2} - \theta\right)}$
(8)

24. The sum of the cubes of the first n positive integers is $\left(\frac{n(n+1)}{2}\right)^2$. Verify this formula for the sum
(R) of the cubes of the first three positive integers. Apply this formula to find the sum of the cubes of the first 40 positive integers.

25. Assuming $x = 2y$, compare the following: A. y^2 B. $0.25x^2$
(1)

LESSON 41 *Graphs of Rational Functions III • Repeated Factors*

41.A
graphs of rational functions III

To review the properties of factors of polynomials, consider $f(x) = x^2 - 4$ and $g(x) = x^2 + 4$. Note that if x equals 2 or -2, $f(x)$ has a value of zero. However, no real value of x causes the polynomial $g(x)$ to equal zero. If x equals zero, the value of $g(x)$ is 4, and if x is any other real number, x^2 is a positive number and $x^2 + 4$ is a positive number greater than 4. The polynomial $f(x)$ can be factored into two linear real factors. The polynomial $g(x)$ cannot be factored into linear real factors, and we remember that this polynomial is called an irreducible quadratic polynomial. Since irreducible quadratic factors never equal zero for any real number value of x, the vertical asymptotes and x-intercepts of rational functions are not affected by irreducible quadratic factors. They do cause "bends" in the graphs but do not affect our rough sketches.

example 41.1 Graph: $y = -\dfrac{(x^2 + 2)(x - 1)}{(x + 3)(x - 2)(x - 3)(x + 2)}$

solution We ignore the irreducible quadratic factor in the numerator, plot the zeros and vertical asymptotes, and graph the function. The ratio of the dominant terms in the two polynomials is

$$-\dfrac{x^3}{x^4}$$

so the graph will begin on the right-hand side as a small negative value of *y*.

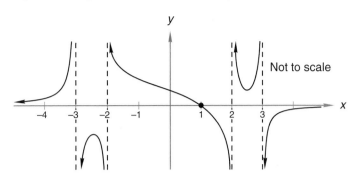

Such graphs were drawn in this right-to-left fashion in Lesson 28. Note that all portions of this graph continue indefinitely, getting close to the asymptotes but never crossing them. Arrowheads are placed on their ends to indicate this. The complete solution is the graph shown below.

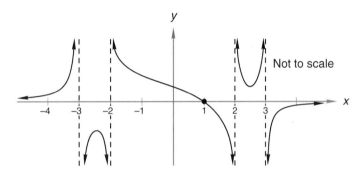

This graph could also be drawn with a graphing calculator. However, the calculator must be used carefully! For example, the graph of this function with `ZStandard` settings is:

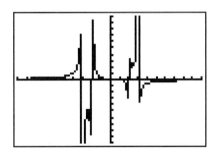

This is certainly not an optimal rendition of the graph.

41.B

repeated factors

If a linear real factor is repeated an even number of times in the numerator or in the denominator of a rational function, the graph of the function is changed. If a factor in the numerator is raised to an even power, the factor can equal zero, but it can never have a negative value. **Thus the graph of a rational function does not cross the *x*-axis at a zero caused by a factor raised to an even power.** It touches the *x*-axis at this zero and goes back in the vertical direction from whence it came. In the same way, even-powered linear factors in the denominator still cause vertical asymptotes, but the graph does not "jump" across the *x*-axis at the vertical asymptotes.

example 41.2   Graph: (a) $y = \dfrac{4}{(x - 3)^2}$ (b) $y = -\dfrac{4}{(x - 3)^2}$

solution   The number 3 makes the denominator zero in both functions, so there is a vertical asymptote at $x = 3$ in each graph. However, the value of $(x - 3)^2$ is never negative, so this factor does not change sign when x goes from a value less than 3 to a value greater than 3. The graph "jumps" across the vertical asymptote, but not across the x-axis.

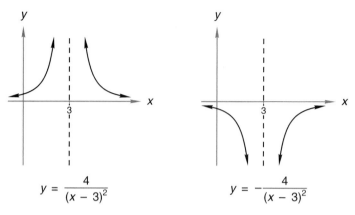

$$y = \frac{4}{(x-3)^2} \qquad\qquad y = -\frac{4}{(x-3)^2}$$

The graph on the left-hand side resembles a volcano, and the graph on the right-hand side resembles a volcano that is upside down. Whenever there is a "volcano" in the graph of a rational function, we know that the denominator of the function contains a linear real factor raised to an even power.

example 41.3   Graph: $y = \dfrac{(x-1)^2(x^2+1)}{(x+2)(x-3)^2(x-6)^2}$

solution   Note that the ratio of the lead terms of the numerator and denominator polynomials is x^4 over x^5. Thus, when x is a large positive number, the function has a small positive value, which gives us a starting point for the graph. We ignore the irreducible quadratic factor in the numerator and locate the zeros and vertical asymptotes.

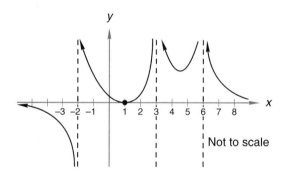

The $(x-3)^2$ and $(x-6)^2$ in the denominator cause "volcanos" in the graph around the asymptotes at $+3$ and $+6$, and the $(x-1)^2$ in the numerator causes the graph to touch but not cross the x-axis at the zero of $+1$.

Therefore the final solution is the graph shown below.

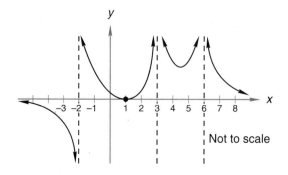

problem set
41

1. The volume of liquid decreased exponentially. At midnight there were 3 liters of liquid, and
(26) 1 hour later there was only 1 liter of liquid. How many liters of liquid were there at 7 a.m.?

Sketch the functions whose equations are given in problems 2 and 3. Clearly show the asymptotes and
x-intercepts of the graphs. Other than these features, the graphs need not be precise.

2. $y = \dfrac{(x + 1)^2(x^2 + 1)}{(x - 3)(x - 1)^2(x - 5)^2}$
(41)

3. $y = -\dfrac{(x^2 + 1)(x - 1)}{x(x + 1)^2(x - 2)}$
(41)

4. The population P at any time t is given by the equation $P(t) = 20{,}000e^t$. Find the rate of change
(40) of the population when $t = 3$.

5. Find the equation for the rate of change of the volume $\frac{dV}{dt}$ if $V = \frac{4}{3}\pi r^3$ and both V and r are
(34) functions of time t.

6. Write the equation of the line normal to the graph of $y = x + \ln x$ at $x = 1$.
(40)

7. (a) Find all the critical numbers of $y = \dfrac{1}{4}x^4 + \dfrac{4}{3}x^3 - \dfrac{1}{2}x^2 - 4x + 9$.
(36)

   (b) Use this equation and a rough sketch of the graph of the function to determine the local
   maximum and minimum values of y and where they occur.

8. Sketch the graph of $y = \sin x$ where $0 \le x \le \pi$. Partition the interval $[0, \pi]$ into four equal
(39) subintervals, and estimate the area between the graph of $y = \sin x$ and the x-axis on the
interval $[0, \pi]$ by computing a lower sum. (No calculator is necessary.)

9. Use four midpoint rectangles of equal width to estimate the area under $y = \sin x$ on the
(39) interval $[0, \pi]$.

10. Use upper rectangles to estimate the area under $y = -x^2 + 9$ on the interval $[-3, 3]$ with
(39) $n = 6$ subintervals.

11. Approximate the value of the derivative of $y = \sin \frac{1}{x}$ at $x = 0.2$ by using a graphing
(29) calculator.

12. Let $f(x) = 1 + x \sin x + (\ln x)(\cos x)$ where $1 \le x \le 10$.
(40)

   (a) Graph f on a graphing calculator.

   (b) Approximate the coordinates of all local minimum and maximum points, excluding
   endpoints.

   (c) Approximate the zero of f that lies in the interval $[2, 4]$.

Integrate in problems 13–15.

13. $\displaystyle\int \left(2 \sin u - \dfrac{3}{u^3}\right) du$
(38)

14. $\displaystyle\int -\dfrac{3}{t}\, dt$
(38)

15. $\displaystyle\int \left(\dfrac{2}{\sqrt{x}} - 4\right) dx$
(38)

Differentiate the functions given in problems 16–20 with respect to x.

16. $f(x) = \dfrac{1}{\sqrt{x^2 + 1}}$
(37)

17. $y = \ln \left|x^2 + 1\right|$
(37)

18. $y = \ln \left|\sin x\right|$
(37)

19. $y = x^2 e^x$
(31)

20. $y = x \ln \left|x\right|$
(31)

21. Let $f(x) = \left|x\right|$ and $g(x) = 1 + f(x - 3)$. Sketch the graphs of f and g on the same
(21) coordinate plane.

22. Let $f(x) = \ln x$ and $g(x) = \dfrac{1}{x}$. Write the equation of fg and determine the domain of fg.
(18)

23. Evaluate $\displaystyle\lim_{x \to 1^-} f(x)$ and $\displaystyle\lim_{x \to 1^+} f(x)$ where $f(x) = \begin{cases} x & \text{when } x \geq 1 \\ -x + 1 & \text{when } x < 1. \end{cases}$
(11)

24. Solve for r in terms of h in the figure shown.
(8)

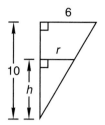

25. What is the sum of the first 200 positive integers?
(R)

LESSON 42   *The Derivative of a Quotient • Proof of the Quotient Rule*

42.A
the derivative of a quotient

We remember the rule for the derivative of a product by saying

> first dee second plus second dee first

The rule for the derivative of the quotient of two functions is a little more complicated. **The derivative of a quotient of two functions equals the denominator times the derivative of the numerator, minus the numerator times the derivative of the denominator, all divided by the square of the denominator.** Symbolically, this can be represented as in the following box:

$$d\left(\frac{u}{v}\right) = \frac{v\,du - u\,dv}{v^2}$$

A mnemonic can also be used to remember the derivative of a quotient.

> low dee high minus high dee low, over the square of what's below

example 42.1   Let $f(x) = \dfrac{\ln x}{2x + 3}$. Find $f'(x)$.

solution   We remember "low dee high minus high dee low, over the square of what's below" and write

$$f'(x) = \frac{\overbrace{(2x + 3)}^{\text{low}}\overbrace{\left(\dfrac{1}{x}\right)}^{\substack{\text{dee} \\ \text{high}}} - \overbrace{(\ln x)}^{\text{high}}\overbrace{(2)}^{\substack{\text{dee} \\ \text{low}}}}{(2x + 3)^2}$$

We rearrange this result by multiplying both top and bottom by x.

$$f'(x) = \frac{(2x + 3) - 2x\,\ln x}{x(2x + 3)^2}$$

example 42.2   Find $D_x \dfrac{x^3 - 2x + 2}{\sin x}$.

solution   Writing the denominator times the derivative of the numerator minus the numerator times the derivative of the denominator, all divided by the square of the denominator gives us

$$D_x \frac{x^3 - 2x + 2}{\sin x} = \frac{(\sin x)(3x^2 - 2) - (x^3 - 2x + 2)(\cos x)}{\sin^2 x}$$

There are many ways this derivative can be written, and all are rather complicated. Therefore, we leave it as it is.

example 42.3   Let $y = \dfrac{\cos x}{e^x + x}$. Find $\dfrac{dy}{dx}$.

solution   Using the rule for the derivative of a quotient lets us write

$$\frac{dy}{dx} = \frac{(e^x + x)(-\sin x) - (\cos x)(e^x + 1)}{(e^x + x)^2}$$

The derivative could be left in this form, but we decide to rearrange the expression and write

$$\frac{dy}{dx} = \frac{(-\sin x)(e^x + x) - (\cos x)(e^x + 1)}{(e^x + x)^2}$$

example 42.4   Find the differential dy of $y = \dfrac{x}{\cos x}$.

solution   We use low dee high, etc., but with differentials instead of derivatives.

$$dy = \frac{(\cos x)(dx) - (x)(-\sin x\, dx)}{(\cos x)^2} = \left(\frac{\cos x + x \sin x}{\cos^2 x}\right) dx$$

42.B
proof of the quotient rule

The derivatives of two functions, f and g, are defined as follows:

$$f'(x) = \lim_{\Delta x \to 0} \frac{f(x + \Delta x) - f(x)}{\Delta x} \qquad g'(x) = \lim_{\Delta x \to 0} \frac{g(x + \Delta x) - g(x)}{\Delta x}$$

If $h(x)$ is equal to $f(x)$ over $g(x)$, we need to show that

$$h'(x) = \frac{g(x) \displaystyle\lim_{\Delta x \to 0} \dfrac{f(x + \Delta x) - f(x)}{\Delta x} - f(x) \displaystyle\lim_{\Delta x \to 0} \dfrac{g(x + \Delta x) - g(x)}{\Delta x}}{[g(x)]^2}$$

By definition, the derivative of the function h is

$$h'(x) = \lim_{\Delta x \to 0} \frac{h(x + \Delta x) - h(x)}{\Delta x} = \lim_{\Delta x \to 0} \frac{\dfrac{f(x + \Delta x)}{g(x + \Delta x)} - \dfrac{f(x)}{g(x)}}{\Delta x}$$

Adding the two terms in the numerator and then dividing by Δx as indicated, we get

$$\lim_{\Delta x \to 0} \frac{f(x + \Delta x) \cdot g(x) - f(x) \cdot g(x + \Delta x)}{\Delta x \cdot g(x) \cdot g(x + \Delta x)}$$

To get the desired form, an algebraic trick is needed. We subtract *and* add $f(x) \cdot g(x)$ in the numerator to get

$$h'(x) = \lim_{\Delta x \to 0} \frac{f(x + \Delta x) \cdot g(x) - f(x) \cdot g(x) - f(x) \cdot g(x + \Delta x) + f(x) \cdot g(x)}{\Delta x \cdot g(x) \cdot g(x + \Delta x)}$$

Now the numerator can be factored and rewritten as

$$h'(x) = \lim_{\Delta x \to 0} \frac{g(x)[f(x + \Delta x) - f(x)] - f(x)[g(x + \Delta x) - g(x)]}{\Delta x \cdot g(x) \cdot g(x + \Delta x)}$$

Because the limit of a sum or product or quotient equals the sum or product or quotient of the respective individual limits, this can be rearranged as

$$\frac{\lim\limits_{\Delta x \to 0} g(x) \cdot \lim\limits_{\Delta x \to 0} \dfrac{f(x + \Delta x) - f(x)}{\Delta x} - \lim\limits_{\Delta x \to 0} f(x) \cdot \lim\limits_{\Delta x \to 0} \dfrac{g(x + \Delta x) - g(x)}{\Delta x}}{\lim\limits_{\Delta x \to 0} g(x) \cdot \lim\limits_{\Delta x \to 0} g(x + \Delta x)}$$

(The properties of limits that are applied here are discussed in greater detail in Lesson 70.) The limits of $g(x)$ and $f(x)$ as Δx approaches zero are $g(x)$ and $f(x)$, because these expressions are independent of Δx. Also, as Δx approaches zero, the value of $g(x + \Delta x)$ in the denominator approaches $g(x)$. So the denominator approaches $[g(x)]^2$. Thus the proof is complete.

problem set 42

$(5,6,40)$

1. Squares are cut from the corners of a sheet of metal that is 8 inches wide and 10 inches long. The resulting flaps are folded up to form a box that has no top.

   (a) Express the volume of the box formed in terms of the variable x, which represents the lengths of the sides of the squares that are cut away.

   (b) Graph the equation you found in (a) on a graphing calculator. Choose window settings that show the local maximum and minimum of this volume function.

   (c) Use the CALCULATE menu to approximate the local maximum of the volume function. For what value of x is the volume a maximum? What is the corresponding value of the volume?

   (d) What are the values of x that make sense for this problem? In other words, what is the domain of this real-world problem?

Differentiate the functions in problems 2 and 3 with respect to x.

2. $y = \dfrac{\sin x}{e^x - x}$
(42)

3. $f(x) = \dfrac{\sin x}{\cos x}$
(42)

4. Write the differential dy in terms of u, v, du, and dv given $y = \dfrac{u}{v}$.
(42)

5. Sketch the graph of $y = \dfrac{(x^2 + 3)(x - 1)}{x(x + 4)^2(x + 2)}$. Do not use a graphing calculator. Clearly indicate all zeros and asymptotes.
(41)

6. Use implicit differentiation to find the equation for the rate of change of volume V, where $V = \frac{1}{3}\pi r^2 h$ and the radius r and the height h are both functions of time t.
(34)

7. Use five left rectangles to estimate the area under $y = e^x$ on the interval $[-1, 1]$.
(39)

8. Sketch a graph of $y = x$ where $0 \le x \le 5$. Partition the interval $[0, 5]$ into five subintervals of equal length.
(39)

   (a) Estimate the area under the graph of $y = x$ by computing an upper sum.

   (b) Estimate the area under the graph of $y = x$ by computing a lower sum.

   (c) Use geometry to compute the actual area of the described region.

   (d) Suppose the interval $[0, 5]$ is divided into n equally long subintervals. Estimate the area under the graph of $y = x$ by computing an upper sum. (*Note:* The answer should be given in terms of n.)

9. Find the equation of the line normal to the graph of $y = \cos x$ at $x = \pi$.
(40)

10. (a) Find the critical numbers of the function $f(x) = -\frac{1}{4}x^4 + \frac{1}{2}x^2 - 3$.
(36)

(b) Use this equation and a rough sketch of the graph of f to determine the local maximum and minimum values of f and where they occur.

Integrate in problems 11 and 12.

11. $\int \left(2x^2 - \frac{1}{\sqrt{x}} + e^x + \frac{1}{x} - \sin x \right) dx$
(38)

12. $\int -\frac{4u}{\sqrt{u}} \, du$ (*Hint:* First simplify the integrand.)
(35)

Differentiate the functions in problems 13 and 14 with respect to x.

13. $y = \ln \left| x^2 + \sin x \right|$ **14.** $y = \dfrac{1}{\sqrt{x^3 + 3}}$
(37)   (37)

15. The pressure P at any time t is given by $P(t) = 16e^{-4t}$. Find the rate of change of P when $t = 4$.
(40)

16. Find $s'(t)$ where $s(t) = \dfrac{2}{\sqrt{t}} + \ln |t|$.
(26)

17. Let $y = 2u^3 e^u$. Find $\dfrac{dy}{du}$.
(31)

18. Let $f(x) = \sin(2x)$ $(0 \le x \le 2\pi)$. Use interval notation to indicate when f is increasing.
(15)

19. The base of a right circular cone has a radius of 3 cm, and the height of the cone is 6 cm. What is the volume of the cone?
(R)

20. Use the key trigonometric identities to develop identities for $\cos \dfrac{x}{2}$ and $\sin \dfrac{x}{2}$.
(12)

21. Use interval notation to describe the values of x for which $|x - 1| < 0.01$.
(9)

22. Graph $f(x) = [x]$ and evaluate $f(1.2)$, $f(-1.5)$, and $f\left(-2\frac{1}{2}\right)$.
(9)

23. Find the radius of the circle shown. In the figure, $AB = 8$ and $OD = 3$.
(2)

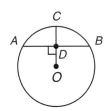

24. Calculate the sum of the first 300 positive integers.
(R)

25. Compute $\lim\limits_{n \to \infty} \dfrac{\frac{1}{2}n(n+1)}{n^2}$. The numerator of this fraction is the sum of the first n natural numbers (also called the nth *triangular* number), while the denominator is obviously the nth square number. (The point of this problem is to relate the sum of the first n numbers to n^2.)
(17)

LESSON 43 *Area Under a Curve as an Infinite Summation*

The discussion in Lesson 39 on upper and lower sums contained the idea that, as the number of equal-width subintervals increases, the error in the approximation of the area under the curve diminishes. This reduction in error is pictured in the graphs below. The shaded areas indicate the errors in the lower sum of the area under the graph of $y = x + 2$ on the interval from 0 to 6. As the number of subintervals increases from 2 to 3 to 6, the error decreases from 9 to 6 to 3.

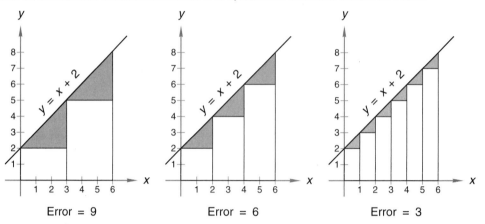

Error = 9   Error = 6   Error = 3

To write a general expression for the lower- or upper-sum estimate of the area under a curve on an interval $[a, b]$, we partition the interval into n nonoverlapping subintervals of equal width, $\Delta x = \frac{b - a}{n}$. A lower sum is computed using lower, or *inscribed*, rectangles, while an upper sum is computed using upper, or *circumscribed*, rectangles.

It is not known where minimum or maximum values are attained in the subintervals, so we say that $f(x_{L1})$ represents the least value of $f(x)$ on the first subinterval. Thus the area of the first rectangle in a lower sum is $f(x_{L1})\Delta x$. Similarly, $f(x_{L2})$ represents the minimum value of $f(x)$ on the second subinterval, so the area of the second rectangle in a lower sum is $f(x_{L2})\Delta x$. Thus the lower sum of all n rectangles can be written as

$$S_L = f(x_{L1})\Delta x + f(x_{L2})\Delta x + f(x_{L3})\Delta x + \cdots + f(x_{Ln})\Delta x \qquad \text{or}$$
$$S_L = \Delta x[f(x_{L1}) + f(x_{L2}) + f(x_{L3}) + \cdots + f(x_{Ln})]$$

We can use summation notation to write this sum as $S_L = \Delta x \sum_{i=1}^{n} f(x_{Li})$.

If $f(x_{G1})$ represents the greatest value of $f(x)$ in the first subinterval and $f(x_{G2})$ represents the greatest value of $f(x)$ in the second subinterval and so on, we can write a general expression for the upper sum.

$$S_U = f(x_{G1})\Delta x + f(x_{G2})\Delta x + f(x_{G3})\Delta x + \cdots + f(x_{Gn})\Delta x \qquad \text{or}$$
$$S_U = \Delta x[f(x_{G1}) + f(x_{G2}) + f(x_{G3}) + \cdots + f(x_{Gn})]$$

This sum can also be written in summation notation as $S_U = \Delta x \sum_{i=1}^{n} f(x_{Gi})$.

The actual area under the curve, A, is a number greater than or equal to any lower sum and less than or equal to any upper sum.

$$S_L = \Delta x \sum_{i=1}^{n} f(x_{Li}) \leq A \leq \Delta x \sum_{i=1}^{n} f(x_{Gi}) = S_U$$

We define the area on the interval $[a, b]$ between the curve and the x-axis to be A, the number approached by both S_L and S_U as n approaches infinity.

$$A = \lim_{n \to \infty} \Delta x \sum_{i=1}^{n} f(x_{Li}) = \lim_{n \to \infty} \Delta x \sum_{i=1}^{n} f(x_{Gi})$$

In this text we simply assume that both of these limits exist and are equal. This is quite an assumption, but not a false one. However, the proof of the existence and equality of these limits is beyond the scope of this text.

Now, look carefully at the two-limit definition above. Note that it makes no reference to a graph nor to area in the usual sense. The definition contains only the limits of the sums of products of a partitioned function. Rectangles are not mentioned. We have defined the area under the graph of f between a and b to be the limit of either of two sums and note that this definition of area has absolutely nothing to do with area as we normally think of it. **We used a graph to get started, but this definition of area stands alone without any graph!**

So, is it actually possible to find an upper or lower sum as the number of rectangles approaches infinity? As we begin to investigate this idea, keep in mind that as n approaches infinity, Δx must approach zero because $\Delta x = \frac{b-a}{n}$.

The following example uses continuous functions that are increasing and nonnegative on the interval. The result is also valid for continuous functions that are not everywhere increasing, and this is discussed in a later lesson. The discussion of the extension of this procedure to functions that are negative on the interval will lead to the development of a limit that is called the *definite integral*.

example 43.1   Use inscribed rectangles to find the exact area under $y = 2x$ on the interval $[0, 2]$ by allowing the number of rectangles to increase without bound.

solution   We partition the interval $[0, 2]$ into n subintervals, each of length $\Delta x = \dfrac{2-0}{n} = \dfrac{2}{n}$.

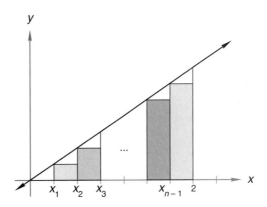

The endpoints of the subintervals and the heights of the rectangles are easily found.

i	x_i	$f(x_i)$
0	0	0
1	$\dfrac{2}{n}$	$2\left(\dfrac{2}{n}\right)$
2	$2\left(\dfrac{2}{n}\right)$	$2\left(\dfrac{4}{n}\right)$
3	$3\left(\dfrac{2}{n}\right)$	$2\left(\dfrac{6}{n}\right)$
$\vdots$	$\vdots$	$\vdots$
$n-1$	$(n-1)\left(\dfrac{2}{n}\right)$	$2\left(\dfrac{2(n-1)}{n}\right)$
n	$n\left(\dfrac{2}{n}\right) = 2$	$2(2)$

Since the width of each rectangle is the same, the lower sum is the product of the width, which is Δx, and the sum of the heights of the rectangles.

$$S_L = \Delta x\left(f(x_0) + f(x_1) + f(x_2) + \cdots + f(x_{n-1})\right)$$

$$= \Delta x\left(0 + \frac{4}{n} + \frac{8}{n} + \frac{12}{n} + \cdots + \frac{2(2(n-1))}{n}\right)$$

Note that we stop with $f(x_{n-1})$ because x_{n-1} is the left endpoint of the last subinterval. To include $f(x_n)$ in the above would be incorrect in this problem. We factor a 4 out of each term in the parentheses and move the common denominator n outside the parentheses to get

$$S_L = \frac{4(\Delta x)}{n}(0 + 1 + 2 + 3 + \cdots + (n-1))$$

Since $1 + 2 + \cdots + m$ equals $\dfrac{m(m+1)}{2}$, $1 + 2 + \cdots + (m-1) = \dfrac{(m-1)m}{2}$. Therefore

$$S_L = \left(\frac{4}{n}\right)\left(\frac{2}{n}\right)\left[\frac{(n-1)n}{2}\right] \qquad \text{since } \Delta x = \frac{2}{n}$$

$$= \frac{4(n-1)}{n}$$

The exact area is found by taking the limit of S_L as n goes to infinity. (Remember, n is the number of rectangles used to approximate the area.)

$$A = \lim_{n \to \infty} S_L$$

$$= \lim_{n \to \infty} \frac{4(n-1)}{n}$$

$$= 4 \lim_{n \to \infty} \frac{n-1}{n}$$

$$= \mathbf{4 \ units^2}$$

A simple check with geometry confirms that this is the correct answer because the region whose area we are trying to find is a triangle with a base of 2 and a height of 4.

example 43.2 Use upper rectangles to estimate the area under an increasing function f on the closed interval $[a, b]$ using n subintervals.

solution

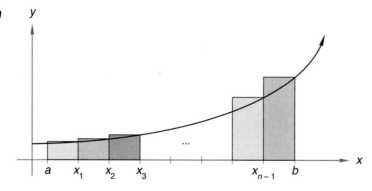

The height of each rectangle is the length of its right edge.

$$\text{Area of the first rectangle} = f(x_1) \cdot \Delta x$$

$$\text{Area of the second rectangle} = f(x_2) \cdot \Delta x$$

$$\text{Area of the third rectangle} = f(x_3) \cdot \Delta x$$

$$\vdots$$

$$\text{Area of the } n\text{th, and last, rectangle} = f(x_n) \cdot \Delta x$$

Adding the areas of these upper rectangles gives an approximation of the area under the curve.

$$A \approx S_U = f(x_1) \cdot \Delta x + f(x_2) \cdot \Delta x + f(x_3) \cdot \Delta x + \cdots + f(x_n) \cdot \Delta x$$

$$= \Delta x[f(x_1) + f(x_2) + f(x_3) + \cdots + f(x_n)]$$

$$= \Delta x \sum_{i=1}^{n} f(x_i)$$

example 43.3   Use circumscribed rectangles to find the exact area under $y = x^2$ on the interval $[0, 3]$ by allowing the number of rectangles to increase without bound.

solution

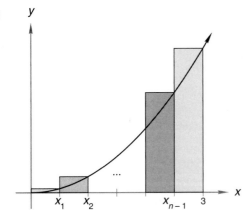

The width of each rectangle is

$$\Delta x = \frac{3 - 0}{n} = \frac{3}{n}$$

The height of each rectangle is determined by the right endpoint of the interval.

i	x_i	$f(x_i)$
1	$\left(\dfrac{3}{n}\right)$	$\left(\dfrac{3}{n}\right)^2$
2	$2\left(\dfrac{3}{n}\right)$	$\left[2\left(\dfrac{3}{n}\right)\right]^2$
3	$3\left(\dfrac{3}{n}\right)$	$\left[3\left(\dfrac{3}{n}\right)\right]^2$
$\vdots$	$\vdots$	$\vdots$
n	$n\left(\dfrac{3}{n}\right)$	$\left[n\left(\dfrac{3}{n}\right)\right]^2$

The upper sum is the product of the uniform width Δx and the sum of the heights of the rectangles.

$$S_U = \Delta x(f(x_1) + f(x_2) + f(x_3) + \cdots + f(x_n))$$

$$= \frac{3}{n}\left[(1^2)\left(\frac{3}{n}\right)^2 + (2^2)\left(\frac{3}{n}\right)^2 + (3^2)\left(\frac{3}{n}\right)^2 + \cdots + (n^2)\left(\frac{3}{n}\right)^2\right]$$

$$= \left(\frac{3}{n}\right)\left(\frac{3}{n}\right)^2[1^2 + 2^2 + 3^2 + \cdots + n^2]$$

$$= \frac{27}{n^3}\left(\frac{n(n+1)(2n+1)}{6}\right) \qquad \text{since } 1^2 + 2^2 + \cdots + n^2 = \frac{n(n+1)(2n+1)}{6}$$

$$= \frac{9}{2}\left(\frac{n(n+1)(2n+1)}{n^3}\right)$$

To calculate the exact area, we must find the limit of S_U as n approaches ∞.

$$A = \lim_{n \to \infty} S_U = \lim_{n \to \infty} \frac{9}{2}\left(\frac{n(n+1)(2n+1)}{n^3}\right)$$

$$= \lim_{n \to \infty} \frac{9}{2}\left(\frac{2n^3 + 3n^2 + n}{n^3}\right)$$

$$= \frac{9}{2}(2) = \textbf{9 units}^2$$

Therefore the exact area of this "oddly" shaped region is simply 9 units².

problem set 43

1. A window has the shape of a rectangle
(5,40) topped by a semicircle, as shown. The perimeter of the entire window is 20, the length of one side of the rectangle is h, and the radius of the semicircular part is r.

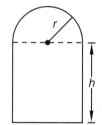

(a) Find h in terms of r.

(b) Express the area of the entire window in terms of r.

(c) Graph the function you found in (b) on a graphing calculator using settings that show the graph's maximum.

(d) Use the appropriate features of the graphing calculator to find the maximum area of the window. What value of r maximizes the area? What is the maximum area?

2. Find the exact area under $y = 2x$ on the interval $[0, 2]$ with an infinite number of
(43) circumscribed rectangles. Check your answer using geometry.

3. Find the exact area under $y = x^2$ on the interval $[0, 2]$ with an infinite number of inscribed
(43) rectangles.

4. Sketch the graph of $f(x) = 1 + \sin x$. Partition the interval $[0, 1.2]$ into six subintervals of
(39) equal width. Use a calculator as necessary to estimate the area under the curve on the interval by calculating a right sum.

5. For $f(x) = 1 + \sin x$, use summation notation to indicate a general lower sum for $f(x)$ on the
(39) interval $[0, 1.2]$ with a partition of 10 subintervals.

Differentiate the functions in problems 6 and 7 with respect to x.

6. $y = \dfrac{e^x + x}{\cos x}$
(42)

7. $y = \dfrac{x^2 + 3}{x^3 - 2x}$
(42)

8. Use the quotient rule to find $d\left(\dfrac{u}{v}\right)$.
(42)

9. Sketch the graph of $y = \dfrac{(x-1)^2(x+2)}{(x+1)(x+2)(x+3)^2(x^2+1)}$. Do not use a graphing calculator. Clearly
(41) indicate all zeros and asymptotes.

10. A particle moves along the number line so that its distance from the origin at any time t
(40) (measured in seconds) is given by $s(t) = \sin t$. Find the velocity of the particle when $t = \pi$ seconds.

11. (a) Find the critical numbers of $f(x) = x^3 - \dfrac{9}{2}x^2 + 6x + 2$.
(36)

(b) Use a rough sketch of the graph of f and its equation to determine the local maximum and minimum values of f and where they occur.

Differentiate the functions in problems 12 and 13 with respect to x.

12. $y = \sqrt{e^x - 1}$
(37)

13. $f(x) = \dfrac{1}{\sqrt[3]{x^2 - 1}}$
(37)

Integrate in problems 14 and 15.

14. $\displaystyle\int \frac{3}{\sqrt{u}}\, du$
(35)

15. $\displaystyle\int \left(\frac{3}{x} + \sqrt{2}x^{4/3} + \cos x - 4e^x \right) dx$
(38)

16. Make a rough sketch of the graph of $f(x) = (x - 1)(x + 1)(2 - x)$. Do not use a graphing
(33) calculator.

17. Let $g(x) = \frac{1}{f(x)}$, where $f(x) = (x - 1)(x + 1)(2 - x)$. Sketch the graph of g without using a
(30) graphing calculator.

18. Graph the function $f(x) = (x - 1)(x + 1)(2 - x)$ on a graphing calculator, and find the
(40) coordinates of all the relative maximum and minimum points.

19. Graph: $f(x) = \ln |x|$
(26)

20. What is $\displaystyle\lim_{x \to 0^+} \ln |x|$?
(16)

21. (a) Express the area A of a rectangle whose perimeter is 50 in terms of the variable x, which
(5,6,40) represents the length of one side of the rectangle.

(b) What is the domain of the function A? (That is, what values of x yield possible rectangles? Include the "degenerate" rectangle of area 0 as a possibility.)

(c) Use a graphing calculator to graph the function A. Set the viewing screen so the x-values range over the domain of A determined in (b) and the y-values show the maximum value for the function.

(d) Find the coordinates of the highest point on the curve.

22. Find the equation of the quadratic function whose zeros are $x = 1$ and $x = -2$ and whose
(10) graph has the y-intercept $y = -4$.

23. (a) Identify the conic section determined by $x^2 + y^2 = 4$.
(22,23)

(b) What two functions must be used to graph this equation on a graphing calculator?

24. Show that $\left[-\sin \left(\dfrac{\pi}{2} - x \right) \right](\cos -x) + 1 = \sin^2 x$ for all x.
(8)

25. Assuming $a - b = 2$, compare the following: A. a^2 B. $b^2 + 4b + 3$
(1)

LESSON 44 *The Chain Rule • Alternate Definition of the Derivative • The Symmetric Derivative*

44.A

the chain rule   If the first function machine shown here multiplies any input by 3 and the second function machine multiplies any input by 2, then the two machines linked together multiply any input of the first machine by 6.

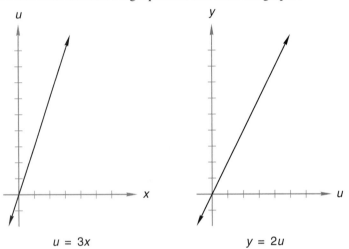

If we call the input of the first machine *x*, the output of the first machine *u*, and the output of the second machine *y*, then we can write the following equations and draw the graphs.

$$u = 3x \qquad\qquad y = 2u$$

The rate of change of *u* with respect to *x* is the slope of the left-hand graph, which is 3. The rate of change of *y* with respect to *u* is the slope of the right-hand graph, which is 2. If *x* changes 1 unit, *u* will change 3 units. But if *u* changes 3 units, then *y* will change 3 times 2, or 6, units. Thus a change of 1 unit in *x* causes a change of 6 units in *y*, and the rate of change of *y* with respect to *x* is 6, which is the product of the two rates of change. We used linear functions for this example, but the rule is true for any two functions if the derivatives exist for the values of *x* and *u* being considered. This rule is called the **chain rule.** The chain rule contains a nuance that is not obvious. It states that the derivative of a composite function equals the product of the slope of the second machine evaluated at *u* times the slope of the first machine evaluated at *x*.

The chain rule is easy to remember when written using Leibniz's notation.

$$\frac{dy}{dx} = \frac{dy}{du} \cdot \frac{du}{dx}$$

The first part of the product is the rate of change of the second function, and the second part of the product is the rate of change of the first function. This product can be extended to define the derivative of any number of functions linked together in this fashion. If *x* is a function of *s* and *s* is a function of *t*, then this notation can be extended to write

$$\frac{dy}{dt} = \frac{dy}{du} \cdot \frac{du}{dx} \cdot \frac{dx}{ds} \cdot \frac{ds}{dt}$$

Each new dependence adds another link to the chain. The notation of Leibniz, which considers *dy*, *du*, *dx*, *ds*, and *dt* as infinitesimals, allows us to check our expression by canceling numerators and denominators.

$$\frac{dy}{dt} = \frac{dy}{d\!\!\!/u} \cdot \frac{d\!\!\!/u}{d\!\!\!/x} \cdot \frac{d\!\!\!/x}{d\!\!\!/s} \cdot \frac{d\!\!\!/s}{dt}$$

We can also state the chain rule using the modern variant of Newton's notation.

$$\text{If } h(x) = f(g(x)), \text{ then}$$
$$h'(x) = f'(g(x))g'(x).$$

While this definition is less intuitive, it highlights the fact that the derivative of the second function in the composition must be evaluated at the output of the first function. Then this result must be multiplied by the derivative of the first function in the composition evaluated at x.

example 44.1   Let $y = u^2 + 4u$ and $u = 5x^3$. Find $\dfrac{dy}{dx}$.

solution   The first step is to compute the individual derivatives.

$$\frac{dy}{du} = 2u + 4 \qquad \frac{du}{dx} = 15x^2$$

Then we use the notation of Leibniz to write the chain rule and substitute.

$$\frac{dy}{dx} = \frac{dy}{du} \cdot \frac{du}{dx} = (2u + 4)(15x^2)$$

Since $u = 5x^3$, we substitute $5x^3$ for u and simplify.

$$\frac{dy}{dx} = \left[2(5x^3) + 4\right](15x^2)$$
$$= (10x^3 + 4)(15x^2)$$
$$= \mathbf{150x^5 + 60x^2}$$

We can also compute $\frac{dy}{dx}$ without using the chain rule. Notice that, in the above example, $y = (5x^3)^2 + 4(5x^3)$, or $y = 25x^6 + 20x^3$. Then $\frac{dy}{dx} = 150x^5 + 60x^2$, which confirms the result. While this is a nice way to check our answer in this problem, it is not always possible to compute the derivative of a composition without using the chain rule.

example 44.2   For $y = 2 \ln v$ and $v = u^2$, find $\dfrac{dy}{du}$.

solution   First the individual derivatives must be found.

$$\frac{dy}{dv} = \frac{2}{v} \qquad \frac{dv}{du} = 2u$$

Next we use the chain rule.

$$\frac{dy}{du} = \frac{dy}{dv} \cdot \frac{dv}{du} = \left(\frac{2}{v}\right)(2u) = \frac{4u}{v}$$

Since $v = u^2$, we substitute u^2 for v.

$$\frac{dy}{du} = \frac{4u}{u^2} = \frac{4}{u}$$

example 44.3   If $y = \sin t$ and $t = \dfrac{1}{\sqrt{x}}$, what is $\dfrac{dy}{dx}$?

solution   Finding the individual derivatives is the first step.

$$\frac{dy}{dt} = \cos t \qquad \frac{dt}{dx} = \frac{d}{dx}(x^{-1/2}) = -\frac{1}{2}x^{-3/2}$$

Then we write the chain rule and substitute.

$$\frac{dy}{dx} = \frac{dy}{dt} \cdot \frac{dt}{dx} = (\cos t)\left(-\frac{1}{2}x^{-3/2}\right)$$

Since $t = \dfrac{1}{\sqrt{x}}$, we substitute $\dfrac{1}{\sqrt{x}}$ for t.

$$\frac{dy}{dx} = \left(\cos \frac{1}{\sqrt{x}}\right)\left(-\frac{1}{2}x^{-3/2}\right) = -\frac{1}{2\sqrt{x^3}}\cos \frac{1}{\sqrt{x}}$$

Notice the usefulness of the chain rule. Before this lesson, it would have been difficult to find $\frac{dy}{dx}$ for $y = \sin \frac{1}{\sqrt{x}}$, but with the chain rule, we quickly found

$$\frac{dy}{dx} = -\frac{1}{2\sqrt{x^3}}\cos \frac{1}{\sqrt{x}}$$

by breaking the composite function $\sin \dfrac{1}{\sqrt{x}}$ into two parts.

44.B
alternate definition of the derivative

We are familiar with the two forms shown below for the definition of the derivative. The notation on the left-hand side defines the derivative to be a limit as Δx approaches zero. The definition on the right-hand side makes the same statement but uses h as the variable that approaches zero.

$$f'(x) = \lim_{\Delta x \to 0} \frac{f(x + \Delta x) - f(x)}{\Delta x} \qquad f'(x) = \lim_{h \to 0} \frac{f(x + h) - f(x)}{h}$$

An alternative definition uses the value of the function at some constant a and at x and finds the limit as x approaches a.

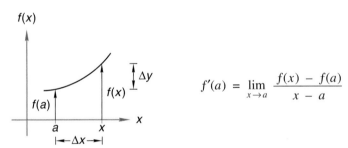

$$f'(a) = \lim_{x \to a} \frac{f(x) - f(a)}{x - a}$$

The value of $f(x) - f(a)$ equals Δy, and the value of $x - a$ equals Δx, so this is a different way to express the same statement made by both notations above.

example 44.4 Use the alternate definition of the derivative to find $f'(a)$ where $f(x) = x^2 + 1$ and a is some constant.

solution We know from the rule for the derivative of x^n that the answer will be $2a$. We are doing this problem to enhance our understanding of the definition of the derivative and to acquaint ourselves with the thought processes and procedures necessary for success in mathematics. The height of the curve at x is $f(x)$, or $x^2 + 1$. The height of the curve at a is $f(a)$, or $a^2 + 1$. The difference between x and a is $x - a$. Thus we write the definition for the slope at a, which is $f'(a)$, as follows:

$$f'(a) = \lim_{x \to a} \frac{(x^2 + 1) - (a^2 + 1)}{x - a} \qquad \text{definition}$$

We have $x - a$ in the denominator, and as x approaches a the denominator approaches zero. **We must find a way to get the $x - a$ factor out of the denominator.** The numerator simplifies to $x^2 - a^2$, which can be factored into $(x + a)(x - a)$. Therefore

$$f'(a) = \lim_{x \to a} \frac{(x + a)(x - a)}{x - a} = \lim_{x \to a} (x + a)$$

> **Since $x - a$ is no longer a factor of the denominator, we can let x approach a without causing division by zero.**

$$f'(a) = \lim_{x \to a} (x + a) = a + a = 2a$$

example 44.5   Let $f(x) = x^2$. Use the alternate definition of the derivative to find $f'(1)$.

solution   If we use the power rule, the derivative of x^2 is $2x$, and when x equals 1, $2x$ equals $2(1)$, which equals 2. In this problem we are playing a calculus game rather than just trying to find the answer.

The height of the curve at x is x^2, and the height of the curve at 1 is $(1)^2$. Using the alternate definition of the derivative, we have

$$f'(1) = \lim_{x \to 1} \frac{x^2 - (1)^2}{x - 1}$$

Again we have a denominator that goes to zero. This is not permitted, so we manipulate the numerator to compensate. Fortunately the numerator can be factored.

$$f'(1) = \lim_{x \to 1} \frac{x^2 - 1}{x - 1}$$

$$= \lim_{x \to 1} \frac{(x + 1)(x - 1)}{x - 1}$$

$$= \lim_{x \to 1} (x + 1) = 2$$

example 44.6   Assume $f(x) = \sqrt[3]{x}$. Use the alternate definition of the derivative to find $f'(-1)$.

solution   We know that

$$f'(x) = \frac{1}{3}x^{-2/3} \qquad \text{and} \qquad f'(-1) = \frac{1}{3}(-1)^{-2/3} = \frac{1}{3}$$

But we have been instructed to obtain the answer another way, so we shall.

$$f'(-1) = \lim_{x \to -1} \frac{f(x) - f(-1)}{x - (-1)}$$

$$= \lim_{x \to -1} \frac{x^{1/3} - (-1)}{x + 1}$$

$$= \lim_{x \to -1} \frac{x^{1/3} + 1}{x + 1}$$

Now we have to get the factor of $x + 1$ out of the denominator. This requires a trick. The denominator, $x + 1$, can be written as the sum of two cubes, $(x^{1/3})^3 + (1)^3$, which is a factorable expression.

$$\frac{x^{1/3} + 1}{x + 1} = \frac{(x^{1/3} + 1)}{(x^{1/3} + 1)[(x^{1/3})^2 - (x^{1/3})(1) + (1)^2]}$$

Now we have

$$f'(-1) = \lim_{x \to -1} \frac{1}{x^{2/3} - x^{1/3} + 1}$$

The $x + 1$ factor is no longer in the denominator. Substituting -1 for x, we get

$$f'(-1) = \frac{1}{(-1)^{2/3} - (-1)^{1/3} + 1} = \frac{1}{1 - (-1) + 1} = \frac{1}{3}$$

Problems like this one are carefully contrived so that students can find a solution using the skills and concepts that they have studied thus far. If the function had been $g(x) = \sqrt[14]{x}$, the trick we used in this problem would not have worked.

44.C

the symmetric derivative

One last form of the derivative is worth mentioning at this time. It is called the symmetric form of the derivative or the **symmetric derivative.** If $f(x)$ is a function, then its derivative $f'(x)$ can be found as

$$f'(x) = \lim_{h \to 0} \frac{f(x + h) - f(x - h)}{2h}$$

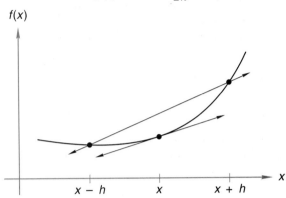

$f(x)$

$x - h$ x $x + h$ x

The idea is that, as h approaches 0, the secant line connecting $(x + h, f(x + h))$ and $(x - h, f(x - h))$ approaches the tangent line at $(x, f(x))$. So their slopes become equal. The slope of the tangent line through $(x, f(x))$ is $f'(x)$, while the slope of the secant line is

$$\frac{\Delta y}{\Delta x} = \frac{f(x + h) - f(x - h)}{(x + h) - (x - h)}$$

$$= \frac{f(x + h) - f(x - h)}{2h}$$

Hence

$$f'(x) = \lim_{h \to 0} \frac{f(x + h) - f(x - h)}{2h}$$

example 44.7   Use the symmetric derivative to find $f'(x)$ where $f(x) = x^2 + 15$.

solution

$$f'(x) = \lim_{h \to 0} \frac{f(x + h) - f(x - h)}{2h}$$

$$= \lim_{h \to 0} \frac{[(x + h)^2 + 15] - [(x - h)^2 + 15]}{2h}$$

$$= \lim_{h \to 0} \frac{x^2 + 2hx + h^2 - (x^2 - 2hx + h^2)}{2h}$$

$$= \lim_{h \to 0} \frac{4hx}{2h} = \lim_{h \to 0} 2x = \mathbf{2x}$$

So $f'(x) = 2x$, which is what we would expect.

problem set 44

1. *(26)* The number of troubles Dot experienced increased exponentially. On the first of the month, Dot experienced 6 troubles, and on the fourth of the month Dot experienced 48 troubles. How many troubles would Dot experience on the fifteenth of the month?

2. *(5,6,40)* A rectangular box with a square base has a volume of 27. The length of a side of the square base is x, and the height of the box is y.

(a) Write an equation that expresses the volume of the box in terms of x and y.

(b) Write an equation that expresses the surface area of the box in terms of x and y.

(c) Use the equation in (a) to express the surface area in terms of x.

(d) What is the domain of the surface area function? (That is, for what values of x does this problem make sense?)

(e) Graph the surface area function on a graphing calculator. Use the appropriate features of the calculator to find the value of x that minimizes the surface area. What are the values of x and the minimal surface area?

Find $\dfrac{dy}{dx}$ in problems 3 and 4.

3. $y = \sin u, \quad u = 5x^3$
(44)

4. $y = \ln |u|, \quad u = x^3 + e^x$
(44)

5. Use the symmetric derivative to find $f'(x)$ where $f(x) = -3x + 2$.
(44)

6. Use the definition $f'(a) = \lim\limits_{x \to a} \dfrac{f(x) - f(a)}{x - a}$ to find $f'(1)$ where $f(x) = -x^2$.
(44)

7. Find the exact area under $y = 3x$ on the interval $[0, 4]$ by using an infinite number of inscribed rectangles. Check your answer by using geometry.
(43)

8. Find the exact area under $y = x^2$ on the interval $[0, 3]$ by using an infinite number of circumscribed rectangles.
(43)

Differentiate the functions in problems 9 and 10 with respect to x.

9. $f(x) = \dfrac{\sin x}{e^x + x^2}$
(42)

10. $y = \dfrac{\ln x}{\sin x + \cos x}$
(42)

11. Sketch the graph of $y = \dfrac{(x^2 + 1)(x - 1)}{(x + 2)^2 x^2}$. Do not use a graphing calculator. Clearly indicate all zeros and asymptotes.
(41)

12. A particle moves along the number line so that its position at any time t (in seconds) is given by $s(t) = -2 \ln (t + 1)$. Find the velocity of the particle at $t = 2$ seconds.
(40)

13. Find the equation of the line normal to the graph of the function $y = \sin x$ at $x = \dfrac{\pi}{2}$.
(40)

Integrate in problems 14 and 15.

14. $\displaystyle\int \left(\dfrac{3}{\sqrt{t}} + 4 \cos t + 6t^2 + 6 \right) dt$
(38)

15. $\displaystyle\int \left(\dfrac{3}{x} + 4 \sin x + 5e^x + x^{-6} \right) dx$
(38)

16. Find $(fg)'(x)$ where $f(x) = 3e^x$ and $g(x) = 4 \sin x$.
(25,31)

17. Find $\dfrac{dy}{dx}$ where $y = \dfrac{2}{x} + 3x \ln |x| - 6$.
(26)

18. Find $h'(x)$ where $h(x) = \dfrac{1}{\sqrt{x^2 - 4}}$.
(37)

19. Suppose L and x are both functions of time. Find $\dfrac{dL}{dt}$ given that $\dfrac{10}{L + x} = \dfrac{5}{L}$.
(34)

Evaluate the limits in problems 20 and 21.

20. $\lim\limits_{t \to \infty} \dfrac{2t - t^3}{14t^3 - 4t^4}$
(17)

21. $\lim\limits_{x \to -1} \dfrac{2x + 2}{x^2 + 2x + 1}$
(17)

22. Sketch the graph of $y = (x - 2)^2$.
(21)

23. Use a graphing calculator to graph the functions $y = \dfrac{1}{x}$ and $y = e^x$. Then approximate the coordinates of the point(s) of intersection of the two curves.
(2)

24. Assuming $0 < y < 1$, compare the following: A. $\dfrac{1}{y^2}$ B. $\dfrac{1}{y^3}$
(1)

25. Use the fact that $1^3 + 2^3 + \cdots + (n - 1)^3 = \left[\dfrac{(n - 1)n}{2} \right]^2$ to find the sum of the cubes of the first 200 positive integers.
(R)

LESSON 45 *Using f′ to Characterize f • Using f′ to Find Maximums and Minimums*

45.A
using f′ to characterize f

We know that a function is an increasing (decreasing) function on an interval I if every greater value of x is paired with a greater (lesser) value of $f(x)$.

> A function f is **increasing** on an interval I if
>
> $$f(x_1) < f(x_2) \qquad \text{whenever } x_1 < x_2 \text{ in } I.$$
>
> It is **decreasing** on I if
>
> $$f(x_1) > f(x_2) \qquad \text{whenever } x_1 < x_2 \text{ in } I.$$

Often the derivative can be used to check whether or not a function is increasing or decreasing. **If $f′(x)$ is greater (less) than zero for every value of x on an interval I, then f is an increasing (decreasing) function on I.** The graph shown below is the graph of $f(x) = x^3 + 2x$. The equation of $f′$ is $f′(x) = 3x^2 + 2$, and we see that for any real value of x, $f′$ is positive because x^2 is at least zero and thus $3x^2 + 2$ is always positive. Hence f is increasing on the entire interval $(-\infty, \infty)$.

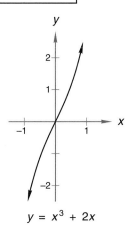

$$y = x^3 + 2x$$

The converse of the statement in boldface above is not necessarily true. If f is increasing on an interval I, $f′(x)$ does not have to be greater than zero (positive) for all values of x in I. An example of this is the function $f(x) = x^3$. For this function, f is increasing for all real values of x; yet $f′(x)$ is not greater than zero for every value of x because the derivative $3x^2$ equals zero when $x = 0$.

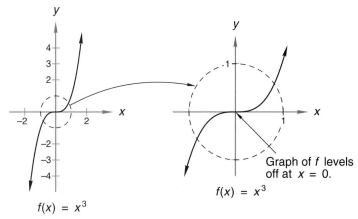

$$f(x) = x^3$$

Graph of f levels off at $x = 0$.

$$f(x) = x^3$$

The box below summarizes how derivatives can be used to characterize functions. Only the final statement is reversible. The converses of the other two are not necessarily true.

> If $f′(x) > 0$ for all x on an interval I, then f is **increasing on I.**
>
> If $f′(x) < 0$ for all x on an interval I, then f is **decreasing on I.**
>
> If $f′(x) = 0$ for all x on an interval I, then f is **constant on I.**

example 45.1   Shown is the graph of a function f. From among the points labeled, choose those at which f' appears to be positive.

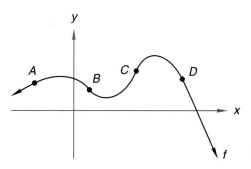

solution   At points A and C, the slope of the graph of f is positive and hence f' **is positive at the x-coordinates of A and C.**

example 45.2   If f is a function such that $f'(x) > 0$ for all x, then describe the graph of f. Sketch how f could possibly look.

solution   If $f'(x)$ is positive (greater than zero) for all values of x, then f must have positive slope for all values of x. Thus the graph of f could look like one of the graphs shown below.

Of course, this list is not exhaustive.

example 45.3   Shown is the graph of some quadratic function f. Sketch the graph of f'.

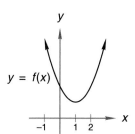

solution   We see that the slope of the graph of f is negative for all $x < 1$ and that the slope of the graph of f is positive for all $x > 1$. At $x = 1$ the slope of the graph is 0. Since f is a quadratic function, f' must be a linear function. Thus the graph of f must be a line that passes through $(1, 0)$ and lies below the x-axis when $x < 1$ and above the x-axis when $x > 1$.

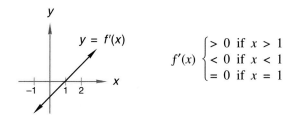

$$f'(x) \begin{cases} > 0 \text{ if } x > 1 \\ < 0 \text{ if } x < 1 \\ = 0 \text{ if } x = 1 \end{cases}$$

The slope of the line cannot be determined, since we are unable to determine the value of f' at any other value of x. If $f(x) = x^2 - 2x + 1$, then $f'(x) = 2x - 2$; while if $f(x) = 7x^2 - 14x + 8$, then $f'(x) = 14x - 14$, which is a much different derivative.

example 45.4   Assuming $f'(x)$ exists for all values of x, sketch the basic shape of the graph of the function f with the following properties:

$$f'(x) \begin{cases} < 0 & \text{when } x < 1 \\ = 0 & \text{when } x = 1 \\ > 0 & \text{when } 1 < x < 2 \\ = 0 & \text{when } x = 2 \\ < 0 & \text{when } x > 2 \end{cases}$$

solution   We use the fact that the graph of f must have a positive slope on intervals where $f' > 0$, a negative slope on intervals where $f' < 0$, and no slope at points where $f' = 0$.

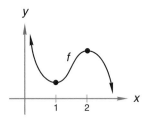

Note that we can shift the graph of f vertically and not change the properties of f'. The next two figures illustrate how the slope of the tangent line to the graph of a function f remains the same as the graph shifts vertically a distance of c.

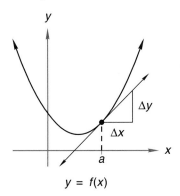

$$y = f(x)$$

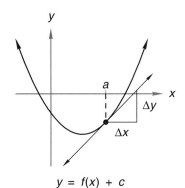

$$y = f(x) + c$$

example 45.5   Assume the graph of f' is the graph at right.

Determine the basic shape of the graph of f.

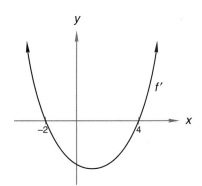

solution   We first notice that $f'(-2) = 0$ and $f'(4) = 0$. So the graph of f at $x = -2$ and $x = 4$ must be local maximum or minimum points. Also, the graph of f' is positive on the intervals $(-\infty, -2)$ and $(4, \infty)$. Hence, over these two intervals, f must be increasing. On the interval $(-2, 4)$, $f' < 0$. On this interval, f must be decreasing. Therefore, the basic shape of the graph must be the following:

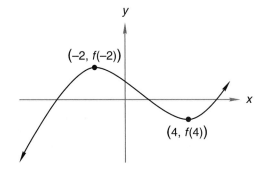

45.B

using *f′* to find maximums and minimums

If the first derivative f' of a function f equals zero for a particular value of x—say x_1—we know that the slope of the graph of f is zero at x_1. If the slope is positive just to the left of x_1 and negative just to the right of x_1, then x_1 is a local maximum. If the slope is negative just to the left of x_1 and positive just to the right of x_1, then x_1 is a local minimum.

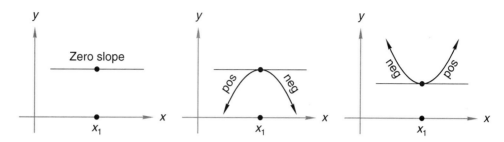

Since the slope is positive when the value of the derivative f' is positive and negative when the value of the derivative is negative, a local maximum can be defined using the input-output concept without using a graph. First we must find some value of x, which we call c, for which the value of f' equals 0.

$$c \longrightarrow \boxed{\;f'\;} \longrightarrow f'(c) = 0$$

Now if the numbers c^-, which are numbers close to but less than c, have positive values of f' and numbers c^+, which are numbers close to but greater than c, have negative values of f', then the number c is a **stationary number** at which f has a local maximum value.

$$
\begin{aligned}
c^- &\longrightarrow \\
c &\longrightarrow \boxed{\;f'\;} \\
c^+ &\longrightarrow
\end{aligned}
\quad
\begin{aligned}
&\longrightarrow f'(c^-) > 0 \\
&\longrightarrow f'(c) = 0 \\
&\longrightarrow f'(c^+) < 0
\end{aligned}
$$

Local maximum

For f to have a local minimum value, the derivative $f'(c)$ must be zero. In addition, numbers close to but less than c must have negative values of f', and numbers close to but greater than c must have positive values of f'.

$$
\begin{aligned}
c^- &\longrightarrow \\
c &\longrightarrow \boxed{\;f'\;} \\
c^+ &\longrightarrow
\end{aligned}
\quad
\begin{aligned}
&\longrightarrow f'(c^-) < 0 \\
&\longrightarrow f'(c) = 0 \\
&\longrightarrow f'(c^+) > 0
\end{aligned}
$$

Local minimum

example 45.6   Suppose f is a function such that $f'(1) = 0$, f' is positive on the interval $(-3, 1)$, and f' is negative on the interval $(1, 4)$. Sketch the graph of f for values of x near $x = 1$, and indicate any special characteristics of f.

solution   We use the information given to sketch the graph of f for values of x between -3 and 4.

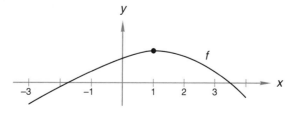

Note that the graph of f has a relative maximum point at $x = 1$, and hence the function f has a relative maximum value at $x = 1$. The problem does not give enough information to determine the x-intercepts, the y-intercept, or the vertical placement of the graph.

example 45.7   Use the first derivative to demonstrate that the function $f(x) = x^2 + 2x + 3$ attains a relative minimum at $x = -1$.

solution   First we find the derivative.

$$f(x) = x^2 + 2x + 3 \qquad \text{equation for } f$$
$$f'(x) = 2x + 2 \qquad \text{differentiated}$$

Setting $f'(x) = 0$ gives $2x + 2 = 0$. Solving for x yields $x = -1$. Thus, $f' = 0$ at $x = -1$. From the equation of f' above, we see that $f'(x) > 0$ for all x greater than -1, and $f'(x) < 0$ for all x less than -1. Thus the graph of f is rising for all $x > -1$ and falling for all $x < -1$. **Since the slope of the graph of f is zero precisely at $x = -1$, the function f must attain a relative minimum at $x = -1$.**

problem set 45

1. A 10-foot-long ladder leans against a vertical wall. If the base of the ladder is x feet away from
   (5) the wall, how high above the ground is the top of the ladder?

2. Shown is the graph of a function f. At which of the points A, B, C, and D is f' positive?
   (45)

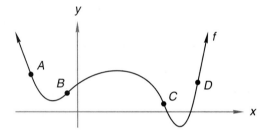

3. Assuming $f'(x)$ exists for all real values of x, sketch the basic shape of the graph of f where
   (45)

$$f'(x) \begin{cases} < 0 \text{ when } x < 1 \\ = 0 \text{ when } x = 1 \\ > 0 \text{ when } 1 < x < 2 \\ = 0 \text{ when } x = 2 \\ < 0 \text{ when } x > 2 \end{cases}$$

4. Suppose f is a function such that $f'(-1) = 0$, f' is negative on the interval $(-3, -1)$, and f' is
   (45) positive on the interval $(-1, 2)$. Sketch the graph of f for values of x near $x = -1$. Indicate where f attains a local maximum value or a local minimum value.

Determine $\dfrac{dy}{dx}$ in problems 5 and 6.

5. $y = \sin t, \ t = \sqrt{x}$
   (44)

6. $y = \dfrac{1}{u}, \ u = x^2 + 1$
   (44)

7. Use the symmetric derivative to find $f'(x)$ where $f(x) = x^2 + 3x$.
   (44)

8. Use the definition $f'(a) = \lim\limits_{x \to a} \dfrac{f(x) - f(a)}{x - a}$ to find $f'(1)$ where $f(x) = x^3$.
   (44)

9. Sketch the graph of $y = \sin x$ $(0 \le x \le \pi)$. Partition the interval $[0, \pi]$ into four equal
   (39) subintervals, and estimate the area between the graph of $y = \sin x$ and the x-axis on the interval $[0, \pi]$ by computing a lower sum.

10. Sketch the graph of $y = \sin x$ $(0 \le x \le \pi)$. Partition the interval $[0, \pi]$ into four equal
    (39) subintervals, and estimate the area between the graph of $y = \sin x$ and the x-axis on the interval $[0, \pi]$ by using rectangles whose heights are determined by $\sin(x_m)$ where x_m is the midpoint of each subinterval.

11. Find the exact area under $y = x^3$ on the interval $[0, 4]$ by using an infinite number of lower
    (43) rectangles.

12. Let $y = \dfrac{\cos x}{\sin x}$. Find y' .
(42)

13. Let $f(x) = \dfrac{e^x}{1 + x^2}$. Find $f'(x)$.
(42)

14. (a) Find the critical numbers of f where $f(x) = \dfrac{1}{3}x^3 + \dfrac{3}{2}x^2 + 2x + 2$.
(36)

(b) Use the equation of f and a rough sketch of the graph of f to determine the local maximum and minimum values of f and where they occur.

15. Use a graphing calculator to graph $f(x) = \dfrac{1}{3}x^3 + \dfrac{3}{2}x^2 + 2x + 2$.
(2,40)

(a) Find all the real roots of f .

(b) Approximate the x - and y -coordinates of all the local maximum and minimum points.

(c) How do these answers compare to those in problem 14?

Differentiate the functions in problems 16–18 with respect to the independent variable.

16. $y = \dfrac{1}{\sqrt{x^3 + 5}}$
(37)

17. $f(x) = x - x \ln |x|$
(31)

18. $s(t) = s_0 + v_0 t + \dfrac{1}{2}gt^2$ (s_0 , v_0 , and g are constants)
(25)

Integrate in problems 19 and 20.

19. $\displaystyle\int \left(\pi e^t - 2 \sin t + 1 \right) dt$
(38)

20. $\displaystyle\int \left(\dfrac{4}{u} + 3u^{-15} \right) du$
(38)

21. Let $f(x) = \sqrt{x}$ and $g(x) = x^2 - 1$. Write the equation of $f \circ g$.
(18)

22. Find the domain and range of $f \circ g$ where f and g are as defined in problem 21.
(18)

23. Evaluate: $\displaystyle\lim_{x \to -1} \dfrac{x^3 + 1}{x + 1}$
(17)

24. Find the sum of the first twenty terms of the arithmetic sequence whose first three terms are
(R) -2 , 1, and 4.

25. Find the radius of the circle that can be circumscribed about a rectangle whose length is 3 units
(R) and whose width is 4 units.

LESSON 46 *Related-Rates Problems*

A **related-rates problem** is a problem that presents a situation where one or more related quantities are changing and asks for the rate at which one of the quantities is changing. The first step to solving such a problem is writing an equation that relates the variable quantities of the problem. This equation is called the **relating equation.** Differentiating the relating equation produces an equation that tells how the rates of change of all the variable quantities relate to each other. Specific information given in the problem can be substituted into the differentiated equation to solve for the desired quantities. A general principle applies for related-rates problems.

> The sum of the number of rates given and sought should equal the number of variables in the relating equation before differentiation is performed.

The following problems are classic examples of the kinds of related-rates problems that appear in virtually every calculus book.

example 46.1 A 13-meter-long ladder leans against a vertical wall. The base of the ladder is pulled away from the wall at a rate of 1 meter per second. Find the rate at which the top of the ladder is falling when the base of the ladder is 5 meters away from the wall.

solution **The first task in a related-rates problem is to find the equation that relates the variables.** We begin by drawing a diagram of the problem. Let x represent the distance from the base of the ladder to the wall, and let y represent the distance from the ground to the top of the ladder. The distances x and y form the sides of a right triangle, and 13 is the hypotenuse. Thus we use the Pythagorean theorem to write the equation that relates x and y.

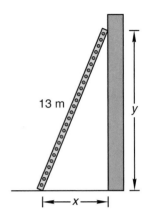

$$x^2 + y^2 = 13^2 \quad \longrightarrow \quad x^2 + y^2 = 169$$

Note that the relating equation contains two variables. Because the sum of the number of rates given and sought equals two (we are given $\frac{dx}{dt}$ and are asked to find $\frac{dy}{dt}$), we know that we can proceed to solve the problem. To find an equation that relates $\frac{dx}{dt}$, $\frac{dy}{dt}$, x, and y, we differentiate the relating equation implicitly with respect to time t.

$$x^2 + y^2 = 169 \qquad \text{relating equation}$$
$$2x\,dx + 2y\,dy = 0 \qquad \text{differentials}$$
$$2x\frac{dx}{dt} + 2y\frac{dy}{dt} = 0 \qquad \text{divided by } dt$$

We want to find $\frac{dy}{dt}$, so we solve this equation for $\frac{dy}{dt}$.

$$2y\frac{dy}{dt} = -2x\frac{dx}{dt} \qquad \text{rearranged}$$
$$\frac{dy}{dt} = -\frac{x}{y}\frac{dx}{dt} \qquad \text{divided}$$

To get a numerical answer for $\frac{dy}{dt}$, we need to know values of x, y, and $\frac{dx}{dt}$. We were given that $\frac{dx}{dt} = 1$ and that $x = 5$. We can use the Pythagorean theorem to find y when $x = 5$.

$$5^2 + y^2 = 13^2 \qquad \text{Pythagorean theorem}$$
$$y^2 = 169 - 25 \qquad \text{rearranged}$$
$$y = 12 \qquad \text{solved}$$

13 m

y

|← 5 m →|

Next, we replace $\frac{dx}{dt}$ with 1, x with 5, and y with 12.

$$\frac{dy}{dt} = -\frac{5}{12}(1) = -\frac{5}{12} \text{ meter per second}$$

The negative sign indicates that the value of y is decreasing as time increases.

example 46.2   A 6-foot-tall man is walking straight away from a 15-foot-high streetlight. At what rate is his shadow lengthening when he is 20 feet away from the streetlight if he is walking away from the light at a rate of 4 feet per second?

solution   The first task in a related-rates problem is to find the equation that relates the variables. We begin by drawing a diagram of the problem, using x to represent the distance of the man from the streetlight and L to represent the length of the shadow.

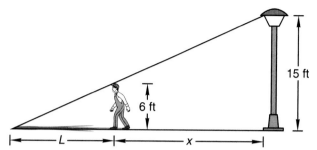

By similar triangles,

$$\frac{L + x}{L} = \frac{15}{6}$$

Since the relating equation contains two variables, we should verify that the sum of the rates given and sought equals two before proceeding. This is the case, as we are given $\frac{dx}{dt}$ and asked to find $\frac{dL}{dt}$. We rearrange the equation and find the differential of every term.

$$L + x = \frac{15}{6}L \qquad \text{multiplied by } L$$

$$x = \frac{3}{2}L \qquad \text{subtracted } L$$

$$dx = \frac{3}{2}\,dL \qquad \text{found differential}$$

Next we divide every term by dt and solve for $\frac{dL}{dt}$.

$$\frac{dx}{dt} = \frac{3}{2}\frac{dL}{dt} \qquad \text{divided by } dt$$

$$\frac{dL}{dt} = \frac{2}{3}\frac{dx}{dt} \qquad \text{solved for } \frac{dL}{dt}$$

It is given that $\dfrac{dx}{dt} = 4$ feet per second, so we substitute 4 for $\dfrac{dx}{dt}$.

$$\frac{dL}{dt} = \frac{2}{3}(4) = \frac{8}{3} \textbf{ feet per second}$$

The variables of x and L did not appear in the equation for $\frac{dL}{dt}$, so these values were not needed in the last step. Thus the rate at which the man's shadow is lengthening is $\frac{8}{3}$ feet per second regardless of his distance from the light.

example 46.3   A conical container has a height of 9 centimeters and a diameter of 6 centimeters as shown. It is leaking water at the rate of 1 cubic centimeter per minute. Find the rate at which the water level h is changing when h equals 3 centimeters.

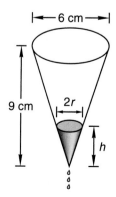

solution   The volume is decreasing at a rate of 1 cubic centimeter per minute, so $\frac{dV}{dt} = -1$. We are asked to find $\frac{dh}{dt}$. Thus we need an equation that relates the volume V and the height of the water h. The formula for the volume of a cone is

$$V = \frac{1}{3}\pi r^2 h$$

In this equation we have V as a function of both r and h. Note that the relating equation has three variables. However, the total number of rates given and sought only equals two (given $\frac{dV}{dt}$ and seeking $\frac{dh}{dt}$), which means we should work to eliminate one of the variables in the relating equation. Since the shape of the cone is known, the similar triangles found in a side view of the cone can be used to write the relationship between r and h. We do this on the left-hand side below. On the right-hand side, we substitute to get the desired relating equation.

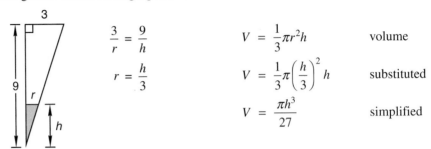

$$\frac{3}{r} = \frac{9}{h} \qquad\qquad V = \frac{1}{3}\pi r^2 h \qquad\qquad \text{volume}$$

$$r = \frac{h}{3} \qquad\qquad V = \frac{1}{3}\pi\left(\frac{h}{3}\right)^2 h \qquad\qquad \text{substituted}$$

$$V = \frac{\pi h^3}{27} \qquad\qquad \text{simplified}$$

The sum of the number of rates given and the number of rates sought now equals the number of variables in the relating equation. We take the differential of both sides, divide every term by dt, and then solve for $\frac{dh}{dt}$.

$$dV = \frac{\pi h^2}{9}\, dh \qquad\qquad \text{differentials}$$

$$\frac{dV}{dt} = \frac{\pi h^2}{9}\frac{dh}{dt} \qquad\qquad \text{divided by } dt$$

$$\frac{dh}{dt} = \frac{9}{\pi h^2}\frac{dV}{dt} \qquad\qquad \text{solved for } \frac{dh}{dt}$$

As the last step, we use -1 for $\frac{dV}{dt}$ and 3 for h, which is information given in the problem.

$$\frac{dh}{dt} = \frac{9}{\pi(3)^2}(-1) = -\frac{1}{\pi} \approx \textbf{−0.3183 centimeter per second}$$

The negative sign indicates that the water level is decreasing as time increases.

example 46.4 Air is pumped into a spherical hot-air balloon at a rate of 25 cubic feet per minute. Find the rate of change of the surface area of the sphere when the radius is 5 feet.

solution First, we need an equation relating the surface area of a sphere to the radius of the sphere.

$$A = 4\pi r^2$$

We are asked to find $\frac{dA}{dt}$, and it is given that $\frac{dV}{dt} = 25$. (Here V represents the volume of the sphere.) The relating equation has two variables, and the sum of the number of rates given and sought is also two. So we proceed with the differentiation of the relating equation.

$$\frac{dA}{dt} = 8\pi r \frac{dr}{dt}$$

To find $\frac{dA}{dt}$, both r and $\frac{dr}{dt}$ are needed. We know $r = 5$ in this problem, but $\frac{dr}{dt}$ is still unknown. This is where the fact that $\frac{dV}{dt} = 25$ can be utilized. We introduce another relating equation involving V and r to determine the value of $\frac{dr}{dt}$ when r is 5.

$$V = \frac{4}{3}\pi r^3$$

$$\frac{dV}{dt} = 4\pi r^2 \frac{dr}{dt}$$

When $r = 5$ we have

$$25 = 4\pi(5)^2 \frac{dr}{dt}$$

$$25 = 100\pi \frac{dr}{dt}$$

$$\frac{dr}{dt} = \frac{1}{4\pi}$$

We can now determine $\dfrac{dA}{dt}$.

$$\frac{dA}{dt} = 8\pi r \frac{dr}{dt}$$

$$= 8\pi(5)\left(\frac{1}{4\pi}\right)$$

$$= 10$$

So the surface area is increasing at a rate of **10 ft²/min** when the radius is 5 feet.

**problem set
46**

1. The number of people listening attentively varied inversely as the indifference index. If P people
(5)   listened attentively when the indifference index was I, how many people would have been
listening attentively if the indifference index had been J?

2. A 10-meter-long ladder leans against a vertical wall. The base of the ladder is pulled away from
(46)   the wall at a rate of 1 meter per second. How fast is the top of the ladder sliding down the wall
when the base of the ladder is 4 meters away from the wall?

3. A 5-foot-tall man walks straight away from a lamppost that is 35 feet tall. How fast is the length
(46)   of his shadow changing when he is 12 feet away from the lamppost if he walks at a rate of 3 feet
per second?

4. Let $f'(x)$ exist for all real values of x. Sketch the basic shape of the graph of f where
(45)

$$f'(x) \begin{cases} > 0 & \text{when } x < 2 \\ = 0 & \text{when } x = 2 \\ > 0 & \text{when } 2 < x < 3 \\ = 0 & \text{when } x = 3 \\ < 0 & \text{when } x > 3 \end{cases}$$

5. Let $f(x) = x^2 + 6x - 4$. Use the first derivative to find the critical number(s) of f. Then use
(45)   the first derivative to determine whether f attains a maximum or minimum value at the critical
number(s) found.

Find $\dfrac{dy}{dx}$ in problems 6 and 7.

6. $y = \sqrt{u}, \ u = x^2 + 1$
(44)

7. $y = e^u, \ u = \sin x$
(44)

8. Use the fact that $f'(a) = \lim\limits_{x \to a} \frac{f(x) - f(a)}{x - a}$ to find $f'(1)$ where $f(x) = \sqrt{x}$. (*Hint:* Factor the
(44)   denominator.)

9. Use the symmetric derivative to find $f'(x)$ where $f(x) = x^2 + 3$.
(44)

10. Find the area under $y = x^3$ on the interval $[0, 3]$ by using inscribed rectangles and letting the
(43)   number of rectangles increase without bound.

Differentiate the functions in problems 11–14 with respect to x.

11. $f(x) = \dfrac{\sin x}{\cos x + \sin x}$
(42)

12. $y = 2x \ln |x| + 5$
(31)

13. $y = \sqrt{x^2 + 1}$
(37)

14. $y = e^{\sin x}$
(37)

15. Use the graphing calculator to graph the conic section given by $x^2 + 2y^2 + 6y - 8 = 0$.
(22)   Determine the center of this conic section.

16. (a) Find the critical numbers of $f(x) = 3x^4 + 4x^3 - 12x^2 + 5$.
(36)
(b) Use this equation and a sketch of the graph of f to determine where f attains a local
maximum or minimum.

Integrate in problems 17 and 18.

17. $\displaystyle\int \left(3x + e^x - \frac{1}{\sqrt{x}} + \frac{1}{3} \right) dx$
(38)

18. $\displaystyle\int \left(t + \frac{1}{t} - 3 + t^5 + t^{-5} - \sin t \right) dt$
(38)

19. Sketch the graph of $y = \tan x$ $(0 \le x \le 2\pi)$.
(30)

20. Let $f(x) = 2 \sin x$. Approximate $f'''(2)$.
(29)

21. Beginning with the key trigonometric identities, develop an identity for tan $(2A)$.
(12)

22. (a) Use a graphing calculator to approximate the value of $f'(2)$ where $f(x) = e^{g(x)}$ and
(44) $\quad\quad$ $g(x) = x^2$.

$\quad\quad$ (b) Evaluate $f(2)$ and $g'(2)$. Approximate the value of $f(2) \cdot g'(2)$.

$\quad\quad$ (c) How do the answers to (a) and (b) compare?

23. Graph f where $f(x) = \begin{cases} \sqrt{x} & \text{when } x > 0 \\ -\sqrt{-x} & \text{when } x < 0. \end{cases}$
(9)

24. For f as defined in problem 23, evaluate the following limits:
(11)

$\quad\quad$ (a) $\displaystyle\lim_{x \to 0^+} f(x)$ $\quad\quad\quad\quad\quad\quad\quad\quad$ (b) $\displaystyle\lim_{x \to 0^-} f(x)$

25. Suppose $a - b = 2$. Compare: A. $a^2 + b^2$ $\quad\quad$ B. $4 + 2ab$
(1)

LESSON 47 *Fundamental Theorem of Calculus, Part 1* • *Riemann Sums* • *The Definite Integral*

47.A
fundamental theorem of calculus, part 1

We have defined the area between the x-axis and the graph of a continuous, nonnegative function f on the interval $[a, b]$ to be the limit of the sum of the areas of the rectangles on a partition of $[a, b]$ between the x-axis and the graph of f as the number of rectangles increases without bound. On the left-hand side below, we show the area under the graph of the function f between x-values of a and b. The width of each rectangle is Δx and the height of each rectangle is the least value of $f(x)$ on each interval, so the sum of the areas of these rectangles is a lower sum. (We could have used an upper sum.) On the right-hand side we take the limit of this sum as the number of rectangles goes to infinity. We have defined the limit of this sum to be the area under the curve, which we designate as A.

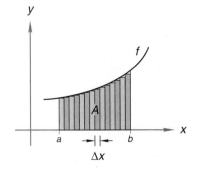

$$A = \lim_{n \to \infty} \sum_{i=1}^{n} f(x_i) \frac{b - a}{n}$$

$$A = \int_a^b f(x)\, dx$$

Underneath the summation notation we have written the integral notation for the same sum. We read this as "the area A equals the integral from a to b of f of x dee x."

The expression $\int_a^b f(x)\,dx$ is called a **definite integral.** Definite integrals will be formally defined in the next section. We introduce it in this section to highlight an extremely important property.

FUNDAMENTAL THEOREM OF CALCULUS, PART 1

Suppose f is a continuous function on the closed interval $[a, b]$. If F is any antiderivative of f, then

$$\int_a^b f(x)\,dx = F(b) - F(a)$$

The statement in the box is a remarkable mathematical fact. It ties together the area under a curve (which is a sum of the areas of an infinite number of rectangles) with antiderivatives. What the statement says is that the area under the graph of a continuous function f can be computed using an antiderivative of f.

example 47.1   Find the area under the graph of $f(x) = 4 \sin x$ between 0 and π.

solution   On the left-hand side the graph of the equation $f(x) = 4 \sin x$ is shown with the area that we want to find shaded. On the right-hand side we show the graph of $F(x) = -4 \cos x + 0$, which is an antiderivative of $4 \sin x$. Arrows in the second figure indicate the distance from the x-axis to the graph when $x = 0$ and when $x = \pi$.

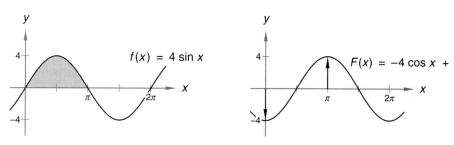

We can see that $F(0) = -4$ and $F(\pi) = 4$. By the Fundamental Theorem of Calculus, the area must be

$$\int_0^\pi 4 \sin x\,dx = 4 - (-4) = 8$$

Rather than drawing pictures, it is customary to proceed as follows:

$$A = \int_0^\pi 4 \sin x\,dx = 4[-\cos x]_0^\pi = -4[\cos x]_0^\pi$$

The notation to the right-hand side is used to indicate that the value of x at the left end of the interval is zero, and zero is called the **lower limit of integration.** The value of x at the right end of the interval is the **upper limit of integration,** which is π in this example. We note that here the word *limit* has a different meaning than it does in the phrase *limit of a function.* Here the word *limit* is used to designate the values of x at the ends of the interval $[0, \pi]$. **We always evaluate the antiderivative at the upper limit first and subtract from it the value of the same antiderivative evaluated at the lower limit.**

$$-4[\cos x]_0^\pi = -4(\cos \pi - \cos 0)$$
$$= -4[(-1) - (1)] = -4(-2) = \textbf{8 units}^2$$

example 47.2   Evaluate: $\int_1^3 (x^2 + 2x + 5)\,dx$

solution   The definite integral equals the area of the shaded region shown.

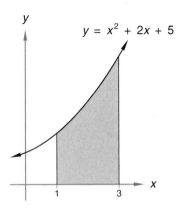

We begin by writing the integral of the sum as the sum of integrals.

$$A = \int_1^3 (x^2 + 2x + 5)\,dx = \int_1^3 x^2\,dx + \int_1^3 2x\,dx + \int_1^3 5\,dx$$

Now we find an antiderivative and evaluate this antiderivative at the endpoints of the interval to determine the integral.

$$\left[\frac{x^3}{3} + x^2 + 5x\right]_1^3 = [9 + 9 + 15] - \left[\frac{1}{3} + 1 + 5\right] = 33 - \frac{19}{3} = \frac{80}{3}$$

example 47.3   Evaluate: $\int_1^2 \left(3e^x + \frac{2}{x} + x^2\right)dx$

solution   The definite integral equals the area of the shaded region shown.

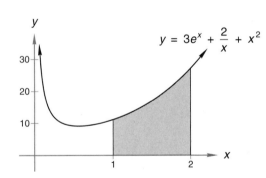

We write the integral of a sum as the sum of the integrals.

$$\int_1^2 \left(3e^x + \frac{2}{x} + x^2\right)dx = 3\int_1^2 e^x\,dx + 2\int_1^2 \frac{1}{x}\,dx + \int_1^2 x^2\,dx$$

We find appropriate antiderivatives and evaluate at the endpoints.

$$\left[3e^x + 2\ln|x| + \frac{x^3}{3}\right]_1^2 = \left[3e^2 + 2\ln 2 + \frac{8}{3}\right] - \left[3e + 0 + \frac{1}{3}\right]$$

$$= \left(3e^2 + 2\ln 2 - 3e + \frac{7}{3}\right)$$

To four decimal places, the area of the shaded region shown above is **17.7320**.

47.B

Riemann sums   The area between the graph of a positive-valued function f and the x-axis over the interval $[a, b]$ is defined by the expression $\int_a^b f(x)\,dx$. This expression is called a definite integral. In the previous section we saw how the Fundamental Theorem of Calculus can be applied to easily compute $\int_a^b f(x)\,dx$. This section formally defines what we mean by the definite integral $\int_a^b f(x)\,dx$. For the purposes of this discussion, no assumptions are made about f. That is, we do **not** assume that f is continuous, that f is positive-valued, or that f has an easily expressible antiderivative F.

The definition we provide was developed by the German mathematician G. F. B. Riemann (1826–1866) and the French mathematician A. L. Cauchy (1789–1857) and named after Riemann. **Instead of using upper sums and lower sums, they defined a single sum. For this sum any point in a subinterval can be used to determine the height of the rectangle drawn on the subinterval.** Thus some of the rectangles can have all portions either below the curve or above the curve, and some of the rectangles can have portions both above and below the curve. However, the top of each rectangle must touch the graph of the function at least once. **Another important distinction for these sums is that the widths of the subintervals can be different.** If we use $f(x_1)$ to designate the value of $f(x)$ at any chosen point in the first subinterval and Δx_1 as the length of this subinterval, the area of the first rectangle would be $f(x_1)\,\Delta x_1$. Using the same notation, the area of the second rectangle would be $f(x_2)\,\Delta x_2$, and the sum of the areas of n rectangles could be expressed as follows.

$$\text{Riemann sum} = f(x_1)\Delta x_1 + f(x_2)\Delta x_2 + f(x_3)\Delta x_3 + \cdots + f(x_n)\Delta x_n$$

Below we show six rectangles drawn on a partition of six subintervals of $[a, b]$. We use summation notation to indicate the sum of the areas of these six rectangles.

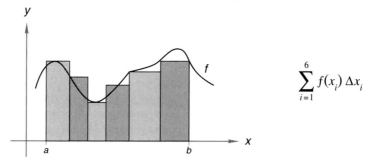

$$\sum_{i=1}^{6} f(x_i)\,\Delta x_i$$

The width of the largest subinterval of a partition $\mathcal{P}$ is called the **norm** of the partition and is designated by $\|\mathcal{P}\|$. The work of Cauchy and Riemann included a proof that if $\|\mathcal{P}\|$ approaches zero as the number of subintervals n increases without bound, then the limit of this sum exists for any continuous function and is unique (i.e., the limit is the same for any partition). The limit of this sum is called the **Riemann integral.** The notation $\|\mathcal{P}\| \longrightarrow 0$ indicates that the norm of $\mathcal{P}$ approaches zero as n increases without bound.

$$\text{Riemann integral} = \lim_{\|\mathcal{P}\|\to 0} \sum_{i=1}^{n} f(x_i)\Delta x_i = \int_a^b f(x)\,dx$$

If the limit of this sum exists for a function f, then that function is said to be *integrable on $[a, b]$ in the sense of Riemann,* which means that $\int_a^b f(x)\,dx$ exists and is a uniquely determined real number.

example 47.4   Express the value of $\int_0^2 e^x\,dx$ as a Riemann sum.

solution $\int_0^2 e^x\,dx = \lim\limits_{\|\mathcal{P}\|\to 0} \sum\limits_{i=1}^{n} f(x_i)\Delta x_i$

Using the definition of a Riemann integral, we obtain the Riemann sum. Here $f(x) = e^x$, $\mathcal{P}$ is a partition into n subintervals of the interval $[0, 2]$, and x_i is some arbitrary point in the ith subinterval. We may write the answer as

$$\lim_{\|\mathcal{P}\|\to 0} \sum_{i=1}^{n} e^{x_i}\Delta x_i$$

47.C
the definite integral

Our search for a precise definition of the word *area* when applied to a closed geometric figure has led us to the Riemann integral. Look at the Riemann integral closely.

$$\int_a^b f(x)\,dx = \lim_{\|\mathcal{P}\|\to 0} \sum_{i=1}^{n} f(x_i)\Delta x_i$$

Note that the definite integral simply describes a number that is the limit of a sum of products that involve values of a function. Thus it is applicable to functions that are negative for some portion of an interval as well. For negative-valued functions, the definite integral no longer describes the area between the graph of the function and the x-axis. Rather, if f is negative-valued on the interval $[a, b]$ (meaning the graph of f is below the x-axis on the interval $[a, b]$), then $\int_a^b f(x)\, dx$ is negative. In fact, the negative of $\int_a^b f(x)\, dx$ is the area of the region between the graph of f and the x-axis on the interval $[a, b]$.

In the following exercises we explore the geometric interpretations of the definite integral.

example 47.5   Find $\int_0^{2\pi} \sin x\, dx$ geometrically.

solution   We begin by graphing the function and shading the region described.

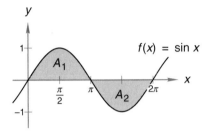

The geometric interpretation of this definite integral is that it equals $A_1 - A_2$, as denoted in the graphic above. So it does **not** represent the shaded area, but the difference of the two areas (since one is above the x-axis and the other is below).

By symmetry, we see that $A_1 = A_2$, which means

$$\int_0^{2\pi} \sin x\, dx = A_1 - A_2 = \mathbf{0}$$

Obviously, $\int_0^{2\pi} \sin x\, dx$ cannot represent the shaded area if its value is 0. To compute the area of the shaded region, we would have to find $A_1 + A_2$.

example 47.6   Evaluate: $\int_0^4 (8 - 2x)\, dx$

solution   We consider the graph of $y = 8 - 2x$ over the interval $[0, 4]$.

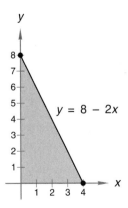

Since the graph of $y = 8 - 2x$ is completely above the x-axis, the integral $\int_0^4 (8 - 2x)\, dx$ actually does yield the area between the x-axis and the diagonal line. This is obviously the area of a triangle with height 8 and base 4. So the area is 16. Therefore,

$$\int_0^4 (8 - 2x)\, dx = \mathbf{16}$$

problem set
47

1. A 13-meter-long ladder leans against a vertical wall. The base of the ladder is pulled away from
(46) the wall at a rate of 2 meters per second. How fast is the top of the ladder moving when the base
of the ladder is 5 meters away from the wall?

2. The volume of a spherical ball is increasing at a rate of 1 cubic centimeter per second. At what
(46) rate is the radius increasing when the radius of the ball is 10 centimeters?

Use the Fundamental Theorem of Calculus to compute the areas of the shaded regions shown in
problems 3–6.

3.
(47)

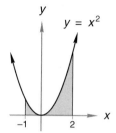

$y = x^2$

4.
(47)

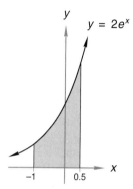

$y = 2e^x$

5.
(47)

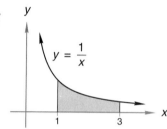

$y = \dfrac{1}{x}$

6.
(47)

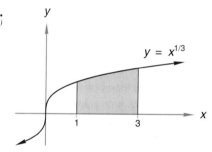

$y = x^{1/3}$

7. (a) Find all the critical numbers of f where $f(x) = -2x^3 - 3x^2 - 4$.
(36)
   (b) Use the equation and a rough sketch of the graph of f to find the values of x at which f
       attains local maximum or minimum values.

8. Use the first derivative to justify your answers to problem 7.
(45)

Find $\dfrac{dy}{dx}$ in problems 9 and 10.

9. $y = e^u$, $u = x + \cos x$
(44)

10. $y = \dfrac{1}{\sqrt{u}}$, $u = e^x + 1$
(44)

11. Use the definition $f'(a) = \lim\limits_{x \to a} \dfrac{f(x) - f(a)}{x - a}$ to compute $f'(2)$ where $f(x) = x^2 + 1$.
(44)

12. Use the symmetric derivative to find $f'(x)$ where $f(x) = 2x^2 + 3x + 2$.
(44)

Differentiate the functions in problems 13–16 with respect to the independent variable.

13. $y = 3e^{x + \sin x}$
(44)

14. $y = 4t^3 \ln t$
(31)

15. $y = 6u - \dfrac{1}{\sqrt{u}}$
(25)

16. $y = \dfrac{\sin x}{x^2 + 1}$
(42)

17. Find the area under $y = 4x$ on the interval $[1, 5]$ by using circumscribed rectangles and letting
(43) the number of rectangles increase without bound. Check your answer using geometry.

18. Approximate the coordinates of the relative maximum and relative minimum points of the graph
(45) of the function $y = \frac{\sin x}{x^2 + 1}$. You may assume that the only portion of the graph you need to examine lies in the interval $-5 < x < 5$.

Sketch the graphs of the equations given in problems 19 and 20. Clearly indicate all x-intercepts and asymptotes of the graphs.

19. $y = \dfrac{2}{(x - 2)^2}$
(41)

20. $y = x^2(x - 1)(x + 1)^2$
(33)

21. Determine the domain and range of the inverse trigonometric function $y = \arccos x$.
(13)

22. Express $\sin^2 x$ in terms of $\cos (2x)$.
(12)

23. Integrate: $\displaystyle\int \left(4e^x + 2 \cos x + x^{-5} + \frac{1}{x} + \sqrt{x} \right) dx$
(38)

24. Assuming x and y are real numbers, compare the following: A. $(x + y)^2$ B. $x^2 + y^2$
(1)

25. Let $f(x) = x - \frac{x^3}{3!} + \frac{x^5}{5!} - \frac{x^7}{7!} + \frac{x^9}{9!} - \frac{x^{11}}{11!} + \frac{x^{13}}{13!}$. Use a calculator to approximate $f(1)$ to
(R) ten decimal places. Also, evaluate $\sin (1)$ where 1 is a radian measure. How do the two answers compare?

LESSON 48 *Derivatives of Trigonometric Functions • Summary of Rules for Derivatives and Differentials*

48.A

derivatives of trigonometric functions

When we try to use the definition of the derivative to find the derivatives of $\sin x$, $\cos x$, $\tan x$, and other trigonometric functions, we encounter limits of expressions that cannot be evaluated by using elementary algebraic manipulations. There is a way to prove that the derivative of $\sin x$ with respect to x is $\cos x$ using the limits of geometric areas as a part of the proof. This proof is presented in Lesson 101.

We can use the fact that the derivative of $\sin x$ with respect to x is $\cos x$ to find the derivatives of other trigonometric functions. We begin by using this fact to find the derivative of $\cos x$ with respect to x. To find the derivative of $\cos x$, all we have to do is remember that $\cos x$ is the cosine of x, which means that $\cos x$ is the sine of the other angle. From the diagram we see that the other angle is $\frac{\pi}{2} - x$.

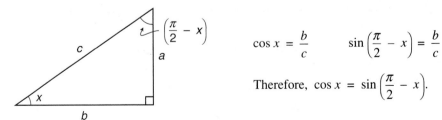

$$\cos x = \frac{b}{c} \qquad \sin\left(\frac{\pi}{2} - x\right) = \frac{b}{c}$$

$$\text{Therefore, } \cos x = \sin\left(\frac{\pi}{2} - x\right).$$

It is also useful to note that $\sin x = \cos\left(\dfrac{\pi}{2} - x\right)$. We can see this from the figure above.

$$\sin x = \frac{a}{c} \qquad \cos\left(\frac{\pi}{2} - x\right) = \frac{a}{c}$$

example 48.1   Use the fact that the derivative of $\sin x$ with respect to x is $\cos x$ to find the derivative of $\cos x$ with respect to x.

solution   We know how to differentiate the sine function, so we will substitute $\sin\left(\frac{\pi}{2} - x\right)$ for $\cos x$. Then we will use u substitution to differentiate this function. We begin by writing

$$y = \cos x$$

Next we replace $\cos x$ with its cofunction, $\sin\left(\dfrac{\pi}{2} - x\right)$.

$$y = \sin\left(\frac{\pi}{2} - x\right) \qquad \text{cofunction}$$

We note that this expression has the form $y = \sin u$. We can find the differential of this form.

$$dy = \cos u \, du \qquad \boxed{\begin{array}{l} u = \dfrac{\pi}{2} - x \\[2mm] du = (-1)\,dx \end{array}}$$

Now we use the box to substitute again. We simplify the expression and divide both sides by dx to find the derivative.

$$dy = \cos\left(\frac{\pi}{2} - x\right)(-1)\,dx \qquad \text{substituted}$$

$$dy = -\cos\left(\frac{\pi}{2} - x\right)dx \qquad \text{simplified}$$

$$\frac{dy}{dx} = -\cos\left(\frac{\pi}{2} - x\right) \qquad \text{divided by } dx$$

We began by replacing $\cos x$ with its cofunction, $\sin\left(\frac{\pi}{2} - x\right)$. We finish by replacing $\cos\left(\frac{\pi}{2} - x\right)$ with its cofunction, $\sin x$.

$$\frac{dy}{dx} = -\sin x$$

Therefore $\dfrac{d}{dx}(\cos x) = -\textbf{sin } \textbf{x.}$

example 48.2   Use the quotient rule and the derivatives of $\sin x$ and $\cos x$ to find the derivative of $\tan x$ with respect to x.

solution   We begin by writing the derivatives (with respect to x) of $\sin x$ and $\cos x$.

$$\frac{d}{dx}\sin x = \cos x \qquad \frac{d}{dx}\cos x = -\sin x$$

Then we write $\tan x$ as a quotient

$$\tan x = \frac{\sin x}{\cos x}$$

Next we use the quotient rule to find the derivative.

$$\frac{d}{dx}(\tan x) = \frac{(\cos x)(\cos x) - (\sin x)(-\sin x)}{\cos^2 x}$$

$$= \frac{\cos^2 x + \sin^2 x}{\cos^2 x}$$

Since $\sin^2 x + \cos^2 x = 1$ and the reciprocal of $\cos^2 x$ is $\sec^2 x$,

$$\frac{d}{dx}(\tan x) = \frac{1}{\cos^2 x} = \textbf{sec}^2\,\textbf{x}$$

example 48.3   Use the quotient rule and the derivatives of $\sin x$ and $\cos x$ to find the derivative of $\cot x$ with respect to x.

solution   Again we begin by writing the derivatives (with respect to x) of $\sin x$ and $\cos x$.

$$\frac{d}{dx}\sin x = \cos x \qquad \frac{d}{dx}\cos x = -\sin x$$

Then we write $\cot x$ in terms of sine and cosine.

$$\cot x = \frac{\cos x}{\sin x}$$

Next we use the quotient rule to find the derivative.

$$\frac{d}{dx}(\cot x) = \frac{(\sin x)(-\sin x) - (\cos x)(\cos x)}{\sin^2 x}$$

$$= \frac{-\sin^2 x - \cos^2 x}{\sin^2 x}$$

$$= \frac{-(\sin^2 x + \cos^2 x)}{\sin^2 x}$$

Since $-(\sin^2 x + \cos^2 x) = -1$ and the reciprocal of $\sin^2 x$ is $\csc^2 x$,

$$\frac{d}{dx}(\cot x) = \frac{-1}{\sin^2 x} = -\csc^2 x$$

example 48.4   Use the fact that $\sec x$ is the reciprocal of $\cos x$ to find the derivative of $\sec x$ with respect to x.

solution   First we rewrite $\sec x$ as a power of $\cos x$.

$$y = \sec x = \frac{1}{\cos x} = (\cos x)^{-1}$$

This equation has the form $y = u^{-1}$.

$$y = u^{-1} \quad \longrightarrow \quad dy = (-1)u^{-2}\,du \qquad \boxed{\begin{array}{l} u = \cos x \\ du = -\sin x\,dx \end{array}}$$

Therefore

$$dy = (-1)(\cos x)^{-2}(-\sin x\,dx) \qquad \text{substituted}$$

$$dy = \frac{\sin x}{\cos^2 x}\,dx \qquad \text{simplified}$$

$$dy = \frac{1}{\cos x}\frac{\sin x}{\cos x}\,dx \qquad \text{rearranged}$$

$$dy = \sec x \tan x\,dx \qquad \text{simplified}$$

$$\frac{dy}{dx} = \sec x \tan x \qquad \text{divided by } dx$$

This shows that

$$\frac{d}{dx}(\sec x) = \sec x\,\tan x$$

example 48.5   Use the fact that $\csc x$ is the reciprocal of $\sin x$ to find the derivative of $\csc x$ with respect to x.

solution   First we rewrite $\csc x$ as a power of $\sin x$.

$$y = \csc x = \frac{1}{\sin x} = (\sin x)^{-1}$$

This equation has the form $y = u^{-1}$.

$$y = u^{-1} \quad \longrightarrow \quad dy = (-1)u^{-2}\,du \qquad \boxed{\begin{array}{l} u = \sin x \\ du = \cos x\,dx \end{array}}$$

Therefore

$$dy = (-1)(\sin x)^{-2}(\cos x \, dx) \qquad \text{substituted}$$

$$dy = -\frac{\cos x}{\sin^2 x} \, dx \qquad \text{simplified}$$

$$dy = -\frac{1}{\sin x} \frac{\cos x}{\sin x} \, dx \qquad \text{rearranged}$$

$$dy = -\csc x \cot x \, dx \qquad \text{simplified}$$

$$\frac{dy}{dx} = -\csc x \cot x \qquad \text{divided by } dx$$

This shows that

$$\frac{d}{dx}(\csc x) = -\mathbf{csc\ x\ cot\ x}$$

We have now developed the derivatives of all six trigonometric functions. These derivatives should be memorized and known well. It is also wise to remember the techniques for deriving them.

48.B
summary of rules for derivatives and differentials

Let c represent a constant and u and v be differentiable functions of x. The rules for derivatives and differentials that we have discussed to this point are as follows:

DERIVATIVES	DIFFERENTIALS
$\dfrac{d}{dx}c = 0$	$d(c) = 0$
$\dfrac{d}{dx}(cu) = c\dfrac{du}{dx}$	$d(cu) = c \, du$
$\dfrac{d}{dx}(u + v) = \dfrac{du}{dx} + \dfrac{dv}{dx}$	$d(u + v) = du + dv$
$\dfrac{d}{dx}(uv) = u\dfrac{dv}{dx} + v\dfrac{du}{dx}$	$d(uv) = u \, dv + v \, du$
$\dfrac{d}{dx}\left(\dfrac{u}{v}\right) = \dfrac{v\dfrac{du}{dx} - u\dfrac{dv}{dx}}{v^2}$	$d\left(\dfrac{u}{v}\right) = \dfrac{v \, du - u \, dv}{v^2}$
$\dfrac{d}{dx}x^n = nx^{n-1}$	$d(x^n) = nx^{n-1} \, dx$
$\dfrac{d}{dx}e^x = e^x$	$d(e^x) = e^x \, dx$
$\dfrac{d}{dx}\ln|x| = \dfrac{1}{x}$	$d(\ln|x|) = \dfrac{1}{x} \, dx$
$\dfrac{d}{dx}\sin x = \cos x$	$d(\sin x) = \cos x \, dx$
$\dfrac{d}{dx}\cos x = -\sin x$	$d(\cos x) = -\sin x \, dx$
$\dfrac{d}{dx}\tan x = \sec^2 x$	$d(\tan x) = \sec^2 x \, dx$
$\dfrac{d}{dx}\cot x = -\csc^2 x$	$d(\cot x) = -\csc^2 x \, dx$
$\dfrac{d}{dx}\sec x = \sec x \tan x$	$d(\sec x) = \sec x \tan x \, dx$
$\dfrac{d}{dx}\csc x = -\csc x \cot x$	$d(\csc x) = -\csc x \cot x \, dx$

**problem set
48**

1. The radius of the base of a right circular cone increases at a rate of 1 centimeter per second
   (46) while its height remains constant at 10 centimeters. Find the rate at which the volume of the
   cone is changing at the instant the base of the cone has a radius of 24 centimeters.

2. Em is using the faucet to force water into her balloon at a rate of 2 cubic centimeters per
   (46) second. Assuming the balloon's shape remains spherical, find the rate of change of the
   surface area of the balloon when its radius is 7 centimeters.

3. Use the fact that the derivative of $\sin x$ with respect to x is $\cos x$ to develop the derivative of
   (48) $\cos x$ with respect to x.

4. Use the quotient rule and the derivatives of $\sin x$ and $\cos x$ to develop the derivative of $\cot x$
   (48) with respect to x.

5. Use the fact that $\csc x$ is the reciprocal of $\sin x$ to develop the derivative of $\csc x$ with respect to x.
   (48)

Find the derivatives of the functions in problems 6 and 7 with respect to x.

6. $y = e^x \csc x$ 7. $y = x^2 \sec x$
   (48)   (48)

Use the Fundamental Theorem of Calculus to compute the exact areas of the shaded regions in
problems 8–11.

8. (47)

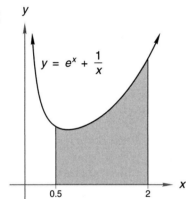

9. (47)

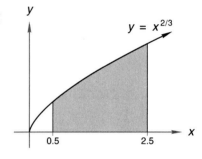

10. (47)

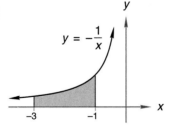

11. (47)

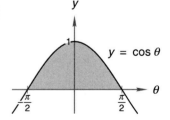

12. Suppose $f(x) = x^2 + bx + c$ where b and c are real numbers. Use the first derivative to
    (45) determine where the minimum value of f occurs. Use a rough sketch of f to justify
    the answer.

13. Let g be a function such that $g'(2) = 0$, $g' < 0$ when x lies in the interval $(0, 2)$,
    (45) and $g' > 0$ when x lies in the interval $(2, 4)$. Determine whether g attains a local maximum
    or minimum value at $x = 2$.

Find $\dfrac{dy}{dx}$ in problems 14 and 15.

14. $y = 4 \sin u$, $u = x^2$ 15. $y = -\dfrac{1}{\sqrt{u}}$, $u = e^x - 1$
    (44)   (44)

16. A particle moves along the number line so that its position at time t is given by the equation
(40) $s(t) = t^3 - t^2 - 12$. Find the velocity of the particle at $t = 3$.

17. Determine: $\int \left(-\dfrac{1}{\sqrt{u}} + 2u^2 - 1 + 3\sqrt{u} + 2\sin u - \cos u + u^{-5} - 4e^u \right) du$
(38)

18. Determine: $\int \dfrac{x^2 + x + 1}{x}\, dx$ (*Hint:* First rewrite the integrand as a sum.)
(38)

19. Solve: $\log_x 3 = 5$
(9)

20. Rewrite $y = \log_2 x$ entirely in terms of the natural logarithm function.
(20)

21. Let $f(x) = x^3$ and $g(h) = \dfrac{f(1+h) - f(1-h)}{2h}$.
(44)

(a) Use the appropriate features of a graphing calculator to find $g(h)$ for values of h near 0. What do you think $g(h)$ approaches as h approaches 0?

(b) Use calculus to determine the value of $f'(1)$.

(c) How do the answers to (a) and (b) compare?

22. Let $f(x) = \dfrac{x^2 + x + 1}{x}$ where $x < 0$. Use a graphing calculator to determine the coordinates of
(40) the relative maximum point of the graph of f.

23. (a) Use a graphing calculator to determine the value of $f'(2)$ where $f(x) = \dfrac{2x + 1}{x^2 + 1}$.
(31)

(b) Suppose $g(x) = 2x + 1$ and $h(x) = x^2 + 1$. Determine the value of $\dfrac{h(2)g'(2) - g(2)h'(2)}{[h(2)]^2}$.

(c) How do the answers to (a) and (b) compare?

24. Graph the set $\{x \in \mathbb{R} \mid |2x - 3| < 4\}$ on a number line.
(9)

25. Assuming $xy = 1$, compare the following: A. $-x$ B. $-\dfrac{1}{y}$
(1)

LESSON 49 *Concavity and Inflection Points • Geometric Meaning of the Second Derivative • First and Second Derivative Tests*

49.A

concavity and inflection points

We begin with a continuous function f that has a derivative at $x = c$ as shown in the figures below. If we can draw a line tangent to the graph of the function f at $x = c$, there are three possibilities for the behavior of the graph near the point of tangency P.

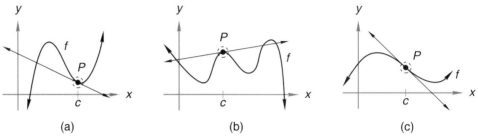

(a)   (b)   (c)

(a) All points on the graph near the point of tangency P lie above the tangent line. In this case the graph moves **up** and away from the tangent line on both sides of P, and we say that the graph of f is **concave upward** at $x = c$.

(b) All points on the graph near the point of tangency P lie below the tangent line. In this case the graph moves **down** and away from the tangent line on both sides of P, and we say that the graph of f is **concave downward** at $x = c$.

(c) The points on the graph near the point of tangency P are above the tangent line on one side of P and below the tangent line on the other side of P. Thus the curve moves up and away (concave upward) on one side and down and away (concave downward) on the other side. In this case we call the point P an **inflection point** and say that f has an inflection point at $x = c$.

example 49.1   Shown at right is the graph of f.

Indicate if the graph appears to be concave upward, to be concave downward, or to have an inflection point at the points labeled.

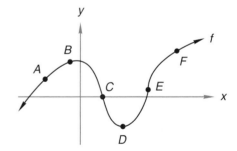

solution   A: **Concave downward**   B: **Concave downward**   C: **Inflection point**

D: **Concave upward**   E: **Inflection point**   F: **Concave downward**

Notice that the graph is concave upward on one side of both inflection points and is concave downward on the other side.

49.B

geometric meaning of the second derivative

The derivative of a function is another function called the **first derivative,** which describes the rate of change of the original function with respect to x. The value of the first derivative where $x = c$ equals the slope of the line tangent to the graph when $x = c$.

If we differentiate the first derivative of a function, we get another function called the **second derivative** of the function. The second derivative describes the rate of change of the first derivative. Thus the value of the second derivative when $x = c$ is the rate of change of the slope of the graph of the original function at $x = c$. **If the second derivative is positive when $x = c$, the slope of the graph of the function is increasing as the x-coordinate increases, and the graph is concave**

upward at that point. In the figure below, we show the graph of a function that is concave upward at every value of x. The numbers near the curve indicate the slope of the tangent line at that point.

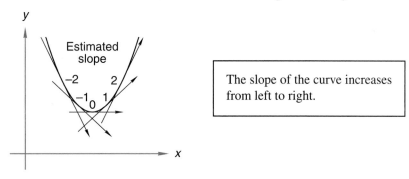

As x increases, we see that the slope goes from −2 to −1 to 0 to +1 to +2. Each value of the slope is greater than the value to its left, and thus the rate of change of the slope is positive.

If the second derivative is negative when $x = c$, the slope of the graph of the function is decreasing as the x-coordinate increases, and the graph is concave downward at that point. In the figure below, we show the graph of a function that is concave downward at every value of x.

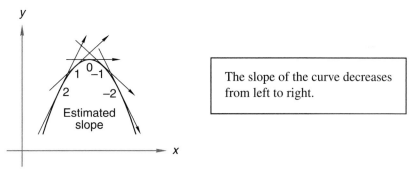

In this graph of a function, as x increases the indicated values of the slope go from +2 to +1 to 0 to −1 to −2. Each value of the slope is less than the one to its left, and thus the rate of change of the slope is negative.

We can remember the connection between values of the second derivative and concavity by using these faces as a mnemonic.

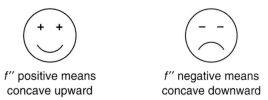

The first derivative tells us whether the slope is positive, negative, or zero and tells us how steep the slope is if the slope is not zero. To illustrate, we show the graphs of the following:

$$y = \frac{1}{3}x \qquad\qquad y = 2x \qquad\qquad y = -\frac{1}{3}x \qquad\qquad y = -2x$$

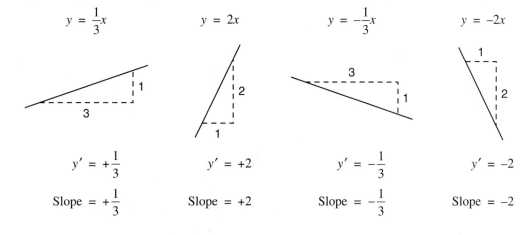

$$y' = +\frac{1}{3} \qquad\qquad y' = +2 \qquad\qquad y' = -\frac{1}{3} \qquad\qquad y' = -2$$

$$\text{Slope} = +\frac{1}{3} \qquad \text{Slope} = +2 \qquad \text{Slope} = -\frac{1}{3} \qquad \text{Slope} = -2$$

If the second derivative is not zero for some value of *x*, its value tells us whether the slope is increasing positively or negatively and tells us how fast the slope is increasing, which is a measure of the "bend" in the graph at that value of *x*.

Here we show tangent lines drawn to the graphs of four different functions. The slopes of the tangent lines are equal, so the values of the first derivatives of these functions are equal at the points of tangency.

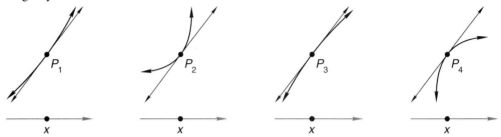

The values of the second derivatives are all different. At P_1 and P_2 the graphs are concave upward, so the slope is increasing from left to right. The bend in the graph at P_2 is greater, so if the value of the second derivative at P_1 were +2, a value of +4 at P_2 would not be unreasonable. At P_3 and P_4 the graphs are concave downward, so the slope is decreasing from left to right. The bend in the graph at P_4 is greater, so if the value of the second derivative at P_3 were –2, a value of –4 at P_4 would not be unreasonable.

example 49.2 At which of the points labeled on the graph shown is $\frac{d^2y}{dx^2}$ positive?

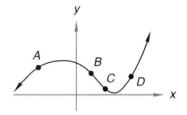

solution The places at which the second derivative is positive are those places where the graph is concave upward. Only two of the indicated points appear to satisfy this condition; they are **C** and **D.**

49.C

first and second derivative tests

Critical points (or critical numbers) are input values for which the value of a function could be a local maximum or a local minimum. Local maximum values and local minimum values are sometimes called **local extrema.** Local extrema can occur at the endpoints of the domain and also at inputs for which the graph of a function has a corner or "sharp point." Local extrema can also exist at inputs for which the first derivative equals zero (the slope of the graph is zero). These critical points are called *stationary points* or *stationary numbers.* **If the function *f* is continuous at *c* and if $f'(c) = 0$, then we can use the first derivative to test whether $f(c)$ is a local maximum or a local minimum or if the graph of *f* has an inflection point at $(c, f(c))$.**

FIRST DERIVATIVE TEST

Suppose the first derivative of *f* equals zero at $x = c$—that is, suppose $f'(c) = 0$.

1. If the derivative of *f* (slope of the graph of *f*) is positive for all values of *x* just to the left of *c* and negative for all values of *x* just to the right of *c*, then $f(c)$ is a local maximum.

2. If the derivative of *f* (slope of the graph of *f*) is negative for all values of *x* just to the left of *c* and positive for all values of *x* just to the right of *c*, then $f(c)$ is a local minimum.

3. If the derivative of *f* (slope of the graph of *f*) has the same sign for all values of *x* just to the left and right of *c*, then $(c, f(c))$ is an inflection point on the graph of *f*.

The three possibilities are shown here.

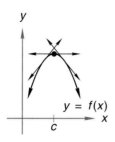 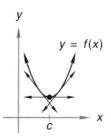 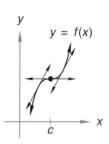 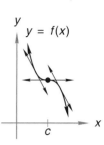

Local maximum   Local minimum   Inflection points

If the value of the second derivative, $f''(x)$, is positive or negative when $x = c$, the second derivative can be used to obviate the requirement for checking the value of the first derivative on both sides of $x = c$. If the value of the second derivative is zero, $f''(c) = 0$, then the second derivative test cannot be used.

SECOND DERIVATIVE TEST

Suppose the first derivative of f equals zero at $x = c$—that is, suppose $f'(c) = 0$.

1. If the second derivative of f is a negative number at $x = c$, then $f(c)$ is a local maximum value.

2. If the second derivative of f is a positive number at $x = c$, then $f(c)$ is a local minimum value.

Note: **A zero value of the second derivative does not necessarily indicate an inflection point. A zero value of the second derivative compels us to use the first derivative test.**

example 49.3   Suppose f is a polynomial function such that $f'(3) = 0$ and $f''(3) = 3$. Sketch the graph of f for inputs close to 3, and indicate the property of the function f at $x = 3$.

solution   With the information given, we can only guess at the shape of the graph in the vicinity of $x = 3$. Since $f'(3) = 0$, we have a critical point at $x = 3$. **Since $f''(3) > 0$, the graph must be concave up there.** Hence, f has a local minimum at $x = 3$.

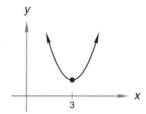

example 49.4   Suppose f is a polynomial function such that $f'(3) = 0$ and $f''(3) = 0$. In addition f' is positive for all values of x near $x = 3$. Sketch the graph of f near $x = 3$, and indicate the significance of the point on the graph of f at $x = 3$.

solution   Since $f'(3) = 0$, $f(3)$ is a local maximum or minimum value of f, or the graph of f has an inflection point at $(3, f(3))$. We cannot use the second derivative test to check this because $f''(3) = 0$, so we resort to the first derivative test instead. The first derivative has the same sign (positive) on both sides of 3, **so the point $(3, f(3))$ must be an inflection point.** We use this information to sketch the graph of f.

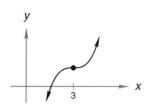

example 49.5   Given $f(x) = x^4$, use f' and f'' to describe the graph of f near $x = 0$.

solution   We begin by finding the equations of f' and f''.

$$f(x) = x^4$$
$$f'(x) = 4x^3 \longrightarrow f'(0) = 4(0)^3 = 0$$
$$f''(x) = 12x^2 \longrightarrow f''(0) = 12(0)^2 = 0$$

At $x = 0$, f' and f'' equal 0. The fact that $f'(0) = 0$ tells us that f has a stationary point at $(0, f(0))$. The second derivative test cannot be used because $f''(0) = 0$. Using the first derivative test, we see that f' is negative when x is negative and f' is positive when x is positive. Thus $f(0)$ is a local minimum value of f.

$$f'(x) = 4x^3 \begin{cases} < 0 \text{ when } x < 0 \\ = 0 \text{ when } x = 0 \\ > 0 \text{ when } x > 0 \end{cases}$$

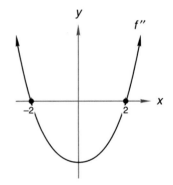

example 49.6   The graph at right represents f'', the second derivative of f.

Discuss the basic shape of the graph of f.

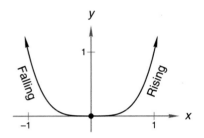

solution   We first notice that $f''(-2) = 0$ and $f''(2) = 0$. So the graph of f has possible inflection points at $x = -2$ and $x = 2$. Next we see that $f''(x) > 0$ for $x < -2$. Therefore, when $x < -2$, the graph of f must be concave up. Similarly, the graph of f must be concave up when $x > 2$. Finally, we see that $f''(x) < 0$ when $-2 < x < 2$. So over this interval, the graph of f must be concave down. Therefore, the basic shape of the graph of f must be the following:

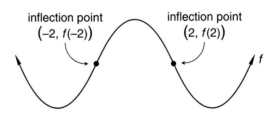

inflection point $(-2, f(-2))$ inflection point $(2, f(2))$

Note that we lack a great deal of information about f. This is only one of the numerous possibilities for the shape of f.

problem set 49

1. *(46)* An inverted right circular cone whose depth is 10 cm and whose base has a radius of 5 cm is dripping liquid at a rate of 1 cm³/s. How fast is the depth of the liquid changing when the depth of the liquid is 5 cm?

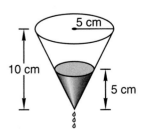

2. Sketch the basic shape of the graph of f where $f''(x)$ $\begin{cases} > 0 \text{ when } x > 1 \\ = 0 \text{ when } x = 1 \\ < 0 \text{ when } x < 1. \end{cases}$
(49)

3. (a) Find all the critical numbers of $f(x) = x^4 - 2x^2$.
(45)

    (b) Use the equation of f and its graph to determine where the extrema of f occur and what their values are.

4. For $f(x) = x^4 - 2x^2$ use the second derivative test to determine whether the graph of f has a
(49) local maximum, a local minimum, or an inflection point at each of the critical numbers of f.

Use the Fundamental Theorem of Calculus to compute the areas of the shaded regions shown in problems 5–8.

5.
(47)

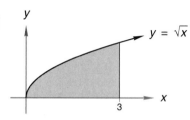

6.
(47)

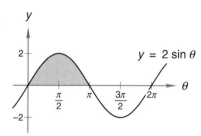

7.
(47)

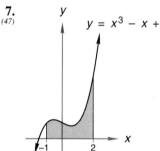

8.
(47)

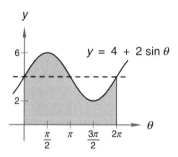

9. Shown is the graph of f'. Make a rough sketch of the graph of f.
(45)

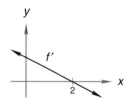

Differentiate the functions in problems 10–12 with respect to x.

10. $y = 4x \csc x$
(48)

11. $g(x) = x \ln |x| - x \tan x$
(48)

12. $y = 13(\sin x + \cos x)^{22}$
(48)

13. Find $\dfrac{dy}{dx}$ where $y = 6u^4$ and $u = \sin x + \cos x$.
(44)

14. Evaluate $f'''(-2)$ where $f(x) = 2 \ln |x| + 3$.
(27)

Sketch the graphs of the equations given in problems 15 and 16.

15. $y = \dfrac{(1 - x)(x^2 + 1)(x - 4)}{(x^2 + 2)(x - 2)(x - 4)x}$
(41)

16. $y = x(x - 1)(x + 1)^3$
(33)

17. Use the fact that the derivative of sin x with respect to x is cos x to prove that the derivative of
(48) cos x with respect to x is $-\sin x$.

18. Find y' where $y = 2e^x - \cos x + 14 \sin x$.
(26)

19. Let $f(x) = \sin x$ and $g(x) = f\left(x - \dfrac{\pi}{4}\right)$. Sketch the graph of g.
(21)

20. Evaluate: $\displaystyle\lim_{h \to 0} \dfrac{3xh - 4h^2}{h}$
(14)

21. (a) Sketch a graph of the region bounded by $y = x$ and the x-axis on the interval $[0, 1]$.
(43)
   (b) Divide the region into n upper rectangles. What is the width of each rectangle?
   (c) What is the height of the first rectangle? The third rectangle? The sixth rectangle? The nth rectangle?
   (d) Write an expression using limit notation that represents the area of the n rectangles as n approaches infinity. Use your answers from (b) and (c) to indicate the width and height of each rectangle.

22. Integrate: $\displaystyle\int \left(\dfrac{4}{\sqrt{x}} - 3\sqrt{x} - x^\pi + x^{-\pi} - 3 \sin x + \cos x - 2e^x \right) dx$
(38)

23. Use the derivatives of sin x and cos x to prove that the derivative of tan x with respect to x
(48) is $\sec^2 x$.

24. Graph the set $\left\{ x \in \mathbb{R} \mid |x - 3| < 4 \right\}$ on a number line.
(9)

25. Suppose $h(x) = \dfrac{f(x)}{g(x)}$ where $f(x) = x + \ln x$ and $g(x) = \sin x + \cos x$.
(42)
   (a) Use the graphing calculator to determine the value of $h'(1)$.
   (b) Determine the values of $f(1)$ and $g(1)$.
   (c) Differentiate to find $f'(x)$ and $g'(x)$.
   (d) Use the equations found in (c) to determine the values of $f'(1)$ and $g'(1)$.
   (e) Find the value of $\dfrac{g(1)f'(1) - f(1)g'(1)}{[g(1)]^2}$ by substituting the values for $g(1)$, $f(1)$, $f'(1)$, and $g'(1)$ found in (b) and (d).
   (f) How do the answers to (a) and (e) compare?

LESSON 50 *Derivatives of Composite Functions • Derivatives of Products and Quotients of Composite Functions*

50.A
derivatives of composite functions

We have been using two methods to find the derivative of a composite function. First we learned to use u substitution, and then we learned to treat the equations separately and use the chain rule. The function

$$y = e^{2x}$$

is a composite function formed by composing two function machines into one as we show here.

The derivative of this composite function is the same whether we use u substitution or the chain rule.

$$\frac{d}{dx} e^{2x} = e^{2x} \frac{d}{dx}(2x) \qquad \text{so} \qquad \frac{d}{dx} e^{2x} = 2e^{2x}$$

We need to differentiate composite functions often, and it is helpful to realize that a shortcut can be used. We treat the argument of the composite function as if it were a single entity and multiply the derivative of this function by the derivative of the argument. Thus if ( ) is the argument of the function, we have:

$$\frac{d}{dx} c(\ ) = c \frac{d}{dx}(\ ) \qquad\qquad \frac{d}{dx}(\ )^n = n(\ )^{n-1} \frac{d}{dx}(\ )$$

$$\frac{d}{dx} e^{(\ )} = e^{(\ )} \frac{d}{dx}(\ ) \qquad\qquad \frac{d}{dx} \ln (\ ) = \frac{1}{(\ )} \frac{d}{dx}(\ )$$

$$\frac{d}{dx} \sin (\ ) = \cos (\ ) \frac{d}{dx}(\ ) \qquad\qquad \frac{d}{dx} \cos (\ ) = -\sin (\ ) \frac{d}{dx}(\ )$$

$$\frac{d}{dx} \tan (\ ) = \sec^2 (\ ) \frac{d}{dx}(\ ) \qquad\qquad \frac{d}{dx} \cot (\ ) = -\csc^2 (\ ) \frac{d}{dx}(\ )$$

$$\frac{d}{dx} \sec (\ ) = \sec (\ ) \tan (\ ) \frac{d}{dx}(\ ) \qquad\qquad \frac{d}{dx} \csc (\ ) = -\csc (\ ) \cot (\ ) \frac{d}{dx}(\ )$$

example 50.1   If $f(x) = \sin (2x^2 + 4x + 6)$, what is $f'(x)$?

solution   We remember that

$$\frac{d}{dx} \sin (\ ) = \cos (\ ) \frac{d}{dx}(\ )$$

Next we write $2x^2 + 4x + 6$ in each of the parentheses.

$$\frac{d}{dx} \sin (2x^2 + 4x + 6) = \cos (2x^2 + 4x + 6) \frac{d}{dx}(2x^2 + 4x + 6)$$

We finish by taking the derivative of the argument and writing either

$$f'(x) = \big[\cos (2x^2 + 4x + 6)\big](4x + 4) \qquad \text{or} \qquad f'(x) = (4x + 4) \cos (2x^2 + 4x + 6)$$

example 50.2   Let $g(x) = \ln (\sin x)$. Find $g'(x)$.

solution   We remember that

$$\frac{d}{dx} \ln (\ ) = \frac{1}{(\ )} \frac{d}{dx}(\ )$$

Next we write $\sin x$ in each of the parentheses.

$$\frac{d}{dx} \ln (\sin x) = \frac{1}{\sin x} \frac{d}{dx}(\sin x)$$

Then we take the derivative of the argument and simplify.

$$g'(x) = \frac{1}{\sin x} \cdot \cos x = \cot x$$

However, this is not true for all x. The derivative is not defined where the function is not defined. So the derivative is not defined at x if $\sin x \le 0$.

example 50.3   Let $h(x) = (x^2 + 4x)^{100}$. Find $h'(x)$.

solution   We remember that

$$\frac{d}{dx}(\ )^{100} = 100(\ )^{99} \frac{d}{dx}(\ )$$

We write $x^2 + 4x$ in each set of parentheses, take the derivative of the argument, and simplify.

$$\frac{d}{dx}(x^2 + 4x)^{100} = 100(x^2 + 4x)^{99} \frac{d}{dx}(x^2 + 4x)$$

$$= 100(x^2 + 4x)^{99} (2x + 4)$$

$$= 200(x + 2)(x^2 + 4x)^{99}$$

$$h'(x) = 200x^{99}(x + 2)(x + 4)^{99}$$

50.B

derivatives of products and quotients of composite functions

The process of finding the derivatives of products and quotients of composite functions can be a little confusing. It is helpful to write the individual derivatives as a first step. This lessens the chance of leaving out part of the answer, and it often saves time that might otherwise be spent on mental bookkeeping.

example 50.4 If $f(x) = e^x(x^2 + 1)^{100}$, what is $f'(x)$?

solution We need to find the derivative of a product, and one of the factors is a composite function. We write the derivatives of both factors of the product as the first step.

$$\frac{d}{dx}e^x = e^x \qquad \frac{d}{dx}(x^2 + 1)^{100} = 100(x^2 + 1)^{99}(2x)$$

$$= \left[200x(x^2 + 1)^{99}\right]$$

The derivative of a product is the first times the derivative of the second, plus the second times the derivative of the first. We have the functions and the derivatives, so we can write the result.

$$f'(x) = e^x\left[200x(x^2 + 1)^{99}\right] + \left[(x^2 + 1)^{100}\right](e^x)$$

We can simplify this expression a little.

$$f'(x) = 200xe^x(x^2 + 1)^{99} + e^x(x^2 + 1)^{100}$$

This answer is satisfactory, but some people prefer that answers be in a fully factored form. We note that e^x is a factor of both terms, and if we look closely, we can see that $(x^2 + 1)^{100}$ can be written as $(x^2 + 1)(x^2 + 1)^{99}$. Since $(x^2 + 1)^{99}$ is a factor of both terms, we can write

$$f'(x) = e^x(x^2 + 1)^{99}(200x + x^2 + 1)$$

It is wise and helpful to write all first derivatives in their fully factored form. It makes the task of finding stationary points rather easy. In the above example, $f'(x) = 0$ when

$$e^x = 0 \qquad \text{or} \qquad (x^2 + 1)^{99} = 0 \qquad \text{or} \qquad 200x + x^2 + 1 = 0$$

We know e^x is never zero, and neither is $x^2 + 1$. To find stationary points, we can spend all of our energy solving $200x + x^2 + 1 = 0$.

example 50.5 Suppose $f(t) = \dfrac{\sin(2t) + \ln t}{(t^3 + 3t)^5}$. Find $f'(t)$.

solution We write the derivatives of the numerator and denominator as the first step.

$$\frac{d}{dt}[\sin(2t) + \ln t] = 2\cos(2t) + \frac{1}{t}$$

$$\frac{d}{dt}(t^3 + 3t)^5 = 5(t^3 + 3t)^4(3t^2 + 3)$$

The quotient rule is the denominator times the derivative of the numerator, minus the numerator times the derivative of the denominator, all over the square of the denominator. We have all the components and just have to write them.

$$\frac{(t^3 + 3t)^5\left[2\cos(2t) + \dfrac{1}{t}\right] - [\sin(2t) + \ln t]5(t^3 + 3t)^4(3t^2 + 3)}{(t^3 + 3t)^{10}}$$

This expression can be simplified a little.

$$f'(t) = \frac{(t^3 + 3t)\left[2 \cos (2t) + \dfrac{1}{t}\right] - 5[\sin (2t) + \ln t](3t^2 + 3)}{(t^3 + 3t)^6}$$ canceled common factor $(t^3 + 3t)^4$

$$= \frac{t(t^2 + 3)\left[2 \cos (2t) + \dfrac{1}{t}\right] - 5[\sin (2t) + \ln t]3(t^2 + 1)}{t^6(t^2 + 3)^6}$$ factored

$$= \frac{(t^2 + 3)[2t \cos (2t) + 1] - 15[\sin (2t) + \ln t](t^2 + 1)}{t^6(t^2 + 3)^6}$$ simplified

problem set 50

1. (46) A particle moves along the circular path determined by the equation $x^2 + y^2 = 9$. Find the rate at which the x-coordinate is changing the instant the particle passes through the point $(2\sqrt{2}, 1)$, assuming the y-coordinate is decreasing at a rate of 2 units per second at that instant.

2. (49) Sketch the basic shape of the graph of f where $f''(x) \begin{cases} < 0 \text{ when } x < 2 \\ = 0 \text{ when } x = 2 \\ > 0 \text{ when } x > 2. \end{cases}$

3. (36) (a) Find all the critical numbers of $f(x) = -12x^4 + 4x^3 + 12x^2 - 1$.

(b) Use the equation of f and its graph to determine the extremum values of f and where they occur.

4. (49) Suppose $f(x) = -12x^4 + 4x^3 + 12x^2 - 1$.

(a) Find where the inflection points of the graph of f occur.

(b) Identify the intervals on which the graph of f is concave upward and the intervals on which the graph of f is concave downward.

Find the derivatives of the functions in problems 5–9 with respect to the independent variable.

5. (50) $f(x) = \tan (3x^2 - 4x + 1)$

6. (50) $y = \ln (\sec x)$

7. (50) $h(x) = (x^2 - 4)^{50}$

8. (50) $y = e^x(x^2 + 4)^{50}$

9. (50) $g(t) = \dfrac{\sin (2t)}{\cos^2 t}$

Use the Fundamental Theorem of Calculus to compute the areas of the shaded regions in problems 10–12.

10. (47)

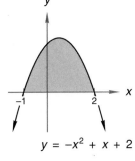

$y = -x^2 + x + 2$

11. (47)

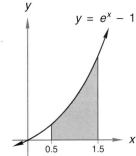

$y = e^x - 1$

12. (47)

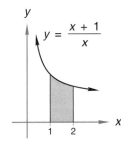

$y = \dfrac{x + 1}{x}$

Antidifferentiate in problems 13 and 14.

13. (25) $\displaystyle\int \sqrt{x}\,(x - 2)\,dx$

14. (25) $\displaystyle\int (x - 2)^2\,dx$

15. (27,34) Use implicit differentiation as required to find the equation of the line tangent to the graph of $x^2 + y^2 = 9$ at $(2\sqrt{2}, 1)$.

16. Approximate $\left.\dfrac{d^2 y}{dx^2}\right|_2$ where $y = -2 \cos x$.
(29)

17. Evaluate: $\lim\limits_{h \to 0} \dfrac{e^{x+h} - e^x}{h} + \lim\limits_{n \to \infty} \dfrac{1}{1 - n^2}$
(17,28)

18. Antidifferentiate: $\displaystyle\int \left(3\sqrt{x} - \dfrac{4}{\sqrt[3]{x}} + \sin x - 2x^{-4} - \dfrac{7}{x} - 3e^x \right) dx$
(38)

Sketch the graphs of the functions given in problems 19 and 20. Clearly indicate all zeros and asymptotes.

19. $y = \dfrac{x(x - 2)}{x(x^2 + 2)(x + 1)}$
(28)

20. $y = -x(x + 1)^2 (x - 1)^3$
(33)

21. (a) Write a definite integral that equals $\lim\limits_{n \to \infty} \dfrac{1}{n}\left[\dfrac{1}{n} + \dfrac{2}{n} + \dfrac{3}{n} + \cdots + 1 \right]$.
(43,47)

   (b) Evaluate the expression in (a) by computing the definite integral.

Use a calculator as necessary to solve the equations in problems 22 and 23 for x.

22. $e^x = 21$
(9)

23. $\log_x (4x) = 2$
(9)

24. Suppose that the function f is differentiable at 0, $g(x) = [f(x)]^2$, $f(0) = -1$, and $f'(0) = -1$.
(44) Evaluate $g'(0)$.

25. In this exercise you will use a graphing calculator to approximate the graph of the
(2) function $f(x) = e^x$ by using polynomials. Enter all of the following equations into your graphing calculator:

$$Y_1 = e^x \qquad Y_2 = 1 \qquad Y_3 = 1 + x \qquad Y_4 = 1 + x + \dfrac{x^2}{2!}$$

$$Y_5 = 1 + x + \dfrac{x^2}{2!} + \dfrac{x^3}{3!} \qquad Y_6 = 1 + x + \dfrac{x^2}{2!} + \dfrac{x^3}{3!} + \dfrac{x^4}{4!}$$

   (a) Graph only Y_1, Y_2, Y_3, and Y_4.

   (b) Graph only Y_1 and Y_5.

   (c) Graph only Y_1 and Y_6.

As you can see from the graphs, Y_2 is not a good approximation of $f(x) = e^x$, but each successive approximation improves upon the previous ones. Evidently, increasing the number of terms increases the accuracy of the approximation. A later lesson shows that the function $f(x) = e^x$ can be easily written as an infinite series (called the Maclaurin series for e^x).

$$e^x = \sum_{n=0}^{\infty} \dfrac{x^n}{n!} = 1 + x + \dfrac{x^2}{2!} + \dfrac{x^3}{3!} + \dfrac{x^4}{4!} + \dfrac{x^5}{5!} + \cdots$$

LESSON 51   *Integration by Guessing*

It can be shown that every continuous function has an antiderivative, and thus the indefinite integral exists for every continuous function. Finding an explicit expression for many of these integrals is difficult, and for some it is impossible. But we know that the integrals do exist. Thus far we have concentrated on integrating carefully contrived expressions that have one of the following basic forms. An explicit expression for each of the following integrals can be written by inspection.

$$\int u^n \, du \qquad \int \frac{du}{u} \qquad \int e^u \, du \qquad \int \sin u \, du \qquad \int \cos u \, du$$

We now extend our investigation to finding integrals of expressions that are differentials of composite functions. **Remember that the basic technique for integrating is guessing the answer then checking that guess by differentiating it.** If the differential of the guess is the expression we are trying to integrate, it is the answer. If not, we guess again and check the new guess. The ability to make good guesses improves with practice.

example 51.1   Integrate: $\displaystyle\int 6(x + 1)^5 \, dx$

solution   We guess that $(x + 1)^5$ is a factor of the differential of an expression whose basic form is u^6, since differentiation of a monomial reduces the power by one. Notice that $d(u^6) = 6u^5 \, du$. The expression on the right-hand side below closely resembles $6(x + 1)^5 \, dx$. The substitution $u = x + 1$ makes them equivalent.

$$\underbrace{d(x + 1)^6}_{u^n} = \underbrace{6(x + 1)^5}_{nu^{n-1}} \underbrace{dx}_{du}$$

Since the differential of $(x + 1)^6$ is the expression on the right-hand side of the equals sign, the integral of that expression is $(x + 1)^6$ plus a constant of integration.

$$\int 6(x + 1)^5 \, dx = (x + 1)^6 + C$$

example 51.2   Integrate: $\displaystyle\int 7 \sin^6 t \cos t \, dt$

solution   Note the exponent 6 in $\sin^6 t$. Because monomials lose a power in differentiation, it is very likely that our basic form u^6 is a result of differentiating u^7. So we guess that $u^7 = \sin^7 t$ and check by differentiating.

$$\underbrace{d\sin^7 t}_{u^n} = \underbrace{7 \sin^6 t}_{nu^{n-1}} \underbrace{\cos t \, dt}_{du}$$

Our guess was a good one. **Since the differential of $\sin^7 t$ is the expression on the right-hand side of the equals sign, the integral of that expression is $\sin^7 t$ plus a constant of integration.**

$$\int 7 \sin^6 t \cos t \, dt = \sin^7 t + C$$

example 51.3   Integrate: $\displaystyle\int \frac{3}{2}\sqrt{x + 7} \, dx$

solution   We begin by rewriting the expression as follows:

$$\int \frac{3}{2}(x + 7)^{1/2} \, dx$$

Noticing the exponent of $\frac{1}{2}$, we guess that the indefinite integral contains the form $u^{3/2} = (x + 7)^{3/2}$, which we check by finding the differential.

$$\underbrace{d(x + 7)^{3/2}}_{u^n} = \underbrace{\frac{3}{2}(x + 7)^{1/2}}_{nu^{n-1}} \underbrace{dx}_{du}$$

So, $\displaystyle\int \frac{3}{2}\sqrt{x + 7} \, dx = (x + 7)^{3/2} + C.$

example 51.4 Integrate: $\int \dfrac{3x^2\,dx}{2\sqrt{x^3+4}}$

solution We begin by rewriting the radical expression with a fractional exponent.

$$\int \frac{3}{2}x^2(x^3+4)^{-1/2}\,dx$$

Note the exponent $-\frac{1}{2}$ on $(x^3+4)^{-1/2}$. It is likely a factor of the differential of an expression whose basic form is $u^{1/2}$. We guess that $u^{1/2}=(x^3+4)^{1/2}$ and check our guess by finding its differential.

$$\underbrace{d(x^3+4)^{1/2}}_{u^n}=\underbrace{\frac{1}{2}(x^3+4)^{-1/2}}_{nu^{n-1}}\underbrace{(3x^2\,dx)}_{du}$$

We made a good guess because the expression on the right-hand side of the equals sign is a rearranged form of the expression we wish to integrate. **Since the differential of $(x^3+4)^{1/2}$ is the expression on the right-hand side of the equals sign, the integral of that expression is $(x^3+4)^{1/2}$ plus a constant of integration.**

$$\int \frac{3x^2\,dx}{2\sqrt{x^3+4}}=(x^3+4)^{1/2}+C$$

example 51.5 Integrate: $\int 8x\left(e^{4x^2}\right)dx$

solution The presence of e^{4x^2} is the key to this problem. We hope this expression is a factor of a differential whose basic form is $e^u\,du$. We guess that the indefinite integral has the form e^{4x^2} and check our guess by finding the differential.

$$\underbrace{de^{4x^2}}_{e^u}=\underbrace{e^{4x^2}}_{e^u}\underbrace{(8x\,dx)}_{du}$$

The differential is a rearranged form of the expression we want to integrate, so we can write the answer by inspection if we remember to include a constant of integration.

$$\int 8x\left(e^{4x^2}\right)dx=e^{4x^2}+C$$

example 51.6 Integrate: $\int 20x(2x^2+4)^4\,dx$

solution First note the exponent 4 on the factor $(2x^2+4)^4$. We guess an expression that has the basic form u^5 and check our guess by finding its differential. If this guess is correct, we will be able to write the answer by inspection. For our first try we guess that u^5 is $(2x^2+4)^5$. Then we find its differential.

$$\underbrace{d(2x^2+4)^5}_{u^n}=\underbrace{5(2x^2+4)^4}_{nu^{n-1}}\underbrace{(4x\,dx)}_{du}$$

The expression on the right-hand side of the equals sign is a rearranged form of the expression we wish to integrate. **Since the differential of $(2x^2+4)^5$ is the expression on the right-hand side of the equals sign, the integral of that expression is $(2x^2+4)^5$ plus a constant of integration.**

$$\int 20x(2x^2+4)^4\,dx=(2x^2+4)^5+C$$

problem set 51

1. (46) A large spherical balloon is deflated at a rate of 3 cubic centimeters per second while retaining its spherical shape. Find the rate at which the radius of the sphere is changing when the radius is 5 centimeters long.

2. (49) Sketch the basic shape of the graph of f, where $f''(x)\begin{cases}>0 & \text{when } x>1\\=0 & \text{when } x=1\\<0 & \text{when } x<1.\end{cases}$ Indicate on the graph of f any points of inflection.

3. (a) Find all the critical numbers of the function $f(x) = 2x^3 - 3x^2 - 12x + 1$.
(36)
  (b) Use the equation of f and its graph (as necessary) to determine the extremum values of f and where they occur.

4. (a) Find all the inflection points of the graph of $f(x) = 2x^3 - 3x^2 - 12x + 1$.
(49)
  (b) Use interval notation to describe the interval(s) on which the graph of f is concave upward.

Integrate in problems 5–10.

5. $\displaystyle\int 12x(x^2 + 4)^5\, dx$
(51)

6. $\displaystyle\int 6\sin^5 t \cos t\, dt$
(51)

7. $\displaystyle\int \frac{x\, dx}{\sqrt{x^2 + 4}}$
(51)

8. $\displaystyle\int 4xe^{2x^2}\, dx$
(51)

9. $\displaystyle\int \frac{6x + 1}{3x^2 + x}\, dx$
(51)

10. $\displaystyle\int 4e^{4\sin x} \cos x\, dx$
(51)

Differentiate each function in problems 11–16 with respect to x.

11. $y = (x^2 + 1)^{30}$
(50)

12. $y = e^x(x^2 - 1)^{30}$
(50)

13. $y = \sec^2(x^2 + 3x)$
(50)

14. $f(x) = \dfrac{\sin x}{(x^2 + 1)^{10}}$
(50)

15. $g(x) = 3\ln|\cos x|$
(50)

16. $y = e^{\tan(\sin x)}$
(50)

Use the Fundamental Theorem of Calculus to compute the area of each shaded region in problems 17 and 18.

17.
(47)

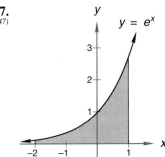

18.
(47)

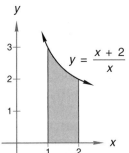

19. Evaluate: $\displaystyle\lim_{x\to 1} \frac{e^x - e}{x - 1}$
(44)

20. (a) Write the definite integral that is represented by $\displaystyle\lim_{n\to\infty} \frac{5}{n}\left[\frac{5}{n} + \frac{10}{n} + \frac{15}{n} + \cdots + 5\right]$.
(43,47)
  (b) Evaluate the sum in (a) by computing the definite integral.

21. We define a **fixed point** for a real-valued
(R) function to be a real number x_0 such that $f(x_0) = x_0$. To find any fixed points for the function $f(x) = 3x - 2$, we write $3x_0 - 2 = x_0$. Upon solving this equation, we find that $x_0 = 1$. Therefore, 1 is a fixed point for the function $f(x) = 3x - 2$. We can illustrate this example more clearly by graphing the function $f(x) = 3x - 2$ and the line $y = x$ in the first quadrant.

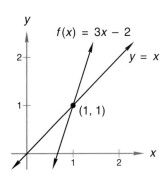

In this example, the graphs of the two functions intersect at only one point, $(1, 1)$. Therefore, the function $f(x) = 3x - 2$ has only one fixed point, $x_0 = 1$. Calculate the fixed points for each function below.

(a) $f(x) = x^2$

(b) $f(x) = 4x^2 + 4x - 1$

(c) $f(x) = \dfrac{1}{x + 1}$

Use a graphing calculator to find the approximate values of the fixed points for the functions in problems 22 and 23.

22. $f(x) = 1 + \sin x$ on $[0, 4]$
(2)

23. $f(x) = -1 + \tan x$ on $\left[0, \dfrac{3}{2}\right]$
(2)

24. Suppose $f(x_1) + f(x_2) = f(x_1 + x_2)$, where x_1 and x_2 are real numbers. Which of the following could be an equation of f?
(R)

    A. $f(x) = e^x$ B. $f(x) = \ln x$

    C. $f(x) = 3x$ D. $f(x) = x^2$

25. Let $f(x) = e^{bx}$ and $g(x) = e^{ax}$. Find the value of b in terms of a such that $\left(\dfrac{f(x)}{g(x)}\right)' = \dfrac{f'(x)}{g'(x)}$.
(26)

LESSON 52 *Maximization and Minimization Problems*

The critical numbers of a function of x on an interval I are the values of x for which the function could have a local maximum value or a local minimum value. Local maximum values and local minimum values are often called local extrema. Critical numbers can be values of x at which the derivative equals zero. For these values of x the tangent to the graph of the function is horizontal. Critical numbers can also be values of x for which the derivative does not exist. The derivative does not exist at endpoints, at values of x for which the graph has a sharp point, or at points where the tangent line to the graph is vertical. This lesson includes applied problems that ask us to find the **absolute maximum (minimum)** value of a function on a designated interval. The absolute maximum (minimum) value is sometimes called the **global maximum (minimum)** value. The absolute maximum (minimum) value must also be a local maximum (minimum) value. **So our search for an absolute maximum (minimum) value of a function on an interval begins by finding all the critical numbers of the function on the interval.** Then we find which of these numbers produces a local maximum (minimum) value. We must also find the function values at the endpoints of the domain. Then we choose the greatest (least) value as our answer.

Suppose we are searching for the maximum area of some region where the area is described by the following equation:

$$A(x) = -3x^2 + 6x + 2$$

We already know that this is the equation of a parabola that opens downward and that the x-value of the vertex is $-b$ over $2a,$ which equals 1.

$$\bar{x} = \frac{-(6)}{2(-3)} = 1$$

Thus the maximum value of this function occurs when $x = 1.$

$$A(1) = -3(1)^2 + 6(1) + (2) = 5$$

Since the parabola opens downward, any other value of x produces a lesser value of $A,$ so 5 is the maximum value of the function.

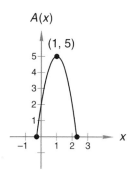

We will pretend that we do not know that 5 is the maximum value, because we are interested in using calculus to find the maximum and minimum values of functions. The first step is to locate the critical numbers of the function.

1. No domain was specified, so we assume that the domain is as large as possible in the context of the problem. In this case, we want

$$\text{Area} \geq 0 \qquad \text{or} \qquad -3x^2 + 6x + 2 \geq 0$$

   This results in two endpoints, which occur at

$$x = 1 - \frac{\sqrt{15}}{3} \qquad \text{and} \qquad x = 1 + \frac{\sqrt{15}}{3}$$

   (These can be calculated from the quadratic formula.) But the area at both of these values is 0, which is clearly *not* the maximum area possible.

2. The graph of a polynomial function is a smooth curve that has no corners and no vertical tangents, so there are no critical numbers for this function that are caused by the failure of the derivative to exist (except for the endpoints, which we already discussed).

3. The only other critical numbers are those numbers for which the first derivative equals zero. Thus we find the first derivative and set it equal to zero.

$$\frac{dA}{dx} = -6x + 6 \qquad \text{first derivative}$$

$$0 = -6x + 6 \qquad \text{set equal to 0}$$

$$x = 1 \qquad \text{solved}$$

Thus this function has only one critical number. The value of this function when $x = 1$ is 5.

$$A(1) = -3(1)^2 + 6(1) + 2 = 5$$

At this point we do not know if 5 is a local maximum value, a local minimum value, or the y-value of an inflection point. Checking x-values on either side of $x = 1$ shows that these numbers produce values of $f(x)$ that are less than 5, so 5 must be a local maximum value of the function. The second derivative test confirms that 5 is a local maximum.

$$A''(x) = -6 \qquad \text{second derivative}$$

$$A''(1) = -6 \qquad \text{evaluated}$$

Since the second derivative is negative at the critical point $x = 1$, the value of A at 1 is a local maximum.

In the applied problems we do not need to go through all the steps, because the functions are polynomial functions. In these problems we just determine the critical numbers for which the derivative equals zero. If the function is a familiar function, such as a second-, third-, or fourth-degree polynomial function, we can use our knowledge of the graph of the function to justify a claim for an absolute maximum or minimum value. Knowledge of the function and its graph can also be used to make a statement about endpoint values of the function. In Lesson 63 we will consider problems in which the endpoint values of the function produce the absolute maximum or minimum values of $f(x)$.

example 52.1   Mr. Wallen has 100 yards of fence. He wants to form a rectangular field enclosed on three sides by the fence and on one side by a river whose banks are straight. Find the greatest area that the fence can enclose.

solution   We begin by making a drawing of the problem. Let x be the width of the rectangle.

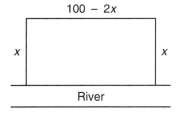

Since the sum of the three legs of the rectangle must equal 100 yards, the length must be $100 - 2x$. The problem directs us to maximize the area, so we must find a formula for it. The area of the field is the length times the width.

$$A(x) = x(100 - 2x)$$
$$A(x) = 100x - 2x^2$$

Now we find the values of x for which the derivative equals zero.

$$\frac{dA}{dx} = 100 - 4x \qquad \text{first derivative}$$
$$0 = 100 - 4x \qquad \text{equals 0}$$
$$x = 25 \qquad \text{solved}$$

This function has only one value of x at which A could be a maximum or a minimum. Using the second derivative test, we find that $A''(25)$ is a negative number.

$$A''(x) = -4 \qquad \text{second derivative}$$
$$A''(25) = -4 \qquad \text{evaluated}$$

Thus $A(25)$ is a local maximum.

$$A(25) = 25[100 - 2(25)] = 1250 \text{ square yards (yd}^2)$$

The graph of the function (a parabola that opens downward) reveals that this function has only one maximum value, so the absolute maximum area that could be enclosed is **1250 yd²**. We did not consider the values 0 and 50, because if x had a value of either 0 or 50, the area enclosed would be zero.

example 52.2   Find two positive numbers whose sum is 8 and whose product is a maximum.

solution   The statement of the problem gives us two equations. We use p to represent the product and use x and y to represent the numbers.

$$p = xy \qquad x + y = 8$$

Since $y = 8 - x$, we can substitute to write p as a function of x.

$$p = x(8 - x) \qquad \text{substituted}$$
$$p = 8x - x^2 \qquad \text{simplified}$$

The extreme value of p occurs when $\frac{dp}{dx}$ equals zero.

$$\frac{dp}{dx} = 8 - 2x \qquad \text{derivative}$$
$$0 = 8 - 2x \qquad \frac{dp}{dx} = 0$$
$$x = 4 \qquad \text{solved}$$

An extreme value of p occurs when $x = 4$. We know that this is a maximum value because the second derivative is negative when $x = 4$.

$$f''(x) = -2 \qquad \text{second derivative}$$
$$f''(4) = -2 \qquad \text{evaluated}$$

Knowing that $x = 4$, we can find y by substituting in our original equation.

$$x + y = 8 \qquad \text{equation}$$
$$4 + y = 8 \qquad \text{substituted}$$
$$y = 4 \qquad \text{solved}$$

Thus the two numbers we are looking for are both **4.**

example 52.3 Make an open-top cardboard box by cutting squares (x inches on a side) from each corner of a 12- by 15-inch piece of cardboard and folding up the edges. Find the value of x that results in the largest possible volume, and find the volume of that box.

solution We make a drawing of the problem and label all the dimensions of the box in terms of x.

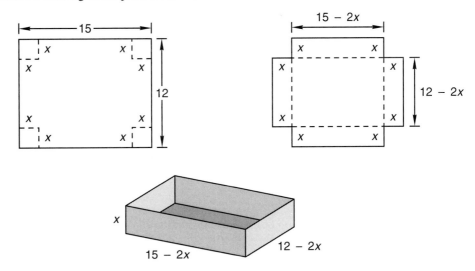

We must express V as a function of x.

$$V = (15 - 2x)(12 - 2x)x$$
$$V = 180x - 54x^2 + 4x^3$$

Next we need to find the value of x that maximizes V.

$$
\begin{array}{lll}
V = 180x - 54x^2 + 4x^3 & & \text{equation for } V \\
V' = 180 - 108x + 12x^2 & & \text{differentiated} \\
0 = 180 - 108x + 12x^2 & & \text{set } V' = 0 \\
0 = x^2 - 9x + 15 & & \text{simplified and rearranged} \\
x = \dfrac{9 \pm \sqrt{81 - 4(15)}}{2} & & \text{solved for } x \\
x \approx 2.2087,\ 6.7913 & & \text{approximated numerically}
\end{array}
$$

The second derivative test indicates whether x-values of 2.2087 and 6.7913 produce local maximum or local minimum values of V.

$$V''(x) = 24x - 108$$
$$V''(2.2087) = 24(2.2087) - 108 = -54.9912$$
$$V''(6.7913) = 24(6.7913) - 108 = +54.9912$$

Since $V''(2.2087)$ is a negative number, $V(2.2087)$ is a local maximum value of the function. Since $V''(6.7913)$ is a positive number, $V(6.7913)$ is a local minimum value of the function. We know that the graph of a cubic can have two turning points and that if the leading coefficient is positive the graph looks like this:

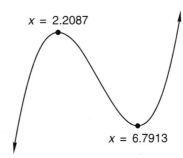

We have found the *x*-values of the two turning points. The box is only 12 inches wide, so **x can be any number between 0 and 6.** The number 6.7913 is greater than 6 and has no meaning in this problem. The values 0 and 6 result in a volume of zero. Thus the maximum volume of the box is found at **x ≈ 2.2087.**

$$V(2.2087) = 180(2.2087) - 54(2.2087)^2 + 4(2.2087)^3 \approx \textbf{177.2341 in.}^3$$

problem set 52

1. (49) (a) Use the first derivative and a rough sketch of *f* to determine the location and the values of the local maxima and minima of $f(x) = -x^3 + 3x - 2$. Use the second derivative test as necessary to justify your answer.

(b) Find the coordinates of any points of inflection.

2. (52) Find two positive numbers whose sum is 10 and whose product is a maximum.

3. (52) Detia wants to enclose a rectangular plot of land that adjoins a straight brick wall. If she has only 200 yards of fence, what should the dimensions of the rectangular plot be so that the area enclosed is a maximum?

4. (52) An open-top box is made by cutting squares from the corners of a rectangular piece of tin that measures 10 cm by 20 cm and then folding up the edges. Find the dimensions of the box that maximize the volume. What is the maximum volume for this box?

Integrate in problems 5–11.

5. (51) $\int 5 \cos x \sin^4 x \, dx$

6. (51) $\int (2x)\left(\frac{3}{2}\right)\sqrt{x^2 + 3} \, dx$

7. (51) $\int 2x e^{x^2} \, dx$

8. (51) $\int \frac{2x \, dx}{x^2 - 1}$

9. (51) $\int 2x \sin (x^2 + 3) \, dx$

10. (38) $\int (x - 1)\sqrt{x} \, dx$

11. (38) $\int (x^{-3} + 1)^2 \, dx$

Differentiate with respect to *x* in problems 12–15.

12. (50) $y = \dfrac{\sqrt{x + 1}}{\sqrt{x - 1}}$

13. (50) $y = (x^2 + 3)^4 \sin x$

14. (50) $y = x e^{x^2 + 1}$

15. (50) $y = \sec^2 x$

Use the Fundamental Theorem of Calculus to compute the area of each shaded region in problems 16 and 17.

16. (47)

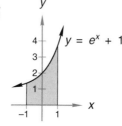

17. (47)

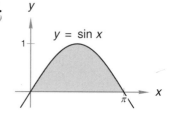

18. (26) Evaluate: $\lim\limits_{h \to 0} \dfrac{e^{x + h} - e^x}{h}$

19. Polynomials can approximate many functions. Complete the following chart to begin to see how
(7)   this works.

x	$1 + x + \dfrac{x^2}{2}$	e^x
0.1		
0.2		
0.3		

20. Determine the domain of the function $f(x) = \dfrac{\sqrt{x}}{x - 1}$.
(6)

21. A cylindrical tin can must be designed to hold 300 cm^3 of liquid. What dimensions for the can
(52)   would require the minimum amount of tin, assuming no waste in construction? Begin by writing
an equation for the volume. Then write the equation for the surface area of the can. Reduce the
number of variables in the surface area equation by making a substitution from the volume
equation. Finally, use the graphing calculator to graph the surface area equation in the first
quadrant using an appropriate window. What value of r minimizes the surface area? What is the
corresponding value for h?

Find the fixed points of the equations given in problems 22 and 23. (Recall problem 21 in Problem
Set 51.)

22. $f(x) = x^3 + 2x - 1$ on [0, 1]
(2)

23. $f(x) = 3x^3 + \sin x - 1$ on [0, 1]
(2)

24. Suppose f is a function such that $f(x_1 x_2) = f(x_1) + f(x_2)$ for all $x_1, x_2 > 0$. Which of the
(16)   following could be the equation of f?

A. $f(x) = \ln x$ B. $f(x) = \dfrac{1}{x}$

C. $f(x) = x^2$ D. $f(x) = \sin x$

25. Suppose g is a function such that for all real values of x and h, $g(x + h) - g(x) = 3xh + \frac{3}{2}h^2$.
(14,19)   Find $g'(x)$.

LESSON 53   *Numerical Integration of Positive-Valued Functions on a Graphing Calculator*

We have seen many integration problems, including definite integrals and their evaluation using the
Fundamental Theorem of Calculus. We have also seen that the area between the x-axis and the curve
of a positive-valued function f on the interval $[a, b]$ is represented by

$$\int_a^b f(x)\, dx$$

It is crucial that you be able to calculate the exact values of such definite integrals with a high
degree of proficiency. Sometimes, however, it is also useful to approximate such values, which can
be done quite readily on a graphing calculator. The command needed to approximate such integrals
numerically can be found on the TI-83 by pressing the **MATH** key and selecting the fnInt(option.

This stands for *function integral,* and it calculates the numerical integral of a function with respect to a variable over a certain interval defined by a and b. For example,

$$\text{fnInt(X}^2\text{+1,X,0,1)}$$

returns a value of 1.333333333, which seems to be an approximation of the number $\frac{4}{3}$. Indeed, thanks to the Fundamental Theorem of Calculus, we know that

$$\int_0^1 (x^2 + 1)\, dx = \left[\frac{x^3}{3} + x\right]_0^1 = \frac{1}{3} + 1 - (0 + 0) = \frac{4}{3}$$

example 53.1   Using a graphing calculator, approximate $\int_2^3 (x + 7)\, dx$.

solution   We simply enter

$$\text{fnInt(X+7,X,2,3)}$$

and the calculator returns **9.5.** This answer can be checked by hand. The value of the integral in question is simply the area of the region pictured here.

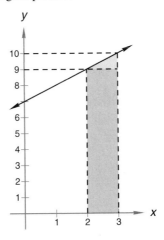

This area can be broken into the area of a triangle and the area of a rectangle. The area of the triangle, whose base and height are length 1, is 0.5, while the area of the rectangle is $9 \cdot 1$, or 9. The sum of these two is 9.5, which is the answer given by the calculator.

example 53.2   Using a graphing calculator, approximate the area under the curve of $y = \sin x$ between $x = 0$ and $x = \frac{\pi}{6}$.

solution   The region in question is completely above the x-axis, so its area is given by $\int_0^{\pi/6} \sin x\, dx$. This is easily approximated by the calculator via

$$\text{fnInt(sin(X),X,0,}\pi\text{/6)}$$

which yields **0.133975** (when the calculator is in RADIAN mode).

While it is nice to obtain accurate approximations with this technique, the disadvantage is that the exact value of this definite integral is simply not discernible from the calculator output. We close by finding the exact value of the integral here.

$$\int_0^{\pi/6} \sin x\, dx = -\cos x\Big|_0^{\pi/6}$$

$$= \left(-\cos \frac{\pi}{6}\right) - (-\cos 0)$$

$$= -\frac{\sqrt{3}}{2} + 1$$

$$= 1 - \frac{\sqrt{3}}{2}$$

This value, according to the graphing calculator, is approximately 0.1339745962.

problem set 53

1. Farmer Yu-Heng wants a rectangular enclosure for 200 square yards of land. Find the amount
(52) of fencing required if the amount of fencing used is to be minimized.

2. Lori snipped square pieces of metal from the corners of a 6- by 6-inch sheet of metal. She then
(52) folded up the flaps to form a box with no top. Find the dimensions of the box of maximum
volume. What is the volume of the box?

3. A square is being enlarged so that each of its sides increases at a rate of 2 cm/s. How fast is the
(46) area of the square increasing when the sides of the square are 6 cm? How fast is the perimeter
of the square increasing at the same moment?

Evaluate the integrals in problems 4–6. (Do not use numerical integration on a graphing calculator.)

4. $\int_{0}^{3\pi/2} \cos x \, dx$
(47)

5. $\int_{1}^{3} (x^3 - e^x) \, dx$
(47)

6. $\int_{\pi/2}^{\pi} (\sin x - \cos x) \, dx$
(47)

7. (a) Use a graphing calculator to find the area of the region bounded by the graph of $y = \frac{1}{x}$ and
(53)   the x-axis on the interval $[1, 5]$.

(b) Use your calculator to evaluate $\ln 5$.

(c) Compare the answers to (a) and (b).

8. Let R be the region bounded by the graph of $y = \sqrt{x}$ and the x-axis on the interval $[c, k]$.
(47)

(a) Find the area of R when $c = 1$ and $k = 8$.

(b) Find the area of R when $c = 1$ and $k = 3$.

(c) Find the area of R when $c = 3$ and $k = 8$.

(d) Add the answers obtained in (b) and (c). Compare this result to the answer obtained in (a).

Use a graphing calculator to approximate the integrals in problems 9 and 10.

9. $\int_{e}^{\pi} 2^x \, dx$
(53)

10. $\int_{\sqrt{2}}^{9.5} \log x \, dx$
(53)

11. (a) Write a definite integral that is equivalent in meaning to $\displaystyle\lim_{n \to \infty} \frac{10}{n} \sum_{i=1}^{n} \left(\frac{10i}{n}\right)^2$.
(43,47)

(b) Evaluate the definite integral written in (a).

Integrate in problems 12–16.

12. $\int 8 \sin^7 x \cos x \, dx$
(51)

13. $\int (4x^3)\left(\frac{1}{2}\right)(x^4 - 3)^{-1/2} \, dx$
(51)

14. $\int 8xe^{4x^2} \, dx$
(51)

15. $\int \frac{4x^3 \, dx}{x^4 - 42}$
(51)

16. $\int \cos (\sin^2 x) \sin (2x) \, dx$
(51)

Differentiate with respect to x in problems 17–19.

17. $y = 2x \ln (x^2 + 1) + 4 \tan x$
(50)

18. $y = -\dfrac{e^x}{\cot^2 x + x}$
(50)

19. $y = \sec (\tan x^2)$
(50)

20. The graph of f is given below.
(45)

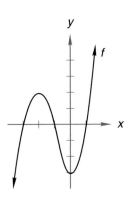

Which of the following graphs most resembles the graph of f'?

A. 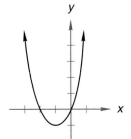   B.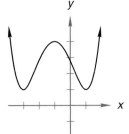

C. 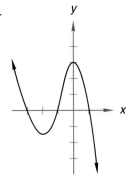   D.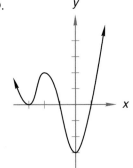

21. Sketch the graph of $y = \dfrac{(x - 2)(x + 3)(x - 1)}{x(x - 3)(x - 1)(x + 1)}$. Clearly indicate all zeros and asymptotes.
(28)

22. Complete the following table to compare polynomial approximations of values of cosine x to the
(4)   actual values of cosine x.

x	$1 - \dfrac{x^2}{2!} + \dfrac{x^4}{4!}$	$\cos x$
0.1		
0.2		
0.3		

23. Evaluate $\displaystyle\lim_{x \to 2} \dfrac{f(x) - f(2)}{x - 2}$ where $f(x) = x^2 - 2$.
(44)

24. Which of the following represents the slope of the line joining the points $(\sin 26°, 0)$ and
(4) $(0, -\cos 26°)$?

    A. $\tan 26°$ B. 1 C. $\cot 26°$ D. $-\cot 26°$

25. Let $g(x) = f(x + 3)$. Which of the following statements is true?
₍₂₁₎

    A. The graph of g is the graph of f shifted 3 units to the right.

    B. The graph of g is the graph of f shifted 3 units to the left.

    C. The graph of g is the graph of f shifted up 3 units.

    D. The graph of g is the graph of f shifted down 3 units.

LESSON 54 *Velocity and Acceleration • Motion Due to Gravity*

54.A
velocity and acceleration

The instantaneous speed of an object tells how fast the position of the object is changing with respect to time. The instantaneous velocity of an object tells how fast the position of an object is changing with respect to time and also designates the direction in which the object is moving. If an object is at the origin when time equals zero and moves to the right at 6 inches per second, it would travel 6 inches in 1 second. It would travel 12 inches in 2 seconds and $6t$ inches in t seconds. Its position in relation to the origin is described by the **position function**

$$x(t) = 6t$$

The velocity is the rate of change of position, and thus the **velocity function** is the derivative of the position function with respect to time.

$$v(t) = x'(t) = \frac{d}{dt}6t = 6$$

If the position function is not a linear function, the velocity is not constant as it is in this example. If the position of an object at time t is given by the equation on the left-hand side below, its velocity at any time t is designated by the velocity function to its right. The velocity function is the derivative of the position function, as we show.

$$x(t) = t^3 + t + 1 \qquad v(t) = x'(t) = 3t^2 + 1$$

The acceleration of an object tells us how fast and in what direction the velocity of the object is changing with respect to time. If time is measured in seconds, acceleration is measured in units per second per second, or units per square second. For example, if the velocity changed 6 inches per second in 2 seconds, then the average acceleration for the 2 seconds is

$$a = \frac{\Delta v}{\Delta t} = \frac{6\ \frac{\text{in.}}{\text{s}}}{2\ \text{s}} = \frac{3\ \frac{\text{in.}}{\text{s}}}{1\ \text{s}} = 3\ \frac{\text{in.}}{\text{s}^2}$$

If the velocity function is not a linear function, the **acceleration function** is not a constant function. If the velocity function is given by the equation on the left below, the acceleration function is the derivative shown on the right.

$$v(t) = x'(t) = 3t^2 + 1 \qquad a(t) = v'(t) = x''(t) = 6t$$

Acceleration is the rate of change of velocity, which in turn is the rate of change of position.

A reference scale is needed to describe the position, velocity, and acceleration of an object. We have used the x-axis for this purpose because this axis is convenient. But this use of the horizontal axis causes a problem because we always use the horizontal axis as the axis of the independent variable.

The independent variable in this context is t. Thus we graph t on the horizontal axis and $x(t)$, $x'(t)$, and $x''(t)$ on vertical axes.

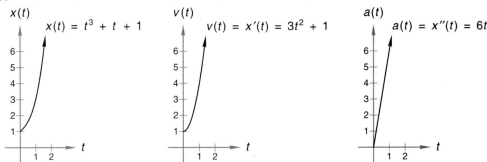

Note: In the first graph, $x(t)$ simply gives the values of the position—the graph is not a depiction of the path.

We define positive velocities to be velocities in the positive x-direction and call velocities in the opposite direction negative velocities. If an object is speeding up in the positive direction, then the object is accelerating, its acceleration is positive, and the object's velocity is increasing. If an object is speeding up in the negative direction, the object is decelerating, the acceleration is negative, and the velocity is decreasing.

example 54.1   The position of a particle moving along the x-axis at any time t in seconds is given by the equation $x(t) = -3t^2 + 4t + 2$. Find the position, velocity, and acceleration of the particle when $t = 3$.

solution   The position when $t = 3$ is $x(3)$.

$$x(3) = -3(3)^2 + 4(3) + 2 = -13$$

The position when $t = 3$ is **13 units to the left of the origin.**

The velocity function is the derivative of the position function.

$$v(t) = x'(t) = -6t + 4$$

The velocity of the particle when $t = 3$ is $v(3)$.

$$v(3) = -6(3) + 4 = -14$$

The velocity when $t = 3$ is **–14 units per second,** which means the object is moving to the left.

The acceleration function is the derivative of the velocity function.

$$a(t) = v'(t) = x''(t) = -6$$

This acceleration is a constant. For $t = 3$ or any other value of t, the acceleration is -6. This means that the acceleration is **6 units per square second in the negative x-direction.**

example 54.2   The position of a particle moving along the x-axis at any time t is given by the equation

$$x(t) = t^2 - 3t + 2$$

Find the times when the particle is momentarily at rest, the times when the particle is moving to the right, and the times when the particle is moving to the left. Also, find the times when the particle is decelerating or accelerating.

solution   We begin by finding the equations of the velocity and acceleration functions.

$$x(t) = t^2 - 3t + 2 \qquad \text{position function}$$
$$v(t) = x(t) = 2t - 3 \qquad \text{velocity function}$$
$$a(t) = v(t) = x(t) = 2 \qquad \text{acceleration function}$$

The particle is momentarily at rest when its velocity is zero.

$$v(t) = 2t - 3 \qquad \text{velocity function}$$
$$0 = 2t - 3 \qquad \text{set equal to zero}$$
$$t = \frac{3}{2} \qquad \text{solved for t}$$

The particle is moving to the right when the velocity is greater than zero and moving to the left when the velocity is less than zero.

MOVING TO THE RIGHT	MOVING TO THE LEFT
$2t - 3 > 0$	$2t - 3 < 0$
$t > \dfrac{3}{2}$	$t < \dfrac{3}{2}$

Thus the particle is moving to the right when $t > \dfrac{3}{2}$ **and moving to the left when** $t < \dfrac{3}{2}$.

The particle decelerates when the acceleration is negative $(a < 0)$ and accelerates when acceleration is positive $(a > 0)$. In this case, $a = 2$ for all values of t, so **the particle is always accelerating.**

54.B
motion due to gravity

If a physical object is released at or near the surface of the earth, the object accelerates toward the center of the earth at 9.8 meters per second per second (m/s^2). This acceleration is caused by the attraction of the mass of the object to the mass of the earth and is called **acceleration due to gravity.** Interestingly, a feather has the same acceleration as a lead ball in the earth's gravitational field (neglecting factors such as air resistance).

It is customary to use the surface of the earth (sea level) as a reference plane and use up as the positive direction and down as the negative direction. Thus positive velocity and acceleration are upward. Note that the acceleration due to gravity is negative since objects released from above the surface of earth accelerate downward (or in a negative direction). We will develop the equations of vertical motion in a later lesson. This lesson investigates the use of these equations.

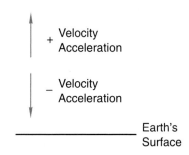

example 54.3   A ball is thrown vertically into the air so that its height in meters at any time t in seconds is

$$h(t) = -4.9t^2 + 20t + 2$$

(a) Find the height of the ball and the velocity of the ball when $t = 1$.

(b) At what time t is the ball the greatest distance above the ground?

(c) How high will the ball go?

(d) What is the greatest value of the acceleration?

solution   We begin by writing the position function and finding the velocity function and the acceleration function.

$$h(t) = -4.9t^2 + 20t + 2 \qquad \text{position function}$$
$$v(t) = h'(t) = -9.8t + 20 \qquad \text{velocity function}$$
$$a(t) = v'(t) = h''(t) = -9.8 \qquad \text{acceleration function}$$

All four answers can be found using these three equations.

(a) The height of the ball when $t = 1$ is $h(1)$, and the velocity of the ball when $t = 1$ is $v(1)$.

$$h(1) = -4.9(1)^2 + 20(1) + 2 = \textbf{17.1 m}$$
$$v(1) = -9.8(1) + 20 = \textbf{10.2 m/s}$$

(b) The velocity is positive on the way up. On the way down the velocity is negative. At the top the velocity equals zero, so we set the velocity function equal to zero and solve for t.

$$-9.8t + 20 = 0 \qquad\qquad \text{set } v = 0$$
$$t \approx 2.0408 \text{ s} \qquad\qquad \text{solved}$$

Thus the ball reaches its high point after about **2.0408 s.**

(c) The distance to the top is approximately $h(2.0408)$.

$$h(2.0408) = -4.9(2.0408)^2 + 20(2.0408) + 2 \approx 22.4082 \text{ m}$$

Thus the distance to the top is about **22.4082 m.**

(d) The acceleration is the acceleration due to gravity and is always **–9.8 m/s²** for any object at or near the surface of the earth. This is consistent with the equation above: $a(t) = -9.8$.

problem set 54

1. A rectangular field that must be 3600 square meters in size must be enclosed in such a manner
    (52)
    so as to minimize the amount of fence used.

    (a) Solve this problem with a graphing calculator. Begin by writing an equation for the area and an equation for the perimeter. Use the area equation to reduce the number of variables in the perimeter equation. Graph the new perimeter equation in an appropriate window. What are the dimensions of the field that minimize the amount of fence? How much fence is required?

    (b) Solve this problem again using calculus.

2. The position of a particle moving along the x-axis at any time t in seconds is given by the
    (54)
    equation $x(t) = -4t^2 + 2t - 1$. Find the position, velocity, and acceleration of the particle when $t = 2$.

3. The position of a particle moving along the x-axis at any time is given by the equation
    (54)
    $x(t) = t^2 + t - 2$. Find the times when the particle is momentarily at rest and when the particle is moving to the right. Also, tell when the particle is accelerating and decelerating.

4. Lacey throws her ball vertically into the air so that its height in meters above the ground at any
    (54)
    time t in seconds is given by $h(t) = -4.9t^2 + 40t + 5$. Find the time when the ball is at its greatest height above the ground. How high above the ground is the ball when it is at its greatest height?

Evaluate the integrals in problems 5–7.

5. $\displaystyle\int_0^4 \sqrt{x}\ dx$
    (47)

6. $\displaystyle\int_1^3 \frac{1}{x}\ dx$
    (47)

7. $\displaystyle\int_{\pi/6}^{\pi/2} \cos x\ dx$
    (47)

Approximate the integrals in problems 8–10 by using a graphing calculator.

8. $\displaystyle\int_1^2 x^{-2}\ dx$
    (53)

9. $\displaystyle\int_{\ln 3}^{e^2} \sqrt{e^x}\ dx$
    (53)

10. $\displaystyle\int_{-1}^1 2\sqrt{1 - x^2}\ dx$
    (53)

11. Use basic geometry to find the area of the region between the graph of $y = x + 2$ and the
    (47)
    x-axis on the interval $[2, 4]$. Then express the area of the region as a definite integral, and evaluate the integral.

Integrate in problems 12–16.

12. $\displaystyle\int 2x\left(\frac{3}{2}\right)\sqrt{x^2 + 1}\ dx$
    (51)

13. $\displaystyle\int (\cos x)e^{\sin x}\ dx$
    (51)

14. $\displaystyle\int \left(\frac{1}{x}\right)(4)(\ln x)^3\ dx$
    (51)

15. $\displaystyle\int 2 \tan x \sec^2 x\ dx$
    (51)

16. $\displaystyle\int \frac{\sin (2x)}{\sin^2 x}\ dx$
    (51)

17. Use implicit differentiation to find $\dfrac{dy}{dx}$ where $x^2 - x\cos y + y^3 = 0$.
(34)

18. Find $\dfrac{dy}{dx}$ where $y = \dfrac{e^{x^2}\cos^2 x}{x^2 + 1} + e^x \csc x$.
(48)

19. Find the equation of the line tangent to the graph of $y = \ln\dfrac{x}{3}$ at $x = e$.
(27)

20. If $\dfrac{dy}{dx} = \sin(2x)$, which of the following is a valid choice for y?
(51)

A. $\cos(2x) + C$ 　　　　　 B. $\dfrac{1}{2}\cos(2x) + C$ 　　　　　 C. $-\dfrac{1}{2}\cos(2x) + C$

D. $\dfrac{1}{2}\sin(2x) + C$ 　　　　　 E. $-\dfrac{1}{2}\sin(2x) + C$

Evaluate the limits in problems 21 and 22.

21. $\displaystyle\lim_{n\to\infty}\dfrac{5n^2}{10{,}000n + n^3}$
(17)

22. $\displaystyle\lim_{h\to 0}\dfrac{e^{e+h} - e^e}{h}$
(44)

23. Complete the following table to compare polynomial approximations of values of $\sin x$ to the
(4) actual values of $\sin x$.

x	$x - \dfrac{x^3}{3!} + \dfrac{x^5}{5!}$	$\sin x$
0.1		
0.2		
0.3		

24. Graph $y = \sqrt{1 - x^2}$. Use geometry to evaluate $\displaystyle\int_{-1}^{1}\sqrt{1 - x^2}\,dx$.
(23,47)

25. Let x and y be two positive numbers such that $x + y = 20$. Find the values of x and y for which
(52) xy is as large as possible.

LESSON 55 *Maclaurin Polynomials*

In recent problem sets you have been asked to verify that certain polynomials can be utilized to approximate values of functions that are not polynomials. These functions, known as **transcendental functions,** include trigonometric, inverse trigonometric, exponential, and logarithmic functions. For years the values of these transcendental functions have been printed in tables so students can reference them as needed. In recent years calculators and computers have been programmed to produce those same values (and often more accurate ones) on demand.

So why study these approximating polynomials? First of all, to be able to represent transcendental functions in terms of polynomials is a significant simplification. Secondly, as you learn to approximate transcendentals with polynomials, you simulate many calculator and computer operations. Have you ever wondered how your calculator approximates a value such as sin (1) with such speed and accuracy?

In this lesson we make no attempt to rigorously explain the theory behind what we are doing nor attempt to prove it—this will be done in future lessons. For now we are content to explore the power of these approximating polynomials, which are called **Maclaurin polynomials.** At this point the only explanation needed is a rather rough geometric description.

It is helpful to remember that the graph of a polynomial is always a smooth curve. If we find a way to make the curves of a polynomial match the curves of the function we are trying to approximate, it will be a step in the right direction. The process can essentially be reduced to the following steps.

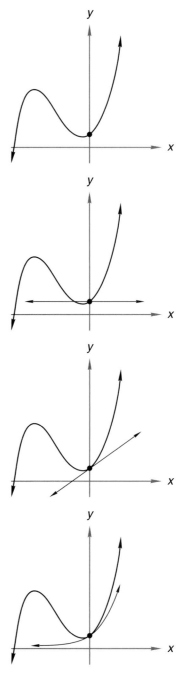

1. Begin by picking an anchor point around which to bend the polynomial to make it fit the function.

2. The approximating polynomial begins as simple as they come—a horizontal line that passes through the anchor point. This means that the polynomial and the function have the same *x*- and *y*-values at the anchor point. **The polynomial is constant.**

3. Next we make the fit better by giving the line some slope—but not just any slope. The slope of the line must be the same as the slope of the function at the anchor point. In other words, the line is tangent to the function at the anchor point. Now the polynomial and the function have the same value and slope at the anchor point. **The polynomial is linear.**

4. Now we bend the polynomial by forcing it to have the same concavity at the anchor point as the function. Thus they have the same value, slope, and concavity at the anchor. Another way of saying this is that their zeroth, first, and second derivatives are like-valued at the anchor point. **The polynomial is quadratic.**

5. Though we have no easily describable geometric meaning to attach to successive derivatives, the process continues. Each successive derivative of the polynomial must have the same value as the corresponding derivative of the function. The further we expand this process the more the shape of the polynomial approximates the curve of the function. How close can we make it? That depends, in most cases, on how much time we want to spend working on it! When is close close enough?

For now, we select all anchor points at *x* = 0. (In future lessons we will allow the anchor point to be away from the *y*-axis.) The polynomial approximation is always most accurate at the anchor point and becomes less accurate as we move away from the anchor point. Without explanation, we simply state at this time that the polynomial we seek is always of the form

$$f(x) = a_0 + a_1x + a_2x^2 + a_3x^3 + \cdots + a_nx^n$$

where

$$a_0 = \frac{f(0)}{0!}, \quad a_1 = \frac{f'(0)}{1!}, \quad a_2 = \frac{f''(0)}{2!}, \quad a_3 = \frac{f'''(0)}{3!}, \quad \ldots, \quad a_n = \frac{f^{(n)}(0)}{n!}$$

Note: The notation $f^{(n)}(0)$ means the nth derivative of f evaluated at 0.

example 55.1   Find the Maclaurin polynomial for $f(x) = 2x^2 + 3x - 4$.

solution   In the table below, $f^{(n)}(x)$ is the nth derivative of f evaluated at x, where $f^{(0)}(x) = f(x)$.

n	$f^{(n)}(x)$	$f^{(n)}(0)$
0	$2x^2 + 3x - 4$	-4
1	$4x + 3$	3
2	4	4
3	0	0

(Note that all remaining derivatives are also 0.) The Maclaurin polynomial is

$$\begin{aligned} p(x) &= -4 + 3x + \frac{4}{2}x^2 + 0 \\ &= -4 + 3x + 2x^2 \\ &= 2x^2 + 3x - 4 \end{aligned}$$

We see that the Maclaurin polynomial that approximates a polynomial is simply the polynomial itself. You will be asked a few times to find the Maclaurin polynomial that approximates a polynomial. For practice, it would be a good idea that you follow the procedure rather than state the answer by inspection.

example 55.2   Find the Maclaurin polynomial of degree 4 for $f(x) = e^x$.

solution   We begin by building a table of derivatives up to $n = 4$.

n	$f^{(n)}(x)$	$f^{(n)}(0)$
0	e^x	1
1	e^x	1
2	e^x	1
3	e^x	1
4	e^x	1

The Maclaurin polynomial is $p(x) = 1 + x + \dfrac{x^2}{2} + \dfrac{x^3}{3!} + \dfrac{x^4}{4!}$.

For demonstration, we compare the graphs of $y = f(x)$ and $y = p(x)$.

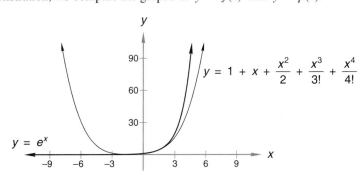

Over the interval $-3 \leq x \leq 3$, the two graphs are almost indistinguishable. However, for x-values outside this interval, the two graphs are quite different. Thus $p(x) = 1 + x + \frac{x^2}{2} + \frac{x^3}{3!} + \frac{x^4}{4!}$ is an excellent approximator of $f(x) = e^x$ over the interval $[-3, 3]$. Notice, for example, that $f(1) = e^1 \approx 2.718$, while $p(1) = 2.708\overline{3}$. Could the Maclaurin polynomial be modified so that it better approximates $f(x)$? Yes, by adding more terms of higher degree. Notice the pattern of the terms. It is fairly obvious that the next few terms in the Maclaurin polynomial would be $\frac{x^5}{5!}$, $\frac{x^6}{6!}$, and $\frac{x^7}{7!}$. We now compare the graphs of $f(x) = e^x$ and the (hopefully) more accurate Maclaurin polynomial, $q(x) = 1 + x + \frac{x^2}{2} + \frac{x^3}{3!} + \cdots + \frac{x^7}{7!}$.

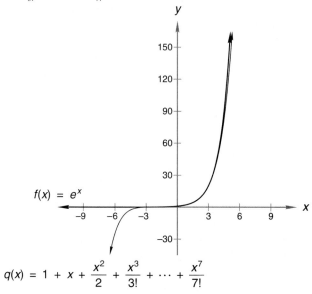

$$q(x) = 1 + x + \frac{x^2}{2} + \frac{x^3}{3!} + \cdots + \frac{x^7}{7!}$$

This Maclaurin polynomial of degree 7 closely approximates $f(x)$ for a wider interval on the x-axis. If we allow the number of terms in the Maclaurin polynomial to go to infinity, we obtain the **Maclaurin series** for e^x, namely

$$1 + x + \frac{x^2}{2} + \frac{x^3}{3!} + \cdots = \sum_{n=0}^{\infty} \frac{x^n}{n!}$$

While this series may be of little practical value (because it contains infinitely many terms), it does hold the distinction of being equal to, and not just an approximation of, e^x.

example 55.3   Find the Maclaurin polynomial of degree 6 for $f(x) = \cos x$.

solution   We again build the table of derivatives.

n	$f^{(n)}(x)$	$f^{(n)}(0)$
0	$\cos x$	1
1	$-\sin x$	0
2	$-\cos x$	-1
3	$\sin x$	0
4	$\cos x$	1
5	$-\sin x$	0
6	$-\cos x$	-1

So the polynomial in question is

$$p(x) = 1 + 0x - \frac{1x^2}{2!} + \frac{0x^3}{3!} + \frac{1x^4}{4!} + \frac{0x^5}{5!} - \frac{1x^6}{6!}$$

$$= 1 - \frac{x^2}{2!} + \frac{x^4}{4!} - \frac{x^6}{6!}$$

It should be clear that the Maclaurin polynomial of degree 12 would follow a similar pattern:

$$q(x) = 1 - \frac{x^2}{2!} + \frac{x^4}{4!} - \frac{x^6}{6!} + \frac{x^8}{8!} - \frac{x^{10}}{10!} + \frac{x^{12}}{12!}$$

Moreover, the Maclaurin series for $\cos x$ is

$$\cos x = 1 - \frac{x^2}{2!} + \frac{x^4}{4!} - \frac{x^6}{6!} + \cdots$$

$$= \sum_{n=0}^{\infty} \frac{(-1)^n x^{2n}}{(2n)!}$$

problem set
55

1. Find the Maclaurin series for $y = 3x^2 + 4x - 3$.
(55)

2. Find the Maclaurin series for $y = \sin x$, and write the answer in summation notation.
(55)

3. A ball is thrown upward from the top of a 100-ft-high building. Its height in feet above the
(54) ground t seconds after it is thrown is given by $h(t) = 100 + 30t - 16t^2$. At what time is the ball falling toward the earth at 46 ft/s?

4. Find the area under one arch of the graph of $y = 3 \sin (3x)$.
(47)

5. Find the area of the region between the x-axis and the graph of $y = \dfrac{1}{x}$ over the interval $[1, e]$.
(47)

Integrate in problems 6–9.

6. $\displaystyle\int \frac{2x + 1}{2\sqrt{x^2 + x + 1}}\, dx$
(51)

7. $\displaystyle\int 4 \tan^3 x \sec^2 x\, dx$
(51)

8. $\displaystyle\int 3(\sec^2 x)(\sec x \tan x)\, dx$
(51)

9. $\displaystyle\int \frac{x + 1}{x}\, dx$
(38)

Differentiate the functions given in problems 10 and 11 with respect to x.

10. $y = e^{2x} \tan^2 x$
(50)

11. $y = \dfrac{\sqrt{x^2 + 1}}{x + \sin x}$
(50)

12. A rectangle is to be inscribed in a semicircle of radius 3 centimeters. Find the largest area that
(52) the rectangle can have. Also, find the dimensions of the rectangle.

(a) Solve this problem with a graphing calculator. Begin by writing an equation for the area of the rectangle in terms of the single variable x, and then graph the function in an appropriate window.

(b) Solve this problem again using calculus.

13. Describe the concavity of the graph of $y = x \ln x$ at $x = e^2$.
(49)

14. The radius of a spherical ball is expanding at a rate of 3 cm/s. How fast is the surface area of the
(46) ball increasing when the radius of the ball is 10 cm?

Evaluate the limits in problems 15–17.

15. $\displaystyle\lim_{x \to \infty} \frac{x^3 - 2x^2}{1 - x^4}$
(17)

16. $\displaystyle\lim_{x \to 2} \frac{e^x - e^2}{x - 2}$
(44)

17. $\displaystyle\lim_{\Delta x \to 0} \frac{\cos (\pi + \Delta x) - \cos \pi}{\Delta x}$
(28)

18. Which of the following integrals could be used to evaluate $\displaystyle\lim_{n \to \infty} \frac{3}{n} \sum_{i=1}^{n} \ln (x_i)$ for $1 \le x_i \le 4$?
(43)

    A. $\displaystyle\int_0^3 \ln x\, dx$ B. $\displaystyle\int_3^{12} \ln x\, dx$ C. $\displaystyle\int_1^4 \ln x\, dx$ D. $3\displaystyle\int_1^4 \ln x\, dx$

19. Find the equation of the line tangent to the graph of the function $y = \ln x^2$ at $x = 1$.
₍₂₇₎

20. Evaluate $\dfrac{d^4 y}{dx^4}$ at $x = \dfrac{\pi}{2}$ where $y = 2 \sin x$.
₍₂₇₎

21. Suppose f is a function whose slope at any point is twice its x-coordinate. If the graph of f passes
₍₃₂₎ through $(1, 1)$, what is the equation of f? (*Hint:* You can solve for the constant of integration by substituting values for x and y in your equation for f.)

22. Sketch the graph of $y = \dfrac{x(x - 2)}{x(x^2 + 1)(x + 1)}$.
₍₄₁₎

23. Suppose $f(x) = ax^3 + bx$. Find a and b given that the graph of f passes through $(1, -1)$ and
_(2,25) that $f'(1) = 3$.

24. If $\dfrac{d}{dx} g(f(x)) = g'(f(x))f'(x)$, then what is $\int g'(f(x))f'(x)\, dx$?
₍₃₂₎

25. Suppose that the sum of the squares of two positive numbers is 200. Their minimum product is
₍₅₂₎

    A. 25   B. 100   C. $28\sqrt{7}$ D. 50   E. None of these

---

LESSON 56 *More Integration by Guessing • A Word of Caution*

56.A

more integration by guessing

Thus far each integration-by-guessing problem in the problem sets has been designed so that the integrand was the exact differential of an expression whose basic form was u^n, e^u, $\ln u$, $\sin u$, or $\cos u$. Now we consider integrands that would be an exact differential of one of these forms if the integrand contained an additional constant factor. We can insert the needed constant factor to the right of the integral sign if we insert its reciprocal as a factor to the left of the integral sign.

example 56.1 Integrate: $\displaystyle\int \sin(3t)\, dt$

solution We guess that the answer is $-\cos(3t)$ and check our guess by finding the differential.

$$d\underbrace{\left[-\cos(3t)\right]}_{\cos u} = \underbrace{\left[\sin(3t)\right]}_{\sin u}\underbrace{(3\, dt)}_{du}$$

This differential differs from our integrand by a factor of 3. Thus we insert a factor of 3 to the right of the integral sign and a factor of $\frac{1}{3}$ in front of the integral sign.

$$\int \sin(3t)\, dt = \frac{1}{3}\int 3 \sin(3t)\, dt$$

We have already seen that constants can be placed on the left or the right of the integral sign with no change in outcome. In this case, multiplication by $\frac{1}{3}$ and 3 is simply multiplication by 1, which does not change the value of the expression. We have chosen to leave the 3 inside the integral because it is needed to make up the du portion of the integral. Hence

$$\int \sin\underbrace{(3t)}_{u}\, dt = \frac{1}{3}\int \underbrace{[\sin(3t)]}_{\sin u}\underbrace{(3\, dt)}_{du} = -\frac{1}{3}\cos u + C = -\frac{1}{3}\cos(3t) + C$$

It is easy to make a mistake when manipulating constants in integrals, so we check our answer by differentiating it.

$$\frac{d}{dt}\left[-\frac{1}{3}\cos{(3t)} + C\right] = -\frac{1}{3}\left[\frac{d}{dt}\cos{(3t)}\right] + 0$$

$$= -\frac{1}{3}[-\sin{(3t)}](3)$$

$$= \sin{(3t)}$$

This was the original integrand, so the answer must be correct.

example 56.2   Integrate: $\int x^2(3x^3 + 4)^4\,dx$

solution   We note the exponent on $(3x^3 + 4)^4$ and guess that this is a factor of the differential of an expression whose basic form is u^5. We guess that the expression is $(3x^3 + 4)^5$ and check our guess by finding its differential.

$$d\underbrace{(3x^3 + 4)^5}_{u^n} = \underbrace{5(3x^3 + 4)^4}_{nu^{n-1}}\underbrace{9x^2\,dx}_{du}$$

The differential is the same as our integrand except for the factors 5 and 9, whose product is 45. Thus we insert a factor of 45 to the right of the integral sign and a factor of $\frac{1}{45}$ in front of the integral sign to get

$$\int x^2(3x^3 + 4)^4\,dx = \frac{1}{45}\int (5)(x^2)(3x^3 + 4)^4(9)\,dx = \frac{1}{45}(3x^3 + 4)^5 + C$$

example 56.3   Integrate: $\int \dfrac{x^2\,dx}{\sqrt{x^3 + 1}}$

solution   We begin by rewriting the integral as

$$\int (x^3 + 1)^{-1/2}(x^2)\,dx$$

We guess that $(x^3 + 1)^{-1/2}$ is a factor of the differential of the expression $(x^3 + 1)^{1/2}$ whose basic form is $u^{1/2}$ and check our guess by finding the differential.

$$d\underbrace{(x^3 + 1)^{1/2}}_{u^n} = \underbrace{\frac{1}{2}(x^3 + 1)^{-1/2}}_{nu^{n-1}}\underbrace{(3x^2)\,dx}_{du}$$

The differential is the same as our integrand except for the factors of $\frac{1}{2}$ and 3. We insert these factors to the right of the integral sign and insert $\frac{2}{3}$, which is the reciprocal of their product, to the left of the integral sign.

$$\int \frac{x^2\,dx}{\sqrt{x^3 + 1}} = \frac{2}{3}\int \left(\frac{1}{2}\right)(x^3 + 1)^{-1/2}(3)x^2\,dx = \frac{2}{3}(x^3 + 1)^{1/2} + C$$

example 56.4   Integrate: $\int \cos^3{(2t)}\sin{(2t)}\,dt$

solution   We note the exponent 3 in $\cos^3{(2t)}$ and guess that the whole expression is the differential of u^4, namely $[(\cos 2t)]^4$.

$$d\underbrace{[\cos^4{(2t)}]}_{u^n} = \underbrace{[4\cos^3{(2t)}]}_{nu^{n-1}}\underbrace{[-\sin{(2t)}](2\,dt)}_{du}$$

The differential of $\cos^4{(2t)}$ has factors of $\cos^3{(2t)}$ and $\sin{(2t)}\,dt$ and has 4, 2, and -1 as additional factors. The product of these factors is -8. The integrand in this problem does not have a factor of -8.

We can circumvent this difficulty by writing the original expression with a factor of -8 to the right of the integral sign and a factor of $-\frac{1}{8}$ to the left of the integral sign. The product of these extra factors is 1, so the value of the expression is unchanged.

$$\int \cos^3 (2t) \sin (2t) \, dt = -\frac{1}{8} \int -8 \cos^3 (2t) \sin (2t) \, dt$$

The integral of $-8 \cos^3 (2t) \sin (2t)$ is $\cos^4 (2t)$, so we have

$$\int \cos^3 (2t) \sin (2t) \, dt = -\frac{1}{8} \int -8 \cos^3 (2t) \sin (2t) \, dt = -\frac{1}{8} \cos^4 (2t) + C$$

example 56.5 Integrate: $\int 4 \sec^2 (3t) \, dt$

solution First we move the 4 to the left of the integral sign and get

$$4 \int \sec^2 (3t) \, dt$$

This time the exponent of 2 does not indicate a form of e^u or u^n. We remember that the derivative of $\tan \theta$ is $\sec^2 \theta$, and this gives us the clue for our guess.

$$d \underbrace{[\tan (3t)]}_{\tan u} = \underbrace{[\sec^2 (3t)]}_{\sec^2 u} \underbrace{(3 \, dt)}_{du}$$

An extra factor of 3 is needed in our original expression, so we insert a factor of 3 to the right of the integral sign and a factor of $\frac{1}{3}$ to the left of the integral sign.

$$\int 4 \sec^2 (3t) \, dt = 4 \left\{ \frac{1}{3} \int \left[\sec^2 (3t) \right](3) \, dt \right\} = \frac{4}{3} \tan (3t) + C$$

example 56.6 Integrate: $\int \dfrac{e^{\sqrt{x}} \, dx}{\sqrt{x}}$

solution As the first step we replace the radicals with fractional exponents and write everything in the numerator.

$$\int e^{x^{1/2}} x^{-1/2} \, dx$$

We guess an answer of $e^{x^{1/2}}$ and check our guess.

$$d \underbrace{\left(e^{x^{1/2}} \right)}_{e^u} = \underbrace{\left(e^{x^{1/2}} \right)}_{e^u} \underbrace{\left(\frac{1}{2} x^{-1/2} \, dx \right)}_{du}$$

The differential on the right-hand side is the same as the integrand in this problem except for the additional factor of $\frac{1}{2}$. Thus, we insert reciprocal constant factors of $\frac{1}{2}$ and 2 and complete the solution.

$$\int \frac{e^{\sqrt{x}} \, dx}{\sqrt{x}} = 2 \int \left(e^{x^{1/2}} \right) \left(\frac{1}{2} \right) x^{-1/2} \, dx = 2 e^{x^{1/2}} + C$$

example 56.7 Integrate: $\int \dfrac{2x^3 + x}{x^4 + x^2} \, dx$

solution We guess that this expression has the form du over u and is the differential of $\ln |x^4 + x^2|$ because we know that the differential of the denominator will involve x^3 and x, which are present in the numerator.

$$d \left(\ln |x^4 + x^2| \right) = \left(\frac{1}{x^4 + x^2} \right)(4x^3 + 2x) \, dx = \left(\frac{1}{x^4 + x^2} \right) 2(2x^3 + x) \, dx$$

We need an additional factor of 2, which we insert to the right of the integral sign, and a factor of $\frac{1}{2}$, which we insert to the left of the integral sign.

$$\int \frac{2x^3 + x}{x^4 + x^2}\, dx = \frac{1}{2} \int \frac{2(2x^3 + x)}{x^4 + x^2}\, dx = \frac{1}{2} \ln \left| x^4 + x^2 \right| + C$$

$$= \ln \sqrt{x^4 + x^2} + C$$

example 56.8 Find $\int \dfrac{\cos (ax)\, dx}{\sqrt{b + \sin (ax)}}$, where a and b are nonzero constants.

solution A good first step in any problem with a radical is to replace the radical with a fractional exponent.

$$\int [b + \sin (ax)]^{-1/2}[\cos (ax)]\, dx$$

We note the fractional exponent of $\frac{1}{2}$ and guess that $[b + \sin (ax)]^{-1/2}$ is a factor of the differential of the expression $[b + \sin (ax)]^{1/2}$ whose basic form is $u^{1/2}$.

$$d\underbrace{[b + \sin (ax)]^{1/2}}_{u^n} = \underbrace{\frac{1}{2}[b + \sin (ax)]^{-1/2}}_{nu^{n-1}}\underbrace{[\cos (ax)](a\, dx)}_{du}$$

The integrand in this problem does not have a factor of $\frac{1}{2}$ or a factor of a, both of which we need. We can correct this by inserting factors of $\frac{1}{2}$ and a to the right of the integral sign and a factor of $\frac{2}{a}$ to the left of the integral sign. The product of these factors is 1, so the value of the expression is unchanged.

$$\frac{2}{a} \int \left(\frac{1}{2}\right)[b + \sin (ax)]^{-1/2}[\cos (ax)](a)\, dx$$

The expression to the right of the integral sign is the differential of $[b + \sin (ax)]^{1/2}$, so $\frac{2}{a}$ times the integral of this expression is $\frac{2}{a}$ times $[b + \sin (ax)]^{1/2}$ plus a constant.

$$\int \frac{\cos (ax)\, dx}{\sqrt{b + \sin (ax)}} = \frac{2}{a} \int \frac{1}{2}[b + \sin(ax)]^{-1/2}[\cos (ax)](a)\, dx = \frac{2}{a}\sqrt{b + \sin (ax)} + C$$

56.B

a word of caution While it is perfectly legitimate to multiply an integral by a constant and its reciprocal to accomplish the integration, it is **not** allowable to multiply an integral by a variable quantity and its reciprocal if one of the factors is placed to the left of the integral. Consider, for example, the following integral:

$$\int x(x^3 + 2)^4\, dx$$

We guess that the integral will involve $(x^3 + 2)^5$, so we take the differential of $(x^3 + 2)^5$.

$$d(x^3 + 2)^5 = 5(x^3 + 2)^4(3x^2)\, dx$$

So we need a factor of 15, but we also need an additional factor of x. We might consider writing

$$\int x(x^3 + 2)^4\, dx \qquad \text{as} \qquad \frac{1}{15x} \int 15x^2 (x^3 + 2)^4\, dx$$

While we now have a friendly integrand, this approach gives an incorrect answer. **You cannot multiply to the left of the integral sign by the variable.**

problem set 56

1. Rectangular boxes shipped via Global Airlines are subject to the condition that the sum of the
(52) three dimensions of the package cannot exceed 16 feet. Find the dimensions for a package with maximal volume and square ends that can be shipped via Global Airlines. What is the volume of the package?

   (a) Solve this problem with a graphing calculator. Begin by expressing the volume of the box as a function of the single variable x, and then graph the function in an appropriate window.

   (b) Solve this problem again using calculus.

2. (46) If x is positive and increasing at a rate of 2 units/s, at what rate is x^4 increasing when $x = 6$?

3. (54) The position of a particle moving along the x-axis at any time t is given by $x(t) = t^3 + 2t^2 - 7t + 4$. Find the times when the particle is momentarily at rest, the times when it is moving to the left, and the times when it is moving to the right.

4. (54) A ball is thrown straight upward from the top of a 100-ft-high building. Its height in feet above the ground t seconds after it is thrown is given by $h(t) = -16t^2 + 40t + 100$. Find the height of the ball above the ground when it is at its highest point.

Evaluate the definite integrals in problems 5 and 6.

5. (47) $\displaystyle\int_{-\pi/2}^{\pi} 2 \sin x \, dx$

6. (47) $\displaystyle\int_{1}^{4} \sqrt{x} \, dx$

Integrate in problems 7–12. In problem 12, a is a constant.

7. (56) $\displaystyle\int 4xe^{x^2} \, dx$

8. (56) $\displaystyle\int \frac{1}{4} \sin^6 t \cos t \, dt$

9. (56) $\displaystyle\int \frac{x \, dx}{2x^2 + 1}$

10. (56) $\displaystyle\int 3x^2(x^3 - 2)^{1/2} \, dx$

11. (56) $\displaystyle\int 4 \cos (3t) \sin^2 (3t) \, dt$

12. (56) $\displaystyle\int \frac{\cos (ax)}{\sqrt{1 + \sin (ax)}} \, dx$

Differentiate the functions in problems 13 and 14 with respect to x.

13. (50) $y = \dfrac{\sin (2x + 1)}{x^2 + 2} + 2 \tan x$

14. (50) $y = \ln |\sin x + x| + \csc (2x)$

15. (55) Find the Maclaurin series for $y = -2x^2 - 7x + 2$.

16. (55) Find the Maclaurin series for $y = \cos x$, and write the answer in summation notation.

17. (34) Find the slope of the line tangent to the hyperbola $\frac{x^2}{9} - \frac{y^2}{4} = 1$ at the point $\left(\frac{9}{2}, \sqrt{5}\right)$. (*Hint:* Begin by differentiating implicitly.)

18. (45) Suppose $f'(1) = 0$, $f'(x) < 0$ when $-2 \le x < 1$, and $f'(x) > 0$ when $1 < x \le 3$. Make a rough sketch of f on the interval $-2 \le x \le 3$.

19. (28) Sketch the graph of $y = \dfrac{x(x + 4)}{(x - 1)(x^2 + 2)(x + 5)}$. Clearly indicate all zeros and asymptotes.

20. (29) Approximate the value of $f'(\sqrt{13})$ where $f(x) = 3^{\sin x} + \sin (\cos x)$.

Approximate the definite integrals in problems 21 and 22.

21. (53) $\displaystyle\int_{-2}^{2} \frac{1}{2}\sqrt{4 - x^2} \, dx$

22. (53) $\displaystyle\int_{\sqrt{3}}^{e^\pi} \sqrt{3^x + \cos x} \, dx$

23. (14) Find $\lim\limits_{x \to 3} f(x)$ where $f(x) = \begin{cases} \dfrac{x^2 - 9}{x - 3} & \text{when } x \ne 3 \\ 0 & \text{when } x = 3. \end{cases}$

24. (20) Express $\log_3 x$ in terms of natural logarithms.

25. (R) Determine the measure of an angle inscribed in a semicircle whose diameter is $\dfrac{3\pi}{2}$ units long.

LESSON 57   *Properties of the Definite Integral*

We remember that the definite integral is a number that is the limit of a Riemann sum. The definite integral of f from a to b in the figure below is –2.

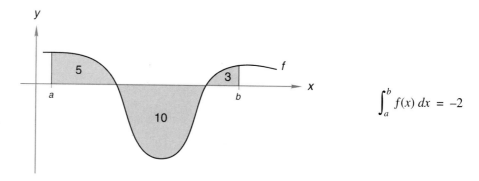

$$\int_a^b f(x)\, dx = -2$$

The definite integral equals the sum of the areas between a and b that are below the graph of f and above the x-axis and the negatives of the areas above the graph and below the x-axis. For the figure above, the sum of the areas above the x-axis is 8, and the sum of the areas below the x-axis is 10, so the value of the definite integral from a to b is –2.

The definition of the definite integral of a function that is continuous on the interval $[a, b]$ requires that a be less than b. We usually evaluate a definite integral by finding the value of some antiderivative of f evaluated at b and subtracting the value of the same antiderivative of f evaluated at a. If F is an antiderivative of f, then

$$\int_a^b f(x)\, dx = F(b) - F(a)$$

The definition of the definite integral and the way we evaluate the definite integral require us to make several definitions that an examination of the following figure can clarify. We show both the graph of $y = x + 2$ and an antiderivative that can be evaluated to get the definite integral from 2 to 4.

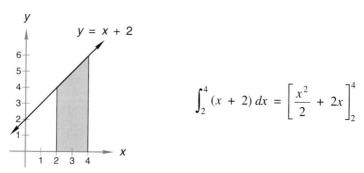

$$\int_2^4 (x + 2)\, dx = \left[\frac{x^2}{2} + 2x \right]_2^4$$

Here 4 is the upper limit of integration, which is evaluated first, and 2 is the lower limit of integration. First we note that

$$\int_2^4 (x + 2)\, dx = \left[\frac{x^2}{2} + 2x \right]_2^4$$

$$= \left[\frac{x^2}{2} \right]_2^4 + \left[2x \right]_2^4$$

$$= \left(\int_2^4 x\, dx \right) + \left(\int_2^4 2\, dx \right)$$

This is an example of the following more general statement:

$$\int_a^b (f(x) + g(x))\, dx = \left(\int_a^b f(x)\, dx\right) + \left(\int_a^b g(x)\, dx\right)$$

This rule leads to

$$\int_a^b k f(x)\, dx = k \int_a^b f(x)\, dx$$

in the case where k is a positive integer, but this fact is actually true for all real numbers k. We have been using this rule for some'time now.

To introduce another rule, we evaluate the integral in question.

$$\left[\frac{x^2}{2} + 2x\right]_2^4 = \left(\frac{16}{2} + 8\right) - \left(\frac{4}{2} + 4\right)$$

$$= 16 - 6$$

$$= 10$$

When we interchange the limits and let 2 be the upper limit and 4 be the lower limit, we find the definite integral from 4 to 2.

$$\left[\frac{x^2}{2} + 2x\right]_4^2 = \left(\frac{4}{2} + 4\right) - \left(\frac{16}{2} + 8\right)$$

$$= 6 - 16$$

$$= -10$$

We see that interchanging the limits of integration changes the sign of the definite integral.

$$\int_4^2 f(x)\, dx = -\int_2^4 f(x)\, dx$$

This illustrates a general fact that is true for any real numbers a and b. If f is integrable between a and b, then

$$\int_a^b f(x)\, dx = -\int_b^a f(x)\, dx$$

We can also find the area between 0 and 2 and the area between 0 and 4.

$$\left[\frac{x^2}{2} + 2x\right]_0^2 = \left(\frac{4}{2} + 4\right) - 0 = 6 \qquad \left[\frac{x^2}{2} + 2x\right]_0^4 = \left(\frac{16}{2} + 8\right) - 0 = 16$$

So we have

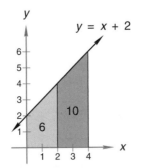

$$\int_0^2 (x + 2)\, dx = 6$$

$$\int_2^4 (x + 2)\, dx = 10$$

$$\int_0^4 (x + 2)\, dx = 16$$

This illustrates the following general property of continuous functions:

$$\int_a^b f(x)\,dx + \int_b^c f(x)\,dx = \int_a^c f(x)\,dx$$

This is true for all real numbers a, b, and c, whether they satisfy $a < b < c$ or not. Since each of the expressions represents a number, we can use the rules of algebra to move the expressions about and write other equivalent expressions, such as

$$\int_b^c f(x)\,dx = \int_a^c f(x)\,dx - \int_a^b f(x)\,dx \qquad \text{and}$$

$$-\int_a^c f(x)\,dx + \int_a^b f(x)\,dx + \int_b^c f(x)\,dx = 0$$

Every definite integral equals some number. Since the sum of a number and its opposite equals zero, we can write

$$\int_b^a f(x)\,dx - \int_b^a f(x)\,dx = 0$$

But $-\int_b^a f(x)\,dx$ can be rewritten as $+\int_a^b f(x)\,dx$ using previous rules, so

$$\int_b^a f(x)\,dx + \int_a^b f(x)\,dx = 0$$

Using the last boxed rule, the expression on the right-hand side above can be rewritten as $\int_a^a f(x)\,dx$, which gives us another rule.

$$\int_a^a f(x)\,dx = 0$$

This fact makes sense if we think geometrically. Thinking of $\int_a^a f(x)\,dx$ as an area, we are finding the area under the curve of f (if f is above the x-axis) between $x = a$ and $x = a$. So the width of the region is zero, and the total area must therefore be zero as well.

We can use the geometric interpretation of the definite integral to justify several other properties. If the graph of the function is on or above the x-axis $(f(x) \geq 0)$ between a and b, then the definite integral from a to b is greater than or equal to zero.

$$\text{If } f(x) \geq 0 \text{ on } [a, b], \text{ then } \int_a^b f(x)\,dx \geq 0.$$

If the graph of the function is on the x-axis everywhere between a and b, the definite integral from a to b is zero.

$$\text{If } f(x) = 0 \text{ on } [a, b], \text{ then } \int_a^b f(x)\,dx = 0.$$

If the graph of the function is on or below the x-axis between a and b, the definite integral from a to b is less than or equal to zero.

$$\text{If } f(x) \leq 0 \text{ on } [a, b], \text{ then } \int_a^b f(x)\,dx \leq 0.$$

If the graph of g is always below the graph of f between a and b, then the definite integral of g on the interval $[a, b]$ is less than the definite integral of f on the same interval.

$$\text{If } g(x) < f(x) \text{ on } [a, b], \text{ then } \int_a^b g(x)\, dx < \int_a^b f(x)\, dx.$$

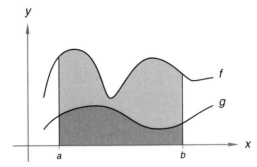

Of course, if $f(x) = g(x)$ on $[a, b]$, the integrals of f and g are equal.

$$\text{If } f(x) = g(x) \text{ on } [a, b], \text{ then } \int_a^b f(x)\, dx = \int_a^b g(x)\, dx.$$

We make a couple of observations about the possible maximum and minimum values of the definite integral of a function on $[a, b]$. If the maximum value of f on an interval is denoted max f, then the maximum possible value of $\int_a^b f(x)\, dx$ is $b - a$ times max f. If max f is greater than zero, then the maximum value of the definite integral equals the area of a rectangle $b - a$ wide and max f high.

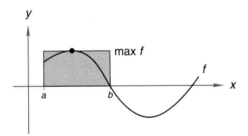

Area of rectangle $= (b - a)(\text{max } f)$

If the minimum value of f on an interval is denoted min f, then the minimum possible value of $\int_a^b f(x)\, dx$ is $b - a$ times min f. If min f is greater than zero, then the minimum value of the definite integral equals the area of a rectangle $b - a$ wide and min f high.

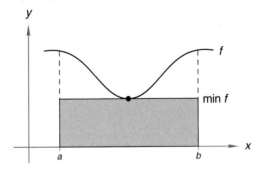

Area of rectangle $= (b - a)(\text{min } f)$

example 57.1   Let $\int_{-1}^1 f(x)\, dx = 7$ and $\int_1^4 f(x)\, dx = 2$. Evaluate $\int_{-1}^4 f(x)\, dx$.

solution   The integral from -1 to 4 equals the integral from -1 to 1 plus the integral from 1 to 4.

$$\int_{-1}^4 f(x)\, dx = \int_{-1}^1 f(x)\, dx + \int_1^4 f(x)\, dx = 7 + 2 = \mathbf{9}$$

Notice that the answer was found without knowing the rule for the function f.

example 57.2   Let f and g be functions such that

$$\int_1^3 f(x)\ dx = 4 \quad \text{and} \quad \int_1^3 g(x)\ dx = -1$$

Evaluate: $\displaystyle\int_1^3 \left[3f(x) - \frac{1}{3}g(x) \right] dx$

solution   First we write the given integral as the sum of two integrals.

$$\int_1^3 \left[3f(x) - \frac{1}{3}g(x) \right] dx = \int_1^3 3f(x)\ dx - \int_1^3 \frac{1}{3}g(x)\ dx$$

Next we move the constants across the integral signs.

$$\int_1^3 3f(x)\ dx = 3\int_1^3 f(x)\ dx \quad \text{and} \quad \int_1^3 \frac{1}{3}g(x)\ dx = \frac{1}{3}\int_1^3 g(x)\ dx$$

We finish by substituting 4 and –1 as the values of the two integrals.

$$3(4) - \frac{1}{3}(-1) = \frac{37}{3}$$

example 57.3   Suppose $\displaystyle\int_{-2}^1 f(x)\ dx = 3$ and $\displaystyle\int_3^1 f(x)\ dx = 7$. Evaluate $\displaystyle\int_{-2}^3 f(x)\ dx$.

solution   The integral of f from –2 to 3 equals the integral of f from –2 to 1 plus the integral of f from 1 to 3.

$$\int_{-2}^3 f(x)\ dx = \int_{-2}^1 f(x)\ dx + \int_1^3 f(x)\ dx$$

The value of the first integral was given as 3. It was also given that the integral of f from 3 to 1 is 7, which means the integral of f from 1 to 3 is –7. Thus

$$\int_{-2}^3 f(x)\ dx = 3 + (-7) = \mathbf{-4}$$

example 57.4   Assume f is a positive-valued, continuous function over the interval [5, 8]. Assume also that the absolute maximum of f over this interval is 12, while its absolute minimum over the interval is 3. Using the properties in this lesson, state the maximum and minimum values possible for

$$\int_5^8 f(x)\ dx$$

solution   A graphic would help here.

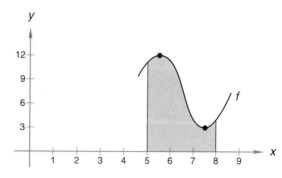

The area of this shaded region is

$$\int_5^8 f(x)\ dx$$

Clearly this area is less than the area of the rectangle shown here:

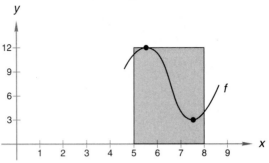

The area of this rectangle is $12(3) = 36$, so $\int_5^8 f(x)\,dx \le 36$.

Similarly, this integral must be greater than the area of the following rectangle:

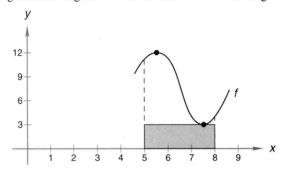

The area of this rectangle is $3(3) = 9$. Therefore we see that

$$9 \le \int_5^8 f(x)\,dx \le 36$$

without knowing anything about f except its maximum and minimum values on an interval.

**problem set
57**

1. A line joins the points $(0, 6)$ and $(4, 0)$ as
(52) shown to the right. Find the coordinates of
the point (x, y) on the line that maximizes
the area of the inscribed rectangle shown.

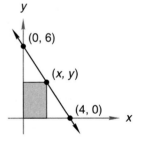

2. Find the Maclaurin series for $y = 2x^3 + 4x^2 - 2x + 6$.
(55)

3. Find the Maclaurin series for $y = e^x$, and write the answer in summation notation.
(55)

4. A particle moves in a circular orbit described by the equation $x^2 + y^2 = 25$. As it passes
(46) through the point $(4, 3)$, its y-coordinate is decreasing at a rate of 3 units/s. What is the rate of
change of the x-coordinate the instant the particle passes through the point $(4, 3)$?

5. An open-topped box is to be made from a square sheet of aluminum 0.3 meter on each side by
(52) cutting a small square with sides of length x from each corner and folding up the resulting flaps.
Find the size of the square that must be cut from each corner to maximize the volume of the box.
What is the maximal volume of the box?

(a) Solve this problem with a graphing calculator. Begin by expressing the volume of the box
as a function of the single variable x, and then graph the function in an appropriate window.

(b) Solve this problem again using calculus.

6. A particle moves along the number line so that its position at time t is given by
(54) $s(t) = -12t + t^3$. Find the time(s) when the particle is momentarily at rest.

7. If $\int_{-1}^{4} f(x)\,dx = -3$ and $\int_{4}^{5} f(x)\,dx = 2$, what is $\int_{-1}^{5} f(x)\,dx$?
(57)

8. If $\int_{1}^{3} f(x)\,dx = -2$ and $\int_{1}^{3} g(x)\,dx = 4$, what is $\int_{1}^{3} \left[-3f(x) + 2g(x)\right] dx$?
(57)

9. If f is a continuous function on $[-1, 3]$ and if f attains a maximum value of 4 on $[-1, 3]$, then
(57) which of the following must be true?

A. $\int_{-1}^{3} f(x)\,dx \leq 16$ B. $\int_{-1}^{3} f(x)\,dx = 4$

C. $\int_{-1}^{3} f(x)\,dx \geq 16$ D. $\int_{-1}^{3} f(x)\,dx \geq 0$

Evaluate the integrals in problems 10 and 11.

10. $\int_{1}^{9} \frac{1}{\sqrt{x}}\,dx$ **11.** $\int_{-\pi/2}^{3\pi} \cos x\,dx$
(47)   (47)

Antidifferentiate in problems 12–15.

12. $\int \frac{3x + 1}{3x^2 + 2x}\,dx$ **13.** $\int (4x + 2)e^{x^2 + x}\,dx$
(56)   (56)

14. $\int \frac{2x + 1}{\sqrt{x^2 + x + 1}}\,dx$ **15.** $\int \tan^3 x \sec^2 x\,dx$
(51)   (51)

16. Sketch the graph of f given that $f'(3) = 0$, $f''(x) < 0$ when $x < 3$, and $f''(x) > 0$
(45) when $x > 3$.

17. Find the number k such that the area between $y = \frac{1}{x}$ and the x-axis from $x = 1$ to $x = k$ is
(47) equal to 1.

18. Given this graph of f',
(45)

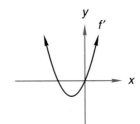

which of the following graphs most resembles the graph of f?

A.   B.   C.   D.

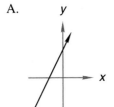 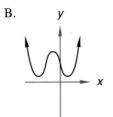 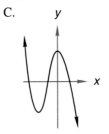 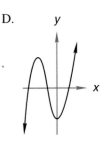

19. Given the following graph of f, sketch the graph of f'.
(45)

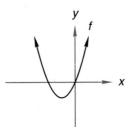

20. Find $\dfrac{dy}{dx}$ where $y = \dfrac{e^{x^2} + x}{x^2 + 2x} + \sec^3(2x) + \csc^3(4x)$.
(50)

21. Find the equation of the line normal to the graph of $y = \dfrac{\sqrt{x+2}}{x}$ at $x = 2$.
(40)

22. Sketch the graph of $f(x) = \dfrac{1-x}{x(1-x)}$.
(21)

23. Find the values of x for which $|2x - 3| < 0.01$.
(9)

24. Evaluate $\displaystyle\int_0^1 \sqrt{1 - x^2}\ dx$ without using calculus. (*Hint:* Consider the integral geometrically.)
(22,47)

25. Find the positive number that exceeds its cube by the greatest amount.
(52)

LESSON 58 *Explicit and Implicit Equations • Inverse Functions*

58.A
explicit and implicit equations

We customarily use x as the input of a function machine, and we call the output y or $f(x)$.

$$x \longrightarrow \boxed{f} \longrightarrow y \qquad\qquad x \longrightarrow \boxed{f} \longrightarrow f(x)$$

If an equation is written in the form "y equals" or "$f(x)$ equals," we say that the equation is written in **explicit form** and is an **explicit equation.** Thus the following equations are all explicit equations:

$$y = 2x + 6 \qquad f(x) = 2x + 6 \qquad y = e^x \qquad y = \log_b x$$

Many equations have forms other than the "y equals" form. These other forms of the equation are called **implicit forms.** Equations that are not "y equals" or "$f(x)$ equals" equations are called **implicit equations.** Three of the many implicit forms of the linear equation $y = 2x + 6$ are

$$2x - y = -6 \qquad x = \frac{1}{2}y - 3 \qquad \frac{x}{-3} + \frac{y}{6} = 1$$

The logarithmic function machine takes the number x as an input and produces the output y, which is the logarithm of the input.

$$\overset{\log_b(\ )}{x \longrightarrow \boxed{f} \longrightarrow y}$$

The equation of this function machine has both an explicit form and an implicit form. If we use 10 as the base, the forms are as follows.

EXPLICIT FORM	IMPLICIT FORM
$y = \log_{10} x$	$10^y = x$

Understand that these two equations are two forms of the same equation and pair the same values of x and y. The equation on the left-hand side says that y is the logarithm and x is the number. The equation on the right-hand side also says that y is the logarithm and x is the number. If we use 2 for y and 100 for x in the equations above, we get two numerical equations that make the same statement.

$$2 = \log_{10} 100 \qquad 10^2 = 100$$

The function machine for the exponential function takes the logarithm x as the input and produces the output y, which is the number that results when the base is raised to the x power.

$$\overset{10^{(\ )}}{x \longrightarrow \boxed{} \longrightarrow y}$$

The equation of this function machine also has both an explicit form and an implicit form. If we use 10 as the base, the forms are

EXPLICIT FORM	IMPLICIT FORM
$y = 10^x$	$\log_{10} y = x$

These equations seem to be the same equations as the two forms of the logarithmic function, but they are not. In these equations the input x is the logarithm, and the output y is the number. If we use 2 as the value of the input x and 100 as the output y, we again get two numerical equations that make the same statement.

$$100 = 10^2 \qquad \log_{10} 100 = 2$$

The explicit forms of the basic sine, cosine, and tangent equations are

$$y = a \sin x \qquad y = a \cos x \qquad y = a \tan x$$

When we divide both sides of these equations by a, we get equations that suggest the triangles shown here:

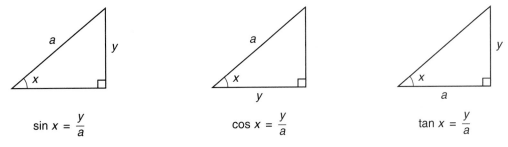

$$\sin x = \frac{y}{a} \qquad\qquad \cos x = \frac{y}{a} \qquad\qquad \tan x = \frac{y}{a}$$

We can use the Pythagorean formula to find the values of the labeled sides of those triangles.

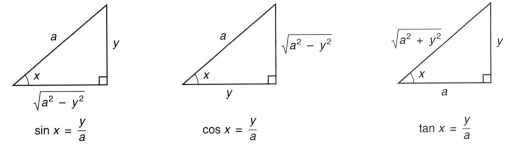

$$\sin x = \frac{y}{a} \qquad\qquad \cos x = \frac{y}{a} \qquad\qquad \tan x = \frac{y}{a}$$

The equations above are implicit equations, and they define y as a function of x implicitly. We can use words to write implicit forms of these equations, and we can use two different symbolic notations that make the same statements as the words. The notations $\sin^{-1}$, $\cos^{-1}$, and $\tan^{-1}$ are read as "the inverse sine of," "the inverse cosine of," and "the inverse tangent of." (The $^{-1}$ is a special notation for inverses and is not a negative exponent.) Each column below lists four ways to designate a particular inverse trigonometric function.

x is an angle whose sine is $\frac{y}{a}$	x is an angle whose cosine is $\frac{y}{a}$	x is an angle whose tangent is $\frac{y}{a}$
x is the inverse sine of $\frac{y}{a}$	x is the inverse cosine of $\frac{y}{a}$	x is the inverse tangent of $\frac{y}{a}$
$x = \arcsin \frac{y}{a}$	$x = \arccos \frac{y}{a}$	$x = \arctan \frac{y}{a}$
$x = \sin^{-1} \frac{y}{a}$	$x = \cos^{-1} \frac{y}{a}$	$x = \tan^{-1} \frac{y}{a}$

Beginners often find the implicit form of these trigonometric equations intimidating. Drawing the triangle defined helps eliminate confusion. For demonstration we draw the triangle determined by

$x = \tan^{-1} 3$. In other words, we draw a right triangle in which $\tan x = 3$. We also show the values of the trigonometric functions evaluated at x, all of which can be deduced from the triangle.

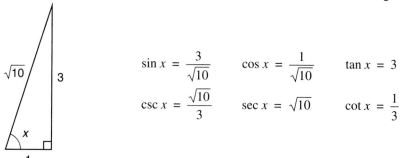

$$\sin x = \frac{3}{\sqrt{10}} \qquad \cos x = \frac{1}{\sqrt{10}} \qquad \tan x = 3$$

$$\csc x = \frac{\sqrt{10}}{3} \qquad \sec x = \sqrt{10} \qquad \cot x = \frac{1}{3}$$

58.B
inverse functions

In Lesson 13 we began investigating inverse trigonometric functions. In this lesson we consider other inverse functions as well, but first we discuss inverse operations. Addition and subtraction are inverse operations because addition undoes subtraction and subtraction undoes addition. On the left-hand side below, we begin with 7 and add 3 to get 10. On the right-hand side we subtract 3 from 10 and get back to 7, where we began.

ADDITION   SUBTRACTION

$7 + (3) = 10 \qquad 10 - (3) = 7$

Inverse function machines perform inverse operations. (*Note:* We use g^{-1} to designate the inverse function of g and h^{-1} to designate the inverse function of h. We read g^{-1} as "g inverse" and h^{-1} as "h inverse.") An inverse function machine is a function machine that takes the output of another function machine and produces that machine's input.

If the f function machine takes inputs of 4 and 5 and produces outputs of 43 and 13, then the inverse function machine f^{-1} would take 43 and 13 as inputs and produce 4 and 5 as outputs.

Not all functions have inverse functions. Consider the function machine for g shown on the left below. It produces exactly one output for each input. The inputs of 3 and 11 both have an output of 5, which is acceptable behavior for a function machine, because 3 and 11 have exactly one output apiece. But when we try to define the g^{-1} machine, we are not successful since the machine does not know where to send 5. It cannot tell whether to send it to 3 or to 11.

Thus, for a function to have an inverse function, each output must correspond to only one input. We call functions of this type **one-to-one** functions. In a one-to-one function, every value of x is paired with exactly one value of y, and every value of y is paired with exactly one value of x.

We can tell whether a function is one-to-one by looking at its graph. **If the slope of the graph of a function is always positive (with the exception of isolated points) or if the slope of the graph of a function is always negative (with the exception of isolated points), then the function is a one-to-one function and has an inverse.**

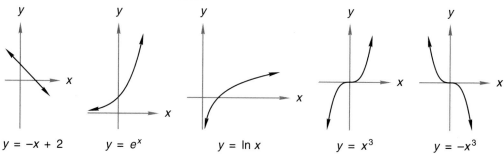

$y = -x + 2 \qquad y = e^x \qquad y = \ln x \qquad y = x^3 \qquad y = -x^3$

The slope of the graph of $y = -x + 2$ is always negative, and thus the function is a one-to-one function and has an inverse. The slopes of $y = e^x$ and $y = \ln x$ are positive everywhere, so these functions are one-to-one functions and have inverses. The slope of $y = x^3$ is positive everywhere except at the isolated point $(0, 0)$, where the slope is zero. Thus this function is a one-to-one function and has an inverse. The slope of $y = -x^3$ is negative everywhere except at the isolated point $(0, 0)$, where the slope is zero. Thus this function is a one-to-one function and has an inverse.

The functions shown below are not one-to-one functions, because some values of y are paired with two or more values of x.

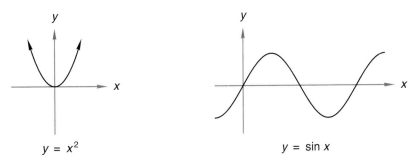

$y = x^2$ $y = \sin x$

We can tell this at a glance because the slopes of these graphs are not everywhere positive or everywhere negative. We could also use a horizontal line test. Restricting the domain of such functions produces a new function that is one-to-one. (Remember that a function is a rule **and** a domain.) So the function $g(x) = x^2$ with domain $[0, \infty)$ is one-to-one.

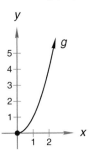

To find the inverse of an equation all we have to do is to interchange x and y in the equation. Suppose we have the equation $y = 2x + 4$ and want to write its inverse. If we interchange x and y, we get the implicit form of the inverse equation, which can be rearranged into the explicit form.

IMPLICIT FORM   EXPLICIT FORM

$$x = 2y + 4 \qquad\qquad y = \frac{1}{2}x - 2$$

Below we show the $f(x) = 2x + 4$ function machine on the left-hand side and the inverse function machine to its right. Using an input of 4 on the left gives an output of 12. An input of 12 in the inverse machine produces an output of 4, which is the original input. More importantly, an input of x on the left returns to x when the output of f is used as an input of f^{-1}.

$$
2(\ ) + 4 \qquad\qquad\qquad \frac{1}{2}(\ ) - 2
$$

$$
\begin{array}{ccccc}
4 \rightarrow & \boxed{\ \ f\ \ } & \rightarrow\ 12 & \rightarrow & \boxed{\ f^{-1}\ } \rightarrow\ 4 \\
x \rightarrow & & \rightarrow\ 2x + 4 & \rightarrow & \qquad\quad \rightarrow\ x
\end{array}
$$

Two comments briefly summarize important aspects of inverse functions. The first deals with the composition of a function f and its inverse function f^{-1}.

> For any one-to-one function f,
>
> $$(f^{-1} \circ f)(x) = x \qquad \text{for all } x \text{ in the domain of } f$$
> $$(f \circ f^{-1})(x) = x \qquad \text{for all } x \text{ in the domain of } f^{-1}$$

The second comment deals with the graphs of f and f^{-1}. The two functions shown here are inverse functions. The function g is the inverse of the function f, and the function f is the inverse of the function g.

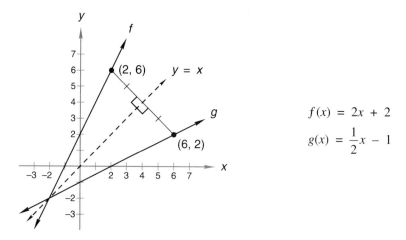

$$f(x) = 2x + 2$$

$$g(x) = \frac{1}{2}x - 1$$

The graph of any function and the graph of its inverse are reflections of each other in the line $y = x$. Because the coordinates of any point and its reflection are the same numbers but in reverse order, the perpendicular distance from a point to the line $y = x$ is the same as the perpendicular distance from the line $y = x$ to its reflection in that line. In the figure above we note that the distance from the point $(2, 6)$ to the line $y = x$ is the same as the distance from the point $(6, 2)$ to the line $y = x$.

In the graph on the left below, we see that the graph of $y = \ln x$ and $y = e^x$ are reflections of each other in the line $y = x$.

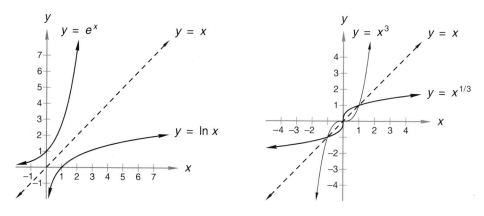

On the right-hand side we note that the graphs of $y = x^3$ and $y = x^{1/3}$ are reflections of each other in the line $y = x$.

example 58.1   Let $f(x) = 2x - 3$. Find $f^{-1}(4)$.

solution   First we replace $f(x)$ with y. To find an implicit form of f^{-1}, we simply interchange x and y as we show in the center. On the right-hand side we rearrange this equation into its explicit form.

EQUATION	IMPLICIT INVERSE	EXPLICIT INVERSE
$y = 2x - 3$	$x = 2y - 3$	$y = \dfrac{1}{2}x + \dfrac{3}{2}$

To find $f^{-1}(4)$, we replace x with 4 and get

$$f^{-1}(4) = \frac{1}{2}(4) + \frac{3}{2} = \frac{7}{2}$$

example 58.2   Find $f^{-1}(8)$ where $f(x) = 4 \ln x$.

solution   First we replace $f(x)$ with y. Then we find an implicit form of f inverse by interchanging x and y in the equation. Since $f^{-1}(8)$ is the value of y when $x = 8$, we also need the explicit form.

EQUATION	IMPLICIT INVERSE	EXPLICIT INVERSE
$y = 4 \ln x$	$x = 4 \ln y$ or $\dfrac{x}{4} = \ln y$	$y = e^{x/4}$

Now we replace x with 8 in the explicit form to get $f^{-1}(8)$.

$$f^{-1}(8) = e^{8/4} = e^2$$

example 58.3   Let $f(x) = 2x - 3$ and $f^{-1}(x) = \frac{1}{2}x + \frac{3}{2}$, as in example 58.1. Find $(f^{-1} \circ f)(6)$ and $(f \circ f^{-1})(6)$.

solution   The notation $(f^{-1} \circ f)(6)$ tells us to put 6 into the f machine and then put the resulting output into the f^{-1} machine. The notation $(f \circ f^{-1})(6)$ tells us to put 6 into the f^{-1} machine and then put the resulting output into the f machine.

$$(f^{-1} \circ f)(6) = f^{-1}(f(6)) = f^{-1}(9) = \frac{1}{2}(9) + \frac{3}{2} = \mathbf{6}$$

$$(f \circ f^{-1})(6) = f(f^{-1}(6)) = f\left(\frac{9}{2}\right) = 2\left(\frac{9}{2}\right) - 3 = \mathbf{6}$$

example 58.4   Find $f^{-1}(9)$ where $y = f(x)$ and $\dfrac{y}{3} = \cot x$.

solution   On the left-hand side below, we interchange x and y to write the implicit form of f^{-1}. Then we write the explicit form on the right-hand side and let $x = 9$ to find $f^{-1}(9)$.

IMPLICIT FORM OF f^{-1}	EXPLICIT FORM OF f^{-1}	EVALUATION OF $f^{-1}(9)$
$\dfrac{x}{3} = \cot y$	$y = \cot^{-1}\dfrac{x}{3}$	$y = \cot^{-1}\dfrac{9}{3} = \cot^{-1}3$

If y is the angle whose cotangent is 3, then the tangent of y is $\frac{1}{3}$. We set the calculator to radians and use the inverse tangent key to get a numerical approximation.

$$y = \tan^{-1}\frac{1}{3} \approx \mathbf{0.3218}$$

problem set 58

1. (52) A rectangle is to be inscribed in a circle whose radius is 2 units. Find the dimensions that maximize the area of the rectangle. What is the maximum area of the rectangle?

   (a) Solve this problem with a graphing calculator. Begin by expressing the area of the rectangle as a function of the single variable x, and then graph the function in an appropriate window.

   (b) Solve this problem again using calculus.

2. (55) Find the Maclaurin series for $y = \sin x$, and write the answer in summation notation.

3. (55) Find the Maclaurin series for $y = \ln(1 + x)$, and write the answer in summation notation.

4. (46) The radius of a spherical ball is expanding at a rate of 3 cm/s. How fast is the surface area of the ball increasing when the radius of the ball is 10 cm?

5. (54) A ball is thrown vertically upward from the top of a 100-ft-high building. Its height above the ground (in feet) at time t (in seconds) is given by $h(t) = 100 + 50t - 16t^2$. At what time is the ball falling toward the earth at 75 ft/s?

6. (58) Let $f(x) = 4x - 3$. Write the equation of f^{-1}. Evaluate $(f \circ f^{-1})(x)$ and $(f^{-1} \circ f)(x)$.

7. Find $f^{-1}(3)$ where $f(x) = 2 \ln x$.
(58)

8. Write an equation that expresses the inverse of $y = \sin x \cos y$ implicitly.
(58)

9. Let $\int_{-1}^{3} f(x)\,dx = 4$ and $\int_{-1}^{3} g(x)\,dx = -2$. Evaluate $\int_{-1}^{3} \left[3f(x) - g(x)\right] dx$.
(57)

10. Suppose f is a continuous function on $[-1, 2]$ whose maximum value is 10 and whose minimum
(57) value is -5. Which of the following must be true?

   A. $-15 \le \int_{-1}^{2} f(x)\,dx \le 30$ B. $-5 \le \int_{-1}^{2} f(x)\,dx \le 10$

   C. $-10 \le \int_{-1}^{2} f(x)\,dx \le 20$ D. $0 \le \int_{-1}^{2} f(x)\,dx \le 30$

11. Given that $\int_{1}^{4} f(x)\,dx = 10$, $\int_{2}^{4} f(x)\,dx = 6$, and f is a continuous function, evaluate
(57) $\int_{1}^{2} f(x)\,dx$.

12. Use implicit differentiation to find $\dfrac{dy}{dx}$ given $\sin(xy) = x$.
(34)

13. Find the equation of the line tangent to the curve $x^3 + y^2 = y$ at $(0, 1)$.
(34)

14. Find the equation of the line normal to the graph of $y = \sqrt{2x}$ at $x = 4$.
(40)

Differentiate the functions in problems 15 and 16 with respect to x.

15. $y = \dfrac{e^{2x} + e^{-x^2}}{x^3 + 1} - 3 \cot x$
(50)

16. $y = \dfrac{1}{\ln 2} \ln(x^2 + 3x - 1) - \dfrac{\sin x}{\cos(ax)}$, where a is constant
(50)

Integrate in problems 17–19.

17. $\displaystyle\int \dfrac{3x^2 + 2}{\sqrt{2x^3 + 4x}}\,dx$ **18.** $\displaystyle\int (\cos x - 1)e^{\sin x - x}\,dx$
(56)   (51)

19. $\displaystyle\int \cos(ax)\sin^4(ax)\,dx$, where a is constant
(56)

20. Evaluate: $\displaystyle\lim_{x \to \infty} \dfrac{x^2 - 3}{3 + x - 5x^2}$
(17)

21. For which of the following functions is $\dfrac{d^3y}{dx^3} = \dfrac{dy}{dx}$?
(27)

   A. $y = \sin x$ B. $y = 2e^x$ C. $y = x^3$ D. $y = \cos x$

22. Evaluate $\dfrac{4}{9}\displaystyle\int_{0}^{3} \sqrt{9 - x^2}\,dx$. Do not use a graphing calculator.
(47)

23. Find $\sec^2(2\theta)$ for the angle θ in this
(13) triangle.

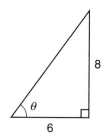

24. Use a trigonometric function to relate h,
(34) 6, and θ in the triangle below. Suppose h
and θ are functions of t. Implicitly
differentiate the equation found with
respect to t.

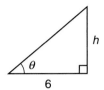

25. The following graph represents $y = e^x$,
(57) and the area of the shaded region is
3 square units. Find the value of k.

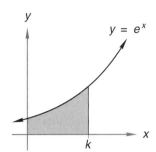

LESSON 59 *Computing Areas* • *More Numerical Integration on a Graphing Calculator*

59.A
computing areas

We have found that the definite integral of a function is related to area.

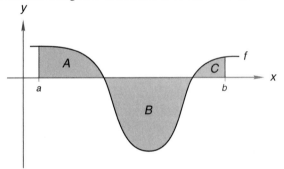

For the function f graphed above, the definite integral of f from a to b is $A - B + C$. A and C are positive in the sum, because the regions whose areas are A and C are above the x-axis. B is negative in the sum, since the region whose area is B lies below the x-axis. To find the total area on an interval, it is often necessary to integrate piecewise as dictated by the graph of the function.

example 59.1 Find the area between the graph of $y = \sin x$ and the x-axis between $x = 0$ and $x = 2\pi$.

solution Evaluating the definite integral of $\sin x$ between 0 and 2π gives us an answer of zero because half of the area is above the x-axis and half of the area is below the x-axis. To get the total area, we must use two integrals, adding the integral of $\sin x$ from 0 to π to the negative of the integral of $\sin x$ from π to 2π.

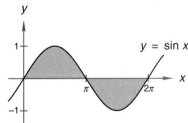

$$\text{Total area} = \int_0^\pi \sin x \, dx - \int_\pi^{2\pi} \sin x \, dx = [-\cos x]_0^\pi - [-\cos x]_\pi^{2\pi}$$
$$= [1 - (-1)] - [-1 - (1)] = 2 + 2 = \textbf{4 units}^2$$

Note that the area of one loop of $y = \sin x$ equals 2. This means that the area of one loop of $y = 42 \sin x$ would be 84, because the integral of $42 \sin x$ equals 42 times the integral of $\sin x$. The area under one loop of $y = k \sin x$ is $2k$.

example 59.2 Find the area of the region bounded by the graph of $y = x^2 - 1$ and the x-axis over the interval $[-2, 2]$.

solution From the graph we see that the area between -2 and -1 is above the x-axis. The area between -1 and 1 is below the x-axis. The area between 1 and 2 is above the x-axis. To find the total area we find the sum of three numbers. The first number is the definite integral from -2 to -1, the second is the negative of the definite integral from -1 to 1, and the third is the definite integral from 1 to 2.

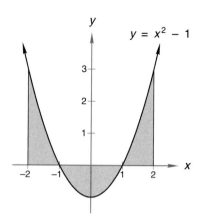

$$\text{Total area} = \int_{-2}^{-1} (x^2 - 1)\, dx - \int_{-1}^{1} (x^2 - 1)\, dx + \int_{1}^{2} (x^2 - 1)\, dx$$

$$= \left[\frac{x^3}{3} - x \right]_{-2}^{-1} - \left[\frac{x^3}{3} - x \right]_{-1}^{1} + \left[\frac{x^3}{3} - x \right]_{1}^{2}$$

We use symbols of inclusion as necessary to guard against making mistakes in signs.

$$\left[\left(-\frac{1}{3} + 1 \right) - \left(-\frac{8}{3} + 2 \right) \right] - \left[\left(\frac{1}{3} - 1 \right) - \left(-\frac{1}{3} + 1 \right) \right] + \left[\left(\frac{8}{3} - 2 \right) - \left(\frac{1}{3} - 1 \right) \right]$$

$$= -\frac{1}{3} + 1 + \frac{8}{3} - 2 - \frac{1}{3} + 1 - \frac{1}{3} + 1 + \frac{8}{3} - 2 - \frac{1}{3} + 1 = \frac{12}{3} = \textbf{4 units}^2$$

We also note that the graph of $y = x^2 - 1$ is symmetric about the y-axis. So the area to the left of the y-axis equals the area to the right of the y-axis. Therefore the total area is twice the area on one side.

$$\text{Total area} = 2 \left[-\int_{0}^{1} (x^2 - 1)\, dx + \int_{1}^{2} (x^2 - 1)\, dx \right]$$

This also yields an answer of 4. The advantage of computing the area in this fashion is that fewer integrals have to be evaluated, leaving fewer opportunities for arithmetic mistakes.

example 59.3 Find the area of the region completely enclosed by the graph of $y = -x^3 - x^2 + 2x$ and the x-axis.

solution We begin by factoring so we can find the zeros of the function.

$$-x^3 - x^2 + 2x = -x(x + 2)(x - 1) \quad\longrightarrow\quad \text{zeros are } -2, 0, +1$$

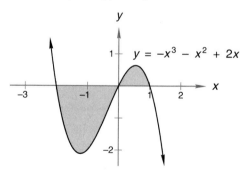

From the graph we see that we can find the total area by adding the negative of the definite integral from $x = -2$ to $x = 0$ to the definite integral from $x = 0$ to $x = 1$.

$$\text{Total area} = -\int_{-2}^{0} (-x^3 - x^2 + 2x)\, dx + \int_{0}^{1} (-x^3 - x^2 + 2x)\, dx$$

$$= -\left[-\frac{x^4}{4} - \frac{x^3}{3} + x^2 \right]_{-2}^{0} + \left[-\frac{x^4}{4} - \frac{x^3}{3} + x^2 \right]_{0}^{1}$$

Again we use symbols of inclusion to help prevent making mistakes in signs.

$$\text{Total area} = -\left[0 - \left(-\frac{16}{4} + \frac{8}{3} + 4\right)\right] + \left[\left(-\frac{1}{4} - \frac{1}{3} + 1\right) - 0\right]$$

$$= -\left(-\frac{8}{3}\right) + \left(\frac{5}{12}\right) = \frac{37}{12} \text{ units}^2$$

59.B
more numerical integration on a graphing calculator

As we have seen in the past, it is possible to use the calculator to approximate areas. However, as with our work done by hand in the previous section, we must take great care to integrate piecewise with some functions.

example 59.4   Using a graphing calculator, approximate the area described in example 59.3.

solution   The incorrect approach would be to calculate

$$\texttt{fnInt(-X}^3\texttt{-X}^2\texttt{+2X,X,-2,1)}$$

Indeed, this yields –2.25, which we know is wrong because area is supposed to be positive. Instead, we need to calculate

$$\texttt{-fnInt(-X}^3\texttt{-X}^2\texttt{+2X,X,-2,0)+fnInt(-X}^3\texttt{-X}^2\texttt{+2X,X,0,1)}$$

This yields 3.083333..., which can be quickly converted to a fraction by pressing **MATH 1 ENTER**. This key sequence yields $\frac{37}{12}$, which is the answer found in example 59.3.

Now we calculate another area that could be problematic without the calculator.

example 59.5   Using a graphing calculator, approximate the area of the region completely enclosed by the graph of $y = x^3 - 7x^2 + 2x + 5$ and the x-axis.

solution   Unlike the function in example 59.3, this function does not factor easily, which makes finding the zeros difficult.

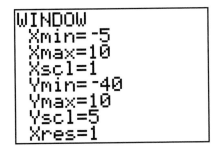
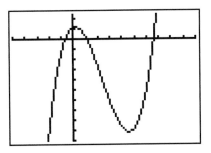

However, the TI-83 has a built-in zero finder in its CALCULATE menu. The TI-83 approximates the three zeros as the following values of x:

$$x = -0.6868446 \qquad x = 1.1062289 \qquad x = 6.5806156$$

We can use these values, along with fnInt, to get the result. Note that the second integral must be subtracted from the first because the second region in the graph is below the x-axis.

$$\texttt{fnInt(X}^3\texttt{-7X}^2\texttt{+2X+5,X,-0.6868446,1.1062289)}$$

$$\texttt{-fnInt(X}^3\texttt{-7X}^2\texttt{+2X+5,X,1.1062289,6.5806156)}$$

The result is approximately **129.9950.**

**problem set
59**

1. A 4- by 8-meter rectangular sheet of cardboard is cut into the shape shown below and folded
(52) along the dotted lines to form a box.

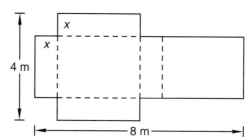

Find the value of x that maximizes the volume of the box. What is the maximal volume of the box?

(a) Solve this problem with a graphing calculator. Begin by expressing the volume of the box
as a function of the single variable x, and then graph the function in an appropriate window.

(b) Solve this problem again using calculus.

2. Find the Maclaurin series for $y = \cos x$, and write the answer in summation notation.
(55)

3. Find the Maclaurin series for $y = \dfrac{1}{x + 1}$, and write the answer in summation notation.
(55)

4. The height of the right triangle shown
(46) increases at a rate of 1 unit per second.
Find $\frac{d\theta}{dt}$ when $h = 8$.

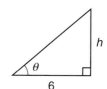

5. The following graph represents the
(59) continuous function $y = f(x)$. A, B, and
C represent the areas of the enclosed
regions. Suppose $A = 6\frac{5}{12}$, $B = \frac{23}{6}$, and
$C = 4\frac{1}{3}$. Find $\int_a^d f(x)\, dx$.

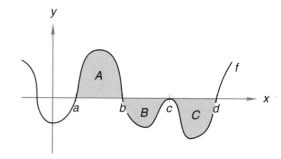

6. Find the area of the region between the graph of $y = \cos x$ and the x-axis on the interval $[0, 2\pi]$.
(59)

7. Express the area of the region completely enclosed by the x-axis and the graph of
(59) $y = (x - 1)(x + 1)(x - 2)$ as the sum of two definite integrals.

8. Use a graphing calculator to find the area bounded by the graph of $f(x) = xe^{\sin(1/x)}$ and the
(59) x-axis over the interval $\left[\frac{\pi}{9}, \frac{\pi}{4}\right]$.

9. Find the equation of f^{-1} where $f(x) = 3x + 2$. Evaluate $f^{-1}(4)$, $(f \circ f^{-1})(x)$, and $(f^{-1} \circ f)(x)$.
(58)

10. Suppose g is the inverse function of f and $f(x) = \dfrac{1}{x}$. Find the equation of g.
(58)

11. Write the implicit form of the inverse of $y = \tan x$.
(58)

12. Suppose f is continuous on $[1, 4]$. Which of the following statements must be true?
(57)

A. $\displaystyle\int_1^2 f(x)\, dx + \int_2^4 f(x)\, dx = \int_1^4 f(x)\, dx$ 　　B. $\displaystyle\int_1^4 f(x)\, dx \geq 0$

C. $\displaystyle\int_1^2 f(x)\, dx \leq \int_2^4 f(x)\, dx$

Integrate in problems 13–15.

13. $\int 2x(x^2 + 2)^3 \, dx$
(51)

14. $\int \dfrac{2x - 1}{\sqrt{x^2 - x + 1}} \, dx$
(51)

15. $\int \pi \cos^2 (2x) \sin (2x) \, dx$
(56)

16. Find the values of x for which the graph of $y = 2x^3 - 3x^2 + 12x + 1$ is concave upward.
(49)

17. Differentiate $y = \dfrac{\cos (3x)}{x^2 + 2} + \tan (2x)$ with respect to x.
(50)

18. Find an equation of the line normal to the graph of the function $y = \dfrac{e^{\pi - x}}{2}$ at $x = 2$.
(40)

19. Find $\dfrac{dy}{dx}$ given $x = \sin (xy)$.
(34)

20. Graph $f(x) = 2^x + 1$ and $g(x) = 2^{-x} + 1$ on the same coordinate plane.
(7)

21. Write the equation whose solution set is all the points that are 3 units away from $(2, 3)$. What is
(9) this geometric figure?

22. Determine the domain and range of $y = 2 - \sin (3x - \pi)$.
(6)

23. If the graph of $y = x - 1$ for positive values of x is reflected about the y-axis, what is the
(9) equation of the reflection?

24. The curves $y = \frac{1}{2}x^2$ and $y = 1 - \frac{1}{2}x^2$ intersect in the first quadrant. Find the angle at which
(13,27) the two curves intersect in the first quadrant. (*Note:* The angle between two curves is defined to be the angle between their tangents at the point of intersection. If the slopes are m_1 and m_2, then the angle of intersection can be obtained from the formula $\tan \theta = \frac{m_1 - m_2}{1 + m_1 m_2}$.)

25. If the function $f(x) = \frac{x^2 + 2x - 3}{x^2 + bx + 4}$ is continuous for every x, then which of the following is true?
(28)

   A. $b = 4$ B. $b = -4$ C. $|b| < 4$

   D. $|b| > 4$ E. $0 < b < 4$

LESSON 60   *Area Between Two Curves • Area Between Curves Using a Graphing Calculator*

60.A

area between two curves

We can find the area bounded by the graphs of two continuous functions on the interval $[a, b]$ by using the limit of a sum of rectangular areas to represent the area and evaluating the sum by using the Fundamental Theorem of Calculus. In the figure on the left-hand side below, to find the area between the graphs of f and g on the interval $[a, b]$, we partition the interval and draw rectangles whose heights are $f(x_i) - g(x_i)$ and whose widths are Δx as shown. (Note that f is the "high" function on the interval and that g is the "low" function.)

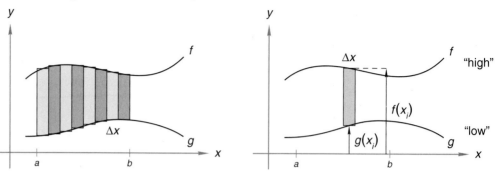

A **representative rectangle** is shown on the right-hand side. The width of the rectangle is Δx, and the height of the rectangle is $f(x_i) - g(x_i)$. The area between $x = a$ and $x = b$ can be represented by the following limit:

$$\text{Area} = \lim_{\Delta x \to 0} \sum_{i=1}^{n} (f - g)(x_i)\Delta x_i$$

This sum is similar to a Riemann sum. We can find the limit by evaluating the following integral using the Fundamental Theorem of Calculus.

$$\int_a^b (f - g)(x)\, dx \qquad \text{which is} \qquad \int_a^b (\text{high} - \text{low})\, dx$$

We must be careful to use $(f - g)(x)$ as the height of the rectangle when $f > g$. If we use $(g - f)(x)$ as the height, we will get the negative of the area that we want to find.

example 60.1   Find the area of the region between the graphs of $f(x) = x^2 + 2$ and $g(x) = -x$ on the interval [0, 1].

solution   We sketch the curves and draw a representative rectangle. The width of the rectangle is Δx, and the height is $(f - g)(x)$. Using this information to set up the integral gives us

$$\text{Area} = \int_0^1 (f - g)(x)\, dx$$

$$= \int_0^1 \left[(x^2 + 2) - (-x)\right] dx$$

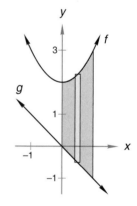

We evaluate the integrals using the fundamental theorem.

$$\int_0^1 (x^2 + x + 2)\, dx = \left[\frac{x^3}{3} + \frac{x^2}{2} + 2x\right]_0^1 = \frac{1}{3} + \frac{1}{2} + 2 - 0 = \frac{17}{6}\ \textbf{units}^2$$

example 60.2   Find the area of the region completely bounded by the graphs of $f(x) = 2 - x^2$ and $g(x) = x$.

solution   Problems like this one are carefully designed so that the coordinates of the points of intersection of the graphs are easy to find. The solution to the system

$$\begin{cases} y = x \\ y = 2 - x^2 \end{cases}$$

is (1, 1) and (−2, −2).

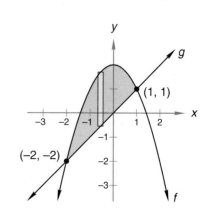

The width of the representative rectangle is Δx, and the height of the rectangle is $(f - g)(x)$, or $(2 - x^2) - (x)$. The width Δx tells us that x is the variable of integration. We integrate from $x = -2$ to $x = +1$.

$$\text{Area} = \int_{-2}^{1} [(f - g)(x)] \, dx = \int_{-2}^{1} (2 - x^2 - x) \, dx = \left[2x - \frac{x^3}{3} - \frac{x^2}{2} \right]_{-2}^{1}$$

$$= \left(2 - \frac{1}{3} - \frac{1}{2} \right) - \left(-4 + \frac{8}{3} - 2 \right) = \frac{9}{2} \text{ units}^2$$

example 60.3   Find the area of the region between the graphs of $f(x) = 2 - x^2$ and $g(x) = x$ on the interval $[1, 2]$.

solution   The boundary functions are the same as in the preceding example, but on this interval the graph of g is above the graph of f. Therefore the height of the rectangle in this example is $(g - f)(x)$.

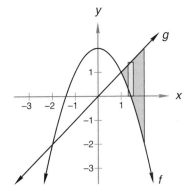

$$\text{Area} = \int_{1}^{2} [(g - f)(x)] \, dx = \int_{1}^{2} [x - (2 - x^2)] \, dx = \int_{1}^{2} (x - 2 + x^2) \, dx$$

$$= \left[\frac{x^2}{2} - 2x + \frac{x^3}{3} \right]_{1}^{2} = \left(\frac{4}{2} - 4 + \frac{8}{3} \right) - \left(\frac{1}{2} - 2 + \frac{1}{3} \right) = \frac{11}{6} \text{ units}^2$$

example 60.4   Find the area of the region bounded by the graphs of $y = x^2$ and $y = 2x^2 - 4$.

solution   On the left-hand side we factor to find the x-coordinates of the points of intersection, and on the right-hand side we show the graphs of the functions and a representative rectangle.

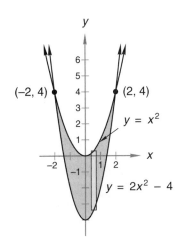

$$x^2 = 2x^2 - 4$$
$$0 = x^2 - 4$$
$$0 = (x + 2)(x - 2)$$
$$x = -2 \quad \text{or} \quad x = 2$$

The width of the representative rectangle is Δx. The height of the representative rectangle is $(x^2) - (2x^2 - 4)$, or $-x^2 + 4$, and the limits of integration are $x = -2$ and $x = +2$.

$$\text{Area} = \int_{-2}^{2} (-x^2 + 4) \, dx = \left[-\frac{x^3}{3} + 4x \right]_{-2}^{2} = \frac{16}{3} - \left(-\frac{16}{3} \right) = \frac{32}{3} \text{ units}^2$$

60.B

area between curves using a graphing calculator

One of the greatest advantages of using a graphing calculator in calculus is the ability to produce the graphs of complicated functions quickly. We demonstrate this here.

example 60.5   Using a graphing calculator, determine the area of the region bounded by the graphs of $y = x^5 - 4x^2 + 1$ and $y = 2x^2 - 4$.

solution   We start by drawing the graphs of these two functions in $\mathtt{ZStandard}$ mode.

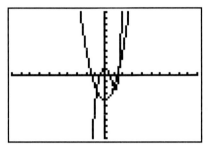

At this point it is difficult to see the shape of the boundary, so we restrict the window to the intervals $-5 \le x \le 5$, $-5 \le y \le 5$ for a better view.

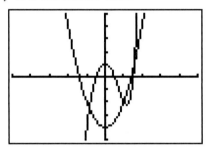

This graph clearly shows that there are two regions. This would have been quite a challenge to show by hand. We need to find the three points of intersection that serve as our limits of integration. Using Option 5 in the $\mathtt{CALCULATE}$ menu, these points are found to occur at the following values of x:

$$x = -0.8669984 \qquad x = 1 \qquad x = 1.5905002$$

Now we set up two definite integrals. For the larger region, the integral is

$$\int_{-0.8669984}^{1} \left[(x^5 - 4x^2) + 1 - (2x^2 - 4) \right] dx$$

since the polynomial of degree 5 is above the binomial. The area of the smaller region is given by

$$\int_{1}^{1.5905002} \left[(2x^2 - 4) - (x^5 - 4x^2 + 1) \right] dx$$

The total area is the sum of these two integrals. We enter

$$\mathtt{fnInt(X^5-4X^2+1-(2X^2-4),X,-0.8669984,1)}$$
$$\mathtt{+fnInt(2X^2-4-(X^5-4X^2+1),X,1,1.5905002)}$$

which yields **6.6905 units^2** as the approximate answer.

problem set 60

1. Find the dimensions of the closed rectangular box that has a square base, has a volume of
   (52) 1000 cubic inches, and requires the least amount of material to construct. (Assume the surface area of the box is a measure of the material used.)

   (a) Solve this problem with a graphing calculator. Begin by expressing the surface area of the box as a function of the single variable x, and then graph the function in an appropriate window.

   (b) Solve this problem again using calculus.

2. Find the Maclaurin series for $y = e^x$, and write the answer in summation notation.
(55)

3. Find the Maclaurin series for $y = \ln (1 - x)$, and write the answer in summation notation.
(55)

4. The position of a particle moving along a straight line is given by $s(t) = e^t \sin t$. Find the
(54) velocity of the particle when $t = \pi$.

Integrate in problems 5–7.

5. $\int \sin^3 (2x) \cos (2x)\, dx$
(56)

6. $\int \dfrac{\sin x}{\sqrt{1 + \cos x}}\, dx$
(56)

7. $\int \dfrac{x^2 + x + 2}{x}\, dx$
(38)

8. Find the area of the region completely enclosed by the graphs of $y = x^2 - 1$ and
(60) $y = -x^2 + 1$.

9. Find the area of the region bounded by the graphs of $y = e^x$, $y = x$, $x = -1$, and $x = 2$.
(60)

10. Find the area of the region completely enclosed by the graph of $y = (x - 1)(x + 2)^2$ and
(59) the x-axis.

11. Use a graphing calculator to find the area of the region between the graphs of
(60) $y = 2^x$ and $y = -2^{-x}$ on the interval $[-3, 3]$.

12. The following graph represents the
(59) continuous function $y = f(x)$. A, B, and C represent the areas of the enclosed regions. $\int_a^d f(x)\, dx$ is equal to which of the following?

A. $A + B - C$

B. $B - (A - C)$

C. $A - B + C$

D. $B - (A + C)$

E. $A + B + C$

13. Find $f^{-1}(2)$ where $f(x) = 2 \ln x$.
(58)

14. Write the explicit inverse equation of $y = \sin x$ for $-\dfrac{\pi}{2} \le x \le \dfrac{\pi}{2}$.
(58)

Differentiate with respect to x in problems 15–17.

15. $y = e^{(\ln 2)(x^2 + 1)}$
(50)

16. $y = \dfrac{\ln |\sin x|}{x^2 - 1}$
(50)

17. $y = e^{x^2 + 2x}(\cot x)^2$
(50)

18. Evaluate $\dfrac{d^2 y}{dx^2}$ at $x = 1$ for $y = x \ln x - x$.
(27)

19. Find the slope of the line tangent to the ellipse $\dfrac{x^2}{4} + \dfrac{y^2}{9} = 1$ at the point $\left(\sqrt{3}, \dfrac{3}{2} \right)$.
(34)

20. Shown is the graph of f. At which point(s) are both $\dfrac{df}{dx}$ and $\dfrac{d^2 f}{dx^2}$ positive?
(49)

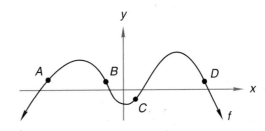

21. Suppose $f(x) = [x]$. Sketch the graph of $y = f(x - 2) + 1$.
(9,21)

22. Simplify: $(\tan -\theta)(\cos -\theta)\left[\sec\left(\dfrac{\pi}{2} - \theta\right)\right]$
(8)

23. Determine the amplitude, phase angle, and period of the function whose equation is
(7) $y = 3 + 2\sin(3x - 45°)$.

24. (a) Solve the equation $\dfrac{10^x - 10^{-x}}{2} = 8$ with the graphing calculator. Begin by graphing the
(2,16)   functions $y = \dfrac{10^x - 10^{-x}}{2}$ and $y = 8$. Find the x-coordinate of their point of intersection.

    (b) Solve the equation $\dfrac{10^x - 10^{-x}}{2} = 8$ again using algebraic methods. Find an exact answer and
        then convert your answer to a decimal number. Check your solution by comparing it to your
        answer to (a). (*Hint:* You can solve this equation by first multiplying it by 10^x and
        rewriting it as a quadratic equation in terms of 10^x. Then the quadratic formula can be
        used—but it will solve for 10^x, not x. So do not forget to solve for x.)

25. Find the angle at which the curves $y = x^3$ and $y = \sqrt{x}$ intersect. (*Hint:* See problem 24 in
(13,27) Problem Set 59.)

LESSON 61 *Playing Games with f, f', and f"*

Problems that permit us to explore the relationships between a function and the first and second
derivatives of the function are designed to enhance our understanding of these relationships. These
problems allow us to play games with concepts. In this lesson we look at problems that let us consider
information about f, f', and f''.

We can determine the constants in the linear equation

$$y = mx + b$$

if we know two points on the line. If the line passes through $(1, 2)$ and $(5, 6)$, we can write

$$\begin{cases} 2 = m(1) + b \\ 6 = m(5) + b \end{cases}$$

and solve this system for m and b.

If we have the equation of a quadratic function

$$y = ax^2 + bx + c$$

three independent equations are needed to find a, b, and c. In the case of a general cubic with four
terms, four pieces of information are needed to solve for the four constants. In general, we need as
many independent pieces of information as we have coefficients in the equation.

example 61.1   Given that $f(x) = ax^3 + b$, that the graph of f passes through $(2, 25)$, and that $f'(3) = 81$, find
a and b.

solution   We get one equation from the fact that $f(2) = 25$.

$$25 = a(2)^3 + b$$
$$25 = 8a + b$$

The second equation comes from the fact that $f'(3) = 81$.

$$f'(x) = 3ax^2$$
$$f'(3) = 3a(3)^2$$
$$81 = 27a$$
$$a = 3$$

Now we replace a with 3 in the first equation and solve for b.

$$25 = 8(3) + b$$
$$b = 1$$

Thus the equation of f is $f(x) = 3x^3 + 1$.

example 61.2   The function f is a real quadratic function whose graph passes through $(2, 9)$ and $(0, 1)$, and the slope of its graph is 6 at $x = 2$. Find the equation of f.

solution   The equation is of the form $f(x) = ax^2 + bx + c$, so we need three independent equations to solve for a, b, and c. The first two equations come from the fact that $(2, 9)$ and $(0, 1)$ are on the graph of f.

$$9 = a(2)^2 + b(2) + c \quad\longrightarrow\quad 9 = 4a + 2b + c \qquad (1)$$
$$1 = a(0)^2 + b(0) + c \quad\longrightarrow\quad 1 = c \qquad (2)$$

The third equation comes from the fact that $f'(2) = 6$.

$$f'(x) = 2ax + b$$
$$6 = 2a(2) + b$$
$$6 = 4a + b \qquad (3)$$

By combining equations (1) and (2) and copying equation (3), we get the following linear system.

$$\begin{array}{ll} \text{(1) and (2)} & \left\{ 8 = 4a + 2b \right. \\ \text{(3)} & \left. 6 = 4a + b \right. \end{array}$$

We have already used the fact that $c = 1$. Solving this system shows that $a = 1$ and $b = 2$. Thus, the equation we want is

$$f(x) = x^2 + 2x + 1$$

example 61.3   If $f''(x) = 10$, $f'(0) = 2$, and $f(0) = 3$, what is the equation of f?

solution   The equation of f'' is $f''(x) = 10$, which is a constant function. We integrate f'' to get f'.

$$f'(x) = \int f''(x)\,dx = \int 10\,dx = 10x + C_1$$

It is given that $f'(0) = 2$, so we can substitute and solve for C_1.

$$\begin{array}{ll} f'(x) = 10x + C_1 & \text{general equation of } f' \\ 2 = 10(0) + C_1 & \text{substituted} \\ 2 = C_1 & \text{solved} \end{array}$$

Now that we have $f'(x) = 10x + 2$, we can integrate $f'(x)$ to get $f(x)$.

$$f(x) = \int f'(x)\,dx = \int (10x + 2)\,dx = 5x^2 + 2x + C_2$$

It is given that $f(0) = 3$, so we can substitute and solve for C_2.

$$\begin{array}{ll} f(x) = 5x^2 + 2x + C_2 & \text{general equation of } f \\ 3 = 5(0)^2 + 2(0) + C_2 & \text{substituted} \\ 3 = C_2 & \text{solved} \end{array}$$

Now we can write the equation for f.

$$f(x) = 5x^2 + 2x + 3$$

problem set
61

1. Find the largest area possible for a right triangle whose hypotenuse is 5 inches long.
(52)

    (a) Solve this problem with a graphing calculator. Begin by writing an equation for the area of the triangle as a function of x, the length of one leg of the triangle. Then graph the equation in an appropriate window and find the maximum.

    (b) Solve this problem again using calculus.

2. Write the Maclaurin series for $y = e^x$ (from memory if possible).
(55)

3. (a) Find the Maclaurin series for $y = e^{-x}$.
(55)

    (b) Substitute $-x$ for x in the Maclaurin series found in problem 2. Compare this result with the answer to (a).

4. A hemispherical bowl has a diameter of 14 inches. If water is poured into the bowl at a rate of 1 cubic inch per second, how fast is the water level rising when the water is 4 inches deep? The formula for the liquid volume of a hemisphere of radius r filled to a height h is $V = \pi r h^2 - \frac{1}{3}\pi h^3$. (*Hint:* r is the radius of the bowl, which is a constant.)
(47)

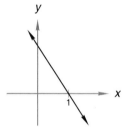

5. The equation of f is $f(x) = ax^3 + b$. The graph of f passes through the point $(1, 5)$ and $f'(2) = 12$. Find a and b.
(61)

6. If f is a real quadratic function whose graph passes through the points $(1, 5)$ and $(-1, -1)$ and if the slope of its graph is 5 at $x = 1$, then what is the equation of f?
(61)

7. Shown is the graph of f''. Sketch a possible graph of f.
(45)

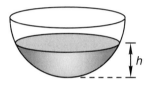

8. If $f''(x) = 6$ and $f'(1) = f(1) = 4$, what is the equation of f?
(61)

Integrate in problems 9–11.

9. $\displaystyle\int \sin(3x)\,dx$
(56)

10. $\displaystyle\int \frac{\cos x}{\sin^2 x}\,dx$
(56)

11. $\displaystyle\int \frac{1}{e^x}\,dx$
(56)

12. Find the area of the region in the first quadrant bounded by the x-axis and the graph of the equation $y = x\sqrt{9 - x^2}$.
(59)

13. Approximate the area bounded by the graph of $f(x) = e^{-x^2}$ and the x-axis over the interval $[-2, 2]$.
(59)

14. Find the area under one arch of the graph of $y = 2\sin(3x)$.
(59)

15. Find the area of the region in the first quadrant that is completely enclosed by the graphs of $y = x^3 + 3$ and $y = x + 3$.
(60)

16. Find k such that $\displaystyle\int_{-2}^{2} (4x^3 + k)\,dx = 15$.
(47)

17. Let k be the number such that the area between $y = \frac{1}{x}$ and the x-axis from $x = 1$ to $x = k$
(47) equals 2. What is k?

18. Suppose $f(x)$ is a polynomial such that $f''(3) = 4$ and $f'(3) = 0$. Sketch the graph of f for
(61) input values near $x = 3$.

19. The graph of f'' is a horizontal line below the x-axis. Describe the graph of f.
(45)

20. Sketch the graph of $y = \dfrac{(x - 2)(x + 1)(x - 1)}{x(x - 3)(x - 1)(x + 2)}$.
(28)

21. Use the definition of the derivative to find f' where $f(x) = \dfrac{1}{x}$.
(19)

22. Differentiate $y = \dfrac{1}{\sqrt{x^3 + x + 1}} + e^{4x - 3} \tan(\pi x)$ with respect to x.
(50)

23. What is the implied domain of the function $y = \arcsin x$?
(13)

24. Suppose f is a function that is defined only on $[1, 3]$. On what interval is g defined if
(21) $g(x) = f(x - 2)$?

25. Find the value of m such that the line $y = mx$ is tangent to the graph of $y = \ln x$.
(26,27)

LESSON 62   *Work, Distance, and Rates*

When a uniform force moves an object in the direction of the force, the **mechanical work** done is force times distance.

> Mechanical work = force × distance

Often in today's science books, distances are given in meters and forces in newtons. If a block that weighs 3 newtons is moved vertically upward a distance of 4 meters, 12 newton-meters of work is done.

$$4 \text{ newtons} \times 3 \text{ meters} = 12 \text{ newton-meters}$$

A newton-meter is called a **joule.** The work done is represented by the area of the rectangle on the left-hand side below, where F is the force in newtons and x is the distance in meters. In this figure the mathematical area, 12, represents the work done, 12 joules.

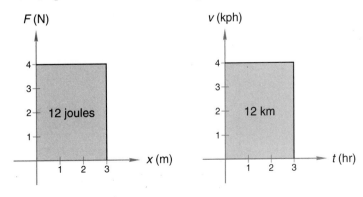

If someone walks at 4 kilometers per hour for 3 hours, the distance traveled is 12 kilometers.

$$\frac{4 \text{ km}}{1 \text{ hr}} \times 3 \text{ hr} = 12 \text{ km}$$

This distance can be represented by the area of the rectangle on the right-hand side above, where v is velocity in kilometers per hour and t is the time in hours. In this figure the mathematical area, 12, represents the distance traveled, 12 kilometers.

The units for any rectangular area equal the product of the units used for the horizontal measurement and the units used for the vertical measurement, as the previous graphs demonstrate. Since we have carefully defined area beneath a curve to be the limit of a sum of rectangles, the units for any area under a curve also equal the product of the horizontal units and the vertical units.

example 62.1   A steady force of 50 newtons (N) is applied to an object to move it 100 meters (m) in the direction of the force. What is the work done by the force?

solution   The area under the curve is the integral of the constant force times the distance.

$$\text{Work} = \int_0^{100} 50 \, dx$$
$$= [50x]_0^{100}$$
$$= \textbf{5000 joules}$$

example 62.2   A variable force $F = \frac{1}{2}x^2$ newtons is applied to an object to move it 6 meters in the direction of the force from $x = 0$ to $x = 6$. What is the work done by the force?

solution   The work done equals the area under the graph of $F = \frac{1}{2}x^2$ newtons between the x-values of 0 and 6 meters.

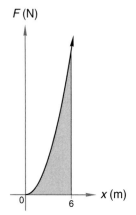

$$\text{Work} = \int_0^6 \frac{1}{2}x^2 \, dx$$
$$= \frac{1}{2} \int_0^6 x^2 \, dx$$
$$= \frac{1}{2}\left[\frac{x^3}{3} \right]_0^6$$
$$= \frac{1}{2}\left(\frac{6^3}{3} - \frac{0}{3} \right) = \textbf{36 joules}$$

example 62.3   In example 62.2 how much work was done by the force in moving the object from the 4-meter mark to the 6-meter mark?

solution   The work done equals the area under the curve of $F = \frac{1}{2}x^2$ newtons between the x-values of 4 and 6 meters.

$$\text{Work} = \int_4^6 \frac{1}{2}x^2 \, dx$$
$$= \frac{1}{2}\left[\frac{x^3}{3} \right]_4^6$$
$$= \frac{1}{2}\left(\frac{6^3}{3} - \frac{4^3}{3} \right)$$
$$= \frac{1}{2}\left(72 - \frac{64}{3} \right) = \frac{76}{3} \text{ joules}$$

example 62.4   Hooke's law for perfectly elastic springs says that the force on a spring is proportional to the displacement of the spring from the position of rest, or $F = kx$. The constant k is called the **spring constant**, and x represents the displacement of the spring. If the spring constant for a spring is $\frac{1}{2}$ newton per meter, how much work is done in stretching the spring from 3 meters to 4 meters?

solution   On the left-hand side we show the spring, and on the right-hand side we show the graph of the force F versus the distance x that the spring has been stretched.

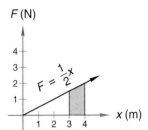

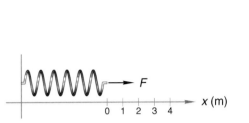

The work done in stretching the spring from its rest position to $x = 4$ equals the area under the graph from $x = 0$ to $x = 4$. The work done between x-values of 3 and 4 is the area under the graph between $x = 3$ and $x = 4$.

$$\text{Work}\Big|_3^4 = \int_3^4 \frac{1}{2}x\,dx = \left[\frac{x^2}{4}\right]_3^4 = \frac{16 - 9}{4} = \frac{7}{4}\ \textbf{joules}$$

example 62.5   Shanna calculated that the velocity of an object would equal $\frac{1}{2}t^2 + t$ meters per second, where t represents elapsed time (in seconds). How far would the object travel between the fifth and the seventh second?

solution   The distance traveled equals the area under the graph of $v = \dfrac{1}{2}t^2 + t$ between $t = 5$ and $t = 7$.

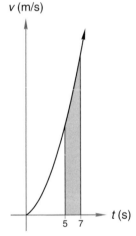

$$\begin{aligned}
\text{Distance} &= \int_5^7 \left(\frac{t^2}{2} + t\right) dt \\
&= \left[\frac{t^3}{6} + \frac{t^2}{2}\right]_5^7 \\
&= \left(\frac{7^3}{6} + \frac{7^2}{2}\right) - \left(\frac{5^3}{6} + \frac{5^2}{2}\right) \\
&= \frac{145}{3}\ \textbf{meters}
\end{aligned}$$

The definite integral represents accumulation of some known quantity, as in the previous examples. In the case of distance accumulation,

$$\int_a^b v(t)\,dt$$

represents the sum of infinitely many quantities of the form velocity × time. This idea of integration as accumulation can be used to solve various problems involving rates and accumulated quantities.

example 62.6   Water leaked from a tank at a rate of $R(t) = e^{-t}$ gallons per hour. How much water leaked from the tank during the first 10 hours?

solution   If the rate was constant, say 7 gallons per hour, then the answer would simply be a product.

$$7\,\frac{\text{gallons}}{\text{hour}} \times 10\ \text{hours} = 70\ \text{gallons}$$

Here the rate of leakage varied with time, so we must consider summing many smaller quantities of the form

$$\text{rate} \times \text{time}$$

This is accomplished with the integral. The total amount that leaked during the first 10 hours is given by

$$\int_0^{10} e^{-t} \, dt = -e^{-t}\Big|_0^{10} = -e^{-10} + e^0$$
$$= -e^{-10} + 1$$

The number $-e^{-10}$ is extremely small. Therefore we say that approximately **1 gallon** of water leaked from the tank during the first 10 hours.

problem set 62

1. Find the area of the largest rectangle with horizontal and vertical sides that can be inscribed in the region bounded by the x-axis and the graph of $y = 12 - x^2$. Begin by drawing a rectangle inscribed in the region bounded by the x-axis and the graph of $y = 12 - x^2$. Write an equation for the area of the rectangle in terms of x, where x represents the distance from the origin to the lower left-hand corner of the rectangle.
(52)

  (a) Solve this problem with a graphing calculator.

  (b) Solve this problem again using calculus.

2. Find the Maclaurin series for $y = \dfrac{1}{1 + x}$.
(55)

3. (a) Find the Maclaurin series for $y = \dfrac{1}{1 - x}$.
(55)

  (b) Substitute $-x$ for x in the Maclaurin series found in problem 2. Compare this with the answer to (a).

4. A steady force of 20 newtons is applied to an object to move it 30 meters in the direction of the force. What is the work done by the force?
(62)

5. A variable force of $F(x) = \frac{1}{2}x^3 + x$ newtons is applied to an object to move it in the direction of the force from $x = 0$ to $x = 3$ meters. Find the work done by the force.
(62)

6. The spring constant for a spring is 3 newtons per meter. How much work is done in stretching the spring from 2 to 4 meters?
(62)

7. Gold is being mined at a rate of $R(t) = 7t^{-1}$ ounces per hour. How much gold is removed between the third hour and the sixth hour of operation?
(38,62)

8. Suppose $f(x) = ax^2 + bx$. Find a and b such that the graph of f passes through $(1, 2)$ and $f'(2) = -1$.
(61)

9. Suppose f is a function whose slope at any point is twice its x-coordinate. If the graph of f passes through $(2, 5)$, what is the equation of f?
(61)

Integrate in problems 10–13.

10. $\displaystyle \int \cos\left(2x - \frac{\pi}{2}\right) dx$
(56)

11. $\displaystyle \int \frac{2x^2 - 3x + 4}{\sqrt{x}} \, dx$
(38)

12. $\displaystyle \int \cos t \sqrt{\sin t} \, dt$
(51)

13. $\displaystyle \int \tan^3 x \sec^2 x \, dx$
(51)

14. Find the area of the region enclosed by the graphs of $y = 2 - x^2$ and $y = -x$.
(60)

15. Find the area between the graph of $y = x(x - 2)$ and the x-axis on the interval $[-1, 2]$.
(59)

16. Let f be a continuous function on $(-\infty, \infty)$. In (a) and (b), find the values of a and b that make
(57) each equation true.

(a) $\displaystyle\int_1^2 f(x)\, dx \;+\; \int_2^3 f(x)\, dx \;=\; \int_a^b f(x)\, dx$

(b) $\displaystyle\int_0^3 f(x)\, dx \;+\; \int_a^b f(x)\, dx \;=\; \int_0^5 f(x)\, dx$

17. Suppose $f(x) = x^3 + x$. Write an implicit equation for f^{-1}.
(58)

18. Suppose $f(x) = \ln x$. Find $f^{-1}(1)$.
(58)

19. A ball is thrown straight up from ground level. Its height above the ground in feet at time t is
(54) given by $h(t) = 200t - 16t^2$. How high will the ball go?

20. Differentiate $y = \dfrac{e^{\sin x}}{\sqrt{2x - 1}} + \ln (2x)$ with respect to x.
(50)

21. Find $\dfrac{d^2y}{dx^2}$ where $y = 2e^{\sin x}$.
(50)

22. The function $f(x) = \ln (\cos x)$ is defined for all x in which of the following intervals?
(6)

A. $-\dfrac{\pi}{2} \le x \le \dfrac{\pi}{2}$ B. $0 < x < \pi$

C. $0 \le x \le \pi$ D. $-\dfrac{\pi}{2} < x < \dfrac{\pi}{2}$

23. A trough 4 feet long has ends that are
(8) equilateral triangles. Find the volume of
water in the trough when the water is
h feet deep.

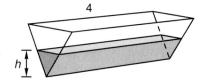

24. Suppose $f(x) = \ln x$ and $(f \circ g)(x) = \ln \sqrt{x^2 + 1}$. Find g.
(18)

25. (a) Solve the equation $\dfrac{e^x - e^{-x}}{2} = 7$ with a graphing calculator. Begin by graphing the
(2,16)   functions $y = \dfrac{e^x - e^{-x}}{2}$ and $y = 7$. Then find the x-coordinate of their point of
intersection.

     (b) Solve the equation $\dfrac{e^x - e^{-x}}{2} = 7$ again using algebraic methods. Find an exact answer and
then convert the answer to a decimal number. (*Hint:* See problem 24 in Problem Set 60.)

LESSON 63 *Critical Number (Closed Interval) Theorem*

The **maximum-minimum value existence theorem** says that a continuous function must have both a maximum value and a minimum value on any closed interval.

> MAXIMUM-MINIMUM VALUE EXISTENCE THEOREM
>
> If f is continuous on the closed interval $I = [a, b]$, then f attains a maximum value M and a minimum value m on I.

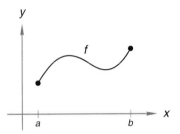

This statement is intuitively obvious, but the proof of the theorem is beyond the scope of an elementary calculus book. This theorem indicates that the maximum and minimum values of a function exist but gives no clue as to how to find them. The clue we need comes from the **critical number theorem** (sometimes called the **closed interval theorem**), which we state below but do not prove. The critical number theorem says that the maximum value and the minimum value must occur either at an endpoint of the domain or at a critical number, which is a value of x for which the derivative does not exist (the graph of the function comes to a corner) or a value of x for which the derivative equals zero (the slope of the graph is horizontal).

> CRITICAL NUMBER THEOREM
>
> If f is a continuous function on a closed interval I and if f attains a maximum or minimum value at $x = c$, where $c \in I$, then either
>
> 1. c is an endpoint,
> 2. $f'(c)$ does not exist, or
> 3. $f'(c) = 0$.

In the applied problems that we have worked thus far, the maximum and minimum values have occurred at values of x for which the derivative equals zero (stationary numbers). It is difficult to find applied problems for which a maximum or minimum value occurs at an endpoint (endpoint numbers). Since absolute value functions do not have a derivative at the values of x where a cusp occurs on the graph (singular points), these functions are often used as examples of functions that have critical points at which $f'(x)$ does not exist. Other continuous functions that do not have derivatives at some values of x are odd roots of even powers of x, such as $y = x^{2/3}$ and $y = x^{4/5}$. To get still more examples, we can devise continuous piecewise functions that do not have derivatives at one or more values of x.

example 63.1   Find the maximum and minimum values of $f(x) = 2x^3 - 3x^2 - 12x + 1$ on the interval $[-2, 4]$.

solution Since this function is continuous on [–2, 4], the maximum-minimum value existence theorem guarantees that f attains a maximum value and a minimum value on [–2, 4]. The closed interval theorem says these maximum and minimum values must occur at critical numbers or endpoints.

We begin by making a list of all the critical numbers. Since a polynomial function has a derivative at every value of x, there are no critical numbers at which the derivative does not exist. It has critical numbers only when $f'(x) = 0$.

$$f'(x) = 6x^2 - 6x - 12$$
$$0 = 6x^2 - 6x - 12$$
$$0 = 6(x - 2)(x + 1)$$

We see that $f'(x) = 0$ at $x = 2$ and $x = -1$. Thus, on the interval [–2, 4], the critical numbers are $x = 2$ and $x = -1$. **The closed interval test consists of finding the values of $f(x)$ for all critical numbers and endpoints then comparing these values.**

$$f(-2) = -3 \qquad f(-1) = 8 \qquad f(2) = -19 \qquad f(4) = 33$$

This test reveals that f attains a **maximum value of 33** at $x = 4$ and a **minimum value of –19** at $x = 2$ on the closed interval [–2, 4].

example 63.2 A 10-inch-long string is to be cut into two pieces. One of the pieces will be bent to form a square, and the other piece will be formed into a circle. Find where the string should be cut to maximize the combined area of the circle and the square.

solution We begin by drawing a picture of the problem and labeling the length of the segment used to form the circle x.

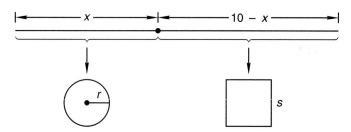

We see that $10 - x$ is the length of the segment used to form the square. Thus the perimeter of the square is $10 - x$, and the circumference of the circle is x. To find the areas, we need to solve for the radius of the circle r and the length of the side of the square s.

$$x = 2\pi r \qquad\qquad 4s = 10 - x$$
$$r = \frac{x}{2\pi} \qquad\qquad s = \frac{10 - x}{4}$$
$$\text{Area of circle} = \pi\left(\frac{x}{2\pi}\right)^2 \qquad \text{Area of square} = \left(\frac{10 - x}{4}\right)^2$$
$$\text{Total area} = A(x) = \pi\left(\frac{x}{2\pi}\right)^2 + \left(\frac{10 - x}{4}\right)^2$$

The graph of the function $A(x)$ is a parabola that opens upward and is chopped off at the endpoints. We do not show the graph, as the closed interval test does not require a graph. Note that the domain of A is the closed interval [0, 10] because x must be equal to or greater than zero and less than or equal to 10.

$$\text{Domain of } A = \{x \in \mathbb{R} \mid 0 \le x \le 10\}$$

(*Note:* If the "cut" occurs at $x = 0$ or $x = 10$, the string is not really cut. Instead it is used entirely to form either a square or a circle.) We now find all the critical numbers of A where $0 \leq x \leq 10$.

$$A(x) = \frac{1}{4\pi}x^2 + \frac{1}{16}x^2 - \frac{5}{4}x + \frac{25}{4} \qquad \text{function}$$

$$A'(x) = \left(\frac{1}{2\pi} + \frac{1}{8}\right)x - \frac{5}{4} \qquad \text{derivative}$$

$$0 = \left(\frac{1}{2\pi} + \frac{1}{8}\right)x - \frac{5}{4} \qquad \text{derivative set equal to 0}$$

$$\frac{5}{4} = \left(\frac{4 + \pi}{8\pi}\right)x \qquad \text{simplified}$$

$$\left(\frac{10\pi}{4 + \pi}\right) = x \qquad \text{solved}$$

$$x \approx 4.3990$$

Thus the critical number for A is $x \approx 4.3990$. By the closed interval theorem, $A(x)$ is maximized either at one of the endpoints or at this critical number.

$$A(0) = 6.25 \qquad A(4.3990) \approx 3.5006 \qquad A(10) \approx 7.9577$$

The value 7.9577 for $A(10)$ is greater than the other values, so the maximum area of 7.9577 in.^{2} is attained at $x = 10$. In this example the maximum value of the function occurs at an endpoint, not a critical number. **None of the string is used to form the square. The entire length of the string is used to form the circle.**

example 63.3 Find the maximum and minimum values of f on the interval $[-2, 3]$ where $f(x) = x^{2/3}$.

solution The maximum and minimum values must occur at critical numbers or endpoints. The critical numbers occur when $f'(x) = 0$ or where f' does not exist. Thus we begin by finding f'.

$$f'(x) = \frac{2}{3}x^{-1/3} = \frac{2}{3x^{1/3}}$$

This derivative can never equal zero, because the numerator can never equal zero. Thus there are no critical numbers caused by the derivative equaling zero. The derivative does not exist when $x = 0$, because $f'(0) = \frac{2}{0}$ is not defined. Thus $x = 0$ is a critical number caused by the failure of f' to exist. Therefore we compute the values of f at 0, -2, and 3.

$$f(0) = 0 \qquad f(-2) \approx 1.5874 \qquad f(3) \approx 2.0801$$

From this we see that the **minimum value of f on $[-2, 3]$ is 0** and the **maximum value of f on $[-2, 3]$ is approximately 2.0801.**

example 63.4 A function f is continuous on the closed interval $[-2, 4]$. Also, $f(-2) = 2$, $f(-1) = -1$, and $f(4) = 5$. Furthermore the functions f' and f'' have the properties indicated in the table below.

x	$-2 < x < -1$	$x = -1$	$-1 < x < 2$	$x = 2$	$2 < x < 4$
$f'(x)$	negative	undefined	positive	0	positive
$f''(x)$	negative	undefined	negative	0	positive

Find the values of x for which f attains absolute maximum and minimum values.

solution We use the information to make a rough sketch of the function.

The function is continuous on the interval $[-2, 4]$ and has critical numbers at $x = -1$ and $x = 2$. The function can only attain extreme values at critical numbers and endpoints. From the graph we see that f **attains an absolute minimum value at** $x = -1$ and an **absolute maximum value at** $x = 4$.

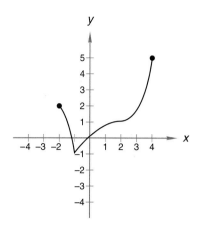

We also see that the graph of f has an inflection point at $x = 2$. Since we are able to sketch the function, we can obtain the maximum and minimum values from the graph. Note that we were able to find the x-values of the extrema in this problem even though we did not have the equation for f.

problem set 63

1.
(46)
A trough 4 feet long has ends that are equilateral triangles, as shown. If water is being poured into the trough at a rate of 1 ft^3/min, how fast is the water rising the instant the water is about to spill over the top?

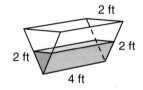

2.
(63)
Use calculus to find the maximum and minimum values of $f(x) = 2x^3 + 3x^2 - 12x + 1$ on the interval $[-3, 1]$. Check the answer with a graphing calculator.

3.
(63)
Find the maximum and minimum values of $f(x) = x^{2/3}$ on the interval $[-1, 8]$ by considering the graph of f.

4.
(63)
The function f is a continuous function on the closed interval $[-1, 4]$, and $f(-1) = 3$ and $f(4) = 6$. In addition, f, f', and f'' have the properties indicated in the table below. Sketch the graph of f, and find the locations on this interval where f attains its maximum and minimum values.

x	$-1 < x < 2$	$x = 2$	$2 < x < 4$
$f'(x)$	negative	undefined	positive
$f''(x)$	negative	undefined	negative

5.
(52)
A rectangle is inscribed in an isosceles right triangle whose hypotenuse is 6 centimeters long, as shown.

(a) Find the y-coordinate of the point (x, y) in terms of x.

(b) Express the area of the rectangle in terms of x.

(c) Find the maximum possible area of the rectangle.

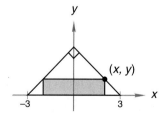

6.
(62)
A variable force of $F(x) = 2x$ newtons (x is measured in meters) is applied to an object. Find the work done in moving the object in the direction of the force from $x = 1$ meter to $x = 3$ meters.

7.
(62)
The velocity (in meters per second) of an object moving along a line is given by $v(t) = 3t^2 + 1$. Find the distance traveled by the object from $t = 0$ seconds to $t = 2$ seconds.

8. Suppose $f(x) = ae^x + b$. If $f'(0) = f(0) = 3$, what are the values of a and b?
(61)

9. For what values of x is the graph of $y = \ln x$ concave upward?
(49)

10. Evaluate: $\int_1^3 \dfrac{x^2 - 1}{x + 1}\, dx$
(38)

Integrate in problems 11–13.

11. $\int \cos(2x)\, e^{\sin(2x)}\, dx$ **12.** $\int e^{-2x}\, dx$ **13.** $\int \dfrac{3x^2 + 2x}{\sqrt{x^3 + x^2}}\, dx$
(56)   (56)   (51)

14. Find the area enclosed by the graph of $y = -x(x - 1)(x + 1)$ and the x-axis.
(59)

Let f be a continuous function on $(-\infty, \infty)$ in problems 15 and 16. Find the values of a and b that make each equation true.

15. $\int_{-1}^1 f(x)\, dx + \int_1^5 f(x)\, dx = \int_a^b f(x)\, dx$
(57)

16. $\int_a^b f(x)\, dx + \int_{-3}^1 f(x)\, dx = \int_{-5}^1 f(x)\, dx$
(57)

17. If $\int_a^b f(x)\, dx = -4$, what is $\int_b^a 2f(x)\, dx$?
(57)

Differentiate the functions in problems 18 and 19 with respect to x.

18. $y = e^{2x} \tan^2 x$ **19.** $y = \dfrac{\sqrt{x^2 + 1}}{x + \sin x}$
(50)   (50)

20. Which of the following statements is true about the function $f(x) = x \ln x$?
(45)
   A. f is decreasing for all positive real values of x.
   B. f is increasing for all positive real values of x.
   C. f is increasing only for all numbers greater than $\frac{1}{e}$.
   D. f is increasing only for all numbers greater than e.

21. Suppose $f(x) = \dfrac{1}{x - 1}$. Evaluate $\lim\limits_{x \to 1^+} f(x)$ and $\lim\limits_{x \to 1^-} f(x)$.
(17)

22. Evaluate: $\lim\limits_{x \to 2} \dfrac{\ln x - \ln 2}{x - 2}$
(44)

23. Suppose $\cos y$ is positive and $\dfrac{x}{a} = \sin y$. Express $\cos y$ in terms of x and a.
(4,58)

24. Find the angle at which the two curves $x^2 + y^2 = 1$ and $(x - 1)^2 + y^2 = 1$ intersect in the
(27,58) first quadrant. (*Hint:* See problem 24 in Problem Set 59.)

25. Economics textbooks often use p for the price of an item and Q for the quantity of items. In a
(63) free market, the number of items sold is price-sensitive. This means that if the price of the item
   is changed, the number of items sold changes. If 4000 items are sold when the price is $16, we
   could write

$$Q(16) = 4000$$

If each price increase of $1 causes the number sold to decrease by 200, we could write

$$Q(p) = 4000 - 200(p - 16)$$

The second term equals zero if $p = \$16$. If the price is $17 per item, the number sold would be

$$Q(17) = 4000 - 200(17 - 16) = 3800$$

The total revenue R would be the number sold, $Q(p)$, times p, the price per item.

$$R(p) = pQ(p) = p[4000 - 200(p - 16)] \qquad \text{revenue}$$
$$R(p) = -200p^2 + 7200p \qquad \text{simplified}$$

Thus the total revenue $R(p)$ is a quadratic function of the price of the item.

Suppose that 10,000 items are sold when the price is \$20 per item and that the number of items sold decreases by 50 for each \$1 increase in unit price. Write an equation that expresses revenue as a function of the price per item.

LESSON 64   *Derivatives of Inverse Trigonometric Functions • What to Memorize*

64.A
derivatives of inverse trigonometric functions

Derivatives of inverse trigonometric functions are studied because of their usefulness in antidifferentiation. The integrands in

$$\int \frac{-2x}{\sqrt{a^2 - x^2}} \, dx \qquad \text{and} \qquad \int \frac{2x}{a^2 + x^2} \, dx$$

can be written in the forms $u^n \, du$ and $\ln u \, du$ respectively (assuming a is an unspecified constant). These are forms we can integrate. Although the integrals

$$\int \frac{dx}{\sqrt{a^2 - x^2}}, \qquad \int \frac{dx}{a^2 + x^2}, \qquad \text{and} \qquad \int \frac{dx}{x\sqrt{x^2 - a^2}}$$

have a similar appearance, they cannot be converted to any familiar form. To integrate these, we must know the differentials (or derivatives) of inverse trigonometric functions. These differentials are shown below.

$$d \sin^{-1} \frac{x}{a} = \frac{dx}{\sqrt{a^2 - x^2}} \qquad\qquad d \cos^{-1} \frac{x}{a} = \frac{-dx}{\sqrt{a^2 - x^2}}$$

$$d \tan^{-1} \frac{x}{a} = \frac{a \, dx}{a^2 + x^2} \qquad\qquad d \cot^{-1} \frac{x}{a} = \frac{-a \, dx}{a^2 + x^2}$$

$$d \sec^{-1} \frac{x}{a} = \frac{a \, dx}{x\sqrt{x^2 - a^2}} \qquad\qquad d \csc^{-1} \frac{x}{a} = \frac{-a \, dx}{x\sqrt{x^2 - a^2}}$$

It is poor practice to memorize things that can be developed quickly and accurately. These differentials fall into that category.

example 64.1   Let $y = \arcsin \dfrac{x}{a}$. Find y'.

solution   We begin by writing the implicit form of this equation and drawing the triangle it defines.

EXPLICIT FORM	IMPLICIT FORM
$y = \arcsin \dfrac{x}{a}$	$\sin y = \dfrac{x}{a}$

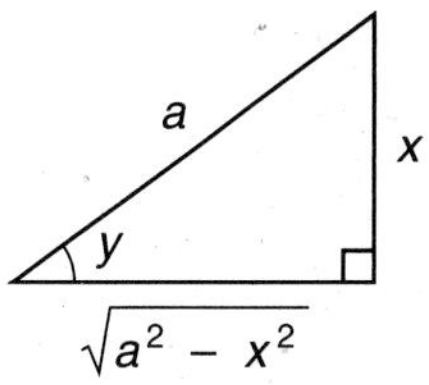

The triangle allows us to write all six trigonometric functions of y by inspection.

$$\sin y = \frac{x}{a} \qquad \cos y = \frac{\sqrt{a^2 - x^2}}{a} \qquad \tan y = \frac{x}{\sqrt{a^2 - x^2}}$$

$$\csc y = \frac{a}{x} \qquad \sec y = \frac{a}{\sqrt{a^2 - x^2}} \qquad \cot y = \frac{\sqrt{a^2 - x^2}}{x}$$

To find y', we take the differential of both sides of the implicit form, divide by dx, and solve for $\frac{dy}{dx}$.

$$y = \arcsin \frac{x}{a} \qquad\qquad \text{equation}$$

$$\sin y = \frac{x}{a} \qquad\qquad \text{implicit form}$$

$$\cos y \, dy = \frac{dx}{a} \qquad\qquad \text{differential}$$

$$\cos y \frac{dy}{dx} = \frac{1}{a} \qquad\qquad \text{divided by } dx$$

$$\frac{dy}{dx} = \frac{1}{a}\left(\frac{1}{\cos y}\right) \qquad\qquad \text{solved for } \frac{dy}{dx}$$

From the triangle we see that

$$\cos y = \frac{\sqrt{a^2 - x^2}}{a} \qquad \text{and} \qquad \frac{1}{\cos y} = \frac{a}{\sqrt{a^2 - x^2}}$$

Substituting for $\dfrac{1}{\cos y}$ gives us

$$y' = \frac{dy}{dx} = \frac{1}{a}\left(\frac{a}{\sqrt{a^2 - x^2}}\right) = \frac{\mathbf{1}}{\sqrt{\mathbf{a^2 - x^2}}}$$

example 64.2   Let $y = \arccos \dfrac{x}{a}$. Find $\dfrac{dy}{dx}$.

solution   We write the implicit form of the equation and draw the triangle it defines.

$$\cos y = \frac{x}{a}$$

We take the differential of both sides of the implicit form, divide by dx, solve for $\frac{dy}{dx}$, and use the triangle to substitute as necessary.

$$-\sin y \, dy = \frac{dx}{a} \qquad\qquad \text{differential}$$

$$-\sin y \frac{dy}{dx} = \frac{1}{a} \qquad\qquad \text{divided by } dx$$

$$\frac{dy}{dx} = \frac{1}{a}\left(-\frac{1}{\sin y}\right) \qquad\qquad \text{solved}$$

$$\frac{dy}{dx} = \frac{1}{a}\left(-\frac{a}{\sqrt{a^2 - x^2}}\right) \qquad\qquad \text{substituted}$$

$$\frac{dy}{dx} = -\frac{\mathbf{1}}{\sqrt{\mathbf{a^2 - x^2}}} \qquad\qquad \text{simplified}$$

Note that the derivative of $\arccos \dfrac{x}{a}$ is the negative of the derivative of $\arcsin \dfrac{x}{a}$.

example 64.3   Let $y = \tan^{-1} \dfrac{x}{a}$. Find y'.

solution   We write the implicit form and draw the triangle.

$$\tan y = \frac{x}{a}$$

Now we find the differential, divide, and solve for $\dfrac{dy}{dx}$.

$$\sec^2 y \; dy = \frac{dx}{a} \quad \longrightarrow \quad \sec^2 y \frac{dy}{dx} = \frac{1}{a} \quad \longrightarrow \quad \frac{dy}{dx} = \frac{1}{a}\left(\frac{1}{\sec^2 y}\right) = \frac{1}{a}\cos^2 y$$

Going back to the triangle, we find an expression for $\cos^2 y$ and substitute.

$$y' = \frac{dy}{dx} = \frac{1}{a}\left(\frac{a}{\sqrt{x^2 + a^2}}\right)^2 = \frac{a}{x^2 + a^2}$$

In examples 64.1 and 64.2 we saw that the derivatives of $\sin^{-1}\frac{x}{a}$ and $\cos^{-1}\frac{x}{a}$ are multiplication opposites. By interchanging the sides a and x in the triangle, we can use the same procedure to show that the derivative of the inverse cotangent of $\frac{x}{a}$ is the negative of the derivative of the inverse tangent of $\frac{x}{a}$.

$$\frac{d}{dx}\cot^{-1}\frac{x}{a} = -\frac{a}{x^2 + a^2}$$

example 64.4   Let $y = \csc^{-1}\dfrac{x}{a}$ with $\dfrac{x}{a} > 0$. Find $\dfrac{dy}{dx}$.

solution   We write the implicit form and draw the triangle.

$$\csc y = \frac{x}{a}$$

Now we find the differentials, divide, and solve for $\dfrac{dy}{dx}$.

$$-\csc y \cot y \; dy = \frac{dx}{a} \qquad\qquad\qquad \text{differentials}$$

$$\csc y \cot y \frac{dy}{dx} = -\frac{1}{a} \qquad\qquad\qquad \text{divided by } -dx$$

$$\frac{dy}{dx} = \left(-\frac{1}{a}\right)\left(\frac{1}{\csc y \cot y}\right) = -\frac{1}{a}\sin y \tan y \qquad \text{solved}$$

The triangle gives expressions for $\sin y$ and $\tan y$.

$$\sin y = \frac{a}{x} \qquad \tan y = \frac{a}{\sqrt{x^2 - a^2}}$$

Now we make the final substitution.

$$\frac{dy}{dx} = \left(-\frac{1}{a}\right)\left(\frac{a}{x}\right)\left(\frac{a}{\sqrt{x^2 - a^2}}\right) = -\frac{a}{x\sqrt{x^2 - a^2}}$$

By interchanging the sides of the triangle, we can show that the derivative of the inverse secant of $\frac{x}{a}$ is the negative of the derivative of the inverse cosecant of $\frac{x}{a}$.

$$\frac{d}{dx}\sec^{-1}\frac{x}{a} = \frac{a}{x\sqrt{x^2 - a^2}}$$

In the statement of the problem, we noted that the value of x over a must be a positive number. If this restriction was not made, the derivative of the inverse secant and the inverse cosecant would contain absolute-value notations, as shown below.

$$\frac{d}{dx}\text{arcsec}\frac{x}{a} = -\frac{a}{|x|\sqrt{x^2 - a^2}} \qquad \frac{d}{dx}\text{arccsc}\frac{x}{a} = \frac{a}{|x|\sqrt{x^2 - a^2}}$$

The absolute-value notation is awkward and could lead to an ambiguous integration formula later. The restriction that x be greater than zero is not unreasonable, because applications of the inverse cosecant (or inverse secant) almost always have values of x that are positive numbers.

64.B

what to memorize

In Lesson 48 we developed the derivatives of tan x, cot x, sec x, and csc x. In the problem sets since that lesson it has been convenient to have these derivatives memorized. In this lesson we have demonstrated that the derivatives of inverse trigonometric functions can be developed easily by drawing the triangles and finding the differentials of the implicit forms of the inverse functions. The derivatives of the inverses of the cosine, secant, cotangent, and cosecant functions are rarely encountered. The derivatives of the inverse sine and inverse tangent appear much more frequently, and it is a good idea to include these derivatives with the list of derivatives in Lesson 48 that should be memorized.

$$\frac{d}{dx}\sin^{-1}\frac{u}{a} = \frac{1}{\sqrt{a^2 - u^2}}\frac{du}{dx} \qquad \frac{d}{dx}\tan^{-1}\frac{u}{a} = \frac{a}{u^2 + a^2}\frac{du}{dx}$$

example 64.5   If $y = \tan^{-1}(\cos x)$, what is $\frac{dy}{dx}$?

solution   This problem requires the chain rule. If ( ) is a function of x, then

$$\frac{d}{dx}\tan^{-1}(\ ) = \frac{1}{(\ )^2 + 1^2}\frac{d}{dx}(\ )$$

We replace ( ) with cos x and finish the problem.

$$\frac{dy}{dx} = \frac{d}{dx}\tan^{-1}(\cos x) = \left(\frac{1}{\cos^2 x + 1}\right)(-\sin x) = -\frac{\sin x}{\cos^2 x + 1}$$

example 64.6   Let $y = \arcsin(2x)$. Find y'.

solution   We have to use the chain rule. If ( ) is a function of x, then

$$\frac{d}{dx}\sin^{-1}(\ ) = \frac{1}{\sqrt{1^2 - (\ )^2}}\frac{d}{dx}(\ )$$

We replace ( ) with $2x$ and finish the problem.

$$y' = \frac{d}{dx}\sin^{-1}(2x) = \frac{1}{\sqrt{1 - (2x)^2}}\frac{d}{dx}(2x) = \frac{2}{\sqrt{1 - 4x^2}}$$

example 64.7 Integrate: $\displaystyle\int \frac{1}{1 + x^2}\, dx$

solution We must identify an expression whose differential is $\dfrac{1}{1 + x^2}$. Note that

$$d(\tan^{-1} x) = d\left(\tan^{-1} \frac{x}{1}\right)$$

$$= \frac{1}{x^2 + 1}\, dx$$

Therefore

$$\int \frac{1}{1 + x^2}\, dx = \tan^{-1} x + C$$

This example demonstrates the need to memorize the derivatives of $\sin^{-1}$ and $\tan^{-1}$.

problem set 64

1. *(52)* If the price of a ticket to the concert is $16, then 4000 tickets will be sold. For each $1 increase in ticket price, the number of tickets sold will decrease by 100. What should the price per ticket be in order to maximize revenue? (*Hint:* See problem 25 in Problem Set 63.)

2. *(52)* A rectangle whose base is the x-axis is inscribed beneath the semicircle $y = \sqrt{9 - x^2}$, as shown.

   (a) Express the area of the rectangle in terms of x.

   (b) Find the dimensions of the rectangle of greatest area that can be inscribed in the region.

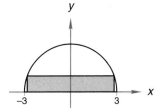

3. *(55)* Find the Maclaurin series for $y = \dfrac{1}{(1 - x)^2}$.

4. *(63)* Use calculus to find the maximum and minimum values of $f(x) = x^3 - 6x^2 + 2$ on the interval $[-1, 5]$. Check the answer with a graphing calculator.

5. *(63)* Use the critical number theorem to determine the maximum and minimum values of $f(x) = x^{3/2} - x$ on the interval $[0, 2]$.

6. *(63)* A function f is continuous on the interval $[1, 5]$. In addition, $f(1) = 2$ and $f(5) = 10$. The properties in the table below also apply. Determine the maximum and minimum values of f.

x	$1 < x < 3$	$x = 3$	$3 < x < 5$
$f'(x)$	positive	0	positive
$f''(x)$	negative	0	positive

7. *(64)* Let $y = \arcsin \dfrac{x}{3}$. Find $\dfrac{dy}{dx}$.

8. *(64)* Let $y = \cos^{-1} \dfrac{x}{5}$. Find y'.

9. *(64)* Let $y = \tan^{-1} \dfrac{x}{2}$. Find $\dfrac{dy}{dx}$.

10. *(64)* Determine: $\displaystyle\int \frac{1}{\sqrt{1 - x^2}}\, dx$

11. *(62)* A force is applied to an object so that the force at any position along the x-axis is given by $f(x) = 2x$ newtons (for x in meters). Find the work done by the force as the object moves in the direction of the force from $x = 2$ to $x = 4$ meters.

12. Let $f(x) = a \sin x + b$. Suppose $f'(0) = 3$ and $f\left(\dfrac{\pi}{2}\right) = 5$. Find a and b.
(61)

13. Find the area between the graphs of $y = 2e^x$ and $y = 3e^x$ from $x = \ln 2$ to $x = \ln 3$.
(60)

14. Find the area in the first quadrant between the x-axis and the graph of $y = 2x\sqrt{4 - x^2}$.
(59)

15. Use a graphing calculator to approximate the area bounded by the graph of $f(x) = e^{x^2}$ and the
(59) x-axis over the interval $[-1, 1]$.

In problems 16 and 17 let f be a continuous function on $(-\infty, \infty)$ such that $\int_1^3 f(x)\,dx = -5$ and $\int_3^7 f(x)\,dx = 6$. Evaluate the given integrals.

16. $\displaystyle\int_1^7 f(x)\,dx$ **17.** $\displaystyle\int_7^1 -5f(x)\,dx$
(57)   (57)

18. Evaluate $\dfrac{d^2 y}{dx^2}$ at $x = 1$ for $y = \sqrt{x}$.
(27)

19. Write the equation of the line tangent to the graph of $y = \sin(\cos x)$ at $x = \dfrac{\pi}{2}$.
(27)

20. Differentiate $y = \sqrt[3]{\sin(2x) + x} + \dfrac{\csc(3x)}{x^3 + 1}$ with respect to x.
(50)

21. Integrate: $\displaystyle\int (3x^2 + 2x + 1)\sqrt{x^3 + x^2 + x}\,dx$
(51)

Evaluate the limits in problems 22 and 23.

22. $\displaystyle\lim_{x \to \infty} \dfrac{x^3 - 2x^2}{1 - x^4}$
(17)

23. $\displaystyle\lim_{\Delta x \to 0} \dfrac{\cos(\pi + \Delta x) - \cos \pi}{\Delta x}$
(28)

24. (a) The following is the equation of an ellipse. Write the equation of the portion of the ellipse
(23,59)   that lies in the first quadrant.

$$\frac{x^2}{a^2} + \frac{y^2}{b^2} = 1 \qquad (a, b > 0)$$

   (b) Use a definite integral to describe the area of the region in the first quadrant that is enclosed by the ellipse described above.

25. Find the angle at which the curves $x^2 + y^2 = 1$ and $(x - 1)^2 + y^2 = 1$ intersect in the
(27,58) fourth quadrant. (*Hint:* See problem 24 in Problem Set 59.)

LESSON 65 *Falling-Body Problems*

In Lesson 54 we began to use calculus to solve problems dealing with the position, velocity, and acceleration of a physical object such as a ball, car, or projectile that moves in a straight line. In this lesson we investigate the motion of bodies falling freely in a gravitational field. These problems are easy because the acceleration is a constant. In a later lesson we will consider problems in which the acceleration is a function of time.

At or near the surface of the earth, the attraction between the earth and any physical object accelerates the object downward at 9.8 meters per second per second (32 feet per second per second). This acceleration is called the **acceleration due to gravity.** The acceleration due to gravity is the same for all objects regardless of their mass or shape, and if we neglect air resistance, a feather and a lead ball fall to the ground in the same time when dropped from the same position.

If an object is released 100 feet above the surface of the earth, it accelerates downward. If another object is released 200 feet above the surface of the earth at the same time, it also accelerates downward and always remains 100 feet above the first object (until the lower object hits the ground), because it was 100 feet higher when it was released. (We are still neglecting air resistance.)

If an object is thrown downward with an initial velocity of 40 meters per second, its downward velocity increases with time, because it accelerates downward at 9.8 meters per second per second. If an object is thrown upward with a velocity of 40 meters per second, its upward velocity decreases, because the object's acceleration is downward at 9.8 meters per second per second. Its upward velocity decreases until the upward velocity becomes zero at the highest point. Then the steady downward acceleration of 9.8 meters per second per second causes it to fall, and its downward velocity increases with time.

For free-falling-body problems, it is often convenient to designate up as the positive direction and measure positive distances upward from the surface of the earth (sea level).

If we use the earth's surface as our reference plane, positive positions are positions above the surface of the earth and negative positions are positions below the surface of the earth. Positive velocities and positive accelerations are upward velocities and upward accelerations, and negative velocities and negative accelerations are downward velocities and downward accelerations. **Since the acceleration due to gravity is always in the downward direction, we use a minus sign and say that the acceleration due to gravity is –9.8 meters per second per second.**

The position function of a body in free fall near the surface of the earth is determined by its initial position, its initial velocity, and its acceleration. Since the acceleration is always –9.8 m/s^2 for any physical object in free fall near the surface of the earth, the only variations in the position, velocity, and acceleration functions are caused by different values of the initial position h_0 and the initial velocity v_0. The position, velocity, and acceleration functions for any free-falling body at or near the surface of the earth are the following:

$$h(t) = -4.9t^2 + v_0 t + h_0 \qquad \text{m}$$
$$h'(t) = v(t) = -9.8t + v_0 \qquad \text{m/s}$$
$$h''(t) = v'(t) = a(t) = -9.8 \qquad \text{m/s}^2$$

In physics, answers to falling-body problems are found by inserting the indicated values of h_0 and v_0 in these equations. In calculus we must learn to develop these equations, because the process uses the same procedures as the ones used to find the velocity and position functions for the motion of particles whose acceleration is not –9.8 m/s^2.

In motion problems the concept of t_{0+} is important. If a ball is released at $t = 0$, the problem begins at t_{0+}, which is the instant after it is released. At t_{0+} the ball has not moved and the ball has no velocity, but it does have a negative acceleration, therefore its velocity increases in the negative direction at 9.8 m/s^2. Whether the ball is thrown upward or downward, at t_{0+} it has not moved (though it has an initial velocity of v_0). Of course, its acceleration at t_{0+} (and at any other time) is –9.8 m/s^2. Since the ball has not moved, its position at t_{0+} is still h_0.

To solve falling-body problems, we always begin by integrating the acceleration function to get the velocity function. Doing this gives us a constant of integration C. To find the value of the constant of integration, we set t equal to zero, let $v(0)$ be the given value of v_0, and solve to find that $C = v_0$. Then we integrate the velocity function to get the position function, which also has a constant of integration C. Thus we substitute h_0 for $h(0)$, set t equal to zero, and solve to find that $C = h_0$.

example 65.1   An object is dropped from a height of 2000 meters. Begin with the acceleration function and develop the position function. How far above the earth will the object be 20 seconds later?

solution   Since h_0 is 2000 and v_0 is zero (because the ball was dropped), we know that the position at time t (in seconds) should be

$$h(t) = -4.9t^2 + 2000$$

But we were instructed to develop this equation, so we begin by integrating the acceleration function to get the velocity function.

$$a(t) = -9.8 \longrightarrow v(t) = \int -9.8 \, dt = -9.8t + C$$

We know that $v(0) = 0$, because the ball was dropped, not thrown. So we replace t with zero and also replace $v(0)$ with zero to solve for C.

$$0 = -9.8(0) + C \longrightarrow C = 0$$

This gives us the velocity function.

$$v(t) = -9.8t$$

Now we integrate the velocity function to get the position function.

$$h(t) = \int -9.8t \, dt \longrightarrow h(t) = -\frac{9.8t^2}{2} + C$$

At t_{0+}, $h(t) = 2000$, so we can substitute and solve for C.

$$2000 = -4.9(0)^2 + C \longrightarrow C = 2000$$

Thus, the position function is

$$\mathbf{h(t) = -4.9t^2 + 2000}$$

To find the position when $t = 20$ seconds, we determine $h(20)$.

$$h(20) = -4.9(20)^2 + 2000 = \mathbf{40\ m}$$

example 65.2   A ball is thrown downward with a velocity of 40 meters per second from a height of 2000 meters. Begin with the acceleration function, and develop the position function for the ball. What will be the position of the ball after 8 seconds?

solution   The equations for freely falling bodies are always the same except that the constants h_0 and v_0 are different. With the data given we know that the velocity function and the position function will be as follows:

$$v(t) = -9.8t - 40 \qquad\qquad \text{velocity function}$$
$$h(t) = -4.9t^2 - 40t + 2000 \qquad \text{position function}$$

But our job is to develop these equations. We begin with the acceleration function. At or near the surface of the earth, the acceleration is always -9.8 m/s^2.

$$a(t) = -9.8$$

The velocity function is found by integrating the acceleration function.

$$v(t) = \int a(t) \, dt = \int -9.8 \, dt = -9.8t + C$$

To solve for C, we let $t = 0$ and remember that $v(0) = -40$, because the ball was thrown downward at 40 meters per second.

$$-40 = -9.8(0) + C \longrightarrow C = -40 \longrightarrow v(t) = -9.8t - 40$$

To find the position function, we integrate the velocity function.

$$h(t) = \int (-9.8t - 40) \, dt \longrightarrow h(t) = -\frac{9.8}{2}t^2 - 40t + C$$

The problem states that when $t = 0$, $h(0) = 2000$. Thus, we substitute.

$$2000 = -4.9(0)^2 - 40(0) + C \longrightarrow C = 2000$$

Now we have the position function h.

$$h(t) = -4.9t^2 - 40t + 2000$$

To find the position after 8 seconds, we determine $h(8)$.

$$h(8) = -4.9(8)^2 - 40(8) + 2000$$
$$= -313.6 - 320 + 2000 = \mathbf{1366.4 \ m}$$

The ball fell 320 meters in 8 seconds because of the initial velocity of 40 meters/second. It fell an additional 313.6 meters because of the acceleration component of the position equation.

example 65.3   A boy stood on top of a building 40 meters high and threw a stone so that it had an initial upward velocity of 20 meters per second. Begin with the acceleration function, and develop the velocity function and the position function for the stone. How high will the stone go? How long after the stone is thrown will it hit the ground?

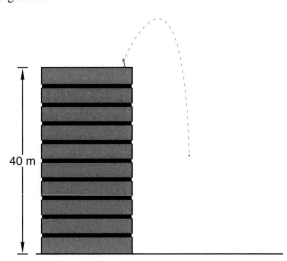

solution   We already know that the velocity function and the position function for the stone will be

$$v(t) = -9.8t + 20 \quad \text{and} \quad h(t) = -4.9t^2 + 20t + 40$$

But our job is to develop these equations. At or near the surface of the earth, the acceleration function is always the same.

$$a(t) = -9.8$$

The velocity function is the integral of the acceleration function.

$$v(t) = \int -9.8 \, dt = -9.8t + C$$

At t_{0+} the velocity is +20.

$$20 = -9.8(0) + C \longrightarrow C = 20$$

Thus, the velocity function is

$$v(t) = -9.8t + 20$$

The position function is the integral of the velocity function.

$$h(t) = \int (-9.8t + 20)\, dt = -\frac{9.8}{2}t^2 + 20t + C$$

At t_{0^+} the position is $h(0) = 40$.

$$40 = -4.9(0)^2 + 20(0) + C \quad\longrightarrow\quad C = 40$$

Thus, the position function is

$$\mathbf{h(t) = -4.9t^2 + 20t + 40}$$

We can answer all the questions by using the velocity function and position function that we have developed. To find out how high the stone goes, we use the velocity function to find the time when the velocity equals zero.

$$0 = -9.8t + 20 \quad\longrightarrow\quad t \approx 2.0408 \text{ seconds}$$

Now we use the position function to find the height at $t = 2.0408$.

$$h(2.0408) = -4.9(2.0408)^2 + 20(2.0408) + 40 \approx \mathbf{60.4082 \text{ meters}}$$

When the stone hits the ground, the elevation will be zero. We can find the time the stone hits the ground by setting the position function equal to zero and using the quadratic formula to solve for t.

$$0 = -4.9t^2 + 20t + 40 \quad\longrightarrow\quad t = \frac{-20 \pm \sqrt{20^2 - 4(-4.9)(40)}}{2(-4.9)} \approx 5.5520, -1.4703$$

The negative number -1.4703 is a solution of the quadratic equation but has no meaning in this problem, since $t = 0$ is our starting point. Thus the time from release to impact with the ground is approximately **5.5520 seconds.**

Since the maximum altitude is 60.4082 meters, we can solve the problem another way by finding the time required for the stone to free-fall from 60.4082 meters and adding this result to 2.0408 seconds. From example 65.1 we see that the position function for a free fall of 2000 meters is

$$h(t) = -4.9t^2 + 2000$$

Thus, the position function for a freefall of 60.4082 meters would be

$$h(t) = -4.9t^2 + 60.4082$$

Since $h(t) = 0$ when the stone hits the ground, we have

$$0 = -4.9t^2 + 60.4082 \quad\longrightarrow\quad t = \sqrt{\frac{60.4082}{4.9}} \approx 3.5112$$

If we add the 3.5112 seconds required to fall 60.4082 meters to the 2.0408 seconds required to get to the height of 60.4082 meters, we get

$$2.0408 + 3.5112 = \mathbf{5.5520 \text{ seconds}}$$

**problem set
65**

1.
(47) An airplane is flying in a horizontal, straight-line path. The speed of the airplane is 100 meters per second, and its altitude is 1000 meters. What is the rate of change of the angle of elevation, θ, when the horizontal distance from a reference point P on the ground is 2000 meters?

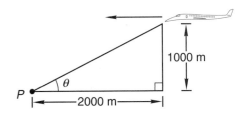

2.
(65) A ball is dropped from a height of 500 meters. Develop an equation that describes the height of the ball at time t after it is dropped. Find the elevation, velocity, and acceleration of the ball 3 seconds after it is released.

3. A ball is thrown straight up from the top of a 100-meter-tall building with an initial velocity of
(65) 30 meters per second. Develop an equation that describes the height of the ball above the ground as a function of time t. What will be the maximum height attained by the ball?

4. Begin with the equation $f(x) = \cos x$. Write the implicit equation of the inverse of f. The
(58) equation of the inverse defines a right triangle. Draw this triangle. Differentiate this equation implicitly and then use the triangle to write the expression for $\frac{d}{dx} f^{-1}(x)$. Evaluate $(f^{-1})'(0.2)$.

5. For $y = \arcsin \dfrac{x}{3}$, evaluate $\dfrac{dy}{dx}\Big|_2$.
(64)

6. For $y = \arctan \dfrac{x}{2}$, find $\dfrac{dy}{dx}$.
(64)

7. Use calculus to find the maximum and minimum values of the function
(63) $f(x) = 2x^3 - 3x^2 - 12x + 7$ on the interval $[-2, 3]$. Check the answer with a graphing calculator.

8. Apply the critical number theorem to determine where the maximum and minimum values of
(63) $f(x) = |x - 1|$ occur and what their values are if f is defined only on the interval $[-1, 3]$.

9. A function f is continuous on the closed interval $[-3, 2]$. In addition, $f(-3) = 4$, $f(-1) = 6$,
(63) $f(1) = 1$, and $f(2) = 2$. The function f also has the properties listed on the chart shown. Sketch a possible graph of f, and determine the maximum and minimum values of f.

x	$-3 < x < -1$	$x = -1$	$-1 < x < 1$	$x = 1$	$1 < x < 2$
$f'(x)$	positive	zero	negative	zero	positive

10. This figure shows an isosceles triangle
(52) drawn with its vertex at the origin, its base parallel to and above the x-axis, and the vertices of its base on the curve $12y = 36 - x^2$.

(a) Express the area of the triangle in terms of x.

(b) Find the maximum possible area of the triangle.

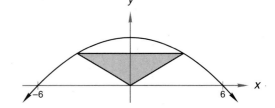

11. The spring constant for a spring is 2 newtons per meter. How much work is required to stretch
(62) the spring from $x = 1$ meter to $x = 2$ meters?

12. Let $f(x) = ax^2 + b$ and $g(x) = x^2 + ax$. Find a and b such that $f'(2) = g'(2)$ and
(61) $f(1) = 5$.

Integrate in problems 13 and 14.

13. $\displaystyle\int \frac{\cos (2x)}{\sqrt{1 + \sin (2x)}}\, dx$
(56)

14. $\displaystyle\int xe^{x^2 + \pi}\, dx$
(56)

15. Find the area enclosed by the graphs of $y = \sqrt{x}$ and $y = x$.
(60)

In problems 16 and 17 let R be the region bounded by the curves $y = 3x^2 - k^2$ and $y = -k^2x^2 + 3$ where $k > 0$.

16. (a) Express the area of R as a function of k.
(60)
(b) Find the value of k for which the area of R is 7 square units.

17. If the area R is increasing at the constant rate of 5 square units per second, at what rate is k
(46) increasing when $k = 15$?

18. Let f be a continuous function on $[1, 5]$. Suppose $\int_1^5 f(x)\,dx = 10$ and $\int_c^5 f(x)\,dx = -2$.
(57) Find $\int_1^c f(x)\,dx$.

19. Evaluate: $\int_1^e \dfrac{1}{x}\,dx$
(47)

20. Evaluate $\dfrac{d^4 y}{dx^4}$ at $x = \dfrac{\pi}{2}$ where $y = 2\sin x$.
(27)

21. Differentiate $y = \sqrt{\sin x} + \dfrac{e^{2x}}{\sec x} + (\ln x)(\csc x)$ with respect to x.
(50)

22. Identify the intervals on which $f(x) = \dfrac{x(x-1)}{(x-2)(x+1)(x+2)}$ is concave upward and the intervals on
(49) which f is concave downward. (*Note:* f'' need not be computed. Only the graph of f is required.)

23. Evaluate: $\lim\limits_{x \to 2} \dfrac{e^x - e^2}{x - 2}$
(44)

24. Suppose f is a function such that $f\left(\dfrac{x_1}{x_2}\right) = f(x_1) - f(x_2)$ for all $x_1, x_2 > 0$. Which of the
(16) following could be the equation of f?

    A. $f(x) = \dfrac{1}{x}$ B. $f(x) = \ln x$ C. $f(x) = x^2$ D. $f(x) = \sin x$

25. Find the set of all values b for which the graphs of $y = 2x + b$ and $y^2 = 4x$ intersect at two
(2) distinct points.

LESSON 66   *u Substitution • Change of Variable • Proof of the Substitution Theorem*

66.A

u substitution   There are procedures and techniques for integration, but guessing the answer is our primary weapon. We have found that it is often necessary to change our first guess by inserting a constant in the integrand and its reciprocal on the other side of the integral sign. This lesson presents a procedure called **u substitution** that obviates the requirement for using the constant and its reciprocal. We can also use u substitution to find some integrals that would be difficult to guess.

example 66.1   Integrate: $\int 40x(x^2 - 4)^5\,dx$

solution   As the first step, we move the constant 40 to the left of the integral sign. Then we let u equal $x^2 - 4$ and record this substitution in the box on the right-hand side below.

$$40 \int x(x^2 - 4)^5\,dx$$
$$\longrightarrow 40 \int x(u)^5\,dx$$

$$\boxed{\begin{aligned} u &= x^2 - 4 \\ du &= 2x\,dx \\ \frac{du}{2} &= x\,dx \end{aligned}}$$

In this problem u has been substituted for $x^2 - 4$, but there is still a factor of $x\,dx$ in the integrand. Thus, we found du and solved for $x\,dx$. We substitute the expression for $x\,dx$ in the integral and antidifferentiate.

$$40 \int u^5 \frac{du}{2} = 20 \int u^5\,du = 20\left(\frac{u^6}{6}\right) + C = \frac{10u^6}{3} + C$$

We use the value of u in the box to make a second substitution.

$$\frac{10u^6}{3} + C = \frac{10}{3}(x^2 - 4)^6 + C$$

example 66.2 Find $\displaystyle\int \frac{20 \cos (ax)\,dx}{\sqrt{b + \sin (ax)}}$ where a and b are constants.

solution We write the constant in front of the integral sign and record our proposed u substitution in a box.

$$20 \int \frac{\cos (ax)\,dx}{\sqrt{b + \sin (ax)}} \qquad \boxed{\begin{array}{l} u = b + \sin (ax) \\[4pt] du = [\cos (ax)](a\,dx) \\[4pt] \dfrac{du}{a} = \cos (ax)\,dx \end{array}}$$

Because there was a factor of $\cos (ax)\,dx$ in the integrand after substituting $u = b + \sin (ax)$, we found du and then solved for $\cos (ax)\,dx$. Now we substitute and integrate.

$$20 \int \frac{\dfrac{du}{a}}{\sqrt{u}} = \frac{20}{a} \int u^{-1/2}\,du = \frac{20}{a} \frac{u^{1/2}}{\dfrac{1}{2}} + C = \frac{40}{a} u^{1/2} + C$$

We look in the box to find that $u = b + \sin (ax)$ and then make this substitution to get

$$\frac{40}{a} u^{1/2} + C = \frac{40}{a}[b + \sin (ax)]^{1/2} + C$$

example 66.3 Integrate: $\displaystyle\int 7x\sqrt{x - 1}\,dx$

solution The derivative of $x - 1$ is 1, not x, so this integrand is not the differential of an expression whose form is $u^n\,du$. But u substitution will still work. We write the constant in front of the integral sign and record the u substitution in a box.

$$7 \int x\sqrt{x - 1}\,dx \qquad \boxed{\begin{array}{l} u = x - 1 \\[4pt] du = dx \\[4pt] x = u + 1 \end{array}}$$

This time the equation $u = x - 1$ had to be solved for x to find the proper substitution.

$$7 \int x\sqrt{x - 1}\,dx = 7 \int (u + 1)(u^{1/2})\,du$$

Now we multiply and integrate.

$$7\left(\int u^{3/2}\,du + \int u^{1/2}\,du \right) = 7\left(\frac{u^{5/2}}{\dfrac{5}{2}} + \frac{u^{3/2}}{\dfrac{3}{2}} \right) + C$$

Simplifying and making a second substitution gives

$$\frac{14}{5}u^{5/2} + \frac{14}{3}u^{3/2} + C = \frac{14}{5}(x-1)^{5/2} + \frac{14}{3}(x-1)^{3/2} + C$$

If we factor out $(x-1)^{3/2}$ and simplify, this can be written as

$$(x-1)^{3/2}\left[\frac{14}{15} \cdot 3(x-1) + \frac{14}{15} \cdot 5\right] + C = \frac{14}{15}(x-1)^{3/2}(3x+2) + C$$

66.B
change of variable

There is a useful alternative procedure for evaluating definite integrals. It is not necessarily easier or simpler but is a procedure that is sometimes helpful. The procedure is called **changing the variable of integration.** When we change the variable of integration, it is usually necessary to change the limits of integration. Suppose we need to evaluate the following integral:

$$\int_0^2 \underbrace{(x^2+1)^3}_{u^3}\,\underbrace{(2x\,dx)}_{du} \qquad \boxed{\begin{array}{l} u = x^2 + 1 \\ du = 2x\,dx \end{array}}$$

Note that we have the form $u^3\,du$, whose integral is $\frac{u^4}{4}$, or $\frac{(x^2+1)^4}{4}$. Thus we have the choice of evaluating

$$\left.\frac{(x^2+1)^4}{4}\right|_{x=0}^{x=2} \qquad \text{or} \qquad \left.\frac{u^4}{4}\right|_{u=1}^{u=5}$$

On the right-hand side we changed (x^2+1) to u. The lower limit of integration was also changed from 0 to 1, because when x equals 0, $u = 0^2 + 1 = 1$. The upper limit was changed from 2 to 5, because when x equals 2, $u = 2^2 + 1 = 5$. Now we evaluate both expressions to demonstrate that the answers are the same.

$$\frac{1}{4}\left[(x^2+1)^4\right]_0^2 = \frac{1}{4}(625-1) = 156 \qquad \frac{1}{4}\left[u^4\right]_1^5 = \frac{1}{4}(625-1) = 156$$

example 66.4   Change the variable to evaluate $\int_0^1 x\sin(\pi x^2)\,dx$.

solution   We note that the form of the integrand is $\sin u\,du$ and that we need the extra factors $\dfrac{1}{2\pi}$ and 2π.

$$\frac{1}{2\pi}\int_0^1 \underbrace{\left(\sin(\pi x^2)\right)}_{\sin u}\underbrace{(2\pi x\,dx)}_{du} \qquad \boxed{\begin{array}{l} u = \pi x^2 \\ du = 2\pi x\,dx \end{array}}$$

This integral can be evaluated by integrating $\sin u\,du$ if we change the lower limit to the value of u when $x = 0$ and change the upper limit to the value of u when $x = 1$.

$$x = 0 \quad\longrightarrow\quad u = \pi(0)^2 = 0$$
$$x = 1 \quad\longrightarrow\quad u = \pi(1)^2 = \pi$$

We make these changes and evaluate the integral.

$$\frac{1}{2\pi}\int_0^\pi \sin u\,du = \frac{1}{2\pi}[-\cos u]_0^\pi = -\frac{1}{2\pi}(\cos\pi - \cos 0) = \frac{-1-1}{-2\pi} = \frac{1}{\pi}$$

example 66.5   Use the method of changing the variable to evaluate $\int_0^\pi e^{\sin(5x)}\cos(5x)\,dx$.

solution   Note that this integral can be written as $e^u\,du$ if we insert the necessary constants.

$$\frac{1}{5}\int_0^\pi \underbrace{\left(e^{\sin(5x)}\right)}_{e^u}\underbrace{[5\cos(5x)\,dx]}_{du} \qquad \boxed{\begin{array}{l} u = \sin(5x) \\ du = 5\cos(5x)\,dx \end{array}}$$

If $x = 0$, then $u = 0$. If $x = \pi$, then $u = 0$. So we have

$$\frac{1}{5} \int_0^0 e^u \, du = 0$$

When the upper and lower limits of integration are equal, the integral is zero. A graph of the original function shows equal areas above and below the x-axis on the x-interval $[0, \pi]$.

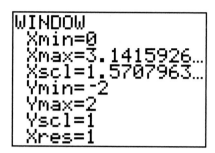
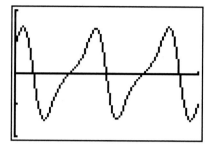

Evaluating the original integral gives us the same result.

$$\frac{1}{5} \int_0^\pi \left(e^{\sin (5x)}\right)[5 \cos (5x)] \, dx = \frac{1}{5}\left[\left(e^{\sin (5x)}\right)\right]_0^\pi = \frac{1}{5}\left(e^0 - e^0\right) = \mathbf{0}$$

66.C

proof of the substitution theorem

The justification for change of variables is straightforward. Before proving it, we state the theorem.

SUBSTITUTION THEOREM FOR DEFINITE INTEGRALS

The following statement of equality is true if the function in the integral on the left is continuous from a to b, inclusive, and the function in the integral on the right is continuous from $u(a)$ to $u(b)$, inclusive.

$$\int_a^b f(u(x))u'(x) \, dx = \int_{u(a)}^{u(b)} f(u) \, du$$

Note that the expression on the left-hand side in the box is the integral of the derivative of a composite function. For a concrete illustration, we use an example from earlier in this lesson.

$$\int_0^2 (x^2 + 1)^3(2x \, dx) = \int_1^5 u^3 \, du$$

To develop our proof, we define an f function and a u function as follows.

$$f(x) = x^3 \quad \text{and} \quad u(x) = x^2 + 1, \quad \text{so} \quad u'(x) = 2x$$

Substituting the equivalent general expression in the concrete example above, we get the following general equality.

$$\int_{x=a}^{x=b} f(u(x))u'(x) \, dx = \int_{u(a)}^{u(b)} f(u) \, du$$

To prove that this is a true statement of equality, we will show that both the left-hand side and the right-hand side of this equality equal $F(u(b)) - F(u(a))$, where F is some antiderivative of f. The right-hand side is easier, because we just substitute $u(a)$ and $u(b)$ for the lower and upper limits of the integral in the general statement of the Fundamental Theorem of Calculus.

FUNDAMENTAL THEOREM   SUBSTITUTED

$$\int_a^b f(x) \, dx = F(b) - F(a) \quad \longrightarrow \quad \int_{u(a)}^{u(b)} f(u) \, du = F(u(b)) - F(u(a))$$

To show that the left side also equals $F(u(b)) - F(u(a))$ for the same antiderivative F, we use the chain rule to find the derivative of $F(u(x))$.

$$\frac{d}{dx}F(u(x)) = F'(u(x))u'(x)$$

Since $F' = f$, we can substitute f for F' and get

$$\frac{d}{dx}F(u(x)) = f(u(x))u'(x)$$

which can be turned around to write

$$\int f(u(x))u'(x)\,dx = F(u(x)) + C$$

If we use the Fundamental Theorem of Calculus to evaluate this definite integral from $x = a$ to $x = b$, we can write the following to finish the proof.

$$\int_{x=a}^{x=b} f(u(x))u'(x)\,dx = F(u(b)) - F(u(a))$$

problem set 66

1. An object is propelled along the x-axis by a force of $x^2 - 3x$ newtons. Find the work done on (62) the object between x-values of 1 meter and 5 meters.

2. A building is 160 meters high. If a ball is dropped from the top of the building, what is the (65) acceleration of the ball when it is 100 meters above the ground?

3. A ball is thrown straight up from the top of a 160-meter-tall building with a velocity of 20 meters (65) per second. Develop an equation that expresses the height h of the ball as a function of time. Find $h(2)$, $v(2)$, and $a(2)$.

Use change of variables to evaluate the integrals in problems 4 and 5.

4. $\displaystyle\int_0^1 x\cos(\pi x^2)\,dx$
(66)

5. $\displaystyle\int_0^\pi [\sin(5x)]e^{\cos(5x)}\,dx$
(66)

6. Write the equation of the inverse of the function $y = \csc x$ where y is defined on $\left[-\frac{\pi}{2}, \frac{\pi}{2}\right]$. (64) Differentiate this equation to find $(f^{-1})'$, and express $(f^{-1})'$ in terms of x.

7. Find the slope of the line tangent to the graph of $y = \arcsin\dfrac{x}{3}$ at $x = \dfrac{3}{2}$.
(64)

8. Find $\dfrac{dy}{dx}$ where $y = \arctan(\sin x)$.
(64)

9. Use calculus to find the maximum and minimum values of the function (63) $f(x) = \frac{4}{3}x^3 - 2x^2 - 15x$ on the interval $[-3, 4]$. Check the answer with a graphing calculator.

10. Suppose f is continuous on $[1, 4]$ and has the properties listed in the table below. Sketch a graph (63) of f, and determine the maximum and minimum values of f.

x	$x = 1$	$1 < x < 2$	$x = 2$	$2 < x < 4$	$x = 4$
$f(x)$	15		10		20
$f'(x)$		negative	0	positive	
$f''(x)$		positive	positive	positive	

11. Find the Maclaurin series for $y = \cos x$.
(55)

12. (a) Find the Maclaurin series for $y = \cos(2x)$.
(55)
   (b) Substitute $2x$ for x in the Maclaurin series found in problem 11. Compare this new series with the answer to (a).

13. Let $f(x) = a\sin x + b\cos x$. Find the values of a and b for which $f'(\pi) = 2$ and $f'\left(\frac{\pi}{2}\right) = 4$.
(61)

Integrate in problems 14–19.

14. $\displaystyle\int x\sqrt{x + 1}\ dx$
(66)

15. $\displaystyle\int (1 + \cos x)(x + \sin x)^3\ dx$
(66)

16. $\displaystyle\int \frac{x^2 + 1}{x}\ dx$
(38)

17. $\displaystyle\int \frac{x}{x^2 + 1}\ dx$
(66)

18. $\displaystyle\int \frac{1}{x^2 + 1}\ dx$
(64)

19. $\displaystyle\int (x^2 + 4)^{-1}x\ dx$
(66)

Differentiate with respect to *x* in problems 20 and 21.

20. $y = \dfrac{\tan (x^3 - 1)}{e^2 + e^x}$
(50)

21. $y = e^{2x}\sec (\pi x)$
(50)

22. Find the equation of the line tangent to the graph of $y = \dfrac{x}{x^2 + 1}$ at $x = 1$.
(27)

23. Suppose $y = f(x)$ is a polynomial function of degree *n*. Which of the following must be true?
(33)
    A. *f* intersects the *x*-axis at least *n* times.
    B. *f* intersects the *x*-axis at least once.
    C. *f* is continuous for all values of *x*.
    D. *f* always has some finite maximum value.

24. In the definite integral shown below, *a* and *b* are positive constants. The integral represents the
(47,58) area of a familiar geometric figure multiplied by *b* over *a*. Evaluate this integral by inspection.

$$\int_0^a \frac{b\sqrt{a^2 - x^2}}{a}\ dx$$

25. Find $\cos^2 \theta$ in terms of *x*, given $\tan \theta = \dfrac{x}{10}$.
(58)

LESSON 67 *Areas Involving Functions of y*

In the area problems we have worked thus far, *y* has been a function of *x*. Thus *x* has been the independent variable. For some problems it is convenient to use *y* as the independent variable and let *x* be a function of *y*. When we do this, *x* is still graphed horizontally. When *x* is a function of *y*, the input axis is the *y*-axis, and the output axis is the *x*-axis.

example 67.1   Find the area of the region completely enclosed by the *y*-axis and the graph of $x = 1 - y^2$.

solution   Solving this equation for *y*, we get $y = \pm\sqrt{1 - x}$. This equation describes two functions: $y = \sqrt{1 - x}$, whose graph is the upper half of the parabola, and $y = -\sqrt{1 - x}$, whose graph is the lower half of the parabola. We could use either of these functions and one of the representative rectangles shown in the left-hand figure below to find half the desired area and double this result to get the whole area.

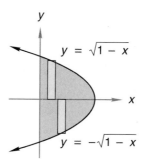

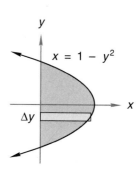

Another way to solve this problem is to let x be a function of y and use the representative rectangle shown in the figure on the right-hand side. When we do this, y is the variable of integration, and the limits of integration are the y-values of the points of intersection of the graph of $x = 1 - y^2$ and the y-axis. First we find the y-values of these points. Since $x = 0$ for all points on the y-axis, we have

$$x = 1 - y^2 \quad \longrightarrow \quad 0 = (1 - y)(1 + y) \quad \longrightarrow \quad y = \pm 1$$

The "height" of the representative rectangle is $1 - y^2$, and its width is Δy. Thus the area equals the following integral:

$$\int_{y=-1}^{y=1} (1 - y^2) \, dy$$

We finish by integrating and evaluating the integral.

$$\text{Area} = \left[y - \frac{y^3}{3} \right]_{-1}^{1} = \left(1 - \frac{1}{3} \right) - \left[-1 - \left(-\frac{1}{3} \right) \right] = \frac{2}{3} - \left(-\frac{2}{3} \right) = \frac{4}{3} \text{ units}^2$$

example 67.2   Find the area of the region completely bounded by the graphs of $x = 3 - y^2$ and $y = x - 1$.

solution   We must be careful when we draw the representative rectangle, as the figure below shows. The left-hand representative rectangle looks all right because it is bounded above by the graph of $y = x - 1$ and below by the graph of $x = 3 - y^2$. Trying to use this representative rectangle to find the area leads to trouble, however, as we see when the rectangle is moved to the right-hand part of the figure. Here it is bounded both above and below by the graph of $x = 3 - y^2$.

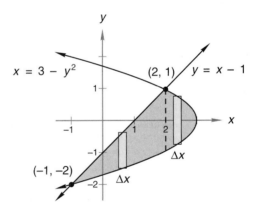

So the area must be calculated as the sum of two different integrals.

$$\text{Area} = \int_{x=-1}^{x=2} \left[(x - 1) - (-\sqrt{3 - x}) \right] dx + \int_{x=2}^{x=3} \left[(\sqrt{3 - x}) - (-\sqrt{3 - x}) \right] dx$$

This is cumbersome at best. There are several ways this difficulty can be overcome. One way is to draw the representative rectangle horizontally and let dy be its width, as shown in the figure below.

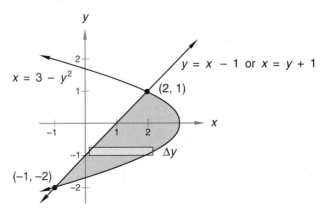

In this figure the right end of the rectangle is bounded by $x = 3 - y^2$, and the left end is bounded by $x = y + 1$. The width of the rectangle is dy, and the limits of integration are the y-values -2 and $+1$.

$$\text{Area} = \int_{y=-2}^{y=1} \underbrace{[(3 - y^2) - (y + 1)]}_{\substack{\text{height of} \\ \text{rectangle}}} \underset{\uparrow}{dy}$$
width

We finish by evaluating the integral.

$$\int_{-2}^{1} (-y^2 - y + 2)\, dy = \left[-\frac{y^3}{3} - \frac{y^2}{2} + 2y \right]_{-2}^{1}$$

$$= \left(-\frac{1}{3} - \frac{1}{2} + 2 \right) - \left(\frac{8}{3} - 2 - 4 \right) = \frac{9}{2}\ \mathbf{units}^2$$

As a reminder, such integrals can be approximated with a graphing calculator. The desired area in example 67.1 equals

$$2 \int_{x=0}^{x=1} \sqrt{1 - x}\ dx$$

Using the TI-83, we press **MATH** **9** to access the $\text{fnInt}($ option. Then we numerically approximate the value of the integral by evaluating

$$2\text{fnInt}(\sqrt{(1-X)},X,0,1)$$

to get 1.333333754. This is an excellent approximation of $\frac{4}{3}$, the exact value found in the example.

problem set 67

1. *(47)* Gaurav is standing 5 meters away from the base of the flagpole on which a flag is being raised at the rate of 1 meter per second. Find the rate of change of the angle of elevation from Gaurav's feet to the flag at the instant the flag is 12 meters above the ground.

2. *(65)* A ball is thrown downward with a velocity of 20 meters per second from the top of a building that is 160 meters tall. After developing the velocity and position functions for the ball, determine how long it will take for the ball to hit the ground.

3. *(52)* The figure to the right shows an isosceles trapezoid inscribed in a semicircle of radius 1 unit. The longer of the two parallel sides of the isosceles trapezoid coincides with the diameter of the semicircle.

   (a) Express the area of the isosceles trapezoid in terms of x.

   (b) Find the maximum possible area of the isosceles trapezoid.

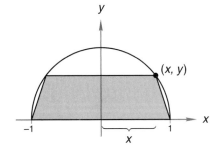

4. *(63)* Use calculus to find the maximum value and the minimum value of the function $f(x) = \frac{2}{3}x^3 - \frac{1}{2}x^2 - 10x - 1$ on the interval $[-3, 5]$. Check the answer with a graphing calculator.

5. *(67)* The area of a region is completely enclosed by the y-axis and the graph of $x = 4 - y^2$. Use y as the variable of integration to write a definite integral that defines this area.

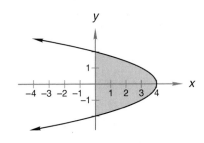

6. Find the area completely bounded by the
(67) graphs of $x = 4 - y^2$ and $x = 3y$.

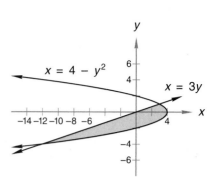

7. Use y as the variable of integration to write a definite integral whose value equals the area
(67) bounded by the coordinate axes and the graph of $y + 2x = 3$.

8. Evaluate $\displaystyle\int_1^5 2x\sqrt{2x - 1}\ dx$ by changing the variable of integration.
(66)

9. Approximate $\displaystyle\int_1^5 2x\sqrt{2x - 1}\ dx$ with a graphing calculator. Compare this answer to the answer
(59) to problem 8.

10. (a) Use calculus to find the area of the region enclosed by the graph of $f(x) = \dfrac{x^2 - 1}{x^2 + 1}$ and the
(59) x-axis. (*Hint:* $\dfrac{x^2 - 1}{x^2 + 1} = 1 - \dfrac{2}{x^2 + 1}$.)

    (b) Check the answer to (a) with a graphing calculator.

11. The definite integral $\displaystyle\int_0^1 x \sin \dfrac{\pi x^2}{2}\ dx$ is equivalent to which of the following?
(66)

    A. $\displaystyle\int_0^1 \dfrac{1}{\pi} \sin u\ du$ B. $\displaystyle\int_0^{\pi/2} \dfrac{1}{\pi} \sin u\ du$

    C. $\displaystyle\int_0^{\pi/2} \sin u\ du$ D. $\displaystyle\int_0^{\pi/2} \pi \sin u\ du$

12. Let $f(x) = \arcsin \dfrac{x}{2}$. Find $f'(1)$.
(64)

13. Find the slope of the line tangent to the graph of $y = \arctan x$ at $x = \dfrac{\sqrt{3}}{2}$.
(64)

14. An object moves along the number line so that its velocity at time t is given by
(62) $v(t) = t\sqrt{t^2 - 1}$. Find the distance the object moves from $t = \sqrt{10}$ to $t = \sqrt{26}$.

Integrate in problems 15–18.

15. $\displaystyle\int \sin^3 x \cos x\ dx$ **16.** $\displaystyle\int \dfrac{\cos x}{\sin^2 x}\ dx$
(66)   (66)

17. $\displaystyle\int \dfrac{3}{\sqrt{9 - x^2}}\ dx$ **18.** $\displaystyle\int \dfrac{3x}{\sqrt{9 - x^2}}\ dx$
(64)   (66)

19. Find the area bounded by the x-axis and the graph of $y = \cos (2x)$ between $x = 0$ and $x = \frac{\pi}{2}$.
(59)

20. Suppose $f(x) \geq 0$ for $2 \leq x \leq 4$. Which of the following statements must be true?
(57)

    A. $\displaystyle\int_2^4 f(x)\ dx \leq 4$ B. $\displaystyle\int_4^2 f(x)\ dx \leq 0$

    C. $\displaystyle\int_2^4 f(x)\ dx = \int_4^2 f(x)\ dx$ D. $\displaystyle\int_2^4 f(x)\ dx = -\int_2^4 f(x)\ dx$

21. Find C and k in $f(x) = Ce^{kx}$ such that $f'(0) = 2$ and $f(0) = 4$.
(61)

22. Differentiate $y = \dfrac{e^{-x} + e^{\cos x}}{2\sqrt{x} + 1}$ with respect to x.
(50)

23. Evaluate $\displaystyle\lim_{h \to 0} \dfrac{f(2 + h) - f(2)}{h}$ where $f(x) = \sin x$.
(28)

24. A monkey cage with a square base and rectangular sides is to be constructed. The volume of the
(5) cage must be 300 cubic feet. The cost per square foot of the top is \$8, the cost per square foot of
the bottom is \$4, and the cost per square foot of each of the walls is \$15. Let the height of the
cage be h and the length of one side of the base be L. Express h in terms of L. Then express the
total cost of the monkey cage in terms of L.

25. Let f be the function defined by $f(x) = x^3 - x^2 - 4x + 4$. The point (a, b) is on the graph of
(27) f, and the line tangent to the graph at (a, b) passes through the point $(0, -8)$, which is not on the
graph of f. Find a and b.

LESSON 68 *Even and Odd Functions*

If a function is an even function, then the value of $f(x)$ where x is a distance to the right of the origin
equals the value of $f(-x)$ where $-x$ is the same distance but to the left of the origin. For an even
function f, if $f(x_1)$ equals $+2$, then $f(-x_1)$ must also equal $+2$. If $f(3)$ equals -5, then $f(-3)$ must also
equal -5. **This means that the same things happen to the graph of an even function at equal
distances to the left and right of the origin.** In general, for any even function f and any value of x
in its domain,

$$f(-x) = f(x)$$

**If a function is an odd function, then the same things happen to the graph of the function at
equal distances to the left and right of the origin but in opposite vertical directions.** If a function
is an odd function and $f(x_1)$ equals 5, then $f(-x_1)$ must equal -5. In general, for any odd function f
and any value of x in its domain,

$$f(-x) = -f(x)$$

The graph of an even function is symmetric with respect to the y-axis, and the graph of an
odd function is symmetric with respect to the origin.** The cosine function is an even function, and
the sine function is an odd function.

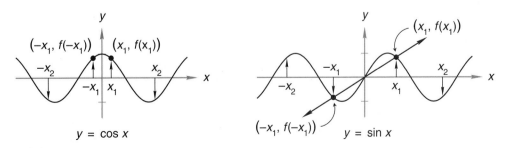

$$y = \cos x \qquad\qquad y = \sin x$$

For the cosine function, the vertical distance and direction from the x-axis to the graph is the same at
x_1 and $-x_1$. The points $(x_1, f(x_1))$ and $(-x_1, f(-x_1))$ are horizontally the same distance from the
y-axis. For the sine function, the vertical distance from the x-axis to the graph at x_1 is the same as at
$-x_1$ but in the opposite direction. The points $(x_1, f(x_1))$ and $(-x_1, f(-x_1))$ lie on a line that passes
through the origin, and these points are equidistant from the origin.

To determine whether a function is odd, even, or neither, the procedure is to replace x with $-x$ in the rule for the function. If the result is the same, the function is an even function. If the magnitude is the same but the sign is different, the function is an odd function. Any other result indicates that the function is neither even nor odd. Recognizing that a function is even or odd can be helpful in graphing the function as well as in evaluating definite integrals involving the function.

example 68.1   Is the function $f(x) = x^4 + x^2 - 6$ an even function, an odd function, or neither?

solution   We compare $f(x)$ and $f(-x)$.

$$f(x) = x^4 + x^2 - 6 \qquad f(-x) = (-x)^4 + (-x)^2 - 6 = x^4 + x^2 - 6$$

Since both $f(x)$ and $f(-x)$ equal $x^4 + x^2 - 6$, the function is an **even function.** Note the symmetry of the graph of f about the y-axis.

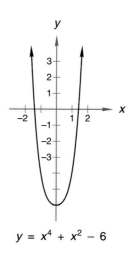

$$y = x^4 + x^2 - 6$$

example 68.2   Is $f(x) = x^3 - x$ an even function, an odd function, or neither?

solution   We consider the expressions for $f(x)$ and $f(-x)$.

$$f(x) = x^3 - x \qquad f(-x) = (-x)^3 - (-x) = -x^3 + x = -(x^3 - x)$$

Since $f(x) = x^3 - x$ and $f(-x) = -(x^3 - x) = -f(x)$, the function is an **odd function.** Notice the symmetry about the origin displayed by the graph of $y = x^3 - x$.

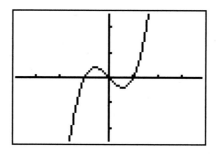

Notice that, in this example, all of the exponents of x were odd, and the function was odd. In example 68.1, all of the exponents were even (-6 can be written as $-6x^0$), and the function was even. This demonstrates a useful rule for polynomial functions: **A polynomial function is even if every exponent of x is even and odd if every exponent of x is odd.** (This is, in fact, the origin of the terms even function and odd function!) To use this rule, remember that it only applies to polynomial functions of a single variable and that constant terms (x^0 terms) have even exponents.

example 68.3   Evaluate: $\displaystyle\int_{-1.5}^{1.5} (x^3 - x)\, dx$

solution   This integral can easily be determined using the Fundamental Theorem of Calculus, but we will do it in a more insightful way.

Since $x^3 - x$ is an odd function, and the lower and upper limits of integration are the same distance from the origin but in opposite directions, we can exploit the symmetry of the graph of $x^3 - x$.

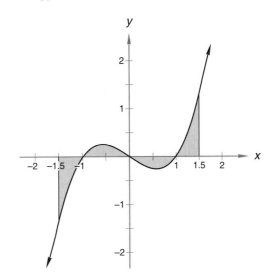

We see from the graph that the regions above the x-axis have exact counterparts below the x-axis. So, in the integral, these areas cancel each other out, giving an answer of 0.

$$\int_{-1.5}^{1.5} (x^3 - x)\, dx = \mathbf{0}$$

example 68.4   Is $g(x) = x^3 - x - 4$ an even function, an odd function, or neither?

solution   We consider the expressions for $g(x)$ and $g(-x)$.

$$g(x) = x^3 - x - 4 \qquad g(-x) = (-x)^3 - (-x) - 4 = -(x^3 - x + 4)$$

We see that $g(-x)$ is not equal to $g(x)$ nor is it equal to $-g(-x)$, because the constant 4 has the wrong sign. Thus the function $g(x)$ is **neither even nor odd.** Of course, we could also have looked at the exponents of x to see by inspection that $g(x)$ is neither even nor odd, because both even and odd exponents are present.

example 68.5   Is $y = -3 \tan (2\pi x)$ an odd function, an even function, or neither?

solution   Every basic trigonometric function is either an odd function or an even function. The coefficient -3 flips the graph upside down but does not affect symmetry. The 2π changes the period, but it does not affect symmetry. A phase shift left or right could affect symmetry, but this function does not have a phase shift. A vertical translation could also affect symmetry, but this function is not translated. Thus we compare $f(x)$ and $f(-x)$.

$$f(x) = -3 \tan (2\pi x) \qquad f(-x) = -3 \tan [2\pi(-x)] = -3 \tan (-2\pi x)$$

$$= 3 \tan (2\pi x) = -[-3 \tan (2\pi x)]$$

In the simplification on the right-hand we used the property $\tan (-kx) = -\tan (kx)$ from Lesson 8. Since $f(x) = -3 \tan (2\pi x)$ and $f(-x) = -[-3 \tan (2\pi x)]$, $f(-x) = -f(x)$. Therefore f is an **odd function.**

example 68.6   Are the following functions even functions, odd functions, or neither?

(a) $f(x) = e^x$ (b) $g(x) = e^{-x^2}$

solution   (a) We compare $f(x)$ and $f(-x)$.

$$f(x) = e^x \qquad f(-x) = e^{-x}$$

For f to be even, $f(-x)$ would have to equal e^x. For f to be odd, $f(-x)$ would have to equal $-e^x$. Since neither of these is true, the function f is **neither even nor odd.**

(b) We compare $g(x)$ and $g(-x)$.

$$g(x) = e^{-x^2} \qquad g(-x) = e^{-(-x)^2} = e^{-x^2}$$

Since $g(x) = g(-x)$, the function g is an **even function.**

These results are also apparent from the graphs of the functions.

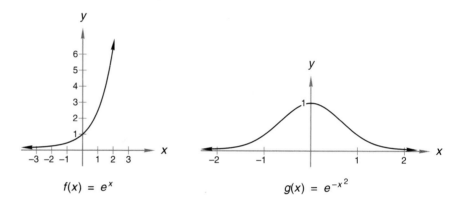

$$f(x) = e^x \qquad\qquad g(x) = e^{-x^2}$$

example 68.7   Is $g(x) = \dfrac{x^2 + \cos x}{\sin x}$ an odd function, an even function, or neither?

solution   We compare $g(x)$ and $g(-x)$.

$$g(x) = \frac{x^2 + \cos x}{\sin x} \qquad g(-x) = \frac{(-x)^2 + \cos(-x)}{\sin(-x)}$$

Since $\cos(-x) = \cos x$ and $\sin(-x) = -\sin x$,

$$g(-x) = \frac{x^2 + \cos x}{-\sin x} = -\left(\frac{x^2 + \cos x}{\sin x}\right)$$

Since $g(-x) = -g(x)$, the function is an **odd function.** Thanks to the graphing calculator, we can quickly visualize this function's symmetry about the origin.

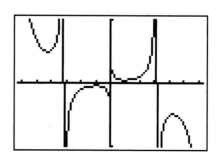

problem set 68

1. A box-shaped building with a square base, a square top, and rectangular sides is to be
(52) constructed. The volume of the building must be 300 cubic meters. The material to be used for
the base costs $8 per square meter, the material for the roof costs $4 per square meter, and the
material for the walls costs $15 per square meter. Let the height of the building be y and the
length of one side of the base be x.

(a) Express the total cost of the building in terms of x.

(b) Use calculus to find the exact dimensions of the building that can be constructed for the
minimal cost.

(c) Check the answer to (b) with a graphing calculator.

2. An object is dropped from a height of 400 feet. Develop an equation that expresses the height of
(65) the object as a function of the time t since the ball is dropped.

Determine whether each of the functions in problems 3–8 is odd, even, or neither.

3. $f(x) = x^6 - x^2 + 5$
(68)

4. $g(x) = x^3 - 2x$
(68)

5. $h(x) = e^x$
(68)

6. $F(x) = e^{-\pi x^2}$
(68)

7. $G(x) = \dfrac{x + \sin x}{\cos x}$
(68)

8. $H(x) = x^2 + \cos x$
(68)

9. The definite integral $\displaystyle\int_0^\pi (\sin x)e^{\cos x}\, dx$ is equivalent to which of the following?
(66)

  A. $\displaystyle\int_0^\pi e^u\, du$ B. $\displaystyle\int_1^{-1} e^u\, du$ C. $\displaystyle\int_{-1}^1 e^u\, du$ D. $-\displaystyle\int_{-1}^1 e^u\, du$

10. Find the Maclaurin series for $y = \sin^2 x$. (*Hint:* Use the trigonometric reduction identity
(55) $\sin^2 x = \frac{1}{2} - \frac{1}{2}\cos(2x)$ to simplify this process.)

Differentiate in problems 11 and 12.

11. $\dfrac{d}{dx}\left[\dfrac{2\sqrt{x+1}}{x^2 + \sin^3(2x)}\right]$
(50)

12. $\dfrac{d}{dx}\left[\arcsin(3x) - \dfrac{1}{4}\sin^4(3x)\right]$
(64)

Integrate in problems 13–15.

13. $\displaystyle\int \cos(3x)\sin^3(3x)\, dx$
(66)

14. $\displaystyle\int x(x^3 + 1)\, dx$
(38)

15. $\displaystyle\int \dfrac{6}{4 + 9x^2}\, dx$
(64)

16. Find the area enclosed by the graphs of
(67) $x = 1 - y$ and $x = -1 + y^2$.

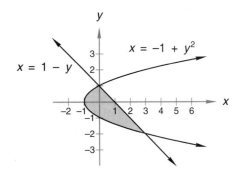

17. Let f be a continuous function on $(-\infty, \infty)$. In each of the following equations, find the values of
(57) a and b that make the equation true.

(a) $\displaystyle\int_a^b f(x)\, dx - \int_3^1 f(x)\, dx = \int_0^3 f(x)\, dx$

(b) $\displaystyle\int_0^4 f(x)\, dx + \int_4^2 f(x)\, dx = \int_a^b f(x)\, dx$

18. Find the maximum value and the minimum value of $f(x) = x(x - 2)(x - 5)$ on the
(63) interval $[0, 5]$.

19. Suppose f is continuous on $[-1, 4]$ and has the properties listed in the table below. Sketch a
(63) graph of f, and determine the maximum and the minimum values of f.

x	$x = -1$	$-1 < x < 2$	$x = 2$	$2 < x < 4$	$x = 4$
$f(x)$	3		-3		-6
$f'(x)$		negative	-1	negative	
$f''(x)$		positive	0	negative	

20. Suppose $f(t) = Ae^t + B$, $f(0) = 5$, and $f'(0) = 10$. Find the values of A and B.
(61)

21. Both f and g are functions that are continuous on $[1, 4]$ with $f(x) > g(x)$ on $[1, 4]$. Express the
(60) area bounded by the graphs of f and g on $[1, 4]$ as a definite integral.

22. The equation of f is $f(x) = x^3 + x$. Find $f^{-1}(2)$.
(58)

23. A rectangle's area remains constant at 200 m^2 as both its width W and length L change with
(46) respect to time.

    (a) Find an equation that relates W, $\dfrac{dL}{dt}$, and $\dfrac{dW}{dt}$, but does not contain L.

    (b) If the length L is increasing at the constant rate of 15 units per second, at what rate is the width W changing when $W = 10$?

24. Express $y = 2^x$ as an exponential whose base is e.
(16)

25. Find the value of x for which lines tangent to $y = \ln x$ and $y = 2x^2$ will be parallel to
(25,26) each other.

LESSON 69   *Integration by Parts I*

Integration by parts is a procedure that permits us to find the integrals of products in some cases. This rule is simply a rearrangement of the results of finding the differential of a product. If u and v are both functions, the differential of the product uv is

$$d(uv) = u\,dv + v\,du$$

Integrating both sides gives us

$$\int d(uv) = \int u\,dv + \int v\,du$$

Since the integral of $d(uv)$ is uv, we can write

$$uv = \int u\,dv + \int v\,du$$

This can be rearranged to yield the following expression:

$$\int u\,dv = uv - \int v\,du$$

    This equation provides a method of finding the integral of $u\,dv$. We find the product of u times v and subtract from this product the integral of $v\,du$. When using this rule, the trick is selecting u and *dv.* Making the wrong choice can lead to expressions that are more difficult to integrate than the original integral. Depending on the integrand, integration by parts may require one step or several steps, or it might not work at all. Because it does not work for all products, it is not called the product rule for integration. In this lesson we consider expressions that can be integrated in one step.

Integration by parts works especially well for expressions such as

$$\int xe^x \, dx, \qquad \int xe^{2x} \, dx, \qquad \text{and} \qquad \int 2x \sin x \, dx$$

In the first two expressions the prudent choice is to let u equal x and to let dv equal the rest of the expression. In the third expression the prudent choices for u and dv are $u = 2x$ and $dv = \sin x \, dx$.

example 69.1   Integrate: $\int x \sin x \, dx$

solution   None of the integration techniques encountered before this lesson appear useful, so we use integration by parts. On the left-hand side we draw a box and let u equal x and dv equal the rest of the expression. Then we find du and v and put them in the box, as shown on the right-hand side.

$u = x$	
	$dv = \sin x \, dx$

$u = x$	$v = -\cos x$
$du = dx$	$dv = \sin x \, dx$

Now we can use the rule for integration by parts.

$$\int u \, dv = uv - \int v \, du$$

We substitute as indicated and get

$$\int x \sin x \, dx = (x)(-\cos x) - \int -\cos x \, dx$$
$$= -x \cos x + \sin x + C$$

Notice that we went from the integral of a product ($x \sin x$) to the integral of a much simpler function ($-\cos x$). To rewrite integrals involving products in such a way that they become easier to evaluate is the primary goal of integration by parts.

One other issue in this example is worth noting. After setting $dv = \sin x \, dx$, we set $v = -\cos x$. We could have set $v = -\cos x + C_1$ for any constant C_1. Notice that this is unnecessary, as terms involving C_1 sum to zero, as shown below.

$$\int u \, dv = uv - \int v \, du$$
$$= x(-\cos x + C_1) - \int (-\cos x + C_1) \, dx$$
$$= -x \cos x + C_1 x + \sin x - C_1 x + C$$
$$= -x \cos x + \sin x + C$$

This was the original answer.

As always, we can check the answer by differentiating.

$$\frac{d}{dx}(-x \cos x + \sin x + C) = -[x(-\sin x) + \cos x] + \cos x$$
$$= x \sin x - \cos x + \cos x$$
$$= x \sin x$$

Checking is wise anytime you use a new technique.

example 69.2   Integrate: $\int \ln x \, dx$

solution   The correct choice in this problem is to let u equal $\ln x$, as shown on the left.

$u = \ln x$			$u = \ln x$	$v = x$
	$dv = dx$		$du = \dfrac{dx}{x}$	$dv = dx$

On the right we complete the box by finding du and v. Then we write the rule for integration by parts and substitute.

$$\int u \, dv = uv - \int v \, du$$

$$\int \ln x \, dx = x \ln x - \int (x)\left(\frac{dx}{x}\right)$$

$$= x \ln x - \int dx$$

$$= x \ln x - x + C$$

example 69.3   Integrate: $\int xe^{2x} \, dx$

solution   We let u equal x and let dv equal $e^{2x} \, dx$.

$u = x$			$u = x$	$v = \dfrac{1}{2}e^{2x}$
	$dv = e^{2x} \, dx$		$du = dx$	$dv = e^{2x} \, dx$

On the right we complete the box by finding du and v. Then we write the rule for integration by parts and substitute.

$$\int u \, dv = uv - \int v \, du \qquad \text{integration by parts}$$

$$\int xe^{2x} \, dx = (x)\left(\frac{1}{2}e^{2x}\right) - \frac{1}{2}\int e^{2x} \, dx \qquad \text{substituted}$$

$$= \frac{1}{2}xe^{2x} - \frac{1}{2}\left(\frac{1}{2}\right)\int e^{2x}(2) \, dx \qquad \text{rearranged}$$

$$= \frac{1}{2}xe^{2x} - \frac{1}{4}e^{2x} + C \qquad \text{integrated}$$

$$= \frac{1}{4}e^{2x}(2x - 1) + C \qquad \text{factored}$$

example 69.4   Integrate: $\int x \ln x \, dx$

solution   There are at least two possible choices for u and dv in the problem. We could (1) let $u = x$ and $dv = \ln x \, dx$, or (2) let $u = \ln x$ and $dv = x \, dx$. We have seen the first option used in previous examples because $du = dx$ often simplifies the integrals in question. So we choose option (1) here.

$u = x$			$u = x$	$v = x \ln x - x$
	$dv = \ln x \, dx$		$du = dx$	$dv = \ln x \, dx$

The fact that $v = x \ln x - x$ follows from example 69.2. We write the rule for integration by parts and substitute.

$$\int u \, dv = uv - \int v \, du$$

$$\int x \ln x \, dx = x(x \ln x - x) - \int (x \ln x - x) \, dx$$

This is a more complicated integral! Rather than continuing, we stop and question our choice of u and dv. Instead of picking option (1) with $u = x$ and $dv = \ln x \, dx$, we try option (2).

$u = \ln x$	
	$dv = x \, dx$

$u = \ln x$	$v = \dfrac{x^2}{2}$
$du = \dfrac{dx}{x}$	$dv = x \, dx$

Integration by parts gives

$$\int x \ln x \, dx = \frac{x^2}{2} \ln x - \int \frac{x^2}{2} \frac{dx}{x}$$

$$= \frac{x^2}{2} \ln x - \int \frac{x}{2} \, dx$$

The difficulty of the integral decreased. This indicates that we are probably on the right track. The remainder of the solution is shown below.

$$\int x \ln x \, dx = \frac{x^2}{2} \ln x - \int \frac{x}{2} \, dx$$

$$= \frac{x^2}{2} \ln x - \frac{x^2}{4} + C$$

$$= \frac{1}{4}x^2(2 \ln x - 1) + C$$

Usually when an integrand is a product of a polynomial and another function, we let u equal the polynomial. This example, however, shows that there are exceptions to this rule.

problem set
69

1. (47) The area of a rectangle remains constant at 1000 square meters as both its length L and width W change with respect to time.

   (a) Find an equation that relates L, $\dfrac{dL}{dt}$, and $\dfrac{dW}{dt}$, but does not contain W.

   (b) Find the length of the rectangle when its width is decreasing at a rate of 1 m/s and its length is increasing at a rate of 10 m/s.

2. (26) The interest was compounded continuously, so the growth of the money in the bank account was exponential. The initial deposit was $1000, and $1100 was in the account one year later. How much money will be in the account 10 years from the time of the initial deposit, assuming no extra deposits or withdrawals are made?

Integrate in problems 3–7.

3. (69) $\displaystyle\int xe^x \, dx$ 4. (69) $\displaystyle\int \ln x \, dx$ 5. (69) $\displaystyle\int x \ln x \, dx$

6. (69) $\displaystyle\int 2x \cos x \, dx$ 7. (69) $\displaystyle\int x \sin x \, dx$

8. (68) Determine whether the function $y = \dfrac{\sin x \cos x}{x^2}$ is even, odd, or neither.

9. Is the graph of $y = x^2 + \cos x$ symmetric about the y-axis, the origin, or neither?
(68)

10. Find: $\dfrac{d}{dx}\left(\dfrac{xe^{\cos(3x)}}{x^3 + 1}\right)$ **11.** If $y = \arcsin x^2$, what is y'?
(50)   (64)

12. Integrate: $\displaystyle\int \dfrac{\cos x}{\sqrt{\sin x + 1}}\,dx + \int x^{-5}\,dx + \int \dfrac{x}{\sqrt{1 - x^4}}\,dx$
(66)

13. Evaluate $\displaystyle\int_0^{\pi/4} [\cos(2x)](e^{\sin(2x)})\,dx$ by changing the variable of integration.
(66)

14. Approximate $\displaystyle\int_0^{\pi/4} [\cos(2x)](e^{\sin(2x)})\,dx$ with a graphing calculator. Compare this answer to the
(59) answer to problem 13.

15. Find the area of the region bounded by the graphs of $y = 1 + x$, $y = -x^2$, $x = 1$, and $x = 3$.
(60)

16. Find the area of the region enclosed by the graphs of $y = 2 - x^2$ and $y = x$.
(60)

17. (a) Use calculus to find the area of the region enclosed by the graphs of $y = \dfrac{2}{1+x^2}$
(60)   and $y = x^2$.

    (b) Check your answer to (a) with a graphing calculator.

18. Write a definite integral whose value equals the area of the region in the fourth quadrant bounded
(67) by $x = y(y - 1)(y + 2)$ and the coordinate axes.

19. Find the Maclaurin series for $y = \cos^2 x$. (*Hint:* Use the trigonometric reduction identity
(55) $\cos^2 x = \frac{1}{2} + \frac{1}{2}\cos(2x)$.)

20. Evaluate $f^{-1}(3)$ where $f(x) = 4x - 12$.
(58)

21. Let R be the region in the first quadrant bounded by $y = 6x^2$, $y = \frac{6}{x}$, the x-axis, and $x = k$,
(60) where $k > 1$.

    (a) Express the area of R as a function of k.

    (b) Find the value of k so that the area of R is 20 square units.

    (c) If the area of R is increasing at the constant rate of 8 square units per second, at what rate is
         k increasing when $k = 27$?

22. Let f be a continuous function on $(-\infty, \infty)$ such that $\int_{-1}^5 f(x)\,dx = 7$ and $\int_{-1}^3 f(x)\,dx = -3$.
(57) Find the following:

    (a) $\displaystyle\int_3^5 f(x)\,dx$ (b) $\displaystyle\int_5^{-1} f(x)\,dx - \int_5^3 f(x)\,dx$

23. The function $f(x) = \ln(\cos x)$ is defined for all x in which of the following intervals?
(12,18)

    A. $0 < x < \dfrac{\pi}{2}$ B. $-\dfrac{\pi}{2} \le x \le \dfrac{\pi}{2}$ C. $0 < x \le 2\pi$ D. $-\pi \le x \le \dfrac{\pi}{2}$

24. Indicate the equation that describes a curve with the following property: For every point (x, y)
(68) on the curve, $(-x, -y)$ also lies on the curve.

    A. $x^2 + y = x$ B. $x^2 + y^2 = 1$ C. $y = 2x + 1$ D. $x^3 + y^3 = 1$

25. Let f be the function defined by $f(x) = \ln(x^2 - 9)$.
(58,68)

    (a) Determine whether the graph of the function is symmetric with respect to the x-axis, the
         y-axis, or the origin.

    (b) Find the domain of the function.

    (c) Find all values of x such that $f(x) = 0$.

    (d) Find the inverse function f^{-1} for $x > 3$.

LESSON 70   *Properties of Limits • Some Special Limits*

70.A
properties of limits

The limit of a function f as x approaches c is a **number,** the number that $f(x)$ approaches as x gets closer and closer to c. What we have learned about the limits of functions can be extended to the limits of sums, differences, products, and quotients of functions. The rules for these extensions are presented without proof. For concrete illustrations of the rules, we use the functions f and g as defined below.

$$f(x) = x + 1 \qquad g(x) = x^2 + 3$$

The limit of f as x approaches 2 is 3, and the limit of g as x approaches 2 is 7.

$$\lim_{x \to 2} (x + 1) = 3 \qquad \lim_{x \to 2} (x^2 + 3) = 7$$

To make a general statement, we let x approach c, the limit of f be L, and the limit of g be M.

$$\lim_{x \to c} f(x) = L \qquad \lim_{x \to c} g(x) = M$$

1. **The limit of the sum of two functions equals the sum of the limits of the individual functions.**

$$\lim_{x \to 2} \left[(x + 1) + (x^2 + 3) \right] = 3 + 7 \qquad \lim_{x \to c} (f + g)(x) = L + M$$

It is important to realize that $(f + g)(x)$ is a new function that equals the sum of the original functions. In this example if we add the f function to the g function, we get $f + g$,

$$(f + g)(x) = x^2 + x + 4$$

and the limit of this new function as x approaches 2 is 10, which equals the sum of the individual limits 3 and 7.

$$\lim_{x \to 2} (x^2 + x + 4) = 10$$

2. **The limit of the difference of two functions equals the difference of the limits of the individual functions.**

$$\lim_{x \to 2} \left[(x + 1) - (x^2 + 3) \right] = 3 - 7 \qquad \lim_{x \to c} (f - g)(x) = L - M$$

3. **The limit of the product of two functions equals the product of the limits of the individual functions.**

$$\lim_{x \to 2} \left[(x + 1)(x^2 + 3) \right] = 3 \cdot 7 \qquad \lim_{x \to c} (f g)(x) = LM$$

4. **The limit of the product of a constant and a function equals the product of the constant and the limit of the function.**

$$\lim_{x \to 2} 9(x + 1) = 9 \cdot 3 \qquad \lim_{x \to c} k f(x) = kL$$

5. **If the limit of the denominator does not equal zero, the limit of the quotient of two functions equals the quotient of the individual limits.**

$$\lim_{x \to 2} \frac{x + 1}{x^2 + 3} = \frac{3}{7} \qquad \lim_{x \to c} \left(\frac{f}{g} \right)(x) = \frac{L}{M}$$

In addition to the limits of arithmetic combinations of functions, two other properties of limits are particularly useful. One is a squeezing principle, and the other is substitution principle.

6. **If the value of a function g is greater than or equal to the value of a second function f and less than or equal to the value of a third function h and if $f(x)$ and $h(x)$ both approach the same limit L as x approaches c, then $g(x)$ also approaches L as x approaches c.** This property is called the **pinching theorem,** the **squeeze theorem,** or the **sandwich theorem,** because the limit of $g(x)$ is pinched, squeezed, or sandwiched between the limits of $f(x)$ and $h(x)$. For example, suppose

$$f(x) \leq g(x) \leq h(x)$$

is true for all x in some interval, and $f(x)$ and $h(x)$ both approach 5 as x approaches some number c in that interval. Since $g(x)$ is greater than $f(x)$ and less than $h(x)$, it is trapped between two expressions that are approaching 5. Thus $g(x)$ must also approach 5.

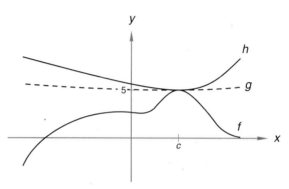

7. **If $\lim\limits_{x \to a} g(x) = L$ and $\lim\limits_{x \to L} f(x) = f(L)$, then**

$$\lim_{x \to a} f(g(x)) = f\left(\lim_{x \to a} g(x) \right) = f(L)$$

This may look intimidating, but it is fairly simple to apply. Its usefulness is that it allows us to evaluate the limit of composite functions under certain conditions. First, the inner function's limit must exist. If it does exist, it has a value. That is what we mean by

$$\lim_{x \to a} g(x) = L$$

Secondly, the value of that limit must be in the domain of the outer function, and the outer function must be continuous at that part of its domain. Those are the conditions captured by the stipulation

$$\lim_{x \to L} f(x) = f(L)$$

Under these circumstances, we can evaluate the limit $\lim_{x \to a} f(g(x))$ by finding $\lim_{x \to a} g(x)$ and then determining $f(\lim_{x \to a} g(x))$.

example 70.1   Let $\lim\limits_{x \to 2} f(x) = 3$ and $\lim\limits_{x \to 2} g(x) = 9$. Find $\lim\limits_{x \to 2} [2f(x) + \pi g(x)]$.

solution   This problem requires that we use two rules. The first is that the limit of a sum equals the sum of the limits.

$$\lim_{x \to 2} [2f(x) + \pi g(x)] = \lim_{x \to 2} 2f(x) + \lim_{x \to 2} \pi g(x)$$

The second is that the limit of the product of a constant and a function equals the product of the constant and the limit of the function. Thus the limit of $2f(x)$ is 2 times the limit of $f(x)$, or $2 \cdot 3$, and the limit of $\pi g(x)$ is π times the limit of $g(x)$, or $\pi \cdot 9$.

$$\lim_{x \to 2} 2f(x) + \lim_{x \to 2} \pi g(x) = 2 \cdot 3 + \pi \cdot 9 = \mathbf{6 + 9\pi}$$

example 70.2   If $\lim_{x \to a} f(x) = L$, can we say that $f(a)$ exists?

solution   This problem is typical of problems that appear on standardized tests requiring calculus. In order to answer these questions, a complete understanding of the concept is required. The limit of $f(x)$ as x approaches a is an indication of what happens at values of x close to a and has nothing to do with $f(a)$, which is the value of f when $x = a$. **The fact that the limit exists does not imply that $f(a)$ exists.** For example, suppose $f(x) = \frac{x^2 - 1}{x - 1}$. Then $\lim_{x \to 1} f(x)$ exists and equals 2, while $f(1)$ does not exist.

example 70.3   Is the following statement true? Why or why not?

$$\text{If } \lim_{x \to 3} f(x) = L, \text{ then } f(3) = L.$$

solution   **The statement is false because the value of the function when $x = 3$ does not have to equal the limit of the function as x approaches 3.** Consider the following graph.

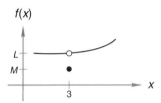

The graph shows that the limit as x approaches 3 is L, but $f(3)$ equals M, not L.

example 70.4   If f is a function such that $-x^2 \le f(x) \le x^2$ for all values of x, what is $\lim_{x \to 0} f(x)$?

solution   The function f is sandwiched between $-x^2$ and $+x^2$. As x approaches zero, both of these functions approach zero, so $f(x)$ **must also approach zero.**

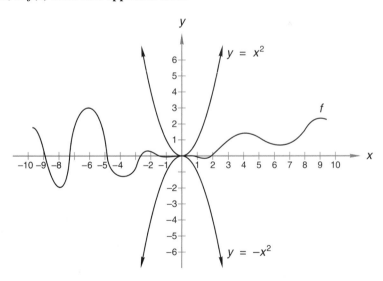

example 70.5   Evaluate: $\lim_{x \to \pi/4} \ln (\tan x)$

solution   Our inclination is to evaluate the expression $\ln (\tan \frac{\pi}{4})$. Indeed, that is what we will do. However, we must apply the substitution principle to ensure that we may. First, we look at $\lim_{x \to \pi/4} \tan x$. From experience with trigonometric functions (in particular, experience with the graph of the tangent function), we know that $\lim_{x \to \pi/4^-} \tan x = \lim_{x \to \pi/4^+} \tan x = \tan \frac{\pi}{4} = 1$. Thus, the first condition of the substitution principle is met. Now we consider the domain of the natural logarithm function. Since its domain is the positive real numbers, 1 is in the domain. We know the natural logarithm function is continuous on its domain (and in particular, at 1), so the second condition is also met. Therefore

$$\lim_{x \to \pi/4} \ln (\tan x) = \ln \left(\lim_{x \to \pi/4} \tan x \right)$$

$$= \ln \left(\tan \frac{\pi}{4} \right)$$

$$= \ln 1$$

$$= \mathbf{0}$$

70.B
some special limits

The limit of a function is a number **unless** the limit is $\pm\infty$. The function $\frac{1}{x}$ has no limit as x approaches zero because the left-hand limit does not equal the right-hand limit.

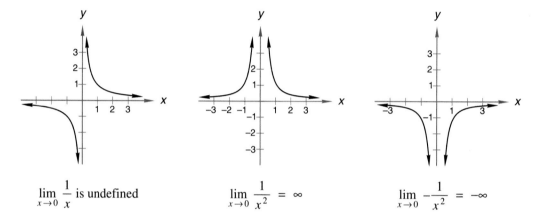

$$\lim_{x \to 0} \frac{1}{x} \text{ is undefined} \qquad \lim_{x \to 0} \frac{1}{x^2} = \infty \qquad \lim_{x \to 0} -\frac{1}{x^2} = -\infty$$

The function $\frac{1}{x^2}$ has a limit of $+\infty$ as x approaches zero, because the value of the function increases positively without bound as x approaches zero from both the left and the right. Similar reasoning can be used to say that the limit of $-\frac{1}{x^2}$ is $-\infty$ as x approaches zero.

Most of the functions that we work with are well-behaved functions. If we need a function whose behavior is somewhat aberrant, we usually design a piecewise function that has the desired behavior, but this is not always necessary. The following two functions are famous for not having limits as x approaches zero.

$$y = \frac{|x|}{x} \qquad y = \sin \frac{1}{x}$$

The graphs of the functions allow us to see why. If x is a positive number, then the graph of the absolute value of x divided by x is the line $y = 1$, and if x is a negative number, then the graph is the line $y = -1$. When $x = 0$, the function is not defined.

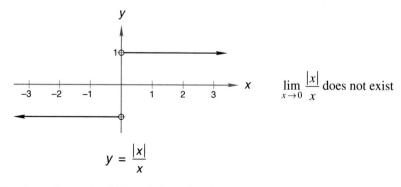

$$\lim_{x \to 0} \frac{|x|}{x} \text{ does not exist}$$

$$y = \frac{|x|}{x}$$

Thus, for all values of $x > 0$, $f(x) = 1$. For all values of $x < 0$, $f(x) = -1$. This means

$$\lim_{x \to 0^+} f(x) = 1 \qquad \text{and} \qquad \lim_{x \to 0^-} f(x) = -1$$

Since the left-hand limit and the right-hand limit are not equal, the function does not have a limit as x approaches zero.

The limit of $\sin \frac{1}{x}$ as x approaches zero does not exist either. The value of the sine function is never greater than $+1$ or less than -1. As x gets closer to zero, a small change in x produces a large change in $\frac{1}{x}$. As x gets closer to zero, the value of $\sin \frac{1}{x}$ fluctuates more rapidly between -1 and $+1$.

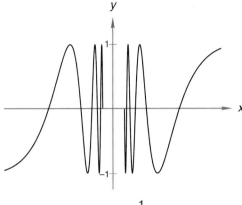

$$\lim_{x \to 0} \sin \frac{1}{x} \text{ does not exist}$$

$$y = \sin \frac{1}{x}$$

The graph of the function was terminated abruptly on both sides of zero, because the continuation would be impossible to draw. The curve becomes indistinguishably dense.

Another way to prove that the limit does not exist is to use a change of variables. If $t = \frac{1}{x}$, then t approaches ∞ as x approaches 0^+.

$$\lim_{x \to 0^+} \sin \frac{1}{x} = \lim_{t \to +\infty} \sin t$$

But $\sin t$ simply oscillates between -1 and $+1$ as t increases. So $\lim_{t \to +\infty} \sin t$ does not exist, meaning $\lim_{x \to 0^+} \sin \frac{1}{x}$ does not exist. Therefore $\lim_{x \to 0} \sin \frac{1}{x}$ cannot exist either.

problem set
70

1. (52) Carmen has 340 meters of fencing that she can use to enclose two separate fields. Let x be the width of a rectangular field that must be twice as long as it is wide and have an area of at least 800 square meters. Let y be the length of a side of a square field that must contain at least 100 square meters.

   (a) Find the minimum and maximum values of x. (*Hint:* No calculus is necessary.)

   (b) Express the sum of the areas of the two fields in terms of x.

   (c) Find the maximum area that Carmen can enclose in the two fields.

2. (65) A ball is thrown straight up from the top of a 100-meter-tall building with an initial velocity of 10 meters per second.

   (a) Develop an equation that expresses the height of the ball $h(t)$ above the ground as a function of time t, and find $h(3)$.

   (b) How long will it take for the ball to hit the ground? (Assume the ball is thrown just away from the edge of the building so that it does not hit the building during its descent.)

3. (63) Use the critical number theorem to find the absolute maximum value and the absolute minimum value of $y = x^{2/3}$ on the interval $[-1, 2]$.

4. (61) Suppose f is a real quadratic function whose graph passes through $(0, 2)$ with a slope of 5 at $x = 1$ and a slope of -1 at $x = -1$. Find the equation of f.

Evaluate each of the limits in problems 5–8 if they exist. Limits of ∞ and $-\infty$ are acceptable.

5. (70) $\lim_{x \to 0} \sin \frac{1}{x}$

6. (70) $\lim_{x \to 0^+} \frac{|x|}{x}$

7. (70) $\lim_{x \to 0} \frac{1}{x}$

8. (70) $\lim_{x \to 0} \frac{1}{x^2}$

Suppose f and g are functions such that $\lim_{x\to 2} f(x) = 3$, $\lim_{x\to 2} g(x) = -2$, $\lim_{x\to 1} f(x) = \pi$, and $\lim_{x\to -1} g(x) = 5$. Evaluate the limits in problems 9–11.

9. $\lim_{x\to 2} f(x)g(x)$
(70)

10. $\lim_{x\to 1} 2[f(x)]^2$
(70)

11. $\lim_{x\to 2} \dfrac{f(x) + g(x)}{f(x)g(x)}$
(70)

12. Suppose $-x^2 + 1 \le f(x) \le x^2 + 1$ for all real values of x. Evaluate $\lim_{x\to 0} f(x)$.
(70)

13. Suppose that g is a function and that $\lim_{x\to 2} g(x) = 4$. Does $g(2) = 4$? Explain your answer.
(70)

Integrate in problems 14–17.

14. $\int 3x \sin x \, dx$
(69)

15. $\int 2xe^{2x} \, dx$
(69)

16. $\int \ln x \, dx$
(69)

17. $\int \dfrac{e^x}{9 + e^{2x}} \, dx$
(66)

18. Which of the following equations describes a curve that is symmetric about the y-axis?
(68)
    A. $y = e^{x^2}$ B. $y = x^3$ C. $y = \sin x$ D. $y = e^x$

19. Find the area of the region enclosed by the graphs of $y = 1 - x^2$ and $y = x + 1$.
(60)

20. Find an equation of the line tangent to the graph of $y = \arctan x$ at the following x-values:
(64)
    (a) $x = 1$ (b) $x = -1$

21. Let $y = \dfrac{e^{\cos x} \sin x}{\ln (2x)} - \arctan (2x)$. Find y'.
(50,64)

Integrate in problems 22 and 23.

22. $\int (x + 1)e^{x^2 + 2x} \, dx$
(66)

23. $\int x \sin (x^2 + \pi) \, dx$
(66)

24. A rectangle of width w and height d is inscribed in a circle of radius 6. Express wd^2 entirely in terms of w.
(R)

25. Express $y = \log_3 x$ in terms of the natural logarithm.
(20)

LESSON 71   *Solids of Revolution I: Disks*

If a planar region is revolved about a line in the same plane, it forms a figure called a **solid of revolution**. The line is called the **axis of revolution**. We begin this lesson by looking at solids with circular cross sections that are formed by rotating planar regions about either the x-axis or the y-axis. The volume of these solids can be approximated by the sum of the volumes of n circular disks. The area of each disk is πr^2. The thickness is Δx if the x-axis is the axis of revolution. The thickness is Δy if the y-axis is the axis of revolution. Thus the volume of each disk is either

$$\pi r^2 \Delta x \qquad \text{or} \qquad \pi r^2 \Delta y$$

Below on the left-hand side we show a region bounded by the graph of f. Next we show the solid of revolution swept out as the region is rotated about the x-axis. The third figure shows the disk approximation of this volume.

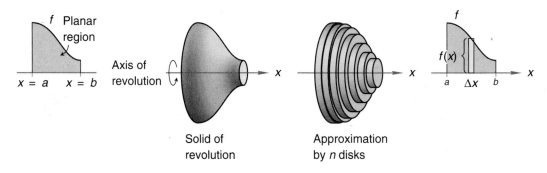

The right-hand figure shows a representative rectangle that generates one of the representative disks. The width of the disk is Δx, and the radius r of the disk is $f(x)$. The sum of the volumes of n disks is represented in summation notation below on the left-hand side. The exact volume is represented by the limit of this sum as n approaches infinity, which is the integral shown on the right-hand side.

$$\text{Approximate volume} \;=\; \sum_{i=1}^{n} \pi\big[f(x_i)\big]^2\,\Delta x \qquad \text{Exact volume} \;=\; \int_{a}^{b} \pi\big[f(x)\big]^2\,dx$$

example 71.1 Find the volume of the solid formed by revolving this triangular region about the x-axis.

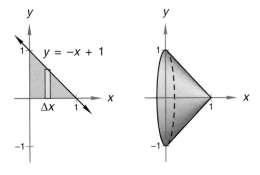

solution The graph shows a side view of half of a cross section of a representative disk. The thickness of the disk is Δx, and the radius of the disk is the height of the rectangle, which is $-x + 1$. We mentally stack these disks from the y-axis to $x = 1$, so the limits of integration are 0 and 1.

$$\text{Volume} \;=\; \int_{0}^{1} \pi r^2\,dx \;=\; \pi \int_{0}^{1} (-x + 1)^2\,dx \;=\; \pi \int_{0}^{1} (x^2 - 2x + 1)\,dx$$

We integrate and evaluate.

$$\text{Volume} \;=\; \pi\left[\frac{x^3}{3} - x^2 + x\right]_0^1 \;=\; \pi\left(\frac{1}{3} - 1 + 1\right) \;=\; \frac{\pi}{3}\ \textbf{units}^3$$

This answer can be confirmed geometrically. We see that the solid is a right circular cone, which means its volume is given by the expression

$$\frac{\pi r^2 h}{3}$$

Substituting $r = 1$ and $h = 1$ into this formula gives

$$\text{Volume} \;=\; \frac{\pi(1)^2(1)}{3} \;=\; \frac{\pi}{3}\ \text{units}^3$$

example 71.2 Find the volume of the solid formed by revolving about the x-axis the region bounded by the graphs $y = e^x$, $x = 0$, $x = 1$, and the x-axis.

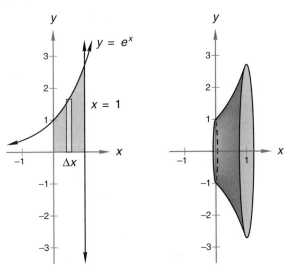

solution   A representative disk has thickness Δx and a radius of $y = e^x$. So the volume of this typical disk is $\pi(e^x)^2 \, \Delta x$. Summing infinitely many such disks gives the volume. This is accomplished by integrating.

$$\text{Volume} = \int_{x=0}^{x=1} \pi(e^x)^2 \, dx$$

$$= \pi \int_0^1 e^{2x} \, dx$$

$$= \pi \left[\frac{1}{2} e^{2x} \right]_0^1$$

$$= \frac{\pi}{2}(e^2 - e^0)$$

$$= \frac{\pi}{2}(e^2 - 1) \text{ units}^3$$

example 71.3   Find the volume of the solid formed by rotating about the y-axis the first quadrant region bounded by the line $y = 3$, the graph of $y = x^2$, and the y-axis.

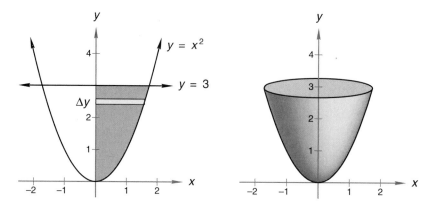

solution   The representative disk has a thickness Δy and a radius equal to the x-value of the right end of the rectangle. Since $y = x^2$, the x-value of the end of the rectangle is $x = \sqrt{y}$. We mentally stack these disks from the x-axis to $y = 3$, so the limits of integration are 0 and 3.

$$\text{Volume} = \int_{y=0}^{y=3} \pi r^2 \, dy = \pi \int_0^3 (\sqrt{y})^2 \, dy = \pi \int_0^3 y \, dy$$

Now we integrate and evaluate to get

$$\text{Volume} = \pi \left[\frac{y^2}{2} \right]_0^3 = \frac{9\pi}{2} \text{ units}^3$$

example 71.4   Find the volume of the solid formed by rotating about the y-axis the first quadrant region of the circle whose equation is $x^2 + y^2 = 9$.

solution

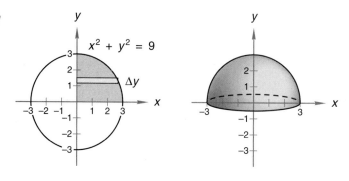

This problem asks for the volume of the top half of a sphere of radius 3. So our volume should be $\frac{1}{2}(\frac{4}{3}\pi(3)^3)$, or 18π, since the volume of a sphere of radius r is $\frac{4}{3}\pi r^3$. Notice that the height of our typical rectangle is an x-value, so we solve the given equation for x.

$$x^2 + y^2 = 9$$
$$x^2 = 9 - y^2$$
$$x = \pm\sqrt{9 - y^2}$$

Since the representative rectangle lies in the first quadrant, we take the positive choice for x.

We now know the following:

$$\text{Volume} = \int_{y=0}^{y=3} \pi r^2 \, dy$$
$$= \int_0^3 \pi(\sqrt{9 - y^2})^2 \, dy$$
$$= \pi \int_0^3 (9 - y^2) \, dy$$
$$= \pi\left(9y - \frac{y^3}{3}\right)\bigg|_0^3$$
$$= \pi(27 - 9)$$
$$= 18\pi \ \textbf{units}^3$$

We now extend this result to find the volume of a sphere of radius k, thus developing the formula for the volume of a sphere.

example 71.5   Find the volume of the solid formed by rotating about the x-axis the region bounded above by the circle whose equation is $x^2 + y^2 = k^2$ and below by the x-axis.

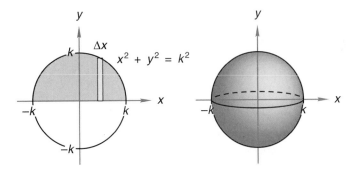

solution   The solid is a sphere whose radius is k. We know the volume of this sphere is $\frac{4}{3}\pi k^3$, and we are using this example to prove that. The thickness of a representative disk is Δx, and we mentally stack the disks from $x = -k$ to $x = k$. The radius of each disk is the y-value of the end of the rectangle, which is $\sqrt{k^2 - x^2}$.

$$\text{Volume} = \int_{-k}^{k} \pi r^2 \, dx = \pi \int_{-k}^{k} (\sqrt{k^2 - x^2})^2 \, dx = \pi \int_{-k}^{k} (k^2 - x^2) \, dx$$

Now we integrate and evaluate to get

$$\text{Volume} = \pi\left[k^2 x - \frac{x^3}{3}\right]_{-k}^{k} = \left(\pi k^3 - \frac{\pi k^3}{3}\right) - \left(-\pi k^3 + \frac{\pi k^3}{3}\right) = \frac{4\pi k^3}{3} \ \textbf{units}^3$$

We have used calculus to develop the formula for the volume of a sphere of radius k.

$$\text{Volume of a sphere} = \frac{4}{3}\pi k^3$$

problem set
71

1. A beam of rectangular cross section is cut
(52) from a log of radius 6, as shown. The
strength of the beam varies jointly with w
and the square of d, where w and d are as
shown. Thus $s = kwd^2$, where k is a
constant. Find the value of w that
maximizes the strength of the beam,
assuming the log is cylindrical with
circular cross section.

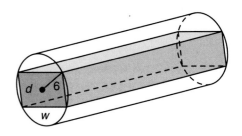

2. A variable force is applied to an object as it moves the object along a number line. The force
(62) applied at a particular value of x (in meters) is $F(x) = \frac{1}{2}x^2$ newtons. What is the work done by the
force on the object to move it in the direction of the force from $x = 1$ meter to $x = 3$ meters?

3. Find the volume of the solid formed when
(71) the triangular region shown is revolved
around the x-axis.

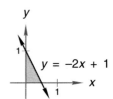

4. Find the volume of the solid formed when
(71) the region shown is revolved around
the y-axis.

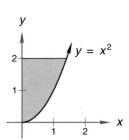

5. Suppose R is the first quadrant region
(71) bounded by the circle $x^2 + y^2 = 4$. Use y
as the variable of integration to write an
integral whose value equals the volume of
the solid formed when R is revolved about
the y-axis.

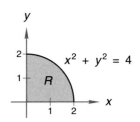

6. The figure shown has a rectangle drawn
(52) with one side along the x-axis and two
vertices on the curve $y = e^{-x^2}$.
  (a) Express the area of the rectangle in
      terms of x.
  (b) Find the exact area of the largest
      possible rectangle that can be so
      inscribed.

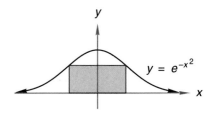

Suppose f and g are functions such that $\lim_{x \to \pi} f(x) = 2$, $\lim_{x \to \pi} g(x) = \frac{1}{3}$, $\lim_{x \to -\pi} f(x) = -2$,
and $\lim_{x \to -\pi} g(x) = 2$. Evaluate the limits in problems 7–9.

7. $\lim_{x \to \pi} \dfrac{2f(x)}{g(x)}$
(70)

8. $\lim_{x \to -\pi} \pi\left[f(x)\right]^2$
(70)

9. $\lim_{x \to \pi} \left[3f(x) - g(x)\right]$
(70)

10. (a) Let $f(x) = -|x|$ and $h(x) = |x|$. Suppose g is a function such that $f(x) \le g(x) \le h(x)$
(70)   for all values of x near 0. Evaluate $\lim_{x \to 0} g(x)$.
  (b) With a graphing calculator, graph $y = |x|$, $y = -|x|$, and $y = x \sin \frac{1}{x}$ in the window
      $-0.2 \le x \le 0.2$, $-0.2 \le y \le 0.2$.
  (c) Find: $\lim_{x \to 0} x \sin \dfrac{1}{x}$

Integrate in problems 11–14.

11.
(66) $\displaystyle\int \frac{3x}{\sqrt{25 - 9x^4}}\, dx$

12.
(69) $\displaystyle\int xe^{2x}\, dx$

13.
(69) $\displaystyle\int 3x \sin x\, dx$

14.
(69) $\displaystyle\int 2x \ln x\, dx$

15. Let R be the region in the first quadrant bounded by the coordinate axes and the graph of the unit
(67) circle whose center is the origin. Use y as the variable of integration to write an integral whose value equals the area of R.

16. Suppose $f(x) = x^3$, $g(x) = x^2 + 1$, and $h(x) = f(x)g(x)$. Determine whether the graph of h
(68) is symmetric about the y-axis, symmetric about the origin, or symmetric about neither.

17. The graph of the function $y = \frac{4}{1 + x^2}$ is
(60) shown. Find the exact area of the shaded region of the rectangle.

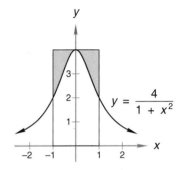

$y = \dfrac{4}{1 + x^2}$

Differentiate with respect to x in problems 18 and 19.

18.
(64) $y = \operatorname{arccsc} \dfrac{x}{4}$ $(x > 0)$

19.
(50,64) $y = \arctan(e^x) + \dfrac{\sqrt{2x + 1}}{\sin x - x}$

Integrate in problems 20 and 21.

20.
(66) $\displaystyle\int x^2 e^{x^3}\, dx$

21.
(66) $\displaystyle\int (\cos x)(\sin^3 x + 1)\, dx$

22. Which of the following definite integrals is equivalent to $\displaystyle\int_1^2 x \ln (x^2 + 1)\, dx$?
(66)

A. $\displaystyle\int_1^2 \ln u\, du$

B. $\dfrac{1}{2}\displaystyle\int_{\ln 5}^{\ln 2} \ln u\, du$

C. $\dfrac{1}{2}\displaystyle\int_2^5 \ln u\, du$

D. $\dfrac{1}{2}\displaystyle\int_{\ln 2}^{\ln 5} u \ln u\, du$

23. Let $f(x) = 4x - 5$. Find the equation for f^{-1}.
(58)

24. Which of the following gives the real number remainder when the polynomial $f(x)$ is divided by
(10) $(x - 3)$?

A. $f(3)$

B. $f(-3)$

C. $f(0)$

D. Cannot be determined unless more information is given

25. Which of the following equations has a graph that is symmetric with respect to the origin?
(68)

A. $y = x^2$

B. $y = \cos x$

C. $y = \dfrac{x - 1}{x}$

D. $y = 2 \sin x$

LESSON 72 *Derivatives of a^x • Derivatives of $\log_a x$ • Derivative of $|f(x)|$*

72.A
derivatives of a^x

The derivative of e^x with respect to x is e^x. If the base is some other positive number, say 42, the derivative with respect to x has another factor, which is the natural logarithm of the base.

$$\frac{d}{dx}42^x = (\ln 42)42^x$$

To see why this additional factor is necessary, we note that e^{kx} has the form e^u, so the derivative of e^{kx} with respect to x is e^{kx} times the derivative of kx with respect to x.

$$\frac{d}{dx}e^{kx} = ke^{kx}$$

Since any positive number can be written as e raised to the appropriate power, we can write 42 as

$$42 = e^{\ln 42}$$

If we substitute $e^{\ln 42}$ for 42 in the expression 42^x, we get an expression whose form is e^{kx}.

$$42^x = (e^{\ln 42})^x = e^{(\ln 42)x}$$

Thus we find the derivative of 42^x with respect to x as follows:

$$\frac{d}{dx}42^x = \frac{d}{dx}e^{(\ln 42)x} = e^{(\ln 42)x}\frac{d}{dx}[(\ln 42)x] = (\ln 42)e^{(\ln 42)x} = (\ln 42)42^x$$

In this illustration we used 42 as the base of an exponential function for a concrete example of the method of finding the derivative of a positive constant raised to the x power. From this development we see that if we use a instead of 42 we can write the rule for the derivative of a^x as follows:

$$\boxed{\frac{d}{dx}a^x = (\ln a)a^x}$$

We should note that a must be a positive constant. If a were negative, the function a^x would not be continuous, and its derivative would not exist.

example 72.1 Let $f(x) = 17^x$. Find $f'(x)$.

solution From the equation just developed,

$$f'(x) = (\ln 17)17^x$$

example 72.2 If $y = 42^{(x^2-5x)}$, what is $\frac{dy}{dx}$?

solution The derivative of 42^x is $(\ln 42)42^x$, but this derivative is in the form of 42^u, so we also need an extra factor, the derivative of $x^2 - 5x$.

$$\frac{d}{dx}42^{(x^2-5x)} = (\ln 42)42^{(x^2-5x)}\frac{d}{dx}(x^2 - 5x)$$
$$= (\ln 42)42^{(x^2-5x)}(2x - 5)$$
$$= (\ln 42)(2x - 5)42^{(x^2-5x)}$$

example 72.3 Let $y = \cos(14^x)$. Find $D_x y$.

solution We use the chain rule.

$$D_x y = -\sin(14^x) \cdot \frac{d}{dx}(14^x)$$
$$= -\sin(14^x) \cdot (\ln 14)14^x$$
$$= -(\ln 14)[\sin(14^x)](14^x)$$

72.B

derivatives of $\log_a x$ The logarithm of a number to any base a can be found by dividing the natural logarithm of the number by the appropriate constant. Before differentiating a logarithmic function, we change the base to e.

$$\log_a x = \frac{\ln x}{\ln a} \qquad\qquad \text{change of base}$$

$$\frac{d}{dx}\log_a x = \frac{d}{dx}\left(\frac{\ln x}{\ln a}\right) \qquad\qquad \text{take derivative of both sides}$$

$$\frac{d}{dx}\log_a x = \frac{1}{\ln a}\frac{d}{dx}(\ln x) \qquad\qquad \text{since } \ln a \text{ is constant}$$

$$\frac{d}{dx}\log_a x = \frac{1}{\ln a}\cdot\frac{1}{x} \qquad\qquad \text{differentiated } \ln x$$

$$\frac{d}{dx}\log_a x = \frac{1}{x\,\ln a} \qquad\qquad \text{simplified}$$

Now we box the formula for reference.

$$\boxed{\frac{d}{dx}\log_a x = \frac{1}{x\,\ln a}}$$

example 72.4   Let $y = \log_{42} x + \log_{10} x$. Find $\dfrac{dy}{dx}$.

solution   We simply twice apply the formula developed above.

$$\frac{dy}{dx} = \frac{1}{x\,\ln 42} + \frac{1}{x\,\ln 10}$$

$$= \frac{1}{x}\left(\frac{1}{\ln 42} + \frac{1}{\ln 10}\right)$$

example 72.5   Let $f(x) = \log_9(x^2 + \sin x)$. Approximate the slope of the tangent line to the graph of f at the point where $x = 1$.

solution   This example is asking for $f'(1)$.

$$f'(x) = \frac{d}{dx}\log_9(x^2 + \sin x)$$

$$= \frac{1}{(x^2 + \sin x)\ln 9}\cdot\frac{d}{dx}(x^2 + \sin x)$$

$$= \frac{2x + \cos x}{(x^2 + \sin x)\ln 9}$$

Using our calculator, we evaluate $f'(x)$ at $x = 1$ to obtain $f'(1) \approx \mathbf{0.6278.}$

72.C

derivative of $|f(x)|$ The absolute value notation changes negative quantities to positive quantities.

$$|-7| = 7 \qquad\qquad |-4.2| = 4.2 \qquad\qquad |-50| = 50$$

Absolute value notation is redundant if the quantities equal zero or exceed it.

$$|0| = 0 \qquad |4| = 4 \qquad \left|\sqrt{x^2 - 4}\right| = \sqrt{x^2 - 4} \qquad |4 - \sin(3x^2)| = 4 - \sin(3x^2)$$

The numbers 4 and 0 are unchanged by the absolute value notation. The expression $\sqrt{x^2 - 4}$ always represents the number zero or a positive number. The value of $-\sin(3x^2)$ varies between $+1$ and -1, and thus $4 - \sin(3x^2)$ is always positive.

Absolute value notation is useful for defining a function that would require a piecewise definition if the notation were not used. **The derivative of the absolute value of a function equals the derivative of the function on the intervals where the function is positive and equals the negative of the derivative of the function on the intervals where the function is negative.** The derivative does not exist at an x-value of c where the derivative of the absolute value function just to the left of c is not approximately equal to the value of the derivative just to the right of c. In particular, the derivative of $|f(x)|$ does not exist at locations where the graph of $|f(x)|$ has a sharp corner.

example 72.6   For $y = |x + 2|$, find $\dfrac{dy}{dx}$.

solution   We redefine the function without using absolute value notation and then graph it.

$$y = |x + 2| \text{ means } \begin{cases} y = x + 2 & \text{if } x > -2 \\ y = 0 & \text{if } x = -2 \\ y = -(x + 2) & \text{if } x < -2 \end{cases}$$

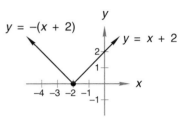

The derivative of $|x + 2|$ where x is greater than -2 is the derivative of $x + 2$, which is $+1$. The derivative of $|x + 2|$ where x is less than -2 is the negative of the derivative of $x + 2$, which is the negative of $+1$ or -1. The derivative does not exist at $x = -2$.

$$\frac{d}{dx}|x + 2| = \begin{cases} 1 & \text{if } x > -2 \\ \textbf{does not exist} & \text{if } x = -2 \\ -1 & \text{if } x < -2 \end{cases}$$

The graph of $\dfrac{d}{dx}|x + 2|$ is the following:

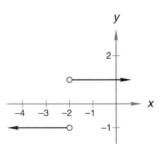

example 72.7   If $f(x) = \left|\sqrt{x^2 - 4}\right|$, what is $f'(x)$?

solution   This use of the absolute value notation is redundant because the expression $\sqrt{x^2 - 4}$ is never negative. This function is not defined for values of x between -2 and 2 and is positive for all values of x less than -2 or greater than 2.

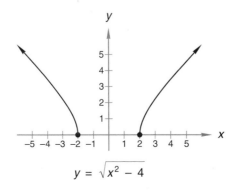

$y = \sqrt{x^2 - 4}$

$$y = \sqrt{x^2 - 4} \quad \text{if } x \leq -2$$
$$y \text{ is not defined} \quad \text{if } -2 < x < 2$$
$$y = \sqrt{x^2 - 4} \quad \text{if } x \geq 2$$

The derivative of $f(x) = \left| \sqrt{x^2 - 4} \right|$ does not exist when x is between -2 and $+2$ inclusive. For other values of x the derivative is the same as the derivative of $y = \sqrt{x^2 - 4}$.

$$\frac{d}{dx}\left| \sqrt{x^2 - 4} \right| = \frac{d}{dx}(x^2 - 4)^{1/2} = \frac{1}{2}(x^2 - 4)^{-1/2}(2x) = \frac{x}{\sqrt{x^2 - 4}}$$

Note that the function is defined at $x = \pm 2$, but the derivative is not defined at $x = \pm 2$.

example 72.8   Let $y = |x^2 - 4|$. Find y'.

solution   A graph is always helpful.

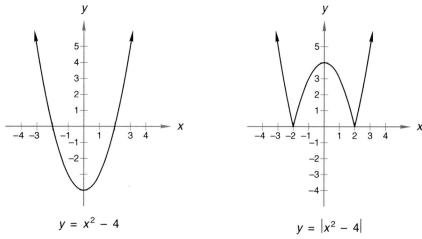

$y = x^2 - 4$ $y = |x^2 - 4|$

First we redefine the function on the open intervals $(-\infty, -2)$, $(-2, 2)$, and $(2, \infty)$. On the intervals $(-\infty, -2)$ and $(2, \infty)$, $y = x^2 - 4$. On the interval $(-2, 2)$, $y = -(x^2 - 4)$. The derivatives on these intervals are as follows. For $(-\infty, -2)$ and $(2, \infty)$, $\frac{d}{dx}|x^2 - 4| = \frac{d}{dx}(x^2 - 4) = 2x$. For $(-2, 2)$, $\frac{d}{dx}|x^2 - 4| = \frac{d}{dx}[-(x^2 - 4)] = -2x$. The derivative does not exist at $x = -2$ or $x = 2$, because the derivatives to the immediate left and right of these values of x are quite different.

$$y' = \begin{cases} 2x & \text{if } |x| > 2 \\ -2x & \text{if } |x| < 2 \\ \text{does not exist} & \text{if } |x| = 2 \end{cases}$$

The graphs of y and y' are given below.

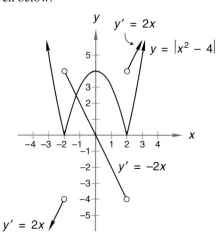

problem set
72

1. The height and radius of the base of a right circular cone are each increasing at a rate of 2 cm/s. Find
(46) the rate at which the volume of the cone is increasing when the radius is 4 cm and the height is 6 cm.

2. An object is thrown straight downward from a height of 160 m with an initial velocity of 48 m/s.
(65)
   (a) Develop the velocity function and the height function.
   (b) How long does it take for the object to strike the ground?
   (c) Find the velocity of the object the instant it strikes the ground.

3. Suppose $x^2 + 2xy + 7y^2 = 8$ where x and y are both functions of time.
(34)

    (a) Differentiate this equation with respect to t.

    (b) Find $\dfrac{dx}{dt}$ at (3, 2) when $\dfrac{dy}{dt} = \dfrac{5}{17}$.

4. Find the slope of the line normal to the graph of $y = \log_2 x$ at $x = 3$.
(72)

5. Find the slope of the line tangent to the graph of $y = 3^x$ at $x = 4$. Write the equation of the tangent line.
(72)

6. Find $\dfrac{dy}{dx}$ where $y = 43^x + 3^x + \log_3 x - \log_{43} x$.
(72)

7. Find the Maclaurin series for $y = 2^x$.
(55)

8. (a) Use calculus to find the maximum value and the minimum value of the function
(63) $f(x) = x^3 - 3x^2 - 9x + 5$ on the interval $[-2, 4]$.

    (b) Check the answers to (a) with a graphing calculator.

9. Let R be the region bounded by $y = x^3$, $y = 1$, and the y-axis. Find the volume of the solid
(71) formed when R is revolved about the y-axis.

10. Let R be the region in the first quadrant bounded by $y = -\frac{1}{2}x + 1$ and the coordinate axes. Use
(71) x as the variable of integration to write a definite integral whose value equals the volume of the solid formed when R is revolved around the x-axis.

11. Let R be the region completely enclosed by the graph of $y = 1 - x^2$ and the x-axis. Use y as
(71) the variable of integration to write a definite integral whose value equals the volume of the solid formed when R is revolved about the y-axis.

Integrate in problems 12 and 13.

12. $\displaystyle\int 3xe^{3x}\,dx$
(69)

13. $\displaystyle\int \pi \sin(\pi x)\,dx$
(66)

14. Evaluate: $\displaystyle\int_0^3 x\sqrt{x+1}\,dx$
(66)

15. Suppose $h(x) = f(x)g(x)$, $\displaystyle\lim_{x\to\pi} h(x) = \dfrac{1}{\pi}$, and $\displaystyle\lim_{x\to\pi} f(x) = 3$. Evaluate $\displaystyle\lim_{x\to\pi} g(x)$.
(70)

16. (a) Let $f(x) = 1 - \frac{x^2}{4}$ and $h(x) = 1$. Suppose g is a function such that $f(x) \le g(x) \le h(x)$
(70)   for all values of x near, but not equal to, 0. Evaluate $\displaystyle\lim_{x\to0} g(x)$.

    (b) On a graphing calculator, graph $y = 1$, $y = 1 - \frac{x^2}{4}$, and $y = \frac{\sin x}{x}$ in the window $-0.5 \le x \le 0.5$, $0.95 \le y \le 1.05$.

    (c) Evaluate: $\displaystyle\lim_{x\to0} \dfrac{\sin x}{x}$

17. Suppose $f(x) = \sin x$, $g(x) = x$, and $h(x) = f(x)g(x)$. Determine whether h is an odd
(68) function, an even function, or neither.

18. Let f be a continuous function on $(-\infty, \infty)$. In (a) and (b), find the values of a and b that make
(57) each equation true.

    (a) $\displaystyle\int_a^b f(x)\,dx - \int_0^2 f(x)\,dx = \int_2^5 f(x)\,dx$

    (b) $\displaystyle\int_6^4 f(x)\,dx + \int_1^6 f(x)\,dx = \int_a^b f(x)\,dx$

19. Differentiate $y = 2\cos^2 x + \arctan(2x) + \dfrac{2\sqrt{2x+1}}{x^2+1}$ with respect to x.
(50,64)

20. Let $y = 2e^{\cos x}$.
(50,46)

(a) Find: $\dfrac{dy}{dx}$ and $\dfrac{d^2 y}{dx^2}$

(b) Suppose x and y both vary with time and that y increases at a constant rate of 5 units per second. Find the rate at which x is changing when $x = \frac{\pi}{2}$.

Integrate in problems 21–23.

21. $\displaystyle\int (x+1)e^{-x^2-2x}\,dx$ **22.** $\displaystyle\int \dfrac{x}{x^2+1}\,dx$ **23.** $\displaystyle\int \dfrac{1}{4x^2+1}\,dx$
(66)   (66)   (66)

24. Boyle's Law states that if the temperature of a quantity of an ideal gas does not change, then the
(5) product of the pressure and the volume is constant. The pressure of a quantity of ideal gas was 5 newtons per square meter when the volume was 1000 cubic meters. What was the volume when the pressure was increased to 15 newtons per square meter and the temperature remained constant?

25. Find the coordinates of the absolute maximum point for the curve $y = xe^{-kx}$, where k is a fixed
(31,49) positive number. Justify the answer with the second derivative test.

LESSON 73   *Integrals of a^x • Integrals of $\log_a x$*

73.A
integrals of a^x

In the previous lesson we developed the formula for the derivative of a^x.

$$\frac{d}{dx}\,a^x = (\ln a)a^x$$

If we integrate both sides of this, we have

$$a^x + C = \int (\ln a)a^x\,dx$$

Upon division by the constant $\ln a$, the equation becomes

$$\frac{a^x}{\ln a} + C = \int a^x\,dx$$

In rewritten form this gives us the following:

$$\int a^x\,dx = \frac{a^x}{\ln a} + C$$

example 73.1   Integrate: $\displaystyle\int 143^x\,dx$

solution   From our developments above, we can substitute 143 for a.

$$\int 143^x\,dx = \frac{143^x}{\ln 143} + C$$

We can easily check the answer.

$$\frac{d}{dx}\left(\frac{143^x}{\ln 143} + C\right) = \frac{1}{\ln 143}\cdot\frac{d}{dx}(143^x)$$

$$= \frac{1}{\ln 143}(\ln 143)143^x$$

$$= 143^x$$

example 73.2   Integrate: $\int xa^{x^2-2}\,dx$

solution   We make a u substitution.

$$
\begin{array}{c}
u = x^2 - 2 \\[4pt]
du = 2x\,dx \\[4pt]
\dfrac{du}{2} = x\,dx
\end{array}
$$

The integral is equivalent to

$$\int a^u \left(\frac{du}{2} \right) = \frac{1}{2} \int a^u\,du$$

We can now apply the formula.

$$= \frac{1}{2} \int a^u\,du = \frac{1}{2}\left(\frac{a^u}{\ln a} + C \right)$$

$$= \frac{1}{2\ln a} a^{x^2-2} + C$$

example 73.3   Find the volume of the solid obtained by rotating about the x-axis the region bounded by the graphs of $y = 5^{x/2}$, $x = 3$, and the coordinate axes.

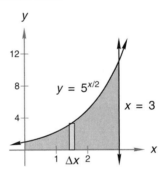

solution   A representative disk has width Δx and radius $y = 5^{x/2}$. The disks must be stacked left to right from $x = 0$ to $x = 3$.

$$\text{Volume} = \int_0^3 \pi r^2\,dx = \int_0^3 \pi (5^{x/2})^2\,dx$$

$$= \pi \int_0^3 5^x\,dx = \pi \left. \frac{5^x}{\ln 5} \right|_0^3$$

$$= \frac{\pi}{\ln 5}(5^3 - 5^0) = \frac{124\pi}{\ln 5}\ \text{units}^3$$

73.B
integrals of $\log_a x$

We now want to determine a formula for $\int \log_a x\,dx$. As in the past, we begin by rewriting the $\log_a x$ in terms of natural logarithms.

$$\int \log_a x\,dx = \int \frac{\ln x}{\ln a}\,dx$$

$$= \frac{1}{\ln a} \int \ln x\,dx \qquad \text{since } \ln a \text{ is constant}$$

We encountered $\int \ln x\,dx$ when studying integration by parts.

$$\int \ln x\,dx = (x\ln x - x) + C$$

Therefore

$$\int \log_a x \, dx = \frac{1}{\ln a} \int \ln x \, dx \qquad \text{implies}$$

$$\boxed{\int \log_a x \, dx = \frac{1}{\ln a}(x \ln x - x) + C}$$

example 73.4   Integrate: $\int \log_{23} x \, dx$

solution   From the above fact,

$$\int \log_{23} x \, dx = \frac{1}{\ln 23}(x \ln x - x) + C$$

**problem set
73**

1. A cylindrical can with a circular base and circular top is to be constructed. The volume of the
   (52) cylindrical can must be 432π mL. The top and bottom are to be made of gold, which will cost
   \$8 per square centimeter. The curved side is to be made of silver, which will cost \$1 per square
   centimeter. (Recall that 1 mL = 1 cm³.) The height of the cylindrical can is y cm and its radius
   is x cm.

   (a) Express the total cost of the cylindrical can in terms of x.

   (b) Use calculus to find the dimensions of the cylindrical can that can be constructed for the
   lowest cost.

   (c) Check the answer to (b) with a graphing calculator, and determine the cost of the least
   expensive can.

2. A variable force of $F(x) = \frac{3}{1+x^2}$ newtons is applied to an object as it moves along a number
   (62) line. Find the exact amount of work done by the force in moving the object in the direction of
   the force from $x = \frac{1}{\sqrt{3}}$ meters to $x = \sqrt{3}$ meters.

3. An object is thrown straight up from the top of a 500-foot-tall building with an initial velocity
   (65) of 20 feet per second. Develop an equation that expresses the height $h(t)$ of the object above the
   ground as a function of time. How long will it take for the object to hit the ground? (Assume the
   ball does not hit the building during its descent.)

4. Find the slope of the line tangent to the graph of $y = \log_3 x$ at $x = 9$. Write the equation of
   (72) the tangent line.

5. Find the slope of the line normal to the graph of $y = 5^x$ at $x = 2$.
   (72)

Differentiate with respect to x in problems 6–10.

6. $y = \log_2 x + 4^x - \log_6 x$
   (72)

7. $y = 2 \cdot 5^x + 3 \log_7 x$
   (72)

8. $y = 24^{(x^2 + 3x)}$
   (72)

9. $y = |x + 1|$
   (72)

10. $y = \left| \sqrt{x^2 - 9} \right|$
    (72)

Integrate in problems 11–15.

11. $\int 13^x \, dx$
    (73)

12. $\int \log_3 x \, dx$
    (73)

13. $\int x \cdot 2^{x^2 + 4} \, dx$
    (73)

14. $\int \tan x \, dx$
    (66)

15. $\int (\sin x)(\cos^3 x + 1) \, dx$
    (66)

16. Use the natural logarithm function to write a definite integral whose value equals the area of the
(20,47) region bounded by the x-axis and the graph of $y = \log_2 x$ between $x = 2$ and $x = 8$.

17. Find the area of the region between the graph of $y = 2^x$ and the x-axis over the interval [1, 5].
(73)

For problems 18 and 19, let R be the region in the first quadrant bounded completely by the graphs of
$f(x) = \tan x$, $g(x) = \sqrt{2} \cos x$, and the y-axis.

18. Use algebraic methods to find the coordinates of the point of intersection of the graphs of f and
(13) g in the interval $0 \le x \le \frac{\pi}{2}$.

19. Find the exact area of R.
(60)

20. Find the volume of the solid formed by rotating about the y-axis the region in the first quadrant
(71) bounded above by $y = 4$ and below by $y = x^4$.

Evaluate the limits in problems 21 and 22 if they exist. Limits of ∞ and $-\infty$ are acceptable.

21. $\lim\limits_{x \to 0^-} \dfrac{|x|}{x}$
(70)

22. $\lim\limits_{x \to 1} \dfrac{1}{(x-1)^2}$
(70)

23. Suppose $f(x) = x^2$, $g(x) = x^3 + \sin x$, and $h(x) = f(g(x))$. Determine whether the graph of
(68) h is symmetric about the x-axis, symmetric about the y-axis, symmetric about the origin, or not
symmetric about any of these.

24. Let f be the function defined by $f(x) = x^3 + ax^2 + bx + c$. Suppose that the graph of f has
(61) a point of inflection at $(0, -2)$ and has a relative maximum at $(-1, 0)$. Determine the values of a,
b, and c, and then use those values to write an expression for $f(x)$.

25. Let $f(x) = x^4 - 3x^2 + 2$.
(27)
    (a) Write an equation for the line tangent to the graph of f at the point where $x = 1$.

    (b) Find the x-coordinate of each point for which the line tangent to the graph of f is parallel to
        the line $y = -2x + 4$.

LESSON 74 *Fluid Force*

The weight of an object in a gravitational field equals its mass times the local acceleration of gravity,
or *mg*. The unit of force in the metric system is the newton, and 1 cubic meter (m^3) of water (fresh
water at a temperature of 4°C) weighs 9800 newtons. The weight density of an object equals its weight
divided by the volume, so the weight density of water is 9800 newtons per cubic meter. On the
left-hand side below, we show a cubic meter of water and note that it weighs 9800 newtons.

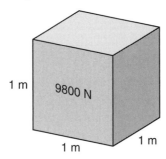
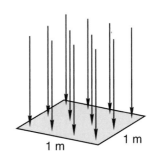

On the right-hand side above, we note that the weight of 9800 newtons is evenly distributed over the
1-square-meter surface at the bottom of the cube, so the average weight of the water at the bottom of
the cube (the water pressure) is 9800 newtons per square meter (N/m^2). If the water is 3 meters deep,

the pressure at the bottom caused by the weight of the water would be 3 m times 9800 N/m³, or 29,400 N/m², as we show on the left below.

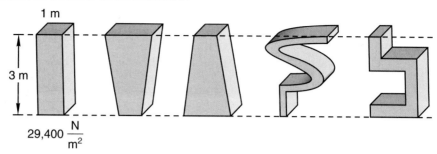

Pascal's Principle is a law of physics named for Blaise Pascal (1623–1662). This law states that **the pressure exerted by a fluid at a depth h below the surface of the fluid is equal in all directions.** The application of this law leads to some rather surprising results. Even though the five containers shown above have different shapes, the pressure at the bottom of all five containers is 29,400 N/m² if all are full of water, because, in each case, the bottom of the tank is 3 meters below the surface of the water.

From this we see that the pressure in a fluid at any depth h depends only on the depth and the weight density w of the fluid.

$$P = wh$$

If the pressure is constant over a particular area, the total force exerted on the area equals the pressure times the area.

$$\text{Total force} = \frac{\text{force}}{\text{area}} \times \text{area} = \text{force}$$

Since the pressure at any depth is the same in all directions, the horizontal pressure at any depth h equals the vertical pressure at that depth, which is wh. This fact allows us to use calculus to calculate the total force exerted by a fluid on a nonhorizontal surface, such as the side of a tank, by adding up the forces on horizontal rectangular strips, each of whose height is Δy. Because the strips are sufficiently narrow, the pressure is practically equal at every point in the strip.

example 74.1 A rectangular tank 6 meters deep is filled with water to a depth of 5 meters as shown in the cross-sectional view. Find the total force exerted by the water on the end of the tank.

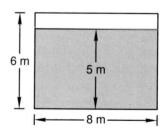

solution Problems like this one can be made harder or easier by the location of the coordinate system. It is often helpful to locate the x-axis at the bottom of the tank, as we do here.

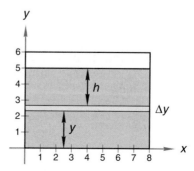

The total force on the rectangular strip equals the weight density w times the depth h times the area.

$$\text{Force} = w \times h \times \text{area}$$

The weight density of water is 9800 N/m³. The distance from the bottom of the tank to the surface is 5, and the distance to the rectangle is y. Thus, $h = 5 - y$. The area of the rectangle is $8\,\Delta y$, so we can write

$$\text{Force} = 9800(5 - y)(8\,\Delta y)$$

To find the total force, we must stack these rectangles from $y = 0$ to $y = 5$.

$$\text{Total force} = \int_0^5 9800(5 - y)(8\,dy)$$

We finish by evaluating the integral.

$$\text{Total force} = 9800\left(\int_0^5 40\,dy - \int_0^5 8y\,dy\right)$$

$$= 9800\left[40y - 4y^2\right]_0^5$$

$$= 9800[(200 - 100) - 0]$$

$$= \mathbf{980{,}000\ newtons}$$

example 74.2   The figure shows the end of a tank 6 meters deep filled with liquid to a depth of 5 meters. Express the total force on the end of the tank as a definite integral given that the weight density of the liquid is 4000 newtons per cubic meter.

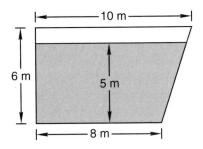

solution   Again we place the x-axis at the bottom of the tank as shown on the right-hand side below.

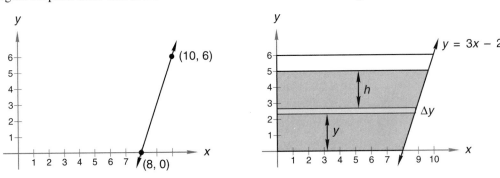

The force on the representative rectangle equals the weight density times the depth h times the area.

$$\text{Force} = w \times h \times \text{area}$$

The depth h is $5 - y$, as in the preceding example, but the length of the rectangle is no longer 8; it is x, where x is determined by $y = 3x - 24$. This line is uniquely determined, because it goes through the points (8, 0) and (10, 6) as shown on the figure on the left-hand side above. Solving this equation for x gives us $x = \frac{1}{3}y + 8$, and thus the area of the representative rectangle equals $\left(\frac{1}{3}y + 8\right)\Delta y$. The rectangles must be stacked from $y = 0$ to $y = 5$, so the total force can be expressed as follows.

$$\text{Total force} = \int_{y=0}^{y=5} wh(\text{area}) = \int_0^5 (4000)(5 - y)\left[\left(\frac{1}{3}y + 8\right)dy\right]$$

After multiplying, we find that the following integral gives the total force:

$$4000 \int_0^5 \left(-\frac{1}{3}y^2 - \frac{19}{3}y + 40\right)dy$$

This evaluation is straightforward but time-consuming. The example is a problem about an application of the definite integral; it is not designed to provide practice evaluating integrals. Thus we consider the solution complete. (For those who wish to do the work for added practice, the answer is 427,777.$\overline{7}$ newtons.)

example 74.3 A cylindrical tank 20 meters long whose radius is 4 meters, as shown, is half-filled with oil whose weight density is 3000 newtons per cubic meter. Set up an integral whose evaluation will yield the total force exerted by the oil on one end of the tank.

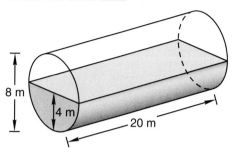

solution The length of the tank need not be considered since the force exerted at any point on the end of the tank is a function of only the weight density of the fluid and the vertical distance h from that point to the surface of the fluid. The length of the tank could be 2 meters, 20 meters, or 2000 meters. The answer would be the same. If we place the origin at the center, the equation of the circle is $x^2 + y^2 = 16$.

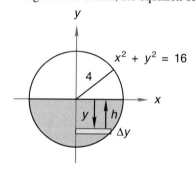

Since the end of the tank is symmetrical, we decide to find the total force on half the tank and double the result. The force on the representative rectangle again equals the weight density w times the depth h times the area.

$$\text{Force} = w \times h \times \text{area}$$

The distance from the x-axis to the rectangle is y, so the depth h, measured in the opposite direction, equals $-y$. The length of the rectangle is x, where x is defined by $x^2 + y^2 = 16$. Thus the length of the rectangle is $\sqrt{16 - y^2}$, and the area is $\sqrt{16 - y^2}\,\Delta y$. We want to stack the rectangles from $y = -4$ to $y = 0$, so the total force on the end of the tank is

$$\text{Total force} = 2 \int_{-4}^{0} 3000(-y)(\sqrt{16 - y^2}\,dy)$$

$$= -6000 \int_{-4}^{0} (16 - y^2)^{1/2}\,y\,dy$$

Inserting the necessary constants gives us

$$\text{Total force} = (-6000)\left(-\frac{1}{2}\right) \int_{-4}^{0} (16 - y^2)^{1/2}(-2y)\,dy$$

This integral has the form of $u^n\,du$, so we can integrate and get

$$\text{Total force} = 3000\left[\frac{(16 - y^2)^{3/2}}{\frac{3}{2}}\right]_{-4}^{0}$$

After doing the arithmetic, we find that the total force equals 128,000 newtons.

We could place the origin at the bottom of the tank to do this problem another way. Then the equation of the circle would be $x^2 + (y - 4)^2 = 16$.

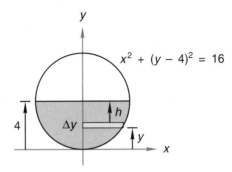

Solving this equation for x, we get $x = \sqrt{16 - (y - 4)^2}$, so the area of the rectangle is $\sqrt{16 - (y - 4)^2}\, \Delta y$. This time the depth h equals $4 - y$, and we want to stack the rectangles from $y = 0$ to $y = 4$. Thus, the total force is given by the following integral:

$$\text{Total force} = 2 \int_0^4 3000(4 - y)\sqrt{16 - (y - 4)^2}\ dy$$

If we simplify the radical, we get

$$\text{Total force} = 2 \int_0^4 3000(4 - y)(-y^2 + 8y)^{1/2}\ dy$$

Placing the x-axis at the bottom of the tank also produces an integral of the form $u^n\, du$.

**problem set
74**

1. Boyle's Law says that, if the temperature of a quantity of ideal gas is unchanged, the product of
   (47) the pressure and the volume is constant. When we have 1000 m³ of gas at a pressure of 5 N/m²,
   the pressure is increasing at a rate of 0.05 N/m² per second. Find the rate at which the volume is
   changing when the pressure is 10 N/m².

2. A variable force $F(x) = x + 2$ newtons (x in meters) is applied to move an object along a
   (62) number line in the direction of the force. Find the work done by the force in moving the object
   from $x = 1$ meter to $x = 4$ meters.

3. A tank 3 meters deep is completely filled
   (74) with fluid whose weight density is
   1000 N/m³. Find the total force exerted on
   one end of the tank if the end of the tank is
   rectangular as shown in the figure.

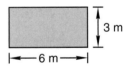

4. A container with a triangular cross section
   (74) as shown is filled with a fluid that has a
   weight density of 3000 N/m³. Find the
   total force exerted against the end of the
   container.

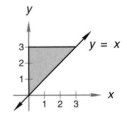

5. A container 1000 meters long has a
   (74) semicircular cross section as shown. The
   container is filled with a fluid whose
   weight density is 1000 N/m³. Write a
   definite integral whose value equals the
   total force against the end of the container.
   Use a graphing calculator to evaluate this
   integral.

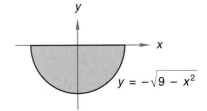

6. Let R be the region bounded by the graph of $y = (x - 1)^2$ and both coordinate axes. Find the
(71) volume of the solid formed when R is revolved about the x-axis.

7. Let R be the region between the graph of $y = x^2$ and the x-axis from $x = 0$ to $x = 2$. Find
(71) the volume of the solid formed when R is revolved around the x-axis.

8. Find the Maclaurin series for $y = 3^x$. Write the answer in summation notation.
(55)

Differentiate with respect to x in problems 9–12.

9. $y = \log_5 x + 7^x + \log_8 x$
(72)

10. $y = 3.5^x - 2 \log_3 x$
(72)

11. $y = \operatorname{arcsec} \dfrac{x}{a} \ (a, x > 0)$
(64)

12. $y = \arcsin (3x) + \dfrac{\sqrt{1 - x}}{x \sin x}$
(64)

Integrate in problems 13–18.

13. $\displaystyle\int \log_5 x \, dx$
(73)

14. $\displaystyle\int 4xe^{2x} \, dx$
(69)

15. $\displaystyle\int x \sin (2x) \, dx$
(69)

16. $\displaystyle\int 3 \tan x \, dx$
(66)

17. $\displaystyle\int \dfrac{x}{\sqrt{x^2 + \pi}} \, dx$
(66)

18. $\displaystyle\int (\sin x)\sqrt{1 + 2 \cos x} \, dx$
(66)

19. Let $f(x) = |\sin x|$ for all x in the interval $[-\pi, 2\pi]$.
(72)

   (a) Find all the zeros of f.

   (b) Graph the function f.

   (c) Find: $f'(x)$

20. Let $f(x) = |\sin x|$ for $-\pi \le x \le \pi$ and $g(x) = x^2$ for all real x.
(18,50)

   (a) Find: $h(x) = g(f(x))$

   (b) Find all the zeros of h.

   (c) Graph the function h.

   (d) Find the domain and range of h.

   (e) Find an equation for the line tangent to the graph of h at the point where $x = \dfrac{\pi}{4}$.

21. Evaluate each of the following limits:
(14,70)

   (a) $\displaystyle\lim_{x \to 1} \dfrac{x^3 - 1}{x - 1}$
   (b) $\displaystyle\lim_{x \to 0^+} \dfrac{|x|}{x}$
   (c) $\displaystyle\lim_{x \to 0} \sin \dfrac{1}{x}$
   (d) $\displaystyle\lim_{x \to 0^-} x \sin x$

22. Write an equation for the line tangent to the graph of $f(x) = \dfrac{x - 1}{x + 1}$ at $x = 1$.
(27,42)

23. One thousand frankfurters can be sold every week at a food stand for \$1 each. For every increase
(63) in price of 20 cents per frankfurter, the number of frankfurters sold decreases by 100. Write an
equation that expresses the number of frankfurters sold as a function of the price p in cents.
What is the total revenue received from the sale of frankfurters per week if the price of each
frankfurter is p?

24. Suppose f is a function that is defined for all real numbers. Which of the following conditions
₍₅₈₎ guarantees that the inverse of f is also a function?

    A. f is a strictly increasing function.

    B. f is an odd function.

    C. f is an even function.

    D. f is continuous and differentiable everywhere.

    E. f is a periodic function.

25. Given the curve $x + xy + 2y^2 = 6$, do the following:
_(27,34)

    (a) Find an expression for the slope of the curve at any point (x, y) on the curve.

    (b) Write an equation for the line tangent to the curve at the point $(2, 1)$.

    (c) Find the coordinates of all other points on this curve with slope equal to the slope at the point $(2, 1)$.

    (d) The equation of the curve $x + xy + 2y^2 = 6$ is written in implicit form. Rewrite this equation in explicit form by using the quadratic formula to solve for y in terms of x. Use a graphing calculator to graph the explicit equation.

LESSON 75 *Continuity of Functions*

The importance of some of the crucial theorems of calculus is difficult for beginners to understand, because the truth of the theorems is so obvious. Two theorems about continuous functions fall into this category. They are the maximum-minimum value existence theorem, which we have already discussed, and the **Intermediate Value Theorem.**

Consider, for example, the graph of the continuous function f given below.

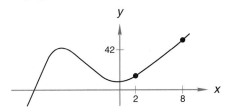

The Intermediate Value Theorem tells us that for any number between $f(2)$ and $f(8)$, there exists a value of x between 2 and 8 inclusive that maps to the number. In this example, 42 is between $f(2)$ and $f(8)$, so there is a number c between 2 and 8 for which $f(c) = 42$.

> **INTERMEDIATE VALUE THEOREM**
>
> If f is continuous on the closed interval $[a, b]$ and N is a number between $f(a)$ and $f(b)$, then there is at least one number c between a and b, inclusive, for which $f(c) = N$.

One of the most useful applications of the Intermediate Value Theorem involves the location of zeros of a continuous function.

example 75.1 Prove that $f(x) = x^3 - 5x + 2$ has a root between $x = 0$ and $x = 1$.

solution We know f is continuous over the interval $[0, 1]$ because it is a polynomial function. Moreover, $f(0) = 2$ and $f(1) = -2$. By the Intermediate Value Theorem, there is a value c between 0 and 1 such that $f(c) = 0$. (Note that the Intermediate Value Theorem cannot locate c, but it does guarantee its existence.) The following graph confirms what the Intermediate Value Theorem guarantees.

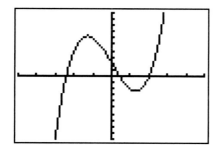
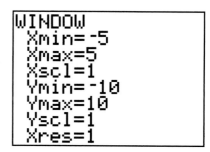

Since continuous functions have such special properties, it is necessary to define **continuous functions** precisely. Below we show the graphs of three functions that are defined for every input value of x between a and b but not for a and b. This means that there is a value of the function for any x on the interval (a, b) and that the domain of each of the functions is (a, b).

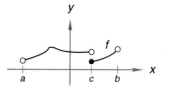
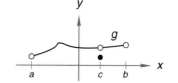
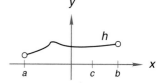

The functions f and g are not continuous on the interval (a, b), because there is a discontinuity at c. There is no discontinuity at any point in the graph of h between a and b, so this function is continuous on (a, b).

For a precise definition of continuity, however, we must avoid the use of graphs. We begin by defining continuity at a point. There are three conditions that must be met for a function to be continuous at $x = c$.

1. Both a left-hand limit and a right-hand limit must exist as x approaches c.

2. The limits must be equal.

3. The value of the function at c, which is $f(c)$, must exist and must equal both the left-hand limit and the right-hand limit.

DEFINITION OF CONTINUITY AT A POINT

A function f is continuous at a point c if f exists at c and

$$\lim_{x \to c^-} f(x) = \lim_{x \to c^+} f(x) = f(c)$$

We know that for a function to have a limit as x approaches c, both the left-hand limit and the right-hand limit must exist and they must be equal; so, if f is defined at c, the notation

$$\lim_{x \to c} f(x) = f(c)$$

suffices to define continuity at that point. For a function to be continuous on an open interval (a, b) it must be continuous at every point between a and b.

DEFINITION OF OPEN-INTERVAL CONTINUITY

A function f is continuous on an open interval (a, b) if it is continuous at every point on the interval.

Sometimes we find it helpful to be able to discuss continuity on a closed interval $[a, b]$. We are not concerned with values of x that are less than a, so the left-hand limit as x approaches a does not matter. We also do not bother with values of x greater than b, so the right-hand limit as x approaches b is of no concern. Thus, for a definition of continuity on a closed interval $[a, b]$, we can modify the definition of continuity on an open interval (a, b) by requiring only that the right-hand limit at a equals $f(a)$ and that the left-hand limit at b equals $f(b)$. All other points on the closed interval must be continuous, as we have defined for the open interval (a, b).

DEFINITION OF CLOSED-INTERVAL CONTINUITY

A function f is continuous on a closed interval $[a, b]$ if it is continuous at every point between a and b, if it is defined at both a and b, and if

$$\lim_{x \to a^+} f(x) = f(a) \qquad \text{and} \qquad \lim_{x \to b^-} f(x) = f(b)$$

---

example 75.2 Suppose the function f is defined on the interval $[1, 3]$, $f(1) = 1$, and $f(3) = 7$. Does a number c exist, $1 \le c \le 3$, such that $f(c) = 3$?

solution **Not necessarily.** The function was not defined to be continuous on $[1, 3]$, so the existence of c in $[1, 3]$ such that $f(c) = 3$ is not guaranteed.

example 75.3 Suppose f is a function that is continuous on the closed interval $[-1, 3]$. Which of the following could be a graph of f?

A.
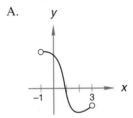

B.
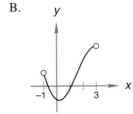

C.
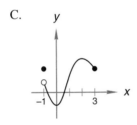

D.
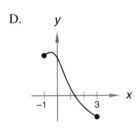

solution For a function to be continuous on the closed interval $[-1, 3]$, it must be defined at the endpoints -1 and 3 and must be continuous at every interior point. Also, the one-sided limits at the endpoints of $[-1, 3]$ must equal $f(-1)$ and $f(3)$. **Graph D** is the only graph that meets all the requirements.

example 75.4 Let f be a piecewise function defined as follows:

$$f(x) = \begin{cases} |x| + 3 & \text{when } x < 1 \\ ax^2 + bx & \text{when } x \ge 1 \end{cases}$$

Find values of a and b such that f is continuous on the interval $(-\infty, \infty)$.

solution We begin with a sketch of f.

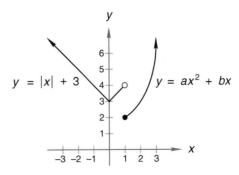

In the sketch we see that f is continuous to the left and right of $x = 1$. The limit of $|x| + 3$ as x approaches 1 from the left is $1 + 3 = 4$. Thus, if $ax^2 + bx = 4$ when $x = 1$, the function will be continuous at $x = 1$. So we let x equal 1 and y equal 4 to get

$$4 = a(1)^2 + b(1) \longrightarrow 4 = a + b$$

Thus any pair of values a and b whose sum is 4 will make f continuous on the interval $(-\infty, \infty)$. For example, $a = 3$ and $b = 1$ yields the following graph.

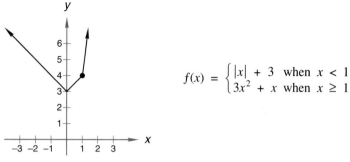

$$f(x) = \begin{cases} |x| + 3 & \text{when } x < 1 \\ 3x^2 + x & \text{when } x \geq 1 \end{cases}$$

Also, $a = -7$ and $b = 11$ satisfy the requirements.

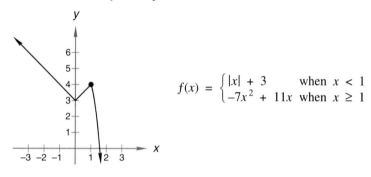

$$f(x) = \begin{cases} |x| + 3 & \text{when } x < 1 \\ -7x^2 + 11x & \text{when } x \geq 1 \end{cases}$$

example 75.5   Let f be a piecewise function defined as follows:

$$f(x) = \begin{cases} \dfrac{x^2 - c^2}{x + c} & \text{when } x \neq -c \\ 2c & \text{when } x = -c \end{cases}$$

Is x continuous on the interval $(-\infty, \infty)$?

solution   When x does not equal c, the function is defined and is continuous for all x, because the equation is the equation of a line.

$$x \neq c: \quad f(x) = \frac{(x + c)(x - c)}{x - c} \longrightarrow f(x) = x + c$$

We were given that $f(c) = 2c$. If the limit of $f(x)$ as x approaches c is also $2c$, the function is continuous at $x = c$.

$$\lim_{x \to c} f(x) = \lim_{x \to c} \frac{(x + c)(x - c)}{(x - c)} = \lim_{x \to c} (x + c) = 2c$$

Since the function is continuous for all $x \neq c$ and is also continuous at $x = c$, **the function is continuous on the interval $(-\infty, \infty)$.**

problem set 75

1.
(63)   One thousand frankfurters can be sold every week if they are sold for $1 each. For every 20-cent increase in price, sales of the frankfurters decrease by 100 per week. This means that $Q(p) = 1500 - 5p$ frankfurters would be sold if the price of each frankfurter was p (measured in cents). Find the price p that maximizes the weekly revenues received from the sale of frankfurters.

2.
(65)   A ball is thrown straight up with an initial velocity of 10 m/s from the top of a 200-meter-high building. Develop an equation that expresses the height of the ball above the ground t seconds after the ball is thrown. How long does it take the ball to reach the ground? (Assume the ball does not hit the building during its descent.)

3. Is the statement below true or false? Explain why.
$^{(75)}$

$$\text{If } f \text{ is a function such that } f(1) = 2 \text{ and } f(4) = 10,$$
$$\text{then there is a number } c, \ 1 < c < 4, \text{ such that } f(c) = 5.$$

4. Suppose f is a function that is continuous on the closed interval $[-1, 4]$. Which of the following
$^{(75)}$ could be a graph of f?

A. y

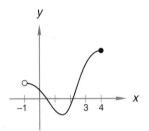

B. y

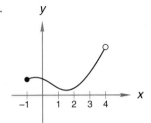

C. y

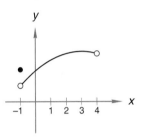

D. y

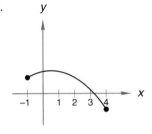

5. Let f be the piecewise function defined as $f(x) = \begin{cases} |x| + 2 & \text{when } x < 2 \\ x^2 + bx & \text{when } x \geq 2. \end{cases}$ Find the value(s) of b for
$^{(75)}$ which f is continuous for all real numbers.

6. Describe the interval(s) on which f is continuous if $f(x) = \begin{cases} \dfrac{x^2 - c^2}{x + c} & \text{when } x \neq -c \\ 2c & \text{when } x = -c. \end{cases}$
$^{(75)}$

7. A rectangular tank 4 m deep is completely filled with a fluid that has a weight density of
$^{(74)}$ 5000 N/m^3. Let F be the total force exerted on a wall that has a width of 5 m. Use y as the
variable of integration to write F as a definite integral.

8. A container with a triangular cross section
$^{(74)}$ as shown is filled with a fluid that has a
weight density of 9000 N/m^3. Find the
total force on one end of the tank.

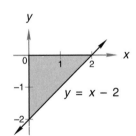

9. Let $f(x) = |x^2 - 9|$ for all real x.
$^{(72)}$
   (a) Find all the zeros of f.
   (b) Graph the function f.
   (c) Find: $f'(x)$

10. Find the maximum value and the minimum value of $f(x) = |x^2 - 2x|$ on the interval $[-2, 3]$.
$^{(63)}$

11. Let R be the region bounded by the graph of $y = 4 - x^2$ and the x-axis. Use y as the variable
$^{(71)}$ of integration to write a definite integral that equals the volume of the solid formed when R is
revolved about the y-axis.

12. Differentiate $y = 5^{x^2 + 1} + \dfrac{2x}{\sqrt{x + 1}}$ with respect to x.
$^{(72)}$

Integrate in problems 13–15.

13.
(73) $\int \left(2^x + \dfrac{1}{\sqrt{x+1}} \right) dx$

14.
(69) $\int -xe^{-x}\, dx$

15.
(66) $\int \dfrac{9x^2}{9+49x^6}\, dx$

16. Let $f(x) = -x^4 + 1$ and $h(x) = x^4 + 1$. Suppose that g is a function such that
(70) $f(x) \leq g(x) \leq h(x)$ for all values of x near, but not equal to, 0. Evaluate $\lim_{x \to 0} g(x)$.

17. Suppose $f(x) = x^2$, $g(x) = e^x$, and $h(x) = g(f(x))$. Determine whether h is odd, even, or
(68) neither.

18. The definite integral $\displaystyle\int_1^4 x\sqrt{x+1}\; dx$ is equivalent to which of the following definite integrals?
(66)

A. $\displaystyle\int_1^4 (u^{3/2} - u^{1/2})\, du$ B. $\displaystyle\int_2^5 (u^{3/2} + u^{1/2})\, du$

C. $\displaystyle\int_2^5 (u^{3/2} - u^{1/2})\, du$ D. $\displaystyle\int_2^5 u(u+1)\, du$

19. Write the equation of the line tangent to the graph of $y = \arcsin(2x)$ at $x = \dfrac{1}{4}$.
(64)

20. Find the area of the first quadrant region beneath the graph of $y = x\sqrt{1-x^2}$.
(66)

In problems 21 and 22 let R be the quasi-triangular region in the first quadrant bounded only by the graphs of $f(x) = \sin x$, $g(x) = \cos x$, and the x-axis over the interval $[0, \frac{\pi}{2}]$.

21. Use algebraic methods to find the coordinates of the point of intersection of the graphs of f and
(13) g in the interval $[0, \frac{\pi}{2}]$.

22. Use calculus to find the area of region R.
(60)

23. The graph of the function $y = x^9 + x^7 + x^5 + x^3$
(49)

    A. is always concave up.

    B. is always concave down.

    C. is concave down when $x > 0$ and concave up when $x < 0$.

    D. has an inflection point at $x = 0$.

24. Suppose f is defined on the closed interval
(21) $[-2, 2]$ and has the graph shown at right.
Sketch the graphs of the following:

    (a) $y = f(x) + 1$

    (b) $y = f(x+1)$

    (c) $y = f(x-1)$

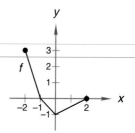

25. Find the point on the curve $y = \sqrt{x}$ nearest to the point $(1, 0)$.
(2,52)

LESSON 76 *Integration of Odd Powers of sin x and cos x*

The derivative of $\sin x$ with respect to x is $\cos x$, and the derivative of $\cos x$ with respect to x is $-\sin x$. The function $\sin x$ and $\cos x$ are also related by the basic Pythagorean identity $\sin^2 x + \cos^2 x = 1$. These relationships allow us to find the integrals of $\sin^n x$ and $\cos^n x$ when n is odd, and they also allow us to find the integrals of $\sin^n x \cos^m x$ when either n or m is odd.

example 76.1 Integrate: $\displaystyle\int \sin^3 x \, dx$

solution The key to integrating odd powers of $\sin x$ is to separate a factor of $(\sin x \, dx)$ to be used later as du. In this case, we replace the remaining factor, $\sin^2 x$, with $(1 - \cos^2 x)$.

$$\int \sin^3 x \, dx = \int (\sin^2 x)(\sin x \, dx) \qquad \text{factored}$$

$$= \int (1 - \cos^2 x)(\sin x \, dx) \qquad \text{substituted}$$

$$= \int \sin x \, dx - \int (\cos^2 x)(\sin x \, dx) \qquad \text{multiplied}$$

The result of the first integral is $-\cos x$. The second integral would have the form $u^2 \, du$ if it had a minus sign, because the differential of $\cos x$ is $-\sin x \, dx$. Thus, we insert the needed minus sign and change the sign in front of the integral from $-$ to $+$.

$$\int \sin^3 x \, dx = -\cos x + \int \underbrace{(\cos^2 x)}_{u^2}\underbrace{(-\sin x \, dx)}_{du}$$

The integral of $u^2 \, du$ is $\dfrac{u^{2+1}}{(2 + 1)}$, so we write

$$\int \sin^3 x \, dx = -\cos x + \frac{1}{3}\cos^3 x + C$$

The difficulty with the minus signs could have been avoided if we had factored $(-\sin x \, dx)$ in the initial step.

$$\int \sin^3 x \, dx = \int (-\sin^2 x)(-\sin x \, dx) \qquad \text{factored}$$

$$= \int -(1 - \cos^2 x)(-\sin x \, dx) \qquad \text{substituted}$$

$$= \int \sin x \, dx + \int (\cos^2 x)(-\sin x \, dx) \qquad \text{multiplied}$$

$$= -\cos x + \frac{1}{3}\cos^3 x + C \qquad \text{integrated}$$

example 76.2 Integrate: $\displaystyle\int \cos^3 x \, dx$

solution The key to integrating odd powers of $\cos x$ is to separate a factor of $(\cos x \, dx)$ to be used later as du. In this case we replace the remaining factor, $\cos^2 x$, with $(1 - \sin^2 x)$.

$$\int \cos^3 x \, dx = \int (\cos^2 x)(\cos x \, dx) \qquad \text{factored}$$

$$= \int (1 - \sin^2 x)(\cos x \, dx) \qquad \text{substituted}$$

$$= \int \cos x \, dx - \int \underbrace{\sin^2 x}_{u^2} \underbrace{\cos x \, dx}_{du} \qquad \text{multiplied}$$

The integral of cos *x* is sin *x*, and the integral of $u^2\, du$ is $\dfrac{u^{2+1}}{(2+1)}$, so

$$\int \cos^3 x\, dx = \sin x - \frac{1}{3}\sin^3 x + C$$

example 76.3   Integrate: $\displaystyle\int \sin^4 x \cos^3 x\, dx$

solution   **The key step is to break up the factor that is raised to an odd power.**

$$\int (\sin^4 x)(\cos^2 x)(\cos x\, dx)$$

We know that (cos *x dx*) is the differential of sin *x*, so it is helpful to have everything else be some form of sin *x*. Thus we replace $\cos^2 x$ with $1 - \sin^2 x$.

$$\int (\sin^4 x)(1 - \sin^2 x)(\cos x\, dx) \qquad\qquad \text{substituted}$$

$$= \int (\sin^4 x - \sin^6 x)(\cos x\, dx) \qquad\qquad \text{multiplied}$$

$$= \int \underbrace{(\sin x)^4}_{u^4}\underbrace{(\cos x\, dx)}_{du} - \int \underbrace{(\sin x)^6}_{u^6}\underbrace{(\cos x\, dx)}_{du} \qquad\qquad \text{two integrals}$$

Since both integrals have the form $\int u^n\, du$, which equals $\frac{u^{n+1}}{(n+1)} + C$, the answer can be written by inspection.

$$\frac{1}{5}\sin^5 x - \frac{1}{7}\sin^7 x + C$$

example 76.4   Integrate: $\displaystyle\int \sin^3 x \cos^7 x\, dx$

solution   Both exponents are odd, so we have a choice. We decide to break up $\sin^3 x$ because its smaller degree makes it easier to handle.

$$\int (\sin^2 x)(\cos^7 x)(\sin x\, dx)$$

The differential of cos *x* is $-\sin x\, dx$, so a negative sign is needed in the last set of parentheses. We choose to take care of this now and remember to write another negative sign to the left of the integral sign.

$$-\int (\sin^2 x)(\cos^7 x)(-\sin x\, dx)$$

Now we substitute $(1 - \cos^2 x)$ for $\sin^2 x$, simplify, and integrate.

$$-\int (1 - \cos^2 x)(\cos^7 x)(-\sin x\, dx) \qquad\qquad \text{substituted}$$

$$= -\left[\int (\cos^7 x)(-\sin x\, dx) - \int (\cos^9 x)(-\sin x\, dx)\right] \qquad\qquad \text{multiplied}$$

$$= -\int \underbrace{(\cos^7 x)}_{u^7}\underbrace{(-\sin x\, dx)}_{du} + \int \underbrace{(\cos^9 x)}_{u^9}\underbrace{(-\sin x\, dx)}_{du} \qquad\qquad \text{simplified}$$

$$= -\frac{1}{8}\cos^8 x + \frac{1}{10}\cos^{10} x + C \qquad\qquad \text{integrated}$$

example 76.5   Integrate: $\displaystyle\int \sin^2 x \cos^5 x\, dx$

solution   Since sin *x* has an even exponent, we work with $\cos^5 x$ and write it as $\cos^4 x \cos x$.

$$\int (\sin^2 x)(\cos^4 x)(\cos x\, dx)$$

The rest of the problem is similar to the previous example, except that it may seem more difficult because the substitution for $\cos^4 x$ is a little more involved. First we express $\cos^4 x$ in terms of $\sin x$.

$$\cos^4 x = (\cos^2 x)^2 = (1 - \sin^2 x)^2 = 1 - 2 \sin^2 x + \sin^4 x$$

Now we substitute this expression for $(\cos^4 x)$ and get

$$\int (\sin^2 x)(1 - 2 \sin^2 x + \sin^4 x)(\cos x \, dx) \qquad \text{substituted}$$

$$= \int \underbrace{(\sin^2 x)}_{u^2}\underbrace{(\cos x \, dx)}_{du} - 2 \int \underbrace{(\sin^4 x)}_{u^4}\underbrace{(\cos x \, dx)}_{du} + \int \underbrace{(\sin^6 x)}_{u^6}\underbrace{(\cos x \, dx)}_{du}$$

All of these have the form $u^n \, du$, and we can write the answer by inspection.

$$\int \sin^2 x \cos^5 x \, dx = \frac{1}{3} \sin^3 x - \frac{2}{5} \sin^5 x + \frac{1}{7} \sin^7 x + C$$

**problem set
76**

1.
(26) The interest was compounded continuously, so the amount of money in the account increased exponentially. The initial deposit was $10,000, and after 3 years $17,000 was in the account. How much money would be in the account after 4 years with no additional deposits or withdrawals?

2.
(74) The shaded area represents the vertical side of a tank that is filled with 100,000 cubic centimeters of water. The measurements shown are in meters. The weight density of water is 9800 newtons per cubic meter. Use y as the variable of integration to write a definite integral whose value equals the total force against the side of the tank.

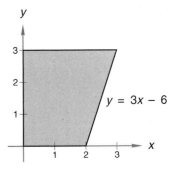

Integrate in problems 3–6.

3.
(76) $\int \sin^3 x \, dx$

4.
(76) $\int \sin^2 x \cos^3 x \, dx$

5.
(76) $\int \sin^3 x \cos^2 x \, dx$

6.
(8) $\int (\sin^2 x + \cos^2 x) \, dx$

7.
(75) Let f be the piecewise function defined below. Find b so that f is continuous for every real value of x.

$$f(x) = \begin{cases} -2x + b & \text{when } x > 0 \\ x^2 + 1 & \text{when } x \leq 0 \end{cases}$$

8.
(75) Determine whether or not f is continuous at $x = 2$ for f as defined below. Justify your answer.

$$f(x) = \begin{cases} \dfrac{x^3 - 8}{x - 2} & \text{when } x \neq 2 \\ 16 & \text{when } x = 2 \end{cases}$$

9.
(61) Suppose f is a cubic function whose equation is $f(x) = x^3 + ax^2 + bx + c$. The graph of f has an inflection point at $x = -\frac{2}{3}$ and a relative minimum point at $x = 0$. If the graph of f passes through the point $(0, 1)$, what are the values of a, b, and c?

10.
(55) Let $f(x) = (1 + e^x)^2$. Show that $f^{(n)}(0) = 2 + 2^n$ for $n = 1, 2, \ldots,$ and write the Maclaurin series for the function.

11.
(70) (a) Use a graphing calculator to graph $y = |x|$, $y = -|x|$, and $y = x \cos \frac{1}{x}$ in the window $-0.2 \leq x \leq 0.2$, $-0.2 \leq y \leq 0.2$.

(b) Assume $-|x| \leq x \cos \frac{1}{x} \leq |x|$ for all values of x near, but different from, zero. Evaluate $\lim_{x \to 0} x \cos \frac{1}{x}$.

12. Find the area of the region between the graph of $y = xe^x$ and the x-axis on the interval [0, 1].
(69)

13. Use x as the variable of integration to write a definite integral whose value is the volume of the
(71) solid formed when the region enclosed by the graph of the equation $x = 1 - y^2$ and the y-axis is revolved around the x-axis.

14. R is the region between $y = x^2$ and the x-axis on the interval [0, 4]. Find the volume of the
(71) solid formed when R is revolved about the x-axis.

15. Differentiate $y = 5^{x^2 + 1} + x \arctan \dfrac{x}{2} + \log_{24} x$ with respect to x.
(64,72)

16. Find all the critical number(s) in the interval $(0, \infty)$ for the function $y = x(\ln x)^2$.
(50)

17. Simplify: $\dfrac{d}{dx}(\arcsin x) + \displaystyle\int \dfrac{dx}{\sqrt{1 - x^2}}$ **18.** Integrate: $\displaystyle\int \left(xe^{2x} + xe^{x^2}\right) dx$
(64)   (69)

19. Find an equation of the line tangent to the curve $xy + y^2 = x + 1$ at the point (2, 1).
(34)

20. Consider the two curves $5y - 2x + y^3 - x^2y = 0$ and $5x + 2y + x^4 - x^3y^2 = 0$. Show
(34) that the tangents to the two curves at the origin are perpendicular.

21. Evaluate: $\displaystyle\int_0^1 \cos x \, e^{\sin x} \, dx$
(66)

22. Use calculus to develop a formula for the volume of a sphere by revolving the semicircle defined
(71) by $y = \sqrt{r^2 - x^2}$ around the x-axis. Use this formula to find the volume of a sphere whose surface area is 16π cm^2.

23. If $f(x) = \dfrac{x^5 - 1}{x - 1}$, then $f(-a)$ equals which of the following?
(10)

    A. $a^4 + a^3 + a^2 + a + 1$ B. $a^4 - a^3 + a^2 - a + 1$

    C. $-a^5 + 1$ D. $-a^4 + a^3 - a^2 + a - 1$

24. Find the exact area of the region beneath $y = \dfrac{1}{x}$ and above the x-axis on the interval [2, 4].
(47)

25. Use numerical integration on a graphing calculator to approximate the area of the region
(53,59) described in problem 24. How does this approximation compare to the answer found in problem 24?

LESSON 77 *Pumping Fluids*

As discussed in Lesson 62, mechanical work is defined as the product of force and distance when the displacement is in the direction of the force.

$$\boxed{\text{Mechanical work} = \text{force} \times \text{distance}}$$

To move a weight of 1 newton vertically a distance of 1 meter requires 1 joule of work. To find the number of joules required to pump a fluid out of a tank, we use a definite integral to sum the products of the weights of thin sheets of fluid and the distances through which the sheets are to be moved.

example 77.1   A rectangular tank is 6 meters high, 10 meters long, and 4 meters wide. If the tank is full of water, how much work is required to pump the water out of the top of the tank?

solution   We need a coordinate system for the physical problem. There are many options, and we decide to place the origin and the axes as shown below.

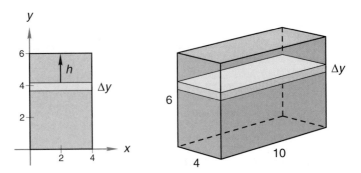

The area of the representative rectangle shown on the left is $4\Delta y$. The volume of the representative rectangular solid on the right is $4\Delta y$ times 10. The weight of the representative rectangular solid is the volume times the weight density of water, which is 9800 newtons per cubic meter.

$$\text{Weight} = \underbrace{(9800)}_{\text{density}}\underbrace{[4(10)\Delta y]}_{\text{volume}}$$

The distance from the x-axis to the top of the tank is 6 meters, and the distance to each representative solid is y. Thus the distance h that each solid must be lifted is $(6 - y)$. The work done equals the distance h times the weight.

$$\text{Work} = \underbrace{(6 - y)}_{h}\underbrace{(9800)}_{\text{density}}\underbrace{[4(10)\Delta y]}_{\text{volume}} = 392{,}000(6 - y)\Delta y$$

We need to sum this work for all the rectangular solids from $y = 0$ to $y = 6$ as the thickness of all solids approaches zero. This sum can be written as the integral shown here.

$$\text{Total work} = 392{,}000 \int_0^6 (6 - y)\, dy$$

$$= 392{,}000\left[6y - \frac{y^2}{2}\right]_0^6$$

$$= \textbf{7,056,000 joules}$$

example 77.2   A tank is 20 meters long, and its cross sections are isosceles triangles with side lengths of 5 meters, 5 meters, and 6 meters as shown. The tank is filled with oil to a depth of 2 meters. Find the work done in pumping the oil out of the top of the tank, assuming the weight density of the oil is 5000 newtons per cubic meter.

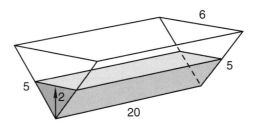

solution   We are using mathematics to solve a physical problem, and there is more than one way to do it. Since the tank is symmetrical, we decide to find the work required to pump the oil out of half the tank and double that amount. We place the origin as shown below so the equation of the line that defines the right-hand side of the tank is a simple equation. We also note that the end of the tank, when cut vertically down the middle, is a 3-4-5 right triangle.

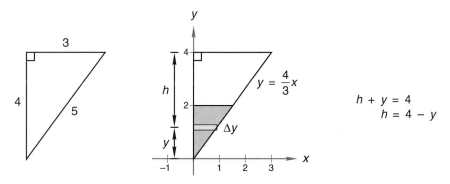

The area of the end of the representative triangle is $x\Delta y$, where $x = \frac{3}{4}y$. Thus the volume of the representative rectangular solid is the width $\frac{3}{4}y$ times the height Δy times the length 20. The weight of the representative rectangular solid is the weight density times the volume. The work to lift this weight a distance $h = 4 - y$ is

$$\underbrace{(5000)}_{\text{density}}\underbrace{(4 - y)}_{h}\underbrace{\left(\frac{3}{4}y\Delta y\right)(20)}_{\text{volume}}$$

This work must be summed for all the rectangular solids from $y = 0$ to $y = 2$. Thus we integrate to solve this problem.

$$\frac{1}{2}\text{Total work} = (5000)(20) \int_0^2 (4 - y)\left(\frac{3}{4}y\right) dy$$

Multiplying gives us

$$\frac{1}{2}\text{Total work} = 100{,}000 \int_0^2 \left(3y - \frac{3}{4}y^2\right) dy$$

$$= 100{,}000\left[\frac{3}{2}y^2 - \frac{y^3}{4}\right]_0^2$$

We evaluate to find that

$$\frac{1}{2}\text{Total work} = 100{,}000(6 - 2) = 400{,}000 \text{ joules}$$

Thus the total work done is **800,000 joules.**

example 77.3 The end of a tank is a semicircle whose diameter is 20 meters. The tank is filled to a depth of 4 meters with a fluid whose weight density is 6000 newtons per cubic meter. Set up an integral that could be evaluated to find the work required to pump the fluid to a point 20 meters above the top of the tank.

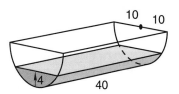

solution We decide to place the origin as shown so the equation of the semi-circle is $x^2 + y^2 = 100$. We compute the work for the right half of the tank and double that result. The area of the end of the representative rectangular solid is $x\Delta y$, where $x = \sqrt{100 - y^2}$. The distance from the rectangular solid to a point 20 meters above the tank is $20 - y$ (y is always negative). Work is the product of volume, weight density, and distance.

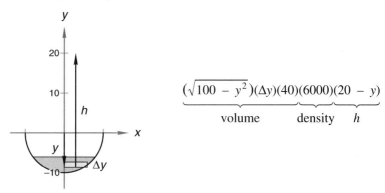

Since the x-axis is at the top of the tank, we must sum the solids from $y = -10$ to $y = -6$.

$$\text{Total work} = 2 \int_{-10}^{-6} (40)(6000)\sqrt{100 - y^2}\,(20 - y)\,dy$$

The additional factor of 2 is required because the integral gives us the work required for only the right-hand half of the tank. In a later lesson we show how to evaluate integrals like this one using a technique called trigonometric substitution. For now we can approximate this integral numerically with $\mathtt{fnInt}$ on the TI-83.

$$\text{Total work} \approx 296,621,705 \text{ joules}$$

problem set 77

1. The volume of a spherical balloon is decreasing at a rate of 3 cm³/s. Find the rate at which the
(46) radius of the balloon is changing when the surface area of the balloon is 16π cm².

2. A rectangular tank is 5 meters deep, 10 meters long, and 4 meters wide. If the tank is full of
(77) water, how much work is required to pump all the water out over the top edge of the tank?

3. A 10- by 10- by 10-meter container is filled
(74) with water. The weight density of water is 9800 newtons per cubic meter. Find the total force against one of the sides of the container.

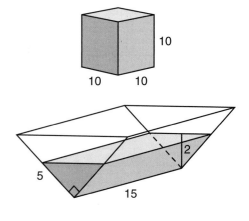

4. A trough 15 meters long, whose cross
(77) section is a right isosceles triangle as shown, is partially filled with a fluid whose weight density is 6000 newtons per cubic meter. The depth of the fluid in the trough is 2 meters. Write a definite integral that expresses the work done in pumping all the fluid out of the trough over its top edge.

Integrate in problems 5–8.

5. $\displaystyle\int \sin^2 x \cos^3 x \, dx$
(76)

6. $\displaystyle\int \cos^3 x \, dx$
(76)

7. $\displaystyle\int \frac{1}{1 + x^2} \, dx + \int \frac{2 \sin x}{\sqrt{\cos x + 1}} \, dx$
(64,66)

8. $\displaystyle\int \frac{x^2 + 1}{x} \, dx$
(38)

9. Let f be the piecewise function defined below. Determine the value(s) of a that make(s) f
(75) continuous everywhere.

$$f(x) = \begin{cases} x^2 & \text{when } x \le 1 \\ ax + 2 & \text{when } x > 1 \end{cases}$$

10. An object is thrown straight up from the top of a 100-meter-tall building with an initial velocity
(65) of 20 meters per second. Develop equations that describe the height and velocity of the object as functions of the time t after the ball is thrown.

11. Find the equation of the line normal to the graph of $y = \log_3 x$ at $x = 3$.
(40,72)

Evaluate the limits in problems 12 and 13.

12. (a) $\displaystyle\lim_{x \to 0^+} \frac{|x|}{x}$ (b) $\displaystyle\lim_{x \to 0^+} \sin \frac{1}{x}$
(70)

13. (a) $\displaystyle\lim_{x \to 0} \frac{\sin x}{\cos x}$ (b) $\displaystyle\lim_{x \to 0} \frac{1}{x}$
(70)

14. Let $f(x) = 3x^2$ and $g(x) = \sin x$. Evaluate $\displaystyle\lim_{x \to \pi} (fg)(x)$.
(70)

15. Suppose f and g are defined as in problem 14 with $h(x) = \frac{f(x)}{g(x)}$. Determine whether the graph
(68) of h is symmetric about the y-axis, symmetric about the origin, or symmetric about neither.

16. Find the area of the region completely enclosed by the graphs of $y = x^3$ and $y = x^2$.
(60)

17. If f is a function that is continuous on $[1, 4]$ and attains a maximum value of 4 and a minimum
(57) value of -6 on this interval, then which of the following statements must be true?

     A. $\displaystyle\int_1^4 f(x)\, dx \geq 0$ B. $\displaystyle\int_1^4 f(x)\, dx \leq 20$

     C. $\displaystyle\int_1^4 f(x)\, dx = 16$ D. $\displaystyle\int_1^4 f(x)\, dx \leq 0$

18. Let $f(x) = |\cos x|$ for all real x on the interval $\left[-\dfrac{3\pi}{2}, \dfrac{3\pi}{2} \right]$.
(72)

     (a) Find all the zeros of f.

     (b) Graph the function f.

     (c) Find: $f'(x)$

19. Let $f(x) = |\cos x|$ and $g(x) = x^2$ for all real x such that $-\frac{3\pi}{2} \leq x \leq \frac{3\pi}{2}$ and let $h = g \circ f$.
(72)
     (a) Find the equaton of h, and determine all the zeros of h.

     (b) Graph the function h.

     (c) Find the domain and range of h.

     (d) Find an equation for the line tangent to the graph of h at the point where $x = \dfrac{3\pi}{4}$.

20. Differentiate $y = \arctan(2x) + \dfrac{2\sin x}{\sqrt{\cos x + 1}} + \sec x \tan x$ with respect to x.
(50)

Evaluate the limits in problems 21 and 22.

21. $\displaystyle\lim_{h \to 0} \dfrac{\sin\left(\dfrac{\pi}{2} + h\right) - \sin \dfrac{\pi}{2}}{h}$ **22.** $\displaystyle\lim_{x \to 4} \dfrac{\ln x - \ln 4}{x - 4}$
(28)   (44)

23. Consider the curve $x^2 - xy + y^2 = 9$.
(34)

     (a) Find an expression for the slope of the curve at any point (x, y) on the curve.

     (b) Find the coordinates of the points on the curve where the tangents are vertical.

     (c) The equation of the curve is written in implicit form. Rewrite the equation of the curve in explicit form by using the quadratic formula to solve for y in terms of x. Use a graphing calculator to graph the explicit equation.

24. Suppose f and g are functions. For a number x to lie in the domain of $f \circ g$, which of the
following must be true?
(18)

    A. x is both an element of the domain of f, and an element of the domain of g.

    B. x is an element of the domain of f, and $f(x)$ is an element of the domain of g.

    C. x is an element of the domain of g, and $g(x)$ is an element of the domain of f.

    D. x is an element of the domain of f, and $g(x)$ is an element of the domain of f.

25. Determine the range of $y = \sin(\arctan x)$.
(13,18)

LESSON 78 *Particle Motion I*

We have discussed equations of motion for bodies freely falling in a gravitational field. The
acceleration function is the derivative of the velocity function, which is the derivative of the position
function. If the initial conditions are known, we can begin with the acceleration function and integrate
to find the velocity function and integrate again to find the position function. In free-falling-body
problems, the acceleration is constant and is always -9.8 m/s^2 (-32 ft/s^2).

In calculus books it is customary to discuss position, velocity, and acceleration of a particle that
moves left and right on the x-axis and whose acceleration is not constant but a function of time. Since
t (time) is the independent variable and we always graph the independent variable on the horizontal
axis, we have to graph $x(t)$ vertically. This means that we are talking about horizontal motion on the
x-axis, but we graph this motion vertically.

example 78.1 A particle moves along the x-axis according to the acceleration function $a(t) = 3t$. The velocity
when $t = 0$ is -10, and the position when $t = 0$ is 6. Find the equation that describes the position
of the object as a function of time. What is the position when $t = 2$?

solution To get the answer, we integrate the acceleration function to get the velocity function and integrate
again to get the position function.

$$v(t) = \int 3t \, dt = \frac{3t^2}{2} + C$$

When $t = 0$, $v(t) = -10$, so we can substitute and solve for C.

$$-10 = \frac{3(0)^2}{2} + C \longrightarrow C = -10$$

Thus the velocity function for this particle is

$$v(t) = \frac{3t^2}{2} - 10$$

The position function is the integral of the velocity function.

$$x(t) = \int \left(\frac{3t^2}{2} - 10 \right) dt = \frac{t^3}{2} - 10t + C$$

When $t = 0$, $x(t) = 6$, so we can substitute and solve for C.

$$6 = \frac{0^3}{2} - 10(0) + C \longrightarrow C = 6$$

Thus the position function for this particle is

$$x(t) = \frac{1}{2}t^3 - 10t + 6$$

The position when $t = 2$ is $x(2)$.

$$x(2) = \frac{1}{2}(2)^3 - 10(2) + 6 = \mathbf{-10}$$

This means that when $t = 2$, the particle is -10 units to the right of the origin, which is the same as being 10 units to the left of the origin.

example 78.2   A particle moves along the x-axis such that the acceleration function is $a(t) = -3t$. Its position when $t = 3$ is 20, and its velocity at $t = 1$ is 5. What is its position when $t = 4$? Also, at what times is the particle changing direction?

solution   This problem is slightly different because it does not give initial conditions for $t = 0$, but we are given the position when $t = 3$ and the velocity when $t = 1$. We begin by integrating the acceleration function to get the velocity function.

$$v(t) = \int a(t)\, dt = \int -3t\, dt = -\frac{3t^2}{2} + C$$

When $t = 1$, $v(t) = 5$, so we can substitute to find C.

$$5 = -\frac{3(1)^2}{2} + C \quad \longrightarrow \quad C = \frac{13}{2}$$

This gives us the velocity function.

$$v(t) = -\frac{3t^2}{2} + \frac{13}{2}$$

We integrate the velocity function to find the position function.

$$x(t) = \int \left(-\frac{3t^2}{2} + \frac{13}{2} \right) dt = -\frac{t^3}{2} + \frac{13}{2}t + C$$

When $t = 3$, $x(t) = 20$, so we can substitute to find C.

$$20 = -\frac{(3)^3}{2} + \frac{13}{2}(3) + C \quad \longrightarrow \quad C = 14$$

Thus the position function is

$$x(t) = -\frac{t^3}{2} + \frac{13}{2}t + 14$$

When $t = 4$, the position is

$$x(4) = -\frac{(4)^3}{2} + \frac{13}{2}(4) + 14 = \mathbf{8}$$

This means that when $t = 4$, the particle is 8 units to the right of the origin.

The particle changes direction exactly when the sign of the velocity changes from positive to negative or vice versa, which only happens when $v = 0$.

$$v(t) = -\frac{3t^2}{2} + \frac{13}{2} = 0$$

$$\frac{3t^2}{2} = \frac{13}{2}$$

$$t^2 = \frac{13}{3}$$

$$t = \pm\sqrt{\frac{13}{3}}$$

We must check that both values make sense as answers to this question. Looking back at the problem, no restrictions are given on the domain of the acceleration function, so we can assume $a(t)$ is defined for all real values of t. This means that negative values of time are perfectly acceptable—they simply refer to times before some particular reference point in time called zero. Therefore the particle changes directions at both $t = -\sqrt{\frac{13}{3}}$ and $t = \sqrt{\frac{13}{3}}$.

example 78.3 A particle moves along the x-axis so that its velocity at time t is given by $v(t) = \frac{1}{t}$ for $t > 0$, and its position is 5 when $t = 2$. Find the time when the particle is 10 units to the right of the origin.

solution The velocity function is given, so we can take its derivative to get the acceleration function or integrate to find the position function. The question is about position, so we integrate to find $x(t)$.

$$x(t) = \int \frac{1}{t}\, dt \quad \longrightarrow \quad x(t) = \ln t + C$$

When $t = 2$, $x(t) = 5$, so we can solve for C.

$$5 = \ln(2) + C \quad \longrightarrow \quad C = 5 - \ln(2)$$

Thus, the position function is

$$x(t) = \ln t + 5 - \ln(2)$$

To find the time when the particle is 10 units to the right of the origin, we let $x(t)$ equal 10 and solve for t.

$$10 = \ln t + 5 - \ln 2 \quad \longrightarrow \quad \ln t = 5 + \ln 2 \quad \longrightarrow \quad t = e^{5 + \ln 2} = \mathbf{2e^5}$$

Using our calculator, we can approximate this value of t.

$$t \approx 296.8263$$

problem set 78

1. Allied Materials Inc. has been contracted to build rectangular crates that have a square base and
   (52) top. The material for the top and bottom of the crates costs \$2.40 per square meter. The material for the four sides of the crates costs \$1.50 per square meter. The total cost of each rectangular crate can be no more than \$360.

   (a) Let the height of the crate be y meters and the length of one side of the base be x meters. Express the volume of the crate in terms of x.

   (b) Find the dimensions of the largest crate (by volume) that Allied can construct.

   (c) Check the answer to (b) with a graphing calculator.

2. A particle moves along the x-axis so that its acceleration at time t is given by $a(t) = 2t$. The
   (78) velocity of the particle at $t = 0$ is -10, and its position at $t = 0$ is 4.

   (a) Find the equations that express the velocity and the position of the particle as functions of t.

   (b) Find the velocity and position of the particle at $t = 2$.

3. A particle moves along the x-axis so that its acceleration is given by $a(t) = 6t - 4$. Its velocity
   (78) at $t = 1$ is -1, and its position at $t = 0$ is $x = -4$. Develop the equations that express the particle's position and velocity as functions of time.

4. A rectangular tank 4 meters deep, 5 meters wide, and 6 meters long is completely filled with a
   (77) fluid whose weight density is 5000 newtons per cubic meter. Find the work done in pumping all the fluid out of the top of the tank.

5. A 20-meter-long trough whose cross
   (77) section is a semicircle with a diameter of 10 meters is partially filled with a fluid whose weight density is 6000 newtons per cubic meter. The depth of the fluid in the trough is 2 meters. Find the work done in pumping all the fluid out of the top of the trough.

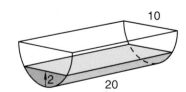

6. Is the following statement true or false: "If $\lim_{x \to 0} f(x) = 5$, then $f(0) = 5$"? Explain
(75) your answer.

7. Find the area of the region between the graph of $y = 3^x$ and the x-axis from $x = 1$ to $x = 3$.
(73)

Integrate in problems 8–13.

8. $\int xe^{2x}\,dx$
(69)

9. $\int \dfrac{x + 1}{\sqrt{x}}\,dx$
(38)

10. $\int \dfrac{4x}{x^2 + 1}\,dx$
(66)

11. $\int \dfrac{4}{x^2 + 1}\,dx$
(64)

12. $\int \sin^6 x \cos^3 x\,dx$
(76)

13. $\int (\cos x)(\sin x + \pi)^3\,dx$
(66)

14. Use y as the variable of integration to write a definite integral whose value equals the area of the
(67) region in the first quadrant bounded by $y = x^2$, $y = 4$, and the y-axis.

15. (a) Use calculus to find the exact maximum value and the exact minimum value of the
(63) function $f(x) = \frac{1}{2}(x - 2)(6x^2 + 21x - 14)$ on the interval $[-4, 2]$.

(b) Check the answer to (a) with a graphing calculator.

16. A function f is continuous on $[0, 3]$ with
(63) $f(0) = 8$ and $f(3) = 2$. The functions f, f', and f'' have the properties shown in the table. Sketch f and indicate any absolute maximum and minimum values that f attains. Also, indicate the coordinates of any inflection points of f.

x	$x < 1$	$x = 1$	$x > 1$
f		5	
f'	negative	zero	negative
f''	positive	zero	negative

17. Suppose $f(x) = e^x + x$. Write an equation that expresses the inverse of f implicitly.
(58)

18. Suppose $f(x) = x^2 + \cos x$, $g(x) = -x$, and $h(x) = f(g(x))$. Determine whether the graph
(68) of h is symmetric about the x-axis, symmetric about the y-axis, symmetric about the origin, or symmetric about none of these.

19. Differentiate $y = x \tan x^2 + \csc(15x) + \dfrac{x}{\sin x + \cos x}$ with respect to x.
(50)

20. Simplify: $\dfrac{d}{dx}[\arcsin(2x)] + \int \dfrac{2}{\sqrt{1 - 4x^2}}\,dx$
(64)

21. Suppose that f is a continuous function on the closed interval $[-1, 1]$ and that $1 \le f(x) \le 5$.
(57) The greatest possible value for $\int_{-1}^{1} f(x)\,dx$ is which of the following?

A. 0   B. 2   C. 10   D. 25

22. Let f be the function defined for all real numbers and having the following properties:
(61)

(i) $f''(x) = 12x^2 - 10$ for all x in the domain of f.

(ii) The line tangent to the graph of f at $(-1, 0)$ has a slope of -6.

Find an expression for $f(x)$, and use a graphing calculator to graph this function.

23. Sketch the graph of $y = \dfrac{(x - 1)^2(x + 3)}{x(x - 3)^2(x^2 + 5)}$. Clearly indicate all zeros and asymptotes.
(41)

24. If the graph of $y = \ln x$ is the dotted curve, which figure's solid curve could depict $y = \ln(x^3)$?
(16)

A.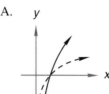

B.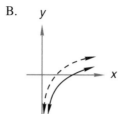

C.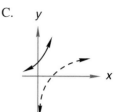

D.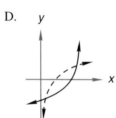

E.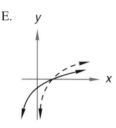

25. Suppose f is a continuous function with $f(-1) = -2$ and $f(2) = 3$. Which of the following
(75)   statements must be true?

A. $f(0) = 0$

B. There exists a number c, where $-1 < c < 2$, such that $f(c) = 0$.

C. f attains no value greater than -2 and no value less than 3 when $-1 < x < 2$.

D. f attains a local minimum at $x = -1$ and a local maximum at $x = 2$.

LESSON 79   *L'Hôpital's Rule*

In mathematics we often study topics that enhance our understanding of a broader concept. **L'Hôpital's Rule** (lō-pē-tâls rül) falls into this category.[†] This rule extends our knowledge of the limit of a quotient, and since calculus is based on the idea of the limit of a function, L'Hôpital's Rule broadens our knowledge of calculus. This rule was discovered by a Swiss mathematician, Johann Bernoulli (1667–1748), but was named for his French associate G. F. A. M. de L'Hôpital (1661–1704).

If the numerator and the denominator of a fraction of polynomials both approach zero as x approaches a, then $x - a$ must be a factor of both the numerator and the denominator. Both the numerator and the denominator of the following expression have a factor of $x - 2$, and the limit of the expression as x approaches 2 is 4.

$$\lim_{x \to 2} \frac{x^2 - 4}{x - 2} = \lim_{x \to 2} \frac{(x - 2)(x + 2)}{x - 2} = \lim_{x \to 2} x + 2 = 4$$

If we attempt to find the limit below, we get the indeterminate form zero over zero. We use the symbol [≠] because we do not wish to indicate that zero over zero is the limit. The substitutions made result in an indeterminate form that is not the limit.

$$\lim_{x \to 0} \frac{\cos x - 1}{x} \;[\neq]\; \frac{1 - 1}{0} = \frac{0}{0}$$

_____

[†] Shown in this sentence is the modern spelling of the name L'Hospital. In mathematics literature, L'Hôpital and L'Hospital are equally used.

In this example the numerator and the denominator do not have a common factor, so an algebraic determination of the limit is not possible; but we can use L'Hôpital's Rule instead. L'Hôpital's Rule tells us to evaluate the limit of the derivative of the numerator divided by the limit of the derivative of the denominator.

$$\lim_{x \to 0} \frac{\cos x - 1}{x} = \lim_{x \to 0} \frac{\dfrac{d}{dx}(\cos x - 1)}{\dfrac{d}{dx}x} = \lim_{x \to 0} \frac{-\sin x}{1} = \frac{0}{1} = 0$$

Our first try at finding the limit resulted in zero over zero, which is an indeterminate form. By using L'Hôpital's Rule, we get a limit of zero over 1, which is determinate because it equals zero.

L'Hôpital's Rule can be used to find

$$\lim_{x \to a} \frac{f(x)}{g(x)}$$

if this limit produces any of the following forms:

$$\frac{0}{0} \qquad \frac{\infty}{\infty} \qquad \frac{-\infty}{\infty} \qquad \frac{\infty}{-\infty} \qquad \frac{-\infty}{-\infty}$$

These quotients are known as **indeterminate forms.** If an application of the rule results in one of these forms, the rule may be used again. Of course the first derivatives must exist for the first application, and the second derivatives must exist for the second application, and so on.

L'HÔPITAL'S RULE

If $\lim\limits_{x \to a} \dfrac{f(x)}{g(x)}$ is an indeterminate form and if $\lim\limits_{x \to a} \dfrac{f'(x)}{g'(x)}$ exists, then

$$\lim_{x \to a} \frac{f(x)}{g(x)} = \lim_{x \to a} \frac{f'(x)}{g'(x)}$$

---

example 79.1   Evaluate: $\lim\limits_{x \to 0} \dfrac{\sin x}{x}$

solution   Since $\sin 0 = 0$, the limit has indeterminate form $\dfrac{0}{0}$. Thus we apply L'Hôpital's Rule.

$$-\lim_{x \to 0} \frac{\sin x}{x} = \lim_{x \to 0} \frac{\dfrac{d}{dx}\sin x}{\dfrac{d}{dx}x}$$

$$= \lim_{x \to 0} \frac{\cos x}{1}$$

$$= 1$$

example 79.2   Evalute: $\lim\limits_{x \to 0} \dfrac{\cos x - 1}{x^2}$

solution   Since $\cos x - 1$ and x^2 approach 0 as x approaches 0, this limit has the indeterminate form zero over zero. The derivative of $\cos x$ exists, as does the derivative of x^2, so we try to compute the limit of the ratio of the first derivatives.

$$\lim_{x \to 0} \frac{f'(x)}{g'(x)} = \lim_{x \to 0} \frac{-\sin x}{2x}$$

This result also has the form zero over zero. Since the second derivatives also exist, we apply the rule again, and this time we find the limit.

$$\lim_{x \to 0} \frac{f''(x)}{g''(x)} = \lim_{x \to 0} \frac{-\cos x}{2} = \frac{-\cos 0}{2} = -\frac{1}{2}$$

We can confirm this result in a couple of ways with the TI-83. The first way uses a table. This almost always requires two button sequences:

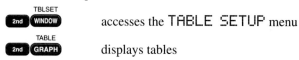

accesses the TABLE SETUP menu

displays tables

After defining $Y_1 = (\cos(X)-1)/X^2$, we access the TABLE SETUP menu. The limit involves x-values close to 0, so we set TblStart=0.5 and $\triangle$Tbl=-0.1. Then we display the table:

X	Y₁
.5	-.4897
.4	-.4934
.3	-.4963
.2	-.4983
.1	-.4996
0	ERROR
-.1	-.4996

X=.5

Note that, as the x-values approach 0, the values of the function get close to −0.5, or $-\frac{1}{2}$. We could confirm this more reliably by changing the values of TblStart and $\triangle$Tbl to get a more accurate account of the behavior of the function when x is close to 0. We set TblStart equal to 0.05 and $\triangle$Tbl equal to −0.01.

X	Y₁
.05	-.4999
.04	-.4999
.03	-.5
.02	-.5
.01	-.5
0	ERROR
-.01	-.5

X=.05

There is no need to be concerned over the ERROR when $x = 0$. Indeed, the function is not defined at $x = 0$. Besides, the limit only reflects the behavior of the function for x-values near 0, not at 0.

We can also confirm this answer graphically.

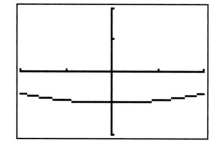

WINDOW
Xmin=-2
Xmax=2
Xscl=1
Ymin=-1
Ymax=1
Yscl=.5
Xres=1

Notice that the graph approaches a y-value of −0.5 as the x-values approach 0 from the left and from the right.

example 79.3   Evalute: $\lim\limits_{x \to 0} \dfrac{x^3 - 4x}{x^2 - 2x}$

solution   Note that

$$\lim\limits_{x \to 0} (x^3 - 4x) = (0)^3 - 4(0) = 0 \quad \text{and} \quad \lim\limits_{x \to 0} (x^2 - 2x) = (0)^2 - 2(0) = 0$$

The limit as x approaches 0 of the expression $\frac{x^3 - 4x}{x^2 - 2x}$ yields the indeterminate form $\frac{0}{0}$. Since there does exist a limit (as x approaches 0) of the quotient of the derivatives of the numerator and denominator, we apply L'Hôpital's Rule.

$$\lim\limits_{x \to 0} \dfrac{x^3 - 4x}{x^2 - 2x} = \lim\limits_{x \to 0} \dfrac{3x^2 - 4}{2x - 2} = \dfrac{0 - 4}{0 - 2} = \mathbf{2}$$

example 79.4   Evaluate: $\lim\limits_{x \to 1} \dfrac{\ln x}{2 - 2x}$

solution   The value of $e^0 = 1$, so ln 1 is 0. Thus we see

$$\lim\limits_{x \to 1} \ln x = 0 \quad \text{and} \quad \lim\limits_{x \to 1} (2 - 2x) = 2 - 2(1) = 0$$

We again have the indeterminate form $\dfrac{0}{0}$. Applying L'Hôpital's Rule gives the answer.

$$\lim\limits_{x \to 1} \dfrac{\ln x}{2 - 2x} = \lim\limits_{x \to 1} \dfrac{\dfrac{d}{dx} \ln x}{\dfrac{d}{dx}(2 - 2x)}$$

$$= \lim\limits_{x \to 1} \dfrac{\dfrac{1}{x}}{-2}$$

$$= \lim\limits_{x \to 1} -\dfrac{1}{2x} = -\dfrac{1}{2}$$

example 79.5   Evaluate: $\lim\limits_{x \to \infty} \dfrac{\cos x + 2x}{6x^2}$

solution   As x approaches ∞, $\cos x$ oscillates between $+1$ and -1, while $2x$ and $6x^2$ go to $+\infty$. Thus we have the indeterminate form $\frac{\infty}{\infty}$. Applying L'Hôpital's Rule yields

$$\lim\limits_{x \to \infty} \dfrac{\cos x + 2x}{6x^2} = \lim\limits_{x \to \infty} \dfrac{-\sin x + 2}{12x}$$

The value of $-\sin x$ is always between -1 and $+1$; so, as x increases, the numerator has a value between 1 and 3. The denominator increases without bound, however, so the limit is a number between 1 and 3 divided by a quantity that is increasing without bound. Thus the limit as x approaches ∞ is zero.

$$\lim\limits_{x \to \infty} \dfrac{-\sin x + 2}{12x} = 0 \quad \text{so} \quad \lim\limits_{x \to \infty} \dfrac{\cos x + 2x}{6x^2} = \mathbf{0}$$

problem set 79

1.
(78)   A particle moves along the x-axis so that its acceleration at time t is given by $a(t) = 2 \cos t$. The velocity of the particle at $t = \frac{\pi}{2}$ is -4, and the position of the particle at $t = 0$ is 8. Develop equations that express the particle's velocity and position as functions of t.

2.
(78)   A particle moves along the x-axis so that its acceleration function is $a(t) = -6t$. Furthermore, its velocity at $t = 1$ is -1, and its position at $t = 2$ is -3. Find the velocity and position of the particle at $t = 3$.

3. A rectangular tank 2 meters deep, 4 meters wide, and 10 meters long is completely filled with
(77) water. Find the work done in pumping enough water out of the tank to decrease the depth of the
water to 1 meter.

4. A trough 6 meters long with cross section
(77) as shown is filled with a fluid whose
weight density is 1000 newtons per cubic
meter. Find the work done in pumping all
the fluid out of the trough.

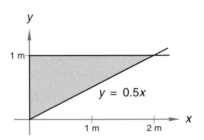

5. The side of a large tank filled with a fluid
(74) whose weight density is 2000 newtons per
cubic meter contains a 1- by 1-meter
square door at its base. Find the total force
against the door if the top of the door lies 5
meters below the surface of the water.

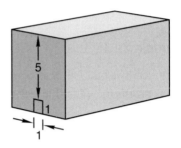

Evaluate the limits in problems 6–10.

6. $\lim\limits_{x \to 0} \dfrac{\sin x}{x}$
(79)

7. $\lim\limits_{x \to 0} \dfrac{2 - 2 \cos x}{\sin x}$
(79)

8. $\lim\limits_{x \to \infty} \dfrac{x}{(\ln x)^2}$
(79)

9. $\lim\limits_{x \to \infty} \dfrac{x + \sin x}{x^2}$
(79)

10. $\lim\limits_{x \to 0} \dfrac{e^x - x}{\sin x}$
(79)

11. Let $f(x) = -\cos x$ and $h(x) = 2 + \cos x$. Suppose that g is a function such that
(70) $f(x) \le g(x) \le h(x)$ for all values of x near, but different from, π. Evaluate $\lim\limits_{h \to \pi} g(x)$.

Integrate in problems 12–14.

12. $\displaystyle\int \sin^3 x \, dx$
(76)

13. $\displaystyle\int \cos x \sin^3 x \, dx$
(76)

14. $\displaystyle\int (\log x + 43^x) \, dx$
(73)

15. Let $f(x) = |x^2 - 8|$ for all real x.
(72)
    (a) Find all the zeros of f.   (b) Graph: f (c) Find: $f'(x)$

16. The definite integral $\displaystyle\int_1^2 x\sqrt{2x - 1} \, dx$ is equivalent to which of the following?
(66)

    A. $\displaystyle\int_1^2 \frac{1}{2}(u^{3/2} - u^{1/2}) \, du$ B. $\displaystyle\int_1^2 \frac{1}{2}(u^{3/2} + u^{1/2}) \, du$ C. $\displaystyle\int_1^3 \frac{1}{2}(u^{3/2} - u^{1/2}) \, du$

    D. $\displaystyle\int_1^3 \frac{1}{2}(u^{3/2} + u^{1/2}) \, du$ E. None of these

17. Suppose $f(x) = \tan x$, $g(x) = 3 \sin x$, and $h(x) = (fg)(x)$. Is the graph of h symmetric about
(68) the y-axis, symmetric about the origin, or symmetric about neither?

18. Find the equation of the line tangent to the graph of the function $y = x^3 + 6x^2 + 1$ at its point
(27,49) of inflection.

19. Suppose $f(x) = a \sin x + b \cos x$ and the slope of the graph of f at $(0, 2)$ is 2. Find $a + b$.
(61)

20. (a) Write a single definite integral whose value equals the area of the region between the graph
(59)   of $y = x^2 + x - 2$ and the x-axis over the interval $[-3, 2]$.

    (b) Find the area of the region described in (a) by using a graphing calculator to evaluate the integral.

21. (a) Find the Maclaurin series for $y = \sin x$. Write the answer using summation notation.
(55)

    (b) Find the Maclaurin series for $y = \sin x^2$.

    (c) Substitute x^2 for x in the Maclaurin series found in (a). Compare your answer with the answer of (b).

22. Find $\dfrac{dy}{dx}$ where $y = \dfrac{x + \sin x}{\cos x} + \arctan(x^2) + e^x \csc(2x)$.
(50)

23. Find $h'(x)$ where $h(x) = f(g(x))$, $f(x) = x^2$, and $g(x) = \sin x$.
(44)

24. If f is a function that is differentiable for all real values of x, then $\lim_{h \to 0} \dfrac{f(a+h) - f(a)}{h}$ equals which of the following?
(44)

    A. $f(a)$ B. $\displaystyle\lim_{x \to a} \dfrac{f(x) - f(a)}{x - a}$

    C. 0   D. undefined

25. Let f be the function defined by $f(x) = 2x^3 - 3x^2 - 12x + 20$.
(27)

    (a) Graph the function f on a graphing calculator.

    (b) Use calculus to find the x- and y-coordinates of all points on the graph of f where the line tangent to the graph is parallel to the x-axis.

LESSON 80 *Asymptotes of Rational Functions*

We can sketch the graph of a rational function quickly and easily if we first mark the locations of the asymptotes and zeros of the function. The asymptotes of the function are the zeros of the linear real factors of the denominator, and the zeros of the function are the zeros of the linear real factors of the numerator. The functions we have sketched have permitted us to study the behavior of rational functions, but since both polynomials must first be factored into a product of linear real factors and irreducible quadratic factors, the possible applications of this method are restricted. To use asymptotes and zeros to graph the function

$$y = \frac{3x^{10} - 2x^5 + 7x^4 + x^3 - x + 5}{5x^8 - 4x^4 + 3x^3 - x^2 + x + 2}$$

would require that we first factor both polynomials. Gauss proved that both of these polynomials can be factored, but unfortunately he did not come up with a method for determining the factorizations. Modern computers and calculators, however, can be programmed to graph functions and to approximate the zeros of functions to any number of decimal places.

There are ways to determine the asymptotic behavior of a rational function even though the two polynomials have not been factored. **If the degree of the numerator is less than the degree of the denominator, the x-axis is the horizontal asymptote. If the degree of the numerator is equal to the degree of the denominator, the horizontal asymptote is a constant function whose value equals the coefficient of the highest-power term in the numerator divided by the coefficient of the highest-power term in the denominator. If the degree of the numerator is greater than the degree of the denominator, the first step is to divide the numerator by the denominator and consider the expression that results.** We look at these cases in the following examples.

example 80.1 Find the equation of the horizontal asymptote of $y = \dfrac{4x^4 + 3x^2 + 2x}{3x^5 + x^3 - 4}$.

solution The degree of the denominator is greater than the degree of the numerator, so the horizontal asymptote is the *x*-axis. To show this, we divide every term in the numerator and denominator by the highest power of *x* in the denominator, which is x^5.

$$y = \frac{\dfrac{4x^4}{x^5} + \dfrac{3x^2}{x^5} + \dfrac{2x}{x^5}}{\dfrac{3x^5}{x^5} + \dfrac{x^3}{x^5} - \dfrac{4}{x^5}} \quad\longrightarrow\quad y = \frac{\dfrac{4}{x} + \dfrac{3}{x^3} + \dfrac{2}{x^4}}{3 + \dfrac{1}{x^2} - \dfrac{4}{x^5}}$$

As *x* increases without limit positively or negatively, the value of each of the fractions approaches zero and the value of the function approaches $\frac{0}{3}$, which equals zero. This means that the graph of the function approaches the *x*-axis (**$y = 0$**) for both large positive values and large negative values of *x*.

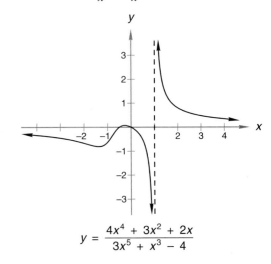

$$y = \frac{4x^4 + 3x^2 + 2x}{3x^5 + x^3 - 4}$$

example 80.2 Graph: $y = \dfrac{-5x + x^2}{2x^2 - 8}$

solution In this example the degree of the polynomial in the numerator equals the degree of the polynomial in the denominator, so the horizontal asymptote is some constant other than zero. To find the constant, we divide above and below by x^2, which is the highest power of *x* in the denominator.

$$y = \frac{-\dfrac{5x}{x^2} + \dfrac{x^2}{x^2}}{\dfrac{2x^2}{x^2} - \dfrac{8}{x^2}} \quad\longrightarrow\quad y = \frac{-\dfrac{5}{x} + 1}{2 - \dfrac{8}{x^2}}$$

As *x* increases without bound positively or negatively, the value of the fractions in the numerator and denominator approach zero and the value of the whole expression approaches $\frac{1}{2}$. Thus the horizontal asymptote is $y = \frac{1}{2}$. We write the factored form and show the graph here.

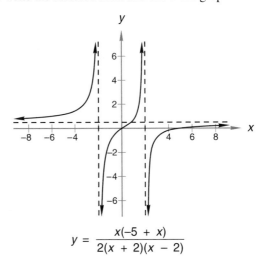

$$y = \frac{x(-5 + x)}{2(x + 2)(x - 2)}$$

In the following examples we concentrate on rational functions like this one, which are easy to factor, so that the vertical asymptotes and zeros are easy to find. **Note that the graph can cross the horizontal asymptote at some values of x; but as the value of x approaches $-\infty$ or ∞, the graph of f approaches but does not cross the horizontal asymptote.**

example 80.3   Graph: $y = \dfrac{x^2 + 1}{x}$

solution   The degree of the polynomial in the numerator is greater than the degree of the polynomial in the denominator. When this occurs, there is no horizontal asymptote because the graph approaches some nonconstant function of x.

The first step is to divide the numerator by the denominator.

$$y = \frac{x^2 + 1}{x} \longrightarrow y = x + \frac{1}{x}$$

For large values of x, the fraction $\frac{1}{x}$ has negligible value, so the value of y is approximately equal to the value of x.

$$y \approx x \quad \text{for large values of } x$$

This means that the line $y = x$ is the asymptote. Such a nonhorizontal linear asymptote is called a **slant asymptote.**

Looking at the original function, we see that it has a vertical asymptote when $x = 0$. Since no value of x makes $x^2 + 1$ equal zero, the function has no zeros and thus the graph of the function never touches the x-axis.

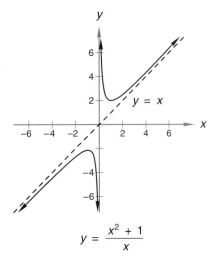

$$y = \frac{x^2 + 1}{x}$$

example 80.4   Graph: $y = \dfrac{x^2 - 1}{x - 2}$

solution   Since the degree of the numerator is greater than the degree of the denominator, the first step is to divide.

$$\begin{array}{r} x + 2 \\ x - 2 \overline{) x^2 \qquad - 1} \\ \underline{x^2 - 2x} \\ 2x - 1 \\ \underline{2x - 4} \\ 3 \end{array} \qquad y = \frac{x^2 - 1}{x - 2} = x + 2 + \frac{3}{x - 2}$$

For large values of x, the value of 3 divided by $x - 2$ becomes negligible. The value of y then approaches $x + 2$, so the asymptote is the line

$$y = x + 2$$

To find the vertical asymptotes and the zeros of the function, we write the function in factored form and see that the function has a vertical asymptote at $x = 2$ and has zeros at x-values of 1 and -1.

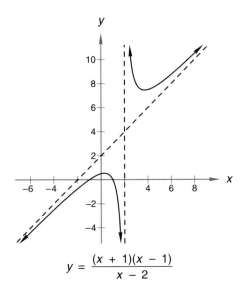

$$y = \frac{(x + 1)(x - 1)}{x - 2}$$

problem set 80

1. *(78)* A particle moves along the number line so that its acceleration at any time t is given by $a(t) = 2t$. The velocity of the particle is 10 at $t = 3$. Find the time when the particle has a velocity of 17.

2. *(77)* A rectangular tank is 4 meters high, 1 meter wide, and 3 meters long. The tank is half full of a fluid that has a weight density of 2000 newtons per cubic meter. Find the work done in pumping all the fluid out of the top of the tank.

3. *(65)* A ball is thrown straight upward from a height of 160 meters with an initial velocity of 50 meters per second.

(a) Write equations that express the height of the ball above the ground and its velocity as functions of the time t after the ball is thrown.

(b) How long after the ball is thrown will it reach its peak?

(c) How long after it is thrown will it hit the ground? (Assume the ball will not hit anything before reaching the ground.)

4. *(52)* A right circular cone of radius x cm and height y cm has a slant height of $4\sqrt{3}$ centimeters.

(a) Express the volume of the right circular cone in terms of x.

(b) Find the dimensions of the right circular cone of maximum possible volume.

(c) Check your answer to (b) with a graphing calculator.

(d) Find the maximum possible volume of the right circular cone. Your answer should be exact.

5. *(80)* Find the equation of the horizontal asymptote of the graph of $y = \dfrac{3x^5 - 2x^3 + 1}{2x^5 - 1}$.

Sketch the graphs of the functions in problems 6–9. Clearly indicate all asymptotes and x-intercepts.

6. *(80)* $y = \dfrac{x + 1}{x}$

7. *(80)* $y = \dfrac{-24x + 6x^2}{3x^2 - 27}$

8. *(80)* $y = \dfrac{x^2 - 1}{x}$

9. *(80)* $y = \dfrac{x^2 - 1}{x - 3}$

Evaluate the limits in problems 10–13.

10. $\displaystyle \lim_{x \to 0} \frac{x}{\sin (45x)}$
(79)

11. $\displaystyle \lim_{x \to \infty} \frac{x^2}{\ln x}$
(79)

12. $\displaystyle \lim_{x \to 0} \frac{\cos x - 1}{52 \sin x}$
(79)

13. $\displaystyle \lim_{x \to 1} \frac{x^2 - 3}{2x - 1}$
(70)

14. Let R be the region completely enclosed by the graph of $y = \sqrt{x}$, the x-axis, and the
(71) line $x = 4$. Find the volume of the solid formed when R is revolved about the x-axis.

15. Find the area of the region completely enclosed by the graphs of $y = x^3$ and $y = x$.
(60)

16. Find the two points on the circle $x^2 + y^2 = 25$ at which the slope of a tangent line is 2.
(34)

17. Suppose $b > c > 1$ and f is continuous for all real numbers. If $\int_1^c f(x)\, dx = 3$ and
(57) $\int_1^b f(x)\, dx = 5$, what is $\int_c^b f(x)\, dx$?

18. Differentiate $y = \arctan (\sin x) + x^2 \ln |\sin x| + e^{\sec x}$ with respect to x.
(50,64)

19. The area of a rectangle remains constant at 100 square centimeters while both its length L and
(46) width W change with respect to time. Find the width W and length L of the rectangle at the instant the width W is decreasing at the rate 0.8 centimeters per second and the length L is increasing at the rate of 5 centimeters per second.

Integrate in problems 20–23.

20. $\displaystyle \int \frac{3x^2 + e^x}{x^3 + e^x}\, dx$
(66)

21. $\displaystyle \int (\ln x + 43^x)\, dx$
(69,73)

22. $\displaystyle \int \frac{x}{\sqrt{6 - 4x^4}}\, dx$
(64,66)

23. $\displaystyle \int \frac{x}{6 + 4x^4}\, dx$
(64,66)

24. Let $f(x) = \sin (\arctan x)$. Determine the range of f.
(13,18)

25. Suppose the function f is defined as below. Find the value of a for which f is continuous
(75) everywhere.

$$f(x) = \begin{cases} 2x + 1 & \text{when } x < 1 \\ ax^2 + 1 & \text{when } x \geq 1 \end{cases}$$

LESSON 81 *Solids of Revolution II: Washers*

Some solids of revolution have cavities, and their volumes can be computed as the difference of two volumes, each of which can be found by stacking disks. These volumes can also be found by stacking washers. The volume of the solid formed by rotating the first-quadrant region shown below about the y-axis is the volume formed by revolving the region bounded by the graph of $f(x) = x^2$ about the y-axis, and then removing the volume formed by revolving the graph of $g(x) = 2x^2$ about the y-axis.

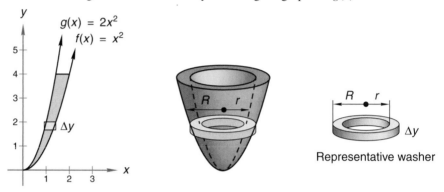

The solid formed is depicted in the center figure, and its volume can be approximated by a stack of circular washers similar to the representative washer shown. The volume of the representative washer is the product of its thickness (Δy) and the area of the whole disk (πR^2) reduced by the area of the hole in its center (πr^2).

$$\text{Volume} = (\pi R^2 - \pi r^2)\Delta y$$

Since this result is exactly the same as the difference in the volumes of two representative disks,

$$\text{Volume} = \pi R^2 \Delta y - \pi r^2 \Delta y$$

we see that the volume-by-washer method is a difference-of-two-disks method in disguise. The washers make it easier to visualize the problem, which is why we use them. The total volume is given by a definite integral that sums all of these smaller volumes.

$$\text{Volume} = \int_a^b (\pi R^2 - \pi r^2)\, dy$$

This is the case when the region has been rotated about the y-axis. R and r are represented in terms of y, and a and b are the smallest and largest y-values denoting the locations of the vertically stacked washers.

We can write a similar integral for volumes of solids of revolution rotated about the x-axis:

$$\text{Volume} = \int_a^b (\pi R^2 - \pi r^2)\, dx$$

Here, R and r are in terms of x, and the washers are stacked along the x-axis from a to b.

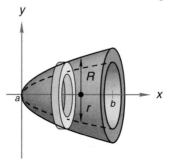

example 81.1   Find the volume of the solid formed by revolving the region shown about the y-axis.

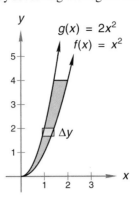

solution   First we generate the solid and draw a representative washer.

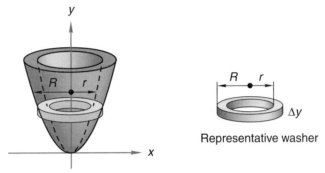

Representative washer

The volume of the representative washer is $(\pi R^2 - \pi r^2)\Delta y$ where R is the outer radius and r is the inner radius of the washer. In this case R is determined by the input for the function f, so $y = R^2$. On the other hand, r is determined by the input for the function g, so $y = 2r^2$ or $r^2 = \frac{y}{2}$. These washers are stacked from $y = 0$ to $y = 4$. Thus the volume of the solid in question is

$$V = \int_a^b \left(\pi R^2 - \pi r^2 \right) dy$$

$$= \int_0^4 \left(\pi y - \pi \frac{y}{2} \right) dy$$

$$= \frac{\pi}{2} \int_0^4 y \, dy$$

$$= \frac{\pi}{2} \left[\frac{y^2}{2} \right]_0^4$$

$$= 4\pi \ \mathbf{units}^3$$

example 81.2   Find the volume of the solid formed by revolving about the y-axis the region bounded by $y = x$, $x = 4$, and the x-axis.

solution   First, we draw the graphs and the solid formed.

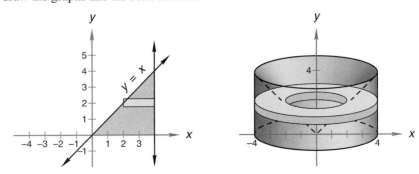

Note that the volume in question is that of a cylinder with a cone removed. The volume of the entire cylinder is

$$V_{cyl} = \pi r^2 h = \pi (4)^2 4 = 64\pi$$

while the volume of the removed cone is

$$V_{cone} = \frac{1}{3}\pi r^2 h = \frac{1}{3}(64\pi) = \frac{64\pi}{3}$$

Therefore, the volume of the resulting object is $V_{cyl} - V_{cone} = 64\pi - \dfrac{64\pi}{3} = \dfrac{128\pi}{3}$.

To confirm this, we compute a definite integral that describes the volume of the object.

$$V = \int_{y=0}^{y=4} (\pi R^2 - \pi r^2)\, dy$$

Here $R = 4$ for all washers, while $r = x$. But since this region is revolved about the y-axis, we must write the equations for R and r in terms of y.

$$R = 4$$

$$r = y \qquad \text{(since } y = x)$$

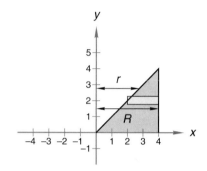

Now we find the volume.

$$V = \int_0^4 \pi (4^2 - y^2)\, dy$$

$$= \pi \left[16y - \frac{y^3}{3} \right]_0^4$$

$$= \pi \left[64 - \frac{64}{3} \right]$$

$$= \frac{128\pi}{3} \text{ units}^3$$

example 81.3   Find the volume of the solid formed by revolving the region shown about the x-axis.

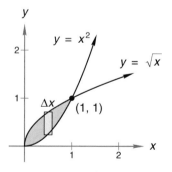

solution   First we draw the solid and show a representative washer.

The volume of the representative washer is

$$V = (\pi R^2 - \pi r^2)\, \Delta x$$

$$= \left[\pi (\sqrt{x})^2 - \pi (x^2)^2 \right] \Delta x$$

$$= (\pi x - \pi x^4)\, \Delta x$$

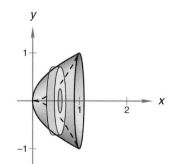

Moreover, the washers are stacked from $x = 0$ to $x = 1$. Therefore the volume in question is

$$V = \int_0^1 (\pi x - \pi x^4)\, dx$$

$$= \left[\frac{\pi x^2}{2} - \frac{\pi x^5}{5}\right]_0^1$$

$$= \pi\left(\frac{1}{2} - \frac{1}{5}\right)$$

$$= \frac{3}{10}\pi \text{ units}^3$$

example 81.4 The region between the graphs of $y = x^2 + 2$ and $y = \frac{1}{2}x + 1$ on the interval $[0, 1]$ is revolved about the x-axis. Find the volume of the solid of revolution generated.

solution We begin by drawing the graph and shading the region to be revolved. Next we show the solid that is generated, as well as a representative washer.

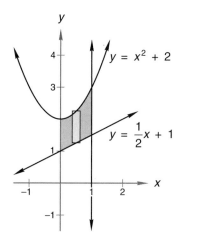  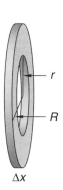

The rectangle in the graph is a profile of a section of the washer on the right. The width of the washer is Δx, and we stack these washers from $x = 0$ to $x = 1$. The radius r of the inside of the washer is $\frac{1}{2}x + 1$, and the radius R of the outside of the washer is $x^2 + 2$. So the volume in question is

$$V = \int_0^1 (\pi R^2 - \pi r^2)\, dx$$

$$= \int_0^1 \left[\pi(x^2 + 2)^2 - \pi\left(\frac{1}{2}x + 1\right)^2\right] dx$$

$$= \pi \int_0^1 \left[x^4 + 4x^2 + 4 - \left(\frac{x^2}{4} + x + 1\right)\right] dx$$

$$= \pi \int_0^1 \left(x^4 + \frac{15}{4}x^2 - x + 3\right) dx$$

$$= \pi\left[\frac{x^5}{5} + \frac{5x^3}{4} - \frac{x^2}{2} + 3x\right]_0^1$$

$$= \pi\left[\frac{1}{5} + \frac{5}{4} - \frac{1}{2} + 3\right]$$

$$= \frac{79\pi}{20} \text{ units}^3$$

**problem set
81**

1. A 10-meter-long trough with a right
(77) triangular cross section is partially filled
with a fluid whose weight density is
9000 newtons per cubic meter. The level
of the fluid is 1 meter below the top rim of
the trough. Find the work done in pumping
all the fluid out of the top of the tank.

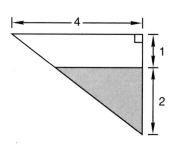

2. Suppose the function f is defined as $f(x) = \begin{cases} x^3 + 2x & \text{when } x \le 2 \\ 3x + b & \text{when } x > 2 \end{cases}$. Find the value of b for which f is
(75) continuous everywhere.

3. Let f be a quadratic function. The slope of the line tangent to the graph of f at $x = 1$ is 1, and
(61) the slope of the line tangent to the graph of f at $x = 2$ is 5. The graph of f passes through the
point $(0, 1)$. Find the equation of f.

In problems 4 and 5, let R be the region in the first quadrant between $y = x^2$ and the x-axis on the
interval $[0, 3]$.

4. Find the volume of the solid formed when R is revolved about the x-axis.
(71)

5. Find the volume of the solid formed when R is revolved about the y-axis.
(81)

6. Let R be the region in the first quadrant enclosed by the graphs of $y = x^2$, $y = \frac{1}{4}x^2$, and
(81) $y = 4$. Find the volume of the solid formed when R is rotated around the y-axis.

7. Let R be the first-quadrant region completely bounded by the graph of $y = \sqrt{x}$ and $y = x^3$.
(81) Find the volume of the solid formed when region R is revolved about the x-axis.

8. Let R be the region bounded by the graphs of $y = x^2 + 1$, $y = x$, $x = 0$, and $x = 2$. Find
(81) the volume of the solid formed when region R is rotated around the x-axis.

9. Write the equations of the asymptotes of the graph of the function $y = \dfrac{2x^2 - 2x - 4}{x - 1}$.
(80)

Graph the functions in problems 10 and 11. Clearly indicate all zeros and asymptotes.

10. $y = \dfrac{x^2 + 1}{2x}$
(80)

11. $y = \dfrac{x^2 + x - 2}{x + 1}$
(80)

Evaluate the limits in problems 12 and 13.

12. $\lim\limits_{x \to 0} \dfrac{\sin (3x)}{x}$
(79)

13. $\lim\limits_{x \to 2} \dfrac{x^3 - x^2 - x - 2}{x - 2}$
(79)

14. Write the equation of the line tangent to the graph of $y = 2^x$ at $x = 2$.
(72)

15. If $\lim\limits_{x \to 2} f(x) = 7$, which of the following must be true?
(75)

  A. f exists at $x = 2$.   B. $f(2) = 7$

  C. f is continuous at $x = 2$.   D. None of the above

16. Differentiate $y = x \ln |x^3 - x| + 2^{2x - 3} + \arctan x$ with respect to x.
(64,72)

17. Antidifferentiate: $\displaystyle \int \left(2^x + \dfrac{1}{1 + x^2} \right) dx$
(64,73)

18. Evaluate $\displaystyle\int_0^\pi \frac{\cos x}{\sqrt{\sin x + 1}}\, dx$ by changing the variable of integration.
(66)

19. Which of the following functions has a graph that is concave upward everywhere?
(49)

A. $y = x^3$ B. $y = -x^2$ C. $y = e^x$ D. $y = \sin x$

20. If f is a function that is continuous and increasing for all real values of x, which of the following
(45) must be true?

A. The graph of f is always concave up.   B. The graph of f is always concave down.

C. $f(x_1) < f(x_2)$ if $x_1 > x_2$ D. $f(x_2) > f(x_1)$ if $x_2 > x_1$

21. Let $f(x) = e^{3x}$. Find the value of $f^{-1}(1)$.
(58)

22. For what values of k does the graph of $y = \frac{4}{3}x^3 + 2kx^2 + 5x + 3$ have two tangent lines
(15,27) parallel to the x-axis.

23. The graph of the function f is shown at the
(21) right. The graph of $g(x) = f(x + 2)$ most
resembles which of the following graphs?

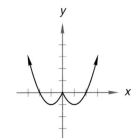

A.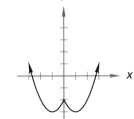

B.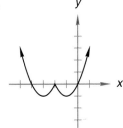

C.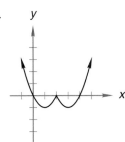

D.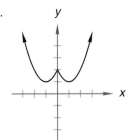

24. Determine the domain and range of $y = \sin\left(\sqrt{x - 1}\right)$.
(18)

25. Let $f(x) = -x^2 - 4x + 12$ on the interval $[-3, 1]$. Find the point(s) on the curve where the
(2,27) tangent line is parallel to the line segment joining the point corresponding to $x = -3$ to the
point corresponding to $x = 1$.

LESSON 82 *Limits and Continuity • Differentiability*

82.A

limits and continuity

The limit of a function as x approaches c is the number that the value of the function approaches as x approaches c. The definition of the limit of a function requires that both the right-hand and left-hand limits exist and requires that these limits be equal. If the one-sided limits exist and are equal at $x = c$ and if $f(c)$, the value of the function at c, exists and equals the one-sided limits, then the function is continuous at c.

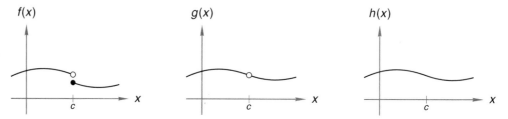

The function f (graphed on the left) has both a right-hand limit and a left-hand limit as x approaches c, but the one-sided limits are not equal, so the limit of the function as x approaches c does not exist. The function g has both one-sided limits equal, so the function has a limit as x approaches c, but the function is not continuous at $x = c$, because these limits do not equal $g(c)$, which is not defined. The function h has a limit as x approaches c and this limit equals $h(c)$, so this function is a continuous function at $x = c$.

The derivative of a function is a special limit. Remember that the graphical interpretation of the derivative of f when $x = c$ is the limit of the slope of a secant line drawn through two points P_1 and P_2 on the graph of f as P_2 approaches P_1 and as the horizontal distance $x - c$ between the points approaches zero. Point P_2 can be to the right of P_1 or to the left of P_1, as we show in the following figures.

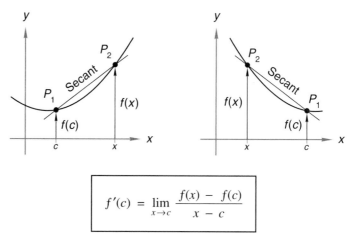

$$f'(c) = \lim_{x \to c} \frac{f(x) - f(c)}{x - c}$$

It is not obvious, but for a function to have a derivative at $x = c$ it is necessary that the function be continuous at $x = c$. We can see that this might be true if we look at an example of a function that is obviously discontinuous at $x = c$.

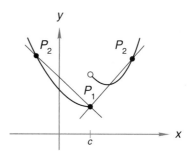

As the point P_2 to the left of P_1 moves down the curve and approaches P_1, the limit of the slope of the secant approaches the slope of the tangent to the curve at P_1. This is obviously not the same limit as the slope of the line through P_1 and the right-hand point P_2 as P_2 moves down the curve.

An algebraic proof of the fact that the existence of the derivative implies continuity requires a trick. We want to show that if the derivative of f at c exists (is some real number and thus is not infinite), then the limit of $f(x)$ as x approaches c is $f(c)$.

$$\boxed{\text{If } f'(c) \text{ exists, then } \lim_{x \to c} f(x) = f(c).}$$

In other words, if f is differentiable at $x = c$, then f is continuous at $x = c$.

We begin by assuming that $f'(c)$ exists and noting that $f(x)$ equals $f(x)$.

$$f(x) = f(x)$$

On the right side we add and subtract $f(c)$ to get

$$f(x) = f(c) + f(x) - f(c)$$

Next we multiply and divide the last part of the sum on the right-hand side by $x - c$. Note that x must not equal c, because division by zero is not allowed.

$$f(x) = f(c) + \frac{f(x) - f(c)}{x - c}(x - c) \qquad x \neq c$$

Next we find the limit of both sides as x approaches c.

$$\lim_{x \to c} f(x) = \lim_{x \to c} \left[f(c) + \frac{f(x) - f(c)}{x - c}(x - c) \right]$$

We expand the limit on the right-hand side of the equals sign by remembering that, if all the individual limits exist, the limit of a sum is the sum of the individual limits and the limit of a product is the product of the individual limits.

$$\lim_{x \to c} f(x) = \lim_{x \to c} f(c) + \lim_{x \to c} \frac{f(x) - f(c)}{x - c} \cdot \lim_{x \to c} (x - c)$$

To the right of the equals sign, the limit of $f(c)$ as x approaches c is $f(c)$. The next limit is $f'(c)$, and the limit of $x - c$ as x approaches c is zero. Now we have

$$\lim_{x \to c} f(x) = f(c) + [f'(c)](0)$$

If $f'(c)$ exists, $f'(c)$ equals some real number, and the product of any real number and zero is zero. Finally we have

$$\lim_{x \to c} f(x) = f(c) + 0 = f(c)$$

We began by assuming that $f'(c)$ existed and were able to prove that the limit of the function as x approaches c exists and equals $f(c)$. **Thus the existence of the derivative at c tells us that the function is continuous at c.**

We must note that the converse of this statement is not true. Namely, a function can be continuous at $x = c$ without being differentiable at $x = c$. The function $f(x) = |x|$ is continuous at $x = 0$, but $f'(0)$ does not exist.

82.B
differentiability   A continuous function is differentiable on an interval if the derivative exists at every point on the interval. A function is not differentiable at $x = c$ if the graph of the function comes to a sharp point when $x = c$. A function is also not differentiable at $x = c$ if the graph has a vertical tangent line at $x = c$. Remember that the values of x for which the derivative does not exist are called **singular numbers.**

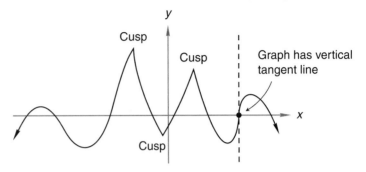

We define the limit on the left-hand side below to be the left-hand derivative at $x = c$ and the limit on the right-hand side to be the right-hand derivative at $x = c$.

$$\lim_{x \to c^-} \frac{f(x) - f(c)}{x - c} \qquad \lim_{x \to c^+} \frac{f(x) - f(c)}{x - c}$$

If these limits exist and are equal for a continuous function f, then the derivative of f exists at $x = c$ (that is, f is differentiable at $x = c$).

example 82.1   Use left-hand and right-hand derivatives to determine if $f(x) = |x - 2|$ is differentiable at $x = 2$.

solution   An absolute-value function can be redefined as a piecewise function that does not use absolute value.

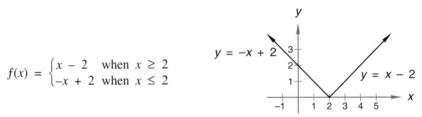

$$f(x) = \begin{cases} x - 2 & \text{when } x \geq 2 \\ -x + 2 & \text{when } x \leq 2 \end{cases}$$

We find the derivatives of $y = x - 2$ and $y = -x + 2$.

$$g(x) = x - 2 \qquad\qquad h(x) = -x + 2$$
$$g'(x) = 1 \qquad\qquad h'(x) = -1$$
$$g'(2) = 1 \qquad\qquad h'(2) = -1$$

The left-hand derivative does not equal the right-hand derivative when $x = 2$, so f **does not have a derivative at $x = 2$.**

example 82.2   For what values of x is the piecewise function shown below differentiable?

$$f(x) = \begin{cases} x^2 & \text{when } x \geq 1 \\ 2x - 1 & \text{when } x < 1 \end{cases}$$

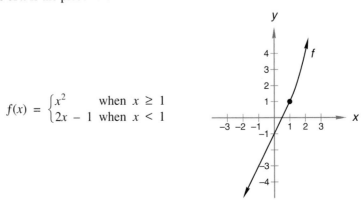

solution First we look at the left-hand and right-hand derivatives.

LEFT-HAND DERIVATIVE   RIGHT-HAND DERIVATIVE

$g(x) = 2x - 1 \longrightarrow g'(x) = 2$ $h(x) = x^2 \longrightarrow h'(x) = 2x$

The derivative of f for every value of x less than 1 is 2, and the derivative of f for every value of x greater than 1 is $2x$. So f is clearly differentiable for all $x \neq 1$. Now we check the values of the left-hand and right-hand derivatives when $x = 1$.

LEFT-HAND DERIVATIVE   RIGHT-HAND DERIVATIVE

$g'(1) = 2$ $h'(1) = 2(1) = 2$

Since f has a derivative for all values of x greater than 1 and for all values of x less than 1, and since the left-hand and right-hand derivatives are equal when $x = 1$, **f is differentiable for all real values of x.**

example 82.3 Let f be defined as follows:

$$f(x) = \begin{cases} |x| + 3 & \text{when } x < 1 \\ ax^2 + bx & \text{when } x \geq 1 \end{cases}$$

Find the values of a and b such that f is continuous and differentiable at $x = 1$.

solution This example is a continuation of example 75.4 on continuity. It is possible for f to be discontinuous, as the graph below shows.

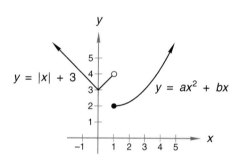

From the graph and equation of f, we see that

$$\lim_{x \to 1^-} f(x) = 4 \qquad \text{and} \qquad \lim_{x \to 1^+} f(x) = a + b$$

For f to be continuous at $x = 1$, these limits must be equal.

$$\lim_{x \to 1^-} f(x) = \lim_{x \to 1^+} f(x)$$
$$4 = a + b$$

If we choose a and b so that $a + b$ is 4, then we are guaranteed that the two branches of the graph connect. So continuity at $x = 1$ is not difficult to achieve.

However, to be differentiable at $x = 1$, the connection cannot create a cusp; it must be smooth. We must choose a and b such that the left-hand derivative of f at $x = 1$ equals the right-hand derivative of f at $x = 1$. The equation of f just to the left of $x = 1$ is $y = x + 3$, and the equation of f just to the right of $x = 1$ is $y = ax^2 + bx$.

LEFT-HAND DERIVATIVE   RIGHT-HAND DERIVATIVE

$g(x) = x + 3$ $h(x) = ax^2 + bx$

$g'(x) = 1$ $h'(x) = 2ax + b$

$g'(1) = 1$ $h'(1) = 2a + b$

Equating these values gives us our second equation for a and b, $1 = 2a + b$. Now we have

$$\begin{cases} 4 = a + b \\ 1 = 2a + b \end{cases}$$

The solution to this system is $a = -3$ and $b = 7$. Thus, for the function to be continuous and differentiable at $x = 1$, the equation of the quadratic function must be

$$y = -3x^2 + 7x$$

Here we see the graph of

$$f(x) = \begin{cases} |x| + 3 & \text{when } x < 1 \\ -3x^2 + 7x & \text{when } x \geq 1 \end{cases}$$

Note the smooth connection at $x = 1$.

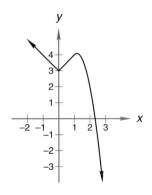

problem set
82

1. A 10-foot ladder leans against a vertical
(47) wall, and the bottom of the ladder slides
away from the wall at a rate of 2 feet per
second. At what rate is the angle between
the ladder and the ground changing when
the top of the ladder is 5 feet above
the ground?

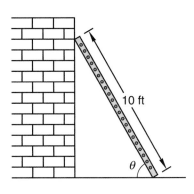

2. The figure to the right shows a rectangle
(52) inscribed in a region bounded by the graph
of $y = 4 - |x|$ and the x-axis.

(a) Express the area of the rectangle in
terms of x without using
absolute value.

(b) Find the maximum possible area of
the rectangle.

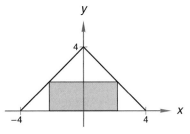

3. A particle moves along the x-axis so that its position at time t is given by the
(78) equation $x(t) = t^2 - 6t + 5$. Find the time(s) at which the particle is momentarily at rest, the
times at which it is moving to the right, and the times at which it is moving to the left.

4. A ball is thrown straight down from the top of a 100-meter-high building with an initial velocity
(65) of 25 meters per second. Develop the velocity function and the height function for the ball. How
long will it take the ball to hit the ground? (Assume the ball does not hit the building during its
descent.)

5. A 100-meter-long cylindrical tank whose
(74) radius is 2 meters is half-filled with a fluid
whose weight density is 9000 newtons per
cubic meter. Determine the total force
exerted by the fluid against one end of
the tank.

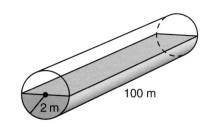

6. A function f is defined as $f(x) = \begin{cases} x^2 + x + 1 & \text{when } x \leq 1 \\ 2x + 1 & \text{when } x > 1. \end{cases}$ Determine the left- and right-hand
(82) derivatives of f at $x = 1$.

7. For what value(s) of x is the function $f(x) = \begin{cases} x^2 + x + 1 & \text{when } x \leq 1 \\ 2x + 1 & \text{when } x > 1 \end{cases}$ not differentiable?
(82)

8. Let g be a function defined as $g(x) = \begin{cases} 3x & \text{when } x \leq 1 \\ ax^2 + b & \text{when } x > 1. \end{cases}$ How must a and b be related for g to be
(75) continuous everywhere?

9. If $g(x) = \begin{cases} 3x & \text{when } x \leq 1 \\ ax^2 + b & \text{when } x > 1. \end{cases}$ what numerical values of a and b make g both continuous and
(82) differentiable for all values of x?

10. Let $f(x) = x^2 - 2$ and $h(x) = -\frac{2}{x} \sin x$. Suppose that g is a function such that
(70) $f(x) \geq g(x) \geq h(x)$ for all values of x near, but not equal to, 0. Evaluate $\lim_{x \to 0} g(x)$.

11. Find the volume of the solid formed when the region in the first quadrant between $y = 2^x$ and
(71) the x-axis on the interval $[0, 2]$ is rotated around the x-axis.

12. Let R be the region completely bounded by the graphs of $y = x^2 + 1$ and $y = x + 1$. Write
(81) a definite integral whose value equals the volume of the solid formed when R is revolved about
the x-axis.

13. Let R be the region in the first quadrant completely enclosed by the graphs of
(81) $y = x$ and $y = x^2$. Compute the volume of the solid formed when R is revolved around
the y-axis.

14. Let $f(x) = \dfrac{x^2 + x - 6}{x - 1}$.
(80)

    (a) Write the equations of all asymptotes of the graph of f.

    (b) Sketch the graph of f.

Evaluate the limits in problems 15–17.

15. $\displaystyle\lim_{x \to \pi} \dfrac{\sin (x - \pi)}{2x - \dfrac{\pi}{2}}$
(70)

16. $\displaystyle\lim_{x \to \infty} \dfrac{x \ln x}{e^x}$
(79)

17. $\displaystyle\lim_{x \to 0^+} \left(1 - \dfrac{|x|}{x} \right)$
(70)

Integrate in problems 18–22.

18. $\displaystyle\int \cos^3 x \, dx$
(76)

19. $\displaystyle\int (\sin x \cos^3 x - \sin x \cos^5 x) \, dx$
(76)

20. $\displaystyle\int 2^x \, dx$
(73)

21. $\displaystyle\int xe^x \, dx$
(69)

22. $\displaystyle\int \dfrac{e^x + \cos x}{\sqrt{e^x + \sin x}} \, dx$
(66)

23. Find $\dfrac{dy}{dx}$ where $y = \dfrac{x}{\sin (1 + x^2)} + \arcsin \dfrac{x}{2} + \log_7 x - 14^x$.
(72)

24. Suppose f and g are functions such that $f(g(x)) = x$. Which of the following are possible
(18) choices for the functions f and g?

    A. $f(x) = \ln x$, $g(x) = \dfrac{1}{x}$ B. $f(x) = 2x - 1$, $g(x) = \dfrac{1}{2}x + 1$

    C. $f(x) = \ln x$, $g(x) = e^x$ D. $f(x) = x^3$, $g(x) = 3x^2$

25. Find the domain and range of $y = \sqrt{1 - \sin x}$.
(6)

LESSON 83 *Integration of Even Powers of sin x and cos x*

To integrate even powers of sin x and cos x, we use the following identities:

$$\sin^2 x = \frac{1}{2} - \frac{1}{2}\cos(2x) \qquad\qquad \cos^2 x = \frac{1}{2} + \frac{1}{2}\cos(2x)$$

A close look at the graphs of $y = \sin^2 x$ and $y = \cos^2 x$ gives us a better understanding of these identities. The graph of $y = \sin x$ is shown on the left-hand side below. In the center we see the effect of squaring. All negative values become positive. The curve still has a maximum value of 1, but the square of any number between 0 and 1 is less than the number, and this causes every other value of $\sin^2 x$ between 0 and π to be less than the value of sin x. The result is the curve shown.

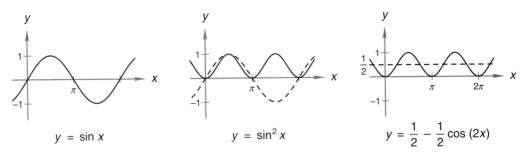

$$y = \sin x \qquad\qquad y = \sin^2 x \qquad\qquad y = \frac{1}{2} - \frac{1}{2}\cos(2x)$$

In the right-hand figure we draw a dotted centerline at $y = \frac{1}{2}$, and we see that the graph of $y = \sin^2 x$ looks like the graph of $y = \frac{1}{2} - \frac{1}{2}\cos(2x)$.

In the first two figures below, we show the corresponding graphs for the square of the cosine function. The graph of $\cos^2 x$ looks like the graph of $y = \frac{1}{2} + \frac{1}{2}\cos(2x)$.

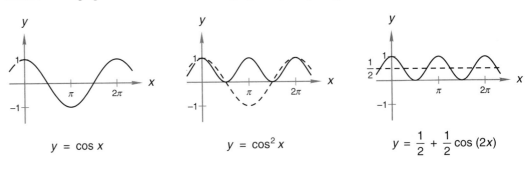

$$y = \cos x \qquad\qquad y = \cos^2 x \qquad\qquad y = \frac{1}{2} + \frac{1}{2}\cos(2x)$$

example 83.1 Integrate: $\displaystyle\int \cos^2 x\,dx$

solution We substitute $\dfrac{1}{2} + \dfrac{1}{2}\cos(2x)$ for $\cos^2 x$ and find that this leads to two integrals.

$$\int \cos^2 x\,dx = \int \left[\frac{1}{2} + \frac{1}{2}\cos(2x)\right]dx = \frac{1}{2}\int dx + \frac{1}{2}\int \cos(2x)\,dx$$

The second integral needs an additional factor of 2 on the right-hand side of the integral sign and an additional factor of $\frac{1}{2}$ in front, which we supply. Then we integrate.

$$\frac{1}{2}\int dx + \frac{1}{2}\cdot\frac{1}{2}\int \underbrace{[\cos(2x)]}_{\cos u}\underbrace{(2\,dx)}_{du} = \frac{x}{2} + \frac{1}{4}\sin(2x) + C$$

example 83.2   Integrate: $\int \sin^2 x \cos^2 x \, dx$

solution   Integration of expressions that contain only even powers of the sine and cosine is not difficult but is tedious because of the algebra involved. In this problem we must substitute for both $\sin^2 x$ and $\cos^2 x$ and multiply. Then, to our dismay, we encounter a $\cos^2 (2x)$, which requires another substitution.

$$\int \left[\frac{1}{2} - \frac{1}{2} \cos (2x) \right]\left[\frac{1}{2} + \frac{1}{2} \cos (2x) \right] dx \; = \; \int \left[\frac{1}{4} - \frac{1}{4} \cos^2 (2x) \right] dx$$

For $\cos^2 2x$ we substitute $\dfrac{1}{2} + \dfrac{1}{2} \cos (4x)$ to get

$$\int \left\{ \frac{1}{4} - \frac{1}{4}\left[\frac{1}{2} + \frac{1}{2} \cos (4x) \right] \right\} dx \; = \; \int \left[\frac{1}{4} - \frac{1}{8} - \frac{1}{8} \cos (4x) \right] dx$$

Now we simplify and integrate. In the second integral additional factors of 4 and $\frac{1}{4}$ are needed, so we supply them.

$$\int \left(\frac{1}{4} - \frac{1}{8} \right) dx - \frac{1}{8} \cdot \frac{1}{4} \int \underbrace{[\cos (4x)]}_{\cos u}\underbrace{(4 \, dx)}_{du} = \frac{x}{8} - \frac{1}{32} \sin (4x) + C$$

example 83.3   Integrate: $\int \sin^4 x \, dx$

solution   First we write $\sin^4 x$ as $(\sin^2 x)^2$. Then we substitute for $\sin^2 x$ and expand the resulting expression.

$$\sin^4 x = (\sin^2 x)^2 = \left[\frac{1}{2} - \frac{1}{2} \cos (2x) \right]^2 = \frac{1}{4} - \frac{1}{2} \cos (2x) + \frac{1}{4} \cos^2 (2x)$$

Next for $\cos^2 (2x)$ we substitute $\left[\dfrac{1}{2} + \dfrac{1}{2} \cos (4x) \right]$.

$$\sin^4 x = \frac{1}{4} - \frac{1}{2} \cos (2x) + \frac{1}{4}\left[\frac{1}{2} + \frac{1}{2} \cos (4x) \right] = \frac{3}{8} - \frac{1}{2} \cos (2x) + \frac{1}{8} \cos (4x)$$

We have reduced $\sin^4 x$ to an expression containing $\cos (2x)$ and $\cos (4x)$, which can be integrated after inserting appropriate constants.

$$\int \sin^4 x \, dx = \int \left[\frac{3}{8} - \frac{1}{2} \cos (2x) + \frac{1}{8} \cos (4x) \right] dx$$

$$= \frac{3}{8} \int dx - \frac{1}{2} \cdot \frac{1}{2} \int [\cos (2x)](2 \, dx) + \frac{1}{8} \cdot \frac{1}{4} \int [\cos (4x)](4 \, dx)$$

$$= \frac{3x}{8} - \frac{1}{4} \sin (2x) + \frac{1}{32} \sin (4x) + C$$

**problem set
83**

1. A 3-meter-long trough whose cross section
(77) is that of the inverted isosceles triangle shown is full of water. Determine the work done in pumping the water out of the top of the trough. Dimensions are in meters. The density of water is 9800 newtons per cubic meter.

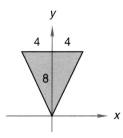

2. Suppose f is defined as $f(x) = \begin{cases} ax^3 + b & \text{when } x \le 1 \\ x^2 & \text{when } x > 1. \end{cases}$ What relationship between a and b will cause
(75) f to be continuous everywhere?

3. Determine the numerical values of a and b that will make $f(x) = \begin{cases} ax^3 + b & \text{when } x \le 1 \\ x^2 & \text{when } x > 1. \end{cases}$ continuous
(82) and differentiable everywhere.

4. Let $f(x) = \begin{cases} ax^3 & \text{when } x \le 1 \\ 2x^2 + bx & \text{when } x > 1. \end{cases}$ Determine the values of a and b that make f differentiable for all
(82) values of x.

5. Determine the maximum value and the minimum value of the function $f(x) = x^{2/3}$ on the
(63) closed interval $[-1, 8]$.

6. Find the volume of the solid formed when the region in the first quadrant bounded
(71) by $y = e^x$ and $x = 3$ is revolved around the x-axis.

In problems 7 and 8, let R be the region enclosed by the graphs of $y = \sqrt{x}$ and $y = x$.

7. Find the volume of the solid formed when R is rotated about the x-axis.
(81)

8. Find the volume of the solid formed when R is revolved around the y-axis.
(81)

9. (a) Find the Maclaurin series for $y = \cos x$. Write your answer in summation notation.
(55) (b) Find the Maclaurin series for $y = \cos x^2$.

Integrate in problems 10–15.

10. $\displaystyle\int \frac{1}{4} \cos^2 x \, dx$
(83)

11. $\displaystyle\int \sin^2 (3x) \, dx$
(83)

12. $\displaystyle\int \sin^3 x \cos^2 x \, dx$
(76)

13. $\displaystyle\int \frac{x - 3}{x^2} \, dx$
(38)

14. $\displaystyle\int (\pi \cos x) e^{\sin x} \, dx$
(66)

15. $\displaystyle\int \frac{x}{x^2 - 1} \, dx$
(66)

Evaluate the limits in problems 16–18.

16. $\displaystyle\lim_{x \to 0} \frac{3 \sin (2x)}{4x}$
(79)

17. $\displaystyle\lim_{x \to 0^+} \frac{x + \sin x}{\ln x}$
(70)

18. $\displaystyle\lim_{h \to 0} \frac{e^{x+h} - e^x}{h}$
(28)

19. Let $f(x) = \frac{x^2 - x - 2}{x - 2}$ and $h(x) = 2|x - 2| + 3$. Suppose that g is a function such that
(70) $f(x) \le g(x) \le h(x)$ for all values of x near, but not equal to, 2. Evaluate $\lim_{x \to 2} g(x)$.

20. Let f be a continuous function for all real numbers. Suppose $\int_{-3}^{0} f(x) \, dx = 4$ and
(57) $\int_{0}^{1} f(x) \, dx = -1$. Find $\int_{1}^{-3} f(x) \, dx$.

21. Find the area of the region between the graph of $y = xe^x$ and the x-axis over the interval $[1, 3]$.
(69)

22. Use y as the variable of integration to write a definite integral whose value is the area of the
(67) region bounded by $x = \sqrt{1 - y^2}$ and the y-axis. What is the value of this integral?

23. Find the equation of the line normal to the graph of $f(x) = \dfrac{x - 2}{x + 1}$ at $x = 3$.
(40)

24. Let $f(x) = x^2$. Divide the interval $[0, 3]$ into three equally long subintervals, and draw
(39) rectangles over each of these subintervals. From left to right, the heights of the three rectangles
must be $f(0)$, $f(1)$, and $f(2)$. Which of the following must be true?

   A. The sum of the areas of the rectangles is less than $\displaystyle\int_{0}^{3} x^2 \, dx$.

   B. The sum of the areas of the rectangles is greater than $\displaystyle\int_{0}^{3} x^2 \, dx$.

   C. The sum of the areas of the rectangles equals $\displaystyle\int_{0}^{3} x^2 \, dx$.

   D. The sum of the areas of the rectangles equals 27.

25. Let $f(x) = x^2 - 3x - 10$ on the interval $[-1, 5]$. Find the point(s) on the curve where the
(2,27) tangent line is parallel to the line segment joining the point $(-1, f(-1))$ to the point $(5, f(5))$.

LESSON 84   *Logarithmic Differentiation*

Logarithms can simplify the process of finding derivatives of complicated expressions. The process of logarithmic differentiation involves no new theory. Logarithmic differentiation is just a manipulative procedure that makes differentiation simpler because the laws of logarithms are used to turn products into sums, quotients into differences, and exponents into coefficients.

example 84.1   If $y = \dfrac{x^2}{(3x + 2)^4}$, what is $\dfrac{dy}{dx}$?

solution   The derivative could be found using the quotient rule, but we will use logarithmic differentiation. We are going to take the logarithm of both y and x^2 divided by $(3x + 2)^4$. Since the domain of the logarithmic function is the set of positive numbers, certain restrictions are placed on these expressions. We discuss that later.

The first step is to take the logarithm of both sides. Remember that the logarithm of a quotient is the difference of the logarithms.

$$\ln y = \ln \left[\frac{x^2}{(3x + 2)^4} \right] \qquad \text{ln of both sides}$$

$$\ln y = \ln x^2 - \ln (3x + 2)^4 \qquad \text{property of logs}$$

$$\ln y = 2 \ln x - 4 \ln (3x + 2) \qquad \text{property of logs}$$

Next we find the differential of every term and then divide by dx.

$$\frac{dy}{y} = \frac{2\,dx}{x} - \frac{4(3\,dx)}{3x + 2} \qquad \text{differential}$$

$$\frac{1}{y}\frac{dy}{dx} = \frac{2}{x} - \frac{12}{3x + 2} \qquad \text{divided by } dx$$

After multiplying both sides by y, we can solve for $\dfrac{dy}{dx}$.

$$\frac{dy}{dx} = y\left(\frac{2}{x} - \frac{12}{3x + 2} \right) \qquad \text{solved for } \frac{dy}{dx}$$

As the final step, y is replaced with $\dfrac{x^2}{(3x + 2)^4}$ to get

$$\frac{dy}{dx} = \frac{x^2}{(3x + 2)^4}\left(\frac{2}{x} - \frac{12}{3x + 2} \right)$$

Whenever logarithmic differentiation is used to find the derivative of a quotient $y = f(x)$, the answer has this form

$$\frac{dy}{dx} = f(x) \times \text{(a sum of fractions)}$$

If the quotient rule is used to differentiate the function, we obtain the following:

$$\frac{dy}{dx} = \frac{(3x + 2)^4(2x) - x^2(4)(3x + 2)^3(3)}{(3x + 2)^8} \qquad \text{quotient rule}$$

$$= \frac{(3x + 2)^3(2x)[(3x + 2) - 6x]}{(3x + 2)^8} \qquad \text{factored}$$

$$= \frac{2x(-3x + 2)}{(3x + 2)^5} \qquad \text{simplified}$$

While this version of the derivative looks quite different than the solution in the example, algebraic manipulation can be employed to show they are equal.

The validity of this procedure might be questioned at this point. We made the mental condition that x be greater than 0 (making x and $3x + 2$ positive) so that $\ln (3x + 2)$ and $\ln x$ would be defined. **But the result we get is the same result we obtain using the quotient rule and is therefore valid for any value of x that does not cause the denominator of the final result to equal zero.** It is certainly strange that the process eliminated part of the domain and recovered it seemingly without explanation. However, this is a valid procedure, though the proof of this is beyond the scope of this book. We present the technique because it greatly simplifies finding some derivatives.

example 84.2   Let $y = \dfrac{x^3 \sqrt{x^2 + 1}}{(x + 2)^6}$. Find $\dfrac{dy}{dx}$.

solution   We rewrite $\sqrt{x^2 + 1}$ using $\dfrac{1}{2}$ as an exponent.

$$y = \frac{x^3 (x^2 + 1)^{1/2}}{(x + 2)^6}$$

Next we take the logarithm of both sides, remembering that the logarithm of a product is the sum of the logarithms and the logarithm of a quotient is the difference of the logarithms. We also apply the property $\ln (a^b) = b \ln a$.

$$\ln y = 3 \ln x + \frac{1}{2} \ln (x^2 + 1) - 6 \ln (x + 2)$$

Now we take the differential of every term and divide by dx.

$$\frac{dy}{y} = \frac{3 \, dx}{x} + \frac{\frac{1}{2}(2x) \, dx}{x^2 + 1} - \frac{6 \, dx}{x + 2} \qquad \text{differentials}$$

$$\frac{1}{y}\frac{dy}{dx} = \frac{3}{x} + \frac{x}{x^2 + 1} - \frac{6}{x + 2} \qquad \text{divided by } dx$$

Next we solve for $\dfrac{dy}{dx}$ and finish by replacing y with the original function.

$$\frac{dy}{dx} = y\left(\frac{3}{x} + \frac{x}{x^2 + 1} - \frac{6}{x + 2}\right) \qquad \text{solved for } \frac{dy}{dx}$$

$$\frac{dy}{dx} = \frac{x^3 \sqrt{x^2 + 1}}{(x + 2)^6}\left(\frac{3}{x} + \frac{x}{x^2 + 1} - \frac{6}{x + 2}\right) \qquad \text{substituted}$$

example 84.3   If $y = \dfrac{\sqrt{3x + 2}\,(x^3 + 1)^4 (5x - 3)^2}{(x^3 - 2)^5}$, what is $\dfrac{dy}{dx}$?

solution   This derivative is tremendously difficult to find without using logarithmic differentiation. The first step is to rewrite $\sqrt{3x + 2}$ as $(3x + 2)^{1/2}$.

$$y = \frac{(3x + 2)^{1/2} (x^3 + 1)^4 (5x - 3)^2}{(x^3 - 2)^5}$$

In our mind we temporarily restrict x to values that cause $3x + 2$, $x^3 + 1$, $5x - 3$, and $x^3 - 2$ to represent positive numbers. Taking the logarithm of both sides yields

$$\ln y = \frac{1}{2} \ln (3x + 2) + 4 \ln (x^3 + 1) + 2 \ln (5x - 3) - 5 \ln (x^3 - 2)$$

Next we find the differential of every term, divide by dx, and solve for $\dfrac{dy}{dx}$.

$$\frac{dy}{y} = \frac{\frac{3}{2}\,dx}{3x+2} + \frac{12x^2\,dx}{x^3+1} + \frac{10\,dx}{5x-3} - \frac{15x^2\,dx}{x^3-2} \qquad \text{differential of both sides}$$

$$\frac{1}{y}\frac{dy}{dx} = \frac{\frac{3}{2}}{3x+2} + \frac{12x^2}{x^3+1} + \frac{10}{5x-3} - \frac{15x^2}{x^3-2} \qquad \text{divided by } dx$$

$$\frac{dy}{dx} = y\left(\frac{\frac{3}{2}}{3x+2} + \frac{12x^2}{x^3+1} + \frac{10}{5x-3} - \frac{15x^2}{x^3-2}\right) \qquad \text{solved for } \frac{dy}{dx}$$

Now we complete the solution by replacing y with the original function.

$$\frac{dy}{dx} = \frac{\sqrt{3x+2}\,(x^3+1)^4(5x-3)^2}{(x^3-2)^5}\left(\frac{3}{6x+4} + \frac{12x^2}{x^3+1} + \frac{10}{5x-3} - \frac{15x^2}{x^3-2}\right)$$

Since this is the same derivative that is found using the product, quotient, and composition rules, it is valid for every value of x that does not cause a denominator to equal zero.

example 84.4   Let $y = x^x$. Find $\dfrac{dy}{dx}$ given that the domain of the function is the set of all positive real numbers.

solution   We have found derivatives of powers such as x^5 that have a variable base and a constant exponent. We have also found derivatives of exponentials such as 5^x that have a constant base and a variable exponent. This function has both a variable base and a variable exponent. It is neither polynomial nor exponential. We need logarithmic differentiation to differentiate it. The exponent can be turned into a coefficient by taking the logarithm of both sides.

$$\ln y = x \ln x$$

Next we take the differential of both sides and then divide by dx.

$$\frac{1}{y}\frac{dy}{dx} = 1 + \ln x \qquad \text{differential}$$

$$\frac{dy}{dx} = y(1 + \ln x) \qquad \text{divided by } dx$$

Now we multiply both sides by y and finish by replacing y with x^x.

$$\frac{dy}{dx} = y(1 + \ln x) \qquad \text{solved for } \frac{dy}{dx}$$

$$\frac{dy}{dx} = x^x(1 + \ln x) \qquad \text{substituted}$$

This result is valid only for positive values of x because $\ln x$ is defined only for positive numbers. This makes sense anyway, because the function was only defined on the positive numbers.

example 84.5   Let $y = x^{x^3+4}$. Find $\dfrac{dy}{dx}$ given that the domain is the set of all positive real numbers.

solution   After finding the logarithm of both sides, we can make $x^3 + 4$ a coefficient.

$$\ln y = (x^3 + 4)(\ln x) \qquad \text{ln of both sides}$$

Taking the differential of both sides gives us

$$\frac{dy}{y} = (x^3+4)\cdot\frac{dx}{x} + (\ln x)(3x^2\,dx)$$

Next we divide by dx and solve for $\dfrac{dy}{dx}$.

$$\frac{1}{y}\frac{dy}{dx} = x^2 + \frac{4}{x} + 3x^2 \ln x \qquad\qquad \text{divided by } dx$$

$$\frac{dy}{dx} = y\left(x^2 + \frac{4}{x} + 3x^2 \ln x\right) \qquad \text{solved for } \frac{dy}{dx}$$

We finish by replacing y with x^{x^3+4}.

$$\frac{dy}{dx} = x^{x^3+4}\left(x^2 + \frac{4}{x} + 3x^2 \ln x\right)$$

This result is valid only for values of x greater than zero, which is consistent with the domain of the function.

problem set 84

1. _(52,63) Hunsinger has 120 meters of fencing with which to enclose two separate fields. One of the fields is square with a side of length y, and the other field is rectangular in shape with a length that is 3 times its width x. The square field must have an area of at least 100 square meters, and the rectangular field must have an area of at least 75 square meters.

   (a) Find the minimum and maximum values of x.

   (b) Express the sum of the areas of the two fields in terms of x.

   (c) Use the critical number theorem as a guide to find the value of x that maximizes the sum of the areas of the two fields.

   (d) Find the greatest total area that can be enclosed in the two fields.

2. ₍₆₂₎ A spring whose spring constant is 2 newtons per meter is stretched from $x = 2$ meters to $x = 4$ meters. Find the work that was done to the spring.

3. ₍₆₅₎ A ball is thrown **horizontally** from the top of a 100-meter-tall building. It is a physical fact that the height of the ball above the ground at a given time t after the ball has been thrown horizontally is exactly the same as if it had been dropped.

   (a) Find the equation that describes the height of the ball as a function of t.

   (b) How long will it take the ball to reach the ground?

   (c) If the horizontal velocity is 20 meters per second, what is the horizontal distance the ball will travel? (The horizontal distance the ball will travel equals the horizontal velocity times the time the ball is in the air.)

4. ₍₇₇₎ A cylindrical container 1 meter high with a circular base whose radius is 1 meter is filled with a fluid whose weight density is 100 newtons per cubic meter. Find the work performed in pumping the fluid out of the cylinder.

5. ₍₈₂₎ Let f be a function defined as $f(x) = \begin{cases} x^3 & \text{when } x \le -1 \\ ax + b & \text{when } x > -1 \end{cases}$. Determine the values of a and b that will make f both continuous and differentiable everywhere.

Use logarithmic differentiation to find $\dfrac{dy}{dx}$ in problems 6–9.

6. ₍₈₄₎ $y = x^x$ **7.** ₍₈₄₎ $y = x^{\sin x}$

8. ₍₈₄₎ $y = \dfrac{x^2\sqrt{x^2+1}}{(x-1)^4}$ **9.** ₍₈₄₎ $y = \dfrac{\sqrt{x-1}(x^3-1)(\sin x)}{(x^2+1)(x^4+1)}$

Integrate in problems 10–14.

10. $\int 2 \sin^2 x \, dx$
(83)

11. $\int 4 \sin^2 x \cos^2 x \, dx$
(83)

12. $\int 2 \sin^3 x \, dx$
(76)

13. $\int 2 \sin^2 x \cos^3 x \, dx$
(76)

14. $\int (\cos x)\sqrt{1 - \sin x} \, dx$
(66)

15. Let $f(x) = \dfrac{x + 1}{x^3 - x^2 + x - 1}$.
(80)

    (a) Write the equations of all asymptotes of the graph of the function.

    (b) Sketch the graph of f.

Evaluate the limits in problems 16 and 17.

16. $\displaystyle\lim_{x \to 0} \frac{2 \sin (3x)}{4x}$
(79)

17. $\displaystyle\lim_{x \to \infty} \frac{x^2}{1 - x^2}$
(79)

18. Determine the slope of the line tangent to the graph of $y = \log x$ at $x = 2$.
(72)

19. Write an equation for the line tangent to the graph $y = \sin (\cos x)$ at $x = \dfrac{\pi}{2}$.
(27,50)

20. Determine the area of the region between $y = xe^x$ and the x-axis on the interval $[1, 2]$.
(69)

21. Determine the area of the region between $y = x^2 - x$ and the x-axis on the interval $[-2, 1]$.
(59)

22. Suppose $f(x) = e^x$ and $g(x) = 5$. Determine whether $h(x) = g(f(x))$ is an odd function, an even function, or neither.
(68)

23. Differentiate $y = \dfrac{\sin (x^2 + 1)}{e^x - e^{-x}} - \arctan (2x)$ with respect to x.
(50,64)

24. The graph of the function $y = x^3 - 27x$ has
(49)

    A. no inflection points.   B. one inflection point.

    C. two inflection points.   D. exactly two local maxima.

25. Let $f(x) = x^3$ on the interval $[-3, 3]$. Find the point(s) on the curve where the line tangent to the graph of f is parallel to the line segment joining the point $(-3, f(-3))$ to the point $(3, f(3))$.
(2,27)

LESSON 85 *The Mean Value Theorem • Application of the Mean Value Theorem in Mathematics • Proof of Rolle's Theorem • Practical Application of the Mean Value Theorem*

85.A
the mean value theorem

Existence theorems are crucial in mathematics, but the attention that they are given is often confusing to the beginner, because the truth of the theorems is sometimes so obvious. It is hard to understand why theorems that are so obvious could be so important. Existence theorems are often used to prove other theorems. Two existence theorems that we have discussed but have not proved are the **maximum-minimum value existence theorem** and the **Intermediate Value Theorem.**

> MAXIMUM-MINIMUM VALUE EXISTENCE THEOREM
>
> If f is continuous on the closed interval $I = [a, b]$, then f attains a maximum value M and a minimum value m on I.

> INTERMEDIATE VALUE THEOREM
>
> If f is continuous on the closed interval $[a, b]$ and N is a number between $f(a)$ and $f(b)$, then there is at least one number c between a and b, inclusive, for which $f(c) = N$.

The **Mean Value Theorem** is another important existence theorem and is useful in proofs. We first present a graphical interpretation of the Mean Value Theorem. Refer to the figure below as needed. If the graph of a function between x-values of a and b inclusive is a smooth continuous curve that has no corners and is never vertical, a tangent line can be drawn to the graph somewhere between a and b that is parallel to the line through A and B.

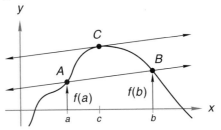

This means that a value of x between a and b **exists** such that the derivative of the function at this value of x equals the slope of the line through A and B.

$$f'(c) = \frac{f(b) - f(a)}{b - a} \qquad \text{for some value } c \text{ between } a \text{ and } b$$

We must be careful in stating the conditions that are necessary for the Mean Value Theorem to be applied. The function must be continuous and must have a defined slope (be differentiable) for every x-value between a and b. Differentiability on an open interval (a, b) implies continuity on the interval, so we are tempted to simply stipulate that the function be differentiable on the open interval (a, b). However, the interval (a, b) is between a and b and does not include a and b. We also need to require that the functions be continuous at their endpoints, like the one on the left-hand side below.

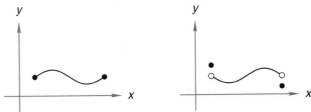

Functions that are discontinuous at one or both endpoints (for example, the one on the right-hand side above) must be excluded. This is customarily done by listing two requirements that are somewhat redundant.

1. **The function must be continuous on the closed interval [a, b].** This requirement takes care of continuity at the endpoints and ensures that the function is defined on the interval.
2. **The function must be differentiable on the open interval (a, b).** This requirement prohibits sharp corners and vertical tangents on the graph and again requires that the function be defined and continuous between a and b.

MEAN VALUE THEOREM

If the function f is continuous on the closed interval $[a, b]$ and is differentiable on the open interval (a, b), then there exists at least one number c in (a, b) such that

$$f'(c) = \frac{f(b) - f(a)}{b - a}$$

The Mean Value Theorem states that the number c exists but does not tell how to find it. Even so, the Mean Value Theorem is a highly important theorem.

example 85.1 Demonstrate an understanding of the Mean Value Theorem by applying it to the function $f(x) = x^2 - 2x - 8$ on the interval $[-2, 1]$.

solution First we must see if the Mean Value Theorem can be applied to this function.

1. Is the function continuous on the interval $[-2, 1]$? Yes. Polynomial functions are continuous for all real values of x. Thus this function is continuous on the open interval $(-2, 1)$ and is also continuous at the endpoints.
2. Is the function differentiable everywhere between the endpoints? Yes. A polynomial function has a defined derivative for all real values of x. Thus the graph has no sharp corners or places where the tangent is vertical.

Both conditions are met, so the theorem can be applied.

To find the slope of the line that passes through the points whose x-values are -2 and 1, we need to find $f(-2)$ and $f(1)$.

$$f(-2) = (-2)^2 - 2(-2) - 8 = 0$$
$$f(1) = (1)^2 - 2(1) - 8 = -9$$

Now we find the slope.

$$\frac{f(-2) - f(1)}{-2 - 1} = \frac{0 - (-9)}{-3} = -3$$

The Mean Value Theorem only guarantees that for some number c between -2 and 1 the value of the derivative (the slope of the graph) equals -3. It does not say what that number is.

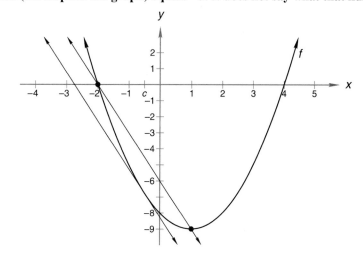

This value of c can be found, but not from the Mean Value Theorem. First we find the derivative of the function.

$$f'(x) = 2x - 2$$

Now we set $f'(x)$ equal to -3 and solve for c.

$$-3 = 2c - 2 \qquad f'(c) = -3 \text{ at } x = c$$
$$-1 = 2c \qquad \text{added } +2$$
$$c = -\frac{1}{2} \qquad \text{solved}$$

Thus the slope of the graph of $f(x)$ is -3 when $x = -\frac{1}{2}$.

example 85.2   The value of the function

$$f(x) = \frac{1}{x^2} - 1$$

equals zero at $x = -1$ and $x = 1$. The line connecting the points $(-1, 0)$ and $(1, 0)$ is horizontal, so the slope of this line is zero. Determine whether the Mean Value Theorem can be applied to prove the existence of a point between x-values of -1 and $+1$ for which the slope of the tangent to the graph of the function (the value of the derivative) equals zero.

solution   The Mean Value Theorem is an existence theorem and cannot be used to find anything. All it does is state that if certain requirements are met, a derivative of a particular value exists. We check the requirements.

1. The function must be continuous on the closed interval $[-1, +1]$.

   If we attempt to find $f(0)$, we see that the function is not defined when $x = 0$.

   $$\frac{1}{0^2} - 1 = ?$$

The function is not continuous on the interval $[-1, 1]$, so the Mean Value Theorem **cannot be used.** We do not need to check the second requirement, differentiability on the open interval (a, b). A quick look at the graph of f shows that there are no horizontal tangent lines to this graph.

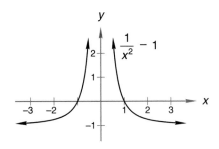

example 85.3   Demonstrate an understanding of the Mean Value Theorem by applying it to the function $f(x) = x^{2/3}$ on the interval $[-8, 27]$.

solution   First we see if the function is continuous between x-values of -8 and 27 inclusive. By inspection we can see that $x^{2/3}$ equals a real number for any x-value between -8 and 27 inclusive, so the requirement for continuity is met. Now we check for differentiability.

$$f'(x) = \frac{2}{3}x^{-1/3} = \frac{2}{3\sqrt[3]{x}}$$

This derivative has no value when $x = 0$, so the function is not differentiable at $x = 0$ and thus is not differentiable everywhere on the interval $(-8, 27)$. Therefore, the Mean Value Theorem **cannot be used.** That is, we cannot guarantee the existence of a value c between -8 and 27 such that

$$f'(c) = \frac{f(27) - f(-8)}{27 - (-8)} = \frac{1}{7}$$

via the Mean Value Theorem.

It should be noted that there is a value of c for which $f'(c) = \frac{1}{7}$.

$$f'(c) = \frac{2}{3c^{1/3}} = \frac{1}{7}$$

$$3c^{1/3} = 14$$

$$c = \left(\frac{14}{3}\right)^3$$

However, this value of c is outside the required interval $(c > 100)$.

example 85.4 The function $f(x) = |x| - 1$ is equal to 0 at $x = -1$ and $x = 1$. Does the Mean Value Theorem imply that $f'(c) = 0$ for some number c between $x = -1$ and $x = 1$?

solution First, we check to see if the requirements of the Mean Value Theorem are met.

1. Is f continuous on $[-1, 1]$? Yes.
2. Is f differentiable on $(-1, 1)$? No.

The derivative does not exist everywhere on the interval $(-1, 1)$ because the left-hand derivative does not equal the right-hand derivative at $x = 0$. Thus the Mean Value Theorem **is not applicable** for this function on the interval $[-1, 1]$.

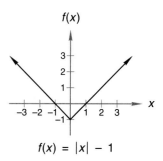

$$f(x) = |x| - 1$$

85.B
application of the mean value theorem in mathematics

As we said before, the primary use of the Mean Value Theorem is to prove other theorems.

> THEOREM
>
> If the derivative of a function equals zero for all real values of x, the function is a constant function. A more formal statement of this is the following:
>
> If $f'(x) = 0$ on a closed interval I,
> then $f(x) = C$ on I for some constant C.

The Mean Value Theorem makes the proof of this theorem almost trivial. We are given that the derivative of the function is zero for any real value of x, so the derivative exists for all x in any open interval (a, b) contained in I. The function is also defined and continuous at the endpoints a and b. Thus the Mean Value Theorem guarantees that for some c between a and b,

$$f'(c) = \frac{f(b) - f(a)}{b - a}$$

But the derivative equals zero everywhere in I, so we can write

$$0 = \frac{f(b) - f(a)}{b - a}$$

Multiplying both sides by $b - a$ gives us

$$0 = f(b) - f(a)$$

which can be rearranged to form

$$f(b) = f(a)$$

This tells us that if we choose any two real numbers a and b in I, $f(a)$ will equal $f(b)$. This is another way of saying that the value of the function described is some constant, and thus the function must be a constant function over this interval. The proof is complete.

THEOREM

If two functions f and g have the same derivative for every real value of x in I, the functions differ by a constant.

$$\text{If } f'(x) = g'(x) \text{ on } I,$$
$$\text{then } f(x) - g(x) = c \text{ on } I \text{ for some constant } c.$$

To prove this theorem, we begin by defining a function h.

$$h(x) = f(x) - g(x)$$

The derivative of a sum equals the sum of the derivatives, so finding the derivative of both sides, we get

$$h'(x) = f'(x) - g'(x)$$

But it was given that the derivatives of f and g were equal, so $f'(x) - g'(x)$ is zero. Therefore

$$h'(x) = 0$$

In the preceding proof we showed that if the derivative of a function is zero on an interval I, the function is a constant function on I. Thus we can substitute c for $h(x)$ and write

$$c = f(x) - g(x)$$

This proves that if f and g have the same derivative on an interval, f and g differ by a constant on the interval.

85.C

proof of Rolle's theorem

Rolle's theorem is a special case of the Mean Value Theorem for which $f(a)$ and $f(b)$ are equal. This theorem is easier to prove than the Mean Value Theorem. Below, we rigorously prove Rolle's theorem without assuming the Mean Value Theorem to be true.

ROLLE'S THEOREM

If (1) f is a continuous function on $[a, b]$, (2) $f(a) = f(b) = 0$, and (3) f is differentiable on (a, b), then some number c exists between a and b such that $f'(c) = 0$.

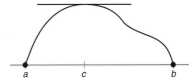

The maximum-minimum value existence theorem tells us that somewhere on the interval $[a, b]$ a maximum value of f exists and a minimum value of f exists. If the maximum and minimum values are the same, the graph of the function would be the graph of a constant function whose slope is everywhere zero. Thus c could be any number between a and b, and the proof is complete for this special case. If the maximum value and the minimum value differ, then an extreme value must occur for some value c that is between a and b. (Since $f(a) = f(b)$ and the extreme values differ, the maximum and minimum cannot both occur at endpoints.) The critical number theorem tells us that maximum and minimum values must occur at critical numbers. Thus c is a critical number and must exist between a and b. We have defined the function to be differentiable on (a, b), so $f'(c)$ must exist. Maximum or minimum values must occur where the slope does not exist or is zero, so $f'(c) = 0$.

The maximum-minimum value existence theorem tells us that a maximum value and a minimum value of the function must exist on $[a, b]$. The process of elimination proves that such value(s) must exist where $f'(x) = 0$, so we know that some number c must exist between a and b such that $f'(c) = 0$.

85.D
practical application of the mean value theorem

We can use the Mean Value Theorem to show that during any trip the speed must at some instant equal the average speed for the whole trip. For example, suppose two stations are 60 miles apart and we drive between the two in exactly 1 hour (i.e., from $t = 0$ hr to $t = 1$ hr). Then the average speed for the whole trip is

$$\text{Average speed} = \frac{f(1) - f(0)}{1 - 0} = \frac{60 \text{ miles}}{1 \text{ hour}} = 60 \frac{\text{mi}}{\text{hr}}$$

The Mean Value Theorem requires that $f'(c) = \frac{f(1) - f(0)}{1 - 0} = 60 \frac{\text{mi}}{\text{hr}}$ at some instant c in $(0, 1)$. However, $f'(c)$ is our speed at time $t = c$, and 60 mph is our average speed for the whole trip. Therefore, the Mean Value Theorem implies that we must have a speed of exactly 60 mph at least once during the trip. If the speed limit between the two stations is 55 mph, then at some instant we must have been traveling in excess of the posted limit. **Therefore the Mean Value Theorem precludes some courtroom defenses from being plausible.**

example 85.5 The speed limit on a highway is 65 mph. At 6:00 p.m. a police officer sees a truck go by at 60 mph. That officer radios another police officer seventy miles down the highway who sees the same truck go by at 7:00 p.m. traveling at 60 mph.

(a) Find the average speed of the truck between 6:00 p.m. and 7:00 p.m.

(b) The truck driver is ticketed for speeding, but he argues that he was never clocked over 60 mph. The truck driver is convicted by a judge who points out that he must have been traveling 70 mph at least once. Is the judge correct?

solution (a) The average speed is the distance traveled divided by the time.

$$\text{Average speed} = \frac{70 \text{ miles}}{1 \text{ hour}} = \textbf{70 mph}$$

(b) **Yes,** the judge is correct. If the driver did not exceed 65 mph for one hour, he could not have traveled more than 65 miles. Certainly, the driver had to have been speeding. By the Mean Value Theorem the driver's speed reached 70 mph at least once between 6:00 p.m. and 7:00 p.m.

problem set 85

1. *(26)* The rate of increase of the bacteria was exponential. When $t = 0$ there were 30 bacteria, and when $t = 10$ there were 100 bacteria. How many bacteria were there when $t = 80$?

2. *(46)* Punch flows into a hemispherical punch bowl whose radius is 14 inches at a rate of 1 cubic inch per second. How fast is the punch rising when the punch is halfway to the top? The equation that gives the volume of the bowl as a function of h is shown to the right.

$$V = \pi r h^2 - \frac{1}{3}\pi h^3$$

3. Suppose $f(x) = \sin x + \cos x$ and f is defined only on the closed interval $[0, \pi]$. Use the
(63) critical number theorem to determine the maximum value and the minimum value of f. Find the x-coordinate of any inflection points in the interval.

4. A particle moves along the x-axis so that its velocity at time t is given by the
(78) equation $v(t) = a \sin t + b \cos t$, where a and b are real numbers. The acceleration of the particle at time t is given by $a(t) = 2 \cos t - 4 \sin t$. Determine the values of a and b.

5. Let $f(x) = \begin{cases} 2x^2 - x & \text{when } x \le 1 \\ ax + b & \text{when } x > 1. \end{cases}$
(82)

   (a) Find the relationship between a and b that ensures the function f is continuous for all values of x.

   (b) Find the numerical values of a and b that will make the function f differentiable for all values of x.

6. Let f be the function defined by $f(x) = x^2 + 1$ on the interval $[1, 3]$. Confirm the Mean Value
(85) Theorem by finding a number c, where $1 < c < 3$, such that $f'(c) = \frac{f(3) - f(1)}{3 - 1}$.

7. Let f be the function defined by $f(x) = 2x^3 - x$ on the interval $[-2, 1]$. Confirm the Mean
(85) Value Theorem by finding a number c, where $-2 < c < 1$, such that $f'(c) = \frac{f(1) - f(-2)}{1 - (-2)}$.

8. Let f be the function defined by $f(x) = |x| - 2$ on the interval $[-2, 2]$. Does the Mean Value
(85) Theorem imply that there exists some number c on the interval $(-2, 2)$ such that $f'(c) = \frac{f(2) - f(-2)}{2 - (-2)}$? Explain why or why not.

9. Let f be the function defined by $f(x) = x^2 - 4x + 3$ on the interval $[1, 3]$. Confirm Rolle's
(85) theorem by finding a number c, where $1 < c < 3$, such that $f'(c) = 0$.

10. Let f be the function defined by $f(x) = x^3 + 3x^2 - 4$ on the interval $[-2, 1]$. Confirm Rolle's
(85) theorem by finding a number c, where $-2 < c < 1$, such that $f'(c) = 0$.

11. Let f be the function defined by $f(x) = 1 - |x|$ on the interval $[-1, 1]$. Does Rolle's theorem
(85) imply that there exists some number c on the interval $(-1, 1)$ such that $f'(c) = 0$? Explain why or why not.

In problems 12 and 13 find $\dfrac{dy}{dx}$.

12. $y = x^x$
(84)

13. $y = \dfrac{x^2 \sqrt{x^3 - 1}}{\sin x \cos x}$
(84)

Integrate in problems 14–18.

14. $\displaystyle\int 6 \cos^2 x \, dx$
(83)

15. $\displaystyle\int 3 \sin^2 x \, dx$
(83)

16. $\displaystyle\int \sin^3 x \, dx$
(76)

17. $\displaystyle\int \sin^3 x \cos x \, dx$
(76)

18. $\displaystyle\int e^{\tan x} (\sec^2 x) \, dx$
(66)

19. Let R be the region bounded by $y = x^2 + 1$, $y = x$, $x = 3$, and the y-axis. Write a definite
(81) integral whose value equals the volume of the solid formed when R is rotated about the x-axis.

20. Sketch the graph of the function $f(x) = \dfrac{1 - x^2}{x}$.
(80)

21. Evaluate: $\displaystyle\lim_{x \to \pi/2} \frac{\sin x - \sin \frac{\pi}{2}}{x - \frac{\pi}{2}}$
(44)

22. Differentiate $y = x \arcsin \dfrac{x}{3} + \dfrac{x}{\sqrt{1+x}} + 3^x - 3 \log_{47} x$ with respect to x.
(64,72)

23. Find the slope of the line normal to the graph of $y = \arcsin \dfrac{x}{3}$ at $x = 1$.
(40,64)

24. Which of the following must be true?
(85)

    A. If f is continuous on the interval $[1, 3]$ and both $f(1)$ and $f(3)$ equal zero, then there exists a number $c \in (1, 3)$ such that $f'(c) = 0$.

    B. If f is continuous on the interval $[0, 3]$ and is differentiable on the interval $(0, 3)$, then there exists a number $c \in (0, 3)$ such that $f'(c) = 0$.

    C. If f is continuous on the interval $[1, 3]$ and is differentiable on the interval $(1, 3)$, and if the graph of f touches the x-axis at $x = 1$ and at $x = 3$, then there exists some number $c \in (1, 3)$ such that $f(c) = 0$.

    D. If a function f has a value of zero at $x = 1$ and at $x = 3$, is continuous on the interval $[1, 3]$, and is differentiable in the interval $(1, 3)$, then there exists some number $c \in (1, 3)$ such that $f'(c) = 0$.

25. Let f and g be functions such that $f(1) = 2$, $f'(1) = 3$, $g(1) = -1$, and $g'(1) = 4$. Evaluate
(18,31) $(fg)'(1)$.

LESSON 86   *Rules for Even and Odd Functions*

Sums of even functions are even functions, and sums of odd functions are odd functions. The product or quotient of two even functions is an even function, and the product or quotient of two odd functions is also an even function. These rules should sound familiar because they are almost exactly like the rules for signed numbers. They are easy to remember if we associate + signs with even functions and – signs with odd functions.

    Sums: $(+) + (+) = (+)$ $(-) + (-) = (-)$

    Products: $(+)(+) = (+)$ $(-)(-) = (+)$ $(+)(-) = (-)$

    Quotients: $\dfrac{(+)}{(+)} = (+)$ $\dfrac{(+)}{(-)} = (-)$ $\dfrac{(-)}{(+)} = (-)$ $\dfrac{(-)}{(-)} = (+)$

    The zero function

$$f(x) = 0$$

is both an even function and an odd function because $f(x)$, $f(-x)$, and $-f(x)$ equal zero for all values of x. Thus

$$f(-x) = f(x) \qquad \text{and} \qquad f(-x) = -f(x)$$

If we exclude the zero function, the sum of an even function and an odd function is neither even nor odd.

example 86.1   Let f be an odd function and g be an even function. Show that fg is an odd function.

solution   Proofs like this one are straightforward. All we have to do is define our notations and substitute. First we note what we mean by $(fg)(x)$ and $(fg)(-x)$.

$$(fg)(x) = f(x)g(x) \qquad (fg)(-x) = f(-x)g(-x)$$

If f is odd, then $f(-x) = -f(x)$ for all values of x. If g is even, then $g(-x) = g(x)$ for all values of x. We use the definition of fg and make these substitutions.

$$\begin{aligned}
(fg)(-x) &= f(-x)g(-x) & &\text{definition of } fg \\
&= [-f(x)][g(x)] & &\text{substituted} \\
&= -[f(x)g(x)] & &\text{associative property} \\
&= -(fg)(x) & &\text{definition of } fg
\end{aligned}$$

We have shown that if f is odd and g is even, then $(fg)(-x) = -(fg)(x)$ for all values of x. So the function fg is an odd function.

example 86.2   Show that the sum of two even functions f and g is an even function.

solution   First we write the expressions for $(f + g)(x)$ and $(f + g)(-x)$.

$$(f + g)(x) = f(x) + g(x) \qquad (f + g)(-x) = f(-x) + g(-x)$$

Now, if f and g are even functions, $f(-x) = f(x)$ and $g(-x) = g(x)$ for all values of x. We use the definition of $f + g$ and make these substitutions.

$$\begin{aligned}
(f + g)(-x) &= f(-x) + g(-x) & &\text{definition of } f + g \\
&= f(x) + g(x) & &\text{substituted} \\
&= (f + g)(x) & &\text{definition of } f + g
\end{aligned}$$

We have shown that if f and g are both even the sum of $f(-x) + g(-x)$ equals the sum $f(x) + g(x)$ for all x, which is the same as $(f + g)(x)$. Thus, the sum of two even functions is an even function.

example 86.3   Show that the quotient $\dfrac{f}{g}$ is an odd function if f is an odd function and g is an even function.

solution   First we recall the definitions of $\left(\dfrac{f}{g}\right)(x)$ and $\left(\dfrac{f}{g}\right)(-x)$.

$$\left(\frac{f}{g}\right)(x) = \frac{f(x)}{g(x)} \qquad \left(\frac{f}{g}\right)(-x) = \frac{f(-x)}{g(-x)}$$

Now if f is odd and g is even, then the following are true for all values of x: $f(-x) = -f(x)$ and $g(-x) = g(x)$. We use the definition of $\frac{f}{g}$ and make these substitutions.

$$\begin{aligned}
\left(\frac{f}{g}\right)(-x) &= \frac{f(-x)}{g(-x)} & &\text{definition of } \frac{f}{g} \\[2mm]
&= \frac{-f(x)}{g(x)} & &\text{substituted} \\[2mm]
&= -\left[\frac{f(x)}{g(x)}\right] & &\text{associative property} \\[2mm]
&= -\left(\frac{f}{g}\right)(x) & &\text{definition of } \frac{f}{g}
\end{aligned}$$

We have shown that, if f is odd and g is even, $\left(\frac{f}{g}\right)(-x) = -\left(\frac{f}{g}\right)(x)$ for all x. Thus, this quotient is an odd function.

example 86.4   Let f be an even function such that $\int_2^4 f(x)\,dx = 7.$ Evaluate $\int_{-4}^{-2} f(x)\,dx.$

solution   This problem requires that the reader know the characteristics of an even function. Since the function is an even function, its graph is a mirror image of itself about the y-axis. If the integral from 2 to 4 is 7, then the integral from -4 to -2 must also be **7.**

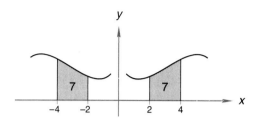

example 86.5   If $\int_{-1}^1 e^{x^2}\,dx = k,$ then what is the value of $\int_0^1 e^{x^2}\,dx?$

solution   This problem is carefully contrived to see if the reader recognizes that e^{x^2} is an even function because $e^{(x)^2} = e^{(-x)^2}.$ This integral cannot be evaluated using a technique of integration with which we are familiar. But since the value of the integral from -1 to 1 equals $k,$ half of this integral occurs from 0 to 1 and must equal $\frac{k}{2}.$

$$\int_0^1 e^{x^2}\,dx = \frac{k}{2}$$

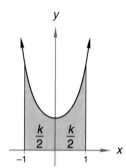

example 86.6   If f is an odd function and $\int_0^2 f(x)\,dx$ is 16, what is the value of $\int_{-2}^2 f(x)\,dx?$

solution   If an odd function defines an area above the axis between 0 and 2, it defines an area of the same size below the axis between -2 and 0, and the definite integral from -2 to 2 must equal **zero.**

We drew the graph of f as one that is above the x-axis on $[0, 2].$ However, the reasoning described still holds true even if $f(x)$ is not always positive over the interval $[0, 2].$ The crucial point is that the graph of f is symmetric about the origin because f is an odd function.

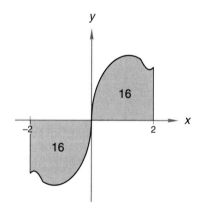

problem set
86   1. A rectangular tank 8 meters deep is half filled with a fluid whose weight density is 3000 newtons
(74,77)   per cubic meter.

   (a) Find the total force exerted by the fluid against one of the walls if the width of the wall is 2 meters.

   (b) Find the work performed in pumping the fluid out of the top of the tank if the length of the tank is 6 meters.

   2. A particle moves along the x-axis so that its acceleration at any time t is given by
(78) $a(t) = 6t + 18.$ At time $t = 0$ the velocity of the particle is 20, and at time $t = 1$ its position is 21. Find the equations for the velocity and position of the particle.

3. Suppose $f(x) = ae^x + b \sin x$, $f'(0) = 4$, and $f'\left(\dfrac{\pi}{2}\right) = 1$. Find a and b.
(61)

4. Let f be the function defined below. Find the numerical values of a and b that make the function
(82) f differentiable for all values of x.

$$f(x) = \begin{cases} x^2 + 1 & \text{when } x \geq 0 \\ ae^x + bx & \text{when } x < 0 \end{cases}$$

5. Let f be a function defined by $f(x) = x^2 + x + 1$ on the interval $[0, 3]$. Find a number c that
(85) confirms the Mean Value Theorem.

6. Let f be the function defined by $f(x) = x^3 + 3x^2$ on the interval $[-2, 1]$. Find a number c that
(85) confirms the Mean Value Theorem.

7. Let f be the function defined by $f(x) = \sin x$ on the interval $[0, \pi]$. Confirm Rolle's theorem
(85) by finding a number c, where $0 < c < \pi$, such that $f'(c) = 0$.

8. Let f be the function defined by $f(x) = x^3 - x$ on the interval $[-1, 1]$. Find a number c that
(85) confirms Rolle's theorem.

9. Prove that if f and g are both odd functions, then fg is an even function.
(86)

10. The function f is an odd function and $\displaystyle\int_0^4 f(x)\, dx = 7$. Evaluate $\displaystyle\int_{-4}^4 f(x)\, dx$.
(86)

11. The function g is an even function and $\displaystyle\int_{-4}^4 g(x)\, dx = 4$. Evaluate $\displaystyle\int_0^4 g(x)\, dx$.
(86)

12. Use logarithmic differentiation to compute $\dfrac{f'(x)}{f(x)}$ where $f(x) = x \sin x \cos x$.
(84)

Evaluate the limits in problems 13 and 14.

13. $\displaystyle\lim_{x \to 0} (x \csc x)$
(79)

14. $\displaystyle\lim_{x \to \infty} \dfrac{x + e^x}{x - e^x}$
(79)

15. Let R be the region between the graph of $y = e^{x^2}$ and the x-axis on the interval $[1, 2]$. Write a
(71) definite integral whose value equals the volume of the solid formed when R is rotated about
the x-axis.

16. Let $y = \arcsin \dfrac{x}{a}$ where a is a constant. Find y'.
(64)

17. Differentiate $y = \arcsin(\cos x) + \dfrac{e^x - x}{\sin(2x) + \cos x} - 2\csc^2 x$ with respect to x.
(50,64)

Integrate in problems 18–20.

18. $\displaystyle\int \dfrac{dx}{\sqrt{9 - x^2}}$
(64)

19. $\displaystyle\int 2xe^x\, dx$
(69)

20. $\displaystyle\int 2xe^{-x^2}\, dx$
(66)

21. Suppose f is a continuous function such that $\displaystyle\int_1^3 f(x)\, dx = \dfrac{5}{2}$ and $\displaystyle\int_1^5 f(x)\, dx = 10$.
(57)

(a) Find the value of $\displaystyle\int_3^5 (2f(x) + 6)\, dx$.

(b) Suppose $f(x) = ax + b$. Find the values of a and b.

22. Suppose both f and g are differentiable everywhere and $f(1) = 4$, $f'(1) = 2$, $g(1) = 1$, and
(42) $g'(1) = 2$. Use the quotient rule to compute $\left(\dfrac{f}{g}\right)'(1)$.

23. Let $f(x) = x^3 + 1$. Find $f^{-1}(2)$.
(58)

24. A function that is continuous and differentiable everywhere passes through the points $(1, 3)$ and
(85) $(6, 2)$. Which of the following **must** be true?

    A. There exists some c such that $1 < c < 6$ and $f'(c) = -\dfrac{1}{5}$.

    B. There exists some c such that $1 < c < 6$ and $f'(c) = -5$.

    C. There exists some c such that $1 < c < 6$ and $f'(c) = 0$.

    D. There exists some c such that $2 < c < 3$ and $f'(c) = -\dfrac{1}{5}$.

25. Let $f(x) = \dfrac{x^3 - 1}{x - 2}$.
(80)

    (a) Find the zero(s) and the vertical asymptote(s) of the function.

    (b) Determine the end behavior of the function.

    (c) Sketch the graph of the function. Clearly indicate all zeros, all asymptotes, and its end behavior.

    (d) Determine the domain and range of the function.

LESSON 87   *Solids of Revolution III: Shells*

The lateral surface area of a right circular cylinder equals the circumference of the cylinder times its height. We can see this if we take the can shown, cut it vertically from top to bottom along the dotted line, and unroll it.

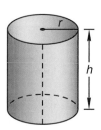

Circumference $= 2\pi r$

Area $= 2\pi rh$

If the can has a thickness of Δx, we can find the volume of metal in the flat sheet by multiplying the area times the thickness Δx.

$$\text{Volume} = (2\pi rh)\Delta x$$

We have already seen that the volume of a solid of revolution can be approximated using disks. The disks are generated by taking representative rectangles in the region to be revolved that are perpendicular to the axis of revolution and revolving those rectangles around the axis. We can also approximate the volume of a solid of revolution by summing the volumes of n concentric sheets, or shells, similar to the can above. The shells are generated using rectangles that are parallel to the axis of revolution.

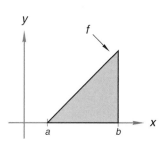

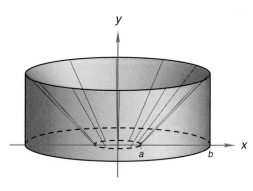

If the triangle in the figure on the left above is revolved about the *y*-axis, the solid represented on the right is generated. To find the volume of the solid, we can use shells. As we see below, a representative rectangle can be revolved to form a shell.

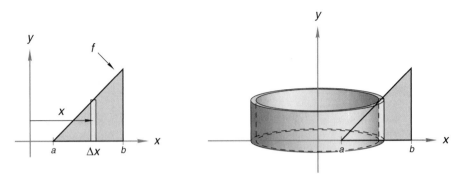

The radius of the representative shell is *x*, the height is $f(x)$, and the thickness is Δx. The sum of the volumes of these shells as *n* increases without bound is an integral.

$$\text{Volume} = \int_a^b 2\pi x \overbrace{\left[f(x) \right]}^{\text{Height}} dx$$

$\underset{\text{Circumference}}{\uparrow} \qquad \underset{\text{Thickness}}{\uparrow}$

We begin with an example whose answer can be checked easily.

example 87.1   The region bounded by the coordinate axes and the lines $y = 5$ and $x = 3$ is revolved about the *y*-axis. Find the volume of the solid generated.

solution   We begin by showing the region and generating the solid.

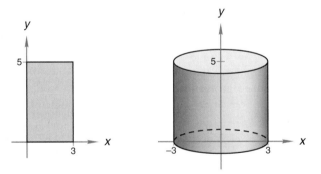

Clearly, we have generated a cylinder of radius 3 and height 5. Thus the volume desired is $\pi r^2 h = \pi(3)^2 5 = 45\pi$.

Now we use the shell method to determine the volume.

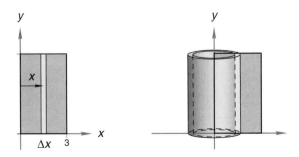

The radius of the shell is x, which means the circumference is $2\pi x$, and the height of the shell is 5. So the volume is

$$\text{Volume} = \int_0^3 2\pi x(5)\,dx$$

$$= 10\pi \int_0^3 x\,dx$$

$$= 10\pi \left[\frac{x^2}{2}\right]_0^3$$

$$= 10\pi \left(\frac{9}{2}\right)$$

$$= 45\pi \text{ units}^3$$

The answer obtained by the shell method is identical to the answer obtained by applying the formula for the volume of a cylinder.

example 87.2   The region bounded by $y = x - 1$, the x-axis, and $x = 4$ is revolved about the y-axis. Use the shell method to find the volume of the solid generated.

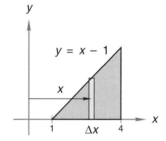

solution   The volume of the representative shell is the circumference $2\pi r$ times the height times Δx. The radius in this problem is x, and the height of the shell is y. The thickness of the shell is Δx, and the shells cover the region between x-values of 1 and 4. Thus

$$\text{Volume} = \int_1^4 2\pi x y\,dx$$

The dx reminds us that x is the variable of integration, so the only variable in the integrand should be x. Therefore we replace y with $x - 1$.

$$\text{Volume} = \int_1^4 2\pi x(x - 1)\,dx$$

We simplify this expression, integrate, and evaluate.

$$\text{Volume} = 2\pi \int_1^4 (x^2 - x)\,dx \qquad\qquad \text{simplified}$$

$$= 2\pi \left[\frac{x^3}{3} - \frac{x^2}{2}\right]_1^4 \qquad\qquad \text{integrated}$$

$$= 2\pi \left[\left(\frac{64}{3} - \frac{16}{2}\right) - \left(\frac{1}{3} - \frac{1}{2}\right)\right] \qquad\qquad \text{evaluated}$$

$$= 27\pi \text{ units}^3$$

example 87.3   Use the shell method to find the volume of the solid formed by revolving about the x-axis the region in the first quadrant bounded by $x = 4 - y^2$ and the x- and y-axes.

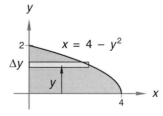

solution   A representative shell is indicated in the figure. The radius of the shell is y, the height of the shell is x, and its thickness is Δy.

$$\text{Volume } = \int_{y=0}^{y=2} 2\pi xy \; dy$$

The dy reminds us that the variable of integration is y, so the only variable in the integrand should be y. Therefore we replace x with $4 - y^2$.

$$\text{Volume } = 2\pi \int_0^2 (4 - y^2)y \; dy$$

Now we simplify this expression, integrate, and evaluate.

$$\text{Volume } = 2\pi \int_0^2 (4y - y^3) \, dy = 2\pi \left[2y^2 - \frac{y^4}{4} \right]_0^2$$
$$= 2\pi(8 - 4) = \mathbf{8\pi \; units^3}$$

example 87.4   Use the shell method to find the volume of the solid formed when the region bounded by the x-axis and $y = -x^2 + 2x$ is revolved about the y-axis.

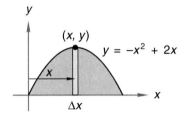

solution   We begin by sketching the problem. On the left-hand side we show the representative shell of the solid, which is formed by revolving the representative rectangle around the y-axis. On the right-hand side we show the solid of revolution.

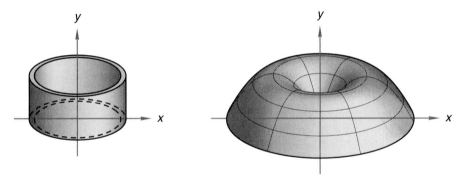

The radius of the shell is its distance from the axis of revolution. Thus the radius is x. The height of the shell is y, the thickness is Δx, and the shells cover the region from $x = 0$ to $x = 2$.

$$\text{Volume } = \int_0^2 2\pi xy \; dx$$

The dx reminds us that x is the variable of integration, so the only variable in the integrand should be x. Therefore, we replace y with $-x^2 + 2x$.

$$\text{Volume } = 2\pi \int_0^2 x(-x^2 + 2x) \; dx$$

Next we multiply and integrate to get

$$\text{Volume } = 2\pi \int_0^2 (-x^3 + 2x^2) \, dx = 2\pi \left[-\frac{x^4}{4} + \frac{2x^3}{3} \right]_0^2$$

We finish by evaluating.

$$\text{Volume } = 2\pi \left(-4 + \frac{16}{3} \right) = \frac{8}{3}\pi \; \mathbf{units^3}$$

problem set
87

1. The money was compounded continuously, so the rate of increase of money was exponential.
(26)   Initially there was $1000. After 100 days there was $1050. Find the amount of money present after 200 days, assuming no additional deposits or withdrawals.

2. Let $f(x) = xe^{-x}$.
(49)
   (a) Find all the critical numbers of f.

   (b) Use the second derivative to determine where f attains local maximum and local minimum values, and find what those values are.

   (c) Find the x-coordinate of any points of inflection.

3. A particle moves along the x-axis so that its acceleration function is $a(t) = -4t + \sin \pi t$. The
(78)   velocity at $t = \frac{1}{2}$ is 4, and the position when $t = 1$ is 4.

   (a) Find the velocity and position functions for the particle.

   (b) Find $v(0)$ and $x(0)$.

4. Any ball thrown horizontally falls at the same rate as a dropped ball. A particular ball is thrown
(65)   horizontally from a height of 200 meters.

   (a) How long will it take for the ball to hit the ground?

   (b) If the horizontal velocity of the ball is 40 meters per second, how far will it travel horizontally before it hits the ground?

5. The slope of the line tangent to $y = x^3 + kx$ is 5 when $x = 1$. Find the value of k.
(27)

6. Let R be the region between $y = \tan x$ and the x-axis on the interval $[0, \frac{\pi}{4}]$. Use the method of
(87)   shells to write a definite integral whose value equals the volume of the solid formed when R is rotated about the y-axis.

7. The region R is bounded by the x-axis and $y = \sin x$ on the interval $[0, \pi]$. Find the volume of
(87)   the solid formed when R is revolved around the y-axis.

8. Let R be the region bounded by $x = y^2$, $x = \frac{1}{4}y^2$, and $x = 4$. Find the volume of the solid
(81)   formed when R is rotated about the x-axis.

9. Let $g(x) = \cos x$ and $\int_{-4}^{-1} g(x)\, dx = k$. Evaluate $\int_{1}^{4} g(x)\, dx$.
(86)

10. If $\int_{0}^{b} e^{x^2}\, dx = L$, what is $\int_{-b}^{b} e^{x^2}\, dx$?
(86)

11. Let f be the function defined by $f(x) = x^3 + x$ on the interval $[1, 3]$. Confirm the Mean Value
(85)   Theorem by finding a number c, where $1 < c < 3$, such that $f'(c) = \frac{f(3) - f(1)}{3 - 1}$.

12. Let f be a function defined by $f(x) = \frac{1}{(x-1)^2}$ on the interval $[0, 2]$. Does the Mean Value
(85)   Theorem imply that there exists some number c in the interval $(0, 2)$ such that $f'(c) = \frac{f(2) - f(0)}{2 - 0}$?
   Why or why not?

13. Let f be the function defined by $f(x) = x^3 - 2x^2 - x + 2$ on the interval $[1, 2]$. Confirm
(85)   Rolle's theorem by finding a number c, where $1 < c < 2$, such that $f'(c) = 0$.

14. Let f be the function defined by $f(x) = x^{2/3} - 1$ on the interval $[-2, 1]$. Does Rolle's theorem
(85)   imply that there exists some number c in the interval $(-2, 1)$ such that $f'(c) = 0$? Why or why not?

15. Lines are drawn through the point $(1, 2)$, each one forming a right triangle with the positive
(52) x-axis and positive y-axis. Find the slope of the line that forms the right triangle of least area.

16. Find $\dfrac{f'(x)}{f(x)}$ where $f(x) = \dfrac{\sqrt{x-1}\,\sin x}{(x^3+1)^{100}(x-1)^5}$.
(84)

Integrate in problems 17 and 18.

17. $\displaystyle\int 4\sin^2(2x)\,dx$
(83)

18. $\displaystyle\int \dfrac{4}{x^2+16}\,dx + \int \dfrac{4x}{x^2+16}\,dx$
(66)

19. Sketch the graph of $y = \dfrac{x(3-x)(x+1)}{(x+1)(x^2+2)(x+3)}$.
(80)

20. Find the area of the region between the graph of $y = 10^x$ and the x-axis on the interval $[-1, 1]$.
(73)

21. Find the area of the region between the graph of $y = x\sin x$ and the x-axis on the interval $[0, \pi]$.
(69)

22. Suppose $f(x) = y = x^3 + x$.
(58)
    (a) Write an equation that expresses the inverse of y implicitly.
    (b) Evaluate $f^{-1}(2)$ by finding the value of x for which $f(x) = 2$.

23. Differentiate $y = \arctan\dfrac{x}{7} + \dfrac{1-e^x}{e^x} + \sin x \cot x$ with respect to x.
(64,72)

24. The point $(1, 3)$ lies on the graph of a function whose inverse is also a function. Which of the
(58) following **must** be true?
    A. The point $(1, 3)$ lies on the graph of the inverse function.
    B. The point $(1, 0)$ lies on the graph of the inverse function.
    C. The graphs of both the function and the inverse of the function pass through the origin.
    D. The point $(3, 1)$ lies on the graph of the inverse function.

25. Let f be the function defined by $f(x) = \dfrac{2x^3 - 4x^2 + 6}{x-2}$.
(28)
    (a) Find all the zeros and vertical asymptotes of the function.
    (b) Determine the end behavior of the function.
    (c) Sketch the graph of the function. Check your graph with a graphing calculator.
    (d) Determine the domain and the range of the function.

LESSON 88 *Separable Differential Equations*

A **differential equation** is an equation that contains one or more derivatives or differentials. The following are examples of differential equations:

$$\frac{dy}{dx} = x\sin x \qquad\qquad dy = 7e^x\,dx$$

The solution to a differential equation is the set of all **functions** that satisfy the differential equation. Without developed procedures, making a good guess is an excellent way to find the solution to a differential equation. Mathematicians have developed procedures that can be used to find the solutions to certain types of differential equations.

If it is possible to use the rules of algebra to put all terms involving x on one side of the equals sign and all terms involving y on the other side of the equals sign, the differential equation is called a **separable differential equation.** We can find the solution to a separable differential equation by integrating both sides of the equation. The differential equation (1) below is a separable differential equation because it can be written with the variables separated, as we show in (2).

$$(1) \quad \frac{dy}{dx} = 4 \qquad (2) \quad dy = 4 \, dx$$

If we integrate both sides of equation (2), we can find a function that is a solution to the original differential equation. Notice that we can combine the constants of integration.

$$\int dy = \int 4 \, dx \quad \longrightarrow \quad y + C_1 = 4x + C_2 \quad \longrightarrow \quad y = 4x + C$$

The function $y = 4x + C$ is called the **general solution** to the differential equation (1), because it contains an unspecified constant C and thus represents a **family of functions.**

Separating the variables and integrating does not work on all differential equations because the variables in some differential equations are not separable. However, the technique did work here. If we had been solving a particular problem and information had been given to allow us to find that the value of C was 15, we could have written

$$y = 4x + 15$$

This would have been the **particular solution** to the particular problem we were solving.

example 88.1   Solve the following differential equation: $\dfrac{dy}{dx} = 4 \cos x$

solution   We guess a function y whose derivative is $4 \cos x$, for example $y = 4 \sin x$. Taking the derivative gives us

$$\frac{dy}{dx} = 4 \cos x$$

Actually, $y = 4 \sin x + 10$ is also a solution to the differential equation, because

$$\frac{dy}{dx} = \frac{d}{dx}(4 \sin x + 10) = 4 \cos x$$

We see that the general solution to this differential equation is

$$y = 4 \sin x + C$$

Some differential equations occur so often that we know just what we should guess to solve them. Many applied problems are modeled by the equation shown in (1) below, where Q represents a function whose value is always positive. If we take the differential of both sides, we get equation (2).

$$(1) \ \ Q = Ae^{kt} \qquad (2) \ \ dQ = Ake^{kt} \, dt \qquad (3) \ \ dQ = kQ \, dt$$

But in (1) we see that $Q = Ae^{kt}$. Thus, we replace Ae^{kt} with Q in (2) to get equation (3). Now, if the statement of a problem says that the rate of change of a quantity is proportional to the amount of the quantity, we can write

$$\frac{dQ}{dt} = kQ \qquad \text{or} \qquad dQ = kQ \, dt$$

The k is necessary because k is the constant of proportionality. To solve this differential equation, we guess that the function Q is

$$Q = Ae^{kt}$$

because if we take the differential of this function, we get

$$dQ = Ake^{kt} \, dt$$

So the **general solution** to this differential equation is

$$Q = Ae^{kt}$$

This is the familiar exponential growth or exponential decay equation. If the necessary information were given in the problem to find that $k = -0.02$ and $A = 75$, we would have

$$Q = 75e^{-0.02t}$$

This would be the **particular solution** to the particular problem.

The discussion thus far permits us to find out that a particular statement about rate can be another way to state the exponential increase or decrease problem. The following statements on the left-hand side imply the differential equations on the right-hand side whose general solutions are the functions indicated by the arrows:

The rate of change of volume at some time t is proportional to the volume at that time t. $\qquad \frac{dV}{dt} = kV \longrightarrow V = Ae^{kt}$

The rate at which the population increases is proportional to the population at time t. $\qquad \frac{dP}{dt} = kP \longrightarrow P = Ae^{kt}$

The rate at which a radioactive substance decays is proportional to the amount present at time t. $\qquad \frac{dS}{dt} = kS \longrightarrow S = Ae^{kt}$

example 88.2 The rate at which a certain bacteria colony is growing at a given time is proportional to the number of bacteria present at that time. At time $t = 0$ there were 1000 bacteria. At time $t = 1$ there were 1050 bacteria. Write an equation that describes the number of bacteria present as a function of time, and determine the size of the bacteria colony at $t = 4$.

solution We write the differential equation indicated by the problem, followed by the function that we know is the general solution to the differential equation. The number of bacteria present at time t is represented by $N(t)$.

$$\frac{dN}{dt} = kN \longrightarrow N(t) = Ae^{kt}$$

First we find A by using zero for t and 1000 for $N(t)$.

$$1000 = Ae^{k(0)}$$
$$1000 = A$$

This means that $N(t) = Ae^{kt} = 1000e^{kt}$.

Now we use the fact that when $t = 1$, $N(1) = 1050$ to solve for k.

$$1050 = 1000e^{k(1)} \qquad \text{substituted}$$
$$1.05 = e^k \qquad \text{simplified}$$
$$\ln 1.05 = k \qquad \text{ln of both sides}$$

Thus the constant k in the differential equation and in the solution is $\ln 1.05$.

$$\frac{dN}{dt} = (\ln 1.05) N \qquad N(t) = 1000e^{(\ln 1.05)t}$$

The particular solution on the right-hand side can be used to find $N(t)$ if t is given or to find t if $N(t)$ is given. The only difference between this problem and the exponential increase problem is that in this problem we began with a differential equation. We solved the differential equation by guessing the general solution and used the general solution to find the particular solution, a process with which we are already familiar.

To find the number of bacteria when $t = 4$, we substitute 4 for t and evaluate.

$$N(4) = 1000e^{[\ln (1.05)4]} \approx 1000(1.2155) = 1215.5$$

So the bacteria colony has a size of approximately **1215** at time $t = 4$. (We did not round up because only whole bacteria count.)

example 88.3 The slope of a certain curve is twice the value of the x-coordinate everywhere. Find the equation of the curve given that it passes through the point $(1, 2)$.

solution The statement of the problem gives the following differential equation:

$$\frac{dy}{dx} = 2x$$

We separate the variables by putting all y-terms on the left and all x-terms on the right.

$$dy = 2x\,dx$$

Now we integrate both sides.

$$\int dy = \int 2x\,dx$$

$$y = x^2 + C$$

This family of functions is the general solution to the given differential equation, since its derivative is $2x$. For this particular problem we can find the particular solution because it is given that the graph passes through $(1, 2)$. Substituting 1 for x and 2 for y gives C.

$$2 = (1)^2 + C$$

$$C = 1$$

The particular function that meets all the stated conditions is

$$y = x^2 + 1$$

example 88.4 Find the general solution to the differential equation $x\,dx + y\,dy = 0$.

solution There is no obvious guess, but the variables are separable, so we put all the x's on one side and all the y's on the other side. Then we integrate.

$$\int x\,dx = -\int y\,dy$$

$$\frac{x^2}{2} = -\frac{y^2}{2} + C$$

$$x^2 + y^2 = C$$

In the center equation C represents some number. If we multiply every term by 2, we get the bottom equation, where C is again some number, which happens to be twice the value of the first C. If we take the differential of each term in $x^2 + y^2 = C$, we get an equation that is algebraically equivalent to the original differential equation. Thus, the equation $x^2 + y^2 = C$ is the general solution since it implicitly defines the family of functions that satisfy the original differential equation.

example 88.5 Given the differential equation $y' = 4x^2y^2$, find the particular solution y that passes through the point $(1, -1)$.

solution The variables are separable.

$$\frac{dy}{dx} = 4x^2y^2 \qquad\qquad \text{differential equation}$$

$$y^{-2}\,dy = 4x^2\,dx \qquad\qquad \text{separated variables}$$

$$\int y^{-2}\,dy = \int 4x^2\,dx \qquad\qquad \text{took integral}$$

$$-\frac{1}{y} = \frac{4x^3}{3} + C \qquad\qquad \text{integrated}$$

If we multiply every term by $3y$ and solve for y, we get an expression that contains $3C$. Then we replace $3C$ with C to get the general solution.

$$-3 = 4x^3y + 3yC \qquad \text{multiplied by } 3y$$

$$-3 = y(4x^3 + 3C) \qquad \text{factored}$$

$$y = -\frac{3}{4x^3 + 3C} \qquad \text{simplified}$$

$$y = -\frac{3}{4x^3 + C} \qquad \text{replaced } 3C \text{ by } C$$

To get the particular solution, we replace y with -1 and x with 1.

$$-1 = -\frac{3}{4(1)^3 + C}$$

$$1 = \frac{3}{4 + C}$$

$$4 + C = 3$$

$$C = -1$$

Now we have the particular solution.

$$y = -\frac{3}{4x^3 - 1} \qquad \text{or} \qquad y = \frac{3}{1 - 4x^3}$$

This function is a solution to the original differential equation. Differentiating y with respect to x yields

$$y = \frac{3}{1 - 4x^3} \qquad \text{solution}$$

$$\frac{dy}{dx} = \frac{0 - 3(-12x^2)}{(1 - 4x^3)^2} \qquad \text{quotient rule}$$

$$\frac{dy}{dx} = \frac{36x^2}{(1 - 4x^3)^2} \qquad \text{simplified}$$

Note that $y^2 = \dfrac{9}{(1 - 4x^3)^2}$, so that

$$4x^2y^2 = 4x^2\frac{9}{(1 - 4x^3)^2} = \frac{36x^2}{(1 - 4x^3)^2}$$

So we see $\dfrac{dy}{dx} = 4x^2y^2$.

problem set 88

1. A force of $F(x) = 3x^2 + 1$ newtons (for x given in meters) is applied to an object to move it
   (62) along the x-axis in the direction of the force. How much work is done between $x = 1$ meter and $x = 5$ meters?

2. A rectangular tank is 3 meters deep and is filled with a fluid whose weight density is
   (74) 2000 newtons per cubic meter. The width of the tank is 4 meters. Find the force exerted by the fluid against one of the faces of the tank.

3. R is the region between the x-axis and $y = e^x$ on the interval $[1, 2]$. Find the volume of the
   (87) solid formed when R is revolved around the y-axis.

4. R is the region between the x-axis and $y = \sec x$ on the interval $\left[0, \frac{\pi}{4}\right]$. Write a definite integral
   (87) whose value equals the volume of the solid formed when R is rotated about the y-axis.

5. Let f be a function defined as $f(x) = \begin{cases} ae^x + \sin x & x \geq 0 \\ bx & x < 0. \end{cases}$ Find the numerical values of a and b that
   (82) make f differentiable for all values of x.

Find a general solution to the differential equations in problems 6 and 7.

6. $x\,dx - y\,dy = 0$
(88)

7. $\dfrac{dy}{dx} = 4x^3 y^2$
(88)

8. The slope of the graph of a function f at any given point is 3 times the value of the x-coordinate
(88) of that point. The graph of the function passes through the point $(2, 3)$. Write the particular solution of f. (*Hint:* Begin by writing the implied differential equation.)

9. Suppose $f(x) = \cos x$ and $g(x) = x^5 - x^3 + x$.
(86)
  (a) Determine whether $(fg)(x)$ is an even function, an odd function, or neither.

  (b) Evaluate: $\displaystyle\int_{-3}^{3} (fg)(x)\,dx$

10. Find the 6th term of the expansion of $(3x + y^2)^9$.
(22)

11. Let f be a function defined by $f(x) = e^{2x}$ on the interval $[0, 1]$. Confirm the Mean Value
(85) Theorem by finding a number c that satisfies the conclusion of the Mean Value Theorem.

12. The volume of a cube decreases at a rate of 6 cubic meters per minute.
(46)
  (a) Find the rate at which the edges of the cube are changing when the volume of the cube is 64 cubic meters.

  (b) Find the rate at which the surface area of the cube is changing at the instant in time described in (a).

13. Find the area of the region between $y = \sin^3 x$ and the x-axis on the interval $\left[0, \dfrac{\pi}{2}\right]$.
(76)

14. Differentiate $y = x\sec(2x) - \dfrac{a - \sin x}{b + \cos x} - \arcsin\dfrac{x}{a}$ with respect to x.
(50,64)

Integrate in problems 15 and 16.

15. $\displaystyle\int x^2 \sqrt{x^3 - 1}\,dx$
(66)

16. $\displaystyle\int \left(\dfrac{1}{\sqrt{a^2 - x^2}} + \dfrac{x}{\sqrt{a^2 - x^2}} \right) dx$
(66)

17. The figures below show the graphs of four functions over the interval $[a, b]$. Which of them are
(85) graphs of functions for which the Mean Value Theorem can be applied on the interval $[a, b]$?

A. y B. y C. y D. y

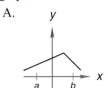 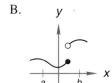 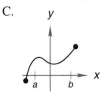

18. Let f be the function defined by $f(x) = x^2 - 9x + 14$ on the interval $[2, 7]$. Show that for the
(85) interval $[2, 7]$ the number c guaranteed by Rolle's theorem is the midpoint of $[2, 7]$.

19. Let f be the function defined by $f(x) = \sqrt{4x - x^2}$ on the interval $[0, 4]$. Confirm Rolle's
(85) theorem by finding a number c that satisfies the conclusion of Rolle's theorem.

Evaluate the limits in problems 20–23.

20. $\displaystyle\lim_{x \to 0} \dfrac{x^3 - 1}{x - 1}$
(14)

21. $\displaystyle\lim_{x \to 0} \dfrac{|x|}{x}$
(70)

22. $\displaystyle\lim_{h \to 0} \dfrac{\ln(x + h) - \ln x}{h}$
(28)

23. $\displaystyle\lim_{x \to 0} [x \csc(3x)]$
(79)

24. Let $y = a\cos x + b\sin x$ where a and b are positive constants. Evaluate: $y + \dfrac{d^2 y}{dx^2}$
(29)

25. The graph of $f(x) = ax^3 + bx^2 + cx + d$ has a relative maximum at $(0, 0)$ and a point of
(49) inflection at $(1, -2)$. Find the equation of f by determining $a, b, c,$ and d.

LESSON 89 *Average Value of a Function • Mean Value Theorem for Integrals • Proof of the Mean Value Theorem for Integrals*

89.A
average value of a function

The average value of a function can be explained graphically by using a side view of a tank made of glass that is sitting on the *x*-axis and is partially filled with water.

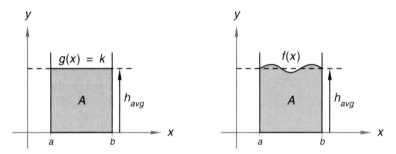

In the figure on the left-hand side above, the surface is smooth and the depth of the water is given by the constant function $g(x) = k = h_{avg}$. The area *A* of the rectangle is the length $b - a$ times the height h_{avg}.

$$\text{Area} = (b - a)h_{avg}$$

In the figure on the right-hand side the water has been disturbed, and the depth of the water against the front glass of the tank is given by $f(x)$. If we assume that the depth of the water is $f(x)$ everywhere from the front of the tank to the back of the tank, the area *A* is unchanged, because the amount of water in the tank is unchanged. This area can be described by the following integral.

$$\int_a^b f(x)\, dx$$

Since the areas are equal, we can write the following equality and solve for h_{avg}, by dividing both sides by $b - a$.

$$(b - a)h_{avg} = \int_a^b f(x)\, dx \quad \longrightarrow \quad h_{avg} = \frac{1}{b - a}\int_a^b f(x)\, dx$$

This tells us that if we divide the area by the length of the tank, the result is h_{avg}, the average value of the height of the water. This value is the same whether the surface is smooth or the surface is not smooth.

We can extend this idea to define the **average value** of any continuous function on a closed interval [*a, b*] where *b* is greater than *a*. Symbolically, there is only one difference: we use v_{avg} to mean *average value* rather than h_{avg} for average height.

DEFINITION OF THE AVERAGE VALUE OF A FUNCTION

If *f* is continuous on the closed interval *I* = [*a, b*], where *b* > *a*, then the average value of *f* is given by

$$v_{avg} = \frac{1}{b - a}\int_a^b f(x)\, dx$$

If the average value computed for a given function on a particular closed interval *I* is negative, we know that more of the area between the *x*-axis and the graph is below the *x*-axis than above the *x*-axis on the interval.

example 89.1   Find the average value of the function $f(x) = x^2 - 10$ on the interval $I = [-1, 2]$.

solution   To find the average value between -1 and 2 inclusive, we divide the definite integral between -1 and 2 by the distance between the x-values of -1 and 2, which is 3.

$$v_{avg} = \frac{1}{2 - (-1)} \int_{-1}^{2} (x^2 - 10) \, dx$$

Now we integrate and evaluate the result at 2 and -1.

$$v_{avg} = \frac{1}{3}\left[\frac{x^3}{3} - 10x\right]_{-1}^{2} = \frac{1}{3}\left\{\left[\frac{2^3}{3} - 10(2)\right] - \left[\frac{(-1)^3}{3} - 10(-1)\right]\right\} = \frac{1}{3}(-27) = \mathbf{-9}$$

We remember that the definite integral assigns a plus sign to areas above the x-axis and a minus sign to areas below the x-axis. The average value of $\frac{1}{3}(-27)$ tells us that the algebraic sum of the areas above the x-axis and the negative of the areas below the x-axis is -27 and that the average value of the function is -9.

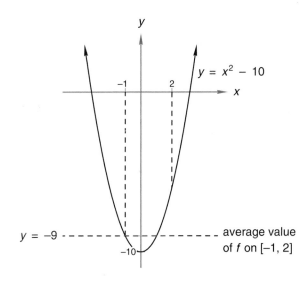

example 89.2   Approximate the average value of the function $f(x) = 4e^{2x}$ on the interval $I = [0, 3]$.

solution   The average value of the function on $[0, 3]$ is the value of the definite integral of the function from 0 to 3 divided by the length of the interval.

$$v_{avg} = \frac{1}{3 - 0} \int_{0}^{3} 4e^{2x} \, dx$$

To integrate, we need a constant factor of 2 to the right of the integral sign.

$$v_{avg} = \frac{4}{3} \int_{0}^{3} e^{2x} \, dx = \frac{4}{3}\left(\frac{1}{2}\right) \int_{0}^{3} e^{2x}(2) \, dx = \frac{2}{3}\left[e^{2x}\right]_{0}^{3}$$

$$v_{avg} = \frac{2}{3}(e^6 - e^0) \approx \mathbf{268.2859}$$

89.B
mean value theorem for integrals

In Lesson 85 we discussed the Mean Value Theorem. In this section we will discuss a different theorem with a similar name, the **Mean Value Theorem for Integrals.** It is an existence theorem that is used in the proof of other theorems. In a later lesson, the Mean Value Theorem for Integrals is used to prove that every continuous function over a closed interval can be integrated. The Mean Value Theorem for Integrals says that if a function is continuous on the interval $[a, b]$, then there exists at least one number c between a and b such that $f(c)$ is equal to the average value of the function on the interval $[a, b]$.

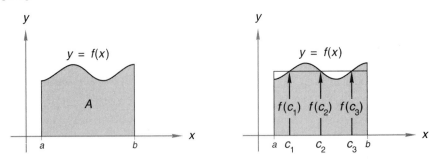

On the left-hand side above, we show the graph of a function f on the interval $[a, b]$. We know that the average value of the function v_{avg} on this interval is the area A divided by $b - a$.

$$v_{avg} = \frac{1}{b - a} \int_a^b f(x)\, dx$$

The Mean Value Theorem for Integrals says that there must be at least one number c between a and b such that $f(c)$ equals the average value of the function on $[a, b]$. For the function graphed above there are three such values of x, which we have labeled c_1, c_2, and c_3 in the right-hand figure.

MEAN VALUE THEOREM FOR INTEGRALS

If f is continuous on the closed interval $I = [a, b]$, there exists at least one number c between a and b such that

$$f(c) = \frac{1}{b - a} \int_a^b f(x)\, dx$$

---

example 89.3   Given that the average value of $f(x) = 2x^3$ on the interval $[0, 3]$ is $\frac{27}{2}$, use the Mean Value Theorem for Integrals to find some number c such that $f(c) = \frac{27}{2}$.

solution   The Mean Value Theorem for Integrals cannot be used to find such a value. The theorem simply states that such a c exists. We use algebra to find the value of c.

$$f(c) = 2c^3 = \frac{27}{2} \quad \longrightarrow \quad c^3 = \frac{27}{4} \quad \longrightarrow \quad c = \sqrt[3]{\frac{27}{4}} \approx 1.8899$$

Note that $0 < c < 3$.

89.C
proof of the mean value theorem for integrals

We now prove the Mean Value Theorem for Integrals.

First note that if f is constant on the interval $[a, b]$, i.e. $f(x) = K$ for all values of x in the interval $[a, b]$ with K constant, then

$$\frac{1}{b - a} \int_a^b f(x)\, dx = \frac{1}{b - a} \int_a^b K\, dx \qquad \text{substituted}$$

$$= \frac{1}{b - a}[(b - a)K] \qquad \text{evaluated the integral}$$

$$= K \qquad \text{simplified}$$

So we can choose c to be any value in the interval, since $f(x) = K$ for all values in the interval.

Next we assume f is not constant on the interval $[a, b]$. By the maximum-minimum value existence theorem (from Lesson 63), we know f attains both a maximum value, $M = f(l)$, and a minimum value, $m = f(k)$, on $[a, b]$. Assume $k < l$ for the remainder of the argument. (If $k > l$, a similar argument will work.) Note that k and l are in the interval $[a, b]$, so $[k, l]$ is completely inside $[a, b]$. So $m \leq f(x) \leq M$ for all x in $[a, b]$. Therefore

$$\int_a^b m \, dx \leq \int_a^b f(x) \, dx \leq \int_a^b M \, dx$$

from the integral properties found in Lesson 57. Since m and M are constants, this system of inequalities becomes

$$m(b - a) \leq \int_a^b f(x) \, dx \leq M(b - a) \qquad \text{or}$$

$$m \leq \frac{1}{b - a} \int_a^b f(x) \, dx \leq M$$

This last system is the same as

$$f(k) \leq \frac{1}{b - a} \int_a^b f(x) \, dx \leq f(l)$$

Since $[k, l]$ is contained in $[a, b]$, we know f must be continuous on $[k, l]$ since it is continuous on $[a, b]$. Therefore, we can apply the Intermediate Value Theorem to conclude there is some c in (k, l) (and therefore in (a, b)) such that $f(c) = N$ for any number N between $f(k)$ and $f(l)$. In particular there is a c such that

$$f(c) = \frac{1}{b - a} \int_a^b f(x) \, dx$$

This completes the proof.

problem set 89

1. (74,77) The end of a triangular trough is shown. The trough is filled with water to a depth of 2 meters.

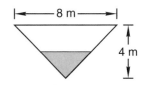

   (a) Find the total force on the end of the trough.

   (b) Find the work required to pump the water out of the trough, assuming the trough is 3 meters long.

2. (63) The function $f(x) = 2x^{2/3}$ is defined on the closed interval $[-1, 8]$. Use the critical number theorem to find the maximum and minimum values of f on this interval.

3. (86) Let the functions f and g be defined for all values of x, and let f be an odd function and g be an even function. Determine whether each of the following functions is an even function, an odd function, or neither.

   (a) $\dfrac{f}{g}$ (b) fg (c) $f^2 g$

4. (89) Find the average value of the function $f(x) = x^2 + 6$ on the interval $[-1, 3]$.

5. (89) Find the average value of the function $f(x) = xe^x$ on the interval $[0, 2]$.

6. (89) Let f be the function defined by $f(x) = x^3 + 4$ on the interval $[-2, 2]$. Find a number $c \in [-2, 2]$ guaranteed by the Mean Value Theorem for Integrals.

7. (89) Suppose that the average value of the function $f(x) = 3x^2$ on the interval $[-1, 2]$ is 3. Is there a number $c \in [-1, 2]$ such that $f(c) = 3$? If so, what is the number?

Find general solutions to the differential equations in problems 8 and 9.

8. (88) $x \, dx + 2y \, dy = 0$

9. (88) $\dfrac{dy}{dx} = 6x^2 y^2$

10. The slope of a curve at any given point on the curve is twice its x-coordinate. Find the equation
(88) of the curve given that it passes through the point $(1, 1)$.

11. If money is compounded continuously, the rate of increase is proportional to the money present.
(88) This statement can be expressed as the following differential equation: $\frac{dB}{dt} = kB$. The solution
to this differential equation is $B = Pe^{rt}$, where B is the balance in the account at some time t,
P is the amount of the initial deposit, and r is the annual interest rate. How much money should
be invested in an account with 8 percent continuous compound interest to reach a value of
$20,000 in 21 years?

12. Let f be the function defined by $f(x) = 4x^2 - 36x + 89$ on the interval $[3, 6]$. Show that, for
(85) the interval $[3, 6]$, the number c guaranteed by the Mean Value Theorem is the midpoint
of $[3, 6]$.

13. Let f and g be continuous functions that are defined for all real numbers x and that have the
(57) following properties:

$$\int_0^2 f(x)\,dx = 2 \qquad \int_1^2 f(x)\,dx = 3 \qquad \int_0^1 g(x)\,dx = -1 \qquad \int_0^2 g(x)\,dx = 4$$

(a) Find the value of $\int_0^2 [f(x) + 2g(x)]\,dx$.

(b) Find the value of $\int_1^2 g(x)\,dx + \int_2^0 g(x)\,dx$.

14. Let R be the region completely bounded by $y = x(1 - x)$ and the x-axis. Write a definite
(87) integral whose value equals the volume of the solid formed when R is revolved about the y-axis.

15. Let R be the region in the first quadrant bounded by $y = 1 - x^2$ and $x + y = 1$. Find the
(81) volume of the solid formed when R is rotated about the x-axis.

16. Let R be the region bounded by the graph of $x + 2y = 3$ and the coordinate axes. Use y as the
(87) variable of integration to write a definite integral whose value equals the volume of the solid
formed when R is rotated about the x-axis.

Differentiate in problems 17 and 18 with respect to x.

17. $f(x) = 2x^{2x}$
(84)

18. $y = \arctan x + \ln|\sin x| + 14^x - \dfrac{\sec x + e^x}{1 + x}$
(50,64,72)

19. Find the area bounded by one arch of the graph of $y = \sin^2 x$ and the x-axis.
(83)

20. Graph: $y = \dfrac{x^2 + 1}{x}$
(80)

Integrate in problems 21 and 22.

21. $\displaystyle\int \cos(2x)\, e^{\sin(2x)}\, dx$ **22.** $\displaystyle\int \dfrac{x^2}{x^3 + 1}\, dx$
(66)   (66)

23. Find $\dfrac{dy}{dx}$ if $x^3 + xy + y^2 = 0$.
(34)

24. Shown at right is the graph of the derivative f' of a function f. Which of the following graphs could be the graph of f?
₍₄₅₎

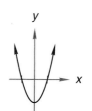

A.
B.
C.
D.

25. Given $f(x) = \sin(2x - \pi)$ and $g(x) = \cos(2x + \pi)$, which of the following statements are true?
_(7,68)

A. The graphs of f and g are identical.

B. Both f and g are even functions.

C. The period of f equals the period of g.

D. The amplitude of g is greater than the amplitude of f.

LESSON 90 *Particle Motion II*

If the graph of a continuous function f is above the t-axis between t_0 and t_1, the definite integral of the function from t_0 to t_1 is a positive number equal to the area between the graph of f and the t-axis between t_0 and t_1. If the graph of f is below the t-axis between t_1 and t_2, the definite integral of the function from t_1 to t_2 is a negative number equal to the negative of the area between the graph of f and the t-axis between t_1 and t_2. The definite integral of f from t_0 to t_2 for the curve shown below is the sum of the area above the t-axis and the negative of the area below the t-axis.

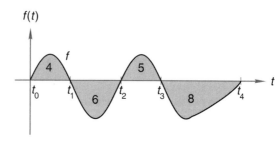

$$\int_{t_0}^{t_1} f(t)\, dt = 4 \qquad \int_{t_1}^{t_2} f(t)\, dt = -6 \qquad \int_{t_0}^{t_2} f(t)\, dt = -2$$

The definite integral of the **velocity function** of a particle moving along the x-axis represents the algebraic sum of the left (−) and right (+) distances traveled by the particle, because

$$\int v(t)\, dt$$

represents the sum of many terms (infinitely many) of the form

$$\underbrace{\text{rate}}_{v(t)} \cdot \underbrace{\text{time}}_{dt}$$

Since distance = rate · time, the net accumulation or change in position is simply $\int v(t)\, dt$.

Assuming the function graphed above is the velocity function of a particle, the particle would travel 4 units to the right during the interval $[t_0, t_1]$ and 6 units to the left during the interval $[t_1, t_2]$ for a net change of position of -2 during the interval $[t_0, t_2]$. The net change of position of the particle in the interval $[t_0, t_4]$ is 5 units to the left, because the value of the definite integral for the function between t_0 and t_4 is -5, which is equivalent to the algebraic sum of the areas between t_0 and t_4.

$$4 - 6 + 5 - 8 = -5$$

example 90.1   The velocity function for a particle moving along the x-axis is $v(t)$. The following is given:

$$\int_1^2 v(t)\, dt = -7 \qquad \int_2^3 v(t)\, dt = 3 \qquad \int_3^4 v(t)\, dt = -2 \qquad \int_4^5 v(t)\, dt = 6$$

(a) How much does the position of the particle change over the interval $[1, 5]$?

(b) If the particle is at $x = 7$ when $t = 2$, what is the position of the particle when $t = 4$?

solution   (a) The sum of the areas above the t-axis between $t = 1$ and $t = 5$ is zero, because $-7 + 3 - 2 + 6 = 0$. Thus the particle moves 7 units to the left, 3 units to the right, 2 units to the left, and 6 units to the right for a **net change in position of zero units.**

(b) Between $t = 2$ and $t = 4$, the particle moves 3 units to the right and 2 units to the left. Thus the particle moves from $x = 7$ to $x = 10$ and returns to $x = 8$ when $t = 4$.

example 90.2   A particle moves along the x-axis so that its position function is

$$x(t) = 2t^3 - 9t^2 + 12t + 1$$

(a) What are the positions of the particle at $t = 0$ and $t = 3$?

(b) What is the total distance the particle travels between $t = 0$ and $t = 3$?

solution   (a) To find the position when $t = 0$ and when $t = 3$, we evaluate $x(0)$ and $x(3)$.

$$x(0) = 2(0)^3 - 9(0)^2 + 12(0) + 1 = \mathbf{1}$$
$$x(3) = 2(3)^3 - 9(3)^2 + 12(3) + 1 = \mathbf{10}$$

(b) The difference in position is 9 units, which is the sum of the areas above the t-axis and the negative of the areas below the t-axis on the graph of $v(t)$ between t-values of 0 and 3. However, some of the areas might have been below the t-axis, representing distances traveled to the left, so 9 is not necessarily the total distance traveled. Thus, we begin by finding $v(t)$.

$$v(t) = \frac{d}{dx}x(t) = 6t^2 - 18t + 12 = 6(t^2 - 3t + 2)$$

It is not necessary to graph the function to find the areas. We just need to know when the graph of the velocity function is above the t-axis and when it is below the t-axis. Thus, we need to find the zeros of the velocity function to know when its graph touches the t-axis. Factoring $v(t)$ gives

$$v(t) = 6(t - 2)(t - 1)$$

From the linear factors $t - 2$ and $t - 1$, we see that the zeros of the velocity function are $+2$ and $+1$. Using 0 as a test point, we see that $v(0) = +12$. This information allows us to deduce that $v(t)$ is positive for t less than 1, is negative between 1 and 2, and is positive for t greater than 2.

sign of $v(t)$

We are interested in the region between $t = 0$ and $t = 3$. We could add the areas above the graph to the negative of the areas below the graph by computing the following integrals.

$$\int_0^1 v(t)\, dt - \int_1^2 v(t)\, dt + \int_2^3 v(t)\, dt$$

Rather than do this, however, we note that between $t = 0$ and $t = 1$ the particle moves to the right. Between $t = 1$ and $t = 2$, the particle moves to the left, and between $t = 2$ and $t = 3$, the particle moves to the right. If we evaluate $x(t)$ at $t = 0, 1, 2,$ and $3,$ we get

$$x(0) = 1 \qquad x(1) = 6 \qquad x(2) = 5 \qquad x(3) = 10$$

During the interval $[0, 1]$ the particle moves from 1 to 6, a distance of 5. During the interval $[1, 2]$ the particle moves from 6 to 5, a distance of 1. During the interval $[2, 3]$ the particle moves from 5 to 10, a distance of 5. Thus, the particle moves a total distance of

$$5 + 1 + 5 = \mathbf{11 \ units}$$

The difference between the initial position and the final position is 9 units, but the total distance traveled is 11 units.

example 90.3 The acceleration of a particle moving on the x-axis is $4\pi \cos t$. If the velocity is 1 at $t = 0,$ what is the average velocity of the particle over the interval $0 \le t \le \pi$?

solution The velocity function is found by integrating the acceleration function.

$$v(t) = \int a(t) \, dt = 4\pi \int \cos t \, dt = 4\pi \sin t + C$$

To find C, we use the fact that $v(t) = 1$ when $t = 0$ and substitute.

$$1 = 4\pi \sin 0 + C \quad \longrightarrow \quad C = 1$$

So the velocity function is

$$v(t) = 4\pi \sin t + 1$$

We can find the instantaneous velocity for any value of t by evaluating the function at that value. To find the average velocity over the interval $0 \le t \le \pi,$ we use the formula from the previous lesson on average values.

$$
\begin{aligned}
\text{Average velocity} &= \frac{1}{\pi - 0} \int_0^\pi (4\pi \sin t + 1) \, dt \\
&= \frac{[-4\pi \cos t + t]_0^\pi}{\pi} \\
&= \frac{4\pi + \pi}{\pi} - \left(-\frac{4\pi}{\pi} \right) \\
&= \frac{9\pi}{\pi} \\
&= \mathbf{9 \ units \ per \ second}
\end{aligned}
$$

example 90.4 The velocity function for a particle moving along the x-axis is given by $v(t) = 2\pi \cos (\pi t)$. For what values of $t, \ 0 \le t \le 2,$ is the particle stationary?

solution The particle is stationary when its velocity equals zero. The coefficient 2π is never zero, since 2π always equals 2π. Thus, the velocity equals zero only when $\cos (\pi t)$ equals zero. This occurs when

$$\pi t = \frac{\pi}{2}, \qquad \pi t = \frac{3\pi}{2}, \qquad \pi t = \frac{5\pi}{2}, \qquad \text{etc.}$$

which is when

$$t = \frac{1}{2}, \qquad t = \frac{3}{2}, \qquad t = \frac{5}{2}, \qquad \text{etc.}$$

Only two of these values, $\frac{1}{2}$ and $\frac{3}{2},$ are between 0 and 2.

example 90.5   What is the total distance traveled to the left by the particle in example 90.4 between times $t = 0$ and $t = 2$?

solution   The velocity is zero when t equals $\frac{1}{2}$ and $\frac{3}{2}$.

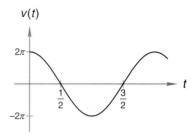

The particle is moving to the left when the velocity is negative. Thus we integrate $v(t)$ from $t = \frac{1}{2}$ to $t = \frac{3}{2}$ to obtain the desired result.

$$2 \int_{1/2}^{3/2} (\cos(\pi t))(\pi \, dt) = 2[\sin(\pi t)]_{1/2}^{3/2} = 2\left(\sin \frac{3\pi}{2} - \sin \frac{\pi}{2} \right) = 2(-1 - 1) = -4$$

The negative sign on the definite integral indicates that the area is below the x-axis and that the particle moved **4 units** to the left between $t = \frac{1}{2}$ and $t = \frac{3}{2}$.

**problem set
90**

1. A cone whose dimensions are as shown
(46) contains water that has a depth of h cm, but
the water is dripping out at a rate of
$\frac{1}{2}$ cm³/s. How fast is the depth of the water
decreasing when the depth of the water
is 2 cm?

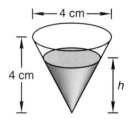

2. Let $v(t)$ be the velocity of a particle moving along the x-axis. Suppose that
(90)

$$\int_1^2 v(t) \, dt = -5 \qquad \int_2^3 v(t) \, dt = 6 \qquad \int_3^5 v(t) \, dt = -3$$

The particle's position at $t = 1$ is 5. Find the particle's position at $t = 5$.

3. A particle moves along the x-axis so that its position as a function of time t is given by
(90) $x(t) = t^2 - 3t + 2$.

(a) What are the positions of the particle at $t = 0$ and $t = 3$?

(b) What is the total distance traveled by the particle between $t = 0$ and $t = 3$?

4. When $\frac{1}{2} \le t \le \frac{3}{2}$ the velocity function for a particle moving along the number line is given
(90) by $v(t) = 2\pi \sin(\pi t)$.

(a) Find the time(s) t for which the particle is momentarily at rest.

(b) Find the total distance traveled in the negative x-direction by the particle.

5. Find the average value of the function $f(x) = \sin(2x)$ on the interval $\left[0, \frac{\pi}{2} \right]$.
(89)

6. Gottfried drops a ball from a height of 576 feet. Find the ball's average height between the time
(89) it is dropped and the time it strikes the ground.

7. The acceleration of a particle moving along a number line is given by the equation
(89) $a(t) = 4\pi \sin t$. The velocity of the particle at $t = 0$ is π. Find the average velocity of the
particle over the interval $0 \le t \le \pi$.

8. Let $f(x) = x^2 + 1$ on the interval [3, 4]. Find the number c guaranteed by the Mean Value
(89) Theorem for Integrals.

9. Given that the average value of the function $f(x) = \frac{x}{\sqrt{x^2 + 16}}$ on the interval $[0, 3]$ is $\frac{1}{3}$, find the
(89) number c guaranteed by the Mean Value Theorem for Integrals.

10. Jan put $1000 in the bank. The money is compounded continuously, which means that the
(88) amount in the account increases at a rate proportional to the amount in the account. After 1 year the account held $1100.

    (a) What annual interest rate did the bank pay?

    (b) If the bank always paid the interest rate found in (a), how much should Jan have deposited to have $90,000 after 20 years?

Find general solutions to the differential equations in problems 11 and 12.

11. $4x\,dx - 2y\,dy = 0$
(88)

12. $\dfrac{dy}{dx} = \dfrac{1}{x}$
(88)

13. The slope of a function f at any given point on the graph of the function equals the reciprocal of
(88) the x-coordinate of the point. Find the equation of f given that its graph passes through $(e, 3)$.

14. Let f be a function defined by $f(x) = 2 \sin x$ on the interval $[0, \pi]$. Find a number $c \in [0, \pi]$
(85) guaranteed by Rolle's theorem.

15. Let f be the function defined below. Find the numerical values of a and b that make the function
(82) f differentiable for all values of x.

$$f(x) = \begin{cases} ax^2 + bx & \text{when } x \geq 1 \\ 2x^2 & \text{when } x < 1 \end{cases}$$

16. Let R be the region between $y = \dfrac{1}{x}$ and the x-axis on the interval $[1, 2]$.
(87)

    (a) Use x as the variable of integration to write a definite integral whose value equals the volume of the solid formed when R is revolved about the y-axis.

    (b) Evaluate this integral.

Integrate in problems 17–21.

17. $\displaystyle\int 3^x\,dx$
(73)

18. $\displaystyle\int x \ln x\,dx$
(69)

19. $\displaystyle\int 3xe^{x^2}\,dx$
(66)

20. $\displaystyle\int \cot x \csc^2 x\,dx$
(66)

21. $\displaystyle\int \dfrac{5\,dx}{1 + x^2}$
(64)

22. Find: $\dfrac{d}{dx}\left[\arctan (\sin x) + \ln (x^2 - 1) + \dfrac{1}{x + 1} \right]$
(64)

23. Let $f(x) = \frac{4x^2 - 16}{x^2 - 9}$. Determine whether f is an odd function, an even function, or neither.
(80,86) Sketch the graph of f. Clearly indicate all zeros and asymptotes.

24. If f is a function whose inverse is also a function, which of the following sets of points could lie
(6,58) on the graph of f?

    A. $\{(1, 3), (-1, 3), (2, 4)\}$ B. $\{(3, 1), (3, 2), (2, 3)\}$

    C. $\{(1, 2), (2, 3), (3, 1)\}$ D. $\left\{\left(\frac{1}{2}, 1\right), \left(-\frac{1}{2}, 1\right), (-1, 2)\right\}$

25. Let f be the function defined by $f(x) = \dfrac{x^3 - 2x - 1}{x + 2}$.
(80)

    (a) Determine the vertical asymptotes and the end behavior of the function.

    (b) Sketch the graph of the function.

    (c) Determine the domain and range of the function.

LESSON 91 *Product and Difference Indeterminate Forms*

We have seen various techniques for finding limits. For example, when we encounter

$$\lim_{x \to 2} \frac{x^2 - 4}{x - 2}$$

we factor the numerator and cancel.

$$\lim_{x \to 2} \frac{x^2 - 4}{x - 2} = \lim_{x \to 2} \frac{(x + 2)(x - 2)}{x - 2} = \lim_{x \to 2} (x + 2) = 4$$

In the special case of the limit of a rational function as x approaches $+\infty$ or $-\infty$, we simply divide all terms by the highest power term in the denominator (coefficient excluded).

$$\lim_{x \to \infty} \frac{5x^2 + 17x - 3}{6x^2 - 4} = \lim_{x \to \infty} \frac{\dfrac{5x^2}{x^2} + \dfrac{17x}{x^2} - \dfrac{3}{x^2}}{\dfrac{6x^2}{x^2} - \dfrac{4}{x^2}} = \lim_{x \to \infty} \frac{5 + \dfrac{17}{x} - \dfrac{3}{x^2}}{6 - \dfrac{4}{x^2}}$$

$$= \frac{5 + 0 - 0}{6 - 0} = \frac{5}{6}$$

Some limits cannot be handled by these techniques. The following are two examples:

$$\lim_{x \to 0} \frac{\sin x}{x} \qquad \lim_{x \to \infty} \frac{\ln x}{e^x}$$

L'Hôpital's Rule was introduced in Lesson 79 to evaluate such limits, and we repeat that rule here.

L'HÔPITAL'S RULE

If $\displaystyle\lim_{x \to a} \frac{f(x)}{g(x)}$ is an indeterminate form and if $\displaystyle\lim_{x \to a} \frac{f'(x)}{g'(x)}$ exists, then

$$\lim_{x \to a} \frac{f(x)}{g(x)} = \lim_{x \to a} \frac{f'(x)}{g'(x)}$$

In this lesson we introduce two new indeterminate forms, $0 \cdot \infty$ and $\infty - \infty$. Handling these forms requires algebraic manipulation. In the case of $0 \cdot \infty$, which involves the product of two terms, we divide by the reciprocal of one of the terms to obtain either of the indeterminate forms $\frac{0}{0}$ or $\frac{\infty}{\infty}$. L'Hôpital's Rule can then be applied. When the indeterminate form $\infty - \infty$ is encountered, we simply find a common denominator and combine the two terms into a single fraction, yielding the form $\frac{0}{0}$ or $\frac{\infty}{\infty}$.

example 91.1 Evaluate: $\displaystyle\lim_{x \to 0} [x(\csc x)]$

solution The form $0 \cdot \infty$ is indeterminate, so we rewrite $x(\csc x)$ as a ratio.

$$x(\csc x) = x \cdot \frac{1}{\sin x} = \frac{x}{\sin x}$$

Now we can use L'Hôpital's Rule.

$$\lim_{x \to 0} [x(\csc x)] = \lim_{x \to 0} \frac{x}{\sin x} \qquad \text{indeterminate form } \frac{0}{0}$$

$$= \lim_{x \to 0} \frac{1}{\cos x} \qquad \text{L'Hôpital's Rule}$$

$$= \frac{1}{1} = \mathbf{1} \qquad \text{evaluated limit}$$

example 91.2 Evaluate: $\lim\limits_{x \to \infty} \left(e^{-x} \ln x \right)$

solution Again we have an instance of the form $0 \cdot \infty$. We can rewrite the function as a ratio and apply L'Hôpital's Rule.

$$\lim_{x \to \infty} \left(e^{-x} \ln x \right) = \lim_{x \to \infty} \frac{\ln x}{e^x} \qquad \text{indeterminate form } \frac{\infty}{\infty}$$

$$= \lim_{x \to \infty} \frac{\dfrac{1}{x}}{e^x} \qquad \text{L'Hôpital's Rule}$$

$$= \lim_{x \to \infty} \frac{1}{xe^x} \qquad \text{simplified}$$

$$= \mathbf{0} \qquad \text{evaluated limit}$$

example 91.3 Evaluate: $\lim\limits_{x \to 0} \left(\dfrac{1}{x} - \dfrac{1}{\sin x} \right)$

solution This is an instance of the indeterminate form $\infty - \infty$, so we rewrite the problem as the limit of a ratio.

$$\lim_{x \to 0} \left(\frac{1}{x} - \frac{1}{\sin x} \right) = \lim_{x \to 0} \frac{\sin x - x}{x \sin x}$$

This rewritten version has the indeterminate form $\dfrac{0}{0}$. Thus we apply L'Hôpital's Rule.

$$\lim_{x \to 0} \frac{\sin x - x}{x \sin x} = \lim_{x \to 0} \frac{\cos x - 1}{x \cos x + \sin x}$$

We again have the indeterminate form $\dfrac{0}{0}$. Thus L'Hôpital's Rule must be applied once more.

$$\lim_{x \to 0} \frac{\cos x - 1}{x \cos x + \sin x} = \lim_{x \to 0} \frac{-\sin x}{x(-\sin x) + \cos x + \cos x} \qquad \text{L'Hôpital's Rule}$$

$$= \frac{0}{0 + 1 + 1} = \frac{0}{2} = \mathbf{0} \qquad \text{evaluated limit}$$

example 91.4 Evaluate: $\lim\limits_{x \to 0^+} \left(\dfrac{1}{x} - \dfrac{1}{\sqrt{x}} \right)$

solution The indeterminate form $\infty - \infty$ arises in this problem. Since we have two fractions, we combine them by using a common denominator.

$$\lim_{x \to 0^+} \left(\frac{1}{x} - \frac{1}{\sqrt{x}} \right) = \lim_{x \to 0^+} \left(\frac{1}{x} - \frac{1}{\sqrt{x}} \cdot \frac{\sqrt{x}}{\sqrt{x}} \right) = \lim_{x \to 0^+} \left(\frac{1 - \sqrt{x}}{x} \right)$$

As x approaches 0 from the right, the numerator approaches 1 and the denominator approaches 0. Thus the quotient approaches $+\infty$. Therefore, $\lim_{x \to 0^+} \left(\frac{1}{x} - \frac{1}{\sqrt{x}} \right) = +\infty$. We confirm this result with a graph of the function $y = \frac{1}{x} - \frac{1}{\sqrt{x}}$.

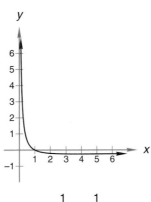

$$y = \frac{1}{x} - \frac{1}{\sqrt{x}}$$

Notice that L'Hôpital's Rule was not needed even though we had an indeterminate form. This usually is not the case. We only avoided having to use L'Hôpital's Rule by choosing the common denominator carefully.

example 91.5 Evaluate: $\lim\limits_{x \to 0} \left(-\dfrac{1}{x} - \csc x \right)$

solution We check the one-sided limits first, beginning with the right-hand limit.

$$\lim_{x \to 0^+} \left(-\frac{1}{x} - \csc x \right) = -\infty - (+\infty)$$

This is not an indeterminate form. There is no ambiguity here, because both terms contribute to the total expression becoming large and negative as x approaches 0 from the right.

$$\lim_{x \to 0^+} \left(-\frac{1}{x} - \csc x \right) = -\infty$$

Now we check the left-hand limit.

$$\lim_{x \to 0^-} \left(-\frac{1}{x} - \csc x \right) = +\infty - (-\infty)$$

Again, this is not an indeterminate form.

$$\lim_{x \to 0^-} \left(-\frac{1}{x} - \csc x \right) = +\infty$$

Since these two one-sided limits differ, we know $\lim\limits_{x \to 0} \left(-\dfrac{1}{x} - \csc x \right)$ **does not exist.**

problem set 91

1. A right circular cylinder is inscribed in a right circular cone of radius 4 cm and height 6 cm, as shown. The radius of the right circular cylinder is r, and the height is h.
   (52)

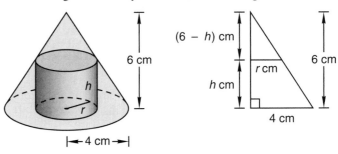

(a) Express the volume of the right circular cylinder in terms of r. (*Hint:* Use the figure on the right-hand side and the properties of similar triangles to find h in terms of r.)

(b) Use calculus to find the radius and height of the right circular cylinder of greatest volume that can be inscribed in the right circular cone.

(c) What is the maximal volume that the inscribed right circular cylinder can have?

2. The time-dependent velocity function for a particle moving along the x-axis is v. Suppose
   (90)

$$\int_1^2 v(t)\, dt = 3 \qquad \int_2^4 v(t)\, dt = -5 \qquad \int_4^6 v(t)\, dt = 10$$

(a) How much does the position of the particle change from $t = 1$ to $t = 6$?

(b) If the particle is at $x = 9$ when $t = 2$, what is the position of the particle when $t = 6$?

3. A particle moves along the x-axis so that its position as a function of time t is given by
   (90) $x(t) = t^3 - 6t^2 + 9t + 2$.

(a) What is the position of the particle at $t = 0$ and at $t = 4$?

(b) What is the total distance traveled by the particle between $t = 0$ and $t = 4$?

4. The velocity function for a particle moving along the number line is $v(t) = 4\pi \cos(2\pi t)$,
(78) where $0 \leq t \leq 1$.

   (a) Find the time(s) t for which the particle is momentarily at rest.

   (b) Find the total distance traveled by the particle in the negative x-direction.

Evaluate the limits in problems 5–8.

5. $\lim\limits_{x \to 0} (x \csc x)$
(91)

6. $\lim\limits_{x \to 0^+} (x \ln x)$
(91)

7. $\lim\limits_{x \to (\pi/2)^-} [\sec x \cos(3x)]$
(91)

8. $\lim\limits_{x \to 0} \left(\dfrac{1}{\sin x} - \dfrac{1}{x} \right)$
(91)

9. Find the average value of the function $f(x) = \cos(2x)$ on the interval $\left[-\dfrac{\pi}{4}, \dfrac{\pi}{4} \right]$.
(89)

10. Isaac drops a ball from a height of 576 feet. Find the ball's average velocity between the time it
(89) is dropped and the time it strikes the ground.

11. The acceleration of a particle moving along a number line is given by the equation
(89) $a(t) = 2\pi \cos(2t)$. If the velocity of the particle at $t = 0$ is 2, what is the average velocity of
the particle over the interval $0 \leq t \leq 2\pi$.

12. Let f be a continuous function on the closed interval $[a, b]$. Suppose that
(89) $\int_a^b f(x)\, dx = 10$, $a = 3$, and the average value of the function f on $[a, b]$ is 5. Find b.

13. Let f be a function defined by $f(x) = \dfrac{1}{x}$ on the interval $[1, e]$. Find the number $c \in [1, e]$
(89) guaranteed by the Mean Value Theorem for Integrals.

14. Let f be a function defined by $f(x) = x$ on the interval $[a, b]$. Show that for the interval $[a, b]$
(89) the number c guaranteed by the Mean Value Theorem for Integrals is the midpoint of $[a, b]$.

15. Let R be the region between $y = x - 2$ and the x-axis on the interval $[2, 5]$. Use the shell
(87) method to find the volume of the solid formed when R is revolved about the y-axis.

16. Let R be the region in the first quadrant bounded by $x = 9 - y^2$ and the coordinate axes. Use
(87) the shell method to find the volume of the solid formed when R is rotated around the x-axis.

17. Find the general solution to the differential equation $\dfrac{1}{y}\, dx - \dfrac{1}{x}\, dy = 0$.
(88)

18. Find the particular solution of $\dfrac{dy}{dx} = 4x^3 y^2$ that intercepts the point $(1, 2)$.
(88)

19. (a) Let f be an even function, and suppose that $\int_0^k f(x)\, dx = 5$. Find the value of $\int_k^{-k} f(x)\, dx$.
(86)

   (b) Let f be an odd function, and suppose that $\int_0^k f(x)\, dx = 5$. Find the value of $\int_k^{-k} f(x)\, dx$.

20. The speed limit on a highway is 65 mph. At 5:00 p.m. a police officer patrolling the highway
(85) sees a truck go by at 60 mph. The officer radios another police officer seventy miles down the
highway who sees the same truck go by at 6:00 p.m. traveling 60 mph.

   (a) Find the average speed of the truck between 5:00 p.m. and 6:00 p.m.

   (b) The truck driver is ticketed for speeding but argues that he was never clocked over 60 mph.
   The truck driver is convicted by a judge who points out that he must have been traveling
   70 mph at least once. Is the judge correct? Explain your answer.

21. Find the equation of the line tangent to the curve $x^3 + y^2 = y$ at $(0, 1)$.
(34)

Integrate in problems 22 and 23.

22. $\int \cos^2 (3x)\, dx$
(83)

23. $\int \cos^3 (3x)\, dx$
(76)

24. Let $f(x) = \sqrt{1 + 6x}$.
(6,27)

    (a) Find the domain and range of f.

    (b) Find the coordinates of the point on the graph of f where the tangent line is parallel to $y = x + 12$.

25. Let $f(x) = 2x^2 + 1$.
(27)

    (a) Find x_0 such that the tangent lines to the graph of f at $\left(x_0, f(x_0)\right)$ and $\left(-x_0, f(-x_0)\right)$ are perpendicular.

    (b) Find the slopes of the tangent lines in (a).

    (c) Find the coordinates of the point of intersection of the tangent lines in (a).

LESSON 92 *Derivatives of Inverse Functions*

We remember that a function is a one-to-one function if no two different input values produce the same output value. Both of the following graphs represent functions, because every value of x is paired with only one value of y. (Any vertical line will touch either graph at only one point.) However, both graphs are not one-to-one. The horizontal line $y = 2$ touches the graph on the left in two places, and both x_1 and x_2 are paired with the y-value of 2. The function graphed on the right is a one-to-one function, since no horizontal line touches the graph twice.

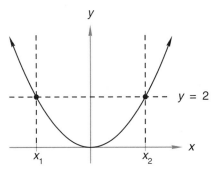
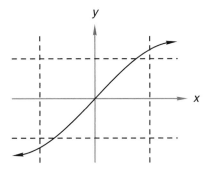

Every one-to-one function has an inverse function whose graph is a mirror image of the function in the line $y = x$. On the left we show the graph of a one-to-one function that we call f and the graph of its inverse function f^{-1}. The symbol f^{-1} is read as "f inverse." If the point (a, b) is on the graph of f, then the point (b, a) must be on the graph of f^{-1}. The slope of f at (a, b) is the reciprocal of the slope of f^{-1} at (b, a) and vice versa.

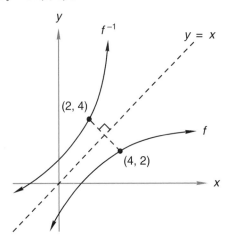
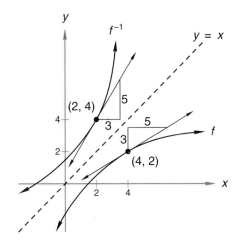

In the figure on the left-hand side above, we show the point $(4, 2)$ on the graph of f and the point $(2, 4)$ on the graph of f^{-1}. For both functions x is the independent (input) variable, and y is the dependent (output) variable, as shown in the function machines below.

$$x \longrightarrow \boxed{f} \longrightarrow f(x)$$
$$4 \longrightarrow \qquad \longrightarrow 2$$

$$x \longrightarrow \boxed{f^{-1}} \longrightarrow f^{-1}(x)$$
$$2 \longrightarrow \qquad \longrightarrow 4$$

From the graph on the right-hand side above, we see that the slope of f^{-1} when $x = 2$ is $\frac{5}{3}$ and that the slope of the graph of f when $x = 4$ is $\frac{3}{5}$. Since 4 is f^{-1} evaluated at 2, we can write $4 = f^{-1}(2)$. Because the slope of the graph of a function of f is determined by its derivative, we can write for this example that the derivative of the inverse function evaluated at $x = 2$ equals the reciprocal of the derivative of the original function f evaluated at 4, which we know is equal to $f^{-1}(2)$.

$$(f^{-1})'(2) = \frac{5}{3} = \frac{1}{\dfrac{3}{5}} = \frac{1}{f'(4)} = \frac{1}{f'(f^{-1}(2))}$$

In general we can say the following:

$$\boxed{(f^{-1})'(x) = \frac{1}{f'(f^{-1}(x))}}$$

Of course, this is only true for those values of x for which both sides of this equation are defined.

The notation can be confusing, but the important thing to remember is that the slope of the inverse function at (c, d) equals the reciprocal of the slope of the original function at (d, c). We investigate this in two steps. First we use the function $f(x) = x^3$ and its inverse function $f^{-1}(x) = \sqrt[3]{x}$.

FUNCTION	INVERSE FUNCTION
$f(x) = x^3$	$f^{-1}(x) = \sqrt[3]{x}$
$f'(x) = 3x^2$	$(f^{-1})'(x) = \dfrac{1}{3(\sqrt[3]{x})^2}$

But what is $\sqrt[3]{x}$ in the lower right-hand equation? It is the output of the f^{-1} machine when the input is x, which is expressed mathematically as $f^{-1}(x)$. If we replace $\sqrt[3]{x}$ with $f^{-1}(x)$, we get the following expression for the derivative of f^{-1} evaluated at x:

$$(f^{-1})'(x) = \frac{1}{3(f^{-1}(x))^2} = \frac{1}{f'(f^{-1}(x))}$$

Following a different approach, consider the one-to-one function f and its inverse function g. We use the definition of inverses and the chain rule to give a general proof of the boxed equation above.

$$f(g(x)) = x \qquad\qquad \text{definition of inverse functions}$$

$$f'(g(x))g'(x) = 1 \qquad\qquad \text{differentiated both sides with respect to } x$$

$$g'(x) = \frac{1}{f'(g(x))} \qquad\qquad \text{divided by } f'(g(x))$$

We use g rather than f^{-1} so that using the chain rule for derivatives to get the second equation does not cause confusion. Replacing g with f^{-1} at this point gives

$$(f^{-1})'(x) = \frac{1}{f'(f^{-1}(x))}$$

example 92.1   The function $f(x) = x^3 + x - 1$ is a one-to-one function. Find the slope of the graph of the inverse function f^{-1} at the point $(-1, 0)$.

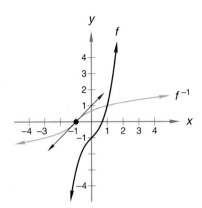

solution   We want to find the slope of the graph of the inverse function at the point $(-1, 0)$. Because there is an abundance of information, the answer can be found in two ways. The first is to find the equation of the inverse function, differentiate, and evaluate at $(-1, 0)$.

$$
\begin{array}{ll}
y = x^3 + x - 1 & \text{function} \\[2mm]
x = y^3 + y - 1 & \text{inverse function} \\[2mm]
dx = 3y^2\, dy + dy & \text{differential} \\[2mm]
\dfrac{dy}{dx} = \dfrac{1}{3y^2 + 1} & \text{simplified} \\[4mm]
(f^{-1})'(x) = \dfrac{1}{3y^2 + 1} & \text{derivative}
\end{array}
$$

Since the point $(-1, 0)$ lies on the graph of the function, we use $x = -1$ and $y = 0$ in the equation above to get

$$
(f^{-1})'(-1) = \frac{1}{3(0)^2 + 1} = 1
$$

Notice that the graph seems to justify this answer.

     The other way to arrive at this answer is to use the equation

$$
(f^{-1})'(-1) = \frac{1}{f'(f^{-1}(-1))}
$$

First we find $f'(x)$.

$$
f'(x) = 3x^2 + 1
$$

We remember that $f^{-1}(-1)$ is the value of $y = f^{-1}(x)$ when $x = -1$, which is 0. Therefore

$$
(f^{-1})'(-1) = \frac{1}{f'(f^{-1}(-1))} = \frac{1}{f'(0)} = \frac{1}{3(0)^2 + 1} = 1
$$

example 92.2   Let $f(x) = x^3 + x$ and let h be the inverse function of f. Find $h'(2)$.

solution   We use h instead of f^{-1} because it is less confusing. The function f must be a one-to-one function because its inverse is a function, and only one-to-one functions have inverses that are functions. We know from this lesson that

$$
h'(x) = \frac{1}{f'(h(x))}
$$

Thus, we begin by finding the derivative of f.

$$f(x) = x^3 + x$$
$$f'(x) = 3x^2 + 1$$

Substituting in the equation for the derivative of h gives us

$$h'(x) = \frac{1}{3(h(x))^2 + 1} \qquad \text{substituted}$$

$$h'(2) = \frac{1}{3(h(2))^2 + 1} \qquad \text{evaluated}$$

But what is $h(2)$? Since h is the inverse function of f, it is the value of x for which $f(x) = 2$. Thus, we need to solve

$$2 = x^3 + x$$

Usually we would have to solve this cubic for x, but the solution is apparent by inspection. We can see that x has to equal 1.

$$2 = (1)^3 + 1$$

So our answer is

$$h'(2) = \frac{1}{3(1)^2 + 1} = \frac{1}{4}$$

Had we been asked to find the value of $h'(12)$, we would have been in trouble, because this would require that we find the roots of the cubic

$$12 = x^3 + x$$

In that case we would use our calculator to approximate the value of x by finding the intersection point of the functions $Y_1 = 12$ and $Y_2 = X^3 + X$ or by finding the root of the function $Y_1 = X^3 + X - 12$. The drawback is that we would not get an exact answer.

problem set 92

1. A particle traveling along the x-axis begins at $x = 4$ when $t = 0$ and moves along the axis so
(90) that when $t > 0$ its velocity is given by $v(t) = \frac{4t}{1 + t^2}$.

  (a) Write the equations that describe the acceleration and position of the particle as a function of time.

  (b) What velocity does the particle approach as t increases without bound?

2. A particle moves along the x-axis so that its position function is given by the equation
(90) $x(t) = 2t^3 - 9t^2 + 12t + 9$.

  (a) Determine the positions of the particle at $t = 0$ and $t = 2$.

  (b) Determine the total distance traveled by the particle between $t = 0$ and $t = 2$.

3. Suppose $f(x) = xe^{-x^2}$. Find all the critical numbers of f, and determine whether f attains a
(49) local maximum or a local minimum at each of the critical numbers found. Use the first derivative test to justify the answer.

4. Suppose that $f(x) = x^3 - x - 1$. Find the slope of the graph of the inverse of f at the
(92) point $(-1, 0)$.

5. Suppose $f(x) = x^3 + 2x$ and h is the inverse function of f. Evaluate $h(3)$ and $h'(3)$.
(92)

6. Suppose $f(x) = x^3 + x$ and h is the inverse function of f. Evaluate $h(0)$ and $h'(0)$.
(92)

Evaluate the limits in problems 7–10.

7. $\lim\limits_{x \to 0} \left[4x \csc (2x) \right]$
(91)

8. $\lim\limits_{x \to \infty} \dfrac{\ln x}{\sqrt{x}}$
(79)

9. $\lim\limits_{x \to \infty} e^{-x} \ln x$
(91)

10. $\lim\limits_{x \to \pi/2^-} (\tan x - \sec x)$
(91)

11. An account continuously compounds interest at an annual rate of 9 percent. How much money
(26) should be deposited in the account so that it will contain $50,000 in 30 years, assuming no
further deposits or withdrawals?

12. Find the general solution to the differential equation $y\, dx - dy = 0$.
(88)

13. A particle moves along the x-axis so that its acceleration at time t is given by $a(t) = 3 \sin t$. If
(90) the velocity of the particle is 3 at $t = 0$, what is the average velocity of the particle on the
interval $0 \le t \le \pi$.

14. Let f be the function defined for all real numbers x by $f(x) = x^3 + ax^2 + bx + c$ with the
(85) following properties:

    (1) The graph of f has a point of inflection at $(0, -3)$.

    (2) The average value of f on the closed interval $[0, 4]$ is -1.

    (a) Find the values of a, b, and c, and write the equation of f.

    (b) Find a number in the interval $[0, 3]$ that confirms the Mean Value Theorem (for derivatives)
for the function f.

15. Let f be the function defined by $f(x) = 3x^2 + 2x + 1$ on the interval $[-1, 2]$. Find a number
(89) c that confirms the Mean Value Theorem for Integrals.

16. At 1:00 p.m. a car traveling 65 mph along an interstate enters a 4-mile speed trap. Exactly
(85) 3 minutes later the car exits the speed trap traveling 65 mph.

    (a) Find the average speed of the car while it is in the speed trap.

    (b) Suppose the posted speed limit along the interstate is 70 mph. Was there some instant when
the driver of the car was speeding while traveling through the speed trap? Explain.

17. Use logarithmic differentiation to compute $\dfrac{f'(x)}{f(x)}$ where $f(x) = \dfrac{\sin x}{(x^3 + 1)^3 (x^4 + 1)^4}$.
(84)

18. Let R be the region bounded by the graph of $y = \sin x$ and the x-axis on the interval $[0, \pi]$. Find
(71) the volume of the solid formed when R is rotated about the x-axis.

19. The definite integral $\int_0^{\pi/2} (\cos x)[\cos (\sin x)]\, dx$ is equivalent to which of the following definite
(66) integrals?

    A. $\displaystyle\int_{-1}^{1} \cos u\, du$ B. $\displaystyle\int_{0}^{\pi/2} \cos u\, du$ C. $\displaystyle\int_{0}^{\pi/2} \sin u\, du$ D. $\displaystyle\int_{0}^{1} \cos u\, du$

20. Suppose $b > a$ and $\displaystyle\int_a^b e^{\cos x}\, dx = k$. Determine the values of the following:
(86)

    (a) $\displaystyle\int_b^a e^{\cos x}\, dx$ (b) $\displaystyle\int_{-b}^{-a} e^{\cos x}\, dx$

21. Find: $\dfrac{d}{dx} \arcsin \dfrac{x}{3} + \displaystyle\int \dfrac{1}{\sqrt{9 - x^2}}\, dx + \dfrac{d}{dx} \arctan \dfrac{x}{3} + \displaystyle\int \dfrac{3}{x^2 + 9}\, dx$
(64)

22. Differentiate $y = \dfrac{1}{\sqrt{x}} + 2 \ln |\sin x + \cos x|$ with respect to x.
(50)

23. Which of the following limits does not exist?
(70,79)

    A. $\displaystyle\lim_{x \to 0} \dfrac{x}{\sin x}$ B. $\displaystyle\lim_{x \to 0} \sin \dfrac{x}{1}$ C. $\displaystyle\lim_{x \to 0} \sin \dfrac{1}{x}$ D. $\displaystyle\lim_{x \to 0} \dfrac{x^2 - 1}{x - 1}$

24. Suppose the points $(4, 2)$, $(3, 4)$, and $(5, 6)$ lie on the graph of the function f. Which of the
$_{(92)}$ following statements must be true?

    A. The points $(-4, -2)$, $(-3, -4)$, and $(-5, -6)$ lie on the graph of the inverse of f.

    B. The points $(4, 2)$, $(3, 4)$, and $(5, 6)$ lie on the graph of f^{-1}.

    C. The points $\left(\frac{1}{4}, \frac{1}{2}\right)$, $\left(\frac{1}{3}, \frac{1}{4}\right)$, and $\left(\frac{1}{5}, \frac{1}{6}\right)$ lie on the graph of f^{-1}.

    D. The points $(2, 4)$, $(4, 3)$, and $(6, 5)$ lie on the graph of f^{-1}.

25. A right circular cone is inscribed inside a hemisphere so that the base of the cone is the same as
$_{(R)}$ the base of the hemisphere. The radius of the hemisphere is r. Find the surface area of the cone
(including the base) and the volume of the cone.

LESSON 93 *Newton's Method*

Since your earliest algebra courses you have used various methods to find the roots of equations.
Simple algebra can be used to solve linear equations, while the quadratic formula can be employed to
solve quadratic equations. Factoring techniques allow us to solve equations of higher degree, but these
are not always applicable. Some rather complicated formulas can be utilized to solve cubic and quartic
equations, but, because of their length and intricacy, these are not often employed. However, it has
been proven that no formulas exist for quintic (5th order) and higher-degree equations. Indeed, the
number of equations for which we can find **exact** roots is quite small. From a practical standpoint, we
need only be able to numerically **approximate** the value of the root of an equation. With this in mind,
we turn to one of the best known methods for approximating roots of equations, **Newton's method.**

The method is developed by considering the following series of graphs.

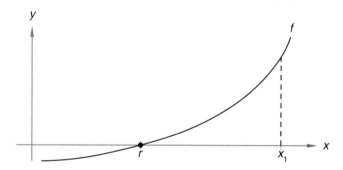

We are interested in approximating the value of r, which is the x-intercept of the graph of f. We begin
this process by choosing a seed value, x_1, near r. (The term "near" is highly relative, which we
discuss later.)

Next we draw the line tangent to the graph of f at the point $(x_1, f(x_1))$. Notice that this tangent
line crosses the x-axis at a point closer to $(r, 0)$ than $(x, 0)$. We call this point $(x_2, 0)$.

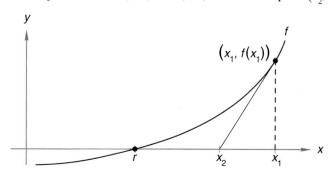

The slope of this tangent line can be written in two different ways. First, we know that its slope is given by $f'(x_1)$, because the slope of a tangent line is given by the derivative of the function. Second, the slope of this tangent line is also equal to

$$\frac{f(x_1) - 0}{x_1 - x_2}$$

from the formula for the slope of any line. Equating these two gives

$$f'(x_1) = \frac{f(x_1) - 0}{x_1 - x_2} = \frac{f(x_1)}{x_1 - x_2}$$

We solve this equation for x_2 in terms of x_1 and obtain the following:

$$x_2 = x_1 - \frac{f(x_1)}{f'(x_1)}$$

Using this value of x_2, we draw the line tangent to the graph of f at the point $(x_2, f(x_2))$. This produces a point $(x_3, 0)$.

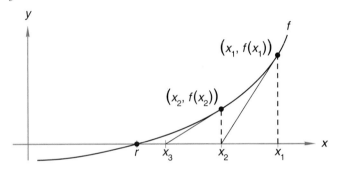

Notice that x_3 is even closer to r than x_2 and x_1. Applying the same reasoning as when calculating x_2, we see that

$$x_3 = x_2 - \frac{f(x_2)}{f'(x_2)}$$

This process can be continued indefinitely to obtain further values, x_4, x_5, ..., which are, in theory, better approximations of the exact value of the root r. From the pattern started above, we see the following formula for the nth approximation of the root $(n \geq 2)$:

$$\boxed{x_n = x_{n-1} - \frac{f(x_{n-1})}{f'(x_{n-1})}}$$

example 93.1 Use Newton's method to approximate the zero of the function $f(x) = \frac{9}{4}x^3 + \frac{3}{4}x^2 + 4$.

solution Notice that $f(-2) = -11$ while $f(0) = 4$. By the Intermediate Value Theorem, the graph of f must cross the x-axis at some value of x between -2 and 0, since it is a continuous function.

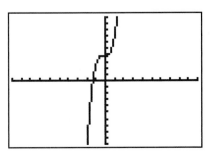

To employ Newton's method we must first find the derivative of the function. In this case, $f'(x) = \frac{27}{4}x^2 + \frac{3}{2}x$. Beginning with a seed value of $x_1 = 0$ gives

$$x_2 = x_1 - \frac{f(x_1)}{f'(x_1)}$$

$$x_2 = 0 - \frac{f(0)}{f'(0)}$$

$$x_2 = -\frac{4}{0}$$

This is undefined! Therefore we cannot use a seed value of $x_1 = 0$.

That is not a problem. We simply choose a different seed value, say $x_1 = -2$. Then we have

$$x_2 = -2 - \frac{-11}{24} = -1.5416666...$$

Our next iteration yields

$$x_3 = x_2 - \frac{f(x_2)}{f'(x_2)}$$

$$= -1.5416666... - \frac{f(-1.5416666...)}{f'(-1.5416666...)}$$

$$= -1.5416666... - \frac{-2.461751...}{13.730471...}$$

$$= -1.362375...$$

Continuing this process yields the following values.

$$x_4 = -1.334007...$$

$$x_5 = -1.333333...$$

The approximations of the root are getting quite close to $-\frac{4}{3}$. Is it the case that $-\frac{4}{3}$ is a zero of the function $f(x) = \frac{9}{4}x^3 + \frac{3}{4}x^2 + 4$? This question can be answered by computing $f(-\frac{4}{3})$.

$$f\left(-\frac{4}{3}\right) = -\frac{16}{3} + \frac{4}{3} + 4 = 0$$

So the zero is $-\frac{4}{3}$. We were only supposed to approximate the zero, but we did much better—we found the exact value.

With the advent of the graphing calculator, such iterative techniques are easier to implement. We demonstrate this in the next example.

example 93.2 Use a graphing calculator to find the zero of the function $f(x) = x^3 - x^2 + 2$.

solution In the function editor screen, we define `Y1=X^3-X^2+2`. Thus `Y1` is simply $f(x)$. Next we let `Y2=nDeriv(Y1,X,X)`. This means that `Y2` is $f'(x)$. In the home screen we use the `STO►` key to enter the initial seed value, or guess, in the variable `X`.

$$-2 \rightarrow X$$

In the home screen we calculate the next approximation of the zero using the formula in Newton's method and store this value as the new value of `X`.

$$X-(Y1/Y2) \rightarrow X$$

Pressing **ENTER** produces the first corrective approximation.

$$-1.375000039$$

Successively pressing **ENTER** yields the next several approximations of the zero prescribed by Newton's method.

$$-1.079313593$$
$$-1.004627413$$
$$-1.000017045$$
$$-1$$

We see that the zero is **–1.** If we continue to press **ENTER**, –1 keeps appearing. The answer can be checked by noting $f(-1) = -1 - 1 + 2 = 0$.

One of the most important aspects of Newton's method is beginning with a good seed value. We noted in example 93.1 that $x_1 = 0$ was not a good guess, because it resulted in a division by 0. In general, care should be taken to avoid using seed values that are equal to or close to critical numbers of the function in question. The number 0 is also a critical number of the function $f(x) = x^3 - x^2 + 2$, which means we cannot use it as a seed value, because it leads to division by 0 in Newton's method.

example 93.3   Approximate the root(s) of the function $y = x^3 - 2x - 1$ to nine decimal places.

solution   A note is in order: It is tempting to use the calculator's zero finder; however, that function is not as accurate as Newton's method, which is why we must use Newton's method instead.

We see from the graph that there are three distinct roots.

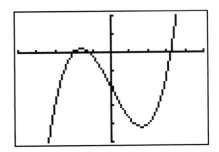

```
WINDOW
 Xmin=-2.5
 Xmax=2.5
 Xscl=.5
 Ymin=-2.5
 Ymax=1
 Yscl=.5
 Xres=1
```

We begin with the seed value $x_1 = -0.5$. We enter this value by using the **STO►** key as in example 93.2. Using the function editor screen, we define $Y_1 = X^3 - 2X - 1$ and $Y_2 = \text{nDeriv}(Y_1, X, X)$. Hence Y_1 represents the function in question, and Y_2 is the derivative of the function. As in example 93.2 we calculate the next approximation of the zero and store this new value as X by using $X - (Y_1 / Y_2) \to X$. This allows us to simply press **ENTER** to obtain successive corrective approximations. The approximations to the roots that appear are as follows:

$$-.5$$
$$-.60000008$$
$$-.6173913287$$
$$-.618033096$$
$$-.6180339887$$
$$-.6180339887$$

So one of the roots is approximately **–0.6180339887.** Using a seed value of 0.5 yields a root of **–1,** while an initial guess of 2 leads to an approximation of **1.618033989** for the third root.

problem set 93

1. A right circular cylinder is inscribed in a
(52) sphere of radius $\sqrt{3}$ meters, as shown.

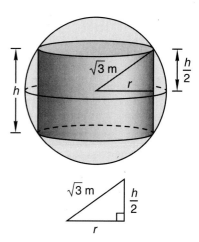

(a) The radius of the right circular
cylinder is r and the height of the
cylinder is h. Express the volume of
the right circular cylinder only in
terms of the variable r.

(b) Find the radius and the height of the
right circular cylinder of greatest
volume that can be inscribed in
the sphere.

(c) What is the maximal volume of this
right circular cylinder.

2. The time-dependent velocity function for a particle moving along the x-axis is v. Suppose
(90)

$$\int_1^3 v(t)\, dt = -4 \qquad \int_3^4 v(t)\, dt = 5 \qquad \int_4^7 v(t)\, dt = -7 \qquad \int_7^8 v(t)\, dt = 3$$

(a) How much does the position of the particle change during the interval [1, 8]?

(b) If the particle is at $x = 3$ when $t = 3$, what is the position of the particle when $t = 7$?

3. A particle moves along the x-axis so that its position as a function of time t is given by
(90) $x(t) = t^3 - 9t^2 + 15t + 3$.

(a) What are the positions of the particle at $t = 0$ and $t = 2$?

(b) What is the total distance traveled by the particle between $t = 0$ and $t = 4$?

4. The velocity function for a particle moving along the number line is $v(t) = 6\pi \sin(3\pi t)$, where
(90) $0 \le t \le 1$.

(a) Find the time(s) t for which the particle is momentarily at rest.

(b) Find the total distance traveled in the negative x-direction by the particle.

5. Use Newton's method to approximate the positive zero of the function $f(x) = x^2 + x - 3$ to
(93) nine decimal places.

6. Use Newton's method to approximate the zero of the function $f(x) = x^3 + x - 1$ in the
(93) interval [0, 1] to ten decimal places.

7. Suppose that $f(x) = x^3 + 2x + 2$ and f^{-1} is the inverse function of f. Find the slope of the
(92) graph f^{-1} at the point (2, 0).

8. Suppose that $f(x) = x^3 + 2x$ and f^{-1} is the inverse function of f. Evaluate $f^{-1}(3)$ and
(92) $(f^{-1})'(3)$.

Evaluate the limits in problems 9 and 10.

9. $\displaystyle\lim_{x \to 0} [4x \csc(3x)]$
(91)

10. $\displaystyle\lim_{x \to 1^+} \left(\frac{3}{x^2 - 1} - \frac{2}{x - 1} \right)$
(91)

11. Find the particular solution to $2\, dx - x\, dy = 0$ that intercepts the point $(e, 2)$.
(88)

12. Find the particular solution to $\dfrac{dy}{dx} = 1 + y^2$ that intercepts the point $\left(\dfrac{\pi}{4}, 1 \right)$.
(88)

13. Find the average value of the function $y = \sin^2 x$ on the interval $\left[0, \dfrac{\pi}{2} \right]$.
(89)

14. Let f be a continuous function on the closed interval $[a, b]$. Suppose that
(89) $\int_a^b f(x)\, dx = 18$, $b = 8$, and the average value of f on $[a, b]$ is 3. Find a.

15. Let $f(x) = (x + 1)^{1/3}$ on the interval $[-2, 0]$. Find a number $c \in [-2, 0]$ that confirms the
(89)   Mean Value Theorem for Integrals.

16. Let $f(x) = \ln |x|$ on the interval $[-1, 1]$. Does Rolle's theorem imply that there exists some
(85)   number c in the interval $(-1, 1)$ such that $f'(c) = 0$? Explain.

Integrate in problems 17–19.

17. $\displaystyle\int \cos^2 x \sin x\, dx$ **18.** $\displaystyle\int \cos (2x) \sin (2x)\, dx$ **19.** $\displaystyle\int \frac{\sin (2x)}{\sin^2 x}\, dx$
(76)   (76)   (66)

20. Let R be the region in the first quadrant bounded by the graph of $y = -x^3 + 3x^2 - 2x$ and the
(87) x-axis. Write a definite integral that can be used to find the volume of the solid formed when R
is revolved about the y-axis.

21. Let f and g be continuous functions that are defined for all real numbers x and that have the
(57)   following properties:

$$\int_0^1 f(x)\, dx = 2 \qquad \int_1^2 f(x)\, dx = 3 \qquad \int_0^1 g(x)\, dx = -1 \qquad \int_1^2 g(x)\, dx = -5$$

Find the value of $\displaystyle\int_0^2 [2f(x) - 3g(x)]\, dx$.

22. Let R be the region in the first quadrant bounded by the y-axis and the graphs of the functions
(46,59) $y = e^x$ and $y = k$ where $k > 1$.

   (a) Express the area of R as a function of k.

   (b) Find the value of k such that the area of R is 1 square unit.

   (c) If the line $y = k$ is moving upward at a rate of 4 units per second, at what rate is the area
of R changing when $k = \sqrt{e}$?

23. Determine the area of the region between $y = 4^x$ and the x-axis on the interval $[-2, 2]$.
(73)

24. Let $f(x) = ax^2 + bx + c$ for all real numbers x. Suppose that $y = 2x$ is tangent to the graph
(27)   of f at the origin and that the graph of f passes through $(2, 1)$. Find the values of a, b, and c, and
write the equation of f.

25. Let f and g be odd functions. Determine which one of the following statements is **not** true:
(68)
   A. $f + g$ is odd

   B. fg is even

   C. $f \circ g$ is even

   D. $f - g$ is odd

LESSON 94   *Solids of Revolution IV: Displaced Axes of Revolution*

Thus far we have considered solids of revolution formed by rotating regions about the y-axis or the
x-axis. If a region is rotated about a line parallel to the x-axis or the y-axis, a different solid is formed
than the one formed when it is rotated about the x- or y-axis. However, we can still use the integration
techniques from previous lessons to calculate the volumes of such solids.

example 94.1 Let R be the region bounded by the coordinate axes and the lines $y = x$ and $x = 5$. Find the volume of the solid generated by rotating R about the line $x = 5$.

solution There are two ways we can find the answer to this example. First, we see that the solid in question is simply a cone of radius 5 and height 5.

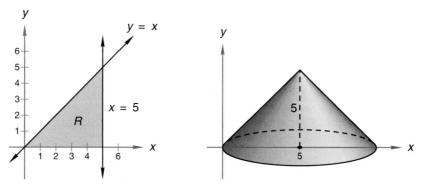

Applying the formula for the volume of a right circular cone, we find the volume to be

$$V = \frac{1}{3}\pi(5)^2(5)$$

$$= \frac{125}{3}\pi \text{ units}^3$$

The volume can also be determined using calculus. We draw the solid, as well as a representative disk.

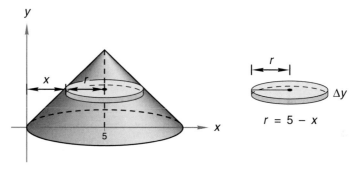

$$r = 5 - x$$

The volume of the representative disk is $\pi r^2 \, \Delta y$, or $\pi(5 - x)^2 \, \Delta y$. Since the disks are stacked from $y = 0$ to $y = 5$, the volume is

$$V = \int_{y=0}^{y=5} \pi(5 - x)^2 \, dy$$

We must write everything in terms of y. Since $y = x$ on the diagonal line, $r = 5 - y$ also.

$$V = \int_0^5 \pi(5 - y)^2 \, dy$$

Now we evaluate the integral.

$$V = \pi \int_0^5 (25 - 10y + y^2) \, dy$$

$$= \pi \left[25y - 5y^2 + \frac{y^3}{3} \right]_0^5$$

$$= \pi \left[125 - 125 + \frac{125}{3} \right]$$

$$= \frac{125}{3}\pi \text{ units}^3$$

The answer confirms the work at the beginning of this example.

example 94.2 Region R is bounded by $y = x^3$, the x-axis, and the line $x = 2$. Use the disk method to write an integral that represents the volume of the solid formed by rotating the region about the line $x = 2$. Evaluate this integral.

solution We show the region described, the solid formed, and a representative disk.

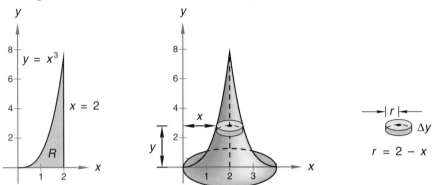

The volume of the representative disk is $\pi r^2 \, \Delta y$, and since r equals $2 - x$, the volume of the disk is $\pi(2 - x)^2 \, \Delta y$. The disks are stacked from $y = 0$ to $y = 8$, so the volume of the solid is

$$V = \int_{y=0}^{y=8} \pi(2 - x)^2 \, dy$$

The dy tells us that y is the variable of integration, so the integrand should have no variable other than y. For this problem, x and y are related by $y = x^3$, which tells us that $x = y^{1/3}$. Thus we replace x with $y^{1/3}$, expand, integrate, and evaluate.

$$V = \pi \int_0^8 (2 - y^{1/3})^2 \, dy \qquad \text{substituted}$$

$$= \pi \int_0^8 (4 - 4y^{1/3} + y^{2/3}) \, dy \qquad \text{expanded}$$

$$= \pi \left[4y - 3y^{4/3} + \frac{3y^{5/3}}{5} \right]_0^8 \qquad \text{integrated}$$

$$= \frac{16\pi}{5} \, \text{units}^3 \qquad \text{evaluated}$$

example 94.3 Region R is completely enclosed by $x = y^2$, $y = 2$, and the y-axis. The region is revolved about the line $y = 2$. Use the disk method to write an integral in terms of x whose value equals the volume of the solid generated.

solution We show the region defined, the solid formed, and a representative disk.

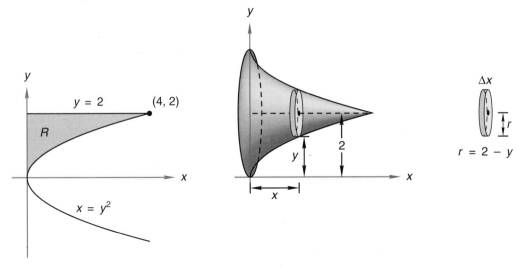

The volume of a representative disk is πr^2 times the thickness Δx. The radius r equals $2 - y$, so the volume of the disk is $\pi(2 - y)^2 \Delta x$. The disks are stacked from $x = 0$ to $x = 4$. Thus the volume of the whole solid is

$$V = \int_{x=0}^{x=4} \pi(2 - y)^2 \, dx$$

The dx tells us that x is the variable of integration, so the integrand should have no variable other than x. In this problem $x = y^2$. Since we are in the first quadrant, this can be rewritten as $y = x^{1/2}$. Substituting $x^{1/2}$ for y gives us the desired integral.

$$V = \pi \int_0^4 (2 - x^{1/2})^2 \, dx$$

A numerical answer, $\dfrac{8\pi}{3}$ units^3, can be found by expanding, integrating, and evaluating the integral.

example 94.4   The region defined in example 94.3 is rotated about the line $y = 3$. Determine the volume of this solid.

solution   We sketch the solid in question.

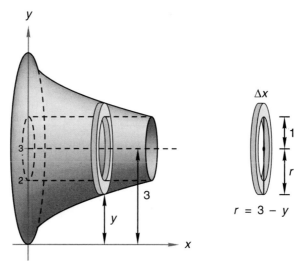

The representative washer has width Δx, outer radius $3 - y$, and inner radius $3 - 2$ (which is 1), so the volume of this washer is $\pi\left[(3 - y)^2 - 1^2\right] \Delta x$. The washers are stacked from $x = 0$ to $x = 4$. Therefore, the total volume of the solid is

$$V = \int_{x=0}^{x=4} \pi\left[(3 - y)^2 - 1^2\right] dx$$

We must write every term in the integrand in terms of x. Since $y = x^{1/2}$ in the example,

$$V = \int_0^4 \pi\left[(3 - x^{1/2})^2 - 1\right] dx$$

We can easily expand this, or we can attempt an approximation via the graphing calculator. Ignoring π for a moment, we look at

```
fnInt((3-√(X))²-1,X,0,4)
```

This expression yields 7.999999554, which appears to be an approximation of 8. Indeed, the correct answer is $V = \mathbf{8\pi}$ **units**^{3}.

example 94.5 Let R be the region bounded by $y = e^x$, the x-axis, $x = 1$, and $x = 2$. A solid of revolution is formed when this region is rotated about the line $x = 3$. Use the shell method to write an integral that could be evaluated to find the volume of this solid.

solution We show the region R, a sketch of the solid of revolution, a representative shell, and a flattened version of the shell.

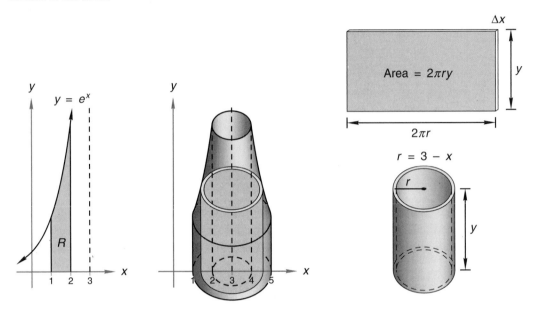

The volume of a representative shell is the area times the thickness.

$$V_{\text{shell}} = 2\pi r y \, \Delta x$$

The shells are stacked from $x = 1$ to $x = 2$. The radius of each shell is $3 - x$, the height is e^x, and the thickness is Δx. Thus, the volume of the solid is

$$V = 2\pi \int_1^2 (3 - x)e^x \, dx$$

When we multiply, we get

$$V = 6\pi \int_1^2 e^x \, dx - 2\pi \int_1^2 xe^x \, dx$$

The value of the first integral is

$$\left[6\pi e^x \right]_1^2 = 6\pi(e^2 - e)$$

and the value of the second integral, which can be found using integration by parts, is $2\pi e^2$.

problem set 94

1. A right circular cone is inscribed in a hemisphere so that the base of the cone is the same as the
    (46) base of the hemisphere. Suppose the surface area of the hemisphere, including its base, is increasing at a constant rate of 24 cm²/s.

    (a) Find the rate at which the radius of the sphere is increasing when $r = 4$ cm.

    (b) Use the information in (a) to find the rate at which the volume of the cone is increasing when $r = 4$ cm.

2. The time-dependent velocity function for a particle moving along the x-axis is v. Suppose
    (90)

$$\int_0^2 v(t) \, dt = -5 \qquad \int_2^3 v(t) \, dt = 7 \qquad \int_3^6 v(t) \, dt = -2$$

    (a) How much does the position of the particle change during the interval $[0, 6]$?

    (b) If the particle is at $x = 5$ when $t = 0$, what is the position of the particle when $t = 6$?

3. A rectangular tank 4 meters wide, 5 meters long, and 4 meters deep is three-quarters full of a
(74,77) fluid whose weight density is 5000 newtons per cubic meter.

    (a) Find the total force on the side of a wall whose width is 4 meters.

    (b) Find the total work done in pumping the fluid out of the top of the tank.

4. At $t = 0$, a ball is 20 meters above ground and moving upward at 20 meters per second.
(54)

    (a) Find the height, velocity, and acceleration functions that describe the ball's motion from
this point until the ball hits the ground.

    (b) Find the height, velocity, and acceleration of the ball at $t = 2$ seconds.

    (c) When does the ball hit the ground?

5. Region R is bounded by the x-axis, $y = x^3$, and $x = 1$. Find the volume of the solid formed
(94) when R is revolved about the line $x = 1$.

6. Region R is bounded by $x = y^2 + 1$ and $x = 2$. Use y as the variable of integration to write
(94) a definite integral whose value equals the volume of the solid formed when R is revolved about
the line $x = 3$.

7. Let R be the region between the x-axis and the graph of $y = \tan x$ on the interval $\left[0, \frac{\pi}{4}\right]$.
(94) Express the volume of the solid formed when R is rotated about the line $x = -1$ as an integral
in the variable x.

8. Let R be the region bounded by $y = e^x$, $x = 2$, $x = 3$, and $y = 0$. Use x as the variable of
(94) integration to write a definite integral whose value equals the volume of the solid formed when
R is rotated about the line $x = 4$.

9. Use Newton's method to approximate the positive zero of the function $f(x) = x^2 - x - 1$ to
(93) nine decimal places.

10. Use Newton's method to approximate the zero of the function $f(x) = x^3 - 3x + 3$ to nine
(93) decimal places.

11. The function $f(x) = x^3 + x + 1$ is a one-to-one function, and thus its inverse f^{-1} is also a
(92) function. Find the equation of the line tangent to the graph of f^{-1} at the point $(1, 0)$.

12. Suppose that $f(x) = \sin x$ where $-\frac{\pi}{2} \le x \le \frac{\pi}{2}$ and that f^{-1} is the inverse function of f.
(92) Evaluate $\left(f^{-1}\right)'$ at $x = \frac{1}{2}$.

Evaluate the limits in problems 13 and 14.

13. $\lim_{x \to 0} (\csc x - \cot x)$
(91)

14. $\lim_{x \to 0} \dfrac{x - \sin x}{x^3}$
(79)

15. Find the particular solution to $\dfrac{dy}{dx} = e^{x-y}$ that intercepts the point $(1, 1)$.
(88)

16. Find the average value of the function $f(x) = \sqrt{9 - x^2}$ on the interval $[0, 3]$. (*Hint:* Find
(89) the value of the definite integral by interpreting it as the measure of the area of a familiar
geometric figure.)

17. Let f be the function defined by $f(x) = x^3 + 2$ on the interval $[0, 2]$. Find a number
(89) $c \in [0, 2]$ that confirms the Mean Value Theorem for Integrals.

18. Let f be the function defined by $f(x) = x^2 + 1$ on the interval $[-1, 1]$. Find a number
(85) $c \in [-1, 1]$ that confirms the Mean Value Theorem (for derivatives).

19. Region R is bounded by the graphs of $x = -y^2 - y + 2$ and $y = -x - 2$. Use y as the
(67) variable of integration to write an integral whose value equals the area of R.

20. Let f be a function defined as $f(t) = \begin{cases} a \sin t - b \cos t & \text{when } t \geq \pi/2 \\ \cos t & \text{when } t < \pi/2. \end{cases}$ Find the values of a and b that
(75) make f continuous for all values of t.

21. Region R is bounded by the graph of $y = \tan x$ and the x-axis on the interval $[\frac{\pi}{6}, \frac{\pi}{4}]$. Find the
(59) exact area of R. (*Note:* The integral can be evaluated if $\tan x$ is rewritten as a quotient of two functions.)

22. Suppose $f(x) = e^x$ and $g(x) = \sin x$. Let $h(x) = f(g(x))$. Evaluate $h'\left(\dfrac{\pi}{2}\right)$.
(50)

23. Evaluate: $\dfrac{d}{dx}\left[\sin(x^2 - 1) + \dfrac{\sin x + 1}{e^x - 2} \right] + \displaystyle\int \dfrac{x^2}{x^3 - 1}\, dx$
(50,66)

24. Suppose f is a function and so is its inverse. Which of the following sets of points could lie on f?
(58)
   A. $\{(1, 2), (2, 3), (3, 4), (4, 5)\}$ B. $\{(1, 2), (2, 3), (1, 3), (4, 5)\}$
   C. $\{(1, 1), (2, 2), (1, 2), (3, 3)\}$ D. $\{(1, -1), (-1, 1), (2, -1), (3, 1)\}$

25. Let $f(x) = \dfrac{2x^3 - x^2 + 3}{2 - x}$.
(6,80)

  (a) Determine the zeros, vertical asymptotes, and end behavior of the function.

  (b) Sketch the graph of the function.

  (c) Determine the domain and range of the function.

LESSON 95 *Trapezoidal Rule • Error Bound for the Trapezoidal Rule*

95.A
trapezoidal rule

We have conducted a rather extensive investigation into evaluating integrals through many different methods of integration. As extensive as it may seem, however, this investigation is far from complete. Even if it were complete, the fact remains that some simple functions do not have simple integrals. Such an example is $\int_1^2 \frac{\cos x}{x}\, dx$. In cases like this we may wish to approximate the definite integral by summing a finite number of areas. Such techniques are usually referred to as **numerical integration.** The methods of upper and lower rectangles, which we have already studied, are methods of numerical integration. You might recall that the upper and lower rectangle methods did not produce results whose accuracy was particularly outstanding. For this reason a great deal of effort has been put into studying other methods of numerical integration.

In this lesson we consider another method, the **trapezoidal rule.** As far as numerical integration techniques go, the trapezoidal rule is quite simple, and it produces results with a fair degree of accuracy. In order to derive the trapezoidal rule, we first recall that the area of the following trapezoid is given by the formula to its right.

$$A = \frac{1}{2}(B_1 + B_2)h$$

Suppose we wish to approximate the definite integral $\int_a^b f(x)\,dx$. (For now, we assume f is a positive-valued function over the interval (a, b).) As before, we divide the interval into n subintervals, each of which has a width of $h = \frac{b-a}{n}$.

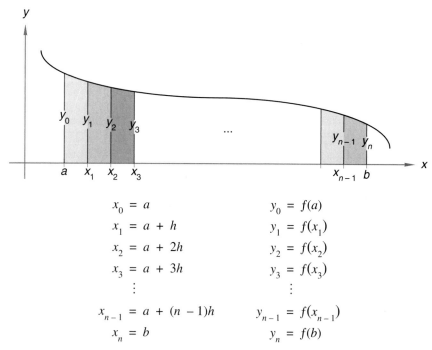

$$x_0 = a \qquad\qquad y_0 = f(a)$$
$$x_1 = a + h \qquad\qquad y_1 = f(x_1)$$
$$x_2 = a + 2h \qquad\qquad y_2 = f(x_2)$$
$$x_3 = a + 3h \qquad\qquad y_3 = f(x_3)$$
$$\vdots \qquad\qquad\qquad \vdots$$
$$x_{n-1} = a + (n-1)h \qquad\qquad y_{n-1} = f(x_{n-1})$$
$$x_n = b \qquad\qquad y_n = f(b)$$

Now, rather than using rectangles to approximate the area under this curve, we use trapezoids.

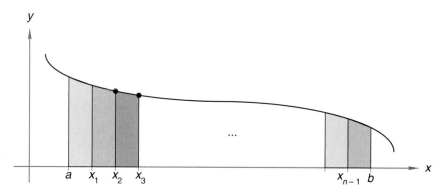

We see that the exact area A is approximately equal to the following:

$$A \approx T = \frac{1}{2}(y_0 + y_1)h + \frac{1}{2}(y_1 + y_2)h + \frac{1}{2}(y_2 + y_3)h + \cdots$$
$$\cdots + \frac{1}{2}(y_{n-2} + y_{n-1})h + \frac{1}{2}(y_{n-1} + y_n)h$$
$$= \frac{1}{2}h(y_0 + 2y_1 + 2y_2 + 2y_3 + \cdots + 2y_{n-2} + 2y_{n-1} + y_n)$$

$$\boxed{T = \frac{b-a}{2n}(y_0 + 2y_1 + 2y_2 + \cdots + 2y_{n-2} + 2y_{n-1} + y_n)}$$

This formula is known as the trapezoidal rule.

example 95.1 Approximate $\int_1^3 x^2\,dx$ using the trapezoidal rule with $n = 4$, and compare the estimate to the exact value obtained using the Fundamental Theorem of Calculus.

solution First we partition the interval into four subintervals.

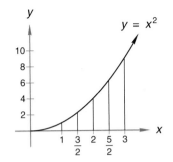

This produces the following data.

x-values	1	$\dfrac{3}{2}$	2	$\dfrac{5}{2}$	3
y-values	1	$\dfrac{9}{4}$	4	$\dfrac{25}{4}$	9

Using these, we can apply the trapezoidal rule to approximate the integral.

$$T = \frac{3-1}{2(4)}\left(1 + 2\left(\frac{9}{4}\right) + 2(4) + 2\left(\frac{25}{4}\right) + 9\right)$$

$$= \frac{1}{4}(18 + 17)$$

$$= \frac{35}{4}$$

Next we find the exact value of the integral.

$$\int_1^3 x^2\,dx = \frac{1}{3}x^3\bigg]_1^3 = 9 - \frac{1}{3} = \frac{27}{3} - \frac{1}{3} = \frac{26}{3} = \frac{104}{12}$$

Notice that our approximation is just $\frac{1}{12}$ **more than the exact value** of the integral $\left(\frac{35}{4} = \frac{105}{12}\right)$. As with upper and lower rectangles, if the number of subintervals increases, the approximation is even closer to the actual value.

example 95.2 Approximate $\int_{3\pi/2}^{2\pi} \dfrac{\cos x}{x}\,dx$ using the trapezoidal rule with $n = 4$.

solution We have introduced no method for finding the exact value of this integral, but we can use the trapezoidal rule to approximate its value.

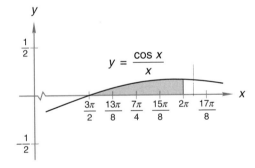

We have the following data:

x-values	$\dfrac{3\pi}{2}$	$\dfrac{13\pi}{8}$	$\dfrac{7\pi}{4}$	$\dfrac{15\pi}{8}$	2π
y-values	0	0.0750	0.1286	0.1568	0.1592

The trapezoidal rule approximation is as follows:

$$T = \frac{2\pi - \dfrac{3\pi}{2}}{2(4)}(0 + 2(0.0750) + 2(0.1286) + 2(0.1568) + 0.1592)$$

$$= \frac{\pi}{16}(0 + 0.15 + 0.2572 + 0.3136 + 0.1592)$$

$$\approx \mathbf{0.1728}$$

95.B

error bound for the trapezoidal rule

With any numerical approximation, it is both useful and important to know how far the approximation can deviate from the actual value. Using advanced techniques beyond the scope of this text, one can show that if f is continuous on $[a, b]$ and twice differentiable on (a, b), then the error E in approximating $\int_a^b f(x)\, dx$ by the trapezoidal rule is bounded as follows:

$$E \leq \frac{b - a}{12} \cdot h^2 \left(\max \left|f''(x)\right|\right)$$

Here, $\max \left|f''(x)\right|$ is the maximum value of $\left|f''(x)\right|$ over the interval $a \leq x \leq b$. Since $h = \frac{b-a}{n}$, we see that

$$E \leq \frac{(b - a)^3}{12n^2}\left(\max \left|f''(x)\right|\right)$$

With this we can state how accurate a trapezoidal rule approximation is without having to know the exact value of $\int_a^b f(x)\, dx$.

example 95.3   Find the largest possible error of the approximation in example 95.1.

solution   Note that $f''(x) = 2$, so $\max \left|f''(x)\right| = 2$. Then

$$E \leq \frac{(b - a)^3}{12n^2}(2)$$

$$E \leq \frac{(3 - 1)^3}{12(4)^2}(2)$$

$$E \leq \frac{16}{12 \cdot 16}$$

$$E \leq \frac{1}{12}$$

That is precisely the difference calculated in example 95.1.

example 95.4   Determine the number of subintervals needed to guarantee a trapezoidal rule approximation of $\int_1^3 (x^3 - x)\, dx$ with an error less than 10^{-3}.

solution   We know $E \leq \frac{(b-a)^3}{12n^2}\left(\max \left|f''(x)\right|\right)$ where $a = 1$ and $b = 3$. Since $f''(x) = 6x$ in this case and $1 \leq x \leq 3$, we see that $\max \left|f''(x)\right| = 6 \cdot 3 = 18$ on this interval. Therefore

$$E \leq \frac{(3 - 1)^3}{12n^2}(18) = \frac{12}{n^2}$$

To guarantee that $E < 10^{-3}$, we must find n such that

$$E \leq \frac{12}{n^2} < 10^{-3}$$

$$\frac{12}{n^2} < \frac{1}{1000}$$

$$n^2 > 12{,}000$$

$$n > \sqrt{12{,}000}$$

So, $n > 109.5445$. Since n must also be an integer, we use $n = $ **110 subintervals.** This guarantees that $E < 10^{-3}$. Note that we could choose an n larger than 110—for example, 111, 112, 250, or 1000—and the trapezoidal rule would still yield an answer with $E < 10^{-3}$.

We note that using the trapezoidal rule with $n = 110$ subinterval yields an approximation of $16\frac{2}{3025}$, whereas

$$\int_1^3 (x^3 - x)\, dx = 16$$

Hence, $E = \dfrac{2}{3025}$, which is less than $\dfrac{1}{1000}$.

These last two examples dealt with integrals that we know how to integrate. Keep in mind that the purpose of the trapezoidal rule is to approximate definite integrals, such as the one in example 95.2, that we cannot evaluate for exact answers.

problem set 95

1. *(52)* A conical tent with no floor is to be shaped like a right circular cone, as shown. The volume of the conical tent must be 100 cubic meters. The radius of the conical tent is r and the height is h.

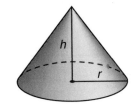

(a) Express the lateral surface area of the conical tent in terms of r.

(b) Find the values of r and h that minimize the tent's lateral surface area (the amount of material used to construct the tent).

2. *(62)* A variable force of $F(x) = \sqrt{16 - x^2}$ newtons (for x measured in meters) is applied to an object, moving it along a number line in the direction of the force. Find the work done by the force in moving the object from $x = 0$ meters to $x = 4$ meters. (*Hint:* Interpret the definite integral geometrically.)

3. *(46)* A point moves along the curve $y = x^2 + 2$ so that its x-coordinate is increasing at the constant rate of $\frac{4}{5}$ units per second.

(a) Find the rate at which the y-coordinate is changing when the point has coordinates $(1, 3)$.

(b) Find the rate at which the distance from the origin is changing when the point has coordinates $(1, 3)$.

4. *(78)* A particle moves along the x-axis so that its position as a function of time t is given by $x(t) = 2t^3 - 21t^2 + 60t + 2$. How many times does the particle reverse its direction of movement between $t = 0$ and $t = 7$?

5. *(90)* The velocity function for a particle moving along the number line is $v(t) = 8\pi \cos\left(4\pi t + \frac{\pi}{2}\right)$.

(a) Find the time(s) t, $0 \le t \le 1$, for which the particle is momentarily at rest.

(b) Find the total distance traveled by the particle in the positive x direction over the interval $0 \le t \le 1$.

6. *(95)* (a) Approximate $\int_1^4 x^2 \, dx$ using the trapezoidal rule with $n = 4$.

(b) Find the exact area under the curve $f(x) = x^2$ on the interval $[1, 4]$ by integrating. Compare this answer to the estimate in (a).

(c) Find the maximum possible error in the answer to (a).

(d) Find the number of equal-width subdivisions required to approximate $\int_1^4 x^2 \, dx$ with an error of less than 0.001.

7. *(95)* Approximate $\int_0^{\pi/4} \sec^3 x \, dx$ using the trapezoidal rule with $n = 4$.

8. *(93)* If $f(x) = x^4 - 3$, then $f(1) = -2$ and $f(2) = 13$. This means f has a zero between $x = 1$ and $x = 2$. Find the zero of f in $[1, 2]$ using Newton's method. Begin with a seed value of 1.5, and find the second approximation without using a calculator.

9. *(92)* Suppose that $f(x) = x^3 - 8$ and that f^{-1} is the inverse function of f. Evaluate $\left(f^{-1}\right)'(0)$.

10. *(92)* Suppose that $f(x) = \cos x$, where $0 \le x \le \pi$, and that f^{-1} is the inverse function of f. Evaluate $\left(f^{-1}\right)'\left(\frac{1}{2}\right)$.

Evaluate the limits in problems 11–14.

11. $\lim\limits_{x \to \infty} \left(e^{-x^2} \ln x \right)$
(91)

12. $\lim\limits_{x \to \pi/2} \sec x$
(70)

13. $\lim\limits_{x \to -3} \left(\dfrac{2x}{x^2 + 2x - 3} - \dfrac{3}{x + 3} \right)$
(91)

14. $\lim\limits_{x \to \infty} \left(x \sin \dfrac{1}{x} \right)$
(91)

15. Let R be the region bounded by $y = \sin x$ and the x-axis on the interval $[0, \pi]$.
(94)

(a) Find the volume of the solid formed when R is revolved about the x-axis.

(b) Find the volume of the solid formed when R is revolved about the line $x = -1$.

16. Find the particular solution to the differential equation $\frac{dy}{dx} = 2xy^2$ that intercepts the point
(88) $(1, -1)$.

17. The general solution to the differential equation $\dfrac{dy}{dx} = \dfrac{1 - 2x}{2y}$ is a family of
(88)

A. Straight lines   B. Circles   C. Parabolas

D. Ellipses   E. Hyperbolas

18. Let f be the function defined by $f(x) = |x|$ on the interval $[-2, 3]$. Find a number $c \in [-2, 3]$
(89) that confirms the Mean Value Theorem for Integrals.

19. In the aftermath of a car accident it is concluded that one car slowed to a stop in 12 seconds while
(85) skidding 600 feet.

(a) Find the average speed of the car during the 12-second interval.

(b) If the posted speed limit along the road is 30 mph, can it be proved that the driver had been speeding? Explain. (*Note:* 1 mile $=$ 5280 feet)

Integrate in problems 20 and 21.

20. $\displaystyle\int \dfrac{3}{x^2 + 16}\, dx$
(64)

21. $\displaystyle\int \dfrac{e^x + \cos x}{e^x + \sin x}\, dx$
(66)

22. Suppose $f(x) = \arctan(x^2)$ and $g(x) = e^x$. Let $h(x) = f(g(x))$. Evaluate $h'(0)$.
(50)

23. Let f be a function defined as $f(x) = \begin{cases} x^2 + 2, & \text{when } x < 2 \\ ax + b, & \text{when } x \geq 2 \end{cases}$ Find the numerical values of a and b that
(82) make f differentiable for all values of x.

24. Let R be the region between $y = \cos x$ and the x-axis on the interval $[0, \frac{\pi}{2}]$. Find the value
(59) of $c \in [0, \frac{\pi}{2}]$ for which the vertical line $x = c$ divides R into two regions of equal area.

25. Which of the following functions shows that the statement "If a function is continuous at
(75,82) $x = 0$, then the function is differentiable at $x = 0$" is **false**?

A. $f(x) = x^2$ B. $f(x) = x^{1/2}$ C. $f(x) = x^{5/2}$

D. $f(x) = x^{3/2}$ E. $f(x) = x^{2/3}$

LESSON 96 *Derivatives and Integrals of Functions Involving Absolute Value*

In Lesson 72 we found that the derivative of $|f(x)|$ equals the derivative of $f(x)$ when $f(x)$ is positive and equals the negative of the derivative of $f(x)$ when $f(x)$ is negative. This rule can be recalled easily by visualizing the graph of $y = \sin x$ and the graph of $y = |\sin x|$.

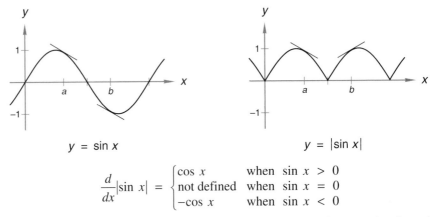

$$y = \sin x \qquad\qquad y = |\sin x|$$

$$\frac{d}{dx}|\sin x| = \begin{cases} \cos x & \text{when } \sin x > 0 \\ \text{not defined} & \text{when } \sin x = 0 \\ -\cos x & \text{when } \sin x < 0 \end{cases}$$

When $x = a$ the lines tangent to the two graphs have the same slopes, because $\sin x$ is positive when x equals a. When $x = b$ the lines tangent to the graphs have different slopes, because $\sin x$ is negative when x equals b.

The derivative of $|f(x)|$ can usually[†] be written as

$$\frac{d}{dx}|f(x)| = \frac{f(x)}{|f(x)|}\frac{d}{dx}f(x)$$

The value of $f(x)$ divided by $|f(x)|$ is 1 when $f(x)$ is positive, -1 when $f(x)$ is negative, and not defined when $f(x)$ equals zero. Thus

$$\frac{d}{dx}|\sin x| = \frac{\sin x}{|\sin x|}(\cos x)$$

makes exactly the same statement as the three-part piecewise definition above.

If the absolute value notation is used only with the independent variable

$$y = f(|x|)$$

the meaning is entirely different. This function is an even function because it has the same value for $-x$ that it has for $+x$. The graph of the function to the left of the origin is a mirror image of the graph to the right of the origin. Graphing the function $y = f(|x|)$ requires that the graph of $y = f(x)$ to the left of the origin be replaced with the mirror image of the graph of $y = f(x)$ to the right of the origin. The graph of $y = f(x)$ is shown in the figure on the left-hand side below.

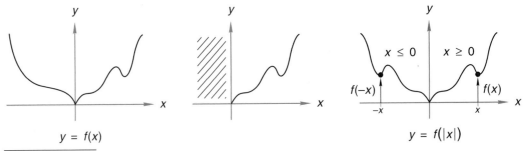

$$y = f(x) \qquad\qquad\qquad\qquad y = f(|x|)$$

[†]The derivative cannot be written as described if $f'(x) = 0$ when $f(x) = 0$. In this case $\frac{d}{dx}|f(x)| = 0$.

In the center figure we discard the portion of the graph to the left of the origin, and in the figure on the right-hand side the discarded portion has been replaced with the graph of $y = f(-x)$ where $x \le 0$. Since x is negative, every value of $f(-x)$ on the left is exactly the same as the corresponding value of $f(x)$ on the right.

To find the derivative of a function of the absolute value of x, we redefine the function as a piecewise function that does not use absolute value.

example 96.1   Let $y = e^{|x|}$. Find $\dfrac{dy}{dx}$.

solution   We begin by redefining the function without using the absolute value notation.

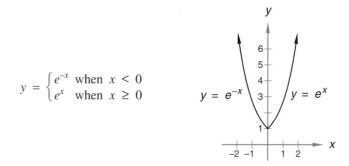

$$y = \begin{cases} e^{-x} & \text{when } x < 0 \\ e^{x} & \text{when } x \ge 0 \end{cases}$$

When x is greater than zero,

$$\frac{d}{dx}e^{|x|} = \frac{d}{dx}e^{x} = e^{x}$$

When x is less than zero, we use the chain rule to get

$$\frac{d}{dx}e^{|x|} = \frac{d}{dx}(e^{-x}) = e^{-x}(-1) = -e^{-x}$$

Because the left-hand derivative at $x = 0$ does not equal the right-hand derivative at $x = 0$, the derivative at $x = 0$ is not defined for this function.

$$\frac{dy}{dx} = \begin{cases} -e^{-x} & \text{when } x < 0 \\ e^{x} & \text{when } x > 0 \end{cases}$$

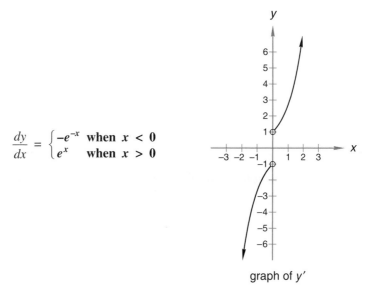

graph of y'

example 96.2   Let $f(x) = \cos |2x|$. Find $f'(x)$.

solution   We redefine the function as a piecewise function to remove the absolute value notation.

$$f(x) = \begin{cases} \cos (2x) & \text{when } x \geq 0 \\ \cos (-2x) & \text{when } x < 0 \end{cases}$$

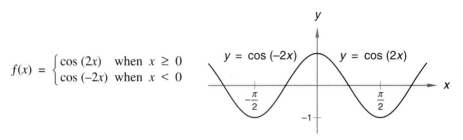

Of course, cosine is an even function, so $\cos (-2x)$ equals $\cos (2x)$, which means the piecewise definition is unnecessary. This is clear from the graph above.

$$f'(x) = \frac{d}{dx}\cos |2x| = \frac{d}{dx}\cos (2x) = -2 \sin (2x)$$

example 96.3   Evaluate: $\int_{-3}^{3} |x + 1| \, dx$

solution   We begin with a graph of the function. On the left-hand side is the graph of the equation $y = x + 1$, and on the right-hand side is the graph of the equation $y = |x + 1|$. We show the regions bounded by the graph and the x-axis on the interval $[-3, 3]$.

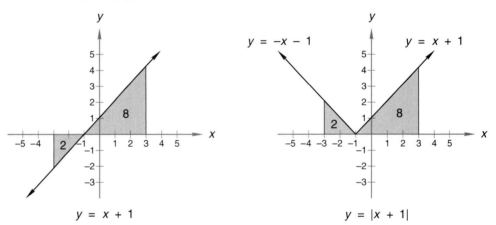

$$y = x + 1 \qquad\qquad\qquad y = |x + 1|$$

We have been asked to find the sum of the two triangular areas. By using $\frac{1}{2}bh$, we find that the area of the small triangle is 2 and the area of the large triangle is 8, as shown. So the answer is 10. To get this answer by using definite integrals, we can add the negative of the integral of $x + 1$ from -3 to -1 to the integral of $x + 1$ from -1 to 3, as shown on the left-hand side below.

$$-\int_{-3}^{-1} (x + 1) \, dx + \int_{-1}^{3} (x + 1) \, dx \qquad \text{or} \qquad \int_{-3}^{-1} (-x - 1) \, dx + \int_{-1}^{3} (x + 1) \, dx$$

$$= -(-2) + 8 = \mathbf{10} \qquad\qquad\qquad\qquad = 2 + 8 = \mathbf{10}$$

On the right-hand side we get the same result by adding the integral of $-x - 1$ from -3 to -1 to the integral of $x + 1$ from -1 to 3.

example 96.4   Evaluate: $\int_{-\pi/2}^{0} \sin |2x| \, dx$

solution   We begin by redefining $\sin |2x|$ without using the absolute-value notation. If $f(x) = \sin |2x|$, then

$$f(x) = \sin (2x) \quad \text{when } x \geq 0$$

$$f(x) = \sin (-2x) \quad \text{when } x < 0$$

A graph of the function is always helpful. To the right of the origin, we show the graph of $y = \sin(2x)$. To the left of the origin, we show the graph of $y = \sin(-2x)$, which is a mirror image of the graph to the right of the origin.

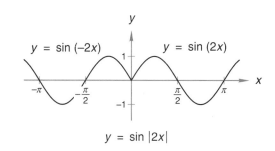

$$y = \sin|2x|$$

Because $\sin|2x| = \sin(-2x)$ over the interval $\left[-\dfrac{\pi}{2}, 0\right]$, we have

$$\int_{-\pi/2}^{0} \sin|2x|\,dx = \int_{-\pi/2}^{0} \sin(-2x)\,dx$$

$$= \frac{1}{2}\int_{-\pi/2}^{0} [-\sin(-2x)](-2\,dx)$$

$$= \frac{1}{2}[\cos(-2x)]_{-\pi/2}^{0}$$

$$= \frac{1}{2}\left\{\cos 0 - \cos\left[(-2)\left(-\frac{\pi}{2}\right)\right]\right\}$$

$$= \frac{1}{2}(1 - \cos\pi) = \frac{1}{2}(2) = \mathbf{1}$$

example 96.5   Evaluate: $\displaystyle\int_{-\pi}^{\pi} |\sin x|\,dx$

solution   The graph of $y = |\sin x|$ indicates that the integral equals the area between the x-axis and the graph from $x = -\pi$ to $x = \pi$. This is twice the area from $x = 0$ to $x = \pi$. Thus we simply find the integral from 0 to π and multiply by 2.

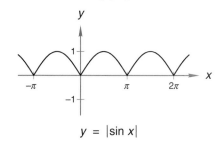

$$y = |\sin x|$$

$$\int_{-\pi}^{\pi} |\sin x|\,dx = 2\int_{0}^{\pi} \sin x\,dx$$

$$= 2[-\cos x]_{0}^{\pi}$$

$$= 2(1 + 1)$$

$$= \mathbf{4}$$

example 96.6   Let $f(x) = \left|\sin x - \dfrac{3}{4}\right|$. Find the maximum value of f.

solution   Since this is a calculus course, we are tempted to try to take the derivative of f and find its value when $f' = 0$. However, we investigate this function by drawing its graph rather than trying to find its derivative. On the left-hand side we show the graph of $y = \sin x - \frac{3}{4}$.

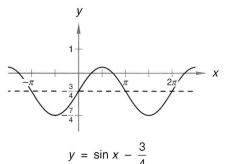

$$y = \sin x - \frac{3}{4}$$

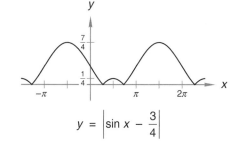

$$y = \left|\sin x - \frac{3}{4}\right|$$

On the right-hand side we show the graph of the absolute value of the function. Its maximum value is $\frac{7}{4}$. The graph on the right-hand side was really not necessary, because the graph on the left-hand side went down to a y-value of $-\frac{7}{4}$, and the absolute value of $-\frac{7}{4}$ is $\frac{7}{4}$. In this example a careful interpretation of the graph, not calculus, was used to find the maximum value of f.

example 96.7   Given that f is a continuous function for all real numbers and given that the maximum value of f is 6 and the minimum value of f is -12, which of the following must be true?

A. The maximum value of $|f(x + 1)|$ is 6.

B. The minimum value of $f(|x|)$ is 0.

C. The maximum value of $|f(x)|$ is 12.

solution   This question is typical of questions that appear on multiple-choice calculus tests. One counterexample is enough to eliminate a choice. We can eliminate A and B by using the graphs shown below.

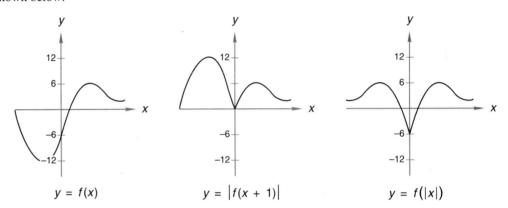

$$y = f(x) \qquad\qquad y = |f(x + 1)| \qquad\qquad y = f(|x|)$$

The graph of f shows that f has a maximum value of 6 and a minimum value of -12. The next graph shows that $|f(x + 1)|$ has a maximum value greater than 6, which eliminates choice A. The final graph shows a minimum value that is less than zero, which eliminates choice B. **Choice C is correct** because the maximum value of the absolute value of a function whose extreme values are 6 and -12 is 12.

problem set 96

1. A particle moves along the x-axis so that its position at time t $(t > 0)$ is given by
    $^{(90)}$ $x(t) = 2t^3 - 9t^2 + 12t + 1$.

    (a) Find the times when the particle is moving to the left.

    (b) Find the total distance traveled by the particle between the times $t = 0$ and $t = 4$.

2. Suppose f is defined on the interval $I = \left[-1, \frac{1}{2}\right]$ by $f(x) = \left|x^2 - 1\right|$.
    $^{(96)}$

    (a) Find all the critical numbers of f on I.

    (b) Use the critical number theorem to determine the maximum and minimum values of f.

Evaluate the definite integrals in problems 3 and 4.

3. $\displaystyle\int_{-2}^{3} |x + 1|\, dx$
    $^{(96)}$

4. $\displaystyle\int_{-2}^{1} \left|x^2 + x\right| dx$
    $^{(96)}$

5. Suppose $f(x) = \left|\cos x - \dfrac{1}{2}\right|$. Determine the maximum value of f.
    $^{(96)}$

6. Let f be a continuous function for all real numbers. Assume the maximum value of f is 7 and
    $^{(96)}$ the minimum value of f is -10. Which of the following statements must be true?

    A. The maximum value of $|f(x)|$ is 7.

    B. The minimum value of $f(|x|)$ is 0.

    C. The maximum value of $|f(x)|$ is 10.

7. (a) Use the trapezoidal rule with $n = 5$ to approximate $\int_0^1 x^3 \, dx$.
(95)

    (b) Find the exact area under the curve $f(x) = x^3$ on the interval $[0, 1]$ by integrating. Compare this answer to the estimate in (a).

    (c) Find an upper bound for the error in approximating the value of $\int_0^1 x^3 \, dx$ using the trapezoidal rule with $n = 5$.

    (d) Find the number of equal-width subdivisions that must be used with the trapezoidal rule to approximate $\int_0^1 x^3 \, dx$ with an error of absolute value less than 10^{-4}.

8. Use the trapezoidal rule with $n = 5$ to approximate $\int_0^1 \sqrt{1 + x^3} \, dx$.
(95)

9. Let R be the region between $y = x^4$ and the x-axis on the interval $[0, 1]$. Express the volume
(94) of the solid formed when R is rotated about the line $x = 1$ as an integral in terms of the variable x.

10. Let R be the region completely enclosed by the graphs of $y = x^2$ and $y = x$. Use x as the
(94) variable of integration to write a definite integral whose value equals the volume of the solid formed when R is rotated about the line $y = -1$.

11. Let R be the region bounded by $y = \sin x$ and the x-axis on the interval $[0, \pi]$. Express the
(94) volume of the solid formed when R is rotated about the line $x = 2\pi$ as an integral in terms of the variable x.

12. Without using a calculator, use Newton's method to approximate the zero of the function
(93) $f(x) = x^4 + x - 3$ on the interval $[1, 2]$. Begin with the seed value $x_1 = 1.5$ and perform one iteration.

13. Suppose that $f(x) = x^3 + 3x - 4$ and f^{-1} is the inverse function of f. Find the slope of the
(92) graph of the inverse function at the point $(-4, 0)$.

Evaluate the limits in problems 14–16.

14. $\lim\limits_{x \to 0^+} (x^2 \ln x)$
(91)

15. $\lim\limits_{x \to \pi/2} \dfrac{1 + \tan x}{\tan x}$
(79)

16. $\lim\limits_{x \to 3} \dfrac{e^x - e^3}{x - 3}$
(44)

17. If interest is compounded continuously, the rate of increase of money in an account is
(26) proportional to the amount of money present. If \$500 is deposited in an account at a particular continuous interest rate and grows to \$911 in 10 years, how much must be deposited in the account for it to reach \$20,000 in 20 years?

18. Suppose that f is an odd function, g is an even function, and both functions are defined for all
(86) real numbers. Determine whether each of the following functions is odd, even, or neither.

    (a) fg (b) $\dfrac{f}{g}$ (c) f^2 (d) $f^2 g^3$

19. Differentiate $y = x^{\sqrt{x}}$ with respect to x.
(84)

20. Find the area under one arch of the graph of $y = 2 \sin^2 x$.
(83)

21. Suppose f is a function that is continuous at $x = 2$. Which of the following statements must
(75) be true?

    A. $\lim\limits_{x \to 2} f(x) = f(2)$ B. f is differentiable at $x = 2$.

    C. $\lim\limits_{x \to 2} \dfrac{f(x) - f(2)}{x - 2} = f'(2)$ D. f attains a maximum value at $x = 2$.

22. Find the interval(s) on which the graph of $y = x^3 - 6x^2 + 6x + 1$ is concave upward.
(49)

23. Compute $\dfrac{d^3 y}{dx^3}$ where $y = (x - 4)^6 + \sin (2x)$.
(27)

24. If f is the function defined by $f(x) = x^3 + kx$ for all real numbers x, then f has one local
(63,75)   minimum value and one local maximum value

    A. for any real value of k.   B. when $k > 0$.   C. when $k = 0$.

    D. for no real values k.   E. when $k < 0$.

25. Which of the following is the inverse function of $y = x$?
(58)

    A. $y = x$ B. $y = -x$ C. $-\dfrac{1}{2}$ D. $y = \sqrt{x}$

LESSON 97 *Solids Defined by Cross Sections*

All of the volumes of solids we have found up to this point have been solids of revolution. In some cases we can find the volume of rather interesting solids that are not solids of revolution. In this lesson we shall investigate solids that have parallel cross sections that are all of the same simple geometric shape, such as squares, circles, or triangles. What you should see as we progress is that problems of this type are simply generalized disk problems. In the disk method the volume of a solid is represented by the following integral:

$$\int_a^b \pi r^2 \, dx$$

(Here we are assuming the solid was formed by revolving a region about the x-axis.) In essence, this integral represents a sum of volumes of arbitrarily thin disks.

$$\int_a^b \pi r^2 \, dx$$

sum   area of   width of
circular   disk
disk

However, there is nothing special about circular disks. In general, it should be possible to find the volume of any solid with well-defined cross sections, which leads to the following general formulas:

$$V = \int_{x=a}^{x=b} A(x) \, dx \qquad \text{or} \qquad V = \int_{y=a}^{y=b} A(y) \, dy$$

The volume formula on the left-hand side is used when the cross-sectional slices are stacked along the x-axis, (i.e., parallel to the y-axis), while the formula on the right-hand side is used when the slices are stacked up the y-axis (i.e., parallel to the x-axis). The functions $A(x)$ and $A(y)$ represent the area of a typical slice, while dx and dy represent the thickness of the slice. The integrals simply sum the volumes of an infinite number of infinitesimally thin slices.

example 97.1 The base of a solid is the region R, which is bounded by $y = \frac{1}{2}x$, $y = -\frac{1}{2}x + 4$, and the y-axis. Every vertical cross section of the solid parallel to the y-axis is a rectangle with a height of 5. Find the volume of the solid.

solution First we draw a picture. The shaded portion represents R as given.

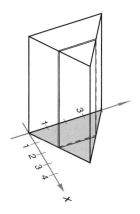

Our procedure is actually quite similar to the disk method. In this particular situation, however, each slice is a rectangle of height 5 instead of a circular disk; but a general formula still applies.

$$V = \int_a^b A(x)\, dx \qquad \text{or} \qquad V = \int_a^b A(y)\, dy$$

Since the slices are parallel to the y-axis, we use the first formula. The plates are stacked from $x = 0$ to $x = 4$. The area of each rectangle is

$$\underbrace{5}_{\text{height}} \times \underbrace{\left(-\frac{1}{2}x + 4 - \frac{1}{2}x\right)}_{\text{base}}$$

So the volume is

$$
\begin{aligned}
V &= \int_a^b A(x)\, dx & \text{general formula}\\[6pt]
&= \int_0^4 5\left(-\frac{1}{2}x + 4 - \frac{1}{2}x\right) dx & \text{substituted}\\[6pt]
&= 5\int_0^4 (-x + 4)\, dx & \text{simplified integrand}\\[6pt]
&= 5\left[-\frac{x^2}{2} + 4x\right]_0^4 & \text{integrated}\\[6pt]
&= 5(-8 + 16) = \textbf{40 units}^3 & \text{evaluated}
\end{aligned}
$$

Since this object is a prism, the result can be confirmed using geometry. The volume of a prism equals the area of the base times the height of the prism. From the diagram we see that the triangle has a base of 4 units in length and that the height (of the triangular base) is also 4 units. The height of the solid is 5, so the volume is $5 \times \left(\frac{1}{2}(4)(4)\right) = 5 \times 8 = 40$ units³, as expected.

example 97.2 The base of a solid is the region enclosed by a circle with a radius of 2 units centered on the origin. All vertical cross sections parallel to the y-axis are squares. Find the volume of the solid.

solution It is particularly important to begin with a picture. We draw the base first. Vertical cross sections perpendicular to the x-axis are squares, as shown.

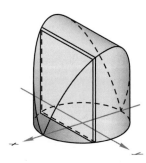

The base of this solid is defined by $x^2 + y^2 = 4$. Each vertical slice is a square whose base is a chord of the circle parallel to the y-axis. So the area of each slice is

$$(2y)^2 = (2\sqrt{4 - x^2})^2 = 4(4 - x^2)$$

We use $V = \int_a^b A(x)\ dx$ since the slices are perpendicular to the x-axis.

$$V = \int_a^b A(x)\ dx \qquad\qquad \text{general formula}$$

$$= \int_{-2}^{2} 4(4 - x^2)\ dx \qquad\qquad \text{substituted}$$

$$= 2\int_{0}^{2} 4(4 - x^2)\ dx \qquad\qquad \text{used symmetry}$$

$$= 8\int_{0}^{2} (4 - x^2)\ dx \qquad\qquad \text{simplified integral}$$

$$= 8\left[4x - \frac{x^3}{3} \right]_0^2 \qquad\qquad \text{integrated}$$

$$= 8\left(8 - \frac{8}{3} \right) = \frac{128}{3}\ \textbf{units}^3 \qquad \text{evaluated}$$

example 97.3   A solid has a circular base of radius 2. Vertical cross sections perpendicular to the base are equilateral triangles. Find the volume of the solid.

solution   We draw a picture as the first step.

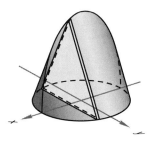

We orient the solid in such a way that the base of the representative cross section (an equilateral triangle) is parallel to the y-axis. The base of the solid is given by $x^2 + y^2 = 4$. We use this equation and a picture of the vertical slice to determine its area.

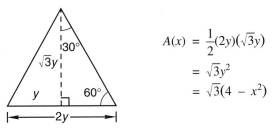

$$A(x) = \frac{1}{2}(2y)(\sqrt{3}y)$$

$$= \sqrt{3}y^2$$

$$= \sqrt{3}(4 - x^2)$$

The area is expressed in terms of x, because the cross sections are parallel to the y-axis, which means the thickness is dx. Now we can determine the volume.

$$V = \int_a^b A(x)\ dx \qquad\qquad \text{general formula}$$

$$= \int_{-2}^{2} \sqrt{3}(4 - x^2)\ dx \qquad\qquad \text{substituted}$$

$$= 2\int_{0}^{2} \sqrt{3}(4 - x^2)\ dx \qquad\qquad \text{used symmetry}$$

$$= 2\sqrt{3}\int_{0}^{2} (4 - x^2)\ dx \qquad\qquad \text{simplified integral}$$

$$= 2\sqrt{3}\left(8 - \frac{8}{3} \right) \qquad\qquad \text{recalled integration in example 97.2}$$

$$= \frac{32\sqrt{3}}{3}\ \textbf{units}^3 \qquad\qquad \text{simplified}$$

**problem set
97**

1. An inverted conical tank has a radius of 5 meters and a height of 15 meters. Water runs into the
(46) tank at the rate of 4 cubic meters per minute. Find the rate at which the water level is rising when
the water in the tank is 9 meters deep.

2. A tank with a rectangular base and rectangular sides is to be open at the top. The tank must be
(52) constructed so that its length is 6 meters and its volume is 72 cubic meters. The material used
for the base of the tank costs $3 per square meter, and the material used for the four sides of the
tank costs $2 per square meter. The height of the tank is y, and the width of the tank is x.

(a) Express the total cost of the tank in terms of x.

(b) Find the width and height of the tank that minimize the cost of the tank.

(c) What is the cost of the least expensive tank?

3. The time-dependent velocity function for a particle moving along the x-axis is v. Suppose
(90)

$$\int_0^2 v(t)\ dt\ =\ 8 \qquad \int_2^3 v(t)\ dt\ =\ -3 \qquad \int_3^5 v(t)\ dt\ =\ 1 \qquad \int_5^6 v(t)\ dt\ =\ -6$$

(a) How much does the position of the particle change during the interval $[0, 6]$?

(b) If the particle is at $x = 4$ when $t = 2$, what is the position of the particle when $t = 6$?

(c) What overall distance does the particle travel during the interval $[0, 6]$?

4. A particle starts at time $t = 0$ and moves along the x-axis so that its position as a function of
(90) time t is given by $x(t) = (t - 1)^3(t - 5)$.

(a) Find the time(s) when the particle is momentarily at rest.

(b) Find the time(s) when the particle is moving to the right.

(c) Find the time(s) when the particle changes its direction of movement.

(d) Find the farthest point to the left of the origin that the particle reaches.

5. The base of a certain solid is the region in the first quadrant bounded by the graphs of
(97) $y = \frac{3}{4}x$, $y = -\frac{3}{4}x + 6$, and the y-axis. Each vertical cross section is a rectangle whose height
is 6 units and whose base is parallel to the y-axis. Find the volume of the solid.

6. The base of a solid is the region enclosed by a circle with a radius of 3 units. Each vertical cross
(97) section is a square whose base is a chord of the circle parallel to the y-axis. Find the volume of
the solid.

7. The base of a solid is the region enclosed by a circle of radius 3 units. Each vertical cross section
(97) is a rectangle with a height of 2 units whose base is a chord of the circle parallel to the y-axis.
Find the volume of the solid.

Evaluate the definite integrals in problems 8 and 9.

8. $\displaystyle\int_{-1}^6 |x - 2|\ dx$
(96)

9. $\displaystyle\int_{-1}^2 |x^2 - x|\ dx$
(96)

10. Let $f(x) = \left|\sin x - \dfrac{1}{2}\right|$. Determine the maximum value of f.
(96)

11. Let f be a continuous function defined for all real numbers. Suppose that the absolute maximum
(96) value of f is 7 and the absolute minimum value of f is -15. Which of the following statements
must be true?

A. The maximum value of $f(|x|)$ is 7.   B. The maximum value of $|f(x)|$ is 7.

C. The minimum value of $f(|x|)$ is 0.   D. The minimum value of $|f(x)|$ is 0.

12. (a) Use the trapezoidal rule with $n = 4$ to approximate $\displaystyle\int_0^2 x^4\ dx$.
(95)

(b) Find the exact value of $\displaystyle\int_0^2 x^4\ dx$ by integrating.

(c) Find an upper bound for the error in the calculations made in (a).

(d) Find the number of trapezoids that must be used to approximate $\int_0^2 x^4\ dx$ with an error
whose absolute value is less than 10^{-3}.

13. Use the trapezoidal rule with $n = 6$ to approximate $\int_0^1 e^{-x^2}\, dx$.
(95)

14. Let R be the region bounded by $y = e^x$, the x-axis, $x = 1$, and $x = 2$. Find the volume of the
(94) solid formed when R is revolved around the line $x = -1$.

15. Approximate, to nine decimal places, the zero of the function $f(x) = x^3 + 2x - 4$.
(93)

16. Suppose $f(x) = x^5 + 2x + 1$ and f^{-1} is the inverse function of f. Evaluate $(f^{-1})'(4)$.
(92)

Evaluate the limits in problems 17 and 18.

17. $\displaystyle\lim_{x \to \infty} \left[x(e^{1/x} - 1) \right]$
(91)

18. $\displaystyle\lim_{x \to 1} \left(\dfrac{x}{\ln x} - \dfrac{1}{\ln x} \right)$
(91)

19. Find $\dfrac{dy}{dx}$ where $y = x^{\sin x}$.
(84)

20. Find the particular solution of $\dfrac{dy}{dx} = y \cos x$ that intercepts the point $\left(\dfrac{\pi}{2}, e \right)$.
(88)

21. Let $f(x) = (x - 1)(x^2 + x + 1)$. Find a number $c \in [-2, 4]$ that confirms the Mean Value
(89) Theorem for Integrals.

22. Evaluate: $\displaystyle\int \dfrac{dx}{\sqrt{9 - x^2}}$
(64)

23. Which of the following limits does not exist?
(70)

    A. $\displaystyle\lim_{x \to 0} \dfrac{\sin (2x)}{x}$ B. $\displaystyle\lim_{x \to 1} \dfrac{x^3 - 1}{x - 1}$ C. $\displaystyle\lim_{x \to 0} \dfrac{\sqrt{1 + x} - 1}{x}$ D. $\displaystyle\lim_{x \to 0} \dfrac{\sqrt{x^2}}{x}$

24. Let $f(x) = \dfrac{x - \sin (2x)}{\sin x}$ for all $x \neq 0$ in the interval $-1 < x < 1$. How should $f(0)$ be defined
(75,82) so that f is continuous for all x in the interval $-1 < x < 1$?

25. Suppose $\displaystyle\int f(x)e^x\, dx = f(x)e^x - \int 2xe^x\, dx$. Find $f(x)$.
(66)

LESSON 98   *Fundamental Theorem of Calculus, Part 2 • The Natural Logarithm Function*

98.A
fundamental theorem of calculus, part 2

We have used the Fundamental Theorem of Calculus to evaluate the integral of a continuous function f on the interval $[a, b]$ by subtracting the value of some antiderivative F evaluated at a from the value of the same antiderivative evaluated at b.

$$\int_a^b f(x)\, dx = F(b) - F(a)$$

The **Fundamental Theorem of Calculus** also guarantees that every continuous function has an antiderivative.

A function is an input-output process that has exactly one output for every input value of x. With the function machine below any input is squared. Thus, if the input is x, the output is x^2; and if the input is 3, the output is 3^2 or 9.

$$x \longrightarrow \boxed{(\ )^2} \longrightarrow x^2$$
$$3 \longrightarrow \qquad \longrightarrow 3^2$$

The next function machine integrates the function f and evaluates it from $t = a$ to $t = x$.

$$x \longrightarrow \boxed{\int_a^x f(t)\,dt} \longrightarrow \ ?$$

But what is the output of this machine? Using the first part of the Fundamental Theorem of Calculus, the output is

$$F(t)\Big|_a^x \ = \ F(x) - F(a)$$

where F is an antiderivative of f. We still have x as the input and as the upper limit, but x is no longer the variable of integration. To use this machine, we must first specify the function f and the lower limit a. To demonstrate, we use the function $f(t) = t$ and a lower limit of 2. In the box we use t instead of x in the integral.

$$x \longrightarrow \boxed{\int_2^x t\,dt} \longrightarrow \frac{t^2}{2}\Big|_2^x = \frac{x^2}{2} - \frac{2^2}{2}$$

For a graphical consideration of such an integral as a function, we let x be a variable on the t-axis.

Shaded area $= \displaystyle\int_2^x f(t)\,dt$

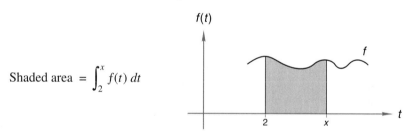

If the graph of a function is above the t-axis on the interval $[2, x]$, as shown, the area between the t-axis and the graph equals the definite integral from 2 to x.

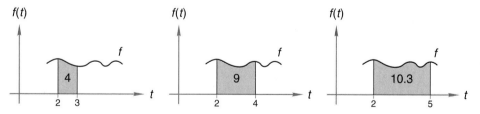

The leftmost figure above shows that if x is 3 the area is 4. The second and third figures show us that if x is 4 the area is 9, and if x is 5 the area is 10.3. The left-hand boundary of each of the areas is fixed at 2, and thus each of the areas under the graph of f is a function of the position of the right-hand boundary x. This is the reason the area can be described by the definite integral

$$A(x) \ = \ \int_2^x f(t)\,dt$$

If we remove the restriction that the graph be above the t-axis, we are no longer describing area but are still describing a definite integral,

$$F(x) \ = \ \int_a^x f(t)\,dt$$

The lower limit a does not have to be 2. It can be 0, –1, 5, or any real number that we choose.

There are functions, such as $y = e^{-x^2}$, whose antiderivatives cannot be expressed in a simple form. However, if f is a continuous function on an interval I, then the second part of the Fundamental Theorem of Calculus both guarantees the existence of an antiderivative of f and describes the antiderivative.

We state the theorem here without proof.

FUNDAMENTAL THEOREM OF CALCULUS, PART 2

If f is a function that is continuous on some closed interval I and c is any number in the interval, then f has an antiderivative F on this interval that can be described as

$$F(x) = \int_c^x f(t)\, dt, \quad x \in I$$

Since F is an antiderivative of f, the derivative of F equals f.

$$\frac{d}{dx}F(x) = \frac{d}{dx}\left(\int_c^x f(t)\, dt\right) = f(x)$$

---

example 98.1   Simplify: $\dfrac{d}{dx}\displaystyle\int_9^x t^2\, dt$

solution   First we find the integral.

$$\int_9^x t^2\, dt = \left[\frac{t^3}{3}\right]_9^x = \frac{x^3}{3} - 243$$

Now we find the derivative and note that the constant –243 is eliminated in differentiation. Thus the value of the lower limit of integration does not affect the derivative, as the contribution of this limit is eliminated when we differentiate.

$$\frac{d}{dx}\left(\frac{x^3}{3} - 243\right) = x^2$$

These two steps were unnecessary, as we could have used the Fundamental Theorem of Calculus to write the answer by inspection.

$$\frac{d}{dx}\int_9^x t^2\, dt = x^2$$

example 98.2   Simplify: $\dfrac{d}{dx}\displaystyle\int_x^4 \frac{\sin t}{t}\, dt \quad (x > 0)$

solution   We know that the integral from x to 4 is the negative of the integral from 4 to x, so we interchange the limits and insert a negative sign to get

$$\frac{d}{dx}\int_x^4 \frac{\sin t}{t}\, dt = \frac{d}{dx}\left(-\int_4^x \frac{\sin t}{t}\, dt\right) = -\frac{d}{dx}\int_4^x \frac{\sin t}{t}\, dt$$

We do not know how to evaluate the integral, but the Fundamental Theorem of Calculus assures us that the integral exists and that its derivative is $\sin x$ divided by x.

$$-\frac{d}{dx}\int_4^x \frac{\sin t}{t}\, dt = -\left(\frac{\sin x}{x}\right) = -\frac{\sin x}{x}$$

Note that we were able to apply the Fundamental Theorem of Calculus because $\frac{\sin t}{t}$ is continuous when $x > 0$. The answer is invalid otherwise.

example 98.3   Simplify: $\dfrac{d}{dx}\displaystyle\int_{17}^{x} e^{-t^2}\, dt$

solution   We do not know how to evaluate the integral, but the Fundamental Theorem of Calculus tells us that it has an antiderivative and that its derivative is e^{-x^2}.

$$\frac{d}{dx}\int_{17}^{x} e^{-t^2}\, dt = e^{-x^2}$$

98.B

the natural logarithm function

In precalculus mathematics you encountered the exponential function whose base is 10, and you used that function to define the common logarithm function whose base is also 10. The common logarithm function is the implicit form of the exponential function whose base is 10.

$$y = 10^x \quad \longrightarrow \quad x = \log_{10} y$$

You also saw the exponential function whose base is e, and you used this function to define the natural logarithm function whose base is also e. The natural logarithm function is the implicit form of the exponential function whose base is e.

$$y = e^x \quad \longrightarrow \quad x = \ln y$$

We have used the laws of exponents to develop the laws of logarithms and have assumed that these laws hold for all real values of x. These laws do hold and they do work, but we have not proven them. However, up to this point, we have not rigorously defined the natural logarithm function. Many mathematicians define the natural logarithm function as an integral. We shall do so as well and then demonstrate that the function so defined possesses the properties expected from the natural logarithm function.

The natural logarithm function is defined as follows:

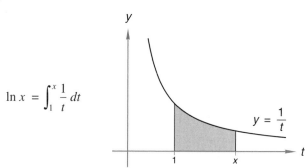

$$\ln x = \int_{1}^{x} \frac{1}{t}\, dt$$

With this definition we see in the figure above that $\ln x$ equals the area under the graph of $\frac{1}{t}$ between 1 and x if x is greater than 1. If x is between 0 and 1, then the expression that defines the integral looks the same, but the integral is the negative of the area.

$$\ln x = \int_{1}^{x} \frac{1}{t}\, dt = -\int_{x}^{1} \frac{1}{t}\, dt$$

The value of this integral is negative because the upper limit is less than the lower limit, and we remember that

$$\int_{a}^{b} f = -\int_{b}^{a} f$$

Two comments are in order here. First, since $\int_1^1 f(t)\, dt = 0$, we see that $\ln 1 = \int_1^1 \frac{1}{t}\, dt = 0$. So we have a well-known result, $\ln 1 = 0$. Second, we can provide a new, qualitative definition for the number e. The number e is the unique number with the property that the integral of $\frac{1}{t}$ from $t = 1$ to $t = e$ is exactly 1. That is, the only solution to the equation

$$\int_1^x \frac{1}{t}\, dt = 1$$

is the value $x = e$.

example 98.4   Differentiate $\ln x = \displaystyle\int_1^x \frac{1}{t}\, dt$ with respect to x.

solution   The Fundamental Theorem of Calculus allows us to write

$$\frac{d}{dx}\ln x = \frac{d}{dx}\int_1^x \frac{1}{t}\, dt = \frac{1}{x}$$

Thus the natural logarithm function has the derivative we expect. We will consider this fact further in Lesson 102.

problem set 98

1. (46)   The length of a rectangle is increasing at a rate of 2 centimeters per second, and the width of the rectangle is decreasing at a rate of 1 centimeter per second. Find the rate at which the area of the rectangle is changing when the length of the rectangle is 12 centimeters and the width of the rectangle is 10 centimeters.

2. (74,77)   A trough 5 meters long whose cross section is as shown is completely filled with a fluid whose weight density is 600 newtons per cubic meter. Dimensions shown in the figure are in meters.

   (a) Find the force against one end of the trough.

   (b) Find the work done in pumping all the fluid out of the top of the trough.

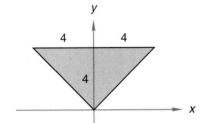

3. (90)   A particle starts at time $t = 0$ and moves along the x-axis so that its position as a function of time t is given by $x(t) = (4t - 1)(t - 1)^2$.

   (a) Find the time(s) when the particle is momentarily at rest.

   (b) Find the interval(s) of time when the particle is moving to the left.

   (c) Find the number of times the particle reverses its direction of movement.

   (d) Find the time during the interval(s) found in (b) when the particle is moving most rapidly (i.e., when the speed is a maximum).

4. (89,90)   The acceleration of a particle moving along the x-axis at time t is given by $a(t) = \pi \sin(\pi t)$. The velocity of the particle at $t = 0$ is 0. Find the average velocity of the particle over the interval $0 \le t \le 1$.

Simplify the expressions in problems 5 and 6, using each of the two following methods:

(a) Evaluate the definite integral first and then differentiate.

(b) Apply the Fundamental Theorem of Calculus.

5. (98) $\dfrac{d}{dx}\displaystyle\int_1^x t^2\, dt$ 6. (98) $\dfrac{d}{dx}\displaystyle\int_x^3 \sin t\, dt$

Simplify the expressions in problems 7 and 8.

7. $\dfrac{d}{dx}\displaystyle\int_{18}^{x} e^{-t^2}\, dt$
(98)

8. $\dfrac{d}{dx}\displaystyle\int_{x}^{5} \dfrac{\cos t}{t}\, dt$
(98)

9. Which of the following equals ln 4?
(98)

    A. ln 3 + ln 1

    B. The area of the region between the graph of $y = \dfrac{1}{x}$ and the x-axis on the interval $[1, 4]$.

    C. The area of the region between the graph of $y = \ln x$ and the x-axis on the interval $[1, \ln 4]$.

    D. The area of the region between the graph of $y = \ln x$ and the x-axis on the interval $[1, 4]$.

10. Let $f(x) = |2 \sin x - 1|$. Find the maximum value of f.
(96)

11. The base of a solid is the region in the first quadrant bounded by the graphs of
(97) $y = -\frac{3}{2}x + 6$, the x-axis, and the y-axis. Each vertical cross section is a rectangle with a height of 6 units whose base is parallel to the y-axis. Find the volume of the solid.

12. The base of a solid is the region enclosed by a circle with a radius of 4 units. Each vertical cross
(97) section is a rectangle with a height of 3 units whose base is a chord of the circle parallel to the y-axis. Find the volume of the solid.

13. The base of a solid is the region enclosed by a circle with a radius of 4 units. Each vertical cross
(97) section is an isosceles triangle with a height of 2 units whose base is a chord of the circle parallel to the y-axis. Find the volume of the solid.

14. Let R be the region between $y = \log x$ and the x-axis on the interval $[1, 10]$. Write a definite
(94) integral whose value equals the volume of the solid formed when R is revolved about the line $y = -1$.

15. (a) Use the trapezoidal rule with $n = 4$ to estimate the value of $\displaystyle\int_{1}^{2} \dfrac{1}{x}\, dx$.
(95)

    (b) Find the exact value of $\displaystyle\int_{1}^{2} \dfrac{1}{x}\, dx$ by integrating.

    (c) Find an upper bound for the error in the calculation made in (a).

    (d) Find the number of trapezoids that must be used to approximate $\int_{1}^{2} \frac{1}{x}\, dx$ with an error whose absolute value is less than 10^{-3}.

16. Use the trapezoidal rule with $n = 6$ to approximate $\displaystyle\int_{0}^{1} e^{x^2}\, dx$.
(95)

17. Find the general solution to the differential equation $\dfrac{dy}{dx} = \sin (2x)$.
(88)

18. Suppose $f(x) = \sin x$ and $g(x) = e^{x^2}$. Determine whether each of the following functions is
(86) even, odd, or neither.

    (a) $f + g$ (b) f^2 (c) $g \circ f$ (d) fg

19. Suppose $\log |f(x)| = \log |x^2 + 1| + \log |\sin x|$. Develop an expression that equals $\dfrac{f'(x)}{f(x)}$.
(84)

20. Use interval notation to indicate the values of x for which $|x - 2| < 3$.
(15)

21. Simplify: $\dfrac{d}{dx}\big[\tan (\sin x) + 3^{x^2}\big] + \displaystyle\int \dfrac{5}{1 + x^2}\, dx$
(50,64)

22. Find $\dfrac{dy}{dx}$ for the curve described by $y = \sin(xy)$.
(34)

23. Evaluate: $\displaystyle\int_0^{\pi/12} \sin^2(2x)\, dx$
(83)

24. Suppose $f(x) = \begin{cases} |x| + 2 & \text{when } x < 1 \\ ax^2 + bx & \text{when } x \ge 1. \end{cases}$ Find the values of a and b for which f is continuous and
(82) differentiable everywhere except at $x = 0$.

25. Two boats leave a buoy at the same time. One of the boats travels due north at a rate of N miles
(5) per hour, while the other boat travels due east at a rate of $4N$ miles per hour. What is the distance between the boats 30 minutes after both boats leave the buoy?

LESSON 99 *Linear Approximations Using Differentials*

One of the most common themes in calculus is approximation. For example, techniques such as Newton's method and the trapezoidal rule are used to approximate roots of equations and values of definite integrals respectively. Now we turn our attention to the approximation of the change of function values as input values change slightly.

Differentials can be used to get a quick approximation for the change in the value of a function Δy caused by a small change in the value of the independent variable. We remember that dy is an approximation for Δy and is defined as the product of the derivative and the change in x, which can be labeled Δx.

$$dy = f'(x)\Delta x$$

Suppose a farmer who has a square field whose sides are 100 meters long idly wonders how much the area of the field would increase if each side was $\frac{1}{4}$ meter longer. With a calculator the farmer could compute the new area and subtract the old area, and the difference would be the increase. However, using a differential can give a quick approximation that is almost as good as the answer from a calculator. The area and the differential of the area are given by

$$\text{Area} = x^2 \qquad \text{and} \qquad dA = 2x\Delta x$$

The change in area dA caused by a $\dfrac{1}{4}$-meter increase in x can be mentally computed.

$$dA = 2(100)\left(\frac{1}{4}\right) = 50 \text{ square meters}$$

Using a calculator, the farmer would find that the exact change in area is

$$(100.25)^2 - (100)^2 = 50.0625 \text{ square meters}$$

As we can see, using the differential quickly produces surprisingly accurate results with little effort.

example 99.1 Leena and Jen have a solid brass ball whose radius is 20 cm. They want to know the change in volume when a 0.02-cm coating is applied. Estimate this change using differentials.

solution We write the equation of the volume of a sphere and find its differential.

$$V = \frac{4}{3}\pi r^3 \quad \longrightarrow \quad dV = 4\pi r^2\, dr$$

We substitute 20 for r and 0.02 for dr to get the estimate.

$$dV = 4\pi(20)^2(0.02) \approx \mathbf{100.5310\ cm^3}$$

The difference between the old volume and the new volume is 100.6315 cm³, which is quite close to the estimate.

example 99.2   If x represents the number of units produced by a company in a given period, the profit p in dollars for the period is given by the equation

$$p(x) = (500x - x^2) - \left(\frac{1}{2}x^2 - 72x + 3000\right)$$

Using differentials, estimate the change in profit when the production is increased from 115 units to 120 units.

solution   All we have to do is find the differential and then use 115 for x and 5 for Δx.

$$dp = [(500 - 2x) - (x - 72)]\Delta x$$
$$dp = [500 - 2(115) - (115 - 72)]5 = 1135$$

Since dp is positive, the change in profit is positive and would be approximately **\$1135.** This is a rather quick and painless calculation.

We can compute the exact change in profit.

$$p(115) = \$42{,}942.50 \qquad \text{and} \qquad p(120) = \$44{,}040$$

So the exact change in profit in this problem is

$$\$44{,}040 - \$42{,}942.50 = \$1{,}097.50$$

Our estimated change is within \$38 of the actual value, an error between 3% and 4%.

example 99.3   Use differentials to approximate $\sqrt{9.4}$.

solution   We noted at the beginning of the lesson that $dy = f'(x)\Delta x$ is an approximation of Δy. To use this, we need a function, a value for x, and a value for Δx. We let $f(x) = \sqrt{x}$ and choose $x = 9$. The input values of 9.4 and 9 differ by 0.4, so $\Delta x = 0.4$.

$$\Delta y = \sqrt{9.4} - \sqrt{9} \approx dy = f'(9)(0.4)$$

Here, $f'(x) = \frac{1}{2}x^{-1/2}$, so $f'(9) = \frac{1}{2} \cdot \frac{1}{3} = \frac{1}{6}$. Thus

$$\sqrt{9.4} - \sqrt{9} \approx \frac{1}{6}(0.4)$$

$$\sqrt{9.4} \approx \sqrt{9} + \frac{1}{6}(0.4)$$

$$\sqrt{9.4} \approx \mathbf{3.0\overline{6}}$$

Note that $\sqrt{9.4} = 3.065941943\ldots$ via the calculator, so the estimate $3.0\overline{6}$ is quite accurate. Moreover, it is a quick calculation that does not require any difficult computations.

problem set 99

1. Find the area of the largest rectangle that can be inscribed in the region bounded by $y = 9 - x^2$
    (52)   and $y = x^2 - 1$.

2. A metal ball 50 centimeters in diameter is coated with a 0.01-centimeter layer of gold. Use
    (99)   differentials to estimate the increase in the volume of the ball.

3. If x represents the number of units produced by a company in a given period, the profit p in
    (99)   dollars for the period is given by $p(x) = (750x - 2x^2) - (x^2 - 99x + 4000)$. Use differentials to estimate the change in profit if the production is increased from 125 units to 130 units.

4. The base of a solid is the region bounded by the coordinate axes and the line $y = -2x + 4$.
    (97)   Every vertical cross section perpendicular to the base and parallel to the y-axis is an equilateral triangle. Find the volume of the solid.

5. A particle moves along the x-axis so that its velocity at time t $(t > 0)$ is given by $v(t) = \frac{t+1}{t}$.
(90) The particle's position at $t = 3$ is $x = 5$. Write an equation for the position function.

6. An object is propelled along the x-axis in the direction of the force $F(x) = \frac{1}{2}x^2$ newtons (for x
(62) given in meters). Find the work done on the object as it is moved from the origin to $x = 6$ meters.

Simplify the expressions in problems 7 and 8.

7. $\dfrac{d}{dx}\displaystyle\int_2^x e^{t^3}\, dt$
(98)

8. $\dfrac{d}{dx}\displaystyle\int_x^2 e^{1/t}\, dt$
(98)

9. Find the volume of the solid formed when the region between $y = e^x$ and the x-axis on the
(94) interval $[0, 2]$ is revolved around the line $x = -1$.

10. Integrate: $\displaystyle\int (\sin^2 x + \sin^3 x)\, dx$
(76,83)

11. Use the trapezoidal rule with $n = 6$ to approximate the area under $y = \frac{1}{x}$ on the
(95) interval $[1, 4]$.

12. Evaluate $\displaystyle\lim_{h \to 0} \dfrac{f(x + h) - f(x - h)}{2h}$, where $f(x) = \sqrt{x}$.
(44)

13. Suppose $f(x) = x^5 + x$ and f^{-1} is the inverse function of f. Evaluate $(f^{-1})'(2)$.
(92)

14. The absolute maximum of $f(x)$ is 4, which occurs when x is 2. The absolute minimum of $f(x)$ is
(96) -6, which occurs when x is -3. What is the absolute maximum value of $|f(x)|$?

Evaluate the definite integrals in problems 15 and 16.

15. $\displaystyle\int_2^4 |x + 2|\, dx$
(96)

16. $\displaystyle\int_{-1}^4 |x^2 + 4|\, dx$
(96)

17. Let R be the region bounded by the hyperbola $xy = 1$, the y-axis, and the lines $y = 1$ and
(67) $y = 2$. Express the area of R as an integral in the variable y.

18. Find the general solution of the differential equation $\dfrac{dy}{dx} = e^{2x - 3y}$.
(88)

19. Given the function f and g such that $\lim_{x \to 2} f(x) = 4$ and $\lim_{x \to 2} g(x) = -1$, evaluate
(70) $\lim_{x \to 2} [f(x)]^2 g(x)$.

20. Use interval notation to indicate the values of x for which $|x + 3| < 1$.
(15)

21. Determine the area between the graph of $y = xe^x$ and the x-axis on the interval $[1, 2]$.
(59)

22. Two boats leave a buoy at the same time. One of the boats travels due north at a rate of N miles
(47) per hour, while the other boat travels due east at a rate of $4N$ miles per hour. At what rate is the distance between the boats changing 30 minutes after both boats leave the buoy?

23. The position of a particle moving along the x-axis is defined by a time-dependent continuous
(75,85) function. The value of $x(t)$ when $t = 1$ is 1, and the value of $x(t)$ when $t = 3$ is 5. Which of the following statements is true?

    A. The velocity of the particle is always positive on the interval $[1, 3]$.

    B. At some time on the interval $[1, 3]$, the velocity of the particle is $+2$.

    C. The velocity of the particle is never zero on the interval $[1, 3]$.

    D. The velocity is zero when $t = 3$.

24. If f is a function such that $f'(x) > 0$ for all real values of x, which of the following statements
(45)   must be true?

    A. $f(x) > 0$ for all values of x.

    B. $f(x_1) > f(x_2)$ for every x_1 and x_2 where $x_1 > x_2$.

    C. The graph of f is concave up everywhere.

    D. The graph of f is concave down everywhere.

25. Suppose f is a function that exists for all real x and $\lim_{x \to a} f(x) = f(a)$ for any real number a.
(14)   Which of the following statements is true?

    A. $f(0) = 0$

    B. $f'(x) = f(x)$ for all real values of x.

    C. The function f is differentiable at all real values of x.

    D. The function f is continuous at all real values of x.

LESSON 100   Integrals of Powers of tan *x* • Integrals of Powers of cot *x* • Integrals of sec *x* and csc *x*

100.A

integrals of powers of tan *x*

The integral of tan x dx can be found because sin x and cos x can be used to write the integral in the form du over u.

$$\int \tan x \, dx = -\int \frac{\overbrace{-\sin x \, dx}^{du}}{\underbrace{\cos x}_{u}} = -\ln |\cos x| + C = \ln \left|\frac{1}{\cos x}\right| + C = \ln |\sec x| + C$$

Now we consider the integral of $\tan^n x \, dx$, where n is an integer greater than 1. If n equals 2, we use the Pythagorean identity

$$\tan^2 x + 1 = \sec^2 x$$

and replace $\tan^2 x$ with $\sec^2 x - 1$. If n is greater than 2, we rewrite $\tan^n x$ as $\tan^{n-2} x \tan^2 x$ and replace $\tan^2 x$ with $\sec^2 x - 1$. Throughout such calculations it is useful to remember that the derivative of tan x is $\sec^2 x$.

example 100.1   Integrate: $\int \tan^2 x \, dx$

solution   Replacing $\tan^2 x$ with $\sec^2 x - 1$ gives two integrals that we can evaluate.

$$\int \tan^2 x \, dx = \int (\sec^2 x - 1) \, dx = \int \sec^2 x \, dx - \int dx = \tan x - x + C$$

example 100.2   Integrate: $\int \tan^3 x \, dx$

solution   First we separate a factor of $\tan^2 x$ and replace it with $\sec^2 x - 1$.

$$\int \tan^3 x \, dx = \int (\tan x)(\tan^2 x) \, dx = \int (\tan x)(\sec^2 x - 1) \, dx$$

When we multiply, we get two integrals.

$$\int \underbrace{(\tan x)}_{u}\underbrace{(\sec^2 x \, dx)}_{du} - \int \tan x \, dx$$

We recognize the form of the first integral as $u\, du$ and know that the integral of $\tan x$ is $\ln|\sec x| + C$.

$$\int \tan^3 x\, dx = \int \tan x \sec^2 x\, dx - \int \tan x\, dx$$

$$= \frac{1}{2}\tan^2 x - \ln|\sec x| + C$$

$$= \frac{1}{2}\tan^2 x + \ln|\cos x| + C$$

example 100.3   Integrate: $\int \tan^4 x\, dx$

solution   We separate a factor of $\tan^2 x$ and substitute.

$$\int \tan^4 x\, dx = \int (\tan^2 x)(\tan^2 x)\, dx = \int (\tan^2 x)(\sec^2 x - 1)\, dx$$

Now we multiply and get

$$\int \tan^2 x \sec^2 x\, dx - \int \tan^2 x\, dx$$

The term $\tan^2 x \sec^2 x\, dx$ has the form $u^2\, du$, so the first integral equals $\frac{1}{3}\tan^3 x$. From example 100.1 we know that the integral of $\tan^2 x\, dx$ is $\tan x - x$, so we have

$$\int \tan^4 x\, dx = \frac{1}{3}\tan^3 x - \tan x + x + C$$

Although we do not consider them in this book, integrals of higher powers of $\tan x$ can be found by repeated use of the process shown in these examples. Each step results in an integral of the form

$$\int \tan^n x\, dx = \int u^{n-2}\, du - \int (\tan x)^{n-2}\, dx$$

This is known as a **power reduction formula.** To illustrate, the first step in the integration of $\tan^{11} x$ would be

$$\int \tan^{11} x\, dx = \int (\tan^9 x)(\sec^2 x - 1)\, dx = \underbrace{\int \underbrace{\tan^9 x}_{u^{11-2}} \underbrace{\sec^2 x\, dx}_{du}} - \int \tan^9 x\, dx$$

The next step would reduce $\tan^9 x$ to $\tan^7 x$, and so forth.

100.B

integrals of powers of cot x   A similar procedure is used to find integrals of $\cot^n x$. We can find the integral of $\cot x\, dx$ by using $\cos x$ and $\sin x$ to write this integral in the form of du over u.

$$\int \cot x\, dx = \int \frac{\overbrace{\cos x\, dx}^{du}}{\underbrace{\sin x}_{u}} = \ln|\sin x| + C$$

To find the integral of $\cot^n x\, dx$, we use the identity $1 + \cot^2 x = \csc^2 x$ and replace $\cot^2 x$ with $\csc^2 x - 1$. Since the derivative of $\cot x$ is $-\csc^2 x\, dx$, the integral of $-\csc^2 x\, dx$ is $\cot x + C$.

example 100.4   Integrate: $\int \cot^2 x\, dx$

solution   We replace $\cot^2 x$ with $\csc^2 x - 1$.

$$\int \cot^2 x\, dx = \int (\csc^2 x - 1)\, dx = \int \csc^2 x\, dx - \int dx$$

A pair of negative signs is needed in the first integral, which we provide.

$$-\int -\csc^2 x\, dx - \int dx = -\cot x - x + C$$

example 100.5   Integrate: $\int \cot^3 x \, dx$

solution   We separate a factor of $\cot^2 x$ and replace it with $\csc^2 x - 1$.

$$\int \cot^3 x \, dx = \int (\cot x)(\cot^2 x) \, dx = \int (\cot x)(\csc^2 x - 1) \, dx$$

Next we multiply, insert two minus signs, and find the integral.

$$\int \cot^3 x \, dx = -\int \underbrace{(\cot x)}_{u}\underbrace{(-\csc^2 x \, dx)}_{du} - \int \cot x \, dx = -\frac{1}{2} \cot^2 x - \ln|\sin x| + C$$

example 100.6   Integrate: $\int \cot^4 x \, dx$

solution   We separate a factor of $\cot^2 x$ and replace it with $\csc^2 x - 1$.

$$\int \cot^4 x \, dx = \int (\cot^2 x)(\cot^2 x) \, dx = \int (\cot^2 x)(\csc^2 x - 1) \, dx$$

Next we multiply, insert two minus signs, and get

$$-\int \underbrace{(\cot^2 x)}_{u^2}\underbrace{(-\csc^2 x \, dx)}_{du} - \int \cot^2 x \, dx$$

From example 100.4 we know that $\int \cot^2 x \, dx$ is $-\cot x - x$, so we have

$$\int \cot^4 x \, dx = -\frac{1}{3} \cot^3 x - (-\cot x - x) + C$$

$$= -\frac{1}{3} \cot^3 x + \cot x + x + C$$

100.C
integrals of sec *x* and csc *x*

Similar reduction techniques can be utilized for integrating powers of sec *x* and csc *x*. For the sake of brevity, we only determine $\int \sec x \, dx$ and $\int \csc x \, dx$ here.

example 100.7   Integrate: $\int \sec x \, dx$

solution   Determining this integral quickly requires a special insight. We multiply the integrand by 1 in the form $\frac{\sec x + \tan x}{\sec x + \tan x}$.

$$\int \sec x \, dx = \int \sec x \, \frac{(\sec x + \tan x)}{(\sec x + \tan x)} \, dx$$

$$= \int \frac{\sec^2 x + \sec x \tan x}{\sec x + \tan x} \, dx$$

Then we note that the differential of the denominator is the numerator.

$$\int \frac{\overbrace{(\sec^2 x + \sec x \tan x) \, dx}^{du}}{\underbrace{\sec x + \tan x}_{u}}$$

Hence this integral is $\ln|u| + C$.

$$\int \sec x \, dx = \ln|\sec x + \tan x| + C$$

For practice it would be wise to check this result by showing

$$\frac{d}{dx}(\ln|\sec x + \tan x| + C) = \sec x$$

example 100.8   Integrate: $\int \csc x \, dx$

solution   As in the case of the integral of sec x, this integral also requires multiplying the integrand by 1, but this time in the form of $\frac{\csc x - \cot x}{\csc x - \cot x}$.

$$\int \csc x \, dx = \int \csc x \, \frac{(\csc x - \cot x)}{(\csc x - \cot x)} \, dx$$

$$= \int \frac{\csc^2 x - \csc x \cot x}{\csc x - \cot x} \, dx$$

The differential of the denominator is the numerator.

$$\int \frac{\overbrace{(\csc^2 x - \csc x \cot x) \, dx}^{du}}{\underbrace{\csc x - \cot x}_{u}}$$

Therefore

$$\int \csc x \, dx = \ln |\csc x - \cot x| + C$$

For summary and reference we display the integrals of all six trigonometric functions.

$$\int \sin x \, dx = -\cos x + C$$

$$\int \cos x \, dx = \sin x + C$$

$$\int \tan x \, dx = \ln |\sec x| + C$$

$$\int \csc x \, dx = \ln |\csc x - \cot x| + C$$

$$\int \sec x \, dx = \ln |\sec x + \tan x| + C$$

$$\int \cot x \, dx = \ln |\sin x| + C$$

**problem set
100**

1. Let R be the region bounded by $y = \sin x$ and the x-axis on the interval $[0, \pi]$.
(94)
   (a) Find the volume of the solid formed when R is revolved around the line $x = -1$.
   (b) Find the volume of the solid formed when R is revolved around the line $y = -2$.

2. The Mean Value Theorem for Integrals says that every continuous function attains its average
(89) value on an interval at some point in the interval. For the function $y = \tan x$, find some number $c \in \left[-\frac{\pi}{4}, \frac{\pi}{4}\right]$ such that $f(c)$ equals the average value of the function on the interval.

3. Determine the slope of the line that joins the points $(1, f(1))$ and $(3, f(3))$ on the graph of
(85) $f(x) = x^3 + 2x + 1$. Illustrate the Mean Value Theorem (for derivatives) for f on the interval $[1, 3]$.

4. Use the trapezoidal rule with $n = 6$ to approximate $\int_0^2 \frac{1}{\sqrt{x^2 + 1}} \, dx$.
(95)

5. Let f be a continuous function whose domain is the set of all real numbers, whose maximum
(96) value is 8, and whose minimum value is -10. Determine the following:
   (a) the maximum value of $|f(x)|$ (b) the maximum value of $f(|x|)$
   (c) the minimum value of $|f(x)|$ (d) the minimum value of $f(|x|)$

Evaluate the limits in problems 6 and 7.

6. $\lim\limits_{x \to 0^+} (\ln x \tan x)$
(91)

7. $\lim\limits_{h \to 0} \dfrac{f(x + h) - f(x - h)}{2h}$, where $f(x) = x^2$
(44)

8. Find the general solution to the differential equation $y' = \sqrt{x}y^2$.
(88)

Integrate in problems 9–14.

9. $\displaystyle\int \tan x \, dx$
(100)

10. $\displaystyle\int \cot x \, dx$
(100)

11. $\displaystyle\int \sec x \, dx$
(100)

12. $\displaystyle\int \tan^2 x \, dx$
(100)

13. $\displaystyle\int \tan^3 x \, dx$
(100)

14. $\displaystyle\int \sec^2 x \, dx$
(100)

15. The base of a solid object is a circle with a radius of 4. Every vertical cross section is an
(97) equilateral triangle. What is the volume of the solid?

16. The base of a solid object is the region in the xy-plane bounded by the graphs of $y = x^2$ and
(97) $y = 4$. Every vertical cross section parallel to the y-axis is a rectangle with a height of 3. What is the volume of the object?

17. Approximate the root of $y = x^3 - x - 7$ to nine decimal places.
(93)

18. Find the volume of the solid formed when the region between $y = \tan x$ and the x-axis on the
(100) interval $[0, \frac{\pi}{4}]$ is revolved around the x-axis.

19. Write an integral in terms of a single variable that can be used to find the volume of the solid
(94) formed when the region between $y = \tan x$ and the x-axis on the interval $[0, \frac{\pi}{4}]$ is revolved around the line $y = -1$.

20. Use differentials to estimate 4.1^4.
(99)

21. Write the equation of the line that is tangent to the graph of $y = 2^x$ at $x = 2$.
(72)

22. Approximate the y-coordinate of the point on the graph of $y = 2^x$ corresponding to $x = 1.9$,
(27) using the tangent line at $x = 2$.

23. Use interval notation to indicate the values of x for which $|2x - 3| < 0.5$.
(15)

24. Simplify: $\dfrac{d}{dx}\left[\sin(x^2 - 1) + \dfrac{\sin x + 1}{e^x - 2}\right] + \displaystyle\int \dfrac{x^2}{x^3 - 1} \, dx$
(50,66)

25. Assume $\displaystyle\int_2^4 2^x \, dx = F(4) - F(2)$. Determine $F(x)$.
(47,73)

LESSON 101 *Limit of $\frac{\sin x}{x}$ for Small x • Proof of the Derivative of sin x*

101.A

limit of $\frac{\sin x}{x}$ for small x

In Lesson 26 we claimed without proof that the derivative of sin x with respect to x is cos x. Then in Lesson 48 we used this fact to prove that the derivative of cos x with respect to x is $-\sin x$, and we showed how to use the derivatives of sin x and cos x to find the derivatives of other trigonometric functions. In this lesson we prove an important fact that is essential in proving that the derivative of sin x is cos x. The key to proving that the derivative of sin x equals cos x is that we be able to evaluate the following limit when x is measured in radians:

$$\lim_{x \to 0} \frac{\sin x}{x}$$

The graphing calculator can be used to estimate this limit. Let `Y1=sin(X)/X`. (Remember to use `RADIAN` mode.) After setting `TblStart=0.1` and `⌂Tbl=-0.01`, we observe the table.

X	Y1
.1	.99833
.09	.99865
.08	.99893
.07	.99918
.06	.9994
.05	.99958
.04	.99973

X=.1

Using ◆, we scroll down to the portion of the table where `X=0` is located. Note that the values of `Y1` are very close to 1 when `X` is close to 0. So it appears the limit is 1.

Using a straightforward geometric proof, we will show that the following inequality is true for small x and then complete the proof by letting x approach zero.

$$\cos x < \frac{\sin x}{x} < 1$$

As x approaches zero, cos x approaches 1. From this we see that sin x over x is between 1 and a quantity that is approaching 1. By the squeeze theorem for limits, the limit of sin x over x as x approaches zero must also be 1.

To prove the inequality, we shade different parts of the same figure, as shown below. Point O is the center of a unit circle, so lengths OA and OC equal 1. We see that the area of the big triangle on the left-hand side is greater than the area of the sector of the circle shown in the center, which is greater than the area of the triangle shown on the right-hand side.

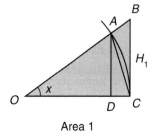

Area 1

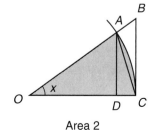

Area 2

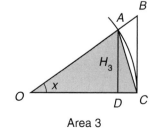

Area 3

Area 1 > Area 2 > Area 3

Area 1 is the area of the big triangle. Since the base of this triangle has length 1, $\tan x$ equals H_1 over 1, or $\tan x = H_1$.

$$\text{Area 1} = \frac{1}{2}BH_1 = \frac{1}{2}(1)(\tan x)$$

$$= \frac{\tan x}{2}$$

Area 2 is the area of a sector of a circle whose central angle is x and whose radius is 1.

$$\text{Area 2} = \frac{x}{2\pi}(\pi r^2) = \frac{x}{2\pi}\pi(1)^2$$

$$= \frac{x}{2}$$

Area 3 is the area of a triangle whose height is H_3 and whose base, OC, has length 1. We can find H_3 because the hypotenuse of the right triangle it forms also has length 1. Thus $\sin x = \frac{H_3}{1}$, which means $H_3 = \sin x$.

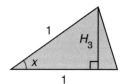

$$\text{Area 3} = \frac{1}{2}BH_3 = \frac{1}{2}(1)(\sin x)$$

$$= \frac{\sin x}{2}$$

Now we substitute the values found for the three areas and get

$$\frac{\tan x}{2} > \frac{x}{2} > \frac{\sin x}{2}$$

Multiplying every term by 2 gives us

$$\frac{\sin x}{\cos x} > x > \sin x$$

Now we divide every term by $\sin x$, knowing $\sin x > 0$, and get

$$\frac{1}{\cos x} > \frac{x}{\sin x} > 1$$

As the last step, we invert each term and reverse the inequality symbols to get

$$\cos x < \frac{\sin x}{x} < 1$$

which squeezes the middle term between $\cos x$ and 1. Because our drawing shows x to be positive and less than $\frac{\pi}{2}$, we know this inequality to be true when

$$0 < x < \frac{\pi}{2}$$

Thus we may only take the right-hand limit of $\frac{\sin x}{x}$ as x approaches 0 if we intend to use this inequality.

$$\lim_{x \to 0^+} \cos x \leq \lim_{x \to 0^+} \frac{\sin x}{x} \leq \lim_{x \to 0^+} 1 \qquad \text{took limit}$$

$$1 \leq \lim_{x \to 0^+} \frac{\sin x}{x} \leq 1 \qquad \text{evaluated bounding limits}^\dagger$$

$$\lim_{x \to 0^+} \frac{\sin x}{x} = 1 \qquad \text{squeeze theorem}$$

---

†*Note:* We assumed that $\lim_{x \to 0^+} \cos x = 1$. However, this is a fact that must be proved. Though there are many ways to do this, we omit the proof here.

If x is a negative angle, we get the same final result. To show this, we let x equal $-u$, where u is a positive number. Then

$$\frac{\sin x}{x} = \frac{\sin (-u)}{-u} = \frac{-\sin u}{-u} = \frac{\sin u}{u}$$

If x approaches 0 from the left, then u must approach 0 from the right. Thus,

$$\lim_{x \to 0^-} \frac{\sin x}{x} = \lim_{u \to 0^+} \frac{\sin u}{u} = 1$$

Since the limit as x approaches 0 from the right and the limit as x approaches 0 from the left both equal 1, we conclude that

$$\lim_{x \to 0} \frac{\sin x}{x} = 1$$

example 101.1   Evaluate: $\displaystyle\lim_{x \to 0} \frac{\sin (4x)}{x}$

solution   L'Hôpital's Rule can be used to find this limit, but the proof above gives us a way to find this special limit almost by inspection. The rule developed can be written as

$$\lim_{(\ ) \to 0} \frac{\sin (\ )}{(\ )} = 1$$

Since the limit of a constant times a function equals the constant times the limit of the function, we can get the form we need by multiplying in front by 4 and by multiplying x in the denominator by 4. Since $4x$ approaches zero as x approaches zero, we can write

$$\lim_{x \to 0} \frac{\sin (4x)}{x} = \lim_{4x \to 0} \frac{4 \sin (4x)}{4x} = 4\left(\lim_{(4x) \to 0} \frac{\sin (4x)}{(4x)} \right) = 4 \cdot 1 = \mathbf{4}$$

The graph of the function $y = \dfrac{\sin (4x)}{x}$ also shows this limit to be 4.

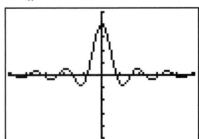

example 101.2   Evaluate: $\displaystyle\lim_{x \to 0} \frac{x}{\sin (47x)}$

solution   The limit of the reciprocal of a function equals the reciprocal of the limit of the function.

$$\lim_{x \to 0} \frac{x}{\sin (47x)} = \frac{1}{\displaystyle\lim_{x \to 0} \frac{\sin (47x)}{x}}$$

We can evaluate $\displaystyle\lim_{x \to 0} \frac{\sin (47x)}{x}$ by multiplying and dividing by 47.

$$\lim_{x \to 0} \frac{\sin (47x)}{x} = 47\left(\lim_{x \to 0} \frac{\sin (47x)}{47x} \right) = 47 \cdot 1 = 47$$

Thus

$$\lim_{x \to 0} \frac{x}{\sin (47x)} = \frac{1}{\displaystyle\lim_{x \to 0} \frac{\sin (47x)}{x}} = \frac{\mathbf{1}}{\mathbf{47}}$$

101.B

proof of the derivative of sin *x*

To prove that the derivative of sin *x* with respect to *x* equals cos *x*, we must show that

$$\lim_{x \to 0} \frac{1 - \cos x}{x} = 0$$

To do this, we first multiply by $1 + \cos x$ over $1 + \cos x$ and mentally restrict *x* to values close to zero, so that $1 + \cos x$ does not equal zero.

$$\lim_{x \to 0} \frac{1 - \cos x}{x} \left(\frac{1 + \cos x}{1 + \cos x} \right) = \lim_{x \to 0} \frac{1 - \cos^2 x}{x(1 + \cos x)}$$

But $1 - \cos^2 x = \sin^2 x$, and this substitution allows us to write the limit as a product.

$$\lim_{x \to 0} \frac{\sin^2 x}{x(1 + \cos x)} = \lim_{x \to 0} \left(\frac{\sin x}{x} \cdot \frac{\sin x}{1 + \cos x} \right)$$

We rewrite the limit of the product as a product of two limits and get

$$\lim_{x \to 0} \frac{\sin x}{x} \cdot \lim_{x \to 0} \frac{\sin x}{1 + \cos x}$$

The limit of sin *x* over *x* as *x* approaches zero is 1, as shown in the previous section. The limit of sin *x* over $1 + \cos x$ as *x* approaches zero is zero, because sin *x* approaches zero and $1 + \cos x$ approaches 2.

$$\lim_{x \to 0} \frac{\sin x}{x} = 1 \qquad \text{and} \qquad \lim_{x \to 0} \frac{\sin x}{1 + \cos x} = \frac{0}{2} = 0$$

Thus the product of these limits is zero, which proves

$$\lim_{x \to 0} \frac{1 - \cos x}{x} = 0$$

The next step in the proof that the derivative of sin *x* with respect to *x* equals cos *x* is to use the definition of the derivative and the identity for $\sin (A + B)$. The rest of the proof is just an application of the algebra of limits. First we use the definition of the derivative to write

$$\frac{d}{dx} \sin x = \lim_{\Delta x \to 0} \frac{\sin (x + \Delta x) - \sin x}{\Delta x}$$

Remembering that $\sin (A + B) = \sin A \cos B + \cos A \sin B$, we let $A = x$ and $B = \Delta x$ to get

$$\frac{d}{dx} \sin x = \lim_{\Delta x \to 0} \frac{[\sin x \cos (\Delta x) + \sin (\Delta x) \cos x] - \sin x}{\Delta x}$$

Then we rearrange the terms in the numerator.

$$\frac{d}{dx} \sin x = \lim_{\Delta x \to 0} \frac{\sin x \cos (\Delta x) - \sin x + \sin (\Delta x) \cos x}{\Delta x}$$

Now we factor the first two terms in the numerator.

$$\frac{d}{dx} \sin x = \lim_{\Delta x \to 0} \frac{(\sin x)[\cos (\Delta x) - 1] + \sin (\Delta x) \cos x}{\Delta x}$$

Since the limit of a sum equals the sum of the individual limits,

$$\frac{d}{dx} \sin x = \lim_{\Delta x \to 0} \left[(\sin x) \frac{\cos (\Delta x) - 1}{\Delta x} \right] + \lim_{\Delta x \to 0} \left[\frac{\sin (\Delta x)}{\Delta x} (\cos x) \right]$$

In these limits the variable is Δx, so sin *x* and cos *x* can be treated as constants and can be written in front of the limit notations. This gives

$$\frac{d}{dx} \sin x = (\sin x) \left[\lim_{\Delta x \to 0} \frac{\cos (\Delta x) - 1}{\Delta x} \right] + (\cos x) \left[\lim_{\Delta x \to 0} \frac{\sin (\Delta x)}{\Delta x} \right]$$

The first of these limits equals zero, and the second equals 1.

$$\frac{d}{dx} \sin x = (\sin x)(0) + (\cos x)(1) = \cos x$$

This completes the proof.

**problem set
101**

1. A square is inscribed inside a circle whose radius is increasing at a rate of 5 cm/min.
(47)

(a) How fast is the area of the circle changing when the radius of the circle is 10 centimeters?

(b) How fast is the area of the square changing at this same instant in time?

(c) Another circle is inscribed inside the square. How fast is the area of this circle changing at the same instant in time?

2. Find the derivative of $y = x^{\sqrt{x}}$.
(84)

3. At the holiday parade Lilly sells 30 drumsticks per hour when she sells them for $2.50 each. For
(63) every 25¢ she decreases the price, she can sell 5 more drumsticks per hour. At what price should Lilly sell her drumsticks to maximize her hourly income?

4. The base of a solid is the region bounded by $y = \sin x$ and the x-axis on the interval $[0, \pi]$.
(97) Every vertical cross section of the object taken perpendicular to the x-axis is a square.

(a) Write the integral used to find the volume of this solid.

(b) What is the volume of the solid?

5. The base of a solid is the region bounded by $y = \sin x$ and the x-axis on the interval $[0, \pi]$.
(97) Every vertical cross section of the object taken perpendicular to the x-axis is a rectangle whose height is the square of its base.

(a) Write the integral used to find the volume of this solid.

(b) What is the volume of the solid?

6. Use the trapezoidal rule with $n = 4$ to approximate $\int_1^4 \frac{e^x}{x^2}\, dx$.
(95)

7. Let $f(x) = e^{|x|}$. Find $f'(x)$.
(96)

8. Evaluate: $\int_{-1}^2 e^{|x|}\, dx$
(96)

Evaluate the limits in problems 9–12.

9. $\lim_{x \to 0} \frac{\sin x}{x}$
(101)

10. $\lim_{x \to 0} \frac{8x}{\sin (3x)}$
(101)

11. $\lim_{x \to 0} \left(\frac{1}{x} - \frac{1}{x^2} \right)$
(91)

12. $\lim_{x \to \infty} xe^{-3x}$
(91)

13. Prove that the derivative of $\sin x$ is $\cos x$.
(101)

Integrate in problems 14–17.

14. $\int \tan x\, dx$
(100)

15. $\int \sec x\, dx$
(100)

16. $\int \sec^2 x\, dx$
(100)

17. $\int \tan^4 x\, dx$
(100)

18. Use differentials to approximate $\sqrt[3]{60}$.
(99)

19. Use Newton's method to approximate $\sqrt[3]{60}$. (*Hint:* Find the zeros of the function
(93) $y = x^3 - 60$.)

20. The position of a particle moving on the x-axis is given by $x(t) = \sin t$.
(89,90)

(a) What is the total distance traveled by the particle from $t = 0$ to $t = 5$?

(b) What is the average velocity of the particle?

21. Given that $f(x) = 3e^{4x}$, find $f^{-1}(e)$.
(58)

22. Determine the area of the region between $y = xe^x$ and the *x*-axis on the interval $[1, 2]$.
(69)

23. The region between $y = xe^x$ and the *x*-axis on the interval $[1, 2]$ is revolved around the line
(94) $x = -1$. What is the volume of the solid formed?

24. Determine the next number in the following sequence: 0, 3, 8, 15, 24, ...
(R)

25. Find the equation of the quadratic function that passes through the points $(-1, -1)$, $(1, 0)$, and
(R) $(3, 6)$. (*Hint:* Use a generic quadratic function such as $y = ax^2 + bx + c$ to set up a system of 3 equations with 3 unknowns.)

LESSON 102   *Derivatives of ln x and eˣ • Definition of e*

102.A

derivatives of ln *x* and *e*ˣ

The natural exponential function is the exponential function whose base is e. The natural logarithm function is the inverse function of the natural exponential function. The base of the natural logarithm function is also e. We designate this function by writing either $\log_e x$ or $\ln x$.

FUNCTION		INVERSE FUNCTION
$y = e^x$	$\xrightarrow{\text{by definition}}$	$y = \log_e x$

In this lesson we use this defined relationship to prove that the derivative of e^x with respect to x is e^x. First we recall from Lesson 98 the alternate definition of $\ln x$:

$$\ln x = \int_1^x \frac{1}{t}\, dt$$

As noted in Lesson 98 the Fundamental Theorem of Calculus implies that

$$\frac{d}{dx} \ln x = \frac{d}{dx}\left(\int_1^x \frac{1}{t}\, dt \right) = \frac{1}{x}$$

We use this to find the derivative of $y = e^x$. Rewriting this equation in terms of the natural logarithm function yields

$$x = \ln y$$

Now y is defined implicitly as a function of x. (This equation is true because $f(x) = e^x$ and $g(x) = \ln x$ are inverse functions.) Next we differentiate implicitly.

$$\frac{d}{dx} x = \frac{d}{dx}(\ln y)$$

$$1 = \frac{1}{y} \cdot \frac{dy}{dx}$$

After rearrangement

$$\frac{dy}{dx} = y$$

Since $y = e^x$, this last equation can be rewritten as

$$\frac{d}{dx}(e^x) = e^x$$

which proves that the derivative of e^x with respect to x is itself.

102.B

definition of *e*   One of the definitions of *e* is

$$e = \lim_{x \to \infty} \left(1 + \frac{1}{x}\right)^x$$

At first it appears that this limit is really just 1, because $\frac{1}{x}$ approaches 0 as *x* approaches ∞, so that

$$\left(1 + \frac{1}{x}\right)^x \longrightarrow 1^x \longrightarrow 1$$

But this is an incorrect set of assumptions, since the $\frac{1}{x}$ term is changing at the same time as the exponent *x*. These two changes combined actually cause the limit to equal a number greater than one. We can see this phenomenon on the TI-83 calculator. Define `Y1=(1+1/X)^X`. In the `TABLE SETUP` menu, set `TblStart` and `ΔTbl` to 100. Accessing the `TABLE` feature we see the tendency of `Y1` as `X` increases.

X	Y1	
100	2.7048	
200	2.7115	
300	2.7138	
400	2.7149	
500	2.7156	
600	2.716	
700	2.7163	

`X=100`

As we scroll down this table, we see that the values of `Y1` are approaching 2.718, a decent approximation of *e*.

It should also be noted that

$$e^a = \lim_{x \to \infty} \left(1 + \frac{a}{x}\right)^x = \lim_{x \to \infty} \left(1 + \frac{1}{x}\right)^{ax}$$

for any real number *a*. Though we omit the proofs, we demonstrate how they might be proved in an example.

example 102.1   Evaluate: (a) $\displaystyle\lim_{x \to \infty} \left(1 + \frac{\pi}{x}\right)^x$ (b) $\displaystyle\lim_{x \to \infty} \left(1 + \frac{1}{x}\right)^{x/4}$

solution   (a) Rather than using the fact above, we use a *u*-substitution, $u = \dfrac{x}{\pi}$.

$$\lim_{x \to \infty} \left(1 + \frac{\pi}{x}\right)^x = \lim_{\pi u \to \infty} \left(1 + \frac{1}{u}\right)^{\pi u} \qquad \text{substituted}$$

$$= \lim_{u \to \infty} \left[\left(1 + \frac{1}{u}\right)^u\right]^\pi \qquad \text{simplified}$$

$$= e^\pi \qquad \text{definition of } e$$

(b) This does not require a *u*-substitution.

$$\lim_{x \to \infty} \left(1 + \frac{1}{x}\right)^{x/4} = \lim_{x \to \infty} \left[\left(1 + \frac{1}{x}\right)^x\right]^{1/4}$$

$$= e^{1/4}$$

problem set
102

1. An equilateral triangle is inscribed inside a circle whose radius is increasing at a rate of 5 cm/s.
(46)

    (a) How fast is the area of the circle changing when the radius of the circle is 8 centimeters?

    (b) How fast is the area of the triangle changing at this same instant in time?

2. The base of a solid is a circle with a radius of 3. Every vertical cross section of the object taken
(94) perpendicular to the base and parallel to the x-axis is a rectangle with a height of 2. Find the volume of the object.

3. The position of a particle moving along the x-axis is given by $x(t) = t^3 - 9t^2 + 24t - 8$.
(89,90)

    (a) Find the total distance traveled by the particle on the interval $[0, 5]$.

    (b) What is the average velocity of the particle?

    (c) What is the maximum velocity of the particle?

4. Find the exact area under $y = 2x + 1$ on the interval $[0, 3]$ by using an infinite number of
(43) circumscribed rectangles.

5. Identify the conic section described by $9x^2 - 18x + y^2 = 18$, and rewrite the equation in
(22) standard form.

6. Prove that the derivative of $\ln x$ with respect to x is $\dfrac{1}{x}$.
(102)

7. Given that the derivative of $\ln x$ with respect to x is $\frac{1}{x}$, prove that the derivative of e^x with respect
(102) to x is e^x.

8. Fast Freeda found that the rubber lost from each tire after a race varied directly with the
(5) temperature coefficient of the tire and inversely with the humidity. The amount of rubber lost was 1.5 mm when the temperature coefficient was 3 and the humidity was 60%. How much rubber did Fast Freeda lose from each tire when the humidity was 75% and the temperature coefficient was 2?

9. Simplify $\dfrac{d}{ds}\displaystyle\int_{\pi}^{s} \cos t \; dt$ using the two following methods:
(98)

    (a) Evaluate the definite integral first and then differentiate.

    (b) Apply the Fundamental Theorem of Calculus.

10. Simplify: $\dfrac{d}{ds}\displaystyle\int_{\pi}^{s} \cos t^2 \; dt$
(98)

11. Use the trapezoidal rule with $n = 5$ to approximate $\displaystyle\int_{0}^{1} \sqrt{1 + x^3} \; dx$.
(95)

Evaluate the limits in problems 12–14.

12. $\displaystyle\lim_{x \to 0} \frac{\sin (7x)}{13x}$ **13.** $\displaystyle\lim_{x \to 0} \left(\frac{1}{x^2} - \frac{1}{x^4} \right)$ **14.** $\displaystyle\lim_{x \to \infty} xe^{-7x}$
(101)   (91)   (91)

Integrate in problems 15–18.

15. $\displaystyle\int \csc x \; dx$ **16.** $\displaystyle\int \cot x \; dx$
(100)   (100)

17. $\displaystyle\int \tan^3 x \; dx$ **18.** $\displaystyle\int \cot^2 x \; dx$
(100)   (100)

19. Find the general solution to the differential equation $\dfrac{dy}{dx} = \sin (2x)$.
(88)

20. Evaluate: $\displaystyle\int_{0}^{\pi/4} \tan x \; dx$
(100)

21. The function $f(x) = x^3 - 6x^2 + 12x - 4$ is reflected about the line $y = x$ to form a new
(92) function. What is the slope of the new function at the reflection of the point $(3, f(3))$?

22. Use interval notation to describe all the values of x for which $|x + 3| < 0.004$.
(15)

23. Evaluate: $\int_0^5 |2x - 4| \, dx$
(96)

24. Use the equation of the line tangent to the curve $x^2y + 6 = xy^3$ at the point $(1, 2)$ to
(27) approximate the coordinates of the point where $x = 1.2$.

25. Let $f(x) = \begin{cases} |x| + 2 & \text{when } x < 1 \\ ax^2 + b & \text{when } x \geq 1. \end{cases}$ Find the values of a and b that make f differentiable everywhere
(82) except at $x = 0$.

LESSON 103 *Proof of the Fundamental Theorem of Calculus •*
Epsilon-Delta Proofs

103.A

proof of the fundamental theorem of calculus

The Fundamental Theorem of Calculus has two parts. We covered one part in Lesson 47 and the other in Lesson 98.

FUNDAMENTAL THEOREM OF CALCULUS

Suppose f is a continuous function on the interval $[a, b]$.

Part 1: If F is any antiderivative of f, then

$$\int_a^b f(x) \, dx = F(b) - F(a)$$

Part 2: If c is any number in the interval $[a, b]$, then f has an antiderivative F that can be defined on $[a, b]$ as

$$F(x) = \int_c^x f(t) \, dt$$

Since F is an antiderivative of f, the derivative of F equals f.

$$\frac{d}{dx} F(x) = \frac{d}{dx}\left(\int_c^x f(t) \, dt\right) = f(x)$$

The easiest way to prove the theorem is to begin with Part 2.

Proof of Part 2: Let $c \in [a, b]$ and let $F(x) = \int_c^x f(t) \, dt$. By the definition of the derivative,

$$F'(x) = \lim_{h \to 0} \frac{F(x + h) - F(x)}{h} = \lim_{h \to 0} \left[\frac{1}{h}\left(\int_c^{x+h} f(t) \, dt - \int_c^x f(t) \, dt\right)\right]$$

From the properties of definite integrals in Lesson 57, we know

$$\int_c^{x+h} f(t) \, dt - \int_c^x f(t) \, dt = \int_x^{x+h} f(t) \, dt$$

Therefore

$$F'(x) = \lim_{h \to 0} \left(\frac{1}{h} \int_x^{x+h} f(t) \, dt\right)$$

By the Mean Value Theorem for Integrals (Lesson 89), there is a number k in the $[x, x + h]$ such that

$$\frac{1}{h} \int_x^{x+h} f(t)\, dt \;=\; f(k)$$

By the squeeze principle, as h approaches zero, k must approach x.

$$F'(x) \;=\; \lim_{h \to 0} \left(\frac{1}{h} \int_x^{x+h} f(t)\, dt \right) \;=\; \lim_{h \to 0} f(k) \;=\; \lim_{k \to x} f(k) \;=\; f(x)$$

Hence F is an antiderivative of f. More explicitly, f has an antiderivative defined as prescribed.

Proof of Part 1: We use Part 2, which tells us that if a function f is continuous on $[a, b]$, then f must have an antiderivative G on $[a, b]$, which can be defined as

(1) $$G(x) \;=\; \int_a^x f(t)\, dt$$

Since both G and F are antiderivatives of f, the derivative of G equals f, and the derivative of F equals f.

$$G' = f \qquad \text{and} \qquad F' = f$$

By a corollary of the Mean Value Theorem, any two functions having the same derivative differ by a constant (as discussed in Lesson 85). Thus F and G differ by a constant, so we can write

(2) $$G(x) \;=\; F(x) + C$$

for some constant C. To find the value of the constant C, we let x equal a and get

$$G(a) \;=\; F(a) + C$$

This allows us to solve for C. By equation (1), $G(a)$ is zero since the integral of $f(x)$ from a to a is zero. (This is another one of the integral properties from Lesson 57.) Thus we have

$$0 \;=\; F(a) + C$$
$$C \;=\; -F(a)$$

We substitute $-F(a)$ for C in equation (2) and get

(3) $$G(x) \;=\; F(x) - F(a)$$

Combining equations (1) and (3) gives

$$\int_a^x f(t)\, dt \;=\; F(x) - F(a)$$

This is true for any real number x in the interval $[a, b]$. If we let x equal b, we can write

$$\int_a^b f(t)\, dt \;=\; F(b) - F(a)$$

At this point, we may replace the dummy variable t with x and write

$$\int_a^b f(x)\, dx \;=\; F(b) - F(a)$$

This completes the proof of the Fundamental Theorem of Calculus.

103.B
epsilon-delta proofs

Consider the function $f(x) = \frac{1}{2}x - 1$. As the value of x gets closer and closer to 8, the value of $f(x)$ gets closer and closer to 3. This happens whether x approaches 8 from the left or from the right, and we say that the limit of $f(x)$ as x approaches 8 is 3.

$$\lim_{x \to 8} \left(\frac{1}{2}x - 1 \right) = 3$$

However, this is not a rigorous definition of the concept of a limit. "Closer and closer" is an ambiguous phrase. To define limits rigorously, we need an explicit treatment of the concept.

For the function above, a student asked how far x could be from 8 for the value of y to be within ± 0.01 of 3. The teacher's answer was that x had to be within $\pm 2(0.01)$ of 8. The student asked how far x could be from 8 for the value of y to be within ± 0.007 of 3. The teacher's answer was that as long as x was within $\pm 2(0.007)$ of 8, the value of y would be within ± 0.007 of 3. The student asked how far x could be from 8 for the value of y to be within $\pm \varepsilon$ of 3. The teacher's answer was that as long as x was within $\pm 2\varepsilon$ of 8, the value of y would be within $\pm \varepsilon$ of 3. The teacher had found a rule that could be used to select values of x that would yield values of y within the limits specified by the student's choice of acceptable error in y. **Since the teacher found the rule that can be used to define a range of acceptable values of x for any choice of error in y, no matter how small, we say that the teacher proved that the limit of $\frac{1}{2}x - 1$ as x approaches 8 is 3.**

We use the Greek letter ε (epsilon) to denote error. The rule for the above example is to multiply the student's choice of acceptable error by 2. The result is the acceptable deviation of x from 8 that ensures y-values are within the prescribed limits of error. The rule defines acceptable deviations in x, symbolized by $\delta(\varepsilon)$, which is read "delta of epsilon." This notation clearly indicates that $\delta(\varepsilon)$ is determined by ε. The process of determining the rule for finding $\delta(\varepsilon)$ is called an **epsilon-delta proof.** To find such a rule is to prove that the limit is the number for which ε sets an error bound.

The following figure allows us to consider the problem graphically. It shows a function whose limit is L as x approaches a. Note that the function is not defined at $x = a$. In determining the limit of a function as x approaches a, it does not matter whether the function is defined at $x = a$. Only the behavior of the function "near" $x = a$ matters.

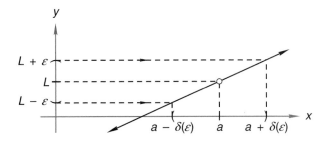

We are accustomed to entering on the x-axis and reading out on the y-axis. For these proofs the thought process requires that we enter on the y-axis with epsilon and read out delta of epsilon on the x-axis. We note in the figure that the acceptable y-error ε determines $\delta(\varepsilon)$ and allows us to give a rigorous definition of the limit of a real function.

DEFINITION OF LIMIT

Let f be a function that is defined for all values in the open interval I, except possibly at the number a in the interval. The limit of $f(x)$ as x approaches a is L, written

$$\lim_{x \to a} f(x) = L$$

if, for any positive number ε (however small), there exists a positive number $\delta(\varepsilon)$ such that

$$L - \varepsilon < f(x) < L + \varepsilon$$

whenever

$$a - \delta(\varepsilon) < x < a + \delta(\varepsilon) \qquad \text{and} \qquad x \neq a$$

Absolute value notation can be used to describe the intervals stated in the definition shown above. Instead of stating

$$L - \varepsilon < f(x) < L + \varepsilon$$

we could use the notation

$$|f(x) - L| < \varepsilon$$

Also, instead of stating

$$a - \delta(\varepsilon) < x < a + \delta(\varepsilon) \qquad \text{and} \qquad x \neq a$$

we could say

$$0 < |x - a| < \delta(\varepsilon)$$

Note that stipulating $|x - a| > 0$ implies that $x \neq a$. We now state the definition of the limit of a function using absolute value notation.

DEFINITION OF LIMIT

Let f be a function that is defined for all values in the open interval I, except possibly at the number a in the interval. The limit of $f(x)$ as x approaches a is L, written

$$\lim_{x \to a} f(x) = L$$

if, for any positive number ε (however small), there exists a positive number $\delta(\varepsilon)$ such that

$$|f(x) - L| < \varepsilon \qquad \text{whenever} \qquad |x - a| < \delta(\varepsilon)$$

It is important to keep in mind that we are given ε and asked to find a $\delta(\varepsilon)$ such that the statement above is true. The task of finding the delta of epsilon rule is not always easy. To illustrate the procedure, we begin with linear functions.

example 103.1   Prove: $\lim_{x \to 2} (2x + 5) = 9$

solution   We are asked to find a rule for $\delta(\varepsilon)$ so that the distance between 9 and $2x + 5$ is less than ε no matter how small a value of ε is chosen. Thus $2x + 5$ must lie between $9 - \varepsilon$ and $9 + \varepsilon$.

$$9 - \varepsilon < 2x + 5 < 9 + \varepsilon$$

We solve for x.

$$4 - \varepsilon < 2x < 4 + \varepsilon \qquad \text{added } -5$$

$$2 - \frac{\varepsilon}{2} < x < 2 + \frac{\varepsilon}{2} \qquad \text{divided by 2}$$

All these steps are reversible. Thus $\delta(\varepsilon) = \frac{\varepsilon}{2}$. Once ε is chosen, an x-value between $2 - \frac{\varepsilon}{2}$ and $2 + \frac{\varepsilon}{2}$ guarantees that the value of $2x + 5$ will be within $\pm\varepsilon$ of 9.

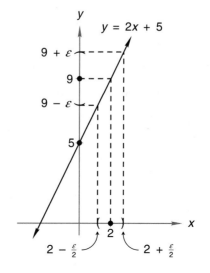

example 103.2   Prove that the limit as x approaches 3 of $3x - 5$ is 4 by finding a $\delta(\varepsilon)$ greater than 0 for every ε greater than 0 such that $0 < |x - 3| < \delta(\varepsilon)$ implies $|(3x - 5) - 4| < \varepsilon$.

solution   We begin by supposing ε is some small real number greater than 0. The value of $3x - 5$ must be between $4 - \varepsilon$ and $4 + \varepsilon$.

$$4 - \varepsilon < 3x - 5 < 4 + \varepsilon$$

We solve for x.

$$9 - \varepsilon < 3x < 9 + \varepsilon \qquad \text{added } +5$$

$$3 - \frac{\varepsilon}{3} < x < 3 + \frac{\varepsilon}{3} \qquad \text{divided by 3}$$

Thus we have found that $\delta(\varepsilon) = \frac{\varepsilon}{3}$. Now we need to confirm that $0 < |x - 3| < \delta(\varepsilon)$ implies $|(3x - 5) - 4| < \varepsilon$.

$$0 < |x - 3| < \delta(\varepsilon) \qquad \text{condition in definition}$$

$$|x - 3| < \frac{\varepsilon}{3} \qquad \text{substituted}$$

$$3|x - 3| < \varepsilon \qquad \text{multiplied}$$

$$|3x - 9| < \varepsilon \qquad \text{simplified}$$

$$|(3x - 5) - 4| < \varepsilon \qquad \text{rewritten}$$

Again the initial steps are reversible. So, if $0 < |x - 3| < \delta(\varepsilon)$, then $|(3x - 5) - 4| < \varepsilon$. Since we have satisfied the definition of limit, the limit is proved.

problem set 103

1. (63) When Forrest sells a tree for $20, he can sell 25 trees a day. For every $1.50 he lowers the price, he sells 7 more trees each day. At what value should he fix the price per tree to maximize his daily revenue? How many trees should he expect to sell at this price?

2. (46) A car travels west through an intersection at 40 miles per hour and continues in this direction at a constant speed. Thirty minutes later a car traveling south at 50 miles per hour passes through the same intersection and continues at a constant speed. How fast is the distance between the cars changing one hour after the south-bound car passes through the intersection?

3. (85) Find the equation of the line that can be drawn tangent to the graph of the function $y = 2^x$ on the interval $[0, 3]$ at the point guaranteed by the Mean Value Theorem.

4. (89) (a) What is the average value of $y = 2^x$ on the interval $[0, 3]$?
   (b) At what value of x is the average value attained?

5. (97) The base of a solid is the region bounded by the graphs of $y = x^2 - 2$ and $y = 2 - x^2$. Find the volume of the solid given that each vertical cross section perpendicular to the base and parallel to the y-axis is a square.

6. (97) The base of a solid is the region in the xy-plane bounded by $y = e^x$, the coordinate axes, and the line $x = 4$. Every vertical cross section of the solid parallel to the y-axis and perpendicular to the base is a semicircle.
   (a) Write the integral that can be used to find the volume of the solid.
   (b) Find the volume of the solid.

Prove that the limits in problems 7 and 8 are correctly stated.

7. (103) $\lim\limits_{x \to 4} (x - 3) = 1$
8. (103) $\lim\limits_{x \to 2} (3x - 1) = 5$

Evaluate the limits in problems 9–12.

9. (101) $\lim\limits_{x \to 0} \dfrac{\cos x - 1}{x}$

10. (102) $\lim\limits_{n \to \infty} \left(1 + \dfrac{1}{n}\right)^n$

11. (91) $\lim\limits_{x \to \infty} x^2 e^{-2x}$

12. (44) $\lim\limits_{h \to 0} \dfrac{f(x + h) - f(x - h)}{2h}$ where $f(x) = 3x^2$

13. Prove that the derivative of ln x with respect to x is $\dfrac{1}{x}$.
(102)

14. Without using L'Hôpital's Rule, prove that $\displaystyle\lim_{x\to0} \dfrac{\sin x}{x} = 1$.
(101)

15. Use the definition of the derivative to prove that the derivative of $\sin x$ with respect to x is $\cos x$
(60)   when x is measured in radians. You may use the fact that $\lim_{x\to0} \frac{\sin x}{x} = 1$.

16. Evaluate: $\displaystyle\int_0^4 |-x + 2|\, dx$
(96)

17. Use the trapezoidal rule with $n = 4$ to approximate $\displaystyle\int_0^{1.4} \sin(x^3)\, dx$.
(95)

18. Evaluate: $\dfrac{d}{dx}\displaystyle\int_0^x \sin k^3\, dk$
(98)

19. Approximate the root of $y = x^3 + 4x - 4$ to ten decimal places.
(93)

20. Sketch the graph of $y = \dfrac{x^2 - 2x}{1 - x^2}$.
(80)

21. Antidifferentiate: $\displaystyle\int \tan^4 x\, dx$
(100)

22. Use the equation of the line tangent to the curve $y = x^3y^3 - 4x^3y^2 + 25$ at the point $(2, 1)$ to
(99)   approximate the coordinates of the point where $x = 1.8$.

23. The function f is quadratic. Find the equation of f given that $f(2) = 0$, $f(-1) = 13$, and
(R) $f(4) = 38$.

24. What is the 40th term in the arithmetic sequence whose first 4 terms are $-5, -2, 1$, and 4?
(R)

25. Form the contrapositive of the following statement: If a building is tall, then it is a skyscraper.
(3)

LESSON 104   *Graphs of Solutions of Differential Equations •*
Slope Fields • Recognizing Graphs of Slope Fields

104.A

**graphs of
solutions of
differential
equations**

A differential equation is an equation that involves derivatives or differentials as discussed in Lesson 88. Some simple examples of differential equations are shown below.

$$V'(t) = kV(t) \qquad \dfrac{dy}{dx} = 2x$$

If k is a constant, the solutions of these differential equations are:

$$V(t) = Ae^{kt} \qquad \text{where } A \text{ is some constant}$$
$$y = x^2 + C \qquad \text{where } C \text{ is some constant}$$

These equations are said to be **general solutions** to their corresponding differential equations. We say that we have determined **explicit** solutions of the differential equations, since the solutions are described as functions of x. (Sometimes, solutions of differential equations cannot be explicitly written as functions and must be defined implicitly.)

Note that $y = x^2 + C$ describes an entire **family of solutions,** including the following:

$$y = x^2 + 1, \qquad y = x^2 - \frac{1}{2}, \qquad y = x^2 + \sqrt{3}, \qquad y = x^2 - \pi$$

Each of the equations listed is called a **particular solution** of the differential equation. We can graph some of the particular solutions of the differential equation to get a sense of the family of solutions. Notice the visual similarity of each of the graphs. We do not graph all of the particular solutions because they would cover every point in the coordinate plane, producing a black blob.

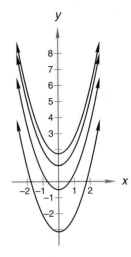

example 104.1   Solve the differential equation $\frac{dy}{dx} = -2x$. Graph four particular solutions to this equation, including one that passes through the point $(1, 1)$.

solution   We solve the differential equations using separation of variables.

$$\frac{dy}{dx} = -2x \qquad \text{equation}$$
$$dy = -2x \, dx \qquad \text{separated variables}$$
$$\int dy = \int -2x \, dx \qquad \text{integrated}$$
$$y + k = -x^2 + c \qquad \text{antidifferentiated}$$
$$\boldsymbol{y = -x^2 + C} \qquad \text{simplified}$$

To find the equation of the graph that passes through $(1, 1)$, we need to find the value of C for which $(1, 1)$ satisfies the equation $y = -x^2 + C$.

$$y = -x^2 + C$$
$$1 = -(1)^2 + C$$
$$2 = C$$

Therefore $y = -x^2 + 2$ is the equation of the graph that passes through $(1, 1)$. We graph this equation and three other arbitrarily chosen equations of the form $y = -x^2 + C$.

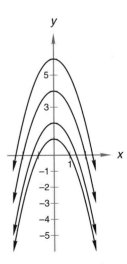

104.B

slope fields   In the previous section we were able to graph equations that satisfied a specific differential equation. With some differential equations it is more difficult (and sometimes impossible) to find the equation of the solutions. In this section we show how to obtain some visual sense of the solution of a differential equation without actually solving the differential equation.

For demonstration we use the differential equation

$$\frac{dy}{dx} = \frac{-x}{y}$$

This equation indicates that the slope of the graph of a solution at the point (x, y) is $\frac{-x}{y}$. For example, at the point $(2, 1)$ the slope of the graph of a solution is $\frac{-(2)}{1}$, or -2. To get some sense of the graph of the solution that passes through $(2, 1)$, we plot a short line segment at $(2, 1)$ that has a slope of -2. For a sense of the general solution, we do this for more points. For convenience we often choose points whose coordinates are integers. At the right we show a coordinate plane with dots at those points whose coordinates are integers.

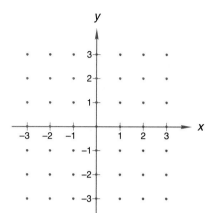

At each of these points we can determine $\frac{dy}{dx}$, since we know $\frac{dy}{dx} = \frac{-x}{y}$. [†]

x	y	Slope
0	0	indeterminate
1	0	undefined
0	1	0
−1	0	undefined
0	−1	0
2	1	−2
2	−1	2
−2	1	2
−2	−1	−2
⋮	⋮	⋮

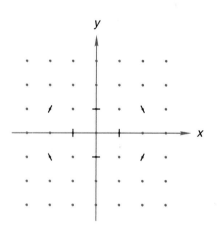

If we continue building the table and plotting the appropriate tangent segments, we get the graph at the right. The solutions appear to have a circular pattern, but note there is no segment at the origin.

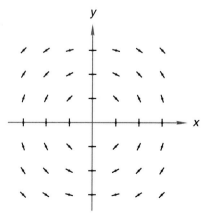

[†]*Note:* An expression like $\frac{1}{0}$ is an undefined expression, but it can be represented with a vertical line segment; however, the expression $\frac{0}{0}$ is indeterminate and cannot be represented by any line segment. Rather than give a rigorous explanation, we provide an intuitive one. Slope can be thought of graphically as "rise over run." $\frac{1}{0}$ can be thought of as rising 1 unit over a run of 0; the result is a vertical segment having infinite slope. The expression $\frac{0}{0}$ unfortunately cannot be expressed graphically as the slope of a line segment, because both the rise and run are 0.

Let us now solve the differential equation. Using separation of variables, we have the following:

$$\frac{dy}{dx} = \frac{-x}{y} \qquad \text{equation}$$

$$y\,dy = -x\,dx \qquad \text{separated variables}$$

$$\frac{y^2}{2} = \frac{-x^2}{2} + C \qquad \text{antidifferentiated}$$

$$\frac{x^2}{2} + \frac{y^2}{2} = C \qquad \text{simplified}$$

$$x^2 + y^2 = k \qquad \text{simplified}$$

This general solution to the differential equation is also the general equation of a circle of radius $\sqrt{k}$.

The graphs of some of the particular solutions to the differential equations are shown at the right. Note that these concentric circles have been traced out by the tangent segments we had drawn earlier. There are an infinite number of such circles we can draw.

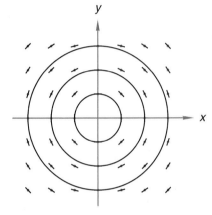

example 104.2 Draw a slope field for the differential equation $\frac{dy}{dx} = x$ by graphing short tangent segments at each dot on the coordinate plane at the right.

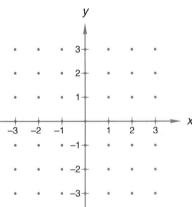

solution At each of the points shown, we draw a short segment that has a slope equal to the x-coordinate of the point. Each column in the slope field has the same slope since $\frac{dy}{dx}$ is independent of y—i.e., the slope $\frac{dy}{dx}$ depends only on x. The table on the left-hand side also indicates this.

x	$\dfrac{dy}{dx}$
−3	−3
−2	−2
−1	−1
0	0
1	1
2	2
3	3

example 104.3   Sketch a graph for the function with the slope field from example 104.2 that satisfies the initial condition (–3, 2). Sketch another graph for the function that satisfies the initial condition (1, 1).

solution   The slope field from example 104.2 represents an entire family of functions that satisfy the given differential equation. By selecting different initial conditions, we can determine different particular solutions of the differential equation.

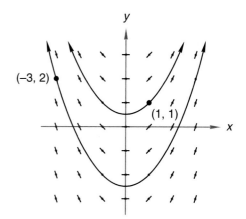

Drawing the particular solutions that satisfy the specific initial conditions may not necessarily be easy. The task seems to be akin to connecting the dots, but without the usual numbering as a guide. To figure out which sequence of dots to connect, we begin at the initial point and use the tangent segment at that point to direct us to another point, because each tangent segment describes the slope of a particular solution to the differential equation at some point. Drawing the solution curves is easier when there are more tangent segments. However, the task of drawing more tangent segments is also tedious.

104.C
recognizing graphs of slope fields

As we noted in the previous example, graphing slope fields and tracing out particular solutions of a differential equation using its slope field can be a lengthy and tedious process. Fortunately, technology makes the process simpler.

example 104.4   To which of the following differential equations could the slope field below correspond? (Assume the dots in the plane are at integer coordinates.)

A. $\dfrac{dy}{dx} = x^2$ B. $\dfrac{dy}{dx} = y - 2$ C. $\dfrac{dy}{dx} = \dfrac{xy}{2}$ D. $\dfrac{dy}{dx} = x + y$

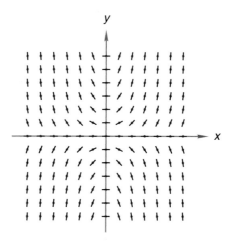

solution   Choice A can be eliminated because the points in any given column in the slope field do not have the same slope. In differential equation A the slope depends only on x but not y. In a similar fashion, since the points in any given row in the slope field do not have the same slope, B can be eliminated. In differential equation B the slope depends on y but not x.

For D we consider a specific point in the plane, such as $(-2, 4)$. At this point $\frac{dy}{dx} = -2 + 4 = 2$, which means the slope of the tangent line at the point $(-2, 4)$ should be positive. However, it is clear from the graph of the slope field that the slope of the line segment at $(-2, 4)$ is negative. Therefore, choice D is eliminated as well.

By process of elimination, the only viable choice is **C.**

Some may feel uncomfortable solving this problem simply by the process of elimination. We take the time to verify that the differential equation in C does indeed give rise to the slope field shown. We see that the differential equation

$$\frac{dy}{dx} = \frac{xy}{2}$$

has positive slope when x and y are both positive or both negative and negative slope when exactly one of the two is negative. Further, as x or y increases in absolute value (meaning as we venture farther and farther from the origin), the slope becomes steeper, either positively or negatively. All these traits are consistent with the slope field.

example 104.5   Shown below are four slope fields. Each slope field arises from a differential equation. For each of the graphs, select the equation that could be a particular solution of the differential equation that determines the slope field. The choices are given below the slope fields.

(a)

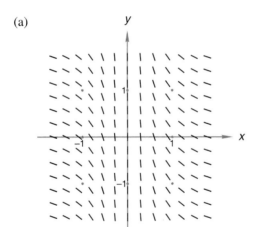

(b)

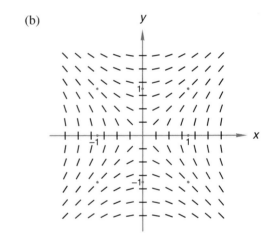

(c)

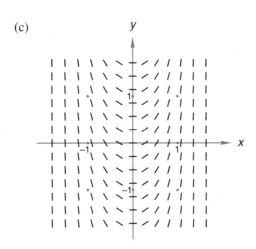

(d)

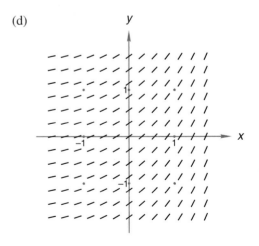

A. $x^2 - y^2 = 1$ B. $y = 2^x$ C. $y = e^{x^2}$ D. $y = \dfrac{1}{x}$

solution   Roughly, what we are trying to do is to identify which equation's graph can be traced out as a curve in each of the slope fields.

(a) The curve $y = \dfrac{1}{x}$ fits in this slope field: (b) $x^2 - y^2 = 1$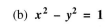

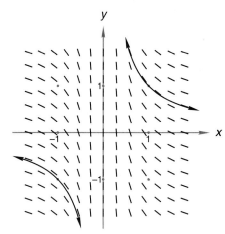   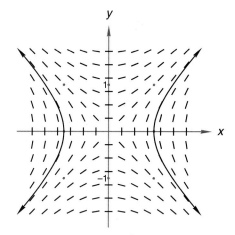

(c) $y = e^{x^2}$ (d) $y = 2^x$

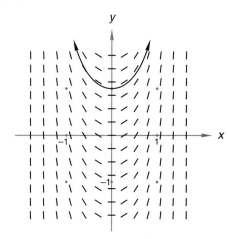   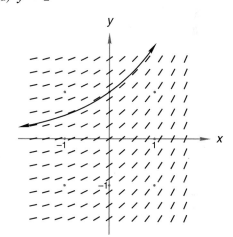

problem set
104

1. The velocity of a particle moving along a straight line at time t is given by the equation
(90) $v(t) = 2t^{1/2} + 4t^3$ meters per second. How many meters does the particle travel from $t = 0$
   to $t = 9$?

2. A cube, each of whose sides is 5 centimeters long, is coated with a thin layer of brass. The thickness
(99)   of the coating is 0.01 centimeters. Use differentials to estimate the volume of the brass layer.

3. The cost in dollars of producing x items is given by $c(x) = x(x - 150)^2 + 140$. Use differentials
(99)   to estimate the cost of producing one more item given that 151 have already been produced.

4. The function f is continuous on the interval $[1, 5]$, $f(1) = 6$, $f(2) = 2$, and $f(5) = 10$. Other
(63)   properties of f are as listed in the table below. Sketch the graph of f.

	$1 < x < 2$	$x = 2$	$2 < x < 5$
f'	negative	undefined	positive
f''	negative	undefined	negative

5. Draw a slope field for the differential equation $\dfrac{dy}{dx} = xy$.
(104)

6. Approximate $\int_0^\pi \sin x^2 \, dx$ using the trapezoidal rule with $n = 6$.
₍₉₅₎

7. To which of the following differential equations could this slope field correspond? (Consecutive slope segments are one unit apart.)
₍₁₀₄₎

A. $\dfrac{dy}{dx} = x^2$

B. $\dfrac{dy}{dx} = y$

C. $\dfrac{dy}{dx} = 3xy$

D. $\dfrac{dy}{dx} = x + 2y$

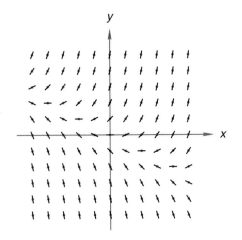

Evaluate the limits in problems 8–11.

8. $\displaystyle\lim_{x \to 0} \frac{\sin (2x)}{x}$
₍₁₀₁₎

9. $\displaystyle\lim_{x \to 0} \frac{4x}{\sin (7x)}$
₍₁₀₁₎

10. $\displaystyle\lim_{h \to 0} \left(1 + \frac{h}{x}\right)^{(x/h)}$
₍₁₀₂₎

11. $\displaystyle\lim_{h \to 0} \frac{e^{2+h} - e^2}{h}$
₍₄₄₎

12. Let $f(x) = \dfrac{d}{dx} \displaystyle\int_3^x e^{t^2 + 4} \, dt$. Find $f(0)$.
₍₉₈₎

13. Simplify: $\dfrac{d}{dx} \displaystyle\int_3^x (\sin t) e^{t^2 + 1} \, dt$
₍₉₈₎

14. Let R be the region completely bounded by $y = x(1 - x)$ and the x-axis. Use x as the variable of integration to write a definite integral whose value equals the volume of the solid formed when R is rotated about the line $x = -1$.
₍₉₄₎

Integrate in problems 15 and 16.

15. $\displaystyle\int \cot^3 x \, dx$
₍₁₀₀₎

16. $\displaystyle\int (\pi \sec^2 x)(e^{\tan x}) \, dx$
₍₆₆₎

17. Evaluate: $\displaystyle\int_{-3}^1 6|(x - 2)(x + 1)| \, dx$
₍₉₆₎

18. If g is the inverse function of f and $f(x) = x^3 + 3x - 1$, what is the value of $g'(35)$?
₍₉₂₎

19. Find the particular solution of $\dfrac{dy}{dx} = x^2 \sqrt{1 - y^2}$ whose graph intercepts the point $(3, 0)$.
₍₈₈₎

20. Differentiate $y = \dfrac{2\sqrt{x^3 - 1}}{\sin x + \cos (2x)} + e^{\sin x}$ with respect to x.
₍₅₀₎

Prove that the limits in problems 21 and 22 are correctly stated.

21. $\displaystyle\lim_{x \to 3} (2x - 5) = 1$
₍₁₀₃₎

22. $\displaystyle\lim_{x \to 4} \left(\frac{3}{2}x - 4\right) = 2$
₍₁₀₃₎

23. Given that the derivative of $\ln x$ with respect to x is $\frac{1}{x}$, prove that the derivative of e^x with respect to x is e^x.
₍₁₀₂₎

24. Let $f(x) = \sin |x|$. Determine the value of $f'\left(-\dfrac{5\pi}{6}\right)$.
(96)

25. Let $f(x) = x^3 + 2x$. Divide the interval $[0, 1]$ into n equal-width subintervals. Let x_i be some
(47) point in the ith subinterval. Write a definite integral whose value equals $\lim_{n \to \infty} \dfrac{1}{n} \sum_{i=1}^{n} f(x_i)$.

LESSON 105 *Sequences • Limit of a Sequence • Graphs of Sequences • Characteristics of Sequences*

105.A
sequences

A **sequence** is an ordered list of numbers. Each number in a sequence is called a **term** of the sequence. Examples of sequences are the sequence of positive integers, the sequence of perfect squares, and the sequence of odd numbers, which we show below.

$$1, 2, 3, 4, \ldots \qquad 1, 4, 9, 16, \ldots \qquad 1, 3, 5, 7, \ldots$$

In each of these examples the sequence has an infinite number of terms. In this book, when we use the word *sequence,* we assume the number of terms is infinite. Also, the sequences we discuss are ones that can be generated by some formula, but a sequence does not have to be generated by a specific mathematical formula. For example, we could consider the sequence of daily high temperatures in Norman, Oklahoma (where we wrote the book) beginning January 1, 1970. The advantage of a formulaic sequence is that the value of each term in the sequence is clearly defined. For example, if we write

$$\frac{1}{2}, \frac{2}{3}, \frac{3}{4}, \ldots, \frac{n}{n+1}, \ldots$$

we are describing a sequence whose nth term is definitely $\dfrac{n}{n+1}$.

Sequences can be denoted in a variety of ways. For example, the last sequence mentioned could be represented by any of the following:

$$a_n = \frac{n}{n+1}, \quad n = 1, 2, 3, \ldots \qquad \left\{\frac{n}{n+1}\right\} \qquad \left\{\frac{n}{n+1}\right\}_{n=1}^{\infty}$$

Any sequence can be represented by the following four notations:

$$a_1, a_2, a_3, \ldots \qquad a_n = f(n), \quad n = 1, 2, 3, \ldots$$
$$\{a_n\} \qquad \{a_n\}_{n=1}^{\infty}$$

example 105.1 List the first four terms of each of the following sequences:

(a) $a_n = 2n, \quad n = 1, 2, 3, \ldots$ (b) $a_n = (n+1)^2, \quad n = 0, 1, 2, \ldots$

(c) $a_n = \dfrac{1}{n}, \quad n = 1, 2, 3, \ldots$ (d) $a_n = (-1)^{n+1} \dfrac{n}{n+1}, \quad n = 1, 2, 3, \ldots$

solution To find the terms of the sequence, we use the generating equations listed on the left-hand side and plug in the numbers on the right-hand side.

(a) $a_n = 2n, \quad n = 1, 2, 3, \ldots$

$a_1 = \mathbf{2}, \ a_2 = \mathbf{4}, \ a_3 = \mathbf{6}, \ a_4 = \mathbf{8}$

(b) $a_n = (n + 1)^2$, $n = 0, 1, 2, 3, \ldots$

Note that the first term of the sequence is a_0, since we specified n to begin with 0.

$a_0 = \mathbf{1}$, $a_1 = \mathbf{4}$, $a_2 = \mathbf{9}$, $a_3 = \mathbf{16}$

(c) $a_n = \dfrac{1}{n}$, $n = 1, 2, 3, \ldots$

$a_1 = \mathbf{1}$, $a_2 = \dfrac{\mathbf{1}}{\mathbf{2}}$, $a_3 = \dfrac{\mathbf{1}}{\mathbf{3}}$, $a_4 = \dfrac{\mathbf{1}}{\mathbf{4}}$

(d) $a_n = (-1)^{n+1}\dfrac{n}{n + 1}$, $n = 1, 2, 3, \ldots$

$a_1 = \dfrac{\mathbf{1}}{\mathbf{2}}$, $a_2 = -\dfrac{\mathbf{2}}{\mathbf{3}}$, $a_3 = \dfrac{\mathbf{3}}{\mathbf{4}}$, $a_4 = -\dfrac{\mathbf{4}}{\mathbf{5}}$

example 105.2   Given the first few terms of the following sequences, determine a generating formula for each sequence. Let the first term of each sequence be indexed by 1 (i.e., let $n = 1, 2, 3, \ldots$).

(a) $2, 4, 6, 8, 10, \ldots$ (b) $1, 3, 5, 7, 9, \ldots$ (c) $0, \dfrac{1}{2}, \dfrac{3}{4}, \dfrac{7}{8}, \dfrac{15}{16}, \ldots$

solution   Notice we asked for *a* generating formula and not *the* generating formula for each of the sequences listed. Many different formulas may generate the same first four or five terms of any sequence. For problems of this sort, we will assume that there is an obvious pattern to each sequence. Our goal is to identify that pattern.

(a)   The sequence $2, 4, 6, 8, 10, \ldots$ looks like the obvious sequence of even numbers. We can describe the nth term of this sequence by the generating formula

$$a_n = 2n$$

For example, the third term, a_3, is simply $2(3) = 6$.

(b)   The sequence $1, 3, 5, 7, 9, \ldots$ is obviously the sequence of odd numbers. The generating formula for the nth term is a little tricky.

$$a_n = 2n - 1$$

For example, the third term, a_3, is simply $2(3) - 1 = 5$. How did we know this formula? Each term is one less than the corresponding term in the previous sequence (the sequence of even numbers).

(c)   This sequence is more difficult to describe. We ignore the first term for now. Note that the denominators of the other terms are powers of two and the numerators are each exactly one less than the denominator. We can therefore describe the nth term as

$$a_n = \frac{2^{n-1} - 1}{2^{n-1}}$$

We see that the first term also conforms to this pattern.

$$a_1 = \frac{2^{1-1} - 1}{2^{1-1}} = \frac{1 - 1}{1} = 0$$

105.B

limit of a sequence   In the previous section we informally defined a sequence as an ordered list of numbers. In this section we present a more formal and rigorous definition.

DEFINITION OF A SEQUENCE

A **sequence** is a function whose domain is the positive integers.

Unfortunately this definition is not very intuitive; however, it has great utility. Since a sequence is a function, we can apply concepts about functions to sequences. A sequence **converges** to a number if all its terms after some specified term are close to the number. A more rigorous definition follows in the box below.

LIMIT OF A SEQUENCE

A sequence $\{a_n\}$ **converges** to L or has the **limit** L, written

$$\lim_{n \to \infty} a_n = L$$

if for any number $\varepsilon > 0$ there exists an integer N such that

$$\left| a_n - L \right| < \varepsilon$$

for all $n \geq N$.

If the sequence $\{a_n\}$ does not converge, then we say it **diverges.**

Some general rules for the limits of sequences follow. They are essentially the same as the rules we have been using for limits of functions.

LIMIT RULES FOR SEQUENCES

If $\{a_n\}$ and $\{b_n\}$ are convergent sequences and if $\lim\limits_{n \to \infty} a_n = K$ and $\lim\limits_{n \to \infty} b_n = L$, then

   1. $\lim\limits_{n \to \infty} (a_n + b_n) = K + L$

   2. $\lim\limits_{n \to \infty} (a_n - b_n) = K - L$

   3. $\lim\limits_{n \to \infty} (a_n \cdot b_n) = K \cdot L$

   4. $\lim\limits_{n \to \infty} \left(\dfrac{a_n}{b_n} \right) = \dfrac{K}{L}$ provided $L \neq 0$

There is also an analogue of the squeeze theorem.

SQUEEZE THEOREM FOR SEQUENCES

If $\{a_n\}$, $\{b_n\}$, and $\{c_n\}$ are convergent sequences with $a_n \leq b_n \leq c_n$ for all n and $\lim\limits_{n \to \infty} a_n = \lim\limits_{n \to \infty} c_n = L$, then $\lim\limits_{n \to \infty} b_n = L$.

Finally, we state a theorem that is very useful in determining the limit of a sequence.

THEOREM

If $a_n = f(n)$ for each positive integer n, then

$$\lim_{x \to \infty} f(x) = L \text{ implies } \lim_{n \to \infty} a_n = L$$

This theorem allows us to determine the limit of a sequence by analyzing the function on an expanded domain rather than as a function on the positive integers; these functions (the ones without restricted domains) are the ones for which we have been finding limits all along.

example 105.3   The generating formulas for four sequences are given below. Determine whether each corresponding sequence converges or diverges. If a sequence converges, state its limit.

(a) $a_n = \dfrac{3n}{5n + 3}$ (b) $a_n = \dfrac{3^n}{n^2}$ (c) $a_n = 1 - \dfrac{1}{2^n}$ (d) $a_n = \dfrac{\cos^2 n}{2^n}$

solution   (a) We want to determine the behavior of the terms $\frac{3n}{5n+3}$ as n grows large. That is, we want to determine

$$\lim_{n \to \infty} \frac{3n}{5n + 3}$$

We divide numerator and denominator by the highest power of n.

$$\lim_{n \to \infty} \frac{3n}{5n + 3} = \lim_{n \to \infty} \frac{3}{5 + \dfrac{3}{n}} = \frac{3}{5}$$

Therefore, the sequence **converges to** $\frac{3}{5}$. Notice that we simply used a technique discussed in Lesson 17.

(b) We begin with the generating formula

$$a_n = \frac{3^n}{n^2}$$

Our familiarity with exponential and polynomial functions should tell us that 3^n grows large much faster than n^2. A quick glance at their graphs also shows this.

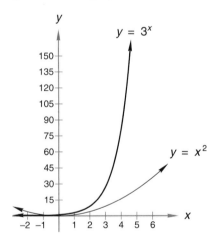

Therefore, as n grows large, $\frac{3^n}{n^2}$ grows large, since the numerator dwarfs the denominator. To approach the problem analytically, we apply L'Hôpital's Rule twice.

$$\lim_{n \to \infty} \frac{3^n}{n^2} = \lim_{n \to \infty} \frac{3^n \ln 3}{2n} \qquad \text{L'Hôpital's Rule}$$

$$= \lim_{n \to \infty} \frac{3^n (\ln 3)^2}{2} \qquad \text{L'Hôpital's Rule}$$

$$= +\infty$$

Therefore the sequence **diverges.**

(c) We can easily see that $\frac{1}{2^n}$ gets small (close to 0) as n gets large. Therefore the sequence generated by the formula $a_n = 1 - \frac{1}{2^n}$ **converges to 1.**

(d) We apply the squeeze theorem here, noting that

$$0 \le \cos^2 n \le 1$$

for all natural numbers n. Likewise,

$$\frac{0}{2^n} \le \frac{\cos^2 n}{2^n} \le \frac{1}{2^n}$$

for all n. Since $\lim_{n \to \infty} \frac{0}{2^n} = 0$ and $\lim_{n \to \infty} \frac{1}{2^n} = 0$, we can use the squeeze theorem to conclude

$$\lim_{n \to \infty} \frac{\cos^2 n}{2^n} = 0$$

Therefore, the sequence **converges to 0.**

105.C

graphs of sequences Contrary to the graphs of continuous functions, the graphs of sequences simply involve a series of discrete points, because the domain of a sequence is just the set of positive integers, not an interval of values.

example 105.4 Graph the sequence defined by $a_n = 2n$, $n = 1, 2, 3, 4, \ldots.$

solution We can easily build the following table of values for this sequence:

n	1	2	3	4	5
a_n	2	4	6	8	10

For example, the table feature on the TI-83, accessed by pressing [2nd] [GRAPH] (TABLE), can be used to construct such a table. This shows that we must plot the points $(1, 2)$, $(2, 4)$, $(3, 6)$, $(4, 8)$, and $(5, 10)$. Additional points can be plotted as desired. The graph of the sequence is below.

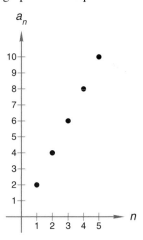

Note that these points are not connected.

example 105.5 Graph the sequence generated by $a_n = \dfrac{10n}{n + 1}$ on the graphing calculator.

solution To be able to produce the graph of this sequence on the TI-83, we need to first press the [MODE] key and select Seq (in the fourth row) and Dot (in the fifth row), as shown.

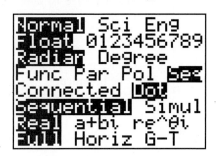

We then press the 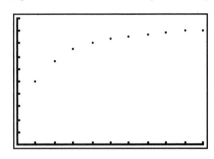 key to access the equation menu. We set `nMin=1` (this is the beginning value for *n* in our sequence) and define `u(n)=10n/(n+1)`. We then press WINDOW to access the window parameters. Since the values of $u(n)$ are positive and range from 0 to no more than 10, we set our window parameters accordingly. Appropriate settings are shown below along with the graph.

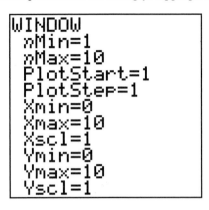

105.D
characteristics of sequences

In this section we define possible characteristics of sequences. After giving the rigorous mathematical definitions, we provide some examples for illustration.

DEFINITION OF INCREASING, DECREASING, AND MONOTONIC

A sequence $\{a_n\}$ is said to be **increasing** if $a_{n+1} \geq a_n$ for all $n > 1$.

A sequence $\{a_n\}$ is said to be **decreasing** if $a_{n+1} \leq a_n$ for all $n > 1$.

A sequence is said to be **monotonic** if it is either increasing or decreasing.

An example of an increasing sequence is the sequence $\{a_n\}$ where $a_n = n$. This is the sequence: 1, 2, 3, 4, …. Not only is this sequence increasing, it can also be said to be **strictly increasing,** since each term is strictly greater than the previous term.

An example of a decreasing sequence is the sequence $\{a_n\}$ where $a_n = \frac{1}{n}$. This is the sequence: $1, \frac{1}{2}, \frac{1}{3}, \frac{1}{4}, \dots$. It is a decreasing sequence, since the terms get smaller and smaller. But we can also say that this sequence is **strictly decreasing,** since every term is strictly less than the previous term. Both of these sequences are monotonic.

DEFINITION OF BOUNDED

A sequence $\{a_n\}$ is said to be **bounded above** if there is some number *M* such that

$$a_n \leq M \text{ for all } n \geq 1$$

A sequence $\{a_n\}$ is said to be **bounded below** if there is some number *m* such that

$$a_n \geq m \text{ for all } n \geq 1$$

A sequence that is both bounded above and bounded below is simply said to be **bounded.**

For example, the sequence $\{a_n\}$ where $a_n = 1 - n$ is bounded above by 0. The terms of this sequence are 0, –1, –2, –3, …. The sequence $\{a_n\}$ where $a_n = n$ is bounded below by 1, since all the terms of the sequence are greater than or equal to 1. (*Note:* We could also have said $\{a_n\}$ is bounded below by –1, since all of its terms are positive and therefore greater than –1.)

The sequence $\{a_n\}$ where $a_n = (-1)^n$ is bounded, since all of the terms are greater than or equal to –1 and less than or equal to 1.

We now state a highly important theorem.

THEOREM

Every bounded, monotonic sequence converges.

What this succinctly stated theorem says is that if a sequence is both bounded and either decreasing or increasing, then it must converge to some limit. For example, the sequence $\{a_n\}$ where $a_n = \frac{1}{n}$ is bounded above by 1 and bounded below by 0. The sequence is decreasing, since as n gets larger, $\frac{1}{n}$ gets smaller. Therefore, by the theorem, the sequence must converge. It turns out that the sequence converges to 0.

example 105.6 Indicate whether each of the following sequences

(1) is increasing, decreasing, or neither.

(2) is bounded above, bounded below, both, or neither.

(3) converges or diverges.

(a) $\{a_n\}$ where $a_n = 1 - \dfrac{1}{2^n}$ (b) $\{b_n\}$ where $b_n = n!$ (c) $\{c_n\}$ where $c_n = \cos(n\pi)$

solution   (a) We list the first few terms of the sequence.

$$a_1 = \frac{1}{2}, \; a_2 = \frac{3}{4}, \; a_3 = \frac{7}{8}, \; \cdots$$

As n increases, $\frac{1}{2^n}$ decreases. Therefore $a_n = 1 - \frac{1}{2^n}$ gets larger as n increases. We conclude that $\{a_n\}$ is an **increasing** sequence. Furthermore the sequence is **both bounded above and below.** It is bounded above by 1 and bounded below by $\frac{1}{2}$. We know by the theorem stated in the lesson that every bounded, monotonic sequence converges. Therefore $\{a_n\}$ **converges.**

(b) Again we list the first few terms of the sequence.

$$b_1 = 1, \; b_2 = 2, \; b_3 = 6, \; \cdots$$

We see immediately that $\{b_n\}$ is an **increasing** sequence, that it is **bounded below** by 1, and that it **diverges** (since the terms increase without bound).

(c) We list the first few terms of the sequence.

$$c_1 = \cos \pi = -1, \; c_2 = \cos(2\pi) = 1, \; c_3 = \cos(3\pi) = -1$$

We see that the sequence $\{c_n\}$ is one whose terms oscillate between –1 and 1. Therefore, it is **neither increasing nor decreasing.** It is, however, **bounded both above and below.** This sequence also **diverges,** because its terms do not get closer and closer to any particular number.

problem set 105

1. A solid has a base bounded by $y = x^2$ and $y = 4$. Find its volume given that every vertical (97) cross section perpendicular to the base and parallel to the x-axis is an equilateral triangle.

2. The rate of change in the number of bacteria is proportional to the number of bacteria present. (26) Initially there were 1000 bacteria, and 10 minutes later there were 3000 bacteria. Write an equation that expresses the number of bacteria as a function of time t.

Write the first four terms of each sequence given in problems 3–5. For each sequence, the domain is $n = 1, 2, 3, \ldots$.

3. $a_n = \dfrac{n+1}{n}$
(105)

4. $a_n = \dfrac{2-n}{n^2}$
(105)

5. $a_n = \dfrac{\ln n}{n}$
(105)

Transform the sequences given in problems 6 and 7 into generator form. Use the domain $n = 1, 2, 3, \ldots$.

6. $\dfrac{1}{2}, \dfrac{2}{3}, \dfrac{3}{4}, \dfrac{4}{5}, \ldots$
(105)

7. $1, -\dfrac{1}{3}, \dfrac{1}{9}, -\dfrac{1}{27}, \ldots$
(105)

Determine whether each sequence in problems 8–10 converges or diverges. If a sequence converges, state its limit.

8. $a_n = \dfrac{\ln n}{\ln (2n)}$
(105)

9. $a_n = \dfrac{e^n}{n^3}$
(105)

10. $a_n = \left(1 + \dfrac{1}{n}\right)^n$
(105)

Evaluate the limits in problems 11–14.

11. $\lim\limits_{x \to 0} \dfrac{7x}{\sin (13x)}$
(101)

12. $\lim\limits_{x \to 0} \dfrac{1 - \cos x}{x}$
(101)

13. $\lim\limits_{x \to 0^+} \dfrac{2x^2 + x}{(\ln x)^2}$
(79)

14. $\lim\limits_{x \to 0} [(1 - \cos x)(\csc x)]$
(91)

15. Use differentials to approximate $(9.3)^2 - \sqrt{9.3}$.
(99)

Simplify the expressions in problems 16 and 17.

16. $\dfrac{d}{dx}\left(\displaystyle\int_7^x (t^3 - 4t^2 + 3t - 7)\, dt\right)$
(98)

17. $\displaystyle\int_3^x \left[\dfrac{d}{dx}\left(\displaystyle\int_3^x (t^3 - 4t^2 + 3t - 7)\, dt\right)\right] dx$
(98)

18. Approximate the negative-valued x-intercept of the graph of the function $y = x^3 - 4x^2 + 6$
(93) to nine decimal places.

19. (a) Draw a slope field for the differential equation $\dfrac{dy}{dx} = y^2$.
(104)

   (b) Draw a possible graph for the function with this slope field that satisfies the initial condition $(1, 1)$.

20. Approximate $\displaystyle\int_{\pi/2}^{\pi} \dfrac{\sin x}{x}\, dx$ using the trapezoidal rule with $n = 4$.
(95)

21. Find an antiderivative of $\ln (x^x x^x x^x x^x)$ with respect to x.
(69)

22. Use an epsilon-delta proof to show that $\lim\limits_{x \to 6}\left(\dfrac{2}{3}x - 1\right) = 3$.
(103)

23. Prove that the derivative of $\ln x$ with respect to x is $\dfrac{1}{x}$.
(102)

24. Evaluate: $\displaystyle\int_1^9 \left|\sqrt{x} - 2\right| dx$
(96)

25. Find the exact area under $y = x^2 + 3$ on the interval $[0, 4]$ by summing the areas of infinitely
(43) many circumscribed rectangles.

LESSON 106   *Introduction to Parametric Equations • Slope of Parametric Curves*

106.A
introduction to parametric equations

Thus far many problems have described the motion of a particle moving along the x-axis. In these instances the independent variable was time (t), and the dependent variable was the position (x). That is, the position of the particle on the x-axis depended on the value of the time variable. This section begins to examine the motion of a particle in two-dimensional space, often the xy-plane.

From your experience graphing, you know a function that defines y in terms of x can be used to describe the path of a particle in the xy-plane. However, when discussing motion, we usually prefer to discuss the position of a particle at a particular instant in time. With a function that defines y in terms of x, this is not possible. In order to do so, both the x- and y-coordinates of the moving particle are expressed in terms of a third variable, time (t). The equations

$$x = f(t) \quad \text{and} \quad y = g(t)$$

which express both x and y in terms of t are called **parametric equations.** The third variable, t in this case, is called the **parameter.** In this pair of parametric equations, both x and y are dependent variables, because they both depend on the value of the independent variable t.

example 106.1   Sketch the path traced by the point $P(x, y)$ given that $x = t + 2$ and $y = 3t - 1$ for every real number t.

solution   The equations can either be graphed in parametric form as they are given, or the parameter can be eliminated so that y is expressed in terms of x (rectangular form). We first examine parametric graphing.

Perhaps the simplest way to graph parametric equations is to set up a table of values and then graph the resulting x- and y-coordinates.

t	−2	−1	0	1	2
x	0	1	2	3	4
y	−7	−4	−1	2	5

From this table of points, we can plot the curve.

It appears the parametric equations $x = t + 2$ and $y = 3t - 1$ simply define a line in the Cartesian plane.

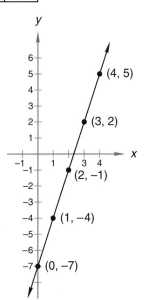

Another method of graphing parametric equations is to express them in rectangular form. This is known as **elimination of parameters.** Here we are attempting to eliminate the presence of t in the description of the curve. The equation $x = t + 2$ can be rewritten as $t = x - 2$. Substituting this expression, $x - 2$, for the value of t in the equation $y = 3t - 1$ gives $y = 3t - 1 = 3(x - 2) - 1$ or $y = 3x - 7$. The parameter t is absent from this equation, but notice that the parametrically determined graph previously drawn is the graph of the line $y = 3x - 7$. Hence the path traced out by the point $P(x, y)$ can be described by the equation $y = 3x - 7$.

Note: Parametric equations can be plotted using the TI-83. To do so, the function **MODE** of the calculator must be changed to Par (for parametric). Once the calculator is in parametric mode, we can press **Y=** and see the following:

```
Plot1  Plot2  Plot3
\X1T=
 Y1T=
\X2T=
 Y2T=
\X3T=
 Y3T=
\X4T=
```

The calculator is requesting both X and Y as functions of T. (The variable T is placed in these equations via the **X,T,θ,n** button.) We enter $\mathsf{T+2}$ for $\mathsf{X1T}$ and $\mathsf{3T-1}$ for $\mathsf{Y1T}$. Then we use the following settings to change the view of the graphing window:

```
WINDOW
 Tmin=-5
 Tmax=5
 Tstep=.1
 Xmin=-10
 Xmax=10
 Xscl=1
 Ymin=-10
 Ymax=10
 Yscl=1
```

Pressing **GRAPH** yields the desired graph.

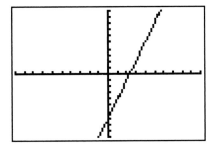

example 106.2   Graph the curve that corresponds to the parametric equations $x = 2t$ and $y = t^2 + 1$.

solution   Once again we can either graph the curve in parametric form or eliminate the parameter and graph it in rectangular form. At this point it is wise to practice both procedures.

First we make a table of values.

t	−2	−1	0	1	2
x	−4	−2	0	2	4
y	5	2	1	2	5

We can then plot points to approximate the shape of the curve.

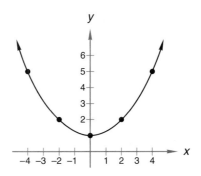

It appears the curve is a parabola symmetric about the y-axis. Note that t is not plotted here. Indeed, if we were simply given the graph without the parametric equations, it would be impossible for us to determine the values of t that correspond to each individual point.

Now we graph the curve by the second method. To eliminate the parameter, we solve for t and then substitute into the equation for y.

$$x = 2t \quad \longrightarrow \quad t = \frac{x}{2}$$

Substitution yields

$$y = t^2 + 1 \quad \longrightarrow \quad y = \left(\frac{x}{2}\right)^2 + 1$$

$$\longrightarrow \quad y = \frac{x^2}{4} + 1$$

Expressing y in terms of x gives an equation that confirms earlier speculation about the graph. The graph is indeed a parabola that is symmetric about the y-axis.

example 106.3   Graph the curve resulting from the parametric equations $x = \cos t$ and $y = \sin t$.

solution   We first graph the curve in parametric form. Here is a table of values generated from the parametric equations.

t	0	$\dfrac{\pi}{4}$	$\dfrac{\pi}{2}$	$\dfrac{3\pi}{4}$	π	$\dfrac{5\pi}{4}$	$\dfrac{3\pi}{2}$	$\dfrac{7\pi}{4}$	2π
x	1	$\dfrac{\sqrt{2}}{2}$	0	$-\dfrac{\sqrt{2}}{2}$	-1	$-\dfrac{\sqrt{2}}{2}$	0	$\dfrac{\sqrt{2}}{2}$	1
y	0	$\dfrac{\sqrt{2}}{2}$	1	$\dfrac{\sqrt{2}}{2}$	0	$-\dfrac{\sqrt{2}}{2}$	-1	$-\dfrac{\sqrt{2}}{2}$	0

These points are graphed at the right with a curve passing through the points.

This appears to be the graph of a circle of radius 1 centered at the origin. Elimination of parameters confirms this supposition. We use the fact that $\sin^2 t + \cos^2 t = 1$ for all values of t. Since $x = \cos t$ and $y = \sin t$, $x^2 = \cos^2 t$ and $y^2 = \sin^2 t$, so that $x^2 + y^2 = 1$. Indeed, this is an algebraic description of a circle.

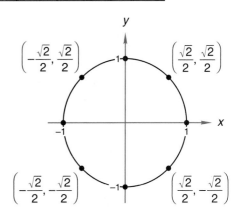

106.B

slope of parametric equations

The previous section examined curves defined by parametric equations. These curves can be called **parametric curves.** This section shows how to find the slope of a tangent drawn to such curves. The slope of a curve drawn in the xy-plane is given by $\frac{dy}{dx}$, which describes the change in y divided by the change in x. The box below shows how $\frac{dy}{dx}$ can be computed for parametric curves.

$$\frac{dy}{dx} = \frac{\frac{dy}{dt}}{\frac{dx}{dt}}$$

This is a consequence of the chain rule, which says $\frac{dy}{dt} = \frac{dy}{dx} \cdot \frac{dx}{dt}$. Dividing both sides of this equation by $\frac{dx}{dt}$ gives the equation in the box above. It is worth noting that $\frac{dy}{dx}$ can be discussed for parametric curves even when y is not a function of x, because $\frac{dy}{dx}$ represents slope, which only depends on the curve.

example 106.4   (a) Find $\dfrac{dy}{dx}$ for the parametric equations $x = \cos t$ and $y = \sin t$.

(b) Find the slope of the curve determined by the given parametric equations at the point where $x = \frac{\sqrt{3}}{2}$ and $y = \frac{1}{2}$.

solution   (a) We simply use

$$\frac{dy}{dx} = \frac{\frac{dy}{dt}}{\frac{dx}{dt}}$$

Here $\dfrac{dx}{dt} = -\sin t$ and $\dfrac{dy}{dt} = \cos t$. Therefore

$$\frac{dy}{dx} = \frac{\frac{dy}{dt}}{\frac{dx}{dt}} = \frac{\cos t}{-\sin t} = \frac{x}{-y} = -\frac{x}{y}$$

The fact that $\frac{dy}{dx}$ involves both x and y is not of concern. Indeed, implicitly differentiating $x^2 + y^2 = 1$ (the rectangular form of the parametric equations in this example) would yield the same result.

(b) To find the slope of the curve at the point $\left(\dfrac{\sqrt{3}}{2}, \dfrac{1}{2}\right)$, remember that

$$\frac{dy}{dx} = \frac{\frac{dy}{dt}}{\frac{dx}{dt}} = -\frac{x}{y}$$

Note that

$$\frac{dy}{dx} = -\frac{\frac{\sqrt{3}}{2}}{\frac{1}{2}} = -\sqrt{3}$$

Here is a picture of the curve and its tangent line at $\left(\frac{\sqrt{3}}{2}, \frac{1}{2}\right)$.

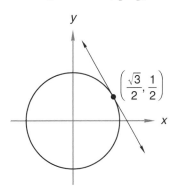

problem set 106

Each pair of equations in problems 1 and 2 represents a parametrically defined curve.

(a) Sketch the curve determined by the equations.

(b) Find $\dfrac{dy}{dx}$ from the parametric form.

(c) Eliminate the parameter to find y as a function of x.

1. $x = 3t + 2,\ y = t^2$
(106)

2. $x = t^3,\ y = t^2$
(106)

3. The profit (in dollars) made from the sale of x items is given by
(99)

$$p(x) = -(x - 100)^2 + 200x$$

Use differentials to estimate the change in profit if 101 items are sold instead of 100 items.

4. Estimate $\sqrt[3]{68}$ using differentials.
(99)

5. Approximate the value of $\sqrt[3]{68}$ to nine decimal places using Newton's method. (*Hint:* Find the zero of the function $y = x^3 - 68$.)
(93)

6. Use the trapezoidal rule with $n = 6$ to approximate $\displaystyle\int_0^1 \sin\left(x^2\right)\,dx$.
(95)

7. Find the exact area under $y = \dfrac{1}{x}$ on the interval $[1, 4]$.
(102)

8. Using the trapezoidal rule, how many intervals are necessary to approximate the area under $y = \frac{1}{x}$ on the interval $[1, 4]$ with an error less than 0.01.
(95)

9. The base of a solid is the region bounded by $y = x^2$ and $y = 4$. Every vertical cross section of the object perpendicular to the base and parallel to the y-axis is an isosceles triangle with a height of 6. Find the volume of the object.
(97)

Evaluate the limits in problems 10–12.

10. $\displaystyle\lim_{x\to 0} \frac{1 - \cos x}{x}$
(101)

11. $\displaystyle\lim_{x\to 0}\left(1 + \frac{x}{3}\right)^{3/x}$
(102)

12. $\displaystyle\lim_{x\to 0}\left(\frac{1}{x} - \frac{1}{2e^x - 2}\right)$
(91)

13. Simplify: $\dfrac{d}{dx}\displaystyle\int_{12}^{x} \frac{\sin k}{k}\,dk$
(98)

Integrate in problems 14 and 15.

14. $\displaystyle\int 2\cot^2 x\,dx + \int \frac{1}{2}\tan^2 x\,dx$
(100)

15. $\displaystyle\int 2\sin^2 x\,dx + \int \sin^3 x\,dx$
(76,83)

16. Let R be the region between $y = e^{-x^2}$ and the x-axis on the interval $[0, 1]$. Find the volume of
(87) the solid formed when R is revolved about the y-axis.

17. The function $f(x) = x^2 + x + 1$ satisfies the conditions of the Mean Value Theorem on the
(85) interval $[1, 3]$. Find a number c that confirms the conclusion of the theorem.

18. Suppose $f(x) = 3x^2 + 2x + 1$. Verify the Mean Value Theorem for Integrals for f on the
(89) interval $[1, 3]$.

19. Suppose $f(x) = a \sin x + b \cos x$. Find a and b such that $f'(\pi) = 2$ and $f'\left(\dfrac{\pi}{2}\right) = 4$.
(61)

20. (a) List the first four terms of the sequence given by $a_n = \frac{3n^2 - 4n}{2 - 5n^2}$, $n = 1, 2, 3, \ldots$.
(105)
    (b) Determine whether the sequence converges or diverges. If the sequence converges, state its limit.

21. Find a generating formula for the sequence whose terms are $\frac{1}{2}, \frac{4}{3}, \frac{9}{4}, \frac{16}{5}, \ldots$, for $n = 1, 2, 3, \ldots$.
(105)

22. Find a generating formula for the sequence $a_3 = \dfrac{1}{2}, a_4 = \dfrac{4}{3}, a_5 = \dfrac{9}{4}, a_6 = \dfrac{16}{5}, \ldots$.
(105)

Determine whether the sequences in problems 23 and 24 converge or diverge. If a sequence converges, state its limit.

23. $a_n = \dfrac{n^2 - 3n + 98}{4^n}$
(105)

24. $a_n = \dfrac{e^n}{n^2}$
(105)

25. Let $x(t) = \dfrac{1}{t}$ and $y(t) = t^2$ for $t > 0$.
(106)

    (a) Graph x as a function of t.
    (b) Graph y as a function of t.
    (c) Graph y as a function of x.

LESSON 107 *Polar Coordinates • Polar Equations*

107.A

polar coordinates

There is only one rectangular form of a point in the xy-plane, but there are multiple ways the polar form of the same point can be written, because both positive and negative angles and magnitudes can be used.

example 107.1 Convert the point $(-3, 2)$ to polar coordinates. Write the four forms of the polar coordinates of this point.

solution On the right-hand side we graph the point and draw a right triangle. Note that one side of the triangle is perpendicular to the x-axis.

By the Pythagorean theorem

$$r^2 = 2^2 + 3^2 = 13$$

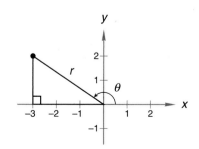

So $r = \sqrt{13} \approx 3.6056$. Moreover, $\tan \theta = -\dfrac{2}{3}$, so $\theta = \arctan\left(-\dfrac{2}{3}\right) \approx 146.31°$.

We can represent the point $(-3, 2)$ in the xy-plane with two new pieces of information, the distance r from the origin to the point $(-3, 2)$ and the angle θ. Thus $(-3, 2)$ in polar form is **3.6056$\underline{/146.31°}$.**[†]

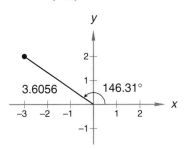

Notice that we can also determine the angle in a clockwise fashion.

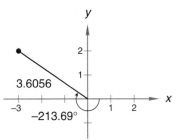

Hence the polar representation of $(-3, 2)$ can also be written as **3.6056$\underline{/-213.69°}$.**

It is also possible to use negative values for r.

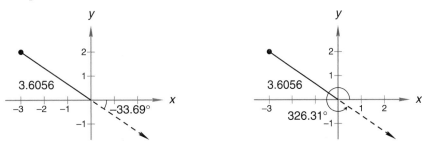

Therefore the point has other representations: **$-3.6056\underline{/-33.69°}$** and **$-3.6056\underline{/326.31°}$.** All of these forms are legitimate because they all describe the point $(-3, 2)$ in the xy-plane.

example 107.2   Let P be the point whose rectangular representation is $(4, 3)$. Express P in polar form.

solution   We first graph P on the coordinate plane. Then we draw a right triangle to determine r and θ.

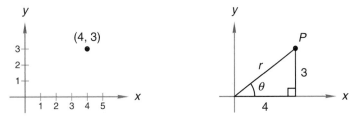

The right triangle establishes relationships for r and θ.

$$r = 5 \quad \text{and} \quad \tan \theta = \frac{3}{4}$$

$$\theta \approx 36.8699°$$

Therefore one polar representation of P is **5$\underline{/36.8699°}$.** Other representations can be used; however, we consider this one the simplest and most obvious.

[†]Another way of writing this is $(3.6056, 146.31°)$. However, we use a nontraditional notation in this textbook to avoid mistaking polar representations for rectangular representations. In this example the degree symbol prevents any ambiguity. When radian measures are used instead of degrees there is potential for confusion.

107.B

polar equations

An equation can be written in rectangular form by using x and y or in polar form by using r and θ. Sometimes one form of an equation is simpler or easier to use than the other. We show a few examples of this phenomenon here.

GRAPH	RECTANGULAR EQUATION	POLAR EQUATION
	$x^2 + y^2 = 4$	$r = 2$
	$(x - 1)^2 + y^2 = 1$	$r = 2\cos\theta$
	$y = x$	$\theta = \dfrac{\pi}{4}$
	$y = x + 1$	$r = \dfrac{1}{\sin\theta - \cos\theta}$
	$y = 4$	$r = 4\csc\theta$

GRAPH (CONTINUED)	RECTANGULAR EQUATION (CONTINUED)	POLAR EQUATION (CONTINUED)
	$x^2 + y^2 - 4x - 4\sqrt{x^2 + y^2} = 0$	$r = 4 + 4 \cos \theta$
	$x^4 + 2x^2y^2 - 2xy + y^4 = 0$	$r^2 = \sin (2\theta)$
	$y = \dfrac{1}{x}$	$r^2 = \dfrac{1}{\sin \theta \cos \theta}$

Converting equations from polar form to rectangular form and vice versa requires the use of the relationships obtained from the illustration at the right.

By the Pythagorean theorem

$$r = \sqrt{x^2 + y^2}$$

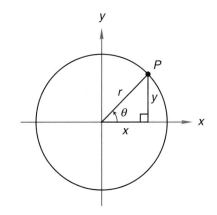

Substituting into the definitions of trigonometric functions,

$$\cos \theta = \frac{x}{r} = \frac{x}{\sqrt{x^2 + y^2}} \qquad \sin \theta = \frac{y}{r} = \frac{y}{\sqrt{x^2 + y^2}} \qquad \tan \theta = \frac{y}{x}$$

These relationships help convert polar equations into rectangular ones. Notice also

$$x = r \cos \theta \qquad y = r \sin \theta$$

These allow conversions from rectangular to polar form.

example 107.3   Write the polar form of $y = x^2$.

solution   We replace y with $r \sin \theta$ and x with $r \cos \theta$.

$$r \sin \theta = (r \cos \theta)^2 \qquad \text{substituted}$$

$$r \sin \theta = r^2 \cos^2 \theta \qquad \text{multiplied}$$

$$r = \frac{\sin \theta}{\cos^2 \theta} \qquad \text{rearranged}$$

$$r = \boldsymbol{\sec \theta \tan \theta} \qquad \text{simplified}$$

Note the implications in going from the second line to the third. In the second equation we see that if $\cos \theta$ is zero, then $r \sin \theta$ must be zero. Since $\sin \theta$ and $\cos \theta$ never equal zero simultaneously, r must be zero when $\cos \theta$ is zero. Therefore, to be precise, $y = x^2$ can be written as $r = \sec \theta \tan \theta$ when $\cos \theta$ is not zero. When $\cos \theta$ is zero, r is also zero.

example 107.4   Write the polar form of $(x - 1)^2 + y^2 = 1$.

solution   We replace y with $r \sin \theta$ and x with $r \cos \theta$. Then we simplify.

$$(r \cos \theta - 1)^2 + (r \sin \theta)^2 = 1 \qquad \text{substituted}$$

$$r^2 \cos^2 \theta - 2r \cos \theta + 1 + r^2 \sin^2 \theta = 1 \qquad \text{multiplied}$$

$$r^2(\sin^2 \theta + \cos^2 \theta) - 2r \cos \theta = 0 \qquad \text{simplified}$$

$$r^2 = 2r \cos \theta \qquad \text{simplified}$$

$$r = \boldsymbol{2 \cos \theta} \qquad \text{divided by}$$

Note that we assumed $r \neq 0$ in the last line. (Otherwise, we would have divided by 0.) However, the case $r = 0$ should not be forgotten. There is one point on the graph of $(x - 1)^2 + y^2 = 1$ that satisfies $r = 0$, namely the origin. We show a graph of $(x - 1)^2 + y^2 = 1$ for illustrative purposes.

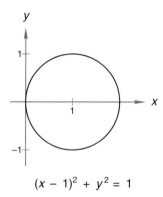

$(x - 1)^2 + y^2 = 1$

example 107.5   Write the rectangular form of the equation $r = 1 - \cos \theta$.

solution   We replace r with $\sqrt{x^2 + y^2}$ and $\cos \theta$ with $\dfrac{x}{\sqrt{x^2 + y^2}}$ and simplify.

$$\sqrt{x^2 + y^2} = 1 - \frac{x}{\sqrt{x^2 + y^2}} \qquad \text{substituted}$$

$$x^2 + y^2 = \sqrt{x^2 + y^2} - x \qquad \text{multiplied by } \sqrt{x^2 + y^2}$$

$$x^2 + y^2 - \sqrt{x^2 + y^2} + x = 0 \qquad \text{rearranged}$$

Note that in the equation

$$\sqrt{x^2 + y^2} = 1 - \frac{x}{\sqrt{x^2 + y^2}}$$

x and y cannot both be zero, because that would result in the term $\frac{x}{\sqrt{x^2 + y^2}}$ not being defined. However, the origin is part of the graph of the polar equation $r = 1 - \cos\theta$, since $r = 0$ when $\theta = 0$. Thus the rectangular point $(0, 0)$ is permissible—not only that, it is required. We eliminated the complication introduced in the intermediate step by multiplying both sides by $\sqrt{x^2 + y^2}$. The final equation $x^2 + y^2 - \sqrt{x^2 + y^2} + x = 0$ allows the point $(0, 0)$ to be included. Therefore we can conclude that the equations $r = 1 - \cos\theta$ and $x^2 + y^2 - \sqrt{x^2 + y^2} + x = 0$ produce the same graph.

problem set
107

1. The base of a solid is the region bounded by $y = \sin x$ and the x-axis on the interval $[0, \pi]$.
(97) Every vertical cross section of the object perpendicular to the x-axis is an equilateral triangle. Find the volume of the solid.

2. The position function of a particle that moves along the x-axis is $x(t) = t^3 - 6t^2 + 9t + 1$.
(90)
(a) Find the velocity function and the acceleration function for this particle.

(b) Determine $v(4)$ and $a(3)$.

3. (a) For what values of t is the particle whose position is described by
(90) $x(t) = t^3 - 6t^2 + 9t + 1$ moving to the left?

(b) For what values of t is the particle moving to the right?

(c) Find the total distance traveled by the particle between $t = 0$ and $t = 4$.

4. The region bounded by $y = \sin^{3/2} x$ and the x-axis on the interval $[0, \pi]$ is revolved around the
(76) x-axis. Find the volume of the resulting solid.

5. The figure shows the triangular end of a
(74) trough that is 20 meters long. The trough is
filled to a depth of 3 meters with a fluid
whose weight density is 3000 newtons per
cubic meter. Find the force of the fluid on
the end of the trough.

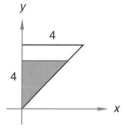

6. Sketch a graph of the curve defined by $x = 2t - 3$ and $y = t^2 + 2$. Find $\frac{dy}{dx}$ for the given
(106) parametric equations, and then eliminate the parameter to write the equation in rectangular form.

7. Convert the point $(-2, 3)$ to polar form.
(107)

8. Convert the point $\left(1, \dfrac{1}{2}\right)$ to polar form. Express the solution four different ways.
(107)

9. Write the polar form of the rectangular equation $y = 2x^2$.
(107)

10. Write the rectangular form of the polar equation $r = \sin\theta$.
(107)

Determine whether the sequences in problems 11 and 12 converge or diverge. If a sequence converges, state its limit.

11. $a_n = \dfrac{2n^2}{(2n + 1)^2}$
(105)

12. $a_n = \dfrac{7}{n!}$
(105)

13. Find a generating formula for the sequence whose terms are $1, -\frac{8}{9}, 1, -\frac{32}{25}, \frac{64}{36}, -\frac{128}{49}, \ldots$ Index
(105) the sequence by $n = 2, 3, 4, 5, \ldots$

14. Use the trapezoidal rule with $n = 6$ to approximate $\displaystyle\int_0^2 \dfrac{dx}{x^2 + 9}$.
(95)

15. Evaluate: $\displaystyle\int_0^2 \frac{dx}{x^2 + 9}$
(64)

16. Use an epsilon-delta proof to show that $\displaystyle\lim_{x \to 1} \left(\frac{3}{4}x + 2 \right) = \frac{11}{4}$.
(103)

Evaluate the limits in problems 17–19.

17. $\displaystyle\lim_{x \to 0} \frac{x - \sin x}{x}$
(79)

18. $\displaystyle\lim_{x \to \infty} \frac{(\ln x)^2}{x}$
(79)

19. $\displaystyle\lim_{x \to \infty} \left(1 + \frac{1}{x} \right)^{4x}$
(102)

20. Find a value of c for $f(x) = \tan x$ on the interval $(0, \frac{\pi}{4})$ that confirms the Mean Value Theorem.
(85)

21. Consider the function $f(x) = ae^x + b \sin x$. If $f'(0) = 4$ and $f''(0) = 7$, what are the values of a and b?
(61)

22. Find the smallest positive solution of $2^x = \tan x$ using a graphing calculator.
(2)

23. If $f(x) = (x - 3)^2 + 1$, what is $\dfrac{d}{dx} f(|x|)$?
(96)

24. Use the definition of the derivative to show that the derivative of $\sin x$ with respect to x is $\cos x$.
(101)

25. Suppose $\displaystyle\int_c^x f(t) \, dt = 4x^4 - 4$.
(98)

    (a) Find the equation of f. (*Hint:* Differentiate both sides of the equation.)

    (b) Use the equation of f to find c.

LESSON 108 *Introduction to Vectors • Arithmetic of Vectors • Unit Vectors and Normal Vectors*

108.A
introduction to vectors

Many physical quantities involve both magnitude and direction. Examples of such quantities include force, velocity, and acceleration. In mathematics these quantities are called *vectors*.

> **DEFINITION OF VECTOR**
>
> A **vector** is a quantity that has both magnitude and direction.

Pictorially, a vector can be represented by a directed line segment. An example is shown below.

This vector is denoted $\overrightarrow{PQ}$, which is read "vector PQ." For the vector shown, P is called the **initial point,** and Q is called the **terminal point.** Its magnitude is the distance between its initial and terminal points, which is denoted by $\left|\overrightarrow{PQ}\right|$.

Often vectors are denoted by boldface lowercase letters such as *v, w,* and *z.* However, it is difficult to draw boldface letters by hand, so many people draw arrows over them instead: for example, $\vec{v}, \vec{w},$ and $\vec{z}.$ We follow that convention in this textbook.

The vector below can be represented numerically in two ways.

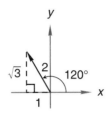

One possible representation is $2\underline{/120°}$. This polar form indicates that the vector's magnitude is 2 and its direction is 120° (measured from the positive *x*-axis). However, the vector can also be represented by $\langle -1, \sqrt{3} \rangle$. This notation indicates that the terminal point of the vector is 1 unit left of its initial point and $\sqrt{3}$ units above it. Unlike the polar notation, the rectangular notation does not explicitly identify the vector's magnitude and direction. However, it is useful in many other respects.

It is important not to confuse the vector $\langle -1, \sqrt{3} \rangle$ with the point $(-1, \sqrt{3})$. Vectors are not bound to physical locations. They only have a specific magnitude and direction according to the definition. Thus each vector in the graph below is correctly described by the notation $\langle -1, \sqrt{3} \rangle$. In fact, all these vectors are equal.

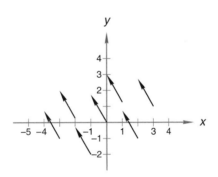

example 108.1   Draw vector $\vec{v}$ in standard position with a terminal point of $(-4, 2)$.

solution   A vector in standard position is one whose initial point is at the origin. We simply draw the directed line segment from the point $(0, 0)$ to the point $(-4, 2)$.

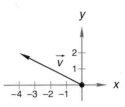

In this case $\vec{v} = \langle -4, 2 \rangle$.

example 108.2   Determine the magnitude $|\vec{v}|$ of the vector $\vec{v} = \langle -4, 2 \rangle$.

solution   We simply find the length of the line segment from the point $(0, 0)$ to the point $(-4, 2)$.

$$|\vec{v}| = \sqrt{(-4 - 0)^2 + (2 - 0)^2} \qquad \text{distance formula}$$
$$= \mathbf{2\sqrt{5}} \qquad \text{simplified}$$

example 108.3   Determine the magnitude $|\vec{v}|$ of the vector $\vec{v} = 6\underline{/42°}$.

solution   Recall that $\vec{v} = 6\underline{/42°}$ is a vector with magnitude of 6 whose direction is 42° from the positive *x*-axis as shown at the right.

So it is easy to determine the length of $\vec{v}$.

$$|\vec{v}| = \mathbf{6}$$

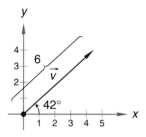

108.B

arithmetic of vectors

We now turn to various arithmetic issues associated with vectors. This section shows how to add and subtract vectors, as well as how to multiply a vector by a **scalar** (a real number).

example 108.4   Let $\vec{v}_1 = \langle -4, 2 \rangle$ and $\vec{v}_2 = \langle 7, 3 \rangle$. Express $\vec{v}_1 + \vec{v}_2$ in component form. That is, express it in the form $\langle a, b \rangle$.

solution   To find this sum, we simply add the corresponding components.

$$\vec{v}_1 + \vec{v}_2 = \langle -4, 2 \rangle + \langle 7, 3 \rangle$$
$$= \langle -4 + 7, 2 + 3 \rangle$$
$$= \langle \mathbf{3, 5} \rangle$$

There is also a graphical approach to the sum of two vectors. We first draw $\vec{v}_1$ and $\vec{v}_2$ in standard position on the *xy*-plane.

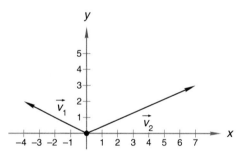

Then we create a parallelogram using these two vectors as its two sides.

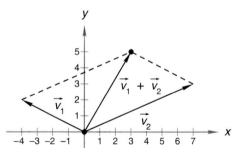

The diagonal of this parallelogram whose initial point corresponds to the initial points of the two vectors is actually the sum vector $\vec{v}_1 + \vec{v}_2$. This method of producing $\vec{v}_1 + \vec{v}_2$ from $\vec{v}_1$ and $\vec{v}_2$ is called the **parallelogram method.**

example 108.5   Determine $\vec{v}_1 + \vec{v}_2$ where $\vec{v}_1 = \langle 2, -3 \rangle$ and $\vec{v}_2 = \langle 3, 5 \rangle$.

solution   As before, the sum is produced by adding corresponding components.

$$\vec{v}_1 + \vec{v}_2 = \langle 2, -3 \rangle + \langle 3, 5 \rangle$$
$$= \langle 2 + 3, -3 + 5 \rangle$$
$$= \langle \mathbf{5, 2} \rangle$$

For illustration, we show another graphical approach, the **triangle method.** First we draw $\vec{v}_1$ in standard position. Then we draw $\vec{v}_2$ with its initial point placed at the terminal point of $\vec{v}_1$.

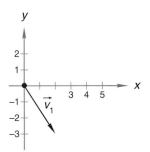
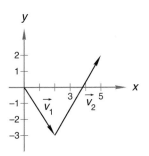

Finally we create a triangle by drawing a vector from the initial point of $\vec{v}_1$ to the terminal point of $\vec{v}_2$. This vector is $\vec{v}_1 + \vec{v}_2$.

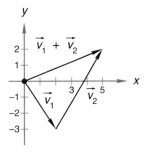

example 108.6   Let $\vec{v}_1 = 3\underline{/37°}$ and $\vec{v}_2 = -4\underline{/290°}$. Express $\vec{v}_1 + \vec{v}_2$ in component form.

solution   We cannot find the sum of these two vectors until we resolve $\vec{v}_1$ and $\vec{v}_2$ into their x- and y-components. We begin with $\vec{v}_1$.

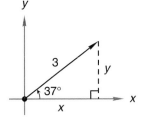

Note   that $x = 3 \cos 37°$ and $y = 3 \sin 37°$. Using a calculator in degree mode, we get the following approximations:

$$x \approx 2.3959 \qquad y \approx 1.8054$$

So $\vec{v}_1 = 3\underline{/37°} \approx \langle 2.3959, 1.8054 \rangle$.

Next we find the components of $\vec{v}_2$.

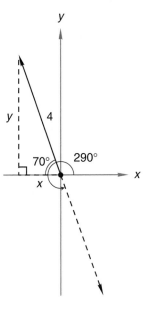

For $\vec{v}_2$, $x = -4 \cos 70°$ and $y = 4 \sin 70°$. The approximations of these values are

$$x \approx -1.3681 \qquad y \approx 3.7588$$

Thus $\vec{v}_2 \approx \langle -1.3681, 3.7588 \rangle$. We add corresponding components to obtain our result.

$$\vec{v}_1 + \vec{v}_2 \approx \langle 2.3959 + (-1.3681), 1.8054 + 3.7588 \rangle$$
$$\approx \langle \mathbf{1.0278, 5.5642} \rangle$$

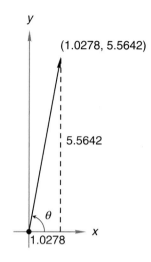

Pictorially $\vec{v}_1 + \vec{v}_2$ is represented at right.

Notice that the length, or magnitude, of this vector is $\sqrt{(1.0278)^2 + (5.5642)^3}$, which is approximately equal to 5.6583. Moreover, the angle θ satisfies

$$\tan \theta = \frac{5.5642}{1.0278} = 5.41369916\ldots$$

which implies $\theta \approx 79.53°$. Therefore we may also say $\vec{v}_1 + \vec{v}_2 \approx 5.6583\underline{/79.53°}$.

example 108.7   Find $\vec{v}_1 - \vec{v}_2$ where $\vec{v}_1 = \langle -4, 2 \rangle$ and $\vec{v}_2 = \langle 7, 3 \rangle$.

solution   The difference $\vec{v}_1 - \vec{v}_2$ is simply $\vec{v}_1 + (-\vec{v}_2)$, where $-\vec{v}_2$ is the "negative" of $\vec{v}_2$, the vector of the same magnitude but in the exact opposite direction.

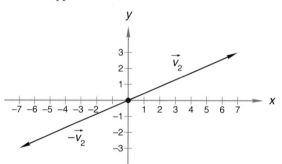

Therefore

$$\vec{v}_1 - \vec{v}_2 = \vec{v}_1 + (-\vec{v}_2)$$
$$= \langle -4, 2 \rangle + \langle -7, -3 \rangle$$
$$= \langle \mathbf{-11, -1} \rangle$$

As with addition, there is a graphical way to subtract vectors. First we graph both vectors in standard position.

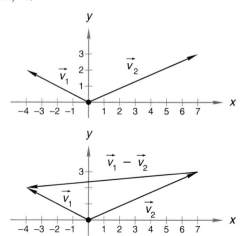

The vector $\vec{v}_1 - \vec{v}_2$ is the vector that can be added to $\vec{v}_2$ to get $\vec{v}_1$. Thus we draw a vector from the initial point of $\vec{v}_2$ to the initial point of $\vec{v}_1$ to get $\vec{v}_1 - \vec{v}_2$.

From the graph we see

$$\vec{v}_1 - \vec{v}_2 = \langle -11, -1 \rangle,$$

which is consistent with our calculation.

example 108.8   Let $\vec{v} = \langle -4, 2 \rangle$. Find $2\vec{v}$ and $-3\vec{v}$.

solution   To determine $2\vec{v}$, we simply multiply each component of $\vec{v}$ by 2.

$$\vec{v} = \langle -4, 2 \rangle$$
$$2\vec{v} = \langle 2(-4), 2(2) \rangle$$
$$\mathbf{2\vec{v} = \langle -8, 4 \rangle}$$

Note the graphical significance of scalar multiplication.

Multiplication of a vector by a positive scalar does not change the direction of the vector, but it does affect the magnitude. The magnitude of $c\vec{v}$ is equal to c times the magnitude of $\vec{v}$.

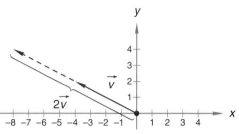

We can perform similar operations to determine $-3\vec{v}$.

$$-3\vec{v} = \langle -3(-4), -3(2) \rangle$$
$$\mathbf{-3\vec{v} = \langle 12, -6 \rangle}$$

Unlike multiplication by a positive scalar, negative scalars change the direction of a vector, as demonstrated below.

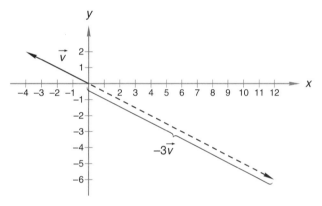

example 108.9   Let $\vec{v} = 3\underline{/37°}$. Find $2\vec{v}$.

solution   Multiplication of $\vec{v}$ by 2 does not affect the direction of the vector, so we retain an angle of 37°.

$$2\vec{v} = 2(3)\underline{/37°} = \mathbf{6\underline{/37°}}$$

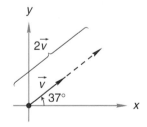

108.C

unit vectors and normal vectors

In light of magnitude and scalar multiplication, a new definition is introduced. A **unit vector** is a vector whose magnitude is 1. For example, the vector in standard position whose terminal point is $(0, -1)$ is a unit vector.

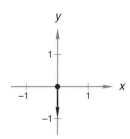

In the Cartesian plane the standard unit vectors are $\langle 1, 0 \rangle$ and $\langle 0, 1 \rangle$, which are denoted $\hat{i}$ (read "i hat") and $\hat{j}$ (read "j hat"). Hats, or carets, are used above these vectors instead of arrows to indicate that they are the standard unit vectors. Any vector in the xy-plane can be expressed in the form $a\hat{i} + b\hat{j}$. For example, the vector $\vec{v} = \langle -2, 4 \rangle$ can also be expressed as $-2\hat{i} + 4\hat{j}$.

From the figure below, it is clear that $\hat{i}$ and $\hat{j}$ are perpendicular to each other.

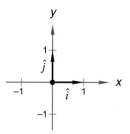

When two vectors are perpendicular to each other, we say they are **normal** to each other.

example 108.10 The initial point of a vector $\vec{v}$ is (3, 1), and its terminal point is (1, –2). Express $\vec{v}$ in the form $a\hat{i} + b\hat{j}$.

solution We begin with a graph of the vector.

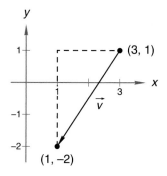

To get from the initial x-coordinate to the terminal x-coordinate, we must move two units left. Thus $a = -2$. To get from the initial y-coordinate to the terminal y-coordinate, we must move 3 units down. Thus, $b = -3$.

$$\vec{v} = -2\hat{i} - 3\hat{j}$$

This problem may be solved another way. We can treat the initial point (3, 1) as a vector $\vec{v}_1 = \langle 3, 1 \rangle$ in standard position and the terminal point (1, –2) as a vector $\vec{v}_2 = \langle 1, -2 \rangle$ in standard position. This leads to the following graph:

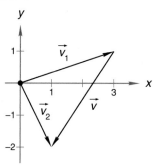

We can see that $\vec{v}$ is the difference of $\vec{v}_2$ and $\vec{v}_1$. Therefore

$$\begin{aligned}
\vec{v} &= \vec{v}_2 - \vec{v}_1 \\
&= \langle 1, -2 \rangle - \langle 3, 1 \rangle \\
&= \langle 1 - 3, -2 - 1 \rangle \\
&= \langle -2, -3 \rangle \\
&= -2\hat{i} - 3\hat{j}
\end{aligned}$$

The answer is the same as before.

example 108.11   Find a unit vector that has the same direction as $\vec{v} = \langle 3, -2 \rangle$.

solution   A unit vector is a vector whose magnitude is 1. If we simply divide $\vec{v}$ by its magnitude, or multiply $\vec{v}$ by $\frac{1}{|\vec{v}|}$, we will obtain a unit vector. Moreover, it will be in the same direction as $\vec{v}$, since it is a scalar multiple of $\vec{v}$.

$$|\vec{v}| = \sqrt{3^2 + (-2)^2} = \sqrt{13}$$

So we multiply $\vec{v}$ by the reciprocal of $\sqrt{13}$.

$$\frac{1}{\sqrt{13}} \vec{v} = \left\langle \frac{3}{\sqrt{13}}, -\frac{2}{\sqrt{13}} \right\rangle$$

This vector is in the same direction as $\vec{v}$ but now has magnitude 1. You should verify this for practice.

example 108.12   Find a unit vector that is normal to $\vec{v} = \langle -4, 5 \rangle$.

solution   First we find a unit vector that is parallel to $\vec{v}$. Note that $|\vec{v}| = \sqrt{(-4)^2 + 5^2} = \sqrt{41}$. So $\vec{u} = \left\langle -\frac{4}{\sqrt{41}}, \frac{5}{\sqrt{41}} \right\rangle$ is a unit vector parallel to $\vec{v}$. Below we show this vector and a unit vector that is normal to it.

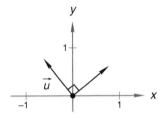

The slope of $\vec{u}$ is

$$\frac{\dfrac{5}{\sqrt{41}} - 0}{-\dfrac{4}{\sqrt{41}} - 0} = -\frac{5}{4}$$

Thus the normal vector has a slope of $\frac{4}{5}$. We got the normal vector by switching the coordinates of the unit vector and removing one negative sign (in other cases we may need to insert one negative sign). Thus a unit vector normal to $\vec{v}$ is $\left\langle \frac{5}{\sqrt{41}}, \frac{4}{\sqrt{41}} \right\rangle$.

example 108.13   Find a unit vector parallel to and a unit vector normal to the line tangent to the curve $y = x^2 - 3x + 1$ at the point $(1, -1)$.

solution   We begin with a sketch of the curve and a unit tangent vector.

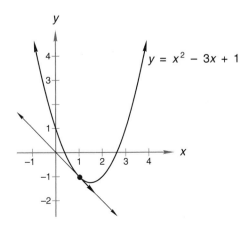

A vector parallel to the tangent line at $x = 1$ is a vector in the same direction as the tangent line at $x = 1$. Observe that $\frac{dy}{dx} = 2x - 3$, so

$$\left.\frac{dy}{dx}\right|_{x=1} = 2(1) - 3 = -1$$

So we first need a vector with such a slope. One such vector is $\vec{v} = \langle 1, -1 \rangle$. This vector is in the same direction as the tangent line, but it is not a unit vector. Notice that $|\vec{v}| = \sqrt{2}$, so $\left\langle \frac{1}{\sqrt{2}}, -\frac{1}{\sqrt{2}} \right\rangle$ **is a unit vector parallel to the tangent line. Thus** $\left\langle \frac{1}{\sqrt{2}}, \frac{1}{\sqrt{2}} \right\rangle$ **is a unit vector normal to the tangent line at (1, –1).**

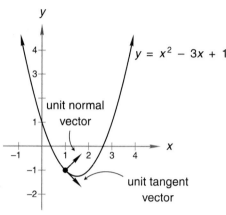

problem set 108

1. The initial point of the vector $\vec{v}$ is (1, 2). Its terminal point is (3, –2). Express $\vec{v}$ in the form $a\hat{i} + b\hat{j}$.
(108)

2. The initial point of the vector $\vec{v}$ is (–3, 4), and its terminal point is the origin. Express $\vec{v}$ in the form $a\hat{i} + b\hat{j}$.
(108)

3. Express the unit vector obtained by rotating $\hat{j}$ counterclockwise 150° in the form $\langle a, b \rangle$.
(108)

4. Express the unit vector having the same direction as $8\hat{i} - 6\hat{j}$ in the form $r\underline{/\theta}$.
(108)

5. Find a unit vector parallel to and a unit vector normal to the line tangent to the curve $y = 3x^2 - 4$ at the point (2, 8).
(108)

6. Indicate whether each of the following statements is true or false. If a statement is false, give a counterexample.
(82,103)

(a) All continuous functions are integrable.

(b) All continuous functions are differentiable.

(c) All integrable functions are differentiable.

(d) All differentiable functions are continuous.

7. Find the volume of the solid formed when the region bounded by $y = \cos x$ and the x-axis on the interval $\left[-\frac{\pi}{2}, \frac{\pi}{2}\right]$ is rotated around the line $x = 3$.
(94)

8. Let R be the region bounded by $y = \sin^2 x$ and $y = 2\sin^2 x$ where $0 \le x \le \pi$. Express the volume of the solid formed when R is rotated about the x-axis as a definite integral.
(81,83)

9. The area between $y = e^x$ and the x-axis on the interval [–1, 1] is the base of a solid. Each vertical cross section of the object parallel to the y-axis is a square. Find the volume of the solid.
(97)

10. Find the equation of the line tangent to the graph of $y = 4^x$ at the point where $x = 1$.
(72)

11. Suppose $\int_0^k e^{x^2}\, dx = c$, where $k > 0$. Evaluate $\int_{-k}^k e^{x^2}\, dx$.
(86)

Determine whether each sequence in problems 12 and 13 converges or diverges. If a sequence converges, state its limit.

12. $a_n = \dfrac{3^n}{n^3}$
(105)

13. $a_n = \left(\dfrac{1}{3}\right)^n$
(105)

14. Find a generating formula for the sequence whose first four terms are $a_1 = -\frac{1}{3}$, $a_2 = \frac{4}{9}$,
(105) $a_3 = -\frac{9}{27}$, and $a_4 = \frac{16}{81}$.

15. What is $\displaystyle\lim_{h \to 0} \frac{f(2 + h) - f(2)}{h}$ if $f(x) = \sin x$?
(28)

16. If $\displaystyle\int_{-1}^{5} f(x)\,dx = 7$ and $\displaystyle\int_{-1}^{3} f(x)\,dx = -3$, what is $\displaystyle\int_{3}^{5} f(x)\,dx$?
(57)

Antidifferentiate in problems 17–19.

17. $\displaystyle\int 2x \ln x\,dx$
(69)

18. $\displaystyle\int \tan^3 (2x)\,dx$
(100)

19. $\displaystyle\int \frac{x^3 + 4x^2 - 3x + 7}{x^2}\,dx$
(38)

20. Simplify: $\displaystyle\frac{d}{dx}[\arcsin (2x)] + \int \frac{2}{\sqrt{1 - 4x^2}}\,dx$
(64)

For problems 21 and 22 a particle is moving in the Cartesian coordinate plane according to the parametric equations $x = 3t$ and $y = t^2 + 1$.

21. As the particle passes through a point whose x-coordinate is 9, what is its y-coordinate?
(106)

22. (a) Sketch a graph of the path that the particle follows based on the parametric equations.
(106)

  (b) Find: $\dfrac{dy}{dx}$

  (c) Eliminate the parameter to express the parametric equations in rectangular form.

23. Write the polar form of the line $y = 2x + 3$.
(107)

24. Find the x-values of all the local maximums, local minimums, and points of inflection of the
(49) curve $y = 3x^4 - 12x^3 - 24x^2$.

25. Find the Maclaurin series of $\ln (1 - x)$. Use the first three terms of the series you find to
(55) estimate $\ln (1.1)$.

LESSON 109 Arc Length I: Rectangular Equations

We have seen integration applied to various applications, including the determination of area, volume, and work. This lesson introduces a new application—finding the length of an arc of a curve. Integration, the summation of infinitely many items, appears again. This investigation of arc length begins by noting the distance formula between two points (x_1, y_1) and (x_2, y_2):

$$d = \sqrt{(x_2 - x_1)^2 + (y_2 - y_1)^2} \quad \text{or}$$
$$d = \sqrt{(\Delta x)^2 + (\Delta y)^2}$$

Unfortunately, finding the length of an arc means dealing with a curve that is not a straight line. This complicates matters, but only slightly. To develop a formula for arc length, we simply break the curve into many small pieces that can be nicely approximated by line segments and add the lengths of those line segments. To eliminate the error, we let the number of such segments go to infinity and the length of each segment approach 0. An integral arises again.

This development is somewhat informal. However, it contains the essential points. We begin with the following diagram:

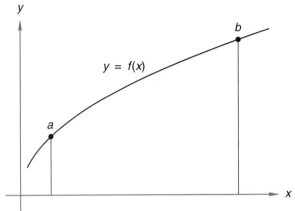

We are interested in calculating the length of this arc from point a to point b, denoted by L_a^b. Next, we cut this arc into several segments and draw in a typical right triangle.

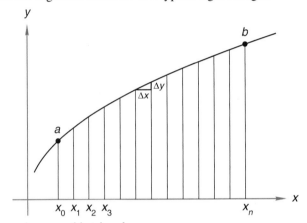

Now we focus on the region near this triangle:

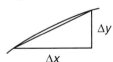

Note that the hypotenuse closely approximates the actual arc, so the length of the arc is approximately $\sqrt{(\Delta x)^2 + (\Delta y)^2}$.

$$L_a^b \approx \sum_{i=1}^{n} \sqrt{(\Delta x_i)^2 + (\Delta y_i)^2}$$

$$\approx \sum_{i=1}^{n} \sqrt{1 + \left(\frac{\Delta y_i}{\Delta x_i}\right)^2} (\Delta x_i)$$

where Δx_i and Δy_i are the change in x and change in y in the ith subinterval. This approximation of L_a^b becomes better as n grows and becomes exact as n approaches ∞.

$$L_a^b = \lim_{n \to \infty} \sum_{i=1}^{n} \sqrt{1 + \left(\frac{\Delta y_i}{\Delta x_i}\right)^2} (\Delta x_i)$$

The Mean Value Theorem implies that

$$\frac{\Delta y_i}{\Delta x_i} = f'(c_i)$$

for some value c_i in the ith subinterval. Therefore

$$L_a^b = \lim_{n \to \infty} \sum_{i=1}^{n} \sqrt{1 + (f'(c_i))^2} (\Delta x_i)$$

In this limit Δx_i approaches 0, yielding a Riemann sum. Thus

$$L_a^b = \int_{x_a}^{x_b} \sqrt{1 + (f'(x))^2} \ dx$$

Hence we have the formula for arc length:

$$L_a^b = \int_{x_a}^{x_b} \sqrt{1 + (f'(x))^2} \ dx \text{ where } x_a \text{ is the } x\text{-coordinate of point } a$$
and x_b is the x-coordinate of point b.

example 109.1   Find the length of the graph of $y = 7x + 5$ between the points $a = (1, 12)$ and $b = (3, 26)$.

solution   From the formula we have

$$L_a^b = \int_1^3 \sqrt{1 + (f'(x))^2} \ dx$$

$$= \int_1^3 \sqrt{1 + (7)^2} \ dx$$

$$= \int_1^3 \sqrt{50} \ dx = \sqrt{50}x\Big|_1^3 = 2\sqrt{50} = \mathbf{10\sqrt{2}}$$

Of course, since this is just straight-line distance, we can check the answer using the distance formula.

$$L_a^b = \sqrt{(3 - 1)^2 + (26 - 12)^2}$$

$$= \sqrt{4 + 196}$$

$$= \sqrt{200} = 10\sqrt{2}$$

example 109.2   Find the length of the curve $y = x^{3/2}$ on the interval from $x = 0$ to $x = 3$.

solution   We begin with a sketch.

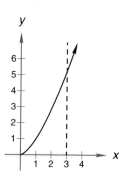

Note that $f(x) = x^{3/2}$ means $f'(x) = \dfrac{3}{2}x^{1/2}$. So the arc length is given by

$$L = \int_0^3 \sqrt{1 + \left(\frac{3}{2}x^{1/2}\right)^2} \ dx$$

$$= \int_0^3 \sqrt{1 + \frac{9}{4}x} \ dx$$

$$= \frac{4}{9} \int_{x=0}^{x=3} \sqrt{u} \ du$$

$$= \frac{4}{9}\left[\frac{2}{3}u^{3/2}\right]_{x=0}^{x=3}$$

$$= \frac{8}{27}\left(1 + \frac{9}{4}x\right)^{3/2}\Big|_0^3$$

$$= \frac{8}{27}\left[\frac{31\sqrt{31}}{8} - 1\right]$$

$$= \frac{31\sqrt{31} - 8}{27}$$

$$\boxed{\begin{array}{l} u = 1 + \dfrac{9}{4}x \\[2mm] du = \dfrac{9}{4} \ dx \end{array}}$$

We close with one last example to emphasize that many straightforward functions yield difficult, or impossible, integrals in arc length problems.

example 109.3 Find the length of the curve $y = x^2$ on the interval $[0, 2]$.

solution From the arc length formula,

$$L = \int_0^2 \sqrt{1 + (2x)^2} \; dx$$

$$= \int_0^2 \sqrt{1 + 4x^2} \; dx$$

We do not know how to evaluate this integral yet. Fortunately, we will learn how to evaluate this integral in an upcoming lesson. However, we can still approximate this integral with some accuracy. For example, using the trapezoidal rule with 10 subintervals, we find that this length is approximately 4.6533. Also, the TI-83 says that

$$\text{fnInt}(\sqrt{(1+4X^2)},X,0,2)$$

is approximately **4.6468**.

problem set 109

1. The amount of water consumed (in gallons) by a particular type of tree is given by
   (99) $w(r) = r(r - 9)^2 + 40$ where r is the radius of the tree in inches. Use differentials to estimate the amount of additional water needed if the tree grows from a 10-inch radius to a 10.5-inch radius.

2. Find the length of the curve $y = x^{3/2}$ on the interval from $x = 0$ to $x = 4$.
   (109)

3. Find the length of the curve $y = x^{2/3}$ on the interval from $x = 0$ to $x = 8$.
   (109)

4. Write an integral expression in terms of a single variable that can be used to find the length of
   (109) the curve $y = x^2 + \sin x$ from the point $(0, 0)$ to the point $(3, 9 + \sin 3)$.

5. A particle moves along the x-axis so that its velocity at time t is given by $v(t) = te^{-t}$. Find the
   (90) acceleration of the particle at $t = 4$. If $x(0) = 0$, what is $x(3)$?

6. Find $\frac{dy}{dx}$ for the parametric equations $x = 3 \sin^2 t$ and $y = 4 \cos^2 t$. Sketch the graph of the
   (106) parametric equations.

7. Convert the polar equation $\theta = \dfrac{\pi}{4}$ to rectangular form.
   (107)

8. Convert the rectangular equation $x^2 + y^2 = 9$ to polar form.
   (107)

Evaluate the limits in problems 9–11.

9. $\displaystyle\lim_{x \to \infty} \frac{x \ln x}{x^2 + 1}$
   (79)

10. $\displaystyle\lim_{x \to 0} \frac{\sin (17x)}{12x}$
    (101)

11. $\displaystyle\lim_{h \to 0} \frac{\sin \left(\dfrac{\pi}{2} + h \right) - \sin \dfrac{\pi}{2}}{h}$
    (28)

12. Evaluate $\dfrac{d}{dx} \displaystyle\int_x^2 \frac{\ln t}{t} \; dt$, assuming $x > 0$.
    (98)

13. Suppose that f is a function defined for all real values of x. The graphs of $y = f(x)$ and
    (96) $y = f(|x|)$ are identical when which of the following statements is true?

    A. $f(x) > 0$ for all values of x.   B. f is an odd function.

    C. f is an even function.   D. f is any polynomial function.

14. Let R be the region between $y = \frac{1}{x}$ and the x-axis on the interval $[1, 2]$. Find the volume of the solid formed when R is revolved about the line $x = -1$.
(94)

Antidifferentiate in problems 15 and 16.

15. $\displaystyle\int \frac{2x\,dx}{\sqrt{25 - x^2}}$
(66)

16. $\displaystyle\int \cot^2 (2x)\,dx$
(100)

17. Rewrite the integral expression $\displaystyle\int_0^1 |e^{2x} - 2|\,dx$ in a way that avoids absolute value notation.
(96)

18. Suppose $f(x) = \sin x$ and f is only defined for all x such that $-\frac{\pi}{2} < x < \frac{\pi}{2}$. Let f^{-1} be the inverse function of f. Evaluate $(f^{-1})'(\frac{1}{2})$.
(92)

19. The Mean Value Theorem for Integrals says that a continuous function must attain its average value on an interval at some number c in the interval. Let $f(x) = \sqrt{x}$. Find some c in $[0, 1]$ such that $f(c)$ is the average value of the function on this interval.
(89)

20. Find the angle between the vectors $\vec{v}_1 = \langle 4, 3\rangle$ and $\vec{v}_2 = \langle-2, 7\rangle$ when they are drawn in standard position.
(108)

21. Find a vector of magnitude 6 that is parallel to the tangent of the curve $y = x^2 - 4$ at the point $(3, 5)$.
(108)

22. Differentiate $y = \arctan \dfrac{x}{2} + e^{\sin x + \cos x} - \dfrac{1 + x}{e^x - \sin x}$ with respect to x.
(50,64)

23. (a) Write the first four terms of the sequence given by $a_n = \dfrac{(-1)^{n+1}\,n}{2^n}$, $n = 1, 2, 3, \ldots$.
(105)

(b) Determine whether the sequence in (a) converges or diverges. If it converges, state its limit.

24. Find a generator for the sequence $a_1 = \dfrac{1}{2}$, $a_2 = \dfrac{3}{4}$, $a_3 = \dfrac{7}{8}$, $a_4 = \dfrac{15}{16}$, $\ldots$.
(105)

25. Let $f(x) = \dfrac{x^2 + x - 2}{x}$.
(80)

(a) Write the equations of all the asymptotes of the graph of f.

(b) When x is large, what monomial expression closely approximates $\dfrac{f(x)}{x}$?

(c) When x is large, what monomial expression closely approximates $xf(x)$?

LESSON 110   Rose Curves

Every point on the rectangular plane can be uniquely represented by an ordered pair of x and y. Thus $(3, -2)$ represents the point whose x-coordinate is 3 and whose y-coordinate is -2. There is no other way to use rectangular coordinates to designate this point. Polar coordinates are different, as $4\underline{/20°}$, $4\underline{/-340°}$, $-4\underline{/200°}$, and $-4\underline{/-160°}$ all designate the same point. This flexibility enhances the usefulness of polar coordinates while at the same time introduces an element of confusion. Polar coordinates can be used to write simple equations whose graphs are very interesting. Some of these figures are so unusual that they have names, as shown here.

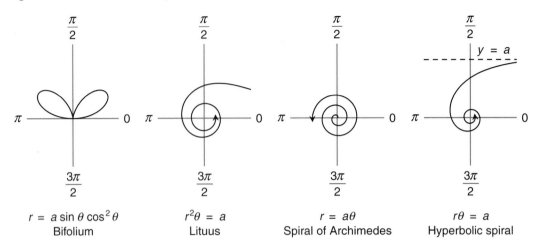

$r = a \sin \theta \cos^2 \theta$	$r^2\theta = a$	$r = a\theta$	$r\theta = a$
Bifolium	Lituus	Spiral of Archimedes	Hyperbolic spiral

These graphs are valid whenever $a > 0$.

Our investigation of polar graphs begins with figures called **rose curves.** The equations of rose curves have the forms

$$r = a \sin (n\theta) \qquad \text{and} \qquad r = a \cos (n\theta)$$

The roses have n petals if n is odd and $2n$ petals if n is even. The figures can be graphed point by point or with a graphing utility. We do both in the examples to follow.

example 110.1   Graph: $r = \sin (2\theta)$

solution   We must use all values of θ between 0 and 2π (or 0° and 360°). For convenience we use degree measure and a calculator to construct the table. First we will examine the behavior of the graph as θ goes from 0° to 180°. In our table we put values of θ, 2θ, and sin (2θ). **Since sin (2θ) has a maximum value when $\theta = 45°$, we are careful to include θ-values of 45° and 135° in the table.**

θ	0°	30°	45°	60°	90°	120°	135°	150°	180°
2θ	0°	60°	90°	120°	180°	240°	270°	300°	360°
sin (2θ)	0	0.8660	1	0.8660	0	−0.8660	−1	−0.8660	0

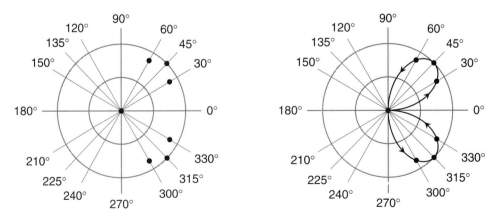

In the figure on the left-hand side above, we have graphed the seven points that arise from the table above. In the figure on the right-hand side we see that as θ increases from 0° to 90°, the leaf in the first quadrant is traced. **As θ increases from 90° to 180°, sin (2θ) is negative; so the angles are in the second quadrant, but the graph is in the fourth quadrant.**

Now we complete our task by considering the behavior of the graph as θ goes from 180° to 360°.

θ	180°	210°	225°	240°	270°	300°	315°	330°	360°
2θ	360°	420°	450°	480°	540°	600°	630°	660°	720°
$\sin(2\theta)$	0	0.8660	1	0.8660	0	−0.8660	−1	−0.8660	0

On the left-hand side we added the new points to the previous graph. Note that when θ is a third-quadrant angle, the graph is in the third quadrant, because $\sin(2\theta)$ is positive when θ is between 180° and 270°. But when θ is a fourth-quadrant angle, the graph is in the second quadrant, because $\sin(2\theta)$ is negative when θ is between 270° and 360°.

Such a task may prove quite difficult for a polar curve that is more complicated or detailed. The process can be simplified by using a TI-83 or similar graphing utility. To graph a polar function on the TI-83, some preliminary steps must be taken. First, the calculator should be in radian mode. Also, the coordinate setting should be Pol (for polar coordinates) rather than Func. (Both of these settings may be selected from the options that arise after pressing MODE.) Finally, the WINDOW settings should be adjusted. This may be the most intimidating step, since the WINDOW menu changes when Func mode is changed to Pol mode. In addition to the usual x and y settings, Pol mode requires θ settings. The settings shown at the right are usually convenient. Note that the calculator automatically computes the decimal equivalents of 2π and $\frac{\pi}{48}$, so the screen will look different than the one shown.

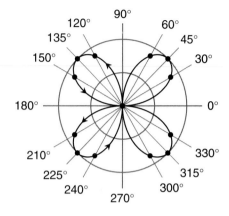

```
WINDOW
 θmin=0
 θmax=2π
 θstep=π/48
 Xmin=-6
 Xmax=6
 Xscl=1
 Ymin=-4
 Ymax=4
 Yscl=1
```

example 110.2   Graph $r = \sin(2\theta)$ on a graphing calculator.

solution   We enter $r = \sin(2\theta)$ as a function definition. This is done with the Y= key.

```
 Plot1  Plot2  Plot3
\r1■sin(2θ)
\r2=
\r3=
\r4=
\r5=
\r6=
```

If the settings specified earlier have been entered, we can press (GRAPH) to get this window.

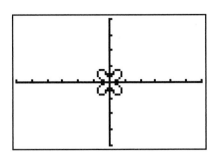

It appears that the ranges of the coordinate axes are too large to obtain an accurate picture, so we press (ZOOM) (2) (ENTER) to zoom in on the origin.

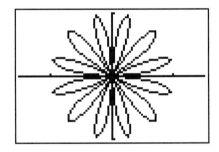

Note that the graph is drawn in exactly the same fashion as in example 110.1. In particular, the petals of the rose are generated in the same order as in the previous example.

example 110.3   Graph $r = \sin(6\theta)$ on a graphing calculator.

solution   Given the previous example, this is easily accomplished by changing the 2 to a 6 in the function definition. This creates the graph at right.

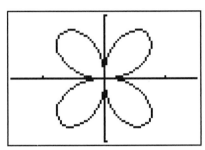

We now see a pattern. In the case of the function $r = \sin(n\theta)$ with n even, the graph is a rose with $2n$ petals.

example 110.4   Graph: $r = 2\cos(3\theta)$

solution   Equations can usually be graphed by plotting points. Plotting points is time-consuming, but we can graph such equations more quickly by plotting a few key points, if we choose them carefully. The given equation is that of a rose that has three leaves, because the argument is 3θ. The maximum and minimum values of cosine are +1 and –1. Thus the maximum value of $2\cos(3\theta)$ is +2, which occurs when 3θ equals 0° or 360°, or when θ equals 0° or 120°. The minimum value of $2\cos(3\theta)$ is –2, which occurs when 3θ equals 180°, or when θ equals 60°.

On the left-hand side we graph $2\underline{/0°}$, $2\underline{/120°}$, and $-2\underline{/60°}$.

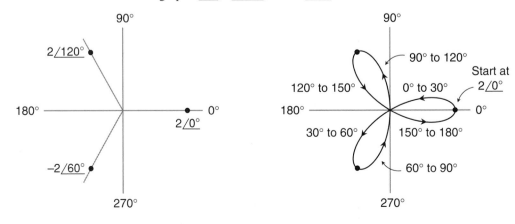

On the right-hand side, after a little more consideration, we draw the graph of the equation. First we consider the trace as θ goes from 0° to 180°. The graph begins at $2\underline{/0°}$ and traces half a petal as θ increases from 0° to 30° and r decreases from 2 to 0. Then, as θ increases from 30° to 60°, r goes from 0 to –2 and traces another half-petal in the third quadrant. Four more half-petals are traced—one between 60° and 90°, one between 90° and 120°, one between 120° and 150°, and one between 150° and 180°. There are six half-petals in all, and the entire figure is formed in 180°. As θ increases from 180° to 360°, the pattern repeats, retracing the three-leafed rose.

example 110.5 Graph $r = \sin(5\theta)$ on a graphing calculator.

solution The TI-83 reveals the graph at right.

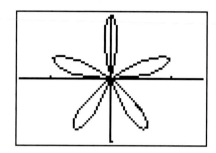

Note that the number of petals is 5, not 10. Moreover, we see that the calculator continues to graph even after the full graph is drawn. (An indicator in the upper right-hand corner of the screen lets us know when the calculator has finished graphing.) The full graph is actually completed as θ goes from 0 to π radians. A second copy is drawn as θ ranges from π to 2π. We must keep this sort of phenomenon in mind whenever we draw graphs of polar curves.

Note: While the graphing utility is helpful, you should begin, after some practice, to recognize the graphs of these rose curves and other polar curves by inspection. This will prove to be a valuable time-saver.

example 110.6 Graph: $r = 4\cos\theta$

solution The maximum value of $\cos\theta$ is +1, so the maximum value of $4\cos\theta$ is 4, which occurs when $\theta = 0°$. The minimum value of $\cos\theta$ is –1, so the minimum value of $4\cos\theta$ is –4, which occurs when $\theta = 180°$. It is no surprise that the points $4\underline{/0°}$ and $-4\underline{/180°}$ (the points for the maximum and minimum) coincide. This is a one-leafed rose since the coefficient of θ is 1. One-leafed roses are actually circles.

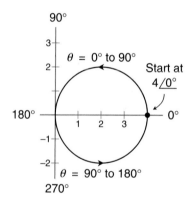

When $\theta = 0°$, $r = 4\cos\theta = 4$, as shown. As θ increases from 0° to 90°, $r = 4\cos\theta$ decreases from 4 to 0 and traces the top half of the circle. As θ goes from 90° to 180°, r is negative because $\cos\theta$ is negative, and r goes from 0 to –4 to trace the bottom half of the circle. As θ goes from 180° to 360°, the pattern repeats and the circle is retraced. To confirm that this graph is truly a circle, we convert the equation $r = 4\cos\theta$ to its rectangular form.

$$
\begin{aligned}
r &= 4\cos\theta && \text{equation} \\
r^2 &= 4(r\cos\theta) && \text{multiplied by } r \\
x^2 + y^2 &= 4x && \text{used conversion identities} \\
x^2 - 4x + y^2 &= 0 && \text{subtracted } 4x \\
x^2 - 4x + 4 + y^2 &= 4 && \text{completed the square} \\
(x-2)^2 + y^2 &= 2^2 && \text{simplified}
\end{aligned}
$$

The graph of this rectangular equation is clearly the circle above.

problem set
110

1. Use differentials to approximate $\sqrt{17}$.
   (99)

2. Let R be the region bounded by $y = e^x$, the coordinate axes, and the line $x = 2$. Find the
   (94) volume of the solid formed when R is revolved around $x = -2$.

3. Find a vector of length 4 that is normal to the vector $\langle 2, -3 \rangle$.
   (108)

4. The slope of the line tangent to the graph of a function f at any point (x, y) on the graph is $\frac{1}{x}$. The
   (61) graph of f passes through the point $(1, 1)$. Find the equation of f.

5. Find the Maclaurin series for $\sin(2x)$. Use the first 3 nonzero terms of the series to estimate the
   (55) value of $\sin(0.4)$.

6. A ball is thrown upward from the top of a 60-meter-high building with an initial velocity of 30
   (54) meters per second.
   (a) Develop the velocity function and the position function for the ball.
   (b) How long does it take the ball to reach its highest point?
   (c) How long does it take the ball to hit the ground after reaching its highest point? (Assume the ball does not hit the building as it falls to the ground.)

7. Write an integral in terms of a single variable that can be used to find the length of the curve
   (109) $y = 2x^2 + 3x - 4$ from $x = 2$ to $x = 6$.

8. Find the length of the curve $y = x^{3/2}$ from $x = 1$ to $x = 4$.
   (109)

9. Find the length of the graph of $(y + 1)^2 = (x - 4)^3$ from the point $(5, 0)$ to the point $(8, 7)$.
   (109)

10. Find $f'(1.4)$ where $f(x) = \int_4^x t^2 \sqrt{1 + t^2} \, dt$.
    (98)

11. Write the rectangular form of $r = 2 + \sin \theta$.
    (107)

12. Write the polar form of $y = 2x + 3$.
    (107)

Graph the equations in problems 13–16.

13. $r = 2$
    (107)

14. $r = 2 \sin \theta$
    (110)

15. $r = 2 \sin(2\theta)$
    (110)

16. $r = 2 \sin(3\theta)$
    (110)

17. A parametric curve has the defining equations $x = e^t$ and $y = e^{-3t}$ where t is a real number.
    (106) Graph the curve, find $\frac{dy}{dx}$, and determine the curve's equivalent rectangular equation.

18. Evaluate: $\int_{-2}^{2} 3|x^2 + x - 2| \, dx$
    (96)

19. Find the area between the graph of $y = \tan^3 x$ and the x-axis on the closed interval $\left[0, \dfrac{\pi}{4}\right]$.
    (100)

Determine whether each sequence in problems 20 and 21 converges or diverges. If the sequence converges, state its limit.

20. $a_n = \dfrac{4n}{\ln n}$
    (105)

21. $a_n = \dfrac{2^n}{3^n}$
    (105)

22. Find the values of x for which $f(x) = x(x - 2)(x - 5)$ attains its maximum and minimum
    (63) values on the interval $[-1, 5]$. What are the maximum and minimum values of f?

23. Suppose that f is a continuous function such that $\int_1^7 f(x) \, dx = 4$ and $\int_3^7 f(x) \, dx = 5$. Find
    (57) $\int_1^3 f(x) \, dx$.

24. Differentiate $y = \tan^3 x - \dfrac{1 + \sin(\pi x)}{1 + cx}$ with respect to x, assuming c is a constant.
    (50)

25. Prove: $\lim\limits_{x \to 0} \dfrac{\sin x}{x} = 1$
    (101)

LESSON 111   The Exponential Indeterminate Forms 0^0, 1^∞, and ∞^0

Previous lessons on limits investigated how to evaluate limits that involve the indeterminate forms $\frac{0}{0}$, $\frac{\infty}{\infty}$, $0 \cdot \infty$, and $\infty - \infty$ using L'Hôpital's Rule. This lesson investigates three additional indeterminate forms: 0^0, 1^∞, and ∞^0. These exponential indeterminate forms cannot be directly transformed into the more familiar $\frac{0}{0}$ and $\frac{\infty}{\infty}$. Therefore a new procedure must be found to evaluate such limits. Fortunately all three cases can be handled following the same procedure. To evaluate $\lim_{x \to a} f(x)^{g(x)}$, we do the following when an exponential indeterminate form arises:

1. Take the logarithm of the limit's argument to obtain $\ln f(x)^{g(x)}$, which equals $g(x) \cdot \ln f(x)$.

2. Evaluate $\lim_{x \to a} \left[g(x) \cdot \ln f(x) \right]$, if it exists.

3. Determine e^L, since $\lim_{x \to a} \left[g(x) \cdot \ln f(x) \right] = L$ implies $\lim_{x \to a} f(x)^{g(x)} = e^L$.

Usually L'Hôpital's Rule is used in the second step. The third step counteracts the effects of taking the logarithm of the expression. The entire process is an application of the substitution principle for limits from Lesson 70. What we are doing is this:

$$
\begin{aligned}
\lim_{x \to a} f(x)^{g(x)} &= \lim_{x \to a} e^{\ln f(x)^{g(x)}} \\
&= \lim_{x \to a} e^{g(x) \cdot \ln f(x)} \\
&= e^{\lim_{x \to a} [g(x) \cdot \ln f(x)]}
\end{aligned}
$$

In this new formulation of the expression, we still have to evaluate a limit whose form is indeterminate, but it is the type of limit discussed in Lesson 79. Therefore we know how to solve it.

example 111.1   Evaluate: $\lim_{x \to 0^+} x^x$

solution   The indeterminate form here is 0^0. The first step is to take the logarithm of x^x.

$$\ln (x^x) = x \ln x$$

Second we determine $\lim_{x \to 0^+} x \ln x$. Note that this has the indeterminate form $0 \cdot -\infty$. We rewrite the limit so that L'Hôpital's Rule can be applied.

$$
\begin{aligned}
\lim_{x \to 0^+} x \ln x &= \lim_{x \to 0^+} \frac{\ln x}{\frac{1}{x}} & &\text{indeterminate form } \frac{-\infty}{\infty} \\
&= \lim_{x \to 0^+} \frac{\frac{1}{x}}{-\frac{1}{x^2}} & &\text{L'Hôpital's Rule} \\
&= \lim_{x \to 0^+} -x & &\text{simplified} \\
&= 0 & &\text{evaluated}
\end{aligned}
$$

The final step is to raise e to this power.

$$e^0 = 1$$

Therefore $\lim_{x \to 0^+} x^x = \textbf{1}.$

The TI-83 calculator confirms this result. Using `Func` mode, we define `Y₁=X^X` and build a table. With `TblStart=.01` and `∆Tbl=-.001` in the `TABLE SETUP` screen. The following is produced:

X	Y1
.007	.96586
.006	.96977
.005	.97386
.004	.97816
.003	.98272
.002	.98765
.001	.99312

X=.001

The function values certainly appear to approach 1 as x approaches 0^+.

example 111.2   Evaluate: $\lim\limits_{x \to \infty} \left(1 + \dfrac{2}{x}\right)^x$

solution   We see the indeterminate form 1^∞ here. The first step is to find the logarithm of the limit's argument.

$$\ln\left[\left(1 + \frac{2}{x}\right)^x\right] = x \ln\left(1 + \frac{2}{x}\right)$$

Second we find the limit of this function as x gets large.

$$\lim_{x \to \infty} x \ln\left(1 + \frac{2}{x}\right) \qquad \text{indeterminate form } \infty \cdot 0$$

$$= \lim_{x \to \infty} \frac{\ln\left(1 + \dfrac{2}{x}\right)}{\dfrac{1}{x}} \qquad \text{indeterminate form } \frac{0}{0}$$

$$= \lim_{x \to \infty} \frac{\dfrac{1}{\left(1 + \dfrac{2}{x}\right)} \cdot \left(-\dfrac{2}{x^2}\right)}{\left(-\dfrac{1}{x^2}\right)} \qquad \text{L'Hôpital's Rule}$$

$$= \lim_{x \to \infty} \frac{2}{1 + \dfrac{2}{x}} \qquad \text{simplified}$$

$$= \frac{2}{1 + 0} = 2 \qquad \text{evaluated}$$

Therefore the original limit is e^2.

$$\lim_{x \to \infty} \left(1 + \frac{2}{x}\right)^x = e^2$$

Indeed, this is consistent with the claim in Lesson 102 that

$$\lim_{x \to \infty} \left(1 + \frac{a}{x}\right)^x = e^a$$

for any constant a.

example 111.3   Evaluate: $\lim\limits_{x \to \infty} x^{1/x}$

solution   This is an example of the indeterminate form ∞^0.

As in the above examples, we take the natural logarithm of the limit's argument.

$$\ln\left[x^{1/x}\right] = \frac{1}{x} \ln x$$

Next we calculate the limit of this function.

$$\lim_{x \to \infty} \frac{1}{x} \ln x = \lim_{x \to \infty} \frac{\ln x}{x} \qquad \text{indeterminate form } \frac{\infty}{\infty}$$

$$= \lim_{x \to \infty} \frac{\frac{1}{x}}{1} \qquad \text{L'Hôpital's Rule}$$

$$= 0$$

Therefore $\lim_{x \to \infty} x^{1/x} = e^0 = \mathbf{1}.$

problem set
111

1. The base of a solid is the region in the xy-plane bounded by the x-axis, $y = \tan^2 x$, and the
(97) line $x = \frac{\pi}{3}$. Every vertical cross section of the object parallel to the y-axis is a square. Find the
volume of the object.

2. Find the distance traveled by a particle between $t = 0$ and $t = 6$ given that its position along
(109) the x-axis is determined by $x(t) = \frac{1}{4}t^4 - \frac{7}{3}t^3 + 5t^2 + 7$.

3. Use the equation of the line tangent to $xy^2 - 4x^2y + 14 = 0$ at the point $(2, 1)$ to
(99) approximate the value of y in $xy^2 - 4x^2y + 14 = 0$ when $x = 2.1$.

4. Sketch the graph of the parametric equations $x = 4 \sin t$ and $y = 3 \cos t$. Find $\dfrac{dy}{dx}$.
(106)

5. Sketch the graph of the parametric equations $x = 4 \sin^2 t$ and $y = 3 \cos^2 t$. Find $\dfrac{dy}{dx}$.
(106)

6. Write the polar form of $x^2 + y^2 - 6x = 0$.
(107)

Graph the equations in problems 7–9 on a polar coordinate system.

7. $r = 3 \cos \theta$ **8.** $r = 3 \cos (3\theta)$ **9.** $r = 3 \cos (4\theta)$
(110)   (110)   (110)

10. Find a vector of magnitude 7 that is normal to $y = 3^{x + \cos x}$ at the point where $x = 2.3$.
(108)

Evaluate the limits in problems 11–19.

11. $\lim\limits_{x \to 0} \left(\dfrac{1}{x^2} - \dfrac{1}{\sin x} \right)$ **12.** $\lim\limits_{x \to (\pi/2)^-} (\cos x \cdot \tan x)$ **13.** $\lim\limits_{x \to 0^+} x^{\tan x}$
(91)   (91)   (111)

14. $\lim\limits_{x \to \infty} x^{1/x}$ **15.** $\lim\limits_{x \to (\pi/2)^-} (\sin x)^{\tan x}$ **16.** $\lim\limits_{x \to \infty} \left(1 + \dfrac{1}{x} \right)^{3x}$
(111)   (111)   (111)

17. $\lim\limits_{x \to 0} \dfrac{\tan \left(\dfrac{\pi}{4} + x \right) - \tan \dfrac{\pi}{4}}{x}$ **18.** $\lim\limits_{x \to \pi/4} \dfrac{\sin x - \sin \left(\dfrac{\pi}{4} \right)}{x - \dfrac{\pi}{4}}$
(28)   (44)

19. $\lim\limits_{x \to 0} \dfrac{\sin (31x)}{13x}$
(101)

20. Write an integral whose value equals the length of the curve $y = \sin x$ on the interval $[0, \pi]$.
(109)

21. Use the trapezoidal rule with $n = 6$ to approximate the length of the curve $y = \sin x$ on the
(95) interval $[0, \pi]$.

22. Determine whether the sequence $a_n = \dfrac{e^{2n}}{e^{3n}}$, $n = 1, 2, 3, \ldots$ converges or diverges. If it
(105) converges, state its limit.

23. (a) Find a generating formula for the sequence whose first four terms are $a_1 = \frac{3}{2}$, $a_2 = \frac{9}{5}$,
(105) $a_3 = \frac{27}{10}$, and $a_4 = \frac{81}{17}$.

   (b) Does this sequence converge or diverge? If it converges, state its limit.

24. Which of the following integrals is equivalent to $\int_0^{\pi/2} \sin^2 x \cos x \, dx$?
(66)

   A. $\int_0^{\pi/2} u^2 \, du$ B. $\int_0^1 u^2 \, du$ C. $\int_0^{\pi/2} u \cos u \, du$ D. $\int_0^1 u \cos u \, du$

25. Integrate: $\int x\sqrt{x+4} \, dx$
(66,69)

LESSON 112 *Foundations of Trigonometric Substitution*

It is fairly simple to integrate $\int \frac{x}{\sqrt{1-x^2}} \, dx$. The most difficult step is the u-substitution $u = 1 - x^2$.

$$\int \frac{x}{\sqrt{1-x^2}} \, dx = \int x(1-x^2)^{-1/2} \, dx$$

$$= -\frac{1}{2} \int u^{-1/2} \, du \qquad \boxed{\begin{array}{l} u = 1 - x^2 \\ du = -2x \, dx \end{array}}$$

$$= -u^{1/2} + C$$

$$= -(1-x^2)^{1/2} + C$$

If the derivatives of the inverse trigonometric functions have been memorized, the integral $\int \frac{1}{\sqrt{1-x^2}} \, dx$ is even easier.

$$\int \frac{1}{\sqrt{1-x^2}} \, dx = \arcsin x + C$$

However, the integral $\int \frac{1}{\sqrt{x^2-1}} \, dx$ is more difficult, and it cannot be determined using the techniques discussed thus far. A new technique called **trigonometric substitution** is required. This lesson focuses on practicing the skills of trigonometric substitution. In Lesson 113 we use the skills to implement the technique.

example 112.1 Simplify the expression $\frac{1}{\sqrt{x^2-a^2}}$ based on the substitution $\sec\theta = \frac{x}{a}$. (Here, a represents a positive constant.)

solution To use the substitution, we must first solve for x.

$$\sec\theta = \frac{x}{a} \quad \longrightarrow \quad x = a\sec\theta$$

Now we make the substitution and simplify.

$$\frac{1}{\sqrt{x^2-a^2}} = \frac{1}{\sqrt{(a\sec\theta)^2 - a^2}} \qquad \text{substituted}$$

$$= \frac{1}{\sqrt{a^2(\sec^2\theta - 1)}} \qquad \text{factored}$$

$$= \frac{1}{\sqrt{a^2\tan^2\theta}} \qquad \text{Pythagorean identity}$$

$$= \frac{1}{a\tan\theta} \qquad \text{square root}$$

example 112.2   Simplify the expression $\dfrac{dx}{\sqrt{x^2 + 4}}$ based on the substitution $\tan\theta = \dfrac{x}{2}$.

solution   First we solve for x in $\tan\theta = \dfrac{x}{2}$.

$$\tan\theta = \frac{x}{2} \quad\longrightarrow\quad x = 2\tan\theta$$

We can substitute this into the expression, but first we should determine dx so that we can substitute for it as well.

$$x = 2\tan\theta \quad\longrightarrow\quad dx = 2\sec^2\theta\, d\theta$$

Now the expression can be rewritten without any x's.

$$\frac{dx}{\sqrt{x^2 + 4}} = \frac{2\sec^2\theta\, d\theta}{\sqrt{(2\tan\theta)^2 + 4}} \qquad \text{substituted}$$

$$= \frac{2\sec^2\theta\, d\theta}{\sqrt{4(\tan^2\theta + 1)}} \qquad \text{factored}$$

$$= \frac{2\sec^2\theta\, d\theta}{\sqrt{4\sec^2\theta}} \qquad \text{Pythagorean identity}$$

$$= \frac{2\sec^2\theta\, d\theta}{2\sec\theta} \qquad \text{square root}$$

$$= \mathbf{\sec\theta\, d\theta} \qquad \text{cancellation}$$

The new expression is noticeably simpler, and it is one that we can integrate.

example 112.3   Draw a reference triangle based on the substitution $\sin\theta = \frac{x}{2}$. Use the triangle to write the expression $\ln\sqrt{|\csc\theta - \cot\theta|} + C$ in terms of x.

solution   In a right triangle the sine of an angle is the ratio of the length of the opposite side to the hypotenuse. The relationship $\sin\theta = \frac{x}{2}$ is true in the triangle on the left-hand side.

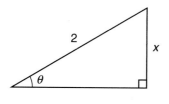   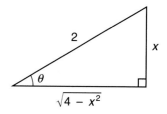

In the triangle on the right-hand side we use the Pythagorean theorem to find the length of the other side. This triangle is the reference triangle required. Now we must use this triangle to write $\ln\sqrt{|\csc\theta - \cot\theta|} + C$ in terms of x. The easiest way to do this is to find substitutions for $\csc\theta$ and $\cot\theta$. From the triangle

$$\csc\theta = \frac{2}{x} \qquad \text{and} \qquad \cot\theta = \frac{\sqrt{4 - x^2}}{x}$$

Therefore

$$\ln\sqrt{|\csc\theta - \cot\theta|} + C = \mathbf{ln}\sqrt{\left|\frac{2 - \sqrt{4 - x^2}}{x}\right|} + C$$

The purpose of this exercise will become clear in Lesson 113.

problem set
112

1. Let R be the region between the graph of
(46) $y = \frac{1}{x}$ and the x-axis from $x = 1$ to
$x = k$ for $k > 1$.

    (a) Determine the area of R.

    (b) Suppose that k is increasing at a rate of
1 unit per second. Find the rate at
which the area of region R is
increasing when $k = 10$.

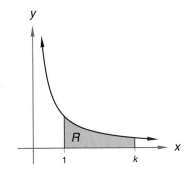

2. Use differentials to approximate $\sqrt{10}$.
(99)

3. The end of a trough has two straight sides
(77) and one curved side, as shown. The trough
is 3 meters long and is filled with a fluid
whose weight density is 3000 newtons per
cubic meter. Express the work required to
pump the fluid out of the trough as a
definite integral.

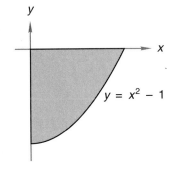

$y = x^2 - 1$

4. (a) Sketch the curve represented by the parametric equations $x = 3 \cos \theta$ and $y = 4 \sin \theta$,
(106) where $0 \le \theta \le 2\pi$.

    (b) Eliminate the parameter and find the corresponding rectangular equation. (*Hint:* Use the
        Pythagorean identity.)

    (c) Find $\frac{dy}{dx}$ for both the parametric and rectangular equations, and verify that they are
        equivalent.

Evaluate the limits in problems 5–7.

5. $\lim\limits_{x \to 0} \left(\dfrac{1}{x} - \dfrac{1}{\sin x} \right)$
(91)

6. $\lim\limits_{x \to 0} \dfrac{\sin (2x)}{4x}$
(101)

7. $\lim\limits_{x \to 0^+} (\sin x)^x$
(111)

8. Convert the polar equation $r = \dfrac{1}{2 \sin \theta - 3 \cos \theta}$ to rectangular form.
(107)

Graph the equations in problems 9 and 10 on a polar coordinate system.

9. $r = 4 \sin \theta$
(110)

10. $r = 4 \sin (3\theta)$
(110)

11. Write an integral whose value equals the length of the graph of $y = e^{x^2}$ on the interval
(109) from $x = -2$ to $x = 2$.

12. Find the length of the graph of $y = x^{2/3}$ on the interval from $x = -8$ to $x = 8$.
(109)

13. Find the magnitude of the vector $3\hat{i} - 2\hat{j}$.
(108)

14. Find a unit vector parallel to the line tangent to the curve $y = x^2 + 2x - 1$ at the point $(2, 7)$
(108) and a unit vector normal to the line tangent to the curve at the same point.

15. Let $f(t) = e^{\sin t + \cos t} - \dfrac{1 + t}{e^t - \sin t}$. Find $f'(0)$.
(50)

Determine whether each sequence in problems 16 and 17 converges or diverges. If a sequence
converges, state its limit.

16. $a_n = (-1)^{n+1} \dfrac{\sqrt{n}}{n}$, $n = 1, 2, 3, \ldots$
(105)

17. $a_n = e^{-n} \ln n$, $n = 1, 2, 3, \ldots$
(105)

18. Find a generating formula for the sequence whose first four terms are $a_1 = \frac{3}{2}$, $a_2 = -\frac{9}{4}$,
(105) $a_3 = \frac{27}{8}$, and $a_4 = -\frac{81}{16}$.

19. Approximate $\displaystyle\int_1^3 \frac{x^2}{\sqrt{x^2 + 1}}\, dx$ using the trapezoidal rule with $n = 4$.
(95)

20. Use Newton's method to approximate to nine decimal places the coordinates of the
(93)   first-quadrant intersection point of the line $y = \frac{1}{4}x$ and the curve $y = \sin x$.

21. Use the substitution $x = \tan\theta$ to simplify the expression $\displaystyle\frac{2\,dx}{(1 + x^2)^3}$.
(112)

22. Evaluate: $\displaystyle\int_{\sqrt{e}}^{e} 2x \ln\left(x^2\right) dx$
(69)

23. Which of the following definite integrals is equivalent to $\displaystyle\int_0^1 \sin\left(\frac{\pi}{2}x\right) \cos\left(\frac{\pi}{2}x\right) dx$?
(66)

    A. $\displaystyle\frac{\pi}{2}\int_0^1 \sin u\, du$ B. $\displaystyle\frac{2}{\pi}\int_0^1 \sin u\, du$ C. $\displaystyle\frac{2}{\pi}\int_0^1 u\, du$

    D. $\displaystyle\int_0^{\pi/2} \sin u\, du$ E. $\displaystyle\frac{2}{\pi}\int_0^{\pi/2} u\, du$

24. According to Rolle's theorem, which of the following statements is true?
(85)
    A. If $f(x) = |x - 3| - 3$, then there must be some $c \in (0, 6)$ such that $f'(c) = 0$.

    B. If $f(x) = 2 - \dfrac{1}{x^2 - 1}$, then there must be a point $c \in (-1, 1)$ such that $f'(c) = 0$.

    C. If $f(x) = (x - 6)(x + 2)(x - 7)$, then there must be a point $c \in (-2, 6)$ such that $f'(c) = 0$.

    D. The function $f(x) = x^2 + 1$ is never zero for any real value of x, so there is no real number such that $f'(c) = 0$.

25. After working with the exponential indeterminate forms, it often seems that 0^∞ should be
(111)   included in the indeterminate list, but this is not true. Prove: If $f(x) > 0$ and $\lim_{x \to a} f(x)^{g(x)}$
has the form $0^{+\infty}$, then the limit **always** equals 0.

LESSON 113   *Trigonometric Substitution*

Consider the following three integrals:

$$\int \frac{dx}{1 + x^2} \qquad \int \frac{dx}{\sqrt{1 - x^2}} \qquad \int \frac{dx}{\sqrt{x^2 - 1}}$$

Because these lack an additional factor of x in the numerator, we cannot determine these integrals using u-substitution. However, a new substitution technique called **trigonometric substitution** can be used. The chart below indicates the kinds of substitutions that are made.

TERM IN INTEGRAND	SUBSTITUTION
$a^2 + x^2$	$x = a\tan\theta$
$\sqrt{a^2 - x^2}$	$x = a\sin\theta$
$\sqrt{x^2 - a^2}$	$x = a\sec\theta$

example 113.1   Integrate: $\displaystyle\int \frac{dx}{1 + x^2}$

solution   When we see an integral involving a power of $a^2 + x^2$ that cannot be integrated via u-substitution, we use the following trigonometric substitutions:

$$x = a \tan \theta$$

$$dx = a \sec^2 \theta \, d\theta$$

Why is this substitution helpful? Notice what happens when $a = 1$.

$$\frac{1}{1 + x^2} = \frac{1}{1 + \tan^2 \theta} \qquad \text{substituted } \tan \theta \text{ for } x$$

$$= \frac{1}{\sec^2 \theta} \qquad \text{Pythagorean identity}$$

$$= \cos^2 \theta \qquad \text{simplified}$$

The integrand is significantly simplified. Once we express dx in terms of θ, the integral is easier to determine. If $x = \tan \theta$, then $dx = d(\tan \theta) = \sec^2 \theta \, d\theta$.

$$\int \frac{dx}{1 + x^2} = \int \frac{\sec^2 \theta \, d\theta}{1 + \tan^2 \theta} \qquad \text{substituted } x = \tan \theta, \; dx = \sec^2 \theta \, d\theta$$

$$= \int \frac{\sec^2 \theta \, d\theta}{\sec^2 \theta} \qquad \text{Pythagorean identity}$$

$$= \int d\theta \qquad \text{simplified}$$

$$= \theta + C \qquad \text{antidifferentiated}$$

To finish the problem, we must rewrite the answer in terms of x. Since $x = \tan \theta$ in this problem, we can draw the following triangle.

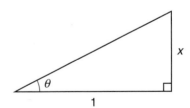

So our solution can be written as

$$\int \frac{dx}{1 + x^2} = \theta + C = \tan^{-1}\left(\frac{x}{1}\right) + C = \mathbf{tan^{-1} x + C}$$

example 113.2   Integrate: $\displaystyle\int \frac{dx}{\sqrt{1 - x^2}}$

solution   Again we see that u-substitution is not useful here. Therefore we apply a trigonometric substitution instead. For terms of the form $a^2 - x^2$, we use the following substitutions:

$$x = a \sin \theta$$

$$dx = a \cos \theta \, d\theta$$

Note that

$$a^2 - x^2 = a^2 - a^2 \sin^2 \theta \qquad \text{substituted } a \sin \theta \text{ for } x$$

$$= a^2(1 - \sin^2 \theta) \qquad \text{factored}$$

$$= a^2 \cos^2 \theta \qquad \text{Pythagorean identity}$$

This often helps to simplify the integrand in question.

$$\int \frac{dx}{\sqrt{1 - x^2}} = \int \frac{\cos \theta \; d\theta}{\sqrt{1 - \sin^2 \theta}} \qquad \text{substituted } x = \sin \theta, \; dx = \cos \theta \; d\theta$$

$$= \int \frac{\cos \theta \; d\theta}{\sqrt{\cos^2 \theta}} \qquad \text{Pythagorean identity}$$

$$= \int \frac{\cos \theta}{\cos \theta} \; d\theta \qquad \text{simplified}$$

$$= \int d\theta \qquad \text{simplified}$$

$$= \theta + C \qquad \text{antidifferentiated}$$

Since $x = \sin \theta$, we draw the triangle at the right.

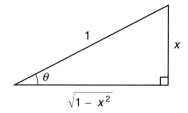

So $\theta = \sin^{-1}\left(\dfrac{x}{1}\right) = \sin^{-1} x$. Therefore,

$$\int \frac{dx}{\sqrt{1 - x^2}} = \theta + C = \mathbf{sin^{-1} x} + C$$

example 113.3   Integrate: $\displaystyle\int \frac{dx}{\sqrt{x^2 - 1}}$

solution   This integrand calls for trigonometric substitution. We choose $x = \sec \theta$, which implies $dx = \sec \theta \tan \theta \; d\theta$. This substitution is chosen because

$$x^2 - 1^2 = \sec^2 \theta - 1 = \tan^2 \theta$$

Using the prescribed substitution,

$$\int \frac{dx}{\sqrt{x^2 - 1}} = \int \frac{\sec \theta \tan \theta \; d\theta}{\sqrt{\sec^2 \theta - 1}}$$

$$\boxed{\begin{aligned} x &= \sec \theta \\ dx &= \sec \theta \tan \theta \; d\theta \end{aligned}}$$

$$= \int \frac{\sec \theta \tan \theta \; d\theta}{\sqrt{\tan^2 \theta}}$$

$$= \int \sec \theta \; d\theta$$

$$= \ln \left| \sec \theta + \tan \theta \right| + C$$

The integral of $\sec \theta$ was discussed in Lesson 100. Now this answer must be written in terms of x. We already know $x = \sec \theta$. This gives the triangle at right.

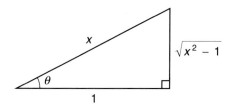

We see that $\tan \theta = \sqrt{x^2 - 1}$. Therefore

$$\int \frac{dx}{\sqrt{x^2 - 1}} = \mathbf{ln} \left| x + \sqrt{x^2 - 1} \right| + C$$

example 113.4   Integrate: $\displaystyle\int \frac{dx}{\left(x^2 - 25\right)^{3/2}}$

solution   The only useful technique we have seen for finding this antiderivative is trigonometric substitution. Terms of the form $x^2 - a^2$ lend themselves to the substitution $x = a \sec\theta$.

$$\int \frac{dx}{\left(x^2 - 25\right)^{3/2}} = \int \frac{5 \sec\theta \tan\theta \, d\theta}{\left(25 \sec^2\theta - 25\right)^{3/2}}$$

$$\boxed{\begin{array}{l} x = 5 \sec\theta \\ dx = 5 \sec\theta \tan\theta \, d\theta \end{array}}$$

$$= \frac{5}{25^{3/2}} \int \frac{\sec\theta \tan\theta \, d\theta}{\left(\sec^2\theta - 1\right)^{3/2}}$$

$$= \frac{5}{125} \int \frac{\sec\theta \tan\theta \, d\theta}{\left(\tan^2\theta\right)^{3/2}}$$

$$= \frac{1}{25} \int \frac{\sec\theta \, d\theta}{\tan^2\theta}$$

$$= \frac{1}{25} \int \frac{1}{\cos\theta} \cdot \frac{\cos^2\theta}{\sin^2\theta} \, d\theta$$

$$= \frac{1}{25} \int \frac{\cos\theta}{\sin^2\theta} \, d\theta$$

Note that this integral is of the form $\displaystyle\int u^{-2} \, du$, so we have

$$\frac{1}{25} \int \frac{\cos\theta}{\sin^2\theta} \, d\theta = -\frac{1}{25}\left(\frac{1}{\sin\theta}\right) + C$$

$$= -\frac{\csc\theta}{25} + C$$

Since $x = 5 \sec\theta$, we draw the triangle below to determine that $\csc\theta = \dfrac{x}{\sqrt{x^2 - 25}}$.

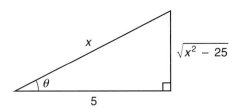

Therefore

$$\int \frac{dx}{\left(x^2 - 25\right)^{3/2}} = -\frac{1}{25}\left(\frac{x}{\sqrt{x^2 - 25}}\right) + C$$

The answer can be checked by differentiation. This is left to the reader.

example 113.5   Integrate: $\displaystyle\int \sqrt{1 + 4x^2} \, dx$

solution   Such an integral arises when we want to know the arc length of the curve defined by $y = x^2$ over some interval. We must be careful with this problem. The integrand contains a term of the form $1^2 + (2x)^2$. We need a trigonometric substitution involving $\tan\theta$, and we must account for the extra factor of 2 in the term. Expressed symbolically, we can say $1^2 + (2x)^2 = a^2 + (\ \ )^2$

where $a = 1$. This motivates the trigonometric substitution ( ) $= a \tan \theta$. We replace ( ) with $2x$ and a with 1. Then we solve for x and determine dx.

$$( ) = a \tan \theta$$

$$2x = 1 \tan \theta$$

$$x = \frac{1}{2} \tan \theta \qquad dx = \frac{1}{2} \sec^2 \theta \, d\theta$$

With these substitutions the integral can be solved.

$$\int \sqrt{1 + 4x^2} \, dx = \int \sqrt{1 + 4\left(\frac{1}{2} \tan \theta\right)^2} \left(\frac{1}{2} \sec^2 \theta \, d\theta\right)$$

$$\boxed{\begin{array}{l} x = \frac{1}{2} \tan \theta \\[2mm] dx = \frac{1}{2} \sec^2 \theta \, d\theta \end{array}}$$

$$= \frac{1}{2} \int \sqrt{1 + \tan^2 \theta} \, \sec^2 \theta \, d\theta$$

$$= \frac{1}{2} \int \sqrt{\sec^2 \theta} \, \sec^2 \theta \, d\theta$$

$$= \frac{1}{2} \int \sec^3 \theta \, d\theta$$

Solving this integral requires the reduction techniques discussed in Lesson 100 and integration by parts. For ease of explanation we momentarily ignore the factor of $\frac{1}{2}$ in front of the integral.

$$\int \sec^3 \theta \, d\theta = \int \sec \theta \sec^2 \theta \, d\theta$$

$$= \int \sec \theta \, (1 + \tan^2 \theta) \, d\theta$$

$$= \int \sec \theta \, d\theta + \int \sec \theta \tan^2 \theta \, d\theta$$

$u = \tan \theta$	$v = \sec \theta$
$du = \sec^2 \theta \, d\theta$	$dv = \sec \theta \tan \theta \, d\theta$

$$= \int \sec \theta \, d\theta + uv - \int v du$$

$$= \int \sec \theta \, d\theta + \sec \theta \tan \theta - \int \sec^3 \theta \, d\theta$$

Now we have

$$\int \sec^3 \theta \, d\theta = \int \sec \theta \, d\theta + \sec \theta \tan \theta - \int \sec^3 \theta \, d\theta$$

Notice that a factor of the term $\int \sec^3 \theta \, d\theta$ appears on both sides of the equation. We add $\int \sec^3 \theta \, d\theta$ to both sides of the equation[†] to obtain the following:

$$2 \int \sec^3 \theta \, d\theta = \int \sec \theta \, d\theta + \sec \theta \tan \theta$$

$$\longrightarrow \quad \int \sec^3 \theta \, d\theta = \frac{1}{2} \int \sec \theta \, d\theta + \frac{1}{2} \sec \theta \tan \theta$$

From Lesson 100 we recall that

$$\int \sec \theta \, d\theta = \ln |\sec \theta + \tan \theta| + C$$

Therefore

$$\int \sec^3 \theta \, d\theta = \frac{1}{2} \ln |\sec \theta + \tan \theta| + \frac{1}{2} \sec \theta \tan \theta$$

$$\longrightarrow \quad \frac{1}{2} \int \sec^3 \theta \, d\theta = \frac{1}{4} \ln |\sec \theta + \tan \theta| + \frac{1}{4} \sec \theta \tan \theta$$

[†]This technique will be discussed more in Lesson 122.

After all this work one is tempted to think we are done; however, we must now write the last expression in terms of x. From the fact that $2x = \tan\theta$, we can draw a triangle to determine substitutions for the trigonometric functions in the expression.

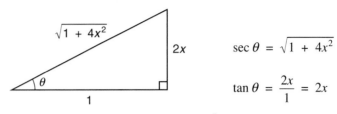

$$\sec\theta = \sqrt{1 + 4x^2}$$

$$\tan\theta = \frac{2x}{1} = 2x$$

Thus $\displaystyle\int \sqrt{1 + 4x^2}\ dx = \frac{1}{2}\int \sec^3\theta\ d\theta = \frac{1}{4}\left(\ln\left|\sqrt{1 + 4x^2} + 2x\right| + 2x\sqrt{1 + 4x^2}\right) + C.$

Note the complexity of both this result and the process of obtaining it.

**problem set
113**

1. The base of a solid is a circle of radius 4. Every vertical cross section of the solid perpendicular
(97) to the base and parallel to a given diameter is a rectangle whose height is half the length of its base. Find the volume of the solid.

2. Explain why $u = a\sin\theta$ is a useful substitution when an integral contains an expression of the
(112) form $\sqrt{a^2 - u^2}$.

3. Find the derivative of $y = \dfrac{x^{3/4}\, 4\sqrt{x}}{(4 + x^3)^6}$ with respect to x.
(84)

4. Use the symmetric derivative to find $f'(x)$ where $f(x) = -5x^2 + \dfrac{1}{2}$.
(44)

Integrate in problems 5 and 7 using methods from Lesson 64. Integrate in problems 6 and 8 using trigonometric substitution. Compare the answers you obtain for problems in the same row. (They should be the same.)

5. $\displaystyle\int \frac{dx}{\sqrt{1 - x^2}}$ **6.** $\displaystyle\int \frac{dx}{\sqrt{1 - x^2}}$
(64)   (113)

7. $\displaystyle\int \frac{dx}{1 + x^2}$ **8.** $\displaystyle\int \frac{dx}{1 + x^2}$
(64)   (113)

Integrate to obtain an exact answer in problems 9–11.

9. $\displaystyle\int \frac{x^3\, dx}{\sqrt{1 - x^2}}$ **10.** $\displaystyle\int \frac{\sqrt{16 - x^2}}{x^2}\, dx$ **11.** $\displaystyle\int 2\sec^3 x\, dx$
(113)   (113)   (113)

12. Find the general solution to the differential equation $y(x^2 + 1)\dfrac{dy}{dx} = xy^2$.
(88)

13. Let $\vec{v}_1 = \langle 6, 5\rangle$ and $\vec{v}_2 = \langle -2, 11\rangle$. Express $\vec{v}_1 + \vec{v}_2$ in the form $\langle a, b\rangle$.
(108)

14. Find $4\vec{v}_1 - 7\vec{v}_2$ when $\vec{v}_1 = \langle 2, 2\rangle$ and $\vec{v}_2 = \langle -1, 3\rangle$.
(108)

15. Add $-4\underline{/150°} + 6\underline{/-200°}$. Express the answer in polar form.
(108)

16. Write the polar form of $y = \dfrac{1}{x}$.
(107)

17. Find the length of the curve $y = \sqrt{16 - (x + 2)^2} + 4$ from $x = 0$ to $x = 2$.
(109,113)

18. Approximate the length of the curve $y = 4^{|x|}$ from $x = -2$ to $x = 4$.
(109)

Evaluate the limits in problems 19–21.

19. $\lim\limits_{x \to \infty} \left(1 + \dfrac{1}{x}\right)^x$ **20.** $\lim\limits_{x \to 0^+} (e^x - 1)^x$ **21.** $\lim\limits_{x \to 1} x^{1/(1-x)}$
(111)   (111)   (111)

22. Draw a slope field for the differential equation $\dfrac{dy}{dx} = x^2$.
(104)

Graph the equations in problems 23 and 24.

23. $r = 4 \cos \theta$ **24.** $r = 4 \cos (2\theta)$
(110)   (110)

25. After working with the exponential indeterminate forms, it often seems that $0^{-\infty}$ should be
(111)   included in the indeterminate list, but this is not true. Prove: If $f(x) > 0$ and $\lim_{x \to a} f(x)^{g(x)}$ has the form $0^{-\infty}$, then this limit **always** equals $+\infty$.

LESSON 114   *Arc Length II: Parametric Equations*

Lesson 109 showed how to compute the arc length of a portion of a curve defined by an equation of the form $y = f(x)$ by developing the following integral formula:

$$L_a^b = \int_{x_a}^{x_b} \sqrt{1 + [f'(x)]^2} \; dx$$

(Here x_a is the x-coordinate of the point a, and x_b is the x-coordinate of point b.) We now wish to find a formula for arc length when the curve is defined by parametric equations of the form $x = f(t)$, $y = g(t)$.

Recall the development in Lesson 109 in which the following curve appeared.

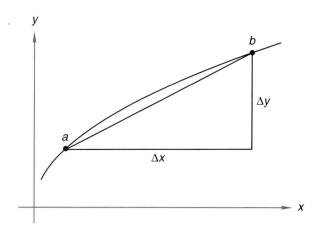

We noted that the actual length of the curve between points a and b is closely approximated by $\sqrt{(\Delta x)^2 + (\Delta y)^2}$ when a and b are quite close. Then we noted that

$$\sum_{i=1}^{n} \sqrt{(\Delta x_i)^2 + (\Delta y_i)^2}$$

closely approximates the arc length and actually equals the arc length as n approaches ∞. We go through this process again, but now include the parameter t.

$$L_a^b = \lim_{n \to \infty} \sum_{i=1}^n \sqrt{(\Delta x_i)^2 + (\Delta y_i)^2}$$

$$= \lim_{n \to \infty} \sum_{i=1}^n \sqrt{\left(\frac{\Delta x_i}{\Delta t}\right)^2 + \left(\frac{\Delta y_i}{\Delta t}\right)^2}\,\Delta t$$

$$= \int_{t_1}^{t_2} \sqrt{\left(\frac{dx}{dt}\right)^2 + \left(\frac{dy}{dt}\right)^2}\,dt \qquad \text{by definition of Riemann sum}$$

Thus we have another nice integral formula for calculating arc length between two points, $a = \big(f(t_1), g(t_1)\big)$ and $b = \big(f(t_2), g(t_2)\big)$:

$$\boxed{L_a^b = \int_{t_1}^{t_2} \sqrt{\left(\frac{dx}{dt}\right)^2 + \left(\frac{dy}{dt}\right)^2}\,dt}$$

It must be noted that this development assumes $f(t)$ and $g(t)$ are differentiable on the open interval (t_1, t_2). If they are not differentiable on (t_1, t_2), the formula cannot be used on the interval. This also assumes the curve does not intersect itself over the interval (t_1, t_2). If it does, then we cannot apply the formula.

example 114.1   A circle of radius r centered at the origin can be defined parametrically by $x = r\cos\theta$ and $y = r\sin\theta$. Find the circumference of the circle based on the parametric description.

solution   The curve is completely traced over the θ-interval $[0, 2\pi]$. By substituting $\frac{dx}{d\theta} = -r\sin\theta$ and $\frac{dy}{d\theta} = r\cos\theta$ into the formula, we find the circumference of the circle.

$$L = \int_{\theta_1}^{\theta_2} \sqrt{\left(\frac{dx}{d\theta}\right)^2 + \left(\frac{dy}{d\theta}\right)^2}\,d\theta \qquad \text{formula}$$

$$= \int_0^{2\pi} \sqrt{(-r\sin\theta)^2 + (r\cos\theta)^2}\,d\theta \qquad \text{substituted}$$

$$= \int_0^{2\pi} \sqrt{r^2\sin^2\theta + r^2\cos^2\theta}\,d\theta$$

$$= \int_0^{2\pi} r\sqrt{\sin^2\theta + \cos^2\theta}\,d\theta$$

$$= \int_0^{2\pi} r\,d\theta \qquad \text{Pythagorean identity}$$

$$= r\theta\big|_0^{2\pi} = 2\pi r - 0 = \mathbf{2\pi r}$$

This confirms a well-known fact: the circumference of a circle of radius r equals $2\pi r$.

example 114.2   Approximate the length of the curve defined by

$$x = 4\cos t - \cos(4t)$$
$$y = 4\sin t - \sin(4t)$$

solution   We use the graphing calculator in parametric-equations mode to graph this function.

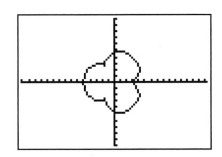

The t-interval from 0 to 2π draws this curve completely; however, the curve is not differentiable over the entire interval. There are three sharp corners regularly distributed over the interval from 0 to 2π. The corners occur at $t = \frac{2\pi}{3}, \frac{4\pi}{3}$, and 2π. To find the arc length, we must sum the lengths of each of the three smooth portions of the curve.

$$L = \int_0^{2\pi/3} \sqrt{\left(\frac{dx}{dt}\right)^2 + \left(\frac{dy}{dt}\right)^2}\ dt + \int_{2\pi/3}^{4\pi/3} \sqrt{\left(\frac{dx}{dt}\right)^2 + \left(\frac{dy}{dt}\right)^2}\ dt$$

$$+ \int_{4\pi/3}^{2\pi} \sqrt{\left(\frac{dx}{dt}\right)^2 + \left(\frac{dy}{dt}\right)^2}\ dt$$

$$= \int_0^{2\pi/3} \sqrt{[-4\sin t + 4\sin (4t)]^2 + [4\cos t - 4\cos (4t)]^2}\ dt$$

$$+ \int_{2\pi/3}^{4\pi/3} \sqrt{[-4\sin t + 4\sin (4t)]^2 + [4\cos t - 4\cos (4t)]^2}\ dt$$

$$+ \int_{4\pi/3}^{2\pi} \sqrt{[-4\sin t + 4\sin (4t)]^2 + [4\cos t - 4\cos (4t)]^2}\ dt$$

$$= \int_0^{2\pi/3} 4\sqrt{2 - 2\sin t \sin (4t) - 2\cos t \cos (4t)}\ dt$$

$$+ \int_{2\pi/3}^{4\pi/3} 4\sqrt{2 - 2\sin t \sin (4t) - 2\cos t \cos (4t)}\ dt$$

$$+ \int_{4\pi/3}^{2\pi} 4\sqrt{2 - 2\sin t \sin (4t) - 2\cos t \cos (4t)}\ dt$$

Using the fnInt option from the MATH menu, we find that the length is **32.**

problem set 114

1.
(97)
When viewed from above, a swimming pool has the shape of an ellipse with the equation $\frac{x^2}{25} + \frac{y^2}{100} = 1$. Every cross section of the pool perpendicular to the ground and parallel to the x-axis is a square. If units are given in feet, what is the volume of the pool?

2.
(109)
Write an integral in terms of a single variable that can be used to find the length of $y = \tan x - 3^x$ from $x = 0$ to $x = 1.5$.

3.
(109)
Find the length of the curve $y = \ln (\sec x)$ from $x = 0$ to $x = 1.5$.

4.
(106)
Graph the parametric curve determined by $x = 4 \cos \theta$ and $y = 4 \sin \theta$.

5.
(109)
Find the length of the curve whose equation is $y = \sqrt{4 - x^2}$. (*Hint:* No calculus is required.)

6.
(114)
Find the length of the curve defined by the parametric equations $x = 2 \cos \theta$ and $y = 2 \sin \theta$ on the interval $[0, \pi]$.

7.
(114)
Find the length of the curve defined by the parametric equations $x = 4 \cos \theta$ and $y = 4 \sin \theta$.

8.
(108)
The initial point of the vector $\langle 2, 0 \rangle$ is at the point $(0, 0)$ and remains stationary at that point. To what point must the terminal point of the vector $\langle 2, 0 \rangle$ be moved so that it has the same direction as the vector $\langle 2, 4 \rangle$?

9.
(93)
Approximate to ten decimal places the x-coordinate of the first-quadrant intersection point of $y = x^2$ and $y = \sin x$.

10. (a) At right is a slope field for the
(104) differential equation $\frac{dy}{dx} = x^2$. The segments indicate slope at integer coordinates for $-5 \le x \le 5$ and $-5 \le y \le 5$. Draw a possible graph for the particular solution to this differential equation that passes through the point $(0, 2)$.

(b) Solve the differential equation $\frac{dy}{dx} = x^2$.

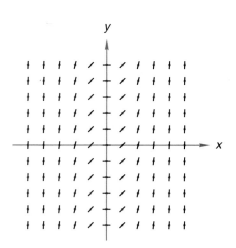

11. Approximate the value of $\int_0^\pi \frac{\cos x}{\sqrt{\sin x + 1}} dx$ using the trapezoidal rule with $n = 6$ subintervals.
(95) Compare this to the actual answer obtained by integrating.

12. Convert the rectangular equation $x^2 + (y - 2)^2 = 4$ to polar form.
(107)

13. Convert the polar equation $r = 3 \csc \theta$ to rectangular form.
(107)

Graph the equations in problems 14 and 15.

14. $r = \cos(3\theta)$
(110)

15. $r = 3 \cos \theta$
(110)

Evaluate the limits in problems 16 and 17.

16. $\lim_{x \to (\pi/2)^-} (\tan x)^{\cos x}$
(111)

17. $\lim_{x \to 0^+} x^{x^2}$
(111)

18. Tell whether the sequence $a_n = \left(\frac{n + 4}{n}\right)^n$ converges or diverges. If it converges, state its limit.
(105)

Integrate in problems 19–22.

19. $\int_0^\pi \frac{-\sin x}{\sqrt{\cos x + 1}} dx$
(66)

20. $\int \frac{dx}{\sqrt{x^2 - 4}}$
(113)

21. $\int \frac{dx}{\sqrt{4 - x^2}}$
(113)

22. $\int_0^1 \frac{1}{\sqrt{x^2 + 6}} dx$
(113)

23. Find the area of the region completely enclosed by the graphs of $y = 1 - x^2$ and $y = x + 1$.
(60)

24. Use a graphing calculator to confirm that $\lim_{x \to 2} (2x^2 - 2x - 3) = 1$ by finding a δ that
(103) guarantees that $2x^2 - 2x - 3$ is within ε of 1 when $\varepsilon = 0.01$.

25. Find the values of a, b, and c so that the graphs of $y = cx - x^2$ and $y = x^2 + ax + b$ are
(24) tangent to each other at the point $(1, 0)$.

LESSON 115 *Partial Fractions I • Logistic Differential Equations*

115.A

partial fractions I

If the numerator of a fraction is the differential of the denominator, the expression has the form du over u, and the integral is $\ln|u| + C$.

$$\int \frac{du}{u} = \ln|u| + C \qquad \int \frac{dx}{x+1} = \ln|x+1| + C$$

In this lesson we consider integrals whose integrands consist of fractions of polynomials in which the denominator's polynomial has only nonrepeating linear real factors and has no irreducible quadratic factors. Examples of such integrals include:

$$\int \frac{1}{x(x+1)}\, dx \qquad \int \frac{x+2}{(x+1)(x-3)}\, dx \qquad \int \frac{x}{x^2-1}\, dx$$

Notice that the third integral can be rewritten in fully factored form as

$$\int \frac{x}{(x-1)(x+1)}\, dx$$

Such factoring is critical to solving the problems in this lesson.

If the degree of the denominator of a fraction of polynomials is greater than the degree of the numerator, and if the denominator can be factored into nonrepeating linear real factors, it is possible to **decompose** the original fraction into a sum of **partial fractions** (i.e., one can write the original fraction as the sum of simpler fractions). The integral of the original fraction equals the sum of the integrals of the partial fractions, which are all in the form du over u. Thus all have integrals of the form $\ln|u|$. For example,

$$\frac{4x^2 + 13x - 9}{x(x+3)(x-1)} \qquad \text{equals} \qquad \frac{3}{x} + \frac{-1}{x+3} + \frac{2}{x-1}$$

Thus the integral of the original fraction equals the sum of the integrals of the partial fractions.

$$\int \frac{4x^2 + 13x - 9}{x(x+3)(x-1)}\, dx = 3\int \frac{dx}{x} - \int \frac{dx}{x+3} + 2\int \frac{dx}{x-1}$$

All three of these integrals are of the form du over u, so the answer is

$$3\ln|x| - \ln|x+3| + 2\ln|x-1| + C$$

Integration by partial fractions is really just an algebraic technique. The difficult step in the example above is determining that

$$\frac{4x^2 + 13x - 9}{x(x+3)(x-1)} = \frac{3}{x} + \frac{-1}{x+3} + \frac{2}{x-1}$$

One procedure for finding the partial fractions is to use letters A, B, and C as the numerators and to use the linear factors of the denominator as the individual denominators, as we show here.

$$\frac{4x^2 + 13x - 9}{x(x+3)(x-1)} = \frac{A}{x} + \frac{B}{x+3} + \frac{C}{x-1}$$

The next step is to multiply every numerator on both sides by the denominator $x(x-3)(x-1)$ to get

$$4x^2 + 13x - 9 = A(x+3)(x-1) + Bx(x-1) + Cx(x+3) \qquad (1)$$

Since we have three unknowns, we need three independent equations. We can get three equations by choosing three different values of x, say 5, 7, and 10. Then we could solve the system for A, B, and C. But if we consider equation (1) carefully, we can see that there are choices of x that allow us to find A, B, and C without solving a system of three equations. We note that x is a factor of the last two terms on the right-hand side in equation (1). If we let x equal zero, these terms are zero, and we can solve for A.

$$4(0)^2 + 13(0) - 9 = A(0 + 3)(0 - 1) + B(0)(0 - 1) + C(0)(0 + 3)$$
$$-9 = A(3)(-1)$$
$$-9 = -3A$$
$$A = 3$$

Two of the terms on the right-hand side of the equals sign in equation (1) have $x - 1$ as a factor. If we let x equal 1, these terms equal zero.

$$4(1)^2 + 13(1) - 9 = A(0) + B(0) + C(1)(1 + 3)$$
$$4 + 13 - 9 = C(1)(4)$$
$$8 = 4C$$
$$C = 2$$

Two of the terms on the right-hand side of the equals sign in equation (1) have $x + 3$ as a factor, and if we let x equal -3, these terms equal zero.

$$4(-3)^2 + 13(-3) - 9 = A(0) + B(-3)(-3 - 1) + C(0)$$
$$36 - 39 - 9 = B(-3)(-4)$$
$$-12 = 12B$$
$$B = -1$$

Thus $A = 3$, $B = -1$, and $C = 2$, which is why

$$\frac{4x^2 + 13x - 9}{x(x + 3)(x - 1)} = \frac{3}{x} + \frac{-1}{x + 3} + \frac{2}{x - 1}$$

example 115.1   Integrate: $\displaystyle\int \frac{dx}{x^2 - 1}$

solution   The denominator of the integrand is factorable, so we use partial fractions.

$$\frac{1}{(x + 1)(x - 1)} = \frac{A}{x + 1} + \frac{B}{x - 1}$$

Next we multiply both sides of this equation by $(x + 1)(x - 1)$.

$$1 = A(x - 1) + B(x + 1)$$

We want to solve for A and B. If $x = 1$ in this equation, then

$$1 = 0x + 2B$$
$$1 = 2B$$
$$B = \frac{1}{2}$$

If $x = -1$, then

$$1 = -2A + 0B$$
$$-2A = 1$$
$$A = -\frac{1}{2}$$

Therefore

$$\frac{1}{(x + 1)(x - 1)} = \frac{A}{x + 1} + \frac{B}{x - 1} = \frac{-\dfrac{1}{2}}{x + 1} + \frac{\dfrac{1}{2}}{x - 1}$$

Now we can find the integral.

$$\int \frac{dx}{x^2 - 1} = \int \left(\frac{-\dfrac{1}{2}}{x + 1} + \frac{\dfrac{1}{2}}{x - 1} \right) dx$$

$$= -\frac{1}{2} \int \left(\frac{1}{x + 1} \right) dx + \frac{1}{2} \int \left(\frac{1}{x - 1} \right) dx$$

$$= -\frac{1}{2} \ln |x + 1| + \frac{1}{2} \ln |x - 1| + C$$

example 115.2   Integrate: $\displaystyle\int \frac{(2x + 3)\, dx}{x(x + 2)(x - 1)}$

solution   We begin by writing

$$\frac{2x + 3}{x(x + 2)(x - 1)} = \frac{A}{x} + \frac{B}{x + 2} + \frac{C}{x - 1}$$

Next we multiply both sides by the denominator on the left-hand side of the equation.

$$2x + 3 = A(x + 2)(x - 1) + Bx(x - 1) + Cx(x + 2)$$

Then we insert specific values of x in order to find A, B, and C.

$$x = 0: \qquad 2(0) + 3 = A(2)(-1)$$
$$3 = -2A$$
$$A = -\frac{3}{2}$$

$$x = 1: \qquad 2(1) + 3 = C(1)(3)$$
$$5 = 3C$$
$$C = \frac{5}{3}$$

$$x = -2: \qquad 2(-2) + 3 = B(-2)(-3)$$
$$-1 = 6B$$
$$B = -\frac{1}{6}$$

Thus the integral can be rewritten as

$$\int \left(\frac{-\dfrac{3}{2}}{x} + \frac{-\dfrac{1}{6}}{x + 2} + \frac{\dfrac{5}{3}}{x - 1} \right) dx = -\frac{3}{2} \int \frac{dx}{x} - \frac{1}{6} \int \frac{dx}{x + 2} + \frac{5}{3} \int \frac{dx}{x - 1}$$

$$= -\frac{3}{2} \ln |x| - \frac{1}{6} \ln |x + 2| + \frac{5}{3} \ln |x - 1| + C$$

115.B
logistic differential equations

In some previous work we encountered **exponential growth models.** In exponential growth, the rate at which a population P grows is proportional to P. This is represented by the following differential equation:

$$\frac{dP}{dt} = kP \qquad \text{for some constant } k$$

This differential equation describes exponential growth, because its solution is $P(t) = P_0 e^{kt}$ where P_0 is the initial size of the population.

Unfortunately, the exponential growth model is flawed. It does not account for factors that limit the growth of a population, including death, disease, famine, and space needs. In an attempt to compensate for this, Pierre François Verhulst (1804–1849) developed the **logistic growth model.** The underlying differential equation in this model is

$$\frac{dP}{dt} = aP(C - P)$$

where P is the time-dependent population size, C is the maximum population attainable in the given environment, and a is a constant of proportionality. The constant C represents the **carrying capacity** of the habitat, and it is constrained by the availability of food, water, space, etc.

This differential equation is separable, as shown.

$$\frac{dP}{P(C - P)} = a\, dt$$

Moreover, the left-hand side of the equation is integrable via partial fractions. We omit that work here but note that the solution of this differential equation is

$$P(t) = \frac{C}{1 + ke^{-Cat}}$$

where k is a constant that arises from integrating both sides of the differential equation.

It is interesting to note the general shape of the graph of this function.

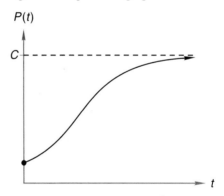

Notice the graph has a horizontal asymptote at the value C. (This can be proved by taking the limit of $P(t)$ as t goes to infinity.) Moreover the graph has an inflection point at $t = \frac{C}{2}$ where its concavity changes from positive to negative.

example 115.3   Suppose 10 moose are placed in an animal preserve. After one year game wardens determine that the moose population has grown to 16 moose. The game wardens estimate that the carrying capacity of the preserve is 150 moose. (a) Assume the moose population is governed by logistic growth. Find a formula for $P(t)$, the number of moose on the preserve t years after the initial placement. (b) Use the formula for $P(t)$ to estimate the number of moose present after 10 years.

solution   (a) The carrying capacity is 150. Thus $P(t) = \frac{150}{1 + ke^{-150at}}$ for some constants a and k. These constants can be determined from the data given in the problem. At $t = 0$ there are 10 moose, so

$$10 = P(0) = \frac{150}{1 + ke^{-150a(0)}} = \frac{150}{1 + k}$$

We solve this for k.

$$10 = \frac{150}{1 + k}$$
$$10(1 + k) = 150$$
$$1 + k = 15$$
$$k = 14$$

Therefore $P(t) = \frac{150}{1 + 14e^{-150at}}$. Now we need to find a. Since there are 16 moose after one year,

$$16 = P(1) = \frac{150}{1 + 14e^{-150a(1)}}$$

which implies the following:

$$16(1 + 14e^{-150a}) = 150$$

$$1 + 14e^{-150a} = \frac{150}{16}$$

$$14e^{-150a} = \frac{150}{16} - 1$$

$$14e^{-150a} = \frac{134}{16}$$

$$e^{-150a} = \frac{134}{224}$$

To obtain a, we convert this equation to logarithmic form and solve.

$$e^{-150a} = \frac{134}{224}$$

$$-150a = \ln\left(\frac{134}{224}\right)$$

$$a = \frac{\ln\left(\frac{134}{224}\right)}{-150}$$

Hence

$$P(t) = \frac{150}{1 + 14e^{-150\left[\frac{\ln(134/224)}{-150}\right]t}} \qquad \text{or} \qquad P(t) = \frac{150}{1 + 14\left(\frac{134}{224}\right)^t}$$

A graph of the function is given here.

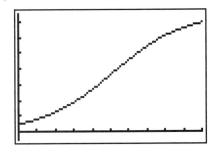 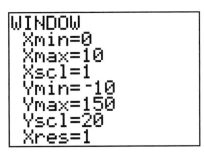

(b) The last task is to estimate the number of moose present after 10 years.

$$P(10) = \frac{150}{1 + 14\left(\frac{134}{224}\right)^{10}} \approx 138.6$$

So we estimate that **138 or 139 moose** will be present after 10 years.

problem set
115

1. The height of a right circular cone is increasing at a rate of 3 cm/s, and the radius of the circular
   (46) base of the cone is decreasing at a rate of 1 cm/s. Find the rate at which the volume of the cone
   is changing when the height of the cone is 10 cm and the radius of the base is 4 cm.

2. Use differentials to approximate the cube root of 9.
   (99)

3. A ball is thrown into the air with an initial velocity of 100 feet per second at a 20° angle of
   (65) elevation. What is the horizontal component of the velocity? What is the horizontal displacement
   of the ball during its first three seconds of flight? (Neglect the effect of air resistance.)

4. The base of a solid is the region in the xy-plane bounded by $y = \sin x$, the x-axis, $x = 0$,
(97) and $x = \frac{\pi}{2}$. What is the volume of the object if every vertical slice of the object parallel to the x-axis is a square?

5. Find the length of $y = \dfrac{x^3}{12} + \dfrac{1}{x}$ from $x = 1$ to $x = 2$.
(109)

Antidifferentiate in problems 6 and 7.

6. $\displaystyle\int \frac{3x}{(x-1)(x+2)}\, dx$ **7.** $\displaystyle\int \frac{x^2 - 2}{x(x-2)(x-1)}\, dx$
(115)   (115)

8. Write an integral whose value equals the length of the curve whose parametric equations
(114) are $x = \sin t + 3$ and $y = 3^t + \cos t$ for t from $t = 2$ to $t = 6$.

9. Find the length of the graph determined by the parametric equations $x = 6 \cos \theta$ and
(114) $y = 6 \sin \theta$ on the interval $\left[\frac{\pi}{2}, 2\pi\right]$.

10. Write the rectangular form of the polar equation $r = 2$.
(107)

Graph the equations in problems 11 and 12.

11. $r = \cos(4\theta)$ **12.** $r = 2 \cos(2\theta)$
(110)   (110)

Antidifferentiate in problems 13–18.

13. $\displaystyle\int \frac{dx}{\sqrt{1 - 4x^2}}$ **14.** $\displaystyle\int \frac{dx}{\sqrt{1 + 4x^2}}$
(113)   (113)

15. $\displaystyle\int \frac{dx}{1 + 4x^2}$ **16.** $\displaystyle\int \frac{dx}{\sqrt{4x^2 - 1}}$
(113)   (113)

17. $\displaystyle\int \frac{x}{1 + 4x^2}\, dx$ **18.** $\displaystyle\int \frac{1 + 4x^2}{x}\, dx$
(66)   (38)

Evaluate the limits in problems 19 and 20.

19. $\displaystyle\lim_{x \to 0} \left[27x \csc(4x) \right]$ **20.** $\displaystyle\lim_{x \to (\pi/2)^-} \left[(\tan x)^{\pi - 2x} \right]$
(91)   (111)

21. Let $g(x) = \dfrac{d}{dx} \displaystyle\int_2^x \sqrt{1 + t^3}\, dt$. Find $g'(x)$.
(98)

22. Suppose f is a function defined for all real values of x. Which of the following conditions
(96) guarantees that the graphs of $y = |f(x)|$ and $y = f(x)$ are identical?

     A. f is an odd function.   B. f is an even function.

     C. $f(x) \geq 0$ for all x.   D. f is continuous for all real x.

23. If f is a function that is everywhere continuous and increasing, which of the following
(58,82) statements must be true?

     A. The inverse of f is also a function.   B. The inverse of f is everywhere decreasing.

     C. f is everywhere differentiable.   D. f^{-1} and f are the same function.

     E. $\dfrac{1}{f}$ and f^{-1} have the same graph.

24. Evaluate: $\displaystyle\int_{0.5}^2 |\ln x|\, dx$
(96)

25. Let f be a continuous function for all real values of x. Suppose $c > a$ and $b > 0$. Which of
(66) the following integrals are equivalent?

     I. $\displaystyle\int_a^c f(x)\, dx$ II. $\displaystyle\int_{a-b}^{c-b} f(x + b)\, dx$ III. $\displaystyle\int_0^{c-a} f(x + a)\, dx$

     A. I. and II. only   B. II. and III. only   C. I. and III. only   D. I., II., and III.

LESSON *116* *Series*

Lesson 105 introduced the concept of a sequence, an infinite and ordered list of terms. We now discuss the concept of the sum of infinitely many terms, which is called an **infinite series** or **series.** If $\{a_i\}$ is a sequence of terms for $i = 1, 2, 3, \ldots,$ we can form a series S by summing these terms.

$$S = a_1 + a_2 + a_3 + \cdots \qquad \text{or} \qquad S = \sum_{i=1}^{\infty} a_i$$

Unfortunately S is represented as an infinite summation. If it has a value, that value cannot be determined by adding all the a_i's, because the process never ends. However, it is possible to add the first n terms. Therefore the nth **partial sum** of $S,$ denoted $S_n,$ is defined by

$$S_n = a_1 + a_2 + a_3 + \cdots + a_n$$

All partial sums are finite, since each is a sum of a finite number of terms.

$$S_1 = a_1$$
$$S_2 = a_1 + a_2$$
$$S_3 = a_1 + a_2 + a_3$$
$$\vdots$$

Notice that the partial sums of S form a sequence $S_1, S_2, S_3, \ldots.$ Thus, we define the **sum** of a series S to be the limit of the sequence of its partial sums.

$$S = \sum_{i=1}^{\infty} a_i = \lim_{n \to \infty} S_n$$

Moreover, we say the infinite series S **converges** if $\lim_{n \to \infty} S_n$ converges. Otherwise S is said to **diverge.**

example 116.1 Let $S = \displaystyle\sum_{n=1}^{\infty} \frac{1}{2^n}.$ Find the first five partial sums of $S.$ That is, find $S_1, S_2, S_3, S_4,$ and $S_5.$

solution The first five terms of S are $\dfrac{1}{2}, \dfrac{1}{4}, \dfrac{1}{8}, \dfrac{1}{16},$ and $\dfrac{1}{32}.$ The partial sums are as follows:

$$S_1 = \frac{1}{2}$$

$$S_2 = \frac{1}{2} + \frac{1}{4} = \frac{3}{4}$$

$$S_3 = \frac{1}{2} + \frac{1}{4} + \frac{1}{8} = \frac{3}{4} + \frac{1}{8} = \frac{7}{8}$$

$$S_4 = \frac{1}{2} + \frac{1}{4} + \frac{1}{8} + \frac{1}{16} = \frac{7}{8} + \frac{1}{16} = \frac{15}{16}$$

$$S_5 = \frac{1}{2} + \frac{1}{4} + \frac{1}{8} + \frac{1}{16} + \frac{1}{32} = \frac{15}{16} + \frac{1}{32} = \frac{31}{32}$$

example 116.2 Does the infinite series $S = \displaystyle\sum_{n=1}^{\infty} \frac{1}{2^n}$ converge or diverge?

solution To answer such a question regarding infinite series, we must consider

$$\lim_{n \to \infty} S_n$$

Therefore we must find a formula for S_n, the nth partial sum of S. We seek a pattern in the partial sums S_1, S_2, S_3, S_4, and S_5. Notice that the denominators are powers of 2.

$$S_1 = \frac{1}{2} = \frac{1}{2^1}$$

$$S_2 = \frac{3}{4} = \frac{3}{2^2}$$

$$S_3 = \frac{7}{8} = \frac{7}{2^3}$$

$$S_4 = \frac{15}{16} = \frac{15}{2^4}$$

$$S_5 = \frac{31}{32} = \frac{31}{2^5}$$

Moreover, the numerators are one less than the denominators.

$$S_1 = \frac{2^1 - 1}{2^1}$$

$$S_2 = \frac{2^2 - 1}{2^2}$$

$$S_3 = \frac{2^3 - 1}{2^3}$$

$$S_4 = \frac{2^4 - 1}{2^4}$$

$$S_5 = \frac{2^5 - 1}{2^5}$$

From these we conjecture that

$$S_n = \frac{2^n - 1}{2^n} = 1 - \frac{1}{2^n}$$

It turns out we can prove that this formula for S_n is correct for all positive integers n. (Usually, it is more difficult to find an explicit formula for S_n.) Thus, we can determine whether the series converges or diverges.

$$\lim_{n \to \infty} S_n = \lim_{n \to \infty} \left(1 - \frac{1}{2^n}\right) = 1 - 0 = 1$$

Hence $\displaystyle\sum_{n=1}^{\infty} \frac{1}{2^n}$ **converges** and $\displaystyle\sum_{n=1}^{\infty} \frac{1}{2^n} = 1$.

example 116.3   Find the first four partial sums of the series $\displaystyle\sum_{n=1}^{\infty} \frac{1}{n}$.

solution   The partial sums are as follows:

$$S_1 = \frac{1}{1} = \mathbf{1}$$

$$S_2 = \frac{1}{1} + \frac{1}{2} = \mathbf{\frac{3}{2}}$$

$$S_3 = \frac{1}{1} + \frac{1}{2} + \frac{1}{3} = \mathbf{\frac{11}{6}}$$

$$S_4 = \frac{1}{1} + \frac{1}{2} + \frac{1}{3} + \frac{1}{4} = \mathbf{\frac{25}{12}}$$

While these partial sums do not appear to grow large, this series actually diverges. The series $\sum_{n=1}^{\infty} \frac{1}{n}$ is known as the **harmonic series.** It will be discussed more in Lesson 127.

**problem set
116**

1. Approximate to ten decimal places the x-coordinate of the first-quadrant point of intersection of
(93)   the graphs of $y = x$ and $y = \cos x$.

2. A solid has a base bounded by $y = 4 - x^2$ and the x-axis. Each cross section perpendicular to
(97)   the base and parallel to the x-axis is a rectangle of height 2. Find its volume.

3. Determine the average value of $f(x) = \sin x$ on the closed interval $[0, \pi]$. Confirm the Mean
(89)   Value Theorem for Integrals using f on this interval.

4. Define: *series*
(116)

5. A variable force $F(x) = xe^{x^2}$ newtons is applied to an object to move it along a straight line in
(62)   the direction of the force. Find the work done by the force on the object in moving it from
       $x = 0$ to $x = 3$ meters.

6. Evaluate: $\lim\limits_{x \to 0^+} [\sin x \ln (\sin x)]$
(91)

Antidifferentiate in problems 7 and 8.

7. $\displaystyle\int \frac{6x + 1}{x(x + 1)(x + 2)} \, dx$
(115)

8. $\displaystyle\int \frac{-x - 7}{(x + 1)(x - 2)} \, dx$
(115)

9. Write the polar form of the rectangular equation $x^2 + y^2 = 4$.
(107)

10. Find the length of the curve whose graph is defined by the parametric equations $x = e^t \sin t$
(114)   and $y = e^t \cos t$ on the interval from $t = 0$ to $t = 2$.

11. A particle moves along the path defined by the parametric equations $x = \frac{t^2}{2}$ and
(114) $y = \frac{1}{3}(2t + 1)^{3/2}$. Find the distance the particle travels between times $t = 0$ and $t = 4$.

Graph the equations in problems 12 and 13 on a polar coordinate system.

12. $r = 2 \sin \theta$
(110)

13. $r = 3 \sin (3\theta)$
(110)

Integrate in problems 14–17.

14. $\displaystyle\int \frac{2x}{4 + 9x^2} \, dx$
(66)

15. $\displaystyle\int \frac{4 + 9x^2}{2x} \, dx$
(38)

16. $\displaystyle\int \frac{2x}{\sqrt{4 + 9x^2}} \, dx$
(66)

17. $\displaystyle\int \frac{2}{\sqrt{4 + 9x^2}} \, dx$
(113)

18. List the first six terms of $\displaystyle\sum_{n=1}^{\infty} \frac{2n}{3}$.
(116)

19. Find the first six partial sums of the series $\displaystyle\sum_{n=1}^{\infty} \frac{2n}{3}$.
(116)

20. Would you guess that the series $\displaystyle\sum_{n=1}^{\infty} \frac{2n}{3}$ converges or diverges? If you say it converges, to what
(116)   would you guess it converges?

21. List the first six terms of $\displaystyle\sum_{n=1}^{\infty} \frac{3}{2^n}$.
(116)

22. Find the first six partial sums of the series $\displaystyle\sum_{n=1}^{\infty} \frac{3}{2^n}$.
(116)

23. Would you guess that the series $\sum_{n=1}^{\infty} \frac{3}{2^n}$ converges or diverges? If you say it converges, to what
(116) would you guess it converges?

24. Differentiate $y = \dfrac{1}{\sqrt{x}} - x \ln |\sin x| + \arcsin \dfrac{x}{2}$ with respect to x.
(50,64)

25. An experiment confirms that there is a relationship between two quantities, which we represent
(95) by the variables x and y. The experiment produced the correspondences between x and y
indicated in the following table:

x	2.0	2.5	3.0	3.5	4.0	4.5	5.0
y	2.7	3.5	4.1	4.0	3.8	3.2	2.4

Though we do not have the equation $y = f(x)$, we know that $\int f(x)\,dx$ has an important
physical meaning. Approximate $\int_2^5 f(x)\,dx$ using this data and the trapezoidal rule with
$n = 6$ subintervals.

LESSON 117 *Geometric Series • Telescoping Series*

117.A

geometric series   A few types of series occur frequently in certain applications. One is called the **geometric series.** A
geometric series is a series of the form

$$a + ar + ar^2 + ar^3 + \cdots + ar^{n-1} + \cdots$$

where a and r are real numbers and $a \neq 0$. One of the most convenient aspects of geometric series is
that a theorem characterizes when they converge.

> The geometric series $a + ar + ar^2 + \cdots + ar^{n-1} + \cdots$
>
> 1. converges to $\dfrac{a}{1-r}$ if $|r| < 1$ or
>
> 2. diverges if $|r| \geq 1$.

The proof of this fact is fairly straightforward. If $r = 1$, then $S_n = a + a + a + \cdots + a = na$.
Because $\lim_{n \to \infty} S_n = \infty$, the series diverges. If $r \neq 1$, then

$$S_n = a + ar + ar^2 + ar^3 + \cdots + ar^{n-1} \qquad \text{and}$$
$$rS_n = ar + ar^2 + ar^3 + ar^4 + \cdots + ar^n$$

If we subtract these two equations and then factor the left-hand side of the resulting equation, we obtain

$$(1 - r)S_n = a - ar^n$$

Dividing both sides of this equation by $1 - r$ produces

$$S_n = \frac{a}{1-r} - \frac{ar^n}{1-r}$$

We take the limit of S_n as n approaches ∞.

$$\lim_{n \to \infty} S_n = \lim_{n \to \infty}\left(\frac{a}{1-r} - \frac{ar^n}{1-r} \right)$$

$$= \lim_{n \to \infty} \frac{a}{1-r} - \lim_{n \to \infty} \frac{ar^n}{1-r}$$

$$= \frac{a}{1-r} - \left(\frac{a}{1-r} \right) \lim_{n \to \infty} r^n$$

At this point we consider two separate cases, $|r| < 1$ and $|r| > 1$.

1. If $|r| < 1$, then $\lim_{n \to \infty} r^n = 0$. Thus, $\lim_{n \to \infty} S_n = \frac{a}{1-r}$ and the series converges to $\frac{a}{1-r}$.

2. If $|r| > 1$, then $\lim_{n \to \infty} r^n$ does not exist. Thus, $\lim_{n \to \infty} S_n$ does not exist and the series diverges.

example 117.1   Find the sum of the series $S = \sum_{n=1}^{\infty} \frac{2}{3^n}$ if it exists.

solution   Note that

$$S = \sum_{n=1}^{\infty} \frac{2}{3^n} = \frac{2}{3} + \frac{2}{3^2} + \frac{2}{3^3} + \frac{2}{3^4} + \cdots$$

$$= \frac{2}{3} + \frac{2}{3}\left(\frac{1}{3}\right) + \frac{2}{3}\left(\frac{1}{9}\right) + \frac{2}{3}\left(\frac{1}{27}\right) + \cdots$$

So S is a geometric series with $a = \frac{2}{3}$ and $r = \frac{1}{3}$. Since $\left|\frac{1}{3}\right| < 1$, the series converges and its sum is

$$\frac{\frac{2}{3}}{1 - \frac{1}{3}} = \frac{\frac{2}{3}}{\frac{2}{3}} = \mathbf{1}$$

example 117.2   A basketball is dropped from a height of 10 feet. Each time the ball hits the floor, it rebounds to a height of $\frac{9}{10}$ its previous fall. What is the total distance the ball travels?

solution   To find the distance the ball travels we break this problem into two situations, the distance the ball *falls* and the distance the ball *rebounds*. The sum of the distances the ball falls forms a geometric series with $a = 10$ and $r = \frac{9}{10}$. Thus the ball falls a total of

$$\frac{10}{1 - \frac{9}{10}} = \frac{10}{\frac{1}{10}} = 100 \text{ ft}$$

The only difference between the distance the ball falls and the distance it rebounds is the first fall. Therefore the ball rebounds $100 - 10$, or 90 feet. Altogether the ball travels a total of $100 + 90$, or **190 feet.**

example 117.3   Find the sum of the series $S = \sum_{n=1}^{\infty} \frac{4}{10^n}$ if it exists.

solution $S = \frac{4}{10} + \frac{4}{100} + \frac{4}{1000} + \cdots$ is a geometric series. Here $a = \frac{4}{10}$ and $r = \frac{1}{10}$. Since $|r| = \left|\frac{1}{10}\right| < 1$, the series converges and

$$S = \frac{\frac{4}{10}}{1 - \frac{1}{10}} = \frac{\frac{4}{10}}{\frac{9}{10}} = \frac{\mathbf{4}}{\mathbf{9}}$$

If we think about this series in a slightly different way, we see that it is a repeating decimal:

$$S_1 = \frac{4}{10} = 0.4$$

$$S_2 = \frac{4}{10} + \frac{4}{100} = 0.44$$

$$S_3 = \frac{4}{10} + \frac{4}{100} + \frac{4}{1000} = 0.444$$

$$\vdots$$

In earlier algebra courses you learned to express repeating decimals as the ratio of two integers to show that they were rational numbers. This was done in the following manner:

Let $n = 0.\overline{4}$; then $10n = 4.\overline{4}$. So,

$$\begin{aligned} 10n &= 4.\overline{4} \\ - \quad n &= 0.\overline{4} \\ \hline 9n &= 4 \end{aligned} \quad \longrightarrow \quad n = \frac{4}{9}$$

This answer agrees with the answer obtained above and shows that this repeating decimal (or any repeating decimal by a similar demonstration) is a rational number. Furthermore, it reinforces the idea that the sum of infinitely many numbers can be a finite number!

example 117.4   Find the sum of $S = \sum_{n=1}^{\infty} \left(\frac{3}{2}\right)^n$ if it exists.

solution   This series is a geometric series with a common ratio $r = \frac{3}{2}$. Since $\left|\frac{3}{2}\right| > 1$, this series actually **diverges.**

117.B

telescoping series   The second type of series we examine in this lesson is called the **telescoping series.** Such series exhibit a collapsing effect (like a sailor's telescope) when the partial sums are studied, which allows us to quickly determine the limit of its partial sums.

example 117.5   Find the value of $S = \sum_{n=1}^{\infty} \frac{1}{n(n+1)}$ if it converges.

solution   This series is not geometric, because it is not of the form

$$a + ar + ar^2 + ar^3 + \cdots$$

We consider the form of the nth term $\frac{1}{n(n+1)}$. This fraction can be decomposed into partial fractions.

$$\frac{1}{n(n+1)} = \frac{1}{n} - \frac{1}{n+1}$$

Thus the individual terms of the series are as follows:

$$a_1 = \frac{1}{1} - \frac{1}{2}$$
$$a_2 = \frac{1}{2} - \frac{1}{3}$$
$$a_3 = \frac{1}{3} - \frac{1}{4}$$
$$a_4 = \frac{1}{4} - \frac{1}{5}$$
$$\vdots$$

To determine whether S converges, we look at its partial sums:

$$S_1 = 1 - \frac{1}{2}$$
$$S_2 = \left(1 - \frac{1}{2}\right) + \left(\frac{1}{2} - \frac{1}{3}\right) = 1 - \frac{1}{3}$$
$$S_3 = \left(1 - \frac{1}{2}\right) + \left(\frac{1}{2} - \frac{1}{3}\right) + \left(\frac{1}{3} - \frac{1}{4}\right) = 1 - \frac{1}{4}$$
$$S_4 = \left(1 - \frac{1}{2}\right) + \left(\frac{1}{2} - \frac{1}{3}\right) + \left(\frac{1}{3} - \frac{1}{4}\right) + \left(\frac{1}{4} - \frac{1}{5}\right) = 1 - \frac{1}{5}$$

Notice the telescoping or collapsing effect in these partial sums. The pattern is obvious.

$$S_n = 1 - \frac{1}{n + 1}$$

Therefore $\lim_{n \to \infty} S_n = \lim_{n \to \infty} (1 - \frac{1}{n+1}) = 1 - 0 = 1$, which means $\sum_{n=1}^{\infty} \frac{1}{n(n+1)}$ converges to **1.**

We close by noting that most telescoping series can be uncovered by decomposing individual terms into partial fractions. You should keep this in mind as you strive to identify telescoping series.

problem set 117

1. Express the repeating decimal $1.\overline{476}$ as a fraction of two integers, thereby showing it is a rational number.
(117)

2. A ball is dropped from a height of 15 feet. Each time the ball hits the floor, it rebounds to a height of $\frac{3}{5}$ its previous fall. What is the total distance the ball falls?
(117)

3. A ball is dropped from a height of 15 feet. Each time the ball hits the floor, it rebounds to a height of $\frac{3}{5}$ its previous fall. What is the total distance the ball travels?
(117)

Determine whether each sequence in problems 4–6 converges or diverges. If a sequence converges, state its limit.

4. $a_n = \dfrac{3}{4^n}$
(105)

5. $a_n = \dfrac{3^n}{5^n}$
(105)

6. $a_n = \dfrac{5^n}{3^n}$
(105)

Determine whether each series in problems 7–9 converges or diverges. If a series converges, state its value.

7. $\displaystyle\sum_{n=1}^{\infty} \frac{3}{4^n}$
(117)

8. $\displaystyle\sum_{n=1}^{\infty} \frac{3^n}{5^n}$
(117)

9. $\displaystyle\sum_{n=1}^{\infty} \frac{5^n}{3^n}$
(117)

10. Explain why the substitution $\sec \theta = \dfrac{x}{a}$ is useful for integrating $\dfrac{dx}{\sqrt{x^2 - a^2}}$.
(112)

11. Determine whether the sequence $a_n = (1 + \frac{3}{n})^n$ converges or diverges. If it converges, state its limit.
(111)

Determine whether each geometric series in problems 12–14 converges or diverges. If a series converges, state its value.

12. $\displaystyle\sum_{n=1}^{\infty} \frac{1}{2^n}$
(117)

13. $\displaystyle\sum_{n=1}^{\infty} 2^n$
(117)

14. $\displaystyle\sum_{n=1}^{\infty} (-1)^{n-1} 2^{n-1}$
(117)

List the first four terms of each series in problems 15–17, and then determine whether the series converges or diverges. If a series converges, state its value.

15. $\displaystyle\sum_{n=1}^{\infty} \frac{1}{(n+1)(n+2)}$
(117)

16. $\displaystyle\sum_{n=1}^{\infty} \ln \frac{n}{n+1}$
(117)

17. $\displaystyle\sum_{n=1}^{\infty} \frac{1}{n(n+1)}$
(117)

Integrate in problems 18–19.

18. $\displaystyle\int \frac{x + 2}{x^2 + 2x - 8}\, dx$
(115)

19. $\displaystyle\int \sqrt{9 - x^2}\, dx$
(113)

20. (a) Evaluate $\displaystyle\int_0^3 \sqrt{9 - x^2}\, dx$ using geometry.
(113)

     (b) Evaluate $\displaystyle\int_0^3 \sqrt{9 - x^2}\, dx$ using the answer to problem 19.

21. Approximate the length of the curve defined by the parametric equations $x = e^{2t}$ and $y = 2e^t$
(114) from $t = 0$ to $t = 5$.

22. Sketch the graph of the polar curve defined by the equation $r = 3 \sin(2\theta)$.
(110)

23. Sketch the graph of the rectangular curve defined by the equation $y = 3 \sin(2x)$.
(7)

24. Write the equation of the curve $(x - 2)^2 + y^2 = 4$ in polar form.
(107)

25. Find the first eleven partial sums of the series $\sum_{n=1}^{\infty} \frac{1}{n}$. Based on the sequence of partial sums, do
(116) you think that the series converges or diverges? If you think it converges, to what do you guess
it converges?

LESSON 118 *Limaçons and Lemniscates*

In this lesson we continue our investigation of the graphs of polar equations by studying limaçons and
lemniscates. We remember that the equation of a rose curve can have one of the following two forms
if n is a counting number.

$$r = c \sin(n\theta) \qquad r = c \cos(n\theta)$$

If we let n equal 1 and insert another constant, we get the equations of **limaçons.**

$$r = a \pm b \sin \theta \qquad r = a \pm b \cos \theta$$

The letters a and b represent positive real numbers. The shape of a limaçon depends on the relative
magnitudes of a and b. The values of $b \sin \theta$ and $b \cos \theta$ change from $+b$ to $-b$ as the values of the
sine and cosine change from $+1$ to -1. If a is less than b, then $|b \sin \theta|$ and $|b \cos \theta|$ are greater than
a for some values of θ, and the limaçon has an inner loop as in the graph on the left-hand side. If a
equals b, the graph is called a **cardioid,** because it looks like a heart. If a over b is a number between
1 and 2, the graph is called a **dimpled limaçon.**

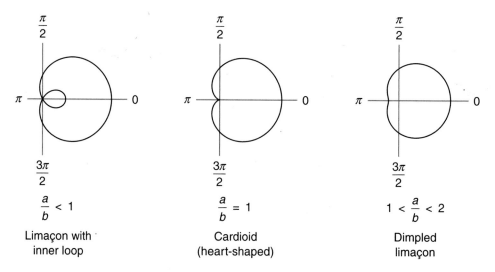

$\dfrac{a}{b} < 1$	$\dfrac{a}{b} = 1$	$1 < \dfrac{a}{b} < 2$
Limaçon with inner loop	Cardioid (heart-shaped)	Dimpled limaçon

If the ratio is greater than or equal to 2, the dimple disappears and we have a flattened circle. As *a* gets greater and greater with respect to *b,* the contribution of *b* sin θ or *b* cos θ diminishes, and the graph approaches the graph of the **circle** *r* = *a*.

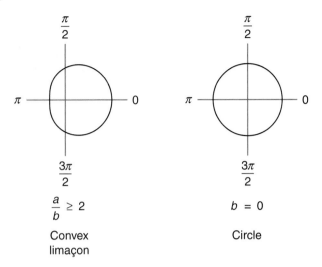

$\dfrac{a}{b} \geq 2$

Convex
limaçon

b = 0

Circle

The graphs of the equations

$$r^2 = a \sin (n\theta) \qquad \text{and} \qquad r^2 = a \cos (n\theta)$$

are called **lemniscates.** In these equations *a* is a constant and *n* is a counting number. If *n* = 2, the graphs look like the graphs of four-leaf roses whose equations are

$$r = a \sin (2\theta) \qquad \text{and} \qquad r = a \cos (2\theta)$$

but they have two leaves missing. To understand why the leaves are missing, we consider the equation

$$r^2 = -1$$

There are no real values of *r* that satisfy this equation, because any real number squared is equal to or greater than zero. The value of r^2 is always positive or zero in the following equations.

$$r^2 = a \sin (2\theta) \qquad r^2 = a \cos (2\theta)$$

Thus, these equations have no solutions whenever sin (2θ) or cos (2θ) is negative. In the equations of the two four-leafed roses shown on the left-hand side below, *r* can be negative and the graphs have leaves for all values of θ. In the equations of the two lemniscates on the right-hand side, r^2 can never be negative, so there is no trace of the curve for values of θ that require r^2 to be negative.

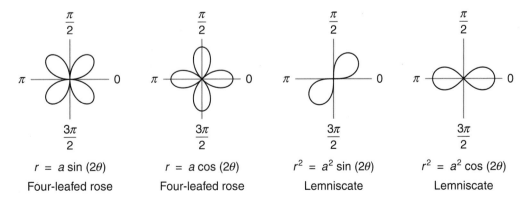

$r = a \sin (2\theta)$

Four-leafed rose

$r = a \cos (2\theta)$

Four-leafed rose

$r^2 = a^2 \sin (2\theta)$

Lemniscate

$r^2 = a^2 \cos (2\theta)$

Lemniscate

As with the roses in Lesson 110, these figures can be graphed point by point, but this is rather time consuming. Often we make use of a graphing utility to graph these kinds of polar equations. After a brief examination the tendencies of these equations become apparent. Then the graphs can be determined by inspection.

example 118.1   Graph: $r = 2 + 2 \sin \theta$

solution   The graph of this function is a cardioid. To draw the graph, it is helpful to begin by visualizing the graph of the following sine function.

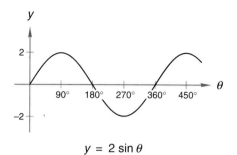

We see that $2 \sin \theta$ equals zero when $\theta = 0°$ and equals 2 when $\theta = 90°$, so $2 + 2 \sin \theta$ goes from 2 to 4 as θ goes from 0° to 90°. We show this in the first figure below. The value of $\sin \theta$ goes from 1 to 0 as θ goes from 90° to 180°, so $2 + 2 \sin \theta$ goes from 4 to 2 between θ-values of 90° and 180°, as shown in the second figure.

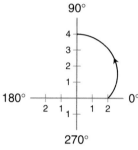
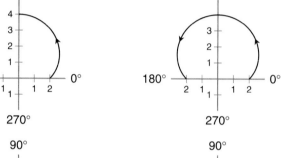

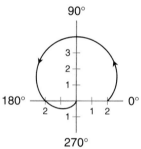
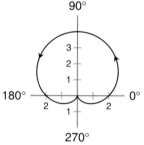

In the next 90° (shown in the third figure) $\sin \theta$ goes from 0 to –1, so $2 + 2 \sin \theta$ goes from 2 to 0. In the fourth figure $2 + 2 \sin \theta$ goes from 0 to +2. Thus the graph is a cardioid whose axis of symmetry is vertical.

We can use a graphing calculator to confirm this result. The first step is to press (MODE) and change to radians and polar coordinates. After pressing the (Y=) key, we set r1=2+2sin(θ). Using the ZTrig option (from the ZOOM menu), we obtain the graph at right.

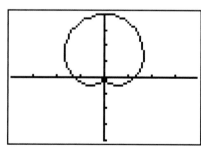

example 118.2   Graph: $r = 3 - 3 \cos \theta$

solution   We begin by visualizing the graph of $y = 3 \cos \theta$.

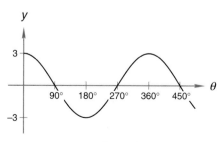

$y = 3 \cos \theta$

Note that $3 \cos \theta$ equals 3 when $\theta = 0°$, so $3 - 3 \cos \theta$ equals zero when $\theta = 0°$. As θ increases from 0° to 90°, $3 \cos \theta$ goes from 3 to 0 and $3 - 3 \cos \theta$ goes from 0 to 3, as we show on the left-hand side below. As θ increases from 90° to 180°, $3 \cos \theta$ goes from 0 to –3, and $3 - 3 \cos \theta$ goes from 3 to 6, as shown in the second figure.

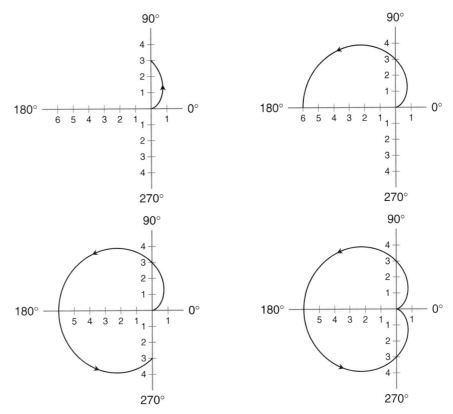

Between 180° and 270°, $3 \cos \theta$ goes from –3 to 0, and $3 - 3 \cos \theta$ goes from 6 to 3, as shown in the third figure. Finally, as θ goes from 270° to 360°, $3 \cos \theta$ goes from 0 to 3, and $3 - 3 \cos \theta$ goes from 3 to 0, as shown in the fourth figure.

Here is the TI-83 graph of this polar function:

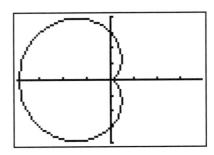

example 118.3 Graph: $r = 2 + 4 \cos \theta$

solution First we visualize the graph of $y = 4 \cos \theta$.

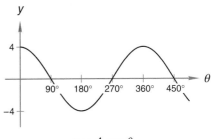

$y = 4 \cos \theta$

Graphing the given equation point by point can be tedious, so we use the fact that the constant 2 in our equation is less than the coefficient 4 to deduce that the graph is a limaçon with an inner loop. We know that $\cos \theta$ equals zero when θ equals 90° and 270°, so $2 + 4 \cos \theta$ equals 2 when θ equals 90° and 270°. The maximum value of $2 + 4 \cos \theta$ is achieved when θ equals 0°, because $\cos \theta$ achieves its maximum value, which is 1, when θ equals 0°. So the maximum value of $2 + 4 \cos \theta$ is $2 + 4 \cos 0° = 6$. We use this to guess the shape of the graph.

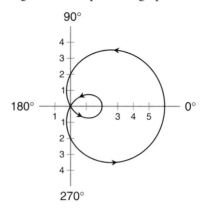

This is confirmed by the TI-83.

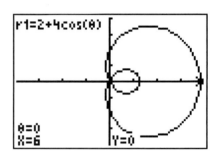

A reminder about the TI-83 is in order here. It is highly important that you know the shape of these graphs based on the functions in question. However, it is also important for you to know where each graph begins (in most cases, when $\theta = 0°$), where the graph intersects itself, where it ends, and so on. The ⬚TRACE button is invaluable in such circumstances. For example, if you graph the function in the previous example and then press ⬚TRACE, you see the graph at right.

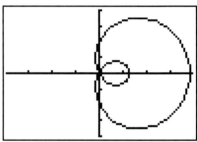

The TI-83 displays the graph, as well as the values of θ, X, and Y that correspond to the highlighted point. As the ⬥ key is pressed, the highlighted cursor moves, updating the θ, X, and Y information for the new point. This proves to be an extremely efficient method for extracting information about polar graphs.

example 118.4   Graph: $r^2 = 4 \cos (2\theta)$

solution   First we visualize the graph of $y = 2 \cos (2\theta)$.

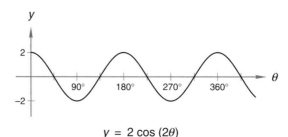

$y = 2 \cos (2\theta)$

We use the graph above as an aid in graphing the equation $r = 2\cos(2\theta)$, which is the four-leafed rose shown on the left-hand side below.

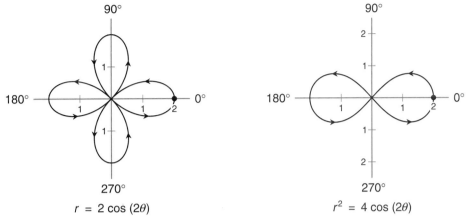

$r = 2\cos(2\theta)$ $r^2 = 4\cos(2\theta)$

The graph of $r^2 = 4\cos(2\theta)$ is a similar graph with blunter ends and without the upper and lower leaves. These leaves are missing because $\cos(2\theta)$ can never be negative in this equation—since r^2 can never be negative. Below is a plot of $r = 2\sqrt{\cos(2\theta)}$ from the TI-83.

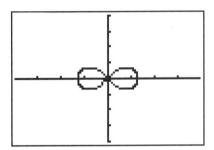

problem set 118

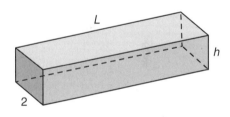

1. (52) A tank, all of whose faces are rectangles, is to be constructed so that the width of its base is 2 meters and its volume is 16 cubic meters. The material for the top and bottom of the tank costs \$8 per square meter, and the material for each of the four sides costs \$4 per square meter. Find the dimensions and the cost of the tank of minimal expense.

2. (114) Find the length of the curve defined by $x = \cos^3\theta$ and $y = \sin^3\theta$ from $\theta = 0$ to $\theta = \dfrac{\pi}{2}$.

3. (99) A solid spherical metal ball is 1 meter in diameter. Use differentials to approximate the increase in the surface area of the ball after applying a 0.01-centimeter coat of gold.

4. (109) Find the length of $y = \dfrac{x^4}{4} + \dfrac{1}{8x^2}$ from $x = 2$ to $x = 4$.

5. (107) Write the polar form of the rectangular equation $x = y^2$.

Graph the equations in problems 6–10.

6. (118) $r = 1 + \sin\theta$

7. (110) $r = 2\cos(3\theta)$

8. (118) $r = 2 + 3\cos\theta$

9. (110) $r = 4\sin(2\theta)$

10. (118) $r = 4 - 2\sin\theta$

11. Find a unit vector that is parallel to and a unit vector that is normal to the line tangent to
(108) $y = x^3 - 3x + 4$ at $(2, 6)$.

Antidifferentiate in problems 12–16.

12. $\int \dfrac{dx}{x^2 - x}$
(115)

13. $\int \dfrac{3x^2 + 9x + 7}{x(x + 1)(x + 2)}\, dx$
(115)

14. $\int \dfrac{dx}{\sqrt{x^2 - 16}}$
(113)

15. $\int \sqrt{16 - x^2}\, dx$
(113)

16. $\int \tan^2 x\, dx$
(100)

Determine whether each series in problems 17–20 converges or diverges. If a series converges, state
its value.

17. $\displaystyle\sum_{n=3}^{\infty} \dfrac{1}{2^n}$
(117)

18. $\displaystyle\sum_{n=3}^{\infty} (-1)^{n-1} \dfrac{1}{2^{n-1}}$
(117)

19. $\displaystyle\sum_{n=3}^{\infty} \dfrac{4^n}{3}$
(117)

20. $\displaystyle\sum_{n=1}^{\infty} \dfrac{1}{n^2 + 3n + 2}$
(117)

Evaluate the limits in problems 21–22.

21. $\displaystyle\lim_{2x \to 0} \dfrac{\sin(137x)}{217x}$
(101)

22. $\displaystyle\lim_{x \to (\pi/2)^-} (1 + \cos x)^{\tan x}$
(111)

23. Find the value of c between 0 and 6 such that $\displaystyle\int_c^x f(t)\, dt = \sin x + 1$.
(98)

24. If $f(2) = 3$, $f'(3) = 2$, and $f'(2) = -4$, then $(f \circ f)'(2)$ equals which of the following?
(50)
  A. -4 B. -8 C. -24 D. -12

25. Let f be defined as $f(x) = \begin{cases} a + bx^2 & \text{when } x \le 2 \\ x^3 & \text{when } x > 2 \end{cases}$ Determine the values of a and b for which f is
(82) differentiable everywhere.

LESSON 119 *Parametric Equations—Second Derivatives and Tangent Lines*

Recall that parametric equations define the dependent variables x and y in terms of a third independent
variable called the parameter. Here we show two variables that are a function of t.

$$x = f(t) \qquad y = g(t)$$

We have seen that the derivative, $\frac{dy}{dx}$, can be found either by eliminating the parameter or by using the
following identity:

$$\frac{dy}{dx} = \frac{\dfrac{dy}{dt}}{\dfrac{dx}{dt}}$$

If $x = \sin t$ and $y = \cos t$, then

$$\frac{dy}{dx} = \frac{\dfrac{dy}{dt}}{\dfrac{dx}{dt}} = \frac{-\sin t}{\cos t} = -\frac{x}{y}$$

Now we wish to consider $\frac{d^2y}{dx^2}$, the second derivative of y with respect to x, where x and y are defined parametrically. Of course, $\frac{d^2y}{dx^2}$ is simply the derivative of $\frac{dy}{dx}$ with respect to x.

$$\frac{d^2y}{dx^2} = \frac{d}{dx}\left(\frac{dy}{dx}\right)$$

This derivative can be rewritten in the following way using the chain rule:

$$\frac{d}{dx}\left(\frac{dy}{dx}\right) = \frac{d}{dt}\left(\frac{dy}{dx}\right) \cdot \frac{dt}{dx}$$

One final revision produces the following identity:

$$\frac{d^2y}{dx^2} = \frac{\dfrac{d}{dt}\left(\dfrac{dy}{dx}\right)}{\dfrac{dx}{dt}}$$

example 119.1   Find $\dfrac{d^2y}{dx^2}$ where $x = \sin t$ and $y = \cos t$.

solution   We know that

$$\frac{dy}{dx} = \frac{-\sin t}{\cos t} = -\tan t$$

Thus $\dfrac{d}{dt}\left(\dfrac{dy}{dx}\right) = \dfrac{d}{dt}(-\tan t) = -\sec^2 t$. Moreover, $\dfrac{dx}{dt} = \cos t$. Therefore

$$\frac{d^2y}{dx^2} = \frac{\dfrac{d}{dt}\left(\dfrac{dy}{dx}\right)}{\dfrac{dx}{dt}} = \frac{-\sec^2 t}{\cos t} = -\sec^3 t$$

If we eliminate the parameter, we get

$$\frac{d^2y}{dx^2} = -\frac{1}{\cos^3 t} = -\frac{1}{y^3}$$

example 119.2   Find $\dfrac{d^2y}{dx^2}$ where $x = e^{-t}$ and $y = e^{2t}$.

solution   Since $\dfrac{dx}{dt} = -e^{-t}$ and $\dfrac{dy}{dt} = 2e^{2t}$, we know

$$\frac{dy}{dx} = \frac{\dfrac{dy}{dt}}{\dfrac{dx}{dt}} = \frac{2e^{2t}}{-e^{-t}} = -2e^{3t}$$

Then we see $\dfrac{d}{dt}\left(\dfrac{dy}{dx}\right) = (-2e^{3t})(3) = -6e^{3t}$. Therefore

$$\frac{d^2 y}{dx^2} = \frac{\dfrac{d}{dt}\left(\dfrac{dy}{dx}\right)}{\dfrac{dx}{dt}} = \frac{-6e^{3t}}{-e^{-t}} = 6e^{4t}$$

We can eliminate the parameter again and write the second derivative in two different ways:

$$\frac{d^2 y}{dx^2} = 6(e^{2t})^2 = 6y^2 \qquad \text{or}$$

$$\frac{d^2 y}{dx^2} = \frac{6}{e^{-4t}} = \frac{6}{(e^{-t})^4} = \frac{6}{x^4}$$

example 119.3   Find the equation of the tangent line corresponding to $t = 0$ for the parametric curve determined by $x = e^t$ and $y = e^{-t}$, and describe the concavity of the curve at the point determined by $t = 0$.

solution   Even parametric curves are drawn in the xy-plane, so the derivatives $\frac{dy}{dx}$ and $\frac{d^2 y}{dx^2}$ yield information about their slope and concavity. To find the equation of the desired tangent line, we must calculate $\frac{dy}{dx}$ when $t = 0$.

$$\frac{dy}{dx} = \frac{-e^{-t}}{e^t} = -e^{-2t} \qquad \left.\frac{dy}{dx}\right|_{t=0} = -e^{-2(0)} = -1$$

Moreover, the point in the xy-plane through which the curve passes at $t = 0$ is (e^0, e^{-0}), or $(1, 1)$. Therefore the equation of the tangent line is

$$y - 1 = (-1)(x - 1) \qquad \text{point-slope form of line}$$
$$y = -x + 2 \qquad \text{slope-intercept form of line}$$

Next we consider the second derivative $\dfrac{d^2 y}{dx^2}$ to study the concavity of the curve.

$$\frac{d^2 y}{dx^2} = \frac{\dfrac{d}{dt}\left(\dfrac{dy}{dx}\right)}{\dfrac{dx}{dt}} = \frac{(-e^{-2t})(-2)}{e^t} = 2e^{-3t}$$

When $t = 0$ we see that the second derivative is $2e^0 = 2$. Since this is positive, we know the curve is **concave up** at this point.

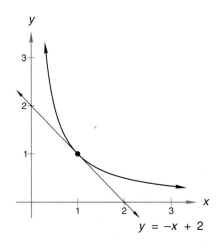

$$y = -x + 2$$

**problem set
119**

1. Find $\dfrac{dy}{dx}$ and $\dfrac{d^2y}{dx^2}$ where $x = 2 + \sin t$ and $y = -1 + \cos t$.
(119)

2. The acceleration at time t of a particle moving along the x-axis is given by the equation
(89) $a(t) = 2\pi \sin t \cos t$. If the velocity of the particle at $t = 0$ is zero, what is the average velocity of the particle over the interval $0 \le t \le \pi$?

3. Find the equation of the line tangent to the curve defined by $x = t^2 + t$ and $y = t + 3$
(119) when $t = 1$. Describe the concavity of the curve at the point where the line is tangent to the curve.

4. Suppose f is defined by $f(x) = \sin^2 x - 2 \sin x$ on the interval $I = [0, 2\pi]$. Find the critical
(45) numbers of f on I, and then determine the maximum and minimum values of f on I.

5. Write an integral whose value equals the length of the curve defined by $x = t + 3$ and
(114) $y = t^3 - 3t^2$ on the interval from $t = 2$ to $t = 5$.

6. Write the rectangular form of the polar equation $r = \sin \theta \cos \theta$.
(107)

7. Let R be the region completely enclosed by $y = 2^x$, $y = 3^x$, and $x = 3$. Write an integral
(81) in one variable whose value equals the volume of the solid formed when R is revolved about the x-axis.

Graph the equations in problems 8–11.

8. $r = 3 \sin \theta$ **9.** $r = 1 - \cos \theta$
(110)   (118)

10. $r = 3 \sin (3\theta)$ **11.** $r^2 = \cos (2\theta)$
(110)   (118)

Determine whether each series in problems 12–14 converges or diverges. If a series converges, state its value.

12. $\dfrac{23}{100} + \dfrac{23}{10{,}000} + \dfrac{23}{1{,}000{,}000} + \cdots$ **13.** $\displaystyle\sum_{n=1}^{\infty} (-1)^n \left(\dfrac{4}{3}\right)^n$
(117)   (117)

14. $\displaystyle\sum_{n=1}^{\infty} \dfrac{n+1}{n}$
(116,117)

15. Sketch the graph of $y = \dfrac{(x-1)(x^2+1)}{(x-2)^2}$. Clearly indicate all zeros and asymptotes.
(80)

Evaluate the limits in problems 16–18.

16. $\displaystyle\lim_{x \to 0} (1 - e^x)^{\tan x}$ **17.** $\displaystyle\lim_{x \to \infty} \left(1 + \dfrac{3}{x}\right)^x$ **18.** $\displaystyle\lim_{x \to \infty} \left(1 + \dfrac{1}{x}\right)^{3x}$
(111)   (111)   (111)

Integrate in problems 19–23.

19. $\displaystyle\int_4^7 \dfrac{3x - 5}{x^2 - x - 6}\, dx$ **20.** $\displaystyle\int \dfrac{dx}{x^2 + 16}$ **21.** $\displaystyle\int \dfrac{dx}{x^2 - 16}$
(115)   (113)   (113)

22. $\displaystyle\int \sin^3 x\, dx$ **23.** $\displaystyle\int \log_3 x\, dx$
(76)   (73)

24. Find $\dfrac{dy}{dx}$ where $y = \arcsin \dfrac{x}{2} + e^x \sin x - \dfrac{\sin (2x)}{x^2 + 1}$.
(50,64)

25.
(95)

The table below shows the relationships between specific values of the variables x and y. Assuming $y = f(x)$ is a continuous function over the given interval, use the table to approximate $\int_3^7 f(x)\, dx$ with the trapezoidal rule.

x	3.0	3.4	3.8	4.2	4.6	5.0	5.4	5.8	6.2	6.6	7.0
y	3.5	3.8	4.5	5.5	6.8	7.5	8.0	8.4	8.6	8.7	8.8

LESSON 120 *Partial Fractions II*

In this lesson we revisit the issue of integrating fractions of polynomials. Specifically, we are interested in fractions of polynomials whose denominators are of higher degree than the numerators and whose denominators have only real linear factors (which may be repeated). Examples of such integrands are the following:

$$\frac{1}{x(x+2)^2} \qquad \frac{1}{x^3(x-7)^2} \qquad \frac{1}{(x+2)(x+1)(x+3)^5}$$

Note: x^3 may be written as $(x-0)^3$, so it is a linear factor repeated three times.

When a linear factor is repeated in the denominator, additional terms are required in its partial fractions decomposition. If a factor appears twice, two terms are required for the factor in the decomposition.

$$\frac{1}{x(x+2)^2} = \frac{A}{x} + \frac{B}{x+2} + \frac{C}{(x+2)^2}$$

If a factor appears three times, three terms are required for the factor in the decomposition.

$$\frac{1}{x(x+2)^3} = \frac{A}{x} + \frac{B}{x+2} + \frac{C}{(x+2)^2} + \frac{D}{(x+2)^3}$$

If a factor appears n times, n terms are required for the factor. The denominators of these factors are simply subsequent powers of the factor in question. The numerators of each of these terms are still constants.

example 120.1   Integrate: $\displaystyle\int \frac{4}{x(x+1)^2}\, dx$

solution   First we find a partial fraction decomposition of the integrand.

$$\frac{4}{x(x+1)^2} = \frac{A}{x} + \frac{B}{x+1} + \frac{C}{(x+1)^2}$$

We simply need to find A, B, and C and then integrate. Multiplication by $x(x+1)^2$ on both sides of the equation yields

$$4 = A(x+1)^2 + Bx(x+1) + Cx$$

Setting $x = -1$ in this equation gives us

$$4 = C(-1)$$
$$C = -4$$

Next we let x equal 0.

$$4 = A(0 + 1)^2$$
$$A = 4$$

With these values for A and C, we update the equation.

$$4 = 4(x + 1)^2 + Bx(x + 1) - 4x$$

We simply let x be some other value and solve for B. If $x = 1$, then

$$4 = 4(2)^2 + B(1)(2) - 4(1)$$
$$B = -4$$

Then we rewrite the integral using the partial fractions decomposition.

$$\int \frac{4}{x(x + 1)^2}\, dx = \int \left(\frac{A}{x} + \frac{B}{x + 1} + \frac{C}{(x + 1)^2} \right) dx$$

$$= \int \left(\frac{4}{x} + \frac{-4}{x + 1} + \frac{-4}{(x + 1)^2} \right) dx$$

$$= 4 \int \frac{dx}{x} - 4 \int \frac{dx}{x + 1} - 4 \int \frac{dx}{(x + 1)^2}$$

The first two integrals have the form du over u, but the third has the form $u^{-2}\, du$. Therefore

$$\int \frac{4}{x(x + 1)^2}\, dx = 4 \ln |x| - 4 \ln |x + 1| - \frac{4(x + 1)^{-1}}{-1} + C$$

$$= \mathbf{4\ \ln\ |x| - 4\ \ln\ |x + 1| + \frac{4}{x + 1} + C}$$

example 120.2   Integrate: $\int \dfrac{x + 1}{x^2 (x + 2)}\, dx$

solution   We begin with the partial fractions decomposition.

$$\frac{x + 1}{x^2 (x + 2)} = \frac{A}{x} + \frac{B}{x^2} + \frac{C}{x + 2}$$

We then multiply by $x^2(x + 2)$ to remove the denominators.

$$x + 1 = Ax(x + 2) + B(x + 2) + Cx^2$$

Next we replace x with strategic values to solve for the constants A, B, and C.

$$x = 0: \qquad 0 + 1 = B(0 + 2)$$
$$\frac{1}{2} = B$$

$$x = -2: \qquad -2 + 1 = C(-2)^2$$
$$-\frac{1}{4} = C$$

$$x = 1: \qquad 1 + 1 = A(1)(1 + 2) + B(1 + 2) + C(1)^2$$
$$2 = 3A + 3B + C$$

Substituting $B = \dfrac{1}{2}$ and $C = -\dfrac{1}{4}$ gives us

$$2 = 3A + 3\left(\frac{1}{2} \right) + \left(-\frac{1}{4} \right)$$

$$A = \frac{1}{4}$$

Therefore

$$\int \frac{x + 1}{x^2(x + 2)}\, dx = \int \left(\frac{A}{x} + \frac{B}{x^2} + \frac{C}{x + 2} \right) dx$$

$$= \int \left(\frac{\frac{1}{4}}{x} + \frac{\frac{1}{2}}{x^2} + \frac{-\frac{1}{4}}{x + 2} \right) dx$$

$$= \frac{1}{4} \int \frac{1}{x}\, dx + \frac{1}{2} \int \frac{1}{x^2}\, dx - \frac{1}{4} \int \frac{1}{x + 2}\, dx$$

The second integral is of the form $u^{-2}\, du$, so the result is

$$\frac{1}{4} \ln |x| - \left(\frac{1}{2} \right)\left(\frac{1}{x} \right) - \frac{1}{4} \ln |x + 2| + C$$

problem set 120

1. *(26)* The rate at which a rabbit colony grows at a particular time t is proportional to the number of rabbits present at that time. Initially there were 2000 rabbits, and at $t = 1$ year, there were 3000 rabbits. Write an equation that expresses the number of rabbits present as a function of t.

2. *(77)* A cubical tank, each of whose sides has a length of 5 meters, is filled with a fluid having a weight density of 5000 newtons per cubic meter. Find the work done in pumping the fluid out of the tank.

3. *(99)* Use differentials to estimate the cube root of 28.

Integrate in problems 4–6.

4. *(120)* $\displaystyle\int \frac{5x - 9}{(x - 3)(x - 3)}\, dx$ **5.** *(120)* $\displaystyle\int \frac{8}{x(x + 2)^2}\, dx$ **6.** *(120)* $\displaystyle\int \frac{dx}{x^2(x - 1)}$

7. *(108)* Find a unit vector parallel to and a unit vector normal to the line tangent to the curve $y = 3x^2 - 4x + 1$ at the point $(1, 0)$.

Graph the equations in problems 8–10.

8. *(110)* $r = 2 \cos (2\theta)$ **9.** *(118)* $r = 3 + 3 \sin \theta$ **10.** *(118)* $r = 2 - 2 \cos \theta$

For problems 11–13, $x = 4t$ and $y = t^2 + t$.

11. *(119)* Find $\dfrac{dy}{dx}$ and $\dfrac{d^2y}{dx^2}$.

12. *(119)* Find the equation of the line tangent to the curve defined by the given equations at $t = 2$. Describe the concavity of the curve at the point of tangency.

13. *(114)* Write an integral that could be used to find the length of the curve from $t = 0$ to $t = 5$.

Determine whether each series in problems 14–16 converges or diverges. If a series converges, state its value.

14. *(116)* $\displaystyle\sum_{n=1}^{\infty} n$ **15.** *(117)* $\displaystyle\sum_{n=1}^{\infty} \frac{1}{(n + 3)(n + 4)}$ **16.** *(117)* $\displaystyle\sum_{n=1}^{\infty} \frac{2}{3^n}$

17. *(109)* Find the length of the graph of $y = \dfrac{1}{3}(x^2 + 2)^{3/2}$ from $x = 0$ to $x = 4$.

Integrate in problems 18–20.

18. *(113)* $\displaystyle\int \sqrt{25 - x^2}\, dx$ **19.** *(113)* $\displaystyle\int_{-4}^{4} \sqrt{25 - x^2}\, dx$ **20.** *(113)* $\displaystyle\int \frac{dx}{x^2 - 25}$

21. Simplify: $\dfrac{d}{dx}\displaystyle\int_1^x \sin\left(t^2\right)\,dt$
(98)

22. Suppose $y = f(x)$ is a continuous function. Which of the following statements must be true?
(96)
   A. The graph of $y = f(|x|)$ lies above the x-axis.
   B. $y = f(|x|)$ is an even function.
   C. $y = f(|x|)$ is an odd function.
   D. $\displaystyle\int_{-c}^c f(|x|)\,dx = 0$ for any real value of c.

23. Let $f(x) = x^3 + x - 1$. Find the value of $(f^{-1})'(1)$.
(92)

24. Find $\dfrac{dy}{dx}$ where $y = 3^{x^2} + \dfrac{2x-1}{\sqrt{x-2}} + \ln|1 + \sin x|$.
(50,72)

25. Let $a < d < b$. Suppose f is differentiable on (a, b) and continuous on $I = [a, b]$. Which of
(89) the following statements is not necessarily true?

   A. There exists a number c in I such that $f'(c) = \dfrac{f(b) - f(a)}{b - a}$.

   B. $\displaystyle\int_a^d f(x)\,dx + \int_d^b f(x)\,dx = \int_a^b f(x)\,dx$

   C. $\displaystyle\int_a^b f(x)\,dx \geq 0$

   D. There exists a number c in I such that $f(c) = \dfrac{1}{b-a}\displaystyle\int_a^b f(x)\,dx$.

LESSON 121   *Convergence and Divergence • Series Indexing • Arithmetic of Series*

121.A

convergence and divergence

Up to this point we have examined two types of series in depth, geometric and telescoping. These two types of series are unique in at least two ways. First it is relatively straightforward to determine whether such series converge. Secondly when they do converge, their exact sum can actually be determined. This is not the case with most other series. As we continue to investigate series, questions of convergence and divergence remain important. However, in most situations, it is quite difficult (if not impossible) to determine the actual sum of convergent series.

We now turn to a powerful theorem for checking whether a series diverges. Initially, we state the theorem as follows:

$$\text{If the series } \sum_{n=1}^{\infty} a_n \text{ converges, then } \lim_{n\to\infty} a_n = 0.$$

Though its meaning is clear, this fact is not useful as written. We need criteria that determine whether a series converges or diverges. This statement simply relates a necessary consequence of convergence. However, its contrapositive is more useful.

DIVERGENCE THEOREM

If $\lim_{n\to\infty} a_n \neq 0$, then the series $\displaystyle\sum_{n=1}^{\infty} a_n$ diverges.

The simplicity of this theorem cannot be overstated. The theorem states that if the **terms** of a series do not tend to 0 as n goes to $+\infty$, then the series must diverge.

Before going to examples, a word of caution is in order. This theorem does **not** imply the following:

$$\text{If } \lim_{n \to \infty} a_n = 0, \text{ then } \sum_{n=1}^{\infty} a_n \text{ converges.} \qquad \text{NO! NO! NO!}$$

This is the converse of the first conditional stated above. Since the converse of a conditional statement is not equivalent to the conditional itself, the converse is not necessarily true. That is exactly the case here.

example 121.1   Determine whether each of the following series converges or diverges.

(a) $\displaystyle\sum_{n=1}^{\infty} n$
(b) $\displaystyle\sum_{n=1}^{\infty} \frac{1}{n}$
(c) $\displaystyle\sum_{n=1}^{\infty} \frac{2n-3}{3n}$

solution   (a) We note that $a_n = n$ here and that $\lim_{n \to \infty} a_n = \lim_{n \to \infty} n = +\infty$. So we see that $\lim_{n \to \infty} a_n \neq 0$. Therefore, by the divergence theorem, $\sum_{n=1}^{\infty} n$ **diverges.**

(b) Here $a_n = \frac{1}{n}$ and $\lim_{n \to \infty} a_n = \lim_{n \to \infty} \frac{1}{n} = 0$. While it would be tempting to conclude that $\sum_{n=1}^{\infty} \frac{1}{n}$ converges, this would be an incorrect conclusion. **No conclusion can be made regarding the convergence or divergence of $\sum_{n=1}^{\infty} a_n$ based on the fact that** $\lim_{n \to \infty} a_n = 0$. In a future lesson we will show that $\sum_{n=1}^{\infty} \frac{1}{n}$ actually diverges.

(c) Note that $\lim_{n \to \infty} a_n = \lim_{n \to \infty} \frac{2n-3}{3n} = \frac{2}{3}$. Since this limit is not 0, we conclude that the series $\sum_{n=1}^{\infty} \frac{2n-3}{3n}$ **diverges.**

Another tool for determining convergence or divergence is the following:

> A finite number of terms can be added to (or subtracted from) a series without affecting whether it is convergent or divergent.

An additional note is appropriate at this point. Even though adding a few terms to (or subtracting a few terms from) a series does not affect its basic nature, it does affect the value of a convergent series.

example 121.2   Determine whether each of the following series converges or diverges. If a series converges, determine its value.

(a) $300 + 25 + 1000 + \displaystyle\sum_{n=1}^{\infty} \frac{1}{2^n}$
(b) $\left(\displaystyle\sum_{n=1}^{\infty} 3^n \right) - 1{,}000 - 1{,}000{,}000$

solution   (a) Since $\sum_{n=1}^{\infty} \frac{1}{2^n}$ is a geometric series with a common ratio of $r = \frac{1}{2}$, it converges. Therefore, $300 + 25 + 1000 + \sum_{n=1}^{\infty} \frac{1}{2^n}$ also **converges,** but to **1326**, not 1.

(b) $\sum_{n=1}^{\infty} 3^n$ is a geometric series with $r = 3$. Since this value is larger than 1, $\sum_{n=1}^{\infty} 3^n$ diverges. Subtracting 1,001,000 cannot reduce $\sum_{n=1}^{\infty} 3^n$ to a finite number, so the series $\left(\sum_{n=1}^{\infty} 3^n \right) - 1{,}000 - 1{,}000{,}000$ also **diverges.**

121.B

series indexing

The **index** of a series is the set of values in the domain of the sequence of terms. For example, the index of the series $\sum_{n=1}^{\infty} \frac{2}{3^n}$ is $n = 1, 2, 3, 4, \ldots$. The index of the series $\sum_{n=-2}^{\infty} \frac{2}{3^{n+3}}$ is $n = -2, -1, 0, 1, \ldots$. A closer look at these two series reveals that they are the same.

$$\sum_{n=1}^{\infty} \frac{2}{3^n} = \frac{2}{3} + \frac{2}{9} + \frac{2}{27} + \frac{2}{81} + \cdots$$

$$\sum_{n=-2}^{\infty} \frac{2}{3^{n+3}} = \frac{2}{3} + \frac{2}{9} + \frac{2}{27} + \frac{2}{81} + \cdots$$

As with the series above, any series can be rendered differently by rewriting the form of the nth term and changing the index appropriately.

example 121.3

Rewrite the series $\sum_{n=1}^{\infty} \frac{n+2}{2^n}$ as a series beginning with $n = -4$.

solution

We want to write the series in the form $\sum_{n=-4}^{\infty} a_n$, but we cannot simply write the series as $\sum_{n=-4}^{\infty} \frac{n+2}{2^n}$, because this includes several extra terms. Since the starting value of the index has *decreased* by 5, we must *increase* every instance of n in the nth term by 5. Thus the series $\sum_{n=-4}^{\infty} \frac{(n+5)+2}{2^{n+5}} = \sum_{n=-4}^{\infty} \frac{n+7}{2^{n+5}}$ is the same series as $\sum_{n=1}^{\infty} \frac{n+2}{2^n}$.

121.C

arithmetic of series

This lesson closes with facts about the arithmetic of series. Most of the facts are intuitive and can be stated without proof. The statements in the following box relate to sums and differences of convergent series:

If $\sum a_n$ and $\sum b_n$ **both converge** and if

$$\sum_{n=1}^{\infty} a_n = A \quad \text{and} \quad \sum_{n=1}^{\infty} b_n = B, \text{ then}$$

1. $\displaystyle\sum_{n=1}^{\infty} (a_n + b_n) = A + B$ 2. $\displaystyle\sum_{n=1}^{\infty} (a_n - b_n) = A - B$

When exactly one of the series diverges, the results differ.

If $\sum a_n$ **converges** and $\sum b_n$ **diverges,** then

1. $\displaystyle\sum_{n=1}^{\infty} (a_n + b_n)$ diverges   2. $\displaystyle\sum_{n=1}^{\infty} (a_n - b_n)$ diverges

---

When both series diverge, it is possible for the sum of the series to converge. For example, if $\sum a_n$ diverges and $b_n = -a_n$ for all n, then

$$\sum_{n=1}^{\infty} (a_n + b_n) = \sum_{n=1}^{\infty} (a_n - a_n) = 0$$

Of course, the sum of two divergent series can easily diverge as well. **When both series diverge, other tests are necessary to determine whether the sum or the difference of the series converges or diverges.**

The rules for multiples of series can be stated more quickly.

---

1. If $\displaystyle\sum a_n$ converges to A and c is a constant, then

$$\sum_{n=1}^{\infty} ca_n = c\sum_{n=1}^{\infty} a_n = cA$$

2. If $\displaystyle\sum a_n$ diverges and c is a nonzero constant, then

$$\sum_{n=1}^{\infty} ca_n \text{ diverges}$$

3. If $\displaystyle\sum a_n$ diverges and c is zero, then

$$\sum_{n=1}^{\infty} ca_n = \sum_{n=1}^{\infty} 0 = 0$$

---

example 121.4   Find the sum of the series $\displaystyle S = \sum_{n=1}^{\infty} \frac{4 - 2^n}{4^n}$.

solution   Note that $\sum_{n=1}^{\infty} \frac{4}{4^n}$ and $\sum_{n=1}^{\infty} \frac{2^n}{4^n}$ are both geometric series with ratios less than 1, so both converge, which means $\sum_{n=1}^{\infty} \frac{4 - 2^n}{4^n}$ can be split into two convergent series.

$$\sum_{n=1}^{\infty} \frac{4 - 2^n}{4^n} = \sum_{n=1}^{\infty} \frac{4}{4^n} - \sum_{n=1}^{\infty} \frac{2^n}{4^n}$$

Now we compute the sums of these two series.

$$\sum_{n=1}^{\infty} \frac{4}{4^n} = 4\sum_{n=1}^{\infty} \frac{1}{4^n} \qquad\qquad \sum_{n=1}^{\infty} \frac{2^n}{4^n} = \sum_{n=1}^{\infty} \frac{1}{2^n}$$

$$= 4\left[\frac{\frac{1}{4}}{1 - \frac{1}{4}}\right] \qquad\qquad\qquad\qquad = 1$$

$$= 4\left(\frac{1}{4}\right) \cdot \frac{4}{3}$$

$$= \frac{4}{3}$$

Therefore

$$\sum_{n=1}^{\infty} \frac{4 - 2^n}{4^n} = \frac{4}{3} - 1 = \frac{1}{3}$$

problem set 121

1. Find the equation of the line tangent to the curve determined by $x = t^2 + 1$ and
(106) $y = t^3 + 1$ at the point corresponding to $t = 4$.

2. Describe the concavity of the curve in problem 1 at the point of tangency.
(119)

3. Find all the points at which the curve defined by the parametric equations $x = t + 3$ and
(106) $y = t^3 - 3t^2$ has a horizontal or vertical tangent.

4. Write the polar equation $r = \sin\theta + \cos\theta$ in rectangular form.
(107)

5. Graph $r = 1 + 2\cos\theta$ in the polar coordinate plane.
(118)

6. Find the area of the region between $y = \cos^2 x$ and the x-axis on the interval $\left[0, \dfrac{\pi}{4}\right]$.
(83)

Integrate in problems 7–16.

7. $\displaystyle\int \tan^3 x \, dx$
(100)

8. $\displaystyle\int \dfrac{-x + 26}{x^2 + 2x - 8} \, dx$
(115)

9. $\displaystyle\int \dfrac{x^2 - x - 1}{x^3 - x^2} \, dx$
(120)

10. $\displaystyle\int \dfrac{-x^3 + 2x^2 + 4x + 2}{x^2(x + 1)^2} \, dx$
(120)

11. $\displaystyle\int \dfrac{dx}{\sqrt{4 + x^2}}$
(113)

12. $\displaystyle\int \dfrac{dx}{\sqrt{x^2 - 4}}$
(113)

13. $\displaystyle\int \dfrac{2 \, dx}{\sqrt{4 - x^2}}$
(64)

14. $\displaystyle\int \dfrac{3 \, dx}{9 + x^2}$
(64)

15. $\displaystyle\int \dfrac{\cos^3 x \sin x}{\cos^4 x + 1} \, dx$
(66)

16. $\displaystyle\int 2x \cos x \, dx$
(69)

Evaluate the limits in problems 17–19.

17. $\displaystyle\lim_{x \to 0} \dfrac{\cos x - 1}{3x}$
(101)

18. $\displaystyle\lim_{x \to \infty} \left(1 + \dfrac{3}{x}\right)^x$
(111)

19. $\displaystyle\lim_{x \to 0} \left(1 + \dfrac{x}{3}\right)^{3/x}$
(111)

Determine whether each series in problems 20–23 converges or diverges. If a series converges, state its value.

20. $\displaystyle\sum_{n=1}^{\infty} \dfrac{n}{n + 1}$
(121)

21. $\displaystyle\sum_{n=1}^{\infty} \dfrac{4}{(4n - 3)(4n + 1)}$
(117)

22. $\displaystyle\sum_{n=1}^{\infty} (-1)^n \dfrac{4}{2^n}$
(117)

23. $\displaystyle\sum_{n=1}^{\infty} \dfrac{5n}{4n + 7}$
(121)

24. If $a^3 + b^3 = 10$ and $a + b = 5$, what is the value of $a^2 - ab + b^2$?
(10)

25. The table below shows the relationships between specific values of the variables x and y.
(95) Assuming $y = f(x)$ is a continuous function, approximate $\int_4^7 f(x) \, dx$ using the trapezoidal rule.

x	4.0	4.3	4.6	4.9	5.2	5.5	5.8	6.1	6.4	6.7	7.0
y	3.5	3.8	4.5	5.5	6.8	6.7	5.6	5.1	4.8	4.5	4.3

LESSON 122 *Integration by Parts II*

We revisit the technique known as integration by parts.

$$\int u \, dv = uv - \int v \, du$$

Lesson 69 presented straightforward uses of this technique. Now we utilize the technique in more complicated situations, such as the integrals below.

$$\int x^2 e^x \, dx \qquad \int e^x \sin x \, dx$$

example 122.1   Integrate: $\int x^2 e^x \, dx$

solution   A wise substitution is $u = x^2$, $dv = e^x \, dx$. Differentiating u produces a polynomial term with a smaller power, and antidifferentiating dv introduces no complications.

$u = x^2$	
	$dv = e^x \, dx$

$u = x^2$	$v = e^x$
$du = 2x \, dx$	$dv = e^x \, dx$

So we have

$$\int x^2 e^x \, dx = \overbrace{x^2 e^x}^{uv} - \int \overbrace{e^x (2x) \, dx}^{v \, du}$$

$$= x^2 e^x - 2 \int x e^x \, dx$$

Now we must determine $\int x e^x \, dx$, which involves integrating by parts again.

$u = x$	
	$dv = e^x \, dx$

$u = x$	$v = e^x$
$du = dx$	$dv = e^x \, dx$

$$\int x e^x \, dx = x e^x - \int e^x \, dx = x e^x - e^x$$

Therefore

$$\int x^2 e^x \, dx = x^2 e^x - 2 \int x e^x \, dx$$

$$= x^2 e^x - 2[x e^x - e^x] + C$$

$$= x^2 e^x - 2x e^x + 2e^x + C$$

Often integrals involving the product of x^n and another function, for example, $\int x^n e^x \, dx$, $\int x^n \sin x \, dx$, or $\int x^n \cos x \, dx$, can be determined by applying integration by parts n times and letting u equal the polynomial factor in each integrand.

example 122.2   Integrate: $\int e^x \sin x \, dx$

solution   The integrand is a product of the form $e^{ax} \sin bx$. We integrate by parts twice and then use algebra to find the answer. Either e^x or $\sin x$ can be chosen for u, but we select $u = e^x$.

$u = e^x$	
	$dv = \sin x \, dx$

$u = e^x$	$v = -\cos x$
$du = e^x \, dx$	$dv = \sin x \, dx$

$$\int e^x \sin x \, dx = -e^x \cos x - \int -e^x \cos x \, dx$$

$$= -e^x \cos x + \int e^x \cos x \, dx$$

Now we must integrate by parts again to find $\int e^x \cos x \, dx$. Since we let $u = e^x$ in the first step, we do so again here. If we had let u be the trigonometric function in the first step, we would do so here as well.

$u = e^x$	
	$dv = \cos x \, dx$

$u = e^x$	$v = \sin x$
$du = e^x \, dx$	$dv = \cos x \, dx$

$$\int e^x \cos x \, dx = e^x \sin x - \int e^x \sin x \, dx$$

Now we combine the results of the first integration by parts and the second integration by parts to get

$$\int e^x \sin x \, dx = -e^x \cos x + e^x \sin x - \int e^x \sin x \, dx$$

It is important to notice that $\int e^x \sin x \, dx$ appears on both sides of the equation. We need to isolate this term, so we add it to both sides of the equation.

$$2 \int e^x \sin x \, dx = -e^x \cos x + e^x \sin x + C$$

$$\longrightarrow \quad \int e^x \sin x \, dx = -\frac{1}{2}e^x \cos x + \frac{1}{2}e^x \sin x + C$$

example 122.3 Integrate: $\int e^x \cos x \, dx$

solution A good choice for u in example 122.2 was e^x. In this example we show that this choice for u is not necessary by letting $u = \cos x$ in the first step and letting $u = \sin x$ in the second step. The important thing is that u must be chosen similarly in both steps, either as the trigonometric function or as the exponential function.

$u = \cos x$	
	$dv = e^x \, dx$

$u = \cos x$	$v = e^x$
$du = -\sin x \, dx$	$dv = e^x \, dx$

$$\int e^x \cos x \, dx = e^x \cos x - \int e^x (-\sin x) \, dx$$

$$= e^x \cos x + \int e^x \sin x \, dx$$

It seems we are going in circles; however, if we choose u and dv correctly in the second integration by parts, we can find the desired integral.

$u = \sin x$	
	$dv = e^x \, dx$

$u = \sin x$	$v = e^x$
$du = \cos x \, dx$	$dv = e^x \, dx$

Now we have

$$\int e^x \cos x \, dx = e^x \cos x + e^x \sin x - \int e^x \cos x \, dx$$

Adding $\int e^x \cos x \, dx$ to both sides and then dividing by 2 gives the answer.

$$2 \int e^x \cos x \, dx = e^x \cos x + e^x \sin x + C$$

$$\longrightarrow \quad \int e^x \cos x \, dx = \frac{1}{2}e^x \cos x + \frac{1}{2}e^x \sin x + C$$

problem set 122

1. A particle moves along the hyperbola $\frac{x^2}{4} - \frac{y^2}{9} = 1$ so that its x-coordinate is always
(46)   increasing at a rate of 2 units per second. How fast is the y-coordinate of the particle changing the instant it passes through the point $\left(\frac{2\sqrt{10}}{3}, 1\right)$?

2. When t is greater than zero, the acceleration function for a particle moving along the x-axis
(54)   is $a(t) = \frac{1}{t}$. Suppose $v(1) = 4$ and $x(1) = 5$.

(a) Find the velocity and position functions of the particle.

(b) Find $x(3)$ and $v(3)$.

3. Find a vector of length 5 normal to $y = 3x^3 - 6x + 2$ at the point $(2, 14)$.
(108)

4. A ball is dropped from a height of 8 meters. Each time the ball hits the pavement it rebounds to
(117) a height of three-fifths its previous fall. What is the total distance the ball travels?

Integrate in problems 5–10.

5. $\displaystyle\int x^2 \cos (2x)\, dx$
(122)

6. $\displaystyle\int e^x \sin x\, dx$
(122)

7. $\displaystyle\int \frac{2x}{(x-1)(x+1)^2}\, dx$
(120)

8. $\displaystyle\int \frac{4+2x}{x^3(x-1)}\, dx$
(120)

9. $\displaystyle\int \frac{dx}{\sqrt{9-x^2}}$
(64)

10. $\displaystyle\int \frac{dx}{\sqrt{x^2-9}}$
(113)

Determine whether each series in problems 11 and 12 converges or diverges. If a series converges, state its value.

11. $\displaystyle\sum_{n=3}^{\infty} \frac{2^n}{n^3}$
(121)

12. $\displaystyle\sum_{n=3}^{\infty} \frac{6-2^n}{3^n}$
(117)

13. Graph the equation $r = 3 + 2\sin\theta$ on a polar coordinate plane.
(118)

14. Convert the rectangular equation $(x-3)^2 + y^2 = 9$ to polar form.
(107)

15. Graph the curve defined by the parametric equations $x = 4\sin^2\theta$ and $y = 5\cos^2\theta$ on the
(106) xy-plane.

16. Find the length of the curve defined by the parametric equations $x = \sin^2 t$ and $y = \cos^2 t$
(114) from $t = 0$ to $t = \frac{\pi}{2}$.

17. Which of the following integrals is equivalent to $\displaystyle\int_{\pi}^{2\pi} (\sin x)(e^{2\cos x})\, dx?$
(66)

    A. $-\displaystyle\int_{-1}^{1} e^u\, du$ B. $-\displaystyle\int_{-1}^{1} e^{2u}\, du$ C. $-\displaystyle\int_{-1}^{1} \frac{1}{2}e^u\, du$ D. $\displaystyle\int_{\pi}^{2\pi} e^{2u}\, du$

18. Describe the concavity of the parametric curve defined by $x = te^t$ and $y = t\sin t$ at $t = 2$.
(119)

19. Suppose k is a positive real number such that $\displaystyle\int_{1}^{k} \frac{\sin x}{x}\, dx = 1$. Evaluate $\displaystyle\int_{-k}^{-1} \frac{\sin x}{x}\, dx$.
(86)

20. Suppose $h(x) = f(x)g(x)$, $\displaystyle\lim_{x\to\pi} h(x) = \frac{1}{\pi}$, and $\displaystyle\lim_{x\to\pi} f(x) = 3$. Evaluate $\displaystyle\lim_{x\to\pi} g(x)$.
(70)

21. Write the equation of the tangent line to the graph of $f(x) = \dfrac{x-1}{x+1}$ at $x = 1$.
(27,42)

22. Find the exact length of the curve $y = x^2$ from $x = -3$ to $x = 3$.
(109)

23. Use the equation of the line tangent to $xy^3 - x^2y + 3x = 4$ at the point $(2, 1)$ to approximate
(99) the value of y in $xy^3 - x^2y + 3x = 4$ when $x = 1.95$.

24. Find y' where $y = (e^x)^{\sin x}$.
(84)

25. Which of the following definite integrals has a value of zero?
(86)

    A. $\displaystyle\int_{0}^{\pi} \sin^2 x\, dx$ B. $\displaystyle\int_{0}^{\pi} \cos^2 x\, dx$

    C. $\displaystyle\int_{-\pi}^{\pi} \sin^3 x\, dx$ D. $\displaystyle\int_{-\pi}^{\pi} x^2 \sin^2 x\, dx$

LESSON *123*   *Vector Functions*

We now introduce a new kind of function known as a **vector function** or a **vector-valued function.**

If $x(t)$ and $y(t)$ are both real-valued functions of the real variable t and $\hat{i}$ and $\hat{j}$ are the unit vectors in the positive x- and y-directions, then

$$\vec{f}(t) = x(t)\hat{i} + y(t)\hat{j}$$

is called a **vector function.**

Vector functions can be used to describe the position of a moving particle. As with parametric equations, one advantage of vector functions is that the x- and y-coordinates and the time parameter are evident.

There is a strong similarity between the abilities of parametric functions and vector functions to describe the path of a moving particle. One significant difference between the two is that parametric equations describe the location of the particle in the plane using its xy-coordinates, while vector functions describe the particle's location as a vector drawn from the origin.

example 123.1   Sketch the curve defined by the vector function $\vec{f}(t) = (t - 3)\hat{i} + (2t + 1)\hat{j}$.

solution   We can choose individual values of t and plot the curve point by point, or we can eliminate the variable t and graph the resulting nonvector function. In this example we apply both techniques. To eliminate the variable t, we treat the components of the vector function as if they were a set of parametric equations.

$$x = t - 3 \qquad y = 2t + 1$$

The equation $x = t - 3$ can be rearranged as $t = x + 3$, so we substitute $x + 3$ for t in the second equation.

$$y = 2(x + 3) + 1 \quad \longrightarrow \quad y = 2x + 7$$

We can now graph the resulting linear equation.

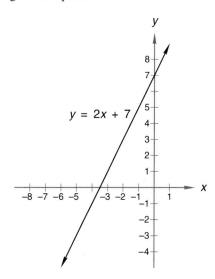

The weakness of this graph is that we only see the path traced by the particle; we know little about the motion of the particle.

In the figure below we see the same graph again, but this time we graph it based on the parametric equations and show where the particle is at particular values of *t*.

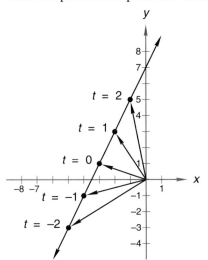

One of the most important concepts in calculus is continuity of functions. Because a vector function is made up of two functions, the continuity of both of these component functions must be taken into consideration in order to discuss the continuity of the vector function. A vector function $\vec{f}(t) = x(t)\hat{i} + y(t)\hat{j}$ is **continuous** at a value of *t* when both $x(t)$ and $y(t)$ are continuous at *t*.

example 123.2   Find the values of *t* at which $\vec{f}(t) = (t + 3)\hat{i} + \left(\dfrac{2t^2 - 4t + 3}{t}\right)\hat{j}$ is continuous.

solution   To determine these values, we simply consider the continuity of the component functions $x(t) = t + 3$ and $y(t) = \frac{2t^2 - 4t + 3}{t}$. Since $x(t)$ is a polynomial in the variable *t*, it is continuous for all real values of *t*. The function $y(t) = \frac{2t^2 - 4t + 3}{t}$ is continuous for all real values of *t* except $t = 0$, since $y(0)$ is undefined. Therefore, the set of values of *t* at which $\vec{f}(t)$ is continuous is the set of all real numbers except $t = 0$.

$$\{t \in \mathbb{R} \mid t \neq 0\}$$

Another issue to consider is differentiability of vector functions. A vector function $\vec{f}(t) = x(t)\hat{i} + y(t)\hat{j}$ is **differentiable** at some value of *t* when both $x(t)$ and $y(t)$ are differentiable at *t*. In this case the derivative of $\vec{f}(t)$ is defined as

$$\vec{f}\,'(t) = x'(t)\hat{i} + y'(t)\hat{j}$$

example 123.3   Let $\vec{f}(t) = (t + 3)\hat{i} + (2t^2 - 4t + 3)\hat{j}$. Find the derivative of this vector function.

solution   We first need to find $\dfrac{d}{dt}(t + 3)$ and $\dfrac{d}{dt}(2t^2 - 4t + 3)$.

$$\frac{d}{dt}(t + 3) = 1 \qquad \frac{d}{dt}(2t^2 - 4t + 3) = 4t - 4$$

Therefore, $\vec{f}\,'(t) = \hat{i} + (4t - 4)\hat{j}.$

example 123.4   Find $\vec{f}\,'(t)$ where $\vec{f}(t) = \ln(2t)\,\hat{i} + 3\cos(2t)\,\hat{j}.$

solution   We see that

$$\frac{d}{dt}(\ln(2t)) = \frac{1}{2t} \cdot 2 = \frac{1}{t}$$

$$\frac{d}{dt}(3\cos(2t)) = 3(-\sin(2t))(2) = -6\sin(2t)$$

Hence, $\vec{f}\,'(t) = \dfrac{1}{t}\hat{i} - 6\sin(2t)\,\hat{j}.$

problem set 123

1. A particle moves along the path defined by the equation $y = x^2$. Find the distance the particle travels from $x = 0$ to $x = 6$.
(109)

2. Describe the concavity of the curve whose parametric equations are $x(t) = 2e^{3t}$ and $y(t) = 2 \ln (3t)$ at the point corresponding to $t = 4$.
(119)

3. A cubical tank, each of whose sides has a length of 5 meters, is filled with a fluid whose weight density is 5000 newtons per cubic meter. Find the total force against one of the vertical sides of the tank.
(74)

4. The acceleration due to gravity on planet X is $15 \frac{m}{s^2}$ toward the center of the planet. A ball is thrown upward from the surface of the planet with an initial velocity of $40 \frac{m}{s}$.
(65)

    (a) Develop the velocity and position functions that apply to this ball from the moment it is released to the moment just before it hits the ground.

    (b) How long after the ball is thrown does it hit the surface of the planet?

Integrate in problems 5–8.

5. $\displaystyle \int \frac{2x + 5}{x^2 + 2x + 1} \, dx$
(120)

6. $\displaystyle \int e^x \sin (2x) \, dx$
(122)

7. $\displaystyle \int x^2 e^x \, dx$
(122)

8. $\displaystyle \int \frac{2x + 1}{(x - 3)(x + 2)} \, dx$
(115)

Find $\overrightarrow{f}'(t)$ for the vector functions in problems 9 and 10, and state the domain of each derived function.

9. $\overrightarrow{f}(t) = 2 \cos (t) \, \hat{i} + \ln (t) \, \hat{j}$
(123)

10. $\overrightarrow{f}(t) = 3^{2t^2} \hat{i} + \dfrac{2t - 3}{2t + 4} \hat{j}$
(123)

Graph the equations in problems 11 and 12.

11. $r = 3 \cos (3\theta)$
(110)

12. $r = 1 + 3 \cos \theta$
(118)

13. Determine the average value of the function $f(x) = (\sin x)(e^{2 \cos x})$ on the interval $[\pi, 2\pi]$.
(89)

14. Let R be the region between the graph of $y = \tan x$ and the x-axis on the interval $[0, 1]$. Find the volume of the solid formed when R is revolved about the x-axis.
(71)

15. Let R be as defined in problem 14. Use one variable to write a definite integral whose value equals the volume of the solid formed when R is rotated around the line $x = -1$.
(94)

Determine whether each series in problems 16–18 converges or diverges. If a series converges, state its value.

16. $\displaystyle \sum_{n=3}^{\infty} e^{-n}$
(117)

17. $\displaystyle \sum_{n=1}^{\infty} \frac{2^n - 5}{3^{n+1}}$
(117)

18. $\displaystyle \sum_{n=1}^{\infty} \frac{2^n + 4}{n^3}$
(121)

19. Find the area of the region between $y = \sqrt{x^2 - 1}$ and the x-axis on the interval $[1, 5]$.
(59)

20. Find $\dfrac{dy}{dx}$ where $y = \arcsin (\tan x) + \dfrac{3 - x}{\sin x + \cos x}$.
(50,64)

21. Find $\dfrac{dy}{dx}$ where $x^2 y^3 - 4y^2 + 3x = 6xy^4$.
(34)

22. Show that $\displaystyle \lim_{x \to \infty} \left(1 + \frac{c}{x} \right)^x$ equals e^c for any constant c.
(102)

Evaluate the limits in problems 23–25.

23. $\displaystyle\lim_{x\to\infty}\left(1+\frac{5}{x}\right)^x$
(102)

24. $\displaystyle\lim_{x\to\infty}\left(1+\frac{1}{x}\right)^{5x}$
(102)

25. $\displaystyle\lim_{x\to0}\left(1+\frac{x}{5}\right)^{5/x}$
(102)

LESSON 124 *Implicit Differentiation II*

We have used differentials to find the derivatives of implicit equations. To find $\frac{dy}{dx}$ for the equation on the left-hand side below, we find the differential of each term as the first step.

$$2x^3 - y^2 = 7 \quad\longrightarrow\quad 6x^2\,dx - 2y\,dy = 0$$

Then we divide every term by dx and algebraically solve for $\frac{dy}{dx}$.

$$6x^2 - 2y\frac{dy}{dx} = 0 \qquad\text{divided by } dx$$

$$\frac{dy}{dx} = \frac{3x^2}{y} \qquad\text{solved for } \frac{dy}{dx}$$

We now consider an alternative approach to implicit differentiation. We do not have to use differentials to differentiate implicit functions if we remember that y represents some function of x and that the derivative of a function of y, say $g(y)$, with respect to x is $g'(y)\frac{dy}{dx}$. To review, let $g(y) = y^2$. Using the chain rule to find the derivative of g with respect to x, we get

$$g'(y) = \frac{d}{dx}(g(y)) = \frac{d}{dx}y^2 = 2y\frac{dy}{dx}$$

Differentiating each term in the equation $2x^3 - y^2 = 7$ with respect to x, we get

$$\frac{d}{dx}(2x^3) - \frac{d}{dx}(y^2) = \frac{d}{dx}(7) \qquad\text{or}\qquad 6x^2 - 2y\frac{dy}{dx} = 0$$

Solving this equation for $\frac{dy}{dx}$, we obtain the same result as above by using differentials.

$$\frac{dy}{dx} = \frac{3x^2}{y}$$

example 124.1   Find $\frac{dy}{dx}$ where $x^5 + 4xy^3 - 3y^5 = 2$.

solution   We differentiate each term with respect to x and solve for $\frac{dy}{dx}$.

$$\frac{d}{dx}x^5 + \frac{d}{dx}4xy^3 - \frac{d}{dx}3y^5 = \frac{d}{dx}2$$

$$5x^4 + 4\left[x(3y^2)\frac{dy}{dx} + y^3\right] - 15y^4\frac{dy}{dx} = 0$$

$$5x^4 + 12xy^2\frac{dy}{dx} + 4y^3 - 15y^4\frac{dy}{dx} = 0$$

$$\frac{dy}{dx}(12xy^2 - 15y^4) = -5x^4 - 4y^3$$

$$\frac{dy}{dx} = \frac{-5x^4 - 4y^3}{12xy^2 - 15y^4}$$

example 124.2 Find $\dfrac{d^2y}{dx^2}$ where $x^2 + y^2 = 100$.

solution We begin by finding the first derivative, which we put in a box for later use.

$$2x + 2y\frac{dy}{dx} = 0 \qquad \text{differentiated}$$

$$\boxed{\frac{dy}{dx} = \frac{-x}{y}} \qquad \text{solved for } \frac{dy}{dx}$$

Now we use the quotient rule and differentiate again.

$$\frac{d^2y}{dx^2} = \frac{y(-1) - (-x)\dfrac{dy}{dx}}{y^2} \qquad \text{quotient rule}$$

$$\frac{d^2y}{dx^2} = \frac{-y + x\dfrac{dy}{dx}}{y^2} \qquad \text{simplified}$$

The box above contains an expression for $\dfrac{dy}{dx}$. We make this substitution and then simplify.

$$\frac{d^2y}{dx^2} = \frac{-y + x\left(\dfrac{-x}{y}\right)}{y^2} \qquad \text{substituted}$$

$$\frac{d^2y}{dx^2} = \frac{-1}{y} - \frac{x^2}{y^3} \qquad \text{simplified}$$

This answer is correct, but it is a good idea to write the answer as a single fraction and to look at the original equation to see if it can be used for additional simplification. After finding a common denominator, we combine the terms in the numerator to get

$$\frac{d^2y}{dx^2} = \frac{-y^2 - x^2}{y^3} = \frac{-(y^2 + x^2)}{y^3}$$

The original equation tells us that $x^2 + y^2 = 100$, so

$$\frac{d^2y}{dx^2} = \frac{-100}{y^3}$$

example 124.3 Use implicit differentiation to find $\dfrac{d^2y}{dx^2}$ given $4y^2 = x^3$.

solution We begin by finding the first derivative and putting it in a box for later use.

$$8y\frac{dy}{dx} = 3x^2 \qquad \text{differentiated}$$

$$\boxed{\frac{dy}{dx} = \frac{3x^2}{8y}} \qquad \text{solved for } \frac{dy}{dx}$$

Now we use the quotient rule to find the second derivative.

$$\frac{d^2y}{dx^2} = \frac{(8y)(6x) - (3x^2)\left(8\dfrac{dy}{dx}\right)}{64y^2}$$

Next we substitute for $\dfrac{dy}{dx}$ and simplify.

$$\frac{d^2y}{dx^2} = \frac{48xy - (24x^2)\left(\dfrac{3x^2}{8y}\right)}{64y^2} \qquad \text{substituted}$$

$$= \frac{48xy - \dfrac{9x^4}{y}}{64y^2} \qquad \text{simplified}$$

$$= \frac{48xy^2 - 9x^4}{64y^3} \qquad \text{simplified}$$

This answer is correct, but the original equation $4y^2 = x^3$ can be used to further simplify the answer. By rearranging the answer, we can write it with factors of $4y^2$ and x^3.

$$\frac{d^2y}{dx^2} = \frac{(4y^2)(12x) - 9x(x^3)}{(4y^2)(16y)}$$

We simplify by replacing $4y^2$ with x^3.

$$\frac{d^2y}{dx^2} = \frac{(4y^2)(12x) - 9x(x^3)}{(4y^2)(16y)} \qquad \text{equation}$$

$$= \frac{(x^3)(12x) - 9x(x^3)}{(x^3)(16y)} \qquad \text{substituted}$$

$$= \frac{12x - 9x}{16y} \qquad \text{canceled}$$

$$= \frac{3x}{16y} \qquad \text{subtracted}$$

Simplification of the answer is not always easy, and it can be time-consuming. In some cases significant algebraic simplification is not even possible.

problem set 124

1. *(71)* The region R is bounded by the x-axis and the graph of $y = \dfrac{1}{\sqrt{x^2 + 10}}$ on the interval $[2, 5]$. Find the volume of the solid formed when R is revolved around the x-axis.

For problems 2 and 3, let f be the function defined on the closed interval $I = [-8, 8]$ by $f(x) = \frac{3}{4}x^{4/3} + 3x^{1/3}$.

2. *(36,45)* (a) Find f' and write the equation of f' as an expression with a single denominator.

   (b) Determine the critical numbers of f on I.

   (c) Find the critical numbers at which the tangent(s) to the graph of f are horizontal or vertical.

3. *(49)* (a) Find the x- and y-coordinates of all the relative maximum and minimum points of the graph of f.

   (b) Determine the intervals on which f is concave upward and the intervals on which f is concave downward.

   (c) Indicate the x-coordinates of all inflection points.

   (d) Sketch the graph of f.

In problems 4 and 5 find $\dfrac{dy}{dx}$ and $\dfrac{d^2y}{dx^2}$.

4. *(124)* $x^3 + y^3 = 100$

5. *(124)* $y^3 + y = x^2$

6. *(116)* Approximate the fourth partial sum of the series $\displaystyle\sum_{n=1}^{\infty} \frac{\sin n}{n}$.

Integrate in problems 7–10.

7.
(122) $\displaystyle\int x^2 \sin x \; dx$

8.
(122) $\displaystyle\int e^{2x} \sin x \; dx$

9.
(120) $\displaystyle\int \frac{8x - 4}{(x - 1)^2 x} \; dx$

10.
(113) $\displaystyle\int \frac{1}{(1 + x^2)^2} \; dx$

11. Find the length of the parametric curve determined by $x = e^t \sin t$ and $y = e^t \cos t$ from
(114) $t = 0$ to $t = \pi$.

12. Write the equation of the hyperbola $x^2 - y^2 = 1$ in polar form.
(107)

13. Graph the equation $r = 2 + 2 \sin \theta$ on a polar coordinate plane.
(118)

Determine whether each series in problems 14 and 15 converges or diverges. If a series converges, state its value.

14.
(121) $\displaystyle\sum_{n=1}^{\infty} \left(1 + \frac{1}{n}\right)^n$

15.
(117) $\displaystyle\sum_{n=4}^{\infty} \frac{3 - \pi^n}{5^n}$

Find the derivative of the vector functions in problems 16 and 17, and state the domain of the derived function.

16.
(123) $\vec{f}(t) = (\ln t)\hat{i} - 2e^{-t}\hat{j}$

17.
(123) $\vec{f}(t) = 3 \tan (2t) \, \hat{i} + \sqrt{t^2 - 4}\, \hat{j}$

18. Find $\frac{dy}{dx}$ and $\frac{d^2 y}{dx^2}$ at $t = -3$ given the parametric equations $x = t^3$ and $y = t^2$. Find the
(119)   equation of the line tangent to the given curve when $t = -3$.

19. Find the Maclaurin series for $\ln (1 - x)$.
(55)

20. Find the area of the region bounded by the graph of $y = x\sqrt{1 - x^2}$ and the x-axis.
(66)

Evaluate the limits in problems 21–23.

21.
(111) $\displaystyle\lim_{x \to \infty} \left(1 + \frac{4}{x}\right)^x$

22.
(111) $\displaystyle\lim_{x \to \infty} \left(1 + \frac{1}{x}\right)^{4x}$

23.
(111) $\displaystyle\lim_{x \to 0} \left(1 + \frac{x}{4}\right)^{4/x}$

24. Let f be the function defined below. Find the values of a and b that make f differentiable
(82)   everywhere.

$$f(x) = \begin{cases} ae^x + b & \text{when } x \geq 0 \\ \pi x & \text{when } x < 0 \end{cases}$$

25. Suppose f is differentiable for all real values of x and $f(x + h) - f(x) = x^2 h + xh^2 + \frac{h^3}{3}$
(19)   for all real values of x and h. Evaluate $f'(3)$. (*Hint:* Review the definition of the derivative.)

LESSON 125 *Infinite Limits of Integration*

This lesson begins the study of **improper integrals.** Consider the integral $\int_2^c f(x)\,dx$ where $f(x) = \frac{1}{(x-1)^2}$ and c is some real number greater than 2. The graph of f is shown at the right.

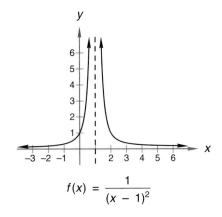

$$f(x) = \frac{1}{(x-1)^2}$$

The value of the integral in question represents the area under the curve between the vertical lines $x = 2$ and $x = c$. The integral is evaluated as follows:

$$\int_2^c \frac{1}{(x-1)^2}\,dx = \left.\frac{-1}{x-1}\right|_2^c = \frac{-1}{c-1} - \frac{-1}{2-1} = 1 - \frac{1}{c-1}$$

The table below shows increasing values of c and the corresponding values of the area under the curve (obtained by evaluating the above expression at each value of c).

c	3	10	100	1000	10,000
area	$\dfrac{1}{2}$	$\dfrac{8}{9}$	$\dfrac{98}{99}$	$\dfrac{998}{999}$	$\dfrac{9998}{9999}$

From these values it should be obvious that, as c becomes larger and larger, the area under the curve gets closer and closer to 1.

$$\lim_{c\to\infty} \int_2^c \frac{1}{(x-1)^2}\,dx = \lim_{c\to\infty}\left(1 - \frac{1}{c-1}\right) = 1$$

This may be a rather startling phenomenon—the area of the **unbounded** region under the graph of f is the **finite** number 1. In other words, **the *infinite* region has a *finite* area!**

This demonstration suggests the need for some definitions. Let f be a continuous function on the interval $[a, \infty)$. Provided the following limit exists,

$$\int_a^\infty f(x)\,dx = \lim_{b\to\infty} \int_a^b f(x)\,dx$$

Similarly, suppose f is a continuous function on the interval $(-\infty, b]$. Provided the following limit exists,

$$\int_{-\infty}^b f(x)\,dx = \lim_{a\to-\infty} \int_a^b f(x)\,dx$$

An integral of either of these forms is called an **improper integral** because one of the limits of integration is not a real number. In either case, if the limit exists, the improper integral **converges.** If the limit is not a finite value, then the improper integral **diverges.**

If an integral has two infinite limits of integration, it is also called an improper integral. In this situation, if f is continuous for all values of x and a is any real number,

$$\int_{-\infty}^{\infty} f(x)\,dx = \int_{-\infty}^{a} f(x)\,dx + \int_{a}^{\infty} f(x)\,dx$$

Here the original integral converges only if **both** of the latter integrals converge. If either of the latter integrals diverges, then the original integral also diverges. Though it is not required by definition, 0 is often the choice for the value of a in the above definition.

example 125.1   Evaluate: $\displaystyle\int_{1}^{\infty} \frac{1}{x}\,dx$

solution   We follow the definition of an improper integral stated previously.

$$\int_{1}^{\infty} \frac{1}{x}\,dx = \lim_{b \to \infty} \int_{1}^{b} \frac{1}{x}\,dx$$

$$= \lim_{b \to \infty} \ln x \Big|_{1}^{b}$$

$$= \lim_{b \to \infty} (\ln b - \ln 1)$$

$$= \lim_{b \to \infty} \ln b$$

Now we must evaluate this limit.

$$\lim_{b \to \infty} \ln b = +\infty$$

Therefore $\displaystyle\int_{1}^{\infty} \frac{1}{x}\,dx$ **diverges.**

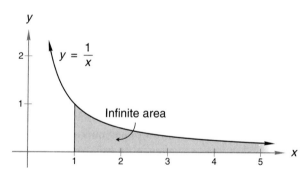

example 125.2   Evaluate: $\displaystyle\int_{1}^{\infty} \frac{1}{x^2}\,dx$

solution   We use the definition of an improper integral again.

$$\int_{1}^{\infty} \frac{1}{x^2}\,dx = \lim_{b \to \infty} \int_{1}^{b} \frac{1}{x^2}\,dx$$

$$= \lim_{b \to \infty} \left[-\frac{1}{x} \right]_{1}^{b}$$

$$= \lim_{b \to \infty} \left[-\frac{1}{b} - \left(-\frac{1}{1} \right) \right]$$

$$= \lim_{b \to \infty} \left(1 - \frac{1}{b} \right)$$

$$= 1 - 0 = 1$$

Therefore $\int_1^\infty \frac{1}{x^2}\,dx$ converges and equals 1. Thus the shaded area shown below, which is unbounded to the right, is exactly 1 square unit.

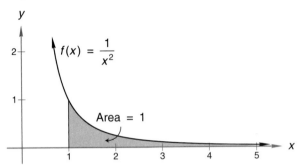

We have now seen that the integral $\int_1^\infty \frac{1}{x}\,dx$ diverges while the integral $\int_1^\infty \frac{1}{x^2}\,dx$ converges to 1, even though the graphs of these two functions are similar on the interval $[1, \infty)$. Notice that $\lim_{x \to \infty} f(x) = 0$ does not imply that $\int_a^\infty f(x)\,dx$ converges. The difference here is that $\frac{1}{x^2}$ approaches zero faster than $\frac{1}{x}$. This is a subtle difference, but an important one.

example 125.3   Evaluate: $\displaystyle\int_{-\infty}^{1} e^x\,dx$

solution   From the previous definitions,

$$\int_{-\infty}^{1} e^x\,dx = \lim_{a \to -\infty} \int_a^1 e^x\,dx$$

We integrate and find the limit as a approaches $-\infty$.

$$\lim_{a \to -\infty} \int_a^1 e^x\,dx = \lim_{a \to -\infty} e^x \Big|_a^1$$

$$= \lim_{a \to -\infty} e - e^a$$

As a approaches $-\infty$, e^a approaches 0. Therefore, $\displaystyle\int_{-\infty}^{1} e^x\,dx$ converges and equals *e*.

example 125.4   Evaluate: $\displaystyle\int_{-\infty}^{\infty} x\,dx$

solution   This is a classic problem involving improper integrals. First we consider the integral as an area.

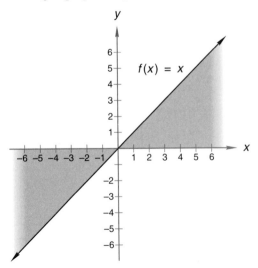

This area appears to be infinite, so we should find that $\displaystyle\int_{-\infty}^{\infty} x\,dx$ diverges.

Next we evaluate the integral **incorrectly.** Many students mistakenly do the following:

$$\int_{-\infty}^{\infty} x \, dx = \lim_{a \to \infty} \int_{-a}^{a} x \, dx \qquad \text{NO! NO! NO!}$$

$$= \lim_{a \to \infty} \frac{x^2}{2} \Big|_{-a}^{a}$$

$$= \lim_{a \to \infty} \frac{a^2}{2} - \left(\frac{(-a)^2}{2} \right)$$

$$= \lim_{a \to \infty} 0 = 0$$

So the integral appears to converge and equal 0, which contradicts the discussion of the graph. The results differ because we did not solve the problem correctly. Remember that, by definition,

$$\int_{-\infty}^{\infty} x \, dx = \int_{-\infty}^{b} x \, dx + \int_{b}^{\infty} x \, dx$$

where b is some real number, provided both of the integrals on the right-hand side converge. We use $b = 0$ here and look at $\int_{0}^{\infty} x \, dx$.

$$\int_{0}^{\infty} x \, dx = \lim_{b \to \infty} \int_{0}^{b} x \, dx$$

$$= \lim_{b \to \infty} \frac{x^2}{2} \Big|_{0}^{b}$$

$$= \lim_{b \to \infty} \frac{b^2}{2}$$

$$= +\infty$$

Since this integral diverges, the original one does too.

$$\int_{-\infty}^{\infty} x \, dx \text{ \textbf{diverges}}$$

This answer is consistent with the conclusion derived from the graph.

problem set 125

1. The acceleration function for a particle moving along the x-axis is $a(t) = 20e^{4t}$. The velocity
(78) when $t = 0$ is 10, and the position when $t = 0$ is 4. Develop the velocity function and the position function of the particle, and find the total distance the particle travels during the time interval [5, 20].

2. Find the length of the curve $y = x^{3/2}$ on the interval from $x = 0$ to $x = \frac{4}{3}$.
(109)

3. Find the derivative of $\vec{f}(t) = 2^t \hat{i} - \log_2 t \, \hat{j}$, and state the domain of the derived function.
(123)

4. The exact shape of the bottom of a 36-foot-long swimming pool is not known and cannot be
(95) figured, because it is full of water. However, beginning at one end of the pool, and then every 6 feet thereafter, depth measurements were made.

Measurement number	1	2	3	4	5	6	7
Depth	10	15	12	9	7	5	3

The pool is 20 feet wide, and its depth is uniform across its width. Approximate the volume of water in the pool using the trapezoidal rule.

Implicitly differentiate the equations in problems 5 and 6 to find $\dfrac{dy}{dx}$ and $\dfrac{d^2y}{dx^2}$.

5. $x^2 - y^2 = 4$
(124)

6. $x^3 + y^2 + y = x$
(124)

Integrate in problems 7–9.

7. $\displaystyle\int \dfrac{-7x - 2}{x^2 - 4}\, dx$
(115)

8. $\displaystyle\int \dfrac{x^2 + 4x + 1}{x^2(x + 2)}\, dx$
(120)

9. $\displaystyle\int \sec^3 x\, dx$
(122)

Evaluate the improper integrals in problems 10–13.

10. $\displaystyle\int_0^\infty \dfrac{1}{x^2 + 1}\, dx$
(125)

11. $\displaystyle\int_1^\infty \dfrac{1}{x^3}\, dx$
(125)

12. $\displaystyle\int_1^\infty \dfrac{1}{\sqrt{x}}\, dx$
(125)

13. $\displaystyle\int_0^\infty (e^{-x} \cos x)\, dx$
(125)

14. Evaluate: $\displaystyle\lim_{x \to 0} \dfrac{2 \cos x - 2}{3x}$
(101)

15. Let $f(x) = \dfrac{d}{dx} \displaystyle\int_x^3 \dfrac{\cos t - 1}{t}\, dt$. Find $f(\pi)$.
(98)

16. Evaluate: $\displaystyle\int_{-3}^4 |2x - 4|\, dx$
(96)

17. Region R is bounded by the y-axis and the graph of $x = 1 - y^2$ on the interval $0 \le y \le 1$.
(94) Use y as the variable of integration to write a definite integral whose value equals the volume of the solid formed when R is revolved about the line $y = -1$.

18. Use logarithmic differentiation to compute $\dfrac{f'(x)}{f(x)}$ where $f(x) = (x)^{x^2}$.
(84)

19. Suppose $b > a$ and $\displaystyle\int_a^b f(x)\, dx > 0$. Which of the following must be true?
(57)

    A. $f > 0$ for all values of x in the interval $[a, b]$.

    B. $\displaystyle\int_b^a f(x)\, dx < 0$

    C. f is an even function.

    D. If $a < c < b$, then $\displaystyle\int_a^c f(x)\, dx > 0$.

20. Find $f'(x)$ where $f(x) = xe^{x^2} - \sqrt{x^3 + 1} - \dfrac{\cot x + x}{e^{-x} - 1}$.
(50)

Determine whether each series in problems 21 and 22 converges or diverges. If a series converges, state its value.

21. $\displaystyle\sum_{n=1}^\infty \dfrac{2n^2 - 3n + 6}{n^2 + 20}$
(121)

22. $\displaystyle\sum_{n=1}^\infty \dfrac{4^n - 2^n}{3^n}$
(117)

Graph the polar equation in problems 23 and 24 on a polar coordinate plane.

23. $r = 4 \sin \theta$
(110)

24. $r = \sin (4\theta)$
(110)

25. Use a graphing calculator to show that $\displaystyle\lim_{x \to 3} 2^x = 8$ by finding a δ-value that guarantees 2^x
(103) is within ε of 8 when $\varepsilon = 0.01$.

LESSON 126 *Partial Fractions III*

Up to this point we have only performed partial-fraction decomposition on fractions whose denominators factor into linear terms. We now consider the situation where the factored denominator contains an **irreducible quadratic** polynomial term, which is a second degree term that cannot be factored over the real numbers. If the denominator of a fraction of polynomials has an irreducible quadratic factor, the numerator of the partial-fraction decomposition must contain one term whose numerator is a linear term of the form $Ax + B$ and whose denominator is the irreducible quadratic factor. For example, the partial-fraction decomposition shown here has a numerator $Ax + B$ for the quadratic denominator $x^2 + 1$ and a numerator of C for the linear denominator $x - 1$.

$$\int \frac{4x^2 - 2x + 2}{(x^2 + 1)(x - 1)}\, dx = \int \frac{Ax + B}{x^2 + 1}\, dx + \int \frac{C}{x - 1}\, dx$$

To find the constants A, B, and C, three independent equations in A, B, and C must be developed. The first step is to find common denominators.

$$\frac{4x^2 - 2x + 2}{(x^2 + 1)(x - 1)} = \frac{Ax + B}{x^2 + 1} + \frac{C}{x - 1} = \frac{(Ax + B)(x - 1)}{(x^2 + 1)(x - 1)} + \frac{C(x^2 + 1)}{(x - 1)(x^2 + 1)}$$

From the two outer expressions:

$$4x^2 - 2x + 2 = (Ax + B)(x - 1) + C(x^2 + 1)$$

As with previous partial-fraction problems, this equation can be used to determine A, B, and C by substituting values for x.

$$x = 1: \qquad 4(1)^2 - 2(1) + 2 = C(1^2 + 1)$$
$$4 = 2C$$
$$C = 2$$

$$x = 0: \qquad 4(0)^2 - 2(0) + 2 = (A(0) + B)(0 - 1) + 2(0^2 + 1)$$
$$2 = -B + 2$$
$$B = 0$$

$$x = -1: \qquad 4(-1)^2 - 2(-1) + 2 = A(-1)(-2) + 2((-1)^2 + 1)$$
$$8 = 2A + 4$$
$$A = 2$$

With these values of A, B, and C, the integral can be determined.

$$\int \frac{4x^2 - 2x + 2}{(x^2 + 1)(x - 1)}\, dx = \int \left(\frac{Ax + B}{x^2 + 1} + \frac{C}{x - 1} \right) dx \qquad \text{partial fractions}$$

$$= \int \left(\frac{2x}{x^2 + 1} + \frac{2}{x - 1} \right) dx \qquad \text{substituted}$$

$$= \ln |x^2 + 1| + 2 \ln |x - 1| + C \qquad \text{integrated}$$

example 126.1 Integrate: $\displaystyle\int \frac{6x^2 - 3x + 1}{4x^3 + x^2 + 4x + 1}\, dx$

solution We check to see whether the numerator is the differential of the denominator. (If so, we have $\int \frac{du}{u}$, which makes the problem relatively simple.)

$$d(4x^3 + x^2 + 4x + 1) = 12x^2 + 2x + 4$$

Unfortunately the numerator is not the differential of the denominator, so we resort to partial fractions. To use partial fractions, we must first factor the denominator completely.

$$4x^3 + x^2 + 4x + 1 = x^2(4x + 1) + (4x + 1)$$
$$= (x^2 + 1)(4x + 1)$$

Therefore

$$\frac{6x^2 - 3x + 1}{4x^3 + x^2 + 4x + 1} = \frac{6x^2 - 3x + 1}{(x^2 + 1)(4x + 1)} = \frac{Ax + B}{x^2 + 1} + \frac{C}{4x + 1}$$

We rewrite the right-hand portion with common denominators and add.

$$\frac{6x^2 - 3x + 1}{(4x + 1)(x^2 + 1)} = \frac{(Ax + B)(4x + 1) + C(x^2 + 1)}{(4x + 1)(x^2 + 1)}$$

Since these fractions are equal and their denominators are the same, the numerators must be equivalent.

$$6x^2 - 3x + 1 = (Ax + B)(4x + 1) + C(x^2 + 1)$$

We substitute values for x to obtain three independent equations involving A, B, and C.

$$x = 0: \qquad 1 = B(1) + C(1)$$
$$1 = B + C$$

$$x = 1: \qquad 6 - 3 + 1 = (A + B)(4 + 1) + C(2)$$
$$4 = 5A + 5B + 2C$$

$$x = 2: \qquad 24 - 6 + 1 = (2A + B)(8 + 1) + C(4 + 1)$$
$$19 = 18A + 9B + 5C$$

Many graphing calculators, including the TI-83, can easily solve such a system of linear equations. The solution of this system is $A = 1$, $B = -1$, and $C = 2$. Thus

$$\int \frac{6x^2 - 3x + 1}{(4x + 1)(x^2 + 1)} \, dx = \int \frac{x - 1}{x^2 + 1} \, dx + \int \frac{2 \, dx}{4x + 1} \qquad \text{partial fraction}$$

$$= \int \frac{x \, dx}{x^2 + 1} - \int \frac{dx}{x^2 + 1} + \int \frac{2 \, dx}{4x + 1} \qquad \text{split fraction}$$

$$= \frac{1}{2} \int \frac{2x \, dx}{x^2 + 1} - \int \frac{dx}{x^2 + 1} + \frac{1}{2} \int \frac{4 \, dx}{4x + 1} \qquad \text{adjusted constants}$$

$$= \frac{1}{2} \ln \left| x^2 + 1 \right| - \tan^{-1} x + \frac{1}{2} \ln \left| 4x + 1 \right| + C \qquad \text{integrated}$$

problem set 126

1. (46) A particle moves along the elliptical path defined by the equation $\frac{x^2}{9} + \frac{y^2}{8} = 1$. Find the rate of change of the y-coordinate of the particle the instant it passes through the point $(1, \frac{8}{3})$ given that the x-coordinate is increasing at a rate of 1 unit per second at that instant.

2. (99) Use differentials to approximate the cube root of 124.

Evaluate the improper integrals in problems 3 and 4.

3. (125) $\int_1^\infty \frac{dx}{x + 1}$ **4.** (125) $\int_1^\infty \frac{dx}{x^2 + 1}$

5. (123) Draw a vector that represents $\vec{f}\,'(2)$ where $\vec{f}(t) = 2^t \hat{i} - t^2 \hat{j}$.

Integrate in problems 6–8.

6. (126) $\int \frac{3x^2 - x}{(x^2 + 1)(x - 1)} \, dx$ **7.** (126) $\int \frac{-x^2 + 2x - 3}{(x^2 + 2)(x + 1)} \, dx$ **8.** (120) $\int \frac{-x^2 + 2}{(x + 1)^2 (x + 2)} \, dx$

9. (107) Convert the polar equation $r = 2 \sin \theta + \cos \theta$ to its rectangular equivalent.

10. (124) Find $\frac{d^2 y}{dx^2}$ where $y^3 - x^2 = y$.

Graph the equations in problems 11 and 12.

11. $r = 1 + 2 \sin \theta$
(118)

12. $r = 2 - 2 \cos \theta$
(118)

13. The Mean Value Theorem says that if f is continuous on $[a, b]$ and differentiable on (a, b), then
(85) there is some number $c \in (a, b)$ such that $f'(c) = \frac{f(b) - f(a)}{b - a}$. For $f(x) = x^3 + 1$, find such a number c in $(-1, 3)$.

14. Find the fourth partial sum of the series $\sum_{n=2}^{\infty} \frac{n^2}{2^n}$.
(116)

15. Determine whether the series $\sum_{n=1}^{\infty} \left(\frac{1}{n(n + 1)} - \frac{3^n}{10} \right)$ converges or diverges. If it converges, state
(117) its value.

16. Find the length of the curve determined by $x = \cos \theta + \theta \sin \theta$ and $y = \sin \theta - \theta \cos \theta$
(114) from $\theta = 0$ to $\theta = \pi$.

Integrate in problems 17–22.

17. $\displaystyle\int \frac{2x + 1}{\sqrt{x^2 + x + 1}}\, dx$
(66)

18. $\displaystyle\int x^2 e^x\, dx$
(122)

19. $\displaystyle\int \frac{4}{\sqrt{4 - x^2}}\, dx$
(64)

20. $\displaystyle\int \frac{4}{\sqrt{x^2 - 4}}\, dx$
(113)

21. $\displaystyle\int \frac{4}{x\sqrt{x^2 - 4}}\, dx$
(64)

22. $\displaystyle\int \sqrt{x^2 - 4}\, dx$
(113)

23. A particle moves along the x-axis so that its position at any time t is given by the
(54) equation $x(t) = t^2 - 3t - 4$. Find the distance the particle moves from $t = -2$ to $t = 5$.

24. A particle moves in the xy-plane along the curve defined by $y = x^2 - 3x - 4$. Approximate
(109) the distance the particle moves from $x = -2$ to $x = 5$.

25. Let p be a cubic function whose equation is $p(x) = x^3 + bx^2 + cx + d$. Suppose that p is an
(68) odd function and that p has local extreme points at $x = q$ and $x = -q$. Find b, c, and d.

LESSON 127 *p-Series*

This lesson considers a family of series called **p-series.** These are series of the form

$$\sum_{n=1}^{\infty} \frac{1}{n^p}$$

where p is a given constant. When $p = 1$, we have the well-studied **harmonic series:**

$$\sum_{n=1}^{\infty} \frac{1}{n}$$

Consider the following partial sums of the harmonic series:

$$S_1 = 1 > 1 \cdot \frac{1}{2}$$

$$S_2 = 1 + \frac{1}{2} > \frac{1}{2} + \frac{1}{2} = 2 \cdot \frac{1}{2}$$

$$S_4 = 1 + \frac{1}{2} + \frac{1}{3} + \frac{1}{4} > \frac{1}{2} + \frac{1}{2} + \frac{1}{4} + \frac{1}{4} = 3 \cdot \frac{1}{2}$$

$$S_8 = 1 + \frac{1}{2} + \frac{1}{3} + \frac{1}{4} + \frac{1}{5} + \frac{1}{6} + \frac{1}{7} + \frac{1}{8}$$

$$> \frac{1}{2} + \frac{1}{2} + \underbrace{\left(\frac{1}{4} + \frac{1}{4}\right)}_{\frac{1}{2}} + \underbrace{\left(\frac{1}{8} + \frac{1}{8} + \frac{1}{8} + \frac{1}{8}\right)}_{\frac{1}{2}} = 4 \cdot \frac{1}{2}$$

While it may not be obvious from these partial sums, a pattern is emerging. The partial sum S_{2^k}, which sums the first 2^k terms, is greater than $(k + 1)\frac{1}{2}$. So, just by considering $S_1, S_2, S_4, S_8, S_{16}, \ldots$, we see that the series diverges.

$$\lim_{k \to \infty} S_{2^k} = \lim_{k \to \infty} (k + 1)\frac{1}{2} = +\infty$$

Since this sequence of partial sums diverges, we know that

$$\lim_{n \to \infty} S_n = +\infty$$

Therefore $\sum_{n=1}^{\infty} \frac{1}{n}$ diverges. This is a fact you should set to memory.

$$\boxed{\text{The harmonic series } \sum_{n=1}^{\infty} \frac{1}{n} \text{ diverges.}}$$

It turns out that we can quickly determine the convergence or divergence of any *p*-series. We state the result here and prove it in the next lesson.

$$\boxed{\text{The } p\text{-series } \sum_{n=1}^{\infty} \frac{1}{n^p} \text{ converges if } p > 1 \text{ and diverges if } p \leq 1.}$$

Though *p*-series with $p > 1$ converge, how to find their exact values is unknown in most cases.

example 127.1   Determine whether $\sum_{n=1}^{\infty} \frac{2}{3n}$ converges or diverges.

solution   Note that

$$\sum_{n=1}^{\infty} \frac{2}{3n} = \frac{2}{3} \sum_{n=1}^{\infty} \frac{1}{n}$$

A nonzero constant times a divergent series still diverges. Since the harmonic series diverges,

$$\frac{2}{3} \sum_{n=1}^{\infty} \frac{1}{n} \text{ must also } \textbf{diverge}$$

example 127.2 Determine whether $\displaystyle\sum_{n=1}^{\infty} \frac{4}{n^3}$ converges or diverges.

solution Note that

$$\sum_{n=1}^{\infty} \frac{4}{n^3} = 4\sum_{n=1}^{\infty} \frac{1}{n^3}$$

Since $\sum_{n=1}^{\infty} \frac{1}{n^3}$ is the *p*-series with $p = 3$ and since $3 > 1$, the series converges. Therefore, $4\sum_{n=1}^{\infty} \frac{1}{n^3}$ also **converges.**

Though we cannot determine the exact value of this series, the TI-83 can approximate its value by summing many of its first terms. For example, the sum of the first 100 terms of $\sum_{n=1}^{\infty} \frac{4}{n^3}$ is approximately 4.80803. This approximation is found by entering

$$\texttt{4*sum(seq(1/N\^3,N,1,100))}$$

in the calculator. The $\texttt{sum(}$ and $\texttt{seq(}$ functions are found using the **STAT** key. They reside in the MATH menu and the OPS menu respectively. The character N is obtained by pressing **ALPHA** **LOG**. The TI-83 shows that the sum of the first 500 terms of the series is approximately 4.80822, which is relatively close to the sum of the first 100 terms. Therefore, both of these estimates are adequate approximations.

problem set 127

For problems 1 and 2 let R be the region between $y = \dfrac{1}{x}$ and the *x*-axis on the interval $[1, \infty)$.

1. Find the area of R.
(125)

2. (a) Find the volume of the solid formed when R is revolved around the *x*-axis.
(125)

    (b) Is the area in problem 1 finite or infinite?

    (c) Is the volume formed by revolving the region finite or infinite?

3. Region R is bounded by $y = e^x$, $x = 0$, and $y = e^2$. Write a definite integral whose value
(94) equals the volume of the solid formed when R is rotated about the line $x = -1$.

4. The slope of the tangent line to the graph of a particular equation at any point (x, y) on its graph
(88) is $\frac{x}{y}$. Find the equation of the curve given that its graph passes through the point $(1, 3)$.

5. A variable force $F(x) = x\sqrt{x^2 - 1}$ newtons propels an object along the *x*-axis in the direction
(62) of the force. Find the work done by the force in moving the object from $x = 1$ to $x = 5$ meters.

6. Find the length of the curve $9x^2 = 4y^3$ between the points $(0, 0)$ and $(2\sqrt{3}, 3)$.
(109)

7. Find $\dfrac{d^2y}{dx^2}$ where $y = \sin(2t)$ and $x = \cos t$.
(119)

Integrate in problems 8–10.

8. $\displaystyle\int \frac{2x^2 + x + 3}{(x^2 + 1)(x + 1)}\, dx$
(126)

9. $\displaystyle\int \frac{3x^2 + 7x + 6}{x^2(x + 2)}\, dx$
(120)

10. $\displaystyle\int e^{3x} \sin(2x)\, dx$
(122)

11. Find the area between the graph of $y = \cot^2 x$ and the *x*-axis on the interval $\left[\dfrac{\pi}{4}, \dfrac{3\pi}{4}\right]$.
(100)

12. Let $f(x) = \dfrac{x + 1}{x}$. Write the equation of f^{-1} and evaluate $(f^{-1})'(2)$.
(92)

13. Find $\dfrac{d^2y}{dx^2}$ where $x^3 - y^3 = x$.
(124)

Integrate in problems 14–16.

14. $\int \sin^2 x \, dx$ **15.** $\int \sin^3 x \cos^2 x \, dx$ **16.** $\int 10^x \, dx$
(83)   (76)   (73)

Determine whether each series in problems 17–22 converges or diverges. Give a reason for each answer. State the value of any convergent series for which it is possible to state a value.

17. $\displaystyle\sum_{n=1}^{\infty} \frac{5}{n}$ **18.** $\displaystyle\sum_{n=1}^{\infty} \frac{1}{5n}$
(127)   (127)

19. $\displaystyle\sum_{n=1}^{\infty} \frac{1}{n^5}$ **20.** $\displaystyle\sum_{n=1}^{\infty} \frac{1}{5^n}$
(127)   (117)

21. $\displaystyle\sum_{n=1}^{\infty} \frac{1 + 2^n}{3}$ **22.** $\displaystyle\sum_{n=1}^{\infty} \frac{1}{(4n - 3)(4n + 1)}$
(117)   (117)

23. Graph the polar equation $r = 3\cos(2\theta)$ on a polar coordinate plane.
(110)

24. Write the equation(s) of the asymptote(s) of $f(x) = \dfrac{x}{1 - x^2}$, and sketch the graph of f.
(80)

25. Find the exact area under $y = x^2 + 2$ on the interval $[0, 4]$ by summing the area of infinitely
(43) many left rectangles.

LESSON 128   *Basic Comparison Test • Integral Test • Proof of p-Test*

128.A

basic comparison test

Up to this point we have seen various results regarding the convergence or divergence of series. However, most of these approaches deal with specific types of series (e.g., geometric series, telescoping series, *p*-series). The only general result we have observed is actually a test for divergence.

> If $\displaystyle\lim_{n \to \infty} a_n \neq 0$, then $\displaystyle\sum_{n=1}^{\infty} a_n$ diverges.

It is helpful to build a repertoire of convergence tests, generic tools that can be used on a given series to check for convergence. The convergence tests we develop in this lesson apply to **positive-termed series.** The first test of convergence we consider is called the **basic comparison test.**

> BASIC COMPARISON TEST
>
> Suppose $\displaystyle\sum_{n=1}^{\infty} a_n$, $\displaystyle\sum_{n=1}^{\infty} c_n$, and $\displaystyle\sum_{n=1}^{\infty} d_n$ are all positive-termed series.
>
> 1. If $a_n \leq c_n$ for every positive integer n and if $\displaystyle\sum_{n=1}^{\infty} c_n$ converges, then $\displaystyle\sum_{n=1}^{\infty} a_n$ also converges.
>
> 2. If $a_n \geq d_n$ for every positive integer n and if $\displaystyle\sum_{n=1}^{\infty} d_n$ diverges, then $\displaystyle\sum_{n=1}^{\infty} a_n$ also diverges.

Both statements above seem quite obvious. In essence they say the following:

1. If a series converges, then a smaller series must also converge.
2. If a series diverges, then a larger series must also diverge.

Notice that we cannot conclude that a smaller series converges by comparing it to a larger divergent series, nor can we conclude that a larger series diverges by comparing it to a smaller convergent series. Hence the comparison test requires some wisdom when used. Moreover, it usually requires some insight on the part of the student in selecting an adequate comparison series.

example 128.1 Determine whether $\sum\limits_{n=1}^{\infty} (2 + 3^n)$ converges or diverges.

solution Each term of the series $2 + 3^n$ is greater than the corresponding term in 3^n. Since $\sum\limits_{n=1}^{\infty} 3^n$ is a divergent geometric series $(r = 3)$, the given series must also **diverge** by the basic comparison test. The basic comparison test was not actually necessary. The divergence theorem also guarantees that this series diverges because its nth term does not approach zero.

example 128.2 Determine whether $\sum\limits_{n=2}^{\infty} \dfrac{1}{n!}$ converges or diverges.

solution Notice that this series begins with $n = 2$. In order to compare it with other familiar series, we rewrite it as a series that begins with $n = 1$.

$$\sum_{n=2}^{\infty} \frac{1}{n!} = \sum_{n=1}^{\infty} \frac{1}{(n + 1)!}$$

The terms of this series are

$$\frac{1}{2}, \frac{1}{6}, \frac{1}{24}, \frac{1}{120}, \cdots$$

They are no greater than the following in one-on-one comparison:

$$\frac{1}{2}, \frac{1}{4}, \frac{1}{8}, \frac{1}{16}, \cdots$$

which are the terms of the series $\sum\limits_{n=1}^{\infty} \frac{1}{2^n}$. We chose this as a comparison series because its ith term involves i factors, just like the given series. Note that $(n + 1)! \geq 2^n$ when $n \geq 1$, so that $\frac{1}{(n + 1)!} \leq \frac{1}{2^n}$ when $n \geq 1$. (We omit a rigorous proof here; however, this should be obvious from the term-by-term comparison of the sequence above.) Since $\sum\limits_{n=1}^{\infty} \frac{1}{2^n}$ is a geometric series with $r = \frac{1}{2}$ (which is less than 1), it must converge. Since $\frac{1}{(n + 1)!} \leq \frac{1}{2^n}$ for all $n \geq 1$, we can conclude that $\sum\limits_{n=2}^{\infty} \frac{1}{n!}$ must also **converge** by the basic comparison test.

The hardest part of this example is choosing to use $\sum\limits_{n=1}^{\infty} \frac{1}{2^n}$ as the comparison series. Skill in choosing an appropriate series is only gained through practice and experience.

example 128.3 Determine whether $\sum\limits_{n=1}^{\infty} |\sec n|$ converges or diverges.

solution Since $|\cos n| \leq 1$ for all $n \geq 1$, we know that $|\sec n| \geq 1$ for all $n \geq 1$. Therefore we compare the given series with $1 + 1 + 1 + \cdots = \sum\limits_{n=1}^{\infty} 1$. It is clear from consideration of its partial sums that $\sum\limits_{n=1}^{\infty} 1$ is a divergent series.

$$S_m = \underbrace{1 + 1 + 1 + \cdots + 1}_{m \text{ times}} = m \qquad \text{and} \qquad \lim_{m \to \infty} S_m = \lim_{m \to \infty} m = +\infty$$

Since $|\sec n| \geq 1$ for all n and since $\sum\limits_{n=1}^{\infty} 1$ diverges, the series $\sum\limits_{n=1}^{\infty} |\sec n|$ **diverges** by the basic comparison test.

128.B

integral test   We now turn to another convergence test, the **integral test.**

> ### INTEGRAL TEST
>
> Suppose $\displaystyle\sum_{n=1}^{\infty} a_n$ is a positive-termed series and that f is a continuous decreasing function such that $f(n) = a_n$ for all $n \geq 1$. Then
> $$\sum_{n=1}^{\infty} a_n \qquad \text{and} \qquad \int_1^{\infty} f(x)\, dx$$
> both converge or both diverge.

However, $\displaystyle\sum_{n=1}^{\infty} a_n$ and $\displaystyle\int_1^{\infty} f(x)\, dx$ usually have two different values when they converge.

example 128.4   Determine whether $\displaystyle\sum_{n=1}^{\infty} ne^{-n^2}$ converges or diverges.

solution   This series does not seem to fit into any of the special types of series we have considered thus far, so we attempt to use the integral test. Let $f(x) = xe^{-x^2}$.

$$\int_1^{\infty} f(x)\, dx = \int_1^{\infty} xe^{-x^2}\, dx$$

If $u = -x^2$, then $du = -2x\, dx$.

$$\begin{aligned}
\int_1^{\infty} xe^{-x^2}\, dx &= -\frac{1}{2}\int_1^{\infty} (-2x)e^{-x^2}\, dx \\
&= -\frac{1}{2}\int_{x=1}^{\infty} e^u\, du \\
&= -\frac{1}{2}e^{-x^2}\Big|_1^{\infty} \\
&= \lim_{b \to \infty}\left(-\frac{1}{2}e^{-b^2} - \left(-\frac{1}{2}e^{-1}\right)\right) \\
&= \lim_{b \to \infty}\left(-\frac{1}{2e^{b^2}} + \frac{1}{2e}\right) \\
&= 0 + \frac{1}{2e} = \frac{1}{2e}
\end{aligned}$$

Since $\displaystyle\int_1^{\infty} f(x)\, dx$ converges, $\displaystyle\sum_{n=1}^{\infty} ne^{-n^2}$ also **converges** by the integral test.

A reminder is in order. We **cannot** conclude that

$$\sum_{n=1}^{\infty} ne^{-n^2} = \frac{1}{2e} \qquad \text{NO! NO! NO!}$$

We can only conclude that the series converges.

128.C

proof of *p*-test   We close this lesson by proving the result stated in the previous lesson regarding *p*-series:

> The *p*-series $\displaystyle\sum_{n=1}^{\infty} \frac{1}{n^p}$ converges if $p > 1$ and diverges if $p \le 1$.

We can prove this with the integral test by considering two cases.

First we consider the case $p = 1$, which gives the harmonic series $\displaystyle\sum_{n=1}^{\infty} \frac{1}{n}$. We set $f(x) = \dfrac{1}{x}$.

$$\int_1^{\infty} f(x)\, dx = \int_1^{\infty} \frac{1}{x}\, dx = \ln x \Big|_1^{\infty}$$
$$= \lim_{b \to \infty} (\ln b - \ln 1)$$
$$= +\infty - 0 = +\infty$$

Since $\displaystyle\int_1^{\infty} f(x)\, dx$ diverges, $\displaystyle\sum_{n=1}^{\infty} \frac{1}{n}$ also diverges by the integral test.

Next we consider the *p*-series with $p \ne 1$. So we have $\sum_{n=1}^{\infty} \frac{1}{n^p}$. Let $f(x) = \frac{1}{x^p}$ where *p* is some fixed constant other than 1. Then

$$\int_1^{\infty} f(x)\, dx = \int_1^{\infty} x^{-p}\, dx = \frac{x^{-p+1}}{-p+1}\bigg|_1^{\infty}$$
$$= \lim_{b \to \infty} \left[\frac{b^{-p+1}}{-p+1} - \frac{1}{-p+1} \right]$$
$$= \lim_{b \to \infty} \left[\frac{1}{p-1} - \frac{1}{b^{p-1}(p-1)} \right]$$

If $p > 1$, then this limit equals $\frac{1}{p-1}$; but if $p < 1$, then $\lim_{b \to \infty} \frac{1}{b^{p-1}(p-1)}$ diverges. Hence the *p*-test follows from the integral test.

**problem set
128**

1. Let R be the region between $y = \frac{1}{x^2 - 3x + 2}$ and the x-axis on the interval $[3, 6]$. Find the
(87)   volume of the solid formed when R is revolved around the y-axis.

2. Let R be the region between $y = \frac{1}{x^2 - 3x + 2}$ and the x-axis on the interval $[3, \infty)$. Is the area of
(125) R finite? If so, determine the area of R.

Determine whether each series in problems 3–11 converges or diverges. Give a reason for each answer. State the value of any convergent series for which it is possible.

3. $\displaystyle\sum_{n=1}^{\infty} \frac{2^n}{3}$
(117)

4. $\displaystyle\sum_{n=1}^{\infty} \frac{3}{2^n}$
(117)

5. $\displaystyle\sum_{n=3}^{\infty} \frac{4}{(4n-3)(4n+1)}$
(117)

6. $\displaystyle\sum_{n=1}^{\infty} \frac{4}{n}$
(127)

7. $\displaystyle\sum_{n=2}^{\infty} \frac{3}{\sqrt{n}}$
(127)

8. $\displaystyle\sum_{n=1}^{\infty} \frac{3}{n^2}$
(127)

9. $\displaystyle\sum_{n=5}^{\infty} \frac{3}{\sqrt{n}-2}$
(128)

10. $\displaystyle\sum_{n=1}^{\infty} \frac{3}{n^2+2}$
(128)

11. $\displaystyle\sum_{n=1}^{\infty} \frac{5}{\sqrt[3]{n^5}}$
(127)

Integrate in problems 12 and 13.

12. $\displaystyle\int \frac{4x^2 - 3x + 5}{(x^2+1)(x-1)}\, dx$
(126)

13. $\displaystyle\int 2e^x \sin x\, dx$
(122)

Evaluate the limits in problems 14–17.

14. $\lim\limits_{x \to 0} \dfrac{\tan (2x)}{3x}$
(79)

15. $\lim\limits_{x \to \infty} \dfrac{x - x \ln x}{1 + x^2}$
(79)

16. $\lim\limits_{x \to \infty} \left(1 + \dfrac{7}{x}\right)^x$
(111)

17. $\lim\limits_{\Delta x \to 0} \dfrac{1}{x} \log_e \left(1 + \dfrac{\Delta x}{x}\right)^{x/\Delta x}$
(111)

18. Determine the concavity of the parametric curve determined by $y = -2t + 3$ and
(119) $x = 2t^2 + 3$ at the point corresponding to $t = 2$.

19. Region R is bounded by the x-axis, $y = \sec x$, $x = -\frac{\pi}{4}$, and $x = \frac{\pi}{4}$. Write an integral in one
(94) variable whose value equals the volume of the solid formed when R is revolved about the
line $x = \frac{\pi}{2}$.

20. A particle is moving on the x-axis. Its velocity at any time t is given by the equation
(89,90) $v(t) = t^2 - 4t + 3$. Find the average velocity of the particle on the interval of time $[0, 5]$. At
what time on this interval does the particle attain its average velocity?

21. A particle is moving on the x-axis. Its velocity at any time t is given by the equation
(89) $v(t) = t^2 - 4t + 3$. Find the average speed of the particle on the interval of time $[0, 5]$.

22. Differentiate $y = \arctan (\sin x) - \dfrac{2^x}{e^{2x} - \sin x}$ with respect to x.
(64,72)

23. Graph the polar equation $r = 3 + 2 \cos \theta$ on a polar coordinate system.
(118)

24. Use a graphing calculator to demonstrate that $\lim\limits_{x \to 8} \log_2 x = 3$ by finding a δ-value that
(103) guarantees $\log_2 x$ is within ε of 3 when $\varepsilon = 0.01$.

25. Find the absolute maximum and the absolute minimum value of $y = x^3 - 12x$ on the
(52) interval $[-3, 5]$.

LESSON 129 *Area Bounded by Polar Curves*

In this lesson we show how to determine the area of a region bounded by polar curves. Because of the
nature of polar functions, we set aside the notion of summing rectangular areas (as in the case of
Riemann sums) and consider summing areas defined by circular sectors.

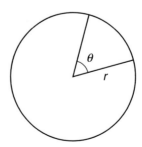

Recall that the area of the sector above equals

$$\text{(area of the circle)} \times \text{(fraction of the circle represented)},$$

or

$$\pi r^2 \cdot \left(\frac{\theta}{2\pi}\right) = \frac{1}{2}\theta r^2$$

To find the area of a polar region, we divide the region into many subregions, each of which can be approximated by a circular sector. The sum of the areas of all these subregions is the area of the whole. As the number of subregions increases without bound, the angle of each region must approach 0. Experience tells us that this can be written as an integral.

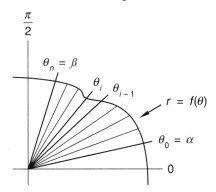

The angle of a typical region is $\theta_i - \theta_{i-1}$, and the "radius" of the region is $f(\theta_{\bar{i}})$, where $\theta_{\bar{i}}$ is somewhere in the interval (θ_{i-1}, θ_i). Thus the area of the region can be approximated by

$$\frac{1}{2}(\theta_i - \theta_{i-1})[f(\theta_{\bar{i}})]^2$$

using the expression mentioned earlier for the area of a circular sector. (*Note:* The regions described are likely not circular sectors. There is no actual radius of the region since the distance from the origin to the curve varies. However, we treat each region as a circular region to get an approximation of its area. As the number of regions increases, the approximation improves.) The sum of the areas of all such regions is

$$\sum_{i=1}^{n} \frac{1}{2}(\theta_i - \theta_{i-1})[f(\theta_{\bar{i}})]^2 = \sum_{i=1}^{n} \frac{1}{2}[f(\theta_{\bar{i}})]^2 \Delta\theta_i$$

The sum has the form of a Riemann sum. By letting the number of sectors increase to ∞ and the angles of all sectors approach 0, we see that

$$\text{Area} = \lim_{n \to \infty} \sum_{i=1}^{n} \frac{1}{2}[f(\theta_{\bar{i}})]^2 \Delta\theta_i = \int_{\theta=\alpha}^{\theta=\beta} \frac{1}{2}[f(\theta)]^2 \, d\theta$$

$$= \int_{\alpha}^{\beta} \frac{1}{2}r^2 \, d\theta$$

example 129.1   Find the area of the region bounded by the polar graph of $r = 2$.

solution   We use the formula above. Since the graph of $r = 2$ is completely drawn from $\theta = 0$ to $\theta = 2\pi$ radians, we have the following:

$$A = \int_{\theta=0}^{\theta=2\pi} \frac{1}{2}r^2 \, d\theta = \int_{0}^{2\pi} \frac{1}{2}(2)^2 \, d\theta$$

$$= \int_{0}^{2\pi} 2 \, d\theta$$

$$= 2\theta \Big|_{0}^{2\pi}$$

$$= 2(2\pi - 0) = \mathbf{4\pi}$$

Indeed, this answer makes perfect sense. The polar graph of $r = 2$ is simply the circle of radius 2 centered at the origin. The area of any circle is πr^2, so the area of this circle must be $\pi(2)^2$, or 4π.

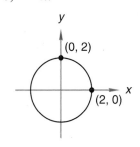

A comment is in order before moving to the next example. It is critical to determine appropriate limits of integration in these problems. If we **incorrectly** used $\theta = 0$ to $\theta = 4\pi$ for the limits, we would obtain an area of 8π, which is twice the correct result.

example 129.2   Find the area bounded by the polar graph of $r = 2 + 2 \sin \theta$.

solution   This curve should be recognized as a cardioid whose graph is completed as θ varies from 0 to 2π.

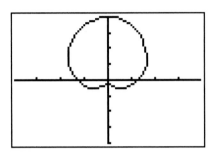

The graph is symmetric about the y-axis, so we can simply find the area of the left-hand side of the region and double it to obtain the answer. The left-hand side is spanned as θ varies from $\frac{\pi}{2}$ to $\frac{3\pi}{2}$ radians. Hence, the total area is given by

$$A = 2 \int_{\pi/2}^{3\pi/2} \frac{1}{2} r^2 \, \theta \, d\theta$$

$$= \int_{\pi/2}^{3\pi/2} (2 + 2 \sin \theta)^2 \, d\theta$$

$$= \int_{\pi/2}^{3\pi/2} (4 + 8 \sin \theta + 4 \sin^2 \theta) \, d\theta$$

We can easily integrate the first two terms of the integrand, but $4 \sin^2 \theta$ requires a trigonometric identity for simplification purposes.

$$A = \int_{\pi/2}^{3\pi/2} \left[4 + 8 \sin \theta + 4 \left(\frac{1}{2} - \frac{1}{2} \cos (2\theta) \right) \right] d\theta$$

$$= \int_{\pi/2}^{3\pi/2} [6 + 8 \sin \theta - 2 \cos (2\theta)] \, d\theta$$

$$= [6\theta - 8 \cos \theta - \sin (2\theta)]\Big|_{\pi/2}^{3\pi/2}$$

$$= (9\pi - 0 - 0) - (3\pi - 0 - 0) = \mathbf{6\pi}$$

example 129.3   Find the area of the region inside $r = 2 + 2 \cos \theta$ and outside $r = 3$.

solution   A graph is certainly a wise first step. We show here the graphs obtained from the TI-83.

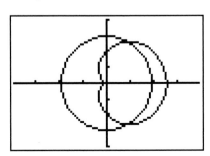

The region is inside the cardioid and outside the circle. To calculate its area, we must find the two points of intersection.

$$2 + 2 \cos \theta = 3$$
$$2 \cos \theta = 1$$
$$\cos \theta = \frac{1}{2}$$
$$\theta = \frac{\pi}{3} \text{ or } \frac{5\pi}{3}$$

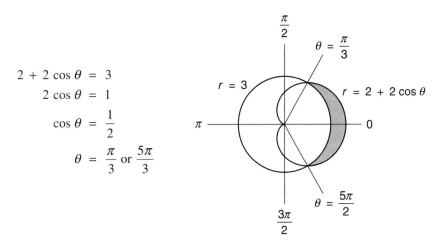

Again we take advantage of symmetry, noting that twice the area from $\theta = 0$ to $\theta = \frac{\pi}{3}$ equals the total area desired. The integrand must involve the difference of $(2 + 2 \cos \theta)^2$ and $(3)^2$, since $2 + 2 \cos \theta$ is the outer radius and 3 is the inner radius.

$$
\begin{aligned}
A &= 2 \int_0^{\pi/3} \frac{1}{2} \left[(2 + 2 \cos \theta)^2 - 3^2 \right] d\theta \\
&= \int_0^{\pi/3} (4 + 8 \cos \theta + 4 \cos^2 \theta - 9) \, d\theta \\
&= \int_0^{\pi/3} \left[-5 + 8 \cos \theta + 4 \left(\frac{1}{2} + \frac{1}{2} \cos (2\theta) \right) \right] d\theta \\
&= \int_0^{\pi/3} \left[-3 + 8 \cos \theta + 2 \cos (2\theta) \right] d\theta \\
&= \left[-3\theta + 8 \sin \theta + \sin (2\theta) \right|_0^{\pi/3} \\
&= \left(-\pi + \frac{8\sqrt{3}}{2} + \frac{\sqrt{3}}{2} \right) - 0 \\
&= \frac{9\sqrt{3}}{2} - \pi
\end{aligned}
$$

problem set 129

1. (119) Given the parametric equations $x = 2t - 1$ and $y = 4t^2 - 2t$, find $\frac{dy}{dx}$, find $\frac{d^2y}{dx^2}$, and graph the curve they define.

For problems 2–4, let R be the fourth-quadrant region bounded by $y = x(x - 3)$ and the x-axis.

2. (94) Write a definite integral in one variable whose value equals the volume of the solid formed when R is revolved about the line $x = 4$.

3. (94) Write a definite integral in one variable whose value equals the volume of the solid formed when R is revolved about the line $y = 1$.

4. (97) Region R is the base of a solid. Every vertical cross section of the solid perpendicular to the base and parallel to the y-axis is an equilateral triangle. Write a definite integral in one variable whose value equals the volume of the solid.

5. Suppose a particle moves along the x-axis so that its position at time t is given by
(78) $x(t) = \frac{1}{3}t^3 - \frac{3}{2}t^2 + 2t + 1$.

(a) Over which time intervals is the particle moving to the right?

(b) What is the total distance traveled by the particle between $t = 0$ and $t = 3$?

6. Find the area of the region bounded by the polar graph of $r = 4 \sin \theta$.
(129)

7. Find the area of the region bounded by the polar graph of $r = 1 + \sin \theta$.
(129)

8. Find the area inside the inner loop of $r = 1 - 2 \sin \theta$.
(129)

Evaluate the limits in problems 9 and 10.

9. $\lim\limits_{x \to 0^+} \dfrac{|x|}{x}$
(70)

10. $\lim\limits_{x \to 0^+} \sin \dfrac{1}{x}$
(70)

Determine whether each series in problems 11–16 converges or diverges. Give a reason for your answer. State the value of any convergent series for which it is possible.

11. $\sum\limits_{n=2}^{\infty} \dfrac{3 - 3^n}{4^n}$
(117)

12. $\sum\limits_{n=1}^{\infty} \dfrac{3}{n^{2/3}}$
(127)

13. $\sum\limits_{n=2}^{\infty} \dfrac{n^3}{\ln n}$
(121)

14. $\sum\limits_{n=2}^{\infty} \dfrac{1}{n \ln n}$
(128)

15. $\sum\limits_{n=2}^{\infty} \dfrac{1}{n - 1}$
(128)

16. $\sum\limits_{n=1}^{\infty} \dfrac{4}{3n}$
(127)

Integrate in problems 17–20.

17. $\displaystyle\int \dfrac{8}{\sqrt{9 - 4x^2}}\, dx$
(64)

18. $\displaystyle\int \dfrac{8}{9 + 4x^2}\, dx$
(64)

19. $\displaystyle\int \dfrac{9 + 4x^2}{8}\, dx$
(38)

20. $\displaystyle\int_1^{\infty} \dfrac{4}{x^{4/5}}\, dx$
(125)

21. Find $\dfrac{dy}{dx}$ where $y = \arcsin (\tan x) - xe^{-x}$.
(64)

22. Find the equation of the line normal to the graph of $y = \ln |x|$ at $x = -\dfrac{1}{2}$.
$(40,96)$

23. Find $\dfrac{dy}{dx}$ where $y = (\sqrt{x})^x$.
(84)

24. Use an epsilon-delta proof to show that $\lim\limits_{x \to 1} (4x - 2) = 2$.
(103)

25. Let $f(x) = x$ and $I = [0, 1]$. Divide I into n equal-width subintervals, and let x_i be a number
(43) in the ith subinterval of I.

(a) Use geometric formulas to find the area of the region between the graph of f and the x-axis on the interval I.

(b) Evaluate $\lim\limits_{n \to \infty} \sum\limits_{i=1}^{n} \dfrac{1}{n} f(x_i)$ using the fact that $1 + 2 + \cdots + n = \dfrac{n(n + 1)}{2}$.

(c) Express $\lim\limits_{n \to \infty} \sum\limits_{i=1}^{n} \dfrac{1}{n} f(x_i)$ as a definite integral. Evaluate this integral.

LESSON 130   *Ratio Test • Root Test*

130.A

ratio test We continue the task of developing convergence tests, looking at two new tests: the **ratio test** and the **root test.** These tests are quite easy to apply to many series, but they do have drawbacks.

RATIO TEST

Suppose $\sum a_n$ is a positive-termed series and $L = \lim\limits_{n \to \infty} \dfrac{a_{n+1}}{a_n}$.

1. The series **converges** if $L < 1$.
2. The series **diverges** if $L > 1$.
3. The **test is inconclusive** if $L = 1$.

The ratio test is particularly helpful in dealing with series whose terms involve factorials, polynomials, or exponentials.

example 130.1 Determine the convergence or divergence of $\displaystyle\sum_{n=1}^{\infty} \frac{1}{n!}$.

solution Note that the integral test is of no use here as there is no integrable $f(x)$ to define as a counterpart to $\frac{1}{n!}$. But we can use the ratio test. Since $a_n = \frac{1}{n!}$ and $a_{n+1} = \frac{1}{(n+1)!}$,

$$
\begin{aligned}
L = \lim_{n \to \infty} \frac{a_{n+1}}{a_n} &= \lim_{n \to \infty} \frac{\dfrac{1}{(n+1)!}}{\dfrac{1}{n!}} \\
&= \lim_{n \to \infty} \frac{n!}{(n+1)!} \\
&= \lim_{n \to \infty} \frac{n!}{(n+1)n!} \\
&= \lim_{n \to \infty} \frac{1}{n+1} = 0
\end{aligned}
$$

Since $L = 0 < 1$, we conclude that $\displaystyle\sum_{n=1}^{\infty} \frac{1}{n!}$ **converges.**

example 130.2 Determine the convergence or divergence of $\displaystyle\sum_{n=1}^{\infty} \frac{n}{2^n}$.

solution We use the ratio test again. Since $a_n = \frac{n}{2^n}$ and $a_{n+1} = \frac{n+1}{2^{n+1}}$,

$$
\begin{aligned}
L = \lim_{n \to \infty} \frac{a_{n+1}}{a_n} &= \lim_{n \to \infty} \frac{\dfrac{n+1}{2^{n+1}}}{\dfrac{n}{2^n}} \\
&= \lim_{n \to \infty} \frac{n+1}{2^{n+1}} \cdot \frac{2^n}{n} \\
&= \lim_{n \to \infty} \frac{n+1}{2n} \\
&= \frac{1}{2}
\end{aligned}
$$

Because $L = \dfrac{1}{2} < 1$, this series also **converges.**

example 130.3   Determine whether $\displaystyle\sum_{n=1}^{\infty} \frac{1}{n^2}$ converges or diverges.

solution   Via the ratio test, we have

$$L = \lim_{n \to \infty} \frac{a_{n+1}}{a_n} = \lim_{n \to \infty} \frac{\dfrac{1}{(n+1)^2}}{\dfrac{1}{n^2}}$$

$$= \lim_{n \to \infty} \frac{n^2}{(n+1)^2}$$

$$= 1$$

Because $L = 1$, the ratio test is inconclusive. However, we recognize this series as a p-series with $p = 2$. We know $\displaystyle\sum_{n=1}^{\infty} \frac{1}{n^2}$ **converges,** since $p > 1$.

130.B

root test   We now consider the second convergence test of this lesson.

ROOT TEST

Suppose $\displaystyle\sum a_n$ is a positive-termed series and $L = \lim\limits_{n \to \infty} \sqrt[n]{a_n}$.

1. The series **converges** if $L < 1$.
2. The series **diverges** if $L > 1$.
3. The **test is inconclusive** if $L = 1$.

This test is highly specialized and is most useful when applied to series whose nth term contains an exponential term, for example 2^n, 3^n, or n^n.

example 130.4   Determine whether $\displaystyle\sum_{n=1}^{\infty} \frac{1}{n^n}$ converges or diverges.

solution   Here $a_n = \dfrac{1}{n^n}$, so we must consider $\displaystyle\lim_{n \to \infty} \sqrt[n]{\frac{1}{n^n}}$.

$$L = \lim_{n \to \infty} \sqrt[n]{\frac{1}{n^n}}$$

$$= \lim_{n \to \infty} \left(\frac{1}{n^n}\right)^{1/n}$$

$$= \lim_{n \to \infty} \frac{1}{n}$$

$$= 0$$

Since $L = 0 < 1$, the root test allows us to conclude that $\displaystyle\sum_{n=1}^{\infty} \frac{1}{n^n}$ **converges.**

example 130.5 Determine whether $\displaystyle\sum_{n=1}^{\infty} \frac{3^n}{n^3}$ converges or diverges.

solution We note the presence of the exponential function 3^n, so we try the root test.

$$L = \lim_{n\to\infty} \sqrt[n]{a_n} = \lim_{n\to\infty} \sqrt[n]{\frac{3^n}{n^3}}$$

$$= \lim_{n\to\infty} \frac{\sqrt[n]{3^n}}{\sqrt[n]{n^3}}$$

$$= \lim_{n\to\infty} \frac{3}{n^{3/n}}$$

$$= \lim_{n\to\infty} \frac{3}{1} = 3$$

(L'Hôpital's Rule shows that $\lim_{n\to\infty} n^{3/n} = 1$.) Since $L = 3 > 1$, the series $\sum_{n=1}^{\infty} \frac{3^n}{n^3}$ **diverges.** (*Note:* The divergence theorem could have produced the same conclusion.)

problem set 130

1. (46) A point moves on the curve $4x^2 - 3y^2 = 36$ so that its y-coordinate increases at a constant rate of 12 meters per second. At what rate is the x-coordinate changing when $x = 6$ meters?

2. (60) Approximate the points of intersection of $y = x^2$ and $y = \sin x$. Use that information to help find the area of the region bounded by the two curves.

Determine whether each series in problems 3–8 converges or diverges. Give a reason for each answer. State the value of any convergent series for which it is possible.

3. (130) $\displaystyle\sum_{n=1}^{\infty} \frac{n+1}{n!}$

4. (130) $\displaystyle\sum_{n=1}^{\infty} \frac{3^n}{n!}$

5. (128) $\displaystyle\sum_{n=2}^{\infty} \frac{1}{n(\ln n)^3}$

6. (128) $\displaystyle\sum_{n=2}^{\infty} \frac{2}{\sqrt{n}-1}$

7. (127) $\displaystyle\sum_{n=1}^{\infty} \frac{4}{n^{3/2}}$

8. (117) $\displaystyle\sum_{n=1}^{\infty} \frac{2^n+2}{3^n}$

9. (103) Using an epsilon-delta proof, show that $\lim_{x\to2} (3x + 2) = 8$.

10. (98) Let $f(x) = \dfrac{d}{dx}\displaystyle\int_x^3 e^{\sin t}\,dt$. Approximate the value of $f(1)$.

11. (118) Graph the equation $r = 4 + 2\cos\theta$ on a polar coordinate plane.

12. (129) Find the area of the region bounded by the graph of $r = 4\cos\theta$.

13. (129) Find the area of the region that is inside both $r = 1$ and $r = 1 + \cos\theta$.

Evaluate the limits in problems 14–17.

14. (70) $\displaystyle\lim_{x\to2} \frac{3x^3 + x^2 - 40x + 52}{2x^2 - 8x + 8}$

15. (111) $\displaystyle\lim_{x\to\infty} \left(1 + \frac{2}{x}\right)^x$

16. (28) $\displaystyle\lim_{h\to0} \frac{\sin(x+h) - \sin x}{h}$

17. (28) $\displaystyle\lim_{h\to0} \frac{\sin(3+h) - \sin 3}{h}$

18. (124) Find $\dfrac{d^2 y}{dx^2}$ for the curve $x^2 + y^2 = 9$.

Integrate in problems 19–21.

19. $\int 2x^2 \cos 2x \, dx$
(122)

20. $\int_1^2 \dfrac{-x^2 - x + 2}{(x + 1)^2 \, x^2} \, dx$
(120)

21. $\int_1^\infty \dfrac{1}{x^2 + 1} \, dx$
(125)

22. Which of the following definite integrals is equivalent to $\int_1^2 \dfrac{e^{\sqrt{x}}}{\sqrt{x}} \, dx\,?$
(66)

A. $\int_1^2 \dfrac{e^u}{u} \, du$ B. $\int_1^{\sqrt{2}} \dfrac{e^u}{u} \, du$ C. $\int_1^{\sqrt{2}} e^u \, du$ D. $\int_1^{\sqrt{2}} 2e^u \, du$

23. Find the third partial sum of $\displaystyle\sum_{n=2}^{\infty} \dfrac{2 + n^2}{2^n}$.
(116)

24. Find the length of the arc determined by $x = 4t^3$ and $y = 3t^2$ from $t = 0$ to $t = 1$.
(114)

25. (a) Graph $f(x) = \dfrac{1}{x}$ in the first quadrant.
(125)

    (b) What is the area between the curve and the x-axis on the interval $[1, \infty)$?

    (c) Use y as the variable of integration to find the area between the graph of the function and the y-axis on the interval from $y = 1$ to $y = \infty$.

    (d) Rewrite the integral in (c) with x as the variable of integration.

LESSON 131 *Infinite Integrands*

In Lesson 125 we introduced improper integrals where one or both of the limits of integration were infinite. Here we shift our attention to improper integrals where the integrand becomes infinite either at one of the limits of integration or at some point between the two limits of integration. One such example would be $\int_{-1}^{1} \frac{1}{x^2} \, dx$, since $\frac{1}{x^2}$ becomes infinite as x approaches 0. Another example is $\int_2^5 \frac{1}{x-2} \, dx$, where $\lim_{x \to 2+} \frac{1}{x-2} = +\infty$.

We now define such improper integrals. If f is a continuous function on the interval $(a, b]$ and f becomes infinite as x approaches a from the right, then

$$\int_a^b f(x) \, dx = \lim_{c \to a^+} \int_c^b f(x) \, dx$$

Similarly, if f is a continuous function on the interval $[a, b)$ and f becomes infinite as x approaches b from the left, then

$$\int_a^b f(x) \, dx = \lim_{c \to b^-} \int_a^c f(x) \, dx$$

Finally, if f has an infinite discontinuity at some number d on the open interval (a, b) but is continuous everywhere else on the closed interval $[a, b]$, then

$$\int_a^b f(x) \, dx = \int_a^d f(x) \, dx + \int_d^b f(x) \, dx$$

The integrals in the sum above would be evaluated using the first two definitions. As before, any integral of the above form is called an **improper integral.** If the limit(s) exist, then the improper integral is said to **converge.** If not, the improper integral is said to **diverge.**

example 131.1   Evaluate: $\displaystyle\int_0^3 \frac{1}{\sqrt{3-x}}\,dx$

solution   As the graph shows, this is an improper integral because $\displaystyle\lim_{x \to 3^-} \frac{1}{\sqrt{3-x}} = +\infty$.

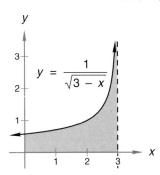

Note the vertical asymptote at $x = 3$. We use the appropriate definition.

$$\int_0^3 \frac{1}{\sqrt{3-x}}\,dx = \lim_{c \to 3^-} \int_0^c \frac{1}{\sqrt{3-x}}\,dx$$
$$= \lim_{c \to 3^-} -2\big[(3-x)^{1/2}\big]_0^c$$
$$= \lim_{c \to 3^-} -2(3-c)^{1/2} + 2(3)^{1/2}$$
$$= \mathbf{2\sqrt{3}}$$

So this improper integral converges and equals $2\sqrt{3}$.

example 131.2   Evaluate: $\displaystyle\int_0^1 \frac{1}{x}\,dx$

solution   Here we must note that $\displaystyle\int_0^1 \frac{1}{x}\,dx = \lim_{c \to 0^+} \int_c^1 \frac{1}{x}\,dx$, since our integrand is undefined when x is 0.

$$\lim_{c \to 0^+} \int_c^1 \frac{1}{x}\,dx = \lim_{c \to 0^+} \ln x \Big|_c^1$$
$$= \lim_{c \to 0^+} (\ln 1 - \ln c)$$
$$= \lim_{c \to 0^+} (-\ln c) = +\infty$$

Remember that $\ln x$ goes to $-\infty$ as x approaches 0 from the right. Therefore $\displaystyle\int_0^1 \frac{1}{x}\,dx$ **diverges.**

example 131.3   Evaluate: $\displaystyle\int_0^2 \frac{1}{(x-1)^2}\,dx$

solution   The graph of this function is always positive. Therefore, $\int_0^2 \frac{1}{(x-1)^2}\,dx$ must also be positive, as a definite integral for a positive-valued function describes the area under the graph of the function. We approach the problem incorrectly first, ignoring the infinite discontinuity at $x = 1$.

$$\int_0^2 \frac{1}{(x-1)^2}\,dx = -(x-1)^{-1}\Big|_0^2 \qquad\qquad \text{NO! NO! NO!}$$
$$= -\big[(2-1)^{-1} - (0-1)^{-1}\big]$$
$$= -[1 - (-1)] = -2$$

This negative answer does not make sense! Note that the graph of $y = \frac{1}{(x-1)^2}$ has an asymptote at $x = 1$.

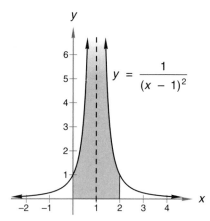

We now solve the problem using proper techniques.

$$\int_0^2 \frac{1}{(x-1)^2}\,dx = \lim_{c \to 1^-} \int_0^c \frac{1}{(x-1)^2}\,dx + \lim_{k \to 1^+} \int_k^2 \frac{1}{(x-1)^2}\,dx$$

Both of the integrals on the right-hand side must converge in order for the integral on the left-hand side to converge. If either of the integrals on the right-hand side diverge, then our original integral diverges.

$$\lim_{c \to 1^-} \int_0^c \frac{1}{(x-1)^2}\,dx = \lim_{c \to 1^-} -[(x-1)^{-1}]_0^c$$

$$= \lim_{c \to 1^-} -\left(\frac{1}{c-1} + \frac{1}{1}\right)$$

$$= +\infty$$

Since this integral diverges, it is unnecessary to evaluate the other integral.

$$\int_0^2 \frac{1}{(x-1)^2}\,dx \text{ \textbf{diverges}}$$

problem set 131

1. A container must have a rectangular base with a width of 4 meters, rectangular sides, no top, and a volume of 36 cubic meters. If the construction materials cost \$15 per square meter for the base and \$12 per square meter for the sides, what is the lowest possible cost of the container?
(52)

2. Curve C is determined by the parametric equations $x = 2 \cos \theta$ and $y = 3 \sin \theta$. Find the equation of the line tangent to C at $\theta = \frac{\pi}{4}$, and describe the concavity of C at the point of tangency.
(119)

3. Find the length of the parametric curve determined by $x = 3(t-1)^2$ and $y = 8t^{3/2}$ from $t = 0$ to $t = 1$.
(114)

4. Find the length of $y = \frac{x^2}{8} - (\ln x)$ from $\left(1, \frac{1}{8}\right)$ to $\left(2, \frac{1}{2} - \ln 2\right)$.
(109)

5. Find the area of the region bounded by the graph of $r = 4 \cos (3\theta)$.
(129)

6. Find the area of the region **inside** $r = 1 + \sin \theta$ and **outside** $r = 1$.
(129)

7. Evaluate: $\lim_{x \to 0} (e^{-x} \sin x)$
(70)

Evaluate the integrals in problems 8–10.

8. $\int_0^8 \frac{1}{\sqrt[3]{x}}\,dx$
(131)

9. $\int_{-1}^1 \frac{1}{x}\,dx$
(131)

10. $\int_{-\infty}^0 e^x\,dx$
(125)

11. Find $\dfrac{d^2 y}{dx^2}$ where $x = \sin y + y$.
(124)

12. Show that $\lim\limits_{x \to 2} 2^x = 4$ by finding a δ that guarantees that 2^x is within ε of 4 when $\varepsilon = 0.01$.
(103)

Determine whether each series in problems 13–18 converges or diverges. Give a reason for each answer. State the value of any convergent series for which it is possible.

13. $\displaystyle\sum_{n=1}^{\infty} \dfrac{n+1}{n \cdot 2^n}$
(130)

14. $\displaystyle\sum_{n=2}^{\infty} \dfrac{1}{n\sqrt{\ln n}}$
(128)

15. $\displaystyle\sum_{n=1}^{\infty} n^{-5/3}$
(127)

16. $\displaystyle\sum_{n=1}^{\infty} \dfrac{2+3^n}{5^n}$
(117)

17. $\displaystyle\sum_{n=2}^{\infty} \dfrac{n^2}{\ln n}$
(121)

18. $\displaystyle\sum_{n=1}^{\infty} \dfrac{3+4n}{5n+2}$
(121)

19. Find the third partial sum of the series $\displaystyle\sum_{n=2}^{\infty} \dfrac{2+n}{n^3}$.
(116)

20. Prove that the derivative of $\sin x$ with respect to x is $\cos x$.
(101)

Integrate in problems 21–23.

21. $\displaystyle\int \dfrac{x^2}{\sqrt{4-x^2}}\, dx$
(113)

22. $\displaystyle\int \dfrac{3x^2 - x + 4}{x(x^2 + 4)}\, dx$
(126)

23. $\displaystyle\int x^2 \ln x \, dx$
(122)

24. Let R be the region bounded by $y = \dfrac{x^2}{\sin x}$ and the x-axis on the interval $[0.2, 1.4]$. Approximate
(95) the area of R using the trapezoidal rule with $n = 4$.

25. (a) Sketch the graph of $y = \dfrac{x^2 + 2x - 8}{x + 1}$. Begin by finding all zeros and asymptotes.
(28,38)

   (b) Find the area of the region bounded by the graph of the function, the x-axis, and the line $x = 4$. (*Hint:* Divide $x^2 + 2x - 8$ by $x + 1$, then use the result in the integrand.)

LESSON 132 *Limit Comparison Test*

In this lesson we examine one final test for the convergence of a positive-termed series. It is known as the **limit comparison test,** and it is quite a powerful technique for determining whether a series converges or diverges.

> **LIMIT COMPARISON TEST**
>
> Let $\displaystyle\sum_{n=1}^{\infty} a_n$ and $\displaystyle\sum_{n=1}^{\infty} b_n$ be positive-termed series. Let $L = \lim\limits_{n \to \infty} \dfrac{a_n}{b_n}$.
>
> If $0 < L < +\infty$, then $\displaystyle\sum_{n=1}^{\infty} a_n$ and $\displaystyle\sum_{n=1}^{\infty} b_n$ either both converge or both diverge. If $L = 0$ or $L = +\infty$, then the test is inconclusive.

The limit comparison test is especially useful when studying series where each term is a ratio of polynomials.

example 132.1 Determine whether $\displaystyle\sum_{n=1}^{\infty} \frac{4n - 3}{2n^3 + n^2 - 5n + 7}$ converges or diverges.

solution Before using the limit comparison test, we must select an appropriate comparison series, one whose convergence or divergence is already known. In this case the nth term of the series is a ratio of polynomials. We build the comparison series by retaining the terms of highest degree in the numerator and denominator, so the comparison series is $\sum_{n=1}^{\infty} \frac{4n}{2n^3}$ or $\sum_{n=1}^{\infty} \frac{2}{n^2}$. Note that $\sum_{n=1}^{\infty} \frac{2}{n^2} = 2 \sum_{n=1}^{\infty} \frac{1}{n^2}$, which is a convergent p-series ($p = 2$). Now we apply the limit comparison test. The nth term, a_n, of the series being examined is $\frac{4n - 3}{2n^3 + n^2 - 5n + 7}$, and the nth term, b_n, of the comparison series is $\frac{4n}{2n^3}$.

$$L = \lim_{n \to \infty} \frac{a_n}{b_n} = \lim_{n \to \infty} \frac{\dfrac{4n - 3}{2n^3 + n^2 - 5n + 7}}{\dfrac{4n}{2n^3}}$$

$$= \lim_{n \to \infty} \frac{(4n - 3)(2n^3)}{(4n)(2n^3 + n^2 - 5n + 7)}$$

$$= \lim_{n \to \infty} \frac{(4n - 3)(n^2)}{2(2n^3 + n^2 - 5n + 7)}$$

$$= \lim_{n \to \infty} \frac{4n^3 - 3n^2}{4n^3 + 2n^2 - 10n + 14}$$

$$= \lim_{n \to \infty} \frac{4n^3}{4n^3}$$

$$= \frac{4}{4} = 1$$

Since $0 < L < +\infty$, $\sum_{n=1}^{\infty} \frac{4n - 3}{2n^3 + n^2 - 5n + 7}$ and $\sum_{n=1}^{\infty} \frac{4n}{2n^3}$ must either both converge or both diverge. We already know that $\sum_{n=1}^{\infty} \frac{4n}{2n^3}$ converges. Therefore, $\sum_{n=1}^{\infty} \frac{4n - 3}{2n^3 + n^2 - 5n + 7}$ must also **converge.**

example 132.2 Determine whether $\displaystyle\sum_{n=1}^{\infty} \frac{n + 1}{3n^2 + 2}$ converges or diverges.

solution Similar to the previous example, we use the limit comparison test and compare this sum to $\sum_{n=1}^{\infty} \frac{n}{3n^2}$ or $\frac{1}{3} \sum_{n=1}^{\infty} \frac{1}{n}$. (Note that the comparison series diverges since it is a constant multiple of the harmonic series.)

$$L = \lim_{n \to \infty} \frac{\dfrac{n + 1}{3n^2 + 2}}{\dfrac{1}{3n}} = \lim_{n \to \infty} \frac{3n(n + 1)}{3n^2 + 2} = \lim_{n \to \infty} \frac{3n^2}{3n^2} = 1$$

Since $0 < L < +\infty$, $\sum_{n=1}^{\infty} \frac{n + 1}{3n^2 + 2}$ and $\sum_{n=1}^{\infty} \frac{1}{3n}$ behave in the same fashion — they either both converge or both diverge. Since we already know that $\sum_{n=1}^{\infty} \frac{1}{3n}$ diverges, we can conclude from the limit comparison test that $\sum_{n=1}^{\infty} \frac{n + 1}{3n^2 + 2}$ also **diverges.**

example 132.3 Determine the convergence or divergence of $\displaystyle\sum_{n=1}^{\infty} \frac{n^2 - 1}{(4n^2 - 2n)3^n}$.

solution We compare the given series with $\sum_{n=1}^{\infty} \frac{n^2}{n^2(3^n)}$, or $\sum_{n=1}^{\infty} \frac{1}{3^n}$. (Note that this series converges, because it is a geometric series with common ratio $r = \frac{1}{3}$.)

$$L = \lim_{n \to \infty} \frac{\dfrac{n^2 - 1}{(4n^2 - 2n)3^n}}{\dfrac{1}{3^n}}$$

$$= \lim_{n \to \infty} \frac{(n^2 - 1)3^n}{(4n^2 - 2n)3^n}$$

$$= \lim_{n \to \infty} \frac{n^2 - 1}{4n^2 - 2n} = \frac{1}{4}$$

Since $0 < L < +\infty$, both series converge or both diverge according to the limit comparison test. Since $\sum_{n=1}^{\infty} \frac{1}{3^n}$ converges, the original series $\sum_{n=1}^{\infty} \frac{n^2 - 1}{(4n^2 - 2n)3^n}$ **converges** as well.

problem set 132

1. Find the area of the largest rectangle that can be drawn so that its base is on the x-axis and its
(52) upper vertices are on the parabola $y = 15 - 3x^2$.

2. The base of a solid is a unit circle. Each vertical cross section of the object taken perpendicular
(97) to the base and parallel to the y-axis is an isosceles right triangle with its hypotenuse as the base. Find the volume of the object.

3. Approximate the area of the region bounded by the curves $y = 2^x$ and $y = x^3$ and the y-axis.
(87)

4. On the same polar coordinate plane, graph both $r = \sin \theta$ and $r = \sin (2\theta)$.
(110)

5. Find the area of the region that is inside both $r = \sin \theta$ and $r = \sin (2\theta)$.
(129)

6. Prove that the derivative of $\ln x$ with respect to x is $\dfrac{1}{x}$.
(102)

Determine whether each series in problems 7–14 converges or diverges. Justify each answer. State the value of any convergent series for which it is possible.

7. $\sum_{n=1}^{\infty} \dfrac{n}{n + 1}$
(121)

8. $\sum_{n=1}^{\infty} \dfrac{1}{n + 1}$
(132)

9. $\sum_{n=1}^{\infty} n^{-4/3}$
(127)

10. $\sum_{n=1}^{\infty} \dfrac{2n + 1}{(n + 1)^2}$
(132)

11. $\sum_{n=1}^{\infty} \dfrac{2^{n+1}}{3^n}$
(117)

12. $\sum_{n=1}^{\infty} \dfrac{1}{(2 + 3n)^3}$
(132)

13. $\sum_{n=1}^{\infty} \dfrac{2^n}{n!}$
(130)

14. $\sum_{n=1}^{\infty} \dfrac{7}{4n}$
(127)

Evaluate the integrals in problems 15–20.

15. $\displaystyle\int_3^{\infty} \dfrac{1}{(x - 1)^3} \, dx$
(125)

16. $\displaystyle\int_0^1 \dfrac{1}{(x - 1)^{2/3}} \, dx$
(131)

17. $\displaystyle\int_0^1 2x^2 \cos (2x) \, dx$
(122)

18. $\displaystyle\int \dfrac{x^2 + 5x + 2}{(x - 1)(x + 1)^2} \, dx$
(120)

19. $\displaystyle\int \dfrac{x^3 + x^2 + x + 3}{x^2 + 1} \, dx$
(126)

20. $\displaystyle\int \dfrac{-x^2 + x - 10}{(x^2 + 9)(x - 1)} \, dx$
(126)

Evaluate the limits in problems 21–23.

21. $\displaystyle\lim_{x \to 0} [x + \cos (2x)]^{\csc (3x)}$
(111)

22. $\displaystyle\lim_{x \to \infty} \left(1 + \frac{1}{x}\right)^x$
(111)

23. $\displaystyle\lim_{x \to \infty} \left(\frac{x + 4}{x}\right)^x$
(111)

24. Estimate $\sqrt[5]{30}$ using differentials.
(99)

25. Let $f(x) = x^3 + x$. If g is the inverse function of f, what is $g'(10)$?
(92)

LESSON 133 *Euler's Method*

Lesson 104 introduced slope fields as an aid in visualizing solutions of differential equations. In this lesson we concentrate on finding quantitative information about these solutions using **Euler's method.** Given a differential equation and a point through which a particular solution passes, the goal is to approximate other points on the graph **without** knowing the specific solution. This is a worthwhile goal, as many differential equations are difficult (if not impossible) to solve using integration techniques.

Suppose $\frac{dy}{dx} = f(x, y)$ and that the function $y = g(x)$ is a solution that passes through the point (x_0, y_0). Then the known slope of the tangent line at (x_0, y_0) can be used to estimate the solution function at another x-value, say x_1.

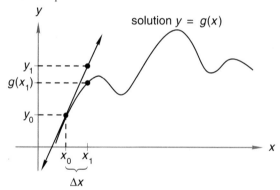

Notice that y_1 lies on the tangent line through the point (x_0, y_0) and closely approximates $g(x_1)$. Moreover, this value of y_1 can easily be determined. We simply equate two different versions of the slope of the tangent line.

$$\frac{y_1 - y_0}{x_1 - x_0} = f(x_0, y_0)$$

The left-hand side of this equation is the usual slope formula expression for a line going through two points. The right-hand side follows from the initial value of the differential equation

$$\frac{dy}{dx} = f(x, y)$$

We solve for y_1 in the equation above.

$$\frac{y_1 - y_0}{x_1 - x_0} = f(x_0, y_0)$$

$$y_1 - y_0 = f(x_0, y_0)(x_1 - x_0)$$

$$y_1 - y_0 = f(x_0, y_0)\Delta x$$

$$\boxed{y_1 = y_0 + f(x_0, y_0)\Delta x}$$

This process can be repeated to approximate other values of the solution g.

$$y_1 = y_0 + f(x_0, y_0)\Delta x$$
$$y_2 = y_1 + f(x_1, y_1)\Delta x$$
$$y_3 = y_2 + f(x_2, y_2)\Delta x$$
$$\vdots$$

Each of these steps is known as an **iteration.** (It should be noted that $x_1 = x_0 + \Delta x$, $x_2 = x_1 + \Delta x$, $x_3 = x_2 + \Delta x$, and so on.)

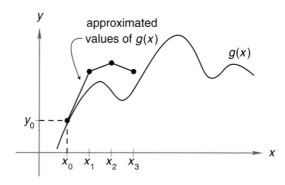

As with any approximating technique, the values determined by Euler's method are not exact. A slight amount of error exists. The best way to minimize this error is to reduce the size of Δx.

example 133.1   Use Euler's method with 5 iterations to approximate the value of y when $x = 1.5$ given the initial condition $y = 1$ when $x = 1$ and the differential equation $\frac{dy}{dx} = 2x$.

solution   Observe that

$$\Delta x = \frac{1.5 - 1}{5} = 0.1$$

Moreover, $y_0 = 1$ when $x_0 = 1$ and $f(x, y) = 2x$. Therefore

$$\begin{aligned} y_1 &= y_0 + f(x_0, y_0)\Delta x \\ &= 1 + 2(1)(0.1) \\ &= 1.2 \end{aligned}$$

$$\begin{aligned} y_2 &= y_1 + f(x_1, y_1)\Delta x \\ &= 1.2 + 2(1.1)(0.1) \\ &= 1.42 \end{aligned}$$

This process continues until we find that $y_5 = 2.20$ when $x_5 = 1.5$. We summarize the results in the table below.

i	x_i	y_i
0	1	1
1	1.1	1.2
2	1.2	1.42
3	1.3	1.66
4	1.4	1.92
5	1.5	2.2

Thus we estimate that $y(1.5)$ is approximately **2.2.**

We did **not** solve the differential equation in coming to this conclusion. However, this particular differential equation is easy to solve.

$$\frac{dy}{dx} = 2x$$

$$dy = 2x \, dx \qquad \text{separation of variables}$$

$$y = x^2 + C \qquad \text{integration}$$

Since the solution passes through $(1, 1)$,

$$1 = 1^2 + C$$

which means $C = 0$. Thus, the particular solution is $y = x^2$. We can now find the exact value of y when $x = 1.5$. It is simply $(1.5)^2$, or 2.25, which is reasonably close to the approximation of 2.20.

example 133.2 Use Euler's method with 6 iterations to estimate the value of y when $x = 2.3$ given the differential equation $\frac{dy}{dx} = x + y$ and the initial condition that $y = 1$ when $x = 2$.

solution This differential equation is difficult to solve, so it is more typical of the kinds of problems for which Euler's method is used.

$$\Delta x = \frac{2.3 - 2}{6} = \frac{0.3}{6} = 0.05$$

We can utilize the iterative process of Euler's method to estimate y when $x = 2.3$.

$$x_1 = 2.05: \qquad y_1 = y_0 + f(x_0, y_0)\Delta x$$
$$= 1 + (2 + 1)(0.05)$$
$$= 1.15$$

$$x_2 = 2.10: \qquad y_2 = y_1 + f(x_1, y_1)\Delta x$$
$$= 1.15 + (2.05 + 1.15)(0.05)$$
$$= 1.31$$

$$x_3 = 2.15: \qquad y_3 = y_2 + f(x_2, y_2)\Delta x$$
$$= 1.31 + (2.10 + 1.31)(0.05)$$
$$= 1.4805$$

Using six iterations of Euler's method yields the results summarized below.

i	x_i	y_i
0	2	1
1	2.05	1.15
2	2.1	1.31
3	2.15	1.4805
4	2.2	1.662025
5	2.25	1.85512625
6	2.3	2.0603825625

We estimate that when $x = 2.3$ the value of the solution function is **2.0603825625.** Again, Euler's method allowed us to numerically explore a differential equation without solving it, which is helpful when the differential equation is not easy to solve.

problem set 133

1. A particle travels along the *x*-axis with acceleration $a(t) = 16t - 10$. If $v(1) = 1$, what is the total distance the particle travels between $t = 0$ and $t = 2$?
(78)

2. Each time a particular ball bounces it rebounds to $\frac{2}{5}$ of the height from which it fell. If the ball is dropped from a height of 10 meters, what is the total distance the ball travels?
(117)

3. Use Euler's method with 4 iterations to approximate the value of *y* when $x = 1$ given the initial condition $y = 4$ when $x = 0$ and the differential equation $\frac{dy}{dx} = y$.
(133)

4. Solve the differential equation in problem 3 using separation of variables. Compare your results.
(133)

5. Find the length of $y = \dfrac{x^2}{4} - \dfrac{\ln x}{2}$ from $x = 1$ to $x = 4$.
(109)

Determine whether each series in problems 6–11 converges or diverges. Justify each answer. State the value of any convergent series for which it is possible.

6. $\displaystyle\sum_{n=2}^{\infty} \frac{2 + 2^n}{4^n}$
(117)

7. $\displaystyle\sum_{n=1}^{\infty} \frac{n^2 + 10}{n}$
(121)

8. $\displaystyle\sum_{n=1}^{\infty} \frac{n}{n^2 + 10}$
(132)

9. $\displaystyle\sum_{n=1}^{\infty} \frac{1}{n^2 + 10}$
(132)

10. $\displaystyle\sum_{n=1}^{\infty} \frac{100 + n}{n^3 + 2}$
(132)

11. $\displaystyle\sum_{n=1}^{\infty} \frac{27}{n - 21}$
(132)

Evaluate the integrals in problems 12–15.

12. $\displaystyle\int \frac{5x^2 + 3x + 2}{x(x + 1)^2}\, dx$
(120)

13. $\displaystyle\int x^2 \cos x\, dx$
(122)

14. $\displaystyle\int_0^4 \frac{1}{(x - 2)^3}\, dx$
(131)

15. $\displaystyle\int_1^{\infty} \frac{1}{x^3}\, dx$
(125)

For problems 16 and 17, let *R* be the region between $y = \dfrac{1}{x^{3/2}}$ and the *x*-axis on the interval $[1, \infty)$.

16. Find the area of *R*.
(125)

17. Find the volume of the solid formed when *R* is revolved around the *y*-axis.
(125)

18. Find the area of the region inside $r = 3 \sin \theta$ and outside $r = 2 - \sin \theta$.
(129)

19. Find the derivative of $\overrightarrow{f}(t) = \arcsin(e^{2t})\, \hat{i} + 4e^{3t}\hat{j}$ with respect to *t*.
(123)

20. Prove: $\displaystyle\lim_{x \to 4} (-2x + 3) = -5$
(103)

21. Use a graphing calculator to show that $\displaystyle\lim_{x \to 3} 2^x = 8$ by finding an appropriate value for δ such that $0 < |x - 3| < \delta$ implies $|2^x - 8| < 0.01$.
(103)

22. Find the equation of the line tangent to the parametric curve defined by $x = \log_4(t^2)$ and $y = \arctan \frac{t}{4}$ at the point corresponding to $t = 5$.
(119)

23. Find all the critical numbers of the function $y = x(\ln x)^2$ in the interval $(0, \infty)$.
(36)

24. Suppose *f* is a continuous function such that $-x^4 \le f(x) \le x^4$ for all values of *x*. Evaluate $\displaystyle\lim_{x \to 0} f(x)$.
(70)

25. Farmer Long is having an argument with the state about the amount of land he owns and, therefore, the amount of property tax that should be paid. He cannot afford to pay a surveyor, so he does his own calculations. His property is bordered on two sides by perpendicular county roads and on another side by a meandering brook. (See the diagram below.) Using his steel tape
(95)

measure, he takes the measurements indicated in the table below. If the measurements are in feet, what is the approximate area of Farmer Long's property?

East	0	100	200	300	400	500	600	700	800	900	1000
North	600	590	550	470	430	420	250	230	220	200	0

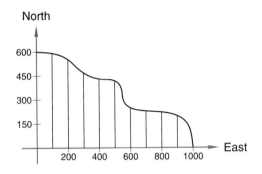

LESSON 134   *Slopes of Polar Curves*

Suppose we wish to find the slope of a polar curve defined by $r = f(\theta)$ or the equation of a line tangent to a polar curve. In order to find the slope of a curve, we must first find its derivative. But in this context, which derivative gives the slope of the curve at a specific point? Is it $\frac{dr}{d\theta}$? Is it still $\frac{dy}{dx}$? We can answer this question once we realize that these curves are still drawn in the xy-plane and that the slope of a line is given by the change in y over the change in x. A tangent line in this context still has the slope $\frac{dy}{dx}$.

In this lesson we explore three options for finding the slope of a polar curve. Depending on the situation, any of the three methods might be preferred. The first option for finding $\frac{dy}{dx}$ is to convert the polar equation $r = f(\theta)$ to a set of parametric equations. Recall from the diagram below that $x = r \cos \theta$ and $y = r \sin \theta$.

Therefore the polar equation easily converts to parametric equations as follows:

$$x = r \cos \theta = f(\theta) \cos \theta \quad \text{since } r = f(\theta)$$
$$y = r \sin \theta = f(\theta) \sin \theta \quad \text{since } r = f(\theta)$$

Finding $\dfrac{dy}{dx}$ simply involves the ratio of $\dfrac{dy}{d\theta}$ over $\dfrac{dx}{d\theta}$.

The second option is to convert the polar form of the equation into a rectangular equation involving only x and y as variables. Then $\frac{dy}{dx}$ can be found from differentiating this equation. (Implicit differentiation may be required.)

The third option is only approximative. The TI-83 can be used to numerically approximate $\frac{dy}{dx}$ at a certain point.

example 134.1 Find the slope of the curve defined by $r = 4 \cos \theta$ when $\theta = \dfrac{\pi}{4}$.

solution Using the first method, we convert this polar equation into parametric equations.

$$r = 4 \cos \theta: \qquad x = (4 \cos \theta) \cos \theta = 4 \cos^2 \theta$$
$$y = (4 \cos \theta) \sin \theta = 4 \cos \theta \sin \theta$$

Since $\dfrac{dy}{dx} = \dfrac{dy}{d\theta} \div \dfrac{dx}{d\theta}$, we must determine $\dfrac{dy}{d\theta}$ and $\dfrac{dx}{d\theta}$.

$$y = 4 \cos \theta \sin \theta \qquad\qquad\qquad x = 4 \cos^2 \theta$$
$$dy = 4[\cos \theta\,(\cos \theta) + \sin \theta\,(-\sin \theta)]\,d\theta \qquad dx = 4[2 \cos \theta\,(-\sin \theta)]\,d\theta$$
$$\frac{dy}{d\theta} = 4(\cos^2 \theta - \sin^2 \theta) \qquad\qquad \frac{dx}{d\theta} = -8 \cos \theta \sin \theta$$

So the slope function is

$$\frac{dy}{dx} = \frac{\dfrac{dy}{d\theta}}{\dfrac{dx}{d\theta}} = \frac{4(\cos^2 \theta - \sin^2 \theta)}{-8 \cos \theta \sin \theta}$$

This expression can be simplified using double angle formulas for $\sin(2\theta)$ and $\cos(2\theta)$. However, this is unnecessary as we only care about $\left.\dfrac{dy}{dx}\right|_{\theta = \pi/4}$.

$$\left.\frac{dy}{dx}\right|_{\theta = \pi/4} = \frac{4\left[\cos^2\left(\dfrac{\pi}{4}\right) - \sin^2\left(\dfrac{\pi}{4}\right)\right]}{-8 \cos\left(\dfrac{\pi}{4}\right) \sin\left(\dfrac{\pi}{4}\right)} = 0$$

Thus, the slope of the curve $r = 4 \cos \theta$ at $\theta = \frac{\pi}{4}$ is **0**, which means the tangent line at this point is horizontal.

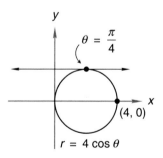

$r = 4 \cos \theta$

Although we have the answer already, for illustrative purposes we still demonstrate the other ways to find $\frac{dy}{dx}$. First we convert $r = 4 \cos \theta$ into a rectangular equation. Note that $r = \sqrt{x^2 + y^2}$ and $\cos \theta = \dfrac{x}{r} = \dfrac{x}{\sqrt{x^2 + y^2}}$.

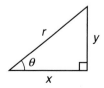

Thus $r = 4 \cos \theta$ converts to

$$\sqrt{x^2 + y^2} = \frac{4x}{\sqrt{x^2 + y^2}} \qquad\qquad \text{or} \qquad\qquad x^2 + y^2 = 4x$$

We implicitly differentiate this equation to find $\dfrac{dy}{dx}$.

$$2x + 2y\,\frac{dy}{dx} = 4 \qquad\qquad \text{implicit differentiation}$$

$$2y\,\frac{dy}{dx} = 4 - 2x \qquad\qquad \text{subtracted}$$

$$\frac{dy}{dx} = \frac{4 - 2x}{2y} \qquad\qquad \text{divided by } 2y$$

To compute $\frac{dy}{dx}$ evaluated at $\theta = \frac{\pi}{4}$, we must find the values of x and y that correspond to $\theta = \frac{\pi}{4}$, so x and y must be expressed in terms of θ. We did this in our first attempt to find the slope, which leads us to believe it is the preferred method for this problem. Nonetheless, the point of tangency in terms of x and y is determined as follows:

$$x = 4\cos^2\left(\frac{\pi}{4}\right) = 2$$

$$y = 4\cos\left(\frac{\pi}{4}\right)\sin\left(\frac{\pi}{4}\right) = 2$$

Therefore the point of tangency is (2, 2) in the xy-plane.

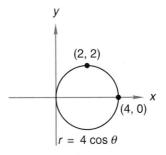

We compute $\dfrac{dy}{dx}$ based on these values of x and y.

$$\left.\frac{dy}{dx}\right|_{\theta=\pi/4} = \left.\frac{4 - 2x}{2y}\right|_{x=2,\,y=2}$$

$$= \frac{4 - 2(2)}{2(2)} = \frac{0}{4} = 0$$

This confirms the previous result.

The third option is numerical approximation. First we graph $r = 4\cos\theta$ on the TI-83.

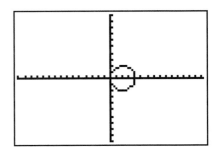

Then we go to the $\mathtt{CALCULATE}$ menu by pressing $\boxed{\mathtt{2nd}}\ \boxed{\mathtt{TRACE}}$. Three options appear: $\mathtt{1\!:value}$, $\mathtt{2\!:dy/dx}$, and $\mathtt{3\!:dr/d\theta}$. We want $\mathtt{dy/dx}$, so we choose option 2.

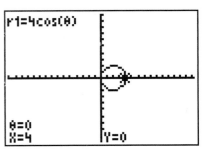

Pressing ◐ moves the cursor. We want it to be on the point (2, 2). Once the cursor is located there, we press ENTER .

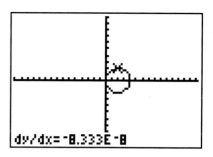

The calculator gives an answer of ⁻8.333E⁻8 for the slope, which is an approximation of 0. (*Note:* −8.333E−8 = −0.00000008333.) Thus the calculator confirms the result. However, this problem demonstrates that the calculator cannot always recognize whether an answer is exactly 0 or simply close to it.

example 134.2   Find an equation of the line tangent to $r = 1 + \cos \theta$ at $\theta = \dfrac{\pi}{6}$.

solution   We only solve the problem one way this time. We convert the polar equation to a pair of parametric equations.

$$r = 1 + \cos \theta: \qquad x = r \cos \theta = (1 + \cos \theta) \cos \theta$$
$$y = r \sin \theta = (1 + \cos \theta) \sin \theta$$

Next we find $\dfrac{dy}{d\theta}$ and $\dfrac{dx}{d\theta}$.

$$\frac{dy}{d\theta} = (1 + \cos \theta) \cos \theta + \sin \theta \,(-\sin \theta) = \cos \theta + \cos^2 \theta - \sin^2 \theta$$

$$\frac{dx}{d\theta} = (1 + \cos \theta)(-\sin \theta) + \cos \theta \,(-\sin \theta) = -\sin \theta - 2 \sin \theta \cos \theta$$

The slope function is the quotient of these two.

$$\frac{dy}{dx} = \frac{\dfrac{dy}{d\theta}}{\dfrac{dx}{d\theta}} = \frac{\cos \theta + \cos^2 \theta - \sin^2 \theta}{-\sin \theta - 2 \sin \theta \cos \theta}$$

$$= \frac{\cos \theta + \cos (2\theta)}{-\sin \theta - \sin (2\theta)}$$

The slope of the tangent line is given by the following:

$$x\big|_{\theta = \pi/6} = (1 + \cos \theta) \cos \theta\big|_{\theta = \pi/6} = \left(1 + \frac{\sqrt{3}}{2}\right)\left(\frac{\sqrt{3}}{2}\right) \approx 1.616$$

$$y\big|_{\theta = \pi/6} = (1 + \cos \theta) \sin \theta\big|_{\theta = \pi/6} = \left(1 + \frac{\sqrt{3}}{2}\right)\left(\frac{1}{2}\right) \approx 0.933$$

Now that we have the slope, we need the *x*- and *y*-coordinates of the point of tangency.

$$x\big|_{\theta = \pi/6} = (1 + \cos \theta) \cos \theta\big|_{\theta = \pi/6} = \left(1 + \frac{\sqrt{3}}{2}\right)\left(\frac{\sqrt{3}}{2}\right) \approx 1.616$$

$$y\big|_{\theta = \pi/6} = (1 + \cos \theta) \sin \theta\big|_{\theta = \pi/6} = \left(1 + \frac{\sqrt{3}}{2}\right)\left(\frac{1}{2}\right) \approx 0.933$$

So an equation of the tangent line when $\theta = \dfrac{\pi}{6}$ is approximately

$$y - 0.933 = -1(x - 1.616) \qquad \text{or}$$

$$y = -x + 2.549$$

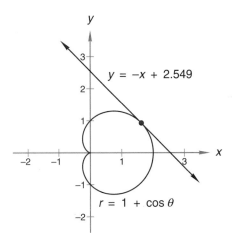

problem set
134

1. The cross section of a 3-meter-long water trough is a semicircle with a radius of 1 meter. If the water trough is full, how much force does the fluid exert on the end of the trough?
   (74)

2. How much work is done in pumping all of the fluid out of the trough described in problem 1?
   (77)

In problems 3–6 let R be the region in the xy-plane bounded by $y = 2^x$, $x = 2$, and the coordinate axes.

3. Find the volume of the solid formed when R is revolved around the x-axis.
   (71)

4. Find the volume of the solid formed when R is revolved around the y-axis.
   (87)

5. Find the volume of the solid formed when R is revolved around the line $x = 2$.
   (94)

6. Find the volume of a solid given that R is its base and that every cross section of the solid perpendicular to its base and parallel to the y-axis is a square.
   (97)

7. Convert $y = 2x + 1$ to polar form.
   (107)

8. Convert the polar equation $r = 2 + 2 \cos \theta$ to rectangular form.
   (107)

9. Find the area of the region bounded by the polar curve $r = 2 + 2 \cos \theta$.
   (129)

10. Use Euler's method with 5 iterations to approximate the value of y when $x = 1.1$ given the initial condition $y = 2$ when $x = 1$ and the differential equation $\frac{dy}{dx} = 7x$.
    (133)

11. Find the slope of $r = 2 + 2 \cos \theta$ at $\theta = \dfrac{4\pi}{3}$.
    (134)

12. Find the equation of the line tangent to the graph of $r = 2 + 2 \cos \theta$ at $\theta = \dfrac{4\pi}{3}$.
    (134)

13. Approximate the slope of $r = 4 \cos (3\theta)$ at $\theta = 2$.
    (134)

14. Approximate the equation of the line tangent to the graph of $r = 4 \cos (3\theta)$ at $\theta = 2$.
    (134)

Determine whether each series in problems 15–20 converges or diverges. Justify each answer. State the value of any convergent series for which it is possible.

15. (132) $\displaystyle\sum_{n=1}^{\infty} \frac{4}{n^{3/2} + 3}$

16. (130) $\displaystyle\sum_{n=1}^{\infty} \frac{n^{3/2}}{3^n}$

17. (130) $\displaystyle\sum_{n=1}^{\infty} \frac{3^n}{n!}$

18. (128) $\displaystyle\sum_{n=1}^{\infty} \frac{\ln n}{n^2}$

19. (117) $\displaystyle\sum_{n=1}^{\infty} \frac{7 + 3^n}{4^n}$

20. (132) $\displaystyle\sum_{n=2}^{\infty} \frac{2}{n^{3/2} - 3}$

Integrate in problems 21 and 22.

21. (115) $\displaystyle\int \frac{(x + 1)^3}{x^2 + x - 2}\,dx$

22. (100) $\displaystyle\int_0^{\pi} \sec x\,dx$

23. (60) Suppose f and g are continuous functions. On the interval $[1, 3]$, let $f(x) \geq g(x)$, and on the interval $[3, 6]$, let $f(x) \leq g(x)$. Which of the following definite integrals equals the area of the region between the graphs of f and g in the interval $[1, 6]$?

A. $\displaystyle\int_1^3 \left[f(x) - g(x)\right]^2 dx + \int_3^6 \left[g(x) - f(x)\right]^2 dx$

B. $\displaystyle\int_1^3 \left[f(x) - g(x)\right] dx + \int_3^6 \left[g(x) - f(x)\right] dx$

C. $\displaystyle\int_1^3 \left[g(x) - f(x)\right] dx + \int_3^6 \left[f(x) - g(x)\right] dx$

D. $\displaystyle\int_1^6 \left[f(x) - g(x)\right] dx$

E. $\displaystyle\int_1^6 \left[g(x) - f(x)\right] dx$

24. (111) Evaluate: $\displaystyle\lim_{x \to 0} \left(e^x + x\right)^{1/x}$

25. (117) Misdirected Darius starts early in the morning at one end of a 100-meter-long field (call this the 0-meter line) and walks to the opposite end (call this the 100-meter line). When he gets to the end he does an about-face and walks halfway back to where he started (i.e., he walks to the 50-meter line). When that leg is completed he does an about-face and walks halfway back to where he started the previous trip (i.e., he walks to the 75-meter line). If this process continues indefinitely, where will Darius be? How far will he have walked?

LESSON 135 *Absolute Convergence*

In most of the tests regarding convergence and divergence of series, it has been assumed that the series in question are positive-termed series. Now we broaden the investigation of series to include some with negative terms as well, such as the ones below.

$$\sum_{n=1}^{\infty} \frac{(-1)^n}{n^2} \qquad \sum_{n=1}^{\infty} \frac{(-1)^{n+1}\sqrt{n}}{n + 3} \qquad \sum_{n=1}^{\infty} \frac{\cos n}{n^2}$$

An extremely important theorem regarding such series follows:

> If $\displaystyle\sum_{n=1}^{\infty} |a_n|$ converges, then $\displaystyle\sum_{n=1}^{\infty} a_n$ converges also.

The theorem is stated without proof, but we provide an intuitive argument for it. Note that $\sum_{n=1}^{\infty} |a_n|$ is a positive-termed series thanks to the absolute value function. Note also that $|a_n| \geq a_n$ for all $n \geq 1$. Hence, in some sense, $\sum_{n=1}^{\infty} |a_n|$ must be greater than $\sum_{n=1}^{\infty} a_n$. If $\sum_{n=1}^{\infty} |a_n|$ converges, it seems that $\sum_{n=1}^{\infty} a_n$ should also converge, because it is smaller. This is only an intuitive way of thinking about the theorem, but it encapsulates the basic idea of the theorem.

Now we state the main definition of this lesson.

> A series $\sum_{n=1}^{\infty} a_n$ is said to **converge absolutely** if $\sum_{n=1}^{\infty} |a_n|$ converges.

You should think about this definition before continuing. The statement that $\sum_{n=1}^{\infty} a_n$ converges absolutely is actually a statement about $\sum_{n=1}^{\infty} |a_n|$, not $\sum_{n=1}^{\infty} a_n$.

example 135.1   Determine whether $\displaystyle\sum_{n=1}^{\infty} \frac{(-1)^{n+1}}{n^3}$ converges or diverges.

solution   If $a_n = \frac{(-1)^{n+1}}{n^3}$, then $\sum_{n=1}^{\infty} |a_n| = \sum_{n=1}^{\infty} \left| \frac{(-1)^{n+1}}{n^3} \right| = \sum_{n=1}^{\infty} \frac{1}{n^3}$. This is a p-series with $p = 3$, which means it converges. Therefore $\sum_{n=1}^{\infty} \frac{(-1)^{n+1}}{n^3}$ converges absolutely. Moreover, from the theorem, $\sum_{n=1}^{\infty} \frac{(-1)^{n+1}}{n^3}$ must **converge.**

example 135.2   Determine the convergence or divergence of $\displaystyle\sum_{n=1}^{\infty} \frac{\cos n}{n^2}$.

solution   We consider the corresponding series $\sum_{n=1}^{\infty} \left| \frac{\cos n}{n^2} \right|$, which equals $\sum_{n=1}^{\infty} \frac{|\cos n|}{n^2}$. Since $|\cos n| \leq 1$ for all $n \geq 1$, we can apply the basic comparison test to $\sum_{n=1}^{\infty} \frac{|\cos n|}{n^2}$ by comparing it to $\sum_{n=1}^{\infty} \frac{1}{n^2}$. This p-series with $p = 2$ converges, so $\sum_{n=1}^{\infty} \frac{|\cos n|}{n^2}$ must also converge since $\frac{|\cos n|}{n^2} \leq \frac{1}{n^2}$ for all $n \geq 1$. Therefore $\sum_{n=1}^{\infty} \frac{\cos n}{n^2}$ converges absolutely, which implies that $\sum_{n=1}^{\infty} \frac{\cos n}{n^2}$ **converges.**

example 135.3   Determine the convergence or divergence of $\displaystyle\sum_{n=1}^{\infty} (-1)^{n+1} \frac{1}{n}$.

solution   We attempt to use the theorem of this lesson by considering $\sum_{n=1}^{\infty} \left| (-1)^{n+1} \frac{1}{n} \right|$. Note that $\sum_{n=1}^{\infty} \left| (-1)^{n+1} \frac{1}{n} \right| = \sum_{n=1}^{\infty} \frac{1}{n}$, which is the harmonic series. Since the harmonic series diverges, we cannot draw any conclusion about the convergence or divergence of $\sum_{n=1}^{\infty} \left| (-1)^{n+1} \frac{1}{n} \right|$ based on this approach. The theorem of this lesson states that if the series of the absolute values of the terms of a series converges, then the original series converges. It says nothing about the situation when the absolute value series diverges. **We cannot draw a conclusion about the convergence of the original series except that it does not converge absolutely.** More will be said about this series in Lesson 138.

problem set 135

1.
(46)   It was determined using radar tracking that a plane was in level flight at an altitude of 4000 feet. When the plane was 10,000 feet downrange, its angle of elevation was changing at a rate of 0.1 radians per second. What was the velocity of the plane at that time?

2.
(78)   A particle moves along the x-axis so that its velocity is given by the equation $v(t) = 24 \sin t + 7 \cos t$. Approximate the maximum velocity of the particle.

3.
(107)   Write the rectangular form of the polar equation $r^2 = \sin^2 \theta - 2 \cos^2 \theta$.

4.
(133)   Use Euler's method with 3 iterations to approximate the value of y when $x = 2.3$ given the initial condition $y = 4$ when $x = 2$ and the differential equation $\frac{dy}{dx} = x^2$.

5. Find the area of the region inside $r = 3$ and outside $r = 3 - 3 \cos \theta$.
(129)

6. Find the derivative of the vector function $\vec{f}(t) = \frac{\sin (2t)}{\cos t} \hat{i} + t \sin t \, \hat{j}$ with respect to t and state
(123) its domain.

Determine whether each series in problems 7–12 converges or diverges. Justify each answer. State the value of any convergent series for which it is possible.

7. $\displaystyle\sum_{n=1}^{\infty} \frac{3^n}{n!}$
(130)

8. $\displaystyle\sum_{n=1}^{\infty} \frac{2^n}{n^n}$
(130)

9. $\displaystyle\sum_{n=1}^{\infty} \frac{(-1)^{n+1}}{n^2}$
(135)

10. $\displaystyle\sum_{n=1}^{\infty} \frac{1}{2^n - 1}$
(132)

11. $\displaystyle\sum_{n=1}^{\infty} \frac{(-1)^{n+1}}{2n}$
(135)

12. $\displaystyle\sum_{n=1}^{\infty} \frac{3}{\left(\dfrac{1}{4}\right)^n}$
(117)

Evaluate the limits in problems 13–15.

13. $\displaystyle\lim_{x \to \infty} (x^2 - 1)e^{-x^2}$
(91)

14. $\displaystyle\lim_{x \to \infty} \left(\frac{x+1}{x}\right)^{7x}$
(111)

15. $\displaystyle\lim_{h \to 0} \left(1 + \frac{h}{7}\right)^{7/h}$
(111)

16. Find $\dfrac{d^2 y}{dx^2}$ where $y^2 = x^2 + 4$.
(124)

17. Find the equation of the line tangent to $r = 3 + 2 \sin \theta$ at $\theta = 0$.
(134)

Evaluate the integrals in problems 18–23.

18. $\displaystyle\int_2^4 \frac{x^2 + 6x - 4}{x^3 + x^2 - 2x} \, dx$
(115)

19. $\displaystyle\int_2^4 \frac{-4}{(x+1)^2(x-1)} \, dx$
(120)

20. $\displaystyle\int_0^4 \frac{-7}{(x^2 + 3)(x + 2)} \, dx$
(126)

21. $\displaystyle\int_0^1 \frac{x+2}{\sqrt{x^2 + 4}} \, dx$
(113)

22. $\displaystyle\int_0^\pi e^{2x} \sin (2x) \, dx$
(122)

23. $\displaystyle\int_0^4 \frac{1}{(x-2)^2} \, dx$
(131)

24. Approximate $2.02^3 + 2.02^2$ using differentials.
(99)

25. Whether an object is dropped, thrown horizontally, or thrown at some angle of elevation or
(54) depression, acceleration of the object during its flight will be due to gravity. Nolan can throw a ball with a velocity of 150 ft/s. If he throws the ball horizontally and his release point is 6 feet above the ground, what is the horizontal distance the ball travels before hitting the ground? (Assume level ground and no air resistance.)

LESSON 136 *Using the Chain Rule with the Fundamental Theorem of Calculus*

Lesson 98 discussed the second part of the Fundamental Theorem of Calculus.

FUNDAMENTAL THEOREM OF CALCULUS, PART 2

If f is a function that is continuous on some closed interval I and c is any number in the interval, then f has an antiderivative F on this interval that can be described as

$$F(x) = \int_c^x f(t)\, dt,\ x \in I$$

Since F is an antiderivative of f, the derivative of F equals f.

$$\frac{d}{dx}F(x) = \frac{d}{dx}\left(\int_c^x f(t)\, dt\right) = f(x)$$

We have used this theorem to differentiate definite integrals. For example,

$$\frac{d}{dx}\int_3^x \sin(t^2)\, dt = \sin(x^2) \qquad \frac{d}{dx}\int_x^7 \frac{\cos t}{t}\, dt = -\frac{d}{dx}\int_7^x \frac{\cos t}{t}\, dt$$

$$= -\frac{\cos x}{x}$$

The problems can be more difficult if limits of integration are functions of x other than the function $u(x) = x$. These more complicated situations require the chain rule.

example 136.1 Simplify: $\dfrac{d}{dx}\left(\displaystyle\int_4^{2x} \sin(t^2)\, dt\right)$

solution It is tempting to simply say that the answer is $\sin(2x)^2$, but this is incorrect. To demonstrate, let $h(u) = \int_4^u \sin(t^2)\, dt$ and $u(x) = 2x$. By the chain rule

$$\frac{d}{dx}\big(h(u(x))\big) = h'(u(x))u'(x)$$

$$= \left(\frac{d}{du}\int_4^u \sin(t^2)\, dt\right)\left(\frac{d}{dx}2x\right)$$

$$= \sin(u^2)\cdot 2$$

$$= \mathbf{2\sin(4x^2)}$$

example 136.2 Find $f'(x)$ where $f(x) = \displaystyle\int_{3x^2}^7 \ln\left(\frac{1}{t}\right)\, dt$.

solution First note that

$$f'(x) = \frac{d}{dx}\left(\int_{3x^2}^7 \ln\frac{1}{t}\, dt\right)$$

$$= -\frac{d}{dx}\left(\int_7^{3x^2} \ln\frac{1}{t}\, dt\right)$$

We let $u = 3x^2$ and use the chain rule.

$$-\frac{d}{dx}\left(\int_7^{3x^2} \ln \frac{1}{t}\, dt\right) = -\left(\frac{d}{du}\int_7^u \ln \frac{1}{t}\, dt\right) \cdot \frac{du}{dx}$$

$$= -\ln \frac{1}{u} \cdot 6x$$

$$= -6x \ln \left(\frac{1}{3x^2}\right)$$

$$= 6x \ln (3x^2)$$

example 136.3 Simplify: $\dfrac{d}{dx}\left(\displaystyle\int_{3x}^{\sin x} \cos (t^3)\, dt\right)$

solution In this case both limits of integration are functions of x. An algebraic trick bypasses this problem.

$$\int_{3x}^{\sin x} \cos (t^3)\, dt = \int_a^{\sin x} \cos (t^3)\, dt + \int_{3x}^a \cos (t^3)\, dt$$

$$= \int_a^{\sin x} \cos (t^3)\, dt - \int_a^{3x} \cos (t^3)\, dt$$

We use the chain rule on each expression. For the first expression

$$\frac{d}{dx}\left(\int_a^{\sin x} \cos (t^3)\, dt\right) = \left(\frac{d}{d\sin x}\int_a^{\sin x} \cos (t^3)\, dt\right)\left(\frac{d\sin x}{dx}\right)$$

$$= \cos (\sin^3 x) \cdot \cos x$$

For the second expression

$$\frac{d}{dx}\left(-\int_a^{3x} \cos (t^3)\, dt\right) = -\left(\frac{d}{d(3x)}\int_a^{3x} \cos (t^3)\, dt\right)\left(\frac{d(3x)}{dx}\right)$$

$$= -\cos (27x^3) \cdot 3$$

Therefore

$$\frac{d}{dx}\left(\int_{3x}^{\sin x} \cos (t^3)\, dt\right) = [\cos (\sin^3 x)](\cos x) - 3 \cos (27x^3)$$

**problem set
136**

1.
(109)
A particle moves in the xy-plane following the path defined by the function $y = \frac{x^3}{6} + \frac{1}{2x}$. Find the distance the particle moves as x varies from $x = 1$ to $x = 3$.

2.
(63)
Determine the absolute maximum and the absolute minimum values of the function $f(x) = xe^{-2x}$ on the interval $[0, 10]$.

3.
(74)
A closed cylindrical barrel whose radius is 1 meter rests on its side. The barrel is half filled with a fluid that has a weight density of 400 newtons per cubic meter. Find the force of the fluid against one circular end of the barrel.

4.
(119)
Find an equation of the line tangent to the curve defined by the parametric equations $x = e^t + 1$ and $y = e^t + e^{-t}$ at the point corresponding to $t = 0$.

5.
(119)
Describe the concavity of the curve described in problem 4 at the point corresponding to $t = 0$.

6.
(134)
Find the equation of the line tangent to the polar curve $r = 2 + 3 \sin \theta$ at $\theta = \pi$.

7.
(98)
Find $f'(x)$ where $f(x) = \displaystyle\int_2^x \frac{\sin t}{t}\, dt$.

8. Find $f'(x)$ where $f(x) = \displaystyle\int_3^{\cos x} \sin(t^2)\, dt$.
(136)

Determine whether each series in problems 9–14 converges or diverges. Justify each answer. State the value of any convergent series for which it is possible.

9. $\displaystyle\sum_{n=1}^{\infty} \frac{(-1)^{n+1}}{n^2 + 1}$ **10.** $\displaystyle\sum_{n=1}^{\infty} \frac{(-1)^{n+1}}{n!}$ **11.** $\displaystyle\sum_{n=1}^{\infty} \frac{4}{3n + 1}$
(135)   (135)   (132)

12. $\displaystyle\sum_{n=1}^{\infty} \frac{3^n}{n \cdot 2^n}$ **13.** $\displaystyle\sum_{n=1}^{\infty} \frac{1}{3^n + 3}$ **14.** $\displaystyle\sum_{n=1}^{\infty} \frac{3^n}{2^n + 3}$
(130)   (128)   (128)

15. Write an integral in one variable that could be used to find the length of the curve determined by the
(114)   parametric equations $x = 2t^2 + 3$ and $y = -2t + 3$ on the interval from $t = 2$ to $t = 6$.

16. (a) Use Euler's method with 4 iterations to approximate the value of y when $x = 1.4$ given the
(133)   initial condition $y = 3$ when $x = 1$ and the differential equation $\frac{dy}{dx} = \frac{x}{y}$.

   (b) Solve the differential equation $\frac{dy}{dx} = \frac{x}{y}$ using separation of variables, and verify the
        answer to (a).

17. Find the area of the region inside $r = 4 \sin\theta$ and outside $r = 2$.
(129)

Evaluate the integrals in problems 18–20.

18. $\displaystyle\int_2^{\infty} \frac{1}{(x + 2)^2}\, dx$ **19.** $\displaystyle\int_0^{\infty} \frac{1}{(x - 1)^3}\, dx$ **20.** $\displaystyle\int_4^6 \frac{x^2 - 3x - 1}{x^3 - 2x^2 + x}\, dx$
(125)   (125,131)   (120)

21. Use the trapezoidal rule with $n = 6$ to approximate $\displaystyle\int_3^4 x^3 \sqrt{x^2 - 4}\, dx$.
(95)

22. Use trigonometric substitution to write an integral in terms of θ that can be used to evaluate the
(113)   integral given in problem 21.

23. Use a graphing calculator to find an approximate value for the integral in problem 21. Use the
(59)   calculator to approximate the answer to problem 22. How do these two numerical solutions
        compare?

24. (a) Create a slope field for the differential equation $\dfrac{dy}{dx} = 3$.
(104)

   (b) Solve the differential equation $\dfrac{dy}{dx} = 3$.

25. Find the volume of the solid formed when the region bounded by $y = x^2 + x - 2$ and the
(94) x-axis is revolved around the line $x = 4$.

LESSON 137 *Piecewise Integration*

For most of this text we have discussed integrals of the form $\int_a^b f(x)\, dx$ where f is a **continuous** function over the interval $[a, b]$. In this lesson we investigate certain noncontinuous functions that are integrable. These are known as **piecewise continuous** functions. A piecewise continuous function g is a function whose domain can be broken into a finite number of nonoverlapping subintervals such that the function is continuous over each subinterval. Initially we require that each piece of the graph of the function is bounded so that no portion goes to $+\infty$ or $-\infty$ on any subinterval.

example 137.1   Find $\int_0^4 f(x)\ dx$ where $f(x) = \begin{cases} x^2 & \text{when } -1 \le x \le 2 \\ x+2 & \text{when } x > 2. \end{cases}$

solution   We begin by graphing the integrand. In this case the piecewise continuous function is actually continuous over the entire interval [0, 4].

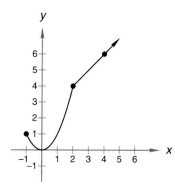

Now we split the integral.

$$\int_0^4 f(x)\ dx = \int_0^2 f(x)\ dx + \int_2^4 f(x)\ dx$$

$$= \int_0^2 x^2\ dx + \int_2^4 (x+2)\ dx$$

Technically, the second integral to the right of the equals sign is $\lim_{a \to 2^+} \int_a^4 (x+2)\ dx,$ since the second piece of the function is not defined at $x = 2$. However, this improper integral can be handled easily.

$$\int_0^4 f(x)\ dx = \int_0^2 x^2\ dx + \lim_{a \to 2^+} \int_a^4 (x+2)\ dx$$

$$= \frac{x^3}{3}\Big|_0^2 + \lim_{a \to 2^+} \left(\frac{x^2}{2} + 2x\right)\Big|_a^4$$

$$= \frac{8}{3} + \lim_{a \to 2^+} \left(8 + 8 - \frac{a^2}{2} - 2a\right)$$

$$= \frac{8}{3} + 10 = \frac{38}{3}$$

example 137.2   Evaluate: $\int_{-2}^3 \frac{|x|}{x}\ dx$

solution   We must break this integral into two integrals at $x = 0$.

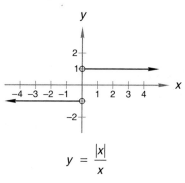

$$y = \frac{|x|}{x}$$

So we have

$$\int_{-2}^3 \frac{|x|}{x}\ dx = \int_{-2}^0 \frac{|x|}{x}\ dx + \int_0^3 \frac{|x|}{x}\ dx$$

Again, to be technically correct, $\dfrac{|x|}{x}$ is not defined when $x = 0$, so we actually have

$$\int_{-2}^{3} \frac{|x|}{x}\, dx = \lim_{b \to 0^-} \int_{-2}^{b} \frac{|x|}{x}\, dx + \lim_{a \to 0^+} \int_{a}^{3} \frac{|x|}{x}\, dx$$

These simplify easily since $\dfrac{|x|}{x} = -1$ for $-2 \le x < 0$ and $\dfrac{|x|}{x} = 1$ for $0 < x \le 3$.

$$\int_{-2}^{3} \frac{|x|}{x}\, dx = \lim_{b \to 0^-} \int_{-2}^{b} (-1)\, dx + \lim_{a \to 0^+} \int_{a}^{3} 1\, dx$$

$$= \lim_{b \to 0^-} (-x)\Big|_{-2}^{b} + \lim_{a \to 0^+} x\Big|_{a}^{3}$$

$$= (-2) + 3 = \mathbf{1}$$

problem set 137

1. *(26)* A rabbit population increases at a rate proportional to the number of rabbits present. On January 1, 1993, there were 1200 rabbits, and on January 1, 1994, there were 4800 rabbits. How many rabbits will there be on January 1, 2007?

2. *(75)* If the function f is defined for all real values of x and $f(2) = 7$, is it true that $\lim_{x \to 2} f(x) = 7$? Explain.

3. *(101)* Prove that the derivative of $\cos x$ with respect to x is $-\sin x$.

4. *(103)* Show that $\lim_{x \to 2} 3^x = 9$ by finding a δ that guarantees that 3^x is within ε of 9 when $\varepsilon = 0.01$.

5. *(137)* Evaluate $\displaystyle\int_{-4}^{4} f(x)\, dx$ where $f(x) = \begin{cases} x + 4 & \text{when } x < -2 \\ x^2 & \text{when } -2 \le x \le 1 \\ 3 & \text{when } x > 1. \end{cases}$

6. *(136)* Find $f'(x)$ where $f(x) = \displaystyle\int_{3x^2}^{\ln x} \sin\left(t^2\right)\, dt$.

7. *(136)* Find the slope of the line tangent to $f(x) = \displaystyle\int_{x}^{\cos x} \sqrt[3]{t^4 - 4}\, dt$ at $x = 2$.

Determine whether each series in problems 8–13 converges or diverges. Justify each answer. State the value of any convergent series for which it is possible.

8. *(128)* $\displaystyle\sum_{n=1}^{\infty} \frac{\sin n}{n}$

9. *(135)* $\displaystyle\sum_{n=1}^{\infty} (-1)^n \frac{n^3}{2^n}$

10. *(132)* $\displaystyle\sum_{n=1}^{\infty} \frac{2n + 7}{4n^3 - 4n^2 + 2n - 1}$

11. *(130)* $\displaystyle\sum_{n=1}^{\infty} \frac{3^n}{n!}$

12. *(130)* $\displaystyle\sum_{n=1}^{\infty} \frac{2^n + 3}{n^n}$

13. *(117)* $\displaystyle\sum_{n=1}^{\infty} \frac{2^n + 3}{3^n}$

14. *(116)* Find the sixth partial sum of the series $\displaystyle\sum_{n=3}^{\infty} \frac{4}{n^2}$.

15. *(110)* Graph the equation $r = 3 \cos (3\theta)$.

16. *(134)* Find the equation of the line tangent to the polar curve $r = 3 \cos (3\theta)$ at $\theta = \dfrac{\pi}{6}$.

17. To which of the following equations does
(104) this slope field correspond?

A. $x^2 + 3y^2 = 1$

B. $x^2 - 2y^2 = 1$

C. $y = \left(\frac{1}{2}\right)^x$

D. $y = \frac{1}{x^2}$

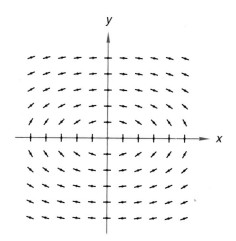

18. Find the area of one petal of the polar curve $r = 3\cos(3\theta)$.
(129)

19. Graph the equation $r = 2 - 2\sin\theta$.
(118)

20. Use Euler's method with 4 iterations to approximate the value of y when $x = 2.2$ given the
(133) initial condition $y = -2$ when $x = 2$ and the differential equation $\frac{dy}{dx} = xy^2$.

Evaluate the integrals in problems 21 and 22.

21. $\displaystyle\int_1^\infty \frac{2}{(x+2)^2}\,dx$
(125)

22. $\displaystyle\int_{-4}^2 \frac{2}{(x+2)^2}\,dx$
(131)

23. Find $\dfrac{dy}{dx}$ where $y = x e^{2x^2}$
(84)

24. Find values of a and b such that the function $f(x) = \begin{cases} ax^2 + b & \text{when } x \geq 1 \\ e^{2x} + 4 & \text{when } x < 1 \end{cases}$ is differentiable
(82) everywhere.

25. Find the coordinates of all the local maximums, local minimums, and inflection points of
(49) $y = 18x^3 + 15x^2 - 16x - 5$. Use the information to graph the function.

LESSON 138 *Conditional Convergence and Leibniz's Theorem*

In Lesson 135 we began a discussion about the convergent or divergent nature of series containing both positive and negative terms. Before that time the only type of series we had examined that had both positive and negative terms were geometric series. The five tests of convergence we have examined—comparison test, integral test, ratio test, root test, and limit comparison test—were used for series with only positive terms. The discussion in Lesson 135 helped us to determine whether or not a series containing positive and negative terms converged by making use of the absolute convergence theorem. If $\sum_{n=1}^\infty a_n$ is a series that contains both positive and negative terms and $\sum_{n=1}^\infty |a_n|$ converges, then $\sum_{n=1}^\infty a_n$ converges absolutely. However, if $\sum_{n=1}^\infty |a_n|$ diverges, we cannot yet determine whether $\sum_{n=1}^\infty a_n$ converges or diverges. We need a test that does not resort to studying $\sum_{n=1}^\infty |a_n|$ but looks at $\sum_{n=1}^\infty a_n$ directly.

Before stating this test we introduce some terminology. Any series of the form

$$\sum_{n=1}^{\infty} (-1)^{n+1} a_n = a_1 - a_2 + a_3 - a_4 + \cdots \qquad \text{or}$$

$$\sum_{n=1}^{\infty} (-1)^{n} a_n = -a_1 + a_2 - a_3 + a_4 - \cdots$$

where each of a_1, a_2, a_3, a_4, ... is positive is called an **alternating series.** When $\sum_{n=1}^{\infty} |(-1)^{n+1} a_n|$ diverges but $\sum_{n=1}^{\infty} (-1)^{n+1} a_n$ converges, the alternating series is said to **converge conditionally.** How is it that we determine when an alternating series converges if it does not converge absolutely? We use the **alternating series test,** or Leibniz's theorem, named after Gottfried Wilhelm Leibniz.

ALTERNATING SERIES TEST

The alternating series

$$\sum_{n=1}^{\infty} (-1)^{n+1} a_n$$

converges if the following are true:

1. $a_n \geq a_{n+1}$ for every n 2. $\lim_{n \to \infty} a_n = 0$

---

example 138.1   Determine whether $\displaystyle\sum_{n=1}^{\infty} (-1)^{n+1} \frac{1}{n}$ converges absolutely, converges conditionally, or diverges.

solution   This example appeared in Lesson 135. We could not determine the convergence of this alternating series, because $\sum_{n=1}^{\infty} |(-1)^{n+1} \frac{1}{n}| = \sum_{n=1}^{\infty} \frac{1}{n}$, which diverges. That means $\sum_{n=1}^{\infty} (-1)^{n+1} \frac{1}{n}$ does **not** converge absolutely; however, it might converge conditionally or it might diverge. We apply the alternating series test to determine which is true. Here $a_n = \frac{1}{n}$.

1. To use this test, we must show that $a_n > a_{n+1}$ for every n. Since $n < n + 1$, we know $\frac{1}{n} > \frac{1}{n+1}$. So the first condition is satisfied.

2. It is obvious that $\lim_{n \to \infty} a_n = \lim_{n \to \infty} \frac{1}{n} = 0$, which satisfies the second condition.

Since both conditions are satisfied, $\sum_{n=1}^{\infty} (-1)^{n+1} \frac{1}{n}$ converges. From our earlier comments, we say it **converges conditionally.**

example 138.2   Determine whether $\displaystyle\sum_{n=1}^{\infty} (-1)^{n-1} n^{1/3}$ converges absolutely, converges conditionally, or diverges.

solution   The second condition of the alternating series test is not satisfied by this series.

$$\lim_{n \to \infty} a_n = \lim_{n \to \infty} n^{1/3} = +\infty$$

No conclusion can be made about this series using the alternating series test; however, the divergence theorem guarantees that the series **diverges** since its terms do not tend to zero.

example 138.3   Determine whether $\displaystyle\sum_{n=1}^{\infty} \frac{(-1)^n}{\sqrt{n}}$ converges absolutely, converges conditionally, or diverges.

solution   This series is not absolutely convergent, because

$$\sum_{n=1}^{\infty} \left| \frac{(-1)^n}{\sqrt{n}} \right| = \sum_{n=1}^{\infty} \frac{1}{\sqrt{n}}$$

is a *p*-series with $p = 0.5 < 1$. Therefore the alternating series in question either diverges or converges conditionally. We determine which using the alternating series test.

1. We know $\sqrt{n} < \sqrt{n + 1}$ because the square root function is an increasing function. Thus $\frac{1}{\sqrt{n}} > \frac{1}{\sqrt{n+1}}$, which means $a_n > a_{n+1}$ for all n.

2. $\lim\limits_{n \to \infty} \dfrac{1}{\sqrt{n}} = 0$

Therefore $\sum\limits_{n=1}^{\infty} \dfrac{(-1)^n}{\sqrt{n}}$ **converges conditionally.**

**problem set
138**

1. (117) (a) Prove that the series $\sum\limits_{n=1}^{\infty} (-1)^{n+1} \dfrac{1}{2^n}$ converges.

(b) Find the value of the series.

(c) How does S_4 compare to the sum?

(d) How does S_4 compare to a_5?

2. (46) A spherical balloon is being inflated with gas at a rate of 110 cubic feet per minute. At the instant when the radius of the balloon is 4 feet, what is the rate of change of the radius of the balloon?

3. (95) MagicLand Carnival has a roller coaster with one section that has a profile similar to the diagram at the right. LandPlus, a local real estate company, would like to drape the side of the roller coaster with canvas and paint an advertisement on it. The MagicLand roller coaster operator provides the measurements (in feet) in the following table to the advertising agent of LandPlus. Approximate the amount of canvas required to cover the whole side.

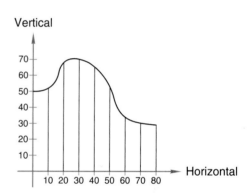

Horizontal	0	10	20	30	40	50	60	70	80
Vertical	50	52	68	70	65	53	34	30	28

4. (104) Create a slope field for the differential equation $\dfrac{dy}{dx} = \dfrac{2x}{3y}$.

5. (129) Find the area of one petal of $r = 3 \cos (2\theta)$.

6. (133) (a) Use Euler's method with 4 iterations to approximate the value of y when $x = 1$ given the initial condition $y = 0$ when $x = 0$ and the differential equation $\frac{dy}{dx} = x$.

(b) Use Euler's method with 8 iterations to approximate the value of y when $x = 1$ given the initial condition $y = 0$ when $x = 0$ and the differential equation $\frac{dy}{dx} = x$.

(c) Solve the differential equation $\frac{dy}{dx} = x$ and compare the exact value of y when $x = 1$ with the approximations from (a) and (b).

7. (134) Find the equation of the line tangent to $r = 3 \cos (2\theta)$ at the point corresponding to $\theta = 2.5$.

8. (136) Find $f'(x)$ where $f(x) = \displaystyle\int_{2}^{3x^4} e^{t^2} \, dt$.

9. (137) Evaluate $\displaystyle\int_{-1}^{1} f(x) \, dx$ where $f(x) = \begin{cases} x & \text{when } x \leq 0 \\ \sin x & \text{when } x > 0. \end{cases}$

680

Determine whether each series in problems 10–15 converges absolutely, converges conditionally, or diverges. Justify each answer. State the value of any convergent series for which it is possible.

10.
(138)
$\displaystyle\sum_{n=1}^{\infty} (-1)^{n+1}\frac{1}{n}$

11.
(132)
$\displaystyle\sum_{n=1}^{\infty} \frac{1}{3n^2 - 4n + 5}$

12.
(138)
$\displaystyle\sum_{n=1}^{\infty} (-1)^{n+1}\frac{2^n}{n^3 + 2}$

13.
(130)
$\displaystyle\sum_{n=1}^{\infty} \frac{3^n}{n^2 \cdot 2^n}$

14.
(132)
$\displaystyle\sum_{n=1}^{\infty} \frac{1}{\sqrt[3]{3n + 2}}$

15.
(138)
$\displaystyle\sum_{n=2}^{\infty} (-1)^n \frac{2}{5^n}$

Integrate in problems 16–19.

16.
(113)
$\displaystyle\int \sec^3 x \, dx$

17.
(113)
$\displaystyle\int \frac{x^2}{x^2 + 1} \, dx$

18.
(131)
$\displaystyle\int_0^4 \frac{1}{x^2 - 4} \, dx$

19.
(131)
$\displaystyle\int_0^1 \frac{x + 1}{x^2 + 1} \, dx$

20. Prove that the derivative of $\ln x$ with respect to x is $\dfrac{1}{x}$.
(102)

21. In an epsilon-delta proof of $\lim\limits_{x \to 2} (5x + 3) = 13$, which of the following choices of δ is the
(103) largest that could be used successfully with an arbitrary value of ε?

   A. $\delta = 5\varepsilon$ B. $\delta = \varepsilon$ C. $\delta = \dfrac{\varepsilon}{4}$ D. $\delta = \dfrac{\varepsilon}{6}$ E. $\delta = \dfrac{\varepsilon}{8}$

22. Find $\dfrac{d^2 y}{dx^2}$ where $x^2 - y^2 = 10$.
(124)

23. Suppose f is a continuous function for all real values of x, a is a constant, and F is an
(136) antiderivative of f. Which of the following statements must be true?

   A. $F(x) = \displaystyle\int_a^x f(t) \, dt$

   B. $F'(x) = \displaystyle\int_a^x f(t) \, dt$

   C. $F(x) = \dfrac{d}{dx}\displaystyle\int_a^x f(t) \, dt$

   D. $F(x)$ and $\displaystyle\int_a^x f(t) \, dt$ differ by a constant.

24. Find the Maclaurin series for $y = \sin x$. Write the series using summation notation.
(55)

25. Find the Maclaurin series for $y = \dfrac{1}{1 + x}$. Write the series in summation notation.
(55)

LESSON 139 *Alternating Series Approximation Theorem*

In the previous lesson we studied the convergence of alternating series and discussed Leibniz's theorem (the alternating series test). As with many of the convergent series that we have studied, it is often difficult (and sometimes impossible) to find the exact value of alternating series; however, approximating the value of an alternating series to any degree of accuracy is always possible.

ALTERNATING SERIES APPROXIMATION THEOREM

Suppose $\sum\limits_{n=1}^{\infty} (-1)^{n+1} a_n$ satisfies the conditions of the alternating series test. Call the value of this sum S. Then the mth partial sum, S_m, approximates S with an error less than or equal to a_{m+1} in absolute value.

That is,

$$\left| \sum_{n=1}^{\infty} (-1)^{n+1} a_n - \sum_{n=1}^{m} (-1)^{n+1} a_n \right| \leq a_{m+1}$$

This theorem allows us to know the accuracy of a partial sum without knowing the actual value of the series!

example 139.1   Consider the series $\sum\limits_{n=1}^{\infty} (-1)^{n+1} \dfrac{1}{2^n}$.

(a) Does this alternating series converge or diverge?

(b) Determine S_4 and discuss the maximum error of this approximation.

(c) Determine S_7 and discuss the maximum error of this approximation.

solution   (a) This series definitely **converges.** Not only does it satisfy the alternating series test, it converges absolutely since $\sum\limits_{n=1}^{\infty} \frac{1}{2^n}$ is a convergent geometric series.

(b) S_4 is the sum of the first four terms:

$$S_4 = \frac{1}{2^1} - \frac{1}{2^2} + \frac{1}{2^3} - \frac{1}{2^4} = \frac{5}{16} = \mathbf{0.3125}$$

According to the alternating series approximation theorem, this approximation of 0.3125 is within $a_5 = \frac{1}{2^5} = 0.03125$ of the actual value of the infinite series.

$$S_4 - a_5 \leq S \leq S_4 + a_5$$
$$0.3125 - 0.03125 \leq S \leq 0.3125 + 0.03125$$
$$\mathbf{0.28125 \leq S \leq 0.34375}$$

We can actually determine the exact sum of $\sum\limits_{n=1}^{\infty} (-1)^{n+1} \frac{1}{2^n}$, since it is a geometric series.

$$\sum_{n=1}^{\infty} (-1)^{n+1} \frac{1}{2^n} = \sum_{n=1}^{\infty} (-1) \left(-\frac{1}{2} \right)^n = \frac{1}{2} - \frac{1}{4} + \frac{1}{8} - \frac{1}{16} + \cdots$$

Here $a = \dfrac{1}{2}$ and $r = -\dfrac{1}{2}$. We apply the formula for the sum of a geometric series to get

$$S = \frac{a}{1-r} = \frac{\dfrac{1}{2}}{1 + \dfrac{1}{2}} = \frac{\dfrac{1}{2}}{\dfrac{3}{2}} = \frac{1}{3} = 0.333\ldots$$

Note that this falls within the range given above.

$$0.28125 \leq S \leq 0.34375$$

(c) By finding a partial sum with more terms, we get a better approximation of the actual sum.

$$S_7 = \frac{1}{2} - \frac{1}{4} + \frac{1}{8} - \frac{1}{16} + \frac{1}{32} - \frac{1}{64} + \frac{1}{128} = \frac{43}{128} = \textbf{0.3359375}$$

From the alternating series approximation theorem, we know that S is within $\pm a_8$ of S_7, where $a_8 = \frac{1}{2^8} = 0.00390625$.

$$S_7 - a_8 \leq S \leq S_7 + a_8$$
$$0.3359375 - 0.00390625 \leq S \leq 0.3359375 + 0.00390625$$
$$\textbf{0.33203125} \leq S \leq \textbf{0.33984375}$$

Because we know that $S = \frac{1}{3}$, we see that these bounds for S are also valid. Most important, we note that these bounds on S were determined **without knowing** the actual value of S.

example 139.2   It can be proven that $\sum\limits_{n=0}^{\infty} \frac{(-1)^n}{(2n+1)!} = \sin 1$. (We will develop this in a later lesson.) Use S_3 to approximate the value of $\sin 1$ and discuss the error in this approximation.

solution   First we find S_3.

$$S_3 = \frac{1}{1!} - \frac{1}{3!} + \frac{1}{5!} = 1 - \frac{1}{6} + \frac{1}{120} = 0.841\overline{6}$$

Because $\sum\limits_{n=0}^{\infty} \frac{(-1)^n}{(2n+1)!}$ satisfies the conditions of the alternating series test, the alternating series approximation theorem tells us that S_3 is at most a_4 from the exact value of $\sin 1$. (Note that $a_4 = \frac{1}{7!}$.) So

$$|\sin 1 - 0.841\overline{6}| \leq 0.000198412698412\ldots$$

The approximation of 0.8416 for sin 1 is accurate to at least three decimal places. Indeed the calculator states that $\sin 1 = 0.8414709848$. (Have you ever pondered how the calculator determines $\sin 1$?)

example 139.3   Using the fact that

$$\sin 1 = \sum_{n=0}^{\infty} \frac{(-1)^n}{(2n+1)!}$$

determine the partial sum S_m with the least terms required so that accuracy within 10^{-6} is guaranteed.

solution   Note the values of the first few terms in the alternating series:

$$a_0 = \left|\frac{1}{1!}\right| = 1$$

$$a_1 = \left|\frac{-1}{3!}\right| = 0.16$$

$$a_2 = \left|\frac{1}{5!}\right| = 0.0083$$

$$a_3 = \left|\frac{-1}{7!}\right| = 1.98 \times 10^{-4}$$

$$a_4 = \left|\frac{1}{9!}\right| = 2.76 \times 10^{-6}$$

$$a_5 = \left|\frac{-1}{11!}\right| = 2.51 \times 10^{-8}$$

Since $\left|\frac{-1}{11!}\right| = 2.51 \times 10^{-8}$ is the first value less than 10^{-6}, we are guaranteed that the partial sum

$$S_5 = \frac{1}{1!} - \frac{1}{3!} + \frac{1}{5!} - \frac{1}{7!} + \frac{1}{9!}^{\dagger}$$

---

†Notice here that $S_5 = a_0 - a_1 + a_2 - a_3 + a_4$ and does not include a_5. In this case the index of the sum begins at 0 rather than 1, so a_5 is not one of the first five terms.

provides the desired accuracy, and it is the partial sum with the least number of terms that can do so. (Note that $S_5 = 0.8414710097\ldots$, which is within 10^{-6} of the actual value of sin 1.)

problem set
139

1. (a) Prove that the series $\displaystyle\sum_{n=1}^{\infty} (-1)^{n+1} \frac{1}{n^2}$ converges.
(139)

(b) Approximate the sum of this series by finding S_4.

(c) How accurate is this approximation?

2. (a) Write the Maclaurin series for cos x in summation notation. (This series converges for all
(55,139) values of x.)

(b) Use this series to approximate cos 1 to six decimal places.

3. A particle moves along the x-axis with acceleration given by $a(t) = 2t - 1$, and it is known
(78,89) that $v(2) = -4$ and $x(0) = 6$. Find the particle's average velocity and average speed from $t = 0$ to $t = 4$.

4. Find the area of the largest rectangle with its lower base on the x-axis that can be inscribed
(52) beneath $y = -x^2 + 9$.

5. Find $f'(x)$ where $f(x) = \displaystyle\int_{-\tan x}^{4} t^2 \sqrt{1 + t^2}\ dt$.
(136)

6. Evaluate $\displaystyle\int_{-2}^{2} f(x)\ dx$ where $f(x) = \begin{cases} x + 1 & \text{when } x < 0 \\ \cos(\pi x) & \text{when } x \geq 0. \end{cases}$
(137)

Determine whether each series in problems 7–12 converges absolutely, converges conditionally, or diverges. Justify each answer. State the value of any convergent series for which it is possible.

7. $\displaystyle\sum_{n=1}^{\infty} (-1)^{n+1} \frac{1}{n^{3/2}}$ **8.** $\displaystyle\sum_{n=1}^{\infty} (-1)^{n+1} \frac{2}{\sqrt{n}}$ **9.** $\displaystyle\sum_{n=1}^{\infty} \frac{n!}{n^2}$
(127,138)   (127,138)   (130)

10. $\displaystyle\sum_{n=1}^{\infty} (-1)^{n+1} \frac{2}{n + 2}$ **11.** $\displaystyle\sum_{n=1}^{\infty} \frac{1}{\sqrt{3n - 2}}$ **12.** $\displaystyle\sum_{n=1}^{\infty} \frac{n}{e^{n^2}}$
(132,138)   (128)   (128)

13. Graph $r = 2 + 2\cos\theta$ and $r = 4\cos\theta$ on the same polar coordinate plane.
(110,118)

14. Find the area of the region inside $r = 2 + 2\cos\theta$ and outside $r = 4\cos\theta$.
(129)

Evaluate the limits in problems 15 and 16.

15. $\displaystyle\lim_{x \to \infty} (1 + x)^{1/x}$ **16.** $\displaystyle\lim_{h \to \infty} \left(1 + \frac{1}{h}\right)^h$
(111)   (111)

Evaluate the integrals in problems 17 and 18.

17. $\displaystyle\int_{\pi/4}^{\pi/2} \cot x\ dx$ **18.** $\displaystyle\int_{2}^{\infty} \frac{1}{(x - 1)^3}\ dx$
(100,131)   (125)

Integrate in problems 19 and 20.

19. $\displaystyle\int \frac{2x^2 - 5x + 2}{x(x - 1)^2}\ dx$ **20.** $\displaystyle\int \frac{e^x + \cos x}{\sqrt{e^x + \sin x}}\ dx$
(120)   (66)

21. Suppose $y = \sin(xy)$. Find $\dfrac{dy}{dx}$.
(34)

LESSON *140* *Projectile Motion*

There has been much discussion regarding parametric equations in previous lessons. In particular we have used parametric equations to represent the motion of a particle in the xy-plane. In many situations parametric equations are preferable to rectangular equations in describing motion, because they not only tell us the path a particle takes but also indicate *where* the particle is at any particular time. In this lesson we use our knowledge of parametric equations to discuss projectile motion.

Suppose an object is launched into motion in the xy-plane from the point $x = 0$, $y = 0$ with an initial velocity of v_0 at an angle of elevation of θ at time $t = 0$. Assume that no forces other than gravity act on the object. It is a physical fact that the horizontal and vertical components of the object's motion are completely independent. For example, an object takes just as long to fall to the ground when dropped as it does when thrown horizontally. Therefore, it is possible to describe the motion of the object using parametric equations.

Because of the assumptions we made, it is evident that

$$\frac{d^2y}{dt^2} = -32 \quad \text{and} \quad \frac{d^2x}{dt^2} = 0$$

where both of these are measured in ft/s². (Acceleration due to gravity is approximately 32 ft/s² downward, and there is no horizontal acceleration.) We integrate these two equations to develop equations for the object's velocity.

$$\frac{dy}{dt} = -32t + C_1 \quad \text{and} \quad \frac{dx}{dt} = C_2$$

By examining the initial conditions, we can compute the value of the constants C_1 and C_2. The following vector diagram should help to make this clear.

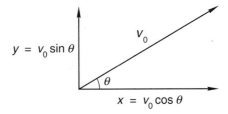

Because C_1 is the initial velocity in the y-direction and C_2 is the initial velocity in the x-direction

$$\frac{dy}{dt} = -32t + v_0 \sin \theta \quad \text{and} \quad \frac{dx}{dt} = v_0 \cos \theta$$

Integrating again gives the following equations to represent the object's position.

$$y(t) = -16t^2 + v_0 t \sin \theta + C_3 \quad \text{and} \quad x(t) = v_0 t \cos \theta + C_4$$

By evaluating both equations at $t = 0$, we find that the constants are the initial positions, which are $x = 0$ and $y = 0$ in this case. Thus the parametric equations that describe the motion of the object in the xy-plane are the following:

$$y(t) = -16t^2 + v_0 t \sin \theta \quad \text{and} \quad x(t) = v_0 t \cos \theta$$

Note that these equations are easily generalizable if the object begins at a height h_0 when $x = 0$. Then the equations are $y = -16t^2 + v_0 t \sin \theta + h_0$ and $x = v_0 t \cos \theta$. We can answer many types of questions pertaining to the motion of an object in the xy-plane using these equations.

example 140.1 An object is propelled with an initial velocity of 200 ft/s at an unknown angle. If the object is to strike a target 800 feet downrange (assuming level ground), what should the angle of elevation be (assuming no air resistance or assistance)?

solution We use the parametric equations developed earlier and substitute the given values. The object begins its flight at (0, 0) and is to land at (800, 0).

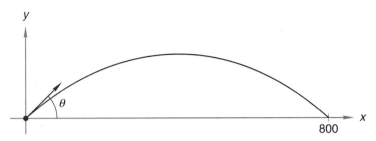

We use the fact that $v_0 = 200$ to solve for t in terms of θ.

$$x(t) = v_0 t \cos \theta$$

$$800 = 200\, t \cos \theta$$

$$t = \frac{4}{\cos \theta}$$

This simplifies the problem. When $x = 800$, $y = 0$. So

$$y = -16t^2 + v_0 t \sin \theta$$

$$0 = -16\left(\frac{4}{\cos \theta}\right)^2 + 200\left(\frac{4}{\cos \theta}\right) \sin \theta$$

$$16\left(\frac{4}{\cos \theta}\right) = 200 \sin \theta$$

$$0.32 = \sin \theta \cos \theta$$

Hence, $2 \sin \theta \cos \theta = \sin (2\theta) = 0.64$. We can now solve for θ, the angle of elevation, which is the goal of the problem. (Note that θ must be between $0°$ and $90°$.)

$$\sin (2\theta) = 0.64$$

$$2\theta \approx 39.7918° \text{ or } 140.2082°$$

$$\theta \approx \mathbf{19.8959°} \text{ or } \mathbf{70.1041°}$$

So two different trajectories are possible, one that causes the object to fly lower and reach the point faster (corresponding to $\theta \approx 19.8959°$) and another that causes the object to fly higher and reach the point in a slower fashion (corresponding to $\theta \approx 70.1041°$).

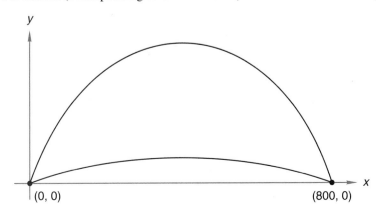

example 140.2   Find the flight time associated with each angle of elevation in example 140.1.

solution   The flight time for each is easily determined.

$$\theta \approx 19.8959°: \qquad t = \frac{4}{\cos \theta} \approx \frac{4}{\cos (19.8959°)} \approx \textbf{4.2539 seconds}$$

$$\theta \approx 70.1041°: \qquad t = \frac{4}{\cos \theta} \approx \frac{4}{\cos (70.1041°)} \approx \textbf{11.7539 seconds}$$

example 140.3   An object is propelled with an initial velocity of 200 ft/s at an unknown angle. If the object is to strike a target 2000 feet downrange (assuming level ground), what should the angle of elevation be (assuming no air resistance or assistance)?

solution   We approach this problem exactly as in example 140.1 except that we now want the object to be propelled from the point (0, 0) to (2000, 0).

$$x = v_0 t \cos \theta$$
$$2000 = 200t \cos \theta$$
$$10 = t \cos \theta$$
$$t = \frac{10}{\cos \theta}$$

Then we substitute into the parametric equation involving y.

$$y = -16t^2 + v_0 t \sin \theta$$

$$0 = -16\left(\frac{10}{\cos \theta}\right)^2 + 200\left(\frac{10}{\cos \theta}\right) \sin \theta$$

$$16\left(\frac{10}{\cos \theta}\right)^2 = 200\left(\frac{10}{\cos \theta}\right) \sin \theta$$

$$0.08\left(\frac{10}{\cos \theta}\right) = \sin \theta$$

$$0.8 = \sin \theta \cos \theta$$
$$1.6 = 2 \sin \theta \cos \theta$$
$$1.6 = \sin (2\theta)$$

At this point we have an insurmountable problem. There is no value of θ for which $\sin (2\theta) = 1.6$, because the sine function never reaches a value larger than 1. Therefore there is **no solution.** Evidently one cannot project an object with an initial velocity of 200 ft/s and expect it to travel 2000 feet downrange, no matter what angle of elevation is used. One can show using previously discussed techniques (Lesson 52) that the maximum distance is obtained when $\theta = 45°$. With an initial velocity of 200 ft/s, the object would then travel a maximum of 1250 feet!

example 140.4   Show that a projectile fired from ground zero on a level plane achieves its maximum height in exactly half of the total flight time.

solution   We begin by finding how long it takes the projectile to reach its maximum height. In other words, we find the critical values of the y-position equation.

$$y(t) = -16t^2 v_0 t \sin \theta \qquad \text{position equation}$$
$$y'(t) = -32t + v_0 \sin \theta \qquad \text{differentiated}$$
$$0 = -32t + v_0 \sin \theta \qquad \text{set derivative to 0}$$
$$32t = v_0 \sin \theta \qquad \text{added}$$
$$t = \frac{v_0 \sin \theta}{32} \qquad \text{solved}$$

This is the time (in seconds) the projectile needs to reach its maximum height (under the conditions of this problem).

Now we find the total flight time. The flight ends when the vertical position becomes zero, so we set the y-position equation equal to zero and solve.

$$y(t) = -16t^2 + v_0 t \sin \theta \qquad \text{position equation}$$

$$0 = -16t^2 + v_0 t \sin \theta \qquad \text{set equation to 0}$$

$$0 = t(-16t + v_0 \sin \theta) \qquad \text{factored}$$

$$t = 0, \frac{v_0 \sin \theta}{16} \qquad \text{solved}$$

The projectile is in flight from $t = 0$ to $t = \frac{v_0 \sin \theta}{16}$, a total of $\frac{v_0 \sin \theta}{16}$ seconds. The maximum height is achieved in exactly half this time, since the maximum height is reached in $\frac{v_0 \sin \theta}{32}$ seconds. This also shows that the rising and falling times are the same.

problem set
140

1. A cannon has a muzzle velocity of 800 feet per second. If a cannon ball is to strike a target
(140) 10,000 feet downrange, at what angle should the barrel of the cannon be placed? Assume no air resistance or assistance, and assume that the cannon and the target are in the same horizontal plane.

2. (a) Write the Maclaurin series for $\sin x$.
(55,139)
    (b) Write this series in summation notation.

    (c) Use S_3 to approximate $\sin 0.5$.

    (d) Discuss what you know about the error of this approximation.

3. How many terms of the series from problem 2 would have to be used to guarantee the accuracy
(139) of $\sin 0.5$ to eight decimal places?

4. The graph of a curve is defined by the parametric equations $x = t^2 + 7$ and $y = t^2 + 1$.
(119) Write the equation of the line tangent to the curve when $t = 2$, and describe the concavity of the curve at this point.

5. Evaluate: $\displaystyle \lim_{x \to \infty} \left(\frac{x + 1}{x} \right)^{6x}$
(111)

Determine whether each series in problems 6–10 converges absolutely, converges conditionally, or diverges. Justify each answer. State the value of any convergent series for which it is possible.

6. $\displaystyle \sum_{n=1}^{\infty} (-1)^{n+1} \frac{n + 2}{n^2}$ **7.** $\displaystyle \sum_{n=1}^{\infty} (-1)^{n+1} \frac{n + 2}{n}$ **8.** $\displaystyle \sum_{n=1}^{\infty} \frac{n!}{n^n}$
(138)   (138)   (130)

9. $\displaystyle \sum_{n=1}^{\infty} \frac{\sin n}{2^n}$ **10.** $\displaystyle \sum_{n=1}^{\infty} \frac{2n^2 + 4n}{4n + 3n^4}$
(128)   (132)

11. Find the area of the region inside both $r = 2$ and $r = 2 + 2 \cos \theta$.
(129)

12. Find the length of $y = \dfrac{x^3}{3} + \dfrac{1}{4x}$ on the interval $[1, 4]$.
(109)

Integrate in problems 13–15.

13. $\displaystyle \int \frac{x^4 + 4x^2 + 2}{x^2 + 2} \, dx$ **14.** $\displaystyle \int \frac{6}{4x^2 + 9} \, dx$ **15.** $\displaystyle \int \frac{3x^2 - x + 8}{(x + 1)(x^2 + 3)} \, dx$
(126)   (113)   (126)

16. Let $f(x) = 4x - 3$ for all real values of x and let $\varepsilon > 0$. What is the largest possible δ such
(103) that $|f(x) - 9| < \varepsilon$ whenever $|x - 3| < \delta$?

    A. 3ε B. ε C. $\dfrac{\varepsilon}{3}$ D. $\dfrac{\varepsilon}{4}$ E. $\dfrac{\varepsilon}{5}$

17. Find $h'(11)$ where $h(x)$ is the inverse of $f(x) = x^3 + 2x - 1$.
(92)

18. Let the closed interval $I = [1, 10]$ be subdivided into n equally long subintervals. Let x_i be the
(43) leftmost endpoint of the ith subinterval. Determine the value of $\lim_{n \to \infty} \frac{9}{n} \sum_{i=1}^{n} \frac{1}{x_i}$.

19. Find $f'(x)$ where $f(x) = \displaystyle\int_{-2}^{e^{x^2}} \cos(t^2)\, dt$.
(136)

20. Find the area of the region bounded by $y = x^3 + 3$ and $y = x + 3$.
(60)

21. Find the area under one arch of $y = 3\sin^2(2x)$.
(83)

LESSON 141 *Taylor Series*

Lesson 55 introduced Maclaurin polynomials, which are polynomials of the form

$$\frac{f(0)}{0!} + \frac{f'(0)}{1!}x + \frac{f''(0)}{2!}x^2 + \frac{f'''(0)}{3!}x^3 + \cdots + \frac{f^{(n)}(0)}{n!}x^n$$

Maclaurin polynomials are a special case of **Taylor polynomials** whose form (shown below) is more general.

$$\frac{f(a)}{0!} + \frac{f'(a)}{1!}(x-a) + \frac{f''(a)}{2!}(x-a)^2 + \frac{f'''(a)}{3!}(x-a)^3 + \cdots + \frac{f^{(n)}(a)}{n!}(x-a)^n$$

Notice that Maclaurin polynomials are Taylor polynomials with $a = 0$. Any function f can be approximated by a Taylor polynomial given that the x-values are close to a. Now that we have worked with series, we can allow the degree of a Taylor polynomial to go to $+\infty$.

$$\frac{f(a)}{0!} + \frac{f'(a)}{1!}(x-a) + \frac{f''(a)}{2!}(x-a)^2 + \frac{f'''(a)}{3!}(x-a)^3 + \cdots$$

This is known as a **Taylor series,** which is a special type of power series. In general a **power series** is a series of the form

$$a_0 + a_1 x + a_2 x^2 + a_3 x^3 + \cdots$$

which can be written in summation notation as $\displaystyle\sum_{n=0}^{\infty} a_n x^n$.

    One of the most interesting facts regarding Taylor series is this: **the Taylor series for a function f is equivalent to the function for all values x in the interval of convergence**[†] **of the Taylor series.**

[†] The interval of convergence of a Taylor series will be discussed in Lesson 145.

Recall that higher degree Maclaurin polynomials are better approximators of $f(x)$ than their counterparts of lower degree. This is also true of Taylor polynomials.

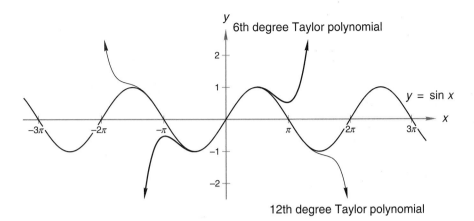

As the degree gets larger, the Taylor polynomial approximates $f(x)$ better. In essence the degree of the Taylor polynomial of $f(x)$ is allowed to go to $+\infty$ in order to mimic the function. This produces a Taylor series that truly equals $f(x)$ in its interval of convergence.

example 141.1   Find the Taylor series about $a = 1$ for $f(x) = \ln(x)$.

solution   We find derivatives of several orders for $f(x)$ and hope that a pattern appears.

n	$f^{(n)}(x)$	$f^{(n)}(1)$
0	$\ln x$	0
1	x^{-1}	1
2	$-x^{-2}$	-1
3	$2x^{-3}$	2
4	$-6x^{-4}$	-6
5	$24x^{-5}$	24

What is the pattern in the column marked $f^{(n)}(1)$? Note that $6 = 3!$ and $24 = 4!$. (Recall that $0! = 1$.) It appears that for $n \geq 1$

$$f^{(n)}(1) = (-1)^{n-1}(n-1)!$$

(Although we can prove this rigorously using a technique called mathematical induction, we elect not to do so, because we intend for students to determine Taylor coefficients by inspection.) Therefore the Taylor series is the following:

$$f(1) + \frac{f'(1)(x-1)}{1!} + \frac{f''(1)(x-1)^2}{2!} + \frac{f'''(1)(x-1)^3}{3!} + \cdots$$

$$= 0 + \frac{1(x-1)}{1!} - \frac{1!(x-1)^2}{2!} + \frac{2!(x-1)^3}{3!} - \frac{3!(x-1)^4}{4!} + \frac{4!(x-1)^5}{5!} - \cdots$$

$$= (x-1) - \frac{(x-1)^2}{2} + \frac{(x-1)^3}{3} - \frac{(x-1)^4}{4} + \frac{(x-1)^5}{5} - \cdots$$

$$= \sum_{n=1}^{\infty} \frac{(-1)^{n-1}(x-1)^n}{n}$$

example 141.2   Find the Taylor series about $a = \dfrac{\pi}{2}$ for $f(x) = \cos x$.

solution   We start by considering $f^{(n)}\left(\dfrac{\pi}{2}\right)$, where $f^{(n)}$ denotes the nth derivative of f.

n	$f^{(n)}(x)$	$f^{(n)}(\pi/2)$
0	$\cos x$	0
1	$-\sin x$	-1
2	$-\cos x$	0
3	$\sin x$	1
4	$\cos x$	0
5	$-\sin x$	-1
6	$-\cos x$	0
7	$\sin x$	1
8	$\cos x$	0

The Taylor series is as follows:

$$f\left(\frac{\pi}{2}\right) + \frac{f'\left(\frac{\pi}{2}\right)\left(x - \frac{\pi}{2}\right)}{1!} + \frac{f''\left(\frac{\pi}{2}\right)\left(x - \frac{\pi}{2}\right)^2}{2!} + \frac{f'''\left(\frac{\pi}{2}\right)\left(x - \frac{\pi}{2}\right)^3}{3!} + \cdots$$

$$= 0 - \frac{\left(x - \frac{\pi}{2}\right)}{1!} + \frac{\left(x - \frac{\pi}{2}\right)^3}{3!} - \frac{\left(x - \frac{\pi}{2}\right)^5}{5!} + \frac{\left(x - \frac{\pi}{2}\right)^7}{7!} - \cdots$$

$$= \sum_{n=1}^{\infty} \frac{(-1)^n \left(x - \frac{\pi}{2}\right)^{2n-1}}{(2n-1)!}$$

problem set 141

1. $_{(140)}$ Show that a projectile's vertical speed is zero at the highest point of its trajectory. (You may assume the flight path starts and ends in the same horizontal plane.)

2. $_{(55)}$ Find the Maclaurin series for $f(x) = x^4 + 2x^2 - 3x - 4$.

3. $_{(141)}$ Find the Taylor series about $a = 1$ for $f(x) = x^4 + 2x^2 - 3x - 4$.

4. $_{(141)}$ Find the Maclaurin series for $f(x) = \sin x$. Write the series in summation notation.

5. $_{(55)}$ Find the Taylor series about $a = \pi$ for $f(x) = \sin x$. Write the series in summation notation.

6. $_{(139)}$ Use the Maclaurin series found in problem 4 to make the S_4 approximation of sin 3. What do you know about the error of this approximation?

7. $_{(139)}$ Use the Taylor series found in problem 5 to make the S_4 approximation of sin 3. What do you know about the error of this approximation? Compare these answers to those found in problem 6. Explain the difference in the answers. In particular explain which answer is more accurate and why.

8. $_{(99)}$ A particle moves along the curve $y = e^x$. Use differentials to approximate the coordinates that give the location of the particle when $x = 0.1$.

9. Determine whether the series $\sum_{n=1}^{\infty} (-1)^{n-1} \frac{n^2}{2^n}$ converges absolutely, converges conditionally, or
(138)   diverges. Justify the answer.

10. Find the slope of the line that is tangent to the curve defined by $f(x) = \int_{x^2}^{\cos x} \frac{\sin t}{t} \, dt$ at the point
(136)   corresponding to $x = 2$.

In problems 11–14 let R be the region between $y = \tan x$ and the x-axis from $x = 0$ to $x = \dfrac{\pi}{2}$.

11. Find the area of R.
(131)

12. Find the volume of the solid formed when R is revolved around the x-axis.
(131)

13. Find the volume of the solid formed when R is revolved around the y-axis.
(131)

14. Suppose R is the base of a solid each of whose vertical cross sections perpendicular to the x-axis
(97)   is square. Find the volume of the solid.

Evaluate the definite integrals in problems 15–18.

15. $\displaystyle\int_0^5 |4 - x| \, dx$
(96)

16. $\displaystyle\int_0^3 |4 - x^2| \, dx$
(96)

17. $\displaystyle\int_0^2 \sqrt{4 - x^2} \, dx$
(113)

18. $\displaystyle\int_0^2 x\sqrt{4 - x^2} \, dx$
(66)

19. Find $\dfrac{d^2 y}{dx^2}$ where $xy + y = x^2$.
(124)

20. Integrate: $\displaystyle\int \frac{x^3 - x^2 + x - 2}{x^2(x^2 + 1)} \, dx$
(126)

21. Find the area of the region inside both $(x - 1)^2 + y^2 = 1$ and $x^2 + (y - 1)^2 = 1$.
(129)   (*Hint:* Think in terms of polar graphs.)

LESSON 142   *Velocity and Acceleration as Vector Functions*

Vector functions are often used to describe the motion of a particle in a plane. In this respect vector
functions are similar to the parametric functions studied in Lesson 140. If the vector function
$\vec{p}(t) = x(t)\hat{i} + y(t)\hat{j}$ describes the position of a particle in a plane, then the derivative of the function
describes the velocity of the particle.

$$\frac{d\vec{p}}{dt} = \vec{v}(t) = x'(t)\hat{i} + y'(t)\hat{j}$$

Moreover the derivative of $\vec{v}$ describes the acceleration of the particle.

$$\frac{d^2\vec{p}}{dt^2} = \frac{d\vec{v}}{dt} = \vec{a}(t) = x''(t)\hat{i} + y''(t)\hat{j}$$

example 142.1   The position function of a particle in the xy-plane is $\vec{p}(t) = (t + 1)\hat{i} + (t^2 + 1)\hat{j}$.

    (a) What is the velocity function of the particle?

    (b) What is the acceleration function of the particle?

    (c) What is the velocity vector at $t = 1$?

    (d) What is the acceleration vector at $t = 1$?

    (e) What is the speed of the particle at $t = 1$?

    (f) Sketch the position, velocity, and acceleration vectors at $t = 1$.

solution   (a) We noted above that the velocity function in this context is

$$\vec{v}(t) = \left[\frac{d}{dt}(t + 1)\right]\hat{i} + \left[\frac{d}{dt}(t^2 + 1)\right]\hat{j}$$

$$\vec{v}(t) = \hat{i} + (2t)\hat{j}$$

    (b) To find the acceleration function $\vec{a}(t)$, we simply differentiate the components of $\vec{v}(t)$.

$$\vec{a}(t) = \left[\frac{d}{dt}1\right]\hat{i} + \left[\frac{d}{dt}(2t)\right]\hat{j}$$

$$\vec{a}(t) = 0\hat{i} + 2\hat{j}$$

$$\vec{a}(t) = 2\hat{j}$$

    (c) The velocity vector at $t = 1$ is simply $\vec{v}(1)$.

$$\vec{v}(1) = \hat{i} + 2\hat{j}$$

    (d) The acceleration vector at $t = 1$ is given by

$$\vec{a}(1) = 2\hat{j}$$

    (For any value of t, $\vec{a}(t) = 2\hat{j}$, so acceleration is constant in this problem.)

    (e) The scalar quantity speed is simply the magnitude of velocity. Hence, at $t = 1$, the speed of the particle is

$$\sqrt{1^2 + 2^2} = \sqrt{5}$$

    (f) The position vector at $t = 1$ is $2\hat{i} + 2\hat{j}$. It is customary to place the position vector with its tail at the origin, so that its head indicates the position of the particle.

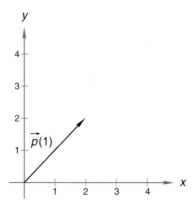

The velocity vector is $\vec{v}(1) = \hat{i} + 2\hat{j}$ and the acceleration vector is $\vec{a}(1) = 2\hat{j}$. The velocity and acceleration vectors are customarily placed with their tails at the head of the position vector.

The intent is to show the magnitude and direction of these two quantities as well as the point at which they apply.

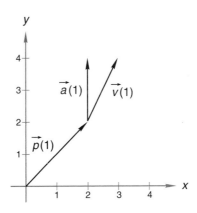

problem set 142

1. If the position of a particle moving in the xy-plane is given by $\vec{p} = (2 \sin t)\hat{i} + (3 \cos t)\hat{j}$, what are the velocity and acceleration functions of the particle?
(142)

2. For the position function described in problem 1, find the velocity vector, the acceleration vector, the speed of the particle, and the acceleration of the particle when $t = \frac{\pi}{4}$. Sketch the position, velocity, and acceleration vectors corresponding to $t = \frac{\pi}{4}$.
(142)

3. Develop the Taylor series about $a = 1$ for $f(x) = x^4 - 3x^2 - 2$.
(141)

4. Write the Taylor series about $a = 0$ for $f(x) = \cos x$ in summation notation.
(141)

5. Find the Taylor series about $a = \dfrac{\pi}{6}$ for $f(x) = \cos x$.
(141)

6. Use the result of problem 5 to find the S_2 approximation of $\cos 0.5$. What do you know about the error in this approximation?
(139)

7. Little Joe stands in the hay mound of the barn and tosses a bale of hay with an initial velocity of 15 feet per second into the corral below. If he tosses the bale at an angle of elevation of 20 degrees from a point that is 14 feet above the ground in the corral, how far from the release point will the bale travel horizontally?
(140)

8. Evaluate: $\lim\limits_{x \to \infty} \left(\dfrac{x + 1}{x} \right)^{7x}$
(111)

9. Prove: $\lim\limits_{x \to -2} (2x + 4) = 0$
(103)

10. Find $f'(x)$ where $f(x) = \displaystyle\int_{-3}^{4x^2} \dfrac{\sin (t^2)}{t^3} \, dt$.
(136)

Evaluate the integrals in problems 11–13.

11. $\displaystyle\int_0^4 [x] \, dx$
(137)

12. $\displaystyle\int_0^\infty e^{-x} \, dx$
(125)

13. $\displaystyle\int_0^\pi \tan x \, dx$
(131)

14. Find the length of the curve defined by the parametric equations $x = e^t \sin t$ and $y = e^t \cos t$ from $t = 0$ to $t = \pi$.
(114)

Integrate in problems 15–17.

15. $\displaystyle\int \dfrac{x^3}{\sqrt{x^2 + 4}} \, dx$
(113)

16. $\displaystyle\int \dfrac{1}{x^3 + x} \, dx$
(120)

17. $\displaystyle\int 3x^2 \cos (4x) \, dx$
(122)

Determine whether each series in problems 18–20 converges absolutely, converges conditionally, or diverges. Justify each answer. State the value of any convergent series for which it is possible.

18. $\displaystyle\sum_{n=1}^{\infty} \frac{3^n + 1}{n!}$
(130)

19. $\displaystyle\sum_{n=1}^{\infty} (-1)^n \frac{3}{4n + 2}$
(138)

20. $\displaystyle\sum_{n=1}^{\infty} \frac{n^{2/3}}{n^{6/7} + 3}$
(132)

21. Find the area of the region bounded by $y = 2x$, $y = \cos x$, and the y-axis.
(60)

22. Approximate $\displaystyle\int_0^2 \sqrt{x^2 + 1}\ dx$ using the trapezoidal rule with $n = 4$. Compare this with an
(95) answer obtained using a graphing calculator.

LESSON 143 *Binomial Series*

One of the special Taylor series that is often encountered in calculus is called the binomial series. The **binomial series** is the Maclaurin series for the function $f(x) = (1 + x)^b$. As noted in Lesson 22, this binomial expansion is finite if b is an integer. In fact it has exactly $b + 1$ terms. However, if b is not an integer, then the expansion is a power series with infinitely many terms. In order to develop this series, we calculate several derivatives of $f(x) = (1 + x)^b$ in hopes of finding a pattern.

n	$f^{(n)}(x)$	$f^{(n)}(0)$
0	$(1 + x)^b$	1
1	$b(1 + x)^{b-1}$	b
2	$b(b - 1)(1 + x)^{b-2}$	$b(b - 1)$
3	$b(b - 1)(b - 2)(1 + x)^{b-3}$	$b(b - 1)(b - 2)$
$\vdots$	$\vdots$	$\vdots$
n	$b(b - 1)(b - 2)\cdots[b - (n - 1)](1 + x)^{b-n}$	$b(b - 1)(b - 2)\cdots[b - (n - 1)]$

So we see that the binomial expansion looks like the following.

$$f(x) = (1 + x)^b = f(0) + \frac{f'(0)}{1!}x + \frac{f''(0)}{2!}x^2 + \frac{f'''(0)}{3!}x^3 + \cdots$$

$$= 1 + bx + \frac{b(b - 1)}{2!}x^2 + \frac{b(b - 1)(b - 2)}{3!}x^3 + \cdots$$

$$+ \frac{b(b - 1)(b - 2) \cdots [b - (n - 1)]}{n!}x^n + \cdots$$

This binomial series can be used to closely approximate nth roots of values near 1.

example 143.1 Use the binomial series to approximate $\sqrt{1.125}$ with an error of less than 0.001.

solution We can write $\sqrt{1.125}$ in an unusual way as

$$(1 + 0.125)^{1/2}$$

This looks like $(1 + x)^b$ with $x = 0.125$ and $b = \frac{1}{2}$. Thus we can use the binomial series expansion with these values of x and b to obtain the approximation.

$$(1.125)^{1/2} = 1 + \frac{1}{2}(0.125) + \frac{\frac{1}{2}\left(-\frac{1}{2}\right)}{2!}(0.125)^2 + \frac{\frac{1}{2}\left(-\frac{1}{2}\right)\left(-\frac{3}{2}\right)}{3!}(0.125)^3 + \cdots$$

$$= 1 + \frac{1}{16} - \frac{1}{512} + \frac{1}{8192} - \cdots$$

Ignoring the first term, we have an alternating series. We need to determine the first value in this alternating series less than 0.001 (in absolute value) and then sum the terms preceding it. Since $\frac{1}{8192}$ is the first such value, the following approximation is within 0.001 of the actual value.

$$(1.125)^{1/2} \approx 1 + \frac{1}{16} - \frac{1}{512} = \frac{543}{512} = \mathbf{1.0605}$$

By Liebniz's theorem this approximation for $(1.125)^{1/2}$ is actually within $\frac{1}{8192}$ of the exact value of $(1.125)^{1/2}$. According to the TI-83 $\sqrt{1.125} \approx 1.060660172$.

problem set
143

1. The light inside a garage is 9 feet above the floor and 8 feet inside the garage door. The garage
(46) door is descending in a vertical plane at a rate of 1 foot per second. The driveway that leads to the garage is flat and is also level with the floor of the garage. At what rate is the garage door's shadow approaching the garage when the door is 3 feet above the floor?

2. A rectangular plot of ground that must include 210,000 square feet is to be enclosed. The plot of
(52) ground must be divided into three equal areas by building a pair of fences that are both parallel to a pair of exterior sides. (See the diagram below.) What is the least amount of fence required to accomplish this task?

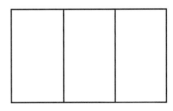

3. A cannon's muzzle velocity is 500 feet per second. If a cannonball is to strike a target
(140) 30,000 feet downrange, at what angle should the barrel of the cannon be placed? How long after firing the cannon will impact occur?

4. Find the binomial series expansion for $y = \sqrt[3]{1 + x}$.
(143)

5. Use the binomial series expansion found in problem 4 to approximate $\sqrt[3]{1.5}$ with an error less
(143) than 0.001.

6. If the position of a particle moving in the xy-plane is given by $\vec{p} = e^{2t}\hat{i} + e^{t}\hat{j}$, what are the
(142) velocity function and the acceleration function for the particle.

7. For the position function defined in problem 6, find the velocity vector, the acceleration vector,
(142) the speed of the particle, and the acceleration of the particle when $t = \ln 2$. Sketch the position, velocity, and acceleration vectors corresponding to $t = \ln 2$.

8. Find the Taylor series about $a = 0$ for $f(x) = \sin x$.
(141)

9. Find the Taylor series about $a = \dfrac{\pi}{6}$ for $f(x) = \sin x$.
(141)

10. Approximate $\sin \frac{\pi}{6}$ using the Taylor series found in problem 9. Compare the approximation to
(141) the actual value of $\sin \frac{\pi}{6}$.

Determine whether each series in problems 11–16 converges absolutely, converges conditionally, or diverges. Justify each answer. State the value of any convergent series for which it is possible.

11. $\displaystyle\sum_{n=1}^{\infty} \frac{4\sqrt{n} - 1}{n^2 + 2\sqrt{n}}$
(132)

12. $\displaystyle\sum_{n=1}^{\infty} \frac{3}{(4n + 5)^2}$
(132)

13. $\displaystyle\sum_{n=1}^{\infty} \frac{n^3}{2^n}$
(130)

14. $\displaystyle\sum_{n=2}^{\infty} \frac{4}{\sqrt[3]{n^2} - 1}$
(132)

15. $\displaystyle\sum_{n=1}^{\infty} (-1)^{n+1} \frac{1}{\sqrt{n}}$
(138)

16. $\displaystyle\sum_{n=1}^{\infty} \frac{(-1)^{n+1}}{2^n}$
(135)

17. Find the length of $x = \dfrac{y^4}{16} + \dfrac{1}{2y^2}$ from $y = -4$ to $y = -1$.
(109)

18. Find the area of the region inside $r = 1 + \sin\theta$ and outside $r = 1$.
(129)

19. A line is drawn tangent to the function defined by $f(x) = \int_{3x^2}^{\sin x} \cos(t^2)\,dt$ at the point
(136) corresponding to $x = 2$. What is the slope of this line?

20. Find $\displaystyle\int_{-b}^{b} e^{x^2}\,dx$ given that $\displaystyle\int_{0}^{b} e^{x^2}\,dx = L$.
(68)

21. What is $\displaystyle\lim_{x \to 0} f(x)$ if $-x^2 + 2 \le f(x) \le x^2 + 2$ for all real values of x?
(70)

LESSON *144* *Remainder Theorem*

While it is impressive that the Taylor series for a function f is actually equal to f, it is often an impractical fact. In most cases one cannot sum infinitely many terms to obtain an exact value of f, so we must discuss the error that arises in using truncated Taylor series to approximate values of a function. We can write

$$f(x) = f(a) + \frac{f'(a)(x - a)}{1!} + \frac{f''(a)(x - a)^2}{2!} + \cdots + \frac{f^{(n)}(a)(x - a)^n}{n!} + R_n$$

where R_n is the **error term** that arises from approximating f using the nth degree Taylor polynomial. In order to know how good an approximation is, we must be able to quantify the error term. This is not an easy task when dealing with Taylor polynomial approximations. The best result comes from Joseph-Louis Lagrange (1736–1813).

LAGRANGE'S FORM OF THE REMAINDER

$$R_n = f^{(n+1)}(c)\frac{(x - a)^{n+1}}{(n + 1)!}, \quad \text{for some number } c \text{ between } x \text{ and } a.$$

Notice the presence of c in this remainder theorem. A similar quantity appears in the error analysis for the trapezoidal rule.

When trying to analyze the error in a Taylor polynomial approximation, we choose the value for c that maximizes R_n. Only in this way can the error be truly bounded. This means that we do not find R_n exactly. Instead we determine that R_n must be less than some number. This means that if an approximation is made and the potential error is determined, then the actual error might be less than that stated.

example 144.1   Approximate e with an error less than 1×10^{-5}.

solution   The Taylor series for $f(x) = e^x$ expanded around zero is

$$e^x = 1 + x + \frac{x^2}{2!} + \frac{x^3}{3!} + \frac{x^4}{4!} + \cdots + R_n$$

If $x = 1$, then $e = 1 + 1 + \dfrac{1}{2!} + \dfrac{1}{3!} + \dfrac{1}{4!} + \cdots + R_n$.

We want the smallest value of n such that $R_n < 1 \times 10^{-5}$. Since $a = 0$ and $x = 1$ in this example, we must consider how large $f^{(n+1)}(c)$ can be on the interval $[0, 1]$. Note that $f^{(n+1)}(x) = e^x$, so $f^{(n+1)}(c) = e^c$ on the interval $[0, 1]$. This value is largest when $c = 1$, so that $f^{(n+1)}(c) \le e^1$ for all c in $[0, 1]$. Therefore

$$R_n \le \frac{e(1 - 0)^{n+1}}{(n + 1)!} = \frac{e}{(n + 1)!}$$

We desire the smallest value of n such that

$$\frac{e}{(n + 1)!} < 1 \times 10^{-5} \qquad \text{or} \qquad (n + 1)! > e \times 10^5$$

We can quickly build a table of values of $(n + 1)!$ by defining $Y_1=(X+1)!$, going to the TABLE SETUP menu, setting $\text{TblStart}=1$ and $\triangle\text{Tbl}=1$, and pressing 2nd GRAPH ^{TABLE}. We see the following after scrolling down:

X	Y1
2	6
3	24
4	120
5	720
6	5040
7	40320
8	362880

X=8

The smallest value of n such that $(n + 1)! > e \times 10^5$ is $n = 8$, since $(8 + 1)! = 9! = 362{,}880 > 3.62 \times 10^5 > e \times 10^5$. Therefore the Taylor polynomial of degree 8 suffices in this problem.

$$e \approx 1 + 1 + \frac{1}{2!} + \frac{1}{3!} + \frac{1}{4!} + \frac{1}{5!} + \frac{1}{6!} + \frac{1}{7!} + \frac{1}{8!}$$

According to the TI-83 this value is approximately 2.71827877.

example 144.2 Use a Taylor polynomial to approximate $\cos 61°$ and discuss the accuracy of the approximation that is made.

solution To approximate $\cos 61°$, which equals $\cos \left(\frac{\pi}{3} + \frac{\pi}{180}\right)$, we use the Taylor polynomial for $\cos x$ expanded around $a = \frac{\pi}{3}$.

$$\cos x = \cos (a) - [\sin (a)](x - a) - \frac{[\cos (a)](x - a)^2}{2!} + R_2$$

We stop at R_2 because this second degree polynomial is quite accurate.

Using $x = \frac{\pi}{3} + \frac{\pi}{180}$ and $a = \frac{\pi}{3}$ gives us

$$\cos 61° = \frac{1}{2} - \frac{\sqrt{3}}{2}\left[\frac{\pi}{180}\right] - \frac{\frac{1}{2}\left(\frac{\pi}{180}\right)^2}{2} + R_2$$

where

$$R_2 = \frac{(\sin c)\left(\frac{\pi}{180}\right)^3}{3!}$$

for some value of c between $\dfrac{\pi}{3}$ and $\left(\dfrac{\pi}{3} + \dfrac{\pi}{180}\right)$. Since $\sin c \le 1$ for all values of c and $\pi < 4$,

$$R_2 \le \frac{1\left(\dfrac{4}{180}\right)^3}{3!} = \frac{1}{546{,}750}$$

Therefore

$$\cos 61° \approx \frac{1}{2} - \frac{\sqrt{3}}{2}\left(\frac{\pi}{180}\right) - \frac{\dfrac{1}{2}\left(\dfrac{\pi}{180}\right)^2}{2}$$

$$\approx \mathbf{0.4848088509}$$

This approximation is guaranteed to be within $\frac{1}{546{,}750}$ of the exact value of $\cos 61°$, and that is an excellent approximation!

problem set 144

1. Find the point on the graph of $y = x^2$ closest to the point (3, 2).
(52)

2. A bow that has a release velocity of 500 feet per second shoots an arrow horizontally from a height of 5.5 feet above level ground. When and where will the arrow hit the ground?
(140)

3. The bow described in problem 3 shoots an arrow at an angle of 30° so that its release point is 7.0 feet above the ground. When and where will this arrow hit the ground? Does this answer seem reasonable? Why or why not?
(140)

4. Use a Taylor polynomial to approximate e with an error less than 10^{-5}.
(144)

5. Use a Taylor polynomial to approximate $\sin 32°$ and estimate the accuracy of this approximation.
(144)

6. Find the Maclaurin expansion of $y = (1 + x)^{2/3}$.
(55)

7. Find the Taylor series expansion about $a = 2$ for $f(x) = \dfrac{1}{x}$.
(141)

8. Use a binomial series to approximate $\sqrt[3]{1.625}$ with an error less than 0.01.
(143)

9. The function $\vec{p} = -3(2^t)\hat{i} + 4\cos(2t)\,\hat{j}$ describes the position of a particle in the xy-plane. What is the speed and the magnitude of the acceleration vector of the particle when $t = 2$?
(142)

10. Sketch the position, velocity, and acceleration vectors of the particle described in problem 9.
(142)

Determine whether each series in problems 11–14 converges absolutely, converges conditionally, or diverges. Justify each answer. State the value of any convergent series for which it is possible.

11. $\displaystyle\sum_{n=1}^{\infty} \frac{\ln(2n+1)}{n(n+2)}$
(132)

12. $\displaystyle\sum_{n=1}^{\infty} \frac{(n+3)!}{3!\,n!\,3^n}$
(130)

13. $\displaystyle\sum_{n=1}^{\infty} \frac{(-1)^{n+1}\,n}{e^n}$
(135)

14. $\displaystyle\sum_{n=1}^{\infty} \frac{(-1)^n(n+1)}{n\sqrt{n}}$
(138)

15. Use Euler's method with 3 iterations to approximate the value of y when $x = 5.3$ given the initial condition $y = -1$ when $x = 5$ and the differential equation $\frac{dy}{dx} = x^3 + y^2$.
(133)

16. Find the area of the region inside $r = 1 - \sin\theta$ and outside $r = 2\cos\theta$.
(129)

Evaluate the integrals in problems 17–19.

17. $\displaystyle\int_{2}^{\infty} \frac{dx}{(x-1)^3}$
(125)

18. $\displaystyle\int_{-2}^{0} \frac{dx}{(2x+1)^{2/3}}$
(131)

19. $\displaystyle\int \frac{dx}{(4x^2-9)^{3/2}}$
(113)

20. Find the equation of the line tangent to the polar curve $r = 2 + 3 \sin \theta$ at $\theta = \dfrac{37}{24}\pi$.
(134)

21. Prove that the derivative of $\ln x$ with respect to x is $\dfrac{1}{x}$.
(102)

22. If f is a function defined for all real numbers and L and a are real numbers, then which of the
(103) following means the same as "if ε is a positive number, no matter how small, then there exists some $\delta > 0$ such that, if $0 < |x - a| < \delta$, then $|f(x) - L| < \varepsilon$"?

A. $\displaystyle\lim_{x \to a} f(x) = 0$ B. $\displaystyle\lim_{x \to 0} f(x) = a$ C. $\displaystyle\lim_{x \to L} f(x) = a$

D. $\displaystyle\lim_{x \to a} f(x) = L$ E. $\displaystyle\lim_{x \to 0} |f(x) - L| = a$

LESSON 145 *Convergence of Power Series*

We have many tests to determine the convergence of a series whose terms are constants. In this lesson we examine the convergence of power series. (Recall that a power series is a series of the form $\sum\limits_{n=0}^{\infty} a_n x^n$.) If the variable is replaced by a constant, then we can decide whether or not the series converges using the tests that we already know. We want to determine the complete set of values of x for which a given power series converges. **To determine the values of x for which a given power series converges, we usually use the ratio test or root test.**

There are two important theorems regarding the convergence of power series.

FIRST CONVERGENCE THEOREM FOR POWER SERIES

1. If a power series converges for some nonzero number, say $x = c$, then it converges absolutely whenever $|x| < |c|$.

2. If a power series diverges for some nonzero number, say $x = d$, then it diverges whenever $|x| > |d|$.

The first convergence theorem for power series leads directly to the following theorem regarding the convergent behavior of power series.

SECOND CONVERGENCE THEOREM FOR POWER SERIES

For any power series, exactly one of the following is true.

1. The series converges only when $x = 0$.

2. The series converges absolutely for all x.

3. There is some positive number r such that the series converges absolutely whenever $|x| < r$ and diverges whenever $|x| > r$. When $|x| = r$, the series may converge or the series may diverge.

If a power series has the type of convergence described in 3, then the number r is called the **radius of convergence.** The interval over which the series converges is called the **interval of convergence.** Since this interval could be an open interval, a closed interval, or a half-open interval, it could take on any one of the following forms:

$$(-r, r), \quad [-r, r], \quad (-r, r], \quad \text{or} \quad [-r, r)$$

example 145.1 Find the interval of convergence of the power series $e^x = \sum_{n=0}^{\infty} \dfrac{x^n}{n!}$.

solution We apply the ratio test to the power series by looking at

$$\lim_{n \to \infty} \left| \frac{a_{n+1}}{a_n} \right|$$

where $a_n = \dfrac{x^n}{n!}$. Notice that

$$\lim_{n \to \infty} \left| \frac{\dfrac{x^{n+1}}{(n+1)!}}{\dfrac{x^n}{n!}} \right| = \lim_{n \to \infty} \frac{|x|}{(n+1)}$$

$$= |x| \lim_{n \to \infty} \frac{1}{n+1} \qquad \text{since } |x| \text{ does not contain } n$$

$$= 0$$

The limit is zero for all values of x.

Since the ratio test requires that

$$\lim_{n \to \infty} \frac{a_{n+1}}{a_n} < 1$$

for convergence and since this limit is 0 for all values of x, we conclude that $\sum_{n=0}^{\infty} \dfrac{x^n}{n!}$ converges for all values of x. Thus the interval of convergence is $(-\infty, \infty)$.

example 145.2 Find the interval of convergence of $\sum_{n=1}^{\infty} n!\, x^n$.

solution We apply the ratio test.

$$\lim_{n \to \infty} \left| \frac{a_{n+1}}{a_n} \right| = \lim_{n \to \infty} \left| \frac{(n+1)!\, x^{n+1}}{n!\, x^n} \right|$$

$$= \lim_{n \to \infty} (n+1)|x|$$

$$= +\infty \qquad \text{if } x \neq 0$$

So, $\lim_{n \to \infty} \left| \frac{a_{n+1}}{a_n} \right| > 1$ for all values of x except the value $x = 0$. Therefore the interval of convergence of $\sum_{n=1}^{\infty} n!x^n$ is the point $x = 0$. (Note that the power series is not exciting when $x = 0$; it is just $\sum_{n=1}^{\infty} n!0^n = 0$.)

example 145.3 Find the interval of convergence of $\sum_{n=1}^{\infty} x^n$.

solution For variety's sake we apply the root test in this problem.

$$\lim_{n \to \infty} \sqrt[n]{|a_n|} = \lim_{n \to \infty} \left(|x^n|\right)^{1/n}$$

$$= \lim_{n \to \infty} |x|$$

$$= |x|$$

According to the root test, $\sum_{n=1}^{\infty} x^n$ converges when $|x| < 1$. Since $|x| < 1$ is equivalent to the interval defined by $-1 < x < 1$, we know the interval of convergence is at least $(-1, 1)$. Before we complete this problem, we must check the endpoints for possible inclusion in the interval of convergence. We do so by plugging in the endpoints in the power series and checking these two series for convergence.

$$x = -1: \qquad \sum_{n=1}^{\infty} (-1)^n = -1 + 1 - 1 + 1 - 1 + 1 - 1 + 1 - \cdots$$

This series diverges, because the partial sums do not converge. (The sequence of partial sums is $-1, 0, -1, 0, -1, 0, \ldots$.)

$$x = 1: \qquad \sum_{n=1}^{\infty} 1^n = \sum_{n=1}^{\infty} 1 = 1 + 1 + 1 + 1 + \cdots$$

This series clearly diverges. Therefore neither $x = -1$ nor $x = 1$ can be included in the interval of convergence. The interval of convergence is **(−1, 1).** (Note that the radius of convergence here is 1.)

example 145.4 Find the interval of convergence of $\sum_{n=1}^{\infty} (-1)^{n+1} \dfrac{x^n}{n}$.

solution We apply the ratio test.

$$\lim_{n \to \infty} \left| \frac{\dfrac{x^{n+1}}{n+1}}{\dfrac{x^n}{n}} \right| = \lim_{n \to \infty} \frac{|x| n}{n+1}$$

$$= |x| \lim_{n \to \infty} \frac{n}{n+1}$$

$$= |x| \cdot 1$$

$$= |x|$$

We know from the ratio test that $\sum_{n=1}^{\infty} \dfrac{x^n}{n}$ converges when the above limit is less than 1.

$$|x| < 1 \qquad \text{or} \qquad -1 < x < 1$$

As in the previous example, we check the endpoints of this interval for possible inclusion in the interval of convergence.

$$x = 1: \qquad \sum_{n=1}^{\infty} (-1)^{n+1} \frac{1^n}{n} = \sum_{n=1}^{\infty} \frac{(-1)^{n+1}}{n}$$

This is the alternating harmonic series, which converges.

$$x = -1: \qquad \sum_{n=1}^{\infty} (-1)^{n+1} \frac{(-1)^n}{n} = \sum_{n=1}^{\infty} \frac{(-1)^{2n+1}}{n} = \sum_{n=1}^{\infty} \frac{-1}{n}$$

This is a scalar multiple of the harmonic series, which diverges. So $x = -1$ is not included in the interval of convergence, while $x = 1$ is. The interval of convergence is exactly **(−1, 1],** and the radius of convergence is 1.

problem set 145

1. Find the interval of convergence of $e^x = \sum_{n=0}^{\infty} \dfrac{x^n}{n!}$.
(145)

2. Find the interval of convergence of $\sum_{n=0}^{\infty} x^n$.
(145)

3. Use a Taylor polynomial to find the S_3 approximation of $\cos 35°$, and estimate the error in this approximation by using Lagrange's form of the remainder.
(144)

4. Use the binomial series to approximate $\sqrt[4]{1.75}$ with an error less than 0.01.
(143)

5. Find the Taylor series expansion about $x = 0$ for $f(x) = \frac{1}{1-x}$. Find the interval of
(145) convergence for the series.

6. Find a unit vector tangent to and a unit vector normal to $y = x^2 + 3x - 4$ at the point $(3, 14)$.
(108)

7. Evaluate $\int_{-2}^{3} f(x)\, dx$ where $f(x) = \begin{cases} x^2 + 1 & \text{when } x < 2 \\ 2x + 1 & \text{when } x > 2. \end{cases}$
(137)

8. Find the slope of the line tangent to $f(x) = \int_{\pi}^{\sin x} \sqrt{1 - \cos t}\, dt$ at $x = \dfrac{\pi}{2}$.
(136)

9. Prove: $\lim\limits_{x \to 3} (3 - 2x) = -3$
(103)

10. Prove that $3.231231231\ldots$ is a rational number by writing it as the ratio of two integers.
(117)

11. What is the sum of $\displaystyle\sum_{n=1}^{\infty} \frac{2^n + 3}{4^n}$?
(117)

12. Approximate $\displaystyle\int_{0}^{2} \sqrt{1 + x^4}\, dx$ using the trapezoidal rule with $n = 4$.
(95)

13. Create a slope field for the differential equation $\dfrac{dy}{dx} = x^2 + y^2$.
(104)

14. Approximate the solution of $x^3 - 3x + 4 = 0$ to nine decimal places.
(93)

Integrate in problems 15 and 16.

15. $\displaystyle\int e^{2x} \sin (3x)\, dx$
(122)

16. $\displaystyle\int \frac{-3x^2 + 2x - 2}{x^2(x - 1)}\, dx$
(120)

17. Find $\dfrac{d^2 y}{dx^2}$ where $x = 2 \sin (3t)$ and $y = 4 \cos (2t)$.
(119)

18. The base of a solid is the region between $y = e^{-x}$ and the x-axis on the interval $[0, \infty]$. If every
(97) vertical cross section of the object perpendicular to the x-axis is a square, what is the volume of
the object?

19. Confirm that $\lim\limits_{x \to 3} (2^x + x^3) = 35$ by finding a δ that guarantees that $2^x + x^3$ is within ε
(103) of 35 for $\varepsilon = 0.01$.

20. Graph: $r = 2 + 2 \sin \theta$
(118)

21. Differentiate $y = xe^{x^2} - \arcsin (x^2)$ with respect to x.
(31,44,64)

LESSON *146* *Term-by-Term Differentiation and Integration of Power Series*

Sometimes a power series representation for a function f can be found without building it from scratch. The following two theorems are remarkably helpful in this regard.

TERM-BY-TERM DIFFERENTIATION OF POWER SERIES

If the power series $f(x) = \displaystyle\sum_{n=0}^{\infty} a_n(x-a)^n$ converges on the

open interval $(a-c, a+c)$, then $\displaystyle\sum_{n=0}^{\infty} na_n(x-a)^{n-1}$ also

converges on the open interval $(a-c, a+c)$ and

$$f'(x) = \sum_{n=0}^{\infty} na_n(x-a)^{n-1}$$

TERM-BY-TERM INTEGRATION OF POWER SERIES

If the power series $f(x) = \displaystyle\sum_{n=0}^{\infty} a_n(x-a)^n$ converges on the

open interval $(a-c, a+c)$, then $\displaystyle\sum_{n=0}^{\infty} \frac{a_n}{n+1}(x-a)^{n+1}$

also converges on the open interval $(a-c, a+c)$ and

$$\int f(x)\, dx = C + \sum_{n=0}^{\infty} \frac{a_n}{n+1}(x-a)^{n+1}$$

for some constant C.

---

example 146.1 Determine the series obtained from term-by-term differentiation of the power series for $f(x) = e^x$.

solution Recall that

$$e^x = 1 + x + \frac{x^2}{2!} + \frac{x^3}{3!} + \frac{x^4}{4!} + \cdots$$

Taking the derivative of each term on the right side yields

$$0 + 1 + \frac{2x}{2!} + \frac{3x^2}{3!} + \frac{4x^3}{4!} + \cdots$$

$$= 1 + x + \frac{x^2}{2!} + \frac{x^3}{3!} + \cdots$$

Notice that this is the same expression with which we began. It should be no surprise that even in series representation

$$\frac{d}{dx}(e^x) = e^x$$

example 146.2 Find a power series representation for $g(x) = \frac{1}{(1+x)^2}$. Find the interval of convergence for the series obtained.

solution First recall the series for $f(x) = \frac{1}{1+x}$. (It is the **binomial** series with $b = -1$.)

$$\frac{1}{1+x} = 1 - x + x^2 - x^3 + x^4 - x^5 + \cdots$$

Next we note that

$$\frac{d}{dx} f(x) = \frac{d}{dx}\left(\frac{1}{1+x}\right) = -\frac{1}{(1+x)^2} = -g(x)$$

Thus $-\frac{d}{dx} f(x) = g(x)$.

$$\begin{aligned}
g(x) &= -\frac{d}{dx}(1 - x + x^2 - x^3 + x^4 - \cdots) \\
&= -(0 - 1 + 2x - 3x^2 + 4x^3 - \cdots) \\
&= 1 - 2x + 3x^2 - 4x^3 + \cdots \\
&= \sum_{n=0}^{\infty} (-1)^n (n+1) x^n
\end{aligned}$$

To determine the interval of convergence of this power series, we apply the ratio test.

$$\lim_{n \to \infty} \left| \frac{(-1)^{n+1}(n+2)x^{n+1}}{(-1)^n(n+1)x^n} \right| = \lim_{n \to \infty} \frac{(n+2)}{(n+1)} |x|$$

$$= |x|$$

Hence this power series converges for x between -1 and 1. To finish the construction of the interval of convergence, we must check both endpoints.

$$\sum_{n=0}^{\infty} (-1)^n (n+1) \qquad \text{and} \qquad \sum_{n=0}^{\infty} (n+1)$$

Both of these series diverge, so the interval of convergence is **$(-1, 1)$.**

example 146.3 Find a power series representation for $h(x) = \ln(1+x)$.

solution Before immediately going to the Taylor series representation and calculating several derivatives of $h(x)$, note that

$$\ln(1+x) = \int \frac{1}{1+x} \, dx$$

Hence, the power series for $h(x)$ can be found by integrating the power series for $\frac{1}{1+x}$ term-by-term.

$$\frac{1}{1+x} = 1 - x + x^2 - x^3 + x^4 - \cdots$$

$$\ln(1+x) = \int \frac{1}{1+x} \, dx = C + x - \frac{x^2}{2} + \frac{x^3}{3} - \frac{x^4}{4} + \frac{x^5}{5} - \cdots$$

When $x = 0$, $\ln(1+x) = \ln(1) = 0$. Therefore $C = 0$ as well. This implies that

$$\ln(1+x) = x - \frac{x^2}{2} + \frac{x^3}{3} - \frac{x^4}{4} + \frac{x^5}{5} - \cdots$$

$$= \sum_{n=1}^{\infty} (-1)^{n+1} \frac{x^n}{n}$$

As noted in the previous lesson, the interval of convergence of this power series is $(-1, 1]$.

problem set
146

1. James heaves the shot at an angle of elevation of $40°$ with an initial velocity of 45 feet per
(140) second. Because he is 6 feet tall, his release point is 7 feet above the ground. What is the
horizontal distance the shot travels before it hits the ground? (Assume level ground and no air
resistance or assistance.)

2. The function $\vec{p} = (\arcsin t)\hat{i} + (\arctan t)\hat{j}$ describes the position of a particle in the xy-plane.
(142) Sketch the position, velocity, and acceleration vector of the particle at $t = 0.5$, and determine
the speed and magnitude of the acceleration of the particle at the same time.

3. Find the Taylor polynomial for the function $y = \sin x$ expanded around $a = \dfrac{\pi}{3}$.
(141)

4. Use the Taylor polynomial found in problem 3 to find the S_3 approximation of $\sin 63°$, and
(139) estimate the error in this approximation by using the alternating series approximation theorem.

5. Use Lagrange's form of the remainder to approximate the error in the S_3 approximation made in
(144) problem 4.

6. Find the Maclaurin series for $f(x) = \dfrac{1}{1 - x}$.
(55)

7. Find the power series for $g(x) = \dfrac{-1}{(1 - x)^2}$.
(146)

8. Find the power series for $h(x) = -\ln(1 - x)$.
(146)

Find the interval of convergence for the power series in problems 9 and 10.

9. $\sin x = \displaystyle\sum_{n=1}^{\infty} (-1)^{n+1} \dfrac{x^{2n-1}}{(2n-1)!}$ **10.** $\displaystyle\sum_{n=1}^{\infty} \dfrac{x^n}{3^n}$
(145)   (145)

11. Use the binomial series to approximate $\sqrt[5]{1.325}$ with an error less than 0.001.
(143)

Determine whether each series in problems 12–15 converges or diverges. Justify each answer.

12. $\displaystyle\sum_{n=1}^{\infty} \dfrac{(-1)^n 2^n}{n!}$ **13.** $\displaystyle\sum_{n=1}^{\infty} \dfrac{\cos^2 n}{n^2}$
(135)   (128)

14. $\displaystyle\sum_{n=1}^{\infty} \dfrac{2^n + 3}{n^2 + 1}$ **15.** $\displaystyle\sum_{n=1}^{\infty} \dfrac{2^n}{n^n}$
(130)   (130)

Evaluate the integrals in problems 16 and 17.

16. $\displaystyle\int_0^4 \dfrac{1}{x^2 - 4}\, dx$ **17.** $\displaystyle\int_0^{\infty} xe^{-x}\, dx$
(131)   (125)

18. "$\displaystyle\lim_{x \to a} f(x) = L$" means that for every $\varepsilon > 0$ there exists a $\delta > 0$ such that,
(103)

     A. if $|f(x) - L| < \delta$, then $0 < |x - a| < \varepsilon$.
     B. if $0 < |x - a| < \varepsilon$, then $|f(x) - L| < \delta$.
     C. $|f(x) - L| < \varepsilon$ and $0 < |x - a| < \delta$.
     D. if $0 < |f(x) - L| < \varepsilon$, then $|x - a| < \delta$.
     E. if $0 < |x - a| < \delta$, then $|f(x) - L| < \varepsilon$.

19. Find the area of one petal of the graph of the polar equation $r = 4\sin(2\theta)$.
(129)

20. Use Euler's method with 5 iterations to approximate the value of y when $x = 5$ given the initial
(133) condition $y = 1$ when $x = 2$ and the differential equation $\frac{dy}{dx} = x^3 y^2$.

21. Use the trapezoidal rule with $n = 4$ to approximate $\displaystyle\int_0^2 \sin(x^2)\, dx$.
(95)

LESSON 147 *Substitution into Power Series*

Several power series expansions have been seen up to this point. For example,

$$\sin x = x - \frac{x^3}{3!} + \frac{x^5}{5!} - \frac{x^7}{7!} + \cdots$$

$$\cos x = 1 - \frac{x^2}{2!} + \frac{x^4}{4!} - \frac{x^6}{6!} + \cdots$$

$$\frac{1}{1 - x} = 1 + x + x^2 + x^3 + x^4 + \cdots$$

There are times when power series expansions are desired for functions similar to those above. What might the power series for the functions below be?

$$\sin(x^2) \qquad \frac{1}{1 - x^3} \qquad \frac{1}{1 + x^2} \qquad \cos(5x)$$

example 147.1 Find the power series representation for $g(x) = \sin(x^2)$.

solution We could begin by performing a Taylor series expansion, which requires the calculation of several higher order derivatives of $\sin(x^2)$.

$$g(x) = \sin(x^2)$$
$$g'(x) = 2x \cos(x^2)$$
$$g''(x) = 2x\left(-2x \sin(x^2)\right) + 2 \cos(x^2)$$

Clearly further derivatives will be difficult to compute, so we choose a different approach to finding the power series representation of $\sin(x^2)$. It is simply **substitution.** Note that

$$\sin u = u - \frac{u^3}{3!} + \frac{u^5}{5!} - \frac{u^7}{7!} + \cdots$$

If we simply think of $\sin(x^2)$ as $\sin u$ with u replaced by x^2, then we have the following:

$$\sin(x^2) = (x^2) - \frac{(x^2)^3}{3!} + \frac{(x^2)^5}{5!} - \frac{(x^2)^7}{7!} + \cdots$$

All that has occurred is the substitution of x^2 for u in every term in the equation. So the power series representation of $\sin(x^2)$ is

$$\sin(x^2) = x^2 - \frac{x^6}{3!} + \frac{x^{10}}{5!} - \frac{x^{14}}{7!} + \cdots = \sum_{n=0}^{\infty} \frac{(x^2)^{2n+1}}{(2n+1)!}$$

example 147.2 Find a power series representation for $f(x) = \dfrac{1}{1 - x^3}$.

solution This is a modification of the series

$$\frac{1}{1 - t} = 1 + t + t^2 + t^3 + t^4 + \cdots$$

We simply make the substitution $t = x^3$ to yield

$$\frac{1}{1 - x^3} = 1 + x^3 + (x^3)^2 + (x^3)^3 + (x^3)^4 + \cdots$$

$$= 1 + x^3 + x^6 + x^9 + x^{12} + \cdots$$

$$= \sum_{n=0}^{\infty} x^{3n}$$

example 147.3   Find a power series representation for $g(x) = \dfrac{1}{1 + x^2}$.

solution   It may not be obvious, but $g(x)$ is also related to

$$\frac{1}{1 - t} = 1 + t + t^2 + t^3 + t^4 + \cdots$$

If we set $-t = +x^2$ or $t = -x^2$,

$$\frac{1}{1 - (-x^2)} = \frac{1}{1 + x^2} = 1 + (-x^2) + (-x^2)^2 + (-x^2)^3 + (-x^2)^4 + \cdots$$

$$= 1 - x^2 + x^4 - x^6 + x^8 - \cdots$$

$$= \sum_{n=0}^{\infty} (-1)^n x^{2n}$$

example 147.4   Find a power series representation of $h(x) = \cos(5x)$.

solution   This problem is fairly straightforward once we see that $\cos(5x)$ is $\cos(x)$ with x replaced by $5x$.

$$\cos x = 1 - \frac{x^2}{2!} + \frac{x^4}{4!} - \frac{x^6}{6!} + \cdots$$

$$\cos(5x) = 1 - \frac{(5x)^2}{2!} + \frac{(5x)^4}{4!} - \frac{(5x)^6}{6!} + \cdots$$

$$= 1 - \frac{25x^2}{2!} + \frac{625x^4}{4!} - \frac{15{,}625x^6}{6!} + \cdots$$

$$= \sum_{n=0}^{\infty} \frac{(-1)^n (5x)^{2n}}{(2n)!}$$

problem set 147

1. Use an appropriate power series and Lagrange's form of the remainder to approximate e to eight decimal places.
(144)

2. Find the Maclaurin series for $\ln(x + 1)$, and use this series to approximate $\ln 1.5$ to four decimal places.
(146)

3. Find the Taylor series for $y = \cos x$ expanded around $\dfrac{\pi}{6}$.
(141)

Find the Maclaurin series for the functions given in problems 4–8.

4. $f(x) = \sqrt{1 + x}$
(143)

5. $g(x) = \dfrac{1}{\sqrt{1 + x}}$
(146)

6. $h(x) = \dfrac{\sqrt{(1 + x)^3}}{3}$
(146)

7. $k(x) = \sin(x^2)$
(147)

8. $l(x) = e^{x^3}$
(147)

Find the interval of convergence of the power series in problems 9 and 10.

9. $\displaystyle\sum_{n=0}^{\infty} n!\, x^n$
(145)

10. $\displaystyle\sum_{n=0}^{\infty} \dfrac{(3x)^n}{n!}$
(145)

11. Find the area of the region outside $r = 2$ and inside $r = 3 - 2\cos\theta$.
(129)

12. Sketch the position, velocity, and acceleration vectors, at $t = \pi$, for a particle that is moving in the xy-plane according to the function $\vec{p} = (\sin t)\hat{i} + (\cos t)\hat{j}$. What is the speed of the particle at this same time?
(142)

13. What is $f'(x)$ if $f(x) = \displaystyle\int_{3x^2}^{\cos x} \sqrt{1 + t^3}\, dt$?
(136)

14. Integrate: $\displaystyle\int \frac{x^3}{\sqrt{4 + x^2}}\, dx$
(113)

15. Evaluate: $\displaystyle\int_0^\pi \sec x\, dx$
(131)

16. Approximate the coordinates of the point of intersection of $y = -x^2 + 4$ and $y = x^3 - 1$ to
(2,93) nine decimal places.

17. Approximate $\displaystyle\int_0^2 e^{x^2}\, dx$ using the trapezoidal rule with $n = 4$.
(95)

18. Use the result of problem 17 to find the average value of e^{x^2} on the interval $[0, 2]$.
(89)

19. Does $\displaystyle\sum_{n=1}^{\infty} (-1)^{n+1}\left(\frac{2^n + 10}{5^n}\right)$ converge or diverge? Explain. If it converges, state its value.
(117)

20. The base of a solid is a circle with a radius of 2. Each vertical cross section perpendicular to the
(97) base and parallel to the y-axis is an equilateral triangle. Find the volume of the solid.

21. Find the area of the region enclosed by the graphs of $y = x^3$ and $y = x^2$.
(60)

LESSON 148 *Integral Approximation Using Power Series*

Throughout this textbook various techniques for approximating definite integrals have been examined: upper and lower sums, the trapezoidal rule, and even the graphing calculator. Such techniques are needed because some antiderivatives are impossible to find. These include

$$\int_0^1 \sin\left(t^2\right) dt \qquad \text{and} \qquad \int_0^2 e^{t^2}\, dt$$

We now combine the ability to determine the power series representation of many functions and the ability to integrate these power series term-by-term to develop yet another way to approximate definite integrals.

example 148.1   Approximate $\int_0^1 \sin\left(x^2\right) dx$ with an error less than 0.0001 using the power series representation of $\sin\left(x^2\right)$.

solution   The power series representation of $\sin\left(x^2\right)$ is

$$\sin\left(x^2\right) = x^2 - \frac{x^6}{3!} + \frac{x^{10}}{5!} - \frac{x^{14}}{7!} + \frac{x^{18}}{9!} - \cdots$$

Thus

$$\int_0^1 \sin\left(x^2\right) dx = \int_0^1 \left(x^2 - \frac{x^6}{3!} + \frac{x^{10}}{5!} - \frac{x^{14}}{7!} + \frac{x^{18}}{9!} - \cdots\right) dx$$

$$= \left. \frac{x^3}{3} - \frac{x^7}{7(3!)} + \frac{x^{11}}{11(5!)} - \frac{x^{15}}{15(7!)} + \frac{x^{19}}{19(9!)} - \cdots \right|_0^1$$

$$= \frac{1}{3} - \frac{1}{42} + \frac{1}{1320} - \frac{1}{75,600} + \cdots$$

This is an alternating series. Hence we can approximate the definite integral to a desired degree of accuracy and have a good idea of the error bound involved.

Since $\left|\frac{1}{1320}\right| = 0.000\overline{75} > 0.0001$ and $\left|-\frac{1}{75,600}\right| = 0.0000\overline{132275}\ldots < 0.0001$, the desired approximation is

$$\int_0^1 \sin(x^2)\,dx \approx \frac{1}{3} - \frac{1}{42} + \frac{1}{1320} = \mathbf{0.31028}$$

Note that using the trapezoidal rule with $n = 4$ subintervals approximates the value of this integral as 0.3159754. However, the error bound for the trapezoidal rule is much more complicated than the error bound for alternating series.

Finally, note that the TI-83 approximates this integral as 0.3102683 via the fnInt function.

example 148.2   Approximate $\int_0^{0.7} \sqrt{1 + x^3}\,dx$ with an error less than 0.0001.

solution   We again use a power series representation. Here we need the binomial series expansion.

$$(1 + x)^{1/2} = 1 + \frac{1}{2}x + \frac{\frac{1}{2}\left(-\frac{1}{2}\right)}{2!}x^2 + \frac{\frac{1}{2}\left(-\frac{1}{2}\right)\left(-\frac{3}{2}\right)}{3!}x^3 + \frac{\frac{1}{2}\left(-\frac{1}{2}\right)\left(-\frac{3}{2}\right)\left(-\frac{5}{2}\right)}{4!}x^4 + \cdots$$

Substituting x^3 for x and simplifying gives:

$$(1 + x^3)^{1/2} = 1 + \frac{1}{2}x^3 - \frac{1}{8}x^6 + \frac{1}{16}x^9 - \frac{5}{128}x^{12} + \cdots$$

Thus

$$\int_0^{0.7} (1 + x^3)^{1/2}\,dx = \int_0^{0.7} \left(1 + \frac{1}{2}x^3 - \frac{1}{8}x^6 + \frac{1}{16}x^9 - \frac{5}{128}x^{12} + \cdots\right) dx$$

$$= x + \frac{1}{8}x^4 - \frac{1}{56}x^7 + \frac{1}{160}x^{10} - \frac{5}{1664}x^{13} + \cdots \Big|_0^{0.7}$$

$$= 0.7 + \frac{1}{8}(0.7)^4 - \frac{1}{56}(0.7)^7 + \frac{1}{160}(0.7)^{10} - \frac{5}{1664}(0.7)^{13} + \cdots$$

$$\approx 0.7 + 0.0300125 - 0.0014706125 + 0.000176547 - 2.911328 \times 10^{-5} + \cdots$$

Because the answer is an alternating series, we obtain an approximation by stopping just before the first term that is less than 0.0001 in absolute value so that the approximation is the sum of the first four terms above.

$$\int_0^{0.7} \sqrt{1 + x^3}\,dx \approx \mathbf{0.7287184345}$$

problem set 148

1. *(140)* On a level baseball field Aaron catches a fly ball 320 feet from home plate and then makes a throw to home plate to try to throw out the runner who is trying to score from third base. If Aaron can throw 120 feet per second, at what angle of elevation should he throw the ball if he hopes to make a perfect throw? Aaron's release point is 6.5 feet above the ground, and the catcher would like to catch the ball one foot above the ground. Assume no air resistance or assistance. (*Note:* If Aaron takes time to calculate the answer, the runner will be safe.)

2. *(147)* Find the Maclaurin series for $f(x) = \dfrac{1}{1 - x}$.

3. *(147)* Find the Maclaurin series for $g(x) = \dfrac{1}{1 - x^2}$.

4. *(146)* Find the Maclaurin series for $h(x) = \dfrac{2x}{(1 - x^2)^2}$.

5. *(147)* Find the Maclaurin series for $\sqrt{1 - x^2}$.

6. Write the Maclaurin series for $\dfrac{x}{\sqrt{1-x^2}}$.
(146)

Evaluate the integrals in problems 7–9.

7. $\displaystyle\int_0^1 \sqrt{1-x^2}\,dx$ **8.** $\displaystyle\int_0^{0.5} e^{-x^2}\,dx$ **9.** $\displaystyle\int_0^1 \cos(x^2)\,dx$
(113)   *(148)*   *(148)*

10. Find the interval of convergence of the power series $\displaystyle\sum_{n=0}^{\infty} \frac{n^2}{2^n}(x+2)^n$.
(145)

Determine whether each series in problems 11–14 converges or diverges. Justify each answer. State the value of any convergent series for which it is possible.

11. $\displaystyle\sum_{n=1}^{\infty} (-1)^{n+1}\frac{3^n}{n!}$ **12.** $\displaystyle\sum_{n=1}^{\infty} \frac{\sin n + 1}{n^2}$
(130)   *(128)*

13. $\displaystyle\sum_{n=1}^{\infty} \frac{\ln n}{n^3}$ **14.** $\displaystyle\sum_{n=1}^{\infty} \frac{n^n}{3^n}$
(132)   *(130)*

15. Find the length of the parametric curve determined by $x = \frac{1}{3}(2t+3)^{3/2}$ and $y = \frac{t^2}{2} + t$ on
(114)   the interval from $t = 0$ to $t = 3$.

16. Write a vector of magnitude 7 that has the same direction as the vector $3\hat{i} - 6\hat{j}$.
(108)

17. Use Newton's method to approximate the root of $y = \sin x + \cos x - e^x + 3x^2$ between
(93) $x = 3$ and $x = 4$ to nine decimal places.

For problems 18 and 19 let R be the region bounded by $y = e^{-x}$, $x = 1$, $x = 4$, and the x-axis.

18. Find the volume of the solid formed when R is revolved around the y-axis.
(87)

19. Find the volume of the solid formed when R is revolved around the line $y = 3$.
(81)

20. Find the area of the region that is bounded by $x^2 + y^2 = 16$ and $(x-4)^2 + y^2 = 16$.
(107,129)

21. Evaluate: $\displaystyle\lim_{x \to 0} \left[4x \csc(3x)\right]$
(101)

22. Antidifferentiate: $\displaystyle\int \left(\frac{5}{1+x^2} - 3^x + \frac{1}{\sqrt{x-1}}\right) dx$
(67,73)

Index

! (factorial), 4–5
⊂ (subset of), 1
Σ (summation), 5

A

Absolute convergence, 669–670
Absolute maximums/minimums, 272
Absolute value, 54–55, 492–496
Absolute-value function, 80–81, 422, 492–496
Acceleration, 281–283
   as vector function, 691–693
   due to gravity, 283, 337
Acceleration function, 281, 337
Addition
   algebraic, 3
   of functions, 105
   of real numbers, 2
   of series, 601, 619–620
   of vectors, 558–560
   See also Sums
Additive inverse, 2
Algebra, concept review, 3–9, 475
Algebraic addition, 3
Algebraic simplification, 3–4
Alternating series approximation
   theorem, 680–683
Alternating series test, 678
Amplitude, 37–38
Angles
   central, 16
   complementary, 49–50
   double-angle identities, 76–77
   half-angle identities, 77–78
   inverse trigonometric functions,
      83–85

Angles (cont.)
   phase, 38
   radian measure of, 16–17
Antiderivatives, 173
Antidifferentiation, 173, 187, 200
   Fundamental Theorem of Calculus,
      246–248
   indefinite integration, 174
Arc length, 16
   parametric equations, 587–589
   rectangular equations, 565–568
Area
   between two curves, 313–316,
      347–349
   bounded by polar curves, 646–649
   definite integrals and, 309
   lateral surface, 445
   subintervals, 205–208, 224, 249
   under a curve
      as infinite summation,
         224–228
      computing, 203–209, 309–311
      Fundamental Theorem of
         Calculus, 246–248
      Riemann sums, 249, 295
Arithmetic
   of functions, 441–443
   of series, 619–620
   of vectors, 558–561
   See also Addition; Division;
      Multiplication; Subtraction
Associative laws, 2
Asymptotes
   horizontal, 125
   linear, 411
   of rational functions, 409–412
   vertical, 70, 126, 164

Average values of functions, 456–459
Axes of revolution, 366
   displaced, 480–484

B

Bases (logarithmic)
   base 10, 58, 505
   base a, 373, 378–379
   base e, 59, 505, 522
   change of base, 118–119
Basic comparison test, 642–643
Bifolium, 570
Binomial
   expansion, 129–130
   series, 694–695
   theorem, 129
Binomials, 125
Bounded sequences, 542–543
Boyle's Law, 21

C

Calculus
   Fundamental Theorem of (*see*
      Fundamental Theorem of
      Calculus)
   history of, 160–161
Cardioid, 604, 606
Carrying capacity, 594
Cauchy, A. L., 249
Centerlines, 37–38
Central angles, 16
Chain rule, 230–232, 264, 334,
     672–673
Changing variable of integration,
     344–345

Circles
    equation of, 131–132
    radian measure of angles, 16–17
    unit, 35–37, 163–164
Circumscribed rectangles, 224, 227
Closed interval, 93
Closed-interval continuity, 387–388
Closed interval theorem, 326
Closure laws, 2
Coefficient, changing, to exponent,
    98–99
Cofunctions, 49–51
Common logarithms, 58
Commutative laws, 2
Complementary angles, 49–50
Completing the square, 7
Composite function machines, 106
Composite functions, 106
    derivatives of, 264–267
    derivatives of products and
        quotients of, 266–267
Composition of functions, 106–109
Concavity, 258, 261
Conditional convergence, 677–679
Conditional statements, 13–15
Conic sections
    equations of, 131–132
    graphs of, 119–121, 135–136
    origin-centered, 119–121
Constant-multiple rule for derivatives,
    141–143
Constant of integration, 174
Constants
    derivatives of, 114
    integrals of, 187
Continuity, 69–70, 386–389
    at a point, 387
    closed-interval, 387–388
    limits and, 420–421
    of differentiable functions, 420–421
    of functions, 69–70, 386–389
    on an interval, 389
    open-interval, 387
Continuous functions, 69
    average value of, 456
    differentiability of, 422–424
    Fundamental Theorem of Calculus,
        502–505
    indefinite integrals, 269
    Intermediate Value Theorem, 386,
        434

Continuous functions (cont.)
    limits of, 88
    maximum-minimum value
        existence theorem, 326, 386
    Mean Value Theorem, 434–439
    Mean Value Theorem for Integrals,
        457–459
    piecewise, 674
Contrapositive, 13–14
Convergence
    absolute, 669–670
    conditional, 677–679
    intervals of, 699–701
    of improper integral, 632–633, 655
    of sequences, 539–540, 543
    of series, 617–618, 639, 669–670,
        677–679
        geometric, 600
        infinite, 597
        p-, 640
        power, 699–701
        telescoping, 602
    radius of, 699
Convergence tests
    alternating series test, 678
    basic comparison test, 642–643
    first convergence theorem for power
        series, 699
    integral test, 644
    limit comparison test, 657–659
    ratio test, 651–652
    root test, 652–653
    second convergence theorem for
        power series, 699
    See also Convergence
Convergent series, sums and
        differences of, 619–620
Converse, 14
Coordinates, 2
    polar, 550–551, 569–570
Cosecant function, 17, 20
    cofunction, 50
    derivatives of, 254–255
    derivatives of inverse of, 333
    graph of, 165–166
    integrals of powers of csc *x*, 514
    Pythagorean identity, 47
Cosine function, 17, 20
    cofunction, 50
    derivatives of, 148–149, 253
    derivatives of inverse of, 332
    double-angle identity, 76–77
    graph of, 37, 351

Cosine function (cont.)
    half-angle identity, 77
    integrals of powers of, 392–394,
        426–427
    inverse, 84, 303, 334
    period of function, 40
    Pythagorean identity, 47
    slope of, 148
    unit circles, 163–164
Cotangent function, 17, 20
    cofunction, 50
    derivatives of, 254–255
    derivatives of inverse of, 333
    graph of, 165–166
    integrals of powers of cot *x*,
        512–513
    Pythagorean identity, 47
Counting numbers, 1
Critical numbers, 191–194, 260, 272
Critical number theorem, 326–329
Critical points, 260
Curves
    arc length of, 16, 565–568, 587–589
    area bounded by (*see* Area)
    parametric, 548
    polar (*see* Polar curves)
    rose curves, 569–573, 605
    slope of, 94–95, 111, 115–116,
        664–668
    tangent function of, 94–95
    tangent line, 152–153
    See also Area
Cusps, 56

D

Decay, exponential, 149–150
Deceleration, 282
Decreasing functions, 95
Decreasing sequences, 542
Definite integrals, 247–250, 295
    area and, 309
    changing variable of integration,
        344–345
    properties of, 295–300
    substitution theorem for, 345–346
Definite integration, 187
Degree of polynomial, 176
Degree-to-radian conversion, 16–17
Delta of epsilon, 526
Denominators
    limits of, 361
    rationalizing, 4

Dependent variables in graphs, 78
Derivatives, 112–115
 absolute-value notation, 492
 alternate definition of, 232–233
 antiderivatives, 173
 chain rule, 230–232, 264, 334,
   672–673
 constant-multiple rule for, 141–143
 first, 153, 236–240, 258–259, 318
 first derivative test, 260
 higher-order, 153–154
 left-hand, 422–424
 Leibniz's notation, 161
 limits and, 158, 420, 516
 maximums, finding with, 239–240
 minimums, finding with, 239–240
 Newton's notation, 161
 notation for, 138, 161
 of a^x, 372
 of differences, 143–144
 of e^x, 146–147, 521–522
 of functions
   composite, 264–267
   implicitly defined, 182
   inverse, 470–473
   involving absolute values,
     492–496
   logarithmic, 373
 of $|f(x)|$, 373–375, 492
 of ln x, 521–522
 of ln $|x|$, 147–148
 of parametric equations, 610–611
 of quotients, 220–222, 429–430
 of sums, 143–144, 200
 of trigonometric functions
   cosine, 148–149, 252
   cotangent, 334
   inverse, 254–255, 331–334
   secant, 254
   sine, 148–149, 252, 516, 519
   tangent, 252
 of x^n, 138–140
 product rule for, 169–172
 right-hand, 422–424
 second, 153, 258–261, 318,
   611–612
 summary of rules for, 255
 symmetric, 234
 third, 153
 units for, 211–212
Difference identities, 74–75

Difference indeterminate forms,
  466–468
Differences
 derivatives of, 143–144
 limits of, 361
 of convergent series, 619–620
 of even functions, 441–443
 of functions, 105
 of odd functions, 441–443
 of vectors, 560
Differentiability
 of continuous functions, 422–424
 of vector functions, 626
Differential equations, 450, 529
 Euler's method, 660–662
 examples of, 529
 explicit solutions to, 529
 general solutions to, 451–452, 529
 graphs of solutions to, 529–530
 logistic, 593–595
 particular solutions to, 451–452,
   530
 separable, 450–454
Differentials, 161
 linear approximations using,
   508–509
 summary of rules for, 255
 use of, 508
Differentiation
 by u substitution, 196–199, 264,
   342–344
 implicit, 182–185, 628–630
 logarithmic, 429–432
 of power series, 703–704
 of relating equations, 241
 techniques of (*see* Techniques of
   differentiation)
 See also Antidifferentiation;
   Integration
Dimpled limaçons, 604
Directed length, 35–36
Discontinuities, 69–70
Discontinuous graphs, 30
Disks, 366–369, 483
Distance, 321
Distance formula, 6
Distributive law, 2
Divergence
 of improper integral, 632–633, 655
 of sequences, 540
 of series, 602, 617–618
   geometric, 600
   infinite, 597
   p-, 640

Divergence (cont.)
 tests, 642, 651
 theorem, 617–618
Division
 of functions, 105
 synthetic, 65
 See also Quotient
Domain, 25–26, 30, 32–33, 106–109
Double-angle identities, 76–77

E

e (number), 42, 522
Elimination of parameters, 545
Ellipses
 equations of, 131–132
 graphs of, 135–136
Endpoints in interval notation, 92–93
Epsilon-delta proofs, 525–528
Equations
 algebra concept review, 3–9
 differential (*see* Differential
   equations)
 explicit, 182, 302–304, 306–307
 exponential (*see* Exponential
   equations)
 functions, 25
 implicit, 182, 302–304, 306–307,
   331–333
 logarithmic, 59–60
 Newton's method for finding roots
   of, 475–478, 508
 nonlinear, 111
 of circles, 131–132
 of conic sections, 131–132
 of ellipses, 131–132
 of hyperbolas, 131–132
 of parabolas, 131–132, 272
 of tangent lines, 152–153
 parametric (*see* Parametric
   equations)
 polar, 552–555, 664
 quadratic formula, 7–8
 quadratic polynomial, 62
 rectangular, 552–553, 565–568
 relating, 241
 roots of, 62, 66–67, 475, 508
 slope of curve, 111
 trigonometric, 85–86
Equivalent statements, 13

Errors
    epsilon-delta proofs, 525–528
    error bound for trapezoidal rule,
        489, 508
    in Taylor polynomial
        approximations, 696
    Lagrange's form of the remainder,
        696–698
Euler's method, 660–662
Even functions, 48, 351–354
    arithmetic of, 441–443
    graphs of, 351
    polynomials, 352
Existence theorems
    Intermediate Value Theorem, 386,
        434
    maximum-minimum value
        existence theorem, 326, 386,
        434, 438–439
    Mean Value Theorem, 434–439
    Mean Value Theorem for Integrals,
        457–459
    Rolle's theorem, 438–439
Explicit equations, 182, 302–304,
    306–307
Explicit expressions, 269
Exponential equations
    of growth and decay, 149–150,
        593–595
    rewriting logarithmic equations as,
        59–60
    solving, 99–100
Exponential functions, 42–44, 505,
    521
Exponential indeterminate forms,
    575–577
Exponents, 4, 98–99
Extrema
    global, 272
    local, 192, 260, 272

F
Factorial, 4–5
Factoring, 4, 475
Falling-body problems, 336–340
Field properties, 2
First convergence theorem for power
    series, 699

First derivatives, 153, 318
    geometric meaning of, 258–259
    to characterize f, 236–238
    to find maximums and minimums,
        239–240
First derivative test, 260
Fluids
    fluid force, 380–384
    pumping fluids, 395–398
Fractional exponents, 4
Fractions, partial, 591–593, 614–616,
    637–638
Free-falling-body problems, 337
Functional notation, 28–29
Function integral, 278
Function machines, 26
    composite, 106
    inverse, 304
Functions, 25–26, 246–248, 502–505
    absolute-value, 80, 422, 492–496
    addition of, 105, 441–443
    average value of, 456–459
    cofunctions, 49–51
    composite, 106, 264–267
    composition of, 106–109
    continuity of, 69–70, 386–389
    continuous (*see* Continuous
        functions)
    decreasing, 95
    derivatives of, 112–115, 318 (*see
        also* Derivatives)
    differences of, 105
    division of, 105
    domains, 30, 32–33
    equations, 25
    even, 48, 351–354, 441–443
    exponential, 42–44, 505, 521
    Fundamental Theorem of Calculus
        (*see* Fundamental Theorem of
        Calculus)
    graphs, 26–30 (*see also* Graphs)
    greatest integer, 57
    increasing, 95
    inverse (*see* Inverse functions)
    limits of (*see* Limits)
    local maximum/minimum (*see*
        Local maximums/minimums)
    logarithmic, 78–81
    multiplication of, 105, 441–443
    natural exponential, 521
    natural logarithm, 505–506, 521
    odd, 48, 351–354, 441–443

Functions (cont.)
    of $-\theta$, 47–48
    one-to-one, 304–305, 470–471
    periods of, 40–41
    piecewise, 58, 422
    piecewise continuous, 674
    polynomial (*see* Polynomials)
    position, 281, 337
    products of, 105–106, 441–443
    quotients of, 105–106
    ranges, 31
    rational (*see* Rational functions)
    reciprocal, 164–167
    relative maximums/minimums, 192,
        214–215
    roots of, 64, 478
    subtraction of, 105
    sums of, 441–443
    transcendental, 285
    translations of, 122–125
    trigonometric (*see* Trigonometric
        functions)
    vector-valued, 625–626, 691–693
    velocity, 281, 337, 461–462
    zero, 441
    zeros of, 10–11, 62, 409, 477
Fundamental Theorem of Calculus
    chain rule with, 672–673
    described, 246–248, 278, 345,
        502–505
    proof of, 524–525

G
Geometric series, 600–602
Global maximums/minimums, 272
Graphing calculator, 9–11
    area computation, 311, 316
    conic sections, 119–121, 135–136
    domains of functions, 32–33
    exponential indeterminate forms,
        576
    functions, 26–28
        absolute value, 80–81
        exponential, 43–44
        increasing and decreasing,
            95–96
        partial, 638
    interval notation, 94
    L'Hôpital's Rule, 406–407
    limit of derivative of sin x, 516
    limits of a function, 90–91
    maximums and minimums,
        214–215

Graphing calculator (cont.)
   numerical integration on, 277–278, 311
   parametric equations, 546
   period of function, 41
   polar curves, 571–572, 606–608, 666–667
   roots of functions, 67, 478
   sequences, 541–542
   sinusoids, 39–40
   slopes of curves, 115–116, 666–667
   zeros of functions, 477
Graphs
   amplitude of, 37–38
   area between two curves, 313–316
   area bounded by polar curves, 646–649
   area under a curve, 203–208
   centerlines of, 37–38
   concept review, 6–9
   cusps of, 56
   dependent variables in, 78
   discontinuous, 30
   Euler's method, 660–662
   independent variable in, 78
   of conic sections, 119–121, 135–136
   of ellipses, 135–136
   of functions, 28–30
       cosecant, 165–166
       cosine, 37, 351
       cotangent, 165–166
       even, 351
       inverse, 306
       logarithmic, 78–81
       odd, 351
       one-to-one, 304–305
       polar, 570–572, 604
       rational, 125–128, 155–158, 216–218, 409–412
       reciprocal, 164–167
       sine, 35, 37, 351
       tangent, 163–164
   of origin-centered conic sections, 119–121
   of parabolas, 62–63
   of parametric equations, 545–549
   of phase angles, 38
   of polynomials, 9–11, 176, 178–180
   of quadratic polynomials, 62–63
   of rose curves, 569–573, 605
   of sequences, 541–542

Graphs (cont.)
   of solutions of differential equations, 529–530
   "sharp point," 260
   slope fields, 530–535, 660
   translations of functions, 122–125
   undefined limits, 103–104
   vertical asymptote, 70, 126, 164
Gravity
   acceleration due to, 283
   falling-body problems, 336–340
Greatest integer function, 57
Growth
   exponential, 149–150, 593–595
   logistic, 594

H

Half-angle identities, 77–78
Harmonic series, 639–640
Hooke's law, 323
Hyperbolas, 131–132
Hyperbolic spiral, 570

I

Identities (*see* Trigonometric identities)
Identity elements, 2
If and only if statements, 14–15
Iff statements, 14–15
If-then statements, 13
Images, 25
Implicit differentiation, 182–185, 628–630
Implicit equations, 182, 302–304, 306–307, 331–333
Improper integrals, 632–633, 654–655
Increasing functions, 95
Increasing sequences, 542
Indefinite integrals, 174–175, 269
Indefinite integration, 174
Indeterminate forms
   difference, 466–468
   exponential, 575–577
   L'Hôpital's Rule, 466–468, 575
   product, 466–468
Indices of series, 619
Infinite integrands, 654–656
Infinite limits of integration, 632–635
Infinite series, 597
Infinitesimals, 161
Infinite summation, area as, 224–228
Infinity, 93, 102–103
Inflection points, 258
Initial points, 556

Inscribed rectangles, 224
Integers, 1
Integrals
   approximation using power series, 708–709
   definite (*see* Definite integrals)
   function, 278
   improper, 632–633, 654–655
   indefinite, 174–175, 269
   numerical, 278
   of $\frac{1}{x}$, 201–202
   of a^x, 377–378
   of constants, 187
   of functions involving absolute values, 492–496
   of $k f(x)$, 188–189
   of logarithms, 378–379
   of powers of cot x, 512–513
   of powers of csc x, 514
   of powers of sec x, 513
   of powers of tan x, 511–512
   of sums, 200–201
   of x^n, 189–190
   Riemann, 249
   See also Integration
Integral symbol, 174
Integral test, 644
Integrands, infinite, 654–656
Integration
   by guessing, 269–270, 290–293
   by parts, 356–359, 621–622
   changing variable of, 344–345
   constant of, 174
   definite, 187
   indefinite, 174
   infinite integrands, 654–656
   infinite limits of, 632–635
   limits of, 247
   numerical, 277–278, 311, 486–489, 508
   of cosine function, 392–394, 426–427
   of power series, 703–704
   of powers of sin x and cos x
       even, 426–427
       odd, 392–394
   of sine function, 392–394, 426–427
   piecewise, 674–676
   techniques of (*see* Techniques of integration)
   using trigonometric substitution, 578–579, 581–586
   u substitution, 342–344
   See also Differentiation; Integrals

Intercepts, 62

Intermediate Value Theorem, 386, 434

Interval notation, 92–94

Intervals

    closed, 93, 326, 387–388

    continuity on, 389

    of convergence, 699–701

    open, 93, 387

    partially closed, 93

Inverse function machines, 304

Inverse functions, 304–307

    derivatives of, 255, 334, 470–473

    graphs of, 306

    one-to-one, 470–471

    trigonometric, 83–85, 255,
        303–304, 331–334

Inverses, 2, 14

Irrational numbers, 1

Irreducible quadratic factors, 176

Iteration, 661

J

Joule (unit), 321

L

Lagrange, Joseph-Louis, 696

Lagrange's form of the remainder,
    696–698

Lateral surface area of right circular
    cylinder, 445

Left-hand derivatives, 422–424

Left-hand limits, 70, 420

Left sums, 208–209

Leibniz, Gottfried Wilhelm, 160

Leibniz's notation, 161

Leibniz's theorem, 678

Lemniscates, 605–609

Length of arc (*see* Arc length)

L'Hôpital's Rule, 404–407, 466–468,
    518, 575

Limaçons, 604–605

Limit comparison test, 657–659

Limit(s), 420, 526–527

    continuity and, 420–421

    derivatives and, 158, 420, 516

    infinity as a, 102–103

    left-hand, 70, 420

    L'Hôpital's Rule, 404–407,
        466–468, 518, 575

    limit comparison test, 657–659

    of denominators, 361

Limit(s) (cont.)

    of difference, 361

    of functions, 70–72, 88–91

    of integration

        infinite, 632–635

        lower and upper, 247

    of products, 361

    of quotients, 404

    of rational functions, 466

    of sequences, 538–541

    of sine function, 365

    of $\frac{\sin x}{x}$, 516–518

    of sums, 361

    pinching theorem for, 362

    properties of, 361–364

    right-hand, 70, 420

    sandwich theorem for, 362

    squeeze theorem for, 362

    undefined, 103–104

Linear approximations using
    differentials, 508–509

Linear asymptotes, 411

Linear factors, products of, 93–94

Lines

    normal, 212–214

    slope of, 7, 111

Lituus, 570

Local extrema, 192, 260, 272

Local maximums/minimums, 192,
    194, 260, 272

    first derivative to find, 239–240

    maximization and minimization
        problems, 272–276

    on graphing calculator, 214–215

Logarithmic differentiation, 429–432

Logarithmic equations, rewriting as
    exponential equations, 59–60

Logarithmic functions, 78–81

Logarithms

    base 10, 58, 505

    base *a*, 373, 378–379

    base *e*, 59, 505, 522

    change of base, 118–119

    common, 58

    derivatives of, 147–148, 373,
        521–522

    integrals of, 378–379

    logarithmic differentiation,
        429–432

    natural, 59, 147–148, 505–506,
        521–522

Logarithms (cont.)

    of powers, 98–99

    of products and quotients, 97–98

    problems involving, 59–60

Logistic differential equations,
    593–595

Logistic growth model, 594

Lower limit of integration, 247

Lower sums, 205, 224

M

Maclaurin polynomials, 285–289, 688

Maclaurin series, 288

Mapping, 30

Maximization problems, 272–276

Maximum-minimum value existence
    theorem, 326, 386, 434, 438–439

Maximums

    absolute, 272

    first derivative to find, 239–240

    global, 272

    local (*see* Local maximums/
        minimums)

    maximization problems, 272–276

    maximum-minimum value
        existence theorem, 326, 386,
        434, 438–439

    on graphing calculator, 214–215

    relative, 192, 214–215

Mean Value Theorem, 434–439

Mean Value Theorem for Integrals,
    457–459

Mechanical work, 321–322, 395

    pumping fluids, 394–398

Midpoint sums, 208–209

Minimization problems, 272–276

Minimums

    absolute, 272

    first derivative to find, 239–240

    global, 272

    local (*see* Local maximums/
        minimums)

    maximum-minimum value
        existence theorem, 326, 386,
        434, 438–439

    minimization problems, 272–276

    on graphing calculator, 214–215

    relative, 192, 214–215

Mnemonic devices
    derivatives of products, 170
    derivatives of quotients, 220
    trigonometric ratios, 17–18
Monomials, 125, 269
Monotonic sequences, 542–543
Motion
    acceleration, 281–283
    due to gravity, 283–284, 337
    falling-body problems, 336–340
    particle, 400–402, 461–464
    projectile, 684–687
    velocity, 281–283, 691–693
Multiplication
    of functions, 105
    of powers, 97
    of real numbers, 2
    of vectors, 561
    See also Products
Multiplicative inverse, 2

N

Natural exponential functions, 521
Natural logarithm functions, 505–506, 521
Natural logarithms, 59, 147–148, 505–506, 521–522
Natural number (e), 42, 522
Natural numbers, 1
Negative infinity, 103
Negative integers, 1
Negative velocity, 282
Newton-meter (unit), 321
Newton, Sir Isaac, 160
Newton's method, 475–478, 508
Newton's notation, 161
Newton (unit), 380
Nonlinear equations, slope of curve, 111
Normal, defined, 212
Normal lines, 212–214
Normal vectors, 561–564
Norms of partitions, 249
Notation
    absolute value, 492
    for derivatives, 138
    functional, 28–29
    interval, 92–94
    Leibniz's, 161
    Newton's, 161

Numbers, 1, 42
    absolute value of, 54–55
    counting, 1
    critical, 191–194, 260, 272
    e, 42, 522
    integers, 1
    irrational, 1
    natural, 1, 42
    pi (π), 42
    rational, 1
    real, 1–2
    sequences, 537–543
    singular, 422
    stationary, 239, 260
    whole, 1
Numerical integral, 278
Numerical integration, 277–278, 486
    on graphing calculator, 277–278, 311
    trapezoidal rule, 486–489, 508

O

Odd functions, 48, 351–354
    arithmetic of, 441–443
    graphs of, 351
    polynomials, 352
One-to-one functions, 304–305, 470–471
Open intervals, 93
Open-interval continuity, 387
Order properties of real numbers, 2
Origin-centered conic sections, 119–121

P

Parabolas
    as functions of y, 347–349
    equations of, 131–132, 272
    graphs of, 62–63
Parallelogram method, 558
Parameters, elimination of, 545
Parametric curves, 548
Parametric equations, 545–549, 610
    arc length, 587–589
    derivatives of, 610–611
    graphs of, 545–549
    polar equations, converting to, 664
    projectile motion, 684–687
    second derivatives of, 611–612
    slopes of, 548
    tangent lines, 612

Partial fractions, 591–593, 614–616, 637–638
Partially closed intervals, 93
Partial sums, 597
Particle motion, 400–402, 461–464
Partitions, 204, 249
Pascal's Principle, 381
Periods of functions, 40–41
Phase angles, 38
Pi (π), 42
Piecewise continuous functions, 674
Piecewise functions, 58, 422
Piecewise integration, 674–676
Pinching theorem for limits, 362
Points
    stationary, 260
    terminal, 556
Point-slope form, 6–7
Polar coordinates, 550–551, 569–570
Polar curves
    area bounded by, 646–649
    graphs of, 570–572, 604
    lemniscates, 605–609
    limaçons, 604–605
    rose curves, 569–573, 605
    slopes of, 664–668
Polar equations, 552–555, 664
Polynomials, 125
    degree of, 176
    errors in approximations, 696
    even functions, 352
    factors of, 176–177
    fractions of, 614
    graphs of, 9–11, 176, 178–180
    L'Hôpital's Rule, 404–407, 466–468
    Maclaurin, 285–289, 688
    odd functions, 352
    quadratic, 62–63, 176
    rational functions, 125–128, 155–158, 216–218, 409–412
    rational roots theorem, 66–67
    real, 176
    remainder theorem, 64–65, 696–698
    roots of, 62
    synthetic division, 65
    Taylor, 688, 696
    turning point theorem, 178
    zeros of, 62, 155, 164
Position functions, 281, 337

Positive integers, 1
Positive velocity, 282
Powers, 4
  integrals of, 511–514
  logarithms of, 98–99
  multiplication of, 97
Power series, 688, 699
  convergence of, 699–701
  convergence theorems for, 699
  integral approximation using, 708–709
  substitution into, 706–707
  term-by-term differentiation and integration of, 703–704
Product indeterminate forms, 466–468
Product rule, 169–172
  mnemonic for, for derivatives, 170
  proof of, 171–172
Products
  limits of, 361
  logarithms of, 97–98
  of composite functions, derivatives of, 266–267
  of even functions, 441–443
  of functions, 105–106, 441–443
  of linear factors, 93–94
  of odd functions, 441–443
  See also Multiplication
Projectile motion, 684–687
Proofs
  epsilon-delta, 525–528
  of continuity being a necessary condition of differentiability, 421
  of derivative of sin x, 519
  of derivative of a sum, 144
  of Fundamental Theorem of Calculus, 524–525
  of Mean Value Theorem for Integrals, 458–459
  of product rule, 171–172
  of p-test, 645
  of quotient rule, 221–222
  of Rolle's theorem, 438–439
  of substitution theorem, 345–346
p-series, 639–641, 645
p-test, 645

Pumping fluids, 395–398
Pythagorean identities, 46–47, 392
Pythagorean theorem, 46, 51

Q
Quadrant signs for trigonometric functions, 18–19
Quadratic formula, 7–8
Quadratic polynomials, 62–63, 176
Quotient rule, 220–222
Quotients
  derivatives of, 220–222, 429–430
  indeterminate forms, 405
  limits of, 404
  logarithms of, 97–98
  of composite functions, derivatives of, 266–267
  of even functions, 441–443
  of functions, 105–106, 441–443
  of odd functions, 441–443
  See also Division

R
Radians, 16–17
Radian-to-degree conversion, 16–17
Radius of convergence, 699
Range, 25–26, 31, 106–109
Rate problems, 323–324
Rational functions, 155
  asymptotes of, 409–412
  graphs of, 125–128, 155–158, 216–218, 409–412
  limits of, 466
Rational numbers, 1
Rational polynomial expressions, 125
Rational roots theorem, 66–67
Ratio test, 651–652
Real numbers, 1–2
Real polynomials, 176
Reciprocal functions, 164–167
Reciprocals, 2
Rectangular equations, 552–553, 565–568
Related-rates problems, 241–245
Relating equations, 241
Relation, 25
Relative maximums/minimums, 192, 214–215
Remainder theorem, 64–65, 696–698

Repeated factors, 217–218
Revolution
  axes of, 366
  displaced axes of, 480–484
  See also Solids of revolution
Riemann integrals, 249
Riemann sums, 248–249, 295
Right circular cylinders, lateral surface area of, 445
Right-hand derivatives, 422–424
Right-hand limits, 70, 420
Right sums, 208–209
Rolle's theorem, 438–439
Roots
  Newton's method, 475–478, 508
  of equations, 62, 66–67, 475–478, 508
  of functions, 67, 478
  of polynomials, 62
  rational roots theorem, 66–67
Root test, 652–653
Rose curves, 569–573, 605

S
Sandwich theorem for limits, 362
Scalars, multiplication of vectors by, 561
Secant function, 17, 20
  cofunction, 50
  derivatives of, 254–255
  derivatives of inverse of, 334
  integrals of powers of sec x, 513
  Pythagorean identity, 47
  slope of, 138
Second convergence theorem for power series, 699
Second derivatives, 153, 318
  geometric meaning of, 258–260
  of parametric equations, 611–612
Second derivative test, 261
Separable differential equations, 450–454
Sequences, 537–538
  bounded, 542–543
  characteristics of, 542–543
  convergence of, 539–540, 543
  divergence of, 540
  graphs of, 541–542

Sequences (cont.)
increasing and decreasing, 542
limits of, 538–541
monotonic, 542–543
squeeze theorem for, 539
Series, 597–598
absolute convergence, 669–670
alternating, approximation theorem, 680–683
alternating, test, 678
arithmetic of, 619–620
basic comparison test, 642–643
binomial, 694–695
conditional convergence, 677–679
convergence of, 597, 600, 602, 617–618, 639–640, 669–670, 677–679, 699–701
convergence tests (*see* Convergence tests)
differences of convergent, 619–620
divergence of, 597, 600, 602, 617–618, 640
geometric, 600–602
harmonic, 639–640
indices of, 619
infinite, 597
Maclaurin, 288
power (*see* Power series)
p-, 639–641, 645
ratio test, 651–652
sums of, 601, 619–620
Taylor, 688–690, 694
telescoping, 602–603
"Sharp point," 260
Shells, 445–448
Similar triangles, 51
Simplification
algebraic, 3–4
of trigonometric expressions, 20
Sine function, 17, 20
cofunction, 50
derivatives of, 148–149, 516
derivatives of inverse of, 331–332, 334
double-angle identity, 76–77
graph of, 35, 37, 351
half-angle identity, 77
integrals of powers of, 392–394, 426–427
inverse, 84, 303, 334
limits of, 365

Sine function (cont.)
period of, 40
proof of derivative of sin *x*, 519
Pythagorean identity, 47
unit circles, 35–37, 163–164
Singular numbers, 422
Sinusoids, 37–40
Slopes
of curves, 94–95, 111, 115–116, 664–668
of lines, 7, 111
of normal lines, 212–214
of parametric curves, 548
of polar curves, 664–668
of tangent lines, 212–213
point-slope form, 6–7
second derivatives and, 258–260
See also Derivatives
Slope fields, 530–535, 660
Slope-intercept form, 6
Solids defined by cross section, 498–500
Solids of revolution, 366
axes of revolution, 366
disks, 366–369, 483
displaced axes of revolution, 480–484
shells, 445–448
volume of, 414, 445, 447, 483
washers, 414–417, 483
Spiral of Archimedes, 570
Spring constant, 323
Squeeze theorem
for limits, 362
for sequences, 539
Stationary numbers, 239, 260
Stationary points, 260
Subintervals, 205–208, 224, 249
Substitution
axiom, 196
into power series, 706–707
theorem for definite integrals, 345–346
trigonometric, 578–579, 581–586
u, 196–199, 264, 342–344
Subtraction
of convergent series, 619–620
of functions, 105
of vectors, 560
See also Differences

Sum and difference identities, 74–75
Summation, 5, 224–228
Sums
derivatives of, 143–144, 200
integrals of, 200–201
left, 208–209
limits of, 361
lower, 205, 224
midpoint, 208–209
of even functions, 441–443
of odd functions, 441–443
of partial fractions, 591
of series, 601, 619–620
of vectors, 558–561
partial, 597
Riemann, 248–249, 295
right, 208–209
upper, 205–206, 224
See also Addition
Symmetric derivatives, 234
Synthetic division, 65

T
Tangent function, 17, 20
cofunction, 50
derivatives of, 253, 255
derivatives of inverse of, 333–334
double-angle identities, 77
graphs of, 163–164
integrals of powers of tan *x*, 511–512
inverse, 84, 303
Pythagorean identity, 47
Tangent lines, 94–95
equations of, 152–153
parametric equations, 612
slope of, 212–213
Taylor polynomials, 688, 696
Taylor series, 688–690, 694
Telescoping series, 602–603
Techniques of differentiation
logarithmic differentiation, 429–432
implicit differentiation, 182–185, 628–630
using the definition, 113–115, 138, 234
u substitution, 196–199, 264

Techniques of integration
    Fundamental Theorem of Calculus, 246–248, 278
    integration by guessing, 269–270, 290–293
    integration by parts, 356–359, 621–622
    partial fractions, 591–593, 614–616, 637–638
    trigonometric substitution, 578–579, 581–586
    using geometry, 250, 353
    using power series, 703–704
    using trigonometric identities, 392–394, 426–427, 511–514
    u substitution, 342–344
Term-by-term differentiation and integration of power series, 703–704
Terminal points, 556
Third derivatives, 153
Transcendental functions, 285
Transitivity, 2
Translations of functions, 122–125
Trapezoidal rule, 486–489, 508
Triangle method, 559
Triangles, similar, 51
Trichotomy, 2
Trigonometric equations, 85–86
Trigonometric expressions, simplifying, 20
Trigonometric functions
    cofunctions, 49–51
    derivatives of, 148–149, 252–255, 331–334
    derivatives of inverse of, 255, 331–334
    even, 353
    implicit forms of, 303
    inverse, 83–85, 255, 303–304, 331–334
    odd, 353
    of $n\theta$, 134–135
    Pythagorean identities, 46–47, 392
    quadrant signs, 18–19
    See also Cosecant function; Cosine function; Cotangent function; Secant function; Sine function; Tangent function

Trigonometric identities, 48–49
    double-angle, 76–77
    half-angle, 77–78
    Pythagorean, 46–47, 392
    sum and difference, 74–75
Trigonometric ratios, 17–18
Trigonometric substitution, 578–579, 581–586
Trinomials, 125
Turning point theorem, 178

U
Undefined limits, 103–104
Unit circles, 35–37, 163–164
Units of force, 380
Units for derivatives, 211–212
Unit vectors, 561–564
Upper limit of integration, 247
Upper sums, 205–206, 224
u substitution
    differentiation using, 196–199, 264
    integration using, 342–344

V
Variables of integration, 174, 344–345
Vectors, 556–558
    arithmetic of, 558–561
    multiplication of, by scalars, 561
    normal, 561–564
    representation of, 557
    subtraction of, 560
    terminology, 556
    unit, 561–564
Vector-valued functions, 625–626, 691–693
Velocity, 281–283, 691–693
Velocity functions, 281
    falling-body problems, 337
    particle motion, 461–462
Verhulst, Pierre François, 594
Volume
    of solids defined by cross section, 498–500
    of solids of revolution, 414, 445, 447, 483
    See also Solids defined by cross section; Solids of revolution

W
Washers, 414–417, 483
Weight, 380
Weight density, 380
Whole numbers, 1
Word problems, 21–23
Work, 321–322, 395
    pumping fluids, 394–398

Z
Zero function, 441
Zero (number), 42
Zeros
    of functions, 409, 447
    of polynomials, 62, 155, 164

Answers

problem set 1
  1. A   **3.** D   **5.** $\frac{R_2 x y}{m R_2 - a x y}$ **7.** $\frac{m x + 1}{a m x + a + m}$ **9.** $\frac{13 - 10\sqrt{2}}{31}$ **11.** $m^{x/3 + 2} b^{5x/2 - 2}$
  13. $(1, -2, 2)$ **15.** $8a^{2m + 3}(2a^{2m} - 1)$ **17.** $(3x + y^2)(3x - y^2)$
  19. $(xy^2 + 2m^4)(x^2 y^4 - 2m^4 x y^2 + 4m^8)$ **21.** $\frac{n}{n + 1}$ **23.** $\frac{49}{4}$ **25.** $\frac{16\pi}{3}$ cm^3

problem set 2
  1. $\sqrt{65}$ **3.** $y = \frac{2}{3}x + \frac{2}{3}$ **5.** $4, -1$ **7.** $\frac{1}{6} \pm \frac{\sqrt{85}}{6}$
  9. $(-1 + \sqrt{5}, -1 - \sqrt{5}), (-1 - \sqrt{5}, -1 + \sqrt{5})$ **11.** $-2.532089, -1.347296, 0.87938524$
  13. $\frac{3bcdk^2 + 18y}{d}$ **15.** $\frac{23\sqrt{10}}{5}$ **17.** $x^{13/6} y^{11/6}$ **19.** $7x^{2b}(2x^{2b - 2} - 1)$ **21.** n **23.** $-\frac{16}{3}$ **25.** D

problem set 3
  1. If the switch is on, then the light is on.   **3.** If the switch is not on, then the light is not on.
  5. $y = -2x + 6$ **7.** $\frac{3}{2} \pm \frac{\sqrt{37}}{2}$ **9.** $x^2 - 12x - 2 - \frac{10}{x - 1}$
  11. $(-1.292402, -2.292402), (0.39729507, -0.6027049), (3.8951065, 2.8951065)$ **13.** 2   **15.** $x^3 y^{11/4}$
  17. $\frac{m^2 - my}{mx - xy + mp}$ **19.** $x(2x - 1)(x + 2)$ **21.** $10,660$ **23.** $\frac{n!}{n + 2}$ **25.** D

problem set 4
  1. $-2.618034, -0.618034, -0.381966, 1.618034$ **3.** $-\frac{1}{4}$ **5.** $-\frac{3\sqrt{3}}{2} + 1$ **7.** $\cos \theta$
  9. If a function is one-to-one, then it is not both increasing and decreasing.
  11. $y + 3 = -\frac{1}{9}(x + 9), \ x + 9y + 36 = 0$ **13.** $x = -\frac{1}{2} \pm \frac{\sqrt{5}}{2}$ **15.** $(2, -2), (-2, 2)$
  17. $(n - 1)n!$ **19.** $x - y$ **21.** $\frac{4}{7}$ **23.** $(5, 5)$ **25.** B

problem set 5
  1. 10 days   **3.** $(L + \frac{200}{L})$ m   **5.** $(-0.7692924, -1.408189)$ **7.** $-2\sqrt{2}$ **9.** $\frac{7}{4}$ **11.** $\sin \alpha$
  13. $1, \frac{1}{2}$ **15.** $(1, 2)$ **17.** $x^2 + ax + a^2$ **19.** $\frac{4x - 4}{mx - m + a}$ **21.** 14
  23. (a) $\frac{3}{4}$ (b) $y = \frac{3}{4}x - \frac{25}{4}$ (c) $(7, -1)$ (d) 5 units   **25.** A

problem set 6
  1. 62.5 newtons per square meter   **3.** $-2.879385, -0.6527036, 0.53208889$ **5.** $90°$
  7. (a) 3 (b) 0 (c) 1   **9.** $2x^2 + 4x(\Delta x) + 2(\Delta x)^2 - 1$
  11. Domain: $\{x \in \mathbb{R} \mid x \geq -1, \ x \neq 0\}$, Range: $\mathbb{R}$ **13.** -1 **15.** $\frac{1}{4}$ **17.** 1   **19.** -1
  21. $\frac{13}{3}$ **23.** 24π cm^2 **25.** 10

problem set 7
  1. 4   **3.** $V = 4x^3 - 28x^2 + 48x$ **5.** $P_1 = (\frac{\sqrt{3}}{2}, \frac{1}{2}), P_2 = (-\frac{1}{2}, -\frac{\sqrt{3}}{2})$ **7.**

  9. $y = 2 + 3 \cos (x + \frac{\pi}{2})$ or $y = 2 - 3 \cos (x - \frac{\pi}{2})$
  11. $x^2 + 2hx + h^2 - x - h$ **13.** $\frac{1}{4}$
  15. $\cos^2 \theta$ **17.** Quadrants I and III
  19. Contrapositive: If $n + 2$ is not an even number,
      then n is not an odd number.
      Converse: If $n + 2$ is an even number, then n is an
      odd number.
      Inverse: If n is not an odd number,
      then $n + 2$ is not an even number.
  21. $-\frac{1}{x(x + h)}$ **23.** No   **25.** C

**problem set
8**

1. $\frac{49}{5}$ 3. (a) $y = (x + 1)^2 - 4$ (b)

(c) upward

(d) $x = -1$

(e) $(-1, -4)$

5. (a) $1 + \cot^2 \theta = \csc^2 \theta$

(b) $\tan^2 \theta + 1 = \sec^2 \theta$

7. 0   9. $-\frac{4}{5}$

11. $\frac{\sin^2 x + 2 + \cos^2 x}{3 \csc^2 - x} = \frac{\sin^2 x + \cos^2 x + 2}{3(-\csc x)^2}$
$= \frac{1 + 2}{3 \csc^2 x} = \frac{1}{\csc^2 x} = \sin^2 x$

13. $(\sin x)\left[\cos\left(\frac{\pi}{2} - x\right)\right]$
$+ (\cos -x)(\cos x)$
$= (\sin x)(\sin x) + (\cos x)(\cos x)$
$= \sin^2 x + \cos^2 x = 1$

15. $x = \frac{3}{4}L$ 17. $\left(\frac{1}{2}, -\frac{\sqrt{3}}{2}\right)$

19. $y = 1 + 11\sin\left(\theta - \frac{\pi}{2}\right)$ or $y = 1 - 11\sin\left(\theta + \frac{\pi}{2}\right)$ 21. $2x + h$ 23. $f(x) = 2x^2 + 10x + 12$

25. $a^2 + b^2 = 90$

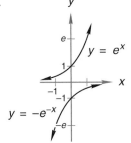

**problem set
9**

1. $V = 10,000 + 300x - 10x^2$ 3. $C = 7x^2 + 1000x^{-1}$

5. $(-2.5, -2)$ 7. B   9. (a) $\log 3 \approx 0.4771$ (b) $\ln 5 \approx 1.6094$ 11. 2, 1

13.

15. $\{x \in \mathbb{R} \mid 2.999 < x < 3.001\}$

17. $y = -5 + 4\sin\left[\frac{2}{3}\left(x + \frac{5\pi}{4}\right)\right]$ or
$y = -5 - 4\sin\left[\frac{2}{3}\left(x - \frac{\pi}{4}\right)\right]$ 19. $\sec x$

21. $y_1 = \frac{1}{2}$, $y_2 = -\frac{1}{2}$, $y_3 = -\frac{\sqrt{3}}{2}$

23. $2hx + h^2$ 25. C

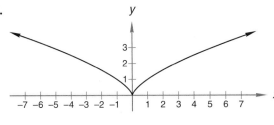

**problem set
10**

1. 100 miles   3. $\sin^2 \theta + \cos^2 \theta = 1$, $1 + \cot^2 \theta = \csc^2 \theta$, $\tan^2 \theta + 1 = \sec^2 \theta$ 5. 3

7. $\pm1, \pm2, \pm4$ 9. (a) 0.6275   (b) –96.2084   (c) –71.5842

11. (a)   (b)   13. $e^{2/3} \approx 1.9477$

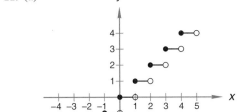

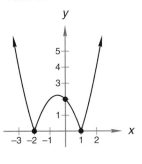

15.   17.

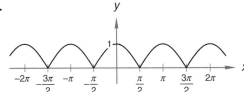

19. $\sec \alpha = \frac{\sqrt{a^2 + b^2}}{b}$ 21. $\sin x - \sin x \cos^2 x = \sin x\left(1 - \cos^2 x\right) = \sin x\left(\sin^2 x\right) = \sin^3 x$

23. $2x + \Delta x$ 25. 25

**problem set
11**

1. 50   3. (a) 2 (b) 1 (c) –1 (d) 0   5. (a) –13 (b) 17 (c) –163

7. $-3, -1.414214, 1.4142136$ 9. $\ln 10 \approx 2.3025$ 11. $5^2 = (x - 1)^2 + (y - 2)^2$

13. $(1.4215299, 0.70346742)$ **15.** $-(\sin -x)(\sec x)\left[\cot\left(\frac{\pi}{2} - x\right)\right] + 1 = \sin x \left(\frac{1}{\cos x}\right)\tan x + 1$
$= \left(\frac{\sin x}{\cos x}\right)\tan x + 1 = \tan^2 x + 1 = \sec^2 x$ **17.** $(1, 3)$

19. 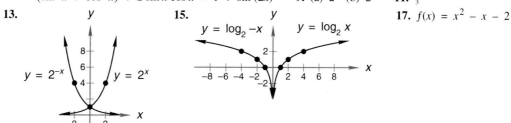   **21.** $f(x) = 2x^2 - 2x - 4$ **23.** $\frac{-1}{x(x + \Delta x)}$

25. B

problem set 12

1. Square: 2×2;   Rectangle: 4×8 **3.** $\sin(2A) = 2 \sin A \cos A;$ $\cos(2A) = \cos^2 A - \sin^2 A;$
$\cos(2A) = 2\cos^2 A - 1;$ $\cos(2A) = 1 - 2\sin^2 A$ **5.** (a) $\tan(A + B) = \frac{\tan A + \tan B}{1 - \tan A \tan B}$
(b) $\tan(A - B) = \frac{\tan A - \tan B}{1 + \tan A \tan B}$ **7.** $(\sin x + \cos x)^2 = \sin^2 x + 2 \sin x \cos x + \cos^2 x$
$= (\sin^2 x + \cos^2 x) + 2 \sin x \cos x = 1 + \sin(2x)$ **9.** (a) 2 (b) 2   **11.** $\frac{1}{3}$

13.

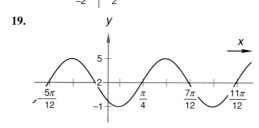

15.

17. $f(x) = x^2 - x - 2$

19.

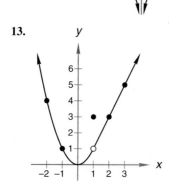

21. (a) $\cos \frac{x}{2} = \pm\sqrt{\frac{1}{2} + \frac{1}{2}\cos x}$
(b) $\sin \frac{x}{2} = \pm\sqrt{\frac{1}{2} - \frac{1}{2}\cos x}$

23. If the sides opposite two angles of a triangle do not have equal lengths, then the two angles do not have equal measures.

25. $2\sqrt{2}$ units ≈ 2.8284 units

problem set 13

1. $\frac{360A}{M^2 P}$ **3.** $-\frac{\pi}{4}$ **5.** $210°, 330°$ **7.** 0

9.

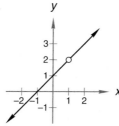

11. $\cos(2A) = \cos^2 A - \sin^2 A,$
$\cos(2A) = 2\cos^2 A - 1,$
$\cos(2A) = 1 - 2\sin^2 A$

13.

15. (a)

(b) $y = \sqrt{9 - x^2}$ represents only the positive square root, which coincides with the portions of the graph of a circle of radius 3 that lie on or above the x-axis.
(c) $Y_1 = \sqrt{(9 - X^2)}$ and $Y_2 = -\sqrt{(9 - X^2)}$

17. $(x - 1)^2 + (y + 2)^2 = 2^2$ **19.** -2.269531 **21.** $\{x \in \mathbb{R} \mid x \geq 2\}$ **23.** 1   **25.** 12

problem set 14

1. $C = 10,000x^{-1} + 70x$ **3.**

5. 5   **7.** 4   **9.** $120°, 180°, 240°$

11.

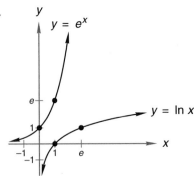

$y = e^x$

$y = \ln x$

13. (a) $\cos (2x) = \cos^2 x - \sin^2 x$;

$\cos (2x) = 1 - 2 \sin^2 x$;

$\cos (2x) = 2 \cos^2 x - 1$

(b) $\cos^2 x = \frac{1}{2} + \frac{1}{2} \cos (2x)$

15. (a) $\tan (A - B) = \frac{\tan A - \tan B}{1 + \tan A \tan B}$ (b) $2 - \sqrt{3}$

17.

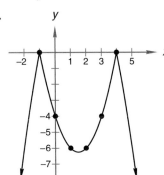

19.

$\begin{array}{ccccccc} & & & & & & \\ -2 & -1 & 0 & 1 & 2 & 3 & 4 \end{array}$

21. $(\sec -x)\left[\sin \left(\frac{\pi}{2} - x\right)\right] + (\sin -x)\left[\cos \left(\frac{\pi}{2} - x\right)\right]$

$= \sec x \cos x + (-\sin x) \sin x = 1 - \sin^2 x = \cos^2 x$

23. $\frac{1}{\sqrt{x + h} + \sqrt{x}}$ **25.** C

problem set 15

1. $\frac{3}{2}$ hr   **3.** (a) $(-\infty, -2)$ and $(2, \infty)$ (b) $(-2, 2)$ (c) $(0, \infty)$ (d) $(-\infty, 0)$ **5.** $-3, 0, 2$
7. $\frac{\pi}{4}, \frac{3\pi}{4}, \frac{5\pi}{4}, \frac{7\pi}{4}$ **9.** $x = \sin y$ **11.** 2   **13.** 2   **15.** 2   **17.** $\sin (2x) = 2 \sin x \cos x$
19. $\frac{5}{7}$ **21.** 1   **23.** $\frac{\sqrt{3}}{4} E^2 L$ cm^3 **25.** $360°$

problem set 16

1. 125 cars   **3.** $\frac{7}{4}$ **5.** $-\frac{1}{6}$ **7.** $\frac{\ln (3/16)}{\ln 12}$ **9.** Increasing: $(-1, 0), (1, \infty)$;
Decreasing: $(-\infty, -1), (0, 1)$ **11.** $+ + + | - - | + | - - | + + +$
$\begin{array}{ccccccc} -3 & -2 & -1 & 0 & 1 & 2 & 3 & 4 \end{array}$
13. $\frac{\pi}{3}, \frac{2\pi}{3}, \frac{4\pi}{3}, \frac{5\pi}{3}$
15. $2x$ **17.** 0
19. $y = 35 + 40 \sin \left[4(\theta - \frac{5\pi}{8})\right]$ or $y = 35 - 40 \sin \left[4(\theta - \frac{7\pi}{8})\right]$
21. Domain: $\{x \in \mathbb{R} \mid x < 0\}$, Range: $\mathbb{R}$ **23.** (a) See Lesson 12.   (b) $-\frac{4}{3}$ **25.** $360°$

problem set 17

1. $\frac{40M + 60B}{M + B}$ mph   **3.** $-\frac{3}{2}$ **5.** $2a$ **7.** ∞ **9.** ∞ **11.** Increasing: $(-\infty, -1)$;
Decreasing: $(-1, 1), (1, \infty)$ **13.** No solution   **15.** $\ln y$ **17.** $\cos^2 A = \frac{1}{2} + \frac{1}{2} \cos (2A)$
19. $f(0.003) = 1.0176$, $f(0.002) = 1.0125$, $f(0.001) = 1.0069$, $\lim_{x \to 0^+} f(x) = 1$ **21.** $\frac{\ln 50,176}{\ln 16 - \ln 343}$
23. $4x$ **25.** 6

problem set 18

1. 2 hr   **3.** 28   **5.** 13   **7.** 3   **9.**
11. 0   **13.** 1

$g(x) = 2x - \pi$

$x \longrightarrow \boxed{\quad g \quad} \longrightarrow (2x - \pi)$

15. Above: $(-3, 0), (2, \infty)$;
Below: $(-\infty, -3), (0, 2)$
17. $(0, \frac{\pi}{2}), (\pi, \frac{3\pi}{2})$ **19.** 3

$f(x) = \cos x$

$(2x - \pi) \longrightarrow \boxed{\quad f \quad} \longrightarrow \cos (2x - \pi)$

21. $\frac{(\sec^2 x - 1)(\cos -x)}{(1 - \cos^2 x)(\tan^2 x + 1)} = \frac{\tan^2 x \cos x}{\sin^2 x \sec^2 x} = \frac{\tan^2 x \cos x}{\tan^2 x} = \cos x$ **23.** Answers may vary: 0.8589   **25.** 16

problem set 19

1. $\frac{25N}{M^2}$ **3.** $3x^2$ **5.** $-\frac{2}{25}$ **7.** $(f \circ g)(x) = \ln \frac{1}{x}$; Domain: $\{x \in \mathbb{R} \mid x > 0\}$; Range: $\mathbb{R}$
9. ∞ **11.** ∞ **13.** $(0, 2)$ and $(4, \infty)$ **15.** 3   **17.** $\frac{1}{2}x^2$ **19.** $\frac{63}{65}$
21. $\sin^2 x = \frac{1}{2} - \frac{1}{2} \cos (2x)$ **23.** 1.3863   **25.** D

problem set 20

1. $\sqrt{5x^2 - 12x + 8}$ **3.** 1.9534   **5.** $6x$ **7.** $Y1 = \int (9 - X^2)$ and $Y2 = -Y1$; The graph does
not look like a circle unless it is graphed in the ZSquare mode on a symmetric axis.

9. (a)

(b) 1   (c) $f'(1) = 1$; They are equal.

11. $(f \circ g)(x) = \sin\left[2\left(x - \frac{\pi}{4}\right)\right]$ **13.** Undefined

15. 0   **17.** $2 \sin y$ **19.** 2   **21.** $5 + 3\sqrt{3}$

23. 0   **25.** 32

problem set 21

1. $A = 50L - \frac{1}{2}L^2$ **3.**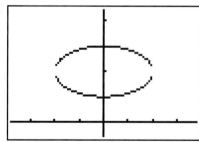

5. $\frac{\ln x}{\ln 10}$

7. $(-2.3553, 0.0949)$, $(-1.3578, 0.2572)$, $(2.2261, 9.2632)$, $(5.1051, 164.8548)$

9. $2x + 2$ **11.** (a) -4

(b) -4; They are the same.

13. For f, Domain: $\mathbb{R}$, Range: $\{y \in \mathbb{R} \mid y \geq 0\}$; for g, Domain: $\mathbb{R}$, Range: $\{y \in \mathbb{R} \mid y > 0\}$;
for $g \circ f$, Domain: $\mathbb{R}$, Range: $\{y \in \mathbb{R} \mid y \geq 1\}$ **15.** ∞ **17.** $\frac{\log 5}{-2} \approx -0.3495$

19. $\sin x - \sin x \cos^2 x = \sin x (1 - \cos^2 x) = \sin x (\sin^2 x) = \sin^3 x$ **21.** $\cos^2 x = \frac{1}{2} + \frac{1}{2} \cos (2x)$

23. Undefined   **25.** 8 units

problem set 22

1. $V = 120x - 44x^2 + 4x^3$

3. $x^6 + 6x^5(\Delta x) + 15x^4(\Delta x)^2 + 20x^3(\Delta x)^3 + 15x^2(\Delta x)^4 + 6x(\Delta x)^5 + (\Delta x)^6$

5. Hyperbola; $(x - 1)^2 - y^2 = 1$ **7.** 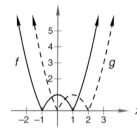   **9.** $\frac{\ln x}{\ln 3}$ **11.** 3

13. f: $\{x \in \mathbb{R} \mid x > 0\}$ g: $\mathbb{R}$

15. $\frac{1}{14}$ **17.** $240°$

19. $\{x \in \mathbb{R} \mid \frac{3}{2} - \frac{\varepsilon}{2} < x < \frac{3}{2} + \frac{\varepsilon}{2}\}$

21. $f(\sqrt{2}) \approx -2.242641$,
$f(\pi) \approx -23.3587$ **23.** 3   **25.** D

problem set 23

1. The circle has the greater area.   **3.** $\frac{5\pi}{24}$, $\frac{11\pi}{24}$, $\frac{17\pi}{24}$, $\frac{23\pi}{24}$, $\frac{29\pi}{24}$, $\frac{35\pi}{24}$, $\frac{41\pi}{24}$, $\frac{47\pi}{24}$

5. 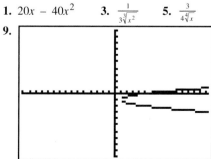   **7.**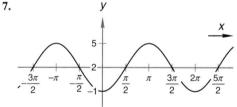

9. $\frac{\ln 17}{\ln 4}$ or $\frac{\log 17}{\log 4}$ or $\log_4 17$ **11.** $3x^2$ **13.** $(f \circ g)(x) = \sin (x^2)$; Domain: $\mathbb{R}$;
Range: $\{y \in \mathbb{R} \mid -1 \leq y \leq 1\}$ **15.** $\frac{3}{2}$ **17.** $(-\frac{1}{2}, \infty)$

19. $(\cot^2 x + 1)(\sin^2 -x) + \left[\cos\left(\frac{\pi}{2} - x\right)\right](\sin -x) = \csc^2 x \sin^2 x + \sin x (-\sin x)$
$= 1 - \sin^2 x = \cos^2 x$ **21.** (a) $\cos^2 x = \frac{1}{2} + \frac{1}{2} \cos (2x)$ (b) $\frac{2 + \sqrt{3}}{4}$ **23.** $(-\frac{\sqrt{3}}{2}, \frac{1}{2})$ **25.** C

problem set 24

1. $20x - 40x^2$ **3.** $\frac{1}{3\sqrt[3]{x^2}}$ **5.** $\frac{3}{4\sqrt[4]{x}}$ **7.** (a)

9.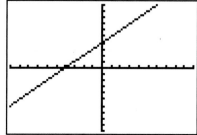

(b) 4   (c) $f'(x) = 2x$; 4   (d) They are the same.

11.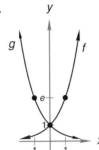

13.

15. $4x$ **17.** 27

19. (a) $(3, \frac{1}{2})$ (b) $y = \frac{3}{2}x - 4$

(c) $y = -\frac{2}{3}x + \frac{5}{2}$

21.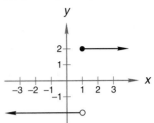

(a) 2

(b) -2

23. $(1 - \cos^2 x)\csc^2 x + \tan^2 x = \sin^2 x \csc^2 x + \tan^2 x = 1 + \tan^2 x = \sec^2 x$ **25.** $40°$

problem set 25

1. $\sqrt{x^4 - 7x^2 - 6x + 25}$ **3.** $\frac{1}{2\sqrt{x}}$ **5.** $-\frac{3}{x^4}$ **7.** $-\frac{1}{2\sqrt{t^3}}$ **9.** $-\frac{8}{u^3} - \frac{3}{2\sqrt{u}}$

11. (a) 0.35 (b) $\frac{1}{2\sqrt{x}}$ (c) 0.35 (d) They are the same.

13.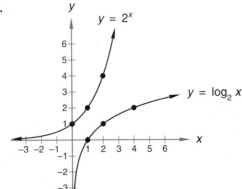

15.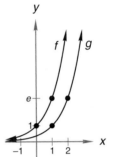

17. Domain: $\{x \in \mathbb{R} \mid -1 \leq x \leq 1\}$; Range: $\{y \in \mathbb{R} \mid -\frac{\pi}{2} \leq y \leq \frac{\pi}{2}\}$

19.
$+ + + + \mid - - - \mid + \mid - - \mid + + + +$

$-6 \ -5 \ -4 \ -3 \ -2 \ -1 \ 0 \ 1 \ 2 \ 3 \ 4$

21. $\frac{\ln 2}{9}$

23. Domain: $\{x \in \mathbb{R} \mid x \geq 0\}$; Range: $\{y \in \mathbb{R} \mid y \geq 1\}$ **25.** $\frac{ac}{a + b}$

problem set 26

1. $W(t) = 150e^{\ln (4/3)t}$; 355.5556 g   **3.** $3{:}31{:}25$ p.m.   **5.** $12x^3 + x^{-3/2}$

7. $\frac{1}{u} - 2e^u + \frac{1}{2}u^{-1/2}$ **9.** $v_0 + at$ **11.** $-6x$

13. $y = \sin (x - 3) + 2$

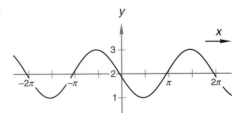

15.

17. $\frac{\ln 4}{\ln 3}$ **19.** 9.5

21. $\frac{\pi}{12}, \frac{5\pi}{12}, \frac{3\pi}{4}, \frac{13\pi}{12}, \frac{17\pi}{12}, \frac{7\pi}{4}$

23. $\frac{(x + 2)^2}{1} + \frac{(y - 3)^2}{4} = 1$

25. $(\frac{a + b}{2}, \frac{c}{2})$

The diagonals of a parallelogram bisect each other.

**problem set
27**

1. $A(t) = 1,530,000\sqrt{0.51}\, e^{-t\ln\sqrt{0.51}}$; $11,534,025.37   3. $-x^{-2} + \frac{2}{x} - 3\cos x$

5. $\frac{1}{x^2}$ 7. $-3\sin t - t^{-2}$ 9. $y = -2x + 2$ 11. $y = 2e^2 x - 2e^2$

13. $67.5°, 157.5°, 247.5°, 337.5°$ 15. (a) $m(x) = \frac{(\sin x - 1)}{x - \frac{\pi}{2}}$ (b)

(c) 0

(d) 0

(e) They are
the same.

17. (a) For f, Domain: $\{x \in \mathbb{R} \mid x \geq 1\}$;
Range: $\{y \in \mathbb{R} \mid y \geq 0\}$.
For g, Domain: $\mathbb{R}$; Range: $\{y \in \mathbb{R} \mid y \geq 0\}$.
(b) $(f \circ g)(x) = \sqrt{x^2 - 1}$; Domain: $\{x \in \mathbb{R} \mid |x| \geq 1\}$; Range: $\{y \in \mathbb{R} \mid y \geq 0\}$

19. $(-\infty, -3), (1, 2)$ 21. 7   23. $y = 2x^2 + 2x - 4$ 25. 22

**problem set
28**

1. On the fifth of the month   3.

5. $\frac{1}{4}$ 7. -0.1089

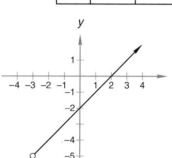

(0, 0)   (3, 0)

Not to scale

9. (a) 0   (b) 0;

y	-0.05	0.05	-0.005	0.005
x	0.1	-0.1	0.01	-0.01

11. $(x + \sqrt{2}), (x - \sqrt{2})$ 13. 5

15. (a)

(b) -5 (c) -5; The answers are the same.   17. C

19. $\frac{(\sin x + \cos x)^2 - 1}{2\sin -x} = \frac{\sin^2 x + 2\sin x\cos x + \cos^2 x - 1}{-2\sin x}$

$= \frac{2\sin x\cos x}{-2\sin x} = -\cos x$ 21. $-2 - 2\sqrt{2} + \sqrt{3} + \sqrt{6}$

23. $y = \frac{1}{4}x^2$ 25. 9

**problem set
29**

1. 197.6424 cm^2 3. $2u^{-1}\,du + 2u^{-3/2}\,du$ 5.

7.

9. -2.8881 11. 2

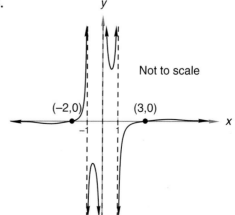

(-2,0)   (3,0)

Not to scale

13. 0.9163, 1.4399, 2.4871, 3.0107; These *x*-values are the same as those in problem 12.   **15.** $\frac{1}{x}$

17.

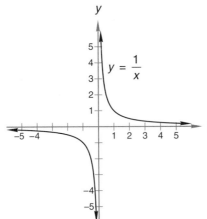

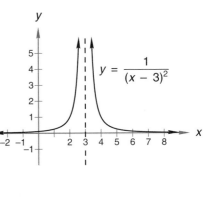

19.

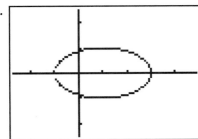

21. Domain: $\mathbb{R}$
      Range: $\{y \in \mathbb{R} \mid -1 \le y \le 3\}$

23. C   **25.** 5050

problem set 30

1. $\frac{MH}{H-2}$ mph   **3.**

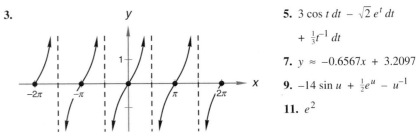

5. $3 \cos t \, dt - \sqrt{2} \, e^t \, dt$
$+ \frac{1}{3} t^{-1} \, dt$

7. $y \approx -0.6567x + 3.2097$

9. $-14 \sin u + \frac{1}{2} e^u - u^{-1}$

11. e^2

13.

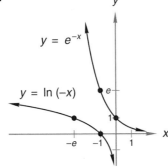

$(1, 0)$ **15.** $\cos \frac{x}{2} = \pm\sqrt{\frac{1}{2} + \frac{1}{2} \cos x}$

17.

$y = e^{-x}$

$y = \ln(-x)$

19. 4   **21.**

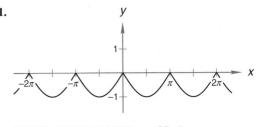

23. $(0.0591, -2.8278), (2.6546, 0.9763)$ **25.** D

problem set 31

1. $V = 4x^3 - 40x^2 + 100x$ **3.** $x^2 e^x(x + 3)$ **5.** $-2 - \ln 16 \approx 4.7726$ **7.** $-\frac{3}{4} x^{-5/2} - 2 \cos x$

9.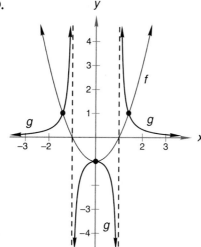

11.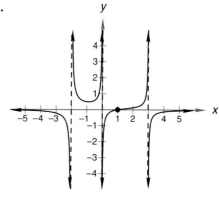

13.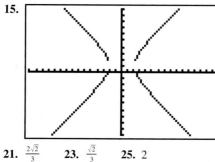

15. 3π cm^3 **17.**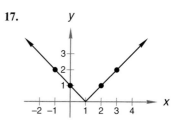

19. 2.4142   **21.** 1   **23.** $\mathbb{Z}$ **25.** $\frac{3}{2}$

problem set 32
1. $2^{2/3} : 1$ **3.** $x^5 + C$ **5.** $\sin x + C$ **7.** $\cos x + C$ **9.** $x(x\,dy + 2y\,dx)$
11. $1 + \ln 2.5 = 1.9163$ **13.**

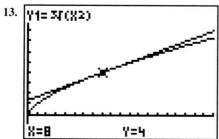

15.

$(0, 1)$ **17.** $-\infty$ **19.**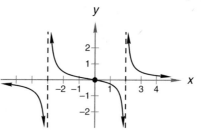

$$\lim_{x \to 0^+} f(x) = 1; \quad \lim_{x \to 0^-} f(x) = 0$$

21. $\frac{2\sqrt{2}}{3}$ **23.** $\frac{\sqrt{2}}{3}$ **25.** 2

problem set 33
1. y units^2 **3.**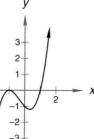

5. C   **7.** $y = e^x + C$ **9.** 1500.2538
11. $2e^x\,dx - \frac{1}{u}\,du + 4\cos t\,dt$
13. $f'(x) = 2\cos x, \; f''(x) = -2\sin x, \; f'''(x) = -2\cos x$
15. e^e **17.** $\tan(2A) = \frac{2\tan(A)}{1 - \tan^2 A}$

19.

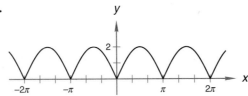

21. $\frac{\pi}{9}$, $\frac{5\pi}{9}$, $\frac{7\pi}{9}$, $\frac{11\pi}{9}$, $\frac{13\pi}{9}$, $\frac{17\pi}{9}$

23. (a) 1 unit (b) $(x - 2)^2 + (y - 3)^2 = 1$

25. $\frac{1}{2}$

problem set 34

1. (a) $(x + 4)^2 + (y + 4)^2 = 144$ (b) $y = \frac{16}{x}$ (c) (2.6808465, 5.9682642), (5.9682642, 2.6808465)

3. $\frac{2y}{2x - \sin x}\frac{dy}{dt}$ **5.**

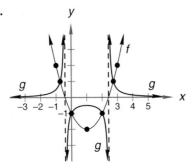

7. $F(x) = x^3 + C$ **9.** $e^t + C$

11. $x^2(-x \sin x + 3 \cos x)$

13. $\frac{2}{x} + \frac{8}{3}x^{-1/3} - \frac{1}{3}e^x$

15.

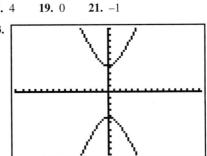

17. 4 **19.** 0 **21.** −1

23.

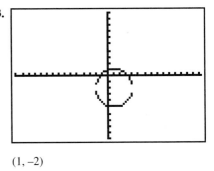

$(0, 4), (0, -4)$

25. $m\angle D = \frac{1}{2}x$, $m\angle B = \frac{1}{2}y$, $m\angle CED = \frac{1}{2}(x + y)$

problem set 35

1. $\left(25L - \frac{1}{2}L^3\right)$ cm^3 **3.** $-3 \cos x + C$ **5.** $\frac{3}{8}u^{4/3} + C$ **7.** $\frac{-\sin x - 4xy}{2x^2 + 2y}$ **9.** $y = 1$

11.

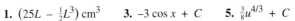

13. e^x **15.** 1 **17.** $\frac{5}{6}$

19.

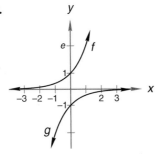

21. $\frac{\pi}{6}$, $\frac{5\pi}{6}$, $\frac{\pi}{2}$ **23.**

$(1, -2)$

25. 25

problem set 36

1. $C = 10(2\pi - x)$ cm, $r = \left(10 - \frac{5}{\pi}x\right)$ cm **3.** Critical numbers: $x = 1, 2$;

Local maximum: $\left(1, \frac{11}{2}\right)$; Local minimum: $(2, 5)$ **5.** $2 \sin t + C$ **7.** $\frac{e^x - y}{x + 3y^2}$

9. $\frac{2xy}{2x-1}\frac{dy}{dt}$ **11.** $4x + 3\cos x + 4\sin x + x^{-1}$ **13.**

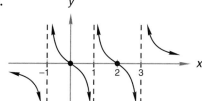

15.

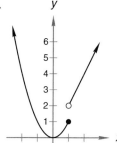

17. (a) 0.73908513   (b) 0.73908513; They are the same.   **19.** 3

21. $\lim\limits_{x\to 1^+} f(x) = 2;\ \lim\limits_{x\to 1^-} f(x) = 1$

23.   **25.** D

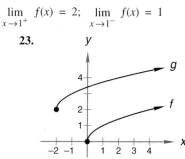

problem set 37

1. (a) $(y+4)^2 + (x+4)^2 = 144$ (b) $\frac{y}{4} = \frac{4}{x}$ (c) $(\frac{16}{x}+4)^2 + (x+4)^2 = 144$

(d) 2.6808465, 5.9682642   **3.** $3t^2\cos(t^3+1)$ **5.** $\frac{2x}{x^2+1}$ **7.** $-x(x^2-1)^{-3/2}$

9. $6u^{1/2} + C$ **11.** $\frac{2}{5}x^{5/2} + C$ **13.** $y = \frac{1}{2}x$

15.

17. $(f \circ g)(x) = \ln\sqrt{x-1}$; Domain: $\{x \in \mathbb{R} \mid x > 1\}$

19. 2.7183   **21.** $y = 2x^2 - 2x - 4$ **23.** -1 **25.** D

problem set 38

1. 5:25:08 a.m.   **3.** $\frac{2}{3}x^3 - 6x^{1/2} + 3x + C$ **5.** $-\sin(x^3 + 2x + 1)(3x^2 + 2)$

7. $-(x+1)^{-2}$ **9.** (a) $-1, 1, 2$ (b) Local minimums: $(-1, -20)$ and $(2, 7)$;

Local maximum: $(1, 12)$ **11.** $\frac{\cos x - y}{x - 3y^2}$ **13.** $\frac{3y^2(dy/dt) + e^t}{3x^2}$

15.   **17.**

19.

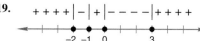

21. 820   **23.** $-\sin^2\theta$ **25.** C

problem set 39

1. 18 units^2 **3.** $\frac{85}{8}$ units^2 **5.** $3e^x - 2\ln|x| - \cos x - \sin x - 8x^{1/2} + \frac{1}{3}x^6 + C$

7. $\cos(x^3 - 4x^2 + 2x - 5)(3x^2 - 8x + 2)$ **9.** (a) $-2, -1, 1$

(b) Local minimums: $(-2, \frac{17}{3})$, $(1, \frac{41}{12})$; Local maximum: $(-1, \frac{73}{12})$ **11.** -0.3647 **13.** 4.2067

15. 3   **17.** ∞   **19.**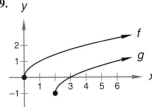

21. Domain: $\{x \in \mathbb{R} \mid -1 \le x \le 1\}$;
     Range: $\{y \in \mathbb{R} \mid -\frac{\pi}{2} \le y \le \frac{\pi}{2}\}$
23. $-\frac{7}{2}$ **25.** 60°

problem set 40

1. $20e^3 \ \frac{cm^3}{s} \approx 401.7107 \ \frac{cm^3}{s}$ **3.** $y = -x - 3 + \ln \frac{1}{27}$ **5.** $\frac{25}{32}$ units²   **7.** $\frac{65}{8}$ units²
9. 12.000001, $y'(2) = 12$ **11.** $\sqrt{2} \ln |t| + 3 \sin t + t + C$ **13.** $\frac{2}{3}x(x^2 + 5)^{-2/3}$
15. $-4 \sin^3 x \cos x$ **17.** $4\pi r^2 \frac{dr}{dt}$ **19.** $e^x(x^{-1} + \ln |x|)$ **21.** 1.4650   **23.** $\cot^2 \theta$ **25.** C

problem set 41

1. $\frac{1}{3^6}$ liter ≈ 0.0014 liter
5. $4\pi r^2 \frac{dr}{dt}$
7. (a) −4, −1, 1
       (b) Local maximum: $(-1, \frac{137}{12})$
           Local minimums: $(-4, -\frac{13}{3}), (1, \frac{73}{12})$
9. 2.0523 units²   **11.** −7.0940
13. $-2 \cos u + \frac{3}{2}u^{-2} + C$ **15.** $4x^{1/2} - 4x + C$
17. $\frac{2x}{x^2 + 1}$ **19.** $xe^x(x + 2)$

21.
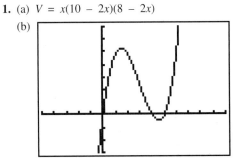

3.
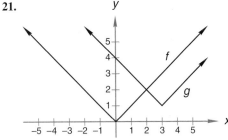
Not to scale

23. $\lim\limits_{x \to 1^-} f(x) = 0, \quad \lim\limits_{x \to 1^+} f(x) = 1$
25. 20,100

problem set 42

1. (a) $V = x(10 - 2x)(8 - 2x)$
     (b)
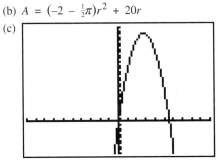
     (c) $x \approx 1.4724754, \ V \approx 52.513804$ in.³
     (d) $\{x \in \mathbb{R} \mid 0 < x < 4\}$
13. $\frac{2x + \cos x}{x^2 + \sin x}$ **15.** $-64e^{-16}$ **17.** $2u^2e^u(u + 3)$
25. $\frac{1}{2}$

3. $\sec^2 x$
5.
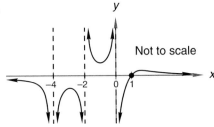
Not to scale

7. 1.9116 units²   **9.** $x = \pi$
11. $\frac{2}{3}x^3 - 2x^{1/2} + e^x + \ln |x| + \cos x + C$
19. 18π cm³   **21.** (0.99, 1.01)   **23.** 5 units

problem set 43

1. (a) $h = 10 - r - \frac{1}{2}\pi r$
     (b) $A = (-2 - \frac{1}{2}\pi)r^2 + 20r$
     (c)
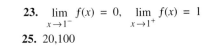

3. $\frac{8}{3}$ units²   **5.** $\sum\limits_{i=0}^{9} 0.12[\sin (0.12i) + 1]$
7. $\frac{2}{x^2 - 2} - \frac{(x^2 + 3)(3x^2 - 2)}{x^2(x^2 - 2)^2}$
     (d) $r \approx 2.8004958$ units, $A \approx 28.004958$ units²

9.

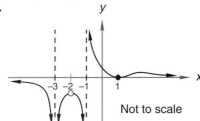

Not to scale

11. (a) 1, 2   (b) Local maximum: $(1, \frac{9}{2})$
          Local minimum: (2, 4)

13. $-\frac{2}{3} x(x^2 - 1)^{-4/3}$

15. $3 \ln |x| + \frac{3\sqrt{2}}{7} x^{7/3} + \sin x - 4e^x + C$

17.

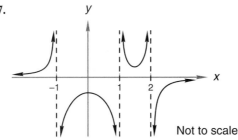

Not to scale

19.

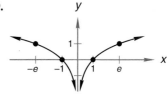

21. (a) $A = 25x - x^2$ (b) $\{x \in \mathbb{R} \mid 0 \le x \le 25\}$ (c)
     (d) (12.5, 156.25)

23. (a) Circle   (b) Y₁=√(4−X²),
     Y₂=−√(4−X²)   **25.** A

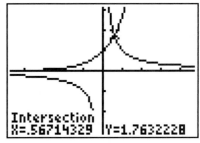

problem set
44

1. 98,304 troubles   **3.** $15x^2 \cos(5x^3)$ **5.** −3   **7.** 24 units²   **9.** $\frac{\cos x}{e^x + x^2} - \frac{\sin x (e^x + 2x)}{(e^x + x^2)^2}$

11.

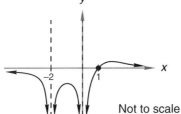

Not to scale

13. $x = \frac{\pi}{2}$ **15.** $3 \ln |x| - 4 \cos x + 5e^x - \frac{1}{5}x^{-5} + C$

17. $-2x^{-2} + 3 \ln |x| + 3$ **19.** $\frac{dx}{dt}$

21. The limit does not exist.

23.

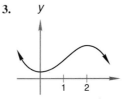

(0.56714329, 1.7632228)   **25.** 404,010,000

problem set
45

1. $\sqrt{100 - x^2}$ feet   **3.**

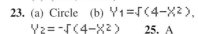

5. $\frac{\cos \sqrt{x}}{2\sqrt{x}}$ **7.** $2x + 3$ **9.** $\frac{\sqrt{2}\pi}{4}$ units²
11. 64 units²   **13.** $\frac{e^x}{1 + x^2} - \frac{2xe^x}{(1 + x^2)^2}$

15.

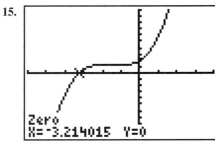

(a) −3.214015
(b) Local maximum: (−1.999998, 1.3333333);
    Local minimum: (−1.000001, 1.1666667)
(c) They are approximately the same.

17. $-\ln |x|$ **19.** $\pi e^t + 2 \cos t + t + C$
21. $(f \circ g)(x) = \sqrt{x^2 - 1}$ **23.** 3   **25.** $\frac{5}{2}$ units

problem set
46

1. $\frac{PI}{J}$ people   3. $\frac{1}{2}$ $\frac{ft}{s}$ 5. Critical number: $x = -3$; Absolute minimum: $x = -3$

7. $e^{\sin x}\cos x$ 9. $2x$ 11. $\frac{1}{1 + \sin(2x)}$ 13. $x(x^2 + 1)^{-1/2}$

15.

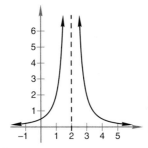

$(0, -\frac{3}{2})$ 17. $\frac{3}{2}x^2 + e^x - 2x^{1/2} + \frac{1}{3}x + C$

19.

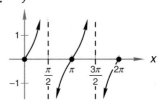

21. $\tan(2A) = \frac{2\tan A}{1 - \tan^2 A}$ 23.

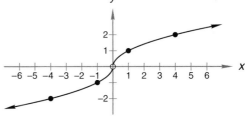

25. C

problem set
47

1. falling at $\frac{5}{6}$ $\frac{m}{s}$ 3. 3 units^2 5. $\ln 3$ units$^2 \approx 1.0986$ units^2 7. (a) $-1, 0$

(b) Local maximum: $(0, -4)$; Local minimum: $(-1, -5)$ 9. $e^{x + \cos x}(1 - \sin x)$

11. 4   13. $3e^{x + \sin x}(1 + \cos x)$ 15. $6 + \frac{1}{2}u^{-3/2}$ 17. 48 units^2

19.

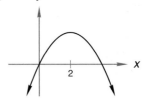

21. Domain: $\{x \in \mathbb{R} \mid -1 \le x \le 1\}$;
Range: $\{y \in \mathbb{R} \mid 0 \le y \le \pi\}$

23. $4e^x + 2\sin x - \frac{1}{4}x^{-4} + \ln|x| + \frac{2}{3}x^{3/2} + C$

25. $f(1) \approx 0.8414709848$; $\sin(1) \approx 0.8414709848$;
They are the same.

problem set
48

1. 160π cm^3/s   3. $-\sin x$ 5. $-\csc x \cot x$ 7. $x \sec x(x \tan x + 2)$

9. $\frac{3}{5}(2.5^{5/3} - 0.5^{5/3})$ units^2 11. 2 units^2 13. Local minimum   15. $\frac{e^x}{2}(e^x - 1)^{-3/2}$

17. $-2u^{1/2} + \frac{2}{3}u^3 - u + 2u^{3/2} - 2\cos u - \sin u - \frac{1}{4}u^{-4} - 4e^u + C$ 19. $3^{1/5} \approx 1.2457$

21. (a) 3   (b) 3   (c) They are the same.   23. (a) -0.4 (b) -0.4 (c) They are the same.   25. C

problem set
49

1. $-\frac{4}{25\pi}$ $\frac{cm}{s}$ 3. (a) $-1, 0, 1$ (b) Relative maximum: $(0, 0)$; Relative minimums: $(-1, -1), (1, -1)$

5. $2\sqrt{3}$ units$^2 \approx 3.4641$ units^2 7. $\frac{33}{4}$ units^2 9.

11. $1 + \ln|x| - x\sec^2 x - \tan x$

13. $24[1 + \sin(2x)]\cos(2x)$

17. See example 48.1.

15.

19.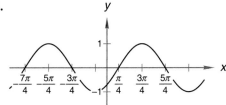

21. (a)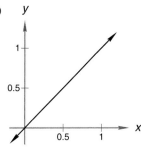

(b) $\frac{1}{n}$ (c) $\frac{1}{n}, \frac{3}{n}, \frac{6}{n}, 1$ (d) $\lim\limits_{n \to \infty} \frac{n+1}{2n}$

23. See example 48.2.   **25.** (a) 1.6052 (b) $f(1) = 1$, $g(1) \approx 1.3818$

(c) $f'(x) = 1 + \frac{1}{x}$, $g'(x) = \cos x - \sin x$ (d) $f'(1) = 2$, $g'(1) \approx -0.3012$ (e) 1.6051

(f) They are approximately the same.

problem set 50

1. $\frac{\sqrt{2}}{2} \frac{\text{units}}{\text{s}}$ **3.** (a) $-0.5931, 0, 0.8431$ (b) Relative maximums: $(-0.5931, 0.9018)$, $(0.8431, 3.8638)$; Relative minimum: $(0, -1)$ **5.** $2 \sec^2(3x^2 - 4x + 1)(3x - 2)$ **7.** $100x(x^2 - 4)^{49}$

9. $2 \sec^2 t$ **11.** $(e^{1.5} - e^{0.5} - 1)$ units$^2 \approx 1.8330$ units^2 **13.** $\frac{2}{5}x^{5/2} - \frac{4}{3}x^{3/2} + C$

15. $y = -2\sqrt{2}x + 9$ **17.** e^x **19.**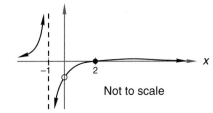

Not to scale

21. (a) $\int_0^1 x\, dx$

(b) $\frac{1}{2}$

23. 4

25. (a)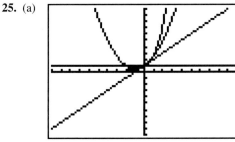

(b)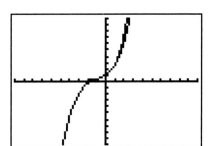

(c)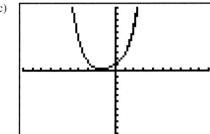

problem set 51

1. $-\frac{3}{100\pi} \frac{\text{cm}}{\text{s}}$ **3.** (a) $-1, 2$ (b) Relative maximum: $(-1, 8)$; relative minimum: $(2, -19)$

5. $(x^2 + 4)^6 + C$ **7.** $\sqrt{x^2 + 4} + C$ **9.** $\ln|3x^2 + x| + C$ **11.** $60x(x^2 + 1)^{29}$

13. $2(2x + 3) \sec^2(x^2 + 3x) \tan(x^2 + 3x)$ **15.** $-3 \tan x$ **17.** $(e - e^{-2})$ units^2

19. e **21.** (a) $(0, 0), (1, 1)$ (b) $\left(\frac{1}{4}, \frac{1}{4}\right), (-1, -1)$ (c) $\left(-\frac{1}{2} + \frac{\sqrt{5}}{2}, -\frac{1}{2} + \frac{\sqrt{5}}{2}\right), \left(-\frac{1}{2} - \frac{\sqrt{5}}{2}, -\frac{1}{2} - \frac{\sqrt{5}}{2}\right)$

23. $(1.1322677, 1.1322677)$ **25.** $\frac{a^2}{a - 1}$

**problem set
52**

1. (a) Local maximum: $(1, 0)$; local minimum: $(-1, -4)$ (b) $(0, -2)$ **3.** $W = 50$ yards, $L = 100$ yards
5. $\sin^5 x + C$ **7.** $e^{x^2} + C$ **9.** $-\cos(x^2 + 3) + C$ **11.** $-\frac{1}{5}x^{-5} - x^{-2} + x + C$
13. $(x^2 + 3)^3 \left[\cos x (x^2 + 3) + 8x \sin x\right]$ **15.** $2\sec^2 x \tan x$ **17.** 2 units^2

19.

x	$1 + x + \dfrac{x^2}{2}$	e^x
0.1	1.105	1.1052
0.2	1.220	1.2214
0.3	1.345	1.3499

21. $r \approx 3.6278$ cm, $h \approx 7.2558$ cm
23. $(0.70635712, 0.70635712)$ **25.** $3x$

**problem set
53**

1. $40\sqrt{2}$ yd   **3.** $\frac{dA}{dt} = 24 \ \frac{\text{cm}^2}{\text{s}}$, $\frac{dP}{dt} = 8 \ \frac{\text{cm}}{\text{s}}$ **5.** $20 - e^3 + e \approx 2.6327$
7. (a) 1.6094 units^2 (b) 1.6094 (c) They are the same.   **9.** 3.2375 **11.** (a) $\int_0^{10} x^2 \, dx$ (b) $\frac{1000}{3}$
13. $\sqrt{x^4 - 3} + C$ **15.** $\ln|x^4 - 42| + C$ **17.** $\frac{4x^2}{x^2 + 1} + 2\ln(x^2 + 1) + 4\sec^2 x$
19. $2x\sec^2 x^2 \sec(\tan x^2)\tan(\tan x^2)$ **21.**
23. 4 **25.** B

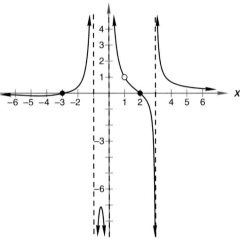

**problem set
54**

1. (a) Dimensions: 60 m $\times$ 60 m; $P_{\min} = 240$ m   (b) Dimensions: 60 m $\times$ 60 m; $P_{\min} = 240$ m
3. At rest when $t = -\frac{1}{2}$; moving right when $t > -\frac{1}{2}$; always accelerating, never decelerating   **5.** $\frac{16}{3}$
7. $\frac{1}{2}$ **9.** 76.9891 **11.** 10 units^2; $A = \int_2^4 (x + 2)\,dx = 10$ units^2 **13.** $e^{\sin x} + C$
15. $\tan^2 x + C$ or $\sec^2 x + C$ **17.** $\frac{\cos y - 2x}{x\sin y + 3y^2}$ **19.** $y = \frac{1}{e}x - \ln 3$ **21.** 0
23.

x	$x - \dfrac{x^3}{3!} + \dfrac{x^5}{5!}$	$\sin x$
0.1	0.0998	0.0998
0.2	0.1987	0.1987
0.3	0.2955	0.2955

25. $x = 10$, $y = 10$

**problem set
55**

1. $-3 + 4x + 3x^2$ **3.** 2.375 s   **5.** 1 unit^2 **7.** $\tan^4 x + C$ **9.** $x + \ln|x| + C$
11. $\frac{x(x^2 + 1)^{-1/2}}{x + \sin x} - \frac{(x^2 + 1)^{1/2}(1 + \cos x)}{(x + \sin x)^2}$ **13.** Positive concavity   **15.** 0 **17.** 0
19. $y = 2x - 2$ **21.** $f(x) = x^2$ **23.** $a = 2$, $b = -3$ **25.** E

**problem set
56**

1. (a) $V_{\max} \approx 151.7037$ ft^3; dimensions: $\frac{16}{3}$ ft $\times$ $\frac{16}{3}$ ft $\times$ $\frac{16}{3}$ ft
(b) $V_{\max} \approx 151.7037$ ft^3; dimensions: $\frac{16}{3}$ ft $\times$ $\frac{16}{3}$ ft $\times$ $\frac{16}{3}$ ft   **3.** At rest when $t = -\frac{7}{3}, 1$;
moving left when $-\frac{7}{3} < t < 1$; moving right when $t > 1$ and when $t < -\frac{7}{3}$ **5.** 2
7. $2e^{x^2} + C$ **9.** $\frac{1}{4}\ln(2x^2 + 1) + C$ **11.** $\frac{4}{9}\sin^3(3t) + C$

13. $\frac{2\cos(2x+1)}{x^2+2} - \frac{2x\sin(2x+1)}{(x^2+2)^2} + 2\sec^2 x$ **15.** $2 - 7x - 2x^2$ **17.** $\frac{2\sqrt{5}}{5}$

19.   *y*   **21.** 3.1416   **23.** 6   **25.** 90°

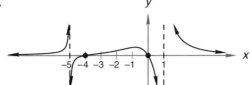

problem set 57

1. $(2, 3)$ **3.** See example 55.2.   **5.** (a) Size of square $= 0.05$ m, $V_{max} = 0.002$ m^3

(b) Size of square $= 0.05$ m, $V_{max} = 0.002$ m^3 **7.** -1 **9.** A   **11.** 1

13. $2e^{x^2+x} + C$ **15.** $\frac{1}{4}\tan^4 x + C$ **17.** $\frac{1}{e}$ or e **19.**

21. $y = \frac{8}{3}x - \frac{13}{3}$ **23.** $\{x \in \mathbb{R} \mid 1.495 < x < 1.505\}$

25. $\frac{\sqrt{3}}{3}$

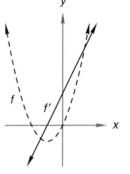

problem set 58

1. (a) Dimensions: 2.8284 units $\times$ 2.8284 units; $A_{max} = 8$ units^2

(b) Dimensions: $2\sqrt{2}$ units $\times$ $2\sqrt{2}$ units; $A_{max} = 8$ units^2 **3.** $\sum_{n=1}^{\infty} (-1)^{n+1} \frac{x^n}{n}$

5. 3.9063 s   **7.** $e^{3/2}$ **9.** 14   **11.** 4   **13.** $y = 1$

15. $\frac{2(e^{2x} - xe^{-x^2})}{x^3+1} - \frac{3x^2(e^{2x}+e^{-x^2})}{(x^3+1)^2} + 3\csc^2 x$ **17.** $\sqrt{2x^3 + 4x} + C$ **19.** $\frac{1}{5a}\sin^5(ax) + C$

21. B   **23.** $\frac{625}{49}$ **25.** $\ln 4$

problem set 59

1. (a) $V_{max} \approx 6.1584$ m^3, $x \approx 0.8453$ m   (b) $V_{max} = \frac{32\sqrt{3}}{9}$ m^3, $x = (2 - \frac{2\sqrt{3}}{3})$ m

3. $\sum_{n=0}^{\infty} (-1)^n x^n$ **5.** $-\frac{7}{4}$ **7.** $\int_{-1}^{1}(x-1)(x+1)(x-2)\,dx + \int_{2}^{1}(x-1)(x+1)(x-2)\,dx$

9. $f^{-1}(x) = \frac{1}{3}x - \frac{2}{3}$; $f^{-1}(4) = \frac{2}{3}$; $(f \circ f^{-1})(x) = x$; $(f^{-1} \circ f)(x) = x$ **11.** $x = \tan y$

13. $\frac{1}{4}(x^2 + 2)^4 + C$ **15.** $-\frac{\pi}{6}\cos^3(2x) + C$ **17.** $\frac{-3\sin(3x)}{x^2+2} - \frac{2x\cos(3x)}{(x^2+2)^2} + 2\sec^2(2x)$

19. $\frac{\sec(xy) - y}{x}$ **21.** $(x-2)^2 + (y-3)^2 = 9$; circle   **23.** $y = -x - 1$ **25.** C

problem set 60

1. (a) Dimensions: 10 in. $\times$ 10 in. $\times$ 10 in.   (b) Dimensions: 10 in. $\times$ 10 in. $\times$ 10 in.

3. $\sum_{n=1}^{\infty} -\frac{x^n}{n}$ **5.** $\frac{1}{8}\sin^4(2x) + C$ **7.** $\frac{1}{2}x^2 + x + \ln x^2 + C$

9. $(e^2 - e^{-1} - \frac{3}{2})$ units^2 **11.** 22.7224 units^2 **13.** e **15.** $e^{(\ln 2)(x^2+1)} x \ln 4$

17. $2\cot x \, e^{x^2+2x}[-\csc^2 x + (x+1)\cot x]$ **19.** $-\frac{3\sqrt{3}}{2}$

21.   *y*   **23.** Amplitude: 2; phase angle: 15°; period: 120°   **25.** 45°, 90°

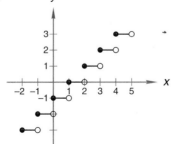

problem set 61

1. (a) 6.25 in.^{2} (b) $\frac{25}{4}$ in.$^2 = 6.25$ in.^{2}

3. (a) $1 - x + \frac{x^2}{2} - \frac{x^3}{3!} + \cdots$ (b) They are the same.   **5.** $a = 1$; $b = 4$

7.

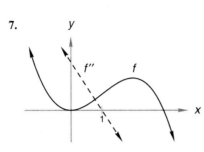

9. $-\frac{1}{3}\cos(3x) + C$ **11.** $-e^{-x} + C$ **13.** 1.7642 units^2

15. $\frac{1}{4}$ unit^2 **17.** e^{-2} or e^2

19. Parabola that opens downward   **21.** $-\frac{1}{x^2}$

23. $\{x \in \mathbb{R} \mid -1 \le x \le 1\}$ **25.** $\frac{1}{e}$

problem set 62

1. (a) 32 units^2 (b) 32 units^2 **3.** (a) $1 + x + x^2 + x^3 + \cdots$

(b) They are the same.   **5.** $\frac{117}{8}$ joules   **7.** 7 ln 2 ounces $\approx$ 4.8520 ounces

9. $f(x) = x^2 + 1$ **11.** $\frac{4}{5}x^{5/2} - 2x^{3/2} + 8x^{1/2} + C$ **13.** $\frac{1}{4}\tan^4 x + C$ **15.** $\frac{8}{3}$ units^2

17. $x = y^3 + y$ **19.** 625 ft   **21.** $2e^{\sin x}(\cos^2 x - \sin x)$ **23.** $\frac{4\sqrt{3}}{3}h^2$ ft^3

25. (a) $x \approx 2.6441208$ (b) $\ln(7 + 5\sqrt{2}) \approx 2.6441$

problem set 63

1. $\frac{1}{8}\frac{\text{ft}}{\text{min}}$ **3.** Maximum: 4; minimum: 0   **5.** (a) $y = -x + 3$ (b) $-2x^2 + 6x$ (c) $\frac{9}{2}$ cm^2

7. 10 meters   **9.** The graph of ln x is never concave upward.   **11.** $\frac{1}{2}e^{\sin(2x)} + C$

13. $2\sqrt{x^3 + x^2} + C$ **15.** $a = -1$, $b = 5$ **17.** 8   **19.** $\frac{x(x^2 + 1)^{-1/2}}{x + \sin x} - \frac{(x^2 + 1)^{1/2}(1 + \cos x)}{(x + \sin x)^2}$

21. $\lim\limits_{x \to 1^+} f(x) = \infty$; $\lim\limits_{x \to 1^-} f(x) = -\infty$ **23.** $\cos y = \frac{\sqrt{a^2 - x^2}}{a}$ **25.** $R(p) = 11{,}000p - 50p^2$

problem set 64

1. $28   **3.** $1 + 2x + 3x^2 + 4x^3 + \cdots$ **5.** Maximum: $2\sqrt{2} - 2$; minimum: $-\frac{4}{27}$

7. $\frac{1}{\sqrt{9 - x^2}}$ **9.** $\frac{2}{x^2 + 4}$ **11.** 12 joules   **13.** 1 unit^2 **15.** 2.9253 units^2 **17.** 5

19. $y = -x + \frac{\pi}{2}$ **21.** $\frac{2}{3}(x^3 + x^2 + x)^{3/2} + C$ **23.** 0   **25.** 60°

problem set 65

1. $\frac{1}{50}\frac{\text{rad}}{\text{s}}$ **3.** $h(t) = -4.9t^2 + 30t + 100$, 145.9184 m   **5.** $\frac{\sqrt{5}}{5}$

7. Maximum: 14; minimum: -13 **9.**   Maximum: 6; minimum: 1

11. 3 joules

13. $\sqrt{1 + \sin(2x)} + C$

15. $\frac{1}{6}$ unit^2 **17.** $\frac{1}{8}\frac{\text{unit}}{\text{s}}$ **19.** 1

21. $\frac{\cos x}{2\sqrt{\sin x}} + e^{2x}(2\cos x - \sin x)$ $+ \csc x\left(\frac{1}{x} - \ln x \cot x\right)$

23. e^2 **25.** $b < \frac{1}{2}$

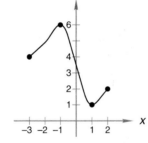

problem set 66

1. $\frac{16}{3}$ joules   **3.** $h(t) = -4.9t^2 + 20t + 160$; $h(2) = 180.4$ m; $v(2) = 0.4$ m/s; $a(2) = -9.8$ m/s^2

5. $\frac{1}{5}\left(e - \frac{1}{e}\right)$ **7.** $\frac{2\sqrt{3}}{9}$ **9.** Maximum: $13\frac{1}{2}$; minimum: $-29\frac{1}{6}$

11. See example 55.3.   **13.** $a = -2$, $b = -4$ **15.** $\frac{1}{4}(x + \sin x)^4 + C$ **17.** $\ln\sqrt{x^2 + 1} + C$

19. $\ln\sqrt{x^2 + 4} + C$ **21.** $e^{2x}\sec(\pi x)[\pi\tan(\pi x) + 2]$ **23.** C   **25.** $\frac{100}{100 + x^2}$

problem set 67

1. $\frac{5}{169}\frac{\text{rad}}{\text{s}}$ **3.** (a) $(1 + x)\sqrt{1 - x^2}$ (b) $\frac{3\sqrt{3}}{4}$ units^2 **5.** $A = 2\int_0^2 (4 - y^2)\,dy$

7. $\int_0^3 \left(-\frac{1}{2}y + \frac{3}{2}\right)dy$ **9.** 57.0667; They are the same.   **11.** B   **13.** $\frac{4}{7}$ **15.** $\frac{1}{4}\sin^4 x + C$

17. $3\arcsin\frac{x}{3} + C$ **19.** 1 unit^2 **21.** $C = 4$, $k = \frac{1}{2}$ **23.** $\cos 2$ **25.** $a = 2$, $b = 0$

problem set 68

1. (a) Cost $= (12x^2 + 18{,}000x^{-1})$ dollars   (b) $5\sqrt[3]{6}$ m $\times$ $5\sqrt[3]{6}$ m $\times$ $2\sqrt[3]{6}$ m

(c) $x \approx 9.0856$, $y \approx 3.6342$ **3.** Even   **5.** Neither   **7.** Odd   **9.** C

11. $\frac{1}{\sqrt{x + 1}\,[x^2 + \sin^3(2x)]} - \frac{4\sqrt{x + 1}\,[x + 3\sin^2(2x)\cos(2x)]}{[x^2 + \sin^3(2x)]^2}$ **13.** $\frac{1}{12}\sin^4(3x) + C$ **15.** $\arctan\frac{3x}{2} + C$

17. (a) $a = 0$, $b = 1$ (b) $a = 0$, $b = 2$ **19.**

Maximum: 3
Minimum: −6

21. $A = \int_1^4 \left[f(x) - g(x) \right] dx$

23. (a) $0 = W \frac{dL}{dt} + 200W^{-1} \frac{dW}{dt}$

(b) $-\frac{15}{2} \frac{\text{units}}{\text{s}}$ **25.** $\frac{1}{2}$

problem set 69

1. (a) $0 = L \frac{dW}{dt} + 1000L^{-1} \frac{dL}{dt}$ (b) 100 m   **3.** $e^x(x - 1) + C$ **5.** $\frac{1}{4}x^2(\ln x^2 - 1) + C$

7. $-x \cos x + \sin x + C$ **9.** y-axis symmetry   **11.** $\frac{2x}{\sqrt{1 - x^4}}$ **13.** $\frac{1}{2}(e - 1) \approx 0.8591$

15. $\frac{44}{3}$ units^2 **17.** (a) $\left(\pi - \frac{2}{3} \right)$ units$^2 \approx 2.4749$ units^2 (b) 2.4749 units^2

19. $1 - x^2 + \frac{2^3 x^4}{41} - \frac{2^5 x^6}{6!} + \cdots$ **21.** (a) $(2 + 6 \ln k)$ units^2 (b) e^3 (c) $36 \frac{\text{units}}{\text{s}}$

23. A   **25.** (a) y-axis symmetry   (b) $\{ x \in \mathbb{R} \mid |x| > 3 \}$ (c) $\pm\sqrt{10}$ (d) $f^{-1}(x) = \sqrt{e^x + 9}$

problem set 70

1. (a) 20 m $\leq x \leq$ 50 m   (b) $A = \frac{17}{4}x^2 - 255x + 7225$ (c) 5100 m^2

3. Maximum: $\sqrt[3]{4}$; minimum: 0   **5.** Does not exist   **7.** Does not exist   **9.** −6

11. $-\frac{1}{6}$ **13.** Not necessarily   **15.** $e^{2x}\left(x - \frac{1}{2} \right) + C$ **17.** $\frac{1}{3} \arctan \frac{e^x}{3} + C$

19. $\frac{1}{6}$ unit^2 **21.** $\frac{e^{\cos x}(\cos x - \sin^2 x)}{\ln (2x)} - \frac{e^{\cos x} \sin x}{x \,[\ln (2x)]^2} - \frac{2}{4x^2 + 1}$ **23.** $-\frac{1}{2} \cos (x^2 + \pi) + C$ **25.** $y = \frac{\ln x}{\ln 3}$

problem set 71

1. $4\sqrt{3}$ units   **3.** $\frac{\pi}{6}$ units^3 **5.** $\pi \int_0^2 (4 - y^2)\, dy$ **7.** 12   **9.** $\frac{17}{3}$

11. $\frac{1}{2} \arcsin \frac{3x^2}{5} + C$ **13.** $-3(x \cos x - \sin x) + C$ **15.** $\int_0^1 \sqrt{1 - y^2}\, dy$

17. $2(4 - \pi)$ units^2 **19.** $\frac{e^x}{e^{2x} + 1} + \frac{1}{\sqrt{2x + 1}(\sin x - x)} - \frac{\sqrt{2x + 1}(\cos x - 1)}{(\sin x - x)^2}$

21. $\frac{1}{4} \sin^4 x + \sin x + C$ **23.** $f^{-1}(x) = \frac{1}{4}x + \frac{5}{4}$ **25.** D

problem set 72

1. $\frac{128\pi}{3} \frac{\text{cm}^3}{\text{s}}$ **3.** (a) $2(x + y) \frac{dx}{dt} + 2(x + 7y) \frac{dy}{dt} = 0$ (b) −1   **5.** $81 \ln 3 \approx 88.9876$;

$y \approx 88.9876x - 274.9504$ **7.** $1 + (\ln 2)x + \frac{(\ln 2)^2 x^2}{2!} + \frac{(\ln 2)^3 x^3}{3!} + \cdots$ **9.** $\frac{3\pi}{5}$ units^3

11. $\pi \int_0^1 (1 - y)\, dy$ **13.** $-\cos (\pi x) + C$ **15.** $\frac{1}{3\pi}$ **17.** Even

19. $-2 \sin (2x) + \frac{2}{4x^2 + 1} + \frac{2}{\sqrt{2x + 1}(x^2 + 1)} - \frac{4x\sqrt{2x + 1}}{(x^2 + 1)^2}$ **21.** $-\frac{1}{2} e^{-x^2 - 2x} + C$

23. $\frac{1}{2} \arctan (2x) + C$ **25.** $\left(\frac{1}{k}, \frac{1}{ke} \right)$

problem set 73

1. (a) $(16\pi x^2 + 864\pi x^{-1})$ dollars   (b) $x = 3$ cm, $y = 48$ cm   (c) \$1357.17

3. $h(t) = -16t^2 + 20t + 500$; $t = 6.25$ s   **5.** $\frac{-1}{25 \ln 5}$ **7.** $5^x \ln 25 + \frac{3}{x \ln 7}$

9. $y' = \begin{cases} 1 & \text{when } x > -1 \\ -1 & \text{when } x < -1 \end{cases}$ **11.** $\frac{13^x}{\ln 13} + C$ **13.** $\frac{2^{x^2 + 4}}{\ln 4} + C$ **15.** $-\frac{1}{4} \cos^4 x - \cos x + C$

17. $\frac{30}{\ln 2}$ units^2 **19.** $\left(1 + \ln \frac{\sqrt{2}}{2} \right)$ units^2 **21.** −1   **23.** y-axis symmetry

25. (a) $y = -2x + 2$ (b) −1.3660, 0.3660, 1

problem set 74

1. −2.5 m^3/s   **3.** 27,000 newtons   **5.** $2000 \int_{-3}^0 -y \sqrt{9 - y^2}\, dy$; 18,000 newtons

7. $\frac{32}{5} \pi$ units^3 **9.** $\frac{1}{x \ln 5} + 7^x \ln 7 + \frac{1}{x \ln 8}$ **11.** $\frac{a}{x\sqrt{x^2 - a^2}}$

13. $\frac{1}{\ln 5}(x \ln x - x) + C$ or $x \log_5 x - \frac{x}{\ln 5} + C$

15. $-\frac{1}{2}x \cos (2x) + \frac{1}{4} \sin (2x) + C$ **17.** $\sqrt{x^2 + \pi} + C$

19. (a) $-\pi, 0, \pi, 2\pi$ (b)

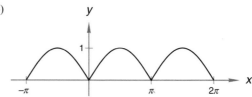

(c) $f'(x) = \begin{cases} \cos x & \text{when } 0 < x < \pi \\ -\cos x & \text{when } -\pi < x < 0 \\ & \text{or } \pi < x < 2\pi \end{cases}$ **21.** (a) 3 (b) 1 (c) Does not exist (d) 0

23. $Q(p) = 1500 - 5p$; $R(p) = 1500p - 5p^2$ **25.** (a) $\frac{-y-1}{x+4y}$ (b) $y = -\frac{1}{3}x + \frac{5}{3}$ (c) $(6, -3)$

    (d) $y = \frac{-x \pm \sqrt{x^2 - 8x + 48}}{4}$

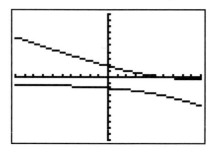

problem set 75

1. $1.50   **3.** Not necessarily true   **5.** 0   **7.** $25{,}000 \int_0^4 (4 - y)\, dy$ **9.** (a) 3, -3

(b)

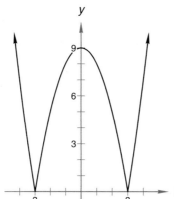

(c) $f'(x) = \begin{cases} 2x, & \text{when } |x| > 3 \\ -2x, & \text{when } |x| < 3 \end{cases}$

11. $\pi \int_0^4 (4 - y)\, dy$

13. $\frac{2^x}{\ln 2} + 2\sqrt{x + 1} + C$

15. $\frac{1}{7} \arctan \frac{7x^3}{3} + C$

17. Even

19. $y = \frac{4\sqrt{3}}{3}x + \frac{\pi - 2\sqrt{3}}{6}$

21. $\left(\frac{\pi}{4}, \frac{\sqrt{2}}{2}\right)$

23. D   **25.** $\left(\frac{1}{2}, \frac{\sqrt{2}}{2}\right)$

problem set 76

1. $20,289.21   **3.** $-\cos x + \frac{1}{3}\cos^3 x + C$ **5.** $-\frac{1}{3}\cos^3 x + \frac{1}{5}\cos^5 x + C$ **7.** 1

9. $a = 2$, $b = 0$, $c = 1$ **11.** (a)   (b) 0

13. $\pi \int_0^1 (1 - x)\, dx$

15. $5^{x^2 + 1} x \ln 25$

    $+ \frac{2x}{x^2 + 4} + \arctan \frac{x}{2}$

    $+ \frac{1}{x \ln 24}$

17. $\frac{1}{\sqrt{1 - x^2}} + \arcsin x + C$

19. $y = 1$ **21.** $e^{\sin 1} - 1$

23. B   **25.** 0.6931 units^2; The answers are the same.

problem set 77

1. $-\frac{3}{16\pi} \frac{\text{cm}}{\text{s}}$ **3.** 4,900,000 newtons   **5.** $\frac{1}{3}\sin^3 x - \frac{1}{5}\sin^5 x + C$

7. $\arctan x - 4\sqrt{\cos x + 1} + C$ **9.** -1 **11.** $y = (-\ln 27)x + \ln(19{,}683e)$ **13.** (a) 0

  (b) Does not exist   **15.** Origin symmetry   **17.** B

19. (a) $h(x) = \cos^2 x$; $-\frac{3\pi}{2}, -\frac{\pi}{2}, \frac{\pi}{2}, \frac{3\pi}{2}$ (b)

  (c) Domain: $\{x \in \mathbb{R} \mid 0 \le x \le 2\pi\}$

    Range: $\{y \in \mathbb{R} \mid 0 \le y \le 1\}$

  (d) $y = x + \frac{2 - 3\pi}{4}$ **21.** 0

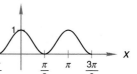

23. (a) $\frac{y-2x}{2y-x}$ (b) $(2\sqrt{3}, \sqrt{3}), (-2\sqrt{3}, -\sqrt{3})$

(c) $y = \frac{x \pm \sqrt{x^2 - 4(x^2 - 9)}}{2}$

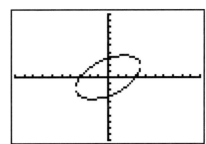

25. $\{y \in \mathbb{R} \mid -1 < y < 1\}$

problem set 78

1. (a) $V = 60x - 0.8x^3$

(b) $x = 5$ m, $y = 8$ m

(c)

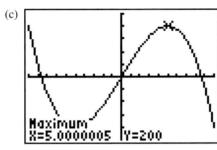

3. $v(t) = 3t^2 - 4t;\ x(t) = t^3 - 2t^2 - 4$

5. 5,120,000 joules   **7.** $\frac{24}{\ln 3}$ units^2

9. $\frac{2}{3}\sqrt{x}(x+3) + C$ **11.** $4 \arctan x + C$

13. $\frac{1}{4}(\sin x + \pi)^4 + C$

15. (a) Maximum: $65\frac{13}{18}$; minimum: $-8\frac{2}{9}$

(b)

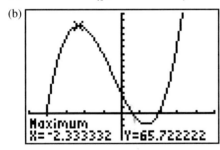
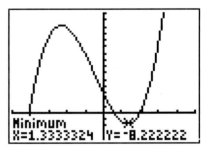

17. $x = e^y + y$ **19.** $2x^2 \sec^2(x^2) + \tan x^2 - 15 \csc(15x) \cot(15x) + \frac{1}{\sin x + \cos x} + \frac{x(\sin x - \cos x)}{1 + \sin(2x)}$

21. C   **23.**   **25.** B

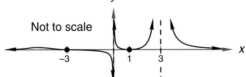

Not to scale

problem set 79

1. $v(t) = 2\sin t - 6;\ x(t) = -2\cos t - 6t + 10$ **3.** 196,000 joules   **5.** 11,000 newtons   **7.** 0

9. 0   **11.** 1   **13.** $\frac{1}{4}\sin^4 x + C$

15. (a) $\pm 2\sqrt{2}$

(b)

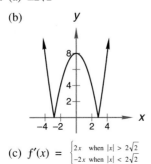

(c) $f'(x) = \begin{cases} 2x & \text{when } |x| > 2\sqrt{2} \\ -2x & \text{when } |x| < 2\sqrt{2} \end{cases}$

17. Symmetric about the y-axis   **19.** 4

21. (a) $\sum\limits_{n=1}^{\infty} (-1)^{n-1}\frac{x^{(2n-1)}}{(2n-1)!}$

(b) $x^2 - \frac{x^6}{3!} + \cdots$

(c) $x^2 - \frac{x^6}{3!} + \frac{x^{10}}{5!} - \frac{x^{14}}{7!} + \cdots$; They are the same.

23. $\sin(2x)$

25. (a)  (b) $(-1, 27)$, $(2, 0)$

problem set 80

1. $-4, 4$ **3.** (a) $v(t) = -9.8t + 50$, $x(t) = -4.9t^2 + 50t + 160$ (b) 5.1020 s   (c) 12.7626 s

5. $y = \frac{3}{2}$ **7.**

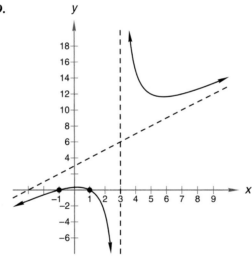

9.

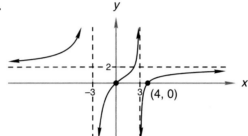

11. ∞ **13.** -2 **15.** $\frac{1}{2}$ unit^2 **17.** 2

19. $L = 25$ cm, $W = 4$ cm

21. $x \ln x - x + \frac{43^x}{\ln 43} + C$

23. $\frac{1}{4\sqrt{6}} \arctan \frac{2x^2}{\sqrt{6}} + C$ **25.** 2

problem set 81

1. $400{,}000$ joules   **3.** $f(x) = 2x^2 - 3x + 1$ **5.** $\frac{81}{2}\pi$ units^3 **7.** $\frac{5}{14}\pi$ units^3

9. Asymptote: $y = 2x$; vertical asymptote: $x = 1$ **11.**

13. 7   **15.** D   **17.** $\frac{2^x}{\ln 2} + \arctan x + C$ **19.** C

21. 0   **23.** B   **25.** $(-1, 15)$

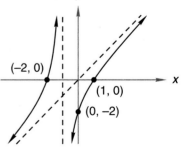

problem set 82

1. $-\frac{2}{5} \frac{\text{rad}}{\text{s}}$ **3.** The particle is at rest when $t = 3$, moving right when $t > 3$, and moving left when $t < 3$.   **5.** $48{,}000$ newtons   **7.** 1   **9.** $a = \frac{3}{2}$; $b = \frac{3}{2}$ **11.** $\frac{15\pi}{\ln 4}$ units^3

13. $\frac{\pi}{6}$ units^3 **15.** 0   **17.** 0   **19.** $-\frac{1}{4} \cos^4 x + \frac{1}{6} \cos^6 x + C$ **21.** $e^x(x - 1) + C$

23. $\csc(1 + x^2)\left[1 - 2x^2 \cot(1 + x^2)\right] + \frac{1}{\sqrt{4 - x^2}} + \frac{1}{x \ln 7} - 14^x \ln 14$ **25.** Domain: $\mathbb{R}$;
Range: $\{y \in \mathbb{R} \mid 0 \le y \le \sqrt{2}\}$

problem set 83

1. 2,508,800 joules   3. $a = \frac{2}{3}$; $b = \frac{1}{3}$ 5. Maximum: 4; minimum: 0   7. $\frac{\pi}{6}$ units^3

9. (a) See example 55.3.   (b) $\sum\limits_{n=0}^{\infty} \frac{(-1)^n x^{(4n)}}{(2n)!}$ 11. $\frac{1}{2}x - \frac{1}{12}\sin(6x) + C$

13. $\ln|x| + 3x^{-1} + C$ 15. $\ln\sqrt{x^2 - 1} + C$ 17. 0   19. 3   21. $2e^3$ units^2

23. $y = -\frac{16}{3}x + \frac{65}{4}$ 25. $(2, -12)$

problem set 84

1. (a) Maximum value of $x = 10$; minimum value of $x = 5$ (b) $7x^2 - 120x + 900$ (c) 5

(d) 475 m^2 3. (a) $h(t) = -4.9t^2 + 100$ (b) 4.5175 s   (c) 90.35 m   5. $a = 3$, $b = 2$

7. $x^{\sin x}\left[\frac{\sin x}{x} + \ln x(\cos x)\right]$ 9. $\frac{\sqrt{x-1}(x^3-1)\sin x}{(x^2+1)(x^4+1)}\left[\frac{1}{2(x-1)} + \frac{3x^2}{x^3-1} + \cot x - \frac{2x}{x^2+1} - \frac{4x^3}{x^4+1}\right]$

11. $\frac{1}{2}x - \frac{1}{8}\sin(4x) + C$ 13. $\frac{2}{3}\sin^3 x - \frac{2}{5}\sin^5 x + C$

15. (a) Asymptote: $y = 0$; vertical asymptote: $x = 1$ 17. -1 19. $y = -x + \frac{\pi}{2}$

(b)

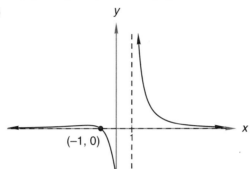

21. $\frac{29}{6}$ units^2

23. $\frac{2x\cos(x^2+1)}{e^x - e^{-x}} - \frac{(e^x + e^{-x})\sin(x^2+1)}{(e^x - e^{-x})^2} - \frac{2}{4x^2+1}$

25. $(\sqrt{3}, 3\sqrt{3})$, $(-\sqrt{3}, -3\sqrt{3})$

problem set 85

1. 457,247 bacteria   3. Maximum: $\sqrt{2}$; minimum: -1; inflection point: $x = \frac{3\pi}{4}$

5. (a) $a + b = 1$ (b) $a = 3$, $b = -2$ 7. -1 9. 2   11. No

13. $\frac{x^2\sqrt{x^3-1}}{\sin x\cos x}\left[\frac{2}{x} + \frac{3x^2}{2(x^3-1)} - \cot x + \tan x\right]$ 15. $\frac{3}{2}x - \frac{3}{4}\sin(2x) + C$ 17. $\frac{1}{4}\sin^4 x + C$

19. $\pi\int_0^3 (x^4 + x^2 + 1)\,dx$ 21. 0   23. $-2\sqrt{2}$ 25. 5

problem set 86

1. (a) 48,000 newtons   (b) 864,000 joules   3. $a = e^{-\pi/2}$, $b = 4 - e^{-\pi/2}$ 5. $\frac{3}{2}$ 7. $\frac{\pi}{2}$

9. $(fg)(-x) = f(-x)g(-x) = -f(x)[-g(x)] = f(x)g(x) = (fg)(x)$ 11. 2   13. 1   15. $\pi\int_1^2 e^{2x^2}\,dx$

17. $-1 + \frac{e^x - 1}{\sin(2x) + \cos x} - \frac{(e^x - x)[2\cos(2x) - \sin x]}{[\sin(2x) + \cos x]^2} + 4\csc^2 x\cot x$ 19. $2e^x(x - 1) + C$

21. (a) 27   (b) $a = \frac{5}{4}$; $b = -\frac{5}{4}$ 23. 1   25. (a) Zero: 1; vertical asymptote: $x = 2$

(b) $y = x^2 + 2x + 4$ (c)

(d) Domain: $\{x \in \mathbb{R} \mid x \neq 2\}$;

Range: $\mathbb{R}$

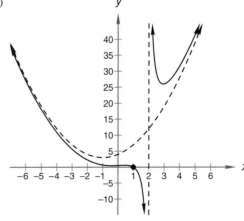

problem set 87

1. $1102.50　　3. (a) $v(t) = -2t^2 - \frac{1}{\pi}\cos(\pi t) + \frac{9}{2}$; $x(t) = -\frac{2}{3}t^3 - \frac{1}{\pi^2}\sin(\pi t) + \frac{9}{2}t + \frac{1}{6}$

(b) $v(0) = \frac{9\pi - 2}{2\pi}\frac{\text{linear units}}{\text{time unit}} \approx 4.1817 \frac{\text{linear units}}{\text{time unit}}$; $x(0) = \frac{1}{6}$ linear unit　　5. 2　　7. $2\pi^2$ units^3　　9. k

11. $\frac{\sqrt{39}}{3} \approx 2.0817$　　13. $\frac{2 + \sqrt{7}}{3} \approx 1.5486$　　15. -2　　17. $2x - \frac{1}{2}\sin(4x) + C$

19.　　　　　　　　　　　　　　　　　　　　　　21. π units^2　　23. $\frac{7}{x^2 + 49} - e^{-x} - \sin x$

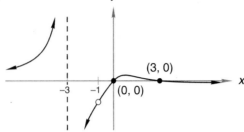

25. (a) Zero: -1; vertical asymptote: $x = 2$　(b) $y = 2x^2$　(c)
(d) Domain: $\{x \in \mathbb{R} \mid x \neq 2\}$,　Range: $\mathbb{R}$

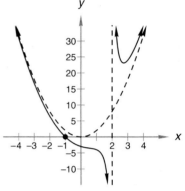

problem set 88

1. 128 joules　　3. $2\pi e^2$ units^3　　5. $a = 0$; $b = 1$　　7. $y = \frac{1}{-x^4 + C}$　　9. (a) Odd function　(b) 0

11. $\frac{1}{2}\ln\left[\frac{1}{2}(e^2 - 1)\right]$　　13. $\frac{2}{3}$ units^2　　15. $\frac{2}{9}(x^3 - 1)^{3/2} + C$　　17. C and D　　19. 2

21. Does not exist　　23. $\frac{1}{3}$　　25. $f(x) = x^3 - 3x^2$

problem set 89

1. (a) $26{,}133\frac{1}{3}$ newtons　(b) 313,600 joules　　3. (a) odd　(b) odd　(c) even

5. $\frac{1}{2}(e^2 + 1) \approx 4.1945$　　7. 1　　9. $y = \frac{1}{-2x^3 + C}$　　11. $3727.48　　13. (a) 10　(b) 1

15. $\frac{\pi}{5}$ units^3　　17. $4x^{2x}(1 + \ln x)$　　19. $\frac{\pi}{2}$ units^2　　21. $\frac{1}{2}e^{\sin(2x)} + C$　　23. $\frac{-3x^2 - y}{x + 2y}$　　25. C

problem set 90

1. $-\frac{1}{2\pi}\frac{\text{cm}}{\text{s}}$　　3. (a) $x(0) = 2$; $x(3) = 2$　(b) $4\frac{1}{2}$ units　　5. $\frac{2}{\pi}$　　7. 5π linear units/time unit

9. $\sqrt{2}$　　11. $y^2 - 2x^2 = C$　　13. $y = \ln|x| + 2$　　15. $a = 2$; $b = 0$　　17. $\frac{3^x}{\ln 3} + C$

19. $\frac{3}{2}e^{x^2} + C$　　21. $5\arctan x + C$　　23. Even;

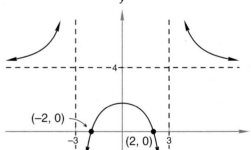

25. (a) Vertical asymptote: $x = -2$;
end behavior: $y = x^2 - 2x + 2$　(b)
(c) Domain: $\{x \in \mathbb{R} \mid x \neq 2\}$
Range: $\mathbb{R}$

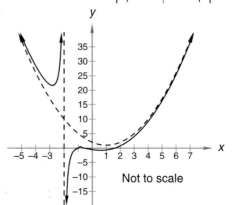

Not to scale

problem set 91

1. (a) $V = 6\pi r^2 - \frac{3}{2}\pi r^3$ (b) $r = \frac{8}{3}$ cm; $h = 2$ cm (c) $\frac{128}{9}\pi$ cm^3 3. (a) $x(0) = 2$; $x(4) = 6$
(b) 12 units 5. 1 7. –3 9. $\frac{2}{\pi}$ 11. 2 linear units/time unit 13. $e - 1$
15. 36π units^3 17. $y^2 - x^2 = C$ 19. (a) –10 (b) 0 21. $y = 1$
23. $\frac{1}{3}\sin(3x) - \frac{1}{9}\sin^3(3x) + C$ 25. (a) $\frac{1}{4}, -\frac{1}{4}$ (b) $f'(\frac{1}{4}) = 1$, $f'(-\frac{1}{4}) = -1$ (c) $(0, \frac{7}{8})$

problem set 92

1. (a) $a(t) = \frac{4 - 4t^2}{(1 + t^2)^2}$; $x(t) = 2\ln(1 + t^2) + 4$ (b) 0 3. $-\frac{\sqrt{2}}{2}$ is a local minimum;
$\frac{\sqrt{2}}{2}$ is a local maximum. 5. $h(3) = 1$; $h'(3) = \frac{1}{5}$ 7. 2 9. 0 11. \$3360.28
13. 6 linear units/time unit 15. $-\frac{1}{3} + \frac{\sqrt{13}}{3}$ 17. $\cot x - \frac{9x^2}{x^3 + 1} - \frac{16x^3}{x^4 + 1}$ 19. D
21. $\frac{1}{\sqrt{9 - x^2}} + \arcsin\frac{x}{3} + \frac{3}{x^2 + 9} + \arctan\frac{x}{3} + C$ 23. C
25. $A = \pi r^2(1 + \sqrt{2})$ units^2, $V = \frac{1}{3}\pi r^3$ units^3

problem set 93

1. (a) $V = 2\pi r^2\sqrt{3 - r^2}$ (b) $r = \sqrt{2}$ m, $h = 2$ m (c) 4π m^3 3. (a) $x(0) = 3$, $x(2) = 5$
(b) 34 units 5. 1.302775638 7. $\frac{1}{2}$ 9. $\frac{4}{3}$ 11. $y = 2\ln|x|$ 13. $\frac{1}{2}$ 15. –1
17. $-\frac{1}{3}\cos^3 x + C$ 19. $2\ln|\sin x| + C$ 21. 28 23. $\frac{255}{16\ln 4}$ units^2 25. C

problem set 94

1. (a) $\frac{1}{\pi}\frac{\text{cm}}{\text{s}}$ (b) 16 cm^3/s 3. (a) 90,000 newtons (b) 750,000 joules 5. $\frac{1}{10}\pi$ units^3
7. $2\pi\int_0^{\pi/4}(1 + x)\tan x\,dx$ 9. 1.618033989 11. $y = x - 1$ 13. 0 15. $y = x$
17. $\sqrt[3]{2}$ 19. $\int_{-2}^{2}(-y^2 + 4)\,dy$ 21. $\ln\frac{\sqrt{6}}{2}$ units^2
23. $2x\cos(x^2 - 1) + \frac{\cos x}{e^x - 2} - \frac{e^x(\sin x + 1)}{(e^x - 2)^2} + \frac{1}{3}\ln|x^3 - 1| + C$
25. (a) Zero: –1; vertical asymptote: $x = 2$; end behavior: $y = -2x^2 - 3x - 6$
(b) (c) Domain: $\{x \in \mathbb{R} \mid x \neq 2\}$
Range: $\mathbb{R}$

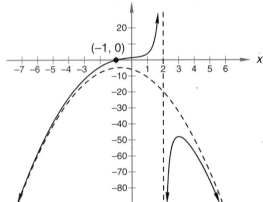

(–1, 0)

problem set 95

1. (a) $A = \pi r\sqrt{r^2 + \left(\frac{300}{\pi r^2}\right)^2}$ (b) $r \approx 4.0721$ m; $h \approx 5.7588$ m 3. (a) $\frac{8}{5}\frac{\text{units}}{\text{s}}$
(b) $\frac{14\sqrt{10}}{25}\frac{\text{units}}{\text{s}} \approx 1.7709\frac{\text{units}}{\text{s}}$ 5. (a) $0, \frac{1}{4}, \frac{1}{2}, \frac{3}{4}, 1$ (b) 8 units 7. 1.1745 9. $\frac{1}{12}$ 11. 0
13. Does not exist 15. (a) $\frac{\pi^2}{2}$ units^3 (b) $2\pi(2 + \pi)$ units^3 17. B 19. (a) 50 ft/s (b) Yes
21. $\ln|e^x + \sin x| + C$ 23. $a = 4$; $b = -2$ 25. E

problem set 96

1. (a) $1 < t < 2$ (b) 34 units 3. $\frac{17}{2}$ 5. $\frac{3}{2}$ 7. (a) $\frac{13}{50} = 0.26$ (b) $\frac{1}{4} = 0.25$
(c) $\frac{1}{50} = 0.02$ (d) 71 9. $2\pi\int_0^1(1 - x)x^4\,dx$ 11. $2\pi\int_0^{\pi}(2\pi - x)\sin x\,dx$
13. $\frac{1}{3}$ 15. 1 17. \$6024.67 19. $x^{\sqrt{x} - 1/2}(1 + \ln\sqrt{x})$ 21. A
23. $120(x - 4)^3 - 8\cos(2x)$ 25. A

problem set 97

1. $\frac{4}{9\pi}\frac{\text{m}}{\text{min}}$ 3. (a) 0 (b) –4 (c) 18 units 5. 72 units^3 7. 18π units^3 9. $\frac{11}{6}$ 11. D
13. 0.7451 15. 1.179509025 17. 1 19. $x^{\sin x}(\frac{\sin x}{x} + \cos x\ln x)$ 21. $\sqrt[3]{10}$ 23. D
25. $x^2 + C$

problem set 98

1. $8\frac{\text{cm}^2}{\text{s}}$ 3. (a) $\frac{1}{2}, 1$ (b) $\frac{1}{2} < t < 1$ (c) 2 times (d) $\frac{3}{4}$ 5. (a) x^2 (b) x^2 7. e^{-x^2}
9. B 11. 72 units^3 13. 16π units^3 15. (a) $\frac{1171}{1680} \approx 0.6970$ (b) $\ln 2$ (c) $\frac{1}{96}$ (d) 13
17. $y = -\frac{1}{2}\cos(2x) + C$ 19. $\frac{2x}{x^2 + 1} + \cot x$ 21. $\sec^2(\sin x)\cos x + 2x(\ln 3)3^{x^2} + 5\arctan x + C$
23. $\frac{2\pi - 3\sqrt{3}}{48} \approx 0.0226$ 25. $\frac{\sqrt{17}}{2}N$ miles

problem set 99

1. $\frac{40\sqrt{15}}{9}$ units^2 3. \$495   5. $x(t) = t + \ln t + 2 - \ln 3$ 7. e^{x^3} 9. $4\pi e^2$ units^3
11. $\frac{787}{560}$ units$^2 \approx 1.4054$ units^2 13. $\frac{1}{6}$ 15. 10   17. $\int_1^2 \frac{1}{y}\, dy$ 19. -16 21. e^2 units^2
23. B   25. D

problem set 100

1. (a) $2\pi(2 + \pi)$ units^3 (b) $\pi(8 + \frac{\pi}{2})$ units^3 3. slope = 15, $c = \frac{\sqrt{39}}{3} \approx 2.0817$ 5. (a) 10
   (b) Cannot be determined   (c) Zero   (d) Cannot be determined   7. $2x$
9. $-\ln|\cos x| + C$ or $\ln|\sec x| + C$ 11. $\ln|\sec x + \tan x| + C$
13. $\frac{1}{2}\tan^2 x - \ln|\sec x| + C$ or $\frac{1}{2}\sec^2 x + \ln|\cos x| + C$ 15. $\frac{256\sqrt{3}}{3}$ units^3
17. 2.086745340   19. $\pi \int_0^{\pi/4} (2\tan x + \tan^2 x)\, dx$ or $2\pi \int_0^1 (1 + y)(\frac{\pi}{4} - \arctan y)\, dy$
21. $y = (\ln 16)x - \ln 256 + 4$ or $y \approx 2.7726x - 1.5452$ 23. $(1.25, 1.75)$ 25. $\frac{2^x}{\ln 2}$

problem set 101

1. (a) 100π cm^2/min   (b) 200 cm^2/min   (c) 50π cm^2/min   3. \$2   5. (a) $\int_0^\pi \sin^3 x\, dx$
   (b) $\frac{4}{3}$ units^3 7. $f'(x) = \begin{cases} e^x & \text{when } x > 0 \\ -e^{-x} & \text{when } x < 0 \end{cases}$ 9. 1   11. $-\infty$ 13. See section 101.B.
15. $\ln|\sec x + \tan x| + C$ 17. $\frac{1}{3}\tan^3 x - \tan x + x + C$ 19. 3.914867641   21. $\frac{1}{4}(1 - \ln 3)$
23. $2\pi(3e^2 - e)$ units^3 25. $y = \frac{5}{8}x^2 + \frac{1}{2}x - \frac{9}{8}$

problem set 102

1. (a) 80π cm^2/s   (b) $60\sqrt{3}$ cm^2/s   3. (a) 28 units   (b) 4 linear units/time unit
   (c) 24 linear units/time unit   5. Ellipse; $\frac{(x - 1)^2}{3} + \frac{y^2}{27} = 1$ 7. See section 102.A.
9. (a) $\cos s$ (b) $\cos s$ 11. 1.1150   13. $-\infty$ 15. $\ln|\csc x - \cot x| + C$
17. $\frac{1}{2}\tan^2 x - \ln|\sec x| + C$ or $\frac{1}{2}\sec^2 x + \ln|\cos x| + C$ 19. $y = -\frac{1}{2}\cos(2x) + C$ 21. $\frac{1}{3}$
23. 13   25. $a = \frac{1}{2}$; $b = \frac{5}{2}$

problem set 103

1. \$12.50; 60 trees   3. $y \approx \frac{7}{3}x - 0.7197$ 5. $\frac{256\sqrt{2}}{15}$ units$^3 \approx 24.1359$ units^3 7. $\delta = \varepsilon$ 9. 0
11. 0   13. $\lim_{h \to 0} \frac{\ln(x + h) - \ln x}{h} = \lim_{h \to 0} \frac{1}{h}[\ln(x + h) - \ln x] = \lim_{h \to 0} \frac{1}{h}\frac{x}{x}[\ln(\frac{x + h}{x})]$
   $= \lim_{h \to 0} \frac{1}{x}\frac{x}{h}[\ln(\frac{x + h}{x})] = \frac{1}{x}\lim_{h \to 0} \ln(\frac{x + h}{x})^{x/h} = \frac{1}{x}\ln e = \frac{1}{x}$
15. $\lim_{h \to 0} \frac{\sin(x + h) - \sin x}{h} = \lim_{h \to 0} \frac{\sin x \cos h + \cos x \sin h - \sin x}{h} = \lim_{h \to 0} \frac{\sin x (\cos h - 1) + \cos x \sin h}{h}$
   $= \sin x \lim_{h \to 0} \frac{\cos h - 1}{h} + \cos x \lim_{h \to 0} \frac{\sin h}{h} = (\sin x)(0) + (\cos x)(1) = \cos x$
17. 0.5210   19. 0.8477075981   21. $\frac{1}{3}\tan^3 x - \tan x + x + C$
23. $f(x) = \frac{14}{3}x^2 - 9x - \frac{2}{3}$ 25. If a building is not a skyscraper, then it is not tall.

problem set 104

1. 6597 m   3. \$303   5.

7. D   9. $\frac{4}{7}$ 11. e^2
13. $(\sin x)e^{x^2 + 1}$
15. $-\frac{1}{2}\cot^2 x - \ln|\sin x| + C$
   or
   $-\frac{1}{2}\csc^2 x + \ln|\csc x| + C$
17. 72
19. $y = \sin(\frac{1}{3}x^3 - 9)$
21. $\delta = \frac{\varepsilon}{2}$
23. See section 102.A.
25. $\int_0^1 (x^3 + 2x)\, dx$

problem set 105

1. $8\sqrt{3}$ units^3 3. $a_1 = 2$, $a_2 = \frac{3}{2}$, $a_3 = \frac{4}{3}$, $a_4 = \frac{5}{4}$
5. $a_1 = 0$, $a_2 = \frac{\ln 2}{2}$, $a_3 = \frac{\ln 3}{3}$, $a_4 = \frac{\ln 4}{4}$ 7. $a_n = (-1)^{n+1}\frac{1}{3^{n-1}}$, $n = 1, 2, 3, \ldots$
9. Diverges   11. $\frac{7}{13}$ 13. 0   15. $83\frac{7}{20} = 83.35$ 17. $\frac{x^4}{4} - \frac{4x^3}{3} + \frac{3x^2}{2} - 7x + \frac{93}{4}$

19. (a)

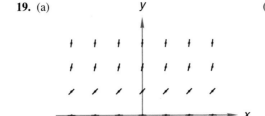

(b)

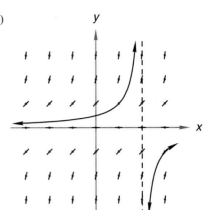

21. $x^2 \ln (x^2) - x^2 + C$ **23.** $\lim_{h \to 0} \frac{\ln (x + h) - \ln x}{h} = \lim_{h \to 0} \frac{1}{h}[\ln (x + h) - \ln x]$

$= \lim_{h \to 0} \frac{1}{h} \frac{x}{x}[\ln (\frac{x + h}{x})] = \lim_{h \to 0} \frac{1}{x} \frac{x}{h}[\ln (\frac{x + h}{x})] = \frac{1}{x} \lim_{h \to 0} \ln (\frac{x + h}{x})^{x/h}$

$= \frac{1}{x} \ln e = \frac{1}{x}$ **25.** $\frac{100}{3}$ units^2

problem set 106

1. (a)

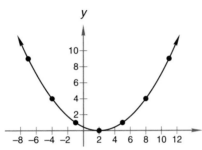

(b) $\frac{2}{9}x - \frac{4}{9}$ (c) $y = \frac{1}{9}x^2 - \frac{4}{9}x + \frac{4}{9}$ **3.** \$200

5. 4.081655102   **7.** ln 4 units^2 **9.** 32 units^3

11. e **13.** $\frac{\sin x}{x}$

15. $x - \frac{1}{2}\sin (2x) - \cos x + \frac{1}{3}\cos^3 x + C$

17. 2   **19.** $a = -2$; $b = -4$

21. $a_n = \frac{n^2}{n + 1}$, $n = 1, 2, 3, \ldots$

23. Converges to 0

25. (a) $x(t)$ (b) $y(t)$ (c) y

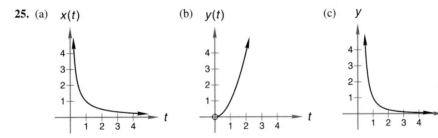

problem set 107

1. $\frac{\sqrt{3}\pi}{8}$ units^3 **3.** (a) $1 < t < 3$ (b) $t < 1$, $t > 3$ (c) 12 units   **5.** 13,500 newtons

7. $\sqrt{13}\ \angle 123.6901°$ **9.** $r = \frac{1}{2}\tan \theta \sec \theta$ **11.** Converges to $\frac{1}{2}$

13. $a_n = (-1)^n \frac{2^n}{n^2}$, $n = 2, 3, 4, 5, \ldots$ **15.** 0.1960   **17.** 0   **19.** e^4

21. $a = 7$; $b = -3$ **23.** $\frac{d}{dx} f(|x|) = \begin{cases} 2x - 6 & \text{when } x > 0 \\ 2x + 6 & \text{when } x < 0 \end{cases}$ **25.** (a) $f(t) = 16t^3$ (b) ± 1

problem set 108

1. $2\hat{i} - 4\hat{j}$ **3.** $\langle -0.5, -0.8660 \rangle$ **5.** Unit parallel vector: $\left\langle \frac{1}{\sqrt{145}}, \frac{12}{\sqrt{145}} \right\rangle$;

unit normal vector: $\left\langle -\frac{12}{\sqrt{145}}, \frac{1}{\sqrt{145}} \right\rangle$ **7.** 12π units^3 **9.** $\frac{1}{2}[e^2 - e^{-2}]$ units^3 **11.** $2c$

13. Converges to 0   **15.** $\cos 2$ **17.** $x^2(\ln x - \frac{1}{2}) + C$ **19.** $\frac{1}{2}x^2 + 4x - 3 \ln |x| - 7x^{-1} + C$

21. 10   **23.** $r = \frac{3}{\sin \theta - 2 \cos \theta}$ **25.** $\ln (1 - x) = -x - \frac{x^2}{2} - \frac{x^3}{3} - \frac{x^4}{4} - \cdots$; $\ln (1.1) \approx 0.0953$

problem set 109

1. 10.5 gallons   **3.** $\frac{8}{27}(10\sqrt{10} - 1)$ units   **5.** $a(4) = -3e^{-4}$; $x(3) = -4e^{-3} + 1$ **7.** $y = x$

9. 0   **11.** 0   **13.** C **15.** $-2\sqrt{25 - x^2} + C$ **17.** $\int_0^{\ln \sqrt{2}} (-e^{2x} + 2)\,dx + \int_{\ln \sqrt{2}}^1 (e^{2x} - 2)\,dx$

19. $\frac{4}{9}$ **21.** $\left\langle \frac{6}{\sqrt{37}}, \frac{36}{\sqrt{37}} \right\rangle$ **23.** (a) $a_1 = \frac{1}{2}$, $a_2 = -\frac{1}{2}$, $a_3 = \frac{3}{8}$, $a_4 = -\frac{1}{4}$ (b) Converges to 0

25. (a) Vertical asymptote: $x = 0$; end behavior: $y = x + 1$ (b) 1   (c) x^2

problem set 110

1. $4\frac{1}{8}$ **3.** $\left\langle \frac{12}{\sqrt{13}}, \frac{8}{\sqrt{13}} \right\rangle$ **5.** $\sin (2x) = 2x - \frac{(2x)^3}{3!} + \frac{(2x)^5}{5!} - \frac{(2x)^7}{7!} + \cdots$; $\sin 0.4 \approx 0.3894$

7. $\int_2^6 \sqrt{16x^2 + 24x + 10}\,dx$ **9.** $\frac{8}{27}(10\sqrt{10} - \frac{13\sqrt{13}}{8})$ units ≈ 7.6337 units

11. $x^2 + y^2 = 2\sqrt{x^2 + y^2} + y$

13.

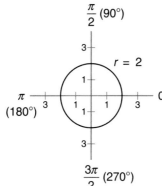

15.

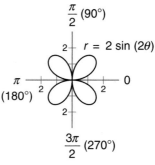

17. $\frac{dy}{dx} = -3x^{-4}$;
     $y = x^{-3}$

19. $\left(\frac{1}{2} - \ln\sqrt{2}\right)$ units^2 **21.** Converges to 0   **23.** -1

25. See section 101.A.

problem set 111

1. $\frac{\pi}{3}$ units^3 **3.** $\frac{7}{8}$ **5.** $-\frac{3}{4}$

7.

$\frac{\pi}{2}$ (90°)

$r = 3\cos\theta$

π (180°)   1   2   0

$\frac{3\pi}{2}$ (270°)

9.

$\frac{\pi}{2}$ (90°)

$r = 3\cos(4\theta)$

π (180°)   3   3   0

$\frac{3\pi}{2}$ (270°)

11. ∞ **13.** 1   **15.** 1
17. 2   **19.** $\frac{31}{13}$
21. 3.8202
23. (a) $a_n = \frac{3^n}{n^2+1}$,
     $n = 1, 2, 3, \dots$
     (b) Diverges

25. $\frac{2}{15}(x + 4)^{3/2}(3x - 8) + C$

problem set 112

1. (a) $\ln k$ units^2 (b) $\frac{1}{10}$ $\frac{\text{units}^2}{\text{s}}$ **3.** $-9000\int_{-1}^{0} y\sqrt{y+1}\,dy$ **5.** 0   **7.** 1

9.

$\frac{\pi}{2}$ (90°)

$r = 4\sin\theta$

π (180°)   2   1   1   2   0

$\frac{3\pi}{2}$ (270°)

11. $\int_{-2}^{2} \sqrt{1 + 4x^2 e^{2x^2}}\,dx$ **13.** $\sqrt{13}$
15. $e - 1$ **17.** Converges to 0   **19.** 3.5673
21. $2\cos^4\theta\,d\theta$ **23.** C
25. $\lim_{x\to a}[f(x)]^{g(x)} = 0^{+\infty}$;
     $\lim_{x\to a} g(x)\ln[f(x)] = \infty \cdot \ln(0^+) = \infty \cdot -\infty$
     $= -\infty$; $\lim_{x\to a}[f(x)]^{g(x)} = e^{-\infty} = 0$

problem set 113

1. $\frac{512}{3}$ units^3 **3.** $\frac{5x^{1/4}(4 + x^3) - 72x^{13/4}}{(4 + x^3)^7}$ **5.** $\arcsin x + C$ **7.** $\arctan x + C$

9. $\frac{(-2 - x^2)\sqrt{1 - x^2}}{3} + C$ **11.** $\ln|\sec x + \tan x| + \sec x \tan x + C$ **13.** $\langle 4, 16 \rangle$

15. $2.1747\underline{/178.6272°}$ **17.** $\frac{4\pi}{3}$ units   **19.** e **21.** $\frac{1}{e}$

23.

$\frac{\pi}{2}$ (90°)

$r = 4\cos\theta$

π (180°)   1   2   3   0

$\frac{3\pi}{2}$ (270°)

25. $\lim_{x\to a}[f(x)]^{g(x)} = 0^{-\infty}$; $\lim_{x\to a} g(x)\ln[f(x)]$
     $= -\infty \cdot \ln(0^+) = -\infty \cdot -\infty = \infty$; $\lim_{x\to a}[f(x)]^{g(x)}$
     $= e^{\infty} = \infty$

problem set 114

1. $1333\frac{1}{3}$ ft^3 3. ln (sec 1.5 + tan 1.5) units   5. 2π units   7. 8π units   9. 0.8767262154

11. $T = 0$; Both methods yield the same answer.   13. $y = 3$ 15.

17. 1   19. $-2\sqrt{2}$ 21. arcsin $\frac{x}{2}$ + C   23. $\frac{1}{6}$ unit^2

25. $a = -3$; $b = 2$; $c = 1$

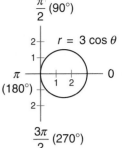

problem set 115

1. $-\frac{32\pi}{3}$ $\frac{cm^3}{s}$ 3. $h \approx 93.9693$ ft/s; $d \approx 281.9079$ ft   5. $\frac{13}{12}$ units

7. $-\ln|x| + \ln|x - 2| + \ln|x - 1| + C$ 9. 9π units   11.

13. $\frac{1}{2}$ arcsin $(2x) + C$ 15. $\frac{1}{2}$ arctan $(2x) + C$

17. $\frac{1}{8}$ ln $(1 + 4x^2) + C$ 19. $\frac{27}{4}$ 21. $\frac{3x^2}{2\sqrt{1 + x^3}}$

23. A   25. D

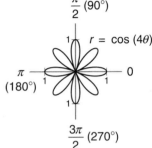

problem set 116

1. 0.7390851332   3. Average $= \frac{2}{\pi}$; $c = $ arcsin $\frac{2}{\pi}$ or $c = \pi - $ arcsin $\left(\frac{2}{\pi}\right)$ 5. $\frac{1}{2}(e^9 - 1)$ joules

7. $\frac{1}{2}$ ln $|x| + 5$ ln $|x + 1| - \frac{11}{2}$ ln $|x + 2| + C$ 9. $r = 2$ 11. 12 units

13.

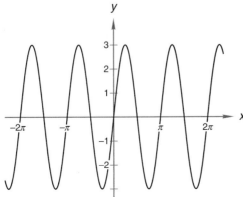

15. 2 ln $|x| + \frac{9}{4}x^2 + C$

17. $\frac{2}{3}$ ln $\left|\sqrt{4 + 9x^2} + 3x\right| + C$

19. $S_1 = \frac{2}{3}$, $S_2 = 2$,
$S_3 = 4$, $S_4 = \frac{20}{3}$, $S_5 = 10$, $S_6 = 14$

21. $a_1 = \frac{3}{2}$, $a_2 = \frac{3}{4}$, $a_3 = \frac{3}{8}$, $a_4 = \frac{3}{16}$,
$a_5 = \frac{3}{32}$, $a_6 = \frac{3}{64}$ 23. Converges to 3

25. 10.575

problem set 117

1. $\frac{1475}{999}$ 3. 60 ft   5. Converges to 0   7. Converges to 1   9. Diverges   11. Converges to e^3

13. Diverges   15. First 4 terms: $\left(\frac{1}{2} - \frac{1}{3}\right), \left(\frac{1}{3} - \frac{1}{4}\right), \left(\frac{1}{4} - \frac{1}{5}\right), \left(\frac{1}{5} - \frac{1}{6}\right)$; converges to $\frac{1}{2}$

17. First 4 terms: $\left(1 - \frac{1}{2}\right), \left(\frac{1}{2} - \frac{1}{3}\right), \left(\frac{1}{3} - \frac{1}{4}\right), \left(\frac{1}{4} - \frac{1}{5}\right)$; converges to 1

19. $\frac{9}{2}$ arcsin $\frac{x}{3} + \frac{x\sqrt{9 - x^2}}{2} + C$ 21. 22,030.3634 units

23.

25. $S_1 = 1$, $S_2 = \frac{3}{2}$, $S_3 = \frac{11}{6}$, $S_4 = \frac{25}{12}$,
$S_5 = \frac{137}{60}$, $S_6 = \frac{49}{20}$, $S_7 = \frac{363}{140}$, $S_8 = \frac{761}{280}$,
$S_9 = \frac{7129}{2520}$, $S_{10} = \frac{7381}{2520}$, $S_{11} = \frac{83,711}{27,720}$;
diverges

problem set
118

1. $L = 2$ m; $h = 4$ m; $C = \$192$ **3.** 4π cm^2 **5.** $r = \cot\theta\csc\theta$

7.

$\frac{\pi}{2}$ (90°)

$r = 2\cos(3\theta)$

π
(180°)

0

$\frac{3\pi}{2}$ (270°)

9.

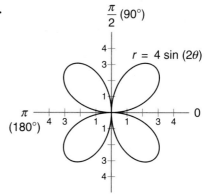

$\frac{\pi}{2}$ (90°)

$r = 4\sin(2\theta)$

π
(180°)

0

$\frac{3\pi}{2}$ (270°)

11. Unit tangent vector: $\left\langle \frac{1}{\sqrt{82}}, \frac{9}{\sqrt{82}} \right\rangle$; unit normal vector: $\left\langle -\frac{9}{\sqrt{82}}, \frac{1}{\sqrt{82}} \right\rangle$

13. $\frac{7}{2}\ln|x| - \ln|x+1| + \frac{1}{2}\ln|x+2| + C$ **15.** $8\arcsin\frac{x}{4} + \frac{x\sqrt{16-x^2}}{2} + C$

17. Converges to $\frac{1}{4}$ **19.** Diverges   **21.** $\frac{137}{217}$ **23.** $\frac{3\pi}{2}$ **25.** $a = -4,\ b = 3$

problem set
119

1. $\frac{dy}{dx} = -\tan t;\ \frac{d^2y}{dx^2} = -\sec^3 t$ **3.** Negative concavity; $y = \frac{1}{3}x + \frac{10}{3}$

5. $\int_2^5 \sqrt{9t^4 - 36t^3 + 36t^2 + 1}\ dt$ **7.** $\pi\int_0^3 (3^{2x} - 2^{2x})\ dx$

9.

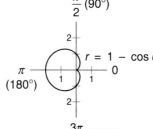

$\frac{\pi}{2}$ (90°)

$r = 1 - \cos\theta$

π
(180°)

0

$\frac{3\pi}{2}$ (270°)

11.

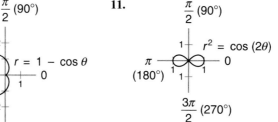

$\frac{\pi}{2}$ (90°)

$r^2 = \cos(2\theta)$

π
(180°)

0

$\frac{3\pi}{2}$ (270°)

13. Diverges

15.

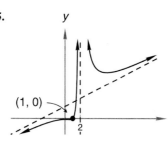

y

(1, 0)

x

17. e^3 **19.** $\frac{4}{5}\ln 4 + \frac{11}{5}\ln\frac{3}{2}$ **21.** $\frac{1}{8}\ln\left|\frac{x-4}{x+4}\right| + C$

23. $x\log_3 x - \frac{x}{\ln 3} + C$ **25.** 27.18

problem set
120

1. $R_t = 2000(1.5)^t$ **3.** $3\frac{1}{27}$ **5.** $2\ln|x| - 2\ln|x+2| + \frac{4}{x+2} + C$

7. Unit tangent vector: $\left\langle \frac{1}{\sqrt{5}}, \frac{2}{\sqrt{5}} \right\rangle$; unit normal vector: $\left\langle -\frac{2}{\sqrt{5}}, \frac{1}{\sqrt{5}} \right\rangle$

9.

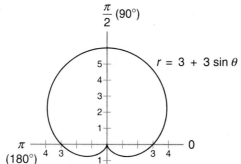

$\frac{\pi}{2}$ (90°)

$r = 3 + 3\sin\theta$

π
(180°)

0

$\frac{3\pi}{2}$ (270°)

11. $\frac{dy}{dx} = \frac{1}{2}t + \frac{1}{4},\ \frac{d^2y}{dx^2} = \frac{1}{8}$

13. $\int_0^5 \sqrt{4t^2 + 4t + 17}\ dt$

15. Converges to $\frac{1}{4}$

17. $\frac{76}{3}$ units   **19.** $25\arcsin\frac{4}{5} + 12$

21. $\sin(x^2)$ **23.** $\frac{1}{4}$ **25.** C

problem set 121

1. $y = 6x - 37$ 3. $(3, 0), (5, -4)$; the curve has no vertical tangents.

5.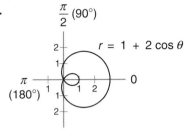

7. $\frac{1}{2} \tan^2 x - \ln |\sec x| + C$ or $\frac{1}{2} \sec^2 x + \ln |\cos x| + C$

9. $2 \ln |x| - \frac{1}{x} - \ln |x - 1| + C$

11. $\ln \left| \sqrt{4 + x^2} \right| + C$ 13. $2 \arcsin \frac{x}{2} + C$

15. $-\frac{1}{4} \ln (\cos^4 x + 1) + C$ 17. 0 19. e

21. Converges to 1   23. Diverges   25. 15.36

problem set 122

1. $3\sqrt{10}$ units/s   3. $\left\langle -\frac{150}{\sqrt{901}}, \frac{5}{\sqrt{901}} \right\rangle$ 5. $\frac{1}{2} x^2 \sin (2x) + \frac{1}{2} x \cos (2x) - \frac{1}{4} \sin (2x) + C$

7. $\frac{1}{2} \ln |x - 1| - \frac{1}{2} \ln |x + 1| - \frac{1}{x + 1} + C$ 9. $\arcsin \frac{x}{3} + C$ 11. Diverges

13.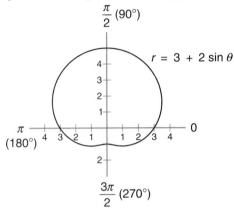

15.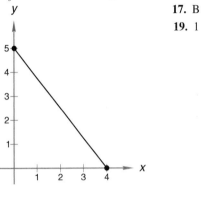

17. B

19. 1

21. $y = \frac{1}{2}(x - 1)$ 23. 1   25. C

problem set 123

1. $\left[3\sqrt{145} + \frac{1}{4} \ln (\sqrt{145} + 12) \right]$ units   3. 312,500 newtons   5. $2 \ln |x + 1| - \frac{3}{x + 1} + C$

7. $e^x(x^2 - 2x + 2) + C$ 9. $\vec{f}\,'(t) = -2 \sin (t)\, \hat{i} + \frac{1}{t} \hat{j}$; Domain: $\{t \in \mathbb{R} \mid t > 0\}$

11.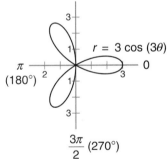

13. $-\frac{1}{2\pi} \left(e^2 - e^{-2} \right)$ 15. $2\pi \int_0^1 (\tan x + x \tan x)\, dx$

17. Converges to $-\frac{1}{6}$ 19. $\left[5\sqrt{6} - \frac{1}{2} \ln (5 + 2\sqrt{6}) \right]$ units^2

21. $\frac{2xy^3 + 3 - 6y^4}{24xy^3 + 8y - 3x^2y^2}$ 23. e^5 25. e

problem set 124

1. $\frac{\pi}{\sqrt{10}} \left[\arctan \frac{\sqrt{10}}{2} - \arctan \frac{\sqrt{10}}{5} \right]$ units^3 3. (a) Relative maximums: $(-8, 6), (8, 18)$; relative minimum: $\left(-1, -2\frac{1}{4}\right)$ (b) Concave up: $(-8, 0), (2, 8)$; concave down: $(0, 2)$ (c) $x = 0, 2$

(d)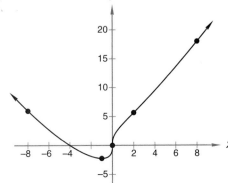

5. $\frac{dy}{dx} = \frac{2x}{3y^2 + 1}$; $\frac{d^2y}{dx^2} = \frac{18y^4 + 12y^2 + 2 - 24x^2y}{(3y^2 + 1)^3}$

7. $-x^2 \cos x + 2x \sin x + 2 \cos x + C$

9. $4\left(\ln |x - 1| - \ln |x| - \frac{1}{x - 1} \right) + C$

11. $\sqrt{2}(e^\pi - 1)$ units

13.

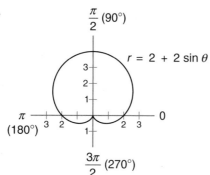

$r = 2 + 2 \sin \theta$

15. Converges to $\frac{3}{500} - \frac{\pi^4}{125(5 - \pi)}$

17. $\vec{f}\,'(t) = 6 \sec^2 (2t)\,\hat{i} + \frac{t}{\sqrt{t^2 - 4}}\,\hat{j}$;

     Domain: $\{ t \in \mathbb{R} \mid t \neq \frac{(2n + 1)\pi}{4}, \; n \in \mathbb{Z},$

          $|t| \geq 2 \}$

19. $\sum\limits_{n=1}^{\infty} -\frac{x^n}{n}$ **21.** e^4 **23.** e **25.** 9

problem set 125

1. $v(t) = 5e^{4t} + 5$; $x(t) = \frac{5}{4}e^{4t} + 5t + \frac{11}{4}$; total distance traveled $= \left[\frac{5}{4}(e^{80} - e^{20}) + 75 \right]$ units

3. $\vec{f}\,'(t) = 2^t \ln 2\,\hat{i} - \frac{1}{t \ln 2}\,\hat{j}$; Domain: $\{ t \in \mathbb{R} \mid t > 0 \}$ **5.** $\frac{dy}{dx} = \frac{x}{y}$; $\frac{d^2 y}{dx^2} = -\frac{4}{y^3}$

7. $-3 \ln |x + 2| - 4 \ln |x - 2| + C$ **9.** $\frac{1}{2}(\sec x \tan x + \ln |\sec x + \tan x|) + C$ **11.** $\frac{1}{2}$

13. $\frac{1}{2}$ **15.** $\frac{2}{\pi}$ **17.** $2\pi \int_0^1 (1 + y)(1 - y^2)\,dy$ **19.** B   **21.** Diverges

23.

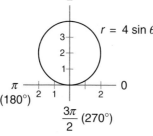

$r = 4 \sin \theta$

                                        25. 0.0002128

problem set 126

1. $-\frac{1}{3} \frac{\text{unit}}{\text{s}}$ **3.** Diverges   **5.**

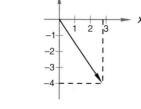

7. $\frac{1}{2} \ln (x^2 + 2) + \frac{1}{\sqrt{2}} \arctan \frac{x}{\sqrt{2}}$
    $- 2 \ln |x + 1| + C$

9. $x^2 - x + y^2 - 2y = 0$

11.

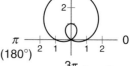

$r = 1 + 2 \sin \theta$

13. $\frac{\sqrt{21}}{3}$ **15.** Diverges   **17.** $2\sqrt{x^2 + x + 1} + C$

19. $4 \arcsin \frac{x}{2} + C$ **21.** $2 \operatorname{arcsec} \frac{x}{2} + C$

23. $24\frac{1}{2}$ units   **25.** $c = -3q^2$; $b = 0$; $d = 0$

problem set 127

1. Infinite   **3.** Shell method: $V = 2\pi \int_0^2 (1 + x)(e^2 - e^x)\,dx$;
    washer method: $V = \pi \int_0^{e^2} [2 \ln y + (\ln y)^2]\,dy$ **5.** $16\sqrt{6}$ joules

7. $-2 \cot t (\csc^2 t + 2)$ **9.** $2 \ln |x| - \frac{3}{x} + \ln |x + 2| + C$ **11.** $(2 - \frac{\pi}{2})$ units^2 **13.** $-\frac{6x^2 + 2}{9y^5}$

15. $-\frac{1}{3} \cos^3 x + \frac{1}{5} \cos^5 x + C$ **17.** Diverges   **19.** Converges   **21.** Diverges

23.

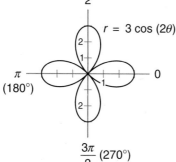

$r = 3 \cos (2\theta)$

                                   25. $\frac{88}{3}$ units^2

problem set 128

1. $2\pi(\ln\frac{32}{5})$ units^3 3. Diverges   5. Converges to $\frac{1}{9}$ 7. Diverges   9. Diverges

11. Converges   13. $e^x(\sin x - \cos x) + C$ 15. 0   17. $\frac{1}{x}$ 19. $2\pi \int_{-\pi/4}^{\pi/4} (\frac{\pi}{2} - x) \sec x \, dx$

21. $\frac{28}{15} \frac{\text{linear units}}{\text{time unit}}$ 23.

25. Absolute maximum $= 65$

Absolute minimum $= -16$

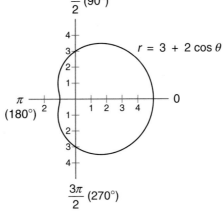

$\frac{\pi}{2}$ (90°)

$r = 3 + 2\cos\theta$

π (180°)

$\frac{3\pi}{2}$ (270°)

problem set 129

1. $\frac{dy}{dx} = 4t - 1$; $\frac{d^2y}{dx^2} = 2$;

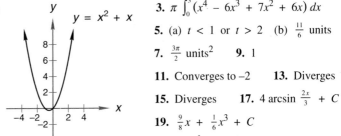

$y = x^2 + x$

3. $\pi \int_0^3 (x^4 - 6x^3 + 7x^2 + 6x) \, dx$

5. (a) $t < 1$ or $t > 2$ (b) $\frac{11}{6}$ units

7. $\frac{3\pi}{2}$ units^2 9. 1

11. Converges to -2 13. Diverges

15. Diverges   17. $4\arcsin\frac{2x}{3} + C$

19. $\frac{9}{8}x + \frac{1}{6}x^3 + C$

21. $\frac{\sec^2 x}{\sqrt{1 - \tan^2 x}} + e^{-x}(x - 1)$

23. $(\sqrt{x})^x(\frac{1}{2} + \ln\sqrt{x})$

25. (a) $\frac{1}{2}$ units^2 (b) $\frac{1}{2}$ (c) $\int_0^1 x \, dx = \frac{1}{2}$

problem set 130

1. If $y = 6$ m, $\frac{dx}{dt} = 9 \frac{\text{m}}{\text{s}}$; if $y = -6$ m, $\frac{dx}{dt} = -9 \frac{\text{m}}{\text{s}}$.   3. Converges   5. Converges

7. Converges   9. $\delta = \frac{\varepsilon}{3}$

11.

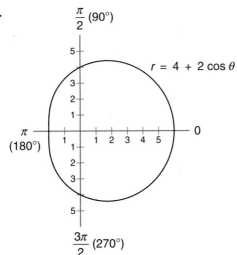

$\frac{\pi}{2}$ (90°)

$r = 4 + 2\cos\theta$

π (180°)

$\frac{3\pi}{2}$ (270°)

13. $(\frac{5\pi}{4} - 2)$ units^2 15. e^2 17. $\cos 3$

19. $x^2 \sin(2x) + x\cos(2x) - \frac{1}{2}\sin(2x) + C$

21. $\frac{\pi}{4}$ 23. 4

25. (a)

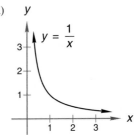

y

$y = \frac{1}{x}$

(b) Diverges   (c) Diverges

(d) $\lim_{b \to 0^+} \int_0^1 (\frac{1}{x} - 1) \, dx$

problem set 131

1. $671.37   3. 9 units   5. 4π units^2 7. 0   9. Undefined   11. $\frac{\sin y}{(\cos y + 1)^3}$ 13. Converges

15. Converges   17. Diverges   19. $\frac{673}{864}$ 21. $2\arcsin\frac{x}{2} - \frac{x\sqrt{4 - x^2}}{2} + C$

23. $\frac{1}{9}x^3(3\ln x - 1) + C$ **25.** (a)   (b) $\left(8 - 9\ln\frac{5}{3}\right)$ units^2

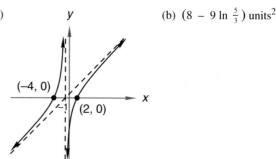

problem set
132
   1. $\frac{20\sqrt{15}}{3}$ units^2 **3.** 1.4056 units^2 **5.** $\left(\frac{\pi}{4} - \frac{3\sqrt{3}}{16}\right)$ units^2 **7.** Diverges   **9.** Converges

   11. Converges to 4   **13.** Converges   **15.** $\frac{1}{8}$ **17.** $\cos 2 + \frac{1}{2}\sin 2$

   19. $\frac{1}{2}x^2 + x + 2\arctan x + C$ **21.** $e^{1/3}$ **23.** e^4 **25.** $\frac{1}{13}$

problem set
133
   1. $\frac{59}{8}$ units   **3.** 9.765625   **5.** $\left(\frac{15}{4} + \ln 2\right)$ units   **7.** Diverges   **9.** Converges   **11.** Diverges

   13. $x^2 \sin x + 2x\cos x - 2\sin x + C$ **15.** $\frac{1}{2}$ **17.** ∞ **19.** $\frac{2e^{2t}}{\sqrt{1 - e^{4t}}}\hat{i} + 12e^{3t}\hat{j}$

   21. 0.0002128   **23.** 1, e^{-2} **25.** 366,000 ft^2

problem set
134
   1. $\frac{19,600}{3}$ newtons   **3.** $\frac{15\pi}{\ln 4}$ units^3 **5.** $2\pi\left[\frac{3 - \ln 4}{(\ln 2)^2}\right]$ units^3 **7.** $r = \frac{1}{\sin\theta - 2\cos\theta}$ **9.** 6π units^2

   11. Undefined   **13.** -0.2968 **15.** Converges   **17.** Converges   **19.** Converges to $\frac{16}{3}$

   21. $\frac{1}{2}x^2 + 2x + \frac{1}{3}\ln|x + 2| + \frac{8}{3}\ln|x - 1| + C$ **23.** B

   25. Darius's location: $66\frac{2}{3}$ m line; total distance: 200 m

problem set
135
   1. -2900 ft/s   **3.** $x^4 + 2x^2y^2 + y^4 + 2x^2 - y^2 = 0$ **5.** $\left(18 - \frac{9\pi}{4}\right)$ units^2 **7.** Converges

   9. Converges absolutely   **11.** No conclusion can be drawn.   **13.** 0   **15.** e **17.** $y = \frac{3}{2}x - \frac{9}{2}$

   19. $\ln\frac{5}{9} + \frac{4}{15}$ **21.** $\sqrt{5} + 2\ln\left(\frac{\sqrt{5} + 1}{2}\right) - 2$ **23.** Diverges   **25.** $\frac{75\sqrt{6}}{2}$ ft ≈ 91.8559 ft

problem set
136
   1. $\frac{14}{3}$ units   **3.** $\frac{800}{3}$ newtons   **5.** Positive concavity   **7.** $\frac{\sin x}{x}$

   9. Converges absolutely   **11.** Diverges   **13.** Converges   **15.** $2\int_2^6 \sqrt{4t^2 + 1}\, dt$

   17. $\left(\frac{4\pi}{3} + 2\sqrt{3}\right)$ units^2 **19.** Diverges   **21.** 129.4366

   23. 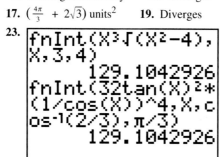   **25.** $\frac{81\pi}{2}$ units^3

problem set
137
   1. 322,122,547,200 rabbits   **3.** See section 48.A.   **5.** 14

   7. $-\sin(2)\sqrt[3]{\cos^4(2)} - 4 - \sqrt[3]{12} \approx -0.8496$ **9.** Converges absolutely   **11.** Converges

   13. Converges to $\frac{7}{2}$ **15.**   **17.** A

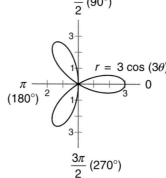

19.

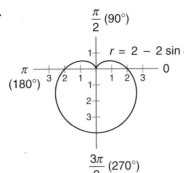

$\dfrac{\pi}{2}$ (90°)

$r = 2 - 2\sin\theta$

π (180°)   3 2 1   1 2 3 0

$\dfrac{3\pi}{2}$ (270°)

21. $\frac{2}{3}$ **23.** $e^{2x^2}x^{e^{2x^2}}\left(\frac{1}{x} + 4x\ln x\right)$

25. Maximum: $\left(-\frac{8}{9}, \frac{683}{81}\right)$; minimum: $\left(\frac{1}{3}, -8\right)$;

inflection point: $\left(-\frac{5}{18}, \frac{35}{162}\right)$ y

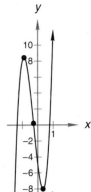

problem set
138

1. (a) $\sum\limits_{n=1}^{\infty}(-1)^{n+1}\frac{1}{2^n} = \sum\limits_{n=1}^{\infty}(-1)(-\frac{1}{2})^n$ is geometric with $a = \frac{1}{2}$ and $r = -\frac{1}{2}$.

Since $|r| < 1$, the series converges.   (b) $\frac{1}{3}$ (c) Error $= \frac{1}{48}$ (d) The error in S_4 is smaller than a_5.

3. 4110 ft^2 **5.** $\frac{9\pi}{8}$ units   **7.** $y \approx -0.5395x + 0.1415$ **9.** $\frac{1}{2} - \cos 1$ **11.** Converges

13. Diverges   **15.** Converges to $\frac{1}{15}$ **17.** $x - \arctan x + C$ **19.** $\ln\sqrt{2} + \frac{\pi}{4} \approx 1.1320$

21. D   **23.** D   **25.** $\sum\limits_{n=0}^{\infty}(-1)^n x^n$

problem set
139

1. (a) $\frac{1}{n^2} \geq \frac{1}{(n+1)^2}$ and $\lim_{n\to 0}\frac{1}{n^2} = 0$, so $\sum\limits_{n=1}^{\infty}(-1)^{n+1}\frac{1}{n^2}$ meets the conditions of Liebniz's theorem and
converges.   (b) $\frac{115}{144}$ (c) Within 0.04   **3.** Average velocity $= -\frac{8}{3}\frac{\text{linear units}}{\text{time unit}}$;

average speed $= \frac{49}{12}\frac{\text{linear units}}{\text{time unit}}$ **5.** $\tan^2 x \sec^3 x$ **7.** Converges absolutely   **9.** Diverges

11. Diverges   **13.**

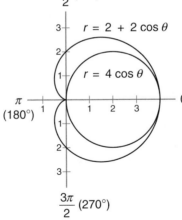

$\dfrac{\pi}{2}$ (90°)

3   $r = 2 + 2\cos\theta$

2

1   $r = 4\cos\theta$

π (180°)   1   1 2 3 0

1

2

3

$\dfrac{3\pi}{2}$ (270°)

15. 1   **17.** $\ln\sqrt{2}$

19. $2\ln|x| + \frac{1}{x-1} + C$

21. 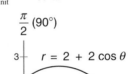 $\dfrac{y}{\sec(xy) - x}$

problem set
140

1. 15°, 75°   **3.** 5 terms   **5.** e^6 **7.** Diverges   **9.** Converges absolutely

11. $(5\pi - 8)$ units^2 **13.** $\frac{1}{3}x^3 + 2x - \sqrt{2}\arctan\frac{x}{\sqrt{2}} + C$ **15.** $3\ln|x+1| - \frac{1}{\sqrt{3}}\arctan\frac{x}{\sqrt{3}} + C$

17. $\frac{1}{14}$ **19.** $\cos\left(e^{2x^2}\right)e^{x^2}(2x)$ **21.** $\frac{3\pi}{4}$ units^2

problem set
141

1. Let $h = f(t)$ be the height of a projectile. Then its vertical speed is given by $v = f'(t)$. The extreme values
of any continuous quadratic function are achieved either at the endpoints of the domain or when the
derivative is zero. At both endpoints of the domain of h (which is a continuous quadratic function), the height
is minimal. Therefore, h is maximal when its derivative is zero. In other words, h is maximal
when $v = f'(t) = 0$.

3. $-4 + 5(x-1) + 8(x-1)^2 + 4(x-1)^3 + (x-1)^4$ **5.** $\sum\limits_{n=1}^{\infty}(-1)^n\frac{(x-\pi)^{2n-1}}{(2n-1)!}$

7. $S_4 \approx 0.1411200081$; Because the next term of this alternating series is positive (the opposite of a negative number), this approximation is too small, but by no more than $|a^5| = \left|\frac{(3-\pi)^9}{9!}\right| = 6.3038 \times 10^{-14}$. In other words this approximation is accurate to the 10 decimal places given. This approximation is more accurate than the one in problem 6, because the series was expanded around $x = \pi$, which is much closer to 3 than 0.

9. Converges absolutely **11.** ∞ **13.** ∞ **15.** $8\frac{1}{2}$ **17.** π **19.** $\frac{2(y-x+1)}{(x+1)^2}$ **21.** $\frac{\pi-2}{2}$ units^2

problem set 142

1. $\vec{v} = (2\cos t)\hat{i} - (3\sin t)\hat{j}$; $\vec{a} = (-2\sin t)\hat{i} - (3\cos t)\hat{j}$

3. $-4 - 2(x-1) + 3(x-1)^2 + 4(x-1)^3 + (x-1)^4$

5. $\frac{\sqrt{3}}{2} - \frac{x - \frac{\pi}{6}}{2} - \frac{\sqrt{3}}{4}(x - \frac{\pi}{6})^2 + \frac{(x - \frac{\pi}{6})^3}{12} + \cdots$ **7.** 15.6374 ft **9.** $\delta = \frac{\varepsilon}{2}$ **11.** 6

13. Diverges **15.** $\frac{1}{3}\sqrt{x^2+4}(x^2-8) + C$ **17.** $\frac{3}{4}x^2\sin(4x) + \frac{3}{8}x\cos(4x) - \frac{3}{32}\sin(4x) + C$

19. Conditionally convergent **21.** 0.2325 units^2

problem set 143

1. 2 ft/s **3.** There is no solution. **5.** 1.1440

7. $\vec{v} = 8\hat{i} + 2\hat{j}$; $\vec{a} = 16\hat{i} + 2\hat{j}$; speed $= 2\sqrt{17}$; acceleration $= 2\sqrt{65}$

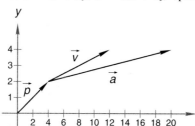

9. $\frac{1}{2} + \frac{\sqrt{3}}{2}(x - \frac{\pi}{6}) - \frac{1}{4}(x - \frac{\pi}{6})^2 - \frac{\sqrt{3}}{12}(x - \frac{\pi}{6})^3 + \cdots$

11. Converges **13.** Converges

15. Converges conditionally **17.** $16\frac{13}{32}$ units

19. $\cos(\sin^2 2)\cos 2 - 12\cos 144$ **21.** 2

problem set 144

1. (1.5675, 2.4571) **3.** 15.6530 s; 6777.9478 ft **5.** $\sin 32° \approx \frac{1}{2} + \frac{\sqrt{3}}{2}(\frac{\pi}{90}) - \frac{1}{4}(\frac{\pi}{90})^2$; error $< \frac{4}{273,375}$ **7.** $\frac{1}{2} - \frac{1}{4}(x-2) + \frac{1}{8}(x-2)^2 - \frac{1}{16}(x-2)^3 + \cdots$

9. Speed ≈ 10.2879; $|\vec{a}| \approx 11.9422$ **11.** Converges **13.** Converges absolutely

15. 199.2325705 **17.** $\frac{1}{2}$ **19.** $\frac{-x}{9\sqrt{4x^2-9}} + C$ **21.** $\lim_{h\to 0}\frac{\ln(x+h) - \ln x}{h} = \lim_{h\to 0}\frac{1}{h}\frac{x}{x}\left[\ln\left(\frac{x+h}{x}\right)\right]$

$= \lim_{h\to 0}\frac{1}{x}\frac{x}{h}\left[\ln\left(1 + \frac{h}{x}\right)\right] = \frac{1}{x}\lim_{h\to 0}\ln\left(1 + \frac{h}{x}\right)^{x/h} = \frac{1}{x}\ln e = \frac{1}{x}$

problem set 145

1. $(-\infty, \infty)$ **3.** $\cos 35° \approx 0.8190945922$; error ≤ 0.0001107620 **5.** $\sum_{n=0}^{\infty} x^n$; $(-1, 1)$ **7.** $15\frac{1}{3}$

9. $\delta = \frac{\varepsilon}{2}$ **11.** 2 **13.**

15. $\frac{1}{13}e^{2x}[2\sin(3x) - 3\cos(3x)] + C$

17. $-\frac{4\cos(2t)}{9\cos^2(3t)} - \frac{2\sin(2t)\sin(3t)}{3\cos^3(3t)}$

19. $\delta = 0.0000638$; Answers may vary.

21. $e^{x^2}(2x^2 + 1) - \frac{2x}{\sqrt{1-x^4}}$

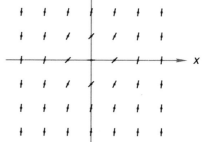

problem set 146

1. 69.6050 ft **3.** $\frac{\sqrt{3}}{2} + \frac{1}{2}(x - \frac{\pi}{3}) - \frac{\sqrt{3}}{4}(x - \frac{\pi}{3})^2 - \frac{1}{12}(x - \frac{\pi}{3})^3 + \cdots$ **5.** $\frac{1}{20,250}$

7. $\sum_{n=0}^{\infty} -(n+1)x^n$ **9.** $(-\infty, \infty)$ **11.** 1.05819775 **13.** Converges

15. Converges **17.** 1 **19.** 2π units^2 **21.** 0.7443

problem set 147

1. 2.718281826 **3.** $\frac{\sqrt{3}}{2} - \frac{1}{2}(x - \frac{\pi}{6}) - \frac{\sqrt{3}}{4}(x - \frac{\pi}{6})^2 + \frac{1}{12}(x - \frac{\pi}{6})^3 + \cdots$

5. $1 - \frac{1}{2}x + \frac{3}{8}x^2 - \frac{5}{16}x^3 + \cdots$ **7.** $\sum_{n=1}^{\infty}(-1)^{n+1}\frac{x^{4n-2}}{(2n-1)!}$ **9.** $x = 0$ **11.** $\left(\frac{14\pi}{3} + \frac{11}{2}\sqrt{3}\right)$ units^2

13. $\sqrt{1 + \cos^3 x}(-\sin x) - \sqrt{1 + 27x^6}(6x)$ **15.** Diverges **17.** 20.6446

19. Converges to $\frac{41}{21}$ **21.** $\frac{1}{12}$ unit^2

problem set 148

1. 21.4745° **3.** $\sum_{n=0}^{\infty} x^{2n}$ **5.** $1 - \sum_{n=1}^{\infty}\frac{x^{2n}}{2^n}$ **7.** $\frac{\pi}{4}$ **9.** 0.9045 **11.** Converges absolutely

13. Converges **15.** $\frac{21}{2}$ units **17.** 3.657758032 **19.** $\pi(6e^{-1} - \frac{1}{2}e^{-2} - 6e^{-4} + \frac{1}{2}e^{-8})$ units^3

21. $\frac{4}{3}$

REFERENCE TABLE OF DERIVATIVES

$$\frac{d}{dx}c = 0$$

$$\frac{d}{dx}u = \frac{du}{dx}$$

$$\frac{d}{dx}u^n = nu^{n-1}\frac{du}{dx}$$

$$\frac{d}{dx}(cu) = c\frac{du}{dx}$$

$$\frac{d}{dx}(u + v) = \frac{du}{dx} + \frac{dv}{dx}$$

$$\frac{d}{dx}(uv) = u\frac{dv}{dx} + v\frac{du}{dx}$$

$$\frac{d}{dx}\left(\frac{u}{v}\right) = \frac{v\frac{du}{dx} - u\frac{dv}{dx}}{v^2}$$

$$\frac{d}{dx}e^u = e^u\frac{du}{dx}$$

$$\frac{d}{dx}\ln|u| = \frac{1}{u}\frac{du}{dx}$$

$$\frac{d}{dx}a^u = (\ln a)a^u\frac{du}{dx}, \; a > 0$$

$$\frac{d}{dx}\log_a u = \frac{1}{u \ln a}\frac{du}{dx}$$

$$\frac{d}{dx}\sin u = \cos u\frac{du}{dx}$$

$$\frac{d}{dx}\cos u = -\sin u\frac{du}{dx}$$

$$\frac{d}{dx}\tan u = \sec^2 u\frac{du}{dx}$$

$$\frac{d}{dx}\cot u = -\csc^2 u\frac{du}{dx}$$

$$\frac{d}{dx}\sec u = \sec u \tan u\frac{du}{dx}$$

$$\frac{d}{dx}\csc u = -\csc u \cot u\frac{du}{dx}$$

$$\frac{d}{dx}|f(x)| = \frac{f(x)}{|f(x)|}\frac{d}{dx}f(x)$$

$$\frac{d}{dx}\sin^{-1}\frac{u}{a} = \frac{1}{\sqrt{a^2 - u^2}}\frac{du}{dx}$$

$$\frac{d}{dx}\cos^{-1}\frac{u}{a} = \frac{-1}{\sqrt{a^2 - u^2}}\frac{du}{dx}$$

$$\frac{d}{dx}\tan^{-1}\frac{u}{a} = \frac{a}{a^2 + u^2}\frac{du}{dx}$$

$$\frac{d}{dx}\cot^{-1}\frac{u}{a} = \frac{-a}{a^2 + u^2}\frac{du}{dx}$$

$$\frac{d}{dx}\sec^{-1}\frac{u}{a} = \frac{a}{u\sqrt{u^2 - a^2}}\frac{du}{dx}$$

$$\frac{d}{dx}\csc^{-1}\frac{u}{a} = \frac{-a}{u\sqrt{u^2 - a^2}}\frac{du}{dx}$$

$$\frac{d^2}{dx^2}u = \frac{d}{dx}\frac{du}{dx}$$

$$\frac{d}{dx}f^{-1}(x) = \frac{1}{\frac{d}{dx}f(f^{-1}(x))}$$

REFERENCE TABLE OF INTEGRALS

$$\int du = u + C$$

$$\int k\,du = ku + C$$

$$\int kf(u)\,du = k\int f(u)\,du$$

$$\int (f(u) + g(u))\,du = \int f(u)\,du + \int g(u)\,du$$

$$\int u\,dv = uv - \int v\,du$$

$$\int u^n\,du = \frac{u^{n+1}}{n + 1} + C, \; n \neq -1$$

$$\int \frac{1}{u}\,du = \ln|u| + C$$

$$\int e^u\,du = e^u + C$$

$$\int \ln u\,du = u \ln u - u + C$$

$$\int a^u\,du = \frac{a^u}{\ln a} + C, \; a > 0$$

$$\int \log_a u\,du = \frac{1}{\ln a}(u \ln u - u) + C$$

$$\int_a^\infty f(u)\,du = \lim_{b \to \infty}\int_a^b f(u)\,du$$

$$\int_{-\infty}^b f(u)\,du = \lim_{a \to -\infty}\int_a^b f(u)\,du$$

$$\int_{-\infty}^\infty f(u)\,du = \int_{-\infty}^a f(u)\,du + \int_a^\infty f(u)\,du$$

$$\int \sin u\,du = -\cos u + C$$

$$\int \cos u\,du = \sin u + C$$

$$\int \tan u\,du = \ln|\sec u| + C$$

$$\int \cot u\,du = \ln|\sin u| + C$$

$$\int \sec u\,du = \ln|\sec u + \tan u| + C$$

$$\int \csc u\,du = \ln|\csc u - \cot u| + C$$

$$\int \sec^2 u\,du = \tan u + C$$

$$\int \csc^2 u\,du = -\cot u + C$$

$$\int \sec u \tan u\,du = \sec u + C$$

$$\int \csc u \cot u\,du = -\csc u + C$$

$$\int \frac{du}{\sqrt{a^2 - u^2}} = \sin^{-1}\frac{u}{a} + C$$

$$\int \frac{du}{a^2 + u^2} = \frac{1}{a}\tan^{-1}\frac{u}{a} + C$$

$$\int \frac{du}{u\sqrt{u^2 - a^2}} = \frac{1}{a}\sec^{-1}\frac{|u|}{a} + C$$

$$\int \frac{du}{\sqrt{u^2 - a^2}} = \ln\left|u + \sqrt{u^2 - a^2}\right| + C$$

REFERENCE GUIDE FOR SERIES

Geometric series: $\sum_{i=0}^{\infty} ar^i = a + ar + ar^2 + \cdots + ar^{n-1} + \cdots$

    1. The series converges to $\frac{a}{1-r}$ if $|r| < 1$.   2. The series diverges if $|r| \geq 1$.

Divergence theorem: If $\lim_{n \to \infty} a_n \neq 0$, then the series $\sum_{n=1}^{\infty} a_n$ diverges.

Harmonic series: $\sum_{n=1}^{\infty} \frac{1}{n}$ diverges.

p-series: $\sum_{n=1}^{\infty} \frac{1}{n^p}$ converges if $p > 1$ and diverges if $p \leq 1$.

Basic comparison test: Suppose $\sum_{n=1}^{\infty} a_n$, $\sum_{n=1}^{\infty} c_n$, and $\sum_{n=1}^{\infty} d_n$ are all positive-termed series.

    1. If $a_n \leq c_n$ for every positive integer n and if $\sum_{n=1}^{\infty} c_n$ converges, then $\sum_{n=1}^{\infty} a_n$ also converges.

    2. If $a_n \geq d_n$ for every positive integer n and if $\sum_{n=1}^{\infty} d_n$ diverges, then $\sum_{n=1}^{\infty} a_n$ also diverges.

Integral test: Suppose $\sum_{n=1}^{\infty} a_n$ is a positive-termed series and that f is a continuous decreasing function such that $f(n) = a_n$ for all $n \geq 1$. Then $\sum_{n=1}^{\infty} a_n$ and $\int_1^{\infty} f(x)$ both converge or both diverge.

Ratio test: Suppose $\sum_{n=1}^{\infty} a_n$ is a positive-termed series and $L = \lim_{n \to \infty} \frac{a_{n+1}}{a_n}$.

    1. The series converges if $L < 1$.   2. The series diverges if $L > 1$.   3. The test is inconclusive if $L = 1$.

Root test: Suppose $\sum_{n=1}^{\infty} a_n$ is a positive-termed series and $L = \lim_{n \to \infty} \sqrt[n]{a_n}$.

    1. The series converges if $L < 1$.   2. The series diverges if $L > 1$.   3. The test is inconclusive if $L = 1$.

Limit comparison test: Let $\sum_{n=1}^{\infty} a_n$ and $\sum_{n=1}^{\infty} b_n$ be positive-termed series. Let $L = \lim_{n \to \infty} \frac{a_n}{b_n}$. If $0 < L < +\infty$, then $\sum_{n=1}^{\infty} a_n$ and $\sum_{n=1}^{\infty} b_n$ either both converge or both diverge. If $L = 0$ or $L = +\infty$, then the test is inconclusive.

Conditional convergence: A series $\sum_{n=1}^{\infty} a_n$ is said to converge conditionally if $\sum_{n=1}^{\infty} |a_n|$ diverges but $\sum_{n=1}^{\infty} a_n$ converges.

Absolute convergence: A series $\sum_{n=1}^{\infty} a_n$ is said to converge absolutely if $\sum_{n=1}^{\infty} |a_n|$ converges.

Alternating series test (Leibniz's theorem): The alternating series $\sum_{n=1}^{\infty} (-1)^{n+1} a_n$ converges if the following are true:

    1. $a_n \geq a_{n+1}$ for every n 2. $\lim_{n \to \infty} a_n = 0$

Alternating series approximation theorem: Suppose $\sum_{n=1}^{\infty} (-1)^{n+1} a_n$ satisfies the conditions of the alternating series test. Call the value of this sum S. Then the nth partial sum, S_n, approximates S with an error less than or equal to a_{n+1} in absolute value.

Power series: $\sum_{n=0}^{\infty} a_n x^n$

First convergence theorem for power series:

    1. If a power series converges for some nonzero number, say $x = c$, then it converges absolutely whenever $|x| < |c|$.

    2. If a power series diverges for some nonzero number, say $x = d$, then it diverges whenever $|x| > |d|$.

Second convergence theorem for power series: For any power series, exactly one of the following is true:

    1. The series converges only when $x = 0$.   2. The series converges absolutely for all x.

    3. There is some positive number r such that the series converges absolutely whenever $|x| < r$ and diverges whenever $|x| > r$. When $|x| = r$, the series may converge or the series may diverge.

Term-by-term differentiation of power series: If the power series $f(x) = \sum_{n=0}^{\infty} a_n(x - a)^n$ converges on the open interval $(a - c, a + c)$, then $\sum_{n=0}^{\infty} na_n(x - a)^{n-1}$ also converges on the open interval $(a - c, a + c)$ and $f'(x) = \sum_{n=0}^{\infty} na_n(x - a)^{n-1}$.

Term-by-term integration of power series: If the power series $f(x) = \sum_{n=0}^{\infty} a_n(x - a)^n$ converges on the open interval $(a - c, a + c)$, then $\sum_{n=0}^{\infty} \frac{a_n}{n+1}(x - a)^{n+1}$ also converges on the open interval $(a - c, a + c)$ and $\int f(x)\,dx = C + \sum_{n=0}^{\infty} \frac{a_n}{n+1}(x - a)^{n+1}$ for some constant C.